Handbook of Jewelry Store
MANAGEMENT

Second Edition

Compiled by the editors of

JCK

JEWELERS' CIRCULAR-KEYSTONE

General Disclaimer:

This edition of the *Handbook for Jewelry Store Management* is a collection of articles published in *Jewelers' Circular-Keystone* from January 1988 through June 1995. Also included are selected articles dating to October 1979 which appeared in the first edition of the *Handbook*. These selections are designed to assist you in handling the day-to-day operations of your store. While these articles were chosen for the overall value of the concepts they present, some of the information in the articles may now be outdated. Wherever possible, we have omitted outdated information without interrupting the flow of the articles. Please excuse any outdated references that remain in the text.

Library of Congress Cataloging in Publication Data
Library of Congress Catalog Card number: 95-81089.

Introduction

In 1985, JCK published the first edition of the *Handbook of Jewelry Store Management*. Jewelers large and small welcomed it with tremendous enthusiasm; for six years running it topped the Jewelers' Book Club best-seller list.

This second edition continues the mission of the first: to provide a single comprehensive management reference designed specifically for the retail jeweler. It offers a wealth of information originally published in JCK issues dating from January 1988 through June 1995. It also includes a handful of selected articles, timeless in content, from the first edition.

Among the highlights of this latest *Handbook* are two new chapters, "Training" and "Your Business Plan"; a broad look at the changing face of "the competition"; and the JCK Management Study Center quizzes (answers are provided, too). In addition, there are idea-filled "Sales Promotion" and "Marketing" chapters.

This edition also is replete with practical guidance on topics of everyday interest such as hiring, firing, legal matters, insurance needs, security issues, financials and computers.

While most of the articles were written by JCK staff editors, some were written by contributors whose names are listed in the acknowledgements.

Acknowledgements

The creation of the *Handbook* was a "community" effort. This second edition bears the mark of about 40 different writers, most of them staff editors at *Jewelers' Circular-Keystone*. Some editors have moved on to other jobs; most continue on the staff today. All used their talents to provide the magazine's readers with the best professional guidance available to help them better manage their stores.

The non-staff contributors brought specific expertise to their work. From working jewelers to industry consultants and observers, each brought the benefit of his or her real life experience to the assignments.

The following individuals contributed to this *Handbook*—each author's business affiliation also is listed: Mark Ebert, Ebert & Co., Los Angeles, CA ("Starting an Estate Jewelry Department"); John Michaels, Michaels Inc., Waterbury, CT ("How to Negotiate the Best Lease"); Mark Moeller, Moeller's Jewelers, St. Paul, MN ("Starting Your Own Estate Jewelry Department"); Jerry Fornell, Chicago Design Group, Northbrook, IL ("Diamond Rooms: Create the Right Atmosphere"); Elly Rosen, Brooklyn, NY ("Why You Need An Appraisal Education"); Maxine Nelson with Juliet George McCleery, QuestComm, Perkasie, PA ("Training Your Staff to Sell Heritage Jewelry"); Edna B. Jacques, Reallyfine Enterprises, Chappaqua, NY ("Man to Woman Selling: Do's and Don'ts for Success"); Suzy Spencer, Austin, TX ("Making the Big Sale: Anyone Can Do It!" "Marketing to Attract Women," "Style, Female Appeal Crucial to Bridal Sales"), V. Michael Williams, Charterhouse & Company, Grosse Pointe, MI ("Market Blindness and How to Cure It"); Cos Altobelli, Altobelli Jewelers, N. Hollywood, CA ("18 Tips For Better Appraisal"); Sharon A. Krimm, Charon Planning Corporation, Doylestown, PA ("Your Benefit Package: The First Steps"); Clayton Bromberg, Underwood Jewelers, Jacksonville, FL ("Retain More Net Profits Before Tax"); Joseph S. Romano, Scull & Co., Union City, NJ ("Sure-Fire Ways to Build Your Bottom Line"); Lynn Clark Bergman, Marketing Solutions, Inc., McLean, VA ("Jewelers Try Coupon Advertising"); Cathleen McCarthy, Philadelphia, PA ("Will It Play in Portland? Understanding Regional Tastes"); Jim Terzian, Terzian International Group, Foster City, CA ("Get To Know the All-Star Customer"); William Hoefer, Jr., Hoefer's Gemmological Services, San Jose, CA ("How to Avoid Problems at Take-In," "Gemstone Justice: How Scam Victims Can Strike Back"); Tom Tivol, Tivol Plaza, Inc., Kansas City, MO ("You, The Law & Your Employees"); Roberta Jacobs-Meadway, Panitch, Schwartz, Jacobs & Nadel, Philadelphia, PA ("Private Right to Act Against False Advertising Strengthened"); Peter Shor, Shor International Corporation, Mt. Vernon, NY ("Choosing Computer Software For Your Business"); Michael Golding, Golding Technologies, Seattle, WA ("The Personal Computer: A Jeweler's Tool"); Richard Laffin, Management Growth Institute, Wellesley, MA ("Know What Your Salespeople Think," "How to Measure Strength & Weakness," "I Can't Buy Now Because"); Helene Huffer, Elaine Cooper & Co., Chestnut Hill, PA ("How to Make That Big Sale"); Willis Cowlishaw, Cowlishaw & Associates, Dallas, TX ("Your Business Plan").

At JCK's headquarters, a handful of people carried this project to completion. Charles M. Bond, publisher, who conceived the idea for the first edition, supported production of the second. Linda Troilo Whitfield, JCK marketing manager, was project director and headed the book's production; Mitch Plotnick, JCK Special Projects Editor, reviewed eight years of JCK issues and made article selections; George Holmes, editor in chief, Deborah Holmes, managing editor, Ren Miller, copy editor, Russ Shor, William G. Shuster, Hedda T. Shupak and Michael Thompson, senior editors; Sandy Alberti and Joe Morris, production editors, contributed the lion's share of the material in this edition. Graphic designers that made the *Handbook* pleasing to the eye include Susanne Williams, Williams & Co. Graphic Design, for the *Handbook* layout and Kathy Singel, Singel Design, for the cover. The project's lone typist, June Kim, delivered copy on time and in order for proofreaders, Ed Killian and Gerald Glenn who worked diligently to complete a tedious task. Christina Perrotta, JCK marketing assistant, cast a critical eye to the final pages before going to the printer.

Contents

Contents

SALES PROMOTION

Contents

LAWS & REGULATIONS

SECURITY & INSURANCE

COMPUTERS

YOUR BUSINESS PLAN

Chapter 1

THE STORE

The Store Is The Center Of The Jewelry Universe

Starting An Estate Jewelry Department

Mark Ebert ◆ *August 1994*

Many jewelry stores dabble in the estate jewelry business. Some broker customers' merchandise as a service; others buy estate pieces over the counter and either stock it or broker it to the trade. But getting serious and starting a full-fledged, professionally managed estate department offers some real advantages.

• It's a great way to grow your business. Indeed, trying to grow without a new department—whether it be estate jewelry or any other merchandise—means increasing the units sold in existing departments. That is a steep climb.

• Estate jewelry allows a greater profit margin than the average in most jewelry departments—if you price wisely. Estate jewelry marked up above keystone often finds ready buyers. In addition, these items often turn faster than the industry's 1-time average.

• Cash flow also may increase. When you advertise an estate department, customers will bring more goods for you to buy over the counter or to accept as trade-in. When these goods fit your inventory and price-point range, you can obtain inventory at attractive prices for a modest cash outlay. When they don't you can sell them to estate dealers in the trade and boost cash flow. As your reputation for handling estate jewelry grows, sales to the trade can become a significant source of cash.

• Accepting estate (previously-owned) jewelry for trade-in may help you close sales in other departments. Most of us know this technique but, unfortunately, rarely use it in our sales presentations.

• Carrying estate jewelry lets you offer different price points than those prevailing in your other departments. Adding higher-end estate goods can help you move up your clientele; adding lower price points may help you close customers you'd otherwise lose. Stay focused on *value* , however, not price. Estate jewelry can't be comparison shopped, and gives you a special niche in your market.

• An estate department lets you tap current interest in the designer market. Estate jewelry is designer jewelry which has withstood the test of time.

Defining the department: An estate jewelry consignment case is not a full-fledged estate department. A department is stocked and priced by plan. A consignment case, by contrast, is stocked by chance, depending on what jewelry owners choose to leave for sale. And its pricing is inconsistent, since the jewelry owners who set those prices often know little about the market. Inconsistent inventory and erratic pricing are no way to create a growth department.

Neither is hosting an annual estate show the same as offering a professional estate department. While such shows can be very successful for a retailer, an annual show offers fewer benefits than a department. Advertising for a show gets only one-time use from your money; it's far better to advertise your estate department over time and reap the accrued benefits of a steady, ongoing campaign. Shows won't help you close sales year-around with trade-ins. Nor do they let you establish a special niche in your market as *the* place to go for estate jewelry.

If you've tried estate shows and they weren't especially successful, consider how hard it would be to develop a successful diamond business without regularly stocking diamonds. If you have had successful shows, consider the potential for much greater success if you maintain a year-around estate department.

Once you decide to launch a full-fledged estate department, be prepared to maintain a balanced inventory in an appropriate range of price points. Just how much inventory is enough will vary; the estate section must be large enough to function effectively as a department in the context of the rest of your store.

You also will need to devote some of your own time to overseeing the department. Or, if your store is too large for you to have hands-on daily involvement in each department, you must appoint a department manager. That manager must be involved in advertising, buying, marketing and training for the estate department and should be compensated in a way that encourages success.

Where to buy: A successful estate department requires an inventory balanced in estate periods, in types of jewelry and in appropriate price points. That takes a lot of time and thought; you can't replace inventory just by calling a manufacturer to reorder item number ZYD-1234. There are a number of resources for obtaining inventory.

Reputable estate jewelry suppliers: These may be the best resource for a retailer looking to open a successful estate department. The reputable supplier provides essential services that will help lay a foundation for your success.

First, the supplier offers reliable information about the item purchased. You should expect gemological identification with appropriate disclosures, accurate information about metal content, and experience-based estimates of total carat weights. Other facts, such as period or designer identification and information about provenance, also may be available. When you buy from other sources, you may have to do all this research yourself.

Second, a reputable supplier offers you a basis for understanding pricing (see below for more information).

The pool of reputable suppliers understands the market and makes offers to buy and sell which fall within a fairly close range and which reflect worldwide supply of and demand for specific types of estate jewelry. When you are just starting out, the relative consistency of pricing by reputable suppliers teaches you how to price your inventory.

Third, reputable estate suppliers can help you balance your inventory. They gather goods from many places and sources to meet the needs of many different clients. This saves you a lot of time and gives you access to a much broader range of merchandise than is available in your market. The supplier also usually will do any restoration needed to make a piece salable as soon as it enters your inventory.

Fourth, reputable suppliers offer specific services which may benefit you. Ebert & Co., for example, offers a same-day turnaround for estimates to purchase pieces from you based even on a faxed photostat of the piece with handwritten notes. We and many other estate jewelry suppliers also offer staff training support to help you launch your department, assistance with advertising and special shows. Terms are available from most suppliers. And, if you experience a problem with a piece or if a piece is not what it was represented to you to be, you have recourse when dealing with reputable suppliers. With other sources, heed the caution—Buyer Beware!

Advantages: Reliable identification and pricing information; balanced inventory; any necessary restoration of the piece; training and education support; payment terms; and recourse if there is a problem.

Disadvantages: Decreased opportunity to purchase an undiscovered treasure.

Buying over the counter: Once you develop a reputation for buying and selling estate jewelry, it will start coming in over the counter from customers who want to sell and trade it in.

Buying over the counter is potentially the retailer's best source of estate jewelry. It is almost like mining precious gems by hand. If you know how to buy and price wisely, you can make a fair purchase from the customer which allows you the maximum profit potential. Often, you'll be able to turn a quick profit. However, it's rare that you can buy enough goods over the counter to keep a fully stocked professional estate department; you'll need to get some merchandise from other sources.

When buying from the public, remember that you're the expert. Even though Aunt Gertie said this was a perfect diamond, Niece Nyleca may have to be told the diamond is an H color, I_1 clarity. Even though the piece may have been in the family for a long time, a gambling uncle may have had the center stone replaced with a simulant. You buy "as is" when you buy from the public.

Before accepting jewelry over the counter, make sure you are aware of and in compliance with all applicable state and local laws and regulations which control buying jewelry.

Also remember that your estate department needs a balanced inventory in a range of price points. Just because you receive something in trade, you don't have to put it in your case. You may choose to sell it to the trade or to break it up for gems and scrap. But check with an estate supplier before you break up merchandise. If you are not fully aware of all periods of estate jewelry, you may destroy a piece which is much more valuable if left intact.

Advantages: Potential to obtain stock for your inventory at the best prices; merchandise comes to you; you may close more sales by encouraging trade-ins; you increase cash flow by selling to the trade.

Disadvantages: You must be the expert on identification; you must decide how to move the piece; you have to write the check that day to buy the item.

Accepting consignment goods: Some customers may ask you to handle goods on consignment. Don't assume that this always is a wise business choice. You must balance the desire to serve your customer with your need to establish and maintain a credible estate jewelry business. Goods which you offer will be taken as a statement of your taste and your quality standards. Further, the price of a consignment piece must reflect a value of consistent with your business image. If a piece offered to you for consignment will not further your business image for taste, quality and value, you may be better off not to accept it.

If you do accept goods on consignment, recognize that your business motive is to be profitable over time. You may accept a piece as a favor to a customer for a long-term business relationship. But you still should set the selling price at a level which allows you to maintain your normal markup.

Advantages: Helps keep a customer satisfied; adds new inventory without tying up your cash.

Disadvantages: Creates potential imbalance in your inventory mix; reduces your potential profit margin.

Buying from banks: Banks which serve as trustees for estates handle estate liquidations and will sell jewelry lots to buyers. If you opt to invest the time and persistence to establish a relationship with bankers who handle estates, be aware that the bank defines what "jewelry" is. Also, as is true for sightholders buying diamonds, you must offer on whatever is tendered and you must accept the entire lot if that offer is accepted.

Anticipate offering on lots ranging from $50 to $50,000+ and be prepared to write a cashier's check or certified check within a day or two of having your offer accepted. You can't predict whether a given estate will contain jewelry which fits your inventory needs, so to avoid cash flow problems you must know how to quickly liquidate unwanted inventory. Be prepared to obtain jewelry lots that may include guns, coins, sterling holloware or flatware.

Advantages: Sometimes an estate contains desirable jewelry which you can obtain inexpensively.

Disadvantages: You must buy what is offered and be able to quickly liquidate what you don't want to keep; you must turn over cash quickly if your offer is accepted; you may invest time and research to make an offer which is rejected.

Buying from auction houses: Christie's, Sotheby's, Butterfields and other large auction houses help determine value and pricing in the worldwide estate jewelry market. Smaller auction houses can be an excellent source of estate jewelry. When you buy at auction, always do your research beforehand so that you are reasonably confident of the content, quality of production and market value of pieces on which you might bid. With that information, set your maximum bid price and don't exceed it.

Advantages: A well-researched purchase may be very good value for the price paid at auction.

Disadvantages: Usually no recourse if you are mistaken about the identification or quality of the item; buyer frenzy may force prices up artificially.

All of these potential sources generally allow enough time for you to use your expertise and conduct the research needed to make prudent purchases. That is both good and bad news, because research is time intensive and may cut into your profit margin.

The following potential sources involve less research time, so they are generally more a shoot-from-the-hip buying experience. Again the caution, Buyer Beware.

Buying from flea markets: With a long history as an excellent source for estate jewelry in Europe, flea markets are gaining importance in the U.S. Some large cities have standing markets, such as the monthly flea market at the Rose Bowl in Los Angeles. Flea market booths will feature merchandise which the vendor has picked up over the last few weeks at garage sales, pawnshops, etc. You might strike out and find nothing. You might end up spending $20,000. Be aware that flea market prices can be nestled at the high end of retail.

Though flea markets have a reputation for being full of fly-by-nighters, over time you'll see repeat vendors who may come to know your taste and cater to it. They'll buy with you in mind or hold items they think you'll offer a fair price on. There is an excitement about shopping flea markets, but buying well there requires wisdom, cash and plain luck. Flea markets are at best a fun and educational outing, though an inconsistent source for inventory.

Advantages: Great buys may be available.

Disadvantages: Buyer beware; time intensive; same day cash; inconsistent resource.

Buying from pawn shops: Traditionally, a pawn shop broker makes a living on the interest on loans given in exchange for collateralized goods. The broker's goal is to get the goods back to the person who took the loan; it may be pawned again, so more interest will be paid. Since the purpose isn't to obtain the piece, the loan is often made on price, not quality.

Most pawn shops already do cycle better quality jewelry to estate jewelry buyers. A jeweler can develop a relationship with a pawn broker to obtain merchandise, especially in an area which serves an upper-end clientele. But with few exceptions, shopping in pawn shops is generally a fun but inconsistent way to find a significant amount of merchandise.

Advantages: An occasional bargain may be found.

Disadvantages: Time intensive and an inconsistent resource.

Buying from "pocket peddlers:" The small dealer who may have a limited but consistent stream of merchandise is essentially a flea market at your door. You still have limited opportunity to research a piece and there are no guarantees. If you like it, you buy it, and if you don't buy wisely, well, maybe next time.

Advantages: You may be able to develop a relationship through which a "pocket peddler" becomes, in effect, a buyer for your department.

Disadvantages: Buyer beware; cash upfront.

Buying at garage sales: This Great American Pastime may give you the chance to find a natural ruby in a collection of costume jewelry, but unless you just like the activity, shopping garage sales is not likely to be very productive.

Flea market vendors will find the merchandise available at garage sales.

Advantages: The occasional real value.

Disadvantages: Time intensive; inconsistent source; cash upfront.

When selecting which sources you will use to obtain inventory, ask yourself:
1. How much time and energy is it reasonable for you to invest?
2. Is your own expertise sufficient to make a wise buy in this situation?
3. What is a realistic potential return for buying from this source?

How to price estate jewelry: When you sell today's jewelry, you can use the price you pay the manufacturer as a touchstone for setting your selling price. It simplifies the situation too much to say that keystone is used across the board for pricing, but keystone is still a useful point of departure.

How can you learn to price estate jewelry so that it sells profitably for you?

A reputable estate supplier's price is a useful place to begin. If you regularly obtain inventory from estate suppliers, you'll get a strong idea of the prevailing selling prices for items in your ideal inventory mix. Most suppliers' prices hover within a fairly modest spread.

The industry expects close harmony on diamond grades reached through the subjective judgment of experienced diamond graders. In the estate jewelry market, the subjective judgment of the pool of experienced reputable suppliers offers a similar consistency. Yes, prices vary—sometimes widely on a given piece. But there is an unplanned, harmonious pricing among estate suppliers who understand the market. Working with this resource helps you understand how the market handles price.

Demand and supply dictate prices for estate jewelry, but so does the power of illusion. How you mark up your inventory—in other words, how much profit you derive from your estate department—depends on your understanding of your store's market. Your supplier also can help you price appropriately and wisely.

Let's say you buy Brooch A from an estate supplier for $200. You sell Brooch A to your customer for $400. You've made $200 and you now know that this type of brooch will sell in your market at $400.

Beth Hopper offers to sell you a similar item, Brooch B. You call your estate supplier who says he would pay $100 to obtain Brooch B. You offer to buy Brooch B from Ms. Hopper for $85-$100 (perhaps even $125), knowing that you can break even if you sell it to your estate supplier. The piece fits well into your inventory mix, however, so you plan to add it to your case. What selling price will you ask?

Some jewelers would go for the traditional keystone and sell Brooch B for $200. Others might look at the $200 profit on the sale of Brooch A and mark Brooch B for $300; that maintains the $200 profit, yet offers "a good value" to their customers. Still others—and this is the strategy I recommend—will realize that Brooch A sold for $400 (a fair price), so that Brooch B also will sell for $400 (a fair price). That gives you a $300 profit, while your customers still get a good value.

Estate jewelry customers usually are more interested in a piece itself than in its price. The customer who likes Brooch B probably will buy it whether it is marked $200, $300 or $400.

Since price is not the main object, and since it is difficult to comparison shop estate jewelry, it is unlikely that many customers will recognize the "good value" of the $200 or $300 tag.

Perhaps you buy most of your inventory from an estate supplier, but buy 20% over the counter. If you price that 20% like the rest of your estate inventory, you can realize a 3- or 4-time markup. This will increase your profits and help you maintain a consistent price range within your estate department. And don't feel guilty—you still are offering a good value at a fair price.

When you buy over the counter, plan for costs to service pieces to make them salable. Many estate items require restorative work, perhaps repair on shanks or replacement of lost melee and certainly cleaning. Price to cover these services.

Don't think you need to offer consumers the same price you would pay a supplier. A reputable supplier gives you added value—such as access to consistent inventory, recourse if an item is not as represented, terms on purchase, research and advertising support. An over-the-counter purchase calls for you to pay money on the spot and to accept all risks in the purchase.

Customers expect to be able to negotiate price on estate jewelry. Your store's pricing policies will dictate how you respond to any request to negotiate price.

With a strong commitment up front in time, energy and willingness to maintain a balanced inventory, an aggressive, professionally managed estate department can help you grow your business. And, handling estate jewelry is a lot of fun.

Reference Books for Your Estate Department

Note: Some books listed are currently out-of-print but may be obtained through specialty bookfinders.

Armstrong, Nancy. *Victorian Jewelry*. New York: Macmillan Publishing Co., 1976.
Becker, Vivienne. *Antique and Twentieth Century Jewellery*. Colchester, Essex: N. AG. Press, 1980.
Art Nouveau Jewelry. New York: E.P. Dutton, 1985.
Egger, Gerhart. *Generations of Jewelry*. West Chester, Pa.: Dorrance & Co., 1984.
Flower, Margaret. *Victorian Jewellery*. London: Cassell & Co., 1951.
Poynder, Michael. *Price Guide to Jewellery*. London: Antique Collectors Club, 1976.
Proddow, Penny; Healy, Debra; and Behl, David. *American Jewelry: Glamour and Tradition*. New York: Rizzoli, 1987.
Raulet, Sylvie. *Art Deco Jewelry*. New York: Rizzoli, 1985.
Jewelry of the 1940s and 1950s. New York: Rizzoli, 1988.
Sataloff, Joseph. *Art Nouveau Jewelry*. Bryn Mawr, Pa.: Dorrance & Co., 1984.
Schiffer, Nancy N. *Handbook of Fine Jewelry*. West Chester, Pa.: Schiffer Publishing, 1991.

JCK Management Study Center: How To Negotiate The Best Lease
John Michaels ◆ May 1994

If you, as an independent jeweler, are thinking of moving to a mall, you'd better realize you'll face a whole different lifestyle. Your store will be open seven days a week—often from 9 in the morning until 10 at night. That's normal in a mall, but it's certainly not what you probably are used to.

The mall will deliver huge numbers of people to your store, but 70% or 80% of them won't be shoppers. In an independent stand-alone store, you'll see one-tenth as many people, but 90% of those who walk through the door are going to be shoppers.

These are two entirely different types of operation. Which is for you? Well, are you a destination? Will people come to you? Or do you need to be in a location where the landlord develops the foot traffic?

When regional malls go in next to downtowns, they kill the downtowns. It's very difficult for an independent to fight

that. We learned that the hard way in several places. But, not every customer wants to go to a mall now. More and more people want good service. They don't want to contend with car jackings, huge mall parking lots, traffic, the poor attitude of sales clerks. They want a different environment.

Are there enough people who want that better service in your market area to sustain a jewelry store outside the mall? Because a huge number of people still go there. Probably three quarters of diamond engagement rings are sold in malls. That's where kids and young people like to go because it's an experience and they can comparison shop easily under one roof.

To consider a mall, your volume should be at least $1 million to $1.2 million. If the basic rent is $120,000 a year, you need to do $1.2 million to make money. The basic figure for jewelers' rent is 5%-6%, but you can afford 10% in a mall if you do enough business. If you don't, you can't afford it; it's that simple.

Location determines whether a particular mall is for you. You may not like the people you have to negotiate with; they may seem intransigent and unreasonable in their negotiating. You just have to learn to live with that; they're in the driver's seat.

A different lease: Leases for mall and downtown stores are very different animals.

You start a mall lease with a letter of intent from a landlord that locks you into all the basics. You see very quickly that you're getting into what is called a triple net lease where the base rent, a percentage of your sales and all the costs of running the entire mall are shared by the tenants. As long as the mall is full, all the landlord's costs are fully covered and he's almost guaranteed a net profit.

A lease for a free-standing downtown store is different. While the landlord might like the same terms, he doesn't have the clout to get them. He isn't drawing tens of thousands of customers to your store. These leases usually are much less expensive because the landlord offers a lot less. They usually don't have percentages or say when you have to be open at night. They're simpler—eight or nine pages double spaced as opposed to a mall lease with its 35 to 50 pages of legal small half-line spaced type along with construction exhibits, rules and regulations.

Once you've decided you do want to enter a mall, you should get the lease, read it and start to work through it item by item. You'll need an advisor to work with you. You could ask your own lawyer, but few hometown lawyers are expert at negotiating a mall lease from a tenant's perspective. They can read a lease, they can think and they know the law. But they don't know how the retail business operates.

You need an advisor who can interpret the lease from a retail point of view, who understands your business and knows the law. The best choice is someone with experience negotiating retail store leases. I'd suggest you ask the International Council of Shopping Centers for a recommendation.

The council, by the way, holds its annual convention in Las Vegas in mid-May. All the major users and developers gather for a weekend to make deals on future malls, current malls and leases are made. We paid $300 to join ICSC so we wouldn't be left out. By spending three days walking the convention we can find out when malls are coming to Connecticut.

When you're reading a lease, be careful. Unethical people occasionally will fiddle around and make changes you haven't approved. It's hard today for that to happen, but we still initial each page of the lease and read it. Most changes are done as an addendum to the basic lease. There is the basic lease, the addenda and then all the changes; all you should have to deal with are the changes. However, the landlord could change a few words in the basic lease before the final signing. So be sure to keep all your notes; then you and your lawyer can show that someone changed something at the 25th hour, which is fraud.

It's good practice to do one final reading with your attorney to make sure everything is okay. This is called conforming the documents. It means making sure the final document you sign conforms with the things that you've been dealing with all along.

Starting off: When I'm negotiating, first I ask for the plot plan, then for the cover sheet which talks about the percentages and dollars and basic terms, and then for the lease. I send a copy of the lease to my lawyer and then I go through it, making notes on what I think we should change. Next, I'll sit with the lawyer and say, "Here's where I think we should ask for changes." We discuss it in concept, not the exact words, because there's no sense wasting a lot of money on wording now with a lawyer.

Next I'll sit down with a lease negotiator and say, "Look, here are the things we need to address." We'll argue about why these are important issues, why "it's only fair" that we change these words.

Remember that these leases weren't designed for a fine retail jeweler. While negotiating, you have to keep saying, "Look, this kind of verbiage doesn't relate to us."

The key points you'll be negotiating include:

• Hours of operation. You can't do much about being open during usual mall hours. But if major stores decide to have a midnight madness sale until 2 in the morning, that's another matter. Security problems and store image may make that inappropriate.

• Base rent and the percentage. You have to be able to live with them.

• The definition of a sale. Deciding what to include in your sales volume—trade-ins, bad debts, low-margin transactions—for purposes of calculating percentage rent often is even more important than the percentage itself.

• The default clause. You want to be sure you have time and opportunity to correct any problems which might cause you to default and lose your lease.

But do they need you? When negotiating a lease, first find out whether the landlord really wants you in his mall—and, if he does, how badly. He's much more likely to compromise if he wants you.

Fifteen years ago, we had a potential lease where the landlord required everyone to be open when the anchors were open—seven days a week, 12 hours a day, all holidays. We weren't willing to do that. But he was about to go to the bank to close on the mortgage to build the place and he wanted us because we were a triple-A tenant, anchor in the community, etc. He wanted our name on his tenant list, so we got concessions that would be impossible to get today.

We wanted to get into a mall that we knew was coming to Danbury, so we stayed in touch with the landlord. They kept saying, "We'll call you, we'll call you." Then, one day we called and they said all the spaces were leased. So we went to the local Rotary Club, where my father happened to be District Governor, we talked to the president and found out who the players were. A mall coming into a community always has tentacles; it uses local lawyers and local architects, because of connections with the zoning and planning commissions, etc. We got these local people to go to the landlord and say, "You made a big mistake in not getting Michaels. You should find a way to fix this one."

Now they wanted us, so all of a sudden a good quality space opened up and we could negotiate. You have to be a big frog in your small pond. You can't just turn on these connections when you need them; you must develop your capital, your chips, all the time.

The rent game: Rents now are all over. A downtown store that the landlord bought from Resolution Trust Company for a third of its construction cost is $12 a foot, which includes base-year taxes. Yet a major developer in one of the country's most accessible East Coast malls is asking $180 a foot for a fine jeweler for a 1,500-sq.-ft. corner store. That's for ten years with a 10 percentage.

That's extreme. A jeweler dealing with a national developer in a super regional mall should expect to pay somewhere between $60 and $100. We are writing new leases anywhere from $60 to $85, depending on the mall and the location.

Even with the base rent, they want natural escalators so they can kick you out if you don't make percentage rent in three years. It's also common in every lease to raise the basic rent 15% rent every time they add another major anchor.

Here's something we've tried. A national operator wanted a $70 rent. We said we'd give him $70—on average. We'd give him $60 for three years, $70 for four and $80 for three. That averages out to $70. One guy took it; one guy didn't.

A landlord is more willing to negotiate on the percentage, because it's all extra, than on the basic rent. He needs that basic rent figure to finance his mortgage. He'll ask for your financial statements because the quality of tenants' financial statements also affects his mortgage.

Some other money matters you'll talk about are the breakpoint (see below) and security deposit. All landlords ask for a security deposit, but if you're a strong enough tenant, you shouldn't have to pay it. If you do pay, ask for it back within a certain time period.

Taxing issues: Taxes are another concern. One problem is the definition of sales taxes, which should be viewed in light of possible changes. If a lease specifically exempts certain types of taxes from sales, then all other taxes are considered sales. That means that if the U.S. passed a Valued Added Tax, with the tax buried in an item's price rather than stated separately, it would become part of sales. You would have to pay percentage rent based on it.

Another problem is that the landlord generally just rebills real estate taxes to tenants, so he has little real incentive to appeal assessments. Something in the lease should require him to do that.

The landlord also assesses a variety of administrative charges to cover his costs. Usually it's 15% of the bill in question. When it comes to common area charges, that makes sense; when it comes to tax bills, it doesn't. How much work is it for a landlord to send out 1,000 tax bills with prearranged percentages for the total taxes? It certainly isn't worth 15% of the total taxes. Landlords are willing to drop administrative charges from 15% to 5% or even 0% in some cases, but you have to ask for it.

Leases usually require that you keep your books on the premises. But if you have a small location, you may want to keep sales records and have audits done at a different location. That's usually a very good idea.

Landlords want a certified public accountant to certify your sales on a monthly basis, but that costs a fortune. Have it sworn to under penalty of perjury by your firm's chief financial officer and president. You can get away with not having to buy a certified statement on the sales.

They also will want you to pay for audits if anything is wrong with your sales. They'll send some internal auditor down to check the definition of sales and the credits and deductions and what did or didn't go through your books. If the sales you reported differ from those the audit says you should have reported by more than 2%, you have to pay for the audit. That's about $750 today. If the difference is more than 5%, there are penalties.

Let's make a deal: Department stores and big owners make their own deals—on common area, on taxes, on everything. If the center has a million square feet and front footage of the big boxes is 10%, they may make a deal to pay 5% of expenses. If they fail to pay even that, other tenants have to make up what they don't send. That's hidden in the lease under words like received and receivable. If your lease says you have to make up the difference if the big owners' payment isn't received by the landlord, then you'll have to pay up. But if you can change the wording to say that overdue payments by the big owners are receivable, that merely says they owe the landlord money. You are off the hook. We've been able to get changes like that made in some leases.

Whoever reads a lease has to understand the King's English extremely well, and know the difference between received and receivable, leased and leasable. If you don't negotiate leases very often, hire someone to do it for you. But stay with them, because they don't know your business. No matter how much money you spend for good advice, you'll save it five times over during the life of the lease.

If you agree in your lease to abide by a certain clause and then see another store violating that clause, call it to the attention of the mall manager if you want. But, remember that you don't know what's in the other guy's lease; he may not have agreed to the same clause. We've tried saying that we will abide by this if all other tenants are similarly obliged. But the landlord won't tell us what everyone else has to do.

In one section of the lease called rules and regulations, the landlord regulates the governance of the mall. We're always able to add a clause saying these rules and regulations will not contravene anything else negotiated in the lease.

What is negotiable? The bigger the developer and the bigger the mall, the less the negotiability because you are less important. That's our experience.

Common area maintenance is an example. The big guys say you must pay your percentage share of common area maintenance on the total leased part of the mall. If a mall with 1 million sq. ft. is 100% leased and you've got 1,000 sq. ft., you must cover 0.1% or one tenth of one percent of the costs. If the place is 80% leased, you'll be assessed .12%. The fact that the mall is 20% under leased becomes your problem as a tenant, because you must pay 20% more to cover all the costs.

We argue that. We'll say we have a very small location, and it's not our fault you've got unleased space; we want to pay a percentage on the leasable space, not the leased. That works in smaller malls, where the people want us and admit that our argument is fair. But a big mall, where you're just 1% or 0.1% of the space, won't go through all the bookkeeping to carve out something special for you. If the place is 100% leased when you go in, then a couple of big people pull out and all of the sudden it's down to 50% leased, your common area charges will double.

We have a mental checklist of things that tend to be negotiable. Experience helps; everything we've been able to negotiate in the past is a clue to what will be negotiable in the future. Every five years or so we also go to an advisor on leasing and ask, "What's going on in the industry? What is negotiable and what isn't?" Finally, we go on the principle that everything is negotiable if they want you. The base rent, the percentage, the hours, the assignment clause, everything. The question is, what is worth negotiating? Sometimes there's no sense in arguing; it just costs too much to dispute fine points when you're paying a lawyer $150 an hour. You might like to see some changes, but 70% of the inequities in the lease aren't worth fussing with. Instead, you end up focusing on the key economic issues.

The empty chair: Always make sure you're not negotiating to an empty chair, just a talking head. You want to talk with someone in authority who can actually make decisions.

One person often is responsible for leasing a center with a hundred retail stores. That person is a salesman, not a negotiator. He probably has never even read the lease. He can't be out prospecting, making deals and selling space and still have the time and skills needed to negotiate all the fine points of a lease. To find someone with authority, you and your lawyer may have to fly someplace and negotiate with a team.

Assignment clause: Can you assign your lease to somebody else? Fewer landlords are willing to let you assign and sublet. They want absolute control of who their tenant is and what the place looks like. We try to put in a statement that permission will not be unreasonably withheld. Sometimes they agree; sometimes they don't.

But is it fair? Administrative issues can make a lease unfair and they're worth arguing over.

Say there's a $100 fee for bounced checks. Period. Even if it's the bank's fault. That's not fair.

Or there's a $50 penalty if you don't report your sales within seven days. If you're late because of computer failure or weather or something beyond your control, that's not fair.

You must keep records for a certain length of time. If you have a percentage rent lease, the landlord has the right to see your sales tax report and sales records, but you'll want to negotiate the extent to which he can come in and take inventory. That has nothing to do with sales.

Once I've gone over changes with my lawyer, I'll sit down with a lease negotiator—hopefully not an empty chair, but someone who really can negotiate. I'll explain why these are important issues and why "it's only fair" that we change the wording from this to this.

What is a sale? Landlords feel they have a right to the proceeds from a sale if any inventory comes into the store and then leaves. R. G. Foster, a professional accounting firm, specializes in auditing leases. It will check your inventory records and if anything leaves the store without documentation it went back to the manufacturer, Foster will go see if it was sold in another store. Then it will try to show that the sale should have come from this store because that's where the merchandise originally was.

The lease will say that every store transaction will be considered a sale when it's recorded in the cash register. Yet when a customer places an order, our accounting system requires that we ring it and its deposit through the cash register. Such orders are not legal sales until they're delivered.

Indeed, our state sales tax and state and federal income tax reports, as well as our financial statements, all are gov-

erned by the rules of commercial transactions that say no sale occurs until there is delivery. But the lease says all transactions are sales. We say, "No. A sale is a sale when our books indicate it's a sale, which is in accordance with GAP [general accounting principles] and the state sales tax department, and the federal and state income tax departments." We always argue that issue.

Other types of transaction we want excluded from sales include low-margin transactions, bad debts, trade-ins and credits. Sometimes they don't want to give you returns, unless the item was sold in that store. But if you accept a return and make another sale, how can you count the sale without crediting the return? Multiple stores can argue this, and usually win.

Trade-ins are another issue. Is the trade-in a reduction in price or a method of payment? The landlord will argue that a trade-in is a payment because you got something of value in return. We argue, "Yeah, we've got inventory which we now have to sell." There is no difference between a trade-in and a credit. It doesn't matter whether it was bought from this store, from another of our stores or from another merchant.

Why buy here? If you have at least two stores, you can try another argument we've had some success with. If one store is in a percentage rent location, the landlord will want all transactions covered. We argue that sales involving short margin dollars—like the $15,000 diamond sale where you'll make maybe $3,000—should be treated differently.

The argument here is, "Look, I've got two stores. I'm at the symphony [or the garden club or the Boy Scouts or a hospital board meeting] and a guy tells me he wants to buy a diamond anniversary necklace for his wife. He wants to spend $15,000. Where do I send him? Do I send him to the mall store, where I've got to pay 6% on the full retail? Or do I send him to another store, where I've got a percentage rate deal or I don't pay percentage rent at all?" That disarms the negotiators, who know they'll get nothing at all if I do the natural thing. They know they have to make a concession on big-ticket sales if they want me to send that necklace buyer to their mall.

Some other transactions should be excluded, too, such as bad debts, layaways until they're delivered, charities, school jewelry (where there's a $5 profit on an $85 class ring), repair business (which truly is done at no profit at all), sales to business at discounts, sales to employees at cost, sales by vendors who come in to do presentations for short profit and have high costs.

What discount? One clause said we had to record something at its full, ticketed price and couldn't take off the discount we gave a customer unless we gave that same discount to every customer. That's a one-price policy; can't make a special price for one person.

I said, "Wait a minute. If we've got an obsolete piece and a chance to sell it for cash, you can't tell me that it's wrong to give someone 10% off for a piece that I'm ready to scrap. Even the American Gem Society won't say that's wrong if you've got this unusual circumstance."

I said, "Go shop in a jewelry store. Find out if you can make a deal on a piece. I'll guarantee that you can buy it for something less in 90% of the stores you go into. And you're telling me you require everyone to pay the full list or a percentage of the full list price?"

This may work for the Gap with its computerized cash register, for people selling clothes. But it doesn't make sense because of the way the jewelry business is done.

Lease % & breakpoint

The big malls are asking for 7% to 10% of total sales volume now, with 5% in the regional shopping centers. We try to define it backwards, and exclude the types of transactions we've discussed.

The percentage starts at what is called a breakpoint. Say your basic rent is $70,000 and your rate is 7%. You divide .07 into the $70,000 and come up with $1 million. That's your breakpoint. And that's where you argue for some relief.

Until your sales hit $1 million, you pay rent of $70,000. At that breakpoint, you start paying 7% of additional sales. What you want to do is extend that to an unnatural breakpoint, so you won't pay any additional rent until you hit, say, $1.2 million. There also is a step breakpoint with a variable percentage. Here you might pay 7% on sales between $1 million and $1.2 million, then 6% for sales between $1.2 million and $1.4 million, and so on. The idea is to lower the percentages as quickly and keep the dollar intervals as small as you can. That's called a stepped percentage with a phased unnatural breakpoint.

How successfully you negotiate the breakpoint depends on how badly the mall really wants you. They need to get their basic rate, but even the big guys often are willing to give you a lower percentage as the sales increase.

Breakpoint problems: The time that your lease starts can be important. We've established that the breakpoint is $1 million, or $83,333 a month. If your sales in any given month exceed $83,333, you'll be subject to percentage rent of 7% of the additional sales.

Jewelry store sales, of course, are concentrated in the last quarter of the year. So if your lease starts in November, you'll certainly have to pay extra percentage rent during the first two months. You'll have to send huge percentage checks to the landlord. And although he says that if you overpay, he will use that as an offset against future months, that's confiscation of cash flow.

To clarify — if you pay percentage rent monthly, you get a credit for 8.3% of the total basic rent because that's 1/2 for each month. In November, when you do 11% of your business, you get an 8.3% credit and end up paying 2.7% extra. In December, when you get 8.3% credit, you do 25% of the business and pay 16.7% extra.

If the lease does start in November and you pay extra in November and December, the landlord will give you credit against future rent payments. But he won't send the cash back. If by next October, at the end of the 12-month period, you haven't made up enough sales, he keeps the money.

If your lease starts Jan. 31, you've got low months where you're doing 4% to 7% or 8% breakpoint. You're going to overpay. That builds up so that when you have to pay for November/December, you get to carry the overpayments forward and don't have to pay anything, or not as much.

When the lease starts, it's up to you whether you agree to monthly or quarterly payments.

Another issue is a short period. Major malls usually want everyone to use a common accounting period, generally ending Jan. 31. if your old lease happens to end or you start up on Oct. 31, they'll want to switch you to a Jan. 31 closing.

So, you'll have 15 months in your first year. You have to make sure the landlord gives you an appropriate base for those 15 months. The base isn't 125%, for a quarter of a year plus a full year; it's 143% because you do 43% of your volume in November, December, January. If you don't do that, you're going to lose out.

Capping your costs: When you're dealing with smaller guys, ask for caps—on escalators, on merchants' association dues, common area maintenance, security, media placement, etc. Ask for half the CPI, the CPI, some arbitrary percentage, whatever.

Four years ago, we negotiated with a local developer for a cap on common area that says the percentage will be between 4% and 11%, but not more than the CPI. With no inflation, he'd still get 4%. But even with hyper inflation or if he had area unrented, 11% would be the maximum increase. We got upside protection; he got downside protection.

We spend a lot of time trying to figure out what our position will be if there is a fire in the mall. The fire may or may not affect our space temporarily or permanently, partially or completely. The landlord decides whether or not you will rebuild and whether the lease continues. But we try to set some parameters. If there is temporary or minor damage to our premises, we want the right to rebuild and to continue the lease.

Don't have a fire: We spend a lot of time trying to figure out what our position will be if there is a fire in the mall. The fire may or may not affect our space temporarily or permanently, partially or completely. The landlord decides whether or not you will rebuild and whether the lease continues. But we try to set some parameters. If there is temporary or minor damage to our premises, we want the right to rebuild and to continue the lease if there's more than two years to go.

The remodeling schedule: Landlords may let you go without remodeling on a seven-year lease, but they'll require you to remodel every five years on a 10-year lease. Remodeling can be as little as change the signs or the carpet or the wall treatment so there's a different look.

Wall treatment costs about $2 a foot; carpet, depending on the quality, is also about $2 a foot. For a 2,000-sq.-ft. store, you're talking $4,000 to $6,000 for carpet, $3,000 for walls and $3,200 for the ceiling. For $15,000 you can make the place look better. You might want to do something with your lighting at the same time. But whatever you do, don't change the ceiling pattern. That's the most expensive thing you can do in any store because you'll get into redistributing the air conditioning and sprinkler systems.

While you can't skip the periodic remodeling, you can negotiate about how much you must do. Fine jewelry stores can argue that this isn't the Gap where we just wheel in some aluminum racks, put plastic milk carton shelving against the wall, and we have a 2-by-4 drop-in ceiling with some fluorescent lights. We're talking about ceilings that are three times more expensive and cases that cost $300 a linear foot without lights. We have huge fixed expenses.

The key is to build a jewelry store that will stand wear and tear and look and be quality. Then you can argue, as we just did, that you've got a huge investment in cherry paneling, walls and cases and it would cost $100,000 to redo all that—two or three times what it would take to redecorate a Gap. Instead, for $25,000, you'll change the carpet, repaint the light cove and put in new signage.

Our landlord bought it, because we had the most beautiful looking store in the place.

Insuring against everything: Insurance is hardly negotiable anymore. The landlord wants you to have rent insurance so he'll get paid if something happens. He wants $5 million of liability. You can get that down to $3 million, but the $1 million that worked in the '70s doesn't count anymore.

You'll need every conceivable kind of insurance he can dream up. There's even disease insurance. Our insurance agent had never heard of it; he called the insurance companies and they said, yeah, that's typical now. And it's not negotiable; you have to be insured against any disease someone might get as a result of visiting your store.

Don't spend a lot of time reading the insurance clause. Send it to your agent. Find out how much more it will cost to comply. Usually, he'll tell you that kind of stuff is covered, so don't worry about it.

The daily grind: Store hours are important. A fine jewelry store can't be open for a midnight madness sale. Every landlord except one has allowed us to adjust hours because this is a fine jewelry operation.

When you talk to them, you have to keep repeating, this business is different. We're not selling handkerchiefs; we're selling emeralds. People making $5 an hour don't sell emeralds; they wait on trade. That's not what goes on in a fine jewelry store. We can't be open more than 11 hours a day. Period. Just can't do it. That's the least to go for. That's 10 a.m. to 9 p.m.

You can try 10 hours—that's 10 to 8—but malls are open longer than that. On Sunday you'll have five hours (12 to 5) or maybe six. Around Thanksgiving and Christmas, the mall will be open 16 hours, but we say we won't be open more than 13 hours a day (9 in the morning to 10 at night) or eight hours on Sunday.
Ask for all legal holidays; little guys will give them to you. The most big guys will give you is Thanksgiving, Christmas, New Years and Easter—and sometimes not even that!

The lease also has to allow us to close for private showings and to do inventory.

Other tenants resent it if we can negotiate shorter hours. But, tough! We have the clout to do it. We're currently in a small strip where the landlord has had so much adverse reaction to our special treatment that now it's non-negotiable. He wants us open every Sunday and six nights a week, not two. When you take the economics of that, the overtime, hiring extra people, fringe benefits and the volume that you do in a stand-alone strip center, it's just not worth doing. So we're leaving.

Common area maintenance: We recently ran into a landlord who wants to include any development costs involved in expanding the shopping center in common area maintenance charges. Say he wants to add a new wing and has to pay an architect $200,000 to draw up plans and present them to the planning commission. He wants to include that in our basic common area charges. My lease negotiator said that was crazy, but word came back that that's the way it is.

Some accountants who used to work for landlords have gone into business on their own. Tenants hire them to audit a landlord's common area bill to be sure it complies with their leases and doesn't include anything it shouldn't. But lease administration told us we couldn't do that. It's OK for them to audit us, but we can't audit them.

The mall adds 15% for administration to our utility, central fresh air supply and exhaust system charges. We try to change that to 0% because it doesn't cost anything to pro rate the bills; they just put it in a computer spreadsheet and it's done.

Some public utility commissions allow malls to act as utilities themselves. They buy power wholesale and sell it at prevailing public utility rate. This doesn't cost us any more, but the mall makes money on it. We have argued that gives them added responsibility. We need power at all times to maintain security. If we lose security, our insurance policy requires that we hire a guard to be in the store 24 hours a day, which costs $50 an hour. We want them to pay for that. But while they're happy to make money as an ersatz public utility, they won't pay us if they make a mistake.

Whose advertising? We've always been successful in limiting how much we must put into mall advertising by proving that we do our own. We argue that we spend 3% to 5% of store sales on advertising the mall, because we have their logo in our ads. They don't want us to stop our own advertising, but they want us in theirs as well. We say we can't afford to do both. Besides, we say, "Look at the last mall leaflet you sent out and then look at our advertising. We can't be in these recycled earth paper things put out by the weekly press; that's not our image."

Default: This is one of the most important points lease negotiation. Always argue for the right and the time to cure any problems that can cause you to lose your lease. Standard leases aren't written that way.

Say you had an electrician install new lighting. The lights he bought are defective and don't work, so you didn't pay him. He wants the money because he has to pay his supplier , so he files a lien on the property to protect his security interest. If you don't cure the mechanics lien within 30 days, you've violated your lease and they can kick you out. You need to negotiate a right to cure, and ask for 120 days to do it. Then if you make a good faith attempt, there is no default.

One time we forgot to file a report with the State of Connecticut. This is a $60 report filed every two years; you just have to send in a computer card. A secretary put the card in a file and forgot it, so we lost our status as a corporation in good standing. That meant default of the lease. We should have a right to cure that.
If you're late sending a rent payment, that's a default. If you catch up and pay it, you've cured the default.

Some things are beyond your control. If the government puts your payroll deposit tax in the wrong account, I challenge you to fix that within five days. It takes months. Meanwhile, you could be in default .

The provisions for cure in most leases are very limited. You want to expand the scope so that if you react within a reasonable time, or are in the process of doing so, that's not a default.

Your store next door: Leases usually won't allow you to put another store within five or seven miles of a mall. We argue for two miles.

Legally, you probably don't even need to argue because this is restraint of trade. But you don't want to go through the legal expense involved in fighting. (Indeed, you should always try to avoid litigation with landlords.

They probably have on-staff legal departments to handle these things, while you have to hire a lawyer at $100 an hour.) So I argue right here that it's not legitimate anyway. If we want to put another store in within two miles, that's our problem. We usually go for two miles, and get it.

Taking out the trash: You usually can't arrange for your own trash removal in a mall. But you should have a right to be sure that the trash removal you must participate in costs no more than you would pay on your own.

Parking: Landlords often require tenants to park in designated areas, which makes a lot a sense. They don't want all the tenants right around the entrance. But we've argued successfully that we need two nearby spaces because of the nature of our business and the high security required. That way, employees who come and go with high-value merchandise don't have to traipse through low security areas.

Sign language: I have a lease here that says any signs in the store that are visible from the mall must be approved by the landlord. He wants control of the aesthetics. We can negotiate that because we have a 15-year track history and the landlord knows the quality and credit of Michaels.

But signs should be in keeping with the mall's overall image. If I were a landlord and wanted a discount mall, fine. I'd have a discount mall. If I wanted a theme, I'd have a theme. But if I wanted a super regional quality mall, then I wouldn't want signage which runs counter to that image. I can understand that. The trouble is that they don't police it.

Do not enter: We usually get a stop on right of entry in the lease. We say, "Fine. If you want to go into the store when we're not there, you have to accept responsibility for the inventory. " All the little guys say, no, I don't want to go into your store, so I won't be responsible.

JCK Management Study Center Quiz

1. The anchor tenant in your mall fails to pay its monthly share of common area expenses. Unless you have a specific clause in your lease which exempts you from any liability, is it probable that you and other small tenants will be required to pay the landlord the cash the anchor did not pay?

    Yes ❏   No ❏

2. Mall landlords usually want a CPA to certify your sales, at your expense. If the store's top officers agree to swear to the accuracy of their sales reports, under penalty of perjury if they have given false information, is the landlord likely to waive the CPA requirement?

    Yes ❏   No ❏

3. When you negotiate for a mall lease, it's critical to have an experienced advisor. Which of the following is likely to be of most help?
    a. Your own attorney
    b. The president of your state jewelers' association
    c. A person recommended by the International Council of Shopping Centers
    d. Your mother-in-law

4. Is it true or false that what you've been able to negotiate in past leases is a clue to what will be negotiable in the future?
    True ❏   False ❏

5. Which of the following transactions should you try to have excluded from the total you report to the mall?
    a. Low-margin transactions
    b. Specials offered as part of a mall-wide promotion
    c. Trade-ins
    d. Returns
    e. Sales on which you give a special discount to a friend or family member

6. What is your breakpoint?
    a. The moment when you and the landlord decide you can't agree on a lease
    b. The halfway mark in your lease

    c. The sales mark at which you start paying a percentage on additional sales
    d. The point at which discounted sales begin to count in your total

7. If your landlord agreed to a stepped percentage with a phased unnatural breakpoint, would this most likely be to your financial advantage or disadvantage?
    Advantage ❏   Disadvantage ❏

8. On a 10-year mall lease, a landlord almost certainly will demand that you remodel your store at some point during the lease. A fine jewelry store with good fixtures should be able to avoid a total makeover. Instead, the landlord may well accept new carpeting and new wall treatments. What is likely to be the cost of an acceptable remodeling of a 2,000 sq. ft. store?
    a. $10,000   b. $25,000   c. $50,000   d. $120,000

9. Disease insurance is one of the newest "extras" to come along. Is this a good issue to try to negotiate out of your lease contract?
    Yes ❏   No ❏

10. If you don't want to participate in the mall's regular advertising, will you usually be able to drop out provided you can prove that you did your own advertising as a mall store?
    Yes ❏   No ❏

11. How important is it to make sure that your lease provides you with adequate time to cure a default?
    a. Extremely important   b. Somewhat important
    c. Slightly important   d. Not important at all

12. A rule of thumb says you ought to have a minimum annual sales volume to make it profitable to operate a mall jewelry store. Which of the following figures represents a realistic minimum?
    a. $500,000   b. $1,000,000
    c. $2,500,000   d. $4,000,000

(Answers to Quiz can be found at the end of this chapter)

Making Displays Work

September 1993

Kurt Merchant is putting more show into the showcases at his two Jacques Jewelers stores in Martinsville, Va.

In July, he hired a design student from a local college to create an eye-catching pearl display case. The result was a display with oyster-shaped baskets spray-painted black and draped with pearls. "It looks interesting," says Merchant. "If it works, I may do more custom showcases."

Merchant says some retailers are attuned to changing showcase displays to maintain consumers' interest. Others spend far more time buying and selling merchandise than creating new ways to display it. But as competition and economic factors combined to dampen sales in the past two years, many more jewelers have started to consider how creative displays can entice consumers to look and buy.

Bottom line effect: "I see retailers becoming a lot more aware of how differences in their store displays affect their bottom lines," says Robert Sherman, president of Bates Display & Packaging, Corona, Cal. "If the displays are not sending a message to the customer, the jeweler is not going to get the sale."

What types of displays are jewelers buying?

The current color favorite is European-inspired white or off-white. White displays used to be hard to maintain because they showed fingerprints easily. But that was before the creation of white Leatherette, a vinyl material that resembles leather and is easily cleaned with a damp cloth. "Over the years, most displays were not easy to clean," says Ed Barks, president of Freehold Display & Packaging, Mukilteo, Wash. "If they got dirty, they were either recovered or thrown away. Now we have something in white that is going to stay clean." (Barks' firm also has sold small numbers of white velvet displays, but he says most retailers avoid it because of the soil factor.)

Manufacturers say many of the latest white displays sport accents ranging from green to teal to black. In fact, solid white may already have peaked. "My impression is that white Leatherette was a fad used by high-end retailers," says Gerald Farnell of the Chicago Design Group, Northbrook, Ill. Ruth Mellergaard, a partner in International Design Group, New York, N.Y., agrees that white will become less popular and predicts that light colors with darker trims will replace the unicolored look.

Among the popular lighter tints are green, gray and pink, says Larry Letz, president of National Box & Display Inc., Spencer, Iowa.

Interest also is rising in multicolored displays, says David Maynard, divisional vice president at International Packaging Corp., Pawtucket, R.I. Retailers often create background scenes using darker colors and place jewelry on lighter-hued props or standard display forms, he says. "We had one retailer recently create a polo playing field in the background of a display case while the jewelry was moved toward the front," he says.

Beyond the rainbow: Even more critical than color is knowing how to arrange displays, says Letz. "Showing tray after tray is not an appropriate way to highlight jewelry," he says. "We see independent jewelers using more individualized display pieces. Instead of showing 15 chains on a tray, they'll show one on a bust display."

By highlighting a few choice pieces, Merchant says he can focus customers' eyes and spark interest in a particular style. He often places a larger, pricier "centerpiece" item among several smaller pieces, leaving the remaining space empty. "Many employees are afraid of that empty space and try to fill it," he says. "But that would just look like a lot of jewelry was set in a case without any real feel to it."

Adds Herb Schottland, owner of Store Design and Fixturing, Fairfax, Va.: "Jewelers used to cram the showcases; now they let the customer take time to really look at a few select items."

A display with a centerpiece establishes a hierarchy for the customer by capturing a wandering eye. Varying the height of each piece or group of pieces is equally critical. "If the elevation is the same throughout the case, the eye gets tired," says Sherman of Bates Display.

Some jewelers prefer to group items by type; others advocate showing an ensemble. Farnell prefers the latter approach. "My clients tell me it helps to sell the merchandise," he says. "They'll do a setting and show an ensemble that tells the story. The merchandise looks more exciting, and it allows a salesperson to talk with the customer sooner by offering to tell the story of the ensemble." The salesperson can bring out other pieces later if needed.

Tell the story, try a prop: Using displays to tell a story is important, says Andrew Macaulay, director of advertising and communications for Chippenhook, Lewisville, Tex. Macaulay, a frequent lecturer on showcase and window design, recommends eye-catching displays that are coordinated with store advertising and decor.

"A prop used to promote a particular seasonal sale or in-store event should be smaller inside the store than in window displays," he says. "And the prop, whatever it is, should be included in the store's newspaper or television ads so there is continuity in the story." Such a unified theme makes it easy for the customer to recognize, he says.

"Big chain stores coordinate their displays and ads all the time," he says. "Small stores rarely have an ad manager or store designer to do the same.

Starting Your Own
Estate Jewelry Department

Mark Moeller ◆ *August 1993 Part I*

Developing an in-store estate and antique jewelry department offers benefits as plentiful as the one-of-a-kind pieces you're likely to discover—literally in your own backyard. Your present customers have untold treasures hidden in their bureau drawers; so do the new customers you can expect to attract by branching into this specialty of the jewelry trade.

The most immediate benefit is the increase in sales you'll enjoy from your existing clients. More and more jewelry customers are coming to expect the full-service jeweler to buy and sell fine antique and estate pieces. This additional service helps strengthen the relationships on which a knowledgeable jeweler builds his or her invaluable client base.

The most dramatic sales growth, however, will come from the additional clients you attract. Who are they likely to be? Extensive marketing studies conducted for our store by students in the Small Business Department at the University of St. Thomas, St. Paul, Minn., produce this profile: they're largely female (70%), ages 40-60 (73%), highly educated and decidedly upscale. A lesser but still significant percentage represents the up-and-coming younger market (ages 25-40) on which the future of your business must be based.

R.F. Moeller Jeweler was a comparatively small player in the retail jewelry trade when we launched our estate and antique jewelry business in 1978. At the time, we were doing about $300,000 in annual sales out of a 500-sq.-ft. store in a commercial strip in the heart of an upper-middle-income neighborhood of St. Paul, Minn.

Today, we occupy 4,400 sq. ft. in the same commercial strip and enjoy annual sales of more than $2 million. One third of that growth is due directly to our entry into the estate and antique jewelry trade, thanks in part to the increased margins these pieces offer and in part to the 40% increase in our customer count attributable to estate and antique jewelry sales.

When wading into uncharted waters, it's always wise to navigate using the KISS Theory (Keep It Simple, Stupid). Our own entrée was almost embarrassing in its simplicity. We just contacted various estate and antique jewelry suppliers about doing a trunk show in our store, advertised the event in a local paper and opened the door. The response was overwhelming and we were soon on our way, carving out an exciting and profitable new market niche.

The following are just a few rules of thumb that we've found to be helpful in developing an estate and antique jewelry department:

1. Start small, one piece at a time if need be.
2. Develop a marketing strategy with specific, measurable goals and ways to track progress toward their achievement.
3. Establish a separate budget for all advertising and promotion tied specifically to estate and antique jewelry sales.
4. Allocate a percentage of all fixed costs to your new department so you can readily determine when you're making a true profit and when you're just turning dollars.

Honing your expertise in the estate and antique jewelry trade is anything but simple. It's vital that you thoroughly understand the universally recognized periods of antique jewelry. Because no organization similar to the Gemological Institute of America has the expressed mission of imparting knowledge in the heritage jewelry field, the store's owner and employees carry the burden for acquiring that expertise solely on their own shoulders. The learning process can be expedited, however, by attending pertinent seminars and courses.

We have found the following three educational alternatives to be especially time- and cost-effective:
1. The University of Maine Antique and Period Jewelry Seminars held each July in Orono, Me.
2. Courses and lectures offered by such nationally recognized experts as Joyce Jonas, Lael Hagan, Christie Romero and Janet Zapata.
3. Seminars sponsored by the American Gem Society and conducted at its annual Conclave.

Organizations such as the International Society of Appraisers and the American Society of Appraisers offer courses in the field. Subscribing to any number of auction house catalogs and, of course, reading the *Heritage* section in JCK also will provide an armchair education.

Though most of the pieces you'll find within their pages will never make their way across your counter, comparative appraisals still provide you with a good working knowledge of how much to pay—and how much to charge—for fine period jewelry.

If you can afford the tuition, the School of Hard Knocks also offers a valuable education in buying or selling. The fact is, you're likely to learn far more from your magnificent failures than from your magnificent successes. It's truly startling how much knowledge you'll retain when you find you've paid way too much for an item or inadvertently acquired a reproduction that you thought was an original.

Acquiring pieces: Buying from trusted antique jewelry suppliers is the least risky way to enter the trade, especially if your shop operates without an on-site repair facility. Virtually none of the pieces you'll acquire from these suppliers will need restoration, whereas nearly half of pieces bought over the counter require some repair work to maximize their price potential. Of course, the profit margins you'll enjoy from over-the-counter purchases are considerably greater than those from suppliers.

If you do choose to buy over the counter, it's imperative that you check with state and local officials to be sure you comply with all governmental statutes applicable to previously owned jewelry. Many state and municipal governments require you to buy a precious metals dealer's license and hold the pieces you buy for a specified time. Consult your local government office.

It's also extremely important to develop a comprehensive purchase agreement and warranty of title and authority. Such documentation will tell you where the bulk of your buys are coming from, how much you're able to realize as an average return on investment from your promotional efforts and how best to target your future marketing strategies.

Another compelling reason to develop a good purchase agreement is the possibility you may inadvertently acquire a piece of stolen property. The problem more or less takes care of itself when you require the seller to provide photo identification and sign off on numerous "herebys," "hold-harmlesses" and other legal niceties.

Advertising your desire to buy is a must if you hope to generate significant estate and antique jewelry sales. In fact, buying can be much harder than selling at first. It certainly was for me. A simple, straightforward ad in your local yellow pages will bring in numerous pieces, as will constant classified advertising in the targeted areas you deem to be most responsive to your offer to buy.

To track actual demand in your local market area, it's wise to develop a waiting list for the kinds of pieces your clients request. That list will prove invaluable in making buying decisions and setting selling prices.

Should you discover there's little local market for some pieces you've acquired, other markets are always available. Early on, I recognized a dual dilemma in our business: not enough of certain kinds of pieces and too many of others. Research, however, showed us that many other antique jewelry dealers had similar problems in other markets. To even the score, we spun off a separate wholesaling subsidiary called The Registry Ltd.

The Registry became an effective clearinghouse for matching supply to demand in markets across the country. For internal reasons we have since folded the wholesale business back into our retail operation, but that marketing network still exists and continues to pay dividends by moving pieces to markets where they are most desirable.

Perhaps the most common concern of those thinking about starting up an over-the-counter antique and estate jewelry department is: "How can I possibly buy a piece from a regular customer, mark it up, put it in my display case and offer it for resale?"

You must understand that most of those who sell to you do not necessarily tend to buy from you. But when it does happen, as it surely will, we have found our clients to be universally understanding. As long as we've dealt ethically and honestly with them in making the buy, they understand our need to make a profit on the resale. In any event, we have found the advantages of providing the service of over-the-counter purchases outweigh any potential disadvantages.

Maximizing sales: As alluded to previously, buying estate and antique jewelry presents a far greater challenge than selling it. At the same time, some tricks of the trade can maximize resales and minimize turnover time.

The in-store display of antique pieces is especially crucial. Just because you have developed a good working knowledge of period jewelry, don't assume that your clients, or potential clients, have done the same.

Set aside some display space with good visibility. Identify the pieces you set out by the historic eras they represent. If the piece has significant provenance you can prove (i.e., it was owned by someone famous or manufactured by Tiffany, Cartier, etc.), be sure to document it. Don't be shy about promoting this aspect. There's a story behind each of the antique pieces you sell and the associated romance adds tremendous value—for you and your customer.

Turning your next sale into a special event will generate by far the biggest return on your promotional dollar. R.F. Moeller Jeweler recently conducted its eighth annual holiday show and sale of estate and antique jewelry, an event that continues to get bigger and better every year. Though we do it up a little differently each time by creating a new theme, the show always involves supplementing our own extensive stock with more than $2 million worth of antique pieces brought in from other suppliers for this exclusive five-day showing.

On the sale's first evening, we stay open three hours later than normal for our 6,000 "preferred customers," each of whom receives a personal invitation in the mail. Appropriate entertainment is booked (this year, a trio performing 18th-century works on period instruments); a spread of hors d'oeuvres, wine and nonalcoholic beverages is provided; a doorman in top hat is in place; and salespeople are decked out in their holiday best.

It's become the highlight of the holiday shopping season in these parts, thanks in no small measure to the complimentary gift (such as a sterling silver snowflake pendant on a chain) we present to all preferred customers who deign to drop by. This year's count: 430 customers in just three hours.

The show and sale, as promoted in the local papers, are open to the general public for the next four days. Sales consistently outstrip anything we ever used to see over the entire preholiday period. As a side benefit, we are helping our rapidly growing customer base acquire the knowledge to match their discriminating taste in fine estate and antique jewelry.

And demand just keeps growing, with no sign of ebbing. In fact, there's every indication the potential for this relatively new field of jewelry merchandising remains largely untapped.

Why the burgeoning interest? I see two reasons, both based on the jewelry customer's changing demands.

First, the romance of bygone eras, captured so exquisitely in the jewelry of the time, increasingly captures the public's imagination. Call it nostalgia if you will, but there's no question that interest in these treasures of yesteryear plays a growing role in jewelry marketing.

Second, and perhaps more to the point, jewelry buyers increasingly appreciate the value unique to estate and antique pieces. They recognize that most of this jewelry simply could not be duplicated today— partly because of the prohibitive costs involved, but also because much of the craftsmanship that went into their creation died with those who made them.

Tapping into this appeal of antique and period jewelry is a challenge for even the most motivated jeweler, requiring a great deal of time and effort. But those with sufficient drive and desire will find their investment in the past paying dividends well into the future.

Sampler of Regional Tastes

Tastes vary by region. What sells well in one area may not move in another. This applies to all discretionary purchases, but perhaps more so to such uniquely personal items as antique, period and estate jewelry. Here is a broad breakdown of regional tastes garnered from 15 years in the trade:

Midwest—Because of this region's Scandinavian background and conservative nature, Victorian jewelry is especially popular.

Northeast—This area tends to be more avant garde, so styles with a more dramatic flair do well. Art Nouveau and Art Deco are particularly popular.

South—Conservative styles are in demand. Larger, lower-color diamonds sell well, especially in Florida.

Southwest—Bigger, flashier pieces seem popular. Jewelry styles from the 1950s move well, and large total-weight white gold and platinum bracelets and earrings are in vogue.

West—Anything with a natural motif, regardless of period, appears to sell well. Jade is especially popular in California, because of its large Asian population. Southern California is a market unto itself where big showy pieces do well. Because of the strong Art Deco architectural influences in and around Southern California, Art Deco jewelry is immensely popular.

Northwest—Victorian jewelry sells well in this relatively conservative area.

Antique and Period Jewelry References

Selections with asterisks are available from the Jewelers' Book Club, *Jewelers' Circular-Keystone*, Chilton Way, Radnor, Pa. 19089; (215) 964-4490/4480. Check libraries or used-book stores for books that are out of print.

American and European Jewelry 1830-1914, Charlotte Gere.

American Jewelry, Glamour and Tradition, Penny Proddow & Deborah Healy.

An Introduction to Sentimental Jewellery, Shirley Bury.

Antique and Twentieth-Century Jewellery: A Guide for Collectors, Vivienne Becker.

Art Deco, A Guide for Collectors, Katherine McClinton.

Art Nouveau and Art Deco Jewelry: An Identification & Value Guide, Lilian Baker.

Art Nouveau Jewelry, Dr. Joseph Sataloff.

Art Nouveau Jewellery & Fans, Gabriel Mourey.

Art Nouveau Style in Jewelry, Metalwork, Glass, Ceramics, Textiles, Architecture and Furniture, Roberta Waddell, editor.

Benedictus' Art Deco Design, introduction by Charles Rahn Fry.

Bradbury's Book of Hallmarks: A Guide to Marks of Origin on British & Irish Silver, 1544 to 1989, originally compiled by Frederick Bradbury, F.S.A.

Collecting Antique Jewelry, Mona Curran.

Collecting Victorian Jewelry, Mary Peter.

Greek and Roman Jewelry, Reynold Higgins.

History of Jewels and Jewelry, Ingrid Kuntzch.

A History of Jewelry, J. Anderson Black (formerly *The Story of Jewelry*).

An Illustrated Dictionary of Jewelry, Harold Newman.

International Hallmarks on Silver Collected, published by Tardy.

Jewellery, Graham Hughes (out of print).

Jewelry from 1900 to 1980, Schmuckmuseum.

Jewelry: History and Techniques from the Egyptians to the Present, Guido Gregorietti (out of print).

Jewelry Through the Ages, Guido Gregorietti (out of print).

Jewelry Through 7000 Years, published by Barron.

Magical Jewels of the Middle Ages and the Renaissance, Joan Evans.

Official 1992 Price Guide to Antique Jewelry, Arthur Guy Kaplan.

Old Jewelry, 1840-1850, Jeanenne Bell.

100 Years of Collectible Jewelry, (1850-1950): An Identification & Value Guide, Lilian Baker.

Original Art Deco Design, William Rowe.

Poinçons d'Or et de Platine, published by Tardy.

The Price Guide to Jewellery: 3000 B.C.-1950 A.D., Michael Poynder.

Renaissance Jewellery, Yvonne Hackenbroch.

Rings Through the Ages, Ward, Cherry, Gere and Cartlidge.

Victorian Jewellery, Nancy Armstrong (out of print).

Victorian Jewellery, Margaret Flowers (out of print).

Victorian Jewellery Design, Charlotte Gere.

19th Century Jewelry, Peter Hicks (out of print).

Bridal Registries: Pain Or Gain?

August 1993 Part I

No matter what the state of the economy, people will get married. While jewelers have always profited from this truism with engagement and wedding ring sales, some also try to capitalize on a greater segment of the bridal market.

The traditional route to the other-than-ring market has been bridal registries—where bride and groom list items they would like well-wishers to buy for them. But the past three decades have seen many changes in the retail jewelry industry and in the way people shop for bridal gifts.

High rents and a need for faster inventory turn have forced many jewelers to cede tableware and some giftware sales to department stores. And numerous jewelers JCK contacted in a spot check in June—the traditional wedding month—did not advise starting a bridal registry now. "It would be like starting a totally new store because registry items are so different from jewelry," says Eleanor Woodruff of J.E. Caldwell Co. in Philadelphia, Pa. The cost of stocking multiple patterns and the space for storage and display would be a major undertaking, she says.

Jewelers also say jewelry stores are not positioned well in the minds of young adults. Most of today's brides and grooms grew up shopping in department and self-service stores. Thorpe and Co. of Sioux City, Iowa, has a successful gift/tabletop operation. But Vice President Karen Thorpe says she still has to educate bridal couples. "It's hard for them to shop in jewelry stores," she says. Couple this with the fact they can register *all* their household items—from stemware to bath mats—at one time in department stores.

This is not to say bridal registries can't succeed in today's jewelry stores. If you have the space, resources and clientele, you can capture more business from wedding ring customers by offering the quality, service and customized selection that bigger stores can't. Wayne Jewelers & Silversmiths, a well-established store on Philadelphia's well-heeled Main Line, does very well with its bridal registry. "For many customers, registering at our store has been a family tradition for generations," says the firm's Jennie St. Clair.

J.M. Edward Fine Jewelry and Diamonds, Cary, N.C., is considering starting a bridal registry as part of an expansion. J.M. Edward feels he "can fill a niche [with a bridal registry] by offering a level of service lacking in department stores." He also feels Southeasterners are interested in the traditional bridal items he offers.

Jewelers say there are other ways to take advantage of the bridal market, too. One involves extensive promotion of fine jewelry as gifts that the bride and groom can give to their attendants, their parents and each other. "This is a good, safe middle ground between a full service bridal department and nothing," says Woodruff.

In recognition of this non-registry bridal market, the National Bridal Service, Richmond, Va., just extended membership to jewelry stores without bridal registries. NBS President Gary Wright recognizes there's a bridal market beyond tabletop items and wants to help these new members capitalize on it by sharing expertise on education, marketing and promotion.

New Luster For Strip Centers

June 1993

Remember when strip shopping centers became poor cousins to enclosed malls? When consumers eagerly spent hours exploring the wide variety of stores gathered under the big roof of a regional mall? When some retailers abandoned downtowns and strip centers to bask in the high-volume traffic of big malls?

Well, the 1960s have turned into the 1990s, and strip centers are starting to lure back the retailers they lost over the past three decades. The centers—which typically offer daily-living goods such as foods and drugs as well as personal services and specialty items—are growing more important for two primary reasons:

• Lower rents and fewer restrictions than malls.

• They attract customers who are more focused on what they want to buy and demand the convenience that malls can't always provide.

Lower rent is a major advantage, says Michael Beyard, senior director of research for the Urban Land Institute, Washington, D.C. "Regional malls charge more to support larger common areas, a higher level of design and—quite often—parking structures," he says. Jewelry stores paid a median $12.78 per square foot in rent at strip centers and $33.88 at regional malls in 1990, according to the latest figures available from the institute.

Restrictions—including advertising and when the store should be open—are another factor with malls, says Rod Miyata, owner of Ace of Diamonds, which has been in a Los Angeles strip center for nine years.

There are other advantages, say retailers.

Customers go to strip center stores to buy—not to pass time, says Miyata. They like the convenience of not having to drive a distance to a regional mall, being able to park close to the store and not having to walk through an entire mall just to find one item.

Strip-center jewelers say they can spend more time with their customers and have fewer security concerns because they don't have to contend with the heavier traffic of a mall. Some say they also attract a better clientele. "Mall shoppers tend to look for off-price and promotional-quality item," says Joe Bilyk, vice president of Leon's Jewelery, which combined three stores (downtown, strip center and mall) in a new strip center in Exton, Pa., last year. "Strip center shoppers look for value and quality. Customers have more faith in a jeweler out of the mall than in a mall."

Is a strip center ideal for every jeweler? Those who sell on price alone will find more comparison shoppers in a mall, says Beyard. And if the only strip center in town is in an undesirable area or has an undesirable mix of stores, customers will shy away from it, says Bilyk. But strip centers are a good way for independent jewelers to distinguish themselves from the big chains that populate malls and attract time-strapped customers whose fascination with big malls is gone.

Superstores Find Size An Advantage

January 1993

In this era of downsizing, some jewelers have found the opposite is the best strategy. JCK asked heads of several jewelry "superstores" why bigger can be better.

"One of our biggest advantages is the selection of merchandise," says Donald Yale of Borsheim's, Omaha, Neb. "We're satisfying a desire, not a necessity, so it's important to answer customer's desires."

"Inventory, service, selection and price," says Robert Smyth Jr. of Albert Smyth & Co., Timonium, Md. "Service is an extremely big part of any business these days, and that's where we shine."

"The public can see the entire inventory of the entire company," echoes Gary Gordon of Samuel Gordon Jewelers, Oklahoma City. Gordon also found distinct advantages in combining his former three stores into a 10,000-sq.-ft. consolidated "superstore"—namely, a drastic drop in overhead expenses and a significantly easier time managing one store instead of three.

"In the old days, if a good customer asked for me in one store and I was in another, it was at least 20 minutes before I could get there," he says. "Now I'm here and I can better serve the customer." Having one store also makes sales training and sales huddles easier. The new store opened in November 1990, and sales have risen 16% over the same relative period before the move, he says.

Like Samuel Gordon, Borsheim's growth in space spurred a tremendous growth in sales. Yale attributes most of the growth to the change in location. Seven years ago, Borsheim's had 7,500 sq. ft. and 35 full-time employees at a downtown location. Now it has 37,000 sq. ft. and 220 full-time employees in an enclosed minimall on the city's west end.

"Being in a smaller location really hindered our ability to grow, plus downtown Omaha wasn't easily accessible," he says. At the new store, Borsheim's gets close to 4,000 visits a day during the holiday season.

Smyth & Co., meanwhile, grew more slowly. "There were no big changes, just steady growth over three generations," says Robert Smyth Jr. "Having a freestanding store is neither an advantage nor disadvantage, but location matters. Luckily, this is a good location."

Smyth says the downside of having only one store (with 7,500 sq. ft.) is that some customers don't shop as often as they might if they had a branch store closer. But the firm has an aggressive mail- and telephone-order business and nationally distributed catalog. So does Borsheim's.

Another disadvantage, says Gordon, is that some vendors hesitate to do business with a single store. "They come to Oklahoma City and decide they are better off selling to our competition because they have more stores than we do," he says. "But it's a mistaken idea that more units necessarily mean more sales. It's not how many stores you have, it's how you market yourself."

Yale doesn't see many disadvantages to superstores, other than logistics. There's that much more merchandise to take out, put away and keep track of, he says, but a good computer system helps. Staffing a large store is another consideration. Borsheim's has an entire department devoted to training employees.

The idea of a superstore is not lost on traditional mall retailers either. The granddaddy of all mall jewelers, Zale, opened a superstore five years ago at The Citadel in Colorado Springs, Colo. Actually, Zale took one of its stores that had operated there for 14 years and converted stock

area into selling space, virtually doubling selling space without doubling the lease cost.

Though at 2,300 sq. ft., this Zale store is one-third the size of Smyth & Co. and one-fourth the size of Samuel Gordon Jewelers, it's more than twice as large as most other Zale stores. Additionally, the renovations included breaking the "threshold barrier" by opening the store on two sides and extending the marble floor from the lease line deep into the interior. Staff also is three times larger than Zale's normal one manager and five associates.

The Citadel branch survived a wave of downsizing in early 1992; Zale executives couldn't be reached for comment about the store's success.

Focus On Fixtures

October 1992

Fixtures—including showcases and lighting—are more than basic necessities for a store. They are essential elements in its image and marketing.

"The best-looking jewelry stores have something in common: a look that is cohesive, fully finished, with a continuity in style," says David Baker of Baker Store Equipment Co. in Cleveland, Ohio. Fixture manufacturers, suppliers and store planners polled by JCK agree.

Yet many jewelers buy the wrong fixtures, scrimp on expenditures or can't find reliable sources. Others treat fixtures as "isolated from store planning when they really should consider them part of the whole planning process," says veteran store designer MariAnn Coutchie of Woodland, California. "They're selling the most expensive product in the market so it behooves them to buy the best fixtures."

The following report offers practical advice on buying fixtures, with a look at trends for the '90s.

Buying Fixtures: 10 Easy Steps

Buying and installing fixtures is as easy as counting from one to ten. Here's how the experts say to do it.

1. Pinpoint your store image. What clientele do you serve? Is yours a small shop for browsers or one designed for upscale, sit-down business?

Your fixtures—lighting, cases, pads, wall hangers, counter lights and other items—should appeal to the market you've chosen and be consistent with your merchandise and price points. A store in an affluent market might use custom-made hardwood cases for example, while one catering to a blue-collar market might opt for metal cases with exterior laminate finishes.

2. Make a floor plan and/or fixture layout. Indicate location and measurements of cases and lighting. This allows you to relate fixture to traffic flow and thus avoid common mistakes such as buying fixture with the wrong dimensions, putting them in the wrong spot of misplacing ceiling lighting. (For example, ceiling lights should be mounted above the

leading edge of showcases so the angle of reflected glare from glass is on the salesperson, not the customer.)

3. Be informed; don't buy or renovate haphazardly. Get information about fixtures' effects on merchandise and store design from suppliers, store designers, trade associations and other retailers.

In lighting, for example, there are real differences between halogen and fluorescent lamps, both used in showcases. Low-voltage halogen lighting penetrates gems, enhances their color and makes them sparkle. But these lamps are spaced in a row with just a few inches between them, so they can produce enough heat to dry out watches or cause gems to crack unless the case has small ventilation holes. Fluorescent lamps are more cost-effective but produce diffused "flood" lighting . This makes jewelry look flat and can create a "downmarket" atmosphere if not planned correctly.

In addition, a jeweler can cut ceiling lighting need in half by lowering and/or using hanging fixtures, says George Halvatzis of Econo-Lite Products, Jersey City, N.J. A fixture lowered from 9' to 6.5', for example, gives three times as much light. Jewelers can get such information easily from lighting and fixture suppliers.

4. Set a realistic budget but don't focus on cost alone. Experts say this is the biggest error jewelers make in buying or renovating fixtures. "Too many jewelers' decisions about fixtures are made on price alone," says Brian Viger, vice president of marketing for Trinity Engineering, Rohnert Park, Cal. "They don't even consider durability, ease of use or design integrity [with the rest of the store]."

Trying to save a buck can backfire. Cheap materials wear out quickly, fade or scar easily. Non-UL lamps may be unreliable. (Underwriters' Laboratory Inc. is an independent organization that tests electrical equipment and appliances for safety and quality. Products that meet UL standards carry a UL approval tag, logo or sticker.) And hiring a "handyman" friend to build or renovate cases can cost more in the long run, says Keely A. Grice III of Grice Showcase & Display Manufacturing Co., Charlotte, N.C. A freelancer unfamiliar with the jewelry trade may cut corners on security and display.

On the other hand, don't buy what you don't need. Some jewelers insist on extensive storage space under showcases when buying for new stores, says Keith Kovar, director of the International Design Group Inc., New York, N.Y. "Yet when I visit them after the store has been open some time, the drawers are usually empty or full of junk. Drawer space is costly to build into cases. A jeweler should look closely at, and budget for, real needs."

5. For large jobs ($100,000+), get a few bids but don't overdo it. "There's an over-reliance on bidding rather than negotiating with a few reliable fixture suppliers," says Bernard Whalen, executive director of the National Association of Store Fixture Manufacturers, Plantation, Fla. "Many assume they'll get a better deal by picking the lowest bids from a lot of firms. But what often happens is they compare apples and oranges or go with a guy who low-balls his bid to get the job, then cuts corners and quality."

6. Get the right fixtures for the right uses! Sit-down cases, for example, are best used with higher-end goods such as diamonds, rings and luxury watches. Wall cases are best for high-visibility items such as giftware, for small stores with little or no space for showcases or for high-volume mall stores where customers can walk up to inspect merchandise.

Pay attention to case dimensions. Many jewelers buy cases that are too deep or too shallow to display jewelry well, say suppliers. And when cases aren't high enough, build-ups won't fit or are easily knocked over when a salesperson reaches inside for jewelry.

Consider what types of in-case and outside lighting will enhance your merchandise and store mood. Convenience counts, too. Remember that track lighting is more versatile and flexible than recessed ceiling lighting because it can be positioned for changing displays and lamps can be added or subtracted.

7. Use professional help. If you're doing a major renovation or opening, retain a store planner, at least as a consultant. He or she will help you to choose between custom-made and catalog-standard fixtures and decide on materials, lighting placement and other issues. Professional advice is useful even if you plan only to refurbish cases or lighting.

Deal only with reputable, reliable manufacturers, suppliers, store designers and lighting consultants—and be sure they are familiar with jewelers' needs. Locate them through trade magazine ads, shows or referrals.

8. Set a time-frame for purchase, production and installation. Manufacturers need time to produce fixtures and ensure they meet your size and space specifications. Too often, say suppliers, retailers wait until the last minute to order, then demand customized options that take weeks.

Be sure your fixtures agreement includes schedule clauses specifying time of delivery and installation. "Progress payments" are recommended for jobs lasting several months, says Whalen, of the National Association of Store Fixture Manufacturers. This gives manufacturers some money to work and gives the retailer more control.

9. Do your fixtures meet the needs of the disabled? The new Americans with Disabilities Act requires easy access to businesses serving the public. This can affect the location and type of fixtures, register stands, counters and even door pulls you use.

Ecological issues likewise have become important to store design. In fact, the Institute of Store Planners has created a Retail Environmental Action Committee to identify products that create a non-toxic retail environment. REAC urges use of paint, carpeting and carpet-padding glues with low VOCs (volatile organic compounds that affect eyes and breathing); development of alternatives to vinyl wall coverings (which release hydrocarbons) and no use of endangered tropical hardwoods (some cities and states ban tropical hardwoods in government-funded projects and are expected to start banning them in retail developments, says REAC, which offers a list of the woods.)

10. Be sure to get what you want. Are your lamps UL-listed? Are fixtures installed according to your plan? Are showcases repairable? Do they have locks on sliding doors and security latches on top glass panels? Do they use safety glass? Are tracks for cases' sliding doors equipped with anti-liftout devices to deter theft?

Money Savers

Cost is a big factor for many jewelers seeking to buy or renovate fixtures. Here are some money-saving ideas from suppliers, designers and manufacturers.

• Consider using local cabinet-makers with solid reputations for good work. If you provide adequate plans, they can make your cases—often at a better price than larger fixture firms. "I've given that idea to many of my clients to their benefit, and they're usually happier to work with people they know in their own communities," notes veteran jewelry store designer MariAnn Coutchie. Be sure the company you use is reliable, licensed and able to provide the jewelry-industry features you need, including security devices and in-case lighting.

• Find out the rated life of your lamps and draw up a regular maintenance plan to clean and replace bulbs rather than do it one at a time. This ensures a consistent level of lighting and a cost-effective return from it.

• Consider standardized rather than custom cases. Mechanical frame cases are cheaper than those with welded frames.

• Existing cases can be refurbished with high-pressure laminate finishes for 35%-75% less than buying new ones.

• Smaller manufacturers, suppliers or consultants sometimes can afford to offer lower rates due to lower overhead.

• You can afford better-quality fixtures by spreading the cost over 10 to 15 years.

• Fixture companies often will cut floor pads for cases and cover them if you provide the fabric. This can be cheaper than having display companies do it.

Diamond Rooms:
Create The Right Atmosphere

Jerry Fornell ◆ *February 1992*

An effective, aesthetically pleasing diamond room can be a great help in displaying high-quality merchandise. And producing one need not strain either your space or financial resources. (To create and furnish a 10 x 12 ft. room typically adds about $25 a sq. ft. to the regular $150-$200 per sq. ft. cost for store design and construction.) Here are a few simple guidelines.

A diamond room should create a private and comfortable area in which to close your most important sales. Its design allows you to show a diamond's characteristics and quality to best advantage. The room should be devoted to a single purpose, and not have to double as workroom or storage area. It can, however, be used for appraisal and employee or customer education.

Locate the room very near your finest quality merchandise. you should be able to ease your customer into the room, taking no more than a few steps. Visually, the room should appear open. Separating it from the rest of the store with translucent panels, smoked glass or vertical blinds provides a nice balance of openness and privacy.

The room should hold at least two customers and a salesperson. Size can range from a minimum 8' x 10' to 10' x 12' for a typical store. Some very large or high-end retailers may opt for two diamond rooms to accommodate demand during peak seasonal and sale periods.

Ambience counts; a diamond room should be inviting, clutter free and simple in form and furnishings. It should be decorated in soft, subtle colors that work with the rest of the store. Decor should be tasteful and not overly elaborate. To create an elegant atmosphere, use quality carpet or, perhaps, a small area rug over highly-polished hardwood floors. High-end fabrics can cover walls and customer chairs; leather is another option for the latter.

If the store has laminated display cases, consider using marble, Corian or Avonite tops for those in the diamond room. A unique ceiling treatment, such as a dome, also can help to distinguish this special room form the rest of the store.

General lighting should be soft, with proper direct highlighting above merchandise presentation areas. A table lamp or task light can supplement overhead lighting. Wall sconces or torch lights are other good indirect-lighting choices. Avoid fluorescent lights on the ceiling and keep it simple.

Don't allow clutter to accumulate. Keep phones and computer equipment out of sight, and tools neatly organized or concealed. Video surveillance cameras and monitors don't belong here, put them elsewhere in the store.

With a little attention, your diamond room can add new sparkle to your sales performance.

Watch Displays:
A Proven Sales-Builder

April 1991

In an effort to catch their customers' eyes, watch marketers are putting more time, talents and dollars into display stands. Most firms, of course, closely monitor their merchandising and revise it every few years. But recently, that process has accelerated.

In the past year, Seiko Time, Citizen's Noblia, TAG-Heuer and Timex have made major changes in their in-store displays. SMH (US)—which sells Swatch, Tissot, Omega, Rado and Hamilton—and North American Watch Co.—whose upscale lines include Piaget, Concord, Corum and Movado—have added merchandising chiefs whose mandates include eye-catching in-store presentations. Pulsar, Citizen and Bulova's Cravelle are studying designs and materials for new displays due out this fall or next year. Meanwhile, Bulova, Pulsar and Lorus have redesigned display cases to make them more efficient.

Last link: Why are watchmakers and suppliers investing in display stands? Because, say vendors, window and in-store displays are the last link in the merchandising chain that brings customer traffic to the point of purchase. Several factors make it more important than ever to ensure that link is not a weak one.

The U.S. watch market has become very crowded, especially at mass- and mid-price levels, with brands both well-known and new. Suppliers and retailers alike need displays that catch the consumer's eye. "As things become more difficult, we're all looking for that extra edge," says Paul Sayegh, executive vice president of Bulova Corp.

The recession has cut sales of big-ticket items like houses, cars or expensive jewelry. This has left some consumers more to spend on affordable but stylish gifts such as watches, say retailers.

Tastes are changing, say demographic researchers; the glitz of the '80s is disappearing. Consumers of the '90s tend to be more mature, and more concerned with quality products at reasonable prices.

Retail conditions, ranging from a weak economy to a growing number of outlets selling watches, also make retailers "more concerned with dressing up the appearance of watch presentations," says Stuart Zuckerman, vice president of merchandising, Citizen Watch Co. of America.

In addition, employee turnover means "watches more and more must sell themselves, because they're more and more in the hands of people new to retailing," says Jonathan Nettlefield, vice president of advertising, Seiko Corp. of America.

These factors combine to make displays more important in watch merchandising. Thus SMH (US) created its new merchandising department to "upgrade our displays and presentation to bring more traffic into stores, get more visibility for our brands and expand our target groups," says president Raymond Zeitoun. Bulova design, sales, marketing and engineering personnel now help create and evaluate display ideas before the firm approaches display manufacturers. Seiko Time's new displays followed a year-long creation, evaluation and production process that was the most comprehensive in its history; the process will be applied next to the display program for its Lasalle brand.

Here are some trends which these factors and efforts are producing.

Highs & lows: The topography of displays is changing.

Display units with risers (i.e., terraced steps), watch collars, ramps and display blocks of varying levels and shapes with collars in them—"ups and downs that catch the eye and create nooks and crannies for various displays," says Nettlefield—are joining or replacing flat pads and trays on which watches are laid or inserted in straight lines.

These features not only let a retailer showcase various models and collections of a brand, but also "force a viewer who is window shopping to look at and study each section, and give more attention to individual watches, " says Andrew McCauley, director of communications for Chippenhook, a leader maker of watch and jewelry displays.

The new displays, such as those for mid-priced Tissot or the Bertolucci luxury line, also let retailers put many pieces in a small area in an attractive way. Their major elements can be added or removed depending on inventory levels, says McCauley. That's important when retail space costs so much and so little is set aside for watches.

Other notable design aspects include curving risers which flow through adjoining units in a display case, pulling the viewer's eye with them; prominent display of the brand name; and flat mini-stages, or "feature areas," which spotlight special merchandise or new models.

Most apparent in these new displays, though, are the watch collars and collar stands of varying shapes and heights for individual watches. These do more than provide variety, says Leslie Gerber, director of visual merchandising for SMH (US).

"By raising up a specific watch and treating it as its own entity," she says, "you subtly tell consumers, 'This timepiece is special. That's why it is on the highest platform.'" Omega and TAG-Heuer, two up-scale brands, now display their watches exclusively on stands. But they aren't limited to expensive watches.

The new first-ever jewelry store displays for Swatch watches use them, too. The aim, says Gerber, is to "highlight Swatch without offending more expensive brands in jewelry stores, [and its] leather [strap] and metal [case] collections, too.

Color & materials: In the 1980s, earth tones and then shades of gray prevailed. Now, "people are using colors more imaginatively and with more daring," says Nettlefield. Today's hues include pastel colors, beiges, peach, pinks and aqua. Still, notes Citizen's Zuckerman, displays can't be too avant garde or transitory. "Designs have to be neutral enough to blend in with many different store environments," he says.

Today's trendiest display color is white. Not just versatile, it also underlines the quality and luxury value of upscale timepieces, many of which feature jewelry, gold or gold-tone bracelets and cases.

The stuff of which displays are made looks classier as well, to accent product quality. There's more suede or leather, and more metal, too. Noblia, for example, is producing solid brass logo plaques in Switzerland for use in windows and cases. Lorus has added brass-colored striping to its new floor stand.

The "stone look" is in, as indicated by more faux granite or marble finishes. Seiko's new display program uses real Portuguese dark marble, while displays for Citizen's upscale Noblia brand use black marbleized wood and Italian-made beige leatherette materials.

Grouping: More manufacturers are developing customized displays for groups of two or three watches within a collection or brand that warrant special merchandising.

Information: Many countertop displays—especially those for multi-functional and specialized models—are becoming silent salesmen, offering more basic information to customers. Examples include the award-winning display for Citizen's sport-tech Promaster and Timex displays using symbols to describe the watches (dress, business, sport, etc.)

New ideas: Some firms are experimenting in other areas.

Cartier and Swatch are among those using "brand corners" (mini-watch shops) in department stores. Both Swatch and Timex are testing pilfer-proof devices—a wall-connected cable for Swatch, a transparent drawer for Timex—which let customers try on watch models without walking away with them.

Timex also is testing an interactive video display unit which helps consumers make buying decisions by printing a list of suggested watch models based on their answers to specific questions (i.e., wearer's gender, desired price, features needed).

Timex's most significant endeavor, however, was its decision to change the packaging in which its watches are displayed from plastic to biodegradable cardboard. Timex so far is the only major watch firm to make the move, effective in February, which cost it at least $8 million just for retooling and new designs. The packaging eliminates annual use of 1,100 tons of plastic.

Nuts & bolts: A number of firms are redoing countertop and/or floor units with revolving vertical displays to make them more efficient.

Pulsar changed the slots into which watches fit in its countertop unit for under-$100 timepieces from horizontal inserts to angular ones. That prevents slippage when customers spin the unit. It also added a tamper-proof lock and anchored security-cable to keep thieves from opening or stealing the unit.

Bulova recently gathered sales, marketing and engineering people to redesign its Caravelle floor tower displays. The result was an aesthetically-pleasing motorized display. A button lets customers stop the display when they want to view specific models. The unit can be turned manually if the motor stops, and the motor itself can be changed easily "without the need of an MIT degree," says a Bulova official.

HOW TO IMPROVE YOUR WATCH DISPLAYS

Multi-million-dollar programs to merchandise watches in jewelry stores often fail, say watch suppliers, due to one major stumbling block: the jeweler.

Many jeweler are lukewarm about watches, contending they consume too much selling space and provide lesser margins than diamonds and gold (although watches can turn more often). And jewelers often misuse—or fail to use—the display materials provided.

"It's frustrating," says a display designer. "A great deal of time, thought and money goes into designing and creating displays for retailers. Then, they're used with other people's merchandise, thrown out after a brief time or not used as intended."

Yet, suppliers contend it's easy for retailers to do a good job in the watch business if they display and merchandise well. Here are some basic tips.

• Use windows. Too many retailers overlook windows for promoting timepieces, notes Gerald Batt, president of Omega Watch (US). Yet, windows can catch the eyes of passers-by, give them an idea of what's inside and pull them in.

But use some imagination; don't simply fill your window with watches. Display them by category or brands. Use a few props and create themes for specific types of watches, such as sport watches or watches for kids. One small town jeweler drew attention—and won an award—with a window display for Jaz Paris watches featuring jazz instruments.

"People tend to create window displays at holidays, like Christmas or Father's Day, but that is when everyone does it," says Sheri McKenzie, general manager of Pulsar's advertising. "But what about the rest of the year," when theme displays would have more impact? Remember to change displays frequently (every four to six weeks) to maintain interest and create anticipation. "It's like theater for passers-by," says McKenzie. "They look forward to it and it can make a lot of difference in business."

• Be neat. Remember the basics

"A retailer can have a beautiful display that looks shoddy because of lack of attention," says Stu Zuckerman of Citizen. "Give displays the attention they deserve. Place watches in pleasing arrangements, not haphazard or cluttered ones. Don't let tags or bracelets hang over the edge."

• Avoid "seas of watches," as Omega's Batt calls them. With retail space expensive and limited, and jewelers assigning less of it to watches, there's a temptation to put as many timepieces into a display as possible. But, say suppliers, retailers tend to display 20% to 30% more watches then they should.

Watch displays should "convey to customers a brand's image—which costs $2,000 and which costs $50—and you don't get that by putting all possible watches in them," says Leslie Gerber, director of visual merchandising for SMH (US).

• Make watches accessible to customers. DO put them where they can be easily viewed—in countertop display cases, stand-alone floor cabinets or counter cases. DON'T put them in wall cases behind the counter where people can't approach or view them easily. Remember, your customers need to *see* the product easily.

Indeed, accessibility and absence of display counters are hallmarks of mall watch shops operated by two successful mass market vendors, Timex and Best of Times, a Woolworth Corp. subsidiary. Their research found customers consider counters intimidating. Instead, they display popular- and mid-priced watches in eye-level wall cases which consumers can approach easily.

• Show watches in their appropriate setting. Countertop units are designed for watches retailing at under $100. Put mid-priced and upscale and watches in your counter cases as you do with jewelry. Indeed, say several watch and marketing execs, fine watches should be presented with the same care and attention as fine jewelry. In Europe, fine watches *are* treated as jewelry, with just a few pieces shown, to emphasize their uniqueness and special qualities.

• Don't mix brands and styles in the same display. Research shows that consumers in the 1990s are increasingly dependent on brands—especially those they know and can easily find—in their purchase choices.

Watches are the one branded jewelry-store product consumers know. Yet, many stores confuse matters by mixing brands A and B in one tray—often designed for brand C.

• Divide by category, as well as brand. Watch firms spend literally millions of dollars to create and maintain brand awareness and consumers do buy by brand. Within those brands, as space allows, segment models by look, lifestyle (dress, sport, business) or type (chronograph, perpetual calendar, jewelry watch, expansion-band model) and by men's, women's and unisex sizes. Display units for many watch vendors are designed to allow this. Be sure to maintain and update presentations as styles and collections change.

• Use suppliers' expertise. Many watch firms not only design displays with jewelers in mind—since department store chains have their own display makers—but also are ready to help in presenting their watches and displays.

"The role of salesman has changed very much in the past 10 years," says Seiko's Nettlefield. "They're doing 50% less selling and 50% more merchandising."

Indeed, if there is one piece of display advice repeated constantly by watch firms it is this. Use the expertise and materials provided—sometimes for free—including display stands, point-of-sale materials, counter cards, even wall clocks.

As one watch company exec puts it, "Retailers can't go to visual merchandising classes, so it's our responsibility to help them display and merchandise the product."

Getting It All From A Mall

August 1990

The major step in getting the most for your money in a mall is to choose the mall carefully.

Bert Foer, chairman of the Silver Spring, Md.-based Melart chain, is an experienced mall jeweler. Although vocal about the pitfalls of malls, Foer is firmly committed to being a mall jeweler. He and several retail consultants offer the following advice on choosing a location and negotiating a lease:

• **Demographics.** Learn the demographics of the mall and town. The mall landlord will have some of this information. Believe some of it, but use common sense, says Foer. Mall landlords typically overstate the size of the market.

If you're opening a branch store in a mall, choose one that's 45 minutes to an hour away from your other store, says Richard Wolf, a retail space consultant in Owings Mills, Md. There, the branch is far enough away not to drain business from the first store and close enough to manage effectively. Wolf cautions that this is not the time to experiment with something new and suggests locating in an area similar to the first.

If you plan to close your first store, don't do it at the same time you move. Be certain your new location is successful before closing the old.

• **Competition.** How much is too much? Four jewelers per hundred non-anchor stores used to be the general limit, but it's now often up to six. In any case, here's how to assess the competition:

If the mall's jewelers don't seem busy, it's a clue there may be too many. Check how many salespeople work in each competitor's store. Two salespeople could indicate little business; if the store has five or six workers, they're there for a reason. Check at different times of day and week—both peak hours (evenings, weekends) and slow.

If some jewelers in the mall seem substantially busier than others, go into their stores and find out why. Look at merchandise, price points, credit terms, service, etc. Judge objectively how your store compares. You may be too upscale or downscale for that mall.

• **Estimate volume.** Ask the leasing agent for some sales figures from other stores and per-square-foot data for the mall itself (excluding anchor stores). Most landlords will give the information; many also provide projected sales figures for your store. Richard Laffin of the Management Growth Institute, Wellesley, Mass., says to discount these figures a minimum 25%. Now balance these figures against expenses to help decide whether the site would be profitable for you.

• **New mall.** For new malls, reliable information is hard to get and projections constitute "crystal ball-gazing at best," says Foer. But through experience, he's gained a general sense of how much business a given size mall should do, and then he figures his projected returns vs. the cost.

Laffin says a new mall has about a two-year establish-ment time. Here again, he says, a jeweler should discount the mall's projected figures by much more than 25%.

• **One's good, two's better.** It's not unusual for the landlord of a new mall to lie about how many other jewelers will be there, claims Foer. One landlord promised him that Melart would be the only jeweler, but then allowed a second one. The landlord's not-very-contrite reasoning: "Sorry, I guess greed won out."

• **Is the mall popular?** How does this mall rate against other area malls? Is it popular? What are the anchor stores? Wolf says to consider not only the anchors' quality, but also their recognition. Robinson's, for example, is a fine store, but not well-known on the East Coast, nor is Strawbridge & Clothier well-known outside the Philadelphia area. A store not familiar to the area won't have the drawing power of one that is.

• **Image consciousness.** If you don't fit the general image of the mall, don't locate there. Melart, for example, generally is a middle-to upper-middle-class jeweler. In some malls it's *the* upscale jeweler; in others it must upscale merchandise to compete. (Foer won't deliberately be the downscale jeweler of a mall.) If you've built a solid working-class clientele, think twice about going into a pricey, upscale center.

NEGOTIATING THE LEASE

After you select a mall, it's time to negotiate the lease. Here are some tips:

• **Location.** Consultants and retailers agree that how much footage you get is fourth in importance behind three primary factors: location, location, location. What good is expensive footage if it's lost in a remote corner next to Bill's Buffalo Burgers?

Foer says the best location is a center court corner. Jeweler Scott Krigel of Kansas City, Mo., concurs, asking whether it's better to do $2 million in sales in an expensive part of the mall (such as center court) or $500,000 in a lesser part of the mall.

Krigel has a 3,500-sq.-ft. mall store that he downsized with false walls because it was too big for his needs. He says it's worth paying for the extra space in order to have the prime location.

If this is your dilemma, ask the landlord to split the space, say Wolf and Foer. Some landlords won't, but they could benefit because per-sq.-foot rent generally is higher for smaller spaces.

Taking more space than you'd planned might prove beneficial, but do it only if you're secure and prepared to grow. Foer once took 2,000 sq. ft. instead of the 1,000 he'd been offered. He built a magnificent store, doubled the inventory and got excellent returns on his investment through increased sales. But if you decide to grow this way, start small and let expansion be driven by volume, says Wolf.

Which is the better choice: a "deal" on a large space in a not-so-good location or a small space that would cramp you even though it's in a good location? Foer and Wolf suggest rejecting both options and trying to negotiate for more space in the better location, waiting until something opens up or looking in a different mall.

• **Radius clause.** The landlord will use this to try to prevent you from opening another store within a certain distance of the mall. If you can't remove a radius clause from the lease, try to reduce the distance as much as possible. You never know when you'll want to open another store, says Wolf.

• **Radius within mall.** Specify that no other jeweler, jewelry cart or kiosk may operate within "X" feet of your store (try to get that "X" as large as possible). It's unlikely to happen, but try to persuade the landlord to agree in writing not to add other jewelry stores, or not add them unless the mall expands.

• **Hours of business.** Most landlords require all tenants to keep mall hours. Don't expect much allowance here. Occasionally, a retailer gets a special dispensation to keep slightly different hours than the rest of the mall, but this is rare and has to be approved before the lease is signed. Remember that mall hours are extended during the holiday season, so if you wish to keep your own hours then, discuss it now.

• **Don't overstate abilities.** Keep your ego out of it and *do not* overestimate what you think you can sell because it will be a factor in your rent, says Wolf. Err on the conservative side when making sales projections to the mall management. It takes about two years to get established and get a true sales potential.

• **Choose your battles.** Remember that negotiation is give and take. Pick your battles carefully and don't fight every point to the death. Give in on the minor to achieve the major. The battles to fight are those that most affect your business.

Finding a Consultant

When choosing an independent retail space consultant, look for one with solid experience in the shopping center business. He or she will likely have built a rapport with local mall developers and landlords.

The consultant will know which of the area malls suit you and which offer the fairest rents. In addition, the consultant will be a big help in negotiating the lease.

Be certain to find a consultant who doesn't stand to gain financially from your choice to enter a given location. A *broker* wants the commission from your lease. A *consultant* should be paid a flat fee—$500 to $1,000 daily—that doesn't change whether or not you choose a particular mall. A reputable consultant should look out for your interests, not just his own.

For help in finding a consultant in your area, contact the International Council of Shopping Centers, 665 Fifth Ave., New York, N.Y. 10022; (212) 421-8181.

Mall Retailing: It's A Different World

January 1990

The displays might look the same and the decor could be similar, but outward appearances mask vast differences between mall and downtown stores.

Before you decide to go into a mall or renew a mall lease, review what lies ahead. How much will you have to pay? How much independence will you surrender to take advantage of the convenience and traffic of a mall store?

The questions become even more pertinent if you are an AGS store. How will mall life affect your community status as a quality-oriented, full-service jeweler?

Costs: No two ways about it—mall space is expensive. Expect to pay $60-$120 per sq. ft. rent in an enclosed mall (these are Connecticut prices, which tend to be 20%-25% above the national average). That's a lot of money, considering most regional malls started out 10-15 years ago at $10-$15 a sq. ft. Strip malls charge $10-$30 per sq. ft., though this varies from region to region. With downtown locations, there is absolutely no way to tell how much rent you'll pay.

In addition to basic rent, you'll pay $6-$12 per sq. ft. for cleaning, heating/air conditioning, security guards and incidentals such as replacing plants and mall services such as baby strollers.

There also will be a marketing charge, generally about 2% of what the mall estimates your sales will be for the year. On average, this amounts to $3-$5 per sq. ft.

This adds up to $69-$137 per sq. ft. If you have a 1,000-sq.-ft. store and your basic mall charge is $100 per sq. ft., you'll pay $100,000 a year. Average rent should be 5% of sales, say Maurice Adelsheim and Jewelers of America, so your store will have to do $2 million volume annually. If you do less, your rent rises as a percentage (to 10% of sales if you do only $1 million, for example). Unless you find another way to get the remaining 5%, you'll work for the landlord and not make a nickel from it.

When your lease ends, you'll be forced to remodel before it's renewed. A complete make-over of a 1,000-sq.-ft. store costs $200,000-$300,000. New cases average $500 a running foot with double lights. You'll need new carpeting and new wallcovering, so the tally quickly reaches $50,000. The mall probably will insist on a new front—count on $75,000. Ceiling work involves big money, and soon you're up to $250,000.

If you do a volume of $1 million and you're sharp enough to net 7% after taxes (I don't know anyone in the industry who does), you have an annual profit of $70,000. If you have to spend $250,000 every seven years to remodel, that takes half your profit.

Limited space: Mall jewelry stores generally are 1,000-1,500 sq. ft. (750-1,200 sq. ft. for national or regional chains). Even AGS jewelers probably won't carry giftware and table-tops in a store this small. In addition to limited display space, there's little room available for storage, packing, boxes and wrapping.

Bench workers and watchmakers take up valuable floor space in a mall store. They also may use bottled gas and oxygen or open flames that mall leases preclude. As a full-service jeweler, you may be able to negotiate a repair shop in your lease. But at $100 per sq. ft., the shop will be very small and will have to do a substantial business. One jeweler did just that by turning his benchman into his storefront. The man sits in the big glass storefront, attracting attention from passers-by. But that's an exception.

You also won't want your bookkeeper using an adding machine, writing checks and doing payroll in space that costs $100 a sq. ft. The same is true for a credit person who calls customers and handles statements. Administrative functions can be performed in less-expensive offices away from the mall. But make sure these support people communicate and relate to the transactions that happen in the store.

Staffing/hours: The normal AGS store, the fine jeweler downtown, has six to eight people on duty each day to take care of anything that happens. In a mall store of 1,000-1,500 sq. ft., however, you'll have three to five people most of the time. This has security ramifications. You'll need to develop different procedures for opening and closing, and you won't have enough workers to take care of customers when they arrive in batches.

Although you'll have fewer employees in the store at a time, you'll need enough to staff two shifts. The downtown AGS jeweler is open 40-50 hours a week: five or six days and one night. In a regional or super-regional mall, however, you'll be open 70-80 hours a week, including Sundays. In November and December, you'll be open longer.

Unfortunately, much of your mall employees' time will be spent waiting for customers. Traffic in malls, regrettably, arrives on Saturdays, Sundays, and Thursday and Friday nights. This has terrible implications for your quality of life because, as the store owner, you'll want to be there at the times of highest traffic. And can you find key people who will work a 40-hour schedule that includes Saturday, Sunday, and Thursday and Friday nights?

How do you solve this problem?

With part-timers. There are school-teachers, there are kids in school, there are police officers. In fact, there are any number of people willing to work 10-20 hours more a week, and weekend work is fine because it won't interfere with their normal schedules. But training is more difficult, and they're at their normal job when you hold store meetings. Turnover among part-timers is high; they're working for economic rea-

sons, not to advance a career. No denigration is intended; part-timers are the backbone of the sales force in some stores. But in general, they aren't career professional gemologists.

Competition: Most regional malls have five to eight fine jewelers just like you, or at least they design their stores to look like yours. To stand apart, you'll have to do battle one-on-one through good service. Cater to customers' needs, teach them about jewelry and show them how to guard against deception.

Most of your competitors will run a 20%- to 70%-off sale every day of the week. Every week. Of every month. For now, we'll forget about undercarating with a "C," under-karating with a "K," disclosure issues, deceptive value, misrepresentation of clarity and color and non-representation of cut. Your competition from fine jewelers will be price discount competition.

Fine jewelry counters in department stores, for example, generate three to five times the sales of other departments. The merchandise will look the same as yours, but it will be lower quality. You'll bear the burden of persuading consumers your merchandise is better quality even though it looks the same to them.

The competition—especially chain and department stores—will try to take your employees as well as your customers. Managers of national chain stores and leased jewelry departments get $40,000-$60,000 a year. That's a lot of money. But they also work 55 hours a week. They don't want to work 55 hours a week forever, so they try to move up the ladder quickly. As a result, chain stores have to look for new managers often, and they may look in your direction. I don't have a solution, but it's something you should be prepared for.

Managers aren't the only ones who can be drawn away. Many of your competitors pay their salespeople $25,000 a year and call them assistant managers. (The administrative title averts paying overtime for anything over 40 hours a week, though federal wage and hours rules may not allow this if the employee doesn't supervise others or have a certain amount of authority.) How many of your salespeople earn that much, and how many would jump elsewhere for an extra $50 a week?

Your competitors' assistant managers often work 55 hours a week, but *your* scheduling may not be much more attractive if it requires a lot of weekend and evening hours. Aside from raising salaries, there are things you can do to keep employees happy, including treating them well and seriously considering their scheduling requests.

Customers: Shoppers are more likely to browse in a mall than downtown. Assuming your diamond close ratio is three in five now, for example, it will drop to one in five in a mall. You'll spend a lot of time educating consumers—and that's great. But a lot of mall consumers aren't yours psychographically. They want to learn a little bit about gemology, and once they figure they know how to buy a diamond, they'll go shopping for price.

According to research at the University of Connecticut on engagement ring customers, 70% are more interested in discount than quality or value. That means 70% will likely shop the chain and discount stores. You still can profit, however, because chain stores use entirely different pricing and merchandising strategies and they look at a different socioeconomic and psychographic market.

The key is teaching consumers about quality and value. Our research shows that until taught differently, consumers generally see value as the lowest price for the lowest acceptable quality, rather than as a good price anywhere along the quality continuum.

Security: Malls are becoming *the* place for thieves. It's easy for four cohorts to occupy salespeople while another one jimmies open a showcase. You'll have to use surveillance cameras as a psychological deterrent—count on a minimum $8,000 investment. You'll also need a very security-conscious staff.

NEGOTIATING THE LEASE

Here are some points of general lease-negotiating advice.

• Don't sign a commitment letter until you and your attorney have read it carefully. If the landlord insists otherwise, add a statement saying, "These items are subject to negotiation." Otherwise, you'll have given up your right to negotiate.

• Guard against unethical practices. I'm sorry to tell you that while you're buying diamonds, training your staff and closing sales, someone somewhere is trying to figure out how to write a lease that will nail you to the wall. He'll make sure his interests are taken care of, even if that means changing wording or switching pages before sending you the final copy.

• Get the landlord to want you in the mall. Don't slap the landlord on the back and say, "You want me in your mall." Instead, show that you have a fine local store with merchandise that sets you apart and that you represent the community. That legitimizes the mall. If the landlord has that in the back of his mind, he'll come to the negotiating table thinking, "How much am I going to have to give in order to get this store?"

A landlord recently wanted a Michaels Jewelers store in his mall because we offer a repair service and we provide a quality product. "Please put in tabletops, please put in gifts; we can't get any jeweler to do that," he said. Our response: "Fine, give us the space for those products at $10 a foot. We'll pay $50 a foot for the other space." He declined, but his interest proved that we had showed ourselves to be more than a jewelry store.

Also, try to get your lawyer and public officials to tell the landlord he needs you in the mall. The only reason we got into two malls was our family's contacts through a business organization and a real estate broker. Because malls wanted us, we were able to get some concessions.

• Nationals come before locals. Most regional shopping centers are leased at a convention of the International Council of Shopping Centers each November in Dallas, Tex. If you're serious about going into malls, you should join ICSC. The $400 membership fee is cheap insurance to make sure you get a shot at being where the action is. But accept the fact that national chains already in one mall will get first chance when the developer builds a new mall. As soon as you become interested in a new mall, get the name of the vice president of leasing and send him or her pictures and a history of your store. Write every six months. That's frequent enough to show strong interest, but not so often the person will think you'd do anything to get space in the mall.

• Get an experienced adviser. A lawyer probably isn't experienced in lease negotiations, but may be able to direct you to someone who is. Or you can ask ICSC in New York (212-241-8181) to recommend someone in your area. If you have to pay someone $5,000 to help negotiate the lease, do it. You'll save the equivalent of $10,000 a year for the life of the lease.

• Read the lease carefully and do the math. Don't depend only on your lawyer and adviser. Give yourself 40 hours to read it the first time, then read it for understanding again. Make sure you understand the sections on insurance, indemnity, eminent domain, construction, tenant responsibilities, storage—everything. Ask questions of your adviser before negotiations begin. If there's math to do about prorations and proportions and indexes and short years, do it.

• During negotiations, read and discuss the lease paragraph by paragraph, not as a whole. If you can't convince the landlord of your position on one item, don't give in right away and don't walk away. Leave it open. At the end, the landlord may be more willing to accept a few of your points once everything else has been settled.

• Most parts of a lease are negotiable. The landlord likely has a big book in his office with 10 alternate paragraphs for each section of the lease. But you'll never know about them if you don't try to negotiate. I admit a few things about mortgages aren't negotiable, but most of the lease is.

• Expect occasional reversals on agreed-upon items. If the landlord checks with his boss and then vetoes an agreed-upon item, use that as an opening to change something else in your favor. You don't want to be unethical, but you've got to be as tough with mall landlords as they are with you. It's a lousy business to be in, on our side anyway.

• Read the amendments carefully. Each amendment—design criteria, construction criteria or whatever else—contains information you must understand.

• Have your architect review the design criteria and negotiate them. Remember that you and the landlord are unusual partners. Your mission in the partnership is to guarantee the landlord's net profit. If there's anything that costs, you pay. And most of those costs are in the design and construction sections. Read them, negotiate them.

• Make the design specifications for your store an integral part of the lease. Otherwise, you'll have no protection if mall officials review the design later and object to something. Add a paragraph to the lease saying, "This lease becomes effective upon agreement between the landlord and the tenant on all issues concerning the plans and specifications." Then if the mall later makes an unreasonable design demand, you can rip up the lease and walk away.

• Initial each page of the lease. When negotiations are concluded and everyone's happy, the lease is finalized, notarized and sent back to you in about a week. Read it carefully to make sure nothing has been changed, initialing each page as you go.

Let's address just a few specific lease issues.

Percentage rent: You'll need an annual volume of $2 million to cover basic minimum rent of $100,000, but the landlord also gets a percentage of any volume over that $2 million breakpoint. Try to negotiate an unnatural breakpoint, such as $2.5 million instead of $2 million. If you didn't have to pay percentage rent on that $500,000 difference, you'd save $25,000 if your rate were 5%. I use 5% because it's easy to work with; in reality, you should expect to be asked to pay 7%-8% percentage rent. Offer 6% up to certain amount and 7% on the rest.

Landlords will try to include all types of transactions when calculating percentage rent. Here are some you should try to exclude through negotiation:

• Trade-ins. If you sell a $10,000 diamond ring and accept a $4,000 trade-in, you actually sold the new ring for $6,000 and bought the trade-in from the customer for $4,000. The landlord, however, will try to say the sale totaled $10,000, even though you haven't sold the trade-in yet.

• Store credit. When you issue credit for a return, make sure it's deducted from gross sales.

• Deposits and undelivered sales. Layaways and deposits on memo requests should be included in gross sales when the transactions are completed, not before.

• Brokerage sales. Only your commission should be counted when you handle a sale for a customer. If you find a buyer for a customer's $50,000 necklace and get 10% commission ($5,000), for example, your books might show a $50,000 sale and $45,000 cost. Be sure that under your lease, you'll pay percentage rent only on the commission, not the entire $50,000.

• Service sales. Tell the landlord that rather than include service receipts in gross sales, you'll give him double your profit from your service department. The reason: if your service sales total $1,000 keystone, for example, it appears you have $500 in direct shop costs and $500 in profits. But you must take into account $200 in labor, $172 in insurance, $30 for transportation and phone calls. Before you know it, you've reduced your profit to nothing. If you pay 5% of service sales at the end of the year, you lose money. But if you pay on double profits (which already have been reduced to zero), you pay nothing and still benefit from your reputation as a full-service jeweler.

• Employee sales. Sales to employees, officers, insurance companies and corporations are loss leaders and deep discounts. Try to get them eliminated from percentage rent calculations. The landlord may agree, but probably will ask you to limit such sales. If you limit them to 2% of sales for employees, 2% for corporations and so on, all the 2's start to add up.

• Donations. Your landlord's auditors will try to include donations and sales to tax-exempt organizations as sales. Try to exclude them.

• Big-ticket sales. Expensive items carry lower margins, so try to persuade the landlord you can't afford to give him 5% on these sales. Try to set this limit at $2,000; if that doesn't work, try $5,000. If he still won't agree, try the biggest 30 sales over $2,000 or one-third of all sales over $2,000.

• Monthly payment of percentage rent. Do not accept this clause in a lease. If you expect to do $1 million volume annually, you'll have to pay $83,333 each month ($1 million divided by 12 months) plus percentage rent on any overage. For example, if you do $250,000 in December, you'll pay your basic rent plus percentage rent on $166,667. When you do only $40,000 in January, February and March, however, the landlord doesn't sent the money back. He holds it as credit for the final accounting. If you don't reach $1 million in volume by the end of the year, he holds the money until you do go on percentage rent.

• Short year. Your first year usually isn't a full year, so make sure your lease allows your accountant to annualize the figures. If you open in September, for example, you'll likely do 24% more business than average between then and the end of the year. Rather than pay full percentage rent on the overage, tell the landlord you want to consider that first short

year as the first four months of a 12-month accounting period. Then calculate the percentage rent for the first 12 months, and pay one-third of that amount for the first four months.

Records and audits: The landlord will want you to keep your records in-store for three years. At $100 per sq. ft., that's pretty expensive storage space. Get permission to keep one year's worth in the store and the rest off-site. And tell the landlord you'll keep only sales records. He has no business seeing salary, advertising, accounts-receivable and similar records.

Under-reporting penalties: Every lease has a clause allowing the landlord to cancel the lease and charge a penalty and auditing expenses if you under-report sales. First, limit penalties and auditing expenses to $500. Then insist on excluding computer or employee error, reasonable misinterpretation or employee fraud.

Construction: The construction documents in your lease probably will be almost as big as the lease itself, and some of the requirements are very costly. The first thing to remember is that you'll get nothing but space—you bear the full cost of interior work. Unless you negotiate exclusions, you'll have to pay the landlord's architect to review your plan, you'll have to pay for his clerk-of-the-works to monitor your contractor during construction and you'll have to accept any changes he wants after your plans are approved.

New developers: Mall openings often are delayed by financial problems of the developer, trouble with unionized construction workers, prolonged bad weather and other reasons. Include a provision in the lease that you don't have to open until 70% of the mall is open. Check with your lawyer for other ways to protect yourself in such cases.

Joint advertising: You'll be expected to participate in mall advertising. Go into the lease negotiation with a little loose-leaf notebook that shows your ads. Tell the landlord that if the mall advertising is of similar quality, you'll participate. If it's not, you won't. The landlord won't let you get away with that, but you can decline to be in an ad and still pay the required amount from your own advertising budget. Then remind the landlord of you 2%-3% contribution to the marketing fund and say you want credit for your own advertising. Just be sure the mall's name is included with your logo in the ads.

Insurance: The landlord will request the craziest types of insurance. Before negotiations begin, check with your insurance agent to be sure what types and limits you will and won't carry. But if the landlord says he will insure any improvements you make, then charge you back for it, it's a good deal. He'll get much lower rates. Just be sure you send him a letter listing increased values every two or three years.

Cancellation: Most leases have a clause allowing the landlord to cancel the agreement if a tenant hasn't attained percentage-rent status in two years. You have two options. If you don't want to risk your investment, tell the landlord you can't build a $250,000 store in his mall unless the clause is removed. Or if you would like the option to get out of the lease, add a clause saying "either party may terminate the lease on six months' notice."

Refuse removal: You would be surprised what it costs to haul garbage from a mall. We pay about $35 a month for a downtown store, but $150 a month for a mall store. This is a small point, but try to limit refuse removal costs to no more than you'd pay to do it yourself.

Parking: Be sure your employees are allowed to park in the mall parking lot. Sound crazy? If parking space is reduced due to a mall addition or some other project, for example, the landlord may rent a remote field for employee parking, using shuttle buses to get them back and forth. Imagine what muggings and vehicle vandalism will do for employee morale?

Remodeling: Leases give the landlord the power to decide when you should remodel your store and to what extent. If he thinks your carpet is a little shabby, your wallpaper doesn't fit the latest earthtone fashions or your counter displays aren't fresh, you'll have about six weeks to change them. You have to do it—it's in the lease! Unless, of course, you were smart enough to eliminate that during negotiations.

Malls, Downtowns, Strip Centers: Which Is Right For You?

January 1990

Consultants say malls rule American retailing, but retailers also can thrive in revitalized downtowns and jazzy strip centers, especially near upscale office and residential developments. In fact, downtowns and strip centers can be especially attractive for specialized retailers such as jewelers. Consumers make specific trips to these "destination stores" to buy specific items.

If you're going to open a branch or relocate, where do you fit in the picture?

Many independent jewelers are "destinations," particularly if they are guild operations serving the affluent or have built loyalty through dedicated customer and community service. These jewelers can flourish in downtowns or upscale strip centers because they don't depend on the high traffic that shopping malls generate.

But before you say, "Yes, that's me," survey your customers—all of them—to get their opinion. "A lot of retailers make the mistake of thinking they are a destination—that there's something truly distinctive about their store—when they are, in fact, not," says Dr. George Lucas, a professor of retailing at Memphis State University.

Accordingly, many jewelers may be surprised at their percentage of business from browsers who had no specific jeweler in mind or from "impulse" purchases by passers-by. If you're among this group that serves the Great Middle Class (with a typical sale of, say, under $200), you may benefit from the high traffic a mall can offer.

Here is a comparison of the different types of retail environments:

MALLS

Recommendation: Don't feel forced into a mall if you've already established a good, strong reputation elsewhere. But if you serve the Great Middle Class, you should benefit from the traffic that a mall generates.

Positive

Convenience & traffic: Well-planned malls offer easy access and attract traffic from a much larger base than downtowns or strip centers. Browsers comprise much of the traffic, but there usually are a fair number of valid shoppers as well.

The Urban Land Institute's 1987 *Dollars and Cents of Shopping Centers* survey examined sales-per-square-foot for different kinds of shopping areas. For super regional malls (three or more anchor stores and a million or more square feet of gross leasable area), the median sales per sq. ft. totaled $541.21 for a local jewelry chain, $439.23 for a national jewelry chain and $433.10 for an independent. In a regional mall (slightly smaller than the super-regional), the figure was $399.59 for a local jewelry chain, $379.94 for a national jewelry chain and $331.62 for an independent. These figures are considerably higher (by at least $200) than for strip centers.

Malls are convenient. They eliminate the hassle of first finding the store, then tracking down a parking spot. But be cautious when considering specialty malls geared to very high income shoppers. They often don't draw enough traffic to support a store that primarily serves the middle-class.

Advertising: Most malls have occasional promotions that retailers can participate in at less cost than individual promotions.

Competition: Not necessarily a bad thing. "Many consumers like to shop around," says Lucas. "If there are five jewelers in a mall, consumers will go there to get a better idea of what they are looking for and how much they will have to spend." Local and regional jewelers can beat the national chains in this game because they have a better knowledge of local tastes, can offer more distinctive merchandise and often have better service. However, try to avoid malls with very strong local or regional chains. These stores can be formidable competitors.

Space: Inventory requirements are much smaller if a suitable location is available. Because mall space is costly, jewelers usually must stick to jewelry and watches, eliminating space-consuming items such as china, crystal and silver. Malls like to see a small repair department because it helps to draw traffic. It also reinforces the "local" jeweler image. But remember a repair department has to do enough business to cover its share of the rent, salaries and benefits, administrative and advertising costs and taxes before it breaks even. To cut costs, consider moving the repair department, administrative offices and storage to a cheaper location outside the mall, perhaps in a nearby office building.

Environment: Most mall developers are selective, so chances are slim that an undesirable store would move next door and drive away "respectable" customers. In addition, most require tenants to replace shopworn fixtures and keep their stores well-maintained.

Security: Most malls have 24-hour patrols on duty. The opportunity remains for smash-and-grab robberies and shoplifting, but the chance is less for an armed holdup. Also, there's a greater chance of apprehending a thief before he gets out of the mall.

Negative

Expense: Mall space is the most expensive retail space available, says Richard Wolf, a retail real estate consultant from Owings Mills, Md. The Urban Land Institute reports the median rent is $31.24 per sq. ft. in a super regional mall, $22.52 in a regional mall, $11.44 in a strip center and $10.16 in a little neighborhood center. Members of the JCK Retail Jewelers Panel reported rents ranging from $8.50 per sq. ft. in South Dakota to $120 per sq. ft. in a posh West Palm Beach, Fla., mall. The average mall rent for panelists: $31.15 per sq. ft.

WARNING!

Don't close your original store simultaneously with a move—particularly a downtown-to-mall move—warns management consultant Richard Laffin. It takes time to get established in a new location and, if the new store fails to meet expectations, you'll still have the original one. If the new store flies, then you can gradually phase out the other one.

In addition, says the Urban Land Institute, most malls levy a 5%-8% charge on monthly gross sales, plus other surcharges (averaging $4 per sq. ft.) to cover expenses such as energy, common area maintenance, taxes and insurance.

These costs force mall retailers to limit inventory and repair and back-room space. This can be difficult if you have, or want to develop, a full-service reputation.

Loss of independence: Many malls become an unwanted business partner, regulating business hours, advertising and decor/remodeling changes.

Advertising: While you can benefit from "piggybacking" the mall's advertising, remember that tenants help to foot the bill for mall ads. The mall management may want your contribution toward advertising at an inconvenient time or may require so much that you have little left for your own advertising. At the outset, you might agree to pay the required percentage but try to negotiate the payment schedule and/or the form of the advertising to your benefit.

Competition: Expect lower margins on some categories. You won't get top price on goods such as gold jewelry and watches, which are always available at low-margin prices in mall department stores and kiosks.

Discounts will come into play also. "Everyone selling jewelry in the mall—especially department stores—will advertise constant sales," says Richard Laffin of the Management Growth Institute, Wellesley, Mass. You can survive without discounting, he says, but you'll have to compensate with hard advertising reinforcing that discounts are illusory.

One compromise, suggests Laffin, is to use midprice watches as loss leaders (items promoted at cost or near cost to generate traffic). Jewelers who use loss leaders say they have one positive effect: "If we heavily promote low prices on some popular items, it gives the impression that all of our prices are lower than our competitors' prices," says one.

DOWNTOWNS

"Downtown" means any commercial district fronting a public street or pedestrian walk. These include central business districts of large cities, neighborhood shopping districts and small town/suburban Main Streets.

Recommendation: Certain types of jewelers get the best results with a downtown location. They usually fall into one of these categories: large, full-service operations; specialized operations catering to the affluent; small custom goldsmiths; small, longtime community jewelers and fashion-oriented stores specializing in lower-cost merchandise.

Large, full-service stores would face exorbitant rent if they moved their full inventory from downtown to a mall. Stores specializing in the affluent market don't need to be in a mall because their income comes from high margins, not volume. Custom goldsmiths may want more traffic, but their clientele usually comprises a relatively small group of loyal customers. Many are "one desk/one showcase" enterprises that couldn't fill the average mall space but require more than a kiosk offers. Longtime community and fashion-oriented stores are long on service and often too oriented toward one area on type of customer to benefit from a mall.

Positive

Cost: Square foot rent usually is lower than in malls, except on ultra-posh streets (Fifth Avenue, Rodeo Drive) or in popular tourist areas. JCK panelists reported costs ranging from $4-$50 per sq. ft., with an average of $11.60.

Because you generally can afford more space downtown, you can stock a greater variety of merchandise than in mall stores.

Clientele: Stores in downtown business centers are close to offices, with access to executives and well-salaried people. Better downtowns also attract shoppers from surrounding communities, especially during the Christmas season.

Negative

Atmosphere: A jeweler has no control over the surrounding businesses and may suffer from undesirable neighbors. Some cities and towns have tight zoning laws to prevent this, but laws are only as good as their enforcement. As a result, downtown jewelers have to be vigilant, contributing time and money to the local merchants' association.

Convenience: Downtown isn't always the easiest place to park and there usually is no free parking like there is at malls. Retailers sometimes offer inducements such as parking vouchers or enticements such as merchandise not available elsewhere.

Weather: Shoppers often choose enclosed malls over downtowns when shopping in bad weather.

Security: Armed robbers are more likely to hit a downtown or strip store than a mall—the street makes getaway easier. Likewise, it's more difficult to apprehend a shoplifter or smash-and-grab thief than in a mall. You can arrange for a security guard, but you'll absorb the cost yourself. Many owners of downtown stores install gates for protection after closing.

STRIP CENTERS

Recommendation: Neighborhood jewelers who rely on service, repairs and "serving their community" can do well in a strip center. High-end jewelers can thrive in an upscale strip center.

Positive

Cost: The median rent for a strip center is $11.44 per sq. ft., says the Urban Land Institute. JCK panelists located in strip centers pay $5-$16 per sq. ft., with an average of $10 per sq. ft. Stores usually are a bit larger (average 1,400 sq. ft., compared with an average 1,200 in a super regional mall). This allows for display of more inventory and more repair and office space. Some strip centers also have upstairs storage space.

Convenience: Strip centers usually offer free parking (unlike downtowns) in lots that usually are uncrowded (unlike malls). Many also are located closer to residential areas.

Independence: Strip centers usually don't dictate store hours, decor and advertising and promotional programs. However, some new upscale centers may be just as restrictive as a mall, behaving basically like a mall without the roof.

Community-oriented: Most strip center patrons are from the immediate area, so you can build a loyal following through service, professional advice and repairs. Many JCK panelists located in strip centers report strong sales of community-related items such as class ring and trophies.

Specialty strip malls can hold their own against malls because they have different types of stores, says Gary Long of Glasscock Village Jewelers, located in the upscale Lincoln Center strip mall in Stockton, Cal. Lincoln Center's 125 independent shops do well despite two major malls in the same area, he says. Speaking for his own store, a guild operation, he says: "We're definitely a destination store: 83% of our customers come to us with a specific purchase in mind."

Negative

Traffic: Strip centers don't attract as much traffic as malls. People go to malls for entertainment but to strip centers with a specific purchase in mind so there's less browsing, say consultants. As a result, strip center retailers find they must advertise more.

Also, in a strip center, a customer must consciously decide to open a store's door, while there are no such barriers in a mall store. But once the door is opened, the jeweler has a better chance of closing the sale, says Bert Foer, chairman of Melart Jewelers, a retail chain based in Silver Spring, Md.

Weather: As with downtowns, strip centers can lose out to malls when people go shopping in bad weather.

Atmosphere: "Strip centers can go downhill very quickly" says Laffin. "One minute they're respectable, the next there's an adult bookstore moving in."

While high mall rents top the list of JCK panelists' complaints, gripes about strip center maintenance, "neighbors" and other environmental problems are prevalent among strip center occupants. Strip centers with a well-known anchor store usually offer a more stable environment than do smaller "community centers" of six or so stores.

Store configuration: Older strip centers usually offer long narrow retail space that isn't conducive to good jewelry store design.

Security: Strip centers have basically the same security concerns as a downtown store. Some centers, especially upscale ones, may provide outside guards to patrol the grounds.

FREE-STANDING/OTHER

Some jewelers have had success with a free-standing store, but it's a risky option because of the huge investment (often $1 million or more) if the store has to be built or an existing building has to be gutted and renovated. Free-standing stores are best suited to a category killer store, catalog showroom or extremely high-end firm.

Some stores locate in office buildings and professional centers. They find their rents are much cheaper, but their business is basically confined to a very limited clientele and very limited hours (lunchtime and perhaps at the end of the workday). This option is best for firms that specialize in insurance replacements, executive gifts, investment gems and those with a high-powered list of private clients.

Wolf, the retail real estate consultant, points out that business-complex stores with retail fronts still may not get much after-work traffic. People want to get out of the office and go home. So unless you generate enough income in those few hours, it may not be worth the trouble.

Know Thy Market: Where To Look Before You Lease

January 1990

In any retail venture, you should study the market you'll be serving. If you're opening a new store, you need to know what customers in the market will buy. If you want to boost your return on rearranging or remodeling existing retail space, you need to keep in touch with market changes. Here's how.

START AT HOME

In an existing store, periodically survey customers, asking:
- What products or services they want that you don't offer.
- If you moved, would they "move with you," and how far?
- Why they prefer you over the competition (or why not?).
- How far they come to shop at your store?

Make silent observations to record after the customer leaves, noting time of sale, approximate age of customer, male or female, whether they're wearing a wedding ring and where their tastes seem to lie.

Next, determine whether you're attracting new customers or if all you see are familiar faces. If you don't see longtime customers as frequently, find out why. Do you have a personnel problem? Do customers find better value or service in a competitor's store?

POPULATION/COMPETITION

To determine how you can best meet the future, research:
- The number of people living within five miles of your intended or existing site (more if you're rural).
- How many other jewelry stores and other luxury-goods firms (such as travel agencies and electronics stores) are within a close driving distance.
- Whether they draw a lot of customers.
- Whether the area is growing (check the 1970, 1980 and 1990 censuses). How has the area changed and where is it heading? In seven years, will your store be in the heart of new growth or left behind.

INCOME

Naturally, you want to know the average salaries of local residents. But here are some other indications of wealth:
- Level of discretionary income (money left after necessary expenses are paid). Example: Columbia, Md., residents are fairly affluent, salary-wise. But expensive housing leaves Columbia residents with little discretionary income.
- Age. Young families have higher housing and education expenses than more established ones. Older residents may be on pensions, but they often have more disposable income because their homes are paid for and their children are on their own.
- Life-style. The average household in a working-class town won't have a lot of extra cash for jewelry. A town of predominantly white collar professionals is a better target for luxury products. Lois Miller, who handles real estate and public relations for the Columbia, Md.-based Barlow & Eaton jewelry chain, suggests driving around an area for indications of its wealth. Do you see a lot of expensive houses and autos?
- Shopping areas. Do more people in the neighborhood shop in middle-market stores (Sears, J.C. Penney) or upscale stores (Macy's, Marshall Field). Watch shoppers, during the day, in the evening and on weekends. Do they *buy* or *look* ? How do they dress? Do they wear jewelry?
- Predominant ethnic background. Some cultures, such as Latin or Mediterranean, traditionally value jewelry and may consider its purchase a priority; others, such as Quaker, eschew overt displays of wealth so you may find you have fewer customers than you thought you would.

ECONOMY

How's the local economy? Examine these factors:
- What industries drive the economy?
- Is the area dependent on one industry and, therefore, susceptible to the ups and downs of that market?
- Are industries moving in, moving out or closing?
- Is there a college or military base (signaling a transient population that may include good customers, but not ones with whom you can build a long-term relationship).

KNOW THYSELF

Now that you know who your customers and potential customers are, know yourself. What kind of jeweler are you? Remember you can't be all things to all people. Richard Wolf of Owings Mills, Md., is a retail space consultant who specializes in retail jewelry stores. He divides jewelers into these categories:
- Guild—High-end, higher-priced merchandise. Guild jewelers frequently offer prestige tableware and gifts as well as jewelry.
- Credit—Fine jewelry, but in a more moderate price range than a guild jeweler and rarely offering tableware or gifts. Many have their own credit system. Most national and major regional chains fall into this category.
- Custom—Usually a small, independent operation that specializes in fine design, custom work and one-of-a-kind pieces.

• Estate—Antique and period jewelry. The estate jeweler's needs are similar to the custom jeweler. Both have a specialized niche, both appeal to a more well-to-do customer who looks for the unusual, both are found frequently in high-traffic tourist areas and both tend to be highly educated independents.

• Costume—Precious metals and semiprecious gemstones. Many of the free-standing kiosks found in malls fall into this category. Similar to the costume jeweler is the "CZ jeweler" whose merchandise features precious metals and man-made stones.

• Category killers—Extremely large specialized stores that haven't been copied successfully. New York-based Fortunoff's is one.

• Catalog showrooms—Best, Service Merchandise, etc.

Space Design: Balancing Beauty And Bottom Line

January 1990

The best retail location in the world won't entice customers if it's not attractive and inviting. Whether you plan to remodel an existing store or open a new one, space design requires careful planning.

Jerry Fornell, president of the Chicago Design Group, and Ken Nisch, president of Jon Greenberg and Associates, are retail space designers with considerable experience in jewelry stores. Both generally break design planning into phases.

Phase One (minimum of two to four weeks):

• Establish jeweler's goals, including market served and image to be projected. You can't be both Kmart and Harry Winston, says Nisch. The way a store is set up will make a statement to the customer.

• Establish the jeweler's perception of how the finished store will appear. Work to make sure the retailer's perception fits the market he serves. Don't rely on your own taste to design a store, adds Keith Kovar, director of International Design Group. Research does a better job.

• Fornell asks about all the product the retailer plans to present. Does the jeweler want to display gold chain hung from a board like an Arab bazaar or show a few elegant samples on a riser? Nisch often suggests investing in one outstanding feature that shoppers will remember (a sensational bridal department with a chandelier and marble would be an example).

• Determine how much space the jeweler will need for each part of the store involved in the project.

• Consult the landlord about the building's mechanical systems. The design could be affected by certain conditions that have to be met. Any extra expense caused by such conditions might be used to negotiate savings in another area. Fornell, for example, asks whether the property has a chilled-air or chilled-water heating/ventilation/air conditioning system (a chilled-water system costs 30%-50% more to operate).

• Check with the local building inspector to be sure the building—old or new—is up to code and to find out any limitations that will be placed on the jeweler. Sometimes, variances can be secured for certain building code requirements, such as handicapped-accessible.

• Consult the jeweler's insurance company to be sure all design ideas comply with its regulations.

• After gathering all the information, Fornell prepares and presents a few different ideas and floor plans to the retailer. The plans then are fine-tuned and reviewed to uncover any hidden costs (such as floor reinforcement under the safe).

Phase Two (minimum of two to four weeks):

The creative fun begins after the floor plans are decided. Fornell presents drawings of how the finished project will look, along with a material board showing samples of all the decor products.

The jeweler and designer further refine plans and discuss dollars. This is where the jeweler's wish list meets with the reality of a budget. Nisch divides the budget in two parts: "have to," including plumbing and electrical work, and "want to," dealing with decor. As an estimated budget is drawn, the jeweler and designer can make modifications in design and materials to keep down the expense.

Phase Three (minimum of four weeks):

• Blueprints for any construction work are drawn and specifications are written. The plans are submitted to the landlord and/or local zoning board for approval.

• After approval, the jeweler can seek bids from construction firms or allow the design firm to choose a contractor. Some design firms have their own construction divisions. Fornell says contractors need at least two weeks to work out bids; any received in less time may reflect shoddy preparation.

• Total cost is broken down and itemized.

Phase Four (minimum of six to eight weeks):

This is the actual construction. If the jeweler is opening a new store, he doesn't have to worry how construction will affect business as long as it doesn't delay the opening.

Remodeling, however, is disruptive and can drive away customers, says Kovar. The store probably will have to close a few days. But people are curious and the savvy jeweler can turn the mess to his or her advantage: hold a renovation sale at some point during the project. Note: check to make sure the jeweler's insurance company (or the landlord's) permits admitting customers during certain phases of construction.

Patrick Murphy: Fixing What Works

Downtown Pottsville, Pa., used to bustle. It's the seat of Schuylkill County, deep in the heart of a once prosperous anthracite coal region. But now the mines are silent, two malls have been built and all that remains downtown are a handful of tenacious merchants and blocks of empty storefronts. Nonetheless, third-generation jeweler Patrick Murphy, president of Murphy Jewelers, decided not to move his thriving business into a mall and refurbished his downtown store instead.

"We thought about moving to the mall, and we thought about keeping this store and opening a second one in the mall," he says. "But we were afraid a second store would be too much competition for this one. We decided to stick with what works and throw our whole hearts into it."

Murphy spent about $50,000 on his remodeling, which included new wallpaper and carpeting, a custom-made center showcase, new display buildups and boxes, some new lighting and refurbishing old cases. He worked with his wife, Kim, and his cousin, Annie Murphy, an interior designer.

The biggest change was replacing three tall shelf islands in the middle of the floor with a jewelry showcase that Murphy designed and a local carpenter built. The islands (which held giftware that's now shown in wall cases) had blocked the back of the store from view and created a traffic jam. The showcase, about 8 feet long and 4 feet wide, has helped to boost sales an reduce pilferage, he says.

The color scheme was changed from gold and dark wood cases to pale green and ivory, giving a much more open feeling. The carpeting is pale seafoam green, the cases were painted pale ivory and the wallpaper is a soft stripe of both colors. Murphy also topped his wall cases and a one-way mirror window between the workshop and store with wooden transoms.

He re-covered hassock chairs at the diamond counter with natural ivory cotton and created two sets of removable backdrops for the wall cases: one has a green-on-white pattern and the other has the reverse. He also bought new display props in green and pale beige.

With the new color scheme, the store's fluorescent lighting was too bright, giving the look of a discount shop. Murphy added recessed spotlights over the center case and track lights over side cases. He left the fluorescent lights in the ceiling, but now turn on only half of them.

Murphy also enlarged his office/workshop in preparation for hiring another jeweler. In his case, the space was easy to obtain because he also owns the Catholic gift shop next door. He simply took a few feet from there to enlarge his office.

Leon Barmache: Magic in Small Spaces

Yes, Virginia, you can fit a diamond salon, a shop, an office and a selling floor into 495 sq. ft. And yes, you can do it without crowding.

The trick, says Leon Barmache, is simplicity. He used mirrors, a monochromatic color scheme and one dramatic round case as a focal point to make tiny Jacqueline et Cie in Palm Springs, Cal., seem much larger than it is.

Paris-born Barmache is the son of Michael Barmache, a noted jeweler who worked under Fabergé in Russia and Cartier in Paris and New York. Leon and his brother were apprenticed to their father, but in 1925 Leon discovered Art Deco and interior design. He earned a degree from the Beaux Arts in Paris, and though he still occasionally makes jewelry for friends, he's happier creating magic with less-than-magical space.

Jacqueline et Cie is one such space. Located in the tony Desert Fashion Plaza Mall, the store had to fit the image of a truly exclusive salon—complete with private diamond room—yet still operate within the confines of 495 sq. ft. Barmache first planned the extra rooms. The only structural change he made was to bring in the side walls, allowing space for the office/shop and diamond room behind. The rest was all optical illusion achieved with careful decor.

Barmache's plan called for mirrored walls (including doors to the hidden salon and office), and varying shades of beige for everything else. He laid a beige carpet, covered the storefront in beige marble and highlighted the back central wall with the same marble. What wasn't covered in mirror or marble (basically the ceiling) was painted pale beige. Brass was the choice for signs and trim. The crowning touch was the store's only floor fixture—a custom, 9-ft.-diameter circular case.

The case was made in four sections from quarter-inch and half-inch glass. Barmache trimmed it in pale oak and brought carpeting up the outside to just below the glass. The carpet on the case makes the floor space look larger and disguises storage cabinets underneath. The jeweler enters through a gateway in the back and gains access to the display areas through sliding doors inside.

Barmache put one small shadowbox case on each side wall and the back wall. The boxes contain just a few dramatic pieces on beige display props. He added two pedestals to flank panels of marble on the back wall, and finished off the corners with tall plants.

He designed a round, recessed cove with about 30 spotlights directly above the case. The top of the cove is white, the outer part and the rest of the ceiling are off-white. He used low-wattage M16 halogen bulbs and ceiling spots throughout the store (no case lights), and put all lights on dimmers. A crystal chandelier over the case gives focal balance but isn't a major light source.

The finishing touch was brass trim and arched tops on the front door. The finished store not only looks twice its size, but it carries an air of exclusivity by the deliberately limited displays. It was a costly endeavor, about $200 per sq. ft. (compared with an average $150 per sq. ft.), but the look had to fit its well-heeled customers.

Barmache says jewelers with similar space limitations but without the tony clientele to make it pay could adapt his ideas. His tips: a monochromatic color scheme and mirrors without marble and custom-designed cases.

Elements of Design

Traffic flow: Jewelers can use lighting, case layouts and floor and wall graphics to entice people to go through the entire store. The layout also should make it easy for the staff to function (example: a salesperson shouldn't have to run the length of the store to retrieve a layaway).

Lease line: A good idea for a mall store is to attract customers with a display at the entrance (lease line), but don't transact business there. People don't feel comfortable buying something expensive when they're standing half in and half out of the store, says space designer Ken Nisch. He recommends perhaps a tall pedestal case highlighting some special merchandise at the lease line.

Initial display: Consultants say front counters and displays should be inviting to targeted customers based on their life-styles. A jeweler with middle-class clientele, for example, should show a range of prices, but without cheapening his image and alienating the high-end customer. A $100 ring and $5,000 ring shouldn't be shown side by side because the contrast could cheapen the look of both, say consultants.

Dr. George Lucas, professor of retailing at Memphis State University, adds this tip for jewelers serving a lower-middle class or blue-collar clientele: Put clearly marked price tags on everything in the front display. People won't go near the store if they don't think they can afford what's inside, he says.

Nonjewelry items, such as mineral specimens or a picture of the Duchess of Windsor to highlight jewelry of that style, also can be used to generate interest.

Case heights: Higher cases, where the customer stands while shopping, are best for impulse items, say consultants. Cases that require the customer to sit down generally indicate higher priced merchandise or bridal sales. Use this concept to emphasize your image; add more seated cases, for example, to upgrade your image or increase your bridal sales.

Nisch and space designer Jerry Fornell don't care for wall cases to display jewelry. It's more like having a stockroom with a window, says Nisch. But they're fine for china or giftware displays.

Salon or diamond room: Fornell doesn't recommend it for jewelers with a low-to-middle-income clientele, but feels it's necessary for a high-end jeweler. Such a room promotes exclusivity and privacy and is more secure than general sales space. However, the room should be in an accessible part of the store so the customer can be ushered in without feeling trapped.

Colors/finishes: Preferences come and go, but the propensity today is toward gray, mauve, marble and chrome. New options are peach, celadon and other shades of pale green. Beige, of course, is classic.

How Much Does Your Space Really Cost?

January 1990

Not all retail space is created equal. Downtown space can rent for as little as $10 per sq. ft., mall space for as much as $100, according to store owners, management consultants and others. Even inside a store, certain selling areas are worth more than others, and certainly more than backroom space. To get the most for your space dollars, don't waste prime selling spots on your least profitable merchandise.

Your best space is the first counter that customers see as they enter the store, say retail consultants. It's worth two times your average per-square-foot rent. Lesser prime spots are worth $1^1/_2$ times the average, other retail space is figured at average and the office, safe and back room are worth half the average. (Aisles are allocated to the department they serve.)

Your best retail spot isn't always obvious if no counters face front. The best spot in rectangular stores with a "horseshoe" layout (counters running parallel to the side

and back walls with aisle in the middle) is the front, to the customer's right, for example. Studies show 90% of customers walk in that direction when they enter a store, says Richard Laffin of he Management Growth Institute, Wellesley, Mass.

Cost vs. profit: You want to make sure no departments lose money. Consider this example:

A store paying basic rent of $20 per sq. ft. filled its prime spot with a 150-sq.-ft. watch department (25 sq. ft. for the counter, 50 for the selling floor space, 75 for the customer aisle in front). As the best spot, it's assessed double the average rent ($40 per sq. ft. or $6,000). The watch department had $50,000 in sales and $20,000 in profits last year. Deductions for the department's share of employee salaries and benefits, administrative and advertising expenses and taxes left $5,250. With its share of rent at $6,000, the department lost $750.

Laffin suggests jewelers evaluate every department this way to determine which don't "earn" their space. If you want to open a new store and base your calculations on projections, you have time to change your plans. But if a department in an existing store doesn't earn its space, it's time to reorganize.

Reorganizing: Options range from simply rearranging merchandise to a complete remodeling, depending on how much you're willing to spend. You can create a "boutique" look with as little expense as a few Oriental fans and a few lighting changes. But adding a private salon where "clients" can view $5,000+ jewelry involves construction and much more expense.

Expense aside, your basic options are:

• Moving less profitable departments to less costly space, but keeping them pretty much intact.

• Expanding profitable departments, downsizing less profitable ones and moving each department to space more closely aligned to its share of total profit.

• The first two options plus eliminating some departments and adding others.

Laffin cautions jewelers not to get carried away and close departments without considering the long-term effect. "Remember you won't lower space costs," he says. "Your goal is to get the maximum return for those costs in the context of other business operations." China, silver and giftware, for example, take more space and offer less return than diamonds and colored stones. But if you're known as a full-service jeweler, eliminating these departments could alienate customers and cut potential traffic.

When it comes time to expand or add lines, consider your options carefully. Should you display more diamond, pearl or colored stone jewelry? "Ask the question: can I sell a lot more?" says Laffin. A 10% sales increase is possible with a little extra effort, he says, but 50% is out of the question without a significant increase in your advertising and promotion budget.

Some research on what's selling, what's not and what customers would like to see more of (ask them), will help to determine which lines to add and which are ripe for expansion.

• Ask customers as they leave what they like best and least about the store, whether they're interested in something the store doesn't carry, whether they've seen similar items elsewhere for less, whether they've bought jewelry in other stores and what you can do to serve them better. Also study your area's demographics.

• Visit competitors. What do they stock that you don't? If they're successful with these items, why can't you be? Check their ads to see what they promote. You may have missed a market they tap.

• If you decide to take on new lines, be sure to advertise and promote them. Laffin cautions that building a new department requires patience and promotion. "Don't put a lot of money into inventory to fill space if you aren't reasonably certain of selling it," he says.

Balances: When deciding how to proceed with your reorganization, balance efficiency with image, says Dr. Dale Lewison, professor of retailing at the University of Ohio in Akron. Also balance efficiency with security, adds Carol Basden, owner of Basden Risk Management, Birmingham, Ala.

Keeping these balances in mind, consultants offer these three space maximizing ideas:

#1: Front counter. The first counter or display customers see should set your image, promote the items you most want to sell and direct traffic.

Remember this is your prime spot, so you want to include the high profit items your store features. But to set your image, you should show a range of items available in your store. Finding the right balance can be tricky.

The solution? Offer a clear picture of your product range, but group it by "life-style." Place some nicely crafted affordable jewelry in one part of the counter and higher-end merchandise in another, showing both types of customers you cater to their needs.

Cost: Front display counters vary widely in cost. A custom-designed counter costs much more than stock counters, but it may be worth the expense. John Garufi, marketing manger for Magic Glass Corp. of San Francisco believes the front display counter is most effective when custom-designed and integrated with the store decor. He and other custom-case designers prefer not to quote prices because each job is so different.

Carefully chosen stock cases can be effective, too, says Larry Gershel of Gershel Bros. Store Fixtures, Philadelphia, Pa. He lists a lighted pedestal display case for $570 (some suppliers offer discounts) and a revolving display case for $1,046. Hexagonal showcases with pedestal storage bases—ideal for islands or front display counters—are $578.

Installation charges are minimal for stock cases. But you also must consider lighting. Overhead two-unit track lights to highlight a display cost $100-$200, depending on type of light. (Note: this cost doesn't include electrical installation.)

#2: Cobweb corners. Potted plants, Oriental urns and elegant grandfather clocks fill corners beautifully, but make no money, says Lewison. He suggests filling corners with "boutiques" featuring such high-profit items as branded merchandise (Rolex watches or Cartier gifts, for example), custom-designed jewelry or seasonal/theme-oriented counters (graduation gifts, Valentine's Day, etc.). Draw attention with special lighting and displays. Have salespeople encourage customers to take a look.

Joe Pfieffer of McDonald Pfieffer Jewelers, Bedford, Ind., took the idea a step further by replacing a big potted plant in one corner with a Merle Norman cosmetics boutique. The boutique make money on its own, he says, but there's a bonus: many women who come in to buy upscale cosmetics often leave with a piece of jewelry, too.

Garufi adds, "Free-standing towers can maximize underused vertical space. For example, a 6 ft. high display tower occupies only 2 sq. ft. of floor space and offers 8 sq. ft. of display space."

Costs: Retailers can build their own boutique or corner unit from stock cases. Gershel says a three-piece corner unit costs about $1,450, plus $168 for case lighting and $250-$350 for three-unit overhead halogen track lighting.

Jewelry suppliers often offer "brand name" boutiques, displays, case "buildups" and signs at cost or reduced price. Magic Glass, for example, offer its "Point of Purchase" boutique program to giftware manufacturers for their retail clients.

Custom displays with special material (such as hardwood paneling) or special sizes are available from contractors and store design and fixture firms. Seek bids from several for the best price.

#3: Diamond room. Jewelers catering to an upmarket clientele can install a private salon or "diamond viewing room" for times when discretion is preferred. "It's a great image-builder," says Laffin. The room should have high-intensity lighting (you may use the low-voltage type if desired), minimal furniture and an elegant look. For securi-ty, says Basden, install a two-way mirror or camera so someone other than the salesperson can view goings-on in the room. She also suggests not keeping your diamond inventory in the room.

Costs: Prices will depend on the contractor. Seek bids from several, and be prepared for wide variations.

Watch Repair: Who Will Do It?

May 1989

Three out of four jewelers say watch repair is impor-tant to their store. Yet, many of them no longer have on-site watchmakers. Instead, they rely on independent watch repair shops.

Such shops range from one-person freelancers to firms with scores of people on repair assembly lines. Whatever their size, jewelers' reliance on these shops has grown signif-icantly in the past few years.

A JCK poll found two out of three jewelers, even many with on-site watchmakers, use repair trade shops. Of those who do, just over half use one shop, the rest use two or more. And this year alone, at least one jeweler in six plans to send more watches to trade shops.

A separate, random JCK study of two dozen indepen-dent watch repair firms of various sizes found most enjoyed 10% to 40% business growth over the past three years. Most say jewelers account for at lest half of their business; one in three depends almost entirely on them.

Jewelers' use of watch repair shops will continue to grow, say jewelers and repair shops "both need each other for survival."

Fewer watchmakers: Trade shops have multiplied as fewer jewelers keep a watchmaker on staff. A generation ago, virtually every jewelry store had an on-site watchmaker. Today, just over a third of those polled by JCK have none.

The simple fact is the number of watchmakers in the U.S. labor market has dwindled from 50,000 in the 1950s to 12,000 or 13,000 now. "Soon all that jewelers will have for watch repair will be trade shops, because the industry is los-ing watchmakers faster than they are coming in," says James Broughton, a senior instructor for the American Watchmakers Institute and operator of a one-man trade shop for 22 years.

Robert Bishop, AWI president, agrees. "With the number of watchmakers decreasing, trade shops are the way to get more production out of fewer people."

Watchmakers' attrition coincides with other factors, including:

• Technological advances such as quartz analog watch-es, which need few repairs.

• The shrinking importance of watches to many jewel-ers as mass merchandisers, discounters and other retailers use them to pull traffic. Explains a Buffalo, N.Y., jeweler who no longer sells or repairs watches, "With everyone in the watch business from beauty shops to grocery stores, it costs more than it's worth to have watches."

• The starting salary of a watchmaker at many jewelry stores hasn't grown enough to entice people, says Henry Fried, a horological expert and JCK editor. Starting salaries at many jewelry stores are $10,000 to $12,000. But experience can double that amount. JCK 's annual salary survey for 1987 showed watchmaker salaries ranging from $8,168 to $33,000, with the median at $22,385.

Many jewelers with watchmakers let them take in trade work to make extra money when off duty. "Almost every watchmaker today moonlights," says Broughton. "When he leaves the store to go home, he often does trade work for other retailers."

Advantages: Even with a steady flow of watch repair business, many jewelers find it cheaper, even profitable, to send out watches rather than keep an on-site watchmaker. That way, they don't have to take up valuable selling space for a bench, maintain a stock of watch parts or pay a watchmak-er's wages, benefits and insurance, say Fried and Broughton.

Sid Rubin of Wood Jewelers, Cleveland, Tenn., started to use a three-man trade shop in Chattanooga when his repair-man left three years ago. Repairs now take less time, and his watch repair service has changed from a break-even opera-tion to a money-maker.

Trade shops let Carl Carstens of Schnack Jewelry Co., Alexandria, La., offer an attractive service without the expense of another employee and watch materials. "Our watch service is profitable and very important to us," says Carstens, who hasn't had an on-site repairman for 15 years. "It brings in traffic. And anything you can do to get people to come in is useful. It also creates opportunities to sell new watches, when the old one isn't worth fixing."

Trade shops also can be a competitive alternative to watch manufacturers' service centers. Says Broughton,

"Factory service centers tend to take longer and their prices are a little higher. Most trade shops try to come in under what factories charge."

As one jeweler says, "They're cheaper and closer."

Even jewelers who have enough work to justify an on-site repairman make more use of trade shops these days. The on-site person can concentrate on special cases while sending routine or overflow repairs to trade shops. Jeweler William Mosher of Port Huron, Mich., for example, uses a trade shop when his on-site watchmaker gets too busy, goes on vacation or finds a problem he can't repair.

Growth industry: The number of trade shops is growing, but specific numbers are hard to pin down. The shops have no separate association (though individual watchmakers have the American Watchmakers Institute), they need no industry certification to operate and many don't even list in phone books or advertise, except by word of mouth. As one shop owner says, "I already have more work than I know what to do with."

But watch repair experts say such shops easily number in the hundreds. A conservative estimate is 400 to 500. It's not a huge industry. But it has almost doubled since the 1970s.

In size, watch repair shops range from one-man freelancers to firms with scores of people on watch repair assembly lines. Most are mom-and-pop firms, operated out of a home by experienced professionals who do all the work on a watch.

Large operations hire professionals and semi-skilled people. The semi-skilled are taught to do specific jobs, such as inserting the balance, putting in the stem and crown of a watch or replacing defective quartz movements.

Large or small, most trade shops (69%) depend on jewelers for at least half their business. One in three gets virtually all its work from jewelers. But the shops also service the watch departments of department stores and catalog showrooms and do contracted warranty work for watch importers.

Quality of work: Generally, jewelers and trade shops have a genial relationship. But a third of jewelers polled by JCK have periodic complaints about service and repairs by trade shops.

The biggest headache (43%) is "comebacks," when annoyed customers return with a complaint about a watch repair. One in eight jewelers (12%) returns a 10th of watch jobs to trade shops because of unsatisfactory workmanship. That exceeds the return rate for factories and in-store watchmakers.

"It's a chronic problem," says David J. Coll of Montclair Jewelers, Oakland, Cal., which uses four trade shops. "We keep changing trade shops, but they all seem to have a high rate of comebacks."

Jewelers place the blame on a lack of experienced watchmakers. "Many of our jobs come back several times because few people do watch repairs anymore, and it's hard to find anyone who does good work," says a Missouri jeweler with a declining watch business.

Unhappy jewelers also blame the way many trade shops operate. "Most take in more than they can handle and don't stick to promised dates [of delivery]," says Coll.

Assembly-line methods of larger repair shops irk some jewelers. "In my experience, trade shops ruin more watch-

es than they repair [because of] short-cut methods," says Ralph M. Fava of Paterson, N.J. "Mass production doesn't produce good work."

A Massachusetts jeweler agrees, based on several bad experiences with a large New York trade shop. In one instance, the firm overhauled an expensive watch for $130, but didn't clean the case and charged $5 for a battery it didn't change. "Only under dire circumstances will we deal with them again," says the jeweler.

Another complaint about trade shops is turnaround time. Routine repairs take on to two weeks; a complex job takes up to three weeks. That's better than service centers and factories, but it's still not fast enough to please a third of jewelers who told JCK they use trade shops.

Remedies: Jewelers suggest these problems could be solved by a few operational changes. They say trade shops should:

• Be more realistic about promised delivery dates and not overextend themselves.

• Pay more attention to quality control, including everything from checking accuracy to cleaning and polishing cases and bracelets. "The outside is almost as important as the inside," says a Memphis, Tenn., jeweler. "A customer who sees a dirty watch immediately thinks the inside hasn't been repaired properly."

• Have a firm policy on repair quality and comebacks. William Mosher tells the trade shop he uses he'll go elsewhere if comebacks become a problem at his Michigan store. "No excuses. We pay cash fast and demand the best service he can give any of his customers," says Mosher. "It works."

• Use only trained employees. "Hire experienced professionals, not apprentices calling themselves watchmakers," says an Illinois jeweler. Because such professionals are scarce, several jewelers suggest that more repair firms set up training programs.

• Talk to jewelers. "If a repair shop has a specific problem with a watch that will take more time, or if parts are back-ordered or discontinued, we should be told right away so we can tell the customer," says Diane Lancaster of Robert Yacovetta Jewelers, Denver, Colo.

Jeweler Thomas J. Kraft of Sheridan, Wyo., agrees. "Advising us that old, 'problem' watches are unrepairable and may never be made to run properly" could eliminate some of the frustration and anger jewelers and customers experience with comebacks, he says.

Bernard Crohn of Dan Marx Jewelers, Portland, Ore., urges trade shops to develop better contact with watch companies. If parts can be acquired more quickly, customers won't have to wait and won't be as likely to lose confidence in the brands they own, he says.

Flip side: Trade shop operators defend their work.

"We do good work, at a reasonable price," says the supervisor of a large Illinois repair shop. "We have established a reputation for quality and quick turnaround. We specialize in large quantities, and yet strive for personal service. These are goals we take seriously."

Most trade shops, of course, do prefer to use experienced watchmakers, preferably ones trained in mechanical and quartz watches. Criteria cited in JCK 's poll range from training in Swiss watchmaking schools to AWI certification.

But the limited supply of watchmakers remains a problem, even though some larger firms have training programs. In fact, Precision Watch Repair, an eight-person Philadelphia firm with a growing business, may have to go overseas to get qualified people, says the owner.

Trade shops also are sensitive to the problem of comebacks. In some larger ones, for example, a watch returned a second time is given to a senior watchmaker for detailed inspection and correction.

But the watch in question may simply be impossible to repair. "If X brand watch doesn't have the right movement to begin with, and its own factory can't fix it, how can you expect the watchmaker to do it? asks Broughton.

In some cases, watch parts aren't available. This is especially true for very old models and gray market watches (legitimate brand names made for overseas markets but imported here for sale at discount). Because gray market watches were made for overseas sale, domestic suppliers sometimes don't have parts needed to repair them.

Communication: Jewelers themselves can cause problems for trade shop owners. Sometimes they pay bills late, complete forms incorrectly or forget to include warranty information with watches. But what really bugs most trade shop operators is jewelers' failure to communicate.

The frequent turnover in jewelry store personnel and no training for new people in watch take-ins complicate matters. Some problems blamed on trade shops actually result from inexperienced jewelry store employees who say and promise things they shouldn't, says a supervisor for a large Illinois watch repair operation.

"[Jewelers] usually don't give us enough information to properly estimate a problem, or they don't relay the customer's problem to us," says the operator of a two-man shop in Florida.

Skill + Service = Profit

The watch repair business is good for F. Martell Grover. He has operated Grover Service Center, a one-man trade shop in Rexburg, Idaho, since finishing watchmaking school in Neuchâtel, Switzerland, in 1970.

In the past three years, his dollar volume has risen 20% and watch take-ins have increased 13% (to 225 a month). Ninety percent of his business is with jewelers, the rest with department stores. About half his 32 clients were referred by salesmen or other clients; he also gets customers by promoting his firm.

Almost two-thirds of the watches he repairs are mechanical. Most of the rest are quartz analog, with a tiny number being digitals.

What's behind all these statistics? Here's what Grover says about being a watch repairman in 1989.

What changes, if any, do you plan to make in your watch service/repair operation this year?

Increase personal contact and mailings. I attend jewelers' conventions and advertise in their program books. Since spring 1988, I've sent out candy bars [with his name and advertising on specially printed wrappers] in follow-up mailings; I also send them to my accounts once a month... At a recent convention, out of 100 packets, I got six new clients.

What is your typical turnaround?

A routine job takes 7 to 14 working days. A complex one takes 10 to 14. American pocket watches take 10 to 30 days. . . Back orders [of parts at supply firms] aren't a great problem for me, because I use material houses with large inventories. (About 5% of parts ordered are back-ordered.) Most back orders are filled in 10 days, and 95% in 30 days.

What are your most common problems with jewelers?

Sometimes instructions aren't clear. For example, [a customer says], "Fix the watch," then gets upset with the jeweler because the parts and work done are more than what he meant. Most of my accounts place price ceilings on work so that doesn't happen very often.

Also, a problem can arise when a customer tells a jeweler he wants his watch back in exactly two weeks. If special parts are needed, they may be back-ordered at the materials house. . . And sometimes no warranty information accompanies a watch. We can't find when it was in for repair or if minor work was done.

Another problem arises when a jeweler gets an estimate for repairs, doesn't respond for three or four weeks, then wants a rush job. This creates a problem if special parts have to be ordered.

How do you keep your business profitable?

Keeping overhead down is very important. That means buying parts at good prices. Parts that are used a lot I buy in volume, and I *ask* for volume discounts. . . I also collect movements from jewelers for spare parts.

Location can also add to the cost of overhead. I just moved my work area to my home last year.

How do you decide what to charge for service / repair jobs?

Cost is based on the time and training needed for the job. After my watch repair training in Switzerland, I worked for several factories to get hands-on training and factory instruction. I also attend special seminars. This training means a higher price because [I have] more training than some other trade shops.

I also keep contact with jewelers on how my prices compare with other trade shops.

What markup do you use?

Keystone is a good rule of thumb, but I don't get as much markup on my materials as some other trade shops. I try to keep my prices within reason so mom-&-pop shops can afford them.

If I pay $10 for a crystal, I charge the jeweler $20. If a set bridge costs me $2, I have a flat fee of $5 to fit it, and cost to the jeweler is $7. A circuit board costs me $22 and just needs to be fitted with three or four screws to the movement. There is a $10 fee for that, so cost to the jeweler is $32.

Some jewelers say they cannot keep their customer happy if the prices are too high. Yet, the [jeweler charges the customer] $64 to $90 for that new circuit board, and the customer complains about the high cost... It is this keystone to triple-keystone markup that some jewelers think they must have that gets me. In Japan and Europe, where all the stores send out watch repairs, they only take a fee of 20% to 25% [over] their cost of the repair.

Watch repair:
Look at It as a Business

Many jewelers say watch repair is more trouble than it's worth. But for William Mosher of Port Huron, Mich., it's a real money-maker.

Retailers who downgrade the value of watch repair "have an attitudinal problem," he says. With that negative attitude, "they'll never do the things necessary to make jewelry and watch repairs—or themselves as jewelers—important to customers."

Mosher's Jewelers has done business in Port Huron since 1906, and watch service is a big reason for the family firm's success. It accounts for 15% to 20% of the firm's dollar business, says Mosher.

And the service is growing. The firm's monthly intake of watches (100 to 150) is up 15% over three years ago. For the first time last fall, in fact, Mosher and his on-site watchmaker started to send overflow repairs to a trade shop.

There's no secret to what makes a successful watch and repair department, says Mosher. "Other jewelers look on watch repair as a necessary evil; we look at it as a business," he says. "It's part of our service and we promote it as though we were selling merchandise."

Here's how:

• Billboards. In a co-op advertising deal with Rolex Watch last year, Mosher posted billboards at 12 locations between July and September (four different locations each month). All promoted his store as the area's authorized Rolex dealer and service center.

"People from all over came in with Rolexes and other fine watches for servicing and repair," he says. In fact, a man from

Lansing, Mich. (150 miles south of Port Huron), brought in his watch after seeing a billboard while driving through town.

The campaign was so successful, Mosher is doing it again this year between March and May. He has an option to renew for three more months if the response is as good as last time.

• Ads. Mosher runs 2"-by-2" ads in local papers in the first quarter of each year to promote his watch and clock repair service for various brands. Why only in the first quarter? "It's a slow time of year for watch and jewelry sales. The ads bring people in with their watches. That keeps our watchmaker's box full and our business up."

• House calls. Mosher offers an at-home service for grandfather clocks he sells. His watchmaker services grandfather clocks in any home within 50 miles of the store.

• Clinics. Periodic free pocket watches are a popular feature of Mosher's watch service.

"We pick a day or two, preferably on weekends, when we advertise that our watchmaker will inspect and give free opinions of value of any pocket watch."

This includes information on when the watch was made, by whom and other relevant details, says Mosher.

"People love it, and if they leave the watch for repair or restoration, they get a typewritten evaluation and free photograph" of the watch.

• Guarantee. The store provides what Mosher calls its own "strong guarantee" on all its watch repairs. "The trade shop guarantee is for six months, but our warranty is for a year," he says. "If anything goes wrong with the watch in that time, there's no charge for repairs."

That doesn't necessarily create traffic, but it "weighs heavily in our customers' decision to get a watch fixed here," he says.

Before You Redesign

April 1986

When Daniel Moyer, a jewelry retailer in Carmel, Ind., decided to open his first store several years ago, a good friend told him, "All you need is an oriental rug, a chandelier and good jewelry."

Those basic elements—something nice underfoot, attractive lighting and good merchandise—still are crucial to a jeweler's success. But there are many more. Today the person—owner or professional outsider—redesigning a jewelry store must consider color schemes, security, layout for proper traffic flow, lighting for enhancement, windows that invite... and the ever-present cost factor.

Moyer learned this lesson with the passage of time. Today he keep his oriental rugs at home; the store floor is covered with heavy plush. The chandelier is gone, replaced with modern and utilitarian track lighting. Only the "good jewelry" element is unchanged.

The total look: Anyone considering a redesign should start with a checklist of eight separate store areas:

• Showcases	• Floors
• Walls	• Ceilings
• Windows	• Lighting
• Color	• Layout

Redesign may involve one, several or all of these elements. Taken together, they project the store's image. Because of their importance, let's begin with...

Showcases: These are what sell your jewelry. They should enhance the merchandise, not distract from it.

First take a look at what you've got. Do you want to upgrade existing cases or start anew? Weight the costs carefully. It's expensive to add security features to old cases; starting from scratch may be more economical.

How about drawers? Do you really need them? Remember, they too are costly. One rough estimate is $50 per drawer.

Of course, materials have much to do with price. A six-foot hand-carved walnut showcase could cost $2600. Minus the hand-carving, the price drops to roughly $1200. Change the walnut to oak, with little or no hand-carving, and the price goes on down to $600 to $800.

Metal cases are the least expensive. But designers and retailers alike are moving away from them for a classier look. This is not to say that metal is *wrong;* rights and wrongs don't exist, only impressions and *effectiveness.*

Should you use riot-proof glass, with it's interwoven plastic membrane, as a showcase option?

Wall cases can display merchandise effectively; they're especially good for showing larger, gift-oriented items. Be sure, though, that customers have easy access to the cases and can get a close-up view of the items on display.

At R.J. Allison Jewelers in Fort Madison, Iowa, attractive wall cases present merchandise and work as a design element, too. The units are sectioned into the perimeter wall while floor cases are grouped in the store's center. Thus customers can browse comfortably and see clearly all the jewelry lines on display.

Flooring it: Carpeting is the unchallenged leader in jewelry stores, with plush cut-piles the most popular. The material actually stands up as opposed to a nap woven into the base (loop type). Avoid very long shags; these record every footstep and require constant raking.

Carpeting can run from $10 to $24 per square foot. Both cut-pile and loop should fall somewhere within this range; good quality cut-pile generally is more costly than loop. There seems little sense in going cheap here; spending more now means a plush look *plus* durability.

For high traffic areas, hard floors of tile, marble or wood are acceptable, even desirable. Quarry tile, known for its toughness and wearability, is used at Warren Hannon Jewelers in Olathe, Kan. The Larry Dowd/Mike Stauder design team, New Concepts and Designs of Pueblo, Colo., redesigned this store.

Hannon's tile walkway is constructed of 12-in. squares placed to form a rectangular walkway. The color closely matches that of the surrounding carpet. The mix of hard and "soft" floors can match other materials.

MariAnn Coutchie, a Woodland Hills, Cal., jewelry store design specialist, likes to integrate hard floors with carpet. She notes that department stores everywhere are doing it, so why not the jeweler? The mix saves on wear and tear and, if properly done, won't detract from the look. She does say that store size is an important consideration. If a store is rather small, putting a hard floor down the middle may make it seem even smaller.

Walls & windows: "There's nothing wrong with a good coat of paint," says Coutchie. In fact it's the cheapest way to enhance walls. Here again, other options can be incorporated for a twist. Fabric-covered panels are an attractive route, though rather costly.

In place of fabric, Mike Manfredi, designer/salesman for American Store Design, Cumberland, R.I., suggests fabric look-alikes made of vinyl. These look so much like fabric you have to touch to tell the difference, he says. "It's as elegant as fabric but priced like vinyl." It also can be wiped clean and, unlike its fabric counterpart, won't snag.

Mirrors may be your wall covering answer. Large posters of gemstones mounted as art also provide an effective cover, suggests Coutchie. Don't overlook wall paper and paneling.

At Warren Hannon Jewelers paneling stops 2 ft. short of the ceiling on 10-ft. walls. As part of the redesign, silver-gray wallpaper now covers that unpaneled upper portion, pulling together the store's blue/gray color scheme.

Windows get mixed reviews. Manfredi says problems with windows occur wherever there is direct sunlight. To avoid a possible glare, he suggests blocking them or closing them off entirely. Others see it differently.

Take, for example, Lawrence Jewelers in Port Huron, Mich. The two floor-to-ceiling windows which flank the doorway are a helpful safety measure, according to local police. To make the open space more attractive, three diamond-shaped wood cubicles are suspended mid-way in each window. These are closed off in back. The boxes add interest but do not block a sidewalk view of the store's interior.

New windows are being made smaller today. The smaller space, says Keith Kovar of New York City's International Design Group Inc., makes displays easier to control. Also, showing a limited number of items causes less consumer confusion. MariAnn Coutchie proposes setting smaller windows within the big as a way to incorporate modern approaches with older store fronts. A strong proponent of effective widow use, she refers to the opening as "your salesman on the street." The Dowd/Stauder design team builds special pedestals and hanging units to add appeal. According to Dowd, windows should work as attractions which draw people into the store.

Ceiling: Don't forget your ceiling. One of the least expensive ways to improve its look is to lower it. The size of the panel squares provides variety. But this look has become so common that Mike Manfredi of American Store Design continues to search for another answer. He suggests trying a plaster ceiling, but remains dissatisfied because the method is expensive.

Keith Kovar and partner Ruth Mellergaard of International Design Group try other overhead variations to pull customers in. They favor a stepped effect using Gypsum board (dry wall) covering metal frames. This method gives a sense of depth to the store. It also can be used in exaggerated form to "echo the flow of the cases," says Mellergaard. The look achieves a dramatic focus on the jewelry.

The light: Lighting may be the least visible design element. Yet it plays a crucial part in any redesign. According to Kovar, "Anything which affects case layout will affect the lighting." Too often, he says, retailers overlook this area, settle for lighting which is too flat.

The nature of the fine jeweler's merchandise calls for special attention. Without proper lighting retailers may be doing themselves (and their jewels) a great injustice.

If the light source comes from the ceiling, as is most often the case, the ceiling should be about 8 ft. to 9 ft. high, says George Stone of Berg Selector Store Fixtures, Lynbrook, N.Y. The lighting must be close enough to be effective, he adds.

Recessed lighting is popular for primary light sources. This type is built-in, providing light without a bulky fixture. The variations are many, from rectangular covered surfaces to circular hollow sources. Recessed is most functional, says Manfredi, and can be manipulated to throw light where necessary.

The chandelier has not died, although some designers are willing to bury it. When Manfredi hunts for one to use in design, he looks for the spectacular. "If I can't find what's exactly right, I'll stick with recessed." Track lighting is a newer light source. The canister-shaped fixtures snap into a tube of metal suspended from the ceiling. The look is extremely modern and suggested only for a very contemporary image.

Regardless of the look, low-voltage lighting is considered the best for highlighting jewelry. This can be used in recessed types as well as track.

Color: Retailers are turning to lighter colors for a warmer look. Neutrals like beige and light gray are being replaced by more interesting shades. Keith Kovar lists "intense peach and strong turquoise" as two examples of today's approach to color. There is no dominant hue; the matter is personal choice.

Keep in mind that jewelry is the vibrant element, says Mike Manfredi. Color should be subdued, and not competitive. He suggests laying jewelry against the color being considered to see how the two work together.

There is an economical edge to this trend. Stores utilizing lighter interiors will require fewer heating and lighting sources.

Layout: The latest word in store layout is snaked cases, where displays are angled to control and dictate customer movement. The idea stems from concern about traffic flow. When the customer is "guided" through the store, no merchandise should remain unseen. But "watch out for dead ends and funny corners," warns Kovar. The customer must be able to wander without getting stuck in any one place.

"Layouts are getting too crazy," concludes Mike Manfredi. He says the excessive emphasis on traffic flow can have ill effects: Layouts that distract from the jewelry or traffic flow which is overly dictated. He prefers the simple approach. One possibility he suggests is a U-shape to pull people in and around merchandise.

Craziness aside, talk of "snaking" and traffic flow continues. It's all part of today's attention to marketing, or "How might I better promote [display] my product?" In support of this trend, fixture specialist George Stone says, "People want to get away from the standard sterile look of store layouts."

Getting It All Together

Give yourself about six months to do a complete interior design, the experts agree. Planning will consume two of those months. Actual work within the store will require an additional 10 to 12 weeks. Don't do yourself the injustice of a rushed redesign; you'll only get less for more.

Business needn't come to a halt during the store's facelift. Consider a renovation sale, says Keith Kovar of International Design Group Inc. Curious customers will want to see what's happening or check for special "deals" on merchandise. "There have been instances," says Kovar, "where some customers were stopping back each week to watch the progress."

Above all, don't panic. Kovar notes that panic often starts when the store is 80% to 95% finished. "The paint may appear brighter than the client anticipated," he says as an example of problems. "But that's without the showcases in position." They'll hide much of the bare wall.

"If there is anything I can recommend, it's to give yourself enough time," says Brian Keith, general manager at Lawrence Jewelers, Port Huron, Mich. "And have a local designer." Keith suggests allowing anywhere from six to eight months for the entire project.

At R.J. Allison Jewelers, Ft. Madison, Iowa, management took nearly four years to plan their redesign. They spent that time, according to store owner Sue Allison, looking at other stores in the state and reading "everything we could get our hands on."

Custom-built, solid oak showcases were commissioned from a local cabinet maker. Each six-foot case cost between $1200 and $1500 (price includes built-in lighting). A plush, cut-pile rug was chosen over cheaper versions for its wearability and ease of care. For general lighting, they chose the latest—halogen track—which lines the showcases and highlights wall displays. Total redesign costs—including a completely new store front—came to roughly $61 per square foot.

Cost figures can vary tremendously. Moyer Jewelers in Carmel, Ind., for example, got a new look—conceived and carried out by management—for about $5.20 a square foot.

That's probably the least one could dream of and Daniel Moyer knows he has it good. He has family in the building business and customers who are a bit artsy. Nothing wrong there; it's called using your resources. That's something to consider when approaching a redesign. Designers' estimates fall between $24 and $90 per sq. ft., for interior work only.

Because of the high costs involved, MariAnn Coutchie urges jewelers to think about the profitable use of space. She lists the "square foot return" of floor space as a key figure, telling jewelers to expand departments (such as diamonds) that bring a high dollar return and to cut back or eliminate those with a poor return.

If Disaster Strikes

April 1985

FLOODS AND FLASH FLOODS

Occurrence: Hundreds of times each year in the U.S. No area in U.S. completely free from flood threat. Average annual losses: 75,000 people driven from homes; 100 killed and more than $1 billion in property damage. Floods can be slow-rising or sudden. They can be seasonal, as when winter or spring rains and melting snow drain down stream beds. Flash floods result from extremely heavy rain or snow and are sudden.

Signs and warnings: Usually during or after periods of heavy precipitation. Look for local streams and rivers flowing more swiftly or water levels noticeably higher than usual. Flash floods strike swiftly and without warning. Listen to radio or TV flood stage forecasts.

Flood warning tells expected severity of flooding (minor, moderate or major), and where it will begin. A flash flood warning is urgent. Radio/TV alerts may be supplemented by door-to-door, loudspeaker and siren warnings. Other information sources: Local police, sheriff, highway patrol and civil defense.

WINTER STORMS

Occurrence: Winter storms vary in size, strength, May affect only part of a state or many states. Three categories:

Blizzard is most dangerous. It combines low temperature, heavy snowfall, high winds, low visibility.

Heavy Snow Storm drops 4 inches or more within 12 hours or 6 inches or more within 24 hours. Also high drifts, low visibility.

Ice Storm occurs when moisture from clouds freezes immediately upon impact. Makes walking and driving extremely hazardous.

Signs and warnings: National Weather Service issues watches and warnings. Keep informed by listening to TV/radio forecasts or reading local papers. Know these terms:

Winter Storm Warning: Severe weather conditions definitely on way to your area.

Blizzard Warning: Large amounts of blowing snow and winds of at least 35 mph expected.

Severe Blizzard Warning: Considerable snow, 45 mph-plus winds, and temperatures 10 degrees F. or lower.

TORNADOES

Occurrences: Highest frequency in Middle Plains and Southeastern states but have struck in every state. Southern states run biggest risk in late winter/early spring; northern states in spring and summer.

Wind funnel rotates at up to 300 mph. Average speed along ground 30 mph; stays on ground about 10 minutes and leaves destructive path several hundred yards wide/2-5 miles long. Most violent of all atmospheric phenomena. Frequently accompany advance of hurricane.

Usually occur on warm muggy days, never without clouds and rarely when temperature below 60 degrees F.

Signs and warnings: National Weather Service issues warnings, using following terms:

• Severe Thunderstorm indicates possible frequent lightning and/or damaging winds in excess of 50 mph.

• Severe Thunderstorm Watch indicates possible tornadoes, thunderstorms, frequent lightning, hail and wind speeds greater than 75 mph.

• Tornado Watch means tornadoes are expected to develop.

• Tornado Warning means one has actually been sighted in area, or is indicated by radar.

EARTHQUAKES

Occurrences: Tend to strike repeatedly along geologic faults. Range in intensity from minor tremors to great shocks; may last from few seconds to five minutes, or occur in a series over several days.

Most of the U.S. is earthquake territory. Western states like Alaska, California, Washington, Oregon, Nevada, Utah and Montana likeliest targets of devastating quakes. Experts predict California's San Andreas Fault area has better than 50% chance of major quake within next 30 years.

People in non-earthquake prone areas subject to highest risk since building codes are lax.

Signs and warnings: Unpredictable and occur without warning. Scientists, however, have produced risk maps showing areas where quakes likely to strike. Earthquake monitoring conducted by U.S. Geological Survey; National Oceanic and Atmospheric Administration, and many universities. Advance warnings of unusual geophysical events issued by local newspapers, radio or TV.

HURRICANES

Occurrences: Begin in North Atlantic, Caribbean and Gulf of Mexico as tropical cyclones (low pressure storm cells). If conditions right, cyclonic air mass grows into hurricane. Term applies when winds reach constant speeds of 74 mph or more.

On average, six Atlantic hurricanes occur per year, most in August, September and October. Not all strike land, but when they do destruction can be tremendous.

Signs and Warnings: Approach signaled by darkening skis, increasing wind velocity. Barometric pressure drops and rain falls in torrents.

The National Hurricane Center, Miami, monitors weather and notifies National Weather Service, which issues forecasts. Many national, state and local officials disseminate hurricane data.

Know the following terminology:
- Hurricane Advisory tells where storm is located; intensity of wind speeds and direction it's heading.
- Hurricane Watch indicates storm close enough for area population to listen for further information and be ready to take precautions.
- Hurricane Warning specifies coastal areas where 74-plus mph winds or dangerously high water expected. Take all precautions, including evacuation, if necessary.

DISASTERS

FLOODS AND FLASH FLOODS

Immediate dangers: Flash flood water surging over river banks sweeps everything before it—houses, bridges, cars, people, even boulders. Torrential currents cause drowning and other injuries. Slower-developing floods interrupt power, disable heat sources and make roads impassable. You could be stranded in store or unable to reach your business.

Long-term dangers: Outbreak of diseases; backed-up sewage systems; widespread water pollution; broken gas lines; downed power lines and fires. Flood water and mud can completely ruin your store. Looting.

Emergency management phases:

Mitigation:
- Add flood insurance to your policy.
- Avoid locating store on floodplain unless you can reinforce it. Check local building codes and ordinances. Special construction costs may be high, but investment may prevent costlier damage.

Preparedness:
- Stockpile emergency building materials, i.e. sandbags, plywood, plastic sheeting and lumber.
- Make store evacuation plans. If store in flash flood area, have several alternate routes to insure rapid evacuation.
- Maintain emergency supplies such as a first aid kit, bottled water, canned foods and other edibles requiring little cooking and no refrigeration. Portable radio, emergency cooking equipment and flashlights should be kept in a safe, dry storage area.
- Keep your insurance policies, inventory listings and names/locations of issuing agents in safe. Periodically review policy requirements. Most warrant you to keep at least 70%-75% of high value items in the safe or vault.

Response:
- If time permits, call insurance agent/underwriter for final instructions on protecting valuables. Agent may recommend locking items in quality safe or vault even if there's risk of minor water damage (mainly to watches). Some agents, however, may lower in-safe warranty requirement and allow evacuation of goods to a bank vault or other secure storage site. But you must call for permission.
- If time too short, slam everything in safe and evacuate immediately. Remember—looting is greater risk than water damage. But life and limb are more important than property.
- If time permits, evacuate all vital records, computer software, etc., or move to higher levels (whether upper floors, shelves, countertops or tables). Safes and vaults aren't waterproof, but can keep records from being crushed or washed away.
- Check emergency food, water and other supplies. Keep them high and dry, too.

- Listen to radio announcements from emergency officials. Evacuate immediately if told to do so. In flash flood alert, all that counts is moving immediately to high ground. A flash flood travels fast, giving you no time to save merchandise or personal possessions.
- If there's time before evacuation, turn off all utilities at main switch. Do not touch office or repair shop electrical equipment unless it's in dry area or you're wearing insulating rubber gloves.
- Use only recommended evacuation routes. Do not attempt to drive over flooded roads to reach your store or home; you can become stranded or trapped. If car stalls in flowing water, abandon it immediately. Floodwaters can rise rapidly and sweep car away.

Recovery:
- Seek all necessary medical care at nearest hospital. Food, shelter and first aid available at Red Cross shelters.
- If store damaged, immediately call insurance agent for further instructions.
- Before re-entering flooded store, check for structural damage; make sure it's not in danger of collapse.
- Let building air out several minutes before entering to remove foul odors or escaped gas.
- Upon entering store, don't use a match or lantern due to possible gas buildup. Check for any electrical shorts and live wires. Make certain power is turned off. Don't use lights/equipment until electrician has checked electrical system.
- Open all doors and windows to help dry premises. Shovel out mud while still moist to give walls and floors chance to dry.

WINTER STORMS

Immediate dangers: Blizzards can trap you in store or car; create major traffic jams. Ice storms can break power lines; cause widespread blackouts. Fire major hazard because of frozen water supplies and blocked roads needed by fire-fighting trucks. Threat of overexertion leading to heart attack and stroke. A big problem among older people.

Long-term dangers: Long storms (more than 1 to 2 days) create snow build-ups that can collapse weak roofs; can cause extreme hardship—even death—from extended exposure to cold.

Emergency management phases:

Mitigation:
- Keep posted on weather conditions. Use radio, TV and newspapers.
- install alternate heat sources such as wood-burning stove.
- Insulate store to make it more energy/efficient.
- Purchase flood insurance policy in event of flood damage during spring thaw.
- Make advance contingency arrangements with local police, fire department, paramedic, emergency management and various relief agencies.
- Establish system for "employee-stay-home" announcements.
- Give staff pamphlets listing safety rules.
- Designate snow emergency routes; place signs in lot/driveway around store.

Preparedness:
- Be prepared to evacuate store and go home, especially in rural area. Severe winter storm could isolate you for one to two weeks.

56

• If remain in store, keep enough heating fuel on hand and use sparingly (regular fuel deliveries may be affected by storm). Keep thermostat down and close off some rooms.

• Keep emergency heating/cooking equipment available, i.e. a camp stove with fuel.

• Stock emergency supply of water and foods requiring little or no preparation.

• Stock battery-powered radio and extra batteries, simple tools and fire fighting equipment. Keep flashlights or lanterns ready for use.

• Remove all inventory from display cases. Store in safe or vault.

Response:
• Don't be fooled if storm seems mild at first. Some take several hours to move into area and last several days.

• Avoid all necessary trips. If you're at home when storm strikes, plan to stay there. Don't go to the store.

• Allow early dismissal of staff if storm imminent.

• Avoid unnecessary physical exertion, especially if you have heart condition. Shoveling snow, walking through deep snow or pushing car can have serious or fatal consequences.

• If trapped in store, do not panic. Telephone for help. If phone out, hang "S.O.S." sign or flashing trouble signal in storefront window. Rescue crews will spot it.

• If outside, wear several layers of loose-fitting, lightweight protective clothing. Mittens warmer than gloves; hoods protect head and face. Cover mouth to protect lungs from cold air.

• If in stuck car, stay inside unless assistance is nearby; turn on emergency blinkers and hang bright cloth from antenna. Wait for help. Run engine to keep warm. Remember to keep snow away from exhaust pipe and open window slightly.

Recovery:
• Check condition of other merchants in immediate area. Make sure they have heat and supplies to get through emergency.

• Avoid overexertion while clearing snow; work slowly and take frequent breaks, particularly if you get dizzy or tired.

• Examine ceiling/roof for any buckling or drooping.

TORNADOES

Immediate dangers: Being blown away; hit by flying debris or trapped in building hit by funnel.
Long-term dangers: Weakened or collapsed buildings; downed power lines; ruptured gas mains.
Emergency management phases:
Mitigation:
• Add storm insurance to your policy.
• Learn community tornado plan, rescue/relief resources, warning and shelter system.
• Stay informed of daily weather conditions and storm alerts.
• Develop itemized disaster plan that includes list of everyone who can help you during preparedness, response and recovery stages.
Preparedness:
• Designate a safe area in or around store as tornado shelter. This may be store basement or protected area in nearby building.
• Educate staff; conduct periodic tornado drills including taking shelter and first aid.
• Look for funnel cloud during violent weather; listen for tornado's roar.

Response:
If you see or hear a tornado, take following action:
• Protect your head and eyes, lie flat and make as small a target as possible.
• Seek shelter inside immediately. If already inside, go to designated shelter area. Take cover under solid furniture, cabinets, etc. If have portable radio, take it with you.
• Open some windows, but don't stay near them because of danger from flying glass or debris.
• If store has no basement seek shelter in interior hallway on lowest floor.
• Do not leave shelter until storm is past.
Recovery:
• Re-enter main store area with extreme caution.
• Be alert for fire hazards.
• Contact insurance agent; have damage/ losses assessed.
• Clean up fallen trees, branches, debris from outside store.
• Clean up interior and repair damage.
• If community declared disaster area by the President, check into eligibility for disaster relief grant or loan. If store destroyed, SBA loan can help pay for temporary quarters and rebuilding/repair.

EARTHQUAKES

Immediate dangers: Actual movement of ground seldom direct cause of death or injury. Earthquake casualties commonly caused by:
• Partial or total building collapse including toppling chimneys or walls; falling ceiling plaster, light fixtures and pictures.
• Flying glass from broken windows and skylights.
• Overturned display cases, fixtures, large furniture and equipment.
• Fallen power lines.
• Drastic human action caused by fear; looting.
• Fires, from broken chimneys and gas lines (especially dangerous since water mains may be broken and fire-fighting equipment unable to reach fire).
Long-term dangers: Earthquakes cause cracks and weaknesses in buildings, utility lines, bridges or dams. Contaminated water supplies; damaged roadways and public transportation systems.
Emergency management phases:
Mitigation:
If store in earthquake prone area:
• Make sure your new building complies with all earthquake codes. If store in high risk area without regulations or codes, support their enactment. Reinforce existing store not already "earthquake safe."
• Prepare adequate contingency plans for minor, moderate and major earthquakes.
Preparedness:
• Inspect store for potential risks: Bolt down or reinforce water heaters and other gas appliances since fire damage can result. Place large heavy equipment/inventory on lower showcase shelves. Securely fasten shelves/cases to walls. Brace or anchor tall or top heavy objects. Know where safest places are in store.
• Educate staff and conduct drills including extinguishing fires and first aid. Show where to turn off gas, electricity and water at main switches and valves (check with loal utility offices for instructions).

Response:

When shaking starts, you and staff should:
• Stay indoors if already there.
• Take cover under sturdy furniture, cabinets or work tables.
• Stay near center of building against a wall.
• Stay away from glass windows and doors.
• Do not run through or near building where there's danger of falling debris.
• If outside, stay in open away from buildings and utility wires.
• In crowded store or mall, do not rush for doorways since hundreds of people may have same idea. Choose exits carefully if you must leave building.

After shaking stops:
• Check for injuries; seek necessary medical help.
• Check for fires or fire hazards.
• You or responsible staff person should turn off utilities at primary control point if water pipes damaged, gas leaking or electrical wires shorting. Open windows if smell gas.
• Leave store and report damage to appropriate utility companies.
• Do not use telephone except for genuine emergency calls. Turn on radio for damage reports and information.
• Do not eat or drink anything from open containers near shattered glass.
• Be prepared for additional tremors (aftershocks). Stay out of damaged buildings; aftershocks can shake them down.

Recovery:

• Check building walls, roof, chimney for cracks and damage. First check from distance, then closer if appears safe.
• If building damaged, contact insurance agent for further instructions or assessment.
• Check inventory and equipment. Open cases and cabinets carefully; watch for items falling from shelves.
• Consult local authorities, newspapers, radio, TV, etc., for disaster assistance information.

HURRICANES

Immediate dangers: Extremely high winds that can demolish houses, uproot trees, collapse bridges and fill air with debris. Tornadoes also can develop as hurricane passes.

Greatest danger is storm surge, a great dome of water, waves and wind up to 50 miles wide traveling with hurricane. Surge sweeps everything in path where storm's eye hits land. Causes 9 out of 10 fatalities.

Long-term dangers: Interrupted gas, water and electric power; fires and explosions from gas leaks; fallen power lines; electrical short circuits; contaminated food and water; looting.

Emergency management phases:

Mitigation:
• Learn about hurricane warnings, dangers and techniques for protecting property.
• Reinforce store to withstand wind and flooding.
• Purchase a flood/hurricane insurance policy from insurance agent.
• Pay special attention to Hurricane Advisories if store in coastal area.

Preparedness:

• Take precautions before start of hurricane season.

Each June recheck windows, shutters, doors and supply of boards, tools, batteries, non-perishable foods and other emergency equipment.
• If area receives hurricane warning, keep calm. Take following actions. Plan time before storm arrives to avoid last minute rush.

1. Board up windows or protect them with shutters or tape. Unplug all electrical equipment. Pack away/protect delicate instruments (microscopes, gem scanning devices, etc.).

2. Remove everything from showcases. Secure merchandise in vault or safe. Move to safer site (i.e. bank vault) only if there's time.

3. Permit all but minimum critical personnel to go home until danger passes. Be prepared to evacuate store if so ordered by authorities.

4. Keep car's gas tank filled. Gas stations may be closed several days due to power outages/flooding.

Response:

• Leave low-lying areas susceptible to storm surge.
• Stay in store if it's sturdy, on high ground and away from shore. If not safe, move to designated shelter; stay there until storm has subsided.
• When hurricane strikes, stay indoors away from windows. Listen to news and weather reports.
• Leave control of looters to police. Contact them at first sign of break-in. But be prepared to defend yourself and store as a last resort.
• Drive/travel on foot only if absolutely necessary. High winds, storm surges and debris extremely dangerous.
• Be wary of hurricane "eye" if storm passes directly overhead. Winds will pick up rapidly again from opposite direction.

Recovery:

• Obtain any necessary medical treatment for self or others.
• Exercise caution in or around store. Avoid broken glass and loose or dangling wires; report them to power company or police. Report broken sewer or water mains to water department.
• Assess damage to store. Consider following recovery checklist:

1. Relocation—square footage available in area; realtors specializing in storage space needed; minimum space needed for temporary operation; remodeling contractors in area; any special electrical needs.

2. Replacing fixtures or equipment—essential special equipment; manufacturers; delivery time required; potential used suppliers.

3. Replacing inventory—primary distributor/wholesale sources; secondary sources.

4. Repair or rebuilding—contractors in area; special material problems; existing store features you'd like to change.

5. Valuable papers & records—are duplicates stored off-site? If not, how will duplicates be prepared?

6. Computer security—storage of critical data and extra copies of software in safe "back-up" site; reciprocal processing agreements with other stores with similar/identical hardware; recovery operations centers run by large computer companies in major cities.

7. Communications—announcement notices to customers re: temporary down-time or location change; advertisements for local papers; other media (i.e. TV, radio).

How To Buy Or Sell A Store

October 1983

Buying or selling a store is one of the most important business deals a jeweler can make.

But too many jewelers botch the job.

They lose important tax benefits; pay more or get less than they should or sign agreements not in their best interests.

"Most jewelers don't realize just how complex the process is," says Richard T. Laffin, senior associate with Management Growth Institute, Wellesley, Mass.

"In too many sales, someone simply walks in, makes an offer to buy, talks with the owner for a couple of hours and, if they agree, they have a contract drawn up. But afterward, there are all sorts of problems involving valuation of assets, how the price was structured, unexpected tax problems."

This article and the following are based on advice from jewelers, lawyers and accountants. They should help you avoid some of the biggest pitfalls in a sale and get the best deal possible.

• **Know when.** Some reasons to buy and sell are obvious: Retirement; declining health; rising rents; need for a new or larger location; a changing or deteriorating market (one jeweler moved when gypsies set up shop next-door).

Your store's fiscal health provides clues. Is it a struggle to make a profit? Is growth rising, declining or flat? What kind of return are you getting on your investment? "Many people don't realize they should be both drawing a salary *and earning* on their investment in the business," says sales consultant Manning Silverman, Westbury, N.Y. If your return is little better than what you would make investing elsewhere, it might be time to sell, he says.

• **Be prepared.** Many jewelers aren't and that's the single biggest mistake they make, say experts. Whether buyer or seller, "plan on doing a lot of work *before* you make your move," says Ian Fuller, Meyers Jewelers, Vallejo, Cal. His firm spent two years preparing before buying a store in a nearby town.

Barring events forcing immediate action, spend several months preparing if you're buying and up to two to five years if you're selling.

As a seller, "you need time to consciously prepare your business for sale," says David T. Barry, MGI president. That means build sales to show earnings; growth; adjust financial statements to show full worth; reduce liabilities; cleanup inventory and plan for maximum tax benefits from the sale. A seller needs time to consider offers—and buyers. "A guy who's put 30 years and his blood into a store wants to spend some time with a prospect to find out his plans for it, his reputation, a little about his background," says Barry.

A buyer, too, better have what Barry calls "a set of specifications." To have that, he needs a clear concept of his own business, customers and goals.

Zale Corp., the world's largest jewelry retailer, for instance, has a very clear idea of what stores it wants to buy and where. "We have a list of specific markets we want to be in and we won't go somewhere if it isn't one of those on the list," says Gene Morphis, Zale vice president of planning. But you don't have to be a retail giant to be prepared: Paul J. Schmitt, Naples, Fla., owner of three stores, has "a long-term growth plan for the next 5 to 10 years, showing where I want to be and the type of store I want."

• **Know where to look.** Classified ads in local papers and jewelry trade journals are obvious places to publicize or find stores for sale. But don't be too quick to publicize your own store for sale, say management experts: It can affect customer traffic; worry employees into seeking work elsewhere and convince creditors to call in their IOUs.

Use other sources, too—bankers and accountants; local merchants and jewelers; business listing services; local jewelry schools, and sales reps.

Don't overlook local or national chains. See if they're interested in buying your location—or if they want to sell poorly run or unproductive stores.

Liquidators (who give the lowest price) and sale consultants can help with quick sales. Even if you can't find a buyer, you still have "arrows in your quiver," says sale consultant Silverman: Sell off your assets separately.

"It's 10 times easier to find someone with $20,000 for some equipment than $200,000 for a store," says Silverman, who always has "at least 20 or 30 jewelers asking for equipment."

Unproductive or financially distressed stores are potential bargains. One Midwest jeweler bought "an excellent store in a high-income area for a small percent of value of its assets: after he learned the bank was going to foreclose. "The price was so low because the bank assumed 100% financing to get out of a bad situation," he says.

Downtown historical buildings are also prime sites for buyers, says James W. Green whose firm bought an historically-registered building in Raleigh, N.C. An historical properties grant helped defray renovation costs and property taxes were reduced.

• **Investigate the location.** Check out the store you want to buy and its community for clues to its profit potential and why the owner is selling.

How is customer traffic? Is parking adequate? Is business in the community going up or down? Is there much competition from other jewelers, discounters or department stores?

Talk to local merchants and banks about the store's reputation and credit rating. Ask local municipal officials about municipal codes or economic changes that might affect the store's business. Do some basic market research to get a profile of community demographics.

What you learn will affect whether you proceed with the purchase and what you offer. Even an unsuccessful store may be a potential money-maker in disguise. One jeweler bought an old, back street shoe store when he learned a nearby mall planned to expand to across the street, bringing thousands of potential customer within a few feet of his new store. And Modesto, Cal., jeweler Roger Marks, after some research, decided a location he was interested in was "poor for the guild-type store there, but excellent, with considerable traffic, for a 'middle-of-the-road operation' like ours."

- **Financing.** Jewelers make two mistakes in funding a purchase, say experts. They either don't borrow at all or they over-extend themselves. "I'm working with at least a dozen jewelers who are sorry they personally signed a note, pledging payment," says Manning Silverman. "Don't be too quick to sign away house and heritage."

- **Using experts.** Many jewelers especially in smaller communities, are "very hesitant about hiring professional consultants" to assist in a sale, says Dr. Bart Basi, attorney and CPA who heads the University of Southern Illinois' accounting department. "They don't bring in a lawyer, public accountant or tax advisor until it is almost too late."

A big reason is cost. A good lawyer or accountant can charge $100 an hour or more. But saving money by scrimping on consultants' fees can be costly in the long run.

"You may find you lose the money you saved at the start because the agreement isn't structured for the best tax advantages or because of serious errors in the acquisition process," says Gene Morphis, Zale vice president.

- **The wrong price.** Some jewelers fumble a sale at the most important point: The purchase price. They ask too little or pay too much because they don't use all the tools available for setting the price.

"The simplest way" is to use a business's book value—the worth of its assets, minus liabilities—says MGI's Dave Barry. "A lot of jewelry stores are sold for book worth, right off the balance sheet," he says.

The majority of JCK panelists who bought or sold a store in the past two years agree. They based the price most often on the market value of the assets.

Fair enough. But, say the experts, there's more to calculating a reasonable price than just book value:

Profitability. Review a store's IRS tax return and profit-and-loss statements for at least the past five years. The figures, when combined with investigation of a store's location and do-it-yourself market research, will help estimate potential profitability.

As a buyer, look at profit margins and trends in sales volume, earnings and costs. What's the ratio of profit to net worth? What's the return on sales? Does this store's financial history justify the investment in money, time and effort you'll make in its future—or would you be wiser to invest your dollars elsewhere?

"If you find you can't improve what a store has done in the past, then don't buy it," says Lester Small, partner in the St. Louis, Mo., accounting firm of Arthur Anderson Inc. And if a buyer refuses to let you see his records, reconsider the deal.

But to prepare for a sale, the seller should adjust the earnings he reports, to get the best price. He can do that in a couple of ways, say experts:

Take fewer tax write-offs in the years just before an expected sale to show earning growth.

Have his accountant prepare an adjusted statement of the company's earnings and worth, with write-offs added back in.

Industry comparisons. Compare your store's profitability by department and size with other jewelry stores in the industry. Such data is available from trade magazines and associations.

Financial descriptions of specific businesses in your community, including the one you may purchase, are available to your accountant and lawyer from credit rating services. Use of these reports cuts both ways. A buyer can get a financial health report on a business he is eyeing, helping him set his offer. But the seller can use such a report to evaluate a potential buyer.

Tax courts are helpful, too, says Bart Basi. A review of their public records, such as estate tax forms or recent tax cases provide comparative prices and valuations of similar-sized, local stores.

Capitalization of earnings projects future growth based on past performance. One current rule of thumb is to multiply earnings for a growing business by a factor (subject buyer/seller negotiation) between 10 and 15, says MGI's Barry, and for a store with flat growth rate by a factor between 5 and 8.

- **How the price is paid** and how it is allocated among the business assets can be even more important than the price itself. Both affect the type and amount of taxes buyer and seller must pay.

Dividing that price among business assets isn't simple, though, because buyer and seller have different ideas about values and opposing goals in terms of tax benefits and liabilities. So, says Zale's Gene Morphis, "It is better to focus on a total package of tax benefits you want, and give up something in order to get as much of it as you can."

The most common forms of payment are cash and deferred. Cash is simpler, with fewer legal or tax complications. But the deferred, or installment, method is used most often. Sellers "want to defer payment for tax reasons, while providing guaranteed income over a period of time," says Laffin. And many buyers "want payments structured to write off future payments as legitimate tax deductions." Purchasers also find it is more convenient to make a small down payment, leaving cash for investment in the business, rather than paying it all up front.

But the seller who takes deferred payment also takes a risk: The buyer may default, leaving the seller with less than a full purchase price.

- **A good contract** is a jeweler's best protection against being cheated.

If you're selling, experts recommend a default clause allowing the business to revert to you if the new owner defaults on payments. Keep some kind of security, too, on the property you sell—such as a lien against assets or inventory—as protection.

If you're buying, don't get stuck with unexpected liabilities left by an unscrupulous seller. Keep part of the purchase price in an interest-bearing escrow account for a couple of years to safeguard against any unexpected claims, liens or liabilities.

Be sure, too, if you're buying a store in a leased location that you can secure the lease *before* you sign the agreement. Otherwise, you may find yourself with a new business—and no place to put it. "make the deal contingent on getting the lease at the same or similar terms" says lawyer Fred S. Steingold, author of *Legal Master Guide for Small Businesses.*

• **Get what you pay for.** It's a good idea for both seller and buyer to have an audit made of all assets, including merchandise, both before and after closing a deal.

One reason is to avoid dispute later about inventory valuation. But a double count of all assets—including fixtures and furniture—also insures the buyer gets everything he paid for. Modesto, Cal., jeweler Roger Marks, for instance, had such a dual inventory taken. "It was a good thing we did," he says. "An employee [for the former owner] thought we didn't want some of the equipment and had it removed. Because of the inventory we made, we knew what should be there and had it brought back."

Tips & Guidelines for Buyer & Seller

WHEN

Seller: Planning to retire. Poor health. Economic factors (projected declines in sales, earnings; insufficient return on investment; unsatisfactory profit margin, volume, inventory turn). Unfavorable changes in neighborhood business or traffic patterns. Other reasons: No family member to continue business; high mall rents.

Worst time to sell: Immediately after a bad year; when sales drop, or just prior to retirement. Don't put yourself in the position of accepting an unsatisfactory offer because of poor timing or insufficient preparation.

Best time to sell: After a couple of good years of growth (based on earnings). Early in the calendar year, to take advantage of Christmas profits in financial statement. Toward the end of fiscal year, to avoid duplication of paperwork (inventory, sales records, etc.) required in a transaction.

Buyer: Expansion needs (additional space or new location). Competition. Changes in neighborhood business or customer traffic. New markets; commercial or residential growth in the area. Starting a new business (less expensive than starting from scratch).

PREPARATION

Seller & Buyer: The biggest mistake jewelers make in a buy/sell transaction is not taking enough time to prepare for it and not knowing how to prepare, say management experts.

TIME FRAME

Seller: Start planning for a sale as early as possible—ideally up to 2 to 5 years in advance, especially if retiring; realistically at least several months before the sale.

Buyer: Expect to spend several weeks to months planning and preparing for a purchase. That includes time to chose a location, investigate it and its profit potential and price negotiations. Some jewelers have taken up to several years before making a purchase. The amount of time depends on the opportunity, financing available and size of the prospective purchase.

PLAN

Seller: Use the time to prepare necessary records; clean-out old, unattractive inventory; make necessary safety or appearance improvements and renovations and boost earnings to get the best possible price.

Tax tip: Incorporate for the best tax advantages from a sale. Incorporation must be done at least a year before a sale. See tax advisor for advice.

Many jewelers depress earnings, (through write-offs of fringes, owners' salaries, company cars) and undervalue inventory for tax reasons. To boost those reported earnings and get a better offer, take fewer write-offs in the 2 to 3 years prior to intended sale to show higher earnings' growth. Or, have an adjusted statement prepared for the prospective buyer showing corporate value and earnings strength, without the write-offs.

Buyer: Evaluate your own business first. Have a long-range business plan, with projected growth (earnings, expansion). Define the type of market you want your stores in and the type of store you would want. This will help you focus your search for a location.

Evaluate your financial ability to make a purchase. What kind of return do you want? Can you afford the purchase? Are you sufficiently capitalized? Can your cash flow and the additional store's projected earnings support the purchase price and initial years' costs. How does the cost of acquisition compare with the cost of starting a new business from scratch?

If your answers indicate you can't afford a purchase, don't overextend yourself. Drop the idea for now.

Tax tip: Investigate during the preparatory period before negotiations even begin, the tax advantages and liabilities of the purchase.

SOURCES

Seller: Potential buyers include family members; long-time employees; other jewelers or merchants, needing new or expanded sites; new or young jewelers or designers; local or national chains. Liquidators (a last resort), provide a quick sale at a low price. Sales or business brokers will sell your business for a fee, a percent of the sale or buy it outright from you.

One possibility: Sell off assets separately (inventory, fixtures, leasehold, etc.). This will attract more buyers than selling the total store.

Don't publicize your store for sale too much; it can effect customer traffic, employee morale, creditors' demands for payment.

To find buyers, consult your banker or accountants; local merchants; jewelers; jewelry schools. Contact officers of local or national chains to see if they are interested in your location. Ask local merchants, friends, sales reps who visit if they know of anyone looking for a store.

To solicit buyers outside your region, place ads in industry trade journals or use business listings services.

Buyer: For potential purchase, consider distressed or bankrupt stores; the firm owned by your employer or relative; an unproductive store or chain outlet; jewelers, without heirs, nearing retirement age. Consider historical buildings or stores inappropriate for their market (i.e., a guild store in a middle class neighborhood).

To find sale prospects, consult the classified sections of local papers or industry trade journals. Talk to other jewelers or sales reps (an excellent source) about stores they know whose owners are dissatisfied with business or looking for buyers.

Use business brokers or consult business sale listings services.

Tax tip: Buying an historical downtown building list in a local, state or federal register can bring a reduction in property taxes and, in some cases, grants to aid in renovation or maintenance. And a locally-known historical building has built-in recognition with the public.

CONSULTANTS

Seller and Buyers: Jewelers try to save money in a buy/sell transaction by not using professional consultants, like lawyers or accountants, or waiting until the last minute to bring them into negotiations.

A jeweler, however, should have a lawyer, a CPA and possibly a tax advisor for any buy/sell transaction involving a store, to advise, assist in preparation (i.e., study financial records, handle legal requirements) and watch over the jeweler's legal and financial interests.

The CPA and attorney should be present at all negotiations. Money "saved" by not using them could be lost later, after the transaction is completed, through substantial tax or legal liabilities, improperly drawn agreements, overlooked tax benefits or other serious errors.

Seller:

Tax tip: Have an accountant prepare an adjusted statement of your store's net worth and earnings, including the equivalent value of any write-offs, such as one-time profits, owner's salary, large fringes, etc.

Have an accountant or tax advisor review your financial position and suggest the best way to structure the sale for the most tax benefits.

Legal tip: A consultant, such as an accountant, can be used as an intermediary in a transaction involving a family business. As a neutral third party, paid by both sides, he can make independent judgments, mediate differences concerning valuation and, based on private consultation with both sides, suggest a reasonable compromise price.

Buyer:

Tax tip: Have an accountant do the necessary financial work to see if you can afford the purchase and at what price.

Legal tip: You may want an engineer or builder to inspect the building to estimate cost of repairs, renovations and compliance with municipal and safety codes.

FINANCING

Seller:

Legal tip: Financing terms are one area where you can bargain for a better price. For example, the buyer may agree to buy some of your corporate stock at your asking price if you accept a smaller down payment in a deferred payment arrangement.

Buyer: Can you afford the purchase? Calculate how much you need for each part of the purchase (assets, fixtures, inventory, leasehold, building, etc.). Add other costs (working capital, payroll, renovations, accounts receivable, consul-

tants' fees), plus continuing costs from the former owner (i.e., maintenance contracts).

Can your cash flow, plus earnings from the new store, support that, or any money you need to borrow? If you have to overextend yourself (i.e. personally sign over assets or home) to support a purchase, or are undercapitalized, reconsider the purchase at this time.

Sources of financing include banks, commercial lenders, insurance companies. The seller is a potential source: He may agree to issue a note as part of the purchase price. But another option—selling part of your equity (though it involves less risk, debt)—is a bad idea: You lose control of your business.

INVESTIGATE

Seller and Buyer: A buyer should study three subjects before negotiations begin, to determine if the purchase is worth the investment; to gather clues to the store's profit potential, and to find reasons, other than the owner's comments, why the owner may be selling.

Those three subjects are location, customers and financial records.

LOCATION

Seller and Buyer: Study the amount of customer traffic over a period of time (i.e. a few weeks) at various times of day.

If in a mall, look at the location. The best sites are near the anchor store, on a corner (where two walkways meet) or in the center.

Study neighborhood business activity. Talk to local merchants, municipal officials. Is business stagnant or going up or down?

Check with municipal officials about local costs (i.e. utility rates or property taxes) and services (i.e. police and fire protection, garbage pick-up).

Consider distance. If you already have one store, is the addition close enough (i.e. less than 30 miles and an hour's drive) to maintain control and include in advertising coverage?

Consider competition in the neighborhood (other jewelers, discounters, department stores) and effect on the store if you take over.

Find out if any municipal, neighborhood or commercial changes are planned which would affect business, (an increase in property taxes; new business tax; building a regional mall in next town; turning your store's street into pedestrian walkway).

CUSTOMERS

Sellers and Buyers: Collect demographic data on the residents and potential customers of the proposed purchase. This is do-it-yourself market research using materials available to any jeweler at little or no cost.

Market research is simply collecting and interpreting facts and figures about the market area which describe residents in dozens of ways.

You want to know residents' income levels; where high income groups live; marital status and family sizes; residential growth or decline; job descriptions. Such information is available from census data, local planning commissions and chambers of commerce.

For economic data (industrial, commercial development, growth, new jobs, real estate values, building growth), check with local chambers of commerce, local economic development authorities, municipal authorities and code enforcers.

Tax tip: Some investigatory and start-up costs, such as travel expenses or consultants' fees, incurred in a buy/sell transaction or in starting a business are deductible. Consult a CPA for details.

Weigh the legal and financial differences of buying your own store or leasing. As your own landlord, your costs are less than in a mall, you control building rules, have a steady tenant and get tax benefits, like depreciation. As a lessee, though, your money isn't tied up in property or renovations, and is more readily available for expansion and reinvestment in business. One possibility: Buy the building, sell to a third party, then lease it back.

FINANCIAL RECORDS

Seller: Review your financial records for the past five years. You need an idea of your store's recent growth and its potential to set a price and deal with the buyer.

Jewelers, like other retailers, often understate inventory value and depress earnings figures (with write-offs of fringe benefits, large owners' salaries, one-time profits, etc.) to keep taxes lower. But to show earnings growth on financial reports and make a store more attractive to the buyer, take fewer write-offs in the 2 or 3 years immediately preceding sale. Also have an adjusted statement (minus write-offs and perks) prepared by your accountant to show the buyer your store's actual worth and profit projections.

Buyers: Review the financial records of the store—IRS tax returns and profit/loss statements—for the past five years.

Look for profit margins, earnings growth, trends; return on investment, sales. Study perpetual inventory records for inventory turn, individual departments' performance.

Develop profit projections based on past five years' performance, location, customer traffic, growth potential.

You want to know if the profit potential is great enough to justify your investment in money, time and effort. If you can't improve on what the store has done in the recent past, then don't make the purchase.

If an owner refuses to let you see his records, it's a warning signal that something may be wrong.

INVENTORY

Seller: Review your inventory prior to sale negotiations. Pull and sell off old, unattractive or slow-moving items.

Have merchandise and departments audited to provide an accurate, current valuation, minus any markdowns on old merchandise, in order to set a reasonable price.

If a buyer doesn't want all or some of the inventory, sell it off at clearance or to a liquidator.

Legal tip: Have the audit of assets, including inventory, done by an auditor mutually acceptable to buyer and seller to prevent the buyer challenging your appraisal of assets' worth during or after sale negotiations.

Buyer: If buying inventory, survey it before negotiations. This will give you a basis for setting a price and show how much, if any, of the inventory is unsuitable to buy. Make another check after closing to be sure you get what you paid for.

Review perpetual inventory records for rate of turn and profitability of each department.

Contact distributors before closing to see if they will agree to continue as the store's suppliers and whether there are any claims or liens against the merchandise.

LEGAL STRUCTURES

Seller and Buyer: The legal status of the business you buy/sell is "extremely important" because it affects your taxes, liabilities and allocation of the price, say experts.

There are three basic forms: Corporation, partnership, sole proprietorship.

CORPORATION

Seller: For the best tax advantages in a sale, a jewelry store, regardless of size, should be incorporated, experts say.

Sale of corporate stock (shares) is preferred to selling assets such as inventory because profit on stock is considered a capital gain, which takes a smaller tax bite than profit on sale of assets, which can be taxed as ordinary income.

If you decide to incorporate, you must do so at least one year prior to a sale. Consult a tax advisor for specifics.

Tax tip: If assets, not corporate stock, are to be sold, investigate the tax advantages and legalities of dissolving the corporation prior to sale negotiations. Also if assets, not stock, are sold, you may have to repay the government for investment credits or depreciations you claimed on your taxes.

Buyer: There are two purchase choices.

A. Buy the existing corporation, meaning all the owner's shares of stock. If you buy the corporation, you inherit all its liabilities, known and unknown, as well as its assets. To the IRS, only ownership has changed, not tax status. Therefore, you are stuck with the older (possibly depleted) depreciation formulas.

Legal tip: Set up some money in escrow for a few years to cover any unknown corporate liabilities (i.e. IRS or insurance claims.)

B. Buy only the assets of the corporation (i.e. fixtures, equipment, inventory, building).

The buyer has no responsibility for the former owner's liabilities or obligations. But the purchase price must be allocated among the various assets (i.e. 10% for inventory, 30% for fixtures), unlike buying the corporate shares, where one price format is sufficient.

Legal tip: Be sure a legal notice of the sale is filed, in compliance with most states' "bulk sales" laws. These require that notice be given to creditors that the former owner is selling his assets and that the new owner isn't responsible for the former owner's liabilities.

PARTNERSHIP

Seller: The partners may be obligated to repay the government for any investment credits or depreciation claimed on assets, now sold. See a tax advisor for specifics.

Buyer: There are two forms of partnership, general and limited. Know the difference.

A. In a general partnership, each partner is personally liable for the partnership's obligations.

B. In a limited partnership, only one partner is liable, regardless of the number of partners involved.

Tax obligations and liabilities depend on the type of partnership you buy into, a situation requiring expert advice.

SOLE PROPRIETORSHIP

Buyer: For all practical purposes, the tax situation of a sole proprietorship (not incorporated) is the same as the purchase of a partnership of purchase of a corporation's assets. The purchase price must be allocated among the assets.

SETTING A PRICE

Seller and Buyer: The final purchase price for a store is based on negotiation between buyer and seller. But both sides should consider several factors before they come to the bargaining table in order to know how much to offer or to ask. Those include:

• The store's "book value" (the value of its assets, minus liabilities).

• Earnings projections and inventory turn, based on review of store's financial documents and books.

• Comparisons of profit and return on sales with the jewelry industry as a whole and with similar categories of stores (see trade associations and trade journals for such data).

• The value and prices asked for similar-sized stores in the community in the past 2 to 5 years. (Check the case records and estate tax forms at the local tax claims court for such data. Request, through accountant, financial reports on specific businesses, including that of the prospective buyer or seller, from credit rating services such as Dun & Bradstreet).

• Profit potential, based on projected future earnings, location, traffic, neighborhood changes or development.

• Capitalization of earnings (a projection of future earnings growth, based on multiplying a growing business's earnings by a factor of 10-15, and a flat or declining earnings rate by 5 to 8, based on accountant's recommendation and both sides' negotiations).

• Good will, which is the store's image, reputation or name.

Tax tip: Since a transaction's tax benefits to buyer and seller are different, what each wants in price allocation and valuation often are opposed. Thus experts recommend you enter negotiations with a "total package of tax benefits" you want to receive from the transaction. You may have to give up some bargaining points to get most of it, but it will strengthen and speed your negotiations.

Generally, the seller wants to allocate as much of the price to capital gains, with its lower tax bite, than to ordinary income. Consult a tax advisor or CPA for specifics on tax implications of sale.

PAYMENTS

Seller and Buyer: Two methods commonly are used to pay for a store. They are cash and deferred, or installment, pay-

ment. Cash has fewer tax complications, but deferred payments are used most often.

Seller: Deferred payment provides the seller with a guaranteed income and lowers the initial tax obligation by spreading it out over a period of time.

Legal tip: In a family business only, deferred payment can take the form of annuity to the former parent-owner, paid for as long as the parent lives.

Tax tip: If the buyer makes deductions in your payment to enforce a non-competitive clause in the agreement, it means more tax for you, since you must report the reduced payments as ordinary income.

Default on payments is a seller's biggest risk in accepting deferred payment.

Be sure your sale agreement includes a default clause (business reverts to you if the new owner can't make payments).

Be sure your agreement is with the principals of the business buying you out, not with the legal entity, the corporation.

Demand some security, such as a lien on the inventory, the buyer's property as collateral or a promissory note, to protect your payments until the debt is paid.

Buyer: Deferred payment enables the buyer to devote much of his cash to investment in the business, by requiring only a down-payment, and lets him write off future payments as legitimate tax deductions.

Tax tip: The IRS requires that the payments include the interest rate paid on each installment. Otherwise, it will deduct the amount itself.

Legal tip: One way of enforcing a non-competitive clause is to have the sale agreement allow deductions from your payments if the seller opens a competing business.

ALLOCATION OF PRICE

Seller and Buyer: When the purchase price is deferred, or paid in installments, the IRS says proceeds must be allocated among the assets. Here is how price generally is allocated among some major assets. See a CPA, tax advisor and attorney for specific advice. Allocation affects amount and type of taxes paid.

INVENTORY

Seller: Seller's gain or loss is taxed as ordinary income (a higher tax bite). He prefers therefore a low allocation.

Buyer: The buyer can write his purchase off as part of the cost of the goods when sold. He prefers a high allocation.

DEPRECIABLE PROPERTY

Seller: The seller may have to repay Uncle Sam part of the depreciation write-off he took on equipment, such as a company car. That affects the allocation.

Buyer: The buyer usually prefers a high allocation, since he can deduct the cost of property like a building or equipment.

GOOD WILL

Seller: This is store image. The seller puts a high value on it. A capital gain.

Buyer: Buyer can't deduct it, so he puts a low value on it.

NON-COMPETITIVE CLAUSE

Seller: The seller obviously puts a low value on this, because of its restriction an because the IRS considers it as ordinary income. Note: See a tax advisor about how payment should be made and reported.

Buyer: The buyer usually wants to allocate a high value to this, since it can be deducted. Note: See a tax advisor about how payment should be made and reported.

LEASEHOLDS

Seller: Profit on this is considered a capital gain (lower tax rate), so the seller prefers a high allocation of price to this.

Buyer: The buyer often also agrees to a high allocation, because he can write it off.

EMPLOYEES

Seller: Once you have a serious buyer, inform employees of your plans to sell the store. Be honest and straight forward about the prospects of a sale and what it means to their future.

Though selling, you still are responsible for people who have worked for you for years. Make their job security and salary a part of the sale agreement, if possible. If the buyer refuses or won't keep the staff, inform workers early enough so they can look for other positions.

Buyer: Employee morale is important to the transaction. Prior to the agreement, investigate how important the staff is to the store's success or failure. If you don't plan to retain the staff, inform them well before their official termination.

If you plan to keep the staff, you must maintain worker morale, especially of key people who might otherwise leave if the store is sold. Establish good relations early. Give them the option of staying or leaving once the sale is made, but tell them there will be no immediate changes because of the sale.

Advise them as early as possible of employee benefit, pension, payroll and insurance plans, etc. Be open, direct and honest. Don't be secretive; an uninformed staff is unproductive and suspicious.

Don't make immediate changes in staff. This reassures workers, keeps up their morale—and helps maintain the store's repeat traffic, especially in smaller towns, where customers are used to dealing with specific salespeople.

Prior to closing, however, request to see all employee-related obligations and pay-roll records, including contracts, pensions, benefits, holidays, etc. You want to know of any employee-related liabilities, such as unfunded pensions or profit-sharing plans which could affect your costs or, if large enough, the sale itself.

FINAL AGREEMENT

Seller: Be sure the contract includes a default clause.

Be sure a "bulk sales" report is filed giving notice to creditors that assets are being sold.

Legal tip: If you plan on retirement, a buyer's insistence on a non-competitive clause may be bargaining chip in your favor—i.e. its inclusion in return for a better price.

A good lease, in time and price, can be a strong selling point.

Legal tip: If the new owners ask you to stay on as a consultant, or advisor, be sure that is included in your final agreement, with payment and duties specified, to cover later dismissal or non-payment.

Buyer: Make the agreement and payment contingent on:
- Compliance with all safety and building codes;
- Clear title to the store;
- Absence of any hidden liens, liabilities, or claims against the business;
- Getting a satisfactory lease for the site from the landlord at the same or similar rates and duration;
- Full access to the premises and all store records between signing and closing.

Be sure the agreement includes:
- A bail-out clause, allowing you to back out if the seller's representations of his store are false or other factors (see above) are not complied with.
- A non-competitive clause prohibiting the former owner from opening a competing business within a certain area and time period.
- A clause prohibiting the former owner from depleting the inventory or doing anything harmful to the store's image between signing and closing the agreement.
- Sufficient time between signing and closing for a final inventory and any final information that might affect the final price.

If this is your first business, or an additional store, you might consider retaining the former owner, if agreed, as an employee, advisor or consultant.

Consider the advantages (image, name recognition) of retaining the store's name.

Legal tip: A clear, detailed agreement is important for transferal of a family business, to prevent later misunderstandings about what each person "assumed" was agreed, and to prevent other relatives from coming in later and claiming a share of business or diluting its earnings.

Be sure a "bulk sales" report has been filed, which gives legal notice that the former owner's assets have been sold.

Be sure all legal forms, documents (policies, titles, leases, mortgages, contracts) have been changed to reflect the new ownership, and that all suppliers, important customers and need-to-know business organizations are informed of the change in ownership.

Be sure insurance coverage is changed to provide proper coverage for the new owners.

Answers To JCK Management Study Center Quiz:
(Questions can be found on page 24)

John A. Michaels of Michaels Enterprises Companies, Waterbury, Conn., wrote this second report for the May 1994 issue. His answers:

1. Yes
2. Yes
3. c
4. True
5. a, b, c, d and e
6. c
7. Advantage
8. $25,000
9. Yes
10. No
11. a
12. b

The most common mistakes here came on #9 and #10. Question #10 asked whether you usually will be able to drop out of a mall's regular advertising if you can prove you did your own advertising as a mall store. While you may be able to *limit* your participation in mall advertising, you won't be able to drop out entirely. And on question #5, which asks what types of transactions you should try to have excluded from the total you report to the mall, Michaels notes that you should *try* to have everything excluded. Thus all 5 choices are correct. However, you are least likely to succeed in having b (specials offered as part of a mall-wide promotion) excluded.

Chapter 2

TRAINING

---

*Well–Educated Employees
Can Keep Your Store
A Notch Above The Competition*

Browsers Present Challenge

January 1993

Recession, competition and consumer savvy have left jewelers facing as much of a challenge as ever in turning browsers into buyers.

Just over 28% of people who enter a jewelry store leave without doing any business, based on a new poll of the JCK Retail Jewelers Panel. That's little changed from 1978, when a JCK poll put the figure at nearly 27%. The polls weren't identical. The 1978 version asked jewelers to track customer information for one day (Feb. 10) while the new one covered a week (Sept. 14-20). But they do allow for comparison in three areas:

• The percentage of people in the store who bought merchandise—28.9% in '92, down from 32.1% in '78.

• The percentage involved in another transaction—42.9%, up from 41%. (The new poll also divided repair/service and other transactions into two categories. Of the 11,950 customers reported that week, 33.5% were involved in a repair or service transaction and 9.4% made some other form of transaction, such as layaway or credit payment.)

• The percentage who left without making any transaction —28.2%, up from 26.9%.

What's the best way to turn lookers into buyers?

Sales training is the clear winner, with many panelists saying salespeople must be able to entice browsers with factual information about how gems are formed, how jewelry is made and how to shop for value rather than price.

Many offer in-store training with sales experts and videos. "We've implemented a long-range sales-training program which encompasses both group and individual training/development plans with related goals and plans of action," says Rob Panowicz of Panowicz Jewelers, Olympia, Wash.

Salespeople should have more than just product knowledge, adds Eileen Eichhorn of Eichhorn Jewelry Inc., Decatur, Ind. "Take time to politely greet customers and mean it," she says. "The real reason most jewelry stores don't meet their potential in sales is lack of sincerity. Salespeople should 'take off' at least one day a month to shop for a fine piece of furniture, draperies, a swimming pool or jacuzzi. Listen to the salespeople who are literally stealing sales from the jewelry industry."

Tom Tinney of Tom's Jewelry, Tallahassee, Fla., meanwhile, relies on heavy advertising and while-you-wait repairs. "Salespeople are regularly trained to turn waiters into buyers. This is a tremendous benefit from while-you-wait repairs."

Other suggestions: telemarketing, show everyone who enters your store a piece of jewelry, give everyone a product or special-event flier, offer quality merchandise in a range of prices so a browser who may have thought you were too expensive will be pleasantly surprised, suggest a gift item for future purchase and have an outside consultant evaluate your business for an objective look at what you do right, what you do wrong and what you can do better.

JCK Management Study Center: Why You Need An Appraisal Education

Elly Rosen ◆ *October 1994*

[Author's note: This article should not be considered a replacement for formal appraisal education. Rather, it is an introduction to some of the basics of appraising, a primer that provides definitions and examples that should be helpful to current practitioners. It is intended to help jewelers assess their proper role in offering appraisal services.]

The appraising profession can provide all the advantages that come with offering professional services. But the benefits and profits often appear overshadowed by ever-growing pitfalls. Rather than scare off a hopeful appraiser, such pitfalls should encourage him or her to gain more knowledge about appraising. This article hopefully will clear up some misconceptions and persuade those who wish to reap the profits to obtain the professional appraisal education they need.

The winds of change: Since the late 1970s, the jewelry industry has experienced an intellectual revolution on the issue of appraising. Many jeweler appraisal practitioners now actively, even aggressively, seek knowledge and standards. An undercurrent of unrest and concern agitates many others. Meanwhile, the number of independent (non-merchant) appraisers has grown markedly over the past decade.

An artist might depict all this activity as a cyclone in which merchant practitioners spin in a cycle of concern and confusion. They hope to find the source of the appraisal problem and a panacea to cure all its woes.

This picture isn't unique to the gem and jewelry trade. It applies equally well to the antiques, fine arts, household contents, machinery and equipment trades, as well as to members of the insurance industry, the legal and business communities and a host of state and federal regulators.

A number of ethical and procedural quandaries have plagued merchants for as long as appraisals have been written. In the late 1980s, for example, inflated donation appraisals drew highly publicized government penalties. Most jewelers never wrote such exotic federal tax appraisals. But court decisions that shot down long-standing beliefs and traditions caused many to wonder about procedural problems with the types of appraisals they did perform.

A barrage of negative appraisal-related problems in the 1980s changed concern and caution to fear. Many jewelry industry leaders tried to fill the void left by a lack of accepted standards in a mad search for panaceas that would answer all appraisal questions and drive away the problems.

Appraisal band-aids: Many well-intentioned solutions were offered; some should sound familiar:

• "We appraise only items that we sold" was one common approach.

• "We appraise any used jewelry, but we will only appraise new jewelry that we sold" was an expanded version of this position.

• "We do appraisals for insurance only" was another approach, sometimes followed with "and an occasional estate or resale appraisal."

• "You should appraise only at your own selling price," proclaimed one jewelry organization.

• "If your appraisal is no more than a restatement of your selling price, then you should call it 'an estimate of replacement cost in our store,'" said one appraisal education program.

• "You should write insurance appraisals at 25% more than your selling price to cover your customer for future inflation," suggested another jewelry organization.

• "You can't appraise items you've sold because you have a conflict of interest," cried a new breed of independent professional appraisers.

• "You can't write accurate appraisals unless you're buying and selling, putting your money where your mouth is," some jewelers retorted.

• "Retail replacement value . . . appraisals must state . . . that appraisers' opinions as to the value of jewelry vary by as much as 25%" became the law in a major metropolitan area.

• "A qualified appraiser is one who is qualified," proclaimed the U.S. Congress in the 1984 Deficit Reduction Act

(which regulates appraisals for charitable contributions of property valued at more than $5,000).

• "When providing appraisals, jewelers are prohibited from charging fees which are based on a percentage of the value," announced the Commonwealth of Pennsylvania in the mid-1980s.

• "You should never appraise a mounted diamond in the setting unless you give a spread of quality grades," claimed a jewelry industry protection organization.

• "Should the guides [for the jewelry industry] be expanded to include appraisals of jewelry in addition to sales and offers to sell jewelry?" asked the Federal Trade Commission in 1992.

• "We no longer do appraisals. There's no way to do them right and we don't need the problems," concluded many jewelers.

An overabundance of such well-intentioned Band-Aid "solutions" plagued the profession. But black-and-white solutions wouldn't solve variable problems. Only one could really treat the disease: professional appraisal education, testing and certification.

The gathering storm: As appraisal issues began to attract headlines and lawyers in the late 1980s, jeweler-appraisers suddenly faced the threat of legal action for violating "express warranties" established by their point-of-sale appraisals. Ever more likely were negligence and damage suits by clients and consumer advocates or charges of appraisal-related disparagement and unfair trade practice from competitors. The merchant-appraiser community also faced a slew of new government regulations and/or penalties.

At the same time, personal property appraisal associations increased their visibility and offered the first professional appraisal courses. While such education was the panacea, it sadly got mired in battles with traditionalists and among the proliferating and competing appraisal groups.

In the early 1980s, I was guilty of panacea-mongering. I was among the many sincere individuals giving well-intentioned but insufficient answers. Specifically, we suggested that appraisals would be more professional if only they were more gemologically intensive, with longer descriptions. Gemology obviously is important to gemological appraising, but many now realize that an understanding of appraising is even more vital.

So why appraise? Considering all the problems, why bother with appraisals? In short, because the needs, benefits and profits outweigh the pitfalls. That's why many jewelers continue to appraise, despite an increase in apparent appraisal hazards.

It helps that the education vacuum is slowly but surely being filled. Although standards for appraising personal property are in the infant stage, good courses and education programs, testing and certification do exist. And more comprehensive advanced courses are being developed.

Here are some specific reasons why jewelers still offer appraisal services:

1. Customer service. Appraisal services often are required by customers who appreciate a full-service establishment.

2. Customer expectations. Customers have come to expect insurance appraisals with items they buy.

3. Traffic building. A well-advertised appraisal service can bring new customers into the store.

4. Competition. The jeweler who fails to offer a point-of-sale appraisal or to recommend the services of an independent appraiser fears a customer may go to the competition for one. Jewelers complain that appraisals by competitors often result in a "killed" sale or a stolen customer.

5. Gemological background. Some jewelers offer appraisals under the misconception that their gemological training alone equips them to do so.

What about the apparent problems? The main ones are lack of professional appraisal education and methodology.

The first step is to recognize that appraising is a profession. Being a competent, safe practitioner requires knowledge of the profession's standards, principles, procedures and methodology. Most apparent problems disappear once the nature of appraisal professionalism and the appraisal process is better understood.

Practitioner or professional? Being an appraisal practitioner and a professional appraiser should be synonymous. But the current state of the profession makes the two quite distinct.

Some argue that full-time independent appraisers are the professionals and that merchants who appraise are simply dabbling with a sideline. Such a definition is nice for the independent and provides an easy answer for some of the troubling questions. But it's too easy and probably wrong, arbitrary and misleading.

Regardless of whether you are a merchant-appraiser or an independent, if you're going to appraise, you should be a professional. You can be an appraiser who also sells the type of items in question or one who does not. You can limit your practice to certain types of appraisals (insurance replacement, for example). Such distinctions don't change the fact that a jeweler can be a professional appraiser or that an independent appraiser can be unprofessional.

Standards make a profession: There are many ways to define a profession and many elements that allow an occupation to be defined as a profession. A profession requires:

• Some degree of standards (a codified body of knowledge encompassing certain principles, procedures and methodology);

• Some medium of education that allows practitioners to learn the standards; and

• At some point, a collective body of practitioners who profess to subscribe to those standards.

Ideally, members of a profession can be formally educated, tested and certified in these standards; can pass on the knowledge learned to others; can promote understanding and growth of the standards; and can develop a procedure to monitor and enforce compliance with the standards.

Despite a lack of government regulation, most of the above exist today in the fragmented, voluntary profession of personal property appraising (which includes gems and jewelry). However, government regulation may be needed to induce groups to agree on one set of uniform standards. Although they shared a similar base and slowly came together on basic principles, groups involved in real estate appraisal took decades to agree on a minimal uniform standard. Federal intervention finally accomplished the task.

While we can glean some founding principles from real property appraising, personal property is different—and more difficult—to appraise, primarily because of its portability. One thing is certain: it will be difficult to convince the client community that appraising is a profession as long as those who do it maintain there are no standards and as long as each practitioner writes appraisals as he or she wishes. Remember that the courts have not considered a lack of uniform opinion sufficient reason for an appraiser to have no formal appraisal education.

Who is an appraiser? Neither the federal government nor any of the 50 states regulates appraisers of personal property. Some states are considering licensing and/or certification. But, appraisal reports and some procedures related to appraising and running an appraisal practice are subject to federal, state and municipal regulations.

There is no such thing as a "licensed appraiser" of personal property in the United States. Some municipalities require appraisal practitioners to obtain a business license, but this doesn't certify any particular qualifications as an appraiser. Until a state does license personal property appraisers, however, it will be difficult to prevent a merchant with a business license from advertising as a "licensed appraiser," though some professional appraisal societies consider such practices unethical.

Many criticize the government for its Band-Aid approach of regulating individual appraisal problems rather than deal with the disease itself by regulating appraisers. However, we can borrow a page from the government and assume that to understand what an appraiser is, we first must understand what an appraisal is.

What is an appraisal? An appraisal is an opinion of value, cost estimate or analysis in a defined market. Appraisals don't exist in a vacuum. Individuals and legal entities seek appraisals for specific reasons, although we often lose sight of the most fundamental one—to serve as a basis for making some financial decision.

It's this simple: two entities want to enter into a relationship or conduct a transaction for which they need an impartial, informed judgment about the worth of an item at a specific time for a particular market level. If appraisers always remembered the purpose of an appraisal and the needs of clients and third parties, many appraisal problems would go away.

More than a decade ago, the North American Conference of Appraisal Organizations (NACAO—primarily an umbrella group of real estate appraisal organizations that reformed as the Appraisal Foundation in 1987) defined an appraisal as: "A [written] statement, independently and impartially prepared, by a qualified appraiser, setting forth an opinion of defined value, of an adequately described property, as of a specific date, and supported by the presentation and analysis of relevant market data."

That definition—since clarified, modified and expanded in personal property appraisal education programs—tells the story. *An appraisal is the opinion of an informed expert. It is prepared to provide meaningful information for the use of clients and third parties.* It explains some of the ingredients without which an appraisal simply will not serve its purpose.

Clients and third parties have every right to believe the appraiser is not an advocate for any party to the transaction or any particular position. And because of market variables, they can expect the appraiser to explain the parameters within which they can rely on the stated value. An appraisal must be based on value in a defined market, not simply on one store's low or high prices.

Appraisal ethics: A jeweler can be very moral and honest and still be considered an unethical appraiser! Appraisal ethics are not the same rules that society applies as a test of moral conduct.

A profession is concerned primarily with behavior that speaks to the professionalism of one of its own and how such behavior reflects on the profession as a whole. If a collective body of practitioners subscribes to a standard of professionalism which one violates, that individual is judged unethical. A lay person who doesn't understand why the professional is required to behave that way might feel that professional ethics contradict society's scale of morality. For example, most people would say it's not immoral or dishonest to advertise. But it used to be against the American Bar Association's agreed-upon standard for lawyers to advertise. That made it unethical for lawyers.

This subject may seem esoteric, but it goes to the heart of the appraisal dilemma. Is appraising a profession whose rules consist of certain principles and procedures for the valuation of property? Or is it just an extension of a trade to be judged by each merchant's notions of morality?

The profession of personal property appraising is young and growing. Opinions abound as to the nature of the profession, its current status and its future direction. This results in a transition stage in which old self-assuring notions will be bandied about as though someone brought them down from a mountain. Much of this activity seems to center on the question of appraisal ethics.

To judge what is and isn't ethical in appraising, we need to look at the right set of rules. Some governmental bodies have adopted minimal standards of conduct for specific types of appraisals. And a number of appraisal organizations have published ethical-conduct codes for appraisers. A cursory look at these codes reveals a consensus on at least minimum guidelines of ethical conduct. This might help a judge decide whether an appraiser acted properly in case of a dispute.

Codes of conduct, standards of practice, and principles and procedures of methodology are all linked in an indivisible package. Such a package has much to offer the practitioner as a guide to professional, ethical appraising.

INTRODUCTION TO PROFESSIONAL APPRAISING: THINGS TO LEARN & DECIDE

We touched earlier on what an appraisal is. Let's expand on that by looking at the meaning of value.

A single item at a certain time can have many different types of values. This often shocks clients and new practitioners. But it gets worse. There also can be many different but equally correct opinions as to what dollar amount most represents value.

It should be obvious that the value of an item can vary as facts relating to the item and the particular transaction vary. It also should be expected that the opinion of appraisers will vary even in the very same scenario.

Value vs. price: Much valuation confusion centers on the failure to distinguish between selling price (or "cost") and value. In a capitalist system (an open market free-enterprise society), the same item often sells at different prices. That's why appraisers are needed.

Within the limits of what the law expects to be "con-

scionable," sellers are free to compete around price levels they feel the market will bear. Conscionable or not, the price paid for an item exists as a fact in the marketplace. Value, however, is not a fact. It's an appraiser's opinion based on the facts—in other words, the prices (usually plural) paid.

When performing appraisals, merchants must be aware of their very different role as an appraiser. Appraisers do not create or influence markets. They do not set prices or establish the conditions for transactions in the marketplace. Their role is to be knowledgeable about the market and its items and to analyze prices in that market, impartially and without advocacy, in order to provide an opinion of value. Appraisers are supposed to base their opinions on knowledge of actual market activity—not on what they feel the market should be.

Undefined value = non-value: Appraisals that define value as "stated value" actually mean "we don't have any particular market or type of transaction in mind. Use this for all of your appraisal needs." This is a typical cause of the appraisal dilemma which exposes the generous appraiser to lawsuits alleging negligence.

Different types of appraisals require different types of value. Failure to identify the type of value or to restrict its use to a particular client need provides a legal document that any party can use for any purpose they wish. If used in the wrong scenario, the appraiser might be held liable for resulting damage.

Appraisers must explain this to clients. Ignoring the problem won't make it go away; an umbrella of ambiguity provides only a false sense of security.
Clients typically request jewelry appraisals for one or more of the following reasons:
- To obtain insurance.
- To confirm they paid a "fair" purchase price.
- To resell an item.

Many appraisers still allow clients to believe an appraisal for any one of these can be used for the other two. Often they do so simply by failing to say otherwise.

Broader misconceptions are that appraisers have a primary role to evaluate (authenticate) a client's property and to make decisions for the client.

Here are examples of decisions that appraisers believe they can make without consulting the client. That an old watch in used condition should be appraised for replacement with a new watch. That an old-mine-cut diamond should be replaced with a scaled-down modern-cut equivalent. That used or old jewelry should be cleaned, that the diamond in a new ring should be removed for grading and that the only market a client should consider for resale is "dumping to the trade."

In reality, an appraiser's primary role is simply to provide information on an item's value. Clients should be told about choices such as those just listed and also told the report will include any limitations related to such areas. But it's up to the client to decide how to proceed.

1.50-ct. old-miner cut = 1.20-ct. modern cut: The notion that old-cut diamonds should arbitrarily be appraised for the replacement cost of modern-cut equivalents is a prime example of decisions an appraiser should not make.

First, it's the client's choice whether to replace with a similar "old" item or a "modern" equivalent.

Second, market reality shows that old-cut value simply is not equal to modern-cut value.

Third, if a client wants a 1.50-ct. G VS_1 old-cut diamond replaced with a modern equivalent, the equivalent is a 1.50-ct. G VS_1 modern-cut diamond, not a 1.20-ct. G VS_1 modern "equivalent!"

This example shows why appraisal methodology should be based on a knowledge of appraisal principles, not just on gemological training or trade experience alone.

It's beyond the scope of this article to debate whether someone must be a gemologist to appraise gemstones or a metallurgist to appraise jewelry. But it's clear that an appraiser should obtain as much product knowledge and market information as possible. It's also clear there's a wide universe of knowledge called for in appraising the multitude of gem and jewelry items.

This article proposes:
• That knowledge of appraisal principles and methodology is an absolute must for appraising.
• That applying this knowledge to each appraisal depends on the needs presented by the item in question and on the needs of the known client and of any foreseeable third party.
• That clients should decide on any options that are theirs to decide.

Take-in: It should be apparent by now that many problems can be resolved at take-in—the time for the critical initial client interview. Widespread gemological training has taught many jewelers the limitations that should be placed on gemstone identification during take-in for cleaning, repairs, modifications and appraising.

Ideally, the appraiser should handle jewelry taken in for appraisal. However, other staff members with fundamental appraising knowledge can handle the basics, perhaps avoiding a final commitment on the scope and fee until the appraiser can speak with the client.

Which services? In deciding to offer appraisals, the jeweler needs to decide on the scope of appraisal services and the background of personnel who will provide them. There are many options to consider.

Which items to appraise
• Only new or old items that you have sold.
• Only new or old items the client acquired elsewhere.
• All of the above or only certain types and categories of gems and jewelry (or of silver, coins, watches, decorative arts, etc.).

Services to be offered
• Basic appraisal (valuation) service.
• Evaluation (gemological) service.
• Full evaluation/valuation (gemological appraisal) service.

Types of appraisals
• Insurance for new, used and/or comparable items.
• Standard consumer services (insurance, confirmation of "fair" purchase price and consumer resale).
• Services for the professional client community. (Note: This category can be very lucrative and attract a new client/customer base, but it also requires more advanced appraisal background and proficiency.) It includes:
– Insurance damage and claims appraisals.
– Divorce, state probate, bankruptcy, etc.
– Federal tax-related appraisals for estate tax, taxable gifts,

charitable contribution deductions, IRS seizure of property, etc.
– Miscellaneous government-related appraisals for the postal service, law enforcement agencies, FDIC/RTC, etc.
– Appraiser expert witness and/or trial consultant services on any of the above.

Options if not offering appraisals
What if you don't offer any appraisal services? You still need to:
• Obtain and maintain fundamental knowledge of the professional appraisal process that still affects you.
• Avoid unconditional "Guarantees of Appraised Value" on items you have sold—a traditional but risky procedure considering the current state of the profession. If you provide such assurance at the point of sale, consult your attorney on how to make the "guarantee" conditional on the background of the appraiser and the type of appraisal obtained.
• Embrace one of the new breed of independent appraisers practicing in your community. Such a non-selling, or limited-selling appraiser can keep your customers from going to another jeweler who does provide appraisals.
• In place of an "appraisal" at the point-of-sale, consider providing your customer with a "Statement (or Estimate) of Replacement Cost in Our Store." This is not an appraisal, but rather a restatement of your selling price, and can be on a form or your own stationery. I have taught and published the concept since 1984, and it is beginning to take hold as an accepted industry procedure. It might also be called, perhaps more properly, "Insurance Replacement Estimate."

You also might consider loose or formal ties with professional appraisers specializing in other types of personal property such as antiques, silver, fine or decorative arts and collectibles, machinery and equipment and even real estate. This gives you access to diverse research sources and information-sharing. In addition, the more lucrative professional appraisal assignments often call for a team of appraisers in a number of specialties. Such could be the case with divorce, estate, tax, liquidation and many other types of appraisals. Often, an appraiser in one specialty contacts one in another specialty for help. It pays to be in the circle.

Background and qualifications: The type and scope of appraisal services you offer affect the training and experience you or your appraiser should have. Background in appraising should include:
• Appraisal education, testing and certification.
• Appraisal experience and/or internship (formal appraisal internship is a relatively new concept).
• Prior experience with specific types of appraisals.
• Knowledge of government regulations relevant to the types of appraisals you offer (also the ability to research and keep up with new and modified regulations).

Background in the jewelry trade should include:
• General trade experience and involvement and/or apprenticeship.
• Gemological and/or other product knowledge education, testing and certification.
• Access to and working knowledge of relevant instrumentation and outside laboratories.
• Experience and/or education related to jewelry arts, fabrication and/or repair techniques.
• Knowledge and background specific to the categories of items to be appraised.

In addition, the appraiser should have access to a library of appraisal texts and maintain an ongoing appraisal education program. Education and experience as a witness/trial consultant will be needed if that's relevant to your practice.

Today, jewelers who appraise have a golden opportunity not available just 15 years ago. Now they can reap the benefits and profits of being part of a profession. If you are going to appraise, make the commitment to really be an appraiser. If you offer appraisal services, be sure you offer nothing less than *professional* appraisal services. Only then will the profits outweigh the pitfalls.

TIMELINE OF SOME IMPORTANT APPRAISAL-RELATED COURT DECISIONS ON SELECTED TOPICS

1941—Guggenheim vs. Rasquin

Subject: Original cost as a measure of fair market value.

Case: "Cost is cogent evidence of value . . . Cost in this situation is not market price in the normal sense of the term. But the absence of market price is no barrier to valuation."— *U.S. Supreme Court*

1962—Hughes vs. Potomac Insurance Co. of the District of Columbia

Subject: Role of appraisers in making an award for damages when serving on an insurance claims panel.

Case: "The function of appraisers [when serving on an insurance claims panel] is to determine the amount of damage resulting to various items submitted for their consideration. It is certainly not their function to resolve questions of coverage and interpret provisions of the policy."—*California Court of Appeal, First District*

1964—Tripp vs. Commissioner

Subject: Appraiser's opinion must be based on facts. (Donation case involving jewelry of antiquity that was bought in Europe).

Case: " . . . the record discloses that the opinion testimony of these witnesses was almost wholly subjective in character. And, opinion evidence which does not appear to be based upon disclosed facts is of little or no value. Petitioner's witnesses failed to support their conclusions as to value with facts of convincing probative value."— *U.S. Court of Appeals, Seventh Circuit*

1967—Goldman vs. Commissioner

Subject: For donations (or estate taxes), the fair market value must be sales to the ultimate consumer.

Case: [paraphrased] "Public" in the fair market value definition means sales to an ultimate consumer. Fair market value cannot be based on sales to a dealer buying for resale.— *U.S. Court of Appeals, Sixth Circuit*

1976—David vs. Commissioner

Subject: Charging a percentage of the appraised value as an appraisal fee creates the appearance of impropriety and questions the credibility of an otherwise qualified appraiser.

Case: "[The petitioner's expert's] fee for making the appraisals was based on a percentage of the values arrived at. While we are not questioning [the appraiser's] integrity, we cannot ignore the fact that a motive existed to arrive at high values. This does not mean the percentage fee arrangement invalidates the appraisal, but rather it simply means we must view the appraisal with added caution."—*U.S. Tax Court*

1980—Stone vs. Those Certain Underwriters at Lloyd's of London

Subject: Failure to disclose that the seller provided an appraisal, at the time of sale, for more than the sales price could be grounds for insurer to cancel the policy after a loss.

Case: "Did the plaintiff's failure to disclose information regarding the wide variation between purchase price and the contemporaneous appraised value and the fact that the seller and appraiser were one and the same person constitute a misrepresentation that affected the materiality of the risk and furnished grounds for recession? Justice and precedent compel an affirmative answer."—*Illinois Appellate Court, Fifth District*

1984—Safeco Insurance Co. of America vs. Sharma

Subject: Appraiser as an impartial provider of information on value. Engaging in issues of authenticity exceeds an appraiser's role when serving on an insurance claims panel.

Case: "In no authority is it suggested that an appraisal panel is empowered to determine whether an insured lost what he claimed to have lost . . . Certainly, an insurer is free to litigate whether the insured has misrepresented what he lost, but it is beyond the scope of an appraisal."— *California Court of Appeal, Second District*

1985—Costa vs. Neimon

Subject: Appraiser has liability for negligence to a third party who the appraiser should foresee would come "within the ambit" of harm that could result from a carelessly done appraisal.

Case: "The duty of any person is to refrain from any act which will cause foreseeable harm to others, even though the nature of that harm and the identity of the harmed person or harmed interest is unknown at the time of the act . . . An appraiser's failure to use due care in performing an appraisal is negligence because it is an act or omission in the face of foreseeable harm. It is not necessary that the appraiser have foreseen the harm to the particular plaintiff [the third-party buyer who relied on the appraisal]. The appraiser should have foreseen that a prospective buyer of the property being appraised was 'within the ambit' of harm which would result from a carelessly done appraisal."—*Wisconsin Court of Appeals*

1985—Lio vs. Commissioner

Subject: Donation or estate tax FMV cannot be based on sales to a dealer who is buying for resale [in purchased form].

Case: " . . . the sale to the ultimate consumer [the 'public'] is any sale to those persons who do not hold the item for subsequent resale."—*U.S. Tax Court*

1985—Price vs. Commissioner

Subject: Original cost isn't necessarily the best evidence of value.

Case: "In many cases, actual sales of property to be valued are the best evidence of fair market value . . . We must also, however, consider reliable opinion testimony as to value . . . The items . . . were sold as tourmalines although some were beryls. They were priced in bulk by average carat value. The likelihood that the price charged to petitioners was inflated is increased by petitioners' apparent lack of knowledge . . . Under all of these circumstances, cost is not the most reliable evidence."—*U.S. Tax Court*

1985—Anselmo vs. Commissioner

Subject: Item must be valued as is, not as though in some other possible form (implication for appraising old-miner as modern cut). Also, donation (and estate and gift tax) FMV definition of "public" is the ultimate consumer, and the "ultimate consumer" could be a manufacturer not buying for resale in the purchased form.

Case: "[Petitioners'] appraisers estimated the retail value of a stone by calculating the portion of a [hypothetical] finished jewelry item's retail price that could be attributed to the [loose commercial quality] gem . . . The commissioner's experts valued the gems on the assumption the 461 stones would be sold together to a single jewelry manufacturer or retail jeweler. The [lower] court concluded the commissioner's experts were correct . . . The Anselmos contend . . . that the Tax Court erred by not valuing the stones as the portion of the jewelry's retail price attributable to the stones . . . The most appropriate purchaser [in a federal tax FMV scenario] is not invariably the individual consumer. For example, the general buying public for live cattle would be comprised primarily of slaughterhouses rather than individual consumers. The fair market value of live cattle accordingly would be measured by the price paid at the livestock auction rather than at the supermarket."—*U.S. Court of Appeals, 11th Circuit* **1987—Hecker vs. Commissioner**

Subject: 1.) Court's distinction of appraiser's evaluation expertise vs. valuation expertise. 2.) Rejection of appraising by price guides and formulae in favor of knowledge of market activity.

Case: "[Petitioner's appraiser's] principal expertise is in evaluating the quality of gemstones rather than their dollar value [and thus he] was forced to value the tourmalines and mineral specimens based on nationally available pricing guides . . . We were unimpressed with [his] experience and credentials . . . We have serious doubts that the methodology he used . . . yielded values that reflected market prices accurately."—*U.S. Tax Court*

'What I Paid is Irrelevant'

It's the mid-1980s and industry concern with the appraisal dilemma is growing. People are looking for answers. A major jewelers' organization presents an interim mitigating policy for its members. "When writing insurance appraisals on items you have sold," says the organization, "the appraised value should be your selling price. What you charged is the best measure of retail value."

During the period of these debates, a customer comes into the store with an item of [new or used] jewelry he recently bought elsewhere. He asks for a "retail replacement value appraisal" to be used in obtaining a floater on his homeowner insurance policy.

In the initial client interview, the jeweler/appraiser asks when the customer bought the item, in what kind of store and how much he paid.

The sudden silence can be cut with a knife; the client tries to retain his composure and, with a knowing and familiar smirk, asks why the jeweler wants to know. "What I paid isn't relevant!" he says. "What am I paying you for? I'm not going to do your job for you! The other jeweler told me

you'd try to kill their sale and I told him that wouldn't happen because I thought you were a professional appraiser!"

With that parting remark, he walks out the door before you can explain the important and valid reasons for your questions, before you can explain that the very reason you asked is that you're a professional.

Two years ago, a jewelry trade press journalist wrote an article about appraisal methodology. The reporter took a piece of jewelry to different jewelry appraisers to see how they would value it. The article told how some of the appraisers had asked what the cost was. In a recurring theme, the author appeared to accuse those who did ask of performing improperly.

Why would one jewelry organization proclaim that appraised values should be equal to the selling price while a journalist decries an appraiser asking about that selling price? Would a client believe it wrong for an appraiser to make such an inquiry if he hadn't gotten that impression from the performance of past appraisers? Why would those other appraisers have shied away from the question?

I think it's safe to say that many in the trade would think asking a client about the cost is wrong—even unethical! Yet many jewelers base their own appraised values on what they themselves charge. Aren't they judging what should be considered ethical against different sets of ethics in different situations?

Many appraisal standards seem unclear to practitioners who haven't gone through formal appraisal education and testing. The standards of many appraisal societies and some government regulations make clear that to determine the value of an item, the appraiser must take into account its recent sales history. The recent sale of an item should be treated just as he or she would consider recent sales of similar items.

I recall one trial in which an expert with many years of trade experience shocked the judge with his view on this issue. In arriving at a value, the expert relied on his own opinion and the opinion of others as to what the item *would* sell for. The item in question had been sold a short time before the valuation date in question. When the judge asked why the appraiser didn't consider this much lower recent sale, he said he would never allow himself to be biased with knowledge of such facts. The judge found against the appraiser's opinion (for many reasons).

Value Defined

A full discussion of the many values an appraiser must consider is far beyond the scope of this article, but we can look at some introductory basics.

Value is the best and impartial opinion of an appraiser as to a dollar amount that is most representative of the fair range of prices typically paid for an item.

For value to have meaning, it must be attached to a particular set of facts, including the quality and condition of the item, the market and/or market level where relevant transactions take place, the position (or desirability) of the item in that market and at a particular time.

Market value generally is intended as a guide to the types of transactions an appraiser is to consider as the basis for forming an opinion of value. The component elements—which are designed to weed out transactions that are extraordinary to the market—are:

• An arm's-length transaction in a free and open market subject to all normal market influences, specifically no private (secret) sales or sales between parties with special relationships.

• Sales between the greatest number of buyers and sellers who are:

– Reasonably well-informed of the facts related to the item and its position in the market.

– Willing to buy or sell but under no particular compulsion to do so.

– Entering the market in a time frame that would be considered normal and reasonable for sellers and buyers in that market or market level.

– Acting prudently and in their own best interest regarding the value of the property (or transaction).

– Typical in their motivation for buyers and sellers normally expected to be transacting business in the relevant market or market level.

• Sales in which payment is:

– In the form of cash or some measurable and consistently definable equivalent.

– Financed, if such financing is typically the method of conducting business for the property in the market and on terms generally available to buyers at the time relevant to the valuation date.

– For the item itself and does not include any atypical add-ons of goods and/or services or special incentives to buy.

• Proper reconciliation and adjustments for atypical forms of payment or for special transaction conditions.

Market value tells an appraiser how to look at transactions and what kind of buyers and sellers to consider. What it usually doesn't do is define the particular market or market level in which the appraiser is supposed to be looking. The assignment does that.

Often, the item itself, the agreed-upon needs of the client and third party or government regulations select the market to be used for market value.

Fair market value or FMV is probably the most misunderstood and misapplied term in the world of appraising! It's usually a legal term that has been defined for the needs of a particular legal "jurisdiction." In this context, jurisdiction can refer to a court, a level or branch of government, and an administrative or regulatory agency.

Most dangerous are the notions that there is a single definition of FMV and that any one definition can be applied arbitrarily to any assignment in which someone wants the fair market value. Law dictionaries do define FMV, but these definitions usually just combine some of the generic elements of "market value."

Individual state or federal agencies typically take these elements and modify or restrict them for application in a particular type of market, perhaps by designating a market level (applicable buyers and sellers) or geographic region to be used in arriving at FMV.

Insurance often confuses practitioners and leads merchants to proceed with all appraisals as though the item were being replaced. A look at the elements of value outlined above should clarify that replacement value (cost) is not a jumping-off point for other appraisal values.

In the strictest sense, replacement value is a major exception to "normal" value. In insurance, the issue often is compensation or the ability to replace rather than value. Usually, an insured person and the insurer sign a contract (policy) in which they agree on a method of making the insured whole and/or on a number to be the basis of compensation in the event of a loss. Insurance companies often accept the buyer's cost or selling price as "value" without any appraisal. However, this approach can change drastically in the event of a dispute following a loss, depending on the language in individual insurance policies.

'I Just Want to Know What it's Worth'

Some appraisal clients so distrust jewelers/appraisers that they believe explaining why they want an appraisal somehow would bias the result.

Having been told by the seller that other jewelers will try to "kill the sale" with a biased appraisal, clients often misstate the real reason for an appraisal or the history of the item. They often will insist that the reason for the appraisal doesn't matter and that they "just want to know what it's worth."

The first thing to clarify is that an item can have many values; which one applies should be defined in the report. You also should explain at the start that the intended use dictates the type of report format to be used, the market level to be examined and the type of transactions selected for comparison, not just the type of value.

Clients should be told the report will be limited to its stated use. It might contain language such as: "'Retail Replacement Cost Estimate—New' stated herein has been provided to assist the client in obtaining insurance for items of like kind and quality in new condition. This report and its stated value(s) are valid for this use only and are invalid for any other use, including, but not limited to, 'consumer resale' or 'confirmation of fair purchase price.'"

It's beyond the scope of this article to explain the differences between these values. However, these are the typical client appraisal needs that many people erroneously believe can be addressed by an appraisal for any one of them.

A paragraph such as the one above should limit any appraisal to just one of these uses. (There are multivalue, multiuse appraisals, but that's another story.)

The Big 'E' in E-Valuation

While the process of valuation can, and often should, include evaluation, the relationship between the two seem to have gone topsy-turvy.

An appraiser's primary role is to provide information on the worth of an item. Depending on the type of appraisal or the defined needs of a known client and a foreseeable third party, varying levels of evaluation might also be required.

These two terms usually are considered synonymous, but have important distinctions in professional appraisal terminology.

A "valuation report" is mainly a vehicle to convey a defined opinion of value (monetary worth); an "evaluation report" offers broader information. Most appraisal valuation reports include some evaluation information. An evaluation report may or may not also include an appraiser's estimate of value.

Evaluation could consist of:
- Identifying and (possibly in-depth) grading of materials.
- Authenticating the background or origin of an item.
- Proposed changes to an item.
- Analysis of available markets for client buying or selling activity.

It is not necessarily the appraiser's role to provide all this information for every item in every appraisal report. Nor should he or she automatically do so and bill the client for the cost. That is for the client to decide after being informed of the options, the pros and cons, possible results, costs, etc.

A classic case involves the question of whether a diamond can be appraised in the setting. Of course it can! To say that a diamond must be removed to be graded (evaluated) for an appraisal is to say that many types and sizes of gem-set jewelry can't be appraised.

The industry deals with gray areas like this by issuing conflicting proclamations of what must always (or never) be done. But there's no need to select an arbitrary extreme. The issue is not whether to do it or not. Instead, the issue is how and when to do it and how to be clear in the report just what was or was not done and why. Like many appraisal questions, it involves report-writing more than procedures.

Similar considerations go into deciding when to use gemological or metallurgical procedures to identify component parts of an item or authenticity procedures to establish its background.

Appraisals often are based on readily apparent identity. This limited valuation procedure must be appropriate for the assignment, and any parties who may rely on the report must know the limitations. (Don't use "readily apparent identity" to run amok with appraising items you don't understand; you might have to justify the background and basis of such a call as well.)

Bottom line: the amount and cost of evaluation procedures to be included in an appraisal assignment usually should be the client's decision and not the appraiser's.

JCK Management Study Center Quiz

1. There are no government regulations pertaining to the appraisal of gems and jewelry.
   True ❏   False ❏

2. Which would be the most accurate source on which to base your appraised value of a new item for consumer insurance?
   a. The price you would charge to replace the item in your own store, regardless of where it was bought.
   b. The price charged by the store which sold the item, if it was bought elsewhere.
   c. 25% higher than your selling price because consumers are accustomed to items being appraised for something over the selling price.
   d. The dollar amount that is most representative of typical selling prices by stores in your area.

3. Most jewelers in your area feel that a certain jeweler-appraiser is unethical in his/her appraisal practices. Identifiable professional groups agree on certain ethical appraisal practices, which would include the areas of your allegation. You go to the attorney general, recognized appraisal standards in hand, to file charges against the unethical appraiser. The attorney general still might be unable to go along with your charges based on the professional appraisal standards you have brought.
   True ❏   False ❏

4. You have been a jeweler and appraiser for 30 years. You have always performed appraisals honestly and without bias. You have no reason to fear that any charge of unethical appraisal conduct on your part could stand up.
   True ❏   False ❏

5. A customer brings in an item he just bought down the street and asks you to appraise it for insurance. It is considered professionally ethical to ask the customer what he paid for the item.
   True ❏   False ❏

6. Which of the following is least true about "value?"
   a. If an appraiser is wrong about the appraised value, he/she is liable for any damage caused to a client who relied on that opinion.
   b. Value is an opinion based on knowledge of actual market activity.
   c. For a value to have meaning it must be defined for a particular market level.
   d. The value of an item can vary for different types of appraisals.

7. The term "Fair Market Retail Value" encompasses all of the regulated elements of value and is the most correct terminology in appraisals for consumer insurance.
   True ❏   False ❏

8. "Market Value" is usually distinguished from "Fair Market Value" by the fact that "Fair Market Value" often adds information on which market to look to for the appraised value.
   True ❏   False ❏

9. "Retail Replacement Value" is the most representative type of value for most types of appraisals where the market to be used is retail.
   True ❏   False ❏

(Continued on next page)

10. Which of the following decisions can be made by an appraiser without consulting the client?

    a. Appraising an old European cut diamond based on the value of a recut modern equivalent.

    b. Cleaning an old ring in order to appraise it.

    c. Appraising an old watch for the value of a new one if the appraisal is for insurance.

    d. None of the above is correct.

11. You are doing an insurance appraisal on an "engagement" ring with an apparently fine-quality 2.00-ct. diamond center stone and the client won't let you remove the diamond from the setting for grading. The client just bought the diamond at a store down the street. Professional appraisal standards require that you pass on the appraisal assignment.

    True ❏   False ❏

12. Which of the following best describes the profession of appraising?

    a. It is an art.

    b. It is a science.

    c. It is an inexact science.

    d. It is a quasi-profession because it has no definable standards.

13. Of the types of appraisals listed below, which one type of appraisal report can be used by clients for the needs encompassed in the other two.

    a. Insurance retail replacement value.

    b. Confirmation of fair purchase price.

    c. Consumer resale.

    d. None of these.

14. The most important aspect of the appraisal "take-in" procedure is interviewing the client to determine the type of appraisal they need.

    True ❏   False ❏

15. An "evaluation report" is synonymous with a "valuation report."

    True ❏   False ❏

16. Until appraisal groups can agree on a uniform standard for all appraisers of gems and jewelry, the pitfalls facing appraisers are not worth the potential profits.

    True ❏   False ❏

(Answers to Quiz can be found at the end of this chapter)

Training Your Staff
To Sell Heritage Jewelry

Maxine Nelson with Juliet George McCleery ◆ *November 1993*

So you've decided to carry antique, period and estate jewelry—heritage jewelry, let's call it—in your store. Congratulations! You've recognized the excellent growth potential this merchandise category offers. Three-quarters of the respondents to a 1992 JCK poll expected heritage jewelry sales to grow 30% by 1995. Besides boosting profits, this jewelry also can enhance your image as a knowledgeable, professional, full-service jeweler who offers something different for value-conscious consumers.

In more than 10 years as a wholesaler and retailer of antique, period and estate jewelry, I have learned the key to success is education—of yourself, your staff and your customers. The more knowledgeable your salespeople, the more excited they can make customers about jewelry.

Before we get into curriculum and methods, let's discuss how to select staff members. I've found that successful heritage jewelry salespeople tend to fit a profile. They are predominantly mature women who have already raised a family and/or been in the work force, though not necessarily in jewelry sales, for some time. Enriched by life experience, they interact confidently and comfortably with customers. They have upbeat, warm personalities and a strong work ethic.

They also own nice jewelry and wear it graciously, and that's important when selling an expensive product.

Of course, there are successful heritage jewelry salespeople who don't fit this description. Let's assume you've hired the best "raw material" in human resources. The first things your new salesperson needs to know are your policies on salaries, commissions, benefits, vacations, returns, repairs and security. Then cover basic selling techniques and the importance of customer development through direct mail or phone contact.

Once you've laid this foundation, you're ready to cover jewelry topics.

How to proceed: Knowledge in the following areas will help you and your staff to sell more heritage jewelry:

• Types of jewelry. Many people believe that estate jewelry means someone died. Make sure your staff explains that estate means previously owned, not necessarily from an actual estate. Other terms they should understand include **antique jewels**, which are more than 100 years old, and **period jewels**, which exhibit the distinct style of a particular era.

• Metals. Salespeople should recognize the characteristics of gold (all karats and colors), gold-filled, silver and platinum.

• Gemology. knowledge of the 4 C's (cut, color, clarity and carat weight) and the Gemological Institute of America's grading system for diamonds is essential. Call the Diamond Promotion Service at (800) 370-6789 for customer handouts.

Staff members also should know the characteristics of pearls and the most commonly seen colored stones including rubies, sapphires, emeralds, opals, amethysts, garnets, citrines and tourmalines. Also acquaint salespeople with special organic materials such as ivory, bone, coral, amber and cameo.

• Manufacturing techniques. Salespeople should understand how jewelry is constructed. Discuss settings, soldering, shank sizing and the most commonly found "art" techniques—filigree, enamelizing and granulation, etc. Explain how the type of catch can help to date a piece.

• Makers and marks. Knowing how to identify marks and interpret their meaning is critical for heritage jewelry salespeople. Teach your staff to use *Bradbury's Book of Hallmarks* (see Bibliography) and encourage them to show it to customers. People are fascinated to learn that different symbols stamped on jewelry stand for dates, cities and makers.

• Care and cleaning. Show your staff how to use a loupe and point out signs of wear and abuse on mountings and catches. Encourage them to teach customers how to view pieces through a loupe. Explain cleaning methods; salespeople must be able to explain that ammonia degrades pearl nacre and that emeralds should be wiped clean with a soft cloth to avoid removing the oils that enhance their beauty. I wrote a pamphlet called *A Guide to Caring for Your Antique Jewelry* that I go over with salespeople and give to customers.

• History. Salespeople should know the design characteristics, motifs, techniques and societal influences of various historical periods. Go over the early periods of ancient, Renaissance and Georgian jewels, but emphasize the periods most commonly traded in the marketplace: Victorian, Edwardian, Art Nouveau, Art Deco and Retro Modern. Explain that from the early Victorian to early Art Deco eras, time periods are longer because styles changed less quickly before the days of TV and mass-market publications.

Inducing desire: The ability to apply historical perspective to the metals, gemology, manufacturing techniques and makers involved is the cornerstone of heritage jewelry sales. Salespeople should be able to explain a technique in such a way that it sticks in the customer's mind and increases the jewel's romantic appeal. When describing foil backing, for example, mention that makers used to place cork and foil behind stones so they glowed when they caught the candlelight. Now, of course, we know to cut holes in the metal mountings to enhance reflection and scintillation. Keep a broken foil-backed garnet on hand as a visual aid.

How do you go about imparting such a breadth of detailed knowledge? It takes time and resources. A basic reference package for an employee might include:

• A historical timeline.
• A comprehensive book on antique and period jewelry such as *Answers to Questions About Old Jewelry* by Jeanene Bell or *Antique & Twentieth Century Jewellery* by Vivienne Becker.

• GIA's small colored stone ID set.
• A colored stone book such as *Gemstones of the World* by Walter Schumann.
• A book on general jewelry store sales techniques such as *A Helping Hand for New Jewelers* from GIA or *More Joy of Selling* from JCK.
• A loupe.

Develop a library of videos, charts, auction catalogs, magazines and books that employees may consult. The most important resource, however, is your own stock. I "case train" my employees by making them familiar with every item in my stock, case by case. They hold each piece and look at it through the loupe. I describe its characteristics and where it fits into the timeline, then relate a story connected to one of its attributes. This teaches the concepts and serves as a reference point for salespeople when they show the piece to customers.

Reinforce what you teach by testing. You can do this formally with written tests or informally, as I do, by pointing out a piece in your case or an auction catalog and quizzing a salesperson about it. Ask your staff to role-play scenarios for selling the value of a particular jewel.

Educating yourself and your staff to sell antique, period and estate jewelry takes time and effort, but following these guidelines should ease the way.

Bibliography

Be sure to check libraries or used-book stores for any items that are out of print.

Antique and Twentieth Century Jewellery: A Guide for Collectors, Vivienne Becker, N.A.G. Press Ltd., London, 1980.
An Illustrated Dictionary of Jewelry, Harold Newman, Thames and Hudson, New York, 1987 (out of print).
Answers to Questions About Old Jewelry 1840-1950, 2nd edition, Jeanene Bell, Books Americana, 1991.
A Helping Hand for New Jewelers, Gemological Institute of America, Santa Monica, Cal., 1986.
A History of Jewellery 1100-1870, Joan Evans, Faber & Faber, London, 1970.
Bradbury's Book of Hallmarks: A Guide to Marks of Origin on British and Irish Silver, 1544-1989, originally compiled by Frederick Bradbury, F.S.A., 1989.
Buying Antique Jewelry, Skipping the Mistakes, Karen Lorene, Lorene Publications, Seattle, Wash., 1987.
Discovering Hallmarks on English Silver, 6th edition, John Bly, Shire Publications Ltd., Bucks, England, 1983.
Gemstones of the World, Walter Schumann, Sterling Publishing Co., New York, N.Y., 1977.
Handbook of Gem Identification, 12th edition, Richard T. Liddicoat Jr., Gemological Institute of America, Santa Monica, Cal., 1990.
Introduction to Precious Metals, Mark Grimwade, Butterworth & Co., Norfolk, England, 1985.

Jewelry 7000 Years, Hugh Tait, The Trustees of the British Museum, British Museum Publications Ltd., London, 1976.

Jewelry Concepts and Technology, Oppi Untracht, Doubleday, New York, N.Y., 1985.

Modern Jewelry: An International Survey 1890-1963, Graham Hughes, Crown Publishers, New York, N.Y., 1963.

More Joy of Selling, Jewelers' Circular-Keystone, Radnor, Pa., 1992.

The Official Price Guide to Antique Jewelry, 6th edition, Arthur Guy Kaplan, House of Collectibles, Random House, New York, N.Y. 1990.

Timeline on Commonly Traded Jewelry Periods

Victorian (1840-1900)
    1840—Queen Victoria begins to reign
    1861—Prince Albert dies
    1900—Footed catch
Art Nouveau (1880-1915)
    1901—King Edward VII begins reign
Edwardian (1900-1913)
Art Deco (1919-1940)
    1920—Spinner catch
    1939—Start of World War II
Retro Modern (1940-1955)

Tips For Successful Design Selling

August 1993 Part II

Because women are attuned to design—and because they're used to seeing apparel promoted by designer—the woman who buys for herself is a good candidate for designer jewelry.

To build a thriving designer jewelry business, you first must know how to select and promote the merchandise correctly. Here are some tips:

1. Walk before you run, suggests Toni Lyn Judd, a designer representative. If you were trying to persuade someone to try new foods, you wouldn't start with frog legs. The same concept holds true here, especially if you're new to selling designer jewelry.

2. Start by looking to fill holes in your merchandise selection. Are you low on pearl jewelry? Colored stone jewelry? Find designers whose work fits your inventory needs, your open-to-buy budget and your customer base in terms of taste and price.

If your customers tend to buy jewelry that retails around $500, don't choose three designers whose jewelry starts at $1,500 retail.

If your customers' tastes run toward pearl strands and diamond studs, look for designers whose work is an updated classic style rather than on the cutting edge of experimental.

If your customers generally spend Saturday night with a pizza and a video instead of at black-tie dinners, choose a designer whose jewelry fits that life-style.

Your customers, not the allure of a top designer's name, should be the determining factor in whose work you stock.

3. As you gain success with your first designer lines, start adding more. You want your customers to grow with you, not run away from their familiar jewelry store that's suddenly anything but familiar.

4. Look for designer jewelry in different places, from the designer sections of major trade shows to craft fairs to the budding designer at your own bench. Read trade magazines for designer profiles and design contest news (especially contests that stress salability and different price points).

5. Be careful of price points. Judd cautions that consumers generally equate the word "designer" with the word "expensive." Educate your staff and let customers know—either by visible pricing or marketing—that it isn't necessarily so.

6. Merchandise your designer jewelry by collection and segregate it from regular stock to give it the aura of being special. Options include dividing a store into "boutiques" for different designers, devoting a case to one designer, highlighting the work of several designers in a single case or even sectioning off a corner of a case for designer jewelry—as long as it's separated from other jewelry.

7. Use signs to identify the designer so customers associate the name with the jewelry.

8. Group pieces to show continuity of design and the ensemble as a whole. You can't represent the scope of a designer's work with only one or two pieces. But don't cram the case full of jewelry—highlight one or two collections and keep the rest in the back to bring out when customers inquire about the designer.

9. Understand what makes designer jewelry special in concept and workmanship. Each designer has a special look to his or her jewelry and all work will reflect that designer's personality. (Some examples: Michael Bondanza's platinum bracelets, David Yurman's nautical cables.)

Some designers handmake and sign each one-of-a-kind piece; some make a prototype and have bench jewelers or a contract manufacturer actually make the line; some are big-business designers who simply oversee styling of the line. In terms of workmanship, designer-made jewelry tends to be more intricate than mass-market goods. It may have special surface treatments such as granulation or etching, it may have unusual clasps or hinges and generally the backs and undersides will be as well-finished as the front.

10. In marketing designer jewelry, promote the designer. Excite your salespeople about the designer so they have a story to tell to customers. Mail designer-supplied postcards showing their newest works (you don't have to stock the pieces as long as you can order them quickly), host personal appearances by designers or schedule a special event dedicated to previewing designer goods.

In general advertising, promote your store as a source for designer jewelry instead of just a good jewelry store. Also encourage customers to become collectors; record which designers' jewelry they collect and look for other designers whose work complements what they already own.

11. BONUS TIP: Wear it and show it! The more people see it, the more they'll be tempted to buy it.

Man-To-Woman Selling: Do's And Don'ts For Success

Edna B. Jacques ◆ August 1993 Part II

1. Don't condescend. This, of course, is a major turnoff when selling to anyone, but especially to a woman who expects to be treated with respect when she is spending her money. Women experience enough of this attitude in the workplace without having to experience it from their jewelers. As a jewelry professional, you must provide information, but be sensitive to your choice of words and gestures. Some tips:

• Keep your eyes and attention focused on the woman and the jewelry you're showing her. Don't look around the store at something else. Avoid interruptions, such as telephone calls and other salespeople.

• Don't say things like, "Women [or ladies] usually like this." That lumps all women into one category and fails to respect individual taste.

• Neither should you say anything like, "Women wear lots of these today." Again, this lumps all women together. It's important to communicate that you're aware of fashion trends, but this is better accomplished by discussing jewelry in terms of how a woman can wear it: "You could wear this necklace with a big white poet shirt or you could wear it with a strapless cocktail dress and it will look just as interesting."

2. Don't make assumptions. You don't know what the customer knows or doesn't know. She might not have much experience buying jewelry, but that doesn't mean she doesn't have opinions and specific tastes.

3. Do pay attention to her image. Does the woman project an image that says, "I care about myself; I value myself"? Is she neatly groomed? Are her clothes well-coordinated? Do they project a color theme? Do they appear moderately priced or expensive? Are they classic, fashion-forward, artsy, casual? Is she wearing fine jewelry? These clues help you to evaluate how a woman perceives herself.

4. Do pay attention to the person. Is she petite? Large? Slim? Are her nails short or long? Is she wearing earrings? Are there any indications she might use her hands or speak by telephone a lot? These kinds of observations can help you in suggesting a certain kind of mounting or type of earring. Showing this kind of awareness also helps to enhance communication with the customer.

5. Don't talk too much. When a situation becomes uncomfortable, there's a tendency to talk too much. Try to talk less and listen carefully to what the woman says. Most women know what they like, even if they don't know exactly what product they want. Give guidance as needed and be ready to offer suggestions. If possible or applicable, try to limit the discussion to a specific type of jewelry, then try—by listening—to determine a price range where the woman feels comfortable. As you suggest a product, you should be able to pick up clues that tell you if she's comfortable with the price.

6. Do be focused. Though women may be unsure what type of jewelry they want, they often have time constraints and appreciate someone who appears to have a focused approach to selling.

7. Do qualify the customer. I've never met a woman who is completely negative on jewelry. So if you're not careful, you can waste a lot of time showing jewelry to someone who is simply having fun looking. Qualifying the purchaser is key in any sales situation, but with women who like jewelry, it's especially important. This is tricky. A lot of women will rely on your instinct and expertise as a salesperson, so don't rush. But make sure she's not taking your time just to amuse herself or to gather information before going elsewhere to buy. At some point, if she's showing no inclination to buy, you'll have to fish or cut bait, especially if other customers need your attention.

8. Don't rush to close the sale. Remember this selling situation may be new and a bit awkward for both of you. If the woman seems unsure, you could suggest things to consider and set up a follow-up appointment. The next meeting should be more comfortable and more conducive to closing the sale. Another option is to stress your liberal return policy, suggesting she take the piece home and try it with her

wardrobe. Encourage her to bring it back if she doesn't like it, and stress that returns are hassle-free. This is a good way to establish trust and to let the woman sell herself on the piece. Once she tries it with her wardrobe and sees the possibilities, she's less likely to bring it back unless she can't afford it. And forcing a sale on someone who really can't afford it accomplishes nothing—except possibly losing a customer for life.

9. Don't be afraid to ask direct questions. One way to show respect is to ask someone's opinion. Ask the woman whether she sees anything she likes. The answer should provide some insight into her preferences. Also, many women are not shy and prefer to deal in a direct manner.

At first glance, you might say these tips are true whether the buyer is male or female. However, there are differences in male and female jewelry purchasers.

For example, many women who buy their own jewelry plan to use it in the workplace. Therefore, the practicality and flexibility of a piece of jewelry are important.

Also, many women—even those with purchasing power—have always received jewelry as a gift and have never thought of buying it for themselves. Because of the sentimentality associated with jewelry gifts, it's easy for some women to lapse into the role of enjoying looking at jewelry. In a sales situation, such women often are unmindful that they're wasting a salesperson's time and don't admit to themselves that they have no intention of buying any jewelry.

The market of women who buy jewelry for themselves is one of the growth opportunities for jewelers in the 1990s. But jewelers must recognize and respond to the needs and differences of the market before their rewards in terms of sales can reach their fullest potential.

Making The Big Sale: Anyone Can Do It!

Suzy Spencer ◆ September 1992 Part II

Johnson & Vaughn Jewellers Ltd. sold a 6-ct. diamond during its $3^1/_2$-hour grand opening party last September. Then the purchaser promptly asked partners Brenda Johnson and John Vaughn to add two 1-ct. pear-shaped diamonds to the package, all to be molded into a gentleman's ring.

That wasn't a one-time fluke. During their first 10 months of business, Johnson and Vaughn made at least a half dozen sales in the $30,000+ category, and "numerous" others in the $20,000 range.

"There is more wealth than people might be aware of," says John Vaughn. "If jewelers would look into their area, they would find such customers."

Indeed. When JCK polled its retail jeweler panelists recently, more than 40% of respondents said they'd made from one to ten sales in the $20,000-$49,999 category during the past year. More than 20% said they'd made from one to ten sales over $50,000 in 1991—a year notable for both unemployment and recession.

Who is making these big sales? Independent jewelers in towns like Alexandria, La.; Carmel, Ind.; and Eatontown, N.J. And independent jewelers in cities like Portland, Ore.; St. Louis, Mo.; and Tulsa, Okla. Independent jewelers just like you.

These jewelers work to create an atmosphere conducive to high-ticket sales. They believe that store appearance, convenient parking, merchandise mix and a knowledgeable sales staff are of extreme importance in creating and making such sales. And many believe that above all, combining these attributes with an impeccable reputation is the crucial element to success.

So how does a new store like Johnson & Vaughn establish a reputation in less than a year of doing business? Indeed, on its very first day?

Through image—and fact.

The owners created an immediate image with the upscale design of their Peoria, Ill., store, and with the performance of a six-piece string ensemble at its grand opening. Adding to that image were John Vaughn's 20 years of local jewelry experience and Brenda Johnson's reputation as a reliable volunteer for charities. Underlining all that is the fact of top-quality merchandise that is never discounted—for anyone—in a town that normally discounts.

Johnson recalls a man who browsed in the store for six to eight weeks, but refused to buy a badly desired item because Johnson & Vaughn would not discount it. Finally, he bought the piece at full price—while saying he'd never do that again.

Johnson says, "He'll be back," adding that their prices "are very competitive."

Also helping is the fact that they usually have merchandise in stock. While memo goods were a factor in their opening months, a majority of sales now come from inventory—24 cases of fine jewelry. Vaughn says $30,000 sales are easier to make during that "magical moment" of desire. It's too easy to miss that moment when goods have to be memoed in.

Memo or no? Though JCK panelists say 30% of their high-ticket sales are due to memo goods, the practice seems to be falling from favor.

Shipping expense is one reason. Shipping in and out 10 memo rings at $60 or more gets costly, especially if the customer walks away without buying, explains Keith Sutton of Sutton's of Park City, Utah.

Nick Greve of Carl Greve Jeweler in Portland, Ore., offers another reason. If you sell memo goods, you are, in essence, selling someone else's inventory—while your own already-paid-for goods lie unsold in your display cases.

But perhaps the biggest reason for owning high-priced items rather than borrowing them on memo is simply that "carrying more expensive pieces makes it easier to see expensive pieces."

That advice comes from a successful Midwestern jeweler who prefers to remain anonymous. Own it, he says, and show it. Don't put it in the vault where no one can see it. If you must lock it in the vault, bring it out with fanfare.

His motive is two-fold. Expensive pieces must be displayed if customers are to believe anyone wears them. And, "you have to have something in stock to perk customers' interest."

At Miss Jackson's Precious Jewels in Tulsa, Okla., Bruce Weber sold a $10,000 diamond pendant to a customer who came in for a watch. That would not have happened if he hadn't had the piece in stock and display. High-ticket impulse sales and frequent at his leased jewelry department in a women's couture store. Yet, he often uses his display items as "starters," then memoes in additional pieces.

Certainly, a combination of stock and memo goods works. Forty years ago, C.A. Schnack Jewelry Company of Alexandria, La., stocked nothing over 1 ct. Now, the store routinely inventories 3-ct. stones and memoes in 4-ct. stones.

Schnack's memoes in two 4-ct. stones at a time, then promotes them in its usual two-column, five-in. local newspaper ad, saying "in stock for a limited time only." Jeweler Carl Carsten explains that he's interested in showing the large stones to customers whether they buy or not. He just wants people to know that Schnack's can get and sell big diamonds. In other words, he's building a reputation.

Schnack's sold a $55,000 5-ct. diamond (plus a couple of anniversary rings, that drove the sale past $60,000), a 7-ct. diamond, and a couple of items in the $20,000 range in 1991. Now, after a brief dry spell, 1992 looks to be at least equally profitable.

Building your image: Schnack's advertises regularly. So does Johnson & Vaughn - about $50,000 worth in seven months. Bruce Weber advertises, and he made "a hell of a lot" of $10,000+ sales last year and "several" in excess of $50,000.

Nick Greve advertises and does special events, and he makes sales of $30,000+ about four to six times a year. He won't reveal his television ad budget, but says, "It's a lot." He's used those ads to transform his store's image. Once it was considered an old-line, downtown guild store competing against "more wedding sets than anyone else" mall stores. Now it's a destination store featuring designer jewelry which, he says, is rarely "knocked off." These 19 designers, including John Atencio and Michael Bondanza, have brought Greve a solid customer base of 30- to 50-year-old consumers.

Greve says socializing has helped him as much as advertising. "We're out all the time, and it's not fun because we're selling all the time when we're out."

He's not alone. While Greve attends the Oregon Ballet and numerous charity balls, Bruce Weber is at the opera and philharmonic "so that people know us." Brenda Johnson not only attends the museum auction, she donates to it and buys from it.

"You do have to be social," she says. "That makes a big difference. I don't think you can sit in your store day in and day out and expect everyone to walk in."

Daniel Moyer of Moyer & Co. Fine Jewelers in Carmel, Ind., agrees it is imperative to put oneself in the right circles—around those with money. So he, too, appears at charity balls and plays golf at country clubs. While there he makes sure that he meets the right people and that they know what he does. He listens carefully to conversations. If he hears someone casually mention a jewelry need, he's there to sell.

We've sold more out there in the country club than anyplace I know," he says. But when you hear something, you must act quickly. "These people may cool off if you don't get them quick."

A Southwestern jeweler learned that lesson the hard way. He once overheard a customer remark, "What I really want someday is a 5-ct. diamond." The jeweler noted the "someday" - not the "I really want" - and didn't pursue the sale.

Three months later, the woman walked into this jeweler's store sporting a shiny new 5-ct. diamond.

"I should kick myself," says the jeweler. "She gave me all the signs." Someday, as this jeweler now knows, often is much sooner than you think.

Learning from that mistake helped this jeweler make a 9-ct. diamond sale last year - simply by calling a woman he thought might like the piece. She'd never expressed an interest in such a piece - but she bought it.

This year, on a whim, the jeweler took a $30,000 stock item to an out-of-town customer. The woman definitely was interested. "It's a segment you have to pursue," says the jeweler. "They don't just come in to browse."

The crucial trust: This Southwestern jeweler often uses his gemscope for half-carat diamond sales - but rarely for big sales. For those, he says, you must have a reputation of trust. "You build trust," he says, "by being a straight-shooter."

Jeweler after jeweler who regularly makes $30,000+ sales stresses that your product must be what you say it is. "We don't go around representing it as something that it's not," says Bruce Weber, whose average sale is $2,500.

"We're not trying to slick them into anything," says Keith Sutton. His sales include a 30-ct. triangle-shaped tanzanite and a $45,000 emerald ring. Now he's working on a $14,000 diamond sale. Yet he tells his customers to shop around!

Jewelers agree you must not prejudge customers. Carl Carstens has sold big-ticket items to tree farmers in baggy pants. Brenda Johnson says her 6-ct. diamond customer wouldn't stand out in a crowd. So what's the secret of selling high-end goods? You must have a reputation for integrity. You must have a reputation for either stocking or being able to obtain expensive pieces and you must socialize and advertise to remind customers of these reputations.

High-Ticket Sales Tips

Nick Greve of Carl Greve Jeweler in Portland, Ore., makes sales of $30,000+ four to six times a year. Here are his selling tips:

1) Study your market.

Find out where people with money live and where they're shopping. "They're buying someplace," he says. If they're buying from one of your competitors, find out why.

2) Cultivate them.

"Send letters over and over again." Greve sends a note every two or three months. If that doesn't work, he tries a gimmick. He sometimes sends flowers to complete strangers just to get them as customers. "But it might take two years," he adds.

3) Believe in your product and believe that the customer can afford it.

Salespeople often think customers can't afford high-priced jewelry simply because the salespeople themselves can't afford it. That's not true. Even when the customer can't afford a $30,000 item, show it anyway; it may encourage the customer to spend more. "A buyer looking for a $10,000 piece suddenly feels the $20,000 item is affordable and a bargain!"

4) Romance the product until it becomes a need.

Talk it up until the jewelry, like a great painting, becomes something the customer simply has to have.

5) Realize that little touches make a big difference.

Greve places a gold doily beneath the cups when he serves coffee. He also serves cookies and sherry. And he spends $1,000 a month on fresh flowers for the store!

Market Blindness
And How To Cure It

V. Michael Williams ◆ July 1992

In the last seven years alone, my staff and I have seen more than 1,000,000 pieces of jewelry offered to us for sale by private owners. We've also had a chance to see the insurance appraisals on many of these items. I'll bet we've seen 30,000 appraisals, and more than half of them were wrong.

Sometimes the identifications were incorrect or the quality descriptions were off, but the biggest problem we found was that the evaluations were terrible. Even when the identification, grading and description were essentially right and the appraiser seemed qualified, the value was often ridiculous.

Why is this happening? I think that jewelers and appraisers have simply lost touch with the reality of the articles they're appraising and with the practical, everyday needs of their customers.

Many of these appraisers are being led astray through false assumptions, the use of abstract formulas, a disregard for the realities of the marketplace and person motives that conflict with those of their customers.

In a way it's hard to blame the appraiser alone. The whole jewelry industry is locked into some ways of thinking about appraisals that breed the very errors that the trade publications are always noting and that the consumer protection agencies are always citing.

Not everyone will agree with what I'm about to say, but I do think every appraiser who stops a minute and considers what I suggest will become a better appraiser as a result.

Appraizo the Magnificent: The problem begins with the fact that most jewelers think they have a magic method for valuing items for replacement appraisals—they just figure the cost to duplicate it. They estimate the weights of stones

and metals. They determine the identity of both and then grade the stones. They compute the cost of the parts, add in the cost of the labor, then apply the markup they think appropriate—and presto, the item is appraised!

Is this method always correct? No! What very important consideration is missing? The style and marketability of the piece. How important are style and marketability? How much should you take them into account when you appraise? I believe that they are the two most important factors needed to properly integrate the individual cost data into a value that applies to the whole.

Jewelry items are symbols of wealth, tokens of sentiment, articles of adornment and products of style and taste. But styles and tastes change and, as they do, so does the value of jewelry. When appraising an item, style and marketability must *always* be taken into account.

Of course, in the case of a diamond solitaire or a simple mounting with two major stones, most of the value is in the stones and the style of the mounting has little effect on the price.

But even when appraising so simple an item as a strand of pearls, the market can affect value. For example, graduated strands haven't been popular since the '50s. So, if the strand you're appraising is graduated, you should reduce the value you compute by analyzing and grading the pearls alone.

On some pieces the market will be silent, but on most it will have a lot to say. Consider three pieces of jewelry all made up from these same essential components: 20 dwt. of platinum and 10 carats of 5-pt. G VS1 full cuts.

The first is an ID bracelet with "Boopsie Gorenflo" in diamonds on the front; the second, a signed Tiffany snowflake brooch; the third, a medallion in the form of a Russian Eagle made by Fabergé for Tsar Nicholas II.

Are each of these worth the same sum of stones, metal and workmanship? Obviously not. A jewelry item isn't just the sum of its parts. Individual gemstones are easy to appraise but, when they become part of a piece of jewelry, then design and marketability complicate the determination of value. . . sometimes adding to the sum, sometimes detracting.

If you consider the effects of market and salability on the three items above, it should be obvious that Boopsie's bracelet has very limited appeal and would be valued for less. The Tiffany pin would command more than a similar one not signed by such a famous firm. And the Fabergé medallion is so rare that it would be worth a small fortune. What's different? The stones? No. The metal? No. The market? Yes.

Now to be fair, most jewelers recognize immediately that some other factor needs to be taken into account with antique pieces like the Russian badge. They recognize that part of the value is tied to the age, desirability, rarity, condition and style of these pieces. But they fail to recognize that all jewelry is style and market related, and that these two factors are crucially important in determining the values of almost everything.

The missing classification: Most appraisers have been dividing jewelry into two general categories—antique jewelry and everything else. They focus on the relevant extra factors when appraising antique goods, but ignore them and just calculate replacement cost on all the rest.

This is a big mistake because there is a very large category being overlooked—used, out-of-style jewelry. A few pieces will qualify as antique, a few more will be new, classic or in style, while all the rest will fall in the used-goods category.

Just as you must research the value of a fine antique and period piece, you must also do the same for a not-so-charming, old, outdated piece. Why? So that the appraisal value really reflects the market for the item.

How would you generally appraise the following item from this rough description? A florentine-finish white gold pin weighing 15 dwt. and set with a central 8mm cultured pearl and eight .03-ct. single cuts in heads that were soldered on the arms of the pin. I would price it very low, since it's an almost unsalable article in today's sleek, yellow gold, contemporary world.

An oddball example: Since many jewelers are hung up on pricing older goods by figuring the cost to make the item new, or by making market comparisons to new goods, let's demonstrate the error in those methods by using an example that doesn't concern jewelry.

Imagine you found an old pair of leather high-button shoes in your grandmother's attic and wanted to know what they were worth. You could approach the evaluation in three ways.

1. You might go to a shoemaker and ask him what it would cost to duplicate the pair—about $500.

2. You could take the shoes with you to a department store and compare them to the price of good new leather shoes and boots—average comparable value $250.

3. You could go to a dealer in vintage clothing and ask what the antique value is—about $25. Which value is correct?

Well, the value in option one is irrelevant. You don't want to pay to have a pair duplicated. That was never the issue. You just wanted to know what the pair you already had was worth.

The value in option two is meaningless since it is a guess at value obtained by comparison with fashionable, currently salable styles.

Only the value in option three reflects the real market value because it includes a proper assessment of the market for these shoes that were popular in 1892, that still exist in great quantities in attics today, and that almost nobody wants.

If you think about it, the correct value is hardly a surprise. The answer would be immediately obvious to you if you had simply looked at the shoes and asked yourself, "Who would want them?"

The value of the shoes, and of anything else for that matter, must be consistent with the identity of the item and with the market that exists for it.

A jewelry example: Now let's apply the same logic to the following item brought in for appraisal by a young woman in her 30s—a lady's diamond watch with diamond band, having a generic mechanical movement. The watch and band are just over 6 in. long and contain 4 cts. of small single-cut melee averaging G SI1. (This article is typical of the millions of such watches made without particular distinction in the 1940s.)

In appraising this, you could follow the first method from the shoe story and value the watch at your best assessment of the cost to duplicate it by hand, from scratch. But if you use this method, you'd better hope she never loses it and wants you to make her a new one. I almost dare you to try. The original watch was cast from a mold with hundreds of others just like it. You'll have to make yours by hand. Can you imagine the difficulty and expense?

Or you could follow method two and take a comparative price survey of the watch dealers you know—Bulova, Seiko, Baume & Mercier, Ebel and Patek. But the catch here is that none of them make watches like this anymore.

Or you could stop a minute and look at the watch. Could you sell such a watch in your store today? Would you even want it in stock? After all, it's only 6 in. long and wouldn't fit anyone, unless they were anorexic. The movement is mechanical, while most new ones are quartz. The dial is too small to be read by the older ladies who still like the style, while the younger ones can't imagine the watch was ever in style. Don't you think these facts ought to affect the value you place on this item?

Sure they should. And so you need to appraise this for what it is—a dead duck. You could call any estate jewelry dealer and ask him what such a duck—excuse me, watch—would cost. It won't be very much. We all get them frequently and would be glad to sell them inexpensively.

Insurance company requirements: "Wait a minute!" you say. "What about the insurance company? Doesn't it want replacement value?" Sure! But it doesn't want to give a brand new handmade watch in replacement for an old mass-produced one. It wouldn't want to do that any more than it would want to give a 1992 Cadillac to a man who smashed up his 1984 Fleetwood.

Now I know the signals are mixed on this issue. Insurance companies don't always apply the same thinking to jewelry that they do to the other articles they insure—like cars, houses and furniture. Maybe they haven't thought it through. Maybe jewelers haven't been helping with their new-for-old replacement appraisals. What I do know is that if older items were insured as such, and replaced with similar older items, the cost of premiums and the payment of claims both would be properly reduced.

Qualify your customer: "Wait a minute again!" you say. "Maybe the customer doesn't want an old watch for her old watch. Maybe she wants it duplicated." That's true, maybe she does. Did you ask her?

When taking in jewelry for appraisal, most jewelers are certain to ask, "Will this be for insurance or estate purposes?" After getting the answer, they explain the appraisal charges and how long it will take. That's it!

Most jewelers would fire a salesman who did so little to qualify a carat diamond customer. You would expect the salesman to do more than just state your price and ask, "Will that be cash or charge?" Yet that is what most appraisal take-in procedures amount to. Few ever bother to ask, "If you lost this item, would you replace it?" Try asking. You'll be surprised at the result.

If you asked the lady with the watch in the above example if she would replace the watch, she'd probably answer, "Heavens, no! It was my mother's and I don't even like it. In fact, I keep it in the safe deposit box at the bank. I'm just insuring it out of sentiment."

That's when I would remind her that appraisals and insurance policies won't get her mom's watch back if she loses it. I'd also point out that if the watch is sitting in the safe deposit box it's not at much risk, and neither insurance nor an appraisal is really necessary.

Of course, aside from the concern over the emotional loss, there is worry of financial loss. Well, what is the financial loss? If she wouldn't replace it, her loss is the amount she would have received for it if she sold it. It wouldn't be the retail charge to make a new one from scratch. Also, if she loses an old out-of-style watch, should she get a new one in its place?

What she *should* receive is a watch of similar style and vintage to the one she lost. Where could you get such a thing? On the second-hand market from an estate jewelry dealer. That's where you could have gotten the best estimate of replacement cost, too.

A new disclaimer: Now if you're thinking, "How can I justify putting down the high retail price of duplication on such a watch when a customer really wants it exactly replaced and then use the lower price for a similar second-hand piece if another customer doesn't?" There is an easy solution.

Just call the latter the "second-hand market value" or "estate market value" along with a footnote that explains that such a value "assures replacement of a similar, but not identical, item obtained on the secondhand market."

This notation will protect customers for replacement of what they actually own, give them a reasonable premium, and allow them realistic compensation if they decide to take the cash should a loss occur.

A very high percentage of the things you appraise are older, not-quite-in-style items and should be appraised on this second-hand market basis.

You also should consider that most of your customers would duplicate only a small percentage of their lost or stolen jewelry. Most would replace the articles they wear every day—such as a diamond engagement ring, a simple gold necklace and a few other basic items of their jewelry wardrobe—but little else. Some might take advantage of the loss and use the insurance proceeds to buy a different article, but most would just take the cash.

Despite this, most jewelers assume that customers would want to replace everything they bring in for appraisal. Maybe their thinking is clouded by counting the profits on the sales they envision they will have when the items become lost or stolen. If you check your own records, you will find that less than 1 in 1,000 pieces you appraise is ever replaced.

Now it may appear to some jewelers that I have brushed aside many important concerns, especially emphasis on gemological training, reliance on price lists like the "Rapp Sheet" and classes in "valuation science."

So, for the record, I want to state that they are of critical importance. But they already are offered to the jeweler/appraiser and so I need not go into them, except to caution you about the proper emphasis to put on them in contrast to market knowledge.

From the ivory tower: No one in our profession is more thoroughly trained than the owners of independent gem labs. But I've known many of these "ivory tower" types who have taken all the gemological courses and own every piece of identification equipment known to man. They belong to every conceivable appraisal organization and have attended all the many lectures on valuation theory. Yet they appraise as if they had never bought or sold a piece of jewelry in their lives.

In fact, many of them proudly proclaim that their opinions are unbiased because they neither buy nor sell jewelry. Yet it is because they have no experience in the market that their prices are somewhere out there in the ozone.

These appraisers often aggravate their error on older pieces by valuing the items senselessly high, based on duplication cost, and then stating that this figure doesn't include antique value. As if that's something added on top of the value, not something that's a part of it. They must sense that they're leaving out market insight and are trying to cover themselves.

Don't get the idea that I think all independent gemologists are guilty of this. I am pleased to say that when one of these experts in identification adds to his skills a thorough knowledge of the market, he or she is among the best in the business.

As these experts will tell you, there is no substitute for thorough gemological training. It's a prerequisite to correct identification and proper grading of gemstones. But, if every jeweler were a Graduate Gemologist, none would be qualified as an appraiser by that fact alone. Identification and grading are not evaluation.

The GIA does a great job training gemologists, most of whom can identify and grade gemstones. Sadly, though, an identifier or a grader is not an appraiser. The missing courses in their education are those on valuation and marketability.

The ASA and the ISA have been insisting rightly that any appraiser know the ins and outs of what is called valuation science. To know the identity and quality of the gemstones in a piece does not tell you the piece's current value from the dozens of other perspectives that can apply.

Too many formulas: Fresh new appraisers, and some old-timers who should know better, often will place too much reliance on formulas, calculations and price lists. Some seem to regard their formulas and price guides as divinely revealed truths. They enshrine then and bow to the altar of formulas and say, "Tell us, Oh Great Formula, what is the value of this ring?" Or, "Give me, Omnipotent Price Guide, the answer I seek."

Try to use some common sense along with your computations and your appraisal will be a lot better. A friend of mine once said that the First Law of Mathematics is, "The answer has to look right." I say the First Law of Appraisal is, "The price has to make sense."

On a weekly basis, every appraiser needs to wade into the market where jewelry is bought and sold. Especially the market for second-hand, estate and antique goods, since most of the jewelry you'll be asked to appraise will be old enough to qualify as second hand.

If you're an independent appraiser, visit various retail jewelers and estate jewelry dealers often, so that you know what the real values are. If you are a staff appraiser for a store and don't buy or sell, talk the boss into letting you into the trenches now and then. It will really help.

Watch the auction market. Subscribe to Sotheby's or Christie's auction catalogs for jewelry. Get some auction catalogs from the regional houses, like Skinner's in Boston, DuMouchelle's in Detroit, or Butterfield's in San Francisco. They'll include the more modestly priced items that you'll be more likely to appraise. (Always rely on actual selling prices rather than the presale estimates.)

Don't just get a few catalogs and then stop your subscription. Staying in constant touch with what's selling, and for how much, is what will help keep you reality focused in your appraising.

Automate your knowledge: One of the best techniques I know to help the appraiser keep his feet on the ground and at least one eye on reality is to automate his knowledge. Most experienced jewelers have a wealth of knowledge that they could bring to bear on their appraisals, but often hold it in separate disconnected fragments.

So, before appraising a piece formally, give a quick estimate of what you think it would retail for. Don't dwell on it, don't analyze it, just put a quick number on it. Then analyze, measure, identify, grade, research the market and

value it. If the two numbers aren't close, you need to readjust your thinking.

The snap judgment suggested above is a way to bring to bear, in an instant, all of your subconsciously held thoughts about style, quality and marketability. By this method, you sum up your experience in a flash.

Anyone over 30 knows that first impressions tell you a lot and can be reliable guides in life if tempered by the facts as they become known. Try it yourself. Next time you're called upon to appraise a complicated piece, write down your first impression of what it would retail for. After doing a thorough appraisal, compare the numbers and explain any discrepancies. After doing this a few times, you'll be surprised how your appraisal "realism index" will increase.

Remember, never tell this impression to the customer. Don't use it alone without verification. Use it to calibrate your appraisal, not as a substitute for it.

I know this will be hard at first. It seems most jewelers have a 150-foot-long umbilical cord that stretches from where they are back to their gem equipment. In order to improve, you need to cut it. Have confidence in your overall appraisal skills, and then back that up with valid technique.

Join the experts: Now, bring your market knowledge to bear on your appraising, and you'll do as a real estate appraiser does by adjusting an estimate of the value of a mansion to reflect that it's located in a ghetto.

Do as the car dealer does when asked for a value on a 10-year-old Cadillac, or for the value of the limousine that used to be Al Capone's. You can bet he won't appraise both those cars at the price of a new one.

Maybe you'll even do what the Ethan Allen Furniture dealer would do when confronted by a request to apprise an antique chest. He'd refer the customer to someone who deals in old things instead of looking up the price of a similar new one in his catalog.

If, like the Ethan Allen Dealer, you find that you have no experience in dealing with a piece you are asked to appraise, be honest and courageous. Don't fake it, just don't appraise it.

I have seen many appraisers let their egos lead them into this fallacy: "When you don't know what you're doing, it's better to appraise high and be safe than low and be sorry."

Instead, admit that you have no experience in appraising such an item. It just might turn out that the customer is flattered that her piece is so unusual that you need special help in valuing it. Then I suggest that you pick up the phone and call for help from someone who understands the market factors and who will help you price it right.

Are Your Appraisals Fair, Accurate And Legally Acceptable?

April 1992

Imagine that a TV news crew doing a "hidden camera" report on jewelry appraisals came to your store. Would the crew record you testing and grading the diamonds and gold, asking proper questions and establishing yourself as a professional? Or would you peer at the item for a few seconds, scribble a price on a slip of paper, then find yourself lumped with the charlatans when the report is aired?

Don't laugh. Many so-called professional jewelers have been skewered publicly in just this way. While good appraisals can make money, bad appraisals can make trouble.

Most jewelers do appraisals, but all too many opt for the "two-second method." Professional appraisers say many jewelers don't take full advantage of this potential profit center because:

• They don't realize it can be so lucrative.

• They're afraid of alienating customers or angering competitors if they disagree with mistaken or deceptive appraisals already in the market.

• They lack the qualifications and/or facilities to do proper appraisals.

All three problems can be solved.

The professional: What makes a professional appraiser? Experience, education and research, say experts. Professional appraisers and members of the JCK Retail Jewelers Panel with a strong appraisal business say consistently accurate appraisals call for at least three to five years of buying, selling and grading gems or jewelry. Some jewelers who've worked with gems and jewelry for decades go further, saying there's no substitute for this experience.

Those who lack such lengthy on-the-job training must take, at the minimum, diamond and colored stone courses such as those offered by the Gemological Institute of America or other recognized educational institutions. A knowledge of jewelry history and fabrication is highly recommended. Also considered critical is thorough instruction in appraisal theory, such as that offered in the International Society of Appraisers' CAPP courses.

Appraising jewelers also need such basic equipment as a microscope, spectroscope, heavy liquids, master diamonds and a color comparison set unless they plan to send all stones to a recognized gem lab for identification and evaluation (see sidebar).

Finally, appraisers must research the requirements for the type of appraisal requested, then research the item and its market to set a value.

Remember that appraising is a science. Using proper procedures, equipment and research will yield predictable, repeatable results. This six-part guide explains how jewelers can adopt the scientific approach and transform their appraisal services into profit centers. It covers:

1. The tools of the trade and take-in procedures and fees.
2. The major types of appraisal and the markets they reflect.
3. How to examine gems and finished jewelry.
4. How to arrive at a value.
5. How to prepare the report.
6. IRS legal requirement and other legal issues.

This guide is not intended to substitute for formal training or on-the-job experience. Instead, it outlines the requirements you must meet in the appraisal process.

STARTING THE APPRAISAL

Here's where jewelers must establish their professionalism and take precautions to protect themselves.

Take in: The first requirement is a good take-in form that gathers information about the customer (name, address, phone), notes the reason for the appraisal (estate, divorce, insurance) and lists each item submitted.

The appraiser should assess the condition of a piece and note any visible damage on the spot. Damage should be discussed with the customer and noted in writing so there is no question later about the condition of gem or jewel upon take-in.

In some cases, the appraiser may want to include a "release of liability" form. This helps protect the appraiser against liability for items that carry higher-than-normal risks in testing or handling. There is no guarantee, however, that a customer won't sue if damage occurs. The customer also should be told how long it will take to perform the necessary tests, to set the value and to write a formal appraisal report.

Some items are beyond a jeweler's expertise. (Green diamonds are one example; even labs find it difficult to tell naturally colored from lab-treated stones.) These should be sent to a recognized gemological lab or a trusted dealer who works with such pieces. But first, get the customer's written permission (incorporated it into the report) and describe the piece in detail to assure the customer he'll get the same piece back.

The fee: "Discuss this openly and up front," says Patti Geolat, a jeweler and appraiser at Geolat & Associates, Dallas, Tex. "Be sure to give as accurate an estimate as possible and tell the client all the fees he may be charged."

There are three basic ways to charge for appraisals.

• A flat rate. This works well for those who do a lot of similar pieces using set procedures, say appraisers. Jerry Ehrenwald of New York's International Gemological Information, which does a volume business for the trade and consumers, offers this schedule: $95 for a 1- to 2-ct. diamond in a ring (including 29 points of side stones); $75 for a .75-

to .99-ct. diamond; $65 for a .50- to .75-ct. diamond; and $50 for a .25- to .50-ct. stone. Bigger diamonds cost more, with a top price of $575 for a 10-ct.- plus stone. Emerald, ruby and sapphire jewelry is $75 for stones under a carat and $95 for 1- to 2-ct. stones, with incremental increases up to $295 for 10-ct.-plus stones. Pearls and watches are $60; gold jewelry is $35. Ehrenwald says his rate structure suits volume work because his staff is experienced at handling many types of jewelry and requires little extra research.

• Hourly charges, often with a minimum. Most jewelers (80% of JCK panelists) and professional appraisers prefer this method, which bases charges on the work required.

"If you charge $25 per item, you'll get a report worth $25," says Geolat. "That may suffice for some pieces, but many require more examination or research than such a flat fee warrants." About a third of JCK panelists combine fees. They generally charge a flat rate (usually $35-$50 for the first item and $10-$25 for subsequent items), but have an hourly rate for pieces that require special attention. Panelists' rate vary widely, from $20 an hour to $200; the majority charge between $40 and $60 an hour.

Some also charge for services such as printouts, gem plotting and lab work.

• Percentage of value. Every appraisal organization in the U.S. considers this method unethical, though 2% of JCK panelists use it. Professional appraisers say the practice represents a potential conflict of interest because it could tempt appraisers to boost their fees by inflating the value of pieces.

TYPES OF APPRAISALS

A piece of jewelry can carry widely different values depending on the type of appraisal needed. Here are the major types and the value levels they carry.

Insurance replacement is the value at which an item can be replaced with a comparable one in new condition at the prevailing retail price in the region.

Most jewelry consumers have insurance policies that allow them to replace lost or stolen jewelry with new items of comparable quality and value. They pay premiums based on this value. The appraiser's job is to determine the value in the light of current market conditions in his or her area.

Insurance replacement is the most common type of appraisal for jewelers; panelists say it provides 82% of their appraisal business. This also is the earliest type of appraisal for retailers because it usually involves simple retail replacement cost, a market they know well.

But the basic rule of appraising still applies. It must be done methodically and accurately. Cos Altobelli, a jeweler in North Hollywood, Cal., who co-authored *Handbook of Jewelry and Gemstone Appraisals,* cautions jewelers against using their own markups as an industry-wide standard. Market research may be time-consuming at first, he says, but becomes less so after the appraiser gains familiarity with the items, sources and routine.

The appraiser must establish a value that ensures clients will get a full replacement from their insurance company. We'll discuss report writing in detail later, but note here that most insurance policies require replacement of like kind and quality. The appraiser's duty is to be complete and accurate, or the customer will get a lot less in replacement.

"It's critical that the appraiser be as explicit as possible on such things as diamond quality," says Carol Basden of Basden Risk Management, Birmingham, Ala., an agent for Jewelers Mutual Insurance and other companies. If someone needs to replace a ring with a 1.5-ct. VVS_1 diamond, she explains, the insurance company will try to get a stone as cheaply as possible from a wholesale dealer. Insurance companies don't seek to spend $5,000 on a piece carrying that appraisal—even if the client paid premiums based on that amount. "A good appraisal is the client's best defense," she says. Some policies provide for cash replacement, but that should make no difference in the appraised value.

Some additional points:

• Stick to the truth. Jewelers are most likely to give inadequate appraisals at the time of initial sale, says Basden. "They accentuate the positive to justify the price. That's OK in the sales talk, but not on appraisals," she says. "If the stone has visible inclusions, the jeweler must note them in the appraisal."

• Inform customers that insurance appraisals don't apply if the customer wants to sell, donate or use the piece as collateral. This problem often arises in divorce cases in which one spouse gets "custody" of the jewelry, then tries to liquidate it. "I've seen people get very angry at their jeweler when they could get only $1,500 for a piece he appraised at $4,000," says Basden. "Jewelers have to tell customers that liquidation value may be a lot lower."

Price/quality confirmation also carries "retail" value. In this type of appraisal, customers bring in items bought elsewhere to see whether they got what they paid for.

The valuing process is similar to insurance replacement, say professional appraisers, but the report should be more thorough. This is because you could face angry competitors if you appraise the piece for far less than the customer expects. Indeed, such a comparison appraisal touched off a series of lawsuits in Columbus, Ohio in which one jeweler sued the appraiser (another jeweler) for defamation, claiming his lower quality grade and appraisal were motivated by competitive jealousy. In such cases, a well-documented appraisal is the best defense.

Jeweler Paul Bischoff of Earth Treasures Jewelers in Eatontown, N.J., says, "We do nothing that would color our judgment of the piece we are examining. If a jeweler calls us to complain that we have denigrated his store, we tell him we do all appraisals objectively and explain in detail how we arrived at our grading and valuation. We usually have no trouble after that."

In appraisals for **estate** or **divorce settlement, collateral, charitable donation** and **liquidation,** values may differ because of differences in the circumstances involved. But the governing principle is *fair market value.* This is defined as the price a willing buyer would pay a willing seller in the most commonly traded market when neither is under duress and both have equal knowledge. This principle reigns because it's what the Internal Revenue Service uses when evaluating such transactions, says IRS spokesman Wilson Fadley. Here's a closer look at each type:

• Estate settlement involves valuing an individual's property for tax and inheritance purposes; it's the second most common type of appraisal for JCK panelists, accounting for 12% of their business.

Appraiser must know or research the most common market in which the item is bought and sold in current condition. In most cases, fair market value is based on these markets: New York's 47th St. for loose diamonds, auction houses for high-value period jewelry, various stone dealers for colored stones, and watch manufacturers, distributors and auction houses for prestige watches.

There is one tricky pitfall in IRS interpretations. If heirs liquidate jewelry through a dealer or auction, the IRS will assess a value based on the dealer or auction *selling* price, because that has become the most common market in which the item is traded, says Jeffrey Schutzman, supervisory appraiser at the IRS in Manhattan.

• Appraisals for divorce settlement are self-explanatory and most states use the fair-market-value standard, though requirements vary. Geolat, the jeweler and appraiser in Dallas, cautions jewelers in border areas to check laws in neighboring states because customers may come from there. Another caveat: jewelers doing divorce appraisals should not work for both parties.

• Loan collateral appraisals should be done at fair market value or even less, says Altobelli, because the bank or other financial institution probably will try to dispose of items quickly in the event of default. "Many jewelers mistakenly give retail replacement value in such cases, but that is not fair to the institution involved because it would never be able to recover that amount in a liquidation sale."

• Donation appraisals determine the value of gems or jewelry given to charity or museums. The IRS insists on fair market value and this is important because such donations are likely to attract a lot of scrutiny (see IRS sidebar). IRS interest stems from rampant abuses of the donation system in the 1970s. As a result of one tax court case, the IRS deeply discounts bulk transactions, requiring that they be valued at wholesale.

Altobelli advises jewelers to be very cautious in taking on such jobs. "If it is very sophisticated or an unusual situation which would likely involve the IRS," he says, "jewelers should stay away unless they've got a lot of experience and education in such matters."

• While less in vogue than during the "hard asset" boom, barter transactions (such as gems for land or barter-club transactions) still occur. Here the rules aren't rigid because valuation depends on how the other party values the item offered in exchange, says Altobelli. Real estate has no "wholesale" or "retail" value, for example. The value of gems depends on the liquidation plans of the person receiving them. A rapid liquidation would require lower value than a slow, orderly sale.

Altobelli advises jewelers doing such appraisals to work for one side only. He also suggests that when bulk parcels are involved, the appraiser keep the gems in their sealed containers unless the owner is there as a witness. "Usually such gems are the type and size that can be easily seen in their containers. Keeping them [there] will protect the jeweler from charges that he switched stones in the event the appraisal is unfavorable."

PRODUCT ANALYSIS

This is the "product knowledge" section. Having a well-educated staff and well-established procedures will yield accurate appraisal results. Procedures will vary a bit, depending on the product.

Loose gemstones

We live in an age of high-quality synthetics and color- and clarity- enhancing gem treatments. The appraiser must be able to identify stones with conventional gemological tools and instruments. He also, where possible, must be able to spot tell-tale clues of laser drilling, heat treatment, irradiation and impregnation with color- or clarity-altering substances. Appraisers must tell customers if they detect such treatments and note them on the report.

The appraiser who lacks knowledge or equipment—particularly to handle unusual or suspect gems (lavender jade or green diamonds, for example)—should send them to a lab or dealer who specializes in them. The client's permission is needed of course.

Here are some guidelines.

1. Carefully clean the stone with a soft gem cloth.

2. Generally turn first to the microscope to identify a gemstone and its characteristics. Even if the microscope provides positive identification, back that up by using a few more gem instruments. If positive ID proves impossible, seek permission to send the stone to an independent gem laboratory.

3. Carefully note on your appraiser's worksheet (not to be given to a client as part of the formal appraisal) the condition and characteristics of the gem and the instruments used to prove its identity.

4. Note gemstone clarity and color. Evaluate the hue, tone and saturation of colored stones. Note whether the stone has any particular phenomena (such as color change or cat's eye). Establish the degree of transparency and plot inclusions. Document the stone's condition inasmuch as it affects beauty or durability. Always use proper lighting; a light source that duplicates north daylight is best for color grading.

5. Note gemstone weight and dimensions.

6. Note the type and quality of cut.

7. Note reference sources if research was necessary.

8. Photograph the gem if necessary or if the client requests it. This visual record of the gem should be given to the client as part of the appraisal process.

9. Establish value.

Finished jewelry

1. Don't always clean jewelry before testing. If cleaning is needed be careful. Check gemstone brittleness and durability before using an ultra-sonic cleaner. Some purists discourage any use of ultrasonic cleaning for colored stones. Neither should you clean any antique metal with a patina because the patina may serve as proof of age. Take extra care with enameled pieces, pearls and mother-of-pearl jewelry, coin jewelry and watches. Consider writing special cleaning instructions on your take-in form.

2. First identify the mounting, stamps and fineness of metal. Mounted stones present some ID problems because the mounting prevents use of some gemological tools. When necessary to remove a stone from its mounting, ask for permission and consider having the client sign a release-of-liability form. On the worksheet, note everything from initial references to equipment used and diagnostic test results.

3. Measure and estimate the weight of the main stones in mountings with a Leveridge gauge and/or screw micrometer and apply appropriate formulas. Note data for all stones on the worksheet. Include estimated metal weight (weight of total piece minus estimated stone weight).

4. Mounted gemstones may show misleading color and clarity. Never grade a diamond "flawless" without first unmounting it. As for diamond color, assign a range instead of a single grade, with the note that value may differ widely within that range.

5. Note in writing the cutting styles and quality of major and minor stones.

6. Note appropriate reference sources, including any research on hallmarks and stamps or on the gemstones themselves.

7. It's optional to photograph jewelry. Many appraisers do so as added documentation and as a service to clients.

8. Establish value.

Antique & period jewelry

1. The cleaning question is especially important with antique pieces. The removal of patina can lessen the value of period jewelry. If accumulated dirt precludes identification of gemstones or hallmarks, discuss the problem with your customer. If cleaning is needed, and you have written consent, be very careful.

Antique and period jewelry certainly is *not* in the domain of every appraiser. "No one can be an expert on everything," says a noted Beverly Hills appraiser. "It is often judicious to defer to the experts in a certain field, such as Art Deco, Edwardian, Victorian or Art Nouveau eras."

2. An appropriate (and growing) reference library is vital. Books should cover specific periods of jewelry, methods of construction, metals and gems most often used, stamps and hallmarks from around the world, design traits and records of typical period jewelry prices. Be aware of watch and findings styles over time, as well as different styles for chains and other forms of jewelry or personal ornamentation.

3. Use an appraisal worksheet for any initial research work. Measure main and satellite gemstones and estimate weights. This may be hard, as older gemstones often weren't cut in a uniform manner. Weight estimation is particularly difficult for unusual cuts mounted in sealed backs. Customers may want to know the value of the stone if recut, so be aware of the formulas for recut weight estimations. Include estimated weight of the item (metals and gems separately), if this directly affects the value of the item.

4. Test the metal. Antique jewelry isn't always stamped or hallmarked, nor do items always match their stamps when assayed. Determine jewelry construction methods, if possible, because these affect value.

5. Photographing jewelry is optional. But every opportunity to examine period jewelry and keep a visual image for your own files further educates you, and it provides a service to the client.

6. Establish value.

WHAT'S IT WORTH?

Establishing value is the meat and potatoes of appraising. Though it seems complex at first, jewelers who know their gems, jewelry and markets—and who have cultivated knowledgeable sources—can arrive at values quickly and easily with practice.

The first places to seek information are price lists, supplier or auction catalogs and trade publications. Then learn what's happening in the market around you. Appraiser Cos Altobelli cautions jewelers against using their own markups as an industry standard. "You can't just say I sell this for X

dollars then put that value on the report," he says. "You must know the market in your area because markups can differ from region to region." As a result, he says, jewelers who do appraisals must know how much their competitors charge for comparable pieces; a mystery shopper trip is one possibility.

Loose diamonds: These are the easiest to value because loose diamonds of comparable weight, quality and make differ little in price.

For wholesale values, use a combination of supplier lists, trade magazines and industry price lists such as *The Rapaport Report* (keep in mind the discounts noted in the trading section), *The Diamond Registry, Diamond Insight, Gemworld Pricing Guide,* and *Diamond Market Monitor.* For retail valuation, use the average markup prevailing in your region. When writing insurance appraisals, be sure you understand your local market; conduct a survey if necessary. Periodic JCK surveys on margins are useful as well.

Colored diamonds are more difficult to value because prices vary enormously depending on hue. Dealer Henry Meyer of New York City says the first rule is to reduce the 4 C's to one: color. "More than anything else, color—not weight or clarity—determines the value of a colored diamond," he says. Price lists give little information on colored diamonds, so have a gem lab grade the stone for origin of color, then call several dealers of such stones. Do your best to describe the color in detail because the grade report lists only the colors comprising the stone's hue, not their attractiveness. This you must convey by words (or photo, if your equipment can reproduce the color accurately).

Auction catalogs are a price source for top specimens. Diamonds colored by treatment (irradiation) usually are valued at their pretreated cost.

Loose colored stones: Fewer pricing resources cover colored gemstones, but they are included in price list such as *Gemworld Price Guide* and *Diamond Market Monitor,* supplier lists and trade magazine reports. These will suffice for valuations at the wholesale level.

The Diamond Trade and Precious Stone Association in New York is one of the few organized bourses in the world actively trading colored stones as well as diamonds. Its members are good sources for arriving at prices of commonly traded, commercial-quality gemstones.

Catalogs and after-sale reports from Christie's, Sotheby's, Butterfield & Butterfield, and Skinner auction houses are a good source for top specimens. Jewelers should request the auction house's presale appraisal as well as the price realized at the sale.

For retail-level valuations, use trade publication markup surveys and be aware of how local competitors price similar gemstones.

Stones in mountings: A vast majority of the gems that appraisers take in are mounted, and most stay that way. Experts say most diamonds and colored stones a jeweler is likely to encounter can be appraised properly in their mountings—as long as the appraiser clearly lists the limitations involved during take-in and in the report. Always remember that mounted diamonds can't be graded exactly, so offer a range of two to three color and clarity grades with the caveat that prices differ among grades, says Geolat, the Dallas jeweler and appraiser. Even sizes can be difficult to pinpoint if the cut is not standard. And the mounting's prongs or bezel will conceal parts of the stone; note this in the report.

A sample appraisal form included in the AGS *Handbook of Jewelry and Gemstone Appraising* includes this cautionary statement: "Most mountings restrict examination of some details of a gemstone; unless specifically stated that stones were removed and graded, statements referring to color and/or internal pureness are provisional; approximate weights are determined by volumetric calculation; estimated replacement cost is based on assumed species, size and quality."

Simon Teakle, who heads Christie's jewelry department in New York City, offers these questions for deciding whether to remove a gemstone from its mounting. "Is the stone worthy of the effort? Can it be easily removed? Would removal jeopardize the stone or the setting?" If the answers are "yes" to the first two and "no" to the third, it's probably worth removing the stone from its mounting for an exacting look.

Geolat adds that common sense is the best guide: "It may be worth removing a diamond to determine whether it's a D fl, but not a commercial grade." Stones should be removed—with permission—if it appears the appraisal could cause a dispute over value, she says.

At the Gemological Institute of America, students now can learn how to grade mounted diamonds and colored stones, says Education Director Dennis Foltz. He says jewelers can detect sophisticated synthetics even in mounted jewelry because magnification is all that's needed in most cases. Synthetic sapphires, emeralds and rubies, for example, show traces of flux material and distinctive growth lines.

Treatments are another matter. Mountings can obscure the tell-tale flash effect in fracture-filled diamonds, say dealers. A spectroscope is needed to detect irradiation, which is used to enhance color. And detecting color enhancement through heat treatment usually requires a clearer view of the stone than mountings permit.

Watches: The manufacturer is the best source of information, though auction houses and estate jewelry experts can help with period watches. Again, jewelers must know their local markets in making retail valuations. Rolex watches often are discounted in the competitive Southwest, for example, so appraisals written there may carry lower values than those written somewhere else.

Finished jewelry: Finished jewelry is appraised for retail value primarily in cases of insurance replacement and price/quality confirmation. And as explained in the "Types of Appraisals" section, retail value is based on prices for comparable merchandise in a jeweler's market area.

Wholesale prices are used primarily in the cases of estate or divorce settlement, collateral and liquidation appraisals. Here's a look at appraising for three types of jewelry:

• For common mass-produced jewelry, appraisal values often are below wholesale because they exclude labor, taxes, duties, shipping costs and distributor markups that are part of the wholesale cost. All that's left is the market price of the metal content and any gemstones, says Jerry Ehrenwald of International Gemological Information.

• For better production-line jewelry, appraisal values are determined by comparing pieces of the same type (ring, brooch, etc.) containing the same kind and total weight of gems and with the same metal fineness and weight. Also look for similar workmanship and design.

• Period/designer jewelry is an altogether different matter, particularly if it's from a classic era or signed by a highly respected designer. "If the customer has a piece by Henry Dunay, Cartier, Tiffany or another famous name, it will carry a premium," says Geolat. "Use common sense and call the company for prices. If that particular piece is no longer manufactured, see if it has a comparable piece in its catalog."

Other price sources include retail jewelers who specialize in period jewelry, guide books (prices are approximate and should be double-checked with period jewelry sellers) and auction catalogs, price lists and newsletters for the higher end of the market (Teakle says auction houses appraise at a dealer-to-dealer level, not retail).

Regardless of the jewelry type, wear and tear must be factored into the value. "Most jewelry will suffer small scratches and abrasions over time," says Geolat. "The appraiser need only note 'ordinary signs of wear' on the report." Larger damages, including "inexpert" repairs or restorations, are a different story. Appraisers must note such damage in their reports and make the appropriate deductions or issue both an "as is" price and a value for the item undamaged. Basden, of Basden Risk Management, says insurance companies will note any damage listed on a report and may challenge appraisals written at full value.

The amount of depreciation depends on the nature of the damage. Jewelers can send a badly chipped diamond or colored stone to a recutting firm for an estimate of weight loss and repolishing charges, then deduct these costs from the value. Goldsmiths and custom manufacturers can provide repair and restoration estimates on gold items, while watch manufacturers can advise on repair costs. (Don't overlook the obvious potential sales in recutting or repairing such items.)

Whatever the situation, cautions Geolat, "appraisers must walk the fine line between giving the customer enough money to replace a lost item but not enough to make a profit on its loss."

THE REPORT

The more detailed and accurate an appraisal report is, the less likely it will be challenged by insurance companies, the IRS, divorce lawyers or even competitors.

Most information in a report is essentially descriptive. Among the most common appraisal outlines is one recommended by the American Gem Society in its widely circulated *Handbook of Jewelry and Gemstone Appraising* by Cos Altobelli and Charlotte Preston. This book is the source of many of the following guidelines:

• The report is a professional document and should be written on your business stationery.

• Provide a cover letter that details your professional appraisal qualifications and specializations.

• A typed or laser-printed (if by computer) report is best. Type should be 8 point or larger, depending on local legal requirements.

• Include a description of the grading scales used. Many retailers insert a cover page that compares the AGS and GIA grading scales. Always state which system you use.

• Clearly note the customer's name and address on the first page, followed by a listing of each item being appraised. If jewelry is paired (two earrings or cuff links), itemize each piece.

• Specify the type of appraisal being performed (such as insurance replacement, estate) because each type may require different valuation methods. A description of "fair market value" (estate or divorce) and "estimated replacement value" (insurance or comparison) often is included on a cover page or accompanying document.

If the item is being appraised for charitable contribution, include your relationship to the donor. The Internal Revenue Service warns that when items are valued at more than $5,000, the appraiser can't be the same person who sold the piece to the consumer.

• Write the report in clear, non-technical language. Never alter the language of the grading system being used; present data simply and without rehashing each procedure used to generate the data. If you are uncertain of the condition or quality of a particular piece, the AGS advises that you qualify the description with a phrase such as "appears to be." Some items can't be identified positively without an expensive or potentially destructive test. Unless the customer agrees to have the test done, a clear qualifier is the best way to handle the description.

• Refer to gemstones by their actual names and sources. The AGS notes that "ruby spinel" and "citrine topaz" are examples of misleading terms. Because a stone's origin can affect its appraised value, any reference to its origin should be accompanied by the evidence that led to the reference.

• When the total value of stones doesn't exceed the value of the mounting plus setting charges, you may refer to the quality of stones in general terms such as "fine," "very good" or "poor." And if stones are of varying sizes, qualities and shapes, you may describe them in more general terms without itemizing.

• Include the pennyweight or gram weight and karatage of the mounting. Note quality marks on the report. In many cases, the mounting represents a significant portion of the item's value.

• Detail the processes listed in the "Product Analysis" section, including condition and quality of gems and mountings, the equipment used, etc. Remember that more significant pieces require more detail.

• Include on each page of the report the page number, total number of pages ("Page 1 of 2," for example) and customer's name. Appraisers often type "End of Appraisal" with a diagonal line drawn underneath after the final description so nothing can be added to the report. Many routinely seal the document with an embossed imprint that covers the total dollar figure. This helps to prevent alteration because any attempt likely would result in torn paper.

Make two copies of the appraisal—one extra copy for the client and one for your records.

The plot: Many appraisers plot all gemstones if their value exceeds that of the mounting; others do so only if requested by the customer or required by the insurance policy.

"Generally it's a good idea," says Deborah Lauer-Toelle, co-owner of Stout & Lauer Jewelers, Springfield Ill. "But if a customer has a piece with 100 stones on it, that's a lot of extra work." Lauer-Toelle, a Certified Gemologist Appraiser, says she plots such items on her worksheets only.

Insurers require a full descriptions of gems in higher-value pieces. This includes type, quality and weight of gemtones (including measurements and inclusions), with all damage noted. The IRS recommends using a photo (or diagram) when appraising for tax purposes, though neither is legally required.

Some appraisers use a prearranged form listing the common characteristics identified during the standard appraisal of specific stones or types of jewelry. But most forms leave much of the page blank to provide room for written description. Most appraisers prefer concise but detailed paragraphs of short sentences. "Don't be flowery," says Lauer-Toelle. "It's not a composition for English class." She says the description for a solitaire ring generally fits on one $8^1/_2$" by 11" page.

Computers: More than 65% of the jewelers on JCK's retail panel don't use a computer in their appraisal business. Not surprisingly, these tend to be less active appraisers, performing fewer than 10 monthly. And only a handful use computer information and trading networks for appraising. Most computer use involves word processing, particularly for legal "boilerplate" such as disclaimers, the appraiser's qualifications, standard formulas and phrases.

Word-processing software has become both inexpensive and user-friendly. Particularly for standard estimate-of-insurance-replacement-cost reports, computers can reduce labor costs by increasing the number of jobs processed each day. Robert A. Lynn, co-owner of Lynn's Jewelry, Ventura, Cal., says he can prepare a six-page estimated-replacement-cost report covering up to six pieces of jewelry in under 15 minutes using computer word processing software (for pieces he had appraised previously).

Michael Golding, manager of Michael & Mark Jeweler and Gemologist, Seattle, adds that a word-processed appraisal report can look more professional than a hand-typed report and is likely to contain fewer typographical errors. Appraisal record-keeping also becomes simpler when past reports are available at the touch of a few keys.

Appraisal software systems vary in complexity and features, but most allow you to input appraisal data onto the computer screen, then generate a report on your own letterhead. For a detailed review of what several appraisal software systems can accomplish, see the February 1991 JCK, pp. 226-236.

Appraisal organizations caution that computer software can't substitute for expertise. "If the data aren't correct, it doesn't matter what program you use," says Lynn, a Certified Appraiser of Personal Property.

The presentation: Once the report is completed, don't simply hand it to your customer, shake hands and say goodbye. Allow time for some discussion. Be sure that the client understands that this report is designed for one purpose only be it insurance coverage, estate settlement, etc. The values established may not be used, for other purposes.

When the appraisal is for insurance purposes, as most done by JCK panelists are, be prepared to advise your client on the types of coverage available. The AGS *Handbook of Jewelry and Gemstone Appraising* includes a section called "Questions customers should ask their insurance agent." Clients might find a copy quite helpful.

YOUR LEGAL LIABILITY

Most appraisers attach to their final reports a list of conditional phrases and definitions designed to limit the possibility of a lawsuit. Called legal "boilerplate," these appear in cover letters or as part of the body of an appraisal. They can be very descriptive and generally are an integral part of how a retailer explains to a customer the nature of an appraisal.

(As an example, one AGS store starts its cover letter with this definition: "THE APPRAISAL: An appraisal is an informed opinion as to the description, quality and value of an item. This appraisal is being issued by a Registered Jeweler of the American Gem Society, an elite group of gemologically trained, professional jewelers who subscribe to a strict code of ethics. Great care has been taken to provide you with complete descriptions and accurate values. Because appraisal and evaluation is subjective, estimates of value may vary from one appraiser to another and such variance does not necessarily constitute error on part of the appraiser.")

Despite appearances, however, the legal phrases in any boilerplate are references only—they don't release an appraiser from liability. "The boilerplate never 100% waives the right of the consumer to dispute the appraisal," says William D. Hoefer Jr., a gemologist and appraiser in San Jose, Cal.

Many jewelers misunderstand the limits of the phrases, says Hoefer. "The danger is not only that the appraiser is not protected, but that he thinks he is," he says. "If the appraiser believes he cannot be sued . . . then what is to prevent him from winging it whenever he feels like it?"

Adds David Coll, a Certified Gemologist Appraiser and owner of Montclair Jewelers, Oakland, Cal., "You can only cover yourself as far as the court may allow, and the court may not allow it." Coll says jewelers who rely heavily on conditional phrases probably aren't qualified to prepare a complete appraisal.

The best defense is a good offense—a thorough, well-researched appraisal report. "The court decides whether the expert was prudent and diligent by having other experts testify as to what is considered standard for the profession," says Hoefer. Personal property appraisal courses available through organizations such as the International Society of Appraisers are typically the basis for these standards. The more thorough and complete, the better, adds Ralph Lerner, general counsel for the Appraisers Association of America and a partner in the New York law firm Sidley & Austin.

What ends up in court most often? "Cases where the appraiser doesn't ask the customer what the appraisal is for," says Hoefer. The customer may use the appraisal for a collateral loan when it was generated by the appraiser for insurance replacement only, for example. The appraisal, completed with the wrong definition of value, can be contested by a third party or even the customer on the basis the appraiser was negligent.

Some cases don't end up in court, says Hoefer. The low value of an item may preclude legal attention, in which case the parties usually settle differences out of court.

Other legal concerns: Comparative appraisals can be a double-edged sword when competitors are involved. Professional appraisers can help consumers avoid being defrauded by jewelers who overstate the value or grading of their merchandise. However, unscrupulous jewelers sometimes use comparative appraisals to discredit competitors. This can be costly.

Called "disparagement of goods" in legal circles, the practice occurs when an appraiser uses his or her report as a tool to undermine the sale of a competitor, and get the business for himself. "Trying to sell to a client seeking an appraisal the very item he brought in to have appraised is dangerous," says Hoefer. "Jewelers who like to 'low ball' values in order to steal a sale risk a lawsuit based on disparagement."

Another concern jewelers who consider re-creating a piece to replace one that an appraisal client has lost should think again, says Geolat. Designs are often copyrighted.

Appraising the IRS Way

If you follow rules set down by the Internal Revenue Service, you can save your client a trip to tax court and a fat penalty. You also can save yourself from fines and a damaged reputation.

The IRS is the federal agency that decides whether your "mistakes" were made intentionally to lower your client's taxes. It's most interested in appraisals done for estate transactions and charitable contributions.

Estate appraisals: Estate appraisals are the more common of the two, says Jeffrey Schutzman, supervisory appraiser for the IRS in Manhattan. Most of these are performed by appraisers with a wide range of expertise.

If an estate is taxable (estates passed on to spouses are not) and is worth more than $600,000, the IRS is likely to be interested in how any jewelry is handled. "If the jewelry is sold we want to know when, by whom and for how much," says Schutzman.

The IRS is particularly interested if the sale price is higher than the appraised value. "If the [new owners of the estate] paid a tax on a claimed value of $100,000 and then sell the piece for $200,000, they owe us tax on the additional $100,000," he says.

The IRS uses retail price as the best indication of value for estate jewelry. Even if the jewelry is sold to a dealer, the taxpayer is accountable for a retail price, which to the IRS is the amount for which the dealer will sell the piece to the public. The exception is when a piece is sold to pay taxes owed by the estate.

If the IRS finds an estate overvalued or undervalued, an appraiser's client will suffer. "Ultimately, it's the taxpayer's responsibility," says Schutzman. But appraisers also can suffer from damaged reputations among exclusive clientele.

Timely reports also are important for correct valuation. For this reason, appraisers should remind their customers to update reports periodically, he adds.

Charitable contributions: Generally, the IRS requires an appraisal for any property valued at more than $5,000 that's donated to charity. If an appraisal of a donated item is deliberately misstated for tax purposes, IRS regulations call for the appraisal to be disregarded, the appraiser to be fined an unspecified amount and the taxpayer to be fined 30% of the amount underpaid in tax. In general, the taxpayer is liable if the value of the item is 150% or more of the correct amount and the taxpayer underpaid taxes by at least $1,000 In general, says Schutzman, appraisers who research, document and follow correct valuation procedures won't face problems. The appraiser doesn't have to belong to any appraisal organization, he says, but the level of expertise and affiliations are contributing factors to the acceptance of an appraiser's opinion. "The opinion is only as good as the evidence that supports it," he says. "Quite frankly, I have experienced people with all kinds of letters after their name who have done a crummy job, and I have seen people who seem to have less certification and designations do a thorough job."

His tips for appraisers:

• Fully identify your qualifications and background, including relationship to the customer.

• State that the appraisal is being completed for tax purposes and list the expected date of donation.

• Include all relevant physical characteristics and descriptions of the piece.

• Document the method used to determine value.

• Use actual sales transactions of similar items to determine fair market value.

• Use photos if possible.

By law, in most cases, you can't appraise a piece that you once sold to someone who now intends to donate it to charity. The exception: if the buyer donates the piece within two months of buying it from you and the appraised value doesn't exceed the purchase price. In addition, you can't be related to or employ the donor and you can't agree to overvalue the item at the donor's request.

For details on estate and charitable contribution appraisals, ask your local IRS office for Publication 561 "Determining the Value of Donated Property," and Publication 559 "Tax Information for Survivors, Executors and Administrators."

APPRAISAL TOOLS

As soon as a client brings you an item to appraise, you begin to use the tools of the trade—starting with your eyes and knowledge. Don't take these for granted. Like any tools, they must be protected and nourished.

Of course, you must know how and when to use technical and mechanical tools as well. Let's look first at tools that let you see the "big picture."

Magnification: No matter how good your vision, certain features in gems and manufactured jewelry can't be seen by the unaided eye. Magnification helps to distinguish jewelry quality or make, natural vs. synthetic and one gem from another that is visually similar.

Assume that two transparent red gems show the same tone, hue and saturation. They might be natural or synthetic ruby, glass, spinel, synthetic spinel, tourmaline or even garnet! Magnification reveals identifying characteristics (or inclusions) for each of these materials. It also reveals the condition and quality of gemstones or metal jewelry. Visual characteristics also help pinpoint a gemstone's origin, which can greatly affect its market value.

Different magnification systems are available:

• The loupe is perhaps the least expensive and most portable of appraisal tools. Skillfully used, the loupe can be an important aid in examining, identifying or separating gems. Loupes most often have 10 power (10x) magnification. Limitations are their single magnification and lack of controlled lighting. They retail for $30-$150 in gemological instrument and jewelry supply shops.

• Binocular microscopes give you a three-dimensional image that helps to determine the relative position and size of inclusions. Microscopes often have controlled light sources, including transmitted, vertical or horizontal illumination. They even may be adapted for polarizing light—an added technique for identifying gemstones.

Microscopes often have variable magnification (typically 10x to 80x), so you can zoom in on smaller inclusions. And many can be adapted for photography. Other uses include detecting gemstone treatments and locating weak areas in gems or jewelry. A microscope may be the largest investment in an appraiser's tool collections, costing $800-$5,000.

Dimensions, weight: Calculating dimensions and weights is an integral part of the appraisal process. These tools will help:

• A Leveridge gauge measures the diameters and depths of mounted or unmounted gemstones. Applying these measurements to known formulas yields estimated weight. Gauges cost about $200.

• Electronic scales are indispensable to a modern appraisal laboratory. They are accurate (check calibration frequently) and save considerable time when weighing loose stones, metal scraps, rings or coins. They may specialize in weighing carats, grams or ounces. Gemological and jewelry supply houses sell scales for $250-$1,000.

Fineness, ID: You'll need technical equipment to test metal fineness and identify loose gems. (The equipment doesn't always work effectively with mounted stones.) This includes:

• Metals testing kit. Confirming gold or silver content is essential because not all jewelry is stamped correctly or at all. These kits contain highly toxic chemicals (hydrochloric and nitric acids) and should be used with great care. Prices range from $50 to $150.

• Refractometer. Many gemstones can be identified by their unique ability to slow down and bend light, a property known as refractivity. A refractometer computes a gemstone's refractive index (the number of times faster light travels in air than in a given material). Used alone or in conjunction with other gemological tests, a refractometer can help identify many gem materials, but it does have some limitations. It can't provide diagnostic key tests on gems with indexes over a certain limit (including diamonds, cubic zirconia and even certain garnets). These must be confirmed by other tests.

• Polariscope. Gemstones from different crystal systems have unique optical characteristics that often may be identified with a polariscope. This piece of equipment helps to determine an optic figure, whether translucent stones have double or single refraction and whether they are uniaxial or biaxial.

• Spectroscope. This measures the way a gem selectively absorbs and emits light. Absorption patterns are unique for given gem materials. These patterns are studied on a spectrum seen when looking through the spectroscope eyepiece. Combined with other gemological tests, the spectroscope is often diagnostic in confirming a gemstone identity. Spectroscopes can be fairly basic, costing as little as $50 for a diffraction-grating spectroscope and as much as $3,000 for fiber-optic illuminated, digital read-out models.

• Specific gravity liquids. A loose gemstone's density, or specific gravity, can be determined using scales and formulas or by immersing it in "heavy liquids." A given gemstone's density will cause it to float, stay suspended or sink in a variety of heavy liquids, so this test can be diagnostic. A set of five liquids costs about $140.

• Diamond master stones and other methods of determining color. Determining and communicating color accurately is vital in appraisals. Different hues, tones and saturations can cause price to fluctuate by thousands of dollars. Gemologists often compare diamonds with GIA's diamond "master stones" to determine a color grade (according to GIA's diamond color grading scale). Systems for colored stones are much more complex and less universally accepted. It's important to adopt a fairly recognized system and to stay with it.

• Lighting, used for different types of testing, includes long and short wave ultraviolet, fiber optic and penlight.

Efficiency: Other equipment can make work more accurate and efficient. For example:

• Smaller items such as tweezers and gem cloths are a must.

• You also may want to invest in a thermal conductivity diamond tester, a thermal reaction tester and camera equipment to document jewelry or gemstones.

• If you do appraisals away from your office, consider a portable gemological laboratory that fits in a briefcase. It contains most of the instruments mentioned, but carries a hefty price tag, ranging from $3,000 to $6,000.

• A proper reference library is essential. Appraisers constantly require updated information. Trips to regular or specialized libraries are time-consuming and expensive, so it's important to build your own collection of useful works. These should deal with such varied topics as appraisal science, gemology, antique/period jewelry and watches, jewelry design and fabrication. You also should stay up-to-date by subscribing to several gem and jewelry trade journals and publications.

SOURCES & RESOURCES

Price information abounds for nearly every type of piece you may be called on to appraise. Here's a list of major price lists and books. Remember these are only a guide to establishing value. Research on specific pieces and the appropriate market are necessary for a complete, accurate value.

PRICE LISTS, NEWSLETTERS, COMPUTER NETWORKS

Diamond Insight, 50 E. 66 St., New York, N.Y. 10021. Auction news and prices from the U.S. and abroad.

Diamond Market Monitor, 650 Washington Rd., Pittsburgh, Pa. 15228.

Diamond Registry Bulletin, 580 Fifth Ave. #806, New York, N.Y. 10036; (212) 575-0444. Weekly newsletter with white and colored diamond prices.

Gemworld Pricing Guide, Gemworld International, 630 Dundee Rd., Suite 235, Northbrook, Ill. 60062; (708) 564-0555. Quarterly report on diamonds, colored stones, jadeite and pearls.

JPR, P.O. Box 35, Rockville, Va. 23146-0035; (804) 749-4367. Quarterly price report on auction sales of antique and period jewelry.

Polygon Network, P.O. Box 1885, Dillon, Colo. 80435; (303) 468-1245. Computer network gem trading.

The Rapaport Report, 15 W. 47 St., New York, N.Y. 10036; (212) 354-0575. Weekly price list and computer network of loose polished diamonds and market news.

APPRAISAL, PRICE REFERENCE & ID WORKS

Appraisal Guidelines, Jewelers of America.

Appraising Diamonds and Jewelry by E.D. Ribacoff (60-minute videotape).

Complete Guide to Watches by Cooksey Shugart and Tom Engle.

Gems: Their Sources, Descriptions & Identification by Robert Webster.

Handbook of Gem Identification by Richard T. Liddicoat Jr.

Handbook of Jewelry and Gemstone Appraising by Cos Altobelli with Charlotte Preston.

Marks of London Goldsmiths and Silversmiths (1697- 1837) by John P. Fallon.

Official Identification and Price Guide to Costume Jewelry by Harrise S. Miller.

100 Years of Collectible Jewelry (1850-1950) by Lillian Baker.

Price Guide to Jewelry 3000 B.C. to 1950 A.D. by Michael Poynder.

Sotheby's International Price Guide, Vol. 2, John Marion, editor.

Sterling Flatware Pattern Index, 4th edition.

Vintage American and European Watch Price Guide, Book 5, by Sherry and Roy Ehrhardt and Joe Demesy.

(These and many other pertinent works are available through the Jewelers' Book Club, (215) 964-4480.)

AUCTION HOUSES

Butterfield & Butterfield, 220 San Bruno, San Francisco, Cal. 94103; (415) 861-7500.

Christie's International, 502 Park Ave., New York, N.Y. 10022; (212) 546-1000. For antique and period jewelry, silver and watches.

Christie's East, 219 E. 67 St., New York, N.Y. 10021; (212) 606-0400.

Habsburg Fine Art Auctioneers, 1 Rue du Mont Blanc, 1201 Geneva, Switzerland. Specializes in watches.

Phillips Auctioneers, 406 E. 79, New York, N.Y. 10021; (212)570-4830.

Skinner Galleries, 2 Newbury St., Boston, Mass. 01740; (617) 236-1700.

Sotheby's, 1334 York Ave., New York, N.Y. 10021; (212) 606-7000. For antique and period jewelry, silver and watches, Sotheby's Arcade Sales at the same location.

Reaching Out To Customers: How To Break The $5,000 Sales Barrier

September 1989

"In my 35 years in business on this corner, we've had but one sale over $5,000—and that was a number of years ago," says an Illinois jeweler.

"I'm good for about thirty $5,000-plus sales a year," says an Iowa jeweler. "That's about one every $2^1/_2$-3 weeks, with several at Christmas."

What's the difference? Why do some stores never handle high-ticket sales, while others call them far from unusual?

Size and type of store, location, local business conditions—all contribute. But jewelers who make high-end sales share one common trait: the personal touch. They know and care about their customers. They listen carefully to find out what customers want, then provide quality products and service that fill their needs. Many build business through referrals by loyal customers who trust them. And many make repeat sales to long-time customers by calling them when a birthday or anniversary approaches, when a piece they'd like comes in, or when a special promotion is planned.

Once salespeople overcome their own initial fear of selling high-priced merchandise, they may find it's no harder to make the $5,000 sale than the $500 one. Some jewelers even say it's easier. But few get the chance to try unless they build the customer relationship from which such business grows.

In the following pages, retailers around the country tell how they've developed such relationships, and describe some of their $5,000-plus sales.

SHOW, TELL & SELL

All jewelry store sales—whether high-dollar or low—are created equal, says Bill Shepherd, manager of Wayne Jewelers and Silversmiths in Wayne, Pa.

"Whether a customer wants to spend $10 or $10,000, we treat the person the same," he says.

But the techniques he and his staff use to make a sale are especially effective in selling high-dollar jewelry, watches and tableware.

'Ask for help': The store in suburban Philadelphia's affluent "Main Line" area has 12 to 13 full-and part-time salespeople. They are divided into two crews—one qualified in jewelry and gemstones, the other knowledgeable in china, crystal and silver flatware. (All are expected to be familiar with the watches and clocks which the store sells.)

All are trained well enough to close a high-end sale, Shepherd says. But each must follow one hard-and-fast

rule automatically: "If you don't know, immediately ask someone who does."

Thus, salespeople who are less knowledgeable about diamonds or have trouble answering a customer's questions about gemstones immediately call on a more experienced staff member for the information. "We don't play games here," says Shepherd. "We want the customer to be correctly informed." That benefits not only the customer but also the store's reputation. And it helps make the sale.

"I've tried to create a sales force that is a team, whose one aim is to make the sale," says Shepherd. "No one—including me—is ashamed to ask for help if they have a question they can't answer or don't know [some information about a product]."

Once help is given, though, the original salesperson takes over. "If a customer starts with a certain salesperson, that individual should be allowed to finish the sale," says Shepherd.

'Show and tell': The Wayne, Pa., store manager doesn't believe high-dollar sales are more difficult than low-dollar ones.

"I've spent as much time closing a $200 sale as I have for a $20,000 sale," he tells nervous new staffers. "The exact same [selling] process is used, except you write down more numbers!"

The key is "finding qualified customers and offering what they can afford.

"We try to know [what] our own customers [can afford]. If we don't know a customer, we ask what price range he or she is looking at, and what they have budgeted," he explains.

Regardless of the amount, Shepherd and his staff always show items more expensive than the customer's price range, "to give them an opportunity to go up." Thus, if a customer's limit is $2,000, Shepherd will show a couple of items valued at $2,000 and $4,000. Customers often will buy higher-priced jewelry than they originally intended, if they're satisfied with the piece shown.

That's why Wayne Jewelers always keeps a small amount of a variety of high-end jewelry—such as diamond rings, ear studs, necklaces or earrings—on hand.

"If you have it available, you can show it. And if you give them the opportunity to see it, they also have the opportunity to buy."

"But we don't pressure our customers. If they're reluctant, I don't push it," says Shepherd. "One of my favorite sayings is, 'I don't sell; I show and tell.'"

Seeking sales: About 75% of the store's high-dollar sales are solicited by its sales staff. They keep current on what their regular customers want or like, and keep them informed of merchandise in which they would be interested.

The store's single biggest recent sale, for example, was an 87-point blue diamond which a regular customer bought for $62,000.

"He's a man who likes unusual stones. He bought a $12,000 alexandrite last year and had it made into a tie tac," says Shepherd. "Whenever we get a line on an unusual stone, we call him, and he asks us to keep watching for certain ones. Right now, he's interested in a natural red diamond."

Some customers who like high-ticket merchandise are reluctant to pay the price. If the salesperson knows the customer can afford an item, he can offer a couple of options.

"Though we're basically a cash store, we'll extend a little credit, up to 90 days," says Shepherd. "We'll also do layaway; the customer leaves a deposit and pays off the price over several months. [The merchandise remains in the store's vault until fully paid.] We often find that works well."

If a customer still is reluctant, salespeople will go for the sale by offering something similar but less expensive.

More sales: Wayne Jewelers & Silversmiths expects to have about 150 sales of merchandise costing more than $5,000 this year. It had nearly 50 by mid-summer, with a few topping $50,000.

"We're getting a much higher percentage of such sales now than a couple of years ago," says Shepherd. The reasons, he suggests, are that "our staff is more experienced, and knows our customers better. Also, we are drawing more and more customers who know we are capable of providing this [merchandise and service]."

Diamond rings account for many of the store's $5,000-plus sales. But it also sells diamond earrings, bracelets, ear studs and necklaces. There are high-dollar sales in tablewares, too, including sterling flatware, china and crystal. And the store sells a number of watches costing $10,000, $15,000 and more, primarily in the Baume & Mercier and Rolex lines.

Excluding Christmas, anniversaries are the single biggest occasion for major purchases, followed by birthdays, says Shepherd. "About 40% of the customers making such purchases are men," he says. "Another 40% are man-and-wife, and the rest are made by anybody" for various reasons.

BY THE WAY, HOW MUCH?

For some reason, folks seem to be much more willing to spend a lot than a little, says Bethesda, Md., jeweler Robert Limon, owner of Robert Limon Inc. He finds it a lot less difficult to sell something over $5,000 than something under $100.

To illustrate, last year one of Limon's customers was looking for a very special sapphire to make a three-stone ring. "I've looked at hundreds of sapphires and they're all so dark!" complained the customer. Limon showed him a picture of a Kashmir sapphire. "That's what I want!" exclaimed the customer.

Not long after, Limon acquired a fine 3.5-ct. Kashmir. The customer took one look; the sale took three seconds.

The customer's exact words were, "That's it! That's the one! I'll have the check here tomorrow. Oh, by the way, how much is it?"

The stone alone was $75,000. Limon later designed a setting incorporating two oval diamonds, each weight more than a carat.

Limon makes about 15 high-end sales per year. He doesn't have a big staff; in fact, he and his grandson are the only two people selling. He does most of the big sales himself, but has no objection to his grandson handling some, too, which he occasionally does. Most high-ticket sales involve custom work, since he specializes in loose stones for which he designs settings.

Most of Limon's big sales involve established customers who want an extra-special gift for some occasion. A number of engagement ring sales also fall into this category. He doesn't do any advertising or make any really special efforts to sell high-ticket items. He will call one of his special customers, however, when he has an extraordinary stone to show.

What happens if a customer hits a financial bind? "Dry their tears, I guess," he says. It happens in all price ranges. He does bend to meet the needs of his established customers, by allowing credit or layaway.

"We don't have any rules about that," he says. "We take it case by case. If we've known the customer for years, know they're good for it, we'll give them time to pay for it." He might require a deposit beforehand from a new customer, however.

If a customer has the money but isn't quite sold, Limon tries to bolster their desire to own the piece. Sometimes it works, sometimes it doesn't.

Limon says he's never had any sales training and doesn't consider himself qualified to offer tips to the budding high-ticket salesperson. But he does remember how frightened he was to make a $100 sale when he was just starting out.

"After all these years, I don't even get nervous at really big sales. There's nothing to differentiate a $1,000 sale from a $5,000 sale from a $75,000 sale. It still depends on whether the customer has the money and wants the piece."

TRUST IS THE KEY

Cartier has thrived on high-market jewelry and watches for decades; quality, attention to customers and service are the reasons.

Brian Lange, Cartier's director of retail development and training, says all of his sales training programs are built around these three factors.

Cartier has two retail jewelry segments. Its main store offers a wide range of products priced from $100 to $40,000, with most over $1,000. In addition, private fine jewelry salons within the store offer pieces costing $40,000 or more. One boutique offers watches from $795 to $35,000. Cartier also has jewelry watches costing as much as $350,000.

Lange says $5,000-plus items comprise 40%-50% of Cartier's jewelry sales. Watches average between $10,000 and $12,000. The main store staff can sell items in any price range, though the private salons employ a separate sales staff.

The key to Cartier's success is trust, says Lange. "Customers are entrusting a lot of money to Cartier," he says, "so they want to work with salespeople they can trust."

The keys to gaining that trust are:
- Product knowledge.

Cartier salespeople are trained to explain to customers why they pay more for Cartier jewelry and watches and to make them feel comfortable that they're getting what they pay for.

Salespeople learn the usual gemological information (the diamond 4 C's and colored stone quality comparisons). But they also learn how Cartier produces its jewelry (gold chain, for example, is hand-crafted and all gold used in jewelry settings is 18k).

People looking for expensive pieces often ask many questions. "Salespeople must give them straight answers," says Lange. "If they don't know the answer, they should tell the customer 'let's find out together' and make a phone call."
- Customer knowledge.

"We tell our salespeople to find out what customers want and don't try to sell them something else," he says. Listening engenders trust and makes a customer more comfortable.

If the customer doesn't ask for something specific, the salespeople find out what significant pieces they already own and find something to complement it. "If someone already has a pair of diamond and sapphire earrings," he says, "we can suggest a diamond-sapphire bracelet."
- Keep poise.

Salespeople who are nervous or reluctant about approaching customers with very expensive pieces will have problems selling them, he says.

Such reluctance can be overcome with experience and training. "The key is product knowledge," he says. "If the salespeople know what they are selling and have confidence in its quality and their ability to covey that message to their customers, they will have no problems."

Because Cartier is *Cartier* , customers generally know the store is expensive territory before they walk in.

Occasionally, however, someone does blanch at the high prices. "Again, the key to turning them around is product knowledge," he says. "If they know our quality standards are much higher than most jewelers, they will often buy from us."
- Keeping promises.

If salespeople, promise to call a customer about a piece they ordered, they must call at the stated time—whether the piece is ready or not. "Keeping promises helps to keep trust," Lange says.

Trust created in the first sale to a customer extends far into the future, stresses Lange. "We have been around for decades," he says. "People trust us because they know our quality and know that we will be there if they need us.

"High jewelry businesses like ours depend upon repeat customers. We couldn't survive on people who make one purchase."

BUILD A LONG-TERM RELATIONSHIP

A retailer's best customers are those most familiar with the store. A customer relationship built up over the years is a wise investment of time and labor.

That's certainly true for Elaine Cooper & Co. Inc., a fine jewelry store in an exclusive area of Philadelphia. "For us," says owner Helene Huffer, "the big sales have occurred where there is a relationship with the customer. It may have been just through a repair and it doesn't necessarily mean that they have been big buyers before."

What really counts is the customer's feeling of trust and confidence in the retailer, she says. Though an appreciable number of large sales have been spontaneous, most occur after a customer has visited the store several times and has built that trust.

"One of my best customers comes in at least seven or eight times before she'll finally say OK." The lesson for her sales representatives: Never "push" a sale.

"If that particular item is not right for that customer, I don't want them to buy it," she adds.

Salespeople should be able to recognize whether a buyer feels comfortable with an item. They also should be able to explain technical details about the piece—at the customer's own level. "Some customers just care that it looks pretty and others want to know every detail," Huffer says. High-end buyers come in both stripes.

Colored diamonds are Huffer's most popular sale at the $5,000-plus level. They seem to appeal to both old and young buyers. "I had a couple in their 90s come in and have a ring cleaned," she explains. "We put the stone under the scope and found some big cracks." But instead of replacing the stone, they bought a new large colored diamond ring.

"I don't have any magic formula," Huffer observes. But she has an edge with colored diamonds that few sales techniques can equal—enthusiasm.

"I wear colored diamonds all the time," she confesses. "I'm addicted to them. I'm mad about them and maybe that's contagious."

NEVER UNDERESTIMATE THE CUSTOMER

Imagine you make $100,000 a year and have a huge disposable income. That's the foundation of Andrew Johnson's advice to sales representatives preparing for their first big sale.

Johnson is vice president and co owner of The Diamond Cellar, a high-end fine jewelry store in Columbus, Ohio. With an average sale "well into the thousands" and a well-heeled clientele, he is familiar with the gap that can exist between customer and new sales clerk.

"The first time they sell a big piece, they may be a bit hesitant," he says. Some may appear surprised or overly excited. "Sometimes they don't believe that someone wants to spend $20,000 or $30,000 on a birthday gift." Often, he says, the salesman may not even show the customer an expensive item. The salesperson assumes the buyer has a lower limit in mind, when in fact he is willing to spend considerably more.

That mindset is natural for sales personnel, who rarely play in the same financial league as their customers. While aware of the difference, salespeople may not be conscious of the way it can affect the sales process.

"You can never underestimate the buying public," Johnson adds. "We find that there are a lot of people for whom $5,000 or more is not a problem." He tells his salespeople to show the customer a very expensive piece and several in other price ranges. A price range can quickly be established without underestimating the buyer.

Many employees are surprised to find that high-ticket items are quite often impulse purchases, says Johnson. Cost for these customers is rarely the deciding factor. "These people have distinctive tastes and it's not dollar amounts that scare them off," he notes. "For them it comes down to design. It's something they fall in love with and buy."

To help new hires avoid undervaluing the customer, Johnson trains them to view the sale from the customer's perspective. "If they put their own financial constraints on the customer, they are not going to sell anything," he says. "They have to mentally get themselves ready for the big sale."

'JUST PART OF THE BUSINESS'

More than half the business at Everhart Jewelers' McLean, Va., store comes form $5,000-plus sales, according to William Everhart. Everyone on the sales staff, whether part- or full-time, has made—and is accustomed to making—high-dollar sales.

"Our philosophy for a $5,000 sale is no different than that for a $500 sale," Everhart says. "We don't consider them special sales. They're just a part of our business."

Everhart says that if high-dollar sales were more the exception than the norm, he would be more selective about who might make such a sale. "It would probably be left to a member of the family or one of the more experienced salespeople," he says.

But the store enjoys a solidly established clientele which includes congressmen and their wives. Everhart notes that about 95% of the people on the firm's mailing list are 50 years or older.

"People in the position to make $5,000 or $10,000 purchases with regularity are accustomed to doing so," Everhart says. "There are times when a $10,000 sale is made in less than a minute, while a $200 sale could take a half hour."

But some customers just aren't aware of what things cost and what they might have to spend for a piece they want. Everhart recalls a customer who wanted an emerald pendant in the $1,000 range for a gift. He soon realized that he wouldn't get the look he desired for that amount.

"Something has to give in a situation like that," Everhart says. "Like when people come looking for a one-carat diamond for $1,000. You just can't get a diamond of quality for that price."

Everhart won't compromise quality for price. "If we miss part of the market, then so be it," he says. The store's customers return frequently and remain long-term patrons because they know they can find pieces of consistent quality and staying power.

The store's inventory does not reflect come an go fashion trends. Everhart notes that efforts are made to "do our own thing," and not necessarily jump into the fashion mainstream.

"We focus on useful pieces for our customers that will survive the ups and downs of fashion," he says.

Customers most frequently seek high-dollar pieces for anniversaries and during the holiday season, Everhart says. Men make virtually all of the purchases, although wives or girlfriends frequently do the legwork.

"It's often a 'find what you want and get it' situation," Everhart says.

Color Enhancement:
How To Tell Your Customer

July 1989

Jewelers know they should disclose color enhancement; they also fear disclosure may be just a quick way to lose a sale.

Most of those who talked with JCK conceded they do not routinely discuss gem enhancement with customers. Their reasons varied. Some admitted they don't know enough about the different treatment processes to explain them comfortably and confidently to customers. Others, surprisingly, don't think disclosure is that important an issue—despite the law that requires it. But the majority said they're scared that telling the truth might turn off customers. One prominent jeweler in the Pacific Northwest admitted, "It's hard to be a leader on this issue. It's like cutting your nose off to spite your face." In other words, you may be up front with your customer about the treatment of gems, but what about the not-so-informed (or not so-honest) jeweler around the corner who claims that his stones are never treated?

Not to be ignored: Gem enhancement has been a critical issue in the industry for nearly a decade—for several good reasons:

• More and more gems now undergo routine enhancement. This is because far too few untreated stones of top color are available to meet growing demand.

• Fueled by media coverage both factual and sensational, consumer knowledge about gemstones is greater than ever. A successful jeweler must be able to answer customer questions, including any on enhancement.

• Finally, the industry now is committed to complete disclosure of gem enhancements.

One indication is the decision by the American Gem Trade Association to require it of all members. Any who don't disclose will be barred from exhibiting at AGTA's all-important Tucson Gem Fair. Another example is the aforementioned *Gemstone Enhancement Manual,* an improved edition of the *Jewelers' Information Manual.* It provides an easy-to-understand shorthand system for labeling various gem enhancements. That's fine. But these efforts still don't answer the question that jewelry store salespeople most ask: "How do I tell *my* customer?" Conversations with many jewelers around the country resulted in some answers. Among them:

- Don't be afraid of the subject and don't feel you have to apologize. This is a standard industry practice and has been for years.
- Stress the positive. Let the customer know that without enhancement, the supply of saleable, attractive colored stones would shrink drastically—and prices for those available would rise equally drastically.

- Take the initiative. Tell the customer up front about color enhancement. Make it clear this is but one of many processing steps involved in preparing a stone for market.
- Don't back off when the customer says a competitor claimed his stones have not been treated. As politely as possible, let the customer know your competitor probably is lying.
- Know your facts. That's the key to discussing disclosure comfortably and confidently.

Secrets Of Selling Clocks

July 1989

Clocks can be a retailer's dream. With new U.S. households forming and demand continuing for clocks as decorative accessories, sales—about $1 billion a year—keep growing at 2%-plus annually. To meet demand, clock firms add new models for every taste and need. In small table clocks alone, clock suppliers this year debuted models by famous artists, models that light up at a touch and models hand-sculpted of Italian marble.

Everyone seems to want a piece of the pie—everyone but jewelers. While gift shops and department stores move high-end clocks to their fine jewelry departments, many jewelers relegate clocks to the bottom of their list of must-sell items.

JCK polled retail jewelers nationally and found more than half (58%) carry clocks. But two out of three say clocks are less than 2% of their business. One in three reports diminishing clock sales over the past three years.

These findings are supported by a 1988 national survey of 5,000 households by the Clock Manufacturers and Marketing Association. It found only 1.1% of clocks bought in the previous 12 months came from jewelry stores.

Bête noire: Why do clocks do poorly in many jewelry stores? Some jewelers blame that handy *bête noire:* competition. "Our business declined [because] everyone—hardware stores, etc.—now sells clocks," laments an Iowa jeweler. Says another in Illinois, "We can't compete with big department stores [that] buy in large quantities and retail for less bucks than we can."

Others say they can't afford to set aside valuable display space for such slow-turning merchandise, even though many clock suppliers offer space-saving stands and petite clocks.

The real problem for many jewelers may be their own attitude or lack of marketing imagination. Too many still think of clocks as just timepieces, like kitchen clocks, rather than as jewelry merchandise, says Tony Rodriquez, CMMA president.

"Kitchen clocks aren't the jeweler's product—or shouldn't be," he says. "People won't come to a jewelry store for a kitchen clock, but they will come for a brass carriage clock or a leather travel clock. They'll buy a mantel clock because it's an attractive accessory, a decoration for the

home, a collectible or a form of art that also tells time. They'll buy a very expensive wall clock and put it where a picture would have gone."

Jewelers who don't cultivate the local clock market miss out on a good way to boost sales, says Rodriquez. Fine clocks can replace watch sales lost to the competitive discount market and are natural add-on sales.

Six who do: Despite overall industry statistics, there are jewelers healthy double-digit rates annually. Their secret: they've found a niche in their local clock market and go after it aggressively. They fill the gap when other retailers drop or reduce clock departments. They cultivate corporate award programs. They track clock sales to see what turns and at what price.

They make sure their sales staff is as knowledgeable about clocks as it is about jewelry and gems. Here are six examples of jewelers who succeed at clock retailing.

Time Shop Jewelers: Corporate clocks

Corporate incentive award programs are the key to success in the clock department at Time Shop Jewelers, Salt Lake City, Utah. Owner Howard Logsdon says clocks account for about 7% of his business, representing a 40% increase in the past three years.

A major reason is his contract to provide 150-200 clocks each year for the corporate award program of a statewide utility. As the utility and its incentive program expand, so does Logsdon's clock business.

He offers some incentives of his own to keep the utility buying from him, including free plating and engraving on all clocks.

The awards create business, too. The warranty that goes with all clocks sold to the utility are imprinted with the store name and address, and that has brought in new customers. In fact, some executives of the utility have become regular Time Shop customers.

Wayne Jewelers: Keep them turning

Clocks are "an easy sell," says Bill Shepherd, manager of Wayne Jewelers & Silversmiths, a three-store suburban Philadelphia firm. "But like anything else in a store, you have to *sell* them."

Clock sales account for about 5% of his business, and they increase at least 10% annually, he says. The main store sells up to 200 clocks a year, and each store keeps 75-130 clocks on hand at all times. The stores have a slightly different market, so they carry slightly different clock stocks. For example, the main store in affluent Wayne stocks more expensive clocks than a mall store. But each store displays clocks in windows and extensively on inside walls and in cases.

Shepherd shakes his head at retailers who say clocks take too much space. "What else could I put there [on the walls] that gives me as much revenue?" he asks. "They're worth the space we give them."

The clocks he stocks aren't cheap—"nothing under $50"—and sales average around $100. The merchandise turns twice a year. "Very little gets old," he says. "We keep putting in different styles and prices that turn in our market; we're always looking for something new and different."

He works closely with suppliers—including Bulova, Hampton-Hadden, Seiko and Matthew Norman—to get quick service and delivery. He makes them track what his stores sell, and supplements that with his own computer printouts and on-the-floor knowledge of what is and isn't moving.

Individuals account for the bulk of clock sales, but about 50 accounts involve corporate award programs. To keep and expand that market, the firm regularly sends mailings to local companies. The staff also keeps in touch with customers who are executives of local firms.

Staff training is important in clock sales, says Shepherd. He periodically talks with staffers, "one or two at a time," to ensure they're familiar with the clocks they sell. Salespeople also have access to loose-leaf binders with the latest clock product information.

Walkers n' Daughters: Floor clock flair

Clocks account for more than 35% of business at the three-store Walkers n' Daughters Jewelers chain, based in Bismarck, N.D. The clock department is so strong (growing 10%-15% in two years), "we pushed out our bridal department to make more space for it," says Louise Walker, vice president and co-owner with her husband and company president, Leroy.

The firm carries more than 125 clocks of numerous types in its downtown store alone. But the big reason for its success is specialization. The Walkers found a niche no one else in their area served—floor clocks—and cultivated it aggressively. They began with just one floor clock more than a decade ago and now show 35 in their downtown store and 10-15 in each of their two mall stores. The average floor clock sale is $1,000, though prices range from $500 to $6,000. The firm sells more than 500 clocks a year, 75-100 of them floor clocks.

Floor clocks are particularly popular because "this market is very conservative, very family-oriented," says Mrs. Walker, and these clocks are closely associated with traditional family-home memories. "We've even had parents come in and buy three or four at a time for their children," she says. That brings business from far beyond Bismarck; the Walkers have sent clocks as far as San Francisco and Hawaii.

In selling clocks, employees stress quality. "We tell customers there are no plastic parts in clocks we carry," she says. "The outsides are all wood and the insides all metal."

The Walkers also provide a free "heritage plaque," a small plate engraved with the customer's name and date. "We tell customers that 100 years from now, their great-grandchildren will want to know to know from which side of the family they inherited this beautiful clock," she says.

The Walkers' marketing program features ads that highlight clocks, including a 30-second TV commercial. They use price-off promotions from a major clock supplier, Howard Miller, and work with corporate award programs. They even turn shipping errors into successful promotions. A few years ago, for example, the firm ordered nine of one model of floor clock but got 18 by mistake. The Walkers held a silent auction, taking bids from anyone who wanted to buy one of the clocks. "We not only sold all 18," she says, "but we had to order six more!"

The Walkers back up their sales with service. They guarantee all clocks for two years; any needed repairs in that period—including houses calls—are done free. There are two clock repairmen: Mr. Walker and son-in-law Larry Weiand (also the firm's clock department manager and buyer for all three stores).

"Our clock repair service bring us lots of business," says Mrs. Walker, including contracts to repair antique clocks in historical buildings.

Mr. Walker helps to deliver the floor clocks and returns a couple of times to ensure they're running properly and to answer any questions. The firm also works with moving companies to install and reset floor clocks.

E.J. Gare & Son: Tell 'em what you've got

It pays to advertise. At least it does for Gare & Son of Northampton, Mass., a store where clock sales account for 12% of business in an area surrounded by malls and shopping centers.

"We put a lot of inventory in and then advertise it to make the public aware of it," says owner E.J. Gare III. He advertises in the local newspaper six times a week, increases that to 10-12 ads each week in November and December and also runs a weekly watch and clock repair ad. In addition, he's sole sponsor of the local 7:30 a.m. radio news program. The advertising features all types of merchandise, but "much of it" is for watches and clocks, he says.

Gare—a traditional full-line jeweler—benefits from the decision of other local retailers to drop or downsize their clock departments. "Not many bother with clocks anymore," he says. "But someone has to sell them because people want them."

The store turns its clock inventory $2^1/_2$ times a year, stocking 200 models and selling more than 500 clocks annually, says Gare. Most are $100-$150 and all are from Seiko. Gare displays clocks in store windows, on walls, in display cases near the doors and on a 6-foot rectangular Seiko display tower that holds several smaller clocks.

Clock sales get a helping hand from an in-house repair service—"a big part of our business"—and the store's reputation. The store has been on Northampton's Main Street at virtually the same location for 204 years. In addition, Gare is known through his work as president of the local retailers' association.

McCormick Jewelers: Clocks on the move

The clock business at McCormick Jewelers is on the move—literally. James G. McCormick, co-owner of the Charlotte, N.C. firm, pulls traffic and builds sales with what he calls motion clocks—any clock with visibly moving parts such as a pendulum or revolving balls.

It's a subtle gimmick, but it works. "We display motion clocks in a storefront window where there is a big walk-by crowd," he says. "People see the motion, stop and look, and many come in."

Before McCormick changed his clock displays three years ago, clock turnover was very slow (0.2 maximum). "We bought clocks sparsely and kept them a long time," he says. "We had to do something to spice up clock sales. No one was asking for clocks. Something had to change."

Since changing displays, clock sales are up 15%-20% in three years and now account for 5% of business. The turn is two to three times a year.

McCormick even uses motion clocks to attract attention to other merchandise. "We put mantel and wall clocks with pendulums in 'dead space' in the store to draw people's attention to items there," he says. "And [we] moved our pearls near a clock display because of increased traffic there."

Herteen & Stocker: Show and sell

Some jewelers complain clocks take up too much display space, but not Herteen & Stocker, Iowa City, Iowa. The firm places clocks in all 13 of its display windows— some showing only clocks, some showing clocks with other merchandise.

"We put clocks where people can see them when they walk by," says assistant manager Terry Dickens. "Seeing them is where most of our [clock] sales come from."

Inside are displays for anniversary clocks, travel clocks and clocks in display cases. "Every available wall has at least one clock on it [so] customers will see clocks wherever they look," he says.

The clock department, accounting for 5% of total sales, has grown 20% in three years, in part because business was so good the firm added Linden clocks to the Seiko line it already carried. The store sells about 100 clocks a year (with sales averaging $75) and has a twice-a-year turn.

"One reason our turnover has increased is we have so many different clocks to choose from [70-80 on-site]," says Dickens. "If customers come in looking for a clock, they usually leave with one."

Other factors that help to boost sales include service and repair by two on-site watchmakers, salespeople who keep up-to-date on new clocks and how to operate them, a 20%-down layaway plan and little competition from area stores.

Herteen & Stocker actively promotes its clocks in radio and newspaper ads at holidays, and makes good use of suppliers' co-op advertising.

"We try to keep clocks in front of people all the time, whether in the windows, the displays or the ads," says Dickens.

How To Shop A Trade Show

July 1988

So you're going to a trade show. Whether it's the Big Apple or a smaller, local show, whether you're a novice or a veteran, these tips can help you make the best buying decisions and get the most return from the time and money you invest.

Before the show

Decide what you want to accomplish. Are you looking for ideas? Inventory fillers? Fresh new looks? Try to write your goals. You'll have an easier time finding what you want and avoiding items you don't need.

Check your inventory. Be objective. Do you still stock items whose popularity has peaked? This is a good time o examine the demographics of your town and clientele. Buying habits change, and your merchandise should reflect the changes.

Make a shopping list. Be specific, but keep your mind open. Example: Rather than go on a blanket search for cocktail rings, focus on the quality, sizes, styles, colors and price ranges that have been successful for you. But don't be afraid to try something new, as long as it fits your general requirements. So what if you've never sold an amethyst/peridot combination? You might hit upon a new winner.

Send enough people. If you usually run yourself ragged at shows, take some qualified staffers to the next one to do some of the legwork. Give each one a category of jewelry to

cover—pearls, colored stones, etc.,—to get the most from comparison shopping. Your helpers may even be able to make a few buying decisions.

Plan your itinerary to fit your budget. Organizations running the show may have information on travel and lodging discounts.

You may find an even better deal yourself. But don't trade too much convenience for the sake of a few dollars. It can be more expensive in the long run.

Call the host city's Chamber of Commerce beforehand for maps and guidebooks. These will help you to find restaurants and spare-time activities to fit your tastes and budget. A few activities outside the show help to keep your mind clear. Also check the show schedule to see what planned activities interest you.

Pack accordingly. Ask the Chamber of commerce about the climate. (If you're going to Europe, take an umbrella!!)

For the show itself, remember exhibition halls can be overheated, overchilled or both. Layer your clothing so you can add or subtract as needed. Note: In the Sunbelt, most buildings have very strong air conditioning, so take a sweater. Make sure you wear comfortable, supportive shoes. If you will attend any industry functions, check ahead to see whether formal dress is required.

Pre-register to save time if you can. If you can't, call the show management beforehand to find out exactly what you will need to register. Double-check to make sure you carry it with you.

Also carry business cards and plenty of identification.

At the show

Plan your strategy. Read the show guide, familiarize yourself with the floor plan and decide how you will work the show. Some buyers like to start at one end and work in order. Others like to see their favorite firms first, then wander. Read the available information and make note of anything that catches your interest. Tip: most buyers who work in order start with the beginning aisle numbers. It's less crowded if you start at the end and work backward.

Compare. Take along some of your merchandise to compare with what you find at the show. (Before you pack it, however, carefully consider the security consequences.) You can choose some finished pieces simply by weight. But when buying pieces that rely on visual impact (especially pearls or colored stones), compare with your own pieces to make sure your standards are met.

Don't rush. When dozens of people crowd around each booth, you may feel pressured to decide quickly and move on. But remember that you are the customer. Take the time you need to decide. Don't worry about monopolizing the sales representative, but keep personal chitchat to a minimum. If you feel pressured by the sales representative, consider whether this is the type of firm you'd like to deal with.

Don't fall victim to shopper's fatigue or the feeling that you must justify your attendance with a purchase. Look at your shopping list. It reflects your customer's tastes, so it's a good guide not only for *what* you should buy, but also whether you should buy.

Pace yourself, especially at a large show. You have a lot of ground to cover and a lot of activities to participate in. Don't tire yourself by doing it all the first day. Allow ample time for work, play and sleep—all are important.

Eat right. Overeating and trade show go hand in hand, but too much overeating, or undereating, makes you sluggish. Eat nutritionally balanced meals. And do remember that food served in hotels and at the shows is usually frightfully expensive—that's the price of convenience.

After the show

Stage a little promotion in your store. Take pictures of the host city, the show and yourself at the show. If you're not handy with the camera, show sponsors are happy to help with pictures. Most city visitor centers also have plenty of stock shots of local scenes. In your store, use a big poster as a backdrop and display the photos with jewelry you bought at the show. Pictures tell a story, and people are always curious to look at them. Tie this promotion into the free publicity mentioned above.

Offer your services as a public speaker. You can relate show anecdotes and offer educational information about jewelry buying and the jewelry industry. Civic groups often look for speakers, and high schools often ask local business owners to speak to business students or during career days.

Take advantage of suppliers who offer promotional assistance with their products. Any time you go to make a purchase, ask what promotional support is offered. After a purchase, don't be afraid to call a supplier and ask for help with advertising.

Travel security

Be careful. There's a reason for the old saying that it's easy to spot a tourist. Keep your extra cash in the hotel safe, use travelers checks when you can, carry only the credit cards you need and keep a record of your numbers. Gents, keep your wallet in a buttoning or inside pocket; ladies, keep a good grip on your purses and keep them close to your body. And everyone remember the most important rule of all: Remove your badge as soon as you leave the show so someone on the street doesn't target you as a jeweler.

Culture shock is inevitable, so when in Rome do as the Romans do. Most people are honest, but beware of anyone who acts suspiciously. Be wary of people on the street who offer to hail a cab for you. Either have the hotel doorman or an officially uniformed employee of the airport or train station hail a cab, or do it yourself. If someone unknown does hail a cab for you, tip him (or her) a dollar, say thanks, take the cab and leave. Don't listen to any "sales pitches" of pre-paying for your trip.

More cab tips. Don't take a chance with a cabbie who seems drunk or acts suspiciously. Confirm with an airport or hotel official if a cabbie demands payment in advance (unless a pre-payment policy is posted in the cab). Try to check a map in case a cabbie seems to take you the long way around (travel within the New York show area should not exceed half an hour). Note the cab company's name and phone as well as the cabbie's name and medallion number, in case you have a complaint or leave something in the cab.

Luggage deserves the same care. Do not surrender your bags to anyone but officially uniformed airline, train or hotel employees. When in doubt, carry it yourself.

If you drive to the show, pay the extra expense to park in a reputable parking lot with 24-hour security. When the hotel or convention center holding the show provides parking, check what security provisions have been made. In all cases, take everything of value out of your car. Don't park in questionable areas, and don't risk onstreet parking, especially in cities. The chance of your car being hit, stolen, burglarized or towed is great.

Tips from suppliers

JCK asked some veteran industry suppliers for suggestions on working trade shows. Virtually all have been on both sides of the display case, as exhibitor and as observer/buyer. Most also make it a point to go to Europe at least once a year to keep up with the trends there.

"Something as important as a trade show should never be rushed," says Murry Shapiro, president of Heirloom 73, Freehold, N.J. Shapiro, who attends various European shows to get ideas, offers his own system: Work the show in order, from right to left, and visit every vendor to see what is offered in terms of price, quality and style. Take notes, and later revisit the vendors with items that caught your eye.

He also suggests coffee breaks every two hours or so. "A ten-minute break, a chance to sit down, catch your breath, have a cup of coffee and look over your notes is very important," he says. "It keeps your rested and your mind clear."

Judy Ban of Leslie's Mfg., New York, also follows the cover-first/visit-later system. She suggests noting particularly interesting exhibits right on the floor map. She also recommends taking the brochures and literature that vendors offer, and discarding any "definite nos" at the end of the day. As for personal comfort, Ban says she drinks lots of water, wears comfortable shoes and accepts the fact that shows are tiring.

Everything else is secondary to just getting up and going to the show, says Tom Chatham, president of Tom Chatham Created Gems, San Francisco, Cal.

"The most important thing, regardless of being open to buy, is going to the show. You can't learn unless you go." Once at the show, he suggests familiarizing yourself with current jewelry fashions and trends. Hindsight, he says, never helped anyone to sell jewelry.

He also stresses the importance of going to the New York show *and* other, smaller shows with smaller vendors. Retailers should always visit their local shows as well, he says.

Chatham sympathizes with retailers who feel intimidated by vendors. Don't be afraid to tell a vendor you don't appreciate his high-pressure sales and don't feel obligated to buy, he says. Retailers also should make sure pieces are returnable in case they don't look the same under store lights.

Richard Korwin, president of Wideband, New Rochelle, N.Y., is a great advocate of teamwork. He brings a group to share the legwork. Walk first, buy later is his general philosophy. Some veterans may be able to buy on their first pass around the show, he says. But novices should compare lines, make notes, then go back to buy. Korwin also cautions first-timers to beware of fly-by-night firms.

Betsy Fuller, a jewelry designer and owner of Betsy Fuller Inc., Hobe Sound, Fla., advises getting an overview before spending all your money in one place. She also advocates knowing what your customers want and keeping a checklist, though she doesn't rule out an occasional impulsive whim. She says some of her most successful merchandise is the result of impulse buying.

Alan Revere, owner of Alan Revere Jewelry Design in San Francisco, Cal., reminds retailers that not every firm has a catalog and traveling representatives. Some firm, his included, exhibit only at shows. Buyers either see the line there or not at all. Allot enough time to see these firms, he suggests.

You've Got To Be Kidding!

Editorial ◆ *June 1988*

Please take a good long look at the young woman in the center of the page. That my friends, is high fashion, 1988-style. Her outfit and her jewelry may seem a bit off-the-wall to some people but don't take one look and turn away. Our business is tied very closely to this woman, or at least it should be.

Clothes like this may not be typical party dress code in Alpena, Michigan, or Lufkin, Texas. They may not even be the right thing to wear to a good restaurant in New York or San Francisco. But their influence is real. The cut of the neckline, the bare arm, the skirt length, the hair style: they'll all influence women's wear on sale at such far-apart fashion stores as Bloomingdales and Filene's Budget Basement. In turn, they'll influence the jewelry women wear and those who buy that jewelry.

Knowing which fashions will filter through the system from high style to ready-to-wear can help any jeweler twice. Once, when ordering inventory and twice when advising uncertain customers what fashion is all about and how to accessorize it.

Sadly, the jewelry industry is not particularly fashion conscious. Ten dollars to the first notarized, sworn statement that not a single green leisure suit (men) or bouffant hairdo (women) showed up at a state jewelry convention this year. But things are getting better. A random check we made last year among fairly small, independent stores found seven of the eight polled declaring, "Yes, fashion is important," and "Yes, we are paying more attention."

What's less encouraging is that a lot of male jewelers believe that fashion is "women's business." That's way out-of-date thinking. If fashion dictates short sleeves are in, the store that doesn't stock and sell bracelets (in styles and prices that suit its customers' tastes) is throwing business away. If green is the season's dominant color, any store that doesn't capitalize on this by stocking promoting and selling a full range of green stones (how familiar are your customers with peridot, tourmaline and tsavorite?) again is throwing business away.

This is not "women's business." This is jewelry business.

How do you cultivate fashion consciousness? Like anything else you want to learn—from accounting to zoology—you study and you practice. There is no magical process through which you become knowledgeable about fashion just because you feel you should be. I'm talking about hard work.

The theory, the home-study lessons, are readily available. Many magazines are heavily dedicated to fashion—*Elle, Glamour* and *Vogue* are among the best. But most new readers should approach them cautiously. All three tend to highlight extremes, fashions and ideas that are closest to the edge of what even the fashion gurus are willing to accept. Some seem deliberately designed to outrage rather than excite or please. These extremes, however, are often the blueprints from which more conventional imitations and derivations will evolve.

Reading magazines is far from enough. You also have to know what people in your area, particularly women, actually buy and wear. About the best way to find out is to go shopping in women's specialty stores and women's clothing sections in department stores. It doesn't take too long to get an idea of what's likely to be popular in colors, fabrics and designs in any coming season.

The advance guidance that clothing gives can be a real plus, by the way. It may exasperate shoppers in search of summer clothes that fall items take over the display racks in July. But the jeweler who places orders at the summer shows can use these early seasonal changeovers to plan some of his or her own buying for fall and Christmas.

So far, I've talked about building a fashion sense. When the talk comes to accessorizing, the jeweler himself can teach, not learn. Only rarely do the fashion books discuss precious jewelry; typically new fashion showings use costume. So the opening is ready-made for any jeweler to display and promote the precious pieces that will adorn the clothing and complete the fashion picture. Even after a particular fashion look passes, the jewelry will keep its appeal and value.

Any store that's not tuned in to the fashion world is letting sales slip away. What sensible store owner wants to be caught in that situation when it is so simple to reverse it?

---

20 Ways To Close The Sale

September 1987

"An objection is the beginning of a sale," says Bette Frazier, diamond department assistant manager at Albert Smyth Co. In Timonium, Md. Why? Because objections let a salesperson recognize, and then resolve, the customer's conflicts.

Frazier, who's in charge of jewelry sales training at Smyth, is excited about selling. For her it's a challenge, an art form and, above all, a source of great satisfaction. One senses she could sell the soot off Santa. But how?

Certainly making the sale requires more than a catchy "close." The sale actually begins when a customer walks through the door, explains John F. Lawhon in his book *Selling Retail,* published last year by J. Franklin, Tulsa, Okla.

The salesperson must expertly execute four key phases before he can hope to successfully close a sale, says this seasoned professional. The four:
1. Greet the customer;
2. Understand fully what his need/problem is;
3. Select the proper solution;
4. Present the solution.

Once a salesperson has fulfilled these obligations, he's ready to close the sale. How can he be sure the time is right? The customer is ready to buy, says Lawhon, when needs have been met and the item's promised benefits exceed its price.

There are more visible signals, however. The customer may keep coming back to a specific item or seem "verbally enthralled" with a piece, says Stuart Packard, owner of Carson's Jewelers in Lancaster, N.Y. Knowing that a customer's ready often is simply intuitive.

Whatever the signal, you can't afford to miss it. If a sale is not "asked for" or closed, there's a good chance the customer won't buy, says Packard. "[A customer] talks herself beyond whatever the item is. She says 'I'll think about it and come back later.' " She never does; the sale is lost.

Here are some practiced techniques for closing in on that treasured sale.

Give 'em what they want: The familiar "We need to think it over" doesn't have to mean customers are heading out. When a couple at Carl A. Doubet Inc. in Wilmington, Del., handed that line to owner J. Edward Doubet, he said, "While you do, why not let me polish those rings you're wearing?"

He took the rings to the back of the store, giving the couple the few private moments they required. "When I came back, the sale was made," recalls Doubet. "They wanted time to think, so I had to think of a way to give it to them," while keeping them in the store.

"Don't be selfish!" Sometimes a mature couple stops in to pick out a nice piece of jewelry for the wife. The husband clearly is enjoying himself, pleased with the idea of giving this gift to his wife. Finally they settle on a beautiful diamond and sapphire ring.

Now that everything seems decided, the trouble begins. "The wife starts saying, 'Honey, we don't need this; it's so expensive,' " says Stuart Packard of Carson's Jewelers. In an instant this sale can be lost. . . or saved.

"I say to the wife, 'You know, you really are being selfish, not letting your husband do this for you.' Once she realizes she is denying her husband pleasure by not accepting the ring, she's ready to buy." Nine times out of ten the sale is won, Packard says.

"Here if you need me": If a customer says she really should confer with her husband before buying, tell her to take the item now with the knowledge that she can return it if necessary.

Say, "I'm so confident your husband will approve of your choice in rings, why not buy it now? If he disapproves in the least, bring it back and I'll refund your money, no questions asked." This ploy is a safe bet for both parties.

Comparison shopping: Similarly, when customers are comparison shopping, suggest they charge the item and take it along. "If they need to compare, that's their right," says Russell Rush, manager of Shuler's in Wayne, Pa. "But tell them, 'Take this with you to shop around.' Even experts can't carry a true [mental] picture of a jewelry item." This gesture also demonstrates your confidence in the item's quality and value.

Moral obligation: Sometimes the customer just isn't ready to buy now. Yet you sense she's really attached to the item. "Hold it for a week," says Larry Hirsch, president of Westerly Jewelry Co., Westerly, R.I. "I tell the customer that I can see how much she really likes the item. So I say, 'Listen, I'll take it out of my showcase for a week. That way no one else can get it before you decide.' "

Will holding the piece press her into buying it? "Typically she's very pleased that I'd do this for her," Hirsch says. "It doesn't really make her feel guilty, but it does create a sense of moral obligation. If for some reason she decides not to buy the piece, the goodwill established almost ensures she'll be back for something else in the future."

List the benefits: If signals are go and the customer voices no objections yet still seems hesitant, what then? "At that point we try to impress upon [customers] the benefits that go along with the purchase," says Larry Hirsch. "We tell them they'll receive a full written appraisal, lifetime service—such as cleaning and checking the setting—and full trade-in value."

Don't forget to note the item's romance as well as its lasting value, both emotional and financial.

Assume the sale is made: "Sometimes I'll just have the sales ticket lying on the counter and casually begin filling it out," says Bette Frazier of Albert Smyth. If the customer doesn't object, the sale is made.

A gentle prodding, like "Would you care to have this wrapped?" also forces a customer beyond the purchase agreement.

Reduce to the ridiculous: "You've been married 20 years. This anniversary ring, costing $2000, comes to under $9 a month over the past 20 years. A small price to pay for something which represents a lifelong commitment. Don't you agree, Mr. Smith?"

Let the customer choose the close: "Will this be cash or credit?" The question, an oldie but goodie, forces the customer to address the issue of buying.

Ask for the sale (the novel approach): A customer needs reinforcement for her buying decision, says David Lahmers, executive vice president-administration for Osterman Jewelers, Sylvania, Ohio. Encourage her; ask her to buy. "Say something like, 'Since you like it so much, go for it,' " suggests Lahmers.

Know when to stop selling: Once the customer agrees to buy, stop selling! Selling beyond the point of sale can turn off the customer . . . and lose the sale. "If you continue to talk, people can get distracted," says Russell Rush of Shuler's. "They may end up saying, 'It's late; I have to get going.'"

If specific information isn't covered during the sale, wait until the transaction is completed, adds Rush; then share that detail. "This makes customers feel good, too, because you're not pushing them out the door."

The firm "no": Here lies the final test of true champions, says Lawhon in *Retail Selling*. If the sale simply can not be made, offer a sincere and gracious thank you. Your job now is to win potential customers as friends and bring them back to your store in the near future.

Customer leads: "Oft times customers tell you where they want to go," says David Lahmers of Osterman's. "If they start looking at something, then bring it out and show it to them. And start building the romance all over again!"

Not over 'til it's over: Add-on sales, whether on the spot or down-the-road, can go a long way to increasing your bottom line.

"You already have the customer in a buying mood," says David Lahmers. "There's no better time to tap him for another purchase." What can you lose?

Playing match-maker: The easiest type of add-on sale is the matching item, says Carson's Stuart Packard. A gold bracelet to go with a chain or a diamond pendant to go with diamond stud earrings are two examples.

Urgent! If there's some reason why the customer should make an additional purchase *now,* be sure to inform him, says Shuler's Russell Rush. Perhaps the color of the stone in a pendant being purchased perfectly matches that in a pair of earrings. "You might say, 'Of course there's a chance I could get earrings to match as well in the future, but I can't guarantee it,' " says Rush. "If the customer doesn't wish to present the gifts together, I offer to hold [the second purchase] until he's ready."

Taking care of number one: If the initial item purchased is obviously a gift, suggest the customer get "a little something" for himself, too. He's selected such a nice gift for his friend/wife/lover. Why not a small reward for doing so well?

One thing leads to another: When a couple or a groom-to-be chooses an engagement ring, the obvious question is "Have you selected your wedding gifts?" Albert Smyth's Bette Frazier even seizes the moment to demonstrate eternity rings. At the least, the presentation plants a seed in the minds of the soon-to-be honeymooners.

Wishful thinking: At Westerly Jewelry Co., Larry Hirsch keeps a "wish list" for every customer. The listing names items bought and specific matching or associated items that the customer might wish to acquire.

"One gentleman who came in wanted 'something different' for his wife," explains Hirsch. "So we showed him a 2-ct. heart-shaped diamond pendant, which he bought.

"Some time later he came back and again wanted something different. This time we were able to show him heart-shaped diamond earrings to match the previously bought pendant," says Hirsch. The wish list instantly let the salesperson helping the customer know what was desirable. And the sale was made. Since then, the same gentleman has returned the ring with three heart-shaped diamonds.

And finally: Following a purchase, reinforce the customer's decision to buy, says Lawhon in *Retail Selling*. Make certain you send each customer off with two business cards (one for a friend). Finally, follow up the transaction with a personalized thank-you note. Even if the sale was not made, let that potential customer know you'll keep him in mind should you see something he'd like. And when you do, give him a call, bring him in, and go for it!

Insurance Replacement: Why Jewelers Are Losing The Business

July 1987

Last year, a regular customer of jeweler Curtis Greenberg reported the loss of her diamond ring to her insurance company, State Farm. Greenberg, an American Gem Society jeweler in Steubenville, Ohio, had provided a detailed appraisal for the ring which he had sold for $2000. He expected the customer to come back for a replacement when her claim was settled.

Greenberg never made that sale. The insurance adjuster gave her a choice: Settle for $1600 cash or accept a "similar" ring from a discount wholesale jewelry outlet in Pittsburgh, 40 miles away.

The woman took the second option and brought the ring back to Greenberg for a look. The ring did have a 60-pt. center stone, as did the ring he'd sold her. But there was still a big difference: Greenberg's diamond was a G color VS_2 clarity, while the replacement was a J SI_2, costing about 40% less on the wholesale market.

Greenberg not only lost that replacement sale, but a customer as well.

"She thinks we overcharged her. Not only that, she was paying premiums on a $2000 ring. The one she got back cost only $1600. It made us look like crooks. She hasn't been back. In fact, I had 12 customers file insurance claims last year and I made zero sales."

Familiar complaint: Sound familiar?

Nearly half of JCK's Retail Jewelers Panel members say they can offer similar tales of losing customers to insurance adjusters who steer claimants to discount operations which offer lower-quality replacements. Discounters and professional insurance replacement companies are taking much of this business from retail jewelers—legitimately and not—though one insurance firm, Jewelers Mutual, does offer policies which require jewelry owners to replace lost or stolen items through the store in which they purchased them.

Insurance executives deny requiring claimants to buy from a particular outlet, especially one as much as 40 mile away, as in Greenberg's case. They also stress that insurance policies stipulate replacement of like quality. And they make no apologies about looking for discounts as long as the customer is well-served.

However, a company's stated policy and the way it is carried out in the field may vary widely, say jewelers who deal with insurance replacements. The majority of jewelers interviewed say that aggressive adjusters, who bend the rules in their efforts to save money, present the real problem.

Thus Louisville, Ky., jeweler William Brundage says adjusters constantly badger him for large discounts to settle claims. His refusal to grant such discounts has cost him a lot of business and, he claims, put him on some adjusters' black list.

"I've had customers inform me that they couldn't do business with me because their insurance adjuster told them I was uncooperative," says Brundage.

Brundage, vice president of the Kentucky Retail Jewelers Association, says he's a fighter, so he carried his complaint against State Farm to the state Insurance Commissioner.

Proof needed: The state took no action against State Farm or its adjusters, says Tom Belt, chief enforcement officer, because Brundage could not prove the adjusters had blacklisted him.

"The company's position was that it would replace items of equal value at the best price possible," says Belt. "They said they had to seek discounts to maintain competitive premium rates. The company also claimed they are one of the area's largest jewelry buyers and are thus entitled to bargain for large volume discounts which Brundage did not offer."

"Poppycock," says Brundage. "They deal with the Perlsteins of Louisville" (a reference to the Philadelphia, Pa., jeweler charged with greatly overstating the quality of the diamonds he sold to customers).

"We sell 'ideal-cut' diamonds, usually G VS quality or better. They replace them with J color 'spread' stones." (Spread stones have a higher crown and larger table, which retains weight with no apparent increase in beauty. Thus, ideal cuts generally carry a higher per-carat cost.)

Brundage also insists he offers professional, detailed appraisals which make little difference when discount retailers lie about the quality of diamonds they provide.

Harassment: Policies which permit claimants a second opinion on replacement jewelry can help reduce the problem of inflated diamond grades, say insurance agents. Jewelers counter that adjusters have tactics against this as well.

Donald Riffe of Wight Jewelers, Ontario, Cal., complains that adjusters will often harass claimants who insist upon comparable replacements.

"First they send people 50 miles away to a discount store. If the customers don't like it, the adjusters start dragging their feet and delaying everything. This forces the claimants to take off from work to write letters, visit jewelers and telephone inquiries."

This tactic works often enough to make it operating procedure in some offices, say jewelers with regular dealings with adjusters.

Charles Zerbe of Zerbe Jewelers in Colorado Springs recalls: "One woman came in with [a replacement stone] which wasn't even close in quality to the one I had sold her. I told her to fight it but she said 'I already went through such hassles with the adjusters that I don't want to fight any more.'"

Playing by the rules: Some insurance executive acknowledge that adjusters can be aggressive in their efforts to cut costs of claims. But they insist they play by the rules.

George Ahrens, State Farms' claims supervisor in Newark, Ohio, says the adjusters generally follow the statements on jewelers' appraisals to determine the quality of stones in replacement pieces. But he adds: "One diamond can have five different appraisals so often there's little credibility there. Adjusters can't grade diamonds so they have to take the seller's word for what they are getting."

Insurance executives also say the information on jewelers' sales slips and appraisals is often very inadequate.

"If we have a sales slip that says only '1 ladies' diamond ring: $1200,' what are we supposed to do?" asks one insurance agent.

Discounting rules: Adjusters contacted by JCK declined to comment. However, Ahrens, whose office supervises activities in Curtis Greenberg's area, says that State Farm's policy is to replace lost jewelry with like kind and quality from a jeweler in the city where the loss occurred. If the claimant wants cash, the company will provide funds *in the amount for which we can replace the items.*

In other words, if the adjuster can get a 20% discount on a $1000 piece of jewelry, the company will give the claimant $800.

Even less aggressive adjusters seek discounts these days. And companies specializing in discount insurance replacement are a fact of life, says Carol Basden, who manages jewelers block insurance programs for the agency of Hilb, Rogal & Hamilton in Birmingham, Ala. Such companies often are run by gemologists or retired retail jewelers, and generally offer insurers lower prices for replacement goods.

"These people have been in business for many years and are fully competent to make certain the customer receives quality replacements," she stresses.

Her company's rule is to allow claims under $3000 to go through retail jewelers. "Over that and the insurers usually insist on taking it to a replacement service."

Replacement firms also provide much of the sterling flatware and giftware to insurance adjusters, says Bob Johnson, consultant and former director of the Sterling Silversmiths Guild, a trade group comprising the major U.S. manufacturers.

"These companies sprang up during the silver boom of 1979-'80, when there were a lot of thefts, and have stayed in business," he says. But even they are starting to lose

business to several silver manufacturers, which now offer factory-direct replacements.

Educating customers: Unfortunately, jewelers can take little direct action against any of these situations. Any complaints or legal action concerning unfair trade practices or inferior replacements must come from the consumer.

The jeweler does have one weapon, however. He or she should educate customers about their rights as policyholders. Retailers who have held their own against adjusters' tactics stress this again and again.

Carol Basden advises jewelers to:

• Know what most homeowners' policies cover and what rights policyholders have.

• Be sure customers' homeowners' policies cover high value items like jewelry. Many policies do not. If not, a separate schedule listing the jewelry is a must.

• Tell customers to speak to their insurance agent about what is covered in their policy.

• Be sure to tell customers that recent, detailed appraisals are a must if jewelry is listed separately in a policy. They should keep photos of their jewelry in a fireproof box or in their office.

• Tell customers they have a right to get independent appraisals for replacement goods.

"Most policies allow this. But jewelers should tell customers to check for this clause. They should also inform customers that they must pay for the appraisal if there is a dispute with the insurance company."

• Advise customers on loss prevention. Tell them to keep expensive jewelry in a safe deposit box. Have settings and clasps checked periodically to be certain they are sound.

"It's surprising how many people don't do this, even with very expensive jewelry," she notes.

• Finally, tell them that if they do not receive a like quality replacement, they have the right to take action in court.

One other remedy, says Basden, is Jewelers Mutual Personal Jewelry Program. This plan requires policyholders to replace jewelry through the retailer who sold them the original piece.

When a customer purchases a piece of jewelry, the retailer provides an application and appraisal form. The customer sends the form on to JM.

"Customers can bring other items [purchased elsewhere] and add them to the JM policy," she explains. "The retailer is protected two ways. First, replacement can be made only through the retailer who provides the appraisal form. Second, the policy provides for replacement jewelry only, not cash restitution."

If customers move, they can maintain coverage by having their jewelry reappraised by a Jewelers Mutual jeweler in their new city. Any replacement business then goes to that jeweler.

Practical Guide
To Appraising Jewelry

April 1987

INSURANCE APPRAISAL:
Granny's Sapphire and Diamond Rings

The take-in

A satisfied customer is a customer for life. So I wasn't surprised when Martha Jones returned to my store with two more jewelry items to appraise.

I remember when she first needed an insurance appraisal. She had heard about my detailed appraisals at a church social. Her friends came to me to provide memories, not just to appraise their jewelry.

And so she came, clutching her mother's ruby ring in her hand. She wanted an appraisal for insurance purposes, but she also wanted to know everything about that ring.

This time Marti, as most everyone calls her, brought two items, a sapphire and diamond ring and a green diamond ring, which her daughters recently received from their grandmother. The grandmother was advanced in age and wanted her granddaughters to enjoy the jewelry during her own lifetime.

Marti was going to include the jewelry on her insurance policy because the daughters still lived at home. So she needed an insurance appraisal, but also wanted to have some photographs to help her remember the jewelry after her daughters left home.

During the take-in, I tested all diamonds to make sure they were real and measured the colored stones. Even though Marti was a repeat customer, I discussed my appraisal fee (a minimum charge, plus a fee for every piece after the first) and the length of time needed to complete the appraisal.

When this was done, I filled out the take-in sheet. I described these two pieces as 1) Lady's blue stone and diamond yellow metal ring, and 2) Lady's green diamond gray metal ring.

The appraisal

Prepared for: Martha Jones
Address: 235 Main St., New Bedford, Mass. 02740
Purpose: Insurance appraisal
Date: Jan. 23, 1987
Item #1: Lady's 14k yellow gold ring, cushion antique-cut sapphire and diamond ring.

A. Sapphire: Natural violetish-blue sapphire, medium tone, medium intensity, even color throughout. It is a fine cushion antique style cut and is of a very good polish. No inclusions are apparent to the unaided eye.

Tests: 10X magnification—fingerprint inclusion; polariscope—double refraction; refractometer—refractive index of 1.76.

Fingerprint inclusion: Fingerprint inclusions take their name from interesting clouds of hollow inclusions filled with liquid and gas that form patterns resembling fingerprints around crystal inclusions.

Measurements: Leveridge gauge—12.50mm length, 8.30mm width, 8.80mm depth.

Estimated carat weight: 9.50 ct.

B. Diamonds: Sixteen full cut of I color and SI_1 clarity, according to the GIA diamond grading system.

Tests: 10X magnification, Diamond Master—diamond indicator. Conclusion: Diamond.

Measurements: Leveridge gauge—2.50mm diameter (average measurement).

Estimated carat weight: .05 ct. each, .80 ct. total weight.

C. Mounting: 14k yellow gold.

The faceted cushion antique-cut blue sapphire stone is set in the center with 16 evenly spaced 15k yellow gold prongs.

The 16 full-cut diamonds are set in multiple 14k yellow gold prongs all around and just below the sapphire stone.

The entire unit is soldered to a scallop design unit approximately 22.30mm long, 18.20mm wide. The scallop unit consists of 16 units with a black enamel finish on the top portion all around.

The under bezel consists of an open work portion approximately 2.70mm wide. The remainder of the under bezel is plain—4.80mm wide on the shoulders tapering down to 3.90mm at the ends.

The shank is 4.20mm wide at the shoulder tapering down to 2.20mm at the bottom.

Black enamel finish approximately 1.50mm down the shank on both sides. The remainder of the shank is plain.

Amount of metal in the mounting: 4.6610 dwts.

D. Estimated replacement value: $2800.

Item #2: Lady's platinum square-style diamond ring with 12 baguettes, finger size 7.

1. *Diamonds:* 13

A. Major: One green, brilliant cut.

Tests: 10X magnification; polariscope—single refraction; refractometer—above the limits; Diamond Master—diamond indicator. Conclusion: Diamond.

Measurements: Leveridge gauge—7.70mm diameter, 4.10mm depth.

Estimated carat weight: 1.48 ct.

Color grade: Dark bluish green (tourmaline shade).

Clarity: Small inclusions. A clover-leaf effect is seen around the culet of a brilliant-cut diamond, the pavilion of which has been subjected to the beams of Deuterons or Alpha particles in a cyclotron to impart a green color to the stone. Since the penetration of such particles is not great, and the color is concentrated at the maximum depth of penetration, the zone of color forms a scalloped "halo" around the culet that has been likened to the shape of a cloverleaf. It is sometimes also referred to as an "umbrella" effect.

The "umbrella" color margin when seen near the culet of a diamond is proof that the stone has been treated in a cyclotron.

In the case of a green colored diamond, the color tends towards the dark bluish green of tourmaline, which is the color of the major diamond in this piece.

B. Minor: 12 baguette cut diamonds, I color and SI$_1$ clarity grade, according to GIA terminology.

Tests: 10X magnification; Diamond Master—diamond indicator, Conclusion: Diamond.

Measurements: Leveridge gauge. Two—4.50mm long, 1.80mm wide, 1.40mm deep. Estimated carat weight: .13 ct. each, .26 ct. total weight.

Four—3.00mm long, 1.80mm wide, 1.40mm deep. Estimated carat weight: .08 ct. each, .32 ct. total weight.

Two—3.50mm long, 1.80mm wide, 1.40mm deep. Estimated carat weight: .09 ct. each, .18 ct. total weight.

Estimated total weight: 1.12 ct.

C. Mounting: Stamping 10% IRD PLAT, finger size 7. The top of the mounting is square in style, approximately 12.00mm.

The green diamond is set in the center in a four-prong head. The baguette diamonds are set all around; looking down at the finger, three baguettes lie end-to-end at the top and at the bottom of the center stone. Two baguettes lie side-by-side on each side of the center stone.

A low basket open-style unit is attached underneath 3.00mm wide in the center opening to 3.80mm at the ends—two sides down the finger. The two side units are 3.80mm all along.

The two tapered baguette diamonds are set one on each shoulder of the mounting.

The remainder of the shank is plain 2.00mm tapering down to 1.50mm at the bottom.

Amount of metal in the mounting: 3.66 dwts.

D. Estimated replacement value: $5700

The appraiser

Paul R. Rousseau of La France Jeweler, New Bedford, Mass.

Retail jeweler, 34 years

Diamond accreditation from Gemological Institute of America, 1958

Diploma in gemology from GIA, 1959

Associate member, American Gem Society, since 1954

Registered jeweler, AGS, 1957

Certified Gemologist, AGS, 1960

Certified Gemologist Appraiser, AGS, 1983

Member of the AGS Appraisal Committee

1982—participated in the First International Gemological Symposium held in Los Angeles in honor of the 50th anniversary of the Gemological Institute of America.

Notes to the appraisal

(usually included in a letter accompanying the appraisal)

Measurements are done using a leverdige gauge, a standard industry practice to measure gemstone size.

Those millimeter measurements of length, width and depth are then used to determine an estimated carat weight,

according to standard formulas. For the sapphire, this formula was used: Length X width X depth X specific gravity X .0026= carat weight. For the green diamond, this formula was used: Diameter^2 X depth X .0061= carat weight.

The amount of metal in the mounting is calculated by this formula: Gross weight of the item—weight of the stones in carats X .13 = net weight of the mounting. This is a standard industry formula.

I didn't try to date the jewelry since the client was not interested in finding out how old the pieces were.

I carefully explain the appraisal with the client. I discuss how all measurements and tests are done and what they mean. Clients appreciate the detailed descriptions of their jewelry.

At this time, I also present a list of questions that the customer should ask her insurance agent before deciding on the type of coverage needed for her jewelry. The questions, included in the AGS Handbook of Jewelry and Gemstone Appraising, cover such topics as types of policies, amounts of deductibles, extent of coverage, amount of depreciation, what is cash value, etc.

Item #1: Under 10X magnification, the sapphire's straight growth lines and a fingerprint inclusion were revealed. That, along with double refraction indicated in the polariscope and a refractive index reading of 1.76, gave me proof that the stone is a natural blue sapphire.

Although I haven't adopted a color grading system, the color description used is one outlined in the AGS appraisal handbook.

The Diamond Master was used both in the take-in process and again during the appraisal process to determine if the diamonds were real. They were.

Diamond cut and clarity grades are done to GIA and AGS standards.

The standard acid test was used to determine if mounting was real gold. It was. The ring was stamped 14k and noted on the appraisal.

The black enamel finish on the baguette diamonds was tested with a pinpoint. Since the pin didn't penetrate the surface, I knew it was very hard and most likely black enamel. Had the pin penetrated the surface, that would have indicated the finish was acrylic.

Setting the value for this item: To determine the value, I looked up the price for that type of blue sapphire and diamonds on suppliers' price lists. The labor and materials for the mounting were calculated at $100 per pennyweight. Then a keystone markup was included. Based on those figures, the value of the sapphire ring was determined to be $2817. Then comparing that value with ones offered by an average fine jewelry store in our area, I determined the average current market price to be $2800. This does not necessarily reflect the price at which the appraised jewelry may be purchased at La France Jeweler.

Item #2: To identify the diamond, I used the Diamond Master tester, but also observed the diamond under 10X magnification. Those observations and the single refraction given by the polariscope and the stone's "above the limits" reading on the refractometer indicated to me that the stone was diamond.

The cloverleaf effect is proof that the diamond was irradiated. This is an important consideration in the value since naturally-occurring green diamonds are rare and extremely expensive.

The baguette diamonds were also tested by the Diamond Master and observed under 10X magnification to make sure they were real diamonds.

The mounting was determined to be 10% iridium platinum by a standard metal test.

Setting the value for this item: This was determined by the individual values of the green diamond, baguettes, the mounting and labor costs. After consulting with suppliers of treated diamonds, the green diamond was valued at $2369 per carat. I consulted with diamond melee suppliers to determine a $750 per carat price for the baguettes. Then a 60% markup was included, before I added in the cost of the labor and materials, to arrive at a cost of $5692.80. I compared this with the average current market price for this item in fine jewelry stores and determined the value to $5700. This is not necessarily the price at which this ring could be purchased at La France Jeweler.

FORENSIC APPRAISAL: *The purloined ring*

The take-in

When Joedoakes Insurance Adjusters called me, I thought it was a prank call. Why would an insurance company need an insurance appraisal, I asked. The reason became clear as the adjuster told his tale.

Client Joan Wellington Smyth of Carmel, Cal., and Newport, R.I., recently filed a claim for $23,000 with her insurance company. She believed something had happened to her diamond ring.

Mrs. Smyth's story: After her jeweler repaired her diamond engagement ring in 1986, she noticed that the diamond was more yellow. She believed it was not her original ring, appraised for $23,000 in 1979. So Mrs. Smyth paid for a new appraisal at the same jewelry store that had been servicing her for many years. (This store also had done the 1979 appraisal.) This time the value was determined to be $7250. Mrs. Smyth gasped, then ordered her secretary to file an insurance claim.

After hearing those details, I knew that the insurance adjuster wanted a forensic appraisal. I was to check over someone else's work. I had to examine the ring and determine if it met the description of the one listed on the 1979 appraisal, since that was the value for which Mrs. Smyth had been insured.

I explained my fee schedule to the adjuster. For this type of appraisal I charge $25 per hour for initial discussions, and $100-$350 per hour for the time I spend outside my store either examining the stone in the client's home or testifying in the courtroom. The adjuster agreed to these fees, knowing he needed a professional to handle the case.

The forensic report

Prepared for: Joedoakes Insurance Adjusters
Address: 9999 Main St., Ventura, Cal. 93999
Purpose: Forensic appraisal
Date: Jan. 20, 1987

The examination was done in the home of Joan Wellington Smyth during the morning hours. The windows of her home face the west beach. In the morning, this location provides lighting reasonably equivalent to north light.

I was asked to examine the diamond ring and determine if it was the one described in a 1979 appraisal.

My observations: One white ring with a butterfly guard inside the shank and set with diamonds. The mass of the ring and microscopic examination of the metal confirms the opinion that the ring is platinum.

The ring is set with one brilliant-style diamond that measures 7.99 to 8.03mm in diameter and 4.82mm in depth. These measurements yield a calculated weight of 1.89 ct. by the ADL formula.

The diamond was compared to my GIA-graded master diamond set and found to match the K color master stone best. The diamond was not checked for fluorescence.

A copy of the plotting diagram is attached. In my examination, I plotted only the significant features without removing the stone from the mounting. I have graded the clarity as SI_2, according to the GIA system.

The ring is also set with two tapered baguette diamonds, one on each side of the center stone. The diamonds measure an average of 2.5mm tapering to 1.75mm wide, by 5.2mm long. The depth was not available. This yields an estimated total weight of approximately .3 ct. by the ADL formula.

I am in agreement with the value of $7250 listed on the appraisal of Oct. 4, 1986.

That appraisal was done by J. Henri, Jeweler. It described the diamond center stone as: 1.88 ct., H-I color, SI_1 clarity. The mounting was listed as platinum, and .33 ct. of baguette diamonds were listed.

My conclusions: The diamond I examined does not meet the description given in the 1979 appraisal, which was: Platinum diamond ring with one full, round-cut diamond. Estimated weight—1.99 ct. Clarity grade—VVS_1. Color grade—fine white. Proportions and finish—excellent. Two tapered baguettes, estimated total weight—.46 ct. Estimated replacement cost—$23,000.

This leads to the conclusion that either the 1979 appraisal was in error or the diamond ring I examined is not the same ring. Since the insurance company accepted the 1979 appraisal as fact, I must conclude that this ring is not the one originally described.

The appraisal done in 1986 was reasonably correct, but incomplete. It didn't include a plotting diagram, measurements, photograph or other supporting and identifying details. The appraisal also didn't include the appraiser's qualifications and procedure.

Although this appraisal was better than many I examine each year, it does not reflect the quality and professionalism consistent with a jeweler of long standing.

While I was examining the ring, Mrs. Smyth asked how a diamond could get changed in a ring like this. She stated that J. Henri was the only jewelry store that had ever handled the ring. She also raised doubts about the jeweler/trade shop that actually did the repair work.

My examination of the ring gives me no indication that it has ever contained any other diamond.

If this is not the original ring and if the change was not made by someone associated with the Smyths, my own inquiries into the reputation of the jeweler and the trade shop suggest that IF substitution occurred, it was done by error rather than deception.

Mr. Smyth described her relationship with the jeweler as very good, to the degree that the ring would sometimes be left without getting a receipt. This sloppy procedure makes the jeweler liable because he is unable to prove that any item left was actually returned to the client. It also leaves the jeweler with no recourse against the trade shop in the event of an error.

There seems to be another series of errors, committed by the insurance company. If I am interpreting the schedules and the statements made by Mrs. Smyth correctly, the insurance company accepted the 1979 appraisal in a completely inadequate form and continued to carry the insurance without doing gemological and appraisal reviews.

This indicates that the standards for an appraisal that is acceptable by the insurance company need to be reviewed and revised. The practice of renewing insurance without a re-examination by a competent appraiser should be questioned. This should be done for the protection of the clients, the insurance company and its agents.

The appraiser

Bob Lynn of Lynn's Jewelry in Ventura, Cal.

Retail jeweler, 16+ years

Graduate Gemologist, Gemological Institute of America, 1979

Registered Jeweler, American Gem Society

Certified Gemologist, AGS, 1979

Certified Gemologist Appraiser, AGS, 1984

Member of the AGS Appraisal Committee

Notes to the appraisal

(usually included in a letter accompanying the appraisal)

I wanted to appraise the piece in the morning to work under the best lighting conditions at Mrs. Smyth's house. North light is considered the best for grading gems. I also asked for a morning appointment because color vision acuity deteriorates as the day goes on.

I used a microscope to identify both the diamonds and the platinum. Under 10X, I found inclusions that identified diamond and indicated its natural origin. I was able to identify the mounting as platinum, using the microscope. Platinum has a much finer grain than does white gold and it is also of a different color than white gold.

After the diamonds were measured with a leveridge gauge, I calculated their weight by the standard ADL formula. [ADL stands for Athos D. Leveridge, inventor of the leveridge gauge. For a round brilliant diamond the formula is radius^2 X depth X .0245 = estimated weight.] I didn't take the stones out of the mounting because I was not asked to do this.

Cut, color and clarity descriptions given are done according to the GIA diamond grading system.

I determined the ring's value by conferring with the principals of three jewelry stores in Mrs. Smyth's upper class neighborhood. I explained what I was doing and asked what they would have to pay for that type of ring, what they would ask for it and finally what they would sell it for. I also checked my own stock and asked two diamond wholesalers for their opinions. The value I determined was very close to that listed on the 1986 appraisal, so I agreed with it.

The diamond this ring contains is its original one since there were no stress marks at the bottom of the prongs, and the prongs were well burnished into the stone.

In this type of appraisal, I was asked to accept the 1979 appraisal as fact since the insurance company had already accepted it and the client had been paying premiums based on that 1979 value. That's why after examining the ring and

comparing it with the 1979 appraisal, I stated that the ring the client now had and the one described in 1979 could not be the same.

But I also had to question the appraisal and how it was done. After examining another of that jeweler's 1979 appraisals and comparing the appraised item to a ring Mrs. Smyth had in her possession, I found that the items in the 1979 appraisals were overgraded. And the appraisals were incomplete.

On a forensic appraisal, I also had to explain what might have happened to Mrs. Smyth's original ring, after determining her present ring didn't match the 1979 appraisal description. I don't believe the ring was switched by domestic help. In most such incidents, a diamond ring is replaced with a cubic zirconia ring, not another platinum diamond ring.

I also don't believe one of Mrs. Smyth's relatives switched the ring. The family is exceedingly wealthy with each having ample jewelry.

Based on my conversations with the competitors of Mrs. Smyth's jeweler and jewelry repair house, I have no questions about their reputations. If the switch did occur at either of those places, it was done by accident not on purpose.

Consequently, any of the parties involved would have a hard time proving anything against each other. There is no chain of evidence which shows continuous custodianship through receipts and logs. The jeweler had holes in his business and appraisal practices, the insurance company had problems in its underwriting, and the client wasn't a good consumer. She didn't demand receipts when she left items in the care of others.

INSURANCE APPRAISAL:
The case of the diamond & pearl bar pin

The take-in

It was a bleak morning when Melanie Montague blew into my store. She wasn't a regular customer, but I recognized the face from her frequent appearances on local TV news. She must have been involved in every civil rights protest since the late '60s.

So I was not surprised when she dumped the contents of her leather knapsack onto my counter top, searching for some pin recently given to her by her parents—"a bribe to make me come to my mother's next garden party."

Montague pulled out a lovely pearl and diamond bar pin. Her parents had suggested she insure it. She agreed, as long as they paid—for both the appraisal and the insurance.

During the take-in procedure, I asked many questions to make sure she knew what an appraisal was all about. I needed to know: What type of appraisal she wanted, if she was willing to pay the cost to test the pearls, and if she wanted to know the age of the pin.

I suggested that she allow me to test the pearls for origin. Their luster and silver-gray color made me think that they were natural. Montague agreed to pay for the xray which would reveal any clues of natural origin.

However, we agreed that the age of the pin wouldn't affect its value a great deal. Its age would be hard to determine in any case, since the piece lacked a trademark or a distinctive style. Although Montague said she often made her parents pay for ignoring her as a child, she agreed that the cost of research would be too high.

I also discussed cost with her. I explained that it would take 1 to $1^1/2$ hours to appraise the pin and told her our hourly rate. She also would have to pay for the xray. The whole process would take about three weeks. All of this was agreed upon before I filled in the take-in form.

Next I tested the pin's diamonds with my diamond tester to make sure they were not cubic zirconia.

Then I completed the take-in form. I described the pin as: One bar pin with 15 graduated pearls, 10 diamond accents, metal stamped PLAT. I included the estimated cost of the appraisal and an approximate completion date: Jan. 24, 1987 (three weeks).

The appraisal

Prepared for: Melanie Montague
Address: 7 Chicago St., Bakersfield, Cal. 93301
Purpose: Insurance appraisal
Date: Jan. 24, 1987
New York gold: $405.00 oz.
New York platinum: $518.00 oz.

One white metal diamond and natural pearl bar pin that is stamped PLAT. This bar pin measures 80mm long, 12.5mm wide in the center which tapers to 3.5mm at the tips.

Set in the existing metal that surrounds the center pearl, are three old European-cut diamonds* set at 12 o'clock and three old European-cut diamonds* set at 6 o'clock.

Also set in the existing metal of the bar pin are two old European-cut diamonds* at each tip. Two of the diamonds set at the tips of the pin are single cuts, but all the other diamonds are full cuts.

Approximate diamond weights are: Two single-cut diamonds .03 ct. each, two full-cut diamonds .06 ct. each, two full-cut diamonds .07 ct. each with four full-cut diamonds .08 ct. each. Approximate total diamond weight: .64 ct.

These diamonds are well-cut and average G-H in color and VS_1-SI_2 in clarity, according to the GIA diamond grading system.

The center section of this bar pin contains 15 graduated natural pearls that are round to semi-button in shape. The exact gradation is as follows:

Center pearl—6.65mm in diameter; two—5.65 and 5.7mm in diameter; two—5.15 and 5.38mm in diameter; two—4.6 and 5.15mm in diameter; two—5 and 3.85mm in diameter; two—3.55 and 3.7mm in diameter; two—3.22 and 3.3mm in diameter; two end pearls—2.85mm in diameter.

These pearls have a light to medium cream body color, slight rose to slight greenish overtones, very good luster with very slight surface markings and no orient. They are excellently matched.

Natural origin of pearls authenticated by xrays done by GBC Gem Lab.

This bar pin was constructed by hand and is in excellent overall condition.

Recommended insurance value: $3500**

*Replace with European-cut diamonds only.
**This value represents what one might expect to pay at the major auction houses or at large antique and collectors' shows, as this is where one is most likely to be able to replace such merchandise.

The appraiser

Carl Saenger of American Jewelry Co., Bakersfield, Cal.
Retail jeweler, 12 years

Registered jeweler, American Gem Society—1977
Certified Gemologist, AGS—1980
Certified Gemologist Appraiser, AGS—1983
Gemology courses taken from the Gemological Institute of America
Member of the AGS Appraisal Committee, Jewelers of America, Jewelers Security Alliance and California Jewelers Association

Notes to the appraisal

(usually included in a letter accompanying the appraisal)

Used terminology "stamped PLAT," and assumed metal was platinum for appraisal purposes.

Measurements are given in millimeters, which is the common jewelry industry practice.

Pearl descriptions are the standard ones listed in the AGS appraisal handbook.

The diamonds are European cut, not the most common cut today. Should my client lose one of the diamonds, she prefers to wait until a European-cut diamond of similar clarity and quality is available. A brilliant cut diamond would stand out too much.

Approximate weights are given for the diamonds, since my client did not want them removed from the setting. Weights were determined by noting the length and width of the diamonds and referring to a diamond-weight chart, listing carat weight for those size stones.

The pin was constructed by hand, which is evidenced by examining the joints. Also, the pearls appear to be uniform when looking down at the pin. However, a side view reveals that some of the pearls are more button-shaped. The only way to make the pearls appear uniform was to construct the pin mounting by hand.

The most common market for this type of item is auction houses and major collectors' houses, as I noted. My client preferred that the value from that market be used, rather than one based on the piece being assembled at today's cost of goods.

Consequently, the pin's value was determined from Sotheby's and Butterfield's catalog listings of pieces sold during their auctions. I have five years' worth of these catalogs, but I was able to determine this pin's value by finding similar bar pins which sold in the past two years.

ESTATE APPRAISAL: *The case of the purplish pins*

The take-in

I had barely finished reading the tribute to Elizabeth Adams when the phone rang. On the line was Bull, Finch & Anderson, the law firm in charge of her estate.

Attorney John Bull was in a tizzy. Adams' three children were in his office demanding that he find an appraiser right away. They all lived in different parts of the country and wanted to know who would appraise their mother's estate before they returned to their homes.

Bull called me because of previous estate appraisals I had done for him. He knew I thoroughly described each piece and provided photographs.

First, I made sure that what he needed was an estate appraisal. Then I went to his office to look over the list of items in Elizabeth Adams' estate. I gave him an estimate of my fee, based on a minimum charge plus a per piece rate for each item. I estimated that I needed five weeks to appraise the whole estate.

I was able to work out an agreement with him to appraise the jewelry in my store. Normally, many estate appraisals take place in a bank vault or the attorney's offices. However, I think I can do a better job in my store with my equipment and references nearby.

The pieces described below are just two of the 35 jewelry items in this estate. They were signed out of the bank vault as: Item #1—yellow metal, purplish stone clip pin, and Item #2—silver metal, purplish stone pin.

The appraisal

Prepared for: Mr. John Bull, Bull, Finch & Anderson, Executor u/w of Elizabeth Adams, 235 Main St., New Bedford, Mass. 02740

Purpose: Estate appraisal

Date: Jan. 5, 1987

Item #1: Lady's yellow metal, purplish colored stone clip pin. The pin consists of the following:

1. Purple stone. One oval faceted purplish stone. Tests: 10X magnification—bubbles; polariscope—single refraction; refractometer—refractive index in 1.50 range. Conclusion: Glass. Stone is 1 in. long, 3/4 in. wide.

2. Mounting: Base metal. The purplish stone is mounted on a four-prong head. A scroll design surrounds three-fourths of the stone. The pin is a clip back.

The entire pin weighs: 8.50 dwts.

Fair market value: No value

Item #2: Lady's sterling amethyst pin.

The pin consists of the following:

1. Amethyst. One oval, faceted natural amethyst that is slightly purplish, of very light tone and dull intensity. Some color zoning is evident. Stone has a fair cut and fair polish.

Tests: 10X magnification—color zoning; polariscope—double refraction; refractometer—refractive index 1.54. Conclusion: Quartz—amethyst.

Measurements: Leveridge gauge—15.50mm long, 11.50mm wide, 7.50mm deep.

Estimated carat weight: For an oval faceted stone (add length and width and divide by two to get the average diameter)—diameter^2 X depth X specific gravity X .0020 = carat weight. Estimated carat weight: 7.27 ct.

2. Mounting: Stamped "Sterling, made in Germany." The stone is set sideways with four prongs. There is an open floral motif, with a pin stem on the back.

Amount of metal in the mounting: Net weight = Gross weight—weight of the stone in carats X .13 = 2.55 dwts.

Estimated fair market value: $25

The appraiser

Paul R. Rousseau of La France Jeweler, New Bedford, Mass. Social Security number: 888-99-1111

Retail jeweler, 34 years

Diamond accreditation from Gemological Institute of America, 1958

Diploma in Gemology, GIA, 1959

Associate member, American Gem Society, since 1954

Registered Jeweler, AGS, 1957

Certified Gemologist, AGS, 1960

Certified Gemologist Appraiser, AGS, 1983

Notes to the appraisal

(usually included in a letter accompanying the appraisal)

Since the total fair market value of this estate exceeded $3000, I had to apply Internal Revenue Service regulations, listed in IRS publication #448, Federal Estate and Gift Taxes, Sept. 1984. Among the requirements are that the appraiser's background and social security number be included on the appraisal.

IRS regulations permit the appraiser of an estate to group items when they do not collectively exceed $100. I prefer to itemize each piece. This thoroughness has built up my appraisal business.

Measurements are made with a leveridge gauge, a standard industry practice to measure gemstone size.

Those millimeter measurements of length, width and depth are then used to determine an estimated carat weight, according to standard formulas.

The amount of metal in the mounting is calculated by subtracting the weight of the stones times .13 from the gross weight of the item. This is a standard industry formula.

The term "fair market value," as used above, is defined as the price at which such property would change hands between willing buyers and willing sellers, neither being under the compulsion to buy or sell, and both having reasonable knowledge of the relevant facts in the most common market which is reasonable and realistic for a purchaser who is an ultimate consumer of the property.

Consequently, fair market value for these two items was to be the collectible jewelry market.

Item #1: While I thought that the stone was glass, I still tested this item. The bubbles seen under magnification, single refraction under the polariscope and refractive index of 1.50 convinced me that the stone was glass.

Standard metal testing of the pin showed that it was base metal.

Setting the value for Item #1: I maintain a well-developed reference library. For this item, I consulted the book *Collectible Jewelry* by Lillian Baker. See plate no. 40 on pages 91-92. Depending on the condition, Baker gives a high value of $10 for similar pieces. Since the pin I was examining was in poor condition and obviously costume jewelry, I determined it to have no fair market value in an estate.

Item #2: The natural origin of the amethyst was determined by examining the stone under 10X magnification, the polariscope and refractometer. Based on those results, I believed the stone to be of natural origin.

The description of the amethyst was done according to that suggested in the AGS appraisal handbook.

The mounting was determined to be sterling from the results of a standard metal test. The pin was stamped "Sterling, made in Germany," which I included on the appraisal.

Setting the value for Item #2: I consulted these books: *Answers to Questions about Old Jewelry, 1840-1950,* by Jeanne Bell, 1st. ed.; *Collectible Costume Jewelry* by S. Sylvia Henzel, *Antique Jewelry Price Guide* by Arthur Guy Kaplan.

Based on values for similar pins, I determined the fair market value of this appraised pin to be $25.

INSURANCE APPRAISAL: *The cultured pearl caper*

The take-in

I have to hold onto my policy and procedures manual when I see Suzanne Austen heading my way.

Suzanne comes in often, always ready to buy. Like any good customer, she thinks of me as a friend. I've been to many a barbecue at her house. But I still make her wait for the receipts.

Recently, she wanted us to appraise a 16-in. strand of pearls. Oh, she tried to get me to do it on the spot. I had to stand firm. Satisfying a customer is one thing, but rushing through an appraisal won't help anyone, I told her.

So I set up an appointment for the next day. I need enough time to review the jewelry carefully during the take-in process.

Why the appraisal, I asked when she came back for the appointment. For insurance? To sell it? Suzanne said she was updating her insurance coverage.

It's very important to look at merchandise at take-in to catch obvious problems. Otherwise, things get complicated later. I recall a customer who brought in a ring for appraisal, assuming its stone was a natural ruby. But when I looked at it during the take-in, I saw it was definitely a synthetic. If I hadn't pointed it out then, she would have thought I switched stones when she received the appraisal later.

For Suzanne's appraisal, I inspected the strand of pearls under a microscope, examining them thoroughly to determine natural or cultured origin and to spot any defects. That helps me set an approximate value.

On the take-in sheet, I noted the pearls were saltwater cultured pearls and listed the number, which I counted, on the strand. It's very important to list the number of pearls so that the customer can't accuse you of shortening her necklace.

While with a gemstone I might write down "red stone" or "blue stone," I can pretty much tell what pearls are when I take them in. But if there had been any uncertainty, I would have written, "Customer claims they are cultured pearls."

Next I asked Suzanne if she had an idea of her pearls' value, then wrote a ballpark figure on the sheet. If a customer doesn't know, we come up together with a rough idea of value.

I told her I charged $40 an hour and gave her an estimate of time and cost, so there would be no surprises later.

The appraisal

Prepared for: Suzanne Austen
Address: El Camino Real, San Diego, Cal. 92101
Purpose: Insurance appraisal
Date: Feb. 3, 1987
One 16-inch strand of cultured pearls, without clasp, knotted with 53 cultured, saltwater pearls. Its description follows:
1. Approximate pearl size—7.5mm to 7.9mm
2. Color—White to rosé, with rosé overtone
3. Luster—Fine
4. Orient—Medium to strong
5. Nacre thickness—Medium to thick.
6. Roundness—Each pearl has a spherical appearance
7. Blemish—Light
8. Match—Good
Estimated replacement value: $2500

The appraiser

Roy Dudenhoeffer of Dudenhoeffer Fine Jewelry Ltd., San Diego, Cal.
Retail jeweler, over 40 years
Certified Gemologist, Gemological Institute of America, 1955
Certified Gemologist Appraiser, American Gem Society, 1983
Member of the AGS Appraisal Committee, Jewelers of America, California Jewelers Association, Jewelers Security Alliance and Jewelers Vigilance Committee

The notes

(usually included in a letter accompanying the appraisal)
We thoroughly examined these pearls under the microscope during the appraisal process. Since we have three people doing appraisals, and the one at take-in isn't always the one doing the appraisal, we are able to check each other.

By examining the pearls under the microscope and looking at the drill holes, I could see that these were cultured pearls. There were separation lines between the mother of pearl beads and actual nacre, indicating their cultured origin.

For their measurements, I used a millimeter gauge, which is more convenient and easier to use than a micrometer.

The other criteria—color, luster, orient, nacre thickness, roundness, blemish and match—are standard ones used to describe pearls and consequently needed to determine value.

The descriptions are ones we use in our store, which we learned from GIA and which we assume are standard in the industry.

Setting the value: We usually have a fairly good supply of pearls in our own stock, and I compared [the ones on the strand against] those.

If I'd had any doubts or had no similar ones in stock for comparison, I would check with one of our several pearl suppliers to get accurate information on values.

The value itself is what it would cost the customer to replace these pearls in a fine jewelry store in our area. It's based on what we know pearls sell for and what we've seen other stores sell them for. It's actually a little higher than what we sell them for in our store.

INSURANCE APPRAISAL: *The sapphire pendant problem*

The take-in

I didn't know Naomi Vanderkeller, but she knew me. By reputation.

"I'm told you do good, fast work," she said. "I try," I answered. I wasn't surprised that she came through my door. Much of my work comes through referrals.

She was a lady with a problem: She needed an appraisal for a sparkling diamond and sapphire pendant—an anniversary gift from her husband. But she had to have it in three days. She was leaving for a cruise and needed to add the pendant to her insurance policy before sailing.

First things first, I thought.

"Was it purchased from us?" I asked. If so, I could check my records for exact weights and measurements. But I knew we hadn't sold the piece. I wouldn't have forgotten a sapphire so lively.

I paused, still taken aback by the sapphire's beauty. I asked about additional testing, but Mrs. Vanderkeller was in a hurry. She needed coverage to be able to take the pendant with her on the cruise.

So I inspected the merchandise, looking closely for defects to note on the take-in form. This usually is a good time to get repair work orders.

But it was good merchandise. I jotted down succinct descriptions. The diamond was described as a "pear-shaped, colorless stone," the sapphire as a "blue transparent stone." Approximate millimeter measurements also were listed.

I explained each action to Mrs. Vanderkeller as I did it. She had no complaints.

"About my fee. It's $75 per hour," I said, giving her a cost and time estimate.

The appraisal

Prepared for: Naomi Vanderkeller
Address: 7984 Buena Vista Dr., Scottsdale, Ariz. 85251
Purpose: Insurance appraisal
Date: Jan. 31, 1987
Lady's diamond and sapphire pendant.

One pear-shaped diamond, AGS provisional color—2, clarity—1, cut—2, 1.67 ct., 9.45 X 6.62 X 4.53mm, faceted girdle, faint blue ultraviolet fluorescence.

One oval, faceted, transparent, natural blue sapphire, medium dark tone, vivid intensity, even color throughout, cut quality—fine, polish—excellent, 4.57 ct., 11.72 by 8.36 by 5.45mm.

Yellow gold, custom-made dangle mounting and butterfly bale. Stamped 14k.

Yellow gold, 2.30mm twist-rope, 18-in. chain with tubular box-plunger clasp, stamped 14k. Figure-eight safety lock.

Estimated replacement value: $33,775.

The appraiser

Thomas H. Hergenroether of Paul Johnson Jewelers, Scottsdale, Ariz.

In the retail jewelry business since 1940
Graduate Gemologist, Gemological Institute of America
Certified Gemologist Appraiser, American Gem Society
Certified Gemologist, AGS
Registered Jeweler, AGS
Two CAPP (Certified Appraiser of Personal Property) courses, offered by the International Society of Appraisers
Member of AGS Appraisal Committee, member of AGS (past-president of the Arizona Guild), member of Arizona Jewelers Association

The notes

(usually included in a letter accompanying the appraisal)
The metal chain and bale both were stamped 14k, as the appraisal form duly noted. I used a standard acid test to determine if the metal was gold.

The stones were measured with a leveridge gauge, a standard industry practice. A micrometer would have been slightly more accurate, but it's only used on unmounted stones or mounted stones with a large enough exposed area. In this case, the leveridge gauge was best suited.

I viewed the diamond under a microscope and saw it was authentic from telltale natural inclusions.

I used AGS Diamond Grading Standards. The qualities of cut, color and clarity are described numerically, from 0 to 10, with "0" being the finest, "10" the poorest. No diamond

may be assigned the AGS grade of "0" in cutting, color or clarity unless it has been graded unmounted.

The "provisional" in "provisional color 2" on the appraisal means the stone was examined in its mounting.

I also included a copy of the AGS chart with comparisons to the GIA diamond grading system with the customer's appraisal.

The diamond was put under an ultraviolet lamp to determine its fluorescence. It's a standard test used for identification purposes.

The sapphire was put under a microscope and a refractometer, and checked for inclusions, angular bandings, crystal formations and other features that indicate natural sapphire.

The sapphire was a clean stone; no inclusions were visible under 10X. So it was described as transparent, a GIA identification term, meaning you can see right through the stone.

The sapphire's color was determined from descriptions listed in the AGS appraisal handbook. I'm still investigating the various color grading systems available to decide which one to use in my appraisal work.

Setting the value: For the sapphire, I contacted two sapphire suppliers—one by phone and another in person. I based the diamond's value on those I have in stock.

Metal value was based on the current gold prices. (I keep a calendar of daily gold prices back to 1979.)

Finally, the piece seemed custom-made. It had to be to accommodate that combination of stones, and the manner in which they were set.

Thus, total value is determined by the value of stones and metal, plus the cost to make the piece. Replacement values are an estimate of the current retail market price at which the appraised jewelry may be purchased in a jewelry establishment in the business of selling such merchandise and do not necessarily reflect the price at which this or similar jewelry may be purchased at Paul Johnson Jewelers. Values include sales tax.

ESTIMATE TO REPLACE: *The dinner ring dilemma*

The take-in

The day hasn't been seen that couldn't be brightened by a visit from Wendy Brimley.

I had to smile when I saw her gracing my doorway. I was thinking back to last month when she finally treated herself to a fine dinner ring.

She had been eyeing that ring for nearly six months. When she finally bought it she was so tickled with her "first piece of fancy jewelry" that she showed it off all over town.

I had to remind her six times to be sure and bring it back in for an estimate to replace. I'd have hated myself if something happened to that ring before she insured it.

Everyone looks out for his neighbor in this small agricultural area. As a retailer, I have to offer very good service, especially since I'm competing with large discounters and department stores in nearby cities. So I give free estimates to replace for jewelry bought in my store.

That doesn't mean I'm not thorough in my work. I follow a specific take-in procedure. The ring I wrote up for Wendy Brimley shows how I do it.

First, I logged it in on a calendar, which helps me keep track of these items. Then, I asked if she needed the estimate to replace for insurance purposes.

I also asked who her agent was. As part of my service, I sometimes hand-deliver photocopies of estimate values directly to the insurance company—it saves my customers an extra trip into town.

The take-in form I use is one I developed while a resident GIA student in 1976. On it, I noted:

• Brimley's name, address, business, person or firm for whom the appraisal is intended, and that she wanted photocopies.

• Under *Ladies and Gents,* I checked the appropriate box for ring.

• Under *Metal,* I checked off the 14k box, because the ring was stamped 14k.

• Under *Condition of mounting,* I wrote new.

• Under *Number of stones on mounting,* I wrote 17.

• Under *Stones stated by customer to be,* I wrote amethyst, diamond, lavender jade, and marked the *Verified* box beneath it. Because we had sold the ring, I knew what these stones were. Still, I checked the stones at take-in under the microscope.

• Under *Description,* I wrote: 8 amethyst melee, 8 diamond melee, 1 oval cab. lav. jade.

• Under *Condition of stones in mounting,* I noted the amethysts had nicks and were slightly worn near the girdle, only seen under 10X.

• Under *Estimated value,* I wrote the purchase price.

At the bottom of the take-in form, I wrote the purpose (insurance); had the customer read the form and sign it. I dated it, and explained how long it would take (in this case, about a week, from take-in to delivery).

The estimate to replace

Prepared for: Wendy Brimley
Address: 2959 Cornsilk Rd., Tulare, Cal. 93271
Purpose: Insurance—estimate to replace
Date: Nov. 12, 1986

Ladies' yellow gold diamond, amethyst and lavender jadeite dinner ring. The ring is stamped "14k" (14 karat). Traditional oval-shaped design featuring one large lavender jadeite center stone, surrounded by one row of diamonds and one row of natural amethysts. See photo exhibits "A" and "B" for top and side views.

The shank splits into three (3) gold wires on each side, which connect near the top to form the gallery. The net weight of the above described mounting is approximately 2.75 dwt (pennyweight).

The ring is a cast piece. Ring size: 6.

The ring contains the following stones:

Eight round faceted natural amethysts, measuring 2.3mm in diameter and weighing approximately .035 ct. each. They are of a purple hue of medium tone and intensity; of poor cut; fair polish and moderately included. Several stones contain nicks, abrasions and cavities, seen under 10X.

Eight round brilliant, full-cut diamonds measuring 2.4mm in diameter and weighing approximately .05 ct. each. The stones are of fair make and I color, VS^2 clarity. AGS grade: 3/4/4.

One oval cabochon-cut natural lavender jadeite center stone. Length: 10.10mm, width: 8.00mm, depth: 15.20mm. Weight: Approximately 10.66 ct.

The jadeite is of violetish/lavender hue, of medium tone and intensity. It is semi-translucent to opaque. The cut and polish are very good. The color is evenly distributed with the exception of some zones of faint white mottling.

Spectroscopic examination/test indicated no color enhancement or treatment.

Estimated replacement cost: $1750.

The appraiser

Richard L. Hammond, Hammond's Jewelry, Tulare, Cal.
Retail jeweler since 1973
Graduate Gemologist, Gemological Institute of America, 1976
Registered Jeweler, American Gem Society, 1978
Certified Gemologist, AGS, 1979
Certified Gemologist Appraiser, AGS, 1984
Member of the AGS Appraisal Committee, AGS, California Jewelers Association, Jewelers of America, Jewelers Security Alliance and Jewelers Vigilance Committee.
AGS zone chairman for membership development

Notes

The ring was stamped 14k, but we did a standard acid test to verify it was gold.

Weights are based on a formula for round faceted stones I learned at GIA. It's approximate weight—since I didn't remove any stones. The formula: Diameter squared, times the depth, times the specific gravity, times .0018.

For measuring, I used a plastic hand-held table gauge which fits under the microscope. A leveridge gauge is cumbersome and can't get in there on accent stones, but I used one to measure the jadeite center stone.

There was microscopic inspection of each stone. And I normally do a spectroscopic exam—at no cost to the customer—on any jade or fancy diamonds, since I so rarely see them. It also reassures a customer that a stone isn't treated or color enhanced, and that they paid a good price.

I used my AGS appraisal handbook for color descriptions. For diamond grades I use GIA grades and include a cover sheet, relating GIA and AGS nomenclature.

As for the piece being cast, I knew that from the gallery underneath. I don't get many custom-made pieces.

Setting the value: In this case, it's based on our retail price (net cost plus markup plus tax).

INSURANCE APPRAISAL: *The lapis lament*

The take-in

The ink on the police report was barely dry when Margaret Rutherford came running into my store.

She, the fashionable wife of the local D.A., had heard about a string of burglaries that happened over the weekend. When she checked over her own insurance coverage, she realized that last year's Christmas gift, a strand of lapis and gold beads, had never been appraised.

That's not unusual. People often come to us for an appraisal after suddenly deciding to insure a piece of jewelry. And they always want the appraisal right away.

During the formal take-in process, I again asked Rutherford the reason for the appraisal—she said it was for insurance—and examined the item for any obvious damage or flaws.

Since she said the beads were lapis, I told her we usually test to determine if they are dyed. No problem, she said, as long as I could do the testing in my store. She wanted the appraisal right away.

On my take-in descriptions, I listed the lapis and gold as "blue beads" and "yellow beads." We won't really know what they are until we've examined them, I explained.

My fee, I explained, was $50 to $75 an hour (depending on items to be appraised and time needed). I gave her an estimate of the cost.

The appraisal

Prepared for: Margaret Rutherford
Address: 3 Park Place, Gloversville, N.Y. 12078
Purpose: Insurance appraisal
Date: Aug. 4, 1986

One 35-in. endless strand of lapis and gold beads. There is no clasp.

There are 72 natural lapis beads, 10mm each. The color is well-matched and the drill holes are well-centered.

There are six sets of yellow gold beads, consisting of one 9mm and two 4mm round yellow gold beads, which follow every 12th lapis bead. (12 lapis, one 4mm gold, one 9mm gold, one 4mm gold, 12 lapis, etc.)

Estimated replacement value: $400

The appraiser

Lou Castiglione, Castiglione Gem Jewelers, Gloversville, N.Y.

Family-operated jewelry store since 1929
Appraiser in the jewelry business since 1971
Graduate Gemologist, Gemological Institute of America, 1978
Registered Jeweler, American Gem Society, 1980
Certified Gemologist Appraiser, AGS, 1983
Accredited Gem Lab, 1980
Member of the American Gem Society. Subcommittee chairman (overseeing publicity) of the AGS Appraisal Committee; past-director and past-treasurer of the New York State Jewelers Association

Notes to the appraisal

(usually included in a letter accompanying the appraisal)

To identify the blue beads, I examined them under the microscope, looking for such distinctive features of lapis—which I found—as metallic inclusions of pyrite and mottling.

To determine if the lapis beads were treated, I used a microscopic hotpoint near the drill hole and pricked the bead. No coating was in evidence. I dabbed the bead in the same area with a small piece of cotton dipped in acetone. No blue color came off, leading me to believe the beads had not been treated.

To identify the yellow metal beads, I found an inconspicuous spot on one, put a small nick in and tested it with acid. It was gold. Though there was no karat marking, we didn't test for quality, because the customer didn't want it.

Bead measurements are given in millimeters, which we got through use of a sliding stone gauge, a micrometer.

Setting the value: The jewelry's value is based on my own experience as a jeweler and buyer. We buy and sell a lot of colored stones. For this piece, I also consulted a colored stone salesman who was in the store at the time.

I use something else, as well, in setting appraised value. I make a point of shopping the competition. I know the wholesale values of jewelry and retail markups. So I try to set a replacement value that is fair to the customer as well as the insurance company.

Consequently, the value listed here is the amount it would most probably cost to replace this necklace at a jewelry store in my area. It's not necessarily the price the customer would pay to replace it at my store.

ESTATE APPRAISAL: *The emerald imbroglio*

The take-in

I set my watch by Joe Greenberg's phone calls. He phones every Tuesday at 3:20 p.m.

Greenberg's law firm and my appraisal business have grown up together. He now has three attorneys handling estates and I do most of their appraisal work. Still, each time I ask why the estate needs an appraisal. Then I remind him of my hourly rate.

This time, Greenberg asked for an appraisal for IRS purposes.

Later, his messenger delivered the jewelry, which I logged in on my take-in form. I described it as a white metal pendant with one green stone and 68 colorless stones.

The appraisal

Prepared for: Estate of Sophie Baker, c/o Joel Greenberg, attorney for the estate, 999 N. Ninth St., Ventura, Cal. 93999
Purpose: Estate appraisal
Date: April 9, 1986

One $16^1/2$ in. hand-made necklace stamped "plat" with a bow [as in bow and arrow] pendant.

The pendant, 2 in. long and $1^1/2$ in. wide contains:

1. One emerald-cut, natural emerald set on four prongs at the bottom center of the pendant. The emerald is of green hue, medium-dark tone, medium-bright intensity, with even color throughout, very good cutting and normal polish. It is moderately included in 10%-15% of the stone.

Measurements: Length, 11.5mm; width, 9.5mm; depth, 4.9mm.

Estimated weight: 3.64 ct.

2. One cultured pearl attached to the bottom of the pendant by a swiveling platinum pearl cap. The pearl is white, round, 7.5mm in diameter with no overtone, no orient, weak luster, slight blemishes and thick nacre.

3. Sixty-eight round diamond melee, used as pavé on the pendant.

1 melee—2.4mm, 0.05 ct., quality 3.49 melee—3.8mm to 1.2mm, 1.56 ct. total weight, quality 3.18 melee—2.0mm, 0.54 ct. total weight, quality 4.

Melee total weight—2.15 ct.

Gross weight: 29.50 grams.
Fair market value: $4000.

The appraiser

Bob Lynn of Lynn's Jewelry in Ventura, Cal. Social Security Number: 959-99-5559

16+ years as a retail jeweler
Graduate Gemologist, GIA, 1979
Registered Jeweler, AGS
Certified Gemologist, AGS, 1979
Certified Gemologist Appraiser, AGS, 1984
Member, AGS Appraisal Committee

Notes on the appraisal

(usually included in a letter accompanying the appraisal)

The necklace was stamped "plat" and noted on the appraisal.

All gem measurements were done with a leveridge gauge.

Microscopic examination of the emerald showed characteristic natural inclusions. That combined with the refractometer reading of the stone identified the gem as natural emerald.

The estimated weight of the emerald was determined by this standard formula: Length X width X depth X specific gravity X .0025.

The gem descriptions are given according to the AGS appraisal handbook guidelines.

The pearl was assumed to be cultured from microscopic examination.

The melee were tested with a diamond tester. Carat weights are taken from tables of estimated weight.

I have developed my own melee grading system, where 0 is flawless and 6 is industrial. My customers wouldn't pay for the time needed to grade each melee to GIA standards.

Setting the value: The value put on the necklace was determined by using the IRS guidelines for fair market value determination. It is the price that would be agreed upon between a willing buyer and seller, with time not being of the essence.

The most common market for this piece was determined to be high-end estate jewelers. I spoke with three of these estate jewelers and asked their opinion of the item's value, their asking price and their selling price.

18 Tips For Better Appraisal

Cos Altobelli ♦ *April 1987*

Appraisals don't have to be a loss leader in your store. You can offer customers a viable service and get paid for your expertise. But you must do it professionally. Here are 18 tips to help you better serve your appraisal customers.

1. Overcome the skeptics. Customers who want an appraisal done while they wait often are afraid that their gems will be switched.

To overcome that fear, first show the customer her stone under magnification, pointing out the internal inclusions and external peculiarities as you plot them. Second, measure the stone with a leveridge gauge and record those measurements on the plotting diagram. Third, determine a value, upon which you both agree, should there be a loss while the piece is in your store. Then allow the customer to take plotting diagram and measurements with her as part of her claim check.

If the customers is still apprehensive, explain what is involved in doing an accurate, detailed appraisal. Show her some examples of your professional appraisals and you'll be sure to overcome the skeptics.

2. Don't judge a piece by its stone. Before you talk your customer out of insuring jewelry with a low-cost center stone, take a good look at the mounting. When such stones are used, most of an item's value comes from the metal in the mounting. Consequently, you must determine the mounting's net weight accurately.

For example, suppose your customer brings in a lady's hand-made ring of 10% iridium-platinum, set with one emerald-cut synthetic spinel. To determine the net weight of the mounting, first compute the weight of the spinel. Let's say it's 40 carats.

Multiply 40 ct. by .13 to get the stone's equivalent weight in pennyweight (5.2 dwt). Then subtract that figure from the gross weight of the ring to get the net weight of the mounting: i.e., 20 dwt—5.2 dwt = 14.8 dwt, net weight.

3. Ask to see the jewelry. Customers often ask for an insurance appraisal update, but don't want to bring in the jewelry. Stress your need to see the items again for the customer's own protection. Point out that there could be damage to the mounting or stones. Advise them that you will be able to clean the items and at least check for any loose stones. That should give them peace of mind and greater enjoyment from having jewelry that "sparkles" again.

Sometimes, however, it is necessary to do an update without seeing the jewelry because of circumstances beyond the customer's control. If the insurance company is willing to accept the appraisal on this basis, you can do the update. But be sure to make a prominent statement on the appraisal that it was performed under this limiting condition. That should protect you from repercussions.

4. Count the pearls. Suppose your customer agrees to have her pearls restrung at the same time an appraisal is done. It is standard practice to count the pearls and measure their millimeter size during an appraisal take-in. It's doubly important to do this when the pearls are to be restrung. Since knots on an old strand will have stretched, a restrung strand will be somewhat shorter. The customer thus may think some of the pearls are missing.

Be sure to explain this during the take-in process. Your customer may even ask you to supply matching pearls to make up the additional length.

5. Watch out for counterfeits. The vast amount of bogus watches on the market today make it vital that your take-in personnel know the telltale signs of imitations. If you don't have a watchmaker in house, visit with one who can explain these and other tips:

• Use an acid test to identify watches that are marked and/or appear to be gold, but are not.

• Check the spelling and/or quality of decals on the dial.

• Look for a rough finish and poor plating quality.
• Inspect the case back—bogus watches often have a snap-on or stainless steel back.

6. Allow for custom work. When taking in a custom-made piece, be sure to ask your client if he wants it replaced with an identical item. If so, you'll have to include in the appraisal the time and cost necessary to custom make that item.

When doing such appraisals, you also should include actual size photos and enlargements of the top, side, front and underside of the item. These will help a jeweler custom make an identical piece.

If the client does not wish to replace the item with an identical piece, your appraisal should state so. In that case, you'll have to allow for the time and cost of new design concepts, renderings and working drawings (top, front, side and underside) for a piece that is still custom-made but not identical.

Be sure to remind your customer that he needs a special endorsement on his policy to cover either of these situations.

7. Keep your customer in mind. Insurance companies usually reimburse only 50% of the value when half of a pair of earrings or cuff links is lost. But to make that replacement, your customer may have to pay 75% to 85% of the total value.

Point this out to your customer during the appraisal take-in. If he wants to be totally covered, he will have to add an endorsement to his policy. And you'll have to state what your customer prefers to do on the appraisal.

8. Stay away from wholesale. Unless a governmental agency requests an appraisal be performed at wholesale, don't do it.

A customer typically requests it in an effort to reduce insurance premiums. His agent tells him to ask for it because that is what the insurance company's replacement cost will be.

Explain to your customer that an insurance appraisal's value is based on what the retail market dictates for replacement of that item, and not the price that item sells for in one outlet.

If your customer is still not convinced, ask him how he will replace his jewelry if that one company goes out of business.

9. Determine who is responsible. During the take-in procedure, work with your customer to determine a mutually-agreed upon value for the merchandise being left with you. Then discuss these two major points:
• If the item is lost, stolen or damaged, *you* want the option of replacing or repairing it at your own cost.

Ask the customer to sign a statement agreeing to that. Then you won't be forced to give cash or allow someone else to make the repair or replacement
• Your customer may believe you are responsible for replacing lost or damaged goods through your insurance company because you asked her to agree on a value. However, primary coverage takes precedence in most states. If a loss occurs and you have acted in a prudent (not careless or negligent) manner with the customer's jewelry, then the customer is required to file the claim with her insurance company. If she has no insurance, then you must make the claim with your carrier.

10. Ask your customer to help. Most insurance companies will accept a new appraisal on a flatware or hollowware service without the appraiser having seen all the items. It is truly an inconvenience because of size, quantity

and weight for a customer to bring in all the pieces. And it is often impractical for an appraiser to keep all of the items on his premises due to lack of space in his vault or safe.

In this case, ask your customer to supply you with:
• A list of the items, sizes, weights, dimensions, trademarks, numbers, stampings, quantities, patterns, manufacturer's names, bills of sale, etc.;
• Simple snapshots of the service;
• A sample place setting for you to inspect. If the insurance company requires that all items be seen, still ask your customer to draw up the list. Then you can check the service against the list, adding your comments and making any necessary tests. This will save you time and perhaps help you avoid keeping the items in your store.

Most customers will provide the list when you explain the amount of time it will save you—which means considerable monetary savings for them.

11. Specify the cut. When taking in pieces that contain more than one old mine-cut or European-cut diamond, counsel your customer about this unusual replacement situation. Tell her that if she replaces that old cut with a modern brilliant cut, the new stone will stand out like a "sore thumb."

If she decides she wants a similarly-cut stone as a replacement, she must be prepared to wait until one can be found. Be sure to state this on the appraisal and have the client add an endorsement to her policy. Otherwise, the insurance company will try to replace the stone with the cut most readily available.

12. Describe damage carefully. Insurance companies sometimes refuse to cover an item containing damaged diamond or colored gemstone.

To help your client get coverage, accurately plot the size, location and configuration of any damage. On the appraisal explain that a recut weight has been computed for the damaged stone. Explain that your net value is based on this recut weight, with considerations for recutting and resetting costs.

The insurance company then may agree to cover any increased damage to the stone or a total loss, based on the recut weight.

13. Be precise in descriptions. Accurately describing the clarity and body appearance of colored gemstones requires more than using the industry clichés, such as lightly, moderately or heavily included.

For example, without a good photograph, a stone which is described as heavily included may be unduly penalized if the inclusions are concentrated in only 30% of the stone. Conversely, a stone may be overrated if you only describe its face-up appearance, although it is colorless when viewed from the side.

To avoid that type of problem, be thorough in your descriptions. For example, you can describe the first stone as: Heavily included in 30% and free of inclusions in 70%. This method should also be applied to descriptions of mottling in jadeite, voids in opal, zoning in sapphires, etc.

14. Paying attention to details. Be sure to consider all the costs in your valuation of a charm bracelet. The replacement cost for a bracelet containing 20 charms, each soldered onto the bracelet and having an average of 20 letters of hand engraving and a safety chain, could increase by $600 when you add all these factors into the value.

15. Give a value, not price. Insurance replacement values should not be predicated on your own selling price. They should be based on the item's selling price at most retail jewelers commonly in the business of selling such merchandise in your area. It is possible that your price and the insurance replacement value will be the same, but that should not be the sole criterion for determining value.

For example, a popular man's watch has a manufacturer's suggested selling price of $9450. However, most merchants, whether they are franchised dealers or not, sell it for $7500. This lower value is the replacement value that should be used.

If you have sold the item and prefer to list your price as the value, you can prepare a document that states it is your "Estimate to Replace" in your establishment and not an "Appraisal for Insurance Replacement Purposes."

In addition, some customers prefer to return to the store where the jewelry was purchased. If their insurance company will accept that replacement situation, the customer will still have to add an endorsement to his insurance policy. And you will have to specify on the appraisal that the customer wants to replace the item at a specific store and that your value is that store's price.

16. Use one of two dates. For an estate tax appraisal, you can use one of two dates as the basis for your fair market value determination—either the date of death or the date six months following the death.

To determine which date to use, look over various items in the estate. If any are part of a market that just experienced an unusual price swing, perhaps gold or silver, you should counsel the executor of the estate to wait six months to see if the price returns to normal.

Remember that fair market value is not fair if it is based on an abnormal market condition.

17. Group low-cost items. When doing an appraisal for estate tax purposes, you can group insignificant items without a definitive description, according to Internal Revenue Service regulations. For example: Costume jewelry: Two pairs of earrings, one pair of cuff links, three neck chains, one anklet, one Timex watch—$90.

But be sure that the total fair market value does not exceed $100 for one or more items collectively.

18. Protect yourself. You don't have to shy away from appraising high-end jewelry or large estates because your basic insurance coverage is inadequate. You have three options.

First, you can discuss this situation with your customer. If she has adequate coverage and/or you can convince her of your own professionalism, she may sign an agreement that you are not responsible provided you are prudent.

Second, you can place all of the items in a bank safety deposit box and remove a few items at a time, exchanging them at intervals until the entire appraisal is completed. If you choose this option, be sure to obtain extra insurance coverage. There have been instances in which bank boxes have been opened without authorization and items have been removed. But the premiums should be reasonable because of the low-loss percentage.

Third, ask the customer to bring in only a few items at a time. Then determine the cost of additional customer goods coverage (per $1000 on a daily rate). The client may be willing to pay the premium for this limited coverage. But be sure to do your appraisal in a timely manner so that you don't subject her to any more costs than necessary.

Answers To JCK Management Study Center Quiz:
(Questions can be found on pages 77 & 78)

WHY YOU NEED APPRAISAL EDUCATION

Elly Rosen a freelance gemological appraisal consultant and appraisal principles educator, prepared this report for the October 1994 issue of JCK. His answers to the quiz:

1. False	9. False
2. d	10. d
3. True	11. False
4. False	12. c
5. True	13. d
6. a	14. True
7. False	15. False
8. True	16. False

Question #1 was most frequently missed. It offered the statement, "There are no government regulations pertaining to the appraisal of gems and jewelry." The answer is false. While neither the federal government nor any of the 50 states regulates *appraisers* of personal property, appraisal reports themselves, as well as some procedures related to appraising and running an appraisal practice are subject to federal, state and municipal regulation.

Chapter 3

PERSONNEL

---

*Solid, Motivated Employees
Are The Fuel
That Powers Your Store*

JCK Management Study Center: Employee Benefits

Sharon A. Krimm ◆ *June 1995*

YOUR BENEFITS PACKAGE: THE FIRST STEPS

Companies that want to keep a solid base of quality employees almost have to offer medical and life insurance. Next, I think, most employees look for disability coverage, with most picking short-term before long-term—though we'll discuss the wisdom of that choice.

If your company is doing well, you also might think about adding a profit sharing plan. A 401(k) is less popular; it involves a lot more administrative cost, and sometimes is hard to sell. While well-paid employees may like it and be able to make the contributions, a 19-year-old is more concerned about making a car payment. That can be a problem because if only high-salaried staff members join your plan, it may become "top heavy" and leave you open to charges of discrimination.

Pension plans often don't rank high for many small businesses, because of the cost and long-term commitment involved. Today, a pension plan must cover anyone who is eligible, namely those who are 19 or older and who work at least 1,000 hours a year. If you want to plan for retirement, you have to take the staff along.

One other benefit to consider is the premium conversion plan (Section 125), which has become very popular with large employers. It lets employees pay for benefits with pretax dollars. If an employee's share of medical insurance costs is $2,000, his or her gross pay is reduced by that amount before federal and FICA—and maybe even state—taxes are levied. For someone earning $30,000 a year, this could mean nearly $500 extra a year in take-home pay, a very tangible benefit.

Here's a detailed look at the options.

MEDICAL AND LIFE

The owner of a small business, say about 10 people, who wants to set up a new medical plan should look at the local Blue Cross organization. Check what the Chamber of Commerce and your business associations may offer. Also look at any small commercial carriers active in your geographic area. Then consider the majors—the companies that operate all across the country, such as Guardian, U.S. Life, Travelers, Aetna, Prudential. They sometimes offer a small-group product.

Most providers offer a combination of medical and life insurance. The life is easy for them; they just tell you the minimum requirement, probably around $10,000 or $15,000. (They'll accommodate you if you want more, of course.)

While traditional commercial carriers require a minimum amount of life insurance, Blue Cross units and health maintenance organizations (HMOs) do not. When there is a minimum life insurance requirement, especially for a small group, you may not be quoted the most competitive rate. You might get a better price by going out into the life insurance market, but if you want medical coverage, you don't have much option—you have to buy life, too. This is one of those little gimmicks of insurance companies.

Today, most employers offer life and medical. However, some employees don't want medical coverage because they're covered elsewhere through a spouse. Insurance carriers allow employees to waive the medical if they can prove coverage elsewhere, but they still require the life insurance. The insurance company wants some money, and it's not a bad policy because $10,000 or $20,000 life coverage can be a real benefit in case of death.

Is it a good buy? To be sure of getting the best deal, any small employer starting up a plan should find an independent broker or agent. Find one that represents more than one insurance company, someone who will put your program out to bid in the marketplace and shop it to about 10 carriers, including your Blue Cross, your Chamber of Commerce and some HMO options.

You'll likely find a lot of price variation. The cost for a small employer would be much higher in urban Philadelphia than in rural Lancaster County two hours to the west, for example. The city has teaching hospitals, too. That tends to add to the expense.

But you can get differences in price even within a metropolitan area. If you have an older group, for example, the Blues will probably be less expensive than going to a commercial carrier—perhaps 10% or more. You could pay a $600 family rate for coverage from a commercial carrier in the Philadelphia area right now, but more like $482 under the Blues. That's a significant difference.

You're also talking significant differences with HMOs because you are willing to stay within a managed care network. There could be a problem with numbers here; some HMOs will accept a group of 10, but two or three may be too few. Still, HMOs are always worth looking into.

Under Blue Cross, a group of two to 29 will put you into what is called a community pool. The advantage here, at least in Philadelphia, is the age makeup of your group isn't taken into consideration. Independence Blue Cross works with a rate structure published each quarter. So if I see a group with a fairly old population, I go right to the Blues.

HMOs also publish rates each quarter, and age does not come into play. But when you look at your commercial marketplace, you need a census of your group—age, sex, whether you are covered as a single or family unit. All these factors are taken into consideration when coming up with rates.

Preexisting problems: Preexisting medical conditions can be a problem, depending where you live. Under medical small-group insurance reform in New Jersey, for example, a person who has a history of participation in one group insurance plan can roll over into a new employer plan with credit for the preexisting condition. He or she has built up a credit and avoids waiting periods of up to one year that some plans have before covering a preexisting condition.

But how preexisting medical conditions are handled differs from state to state. Check this in choosing a provider for medical coverage; it could be very important, particularly if you are starting a new medical plan and some of your employees have been treated for medical problems in the previous months.

If a new employee transfers to your plan from a previous employer plan, there may be a way to handle the preexisting issue, provided the former employer had at least 20 employees. The Consolidated Omnibus Budget Reconciliation Act (COBRA) says affected employers must allow an employee who is leaving to stay on the company group medical plan for a minimum of 18 months. The employee then pays the premiums plus a 2% administration fee. The benefit must be granted whether the employee leaves voluntarily or involuntarily (except in instances where the person is fired for "gross misconduct") and also is available to a surviving spouse for up to 36 months.

Some employers resent offering COBRA to someone they've fired. I've had employers tell me, "I caught this guy stealing—I don't want to offer him COBRA." It's your call. You have to decide whether it's worth the legal fees you would pay if the former employee took you to court—especially when you no longer have to pay his or her premium anyway.

If the departing employee's new employer has a three-month wait before the person qualifies under the company plan, the employee can use COBRA payments to the former employer to cover the three months.

COBRA also can come into play in retirement planning. A person who wants to quit before age 65 may choose to go out 18 months early, take COBRA for those months and then go right into Medicare.

Moves to managed care: With most of my smaller clients, I see a transition to more managed care options. They're doing what bigger employers did five years ago. The only problem is that too often, Mr. Employer doesn't want to be locked into an HMO. He wants the freedom to choose any doctor he wants.

It may be possible for him to get the best of both worlds. In the Philadelphia area, and this may be true elsewhere, Blue Cross will allow a company to have employees in what it calls the Preferred Provider Organization (PPO) and also in the Blue Cross Keystone HMO. It's fine if you have only one in the first and five in the HMO. It's all Blue Cross.

Prudential Insurance has a similar arrangement but requires more employees. So do U.S. Healthcare and Kaiser in California. The concept is now sifting down to the smaller employer, offering cost effective delivery systems and freedom of choice for the employer. Some employers figure they've earned their right to go to any doctor they want while employees generally favor cost-effective plans with low co-pays.

The ultimate option: On medical coverage, let's look at one final option: opting out.

No law requires an employer to offer benefits. But if you decide to drop medical coverage, you'll have a hard time hiring people. Those you want to hire almost surely consider medical insurance a non-negotiable part of their employment contract. As much as you'd like to throw up your hands and say you don't want to be involved in benefits anymore, you almost have to offer life and medical insurance if you want to keep a good base of quality employees.

DISABILITY

It's standard today for a small company to offer short-term disability, typically for 13 or 26 weeks. Normally, the benefit is 60% of the basic weekly earnings up to a maximum amount based on your highest salary or on some other formula. It covers broken legs, appendicitis, maternity and similar short-term situations.

However, long-term probably is a more valuable coverage. Young employees don't ever see themselves getting a serious long-term illness, and they think of accidents as something that happens to someone else. But older employees and those with families realize that if they have only 26 weeks of short-term coverage, then in the 27th week there'll be nothing.

Neither coverage is really expensive. Long-term is cheaper because not that many people become totally disabled and make claims. But it's nice to know you can offer it. If a valued employee becomes disabled, you soon have to ask, "When do I cut off the medical benefits and salary?" If you have long-term disability, you don't have to make that decision.

Many factors affect the cost: the makeup of your group, where you're located, the nature of your industry. I recommend considering self-insuring for short-term coverage. This way, you're not paying short-term premiums for disabilities that never occur. If you know your group and check your records, you may well find that you had only one or two cases—one a maternity, the other a heart attack—where your short-term policy would have come into use. You probably would have paid more in premiums than in a 50% or 60% replacement of those employees' weekly earnings.

Here's how it can work if you self-insure. You set a company policy that if somebody becomes disabled—

with sickness or an injury—he or she first must use up all paid sick days, maybe 10, after which you begin to pay 50% of regular weekly earnings up to 13 weeks, or whatever arrangement you choose. Certainly 13 weeks is not a long time for the employer to be at risk. Of course, you'll want a doctor's note confirming that the illness or injury is disabling and noting the date the employee should return to work.

Your policy, with all its terms and limitations, should be spelled out clearly in a written document given to each employee.

Always insure for long-term disability. There's too much risk not to. You should have an insured contract that goes to age 65 for long-term disability and a salary continuation plan. The policy can kick in on the 90th or 180th day or after one year, whatever you choose. This will depend on how you handle short-term disability.

KEYMAN

The law allows you to offer certain policies to certain key employees. These policies do not violate antidiscrimination rules even though they're not available to every employee.

Such "keyman" policies are written essentially to provide cash to buy out the stock of executives if they die or to provide the resources to hire a talented and highly paid replacement. In the stock buy-out, the goal usually is to prevent the stock—and perhaps control of the company—from passing to an outsider—most often a spouse.

It's also possible, under certain circumstances, to offer your highest-paid people richer group life insurance as well as disability coverage not available to rank-and-file employees.

SICK DAYS AND VACATIONS

Most companies, small or large, base sick days on years of service with the company. Typically, someone starting in January gets five sick days in the first year. If the person starts in July, he or she might get part of a week. After the first year, the employee may get a maximum of 10 sick days and that usually doesn't change.

Vacation days are different. They're also tied to years of service, but in a much stronger fashion. Typically, an employee gets one week in the first year, two weeks for two to five or two to 10 years of service and three weeks after 10. This is a realistic schedule.

I've had some interesting arrangements with employers who have many female employees with young children. They get tired of employees trying to decide, when the kids get sick, whether to take a vacation day, a personal day or a sick day. So they give employees 17 days (10 vacation days, five sick days and two personal days) to use any way they wish. Employees don't have to say which type of free day they're taking.

Some companies allow employees to carry any unused days off into the following year (sometimes with a cap on how many days can be carried over). Or if someone has a lot of days left at the end of the year and it's not practical to use them all in December —certainly true in retailing—they pay the employee

for the days not used. This may not be the full amount, but perhaps 60% of the value of that day. That can be a nice bonus at the end of the year.

Today's workforce needs some flexibility, and your employees will appreciate having it. In return, you'll find they'll support you when you really need them to do a special job.

PENSIONS

A profit-sharing plan can be used to build a retirement benefit. It's a good vehicle because it provides an incentive for employees. If they work hard, the company grows and is able to make a bigger profit-sharing contribution. If there are no profits, the company doesn't have to put any money into the plan, though if no profits are put in for five years, the IRS is likely to ask if it's really a profit-sharing plan.

Profit-sharing allows the company to put aside pretax dollars, with the company's contribution generally based on a percentage of total compensation. The plan is a way for the employer to shelter funds for corporate tax and personal reasons.

Vesting for a profit-sharing plan is strict and usually is set in your plan document. The administrator must follow this schedule. If an employee leaves before being vested, any money put aside on his or her behalf falls back into the pool.

A 401(k) is another retirement option for a small company, even one with only 10 employees. But it's costly to administer and you've really got to shop to find an administrator who does just small-group 401(k)s. It might cost between $1,500 and $2,000 a year to have someone administer a small-group plan.

From the employee's point of view, there are a lot of participation regulations with 401(k)s. There's another potential problem. Highly compensated employees may want to jump in because they see the value, even if the company doesn't put in any matching funds, and they can afford to put aside 3% of their pay. But it may be harder to get the less-well-paid staff members to sign up, especially if there's no company contribution. It may be a real struggle for them to have something like $50 taken out of their paycheck. I think you need at least 25 people for a 401(k); this gives you a better shot at getting a fair mix of salaries. And offering a company match—even if it's 10¢ on the dollar—is a big incentive.

Normally, 401(k)s have a vesting schedule. One formula is 20-40-60-80, which means the employee is 20% vested in the first year and the percentage accumulates each year until it reaches 100%. In a 401(k), employees always get back all money they contribute, even if they leave before being fully vested, but the matching amount from the company is subject to the vesting schedule.

If an employee gets a year-end bonus and wants to spend the money, that's fully taxable. Lower-paid employees, especially younger ones, love getting and spending a bonus at the end of the year. Older employees with families may prefer to shelter some of the bonus. For these staffers, you can arrange to have some or all of the money put into a 401(k).

Defined contribution, defined benefit: Regular pensions fall into two categories:

• Defined contribution, which covers profit sharing and 401(k) plans. The contributions can be made by the employee and employer (in the case of a 401(k) plan) or by the employer alone (in the case of profit sharing). There is no guarantee of what that benefit's going to be at age 65; you just define the contribution the company will make. In a profit-sharing plan, for example, it may be defined as a yearly contribution of 1%, 2% or 5% of total compensation.

• Defined benefit plan, which is the old-fashioned pension plan, one that's most in use at large companies. This plan defines the benefit that each vested employee will qualify for at age 65.

Defined benefit plans are best for employees because the company is required to fund the program every year—whether or not it had a good year. This guarantees that employees will reach retirement age with a nest egg, even if they haven't saved money on their own. Another benefit to the employee: the company puts the handling of its retirement fund into the hands of an expert. Such plans have an investment manager who normally chooses a company such as Merrill Lynch or Smith Barney to manage the money.

But companies probably prefer defined contribution plans, which make no guarantees other than a certain matching contribution in a 401(k) plan and a yearly decision by the board of directors whether the company can afford a contribution to the profit-sharing plan. It's up to the owner and, to some extent, the employees to guide investment policy for defined contribution plans. The owner is rarely an investment expert, so he or she has to pursue due diligence and hire a firm to invest the money, to make it grow and to get the correct asset mix so it shows a steady return in low and high markets. The onus is on the employer to make proper selection of funds and on the employee to invest wisely.

Employees have to make decisions when they participate in a 401(k). Normally, they choose from among three or four investment choices. There may be a number of funds: fixed-income, money market, bond, equity or maybe a balanced fund. It's up to the employees to know what is happening in the finance world so they can make intelligent choices. If they're too conservative—and studies show that many people with little financial know-how are—it will be difficult to turn an investment into a nest egg by age 65.

PASSING THE BENEFITS BUCK

Picture this scene for your 10-person staff.

Thanks to a strategic alliance you've made, they enjoy a benefits package comparable to that available at most of the nation's Fortune 500 companies. You have access to similar coverage for yourself, of course, though you may choose a richer package.

There's more. Under this alliance, you also rid yourself of the agony of payroll paperwork and all the tedious filings required under state and federal work procedures. And for good measure, you also delegate all routine queries and gripes on personnel and payroll issues to someone else.

Where's the catch?

One, the alliance calls for you to cede all your employees to another company and lease them back. Two, you pay for the privilege. The cost can be a charge equal to about 3% to 6% of total payroll, a flat fee of between $500 and $2,000 per person per year or a combination of both.

"Medical usually is the hook that brings them in," says Steven A. Tessler, president of Corporate Management Group, a New York City company that thrives on such alliances. "But six months later, it's the savings in time that keeps them. So often I've heard businesspeople say, 'I can always make another dollar, but I can't make another hour.' "

Corporate Management Group (CMG) represents a business phenomenon that waxed in the late 1980s, then waned and now seems to be waxing again. The premise is simple. A company with expertise in all areas of personnel management becomes the employer-of-record for the staffs of many small to medium-sized businesses and then uses the power of numbers to build benefits packages unavailable (in richness, cost or both) to the individual small companies. At the same time, it has the people-power to take over back-office operations that often are a real burden to the small-time entrepreneur.

CMG has more than 10,000 employees in scores of companies that range in size from three employees to about 1,000. "We are," says Tessler, "the out-source resource."

Emotional obstacle: The biggest issue for business owners is the perception of loss of control. Under such an alliance, your employees may work in your store, but they are employees of a distant, absentee owner.

Tessler likes to allay such fears quickly. He explains that for all practical purposes, the owner continues to run the business just as he or she always did—hiring, firing, promoting, rewarding and disciplining the employees just like before the alliance. All such points are spelled out in a detailed contract.

CMG and potential client companies examine each other diligently before any contract is signed. In fact, CMG rejects about one-third of the companies interested in joining, most often because of employees with bad medical histories or lack of financial stability.

The American Gem Society brought its headquarters staff into the group and, at a recent AGS Conclave in Phoenix, it strongly recommended that members check out CMG. At least one well-known jewelry manufacturer also is now a CMG client.

Once an agreement is signed, CMG requires the new member to put the equivalent of one complete payroll plus taxes on deposit. From then on, payroll is transmitted to CMG's bank in enough time for it to send checks or direct-deposit wages on the due date (CMG performs all payroll functions with appropriate deductions).

CMG sends a two-person team to the new member for a series of one-on-one conversations with employees, primarily to determine their benefits needs and wishes, but also to discuss other personnel issues. Employees may call CMG toll-free any time with payroll or personnel questions.

Tessler says one of the main appeals to employees is the diversity of the health insurance plans available. Among them:

• Cafeteria plans, which allow employees to pick and choose among various benefits at a cost that's within their budget.

• Choice between conventional indemnity medical plans and health maintenance organization plans.

• Flexible spending plans that, among other things, offer coverage for dependent care.

• Various life insurance and savings plans, including 401(k)s.

Many employees like the flexibility, Tessler says. For example, someone who might be covered for medical insurance through a spouse still can pick up dental. And employees who make a personal contribution to their medical coverage (and many do) may do so on a pretax basis under some plans. (Someone with $25,000 annual income who contributes $2,000 toward medical coverage, for example, would have gross taxable income of $23,000.)

"Our goal is to create a plan that's designed to meet individual needs," says Tessler. "They decide how much they want to spend, and we work out a plan to fit that budget."

What it costs: The size of the company seeking to join CMG has a direct bearing on cost. For example, a jeweler with operations in a number of states will have more complex compliance regulations than one with a single store. But in general, the cost is 3%-6% of total payroll or a certain amount per employee (usually $500-$2,000 per person). The dollar charge often is used in the case of a high-salaried employee, possibly the boss.

Tessler estimates that CMG can cut health-care costs 10%-40%. On total service, he estimates that a 50-person company should save about $100,000 a year, after paying its fee, by using all CMG services. He quotes the case of a jewelry company with 80 employees and a $2 million payroll that saved $162,000 by contracting with CMG.

If the savings are so great, why don't more companies use the service and why don't more companies such as CMG get into the business? On the first point, says Tessler, use is limited because the idea of sending off employees to another "boss" and then leasing them back is too big a mental hurdle for a lot of business owners to make. On the second, he offers no particular answer other than it takes a lot of work to learn the business. He launched his company in 1992 and competition still is fairly limited.

There's also the fact that people-leasing companies have had some bad publicity. One major company that was widely publicized in the late 1980s failed when its management allegedly played tricks with finances.

Under the CMG contract, either party may quit with 30 days' notice or immediately if any "gross errors" are uncovered.

Steven A. Tessler, Corporate Management Group, 189 Broadway, New York, N.Y. 10007; (212) 843-6600.

These Jewelers Offer Benefits

JEWELER PROFILE

The jeweler: Single store on fashionable avenue in southern town of about 270,000. Five full-time employees (including owner) and three part-time. Annual volume, $500,000 to $1 million.

The benefits: Medical and life insurance, pension plan, paid sick days and vacations, education financial assistance, merchandise discounts and unpaid family emergency leave. Also pays for lunch for full-time employees. Does not offer 401(k) ("too hard to administer"), dental plan ("still trying to get comfortable with medical") or long-term disability ("just haven't explored it; the staff hasn't asked about it").

Costs: For medical coverage, the owner encouraged the staff to look at many plans and finally picked the local Blue Cross/Blue Shield. Although it was more costly, it offered better benefits, including a "cafeteria plan" under which employees can pick and choose among available levels and types of coverage. Employer and employee split the cost, each paying about $125 a month. Some opt out because they're covered through spouses.

Life insurance and the defined contribution pension plan are offered as part of a Single Employee Pension Plan. The owner picked this plan because it offered the option for profit sharing; the company contributes about $3,000 a year for the entire package. Employees are encouraged to contribute (particularly their Christmas bonus) to shelter the contribution from taxes; younger employees are largely indifferent to this option. The insurance policy has a payout of about $12,000. Employees can take part after two years' service.

The company pays for three sick days a year (either time off or pay) with no monitoring at an annual cost of about $1,000—mostly in cash. "If I trust them with the keys to the store," says the owner, "I can trust them to decide if they are sick or not." Vacation policy is one week after one year, two weeks after two years and an extra day a year for each succeeding year to a maximum of three weeks. The store also allows unpaid leave during slow periods.

The business, a member of the American Gem Society, requires all full-time employees to take Gemological Institute of America and AGS courses to earn the AGS Certified Gemologist Appraiser title. Employees pay their own expenses upfront, get a pay increase on completion and full reimbursement one year after completion. The owner encourages staff members to get outside financial support; a number have received scholarships from Jewelers of America. Total annual cost to the company: about $2,000.

Store merchandise is available to employees at cost with no cap on dollars or units. A house account can run for a maximum of one year; any departing employee must settle the account before leaving. The owner considers this benefit as a service and declines to attach a dollar value.

The annual lunch bill (paid because salespeople must be on the floor during the busy lunch hour) comes to about $3,125 a year.

Owner comment: "When I saw the local White Castle hamburger shop with signs saying it's hiring hamburger flippers for $6 an hour and offering a signup bonus and paid vacations, then I became even more aware of the need to give my employees good benefits."

JEWELER PROFILE

The jeweler: Single store in moderate-size midwestern city with market area of about 50,000. Seven full-time employees. Annual volume, $700,000 to $1 million.

The benefits: Medical, dental and prescription drug insurance, paid sick days and vacation, bonus program, education financial assistance and merchandise discounts. The dental program is about a year old. The company has never had a pension program or any disability insurance (on disability, "it just never arose"). Company policy gives seven sick days. Vacation policy: one week after one year, two weeks for two to five years, three weeks for more than five years.

Costs: The total medical cost is about $165 a month per employee through a group plan with other retailers and with manufacturing companies in the city. "We're very satisfied with the plan we've got," says the owner. "We don't believe in shopping around. We want to stick with what's good." The company pays for 100% of medical coverage for all employees.

The total bonus cost is $30,000 to $35,000 a year.

Owner comments: "If you treat people decently, they'll respond. No one abuses sick days. Good benefits are essential. Employers who take care of their help get loyal help."

JEWELER PROFILE

The jeweler: Three-store company in affluent western community. Immediate market area of more than 100,000; major metropolitan area within easy driving distance. About 40 full-time employees. Annual sales, $5 million-plus.

The benefits: Offers a full range of benefits, including health, dental, vision and life insurance. Also offers 401(k) savings plan, long-term disability, paid sick days and vacation, free parking and unpaid family emergency leave. Has liberal bonus plan under which top producers can earn up to 25% more in total salary.

Also offers vision care, which is about one-quarter the cost of dental care, which is about one-seventh the cost of medical. Sick leave provides six paid days; unused sick days are reimbursed at the end of the year up to four days maximum.

Full-time employees may buy merchandise at cost plus 10% with no limit. This formula was suggested by employees and accepted by management. The company reserves the right to put certain merchandise off-limits, usually one-of-a-kind pieces.

Costs: Total benefit cost is about 8%-10% of payroll, or about $135,000 to $170,000 yearly. Each employee receives an annual accounting of the company contribution for various benefits. Example: an employee with gross income (including commissions and bonus) of $35,000 is told he/she received a company contribution of $3,100 worth of medical, dental and vision care; $108 of life insurance; and $1,350 for education (including attendance at meetings and shows). Employees and the company share medical costs. Employees who take a Gemological Institute of America home-study course are paid half the cost up front and the balance upon completion.

Owner comment: The owner offers a rich benefits package to provide a "good place to work" and to attract and keep well-qualified employees in an intensely competitive market. Other employers in the market offer "humongous" benefits and high pay.

"We don't review our medical plan often enough, but the one we have is good. A change can be very disruptive. People don't like the prospect of going to a new doctor. We don't want to be too restrictive."

Regarding the merchandise benefit: "It's a real advantage to have our associates wearing nice jewelry. And it's great that some of them want to buy real dogs. It cleans out our inventory!"

JEWELER PROFILE

The jeweler: Single store in vital downtown in northeastern town of about 75,000. Eight full-time employees (including owner) and eight part-timers. Uses a salary plus commission compensation plan. Annual volume, $1.1 million.

The benefits: Offers medical, life and dental insurance, short- and long-term disability coverage, paid vacations, education financial assistance and unpaid family emergency leave. Also provides manager and assistant manager with free parking. Considering a pension plan with employee contribution but finds younger staffers are not interested. No savings plan or paid sick days. Owner feels the current benefits level is all the business can afford; employees have not requested any changes.

Costs: Medical coverage provided through local health maintenance organization that the owner contacted in his role as a member of a hospital board. It is a co-pay plan with the cost split 50/50 by employer and employee; each pays about $80 a month. A Travelers Insurance life policy was adopted at the suggestion of a good customer who is a Travelers' agent. The policy ties in with disability insurance, which kicks in the next day for an injury and after one week for an illness. The disability policy pays $175 for the first week, $115 a week for the next four. The total annual cost to the company for this program is $2,580.

Dental coverage is available free to all full-time employees. The cost of this private plan to the company is $2,150.

Paid vacation policy is two weeks after one year and three weeks after 10. The owner encourages employees who want to pursue further education (especially through Gemological Institute of America courses) to apply for scholarships. All have done so successfully. For those who cannot get a scholarship, the company is willing to pay 50¢ on the dollar for out-of-pocket expenses.

Merchandise discounts are cost plus 10%, with purchases restricted to personal use or for members of the immediate family. There is no cap. Unpaid emergency leave can be offered for up to three months—depending on the employee's need—and is restricted to immediate family—mother, father, spouse and child.

JEWELER PROFILE

The jeweler: Single store in high-end shopping district of large eastern metropolitan area. Two full-time and three part-time employees. Annual sales, about $700,000. Targets affluent customers, offers specialized merchandise.

The benefits: Offers full-time staff medical coverage through health maintenance organization, sick and vacation leave, profit-sharing pension plan, unpaid leave for family emergencies, financial help for education and merchandise discounts. Does not offer life or dental insurance.

Costs: The medical plan costs the company about $1,200 yearly; the cost to each participating employee is about $150 a month. Sick leave last year amounted to about 10 days. Figuring hourly pay at about $12, the total sick leave cost ran somewhat over $1,000. The company last year contributed about $6,000 to the defined contribution pension plan; administrative costs were "very, very minor." Vacation policy: 10 days for one to five years of service, 15 days for six to 10 years, and 20 days for more than 10 years.

Education costs average $2,000 to $5,000 a year for courses offered by the Gemological Institute of America and the International Society of Appraisers and/or special seminars offered by the Diamond Promotion Service. Payments to employees are made up front.

Merchandise purchases, at cost, totaled about $2,200 last year. The owner declines to estimate how much extra income the company would have earned had the merchandise been sold at regular retail. "It's important for employees to wear good jewelry."

Owner comment: "We did not try to shop around for benefits. We rely on our accountant for good advice on the pension plan. He recommended Vanguard, which gives us a plan that offers a lot of flexibility.

"We try to be as generous as we can afford to be. Sometimes, we give extra coverage if we can afford it. Of course, we offer unpaid family leave. People have lives, you know. People have emergencies and they have to deal with them. We want to make this a pleasant place to work."

JEWELER PROFILE

The jeweler: Two-store operation in a metropolitan area of about 2.2 million in western U.S. Sixteen full-time employees, including owner. Both units are destination stores in shopping centers. They cater to a retirement market of about 60,000 and a business/professional market of about 200,000. Annual volume, $1 million to $1.5 million.

The benefits: Offers health/medical and life insurance, paid sick days and vacations, profit sharing in a bonus system, education financial assistance, merchandise discounts and unpaid emergency family leave. Does not offer dental insurance because it's too costly in the local market; the staff is unwilling to participate because of the cost. A pension plan was dropped because of the annual administrative cost of about $5,000 and the lack of appeal to the staff. A 401(k) plan is not offered "because of the owner's procrastination."

Costs: Last fiscal year, the company's expense for the life/health package was $10,250. Employees who participate (a total of nine) contribute according to the following formulas: for full-time employees with 20 years or less of service, the company pays 75% of the individual's costs and 25% of dependents'; for those with more than 20 years of service, the company pays all the individual's costs and 75% of dependents'.

When changing providers last year, the owner hired a consultant who brought in five to eight companies to discuss what they offer; employees spoke with the three finalists. The owner also did some personal research among providers "to keep the consultant honest." In the end, the company chose the provider recommended by the consultant. It's a private company—not a health maintenance organization—offering considerable flexibility in choice of doctors.

For life insurance, the company pays 75% of the individual's cost and 25% of dependents'.

The change of insurance provider reduced costs 33% and increased benefit coverage. "The package, especially health insurance, is very important to some employees and for others it is a convenience," says the owner.

In the profit sharing plan, each store has a monthly sales goal. If the store makes the goal, the company pays a percent of gross revenue and of net profits into a pool; if the goal isn't met, only a percent of net profit is paid. At the end of the year, the total pool is split among staff members (75% to the sales staff, 25% to the support staff).

Sick leave is calculated on the basis of one paid day after one year with an additional day added up to the fifth year. The benefit may be taken, without question, in time or cash and does not accumulate past the yearend. Vacation policy: one week after one year, two weeks for two to 10 years, three weeks for 11 to 20 years and four weeks after 20 years. The company allows a mix of time or cash "within reason."

Gemological Institute of America courses or other courses that relate to a person's job are paid for upon successful completion. Merchandise discounts are available, with no cap on purchases, for cost plus 10%.

JCK Management Study Center Quiz

1. A 401(k) is most likely to be welcomed by:

a. A young, newly-married worker anxious to save for a rainy day.

b. The boss's wife because it will help her pay for her new home.

c. The highest-paid people in the business.

2. A premium conversion plan allows employees:

a. To pay for their medical insurance with pre-tax dollars.

b. To convert their insurance premiums into cash to meet an emergency.

c. To change their jobs with the company to a new "premium" level after they reach age 45.

3. One of the big advantages of handling health insurance through a Blue Cross plan is that:

a. The name is so well-known everyone will sign up.

b. If you fall into a Blue Cross community pool the age makeup of your group probably will not be a factor in granting coverage.

c. By joining Blue Cross at the start of the year you automatically qualify for free life insurance as part of your medical policy.

4. The Consolidated Omnibus Budget Reconciliation Act is important in benefit planning because:

a. It helps employers share the cost of medical insurance with their employees.

b. It can provide an employee with a continuation of health care coverage for up to 18 months if the employee quits to take it easy or take another job.

c. It can be invoked if the employee has a row with the boss to bring in an arbitrator who will seek a reconciliation.

5. More employers are moving toward managed-care health plans because:

a. They help control costs.

b. They give the store owner the right to deny any medical expense over a certain limit.

c. They qualify the company using them for matching federal funds.

6. One of the most telling reasons to offer employees a long-term disability plan is that:

a. You only have to pay premiums on the policy after the employee reaches age 50.

b. If a long-term employee becomes too ill to work you won't face having to decide when to cut off his salary as a store expense.

c. It offers you the opportunity to turn over your aging deadwood employees to the insurance company rather than fire them.

7. More companies are disregarding the distinction between vacation, sick or personal days because:

a. It means employees are less likely to take time off to visit the doctor.

b. It offers employees, especially those with small children, more flexibility in handling their time off.

c. It means the employer can cut back vacation time because employees can use sick or personal days for vacations.

8. Profit-sharing plans are popular because:

a. They allow both employers and employees to shelter some of their income from taxes.

b. If the employers don't want to share any of their profits they can tell employees they didn't make any.

c. No matter when an employee quits, he or she knows there'll be a nice payout.

9. The difference between a defined benefit retirement plan and a defined contribution one is:

a. In the defined benefit plan the employer defines the benefit and in the defined contribution plan the employees decide on the contribution.

b. In a defined benefit plan the employer makes a commitment to provide a specific retirement benefit while in the defined contribution plan the employer commits only to make contributions to a retirement fund, provided the resources are available.

c. There is no difference; they both pay the same benefits, only in different ways.

10. What is the most probable reason for a jeweler to discharge and lease back employees?

a. It means that their new employer of record is now responsible for getting and administering the best possible benefits package for the least possible cost.

b. It means the jeweler can rely on someone else to discipline or fire difficult employees.

c. It means that the new employer of record will pay Christmas bonuses instead of the jeweler.

(Answers to Quiz can be found at the end of this chapter)

Important Assets

Editorial ◆ *June 1994*

How often have you heard a company president stand before an industry audience and intone, "The people who work for XYZ Co. are its most important asset"?

Probably four times out of five this is sheer bull.

The ratio seems fair because in about four of every five companies workers rarely are treated as "important assets" when it comes to pay, benefits, recognition for merit, honest communication and real challenge. This may seem like a fairly sweeping statement, but I believe it's supportable.

For the broad picture, let's take a look at corporate America. Over just the past three or four years, close to 1 million workers have lost their jobs largely because management screwed up the companies they were running. Some of these workers got the semi-solace of forced early retirement. The rest were dumped, at best with a brass parachute.

It's true that a fair number of chief executives were axed as well. But their parachutes were at least 14k gold and often pure 24k.

Some of the workers were dumped because their companies were so deeply in trouble they would have gone bankrupt or out of business without draconian cost cuts. But many were let go just so profitable companies could become even more profitable. That may make sense to stockholders; it makes little or no sense to the "important asset" who's given the boot. And no matter why a company "downsizes" (a truly dodge-the-bullet euphemism), the skimming off of workers often has verged on the inhumane. Consider, too, that until the moment of their firing, most of these people really considered themselves company assets.

So much for the picture of big corporate America. How about small corporate America, the land where most jewelers live? Listen well as jewelry-store owners talk and you'll hear a lot about "wonderful people," salespeople who "make the business work," even an occasional "most important asset" eulogy.

Does such talk reflect reality? At best, only marginally. For more than 10 years, JCK has conducted yearly jewelry-store salary and benefit studies, and we've examined literally thousands of jewelry-store pay and benefit records. By and large, it's been a sorry experience. To put it as gently as possible, jewelry-store compensation generally is terrible. Pay often is pathetic—$5 or $6 or $7 an hour for experienced and well-regarded salespeople. That's not too far above the poverty line if the person being paid also is a head of household. The benefits are equally spare.

It's no defense to say that jewelers pay no less than retail as a whole. The truth is that a good retailer—jeweler or otherwise—doesn't have to go third class in compensation. There are living, successful examples to prove that going first class can pay off in spades.

Just as our salary studies paint a widely dismal picture of employee rewards, they also uncover some real stars. I think right away of a half dozen or so participating stores that pay their staffs generously, offer excellent benefits—and are the most financially successful and personally respected in the industry.

That's where we come to the chicken-and-egg issue. Jeweler A says, "I can't afford to pay any more; the business won't support the cost." Jeweler B says, "If I don't pay enough to hire the best people, I'll never build a first-class business."

The industry has a lot of the first type of jeweler. If they don't change their chicken-egg philosophy quickly, they may be condemned to a lifetime of struggle and mediocrity or may even go out of business. A few of the Jewelers Bs may go down in flames, too, because available resources didn't last long enough to get the business on its feet and going in the right direction. But the Bs will succeed provided their attitude to employees is matched by an equally farsighted view of all other parts of their operation. And employee relations have to go far beyond compensation to include open communication, honesty, fairness, good working conditions and more.

Most business leaders dream of hiring and guiding an elite team of top producers. With the right team, a boss knows that nothing is unattainable. If you want such a team, you must aim for the top in everything you do for and with your employees. You mustn't just talk about "important assets." You must prove you mean it.

The rewards can be beyond calculation.

Motivating Non-Family Workers In A Family Business

September 1991 Part II

Motivating employees requires more delicacy in a small family business than in a large corporate environment. Without proper motivation, non-family employees can quickly become resentful, moving from asset to liability.

This resentment typically centers on the appearance—real or imagined—that certain positions will be forever out of their reach. Consider the longtime non-family employee who remembers the boss's child as an irresponsible teenager "working" in the store. Eventually, the child graduates from college and waltzes into a position over the longtime employee, even though he or she doesn't seem at all qualified.

Such resentment can be avoided if a store owner properly motivates employees, is honest from the start about their chances for advancement and doesn't show obvious favoritism to heirs.

"Communication is the key," says François de Visscher, a family business planner in Stamford, Ct. "Non-family members need to know there's no uncertainty about how far up they can go in the firm."

This is particularly critical for managers and other high-level employees. "You want to be sure there is an avenue of growth and promotion for non-family members," de Visscher adds. He suggests that some executive position always be held by a non-family member. There are two major advantages:

• Morale improves when lower-level non-family employees see other outsiders rise through the ranks.

• The non-family executive gives a tight-knit family a valuable outside view of operations.

Non-family employees: Alan Walker at Walkers N' Daughters Jewelers, Bismarck, N.D., says his family's three retail stores often benefit from suggestions by non-family employees. A non-family employee first suggested boosting the firm's custom jewelry work. Today, custom orders are a fast-growing part of the business, and the clerk who made the suggestion has advanced to become one of two non-family employees managing a store.

Walkers N' Daughters has five family and 12 non-family employees. To motivate them, says Walker, the firm keeps the lines of communication open at all times, gives employees greater responsibility as they gain experience and arranges sales competitions and trips to local jewelry shows.

Communication is the key to integrating non-family employees in the business, says Milton H. Stern, author of *Inside the Family Business* and a senior partner at the Hannoch Weisman law firm in Roseland, N.J.

Critical points to pass on to non-family employees include upcoming ownership changes, corporate goals (store growth and profit expectations) and succession plans. Important incentives for non-family employees include:

• Profit-sharing plans.

• Stock-ownership plans.

• Medical and insurance expense reimbursement.

• Perks such as a company car, expense account and executive office (where applicable).

Family employees: When a family member is about to join a firm, the owner should prepare employees to lessen or avoid resentment. Stern suggests the following:

• Encourage the family member to work at another firm first to gain experience. This will quiet charges that he or she has no experience.

• Clearly define the new employee's role.

• Have someone other than parents or siblings train the family member.

"This makes for a more objective and impersonal trainer/trainee relationship," says Stern. "Criticism is not so destructive and the recipient feels there is more substance to praise given by an unrelated party."

• Demand that younger relatives respect veteran employees.

"I have seen a number of instances where very young men, just because they have the same last name as the proprietor, browbeat people who have worked conscientiously for the company for many years," Stern says. "The effect on morale can be terrible."

Employees also can become angry and frustrated because they can't "tell off" the son or complain to the father.

• Make it clear that respect goes both ways. Employees must not constantly remind Junior how little he knows or recall that they remember him in diapers. Both sides should be able to approach the boss if relations among workers become tense.

• Compensate younger family employees on the basis of performance, particularly during their early years in the business.

Selling Sales To Salespeople

September 1991 Part II

There is no such a thing as a "born salesperson," but Nancy, your top achiever, comes close. If she had come into the world with a silver spoon in her mouth, she would have sold it to the doctor and ordered another for the delivery room nurse. She's been a top-notch employee from day one, and you want to make sure she stays that way.

Joe does what you tell him to do—usually. He comes to work on time—barely. He completes assigned tasks, but won't polish a case unless you tell him to. Worst of all, it takes him too long to get up nerve to approach customers; he loses sales because he claims the customer is "just browsing" and doesn't seem to need help.

As the manager of the store, you need to draw excellent performance from the high achiever approaching burnout, the low achiever approaching dismissal, and everyone in between. What do you use? Gifts? Threats? Hypnotism? Baseball bats?

The answer is E: some of the above, but not all. There are ways to motivate your employees to reach and maintain their highest potential, even in the toughest economic times. JCK asked some experts about what works and what doesn't.

Leading the horse: Jewelers often ask, "How can a manager motivate a person to sell jewelry?" Many training experts answer, "A manager can't motivate a person at all."

"It is fundamentally impossible to motivate someone. The best you can do is to inspire someone," claims Orley Solomon, vice president of training and personnel development for the Seattle-based Ben Bridge chain. You can temporarily inspire, he explains, but ultimate motivation has to come from within.

Does that mean a manager has no responsibility to make salespeople want to sell? Quite the contrary. The desire to succeed is intrinsic, like a child's curiosity. But just as a teacher has to stimulate a child's desire to learn, a manager has to draw excitement out of his or her people. Solomon says a manager's job is much like a salesperson's: "You have to find out what the employee's hot buttons are [just as] you have to find out what customers want and give it to them."

Managerial positions require reinforcement and reprimand. But managers must learn to rely less upon *making* an employee do a job; instead, they should try to find out what encourages the employee to *want* to do the job.

Motivation that comes from within lasts, too, according to Dr. Loretta A. Rieser-Danner, assistant professor of psychology at Villanova University, Villanova, Pa.

"Intrinsic motivation over the long term is much more powerful than extrinsic motivation," she says. When external rewards are relied on too heavily, "the [employee's] goal changes. It's no longer self-satisfaction." You don't want them to focus solely on the reward; you want them to enjoy a job well done.

Target management: "You can't throw a bowling ball at a blank sheet and expect to hit the pins behind it," says Kate Peterson, director of training for Akron, Ohio-based Sterling Inc. "Demands must be crystal clear."

Employees can't reach goals if they don't know what they are. That's why managers must clarify performance expectations up front.

David Richardson, a professional speaker with the Richardson Resource Group, Scottsdale, Ariz., says one of the main reasons people leave a job is because they don't know what they are supposed to be doing. "The barrier is that managers won't set specific goals and standards with people."

Get the workers themselves involved in the goal-setting process with good questions, he suggests. Sit down with a person and say something like this: "Last October, you sold $3,000 worth of merchandise. How much do you think you can sell this month?" Then set the employee's own response as his goal for the month.

Conduct structured weekly sales meetings at which a broad range of how-to topics are discussed—how to greet customers, close sales, overcome objections, turn a sale over when necessary. Then at the end of the meeting, go around the room asking for one idea from each employee that they think they can apply to their daily selling strategies.

"Encourage them to think," Richardson says. "That way the ideas become their own."

And don't just let it go at that: *follow up* during the week. If a person has said she will work on greeting customers with more enthusiasm, give specific recognition when you see her doing that.

"Manage each person one-on-one, based on what they've said at the end of the meeting," says Richardson.

Expectations that do come directly from the manager should be extremely challenging, but not be completely unattainable. It's better, however, to err on the side of excellence than to aim too low. Educational psychologists know that students pick up immediately on how a teacher believes they are going to perform. If Johnny is in the "bright" group, he knows he is supposed to excel, and most often does. Put Johnny in the "slow" group next year because of relocation or a change in placement procedure and his performance will decline.

The same is true of a sales staff. If Joe knows you expect Nancy to have the highest dollar figures every month, he's not going to push himself any harder than he must to keep you satisfied.

When setting expectation levels, "You have to strike a balance," says Dr. Peter Kuriloff, professor and former chair of the University of Pennsylvania's Psychology in Education Department. "If the goal is totally ridiculous, it fails. But goals have to be high enough so they're a stretch for people. You have to work with people to know where they are."

If workers constantly reach for specific goals that require a stretch—higher monthly dollar figures, two more add-on sales per day, one fresh sales approach consistently used during a week—the attainment of these goals will build self-esteem. And salespeople need all the confidence they can get when they're out there selling their own image and that of your store to potential customers.

Hot buttons: Higher self-esteem is one reward for good performance in your store. But self-esteem alone doesn't pay the salesperson's bills—and paid bills alone don't convince a salesperson that he or she is important to your company. Although rewards shouldn't be so overused that they replace the inner satisfaction that comes from success, employees do deserve to be recognized both tangibly and intangibly when they live up to or surpass their goals and your expectations. Such recognition, when done right, can significantly increase the desire to succeed again.

Opinion differs across the board as to what rewards are most effective in motivating salespeople.

"No matter what you do, it will never be enough, and they will tell you when it's not enough—about every three months," quips William E. Boyajian, president of the Gemological Institute of America. He believes that employees respond to a system that combines all types of recognition or "stroking" (verbal, written, public, private), money and education. "Contrary to some people's opinion, I don't think the number one way [to motivate] is through money," he says, "it's through giving the emotional, intangible, genuine recognition. Then follow that up with financial benefits."

Jewelers responding to the JCK retail panel survey add to the list of rewards that work: discounts on merchandise, time off from work, promotion, healthy and insurance benefits, sponsorship for courses given by the GIA or the Dale Carnegie Institute, travel, dinners at local restaurants, even company-sponsored parties or free food in the back of the store can be a perk for a sales staff that performs exceptionally well. Sibbings Jewelry in Iowa gave a two-pound box of candy to the person who sold the first 1-ct. or larger diamond this year. Jerry G. Miller of Wink's Jewelry in South Dakota says he puts a $20 bill up on a board every week as a reward for the largest sale in a chosen category and everyone tracks how it changes hands from day to day.

Panelists also list factors such as job satisfaction, fair treatment, respect, a pleasant atmosphere, and involvement in the store among the top factors that motivate salespeople.

Does it really matter what the reward is for a job well done? Only to the extent that it is something the employees want. The important thing is to recognize effort, and the more original the form of recognition, the greater the impact on the minds and spirits of those who receive it.

According to John Michaels, CEO of Michaels Jewelers, Waterbury, Conn., a commission on top of salary is important more for the sense of excitement it adds than for its monetary value. "It lets a salesperson see a light at the end of the tunnel. The next customer can always be a sale." He believes even a modest 1% commission encourages salespeople to learn how to sell higher priced merchandise.

Michaels also believes that trust in the firm motivates a salesperson. He says it is tough for managers when the store is "requiring a person to be absolutely truthful about diamond quality, gold karatage, real prices. Our salespeople lose a lot of sales because they can't lie."

This can be turned around and used to advantage by a good manager. "You have to make them believe in the quality of the store's goods."

When the salesperson sees jewelry that was bought somewhere else "on sale" and is of poor quality, they become motivated by the fact that they are "working for a firm that tells the truth," according to Michaels. Pride in the merchandise makes it much easier to sell jewelry.

The subject of store-wide contests also inspires a broad range of responses, from very positive to very negative. Some experts believe individuals should compete against one another, some believe employees should compete as a team.

Here is a sampling of their ideas:

• John Michaels: Advocates a "store team share." A goal is set for the store every month and the salespeople share in the pot created by whatever is left over after the goal is reached. That way, "once they're over goal, every sale is extra money." The competition exists as a team working against a number rather than people working against other people.

• David Richardson: "A storewide goal does not promote team spirit. It promotes animosity." Good salespeople, he believes, are de-motivated on a team bonus plan when poorer performers drag down the team. Sometimes the real movers will even be asked to slow down their performance by those who don't want the standards to be any higher. "People should be paid upon their ability to perform," he says.

Richardson believes contests based on individual quotas are good, but most fail because of three common mistakes.

First, most are too long. "None should be longer than a month; after that, interest is lost," he explains.

Second, they're not merchandised properly; a thermometer or similar poster on the wall tracking progress makes the contest more visible. Managers must talk it up and make a big deal out of it to keep excitement high.

Finally, too many contests are not fair in standards of measurement because part-timers compete against full-timers. Use percentages for measurement instead of actual dollar figures, he suggests.

• William Boyajian: "I like the team concept." Rather than dragging down the high achievers, he thinks the experience of working on a team "lifts those who aren't pulling their weight . . . raises negative people to be positive."

• Dr. Mary Applegate, assistant professor of education at St. Joseph's University, Philadelphia, says working cooperatively is effective only if "each person is accountable to the group for something." She says projects work when each member has to contribute a finished product to the whole—like a jigsaw puzzle—so it is impossible for one member to do all the work.

Applegate also uses a system whereby each member of the group evaluates the other members in complete confidence on issues of participation and cooperation. The effect is twofold: Those not pulling their weight won't get the same reward the rest of the group earns if negative reports are consistent and valid. Those who are working hard but tend to moan after the project is over that so-and-so was lazy can voice their opinions while the project is still ongoing.

"It makes a big difference in the grumbling afterwards," she says.

• Orley Solomon: Contests are fine, but they are "only for fun," he says. Contests as simple as a spiff for selling a certain item, or a prize drawing for which a chance is earned by making a sale, are important only because having fun on the job is itself a motivator. Other than their potential for fun, he insists, "contests have nothing to do with motivation."

Consistency: No matter what form reward systems or contests take, employees need to know that excellence will be consistently recognized. Simple praise is cited as the reward employees appreciate the most and receive the least. But praise without commensurate compensation wears thin quickly. Solomon sums it up when he says that "at Ben Bridge, if you do a good job, you will be successful. That's motivating." Salespeople need to know the reward for hard work is success, and as a manger you need to find out what "hot buttons" constitute success for each employee in your store.

A gentle reminder: When should reprimand be used instead of reinforcement?

The experts' consensus is, "only when absolutely necessary."

"There's more to a caress than a kick," says Tom Dorman, executive director of the American Gem Society in Los Angeles. "A pat on the back goes further than a kick in the butt."

However, only in an ideal world would a manager never have to put a little foot to flesh, at least in the figurative sense. When a salesperson does need to be called on poor performance or inappropriate behavior, it's important that the manager accomplish the deed without de-motivating the employee. A tough task, but not impossible if a few standards are followed.

"Accolades are paramount and should be announced publicly," says Dorman. When it comes to discipline, though, "never humiliate or reprimand in front of anyone else. Do it in private only." Public

reprimand serves only to lower the self-esteem of the employee. Little of the message you are trying to communicate will reach through the rage and embarrassment created by the rebuke.

Dorman goes on to suggest that every criticism can be tempered by praise. "It's better to be constructive," he claims. "Anytime you reprimand someone, give them a little plus, too." It takes more effort on your part, but if you present a weakness to an employee in a positive way—"You're very strong in your ability to relate to customers, but you need to work on your rapport with your coworkers"—the negative message will fall on much more receptive ears.

You can't always be sweet and kind in a managerial position. "Reprimand with kindness if at all possible," says Boyajian, "but sometimes you need to raise your voice." When that happens, remember it is a means to an end, and not a habit you want to solidify as part of your management style.

Use corrective actions as a second choice only, and use them with care so they don't work against the positive attitude you try to instill in your people. Punishment teaches people to avoid a certain behavior. Dr. Resiser-Danner adds that it is effective in the short term, but eventually you have to ask what it's really teaching. Quite often, it's simply "not to get caught."

"With reinforcement, employees learn a new behavior instead."

Back to basics: Robert Fulghum's best-selling novel, "All I Really Need to Know I Learned in Kindergarten," points out that the lessons we learned as small children would serve us well as adults if we would just remember them. The world would be a better place, he claims, if we would clean up our own messes, share everything and play fair.

The challenge to awaken excitement in employees calls on principles that are just as simple, and just as easily forgotten.

Treat your employees with respect. Learn about their interests and listen to their ideas. If they are involved in decision-making, they will be more committed to the decisions made. "A manager has to be accessible," says Solomon. "An employee has to know that there are no crazy ideas," and that your door is open to suggestions.

Make work fun. Even the most seasoned employee gets into a rut and loses interest sometimes. An interesting, lively environment will help bring them out of it.

Let each employee know where he or she fits into the company, and how important his or her good work is to you.

And most important, lead by example. Be the type of worker you want your employee to be. "Employees need to be convinced that managers are the best at what they do," says Peterson.

Your salespeople will imitate your work ethic if they respect your expertise. They will pick up your enthusiasm because it is, by nature, contagious. And they will find reason within themselves to sell—if you sell excellence as the goal of your store.

10 Certain De-Motivators

- No recognition of jobs well done
- Unenthusiastic management
- Insufficient job training
- Verbal reprimand in front of peers
- Favoritism

- Unrealistic goals
- Unexciting reward system
- Empty threats or promises
- No changes in routine
- No chance for advancement

'90s Staffing: Balancing Employees' Needs With Yours

September 1991 Part II

Jo Erwin likes people. She also likes jewelry. But most of all, she likes living. At age 80, she's not ready to roll up and retire. She works three or four hours every day tracking the 4,000+ repairs done annually at J.A. May Jewelers in Farmington, N.M.

In Modesto, Cal., salesman Joe Chavez bridges the language barrier for the growing Hispanic clientele at Roger's Jewelry. Owner Roger Marks appreciates Chavez's sales skill with a broad range of customers; Hispanics appreciate his ability to speak with them about jewelry in their own language.

Sandy Wade, meanwhile, proves to customers at Chupp Jewelers Inc., Lafayette, Ind., that determination can overcome some limitations of a physical disability. Though she has trouble walking, she does just about everything her coworkers do.

Erwin, Chavez and Wade represent groups that once were among exceptions to retail staffing. But these are the '90s, and demographic shifts are changing the face of the U.S. labor force. Three shifts in particular will account for many changes in the way retailers hire and handle employees through the end of the decade:

• The huge baby boom generation will move into its middle and late middle age, leaving in its place a much smaller succeeding generation to fill a growing number of service-oriented jobs.

• The influx of women into the work force will continue, creating the need for more family-care benefits and placing more emphasis on workplace equality.

• The explosion of ethnic population growth— through immigration and high birth rates—will increase racial and cultural diversity in many neighborhoods. The retailers who cater to these groups— including hiring from among them—will be in a better position to win their loyalty and their business.

John R. Schultz, president of the Retail Services Division of the National Retail Federation, New York

City, says the most critical employee issue of the '90s is how customers perceive employees. "Are employees friendly, helpful, knowledgeable, enthusiastic?" he asks. "If so, you know the employer has made an effort to make those employees happy by meeting their changing needs."

Richard Laffin of the Management Growth Institute, Wellesley, Mass., puts it this way: "People used to live to work; now they work to live. The strength of the independent jeweler will lie in the flexibility to meet the changes this brings."

Here's a more detailed look at why these changes present a growing challenge to employers as they balance their own needs with their employee's needs.

THE PEOPLE

Agewise, the labor force falls into three major categories: baby busters, baby boomers and mature Americans. From young to old, the people behind these life-stage labels will have a profound effect on the work force and labor issues through the '90s and beyond. Will you be able to attract and motivate younger workers? Can you offer enough challenge and compensation to keep middle-agers satisfied as they head into their prime earning years? And what about older workers and retirees? Are you willing to meet their health-care and pension needs in return for dedicated and loyal service?

• **Busters:** The youngest of the three groups—the baby-bust generation—gets its name from the drastic birth-rate drop that began in 1965. Its members present two major challenges to employers:

1) After nearly 20 years of being flooded with job applications from the huge baby-boom generation, employers will receive fewer inquiries from the much smaller baby-bust generation. The number of working-age busters (18-24) will drop 9%, from 26.9 million in

1989 to 24.3 million in 1995, says the U.S. Census Bureau. During the same period, the number of retail sales positions will grow about 20%, from 3.8 million to 4.6 million, says the U.S. Bureau of Labor Statistics.

2) The baby-bust generation has questionable work ethics and limited training, according to surveys of human resource and education experts. Younger workers are motivated by self-interest and are out of touch with the "old-fashioned" notion that working hard has its own, intrinsic value, according to a recent study of 400 large and small firms by the Daniel Yankelovich Group Inc. for the American Association of Retired Persons. And while many people assume that technical skills are the only ones that have declined, a report by the U.S. Department of Labor says young workers also lack "a good work ethic and social skills," both critical to retail sales.

Is there any light in this gloomy picture?

Yes, if you're willing to offer training, better compensation and a better working environment than other service-oriented firms. You still won't attract college graduates, but you'll get the cream of the rest of the crop. You can even start with high-school students. "We're in a partnership program with local schools," says Robert Smyth Jr., vice president of Albert Smyth Co., Timonium, Md. "Students go to school part of the day, then come here for jobs ranging from entry-level filing up to working on the sales floor."

The firm has participated in the program for about 20 years and is pleased overall. "Quite a few students join us full time after graduating," says Smyth. "We've gotten some of our best people this way."

• **Boomers:** Baby boomers, the 80.6 million people born between 1945 and 1964, present a challenge of a different sort.

Younger boomers should be entering their prime earning years. Many will want to move into top management jobs, but there will be more suitors than jobs. If you don't offer alternatives to dead-end jobs, you'll end up with unfilled positions or workers who don't care about their job performance. One alternative is to create positions with top-level pay but not authority. Others include longer vacations, free education or even profit-sharing.

Older boomers, comprising one-fifth of the work force, will be about 10 years from retirement by the end of the 1990s. This is a critical earnings decade for them. But they'll also want efficient health-care, pension and savings plans (see the "Issues" section).

• **Mature:** Jo Erwin remembers the day in 1972 when she walked into J.A. May Jewelers and asked owner Jess May for a job. "I had no retail jewelry experience and was 61 years old, but Mr. May hired me anyway."

She stayed on when May turned over the store to William McGraw in 1989, though now she works just three or four hours a day. "She's a stabilizing force for us," says McGraw. "She's interested in her work, is good with customers and is dependable."

Erwin and store owners interviewed for this article agree that dependability is a major advantage of hiring

older people. "Older people *are* dependable, if not by choice, by circumstance," says Erwin.

Retirees who return to work say they do it to keep active, for companionship and to supplement eager pensions, according to a study by the Federal Reserve Bank of Richmond. Companies rate these "formerly retired" workers high in many categories, according to the AARP study. The respondents said they appreciate older employees' coolness in a crisis, their practical knowledge and their work ethics, including commitment to quality, loyalty, attendance and punctuality. The respondents did note that health costs are higher for older employees (60% offered insurance coverage for previously retired employees, and said it costs 15% more than for average-age workers).

Aside from age, two other significant demographic shifts in the 1990s are working women and the rising tide of ethnic populations.

• **Working women:** Look at the statistics. The number of employed women jumped from 21.8 million in 1960 to 52 million in 1990, a 138% increase. It's clear that women have carved their place in the labor force. It's less clear how well employers have responded.

Family-care benefits are still new or unheard of in some companies. And even the 30-year-old cry of equal pay for equal work continues to fall on deaf ears in some cases. JCK's salary survey for 1989 found that women who manage stores earned 72% of what men in the same position received. That's down from 81% of what male salespeople earned in 1988. Female salespeople earned 81% of what male salespeople earned in1989, up from 70% in 1988.

"Equal pay for equal work simply doesn't exist across the board," says Laffin of the Management Growth Institute. "But it will be an issue of growing importance in this decade."

As the '90s progress, more women will demand an end to wage discrimination and will insist on better day-care options and more flexible work schedules, according to the 1990 Virginia Slims Opinion Poll (see "Issues" section for more details on day care and flexible schedules).

• **Ethnic:** Joe Chavez of Roger's Jewelry represents a type of employee who will become increasingly important to retailers as ethnic populations expand. He was hired because he's knowledgeable and is a good communicator with a broad spectrum of consumers. But he also is valued because he can communicate with a growing Hispanic clientele in its language. "Hispanics are more comfortable speaking with a salesman who speaks their own language," says Marks, who just completed his second and final term as president of Jewelers of America.

Minority groups now account for one in five Americans, says the U.S. Census Bureau. A surge in the U.S. Hispanic population in the 1980s and a doubling of Asian-Americans are two of the major reasons. But before you hire someone who speaks Spanish or an Asian language, remember these groups are diverse. It's better to hire based on skill rather than the language they speak.

Not all languages are spoken either. Randall Chambers of Chambers Fine Jewelry, Fort Worth, Tex., knows the advantages of being able to communicate with sign language. Chambers, who learned to sign because his brother was born deaf, now has about 30 regular deaf customers. "Deaf people get married and celebrate special occasions with gifts just like the hearing population," he says. "They really appreciate someone who can communicate with them in their 'tongue.'"

THE ISSUES

Shifts in employee demographics, as described above, are causing a major change in issues employers will have to face in the 1990s. Gone are the days where it was the employee's responsibility to juggle his home life to fit around his work. Today, employees demand that the workplace adjust itself to fit their home lives.

Many of the emerging issues are family-related, such as day care for children and aging parents. Societal shifts that propelled women into the workplace also have broken apart the extended family structure, leaving a void of support that workers now look to the employer to fill. Additionally, as workers age, they become more concerned with security for their own futures.

Other issues are social, arising from changes in education, expectations and legislation. These, too, must be dealt with—especially since the available labor pool is shrinking and employers who need manpower are going to have to accept some things they may not have in earlier decades.

• **Child care:** More than 29 million children under age 15 have mothers who work, says the Census Bureau. "If a mother pays $100 a week for child care for one child, that takes quite a bite out of her paycheck," says Robert Smyth Jr. of Albert Smyth Co. "Add to that $20 or $30 as the employee contribution to health coverage for the child, plus transportation costs, and some women find they can't afford to work."

One option is to operate a day-care center, but the expense limits this to large firms. Sterling Inc., the second-largest U.S. jeweler, recently added a day-care center at its headquarters in Akron, Ohio, large enough to handle 100 children of headquarters' employees. Such centers are thought to improve productivity and morale, reduce absenteeism and solve problems with the accessibility and quality of care.

If you can't afford this option alone, see if other retailers nearby might be willing to share the expenses, risks and benefits. Joint projects appear to work best in office parks and retail clusters, according to the Bureau of Labor Statistics.

Or you could develop a referral list of child-care programs in your community or offer to set up accounts into which money from paychecks is deposited—pretax—for reimbursement for child-care expenses.

• **Handicapped employees:** Handicapped Americans comprise a diverse group, ranging from the blind, deaf or wheelchair-bound to the learning dis-

abled. Not all of them are able to work. But if you don't make absolutely certain a disability would prevent an applicant from performing the job before you turn him down, you could easily end up the loser in a court battle. The federal Americans with Disabilities Act forbids discrimination against disabled workers by firms with 25 workers or more as of July 26, 1992, and with 15 workers or more as of July 26, 1994. Under the law, employers also must take "reasonable" accommodations to permit workers with disabilities to perform their jobs.

About 33 million Americans have some type of chronic condition that limits their activity, according to the National Center for Health Statistics. But many are able and eager to work. Sandy Wade, for example, has become a valued employee for Leland and Martha Chupp of Chupp Jewelers, Lafayette, Ind. Though she has trouble walking because of problems with her legs, she helps the Chupps with everything from cleaning the store to working the sales floor. "She's got a good sense of humor and is good with customers," says Martha Chupp. "People with disabilities appreciate having a job and are eager to prove themselves worthy."

• **Elder care:** The *Los Angeles Times* got a surprise early this year when it conducted a survey and found more readers interested in getting benefits to care for parents than to care for children. The concern is a growing one as the middle of the baby-boom generation enters its 40s. Their parents are growing elderly and need care but, with the increase in two-income families, no one is left at home to provide it. Few employers have opted to help. The Bureau of Labor Statistics says only 3% of workers were eligible for elder-care assistance in 1989.

As with child care, options include flexible schedules, job sharing, referral services and dependent care reimbursement accounts.

• **Family leave:** Some employers allow workers a defined time off—paid or unpaid—after the birth or adoption of a child or during a family illness. Just over half the states have laws requiring firms to allow some type of family leave; a federal law under consideration would require employers with 50 or more employees to allow 12 weeks per year of unpaid, job-protected family leave.

Many business organizations, including Jewelers of America, have opposed such legislation, saying the expense and problems of finding qualified replacements on a temporary basis would be troublesome. Proponents say the increasing number of working parents makes such legislation inevitable, especially as competition for employees increases.

• **Flex time, job sharing:** With flex time, employees generally work a core of hours during midday and vary the time they begin and end work, with prior approval. This helps employees to juggle the demands of family and work. The disadvantage for jewelers—especially those with few employees—is juggling the schedule to make sure someone is available to open and close the store each day.

Job sharing is another option. Two young parents may want to split a shift so they can be home with a child half of the day.

• **Health care:** The cost of health care is the No. 1 problem facing small businesses today, according to the Small Business Legislative Council, Washington, D.C. Group-policy payments rose from $8.1 billion in 1970 to $70.3 billion in 1987, an astounding 768% increase over the 17 years, or an average 45% increase annually.

"Who's going to pay for it?" says Laffin. Employers pass along some of the cost to customers, absorb some and increase employee contributions, says the SBLC.

Smyth sums up the majority opinion for dealing with the increased cost: "We've moved our policy three times in three years in seeking the very best coverage at a price our employees can afford."

Non-traditional health-care plans—such as health maintenance organizations and preferred provider organizations—have grown in popularity in the past decade, says the U.S. Bureau of Labor Statistics. With these programs, participating health-care providers agree to contain costs in exchange for patient referrals.

Another option is to join your state's high-risk insurance pool (24 states have them). Because premiums are based on usage, a very ill patient can result in higher premiums for every member of your group policy. If you transfer the employee to the high-risk pool, you'll pay an average 1 1/2 times to normal premium for him, but then may negotiate a lower rate for healthy employees. Call your state insurance commissioner for details.

As with child-care and elder-care, you also may set up a pretax savings account from which medical expenses can be reimbursed.

• **Literacy:** Get ready for a wave of illiterate and marginally literate workers. Nearly one-quarter of teens now entering high school won't graduate, and those who do will be less literate than graduates of a decade ago. This warning is reflected in "Literacy in the Work Force," a new study by the Conference Board, a business research group in New York.

About one-fifth of 163 large companies polled nationwide told the Conference Board they already have problems finding people who can read well enough to qualify for entry-level jobs. JCK's own poll of retail jewelers found that 17% encountered problems with illiteracy among job applicants in the past year.

"Illiteracy has become a softly ticking time bomb," says Dr. Leonard Lund, education specialist for the Conference Board. "While precise data are not available, the evidence strongly suggests that the work-force skills of many youngsters are declining at a time when new jobs are becoming increasingly sophisticated."

Who's at fault? You are. As an employer, you should test reading and writing skills (70% of firms in the Conference Board study do not). As a citizen and taxpayer, you should demand and financially support community programs that combat illiteracy.

• **Pension/savings plans:** No doubt about it. Pension plans can be costly. But they can meant the difference between keeping or losing employees. Though savings in general have been slim in the past 20 years, nearly nine Americans in ten between ages 30-50 already have started to save for retirement, according to a Gallup survey.

Contact a financial consultant or lawyer to help you weigh the advantages and disadvantages of various types of plans. The most common type is called a defined-benefit plan, where companies are required to make a set payment each month when the employee retires.

A second type is called the defined-contribution plan, requiring a set contribution yearly, by the employer, the employee or both. Under this category are profit-sharing pension plans, where a portion of profits is placed in the pension plan, and employee stock ownership plans, where employers buy stock for employees.

The 401(k) plan, an increasingly popular defined-contribution plan, calls for a percentage of wages to be placed in a pension fund on a regular basis. Employees pay no income tax or interest until the benefits are distributed. Unlike employer-sponsored plans, employees must pay Social Security taxes on their contributions, however. The major advantage to employers is that they aren't required to contribute to these plans. Fifty-one percent of the firms that sponsor 401(k) plans make contributions, and about half of those are on a dollar-for-dollar basis, says the U.S. General Accounting Office.

• **Substance abuse:** "It nearly breaks my heart," says Roger Marks. "We once employed a young man who had a wonderful future. He was a good salesman, progressed to become assistant manager, then a manager, all while he was still in his 20s. He had ability. He had charisma. Then he got a drug problem." Marks tried to counsel the employee, got him into a rehabilitation program and moved him out of management but gave him another job so he could continue to work. "He's gone now; nothing worked."

Drug and alcohol abuse can take a huge toll in the workplace. Substance abusers were absent 2 1/2 times more often than non-abusers, their productivity was 25%-30% lower, their probability of off-the-job accidents was four to six times higher and their claims for worker compensation were three times greater, according to a study by the Bureau of Labor Statistics. And, as Marks cautions, substance abusers can become thieves to support their habits.

Some firms offer to pay for short-term counseling or refer an employee to community- or state-sponsored programs for longterm counseling or therapy.

Employers also can test for drug use when hiring. Some states have specific laws on testing for drugs, so check with your state's department of labor and industry before proceeding.

Tighter Labor Force vs. Hiring Standards

December 1990

A sort of panic sets in when the labor force shows signs of shrinking. But retailers should be careful to maintain hiring standards to avoid costly mistakes.

Two demographic shifts already have started to reduce the number of job-seekers and will continue to do so in the next few decades, according to government projections.

First, more people are already employed than at any time in the past decade, according to the U.S. Bureau of Labor Statistics. (Though unemployment rose slightly to 5.5% in July, that still was far below the high of 9.5% reached in the early and mid-1980s.)

Second, the U.S. Census Bureau projects that population growth will slow through the end of this decade and begin to decline after 2040. A stagnant or declining population also means fewer people are seeking jobs.

When this happens, human resources officials feel they simply can't afford to screen applicants and risk losing the chance to hire them, says Dr. Jack Jones, an industrial psychologist and vice president of research at London House Inc., Park Ridge, Ill. "Everyone focuses on dropping their standards, and that's the wrong thing to do," he says.

Lower standards can lead to increased employee theft, higher turnover, unskilled or unreliable workers who require more training and supervision and skyrocketing insurance costs from accident-prone employees. The resulting financial burden can be onerous, especially among smaller retailers with small profit margins, he says.

The solutions? Jones suggests using "novel recruitment techniques to build and expand the applicant pool." Among these techniques:

- Reward employees for recruiting peers.
- Offer training and growth opportunities as incentives.
- Attend job fairs.
- Advertise job openings in appropriate media; for example, recruit part-time Christmas help through a high school or college newsletter instead of the city paper.
- Offer benefits that would attract overlooked groups such as senior citizens and minorities.

A majority of jewelers stuck to the high ground when hiring in 1988-'89, according to a recent JCK poll. More than two-thirds of respondents (68%) said their new hires met all their hiring requirements. Eighty-four percent gave their new hires performance ratings of good, very good or excellent. Only 11% said fair, and 5% said poor.

The most frequently mentioned hiring policies were checking all references (mentioned by 35% of respondents) and checking with former employers (29%). Seven percent checked credit references.

Guard Against Negligent Hiring

December 1989

You may try to tell yourself "it won't happen to me." You may convince yourself you've taken every precaution and that your procedures and personnel are sound. But you still could be vulnerable to negligent-hiring lawsuits, as shown in the following fictional illustration:

Sam Smith, owner of Smith Jewelers, thought Steve was basically a good person when he hired him as a sales associate. Steve was vibrant and eager to work; he seemed to have the knack to persuade customers they couldn't go another day without buying a certain piece of jewelry.

True, Smith found some highly negative factors during a standard background check, which involved running the applicant's name past state and local police, checking his driving record with the state transportation department and making a few calls to personal references. Steve had been caught shoplifting as a juvenile. In addition, a previous employer said Steve volunteered to leave the firm when management became suspicious and confronted him about skimming money from several cash registers.

142

These were weighty considerations, indeed. But Smith wasn't worried about the shoplifting; Steve was just a kid then, looking for a little thrill. That he may have dipped into store profits bothered him, but no formal charges were ever filed. Besides, Smith offered incentives for employees who kept an eye out for dishonest co-workers. He discussed the matter with his assistant manager, and the two decided to hire Steve.

Now Smith regrets giving Steve a chance.

Steve sexually assaulted a female co-worker after closing one day, and the woman has sued Smith for negligent hiring. (By definition, a victim can file a negligent-hiring suit when he or she is injured by an employee who wasn't screened properly before hiring and whose position in the company provided an opportunity to cause the injury.)

Similar real-life court cases have resulted in varied decisions.

A recent appellate court decision went against a contract security officer, with a history of petty crimes, who raped a visitor. The prosecution showed that people with minor criminal records are three times more likely to commit violent crimes. The security company was successfully sued for negligent hiring to the tune of $950,000.

But the negligent-hiring argument didn't stand in a 1988 appellate decision in Francioni vs. Rault. In that case, an employee who was convicted of embezzlement at a previous job subsequently murdered a co-worker. The appellate decision found the man's record didn't encompass the risk that he'd commit murder.

Company liability: The decision in the make-believe Smith Jewelers scenario could go either way, said Norman Spain, a director of private security studies and assistant professor of law at Penn State University. But the trend in negligent-hiring cases points to trouble for Smith, especially if the prosecution calls an expert witness who can link minor and violent crime.

"The courts have already charged certain groups, such as common carriers and inn keepers, with an extraordinary duty to screen and train employees," Spain said at the 1989 International Security Conference & Exposition East. "But I predict this extra burden will eventually migrate through all levels of the work force."

Spain led two seminars—"Legal Update for Security Managers" and "Legal Risks of Inadequate Security"—at ISC Expo East, held in New York City Aug. 29-31.

He emphasized that employer liability is targeted in negligence cases because a plaintiff will receive greater compensation from a company or corporation—"Deep Pockets Inc.," as Spain called them—than from an individual. "Lawyers are going to go right after the Deep Pockets."

Due care: But showing negligence on the part of an employer is no easy task, he said. Five "hurdles" must be cleared to "win the race" and prove negligence, he said.

The saleswoman in the Smith Jewelers scenario would have to show that Smith Jewelers had a *duty* to exercise reasonable care in its hiring procedures and that it didn't *exercise this due care.*

Smith's background check was indeed reasonable, with the decision to hire deliberated carefully. But according to Spain, more detailed checks may be necessary should "extraordinary care" become standard throughout the work force.

Several security managers who attended Spain's seminars voiced complaints that police and state-government checks take too long and are impractical.

"There's no leeway there," Spain said. "You either wait or foot the bill for an independent check—or both." Of course, an employer can take the chance of hiring a person without waiting for the results of the check. But should a negligent-hiring suit arise, the company couldn't use excessive time involved with running a check as a defense.

To further illustrate the extra burden of care facing some employers, Spain told of a taxi company that hired a driver after local police ran a background check and declared his record clean. The driver soon assaulted a passenger.

It turned out that the police had checked the wrong records and the driver actually had numerous convictions, including an arrest for sexual assault. In the negligent-hiring suit that followed, the taxi company was successfully sued despite the police error because it didn't conduct an independent check.

'But-for': The plaintiff now must show that this failure to exercise due care was the *cause in fact* of injuries suffered. Spain uses the "but-for" test on this point: "But for the hiring of Steve, would the saleswoman have been assaulted?"

This is a difficult point for employers, Spain said, because the job invariably provides the opportunity for the transgressor to injure someone. If Steve hadn't been hired, he probably wouldn't have met, much less assaulted, the co-worker.

The plaintiff also must show that Smith Jewelers' actions were the *proximate cause* of the assault. This means the store can be held accountable if Smith knew a danger was present and failed to act accordingly, or if a reasonable person in the same situation would have foreseen such an incident.

Vicarious liability: A plaintiff also has the option of proving *vicarious liability,* which means that the transgressor acted within his scope of employment or on behalf of the employer.

This tack is ineffective in cases similar to Smith Jewelers'. Steve obviously was beyond the scope of his duties in assaulting the saleswoman. Vicarious liability is a successful argument for the plaintiff when an individual causes injury in the course of following company policy, or when company policy is violated and the transgressor had no knowledge of the policy, Spain said.

"The liability is still there if you don't document training records or properly record policy memos," he said. "It is the employer's burden to show that an employee knew company policy at the time of the injury."

How To Avoid Hiring Mistakes

April 1989

Joe is the perfect candidate for your vacant sales position. The credentials on his resumé practically dictate on-the-spot hiring. He has all the requisite gemological education, he has seven years of jewelry sales experience and he passed the written security test and personality profile with flying colors. He's personable, knowledgeable and perfectly groomed in a just-right blue suit. He has a winning air about him, and he's convinced you he's what you need. Full confidence, you hire him.

Two months later, you're losing money and sleep. Unfortunately, it seems Joe's true talent was interviewing, not selling jewelry.

It happens. Just ask Paul Lam, owner of California-based Mandarin Gems. When Lam was interviewing applicants for a key position in one of his eight stores, a top candidate presented himself as a GIA graduate and successful manager of a Zales store. The man had three interviews with Mandarin's personnel department, and Lam conducted a final review. Lam says he got a "weird gut feeling" about the candidate but hired him anyway based on the man's references, plus glowing reports from the personnel department. Two months later, Lam fired him. He found the man lazy, shiftless and discourteous to customers. And shortly after his departure, Lam discovered some merchandise was missing.

When a dream interview becomes a real-life nightmare, the consequences can be devastating. Lisa Sands, former owner of a small chain, watched her thriving business go bankrupt after one bad hiring decision.

Fred gave a brilliant interview. References provided glowing reports. The polygraph examiner said "This man would not steal a toothpick." Fred, a churchgoing man in his mid-30s, had a wife and six children. Lisa Sands had no reason to suspect this talented accountant was a master thief.

First, Fred worked to build Lisa's faith in him. But inconsistencies started to show up within three months. Fred always had an excuse and, although puzzled, Lisa took his word. By the time she discovered what he was doing, Fred had taken tens of thousands of dollars worth of jewelry (pawned to area dealers) and even more in cash.

Fred was arrested, and charged with grand theft and dealing in stolen property. Two years later, he pleaded no contest (which means he didn't dispute the charge) and was ordered to repay Lisa $100 a month. At that rate, full restitution would take decades.

The damage, unfortunately, had been done. Fred's actions destroyed Lisa's standing with area banks and in the community. The banks called for a Chapter 7 bankruptcy, and all of Lisa's stores had to be sold to settle debts.

Lisa remains out of business.

Horror stories like these are a sound reason to take a new look at the art of hiring smart. Hiring mistakes can be costly. Says Lee Bowers, author of *No One Need Apply: Getting and Keeping the Best Workers,* a wrong hiring decision can cost a company anywhere from $5,000 for an hourly worker to $75,000 for a manager. These costs mainly cover lost productivity and training. But the toll mounts as you take into account time spent in the hiring process, the person's salary and the time necessary to hire and train a replacement.

Interviews, reference checks and assessment and/or situational tests can minimize the chance of major mistakes. They point out who has the right experience and education, as well as whose attitudes, values and work habits fit those of your company.

A smart hiring process begins with the employer. Brian Dumaine, author of "The New Art of Hiring Smart" (*Fortune,* August 1987), suggests you first list what the position entails. The list should be more than a task description; it should be a "brief, concrete recital" of what the person must be able to do. For a sales position, he says, the list might include: ability to make cold calls, ability to listen well and negotiate effectively, and personal skills to maintain ties with customers. The more concretely you define the job, the less time you'll waste screening candidates.

At Mandarin Gems, the job description for a full-time sales representative lists making sales as the primary function. Secondary functions, to be accomplished during quiet times, include helping with housekeeping, window displays, opening and closing procedures and new store openings, as well as overtime work during the holiday season and attending any sales training sessions held.

Dumaine also suggests that before going to the outside, look through your own ranks, then to employee referrals. Referrals save the cost of job ads and placement agencies. Most employees won't recommend a deadbeat because it would make *them* look bad. And studies show referrals tend to stay with a firm longer than workers found through ads or placement agencies.

Careful review: Whether you go to the outside or not, review applicants' resumés carefully. But never select someone solely on the basis of a resumé! It's a sales document and is likely to be hyped-up. Noted personnel recruitment expert Robert Half calls a resumé "a balance sheet without any liabilities."

Still, resumés can help you choose which applicants to interview. As a first step, toss any gimmicky ones, including video resumés, into the trash. Why would a candidate spend hundreds of dollars on a gimmick unless he's afraid his abilities don't speak for themselves? Half says the best resumé doesn't necessarily come from the best candidate—it may come from the person who's had the spottiest job history and the most practice writing them.

Look for a straightforward approach, a history of job stability, a willingness to work hard and hands-on experience. Half says to beware of the following indicators that a candidate is hiding something:

• Lengthy descriptions of education. Too much emphasis on special seminars attended and courses taken may indicate the candidate lacks the necessary education.

• Phrases such as "exposure to," "knowledge of" and "assisted with" may indicate a lack of hands-on experience.

• No employment dates.

• Bitterness toward previous employers.

• Sloppiness. If a candidate can't take the time to make the resumé letter-perfect, do you think he'll be any more conscientious on the job?

It's hard to determine from a resumé whether someone is a hard worker, says Half, but there are indicators. For example: evaluate the way the candidate describes his past jobs—in terms of duties or in terms of accomplishments? Also look for involvement in civic activities; donating leisure time to work for volunteer organizations is a sign of above-average industriousness.

Now, it's time to interview candidates to see whether they match what their resumés tell you to expect.

Come in, sit down

The face-to-face interview is crucial. This is when you really start to learn whether an applicant will fit into your organization.

There are some questions you can not ask. Marilyn McLaughlin, manger of employment and Equal Employment Opportunity at Chilton Co., Radnor, Pa., offers a simple formula. You may ask everything about a candidate's professional career (salary, duties, etc.). You may ask nothing about his personal life, including age, marital status or children. Nor may you use "back door" questions to elicit the information. For example, you may ask what languages a person speaks fluently, but you may not ask what his native language is. You may ask what days he will be available to work, but you may not ask what holidays he will observe.

If he is not a U.S. citizen, you *must* ask if he has legal permission to work here—and obtain proof—but you may not ask his country of citizenship. (*Note: As of June 1, 1987, federal immigration laws require employers to verify that all applicants, including U.S. citizens, are legally entitled to work in the U.S. The applicant must be able to provide documentation to that effect.*

However, civil rights laws prohibit using the information for discriminatory purposes.)

Clear up questions: Be sure to ask about any employment gaps or frequent job changes noted on a resumé. Some situations—such as layoffs—are certainly excusable. Others—such as repeated job dissatisfaction—can signal problems.

Ask about duties, accountability, responsibilities and roles a candidate took in team projects. If the resumé says a candidate was in charge of a project, ask how many people he supervised. If a candidate says he developed a program, ask whether he did it alone or as part of a team.

Ask open-ended questions so the candidate can't answer just "yes" and "no." Don't ask "why" a candidate made a particular choice; that phrasing may put him on the defensive. Instead, say "please explain your answer further."

Also be certain to ask about a candidate's work style. Good questions are: "What is the environment of your present office?" "What is your boss like?" "Are you comfortable with that style of management?" and "Please describe your ideal boss."

Don't downplay the importance of matching work styles. If yours is a "team" store, you'd better find a candidate with a team mentality. You also have to make sure his style fits your store's image. Some adjustments are necessary in any new job, but you can't expect someone to change his personality radically.

McLaughlin also warns against misrepresenting a position. Don't mislead a candidate about chances for advancement and don't downplay the unpleasant tasks, she says. Applicants at Chilton are told about a job's negative points first so McLaughlin knows whether they're still interested.

McLaughlin says there's no pat formula for conducting an interview. She prefers a relaxed atmosphere, in which a candidate is more likely to reveal things he might not otherwise.

Nor is there a formula to tell when a candidate is lying. Be alert for contradictions, too much hesitation before answering and visual clues such as no eye contact, fidgeting and general discomfort. But McLaughlin warns that a trained sales professional with highly developed interpersonal skills isn't likely to make such slips.

And sometimes, job applicants are just good actors. Jeweler James H. Wallach of Wallach Sons, Manhasset, N.Y., once interviewed an elegant, refined young woman for a sales position in his carriage-trade store. But like Eliza Doolittle in reverse, once hired the woman reverted from lady to street urchin—complete with chewing gum and an irritating twang in her voice.

Going sleuthing

Even Sherlock Holmes would have trouble checking references today. Candidates are suing former employers like never before, so employers are reluctant to speak up. Chilton's McLaughlin says that when asked for a reference, she reveals only the person's title and length of employment. A new employer could go to the person's department supervisor, she says, but supervisors aren't supposed to offer any more information, either.

Jim Echols thinks that's a good idea. Previous employers are too afraid of lawsuits to tell the truth even if the candidate was a lousy worker, he says. Echols himself almost wound up in court when he tried to prevent his $85,000 thief from getting another job. And when Lisa Sands questioned Fred's previous employers, they gave him excellent references even though they'd also fired him for embezzlement. The former employers' decision to hide the facts cost Lisa her business.

Janice Pyle says a former employer still can get the point across. "You can just sense when there's something wrong. If a former employer isn't exuberant about the person, there probably were problems."

When a firm called her about a former employee who was dishonest, Pyle simply said she wouldn't rehire the person. Asked if there were problems, she said "yes" but didn't elaborate. The person wasn't hired.

So how do you get a straight answer? Some firms ask applicants to sign an agreement releasing them and the applicant's former employers from liability before checking references. But attorney Cotlar warns that such a document actually is binding only on the two parties who sign it, so it wouldn't protect former employers. Some such agreements have been upheld in court, he says, but they have a limited application.

If a reference check does result in a lawsuit, the plaintiff must prove the former employer had malicious intent in giving the poor reference.

Proper checking: Reference checking, done effectively, takes time. You have to dig, and you have to ask a lot of people a lot of questions to get enough pieces to form a whole picture. If you can, talk to the applicant's former supervisor to determine work habits and motivation. Also, talk to co-workers.

What should you ask? Follow the same guidelines as you would for the candidate himself—anything about work, nothing about the EEOC-protected information noted earlier.

Rely on networking to get a better picture, especially for higher positions. A person qualified to be your manager probably has been around long enough to have developed some reputation in the industry. Learn to recognize the difference between unfavorable reports and sour grapes, and ask more than one person.

Welcome aboard

You've finally hired your newest employee. Don't stop here—make sure he gets a warm welcome and lot of initial guidance. If you run a large shop, set up a formal "take-in" system. Set ground rules immediately, start to teach the ins and outs of how you do business, outline your disciplinary process, explain your benefits package and, most importantly, make sure he understands everything. Get it in writing!

You might consider having a brief interview a few months later to see if the job is what he expected. If he's happy, his work should make you happy—and that's the bottom line.

Don't Hire Square Pegs for Round Holes

A job applicant's training and experience are easy to determine. His work style, though less tangible, is no less important. The manner in which an employee does his job can make or break a happy workplace.

Some managers want their employees to pace themselves like marathon runners so they're busy every minute. That's not a problem unless you've hired a sprinter, who works feverishly to do a day's work in four hours, then needs to sit back to recharge.

Both types of employee accomplish equal amounts of work, but you judge the sprinter more harshly because he isn't busy all the time. The result: frustration for you and the employee.

To avoid such a mismatch, simply take time during the interview to explore the applicant's work style and pace. Is it compatible with yours?

Apple Computer Inc. knows the advantage of careful interviewing. The firm needed a line manager to reshape a division, define an ambiguous situation but still sell an intangible idea to management. One woman's written qualifications fit the job exactly. But an interviewer found she was extremely uncomfortable with ambiguity and actually was seeking a well-defined routine.

The firm probed deeper and found the woman's current job involved implementing strategies that other people developed—a far different role from what Apple needed. The woman wasn't hired, and a serious mismatch was avoided.

Personality traits don't affect a candidate's intelligence, experience or integrity. They do, however, affect workplace harmony and productivity. Learn about them before trying to fit a square peg into a round hole.

You're Fired!

Firing an employee is never pleasant, but most mangers have to do it at some point. You can't do much to make it easier, but you can make sure it's done legally.

The only legal reasons to fire someone are poor performance and/or obvious breach of discipline. You must be able to prove your charges; courts increasingly favor employees in wrongful-discharge suits.

Extreme situations aside, you should have some sort of "due process" for employees who perform poorly or cause discipline problems. A standard procedure is a verbal warning first, a written warning and probation next, then termination, if necessary.

During probation, the employer must be supportive and willing to help the employee change, and the employee must show a genuine willingness to improve.

Extreme situations—stealing, threatening violence or other criminal acts—may call for immediate dismissal. Drug use is a gray area. If you catch the employee in the act, you can fire him. If you only suspect drug use, you must approach the situation in terms of the worker's lowered performance and use due process.

If termination is the only option after due process, have the sensitivity not to fire the employee on his birthday, anniversary or other significant date. Do it behind closed doors, avoid interruptions, clear your desk and hold all calls.

Many psychologists suggest firing early in the week, and Marilyn McLaughlin of Chilton Co., Radnor, Pa., advocates firing in mid- to late morning. It's not very nice to make an employee work until 4 p.m. and then fire him, she says. Late-morning firings also eliminate dramatic and embarrassing exits. The employee leaves as if to go to lunch, then simply doesn't return.

Here Come The Old Folks!

November 1989

What picture does that headline conjure up for you? An elderly and bent nursing home couple in wheelchairs? Apple-cheeked grandparents doting over a cute pair of tow-headed toddlers? The bravely smiling widow headed for the two-bedroom, 2-bath condo in a spanking new retirement home?

Forget it.

Oh, those old folks exist, all right. But there's another breed of oldster out there. These are men and women who are healthy, energetic and in search of a job either because they're bored with the one they have, they're retired, they need the money or any combination of these three. Believe it or not, when you look at these people, you're looking at a major component of the everyday work force in the '90s and beyond. We're running out of kids.

The demographers have told us about this reality for years. But they've done it in such a dry-as-dust statistical way that the message has glanced off the brain instead of penetrating it. When you've gone through a period of some 30 years with a seemingly endless supply of young people available to take on the starter or routine jobs, it's hard to believe the supply could dry up.

Take a walk around any shopping district and the proof stares you in the face. Help-wanted signs seem to be on permanent display in the fast-food joints and nearly every other store.

Revolution! That's the word the demographers should have used to catch our attention. Because that's what we're facing. Employers across the nation are going to have to do a major overhaul of their thinking about hiring, training, motivating and rewarding the people who work for them. It's not going to be easy and it probably will be costly. The shock is going to be greatest for small businesses, including many jewelers, for they rely on young people more than most.

Several articles in this issue pinpoint the more critical issues. Among them: the special problems that may come in motivating the "senior" worker and, more importantly for the boss, the fringe benefits the older worker considers essential.

Let's look at fringe benefits first. A study of practices among JCK's own retail panelists—a cross-section of all types of stores except major chains—shows fringe benefits are being scaled down, not augmented. Medical care is the principal target. Costs to the employer of providing decent coverage have risen so sharply recently that many have either cut back coverage or passed through a significant amount of the cost to the employee. In extreme cases, some jewelers have dropped health coverage completely.

Cutbacks show up in other areas, too. Our jeweler-panelists report lower company support in seven of 11 popular fringe benefits this year compared with last, with paid sick leave, pensions and long-term disability coverage among the bigger casualties.

If you're fancy-free and twenty-three, this may not seem like a big deal. If you're in your 50s or above, it's a very different story. Simply put, many jewelers will have to put more rather than less money into benefits as they find their new hires are nearing the end of their careers. Older workers will demand a total compensation package that carries generous fringes, knowing they are in a seller's market. In most cases, the jeweler-employer will have to pay up and go along.

There is a rewarding flip side to this situation. The boss may have to pay more, but there's every indication he or she will get much more in return. An older employee, by and large, is more committed to work, is more loyal, has more realistic expectations and is far less likely to job hop than a young counterpart. The critical issue for the employer is to make sure the talents and energies of the older employee are used to their fullest advantage.

A study done by the American Society of Personnel Administrators turned up some problems related to senior workers. Four stood out: complacence or loss of motivation, need for better performance appraisals to identify problems, need for better career pathing and rapidly changing job duties.

Good performance appraisals are the key to forestalling most problems or dealing with them if they do arise. The employer must have a clear understanding of the job to be done, how it should be done and what opportunities there are for the employee to expand the job into something better. This message must be explained clearly to the employee, specific goals must be set and the goals must be met. In all exchanges, there must be frank employer-employee communication.

The boss who can set up standards, who wants top productivity and who is willing and able to measure it will have little trouble motivating the right employees, regardless of age. He or she also will have the mechanism in place to fire the nonproducers. Moreover, if those who really merit employment produce as they should, rewarding them well should follow as a natural consequence.

As we go into the '90s, I expect to see many better-managed jewelry stores employing many older, productive workers—and often achieving better results with fewer people on the payroll.

The Commission Alternative: One Store's Success Story

November 1988

Salespeople at Cleary Jewelers, Greenfield, Mass., work on a commission-only basis, earning 10% on all sales. This policy shocks many jewelers, but it has meant resounding success for Cleary Jewelers. Since 1980, salespeople have doubled their annual earnings while the store's salary/sales ratio dropped more than 50%.

Owner William "Bill" Roberts says the figures proves that commission-only works.

In 1980, Cleary's annual sales totaled $200,000. The store had 6.5 full-time employees, 4.5 of whom were in sales. (Two were the husband and wife who owned the store.) Annual sales averaged $30,769 per employee, and salespeople earned minimum wage ($3.25 an hour at the time). Salaries totaled 22% of sales.

By 1987, Cleary's annual sales had grown to $1,000,015. Full-time employees dropped to six, with only the bookkeeper and the repairman remaining from the old staff. The average annual sales per employee totaled $164,000; the salary/sales ratio, 10%.

How did Roberts do it? The town didn't change much. Greenfield is still a small Main Street, USA, kind of community. Its residents haven't collectively won a lottery, but they're spending a lot more money on jewelry at Cleary's.

Productivity: The key is people, says Roberts. Hire productive people and give them motivation to work hard. The motivation: commission-only sales. That is at the forefront of Roberts' management philosophy.

Cleary Jewelers is one of five prototype stores owned by the Independent Jewelers Organization. Roberts owns the IJO, which provides a buying forum for small independent jewelers and offers consultation in many areas of retail management. It also runs its model stores as places to test new ideas and as living proof of how its management philosophies work. All IJO members are free to examine any of the stores' books, employment policies, advertising, merchandise and design, or spend a few days alongside store personnel. Everything is open for their examination.

To find the best employees, Roberts explains his philosophies right from the first interview. "We offer them a *career*, not just a job," he says. "We tell them right away that we don't want to waste their time and ours. If jewelry is not going to be their lifelong career, they are not for us. We expect them to be ready to relocate and run another jewelry store for us in five years."

Next, says Roberts, all prospective employees take three tests. First is the standard Wonderlic intelligence test, which weeds out people who really don't have enough intelligence. Next comes the Reid Report for basic honesty, which helps to separate those who might have tendencies toward drug abuse or stealing. Finally, Roberts administers the Caliper profile, which assesses a candidate's ego drive, motivation to work without being pushed and ability to sell others to his way of thinking. It also measures a candidate's empathy, another factor in successful sales.

Other basic attributes such as attitude, personality and appearance are taken into consideration as well.

Demonstrate ability: When new employees are hired, they have a three- to six-month test period to demonstrate their selling abilities. During that time, they may work part time, and they have a shot at high-ticket sales just like everyone else. Roberts believes in letting everyone sell everything.

"There's no law that says only the owner or a 25-year veteran male employee can sell diamonds," he says. "Why, one girl sold a carat-plus diamond two days after she started!"

Roberts believes strongly in education. New employees enroll immediately in Gemological Institute of America courses. The firm pays partial costs at first and reimburses the rest when the course is completed. After two years, employees start to go on IJO buying trips, such as a colored stone excursion to mines in Bahia, Brazil.

Employees also take on much responsibility. Within two years, each runs a department, being completely responsible for inventory levels, profits and selection of goods. Within five years, each sales employee is expected to be able to run a store.

Roberts offers more fun-filled motivators as well, such as all-expense-paid cruises (with spouse) to Bermuda. About half the employees win; his object is to get everyone to win.

But the root of his motivational philosophy is commissioned sales.

"Most retail jewelers don't have their personnel machine run efficiently," he says. "Why should an employee take the time to improve skills, build lists, take a JCK home at night and give up many hours of free time to study dry GIA texts if he's not likely to make any more money? If he's commissioned and knows these efforts will help sell more and earn more, he'll be a lot more motivated."

Roberts adds that most jewelers have no idea how much their individual employees produce. In his stores, all of the figures are published and posted, and each employee can see where he stands in relation to his co-workers and the rest of the company as a whole.

Getting started: Changing from salary to commission is fairly simple. Roberts accomplishes it essentially by changing nothing at the outset. Staff salaries are left basically the same.

For example, an employee earning $5 an hour ($200 a week, $10,400 a year) continues to take home that same $200 every week. Except now it is a draw, or advance, on future sales. Roberts settles accounts quarterly. At the end of 13 weeks, the employee has been advanced $2,600. If he has sold $30,000 worth of merchandise, his 10% commission will total $3,000. Thus he'll get a check for an additional $400.

What about a slow quarter, when the employee can't earn even the draw? That's fine, says Roberts. The store doesn't ask for it back.

"We know they'll make it up ultimately. If they don't, they're usually gone," he says. Commission-only sales don't work for everyone, he admits. During

changeovers, he's lost about one employee in four. But this separates the doers from the loafers, he says.

Roberts' credo: "Nothing is as profitable as a productive salesperson, and nothing is as expensive as an unproductive salesperson."

How does he avoid "sharkfights," with employees battling for the same territory? Simple—the store manager settles disputes arbitrarily. Generally, the salespeople take turns—whoever's available serves the customer.

Sometimes a salesperson spends an hour with a customer who decides to "think about it for a while," then returns and buys from a different salesperson. The second salesperson gets the commission. That might seem unfair to some. But Roberts says that until the money is on the table, the salesperson is not *selling,* just *exhibiting.*

Besides, regular customers usually wait for their favorite salesperson, and many customers who return for a purchase often wait for the salesperson who spoke with them the first time. If a salesperson is having little luck with a customer (as, for example, when a young and attractive saleswoman inspires more jealousy than loyalty in older matrons), she might turn over the sale to another staffer. Salespeople usually settle the commission between themselves or if a dispute arises, the manager settles it. Granted, occasional sharks persistently fight over commissions. Roberts solves the problem quickly—he fires them. Firing someone and hiring a replacement costs money, but a persistent shark also can be costly by dragging down morale.

How much to pay: Roberts admits he and every other business owner want to keep down compensation costs. The goal is to pay no more than necessary to keep employees happy and productive.

But how much is that? Aside from the 10% commission rate, Cleary employees' draw rates are based on experience. One new staffer asked for $35,000 to start. He promised to do $300,000 worth of sales in return, and he did it in his first year. At the other end of the scale, an employee with little experience may start out at $10,000 per year.

After one year, employees determine their own pay rates by their sales rates. If an employee's sales warrant, Roberts will increase the draw. He doesn't like an employee to draw all the way up to the limit, however. He prefers to give a nice check at settlement time each quarter.

Voice Barometers

Editorial ◆ November 1988

It's amazing how much you can learn about a company by placing a single telephone call. Here are a few examples of first business contacts I've had recently just by dialing a number. "Hello, Butterworth's." (This was not really the first contact. Before receiving this greeting, I listened to the tail-end of a conversation between the phone answerer and some unknown third party. It sounded dull.)

"Gold mumble mumble and Co."

"This is Shirley."

"4512."

"Good morning, Todbrush Jewelers, Laurie speaking."

"Smithersoon's."

I don't want to beat this point to death so I'll stop the list here. We've all had similar experiences, whether it's dealing with the super-secret (the "4512s" of this world) or the thoughtlessly rude (a toss-up between Butterworth's and Smithersoon's, with Butterworth's slightly ahead). The one feeling I have for both: I don't believe I want to know you any better than I do now.

Considering how much routine day-to-day rudeness we encounter, here's another amazing fact. It's almost a sure bet that when you call a jewelry store, you'll receive a courteous and probably friendly greeting. There is a very simple reason why. Most of the people who work in most jewelry stores are courteous and friendly. This is so because most jewelers hire people like that.

After 20 years of talking with staffs in literally hundreds of jewelry stores in all parts of the country, I feel confident of this opinion. My belief was further strengthened in the past week or so as I read scores of reports in which jewelers discussed how they compensate their staffs. Many stores treat compensation as an extension of normal human relations. Let me share a few comments. From David Coll of Montclair Jewelers in Oakland, Cal.: "If you pay employees more than they are worth, they will be worth more than you can pay them." From Roy Herrud of Herrud Jewelry in Langdon, N.D., on how to keep good people: "Treat them with respect." From Don Kelshelmer of the Bird's Nest in Casey, Ill., on motivation: "The way an employee is treated—such as trust, responsibility, etc.—seems to be the most important." And this from Philip Minsky of Wyman Jewelers in Stoughton, Mass., on which store benefit most appeals to employees: "We care and we prove that we care."

No one is knocking money. The jewelers we polled for our compensation story, members of JCK's retail panel, agree as a group that cash in the paycheck is the No. 1 award to give. But throughout the scores of replies we received is the constantly recurring theme that a good employer goes far beyond offering employees money and medical benefits. "Give praise when they do a good job," says Lee Berg of Lee Michaels Fine Jewelry in Baton Rouge, La. "Involve them in day-to-day decisions of running the business." It's no wonder that when employers think this way of employees, they have little difficulty hiring the top of the crop.

Then they have to keep them. Our panelists agree that TLC, shared responsibilities and an occasional ticket to a ball game all help—often greatly—in keeping top talent. They also agree their best bargaining chip is cash, and they're paying more freely than ever before. A comparison of pay scales the panel recorded in 1985 and those reported in this issue shows median salary improvements of between 30% and 55% for various job categories. The current median for general salesmen is $18,860, an increase of 30% from three years earlier. For general saleswomen, the current median is only $14,000 but that's 40% better than three years ago, and it shows a lessening of the salary discrimination between men and women doing the same job.

One of the more interesting trends to emerge from panel replies is the willingness of more and more jewelers to pay top dollar to the real producers. Performance is the key. Panelists offer various incentives to raise productivity, most often using bonuses tied in some way to the meeting of individual or group goals. Commissions are used widely—and for those of you who continue to say commissions don't belong in the jewelry store, I suggest you read the interview in this issue with Bill Roberts, the president of the Independent Jewelers Organization. The story documents the impact the introduction of commission payment had on a store that had long refused to consider them.

The matter of incentives is very important for those store owners who, when asked how they decide how much to pay for a particular job, reply, "What I can afford." The owner with limited resources certainly can't pay what he hasn't got. But if pay is tied to productivity, an employee may work with more purpose and earn far more than the employer thought possible.

Finally a word on benefits. A recent study by the Washington, D.C.-based Employee Benefit Research Institute reveals that jewelers are much more liberal than other retailers in providing benefits of many types. Our own study shows many jewelers expanding what they already provide, most often in medical/dental coverage. Because benefits typically are worth about one-third of an employee's total cash income, an employer should always stress their value when trying to hire good people.

The American Dream

Editorial ◆ September 1988

What is this dream? A life of independence, of wealth, of pride in work, of ample leisure, of loving family and friends, perhaps a life that will embrace a touch of immortality, a name and a presence carried on to following generations.

Such a life is possible. Most likely it will be found in a family business.

Family businesses are as international as the world. But the U.S. family business enjoys unique opportunities. In no other country is there such freedom to gather a basic investment, start a new company and hope to succeed.

This freedom has a flip side: the freedom to fail, the prospect of the dream becoming a nightmare. In an entrepreneurial society you do a lot of tight-rope walking without a safety net. But that's often where the excitement lies. The person who starts a family business is by nature a risk taker. The one who succeeds is the risk taker who knows how to calculate the odds, how to underpin bravura performance with solid planning.

The jewelry business is the quintessential family affair. By one estimate, close to nine of every ten firms in the industry are family owned and operated. And family embraces whole generations—sons, daughters, in-laws, cousins, uncles, grandparents, the lot. The result is a way of business life as tumultuous, erratic, wonderful, heart-breaking, prosperous and satisfying as any can be. But almost a year of research to gather material for this month's special Part II edition on the family business also showed that too many jewelry family businesses also showed that too many jewelry family businesses think success and succession just happen without real commitment to make them happen. Too many families are pursuing the American dream too carelessly. They don't seem to realize how fragile that dream can be.

Let's look at some specifics. The most fundamental problem is embodied in the phrase, "If I die. . . " If, not when. There speaks the ultimate egoist, the head-of-family and head-of-firm so used to center stage that death itself become irrelevant. If death can be dismissed so readily, what chance is there for a succession plan, training kids to take over, motivating and disciplining employees, putting enough cash by for retirement and making sure that Uncle Sam won't get the biggest bite from the estate?

Far too many jewelry store owners lack even a basic succession plan. In a way that's understandable. When you're working long hours to get a business started or to breath new life into an inheritance, it's hard to worry about adequate insurance or an effective buy/sell agreement with a possible successor. But the owner who neglects such basic planning does so at great peril. Carl Schmieder, a well-known Arizona jeweler, saw the peril first-hand when a friend and fellow flyer was killed in a plane crash. His friend, a young man, had made no provision for untimely death; his family and his business were shattered.

This sudden death jolted Schmieder into action. He thought through what he wants for his family and his business and put his thoughts on paper. That act, getting your plans in writing, is the essential for peace of mind, many jewelers told us. It's so easy for family members who work well together to say, "Who needs a written agreement? We *trust* each other." Unfortunately, those demons called greed, jealousy and selfishness all can knock trust right out of the ring if a family fight starts. But if plans are clearly spelled out in black and white those demons never have a chance.

Children can be a joy and a bane at any time. Multiply the emotions by ten and you have children in the family business. Are there enough jobs to go around? Who gets to do what? What's the pecking order? How about those who want to follow a life outside the business? What claims have they on their parents and on the business?

There are no magical formulas for harmony. But again and again as our editors talked with parents and children in family businesses around the country, they heard similar refrains. Communicate clearly. Be fair. Reward merit. Share responsibility but don't give responsibility without authority. Make decisions that are first good for the family business and, secondly, good for the family (the family *needs* the business). If kids don't want to be part of the business, fine, bid them farewell. Give them a fair shake in any family inheritance but don't let them disturb brothers and/or sisters who decide to stay with the business.

Letting go is the hardest act of all. Without proper planning it can be disastrous. Who knows how many jewelers go on working into their 70s because they can't afford to quit. The tragedy is that it doesn't have to happen. Good planning early in business life can assure adequate retirement income, that there will be a successor waiting in the wings or, failing that, a plan to sell or liquidate the business.

Financial security eases the psychological jolt of retirement. Knowing that well-trained and motivated children will carry on the business can offer sustaining pleasure and pride. That is the dream come true.

Shaping Up A Stagnant Staff

July 1987

Jezebel Jewelers, a mythical Main Street store, is a continuing JCK case study of management problems and solutions. Recently, owner Hiram Jezebel sold this old-line money-losing firm to his repairman, Hamilton Waltham, and Ham's partner, Ebenezer Cheribel. Now the new owners must decide how to reshape their staff for better productivity and profits.

"Hamilton Waltham, store owner."

Ham liked the sound of that. He said it often, quietly, in the days after the purchase as he accustomed himself to his new title.

But with his title came the task of turning around the troubled store. Waltham and his partner and cousin, Ebenezer Cheribel, mulled it over prior to settlement. Cheribel agreed to be a silent partner, leaving Ham to run the store. But he had $50,000 invested—and plenty of "suggestions."

Both agreed sales must rise soon. They way to do it, said Cheribel, is "fire those deadwood employees and hire go-getters. This bunch," he groused, "is getting paid too much for doing too little."

Reducing S/S: Cheribel had a point. Jezebel Jewelers' salary-to-sales ratio was too fat. At time of sale, the firm had annual sales of $432,600 and a staff of eight (including owners) earning $119,500 a year, or 28% of sales. Ham wanted to cut that to 20% (the industry average), and eventually to 10% or 12%. Departure of former owners Hiram and Eustatia Jezebel lowered the s/s ratio, but Ham didn't plow all of their $37,500 salaries back into the firm. He used $5,300 to boost his own salary to $22,500 (since he was doing two jobs, watchmaker and owner). He also wanted a manager—preferably from the staff—to help him. So he set aside another $2,000 (as promotion pay).

That left $30,200 of the old owners' pay for the store, dropping the s/s ratio to about 21%.

Staff chats: But who should Ham fire? To decide he chatted with each of his new employees—which also subtly re-enforced his position as boss.

"I want to learn about the different departments," he said. "What sells well? Any problems with certain items or store operations? Any ideas on how things should change?" He listened closely, noting job attitudes:

Joshua Bullwinkle, the oldest in age (64) and length of employment (since 1944), is a self-taught diamond salesman. He congratulated Ham on buying the store, but said he wanted to "slow down" now he was older. His sales already were slowing. Annual diamond business, while still the store's dollar leader, was 5% under last year. Salary: $18,000.

Henrietta Creekee, 60, a friend of Eustatia Jezebel, has sold watches full-time since 1975. She apologized for poor watch business (down 8%). "My heart's not in it anymore," she said. But she likes working at Jezebel's and, if possible, wants to do some bridal sales. Salary: $10,000.

Company secretary *Marilee Annabelle Smith,* 57, Hiram's cousin has been bridal consultant since 1962. She has a history of absenteeism, missing many days annually for "illness." She was defensive about that ("When you're sick, you're sick") and about poor china and crystal sales (down 17%). "I can't make people buy," she said. Salary $12,000.

Wilson Sharpe, 52, gem salesman and self-styled ladies' man, joined the store in 1979. He's boosted colored gem sales (up 4% last year), and is itching to do diamonds. His ideas to expand the gem department were opposed by Bullwinkle, Hiram and Eustatia. Salary: $16,000.

Ophelia Goodbodie, the newest (1984), youngest (20) full-time employee, sold giftware and tableware. She's an enthusiastic worker who pushed gifts up almost 9% (though tableware fell 6.5%). Salary: $8,800.

His chats convinced Ham that trimming staff—probably Smith, and maybe Bullwinkle—was a quick way to cut costs. But he's a soft-hearted guy; he doesn't like firing a long-time co-worker. Besides, he's not 100% sure firing people is the *only* way to reshape staff and boost productivity.

Getting advice: Before doing anything, Ham sought advice:

• Friend and fellow jeweler Cyrus Smuckmann in Lewiston, 20 miles away, told Ham to keep at least a couple of experienced people for continuity in store operations and with customers. "You don't want to start with a staff unfamiliar with your inventory or procedures," he said.

Also, firing long-time employees without good reason could sour customer relations if disgruntled former workers were to bad-mouth the store. More serious, "they could sue your pants off," said Smuckmann.

• That sent Ham to his attorney, Perry M. Flatbush.

"If you fire someone," warned Flatbush, "be careful who it is and why you do it."

In recent years, he explained, employers' right to fire has been narrowed by court decisions to prevent arbitrary termination. The law also says you can't force someone to retire before 70; make them retire by abolishing their job, or fire them due to age, sex, race or religion.

"If you do fire employees, you'd better have a 'paper trail' of documents to prove it was for performance or operational reasons, like insufficient funds to support full payroll," said Flatbush. "If you abolish jobs, start with the most recent, least senior person, or you may face discrimination suits." But, he added, Ham could make a general offer of early retirement.

• "Okay," thought Ham. "How can I cut staff costs without cutting staff?" He went to accountant Gelda Numerouno for answers.

She offered several:

Reschedule people for peak work hours and use fewer people at slow times. "You can redistribute full-time workers' hours, but you can't reduce them arbitrarily," she said. "Otherwise, they can collect unemployment equal to the amount of reduced hours."

As older employees retire, don't refill their jobs.

Offer more cash-less benefits, like free parking; discounts on store merchandise; more flexible work hours; more days off or vacation time; compensatory time instead of overtime pay.

Pay salaries every two weeks to reduce bookkeeping costs and frequency of tax deposits.

Cultivate workers' money-saving ideas. "Tell them that rather than reduce payroll or jobs, you want to save money elsewhere. Ask them for cost-cutting ideas. Encourage them with rewards for the best idea. Use periodic brainstorming sessions or even a suggestion box."

The staff plan: So, Ham sat down at his desk to create a staff plan. Pencil in hand, he numbered each major point on his yellow legal pad.

1. *Work with people he has.* Any changes that must be made will be apparent in a few months.

2. *Create a work environment where people are motivated to perform well.* That requires that he set business goals for his staff to aim at.

Ham started creating them during purchase negotiations as he and Cheribel reviewed sales overall and by department, then took inventory to see what was in stock. Based on those findings, chats with employees and his own estimates of what the store could do, Ham calculated an annual sales goal for Jezebel Jewelers.

Sales in 1985 were $432,600, down from $510,000 at the start of the 1980s and the end of the region's oil boom. Previous owner Hiram Jezebel did little to promote his store or cultivate new markets (i.e., new housing tracts near the local electronics firms; young marrieds and working mothers; Hispanics). With a lackluster staff and an aging blue-collar customer base, he couldn't maintain sales when oil and farming problems threw the region into an economic tailspin. But Ham believed more promotion, attention to new markets, fresh inventory and a motivated staff with salaries pegged to performance could help the store surpass 1981 figures.

Thus Ham set an ambitious (up 27%) goal of $550,000 for the first year. Next, he defined goals for each department and employee. Diamonds still took the lion's share (35%, or $192,500 of the total), but the target for gems rose to 15% ($82,500).

Based on that, Ham set Joshua's annual goal at $121,000 (keeping him as senior diamond salesman and buyer) and Wilson's at $128,000 (based on more gem sales, plus Ham's decision to let him sell diamonds, too). The remaining $26,000 would be divided among the other salespeople.

3. *Use incentives to encourage people to meet their goals.* Former owner Hiram Jezebel called sales commissions "bribes," saying a good worker didn't need them. He limited incentives to 15% discounts on merchandise and an annual Christmas bonus ($10 for each year with the store).

But Ham learned—from studies in trade magazines and chats with successful retailers—that productive workers are *motivated* workers. He felt good salespeople *should* be rewarded to encourage them.

So he designed some specific rewards. Salespeople will get 1.5% of what they sell. Those exceeding monthly goals will get a bonus equal to the percentage of increase. Thus someone who tops his or her goal by 5% gets 5% more in the next paycheck.

Those topping goals for six straight months also will get theater tickets, dinner at a swanky hotel or their choice of a best-selling book, record or videocassette. Those who sell slow-moving or old merchandise will get 10% of the sale.

If the store tops its goals in all categories, everyone gets an additional bonus equal to the percentage of increase.

During periods when Ham wants top-notch performance (i.e., Christmas), sales goal bonuses double.

As an added "incentive," Ham decided to post "thermometers" for each employee—charting progress on individual goals—and one for the store as a whole in the small employee lounge.

To encourage money-saving ideas, he set up a monthly contest. Any employee whose idea actually trimmed costs would get a $25 bonus.

Here's how Ophelia Goodbodie—whose weekly pretax salary is $169.23 and monthly sales goal is $4,400—could benefit from the incentive plan.

If she met her goal, she'd get $66 (1.5% of her $4,400 monthly goal) added to her next month's first paycheck. If she topped her target by 10%, she'd get another $16.92 (10% of her $169.23 weekly salary), for a total of $82.92 in added incentive pay.

If she stayed 10% over goal for 12 months, she'd get $995.04 (12 times her monthly incentive pay). At Christmas, she'd get a double sales bonus of $33.84 (twice $16.92), plus a $30 holiday bonus ($10 for each year with the store, including her work as a part-timer). That would bring her incentive total for the year to $1,058.84. The amount could climb further if the entire store met its monthly goals and if she sold some slow-moving merchandise.

4. *A salary schedule, based on employee performance and review,* came next. In addition to the specific sales goals, Ham set job standards employees must meet.

Personal traits: Salespeople must be self-starters, friendly and have good communication skills. They must have a neat, clean appearance; be punctual and efficient, and get along with co-workers and management.

Relationship with customers: Employees must be able to create and maintain customer good will and confidence, and do follow-up.

Job skills: Salespeople will be judged on product knowledge (including warranties and guarantees); selling approach (including add-ons, upgrading sales and answering objections); turnover, and store loyalty.

On his accountant's advice, Ham scheduled twice-a-year meetings with each employee to discuss performance and salary. To be considered for a raise during the next two years, a salesperson had to produce sales at least six times his or her pay. Ham planned to raise that to 10 times salary in three years.

Store fringe benefits needed work, too. Under Hiram, they were pretty poor: A week's vacation after a year with the firm; two weeks after 15, three weeks after 25. Health insurance, with employee contributions required. Five days' paid sick leave. No pension. Ham couldn't afford to improve the package yet. But he told his accountant he wanted to review it in a year, assuming sales and profits rose.

5. *Employee discipline.* So much for the carrot; now, the stick. With his attorney's help, Ham prepared clear and specific procedures for employee complaints and discipline.

For each employee problem (such as absenteeism), he set progressive discipline: First, a verbal warning, with time for the employee to correct behavior. Next, written warnings, cosigned by boss and employee, to go into the person's personnel file. Then probation (30 days to improve, with specific, verifiable goals for the employee). Lastly, job termination. The documentation would provide the "paper trail" Ham's attorney suggested.

"Discipline should be done in a positive way," reminded Flatbush, "so the employee feels it's intended to help or improve performance." But some actions—like theft—are cause for immediate discharge, he said.

Who's the boss? Staff plan in hand, Ham took the next step in reshaping his staff—letting them know who was boss.

They knew, of course, he and Cheribel had purchased the store. But the staff had known him for years as "Ham, the store watchmaker," a quiet and good natured co-worker. Now, they had to realize he was no longer a fellow employee but the man paying their salary and expecting them to earn it.

It was also important to reassure them. Ham hadn't discussed his plans with anyone except Hiram and Cheribel. His new staff was curious—and uneasy—about what it meant for them.

So, within a week of settlement, Ham held his first staff meeting after the close of business. It was a happy event; he had it catered with cold cuts and soft drinks. All were in a good mood, as they congratulated him and Cheribel.

Ham was straight forward and honest. Both they and he knew the store had problems, he said. The next three months would be a trial period at the end of which job performances and sales would be evaluated.

"Of course," Ham said, "I hope you can all stay on, at least through the first year."

He outlined plans for the store, such as expanding gem sales and dropping low-profit categories. He explained discipline, salary and incentives, including individual sales goals, which he believed could boost business. Copies of new procedures were given to each employee.

"Running a business isn't new to me," said Ham. "I once had my own repair shop. I want to make this the best jewelry store in town. To do that, I need your help and ideas." He promised to discuss his plans more fully with each of them and listen to their opinions.

Staff chats: In the following week Ham met privately with each employee to review job goals and get reaction to his plans.

Joshua Bullwinkle congratulated him again on buying the store. He was uneasy about the monthly sales quota, he said, since he was getting older. He also questioned Ham's plan to push colored gems. "But it's your store, not mine," he said, promising his support.

Henrietta Creekee wanted to do more bridal work.

Marilee Annabelle Smith criticized his plans, especially employee discipline. "Hiram didn't do that, and we did just fine," she said.

Wilson Sharpe liked Ham's plan to push colored gems and suggested he be put in charge of diamonds, too. "Bullwinkle's a nice old guy, but you need someone younger," he said. He also suggested "our little cutie," Ophelia Goodbodie, be made assistant gem salesperson.

But Ham didn't like Wilson's remarks. "That's discriminatory against Bullwinkle and sexist against Ophelia. I don't want to hear that kind of talk," he warned.

Ophelia was enthusiastic. She bubbled with ideas to promote tableware and gifts, and reach students at local colleges.

Three months later: After the probationary period, Ham's changes seemed to work. Sales inched up in most—though not all—categories.

Joshua Bullwinkle proved a source of real help. Ham found himself relying on Bullwinkle's advice and experience so much—especially in diamond buying and familiarity with long-time customers—he made him store manager, overseeing employee performance.

Wilson Sharpe became the main diamond and gem salesman, though Bullwinkle remained senior salesman and buyer.

Ham reluctantly fired Marilee Annabelle Smith. Despite repeated warnings and requests for a doctor's note, she persisted in calling in sick once or twice a week.

Henrietta Creekee left watches, replacing Marilee Smith as bridal consultant.

Ophelia's enthusiasm was put to good use. She took over watches, continued with gifts, and did some gem sales. She also enrolled in GIA's gemology course, paid for by the store.

Plan For Staff In The Spring

September 1986 Part II

Start thinking about next year's Christmas staff in the spring. Here's a year-long calendar that will help you avoid the hiring crunch next October.

1. Spring—Needs: First, make a staffing plan, based on holiday business you did last year. Which departments were short of staff? What were heavy-traffic times? When did you need more salespeople? Consider effects of new promotions on traffic.

Based on that, calculate how many people you need this year, including part-time or temporary staffers.

Part-timers are hired indefinitely, get some benefits, and work less than full-time. Temporaries work for a limited time—usually a few weeks—get no benefits, and can be full-time.

2. Late spring—Duties: Draw up job specifications. Consider skills and the type of people you need in various departments; the hours you need them for, and how much you can pay.

Specifying job duties enables you to develop training, measure performance, and set wages.

3. Summer—Looking: You have a staffing schedule and job specs. Now, start looking.
   • Consider junior (two-year) or community colleges.
   • Check local chapters of groups for retired people—such as the Association for Retired Persons or local senior citizen centers—who want part-time work.
   • Another source: Relatives of current employees.
   Advertising is simple: Post a notice on your bulletin board; contact the school's student aid office; place ads in the school paper, organization's newsletter, or the local newspaper.

4. Late summer—Interviews: When ready to see applicants, follow this rule to avoid legal hassles later: KEEP the interview work-related.

The reason: Employee selection procedures are scrutinized by state and federal equal employment opportunity agencies.

5. Training: Hire holiday help during the fall, even if you don't use them full-time until Thanksgiving. This gives you time to train them before they start work.

Hiring Interview Checklist

October 1979

Hiring today is no simple matter, whether it is hiring a management employee or a white collar worker, a stock person, a salesperson, or a buyer. There are certain basic principles involved which should be observed carefully. Unless you and your people who do the hiring observe these principles and caveats, you can run afoul of the law and may incur substantial liabilities. The following checklist is designed to help you obtain productive employees without breaking equal opportunity federal laws. It is not all inclusive and it does not cover requirements imposed at the state or local level. However, the checklist is designed to give you some ideas of potential legal pitfalls in the hiring process and to act as a general guide as to what you can and cannot do.

I. Who is involved in the hiring process.

1. The small store owner or manager.
2. The receptionist or telephone operator or whoever else first sees or talks to the applicant.

3. The interviewer who should have training and possibly experience in interviewing.
4. The college recruiter.
5. The supervisor or department head who passes final approval. This person should have some training and practice in interviewing.
6. Executives who will be working with hirees or who may have casual meetings with them during the hiring process.

II. What should the above individuals know about the hiring process.

1. All those listed above should know the legal ramifications in hiring. Often the person doing the actual interviewing is well-trained, but charges of discrimination are brought as a result of casual remarks by others tangentially involved in the hiring process.

2. The interviewers and supervisors and the persons responsible for final hiring should know the content of the job which the applicant is seeking.

155

III. Practical techniques to improve interviewing skills.

1. Do your homework on job content prior to the interview.

2. Avoid over-generalization about the job and the company.

3. Review your own prejudices—don't let them cloud your judgment.

4. Be receptive—both talking and listening.

5. Avoid questions which may be interpreted as an attempt to obtain legally unacceptable information.

6. Never over-question.

7. Use silence—it's hard to do so, but let the applicant be first to break the silence.

8. Keep the interview private.

9. Keep the initiative.

10. Keep your opinions to yourself.

11. Shun the role of the amateur psychologist.

12. Keep an eye on what you want to accomplish.

13. Maintain a steady pace.

14. Don't be misled by appearance of the applicant.

15. Don't shy away from either asking or answering hard questions.

16. At the end of the interview, evaluate carefully the information you have obtained—interpret the facts, weigh them carefully and determine a course of action.

IV. Legal requirements involved in interviewing are complicated.
The two major federal agencies with which the checklist deals are the Wage-Hour Division of the U.S. Department of Labor and the Equal Employment Opportunity Commission. Basic to regulations of both agencies is the concept that discrimination must be avoided. Age, sex, race, national origin and religion are not permissible basis for not hiring an applicant. You can ask whether or not the applicant is a U.S. citizen. Be sure that each person who asks for an application blank gets one whether it be from the receptionist, an executive, an interviewer or any other employee. Save the completed applications for those not hired as well as those hired.

V. What an interviewer must not ask or require on an application before hiring.
(Although many of these questions may be asked after hire if required for fringe benefit programs.)

1. Don't ask the applicant's age.

2. Don't ask the applicant's date of birth.

3. Don't ask the applicant what church he/she attends or the name of his/her priest, rabbi or minister.

4. Don't ask the applicant what his/her father's surname is.

5. Don't ask the female applicant what her maiden name was.

6. Don't ask the applicant whether he/she is married, divorced, separated, widowed or single (but you may ask Mr., Mrs., Miss, or Ms.).

7. Don't ask the applicant who resides with him/her.

8. Don't ask the applicant how many children he/she has.

9. Don't ask the ages of any children of the applicant.

10. Don't ask who will care for the children while the applicant is working.

11. Don't ask the applicant where a spouse or parent resides or works (although you may ask whether relatives of the applicant are or have been employed by the company).

12. Don't ask the applicant if he/she owns or rents his/her place of residence.

13. Don't ask the applicant whether he/she ever had his/her wages garnished.

14. Don't ask the applicant whether he/she was ever arrested.

VI. You can ask questions about the applicant's past job and check his/her suitability for the present position.
The interviewer should do little talking here. The applicant should be encouraged to talk. Try to avoid asking questions which can be answered with "yes" or "no."

1. Job experience

a. Your last job was at the XYZ company. What did you do exactly?

b. How did you like your work?

c. Tell me something about your working relationship with your supervisor.

d. You know we will have to talk to your former employers to check your references. You don't have any objections, do you?

e. In your application you aren't too clear about why you left your last job. How about telling me some of the reasons.

f. How did you find the working atmosphere at your last place of employment?

g. In what accomplishments on your last job did you take the most pride?

h. Did your former boss encourage suggestions or ideas for improvements? Tell me about any suggestions that you made on your own.

i. Discuss your relationship with your associates.

j. For what kind of company do you think you can do your best work?

k. Did you ever become involved in emergency situations and work long hours under pressure? Tell me about such an experience.

2. Suitability for available position

a. I have explained the duties of our job. How do you think your experience fits you for it?

b. Can you tell me about your satisfaction or lack of satisfaction with the rate of advancement at your former company?

c. Suppose you take this job. What are your immediate goals?

d. What do you think are your strong points?

e. Tell me what you consider your greatest abilities and how they will help you in this job.

f. Do you have any weak spots in your work habits? What are you doing to overcome them?

g. Have you taken any courses or home study programs relating to your field of work? Tell me about them.

This checklist was prepared by the National Retail Merchants Association, 100 W. 31st St., New York, N.Y. 10001. It is copyrighted material and is reproduced here with permission.

Know What Your Salespeople Think

September 1982 Part II

The following statements can give a manager a pretty fair grasp on the attitude on his salespeople towards the customer, the store, selling jewelry and themselves.

Simply ask your people whether they agree or disagree with the following statements. Then discuss their answers with them. If you want to check yourself, see if you agree or disagree with us before you look at the answers.

1. I have to know the customer's price range before I can really help her.

2. If I show a customer enough merchandise he'll eventually find something he likes.

3. There's not much I can do for a customer until she decides what she wants.

4. The first fifteen to thirty seconds I'm with a new customer are the most critical.

5. Most customers who leave the store without buying, but say they will come back, do return.

6. When I first meet a customer, it's far more important to be friendly than to find out what he wants.

7. If I have to ask a customer to buy more than one or two times, I'm being pushy.

8. The price of the item is the customer's concern, not mine.

9. "May I help you?" is a good way to greet a customer.

10. Customers want to know all the features of the product.

11. I can tell how much a customer will spend from his appearance.

12. Most of the time a customer knows what she wants from our advertising and display.

13. It's important to know why a customer buys something.

14. Many of the people who come into our store are just looking.

15. It's a good technique to downgrade the competition.

16. Often we lose sales because we don't have the right merchandise in stock.

17. The salesperson who knows the product well is 75% along the way to making the sale.

18. If I'm not getting anywhere, turning a customer over to another salesperson is a good idea.

19. When someone says, "I'm just looking," he should be left alone.

20. When a customer raises an objection to a product or resistance to buying, it's an indication he wants to look at something less expensive.

Here are our answers and our reasons for each one. Whether or not you (or your salespeople) change any of yours is up to you. We will tell you why we feel the way we do and how each of the statements impacts a sale.

1. Disagree. The customer may not be knowledgeable about jewelry values. She may be able and willing to spend more than she had in mind if the salesperson is not blocked by trying to push her into an invalid price range. Your effort should be geared toward finding an item the customer wants, then to work on how she will pay for it. However, be alert for signals from the customer that indicate she is uncomfortable with the price. "Do you have anything smaller, lighter, plainer" are the signals to come down in price.

2. Disagree. Just showing merchandise is not selling. If the statement were true, there really is no need for a salesperson.

3. Disagree. Most people who come into your store have an idea of what they want but have not made a firm decision yet. In fact, one of the salesperson's primary functions is to help the customer decide what he wants.

4. Agree. You get one chance to make a first impression. Many sales are made or lost based on the first impression the customer has of the salesperson. If you blow the greeting badly, you may not have a chance to go any further.

5. Disagree. Even though many people do come back (and those are the ones we remember), the salesperson who lets a customer walk too readily is not trying to make the sale today. We don't advocate a "hard-sell" approach but do feel some attempt at getting the customer to buy should be made before letting a customer leave. You can't make a sale if the customer isn't there.

6. Agree. Most customers need some time to become acclimated to you, you store, your merchandise. The first-time customer, in particular, probably is uneasy until he has developed some measure of trust in you and your store. The customer who wants to get right down to business will let you know.

7. Disagree. While many customers will make their decision on your first attempt to close, many also require multiple opportunities to buy. The salesperson who depends on one or two attempts to make the sale loses those customers who need more opportunities. The good salesperson learns many different types of closes and uses them all because it will appear you are too pushy if you keep saying the same thing when you are asking the customer to buy.

8. Agree. The customer has to pay for it, therefore it's his concern. The salesperson helps the customer resolve the concern and does everything he can to make it easy for the customer to pay for the item.

9. Disagree. The opening gambit in retail selling is "Good morning may I help you no thanks I'm just looking." We don't want a "No" to start off our sale, so why ask for one? Customers hear "May I help you?" wherever they go. It's no particularly friendly and doesn't sound unique. Greet customer with something you think he will respond to in a positive manner.

10. Disagree. There are two reasons we disagree with this. First, some salespeople try to overeducate the customer and wind up confusing him. Second, the customer buys because of the benefit or joy that he derives from the feature of the product, not the feature itself. For example, people don't buy a diamond because it's the hardest surface known. They buy a diamond because they can enjoy the diamond for lifetime.

11. Disagree. Everyone has heard stories of shabbily dressed customers with a big roll of bills in their pockets. However, if we're honest with ourselves, we all have some built-in prejudices. If someone comes in the store who we don't like the look of, for whatever reason, it's better to let someone else wait on him if possible.

12. Disagree. Advertising and display bring people into the store. The decision to buy is generally made only after the customer has actually seen the product and has discussed it with the salesperson.

13. Agree. Not only does knowing why a customer is buying help with the initial sale, it opens the door to an add-on sale by giving a clue to another reason a customer may buy.

14. Disagree. If we feel many people are just looking we tend to treat them that way. The salesperson should treat everyone coming in the store as if they are there to buy something today until they prove otherwise.

15. Disagree. Knocking the competition puts the whole industry in a bad light. Instead, build up your own store and give the customer the advantages of doing business with you.

16. Disagree. No store can carry everything. In helping the customer decide what she wants, steer her toward something you have in stock. You can always special order as a last resort.

17. Disagree. Product knowledge, while extremely important to a salesperson's confidence and certainly needed if you are going to be a professional, is grossly overrated as a *sales* tool. A pleasant personality, interest in the customer, ability to listen and sound sales techniques will make more sales than product knowledge. However, *don't bluff.* If you don't know the answer to a question, say so, even if it loses the sale. Generally you can get the answer from someone else in the store. If not, tell the customer you will get the answer and call him.

18. Agree. No matter how good you are or how pleasant a personality you have, there comes a time when the person across the counter just does not like you and won't buy from you. When that happens, get someone else. Remember, the new salesperson must have a valid reason in the eyes of the customer for coming into the picture. More knowledge, more authority, relates better to the situation, etc.

19. Disagree. "I am just looking" is a complete sentence grammatically. However, it does not express the complete thought. Make the customers tell you whether they are "Just looking for something" or "Just looking around." If they are just looking around, then give them some time and space. Don't accept the first "Just looking." Probe a little further.

20. Disagree. Don't be too quick to go down in price. The customer may be just looking for some reassurance on the item you're discussing. You always have the option of moving to a lower price range but don't do it until it's necessary.

You still may not agree with our answers to some of the statements and that's perfectly all right. When dealing with individual retail customers we are dealing with most unpredictable animals so there are exceptions to every generality.

We hope you've enjoyed the quiz and that somewhere along the line, you and your salespeople make some additional or larger sales because of it.

How To Measure Strength & Weakness

September 1982 Part II

You can use several very objective measurements to assess how well you have developed your sales staff. All have to do with sales made. There are a few subjective guidelines you'll also want to include in your analysis.

You objective is to generate the maximum profitable sales volume you can in your store. As manager, you're not only responsible for your own sales but also for developing the people who work for you and their sales. Whenever we are asked to evaluate a sales force, we compile data which enables us to rate everyone who sells. Next, we try to find how to bring the people on the bottom of the list up to or beyond the people on top while also improving the numbers of the top people.

Often we find the manager (or owner) at or near the top of the list. Generally this means that while the manager is doing his job in selling in relation to the other people, he's not doing the job he's supposed to in terms of training and developing his sales force. You see, the manager (or owner) will make his sales by virtue of his experience, authority and abilities. Look at your own store. If your manager (or you) is near the top, envision what your total store volume would be if his numbers were near the bottom.

Analysis tools and what they mean

1. Total $ volume: This is quite obvious. Tells us who is contributing the most to our total volume.

2. Average $ per sale made: Tells us who is making the higher ticket sales.

3. Gross profit $: Tells us who is able to sell the more profitable items.

4. $ Sold per hours worked: Enables use to measure part timers as well as full timers. Who is the most productive when he is on the floor?

5. Number of sales: The leader is either a good closer or is hustling to get the people who come into the store.

6. % of sales made in relation to customers faced: Measures how effective our people are in making the most of their sales opportunities.

7. % of add-on sales in relation to number of sales: Let's us know who is alert to opportunities for suggestion selling.

8. % of customers who "shop around" who return: Tells us who is most effective in putting a "hook" into people who walk.

9. % of increase over previous period (week, month, year): Who's improving most rapidly?

10. Numbers of regular customers (clients): The real pros develop a regular clientele of good customers they can count on. Who's doing this in our store?

11. Number of new prospects brought into the store: Too many sales people feel they have no responsibility for building traffic. The pros don't feel this way at all. They look for customers. **12. % of merchandise or sales returned:** A high % of returns is an indication of too much sales pressure or a failure to reassure the customer after the sale of the excellent purchase he's made.

In addition to these twelve objective measurements, there are some subjective categories you'll want to consider.

1. Ability to sell all products: The ideal salesperson is comfortable and capable no matter what department he is in in the store.

2. Relations with other sales people: A super salesperson can hurt total store performance if he or she doesn't get along with and/or upsets the rest of the sales force.

3. Performance of non-sales tasks: In any store there are tasks which are not directly related to sales. Administrative, security, cleaning, etc.

4. Willingness to learn: In order to improve, your sales people should be willing to invest some of their time in learning about products, policies and selling.

5. Attitude: The top sales person is positive toward himself, the store, the products, customers and selling.

How To Fire
Without Getting Burned

November 1985

Day after day, a recently hired—and poorly performing—jewelry salesman returned from lunch with liquor on his breath. Management warned verbally that if he didn't stop his apparent lunchtime drinking, he would be fired. Despite the warning, he continued—and was fired.

Besides being a sub-standard salesman, the guy was drinking on the job. Management was clearly justified in firing him. End of story, right? Not quite.

To the chagrin of his boss, the employee eventually was reinstated at the urging of the state board of unemployment. The reason: Management had made mistakes in its termination procedure. Rules governing the use of drugs or alcohol by employees were not included in the firm's personnel manual, which some courts now interpret as actual terms of employment. And management had no written documentation of the warning it issued the employed before his termination. This, coupled with the fact that the man underwent an alcohol rehabilitation program immediately after being terminated, made unemployment officials quite sympathetic to his plight.

Says the jewelry store owner (who requested anonymity): "They didn't quite order us, but they strongly suggested we give this guy a second chance. We're not unreasonable; we said we'd do it. Now, after he's been on the job another year, we're getting ready to fire him again—for his poor sales record."

This time, management is documenting its actions. Managers are giving the employee *written* warnings and reprimands for poor sales performance. (The firm also has rewritten its personnel manual to cover use of alcohol on the job.)

"If I learned anything at all," says the store owner, "Its to leave a paper trail. Being a small family business, I never thought to do that before. But I've learned the hard way."

Although this case did not end up in court, it could have if management had not reinstated an employee who had already proven unsatisfactory. Any time an employee is fired, says a labor relations attorney, his employer should be prepared for a lawsuit.

Employment at will: "You're fired," barked the cigar-chomping manager, pointing towards the door. In old movies—and in earlier times—an employee's response was to hang his head, grab his hat and slink away.

No more. In today's workplace, terminations are a complicated, risky and sometimes costly business. Many former employees who feel they were unjustly fired are bringing lawsuits that cost American companies millions—win or lose. One attorney estimates that any company brought to court will spend a minimum of $20,000 for defense.

This decade has seen significant changes in the right of employees—and an erosion of the common-law doctrine of employment-at-will. That doctrine is simple enough: Absent an agreement to the contrary, employers may terminate an employee at any time for any or, perhaps, no reason. Employees also have the right to terminate their employment at any time.

In 1884, a Tennessee court explained employment-at-will this way: "All may dismiss their employee(s) at-will, be they many or few, for good cause, for no cause, or even for cause morally wrong without being thereby guilty of legal wrong."

Over the years, the doctrine has been limited by federal, state and local laws that prohibit termination because of race, sex, national origin, physical handicap, union activity, age and, in some cities, sexual preference. But no statutes have been enacted that specifically override it. So, terminated employees have turned to the courts for reinstatement or compensation.

A flurry of court decisions in the early 1980s in a number of states, most notably California and Michigan, seriously affected the employment-at-will doctrine, says Francis J. Connell III, a labor relations attorney with the Philadelphia firm of Drinker Biddle & Reath. This past year has seen a decline in the number of cases boosting employees rights. But, he cautions, "any employer in 1985 must be aware that employees and their attorneys are becoming much more aggressive."

Damaging decisions: Courts have used many theories to limit the employer's right to discharge at-will employees, says Connell. Most cases fall into three categories.

1. Unjust dismissal or abusive discharge. "Employees will sue because they feel they have been treated unfairly," says Connell, not because they have been discriminated against per se. "Employees will charge that there was a specific intent to harm them rather than do good for the company."

2. The public policy exception. Some state courts have held that an employer has no right to terminate an at-will employee if doing so would violate a clear mandate of public policy. Although decisions vary from state to state, courts have found that employees cannot be discharged for performing jury duty, for testifying against an employer, for refusing to take a lie detector test, for failing to commit perjury, for refusing to commit acts in violation of anti-trust laws, for reporting violations of the law, or for refusing to engage in political lobbying activity on behalf of an employer (if it is not part of the employee's job).

3. The contract theory. Cases have been tried—and won—based on an implied contract between an employer and an employee. The implied contract can be a casual verbal assurance such as "You'll always have a job here," or "You have a great future here." Or, it can be implied in an employment handbook, personnel policy or even an unwritten custom that specifies terminations only for "just cause."

"No matter what the legal basis of a lawsuit—discrimination, the contract theory, whatever—when these cases go to juries, as more and more of them do, the only thing a jury cares about is if the employee was treated fairly," says Connell. "Juries don't give a damn about legal theories."

Avoid bad blood: Employees sue when they feel they've been treated unfairly, says Connell. Therefore, it's important not to make an employee want revenge.

Consider termination carefully. "An employer has the responsibility to think long and hard about what the employee has been doing unsatisfactorily and then tell the employee," says Connell. Terminating an employee in a moment of anger or frustration is simply poor management.

Instead, use a progressive disciplinary process. Connell recommends these three steps.

1. Issue an oral warning. Let the employee know how he is lacking and give him an opportunity to improve his performance.

2. If the employee continues to flounder, issue a written warning which again details the employee's shortcomings and tells exactly what he must do to perform satisfactorily.

3. As a final step, issue another written warning or suspend the employee for a week without pay.

If termination still seems in the best interest of the employer after these steps have been taken, then dismiss the employee.

But proceed with caution. Make sure employee handbooks and company manuals contain no language that could be construed as a contractual obligation. If they do, change them to disclaim any contractual relationship. (Even if you're not thinking of terminating an employee, check your handbooks and manuals for damaging language and change it now.)

Connell also advises a severance package, "even though the employee may have been lousy." This not only helps you avoid lawsuits but also maintains the goodwill of current employees.

When you offer a severance package, Connell advises getting release of liability from the employee. He warns, however, "The employee who signs such a release may subsequently go to court arguing duress or that he signed the release not knowing what it meant."

An employer's best defense against lawsuits by former employees is a good offense. That involves careful monitoring of the hiring process. Spell out the at-will employment relationship of employment applications. A statement of at-will employment—that an employee can be terminated at any time or with two weeks' notice—just above the signature line on an application may deter a lawsuit. And remember that statement made to a prospective employee during the hiring interview can create contract rights, especially if the applicant can persuade a court that he relied on such statements.

Wielding the Ax

With the exception of Dagwood Bumstead's boss, Mr. Dithers, most managers don't often fire employees nor do they find it easy. But, when the task becomes unavoidable, there are ways to make it more bearable for a manager and less traumatic for an employee.

Robert Half, a nationally-known executive recruiter, offers these tips in his new book "Robert Half on Hiring" (Crown, $15.95).

• Keep your intention to fire to yourself. Firing is a topic that is almost impossible to keep out of the company grapevine. If you tell somebody, the employee is almost sure to find out.

• Fire the employee yourself, don't delegate the task. And do it in private. If your office isn't private enough, find another location. make sure you will not be interrupted.

• Personnel specialists suggest firing late on a Friday afternoon. However, doing it frequently could induce Friday-afternoon anxiety in current employees.

• Deliver the bad news in a tactful but direct manner. Don't beat around the bush with small talk and don't hold out false hope. Be honest, but not brutal.

• Be prepared for a bad reaction. There is no way to gauge exactly how an employee will react, but whatever happens, remain professional.

• Learn from your mistakes. If you have to fire a person, it usually means you made a hiring mistake.

Answers to JCK Management Study Center Quiz:
(Questions can be found on page 132)

EMPLOYEE BENEFITS

1. c	6. b
2. a	7. b
3. b	8. a
4. b	9. b
5. a	10. a

Chapter 4

MANAGEMENT ARTS

*Behind Every Great Store
Is A Great Manager*

JCK Management Study Center: Getting The Most From Your Staff

February 1995

Employee relations.

They're one of the most important—and most troublesome—management issues facing jewelry store owners. After all, employees are the ones doing the work, making the sales, pleasing the customers. Or not.

That's why good employee relations can mean success, while bad ones can lead to a date in bankruptcy court.

But what are good employee relations and how can you maintain them—especially when, as in many jewelry stores, employees are "just like family"?

There are some keys. You might call them the 3 Cs:

• Communication.

You know what you want your employees to do. But do they? You know when you're happy—or unhappy—with their performance. But do they?

• Consistency.

Do you judge all employees by the same standard all the time? Or do you let one employee do something—come in late, use the telephone for personal calls, skip out on housekeeping chores—for which you reprimand others?

• Control.

Is the owner or manager really in charge in your store or does the crew run the ship? Are there clear rules and lines of authority?

Most managers want their employees to like them. And when staffs are relatively small, as they are in most jewelry stores, it's important that people get along with each other. Yet being too friendly with subordinates makes it hard for the boss to maintain discipline and to correct inappropriate behavior. What's a manager to do?

JCK turned to Professional Training Associates Inc., publisher of *Practical Supervision*, for some answers. This monthly newsletter offers non-technical, often simply common sense advice—sometimes based on synopses of management books—on a variety of problems. How can you supervise one worker you dislike or review another who's a friend? How should you handle suspected substance abuse? How do you make long-time employees more productive? How should you respond to charges of sexual harassment or racial bias?

The following edition of the *JCK* Management Study Center features excerpts and adaptations of articles from *Practical Supervision*. Some focus on areas of employee supervision such as performance reviews. Others present scenarios involving problem employees. The advice given often includes no right or wrong answers. Instead, it shows how to apply the keys listed above, especially the first one—communication.

PERFORMANCE REVIEWS

Most managers should welcome the chance to strengthen relationships with employees on a regular basis. That's exactly what performance reviews can do. Yet many bosses regard formal evaluations as a waste of time, a source of stress or both.

It doesn't have to be that way. In *Supervisor's Survival Kit*, author Elwood N. Chapman tells how to turn reviews to everyone's advantage by focusing on the benefits of the process.

Start your positive approach by reviewing the potential payoffs for everyone involved.

Employees profit because reviews clarify what is expected of them and ensure their achievements are recognized. Reviews also identify ways to strengthen weak areas and provide a forum for expressing and resolving concerns.

The company benefits because reviews identify employees worthy of reward or counseling, establish a basis for raises and promotions and allow fairer, more uniform treatment of employees.

Managers profit because reviews offer an opportunity to build better relationships with employees and help them to improve productivity. Proper reviews also make it easier for outstanding employees to get raises and promotions.

No matter what review system you use, it's crucial to give the process the time and energy it deserves. Employees expect a thorough, honest evaluation and will feel cheated if you seem too busy to consider their work carefully. Even a poor system can produce positive results if you take the process seriously and show employees you really care about what they do (and don't do).

Many managers are sensitive about rating their people on a generalized standard (shows initiative) or a numerical scale (rate from 1 to 5). It's hard to pigeonhole people, especially if you must give an unsatisfactory rating to someone you like. Use these tips to decide on ratings that accurately reflect performance:

• Appraise work, not personality. Use objective data such as sales figures, attendance records and customer calls.

• Evaluate according to actual contributions, not potential.

• Base judgment on typical performance—not one good or bad stretch during the period under review.

• Keep various standards separate, rather than allow poor or excellent performance in one area to color your rating in all areas.

• Don't try to save time by simply selecting the middle range on all factors

• If you must give an unsatisfactory rating, have all the facts at your disposal, discuss the problem with the employee, inform your boss (if you have one) of the decision and keep an open mind about the possibility of improvement.

• Discuss ratings openly with the employee. Explain your position and defend it—if necessary. Make it plain that you're interested in helping everyone to succeed.

To make the review process work, you must show employees you believe their work is worthy of thoughtful discussion. Chapman suggests you:

• Choose a time when you and the employee can concentrate on the discussion—preferably not right before lunch, at the end of the day or during peak sales hours.

• Separate salary reviews from performance reviews so concerns about money and benefits don't distract attention from performance issues.

• Let employees do most of the talking and be sure to listen closely to their point of view.

• Make descriptive, specific and non-judgmental statements about performance.

• Reinforce positives while seeking ways to improve below-standard performance.

• Encourage the employee to contribute ideas on how to improve.

• Emphasize future goals and how to reach them rather than dwell on past activities.

• Discuss longer-range career plans, helping employees to consider their progress toward personal goals and what they might do to reach them more quickly.

Always follow up by giving praise or coaching on performance between reviews. The more frequently you communicate with an employee about performance, the easier reviews will become because you'll both have a pretty good idea of where you stand.

POSITIVE REINFORCEMENT

Mark, one of your branch store managers, is frustrated. His sales associates just can't seem to meet their goals. He thinks they could do so easily if only they'd try some of his sales techniques. He's held several staff meetings to explain what he wants, but his ideas don't seem to catch on. Why can't his staff get excited about his way of doing things?

Mark has good ideas and good employees; why isn't he getting the performance he wants? The answer is a lack of positive reinforcement—encouraging desirable behavior by immediately rewarding it. If Mark's sales associates are on commission, he may think that's reward enough. After all, if they sell something, they'll make more money. But what about efforts that don't result in immediate sales—such as patience with a tedious but occasionally good customer no one likes or special attention to keeping the store tidy during busy times? Don't they deserve rewards as well?

Whether you reward good performance with a bonus, a pat on the back or some other recognition, positive reinforcement helps employees to understand what kinds of behavior are desirable and valued in your store. You get what you want and so do your employees. Here are some tips:

• Emphasize the positive, avoid the negative. Everyone prefers cheers to jeers. Positive reinforcement helps to build employees' self-confidence and makes them more self-motivated. Negative reactions (criticism or punishment) motivate them to avoid unpleasant results; they may decrease the chance of undesirable behavior, but they won't encourage people to excel.

When an employee has a performance problem, deal with it quickly, then look for the first chance to recognize improvement. If you have trouble spotting positive performance, start by assuming employees are working toward the same goals you are. Then consciously look for progress toward those goals. Mark's main goal is to boost sales, so he should keep an eye out for anything that will help. When Sally shows a birthstone list to a reluctant customer, for example, he can say, "That was a good idea. Not everyone born in December likes turquoise, but zircon comes in so many nice colors! I think she might want to buy one."

• Act promptly. The shorter the gap between performance and reward, the stronger the reinforcement. Employees learn quickly what kinds of performance are praised or rewarded and start to repeat that performance as soon as possible. Mark can bolster his sales associates' morale by congratulating them when they follow suggested techniques. Thus, Joe would get a pat on the back when he says, "I know you're not looking for a pendant today, Mrs. Jones, but let me show you a stunning designer piece that just came in this morning."

• Make it personal. While recognizing group performance is good, each individual also wants to know that what he/she does is important and appreciated. Start each week by making a list of your employees. As soon as you see one do something that merits recognition, make a note beside the person's name. Add a big check-mark as soon as you congratulate them (hopefully right away). If some names don't have a check mark by Friday morning, pay special attention to these people. Find some contribution each has made and say how much you appreciate it.

• Be specific. Reinforce specific, observable actions so employees know exactly what behavior is being rewarded. Praising Sally for "good work" certainly doesn't hurt, but it doesn't explain what was good about it so she can do it again.

• Be imaginative. There are endless ways to provide positive reinforcement. Being creative in your recognition can give it greater impact. Start an Employee of the Week program and announce the winner at your sales meetings. Give someone an unscheduled afternoon off or give a gift certificate to take his/her family out for pizza. Write a letter thanking a worker for extra effort and send a copy to his spouse. Don't get so carried away, however, that you forget one of the most basic forms of positive reinforcement—a simple "thank you." It's a powerful phrase, and it doesn't wear out with frequent use.

• Keep it up. Providing positive reinforcement is like other management skills—the more you do it, the easier it gets. To stay on track, ask yourself at least once a week:

– "When was the last time I gave each of my employees positive reinforcement?

– "Did I tell each person exactly what he did right?

– "Did I thank the person and encourage her to continue the good performance?"

– "Is someone doing something right now that I can recognize?"

Employees who are rewarded frequently for good performance soon will perform at that level (or better) all the time. And that makes you look good.

FRIENDLY PERSUASION

Several months ago, you became manager of the store where you've worked for five years. Now it's time for performance appraisals of sales associates and you don't know what to do. These people are your friends. How can you criticize them—especially Mary, who's always been so nice but definitely needs some improvement?

Look at the review process as a way to help Mary meet her potential. Sometimes supervisors are afraid to talk about the need for change with coworkers who are friends because they don't want to create tension that could ruin the friendship. But if you already have a good flow of communication, that makes it easier to use a constructive performance review process. You just need to let Mary know the review is supposed to help her.

Explain in advance that you want to cover four points: how well Mary can and does do the job, how well she can and does cooperate with others, the reasons for any current or foreseeable differences between planned and actual performance and anything else she wants to discuss. Remember that performance reviews should be a dialogue.

You don't want to spend the session discussing weekend plans, so write the questions you want to explore and give Mary a copy ahead of time. Focus more than half the discussion on the future, dividing the rest between the past and present. Be sure to present solid examples of any points. Don't assume Mary knows what you're talking about just because you're friends. If you think she's not spending enough time with customers, describe some specific instances and use those examples to set some fresh goals.

Also ask Mary how she thinks you can help her do better. You could be surprised at her answers. As a friend, she may feel free to offer criticism or a suggestion for ways to do things differently—and her ideas may be valid. Always allow time for and encourage this input.

Remember, too, that some of the salespeople may not be your friends. Be sure to follow the same review procedures, even if you find them harder to communicate with. That's the best way to avoid favoritism and build better relationships with your entire team.

FIGHTING CHANGE

Ed, your new store manager, is taking on a staff of seasoned salespeople. He's suggested some procedural changes that he feels will make everyone more productive, but finds after several weeks that nothing has happened. After specifically asking them to use a new take-in form that he feels will reduce errors, he finds they discussed it among themselves and decided to stick with the old form. Their resistance annoys him, and he wonders if he should call a meeting to lay down the law.

Workers who are "set in their ways" pose a special challenge. One key to guiding more experienced workers is to strike a balance between your need to get news ideas up and running quickly and their need to adjust to change. Consider these ideas.

Allow plenty of lead time. Give salespeople as much notice as possible about upcoming changes so they can prepare mentally. By simply announcing changes he wanted and expecting them to happen, Ed set himself up for resistance. Instead, he could have let the staff know he was thinking about changing take-in procedures, described what he had in mind and when it would happen, then asked for input.

• Encourage enthusiasm and ownership. Present new procedures or ideas you have in mind and explain their purpose in practical terms. When you can show employees how they and the store will benefit, they'll be more willing to invest their energy in learning new work habits. Let the staff suggest ways to introduce new procedures. Workers who help to plan their own changes feel more empowered.

• Introduce a new skill or concept in steps. If the new approach is complex, show the whole procedure and then present it in digestible pieces. Have employees practice the first step before moving on to the next one. And blend the old with the new. Look for ways to phase in changes so employees don't have to drop one thing and start something totally new overnight. Dumping changes on people and cutting them off from what's familiar heightens anxiety and resistance.

• Win over group leaders. If you face group resistance, try to get commitments from the informal leaders of the group, who then may influence other staff members in a positive manner.

• Avoid change just for the sake of change. Make sure the new things you expect workers to do are really better than current practices. If an experienced worker is digging in his heels over a change, listen carefully because he may be right. Just because it's your idea doesn't mean it's better.

A MATTER OF DISCIPLINE

You've tried coaching, positive reinforcement and feedback. But Gary, who checks incoming merchandise, remains a problem. You're sure he knows how to do the work, but he keeps making mistakes—on recording stock numbers, checking quality, updating computer files—and his mistakes are costing you money. You're ready to scream. Is there something more constructive you can do?

It's natural to feel like lashing out at problem employees. But as V. Clayton Sherman notes in "From Losers to Winners," emotional reactions are usually futile, and punishment is generally ineffective in getting employees to change.

When a serious performance problem develops, first think for a moment what "discipline" really means. The word comes from "disciple," or follower. And that's what discipline should create: a productive worker on the right path.

Positive discipline doesn't mean getting mad, regarding Gary as an enemy or figuring out how to get even with him. Instead, you must let him know what's expected, help him do it and let him judge for himself the consequences of continuing in the wrong direction.

Analyze performance: Write down exactly what the problem is. Don't settle for "sloppy work" or "bad attitude"; describe specific errors or incidents.

Next, figure out what these mistakes are costing the store. Be as specific as possible; this will help the employee to see the problem really exists. In Gary's case, this probably is easy. Improper computer inventory records may have caused you to order items you didn't need or run short of ones you did; poor quality control may have produced major problems with a customer.

(If you can't assign a cost—if all you can say is that something about the employee annoys you—then discipline, positive or otherwise, isn't appropriate. You can't correct every annoying trait of every employee. It's easier to learn to live with it.)

Finally, analyze your own supervisory performance. Could you do more to help Gary succeed? Have you made your expectations clear, provided enough training and noted mistakes promptly? Try not to feel defensive while doing this self-analysis. If you come up with something new to try, it could make things easier for you and Gary.

Try counseling: In a private session, give Gary some good news along with the bad. Tell him what he's doing right (there must be something), then spell out just what needs to be improved. Use the specifics you've gathered to drive home your points. It's OK to let your feelings about his performance show, as long as you don't become vindictive or abusive.

Ask Gary for his side of the story and for suggestions on how to overcome whatever obstacles are blocking his performance. Tell him you're confident he can do better and that you'll do all you can to help.

The more specifically you describe the problem and the more genuinely you show your support, the more likely he'll be able to turn around his performance. Protect his sense of dignity and let him leave the meeting with a clear idea of both what needs to be done and his ability to do it.

Keep counseling sessions short and to the point. And hold them as soon as possible after a problem appears, before too much damage is done.

Documentation: While you should document every employee's performance, it's especially important with a problem employee such as Gary. If he continues to perform below expectations and you need to take more forceful steps, you'll want proof. And if further discipline should provoke a lawsuit, you'll need to be able to prove you were paying equally close attention to all of your workers, not just picking on this one.

On the plus side, documentation is a big help in objectively analyzing a problem and tracking the progress employees make after coaching.

Some alternatives: If substandard performance continues, consider some alternatives.

• Training. Does Gary really know what he's doing? Maybe he's not comfortable with the computer or lacks the product knowledge needed for proper quality control.

• Referral. If you suspect personal problems are affecting Gary's work, refer him to your company's employee assistance program, if you have one, or to a community resource.

• Restructure the job—perhaps it's simply too demanding. Consider splitting up the duties or reassigning Gary to a job he can perform with success.

• Warning. Tell Gary how much time he has to shape up and what will happen if he meets the deadline—or doesn't.

Finally, offer plenty of feedback. Be sure Gary knows how important it is that his work improve right away. Hold daily or weekly reviews to monitor progress, or lack of it.

If all this fails and you must let Gary go, you'll know you have done everything possible to help him turn things around and that your thorough documentation will cover your legal liabilities. Now you're free to hire someone more capable, more willing or both.

COOPERATIVE COACHING

Coaching is a way to help employees make more of their abilities. As a coach, you help employees to develop and carry out an improvement plan, drawing on their own ideas and your observations of their performance, your understanding of the job and your skill in providing feedback.

Coaching is not directing. Managers who see a need for improvement often think how they would do the job better themselves—and then try to get employees to do it that way. That can frustrate everyone because employees tend to do things their way.

Instead of fighting that tendency, make the most of it. These tips, based on *Coaching and Counseling* by Marianne Minors, show how.

When to coach: Collaborative coaching works when an employee wants or needs to do better and when there's more than one way to do so. It's not the best way to handle infringements of basic work rules. Thus, if Meghan, your new sales associate, arrives late three times a week, you need to tell her exactly what acceptable attendance is, then help her figure out a way to get to work on time. Nor is coaching the right approach for employees whose personal problems interfere with their work; they need counseling.

But what if Meghan is having problems meeting her goal of more add-on sales. Before you talk to her, think through the situation in detail, making notes you can use later. The more you know about what's causing the problem, and the more clearly you can explain why she needs to improve, the more you can help her.

Now you're ready to coach. Here's how:

• Put Meghan at ease. Don't assign blame or give the impression you think she's a poor salesperson. Let her know the purpose of the meeting is to help her do better.

• Pinpoint the problem. Before you start creating solutions, be sure you and Meghan agree on what's wrong. It may come as a surprise to some employees that their performance is lacking—especially if you haven't set specific goals. (Improving add-on ratio sounds like a good goal, but it's vague. Going from one add-on per 10 sales to two is a better goal.)

• Some employees will tell you a different problem is more important than the one you want to talk about. "I know I'm not closing enough add-ons," Meghan may say. "But that's because we're so busy sometimes that I just can't spend enough time with each customer." You may have to take separate action to resolve issues employees bring up.

• Once you agree there's a problem, seek the employee's ideas about improvements—and be willing to put them into practice. It's quite possible that Meghan's complaint about being too busy is valid. Can you rearrange schedules or hire some part-time help to relieve the pressure?

Perhaps Meghan feels she also needs to know more about the products she's selling. Are you willing to pay for—and give her some time to work on—programs such as a home-study course from the Gemological Institute of America?

You, as a supersalesman, may be tempted to insist Meghan try your techniques. But she probably knows her skills and limitations better than you do and will be more comfortable with her own approach. You can make suggestions, but be sure to leave at least some recognizable part of the plan the way the employee suggested it.

• Agree on appropriate actions. Make sure you both understand what's supposed to happen next. Schedule a follow-up meeting and take any support actions you agreed on. Meghan may lose her enthusiasm for studying if she finds you've done nothing about the understaffing problem. After a coaching session, make a special effort to praise signs of improvement. Most employees will do their best to get things right, and your support will reinforce the behavior. If there are no signs of improvement, however, don't let the situation deteriorate. Let Meghan know you're still rooting for her to do better. Ask what part of the plan isn't working and put your heads together to develop a better approach.

Remember that coaching is more about seeking out options than about laying down the law. By focusing on helping employees to develop their own ideas, you can use coaching in many situations—not just when performance needs to be corrected. You can coach good performers who want to do even better or help staff members adjust to changes in policies and procedures.

'BUT I DON'T LIKE HER!'

You have a problem. Mary a long-long employee, constantly monopolizes staff meetings, offers opinions and suggestions quite unrelated to the topics being discussed and comments on other people's statements. Mary may be trying to usurp your authority or just wasting valuable time in needless chatter. But maybe you dislike Mary speaking up so much because you simply don't like her. How can you tell the difference?

Before you say or do anything, spend a few quiet moments considering what really bothers you about Mary's behavior. Be honest with yourself. Then plan to deal with this real issue, whatever it is.

Before you take action, however, find out how the other sales associates view Mary's behavior. If others are upset or dissatisfied, you may have good reason to tackle the problem If they're not—or even think Mary is making valuable contributions—you should reevaluate whether your personal feelings are affecting your judgment.

Give yourself the "friend or foe" test. Ask yourself, "Would I feel this way if a friend were doing the same thing?" If you can honestly say yes, then put your remedial plan into action. But if you realize you'd tolerate the same behavior from Joe, your ace salesman, you can be pretty sure you're upset with Mary rather than her actions. Avoid suing your management position to strike at purely personal targets.

DEMYSTIFYING FEEDBACK

Feedback seems simple. It's defined as communication that lets employees know how well they're doing and what they can do to improve. To work best, it should be timely, specific and frequent.

But if it's really that simple, why are so many people still in the dark about what their bosses think of their work? The reason is that while feedback is simple, it's not easy. The wrong ways of doing it often feel right. Learning to give people helpful information about their performance takes experience and persistence. This look at some common feedback errors should help you to improve your efforts.

Feedback in disguise: Poor feedback often seems so much like the real thing that you look elsewhere for the cause of disappointing results. Be ready to spot the following impostors:

• Describing "your way." Even if your way of closing a sale is very good, explaining it to Sally Salesperson isn't feedback. It doesn't tell her what you think of *her* performance. Instead of describing how you'd do it, tell Sally specifically what you've seen her do and what you'd like to see her do instead.

• Making assumptions. Don't assume you already know how well people perform. If you assume Joe is always excellent, Sally is average and Meghan is a problem, you'll find it hard to make fresh observations about their work. But if you approach each as the changeable individual he/she is, you'll be able to provide feedback on a wider range of triumphs and troubles.

• Keeping it to yourself. Many supervisors avoid feedback because they fear employees will react negatively. Think instead how *you'll* behave if you store up too many concerns about performance. Eventually, you'll lose patience and lash out at Meghan or give up on her. Meanwhile, she'll have had no opportunity to address your concerns.

• Restricting feedback to friends. Some managers give feedback only to those with whom they're comfortable. It's unfair to keep only those you like informed, and it's even worse to give feedback about employees you don't like to other people. Good feedback doesn't require a lot of social smoothing. You can share specific observations with little fanfare. "I like how you're answering the phone, Sally." That's all there is to it. Or if you don't approve of her method: "I'd like you to make sure you use the phone greeting we agreed on, Sally." Make sure the message gets through, then move on. Let Sally's mother worry about her personality; you stick to the specifics of her performance.

• Talking without being heard. Giving feedback in the wrong setting is like having a picnic in the rain. Look for a time and place where employees can understand your comments. Sooner is generally better, but be sure to take people aside to deliver negative feedback. If you're talking to Sally at the sales counter, make sure she has a moment free to concentrate and respond.

Make good feedback better: Once you recognize the mistakes above, it's easier to deliver genuine feedback. Here's how:

• Offer factual information. Don't tell Sally her performance is "good" or "bad." Offer objective data about her performance, then let her draw her own conclusions. When workers see for themselves the need to improve, they're often more motivated to change than when told what to do. And when employees can see they're headed in the right direction, they're usually enthusiastic about continuing. For example, don't tell Sally, "You're 20% below target." Instead say, "You were supposed to make 10 prospecting calls to customers this month, but you made only eight." Once Sally sees the obvious shortfall, you can move on to whatever planning or coaching is needed to help her meet her goal next month. If she exceeds the goal, be sure to recognize that as well.

• Capitalize on mistakes. Perfection is great; obviously, you want everyone to meet their goals. But if people don't feel comfortable discussing their problems in reaching those goals, you'll never know where they really need feedback the most. To help them feel comfortable, handle their mistakes gracefully. Also be up front about your own fallibility; talk with employees about your own problems and challenges occasionally.

• Be creative. One of the hardest things about giving effective feedback is finding fresh ways to note top performance. "Nice" and "good" get pretty tired after a while. The thesaurus is an underrated management tool. A quick glance under "good" in a Pocket Roget's offers "splendid," "stupendous" and "superb"—each a worthy change of pace from more ordinary terms. Listen for ways others express their appreciation. Build a collection of unusual ways to show you value people's efforts.

• Find out what works in your store. Be sure the feedback you offer is relevant to your employees' needs. Be flexible about meeting their preferences for spoken or written comments.

Look at feedback as an ongoing process. It's essential to each worker's continuous growth—which will include successes and setbacks. So don't think of either positive or negative feedback as the last word on performance. Instead, use it to keep people moving forward.

THE OLDER WORKER

Your new manager is taking on a staff that includes two long-time salespeople who are well into their 60s. He's young and has never supervised people so much older. What problems might this cause?

Older workers often are highly motivated to succeed and take a lot of pride in their work. They may bring a wealth of knowledge to the job and require less supervision than less-experienced workers. They are more frequently on time, are more reliable and take fewer days off due to personal problems and child-care emergencies than do younger workers.

However, some are less comfortable with new technologies or have more trouble changing to new work methods. Some have less physical agility and strength, but don't want to admit it. Some no longer operate at their peak of productivity, yet resent any sign that others are becoming more capable than they. And some dislike working for someone who is much younger.

You should understand these differences and tailor your approach to accommodate or capitalize on them. Here are six tips:

1. Appreciate older workers' attributes. Take time to understand and benefit from their mind-set and culture.

2. Build a solid professional relationship. Show a warm, friendly attitude that respects their experiences and contributions.

3. Ask for their input. This not only makes them feel needed, but also gives you the benefit of their experience.

4. Help them to anticipate changes that will affect them. Provide as much advance notice as possible of any shift in schedule, procedures, etc.

5. Give them time to adjust. If you would expect a typical employee to take a month or two to get used to your new computer system, factor in extra time and training for the older worker.

6. Set up teams with their needs in mind. An older employee might view a gung-ho new salesperson as a threat. But if you make the elder a mentor, the pair may function more effectively than either could alone.

FEELING HARASSED

Sally claims that Joe has been sexually harassing her. This is a sensitive situation; it's vital that you know what to do to protect Sally's rights and maintain a productive work environment. Here's what Donald H. Weiss suggests in *Fair, Square and Legal: Safe Hiring, Managing and Firing Practices to Keep You and Your Company Out of Court*:

1. Ask Sally to tell you what happened. Accept complaints at face value without passing judgment. Avoid putting words into her mouth. The less you color the story with your own perceptions, the better able you'll be to understand the situation.

2. Get specifics. Focus on facts, not motives. Encourage Sally to give you as much objective information as possible. Key facts include the frequency of the alleged harassment, how long it's been going on and what she has done to let Joe know his behavior is offensive and should stop.

3. Establish the next steps. Without asking leading questions, find out what Sally wants you to do about her complaint. Ask for permission to conduct a thorough investigation. If she voices a fear of reprisal, assure her that your company won't permit it. Then contact your boss, your personnel department or your lawyer to determine how the investigation should proceed.

Being prepared to deal with harassment complaints should help you to resolve them appropriately. It's better to avoid them altogether, however. Make it clear to everyone in your store you will not tolerate harassment of any kind and, if you're not the boss, encourage whoever is to issue a policy statement to that effect.

NO JOKING

As the work force grows more diverse, the ability to get along with people from different backgrounds becomes ever more crucial. Some employees unfortunately lack this skill. It's your job as a manager to maintain a positive work environment and to ensure that no one behaves in a way that diminishes a sense of mutual respect and dignity.

That's what insensitive racial remarks do. Whether innocent-seeming jokes, repetitions of racial stereotypes or ugly epithets, comments made at the expense of someone's individuality are inappropriate on the job. Such statements are morally wrong and result in lower morale, higher turnover and costly lawsuits.

If an employee makes a racially insensitive remark, don't laugh weakly or pretend you didn't hear. You must respond forcefully. Here's how:

1. Act immediately. The moment you hear a thoughtless or malicious racial comment, ask to speak privately with the employee who made it. Any delay implies that the behavior is acceptable.

2. Be direct. State that you absolutely will not stand for offensive racial remarks and be sure the employee understands what is considered offensive. It's usually OK for employees to discuss coworkers' job-related actions, but it's not OK to demean them because of race.

3. Be sure your company has a policy for dealing with repeated offenses and tell the worker exactly what it is.

4. Explain the benefits of change. Aside from staying out of trouble, the employee will contribute to a more comfortable, productive environment. Tell him you're confident he can avoid making the mistake again and that you expect and appreciate his cooperation.

5. Ask for agreement. Don't end the conversation until the employee signals that he's aware of the problem and willing to change.

6. Follow up. Look for signs of change and praise them. These might include increased cooperation between the previously insensitive employee and coworkers. Remember that behavioral change takes time.

AN 'I DON'T LIKE YOUR ATTITUDE' ADJUSTMENT

Do your comments during performance appraisals always hit the mark? Or do employees sometimes get a funny look on their faces after you've made what you thought was a valid remark? Check your appraisal communication skills by taking this quick quiz, based on *Productive Performance Appraisals* by Randi Toler Sachs. Which of the following sound like constructive comments?

1. Why don't you follow the path Susan took? She started out like you and now she's doing great!

2. You're doing just fine—I can't complain at all. Any comments on your end?

3. That goal simply isn't realistic.

4. Your performance this quarter has really let me down.

5. Sorry to keep you waiting; that was an important call.

6. I wish I could agree that you've met all your deadlines, but these records indicate otherwise.

7. You need to speak to your coworkers with more respect.

8. I know you've got the ability. Why do you think you're having so much trouble meeting goals?

Comments 1-5 are shaky at best. The first talks about another worker, which is irrelevant to the employee under review. The second cuts off discussion too quickly. The third discourages the employee from participating in goal-setting. The fourth makes the issue personal, not performance-based. And the fifth shows disregard for the importance of the discussion.

Comments 6-8 get solid points across. The sixth gives documented feedback. The seventh suggests a constructive change. And the eighth gives workers a chance to explain themselves.

THE HIV EMPLOYEE

Gary just told you the rumor. Apparently Linda, your secretary, was worried about a blood transfusion she had some years ago. She finally got up the nerve to be tested for HIV, and Gary told you the results were positive. How should you handle the situation?

As AIDS and the HIV virus that cause it continue to spread, more and more managers must confront this problem, which requires more than sympathy. You should know your employees' rights and your obligations before it happens.

• Provide education. Experts agree that if you're waiting for an employee to announce having HIV, you've waited far too long to take positive action. Contact a local AIDS service (check the telephone book or ask your state health department) for help in educating your employees about AIDS in

the workplace. Learning the facts—such as the extreme unlikelihood of infection in normal working conditions—can reduce people's anxieties and enhance their ability to function productively if a fellow worker does get the virus. Develop a company policy on disability caused by disease so the same rules apply to everyone—whether they're disabled by a stroke, a heart attack or HIV. (If you're not the boss, encourage your superiors to do this.)

• Know the law. People with HIV are protected from job discrimination under numerous federal, state and local laws. Their rights are strengthened further by the Americans with Disabilities Act, which went into effect for most organizations in July 1992. Basically, the law states that if a person can perform the essential functions of a job, with or without reasonable accommodation, then he or she may not be discriminated against on the basis of disability. In essence, you must treat people with HIV the same way you treat other employees and be ready to make the same kind of accommodations you would make for someone injured in an automobile accident or diagnosed with any other serious illness.

• Suit your actions to the situation. Talk to Linda about her having HIV only if she brings it to your attention. Meanwhile, tell Gary to stop spreading the news; such gossip can destroy a coworker's reputation. And even if the information turns out to be true, Gary could be legally accountable for violating Linda's privacy if he talks about her HIV status without her approval.

• Determine the employee's needs. If Linda does give you the news, ask her what she wants you to do. Many people with HIV have no symptoms and require only your understanding that they're going through a difficult time. Others may require flexible scheduling to receive treatment. Treat requests for HIV accommodation as you would those for any other disability.

• Maintain confidentiality. You must protect the privacy of any employee who confides in you about having the HIV virus. You may be held liable for public disclosure if you notify coworkers, your personnel department or your company's insurer.

If Linda requires more accommodation than you can authorize, get her permission to discuss the situation with your boss. Let her decide how many people she's willing to inform of her situation.

Your responsibility to an employee with HIV or AIDS is to do exactly what you would for all other employees: respect their rights, protect their privacy and give them all the help they need to succeed.

(Information provided by the American Bar Association's AIDS Coordination Project in Washington, D.C.; the National Lawyers' Guild AIDS Network in San Francisco; and the AIDS Legal Resource Project, the Capital Area AIDS Legal Project and Advocacy Inc., all in Austin, Tex.)

THE DRIFTING WORKER

Frank just seems to float along, going wherever the work flow takes him, making few decisions and expending little energy. He usually does what he's told, but not much else. Maybe that's OK. But you'd probably prefer that he be as involved and productive as possible. And he'd probably be happier and work better if inspired to do his best. Here's how to get him on the move.

Put Frank at ease. Let him know you appreciate the work he's doing, but think he might enjoy the satisfaction of using and developing more of his abilities. Say you'd like to help him, if he's interested. If Frank doesn't seem keen to explore the subject, drop it for the time being—but let him know you'd be glad to discuss it further when he's ready. The odds are he'll follow up. If he doesn't, try again.

Clarify goals. Once Frank shows an interest in gaining direction, help him to decide where he wants to go. Ask what he'd like to do that he's not doing now. Draw out his opinions about what he likes and dislikes about the current situation and how he might want to change it.

Make a plan. Look together for ways Frank can grow in your business. Plan steps that would give him a good chance of early success. Determine actions and target dates for achieving his priorities.

Follow up. Keep Frank's momentum going by supporting his efforts and tracking his progress. Give feedback that relates to his new goals. Encourage signs of greater interest and motivation, and provide challenges to keep him from drifting again.

BUILDING CONFIDENCE

You'd love to take a vacation, but you're scared to leave the store. Everything seemed to fall apart the last time you were away at a jewelry show. Can't anybody around here take charge?

If the answer is no, the problem may be lack of confidence, not ability. Managers have more power than anyone else to build or destroy employees' self-confidence. You assign their work, tell them how they're doing and evaluate the quality of their accomplishments. If in the process you

can enhance their confidence in their own abilities, you'll build a team that's ready to take on any task and do it well.

Try these confidence builders:

• When you must be away for a day or two, assign one employee to act as manager in your absence. Select someone who has seemed slightly reluctant to take on new responsibilities, but be sure to prepare him/her well.

• Assign a research project that concludes with a presentation. You might have someone who doesn't usually speak up in meetings investigate a new line you're thinking of carrying and present it to the staff.

• Invite an employee to be a sounding board for you on a difficult project, such as developing next year's advertising budget.

• Ask someone to lead a team of fellow employees in solving a particularly difficult problem that will require several meetings to work out. You're likely to get your problem solved and to get an employee with sharper leadership skills.

• Invite a new or timid employee to go on a buying trip with you. Introduce the person as an important member of your staff and treat him/her with respect.

• When an employee attends a seminar outside the store, have him make a presentation to other salespeople when he returns.

• Make an assignment that requires some creativity—perhaps designing a showcase display or coming up with new ideas for a diamond promotion.

Whatever activities you try, be sure to comment on anything an employee does well—and on areas where improvements are needed. Added responsibilities give employees a chance to grow; your fair, realistic and consistent assessment of results make them genuine confidence-builders.

JCK Management Study Center Quiz

1. Harry tells great jokes; they really cheer things up on a slow afternoon in the store. Sure, they're sort of sexist, but hey, they're just jokes! If Mary or one of the other gals on the staff complains, what should you do?

a. Find something constructive for sales associates to do when business is slow. (And stop referring to female employees as "gals.")   True ❏   False ❏

b. Tell Harry to cool it until Mary gets a life, or at least a sense of humor.   True ❏   False ❏

c. Explain to Harry that sexist, racist or other jokes made at the expense of any group are inappropriate in the workplace and against the store policy.   True ❏   False ❏

2. In conducting a performance review, what are some critical points to keep in mind?

a. It's more important to rate a person's attitude than a person's work.   Agree ❏   Disagree ❏

b. Be sure to talk about potential; it's more important than day-to-day performance.   Agree ❏   Disagree ❏

c. When in doubt about giving a high grade, it's best to settle on something in the middle.   Agree ❏   Disagree ❏

d. If an employee disagrees with your rating, explain your position but don't automatically change it.
    Agree ❏   Disagree ❏

e. Always try to save time by doing performance and salary reviews together.   Agree ❏   Disagree ❏

3. You've always suspected that Bill is gay - though you've never had the nerve to ask - and he's not been looking at all well lately. You're sure he must have AIDS. What should you do?

a. Check if there's some way you can drop him from the company health insurance policy before your claims go sky high.   True ❏   False ❏

b. Quietly let other employees in on your suspicions so they can be careful around Bill.   True ❏   False ❏

c. Find some pretext to fire Bill so you can avoid the whole problem.   True ❏   False ❏

d. Forget about it unless or until Bill comes to you. Why look for trouble?   True ❏   False ❏

e. Start an AIDS education program so that you and your employees know the facts.   True ❏   False ❏

4. The principal matters to consider in coaching an employee are:

a. Seeing that the employee understands how to do the job as you would do it.   True ❏   False ❏

b. Recognizing that an employee wants to be productive but has difficulty getting the job done and is in need of help.   True ❏   False ❏

c. Learning in detail about what problems an employee has and then working with him/her to overcome them.   True ❏   False ❏

d. Making sure that if you and the employee agree on a course action that you follow it up and monitor the program.   True ❏   False ❏

e. Discarding options if you decide it is more efficient merely to "lay down the law."   True ❏   False ❏

5. Feedback is really a matter of keeping open communication with employees. It's best if feedback is:

a. Timely, specific and frequent. True ❏   False ❏

b. Based on assumptions about employee behavior rather than fact.   True ❏   False ❏

c. Kept friendly by withholding any negative comments.   True ❏   False ❏

d. Denied to those employees who you're sure will only use feedback on performance as an opening for argument.   True ❏   False ❏

e. Approached with a fresh and open mind so that you don't sound like a broken record.   True ❏   False ❏

6. Discipline's real purpose is to put a productive worker on the right track. Here's how the owner or manager should go about it:

a. For starters, make sure the employee knows you are very, very angry about some mistake the employee made.   True ❏   False ❏

b. Be very specific in your concerns; know exactly how, when and where the employee went wrong.   True ❏   False ❏

(Answers to Quiz can be found at the end of this chapter)

c. Accept that part of the fault may be yours, as the supervisor, and think about that before confronting the employee.   True ❏   False ❏

d. In an interview with the employee, get right to the heart of the matter at once; don't confuse the issue by bringing up anything the employee has done well.   True ❏   False ❏

e. Have a long-term plan on how to help the employee improve performance and to dismiss him/her if all help fails.   True ❏   False ❏

7. Many long-term employees don't like change, but it often is necessary. Here are points to consider:

a. If you must make a major change, do it without warning so no opposition can develop.   True ❏   False ❏

b. Have your plans complete before announcing them; otherwise employees may want to add their own suggestions.   True ❏   False ❏

c. When you make your announcement, be sure to get the leaders among the staff to endorse your plans.   True ❏   False ❏

d. Never hesitate to change things just for the sake of change; this sort of management keeps people on their toes.   True ❏   False ❏

8. These days when mandatory retirement is largely a thing of the past, most businesses have a number of older workers. In dealing with them day to day:

a. Accept that most of them are dreaming of retirement and look to younger workers for fresh ideas. True ❏   False ❏

b. Consider these employees' long experience a company asset that should be cultivated and tapped often.   True ❏   False ❏

c. Take extra care to give older workers advance warning of impending change.   True ❏   False ❏

d. Be careful not to assign older employees to projects with young staff people because the mixture will only lead to conflict.   True ❏   False ❏

Downsizing Reaches The Jewelry Store (Annual JCK Salary Survey)

November 1994

The national corporate movement to trim staff size and require survivors to work harder and more productively apparently is working its way through the retail end of the jewelry business. JCK's annual salary study, conducted among members of the magazine's retail panel, shows a distinct shift toward use of more part-time employees; the elimination of such positions as office, credit or advertising manager in a number of stores; and a demand for greater employee

173

productivity. Gemologists and appraisers are spending less time behind the microscope and more behind the counter. Benchworkers are doing duty on the sales floor. And the boss often is spending as much or more time selling as managing.

In a further reflection of the times, the study also shows the role of the jewelry-store watchmaker declining in importance while that of the staff benchworker is growing. In the larger reporting stores, those with annual volume of more than $1 million, watchmakers' 1993 pay showed a slight drop from the year before; among stores with volume of less than $1 million, so few reported having watchmakers on the full-time payroll that it's unrealistic to tabulate a median salary.

Meanwhile, however, salaries for benchworkers in stores of all volume categories rose last year. Those in the higher-volume stores showed a particularly good increase, from a median $23,818 in 1992 to $28,000 last year.

There was an interesting development in the salary gender gap. For the first time since JCK started these surveys a decade ago, salaries for women store managers topped those for men doing the same job. In the higher-volume stores, the median salary for women store managers last year was $35,716, just a shade higher ($68) than that reported for men in these larger stores. That occurred because reporting stores showed a fairly sharp decline in men's pay from the year before, coupled with an even sharper increase in women's pay—from 1992's median of $29,000 to 1993's $35,716. (So few of the smaller stores with volume under $1 million reported employing male store managers that it was not possible to come up with a median pay figure for 1993.)

How the salary pie is sliced offers more evidence of an improving pay picture for women managers. Last year, 38% earned more than $40,000 (the top listed category in the study), up from 27% in 1992. The percentage picture for male managers was reversed; while 53% earned more than $40,000 in 1992, only 38% did so last year.

In the category of general sales, which was the only other job category where salaries were recorded by sex, the traditional gender gap prevailed. In all reporting stores, general salesmen earned considerably more than saleswomen; the overall median for men was $26,084 last year while that for women was $16,640.

Not unexpectedly, pay scales in the over-$1 million volume stores generally are higher than in smaller businesses. This shows up quite clearly in the chief executive category. Two in every five bosses (39%) in the larger stores earned more than $100,000 in 1993 while not a single chief executive among those polled in the under-$1 million category

was in the six-figure column. Looking at all stores, salaries for top people changed little; median earnings totaled $55,000 in both 1993 and 1992. But there was significant change when store volume is considered. In the larger stores, median pay rose a couple of thousand dollars to $87,400; in the smaller stores, the median fell sharply—from $48,000 in 1992 to around $34,998 in 1993.

These figures reflect only salary, of course. They do not include expense accounts or income from dividends paid by the corporation.

The benefits package: Panelists reporting for the 1993 study clearly agree that a generous package of benefits is very important in hiring and retaining first-class employees. Two-thirds of them call such a package either "extremely" or "very" important while only 4% called it "somewhat" or "not at all" important. These jewelers definitely backed up their belief with hard cash. In 10 of the 11 benefit categories listed, the percentage of jewelers offering the particular benefit was higher in 1993 than in 1992. The biggest single jump came in the percentage providing financial assistance to staffers who want to improve their education. In the 1993 study, 61% of participating jewelers said they offer such help compared with 50% the year before.

In almost all instances, the higher the store volume, the higher the percentage of stores offering each of the listed benefits.

A number of stores relate the extent of benefits to the value of the employee. For example, the chief executive of a well-managed eastern chain notes that a generous package is "extremely" important for management, "very" important for full-timers but only "somewhat" important for part-timers.

Merchandise discounts and paid vacations continue to be the benefits most universally offered. Not too far behind are the medically related issues. More than three-quarters of the panelists (77%) offer their full-time employees medical insurance and almost as many (70%) offer paid sick leave. In a majority of cases where the company offers medical insurance, the cost is split between employer and employee. The most common split seems to be 50/50. But quite a few panelists, particularly the bigger stores, paid the entire cost of medical insurance.

This generosity appears to be at odds with another finding in the current study. A scant 3% of the panelists said they favor a federal health care plan under which employers would be required to pay for employee care. A number of studies have shown that small business in general is resolutely opposed to the idea of employer-guaranteed medical plans for employees.

Rewards: Who Gets What

Jewelry Store Salaries

Job Title	Median 1993	1992	1993 salary range
Chairman, president, owner, partner			
All reporting stores	$55,000	$55,000	$14,300-$300,000
Stores with annual volume of more than $1 million	$87,400	$85,500	$40,000-$300,000
Stores with annual volume of less than $1 million	$34,998	$48,000	$14,800-$70,000
VP, secretary, treasurer, controller			
All reporting stores	$39,500	$41,000	$19,600-$156,590
Stores with annual volume of more than $1 million	$47,500	$50,000	$30,000-$156,590
Stores with annual volume of less than $1 million	$39,500	$27,200	$19,600-$51,600
All store managers			
All reporting stores	$35,423	$31,000	$17,000-$135,000
Stores with annual volume of more than $1 million	$37,324	$36,400	$22,500-$70,000
Stores with annual volume of less than $1 million	$30,557	$29,500	$17,000-$135,000
Store managers, men			
All reporting stores	$35,648	$31,000	$24,700-$70,000
Stores with annual volume of more than $1 million	$35,648	$40,000	$24,800-$70,000
Stores with annual volume of less than $1 million	(a)	$37,000	(a)
Store managers, women			
All reporting stores	$31,500	$40,000	$17,000-$67,300
Stores with annual volume of more than $1 million	$35,716	$29,000	$22,500-$67,300
Stores with annual volume of less than $1 million	$29,000	$27,000	$17,000-$46,000
Assistant stores managers, buyers			
All reporting stores	$28,240	$22,300	$14,000-$65,000
Stores with annual volume of more than $1 million	$28,500	$25,000	$14,000-$57,180
Stores with annual volume of less than $1 million	$28,000	$22,300	$14,000-$65,000
Jeweler, gemologist, goldsmith, appraiser			
All reporting stores	$25,705	$22,300	$8,674-$75,000
Stores with annual volume of more than $1 million	$31,000	$25,000	$8,674-$75,000
Stores with annual volume of less than $1 million	$22,800	$24,500	$15,000-$35,160
Benchworker, jewelry repair			
All reporting stores	$25,227	$28,000	$12,000-$54,400
Stores with annual volume of more than $1 million	$31,000	$30,000	$13,630-$41,600
Stores with annual volume of less than $1 million	$24,960	$23,658	$12,000-$54,400
Watchmaker, watch repair			
All reporting stores	$24,188	$28,620	$8,244-$47,400
Stores with annual volume of more than $1 million	$30,307	$31,000	$8,244-$47,000
Stores with annual volume of less than $1 million	(a)	$21,590	(a)
General sales, men			
All reporting stores	$26,084	$24,500	$10,400-$48,000
Stores with annual volume of more than $1 million	$28,000	23,818	$13,630-$41,600
Stores with annual volume of less than $1 million	$21,000	$21,000	$10,400-$30,840
General sales, women			
All reporting stores	$16,640	$15,875	$7,360-$55,700
Stores with annual volume of more than $1 million	$17,500	$17,500	$7,360-$55,700
Stores with annual volume of less than $1 million	$15,200	$15,500	$7,500-$30,000
Bookkeeper, accountant			
All reporting stores	$20,868	$29,500	$12,500-$43,080
Stores with annual volume of more than $1 million	$25,000	$20,784	$16,200-$43,080
Stores with annual volume of less than $1 million	$17,400	$15,777	$12,500-$20,800
Other office help			
All reporting stores	$14,560	$15,356	$8,600-$36,160
Stores with annual volume of more than $1 million	$15,250	$15,532	$18,600-$29,000
Stores with annual volume of less than $1 million	$13,500	$14,560	$9,460-$36,160

(a) Sample was too small to tabulate.   Source: JCK Retail Jewelers Panel   **175**

Shares: Who Got What

How the salary pie is sliced for various job categories

Salary range	% earning '93	% earning '92
Chairman, president, etc.		
$100,000+	22%	23%
$50,000-$99,999	41%	41%
$30,000-$49,999	22%	27%
Under $30,000	15%	9%
VPs, treasurers, etc.		
$100,000+	5%	5%
$50,000-$99,999	36%	35%
$30,000-$49,999	41%	38%
Under $30,000	18%	22%
All store managers		
$40,000+	38%	43%
$30,000-$39,999	27%	14%
$20,000-$29,999	31%	28%
Under $20,000	4%	15%
Store managers, men		
$40,000+	38%	53%
$30,000-$39,999	33%	16%
$20,000-$29,999	29%	28%
Under $20,000	0%	3%

Salary range	% earning '93	% earning '92
Store managers, women		
$40,000+	38%	27%
$30,000-$39,999	19%	12%
$20,000-$29,999	35%	29%
Under $20,000	8%	32%
Ass't. stores managers, buyers		
$40,000+	9%	14%
$30,000-$39,999	31%	15%
$20,000-$29,999	43%	31%
Under $20,000	17%	40%
Jeweler, gemologist, etc.		
$40,000+	13%	16%
$30,000-$39,999	23%	22%
$20,000-$29,999	42%	46%
$20,000	22%	16%
Benchworker, jewelry repair		
$40,000+	17%	8%
$30,000-$39,999	23%	22%
$20,000-$29,999	37%	36%
Under $20,000	23%	34%

Salary range	% earning '93	% earning '92
Watchmaker, watch repair		
$40,000+	7%	13%
$30,000-$39,999	28%	32%
$20,000-$29,999	43%	42%
Under $20,000	22%	13%
General sales, men		
$30,000+	33%	32%
$20,000-$29,999	50%	38%
$10,000-1$9,999	17%	30%
Under $10,000	0%	0%
General sales, women		
$30,000+	12%	8%
$20,000-$29,999	23%	28%
$10,000-19,999	57%	60%
Under $10,000	8%	4%
Bookkeeper		
$30,000+	24%	15%
$20,000-$29,999	33%	28%
$10,000-$19,999	43%	57%
Under $10,000	0%	0%

The Benefits Package

% of stores in each sales bracket

Benefit	$300,000-$700,000	$700,000-$1 million	Over $1 million	All
Dental insurance:	6%	26%	41%	27%
Life insurance:	25%	42%	59%	44%
Medical insurance:	75%	74%	83%	77%
Paid sick leave:	81%	53%	79%	70%
Pension plan:	12%	21%	41%	27%
401k savings plan:	6%	21%	21%	12%
Education financial assistance:	56%	63%	62%	61%
Long-term disability:	0%	10%	38%	20%
Merchandise discounts:	100%	100%	100%	98%
Paid vacation:	100%	100%	100%	98%
Unpaid maternity leave:	44%	47%	72%	72%

Employee Benefits
Generosity pays off

% of stores in each sales bracket rating importance of benefits package

	$300,000-$700,000	$700,000-$1 million	Over $1 million	All
Extremely important:	16%	0%	18%	14%
Very important:	32%	79%	49%	51%
Somewhat important:	37%	21%	30%	31%
Not very important:	5%	0%	3%	3%
Not at all important:	0%	0%	0%	1%

Source: JCK Retail Jewelers Panel

Health Care
Keep the government at arm's length

% of stores in each sales bracket favoring the listed option

	$300,000-$700,000	$700,000-$1 million	Over $1 million	All
Plan guaranteeing health care for all:	20%	19%	35%	24%
Plan guaranteeing health care for at least 90% of the population:	12%	19%	22%	16%
Plan in which employer pays for employee health care:	2%	4%	6%	3%
Plan in which government agency pays for health care:	33%	31%	17%	27%
Private insurance pays for plan with government subsidies for those who can't afford private insurance:	33%	31%	17%	27%
Leave health-care system as is:	33%	31%	17%	27%
Other plans:	100%	100%	100%	27%

Source: JCK Retail Jewelers Panel

Forest And Trees

Editorial ◆ *July 1993*

Did you ever get so tied up in day-to-day detail that you forgot to do something really important? If you're human, you probably did. If you're a good manager, chances are you don't let this happen too often. If you're *not* a good manager—or at least not as good as you'd like to be—chances are you run your business by crisis management. That's a system that short-changes everyone in your company—and almost surely the company itself.

These thoughts come up because of a conversation about priorities I had with a jeweler the other day. He worried that he was so busy just running his business that he was mixing up the forest and the trees. Just in case any reader has the same problem, here's a baker's dozen of things to think about or to do to make your business run more smoothly and profitably— and they should help to keep crises to a minimum:

1. Sit down where you can't be disturbed by phone calls or other interruptions and take a look at your priorities. How well are you doing to make sure important tasks take precedence over minor ones? Once the key jobs are identified, it's very important not to let yourself be sidetracked by something that, although pleasant, really isn't that important.

2. Ask yourself how well you delegate. We're not talking about passing the buck. We're talking about getting routine chores and decisions off your list and on to someone else's. If you do delegate, let the other person *do* the job.

3. If you have a good idea (especially at 3 a.m.), be sure you ask a trusted colleague to examine it before you act on it. Most times it's true: two heads are better than one.

4. Walk outside the store and take a long look—the sort of critical look you might expect a stranger to take. Ask yourself realistically: "Is that the sort of store I'd like to shop in?" If not, do something about it.

5. When did you last talk with a customer you didn't know who had just completed a purchase? Did you ask the person if it was a pleasant experience? Was the sales staff

helpful? Was the item purchased just what was wanted? Did the price seem fair?

6. How often do you hold brainstorming sessions with your whole staff—everyone from the boss to the bottle-washer? Properly done, sessions like this can produce a lot of good ideas. If you like the ideas, be sure to say so. And do something to turn them from idea to action.

7. Take your banker to lunch and tell all. Good communication pays great rewards when it comes time to ask for money.

8. Do you read, listen to and/or watch your store's advertising? Really read, listen and watch? Would these ads tempt you to go shopping? If not, why not? If you don't handle your own advertising, how often and how honestly do you talk with the person who does?

9. We all get letters and phone messages we don't want to answer for one reason or another. How many are on your desk? You'll feel better if you do *something*—either answer them or toss them out.

10. Do you always remember to thank people for a job well-done? It's so easy to overlook if you're rushed. The thanks should be for little things as well as big. Criticism for a botched job is less resented if the well-done job is praised.

11. Crime is on every jeweler's mind. But how about insurance? Many times a jeweler doesn't really look at his or her policy until after an attack. A better time to look is before—right now, in fact. Do you have the coverage you really want and need?

12. Talking about crime, when did you last have a good talk with the staff about security? Do you drive the message home every day?

13. Let's end up with a good news item. What have you done recently, or what could you do, to get good publicity for your store? Given a talk? Offered yourself as an expert? Done a great and newsworthy promotion? Remember, good news gets around—and brings in more customers.

The Pain Of Self-Appraisal

Editorial ◆ February 1992

A few years back, a colleague who regularly did performance appraisals of his staff flipped the coin and asked his staff to rate him. He got a D-. So much for the formal appraisal nonsense. He dropped it.

You may or may not ask your staff what they think of you. Admittedly, it's a high-risk proposition for most managers. As a second-best step, there's no harm—and probably much good—in doing a self-appraisal. This should deal with your relationships with your staff as well as people outside your business. To give the performance some shape, let me introduce you to Mary Monica Mitchell, president of Uncommon Courtesies, a Philadelphia firm that helps people to deal more graciously with their business contacts.

After polling a couple of hundred local firms, Mitchell came up with a list of the top 10 business-conduct mistakes. Most of them apply equally well to dealing with insiders or outsiders. I'd like to say I scored a perfect 10. But I can't say that because it's not true, as I'm sure my colleagues will confirm. If you'd like to check your own "good etiquette level," here's your chance. The 10 most common mistakes:

1. *Negative attitudes.* Include here, says Mitchell, rudeness, taking out a problem on someone, bitchiness, surliness, ugly moods, bad temperament, unprovoked anger and unpleasantness. She adds: "People forget that their words ad actions affect others. No one's life is exempt from stress or frustration. . . With a little self-control, the same 'nasty' person might find support and sympathy for whatever is upsetting them. By being rude, they're just making things worse for themselves and the people around them."

2. *Sloppy message taking.* A common gripe from all parts of most businesses. Says Mitchell, "It might be wise to teach everyone in the country how to use a phone properly...If our phone skills improved, we could be saving millions of dollars and hours."

3. *Making people wait.* This can involve being put on hold during a phone conversation or being kept waiting for an appointment. Making people wait, says Mitchell, "creates resentment and sets a hostile tone to the upcoming conversation."

4. *Criticizing people in front of others.* The simple rule: if you have to criticize, do it in private.

5. *Disregarding social courtesies for business functions.* Polite people send RSVPs—and by the date indicated. They do not bring uninvited guests with them.

6. *Errors with names.* Said one respondent: "If a person writing to me can't get something as simple as my name and title right, it makes me wonder what else they'll be careless about." There also were complaints about inappropriate use of first names, assuming familiarity that may not be justified or desired.

7. *Vulgar language.* There was almost unanimous dismay at the common acceptance of cursing in the workplace. Poor grammar and slang also came in for criticism.

8. *Inappropriate clothing.* Says Mitchell: "Every company and industry has a dress code, even though it rarely is in written form. Individual freedom of expression has to be tempered by good judgment."

9. *Forgoing introductions.* Staffers often feel they've been snubbed by the store owner who fails to introduce a colleague. Says Mitchell: "Introductions are another seemingly small thing that make a big difference in everyone's ease and attitude."

10. *Giving someone the runaround.* This had several definitions, among them "not being able to get an answer from anyone, being referred to 10 different people, getting conflicting answers to the same question and people not listening to what is asked."

My guess is that anyone who's not guilty of a single one of these common mistakes or discourtesies is a shoo-in for sainthood. For the rest of us, the list is a useful reminder that periodic self-appraisals of how we deal with others can be very worthwhile.

New Dimensions In Retailing

November 1991

Less retail space, the demise of the discount department store, and the return of customer loyalty are among the projections for retailing by the year 2000 in a new study titled "Retailing 2000" by Management Horizons, Dublin, Ohio.

"Structurally, financially, culturally and competitively, retailing will take on an entirely new set of dimensions," says

Dr. Daniel Sweeney, chairman of Management Horizons and coauthor of the study.

Among the findings of the study:

• Contraction. More than half of today's retailers will be out of business. Total retail square footage will contract significantly, with new retail construction slowing almost to a standstill and a substantial net decrease in retail mall space.

• Discount department store demise. This type of retailing will peak in the mid-1990s, then begin to lose share of total retail sales.

• Return of customer loyalty. As consumers become increasingly time-pressed and shop less frequently, they'll become more destination-oriented and more loyal to the stores that meet their needs.

• Rise of "relationship merchandising." No longer will the retail industry be driven by the homogeneous chain store. Firms will concentrate on serving the demands of the individual customer and develop an ongoing relationship with that customer.

• Disappearance of middle management. The retail organization will be flat, lean and very decentralized as information technology increases senior management's span of control. Middle management will all but disappear as information flows directly up to higher management or down into the organization for analysis and decisions.

"To be prepared for these radical changes," says Sweeney, "retail executives must plan now for the next century." The study suggests these specific management requirements:

• Alliance management. Effectively managing the partnership between retailers and suppliers will be crucial for success.

• Technology management. Executives must demonstrate a mastery of technology and always be willing to integrate technological improvements.

• Speed and time management. Successfully managing the speed with which business is conducted—combined with the proper timing of market penetration—will ensure a powerful competitive advantage.

• Relationship management. Establishing close relationships with individual customers will be crucial.

• Long-term profitability management. Managers will shift their strategic focus from short-term maximization of cash flow to a concentration on long-term profitability and earnings growth.

The Art Of Self-Criticism

Editorial ◆ *September 1990*

Few acts are as potentially rewarding—and as difficult— as honest self-criticism. Robbie Burns, that admirable Scottish 18th century poet whom I've quoted before, caught the difficulties very succinctly when he wrote:

Oh wad some wad some power the giftee gie us
To see ourselves as others see us!

He was right, of course. Seeing ourselves—or our businesses—as we or they really are probably does call for divine intervention. But if, as individuals or businesspeople, we're going to grow and develop, we must at least try to be honest with ourselves about our own strengths and weaknesses. If we feel that we're not up to the task alone, then we should ask for honest opinions from others—and not be upset if we don't like what we hear or, disliking it, reject it.

In business terms, this process is the fundamental building block for a sound marketing plan. It's critical to know who you are and where you are before making plans for what you want to become and where you want to go. For a jeweler, this means a careful examination of every part of the business. Here are just some of the questions you should ask yourself:

• Do I really know the geographic boundaries of my market area?

• Do I really know who my customers are? Just as important, are there potential customers in my market area whom I'm not reaching?

• What perception do people in my marketing area have of my store and my staff?

• What demographic or economic changes are occurring in the market area and what impact will they have on my store?

• How do I perceive the competition and how does it perceive me? How is it changing?

• Are sales, profits and turnover increasing at a satisfactory rate?

• How productive are my staffers and how good a job do I do at motivating them?

A list such as this can be expanded or refined to suit any store owner's needs. Honest answers to the questions can provide what you need to identify the problems and opportunities your business faces and then to take the necessary actions to capitalize on the good and control or overcome the bad.

It's hard to pick out one element in an overall marketing plan and say, "This is the most critical issue." But today if I had to pick, I'd say it's identifying the customers you feel offer the best sales opportunities and then making every effort to satisfy their specific needs. In short, making a commitment to target marketing.

What we're talking about is specialization or, more correctly, multiple specializations. Target marketing is simply identifying various groups with broadly similar needs and then seeing how well you can serve how many of these groups. Let's look at some specifics.

Any one market area might well include some affluent and conservative business executives, the companies which employ them, their marriageable kids, some up-and-coming young executives, an army base and many tourist attractions. Chances are that you won't be able to appeal successfully to all these groups; their interests, tastes, incomes and attitudes are too varied.

179

But you could do very well by zeroing in on those most likely to share many interests and attitudes. The elderly affluent provide marvelous opportunities. They can afford to buy for themselves, which they do, and for others. Their children or even grandchildren probably are part of the bridal market. Meanwhile, young professionals, particularly the women among them, want quality along with that something special a jeweler can offer. No incompatibilities here. All could be very comfortable shopping in the same stores.

And don't overlook the companies which offer entry to the lucrative award market.

In our special issue, we identify about a dozen different markets. Some you may be very familiar with; some may suggest possible new sources of customers. The main point is that the reports on the various demographic groups will stimulate thinking. We hope that when you look closely at your own market, you may see marketing opportunities far beyond the ones mentioned.

How To Choose The Right Attorney

September 1988 Part II

Every jeweler needs legal help sometime. It's a fact of business life. Indeed, the business need for good sound legal counsel is greater today than in the past.

"It's a litigious world," says Herbert E. Rostand, an attorney and AGS jeweler in California. With business and legal obligations becoming more complex, people increasingly use lawyers and courts to handle all sorts of problems, even small ones. As a spokesman for one major insurance company told JCK, "It doesn't take much anymore for people to sue."

Yet, says Rostand, "I'm always surprised, from the number of calls I get, at how many jewelers have no legal contacts at all. Most either don't know a lawyer or don't want to spend the money [for one]."

Leslie E. Grodd, an attorney in Westport, Conn., agrees. "Jewelers are like most people: they're concerned about cost and don't always use a lawyer when they should. But that's penny wise and pound foolish," says Grodd, a former legal and financial counsel to the Independent Jewelers Organization.

Even jewelers who *do* use lawyers often have problems: they go to the wrong ones.

"They'll go to general practice lawyers about a specific problem, like tax planning, when what they need is a specialist," says Grodd.

Sometimes the jeweler needn't worry about legal costs or getting the right attorney. If a customer brings suit against a jeweler who has the right insurance, the insurance firm will provide an attorney, if necessary, and pay any settlements.

But in scores of other instances, from estate planning to contracts, a jeweler has to find a good lawyer himself. If you're in the market for a lawyer, here are guidelines on how to select one—and then keep the lid on legal costs.

Determine needs: Defining your problem is the first step. Too often, says Grodd, a client comes to an attorney disorganized, not knowing exactly what he wants to do.

Identifying what you need helps to determine which type of lawyer you need. The general practice attorney handles a variety of legal problems such as leases, contracts, collections or wills. The specialist is expert in just one aspect of law, such as criminal defense, tax planning or labor relations.

Here are some areas where jewelers definitely should consider legal counsel:

• *Liabilities.* As a jeweler and business person, you need to know your liabilities, for which you can be held financially responsible.

"A jeweler should consult a lawyer to determine the limits of his liabilities, what he should do to limit those liabilities and how he should notify his customers of those limits," says Grodd.

• *Appraisals and repairs.* These are the two most legally sensitive areas for jewelers, say lawyers.

"The legal relationship with customers in appraisal work is daily becoming more complicated, especially with people investing in jewelry and gems as though they were [stock] 'futures,'" says Rostand. A jeweler who gives the wrong appraisal or loses a repair item quickly can find himself on the wrong end of a malpractice suit.

• *Business forms.* A jeweler can spell out what he is and isn't responsible for on business forms. Attorneys should draft "repetitive form contracts" that are used routinely in store business—including credit agreements, purchase orders, collection letters, receipts, appraisal and repair agreements—says Stancly Kalcczyc, an attorney in Helena, Mont., and formerly associate general counsel for the U.S. Chamber of Commerce.

"There's a great desire to save money today by 'doing it yourself,' and repetitive contracts are one area of that," he says. "But that may be more costly in the long run because you'll overlook some coverage" for yourself that an attorney would include.

• *Buying or selling a store.* For these complicated actions, an attorney "covers all contractual bases," says Rostand. "For instance, is the jeweler buying all the business responsibilities [such as unpaid debts] or just the assets? You don't want people coming out of the woodwork after the deal claiming debts."

The need for legal counsel is apparent also in starting a business, according to a report by the American Bar Association (ABA). An attorney can assist in matters of credit, workers compensation, Social Security problems, lease coverage and partnerships. An attorney can guide a new entrepreneur through complicated state and federal business regulations.

• *Leases*. An attorney should review new, renewed or current leases to be sure you aren't tying yourself to unnecessary costs and provisions.

Mall leases, for example, can be tricky. "They're as thick as a good book, and cover everything from real estate and rents to store hours and the number of shifts you must employ," says Rostand. For example, an attorney should check your lease for space at a proposed mall to ensure you can pull out if the anchor store (the mall's main store, usually a department store) doesn't come in.

"Otherwise, you're committed to going into a mall whose success is very uncertain," he says.

Comparison shop: Once you've decided what kind of attorney you want, the next step is actually choosing one.

"Selecting a lawyer is like buying any other service or equipment for your store," says Kaleczyc. "You look around and ask questions."

Here are some sources to check:

• Consult with fellow jewelers, business people, trade associations, your banker and your accountant for suggestions on attorneys.

• Consult the *Martindale-Hubbell Law Directory,* suggests the ABA. The directory, available in most large public libraries, is a roster of U.S. and Canadian lawyers with brief notes on their specialties.

• Use a lawyer referral service, which provides free or low-cost help. These are found throughout the country, usually are operated by local bar associations and are listed in the phone book *Yellow Pages* under "Attorneys."

A legal aide will listen to your problem and refer you to an attorney. The attorney will consult with you free for a half hour or so and suggest a course of action, offer his services (at a mutually agreed-to fee) or recommend a specialist.

If there is a fee for the referral service, it is paid to the bar association, not the lawyer.

• Review lawyers' advertising in local papers, checking for legal specialty, qualifications and type of services.

Interview attorneys: Once you have collected a list of attorneys who interest you, call or visit them. Tell them you're seeking a lawyer and want to talk about services and fees. "Make it very clear in the initial call that you're just interviewing, *not* seeking legal advice," says Kaleczyc. "Otherwise you'll be charged."

When you interview the attorney, go to the law office with specific questions. What type of practice does the attorney have? Has the attorney worked on problems similar to yours? How would the attorney represent you? What type of services would be provided? If you're dealing with a large firm, ask who exactly would do your work, since the partner you talk to isn't necessarily the one who would handle your case.

Some experts advise seeking bar association references or client statements (though the latter are privileged and the lawyer needn't provide them). Ask about the lawyer's qualifications and experience. (One measure of competence, says the ABA, is whether the attorney stays current with changes in laws though continuing education.)

Intuition and "good vibes" play a part in the selection, too, says Rostand. "It's like any confidential relationship you form. You go with the one you feel most comfortable with," he explains.

In the past decade, says Rostand, the field of law has become so specialized, you don't need long to narrow a list of attorneys to those who have experience in the area of law you need help with.

Talk costs: Ask for a clear and detailed explanation of what the attorney charges, what those charges are based on and what they buy.

There are four types of payment to attorneys: a retainer (regular payments for on-call service), hourly rates, contingent or negotiated fees (usually on court-won money settlements) and flat fees (for routine jobs, like wills).

Small businesses most commonly hire an attorney on an hourly basis. The cost can be high (generally from $100 to more than $350 an hour, depending on size, location and reputation of the firm, or the lawyer's experience). Ask the lawyer for written rates and a written estimate of the number of hours he or she will spend on your case.

Remember, too, to ask about "add-ons." These are added to the attorney's fee for such things as serving court papers or property settlement costs.

If your attorney's rate seems too high, check with others to compare. If you and your lawyer dispute a fee for work done, the ABA will arbitrate for free.

How often: Once you choose an attorney, decide how often you might need his or her services and how you will be billed.

Rostand says keeping a lawyer on retainer isn't practical for many jewelers, especially Mom-and-Pop stores. "The typical family-owned store doesn't have that many legal concerns in a year," he says.

But for the time jewelers need legal help, they should know an attorney who is familiar with their business, say the attorneys.

Decide at the start when your legal bills will come and what they will contain. Most jewelers and attorneys prefer monthly billing, if there is enough work to sustain that, because it gives better control over cash flow.

The bill should include the date a task was done, what it involved, who did it, how long it took and the rate or fee, in addition to the total cost.

"Frequent detailed billing makes your lawyer cost-conscious in the work he does for you and lets you know exactly what your legal service is costing you," says Kaleczyc.

Keep in close touch with your attorney so you can be advised on the progress of your case or work. And keep your attorney informed of any developments or changes in your business that might affect what he or she does for you.

Limiting costs: Choosing a lawyer is one problem. Keeping a lid on your business legal costs is another. Here are some tips on how to do that.

• Prepare in advance. Have all the material your attorney needs (receipts, letters, returns, etc.) ready and organized when you meet together.

Write down beforehand any questions or subjects you want to know about. An advance letter or phone call summarizing what you want to discuss helps to prepare the attorney, too.

All this saves time, and "time is what lawyers sell by the hour," says Grodd. "The less time an attorney wastes [going through disorganized material, clarifying vague issues, etc.], the less costly it is to the client.

• Consult with your attorney about several matters during the same visit or phone call.

• See your attorney during regular business hours rather than on weekends or evenings. Overtime is expensive.

• Set a cap on total cost. Get a "good hard estimate of what your work will generate in legal fees," says Kaleczyc. "Depending on the nature and amount of work, how routine or similar it is to other jobs the lawyer has done and factors like inflation, you may be able to get a ceiling price."

Also, guaranteeing a certain amount of hours or work annually (though not a retainer) will get a reduced rate from some attorneys.

Less saves more: Use an associate member of a law firm, if possible, rather than a full or senior partner. Rates are based on who does the work, and associates (who are younger, less experienced or junior members of the firm) charge less.

Also, have your staff do some of the nonlegal work and save on add-on costs. For example, one of your employees can pick up documents your attorney needs from the courthouse.

Use a small law firm rather than a larger one. "Smaller firms are more hungry for your business and more likely to give you more attention and a better rate," says Kaleczyc.

But the best way to avoid unnecessary legal costs, say attorneys, is to take preventive action. "It's much cheaper to solve a problem before it erupts than to get out of a legal bind," says Kaleczyc.

Here are some examples of preventive action:

• Make periodic store inspections for potential hazards such as loose carpet, chipped showcases or glass, and cracked pavement.

• Remind employees to be careful with take-ins, repairs and other routine services. Improperly performed, they can lead to disputes.

• Don't guess at appraisals. If unsure, refuse the piece or send it to an expert.

• Thoroughly review your store's liability insurance with your agent and attorney.

• Spell out, in writing, all store policies on such matters as refunds, layaways, returns and goods left for appraisal or repair.

• Remember that you can be held responsible for negligent actions by your employees if they cause damage to a third party in the course of their job.

• Stay informed on legal developments affecting you, your business and your obligations to customers. Such information is available from trade publications; local, state or national trade associations (via newsletters, booklets, seminars); and groups such as the Better Business Bureau, American Bar Association and U.S. Chamber of Commerce.

Legal Alternatives

Some legal problems can be solved quickly, cheaply—and often without a lawyer.

• "Treat legal problems as though they were public relations problems—which they are," says attorney/jeweler Herbert E. Rostand.

Once a lawsuit hits the newspapers, the jeweler's business and credibility are hurt, regardless of outcome. So use personal initiative and negotiation to solve problems quickly with as little publicity as possible. When an employee stole a diamond from a ring left for repair, for example, the boss replaced the diamond at his own expense, preventing a great deal of adverse publicity.

• Use free or low-cost arbitration to settle disputes with customers or other businesses, without recourse to a lawyer.

Local Better Business Bureaus provide free arbitration. Write the Council of Better Business Bureaus, 1150 17 St., N.W., Washington, D.C. 22209; (703) 276-0100.

The American Arbitration Association provides community and commercial "dispute service" for a fee. Write to the Public Relations Director, American Arbitration Association, 140 W. 51 St., New York, N.Y. 10019.

• If personal negotiation and arbitration doesn't help, consider small claims court. Disputes involving hundreds, sometimes thousands, of dollar are settled there quickly without lawyers. Contact your county courthouse for information.

Advisory Councils Generate New Ideas

September 1988 Part II

Many jewelers could save themselves trouble, headaches and money by setting up an advisory panel of business experts to provide fresh ideas on a regular basis, say business analysts. Why should successful, self-made business people need—or want—a council of advisers?

"Most entrepreneurs are specialists, without experience in other areas of management," explains Dr. Harold W. Fox, professor of marketing at Pan American University in Edinburg, Tex. As a result, "small businesses are constantly in trouble, running from crisis to crisis. Opportunities arise that a small entrepreneur doesn't have time to study or develop. There are specialized problems he doesn't have the skills to handle."

That makes an advisory council useful in a variety of ways. It offers a sounding board for a business person's ideas and plans. It can review corporate policies, budgets, goals, growth strategies and financial structure. It can evaluate corporate and executive performance, arbitrate corporate disputes and provide specific recommendations.

Many businesses don't use an advisory board. That, says Fox, is mainly because they're not aware of them.

One jewelry firm with a successful council is Melart Jewelers Inc., a 19-store chain headquartered in Silver Spring, Md. "A public company has the benefit of outside directors," says Albert A. Foer, Melart chairman. "But a private company doesn't and can become 'in-grown.' It's helpful for us to have periodic meetings with people from outside who bring a different perspective, who watch and evaluate our progress and who help make important decisions."

Specifics: An advisory council *isn't* a board of directors. Unlike a board, it isn't legally accountable for recommendations, and its advice isn't binding on the business owner. It doesn't spend as much time on company-related duties (30 hours annually, versus 122 for a board, according to a *Harvard Business Review* survey). It can't fire company executives and doesn't represent stockholder, family or special interest groups. Members are chosen by the owner (sometimes in concurrence with his board) and replaced when he chooses.

A business person feels freer to discuss problems knowing the council doesn't represent vested interests and has no control over his or her final action—or job. Many business experts will serve on an advisory panel, but not on a board of directors because of the liability question, says Dr. Fred A. Tillman, professor of legal studies at Georgia State University in Atlanta, Ga. "They get the same ego trip, and give the same advice as on a board, but the retailer makes the decisions. So they have freedom to devise without responsibility" for the consequences.

Time for council: It's best to form an advisory council when a business owner prepares for growth or foresees problems.

"Advisory councils are especially good for a dynamic company," says Foer. "They help you think through and prepare for change."

Fox says the councils also are beneficial when a company grows too big to handle alone, or the competition grows too strong. There may be internal disputes between family and non-family managers. Or a management transition may be approaching as a founder nears retirement or turns most operations over to subordinates. An advisory council not only helps the new owners or operators, but also provides the new direction a company needs, says Fox.

It can help in other ways, too. One business owner needed an impartial opinion about his children, who were coming into the business. His council evaluated them and suggested appropriate training. Another owner assigned council members specific duties during the change of management that should occur if he were killed in an accident.

Systematic method: Foer first learned about advisory councils at a Jewelers of America business seminar.

The idea appealed to him. Melart was going through transition. Ill health plagued its co-founders—chairman Melvin Foer (Albert's father) and president Arthur Sheinbaum. The founders, both now deceased, were con-

cerned about the firm's future and delegated more of their duties to younger managers, including Albert. The former antitrust attorney and policy maker at the Federal Trade Commission joined the company as vice president and general counsel, and was groomed to succeed his father.

The firm was growing, but so was competition. Kay Jewelers was based in nearby Alexandria, Va.; Zale Corp. and J.B. Robinson had just entered the Washington market.

"As the company moved into its second generation," says Foer, "we needed a method to deal with vital issues in a systematic way." Working with the council provided that. It also let Foer bring together some consultants—the lawyer, the accountant, the banker—who already met with Melart officials individually, but never with each other.

Melart's council now meets from 8:30 a.m. to 12:30 p.m. three times a year. Members discuss a wide range of topics—from financial reports to advertising strategy. The council just completed its 18th meeting.

"Through the council," says Foer, "our executives are forced to present what they're doing to an outside group that is sympathetic but nonetheless able to ask difficult questions.

"We come out of these meetings feeling stimulated and renewed. To be able to call on these advisers, and to have their brain power and deep understanding of the company available, is one of the great hidden assets of our company."

Foer says he also consults occasionally with council members at other times throughout the year on an as-needed basis.

No ego trip: But before you set up an advisory panel, advises Tillman, "take a personal attitude survey." The retailer himself can be the biggest roadblock to a council's success.

"A business person can't use this as an ego trip," says Tillman. "He doesn't—or shouldn't—want a lot of yes men. He must be able to take criticism. He doesn't have to accept the recommendations, but he should be able to listen."

Fox, who serves on three such panels, adds that being "outspoken" is a top priority for an adviser. "It's my job, as a council member, to point out deficiencies in a company's operations and explain how to improve," he says.

To get full benefit of the advisers' expertise, a retailer has to open up to them. The retailer and his staff must prepare reports for council members, keep them informed of company developments between meetings, devise detailed agendas (a one-day council meeting can cover dozens of topics) and set objectives for the council.

This may seem arduous, but it's necessary, says Foer. "It forces us to look very carefully at what we're doing, and in some cases, rethink our policies. And once we focus attention on a specific subject in a careful and structured way, we can clarify the direction we want to go."

Compensation: When forming a council, Tillman says, you must "lay out the general mechanics." How often will the council meet? How big will it be? Who do you want on it? What should it do? How will members be paid—and can you afford it?

The most obvious payment is a flat fee—anywhere from $100 to $300 per council member for a half-day session, depending on the advisers, the work and the company's size. If you pay a flat fee rather than an hourly rate, you don't have to worry about "the meter running" and you won't have to cut off useful discussion during a meeting to keep expenses in line. But Fox warns the fee shouldn't be large. "You don't want people who do this just for the money," he says.

Compensation can take other forms, too. Pay for a good dinner with cocktails. Hold council meetings at resorts where members can bring families for the weekend, at your expense. Offer price reductions on store merchandise. (Melart lets its advisers buy jewelry "on the best terms authorized for any class of employees.") Some companies are more imaginative. Fox tells of one business owner who rented the local movie theater and invited advisers and their families to an afternoon of free films and popcorn.

Choosing members: When choosing council members, remember these points:

• Keep the panel small—between five and nine people—so meetings are manageable.

• Look for practical people who grasp the problems you deal with, says Fox. An ideal member is a small retailer from another industry, such as hardware or clothing.

• Look for what Fox calls "functional diversity"—people with different, but overlapping, specializations useful to a small business. Melart's council charter, for instance, requires mem bers representing law, accounting, economics, banking, investment banking, retailing and public relations or advertising.

• Don't choose relatives. Too often, says Fox, relatives have "little business experience or simply want to take advantage of the owner." They also can keep an advisory council from being impartial—especially if family disputes are involved.

• Look for candidates at business association meetings, in the local business community, among speakers or fellow registrants at professional trade shows and through recommendations from business associates, friends or other retailers. "The odds are you'll get a few refusals, so be selective," says Tillman. "The idea will intrigue some, flatter others and offer a change of pace to those looking for new, professional challenges."

Melart Welcomes Council's Advice

Melart Jewelers Inc., Silver Spring, Md., has great faith in its advisory council, says chairman Albert A. Foer. Here's a look at the inside workings of the council.

Half-day meetings are held three times a year, enough to involve the members in the business but not so often that it interferes with their schedules.

The council's first meetings were basically get-acquainted sessions. Foer and his staff explained Melart's organization, philosophy and operation; provided reports and memos to keep members informed of company activities; and encouraged "outside " (noncompany) council members to visit Melart stores, ask questions and meet the company's executives.

"Now, when they speak at council meetings, they say 'us' and 'we' instead of 'you.' They identify with the company," says Foer.

Here's a typical agenda:

• The meeting begins at 8:30 a.m. in the board room at corporate headquarters. Outside members report on store visits, then they hear short reports on sales, income and cash.

• Discussion on potential new store locations, renovations and possible acquisitions.

• Discussion on long-term planning (continued from previous meetings).

• Discussion on how the firm oversees work of the merchandise department.

Plan Ahead For Succession

September 1988 Part II

A friend's sudden death in a plane crash two years ago made Phoenix, Ariz., jeweler Carl Schmieder aware of how quickly—and unexpectedly—one's lifeline can snap. Like his friend, Schmieder's hobby was flying. "It could happen to me," he realized

Just as sobering was the tragedy that followed. His friend had been a good businessman. But he made no plans for the smooth continuance of his business in case of his death or disability.

"I saw the agony his family and business went through," says Schmieder. "It tore the family apart, and his estate suffered tremendous loss."

As a consequence, says Schmieder, "I realized I wasn't doing my job if I didn't plan *now* to reduce the trauma, prepare for contingencies and see the family was taken care of should anything happen to me."

After some thought and study, he prepared a written statement outlining his wishes for the operation and ownership of his business, the involvement of his family and key employees and the sale of his business, if necessary. He informed family and key personnel, and began to train a probable successor.

Planning the future: What Schmieder did is called succession planning. All family businesses should do it. Most don't.

The majority of U.S. businesses (80%) are small, family-run operations. But only 40% of them are successfully passed on to a second generation, and only 15% are passed to the third, according to a study by the financial firm of Merrill Lynch, Pierce, Fenner & Smith Inc.

Indeed, a Dun & Bradstreet report found the average family-owned business lasts only as long as the founder's professional lifetime, just 24 years. The reason, say analysts, is inadequate planning. The businesses are wrecked by costly estate taxes, fraternal bickering over to whom Dad would have given the firm, confusion over who's in charge and lack of liquidity to cover debts.

JCK's own survey of jewelers across the country—from mom-and-pops to major regional chains—found only 16% have a formal succession plan.

"It tends to be a major problem in smaller businesses, even though succession planning definitely increases the likelihood of a successful continuation of them," says Roderick Carrell, executive director of the Family Firm Institute in Johnstown, N.Y.

Why it happens: Why do so many entrepreneurs build up successful family firms, only to let them flounder when they leave the scene?

"When the issue isn't being faced in a company, it usually means there's a dilemma," says Dr. Peter Davis, director of executive education at the Wharton School of the University of Pennsylvania.

Many times a succession plan isn't developed because the owner:

• Doesn't want to face his own mortality or acknowledge that his firm can go on without him.

• Has no outside interests and nothing to look forward to if he retires.

• Doesn't want to choose which child will succeed him or decide how to divide ownership among relatives.

• Simply isn't willing to hand over the reins to a younger generation. In one major East Coast firm, older partners had a "tremendous reluctance" to pass control to the next generation, recalled a manager there. They felt the younger generation lacked management skills, and they disagreed with the maverick policies of the incoming president. The impasse ended only when all family members sat down and talked out their problems. The result: the dissident chief executive departed and the remaining family members agreed on the firm's direction.

Comprehensive look: Many family businesses think a smooth succession needs only a properly drawn will or enough insurance to cover the owner's debts when he dies. Wrong. It also means specifying who the owners and operators will be. And it means planning to reduce estate taxes, ensuring the firm has enough liquid assets and providing for the entrepreneur's retirement, assuming he didn't die on the job.

A smooth succession involves looking at the family and its needs, wills, employment agreements, insurance, education funding for children, equity needs, debt coverage and the effects of disablement or divorce, says Jane Scaccetti, a family business adviser and partner in the national accounting firm of Laventhol & Horwath. Carrell says one document should pull this all together.

Adds Davis, "A good succession plan lays out the future of a family business and the steps to get there."

Planning a smooth succession isn't necessarily easy, but it is essential. Without a game plan, says Schmieder, "a business isn't acting on its own initiative. It's only reacting to events, and drifting. It's better to chart your own course."

Here are tips for charting yours.

1. Pinpoint what you want. Before you worry about taxes or debt coverage, consider your personal wishes, family needs and the direction you want your store to go, says Scaccetti.

"The first thing I ask clients is 'What would you *like* to do with the business? Pass it on or sell it? Do you want your kids in it? Do you want any or all to share ownership? Are second spouses or stepchildren involved?'"

Next, decide how you will pass on the business and what your successor will need to be successful. How should the business be disposed of, if that's necessary?

To get a clear fix on where your business should go, decide where it is now, says family business adviser Leon Danco. Make an organizational chart of management, stock ownership, the board of directors, who reports to whom and who is responsible for what major tasks. This helps to show strengths and weaknesses, areas of growth and involvement of current and potential family members.

Once you have some clear ideas, discuss them with other family members in the business, co-owners (if any), key employees and financial and legal advisers. Refine your ideas, if you choose, based on their input.

2. Decide who's in charge. Identifying a successor insures continuity and instills confidence in the firm's staff, vendors and creditors.

"To protect his firm when his leadership is discontinued, an owner *must* have a plan in place to continue leadership at the highest level," says the head of a jewelry firm who came from an outside job when his father died without leaving a plan.

But identifying the successor is only half the job. You also must prepare that successor. "If you don't have a successor trained, it causes tremendous inefficiency, which translates into loss of financial value," says Schmieder.

Instill in that person what one East Coast jeweler calls "a sense of ownership." One way is to give or sell stock to him or her. Another is to give more responsibilities, which helps prepare the successor, your staff and you for the transition. A few years ago, for example, Frank (a pseudonym for a real jeweler in Michigan) began to turn over administration of his store to his son Jim, who has an agreement to buy the store.

When Frank reached 65 and Jim had half ownership, Frank turned over the day-to-day operations. "He's still president and still looks over the numbers," says Jim. "But he's turned over almost exclusive control of daily operations to me."

3. Write it down. Once you've made your plans, put them in writing. This avoids confusion, misunderstandings and other problems later. "When you write something down, you address little nuances that could cause problems later," says Scaccetti. "Expressing them in a concise manner forces you to face issues and deal with them now."

In all matters related to succession, "get it in writing," says Gustav Berle, marketing director of the Service Corps of Retired Executives. "That way you and your heirs know where you're going and you're both committed to it. When you're talking about business and about money, there are always differences of opinion, especially in family businesses."

Families spend little time talking about financial and management details of succession; everyone assumes there's common agreement, says John Michaels, chief executive officer of Michaels Enterprises, Waterbury, Conn. "It's only when you do the buy/sell agreement—when you sit down to dot the i's and cross the t's—that you find everyone has a different slant on the issues," he says.

Paul Stein of Bensons Jewelry Co., Washington, D.C., and his son, Ken, drew up a buy/sell agreement two years ago, even though Paul won't retire until 1995. "Anything could happen," he said. "If I die or become disabled, I didn't want to leave this hanging in the breeze. I wanted my wife protected financially, and I wanted to take some of the burden off Ken's shoulders."

Just as important, "I wanted Ken to know this transfer of ownership is cut-and-dried. I know too many horror stories where a father threw a son out of the business, or kept another for no reason, or the old man developed mental problems. This way, Ken knows I can't do that to him. He has a written agreement, not just my word, that he'll take over."

It isn't always necessary to draw up legal contracts right away. You may not want to formalize an agreement when your kids are toddlers. Schmieder left his plan informal, on a single sheet of paper, because he didn't know whether any of his children would even want to join the firm. "Circumstances can change," he cautions.

But Scaccetti urges at least a brief written analysis of your wishes. Your attorney and family should get copies to ensure your wishes are followed.

4. State a creed. The Old Testament says, "Where there is no vision, the people perish." That's why business advisers say a succession plan should include a statement of mission—what Scaccetti calls a family creed—defining the relationship between the family and business.

John Michaels of Michaels Enterprises mentions this creed: "The purpose of the business is to serve the long-term interests of the family. Therefore, the family exists to serve the business first, so the business can properly serve the family. All decisions are made on what is best for the business, not the family member. Only if there is a strong business, can the family be served."

5. Involve key people in your plans. That way, they already know who's in charge when you retire or withdraw from the business.

Albert Smyth Co., Timonium, Md., practices what vice president Robert Smyth calls deep management. Key employees are fully briefed on their segment of the business, so they're capable of taking over if necessary. Schmieder, meanwhile, insists that his managers train successors "to do the job as well as they." This not only prepares the staff for an emergency, he says, but frees the managers to move up in the company. Gleim the Jeweler, Palo Alto, Cal., holds monthly meetings to keep communication open, says co-owner Georgie Gleim. The sessions include herself; her father Art, founder and co-owner; a store manager, who owns part of the business; and a certified public accountant, who acts as business adviser.

6. Consider money matters. A succession plan reassures bankers who want to know who will repay your business loan if you die.

A good plan also limits tax impact on you now and estate taxes on your heirs later, depending on how and when they divest themselves of ownership. Lack of planning can leave heirs without enough assets to keep the firm afloat, forcing them to sell at a low price to pay taxes.

Following are hints on some financial aspects of estate planning, based on a report by Merrill Lynch, Pierce, Fenner & Smith:

• Get a realistic estimate of your business's value. This can be tough. Dad may want to give the business to the kids at as little cost as possible. Or the kids may think Dad wants an unreasonable amount for the business. Scaccetti suggest setting the business's fair market value for your children the same way you would for an outside buyer.

• Calculate the estate tax bill that would face the business at the time of inheritance. The bigger the business, the higher the estate taxes, says Dan Kachelein, a partner specializing in corporate taxes at Laventhol & Horwath. So you may want to shift much or all of your ownership to your heirs before your death to limit the estate taxes.

• Consider the liquidity of your assets and ways in which the final tax bill could be paid. A common way is with insurance. Do you have enough? Are you and other shareholders adequately covered? Do you have such essential coverage as key man and disability insurance?

7. Start now. Don't postpone succession planning. The sooner you start, the smoother, less costly and more efficient the transition will be. Many owners wait until retirement is pending. But that may be too late, says Dr. John Eldred, co-founder of the family business program at the University of Pennsylvania's Wharton School.

"Succession plans should be made years before the event [retirement or sale]. Start when you're in your 40s or 50s, not when you're 62," he says.

His Wharton colleague Peter Davis agrees: "Entrepreneurs should come to grips with formalizing the succession process—reducing estate taxes and ensuring that potential successors to major positions are in place—by the time kids near 30, and parents are in their 50s." He suggests starting no less than five years before a transition.

If you want your children—or nieces or nephews—in the business, start them early. This involves more than giving them a job in the stock room. "You won't have a successful transition unless you pay a great deal of attention to family relationships right from the beginning," says Davis. "You can't keep your kids close if you develop your firm but pay no attention to them as they grow."

Remember that it takes time to prepare legal paperwork. It took Vicksburg, Minn., jeweler Joseph Canizaro Jr., his father and a tax attorney 18 months to compose their buy/sell agreement. Why so long? "Primarily to work out financial aspects, like setting the value and price of the store, the method of payment, and the tax advantages involved."

8. Inform family members of your plans, even if they aren't directly involved. This can prevent unnecessary friction and bickering. For example, Harold, a Midwest jeweler, has three sons. One of them works in the store and eventually will buy it. Before Harold signed the buy/sell agreement, his accountant met with the entire family to explain exactly what was planned and why. "I didn't want anyone thinking I was giving one son everything and the others nothing," says Harold.

"They learned they'll all share equally in my estate, but that the sale of the business [to one son] is strictly a business proposition, the same as if he were a stranger."

9. Review and update. Once your planing is done, don't shove it in a drawer and forget it. Review it periodically and make any necessary changes. Events that affect a succession plan aren't limited to death or accidents. Among other factors are a change in the value of your business, the resignation of your hand-picked successor or a decision by a child to join the business after all.

10. Get expert advice. Most small-business people are unfamiliar with various tax liabilities, says Davis. And substantial changes in tax laws since 1986 have complicated things. The smart jeweler will ask his attorney and financial adviser for suggestions that benefit both seller and buyer of a family business. Also attend family business seminars and investigate courses at local colleges.

An Employment Contract

Though names are changed, this is an actual employment contract for a jeweler who served his former firm as consultant after retiring.

This agreement made this 31st day of October 1985 by and between Juli Jewelers Inc. (the "Employer") and Wilson Juli (the "Employee").

Whereas, the services of the Employee, his experience and knowledge of the affairs of the Employer and his reputation and contacts in the community are extremely valuable to the Employer, and

Whereas, the Employer desire the Employee to remain in its services and wishes to receive the benefit of his knowledge, experience, reputation and contacts for a period of 10 years after his retirement, and is willing to offer the Employee an incentive to do so in the form of retirement compensation and death and disability benefits.

Now, therefore, it is agreed as follows:

1. Obligations of the Employer.

(a) Employment. The Employer hereby employs the Employee as its president until his retirement from active employment, at an annual salary to be set by the board of directors at their annual meetings. The date of the Employee's retirement should be mutually agreed upon by the Employer and the Employee, but unless modified later by the parties, the retirement date should be Dec. 31, 1986.

(b) Consultation. After the retirement of the Employee, the Employer will employ the employee as a consultant, as hereinafter set forth, for a period of 10 years, at an annual salary equal to the maximum amount the Employee is promoted to receive without reducing the amount he will receive from Social Security benefits, provided the employee performs all the terms and conditions of this Agreement required to be performed by him.

(c) Death or disability. If the Employee dies or becomes totally disabled during the period of his active employment,

his salary shall nevertheless be paid in full. Such payments shall be made to the Employee if living, or to his spouse, if living. If the Employee dies or becomes totally disabled during the period of 10 years after his retirement, the annual salary shall continue to be paid for the balance of 10 years to his spouse, if living.

2. Duties of Employee.

(a) Employment. The Employee accepts the employment for the periods and at the salaries set forth in this Agreement.

(b) Employment duties. During the period of his active employment, the Employee will faithfully perform his duties to the best of his ability and in accordance with the directions of the Employer as given through its board of directors, which duties shall be of substantially the same character as those heretofore performed by the Employee. He will devote to the performance of such duties such time and attention as the Employer and Employee shall agree.

(c) Consultation services. During the period of 10 years after his retirement, the Employee will render to the Employer such services of an advisory or consultative nature as the Employer may reasonably request so that the Employer may continue to have the benefit of his experience and knowledge of the industry, and he will available for advice and counsel to the officers and directors of the Employer at all reasonable times by telephone, letter or in person, provided, however, that his failure to render such services or to give such advice and counsel by reason of his illness or other incapacity shall not affect his right to receive his compensation during such period.

(d) Compensation restriction. During the period of 10 years after his retirement, the Employee will not become associated with, or engage in, or render service to any other business competitive to the business of the employer.

3. Failure to Perform. If the Employee shall fail to substantially perform all the terms and conditions of this Agreement to be performed by him, or if he voluntarily leaves the employment of the Employer during the period of his active employment, or if during such period of active employment he is discharged for proper cause, then all subsequent compensation required to be paid by the Employer to him, or others, or the reminder thereof, as the case may be, shall become forfeited.

4. No assignment. The Employer may not assign his interest in this Agreement without written consent of the Employer.

5. Binding effect. This Agreement shall be binding upon and shall inure to the benefit of the successors and assigns of the Employer.

In witness thereof, the Employee has signed this Agreement, and the president of the Employer has signed, in the name of the Employer, pursuant to a resolution adopted by its board of directors.

All In The Family

Editorial ◆ *May 1987*

Here's a quick true/false mini-test on family-owned business.

Question #1. Family businesses account for 25% of the Gross National Product. True/false.

Question #2. Only large corporations need a written set of company goals. True/false.

Question #3. The owner of a family business should publicly announce plans to quit as chief executive about four years in advance. True/false.

Question #4. When they're being hired, non-family employees should be told that family members always will hold the top jobs. True/false.

The answers, according to Dr. John Eldred of the University of Pennsylvania's Wharton School, are:

#1 False. The figure is around 60% of GNP.

#2 False. All companies, large and small, should have one. Not to have written goals "is merely trying to survive."

#3 True. Succession "should be a process, not an event." To ensure orderly succession, key customers and bankers should be told of the succession plan four to five years before the boss quits. Moreover, said Eldred, a son or daughter succeeding a parent should assume full control of the business no later than age 40.

#4 True. Be upfront with non-family employees, starting with the job interview. Don't lie or be vague about their prospects; that way you avoid future problems.

Eldred, a Wharton specialist in family business operations, was a key speaker at the joint American Jewelry Marketing Association/Jewelry Industry Distributors Association late-March convention in Hilton Head, S.C. His talk was full of challenges to comfortable assumptions.

The heart of his story was that the family-owned and operated business must be professional—and that it can be so without turning into a bureaucracy. This means that the business must have clearly-defined goals and that *all* employees, family or not, should have written job descriptions and performance goals for which they will be held accountable. It also means offering true leadership ("leadership is not a job, it's behavior"), delegating intelligently, motivating through vision, not fear, and pruning the family tree as needed to save the family business from being wiped out in a family war. A bought-out brother, sister or other relative may be the savior of an "over-familied" company.

It's probably fair to say that not one jeweler in a hundred runs a business this way.

We all know the reasons or, more correctly, the explanations why. Either there's "no time" or "no need." No time for planning. No time to teach someone else how to do a job—so the boss does it himself instead of delegating. No need for formal sales training. Just watch the boss at work! No need for job descriptions—"everyone is expected to do a little bit of everything." No need for performance reviews—"I see what they're doing and besides, you can't do that with family."

Sound familiar?

It's so easy for the head of a small organization to feel he or she operates best by instinct. It's so easy for the lines of communication to get blocked, for employees to tell the boss what they believe he wants to hear rather than what he should be told—provided he is willing to listen. It's so easy to have discontent and worse because sister feels brother is not pulling his weight or non-family staffer is sure that's the case with a favored son or daughter. It's so easy to let "upward delegation" overload the boss and stifle employee initiative. That's when the employee passes the buck upward with an "I don't know how to handle this" complaint. So the boss, great guy that he is, steps in to create a lose/lose situation. He gets overloaded; the employee never learns.

Problems, problems. Yet almost all could be quickly and simply solved by using rules, discipline and professionalism. The rules needn't be complex, just adequate for business needs. Their financial cost is minimal; generally it's only the owner's ego that pays.

Many small family businesses—and some surprisingly large ones—have muddled through successfully for years without clear goals or even a suspicion of formal organization. Many others, however, have failed. Today, more than ever before, intensity of competition threatens the poorly-run business. One that also is torn by family dissension is ripe for failure.

The time is now for every family-owned jewelry business to examine critically every aspect of how the company is being run and to take prompt action to deal with trouble spots. If, as owner, you say to yourself, "I don't have the time" or "There are no problems," then find time and take another look to see if you overlooked any problems. Or look at the list of bankruptcies published each month by the Jewelers Board of Trade. As Eldred told his audience, "fear is a powerful motivator." But not a good one.

Earn As You Go

Editorial ◆ *November 1986*

When, we wonder, did some social researcher first report that pay is not a worker's No. 1 motivator? It's one of those pieces of corporate mythology that seems to have been around forever, cherished by generations of employers. The pat on the back, the happy work atmosphere, the open communication with the boss, the being-in-the-know about what's happening and about to happen at the company. *That's* what matters, they say.

They're right—up to a point. The trouble is that this sort of thinking does too much to downgrade the importance of pay. It's true that someone might prefer high job satisfaction and poor pay to poor job satisfaction and high pay. But there comes a point where pay is so poor that no amount of job satisfaction will compensate for it. Firms where this happens end up either with high turnover or a mediocre-or-worse staff.

In times past, too often this was true of jewelry stores. Traditionally a few top people were paid well and the rest badly. As a result the most lowly paid—most often women in general sales—either quit after a year or two if they were good or stayed around as second-raters for ever and ever.

Thankfully this situation is changing. The salary study in this issue shows one of the most dramatic overall increases in pay rates of any we have done over the past 20 years. Not only have the median salaries for the various job categories studied increased substantially from the 1984 study; individual achievements in almost all categories often are outstanding. In the stores studied—a reasonable cross-section of the retail end of the industry—we find reports of store managers earning $85,000 a year, top general salesmen earning $40,000-plus and many benchpeople earning well over $30,000.

The only area of continuing imbalance is the generalist woman salesperson. She still earns little more than half of what her male counterpart does even though, in a majority of cases, her work is judged superior. What's wrong here?

Could it be a failure to link compensation and performance? Early this year a group of JCK staffers sat down with more than a dozen leading jewelers to discuss critical industry issues; what to pay the sales staff emerged as one of the most critical. One strongly-held view was, "We'd like to hire the best but we can't afford them." The opposing view was, "You can't afford *not* to have the best."

Why can't a store afford the best salespeople? The principal argument was that there's so much "dead time" in a jewelry store when traffic dwindles to next-to-none (especially true in mall stores with their long hours) that it's impractical to pay top dollar. That's an argument with holes. It ignores the possibility of linking performance and pay. Salespeople shouldn't be judged on their ability to sell when a customer comes and stands in front of them. They should be judged also on their ability to cultivate a following and to fill a good portion of that "dead time" selling to people they've invited to come into the store to see some particular item.

Jewelers responding to our current salary study offer some guidelines on productivity. One common measure is that total sales should equal at least 10 times total salary. Some stores won't even consider an increase in base pay unless that target is met. One which uses this measure also insists you produce sales at least equal to 7 times total salary if you want to keep your job. Another store figures at annual review time that any employee who has not justified at least a 5% increase in base pay isn't worth keeping.

To judge performance, of course, requires measuring rods. For salespeople, there is a simple starting point: The dollar volume generated in a year. For other jobs possible guides are number of repairs completed, appraisals written or credit applications processed. The point is that important elements of any job can be identified and measured.

The best way to keep tabs on what you, as an employer, want to happen and how well your staff complies is to have regular evaluations. Many jewelers do. This involves sitting down with each employee at the start of a year (or half year or whatever period is most suitable) and agreeing on goals to be accomplished. They must be measurable goals and they must be understood by employer and employee. Performance is judged by how well the goals are met.

Those who don't like such a system have two prime objections. First, that it's impossible to measure precisely some of the intangibles so important in a jewelry store—attitude, ability to smile pleasantly, courteousness and so on. The second is that it's next-to-impossible to use a formal evaluation with a family member and difficult in a small store where employer and employee often have a close, family-like relationship.

These are legitimate objections. But if it's understood that better performance benefits everyone and if evaluations are handled with tact and kid gloves, even these objections can be overcome. This is especially so if there are worthwhile incentives tied to performance. Most of the jewelers we polled don't like commission payments, though those who use them swear by them. But there are many other ways to boost an employee's pay. It's just a matter of picking the one you, as employer, are most comfortable with.

The thing *not* to do is to say you can't afford incentives. They are the very weapons to use to build sales to the point where they become affordable. That way everyone wins.

Answers to JCK Management Study Center Quiz:
(Questions can be found on pages 172 & 173)

GETTING THE MOST FROM YOUR STAFF

1a. True	5a. True
1b. False	5b. False
1c. True	5c. False
2a. Disagree	5d. False
2b. Disagree	5e. True
2c. Disagree	6a. False
2d. Agree	6b. True
2e. Disagree	6c. True
3a. False	6d. False
3b. False	6e. True
3c. False	7a. False
3d. False	7b. False
3e. True	7c. True
4a. False	7d. False
4b. True	8a. False
4c. True	8b. True
4d. True	8c. True
4e. False	8d. False

Chapter 5

MONEY MANAGEMENT

Increasing Profits Does Not Happen By Accident

Fun With Figures

Editorial ◆ *December 1994*

Statistics scare a lot of people. But Jewelers of America has just published a 72-page book full of figures that even the most statistic-shy jeweler ought to acquire and study very carefully. It is JA's *1994 Cost of Doing Business Survey,* produced under the auspices of JA's Center for Business Studies and prepared by Industry Insights Inc., a survey research company in Columbus, Ohio.

The book offers a detailed look at jewelers' financial figures, a synthesis of actual results from 372 participating businesses. The findings are broken down by type of store and by annual store volume.

The most obvious benefit of the book is that a jeweler can compare his or her own figures with those of a larger group. But the book also offers some revealing insights on overall jewelry store operations and marketing. Some of the flavor of what's available shows up in composite figures for jewelry chains and for larger independents (those with sales of more than $1 million a year) reported for 1993 and 1992. The 1993 figures appear in the current book.

One of the first things you notice is that gross margin was significantly higher for chains than for large independents in both years, but it declined from 1992 to 1993 for both groups. For chain stores, the figure dropped from 54.3% to 51.3%. For large independents, it fell from 45.3% to 43.7%.

The big difference in margin between the chains and the independents may come as a surprise. After all, aren't the chains the ones that promote discounts day in and day out? Volume buying by the chains may explain some of the difference. But there's also an inescapable thought that chains employ more aggressive pricing policies. Does this mean independents should raise their prices? Or does it mean they should promote what appear to be their own lower prices? Something to think about.

The chains' higher margins are carried through on all major lines. Let's look at some examples from the new survey, with the chains' figure first and then the independents': loose diamonds, 48% vs. 41.8%; diamond jewelry, 55.2% vs. 47.8%; colored stone jewelry, 59.8% vs. 52.3%; watches, 43.2% vs. 39.1%; and karat gold jewelry, 62.1% vs. 53.2%.

If I were an independent jeweler and my margins were in line with the ones JA has published, I'd certainly take a good look at my buying and pricing records.

Who sells what also is interesting. Last year, for example, the chains made 40.5% of their sales in diamond jewelry and 6.2% in loose diamonds. The independents, perhaps exhibiting their greater gemological expertise and marketing flexibility, made 31.1% of their sales in diamond jewelry and 16.6% in loose diamonds.

The chains have a clear preference for watches. For example, watches accounted for almost 11% of chains' total dollar sales, almost twice the percentage recorded by independents. Chains also did a larger share of business in karat gold jewelry than independents (18.2% vs. 14.1%). For both, karat gold was the best margin producer.

The independents have some good competitive news of their own. Their operating expenses last year typically accounted for 39.9% of net sales, down from 41.1% and well below the chain figure of 48.3%—although the chain figure was a big improvement on the previous year's 52.4%. To a large extent, the chains' higher occupancy and payroll costs accounted for the higher expense percentage. Between 1992 and 1993, however, the chains cut their payroll percentage from 25.7 to 22.7.

The typical large independent also was a bigger sales producer in 1993, with average store volume of $1.3 million compared with average per-store sales of $930,000 for the chains. The average sale per employee was significantly higher for independents—$175 000 vs. $120,000. Payroll per employee (including fringes) also was much higher for independents—$34,099 compared with $28,145 at the chains.

Net profit as a percent of sales was 4.2% at the independents and 3.5% at the chains.

You could peruse the pages and pages of figures in this survey and find endless comparisons and, by checking the 1992 survey, changes from year-earlier figures. Each searcher might look for or find different facts of note.

The main point is that these figures exist and studying them can help any jeweler learn more about how to run a business more efficiently.

Getting Along With Bankers

August 1993 Part I

Off the balance sheet, the key to maintaining a good relationship with bankers is communication.

Bankers and clients agree that many misunderstandings—including some disastrous ones—have arisen because one side failed to fully inform the other of changes or problems. Bankers say they are in business to lend money and are willing to work with clients. But they stress that open communication is an absolute necessity.

First, be specific. "Banking officers must understand the purpose of the loan, whether it's for retailers to remodel or manufacturers to build inventory before their peak season," says Nathaniel Earle, president of the Jewelers Board of Trade.

Second, don't hide problems. Bankers agree that nothing's worse than "surprise" bad news. "If there's a problem, tell your banker and have a plan ready to fix it," says Earle. "Here's an example: 'We've had a disappointing fourth quarter and we're off our projections, so we've reduced some staff and scheduled an inventory clearance sale to get back on track.' "

"This shows your bankers you're a manager, not someone reacting to a situation, so they will be more inclined to work with you than if you attempt to gloss over or hide the problem."

Irene Spector, first vice president at Bank Leumi in New York, calls it a matter of trust. "The worst thing for a banker is to find out from someone else that a client is in trouble. This breaks the bond of trust," she says. "You don't need a complete plan. But we must see some willingness and ability to take action because problems won't go away by themselves."

Bankers caution that more money should not be an integral part of whatever plan a client puts forth. "That's not the problem—that's the symptom," says Spector. "Some manufacturers come to us saying they need more credit because their receivables are slow because of the recession. We ask if they've gotten more aggressive in collections, if they've tightened standards on who they ship to and whether they're too highly leveraged."

Those on the other side of the loan officer's desk say communication has to run two ways.

Larry Simpson, chief financial officer of C.H. Rauch in Lexington, Ky., says he had no clue his bankers were concerned about anything until they called in his loans. He says Rauch executives did "appraise our bank on a monthly basis," but they were mostly general updates without a lot of specifics. He says in retrospect he could have offered more details about potential problems, but the bankers never indicated any concern.

Retain More Net Profits Before Tax

June 1993

Profit is critical to business survival. If you aren't making more profit with your jewelry business than you could make in interest on a CD in the bank, then you might want to consider whether you ought to be in the jewelry business. We have to see ourselves as being in the business of producing gross margin through the vehicle of jewelry.

P – Profit (net) before tax. When you take the cost of goods sold out of your sales figures and you look at the bottom line, you see that you have to do better than the industry average in order to obtain your net profit before tax.

Budget your goal for net profit before tax as your starting point. Look at the industry averages and you'll see that the way to increase your profit is to raise your gross margin.

The pressure for gross margin should lie on your buyers, not on your salespeople. If you can't buy better than your competitors, you can't increase your bottom line. You have to buy at a good price to offer the item at a good price so that you protect your gross margin and give good value to consumers.

Value is perception. You have to price for the value you add to a product. You can't let your pricing be driven solely by your purchase cost.

R – Ratios. You have to know some key ratios in your business to examine and control your profitability trends. Key ratios would include gross margin, return on assets, return on investment and inventory turnover (see box).

Remember, if you can't maintain high margins and if you operate at very low inventory turn, you'll go out of business.

O – Zero based expense budgeting. Plan your expenses, even donations. If you don't plan, you squander your profit. Every day in a recession economy, niches are eroding away in niche-based marketing. Right now there is opportunity, the opportunity to recapture those niches and increase your profit. Justify every expense using the notion that there is to be 0 expense unless it is budgeted and then budget to take advantage of opportunity.

F – Focus. If you focus on profitability, you'll go through your expenses every year and analyze how you spend your money. You may see yourself as in the jewelry business, but you need to focus on the fact that your real business is the business of making your gross margin through the vehicle of the jewelry business.

In order to be profitable, the firm must focus on the plan that will get you to the level of profitability that you want. Your plan has to include your budgeted goal of net profit before tax, and it should include your assessment of all your expenses starting from the assumption of zero as well as your payroll budget for all positions.

I – Imagination generates profit. Use your imagination and the imaginations of the employees to save money and increase your gross margin. Reward your employees when they save you money and you'll continue to reap the benefit of their imagination.

T – Training. Train your people well and then pay them what they are worth to your bottom line in order to keep them. In the best run organizations, people know what they are supposed to do every day and that they are paid to do it. Personnel is the biggest expense in a jewelry store operation. You need to find out what every person costs you, including benefits, and then look at payroll. The team with the best people on the field wins. You can get more productivity out of your people with training.

In many parts of the country, the economy right now isn't the best in which to maximize profit. But now is an excellent time to analyze your business and to get yourself in the position to increase profits when the economy turns.

Industry Averages

Personnel – 20%
Advertising – 5%
Occupancy – 8%
Supplies – 1%
Communication – 1%
All other – 7.5%
Net profit before tax – 10%

Ratios

Gross margin = gross profit ÷ sales
Return on assets = net profit after taxes ÷ total assets
Return on investment = net profit after taxes ÷ net worth
Inventory turnover = sales ÷ average inventory retail
    or = cost of goods sold ÷ average inventory at cost
Cost of goods sold = beginning inventory + purchases + transportation– ending inventory
Average inventory = sum of all inventory counts taken during the year ÷ number of inventory counts taken

Surefire Ways
To Build Your Bottom Line

Joseph S. Romano ◆ *February 1993*

To succeed in the '90s, you must have "problem awareness"—and the decade's problems are many and complicated. Consider that:

• The average increase in sales from 1991 to 1992 was 5%—just about the same as 1992's inflation rate.

• The cost of money (interest rates) is at the lowest point in many years—but it is increasingly difficult to borrow money from the banks.

• Operating expenses are increasing at a rate of at least 4% a year—but the jeweler's average gross profit is declining. Gross profit in 1990, calculated from figures in the Scull Data Bank, was 52.46%; in 1991 it fell to 50.36% (figures for 1992 aren't available yet).

• The average annual inventory turn for the retail jeweler is only 1.0 time a year.

• The jewelry industry is facing increased competition from other industries.

• In today's economy, the term "on sale" hasn't the same impact on consumers as it had in the past.

• The average selling person's close ratio is two out of ten.

All these factors have precipitated a situation where many jewelers are just maintaining the status quo—trying to do what they've always done and expecting the same results. Worse yet, many other jewelers are expending precious energy and not moving forward—they've lost enthusiasm and are not even doing what they did in the past.

These circumstances frustrate many jewelers. As a result, some either are liquidating their businesses or are planning to liquidate. Some even have been forced to file for protection under the Federal Bankruptcy Act.

What's possible, what's not: Can you relate to any of these circumstances? Simple analysis shows that they fall into two categories: those you can control and those you can't.

Controllable	Noncontrollable
• Sales increases/ decreases	• Inflation rate
• Operating expenses	• Cost of money
• Gross profit	• Difficulty borrowing money
• Inventory turn	• Lessening impact of "on sale"
• Salesperson's close ratio	• Increased competition

The purpose of this article is to discuss problems within your control and provide possible solutions. It's beyond our scope to discuss issues outside your control. It's our experience that jewelers who want to talk about problems outside their control often use these problems to justify their firms' poor performance.

However, I would like to point out that the jewelry industry has been subjected to noncontrollable circumstances before—for example, the Depression, two World Wars, other recessions—which precipitated high/low interest rates and, accordingly, new ways of doing business with the banks. The point is, there's nothing new. So what's all the chatter about?

Problem solving: This begins with you. Specifically, your attitude toward a problem should be to solve it—and make a commitment to do whatsoever is necessary to accomplish that goal. The problem needs to be defined, or redefined, and placed in proper perspective. Remember, at least 50% of the circumstances we mentioned are within your control. Let's concentrate on these and see what can happen.

Your openness to change in conjunction with your ability to implement change is the key to your future.

Concomitantly, your resistance to change, and resulting inaction, can lead to your demise.

We live in a time when information is disseminated quickly if not instantly. This affects a person processing information in two ways. First, action, which equals success. Second, inaction, which equals failure. To be successful today, you must do everything right—*all the time!*

Demographic model of the typical retail jeweler
- Annual volume of $1,000,000.
- Christmas is the only season.
- In business for many years.
- Firm passes from generation to generation.
- Eight employees.
- Marketing budget is 4% of sales.
- Marketing style is not consistent with the firm's history.
- Gross profit is 50%.
- Annual inventory turn is less than 1.0 time.
- Owner is a member of Jewelers of America and a buying group.
- Owner's average annual compensation is $50,000 to $75,000.

- Christmas is mortgaged to satisfy debt in January.
- Basic store traffic results from word-of-mouth marketing and repair business.

These factors translate into a typical economic model, which looks like this:

Economic model of the typical retail jeweler

Sales	$1,000,000
Cost of sales	500,000
Gross profit	$500,000
Operating expenses:	
Owner's compensation	$75,000
Human resources	175,000
Marketing	40,000
Plant (rent, real estate, taxes, etc.)	90,000
Supplies	20,000
Communications	10,000
Other	30,000
	$440,000
Net income from operations	$60,000

Let's discuss some possible alternatives to improve the store's performance.

Sales and marketing: Sales cannot be discussed without discussing marketing; they go hand in hand. The most common marketing mistakes are:
- Trying to reach a larger percentage of the city than can properly be reached with the available budget.
- Expecting results right away.
- Advertising what you *wish* the public would buy instead of what they want to buy.
- Foolishly saving all of your budget until the fourth quarter.
- Mistakenly speaking in cliches.
- Making unsubstantiated claims.

Some Scull clients have achieved annual sales growth of as much as 61% with proper marketing and a minimum of at least 15%. Depending on circumstances, typical growth is perhaps 15% to 25% annually.

An ad budget of 4% may not be sufficient to seize the opportunities available in some markets. But an increase in the ad budget should be made only after an experienced advertising professional appraises your situation. Duplicating a campaign that was successful for someone else will not necessarily produce the same success for you. "Don't take another man's medicine. It could become your poison."

In considering sales, you also must ask yourself (and answer) the question: "Is sales training essential?"

To quote A. E. Pearson, former president of Pepsico, "To improve a company fast, develop people fast!"

The most successful companies in the country, such as Xerox and Marriott, to name a couple, have learned to develop their people fast. They spend an average of 2.5% to 3.5% of their annual budget on training and development. They're willing to commit that percentage because they have come to realize that an effective training program can easily return five to 10 times that amount in increased productivity. (About 35 Scull jewelers have instituted formal education programs and preliminary indications are that these are paying off with productivity increases of between 5% and 30%. This information is too fragmentary to offer a reliable indicator.)

Realize that the average retail jewelry store, according to Scull research, commands less than 10% of market share when you include all other retail jewelers, brokers, discounters, department stores and pawnshops. The potential for growth, then, becomes limited only by the amount of effort and resources you put into developing growth opportunities.

Think about the productivity of your sales staff. The average retail jewelry operation has an average closing rate of 2.0 to 2.5 of 10 first-time shoppers looking for a piece of jewelry. That means 7.5 to 8.0 walk out unsatisfied. Imagine your potential for increase if you can teach your staff to win over just one more customer from that group of 10. That one customer alone, sold consistently, represents a 40% to 50% increase in your business.

If you factor in repair customers, the average close rate falls in half to 1.0 to 1.25 out of 10. That means that 8.75 to 9 walk out without buying. If each of your staff can win over just one new customer out of that group of 10, you have the potential for a 100% increase in sales. The real question becomes not "How much does it cost me for training?" but "How much is it costing me if I'm not training?"

The need for training then becomes a given. The most important attributes of an effective training program are *order*, *simplification* and *consistency*. Historically, the most effective trainers have been mentors—individuals with expertise and success in their industry. They possess the ability to share their ideas in a logical, easy-to-comprehend format. These mentors build in strategy for long-term support to sustain the new levels of success.

The most effective trainers expose their charges to new information and help them relate it to their own experience. In this way, participants take personal ownership in the new techniques they've discovered. This allows them to accelerate their training and development curve so they and their companies can enjoy their success sooner and for a much longer time.

Sales and inventory/cost of sales: Cost of sales represents the cost of merchandise/service during a given period. A full discussion of cost of sales involves a comprehensive discussion of inventory management. Key to understanding inventory management is an understanding of inventory turn.

Inventory turn measures the time from when an item of merchandise is placed into stock for sale to the time it is sold. Scull statistics indicate the average inventory turn for jewelers is less than 1.0 time a year—turn being calculated by dividing cost of merchandise sold by average inventory. This means inventory is in stock for 365 days or more.

Let's analyze and draw some conclusions. If your inventory turn is 1.0 time a year, it means that your cash investment in inventory is being invested for 365 days. Does this cost you money? Yes, based on this rationale. This same cash could be placed in another investment—Certificate of Deposit, Treasury bill, etc. Then there's the interest expense if you finance your inventory merchandise by way of a bank or vendor. Also, inventory must be insured and it must be maintained (cleaning, tag replacement, etc.). We estimate that the cost of maintaining inventory is 20% of the inventory cost.

Thus, the real questions relative to inventory management are "How much inventory do I need to maintain current sales volume?" and "How much inventory do I need to sustain growth?"

The answer is to strive for a minimum of 1.5 times a year to a maximum of 2.0 times. This means movement out of your comfort zone. But the benefits are great. Change in inventory turn from 1.0 to 1.5 times a year results in the following model:

	Store with 1.0 turnover		Store with 1.5 turnover	
Sales	$1,000,000	100%	$1,000,000	100%
Cost of goods:				
Beginning inventory	500,000	50%	333,333	33%
Purchases	500,000	50%	500,000	50%
	1,000,000	100%	833,333	83%
Ending inventory	(500,000)	(50%)	(333,333)	33%
	500,000	50%	500,000	50%
Gross profit	$500,000	50%	$500,000	50%
Average inventory	$500,000		$333,333	

Note that the above comparison shows that the store with 1.5 turnover is doing the same volume at the same gross profit as the store with 1.0 turnover but with an inventory investment of only $333,000, while the store with 1.0 turnover carries an inventory of $500,000.

Here's how you make money: Every dollar of inventory reduction is a dollar in your pocketbook. That jeweler increased cash flow by $166,667, as follows:

Average inventory @ 1.0 inventory turn = $500,000
Average inventory @ 1.5 inventory turn = $333,333

Cash available for debt reduction or for owner compensation by reducing the inventory = $166,667.

Operating expenses: Expenses should be analyzed annually to see if they can be eliminated or reduced by better accountability or better purchasing. Specifically:

• Obtain new annual bids on all insurance policies.

• Analyze human resources in light of performance (non-selling people) or productivity (selling people, shop people) against dollars paid.

• Analyze rent in relation to traffic generated. (Rent can be defined as the cost paid for the privilege of transient traffic.)

• Analyze marketing strategies against the results they generate.

• Audit telephone bills to assure there are no internal or external abuses or mistakes.

• Investigate better purchasing techniques. Other expenses (supplies, boxes, etc.) might be grouped generically and negotiated to obtain a lower price.

• And so on.

Operating expenses will differ widely from store to store, depending on many circumstances—and philosophically I can't grade expense control in terms of good or bad. For example, low spending on a marketing program might mean only that the program was being short-changed. But at Scull, we do record low, medium and high averages for various expenses. Here are the figures for 1991:

Expense	Low	Medium	High
Human resources	22.66%	27.62%	32.79%
Marketing	3.04	4.56	7.34
Plant	6.18	7.80	12.38
Supplies	0.61	0.88	1.44
Communications	0.77	1.42	1.87
Other	2.85	4.68	8.12

We have found that 20% of total expenses can be eliminated by implementing the above mentioned procedures as well as others. This translates to 10% greater profit that travels directly to the bottom line and produces more cash.

Summary

By improving inventory turn from 1.0 to 1.5 times per year	$166,667
By a review of expenses and subsequent expense reduction (10% x $440,000)	44,000
Sales increase due to efficient marketing (12% x $1,000,000)	120,000
Sales increase due to more efficient selling people (10% x $1,000,000)	100,000
Total potential	$430,667

Please note that the potential just described falls into two categories. The first represents a one-time benefit; the second, an ongoing benefit.

Improving inventory turn is a one-time benefit. It produces cash only once, when it is achieved. This is why liquidation/retirement sales work. Essentially, inventory is converted into cash, and the cash is used to retire debt or is paid to the store owner.

Alternatively, expense reduction or sales increases due to more efficient marketing and more productive salespeople continue in the long term—so long as the disciplines stay intact. Consider the benefit over a five-year period.

	1 year	5 years
Expense reduction	$44,000	$220,000
Sales increases—marketing	20,000	600,000
Sales increases—sales training	100,000	500,000
Total potential	$264,000	$1,320,000

Recasting the economic model to give effect to these changes results in:

	Original	Recast
Sales	$1,000,000	$1,220,000
Cost of sales	500,000	610,000
*Gross profit	$500,000	$610,000
Operating expenses	440,000	400,000
Net income from operations	$60,000	$210,000

*Model assumes 50% gross profit. Please note that the net income has increased $150,000 ($210,000- $60,000).

In conclusion: Could you afford not to make this money? I think not.

Converting Assets To Cash: The Sale Business Is Booming

February 1992

Business was off about 20% at Jewelcase Diamond Center in 1990, and owner Joe Salkin decided it was time for action. He knew a sale would boost business, but he didn't want to run it by himself. So he hired a sales consulting firm to help.

Working with The Hills Group, Farmington Hills, Mich., he offered customers at his Freehold, N.J., store 30%-60% off the price of old and new merchandise for six weeks in late spring 1990 and again in 1991. The result: annual volume hasn't reached the $700,000-$800,000 levels of the late 1980s, but the 1991 sale did generate 20% more volume than the 1990 sale.

Salkin is among the growing number of retailers opting to hire one of the growing number of firms that conduct sales for jewelers. Three years ago, only two or three professional sales firms advertised in JCK and other industry publications. Today, at least 10 firms specializing in the jewelry industry are active nationally. They are experienced at covering the logistical, supply and legal aspects of sales, providing services that many jewelers aren't trained to handle themselves. Taking advantage of these services are such chain giants as Barry's Jewelers Inc., based in Monrovia, Cal., and Carter Hawley Hale Stores, based in Los Angeles, and such

upscale independents as Argo & Lehne Jewelers, Columbus, Ohio, and Freeman Jewelers, Rutland, Vt.

The potential market for sales-firm services is vast. The Jewelers Board of Trade reported 439 fewer retailers in business this past September than in September 1990. Each of these 439 retailers could well have been interested in going-out-of-business/liquidation sale advice.

Add to that the number of jewelers who are on the brink of bankruptcy, closing a branch or simply striving to improve cash position and you get an idea of the number of potential sales-firm clients.

In fact, a JCK poll found that professional sales firms specializing in the jewelry industry conduct more than 300 sales annually with a total sales volume conservatively estimated at $100 million. (Several professional sales firms decline to reveal figures, so the amount could be much higher.)

How successful are jeweler/sales-firm arrangements? Most appear to end happily, with the jeweler enjoying higher sales volume and the sale firm earning its fee and, in some cases, selling merchandise it acquired from previous liquidations. In some cases, however, jewelers are baffled by the methods used to reach the bottom line. Many aren't acquainted with the large movements of inventory required for such sales, and few know the legal guidelines that govern such movements. (Several recent sales have been tainted by violations of such guidelines.) And as one retailer put it, despite the healthy infusion of cash, "is the jeweler going to be wondering if he sold his soul afterward?"

Here's a guide to common reasons for hiring a professional sales firm, and an outline of what jewelers can expect if they do so.

Financial boost: Jewelers may want to hold a prolonged sale for any number of reasons. "Unfortunately, going-out-of-business sales top the list these days," says Bob Grant, president of The Hills Group.

Other incentives exist, however. Among them are the need to:

• Raise cash quickly to avoid bankruptcy.

• Eliminate unneeded inventory when two stores are consolidated into one.

• Remove old inventory to create a new image for the firm. Such a "restructuring" sale often involves an owner selling to a younger buyer who wants to start fresh with a different image.

"Whether it's called a retirement sale or a moving sale or a promotional sale, the objective almost invariably is to raise cash for survival," says David Barry of the Management Growth Institute, Wellesley, Mass.

Of course, genuine retirements or closings are common, too, as are holiday sales.

Arranging a sale: When arranging a sale, the critical point of negotiation involves payment terms. Jewelers often think sales firms offer a standard package. And indeed, firms seem to follow a standard array of procedures in most instances. " But many of the items are negotiable," Barry says.

The two most common types of arrangements are *acquisition* sales (also called *guaranteed* sales) and *commission* sales.

In an acquisition sale, the sales firm assumes the expense of conducting the sale (including and costs, sales training and, often, jewelry acquisition). Sale prices, the length of sale and fees are negotiated. Generally, the sales firm projects the volume based on its experience with retailers of similar size, type and location. From this estimate, a flat fee and a percentage of sales are negotiated. In some cases, the jeweler and sales firm work out a partnership to share costs and revenue.

In a commission sale, the jeweler and sales firm negotiate responsibility for ad and merchandise costs. Once an estimate of the sales potential is made, the jeweler agrees to receive a percentage of the net proceeds. Sometimes this is a flat percentage, but more often it changes as the sale progresses. The sales firm receives a higher percentage early in the sale, for example, and lower percentages as net proceeds reach agreed-upon levels.

Preparing for a sale: While some sales firms specialize in one type of sale, most appear to offer both commission and acquisition options. A jeweler may find the choice confusing at first.

"In my view, it's a matter of personality," says Mitchell Cohen, an associate at Gordon Brothers Partnership in Boston, which conducts many such sales. "A risk-taker is more willing to share the expenses earlier on," he says. "A conservative retailer will take the guaranteed cash on inventory up front."

Smith Jewelers, Redlands, Cal., teamed with Gordon Brothers in spring 1991 when owner William Junkin retired. The new owners, Junkin's daughter Cindy and her husband Robert Calderon, wanted to start fresh, so they called on Gordon Brothers for help. The Calderons sold the store's inventory to Gordon at a negotiated price and arranged to receive a percentage of gross sales throughout an eight-week sale. They decline to reveal how close to cost Gordon paid for the inventory or to discuss the percentage of gross sales, but Cindy Junkin-Calderon says the figures were "somewhat negotiable."

In some cases, the sales firm becomes as much a jewelry supplier as promotional expert. Salkin, at Jewelcase Diamond Center, simply paid the Hills Group for a cache of jewelry it had bought from a liquidated retailer. "The fact that Hills bought the jewelry at a low price made it profitable for us to buy it from them and sell it," Salkin explains. Salkin then paid The Hills Group a flat percentage of total volume during the six-week sale. Salkin also paid for all ad space and the salary of a Hills employee who worked at his store during the sale. "It was well worth the investment," he says.

Research: Before any deals are struck, most sales firms research a store's history and sales potential thoroughly. "There are many variables," Cohen says. These include the store's age, location and type (guild, chain, etc.), as well as the area's demographics, the competition, time of year and the owner's desired outcome.

"For a store with a fantastic reputation in a small town, the owner may want to consider sharing more of the costs earlier in the sale," Cohen says. "If the store is in a mall with many competitors, the risk is greater and [the owner] may want cash up front."

Rick Hayes, national sales manager for Bobby Wilkerson Sales Innovations, Stuttgart, Ark., says his firm assesses, or "qualifies," a store well before any sales are arranged. If a jeweler seems committed to the sale, Hayes will visit the store to assess the financial goals and gather information on the store's ownership history, sales volume of the past three years, debts and advertising. "Each store is unique," he says. "You can't have a canned operation that fits every situation."

Cohen emphasizes that each store has unique requirements that make it impossible to outline a "typical" sale.

Stuart Fetter, executive vice president of Silverman Jewelers Consultants, a major sales firm with offices in Mt. Pleasant, S.C., and Huntington, N.Y., agrees that each jeweler requires a unique approach. "If a jeweler has already done a series of sales that year, it's a lot harder," he says. "That's why we want to see their recent ads." Fetter says he asks retailers for their mark-up policies and sales figures for the past five years.

Advertising: When jeweler and sales firm agree that a sale is appropriate, the jeweler must scrutinize three areas: advertising, merchandise and image.

Many sales firms create ads in-house to use during sales promotions. These can range from low-key to garish. In all cases, a jeweler should have the right to see (or hear, in the case of radio ads) any ad before it's used, Barry advises. (More on protecting an image later.)

In addition, legal guidelines require specific denotations about the type of sale, its duration and percent-off claims. (See related story titled "Is your sale legal?")

States and the Federal Trade Commission regulate going-out-of-business sales much more strictly than some other types.

And in all situations, the jeweler is responsible for seeing that comparisons between original and sale prices are accurate.

FTC guidelines also require the accuracy of prices representing a discount off "comparative" or "suggested retail " prices. "If no one in the trade area is selling the item at the stated comparative price, then it has no meaning," says Richard Donohue, FTC senior staff attorney. A national jewelry chain (which many jewelers use as a guideline for comparative pricing) may sell an item for $100, but that's not a legitimate comparison if a jeweler's local competitors sell it for less.

Complexities: Sales firms admit that laws governing advertising are complex, but they say they adhere to them scrupulously. In summer 1991, for example, Silverman spent "a fortune" researching laws governing sales in each area where it conducted closing sales for 70 Barry's stores, Fetter says.

Still, errors occur. As Gordon Brothers discovered in 1991, a jeweler who runs a sale faces great scrutiny from competitors. When Gordon failed to list in its ads all the sources of inventory offered at a liquidation sale at Freeman Jewelers, Rutland, Vt., a competitor noted the omission. The state's attorney general issued an assurance of discontinuance to Gordon and assessed the firm $75,000, which it agreed to pay. The quality of the jewelry was never questioned, however, and Gordon explained that the omission was a clerical oversight. In addition, Gordon offered a refund to any customer, as the attorney general requested. Only two or three customers asked for a refund, Gordon reports.

More ad concerns: The look and tone of advertising is especially important if a jeweler intends to remain in business after his sale. Tom Thielman of Rolling Hills Estates, Cal., says frankly that several ads Silverman put together when he closed one of his two Finley's Jewelers stores weren't what he expected. "We approved all of them, but we first had to tone down a few." He admits, however, that the sale was a success and that the ads generated consumer interest and increased store traffic. (However, he later closed his second store also. See "Case study".)

Most sales firms budget ad costs based on revenue expected from the sale. Generally, costs range from 4% to 7% of expected sales (this generally is negotiable). Hayes, of Bobby Wilkerson Sales, says he first canvasses the jeweler's media market to determine the best advertising options. "We generally need about 10 days to research the media and for placement time," he explains. Newspapers, radio stations, cable and network affiliate television stations are assessed as potential ad venues.

In many instances, the sales firm pays all ad costs—but not always. "It depends on which would be best for the jeweler," says Fetter. Retailers with strong ad experience feel more comfortable working with the media directly. They also can save money by not paying a sales firm to handle the ads. But a jeweler with little promotional advertising experience may not be able to direct the media campaign appropriate for a sale. Sales firms are well-versed in media buying and ad development and may be more effective at generating consumer interest. Again, negotiation of terms is advisable.

The merchandise: Jewelers generally work months in advance to stock and sell items in preparation for liquidation or retirement sales. Unless they are consolidating several stores into one, few jewelers are prepared to offer the range and depth of stock that consumers demand at a sale. Yet

laws often say an item must be sold at regular price for 30 days before it can be offered at a reduced sale price. (The time varies among states, cities and types of sales.) And many localities have strict guidelines on how and when new merchandise may be brought in for some types of sales.

Jewelers often prefer that sales firms handle the sourcing of additional merchandise. Junkin-Calderon of Smith Jewelers says that in the few cases where Gordon was unable to furnish merchandise from its own sources, she used her own vendors. She had the final word on all jewelry offered during the sale.

Grant, at The Hills Group, says his firm often buys merchandise at a discount from retailers or manufacturers who are liquidating inventory. He then consigns the merchandise to a store where he's conducting a sale at a price both parties agree on. "The retailer prices it according to what it normally sells for in that market," he says.

Because the jewelry may have been bought at a low price originally, Grant and representatives of other sales firms that use similar sourcing say a jeweler can generate a profit even selling the items at a discount price. "It's the jeweler's profit and he pays us a commission on the whole gross sale," Grant says.

As with jewelry already in stock, jewelry brought in for sale and sold at a discount must have an accurate "comparative retail price." Grant says his firm's pricing conforms to all FTC and local requirements. "We have had those questions [regarding pricing] checked by the Better Business Bureaus and they've found us to be right," he says. "We use comparison shopping."

Image: A jeweler must have a clear view of his goals before hiring a sales firm, Barry cautions. If he plans to retire and wants only to raise cash, he's not likely to look beyond the bottom line. "But if he's going to stay in business, he needs to consider image," he says.

A family-owned guild store with a long history may not be ripe for a banner-waving clearance sale. The danger of "selling down" is very real and can have a long-term impact on business. Likewise, a promotion-minded jeweler may stretch his credibility with too many special sales.

Junkin-Calderon of Smith Jewelers says her goal was to maintain the American Gem Society store's image after her father retired. Other goals were to sell much of the store's old inventory (85% of the old merchandise was sold during the sale), garner publicity and increase the store's customer base. "Those were our objectives, and all were met," she says. Overall, she was pleased with the outcome. "We did a year's worth of business in two months and maintained our AGS image."

Is Your Sale Legal?

What you don't know can hurt your business—even if you're going out of business.

Federal, state and local governments have strict laws, regulations and guidelines on how sales should be advertised and conducted. The rules apply not only to normal sales such as Christmas and Mother's Day, but also to sales for grand openings, closeouts and retirements.

Don't assume you can ignore them. In recent years, the Federal Trade Commission has encouraged states to take more authority in enforcing laws against deceptive pricing, sales and ads, and more states are vigorously doing so in the name of consumer protection.

FTC: At the national level, the FTC is charged with regulating retail sales. Every jeweler should know the FTC's guidelines on gem and jewelry terminology and trade practices. These guidelines are the standards of the industry and are vigorously policed by the Jewelers Vigilance Committee. JVC issues warnings to violators and notifies appropriate federal, state or local authorities.

However, FTC guidelines on pricing and ads—what is and isn't deceptive—are less familiar to retailers. These say, in part, that:

• With in-store price comparisons, the advertised former price must be genuine, not fictitious.

• A genuine price is one at which the product was offered "openly and actively" for sale to the public for a "reasonably substantial period of time."

• If ads don't mention a specific price reduction or percentage discount, the advertiser must ensure the reduction is neither "insignificant" nor "meaningless." It should be sufficiently large that the consumer would believe that a genuine bargain or saving is being offered."

• In ads and sales claiming lower prices than competitors', the competitor's price must be the prevailing price in that market and not be "isolated, unrepresentative, fictitious or misleading."

• Before using a manufacturer's list or suggested retail price in sales, price comparisons or discount ads, the retailer must be sure it is "in fact regularly charged by principal outlets in his [market] area."

• In sales where additional merchandise is offered if a consumer buys one at the regular price (for example, two-for-one or half-price sales), the seller must make conditions of the sale clear at the start. The seller also must not increase the regular price or decrease the amount or quality of articles on sale.

• Retailers can't advertise retail prices as "wholesale" prices or claim to sell at factory prices if they aren't what they paid the manufacturer.

• Seconds, imperfect or irregular items shouldn't be sold at reduced price without disclosing that the advertised higher comparative price is for perfect merchandise.

Guidance: Though not law themselves, the guides are the FTC's official interpretations of the Federal Trade Commission Act, which *is* law. The interpretations "provide guidance to the public on how to conform [to the federal law]," says Bonnie Jansen, director of FTC Public Affairs.

Rick Quaresina, FTC attorney for marketing practices, says the issue in applying the guides to retailers is "a sale, any sale, *cannot* be deceptive."

Failure to comply with the guides can result in what Jansen calls corrective action that includes warnings, formal complaints and lawsuits. FTC discipline applies to anyone the commission believes "knew or should have known" of the deception, she says. Thus a 1990 FTC case against a toy firm with allegedly deceptive ads also named the ad agency that prepared them.

Other sources: There are other sources defining and/or regulating retail prices, advertising and marketing. One is the Uniform Commercial Code (UCC), the legal code for commercial transactions between buyers and sellers. The

UCC is actually a compilation of many commercial codes by the American Law Institute and the Conference of Commissions on Uniform State Laws. The UCC and FTC guides, or parts of them, are the basis for most state and local regulations governing business practices, pricing, marketing and consumer protection.

Another source of what is and isn't acceptable is the advertising code of the Council of Better Business Bureaus, designed to help business regulate itself rather than have Uncle Sam do it. Adherence to the code—based on state and federal provisions and business input—is voluntary and expected only of BBB members. However, its provisions will enable a retailer to comply with most, if not all, local and state regulations covering sales. For example, the BBB code says that words "emergency sale" and "distress sale" shouldn't be used unless these designations are an accurate description of the situation. In addition, such sales should be limited to a stated period of time and only offer merchandise affected by the emergency.

State & local: While the FTC spells out fair pricing policy, it has left enforcement to states and municipalities in recent years. In a 1990 interview with *Women's Wear Daily*, Barry J. Cutler, director of the FTC Bureau of Consumer Protection, noted that more states are policing deceptive retail claims and said it "would not be a good use of our [FTC] resources to duplicate their efforts...[It] is appropriate to let the state handle them."

The type of sale that gets the most legislative attention is the business closeout, which some state officials contend is most liable to abuse.

Roughly a third of the 50 states and many of the 39,000 U.S. municipalities have going-out-of-business statutes. These usually apply to any type of closeout sale. A statute in Memphis, Tenn., for example, includes fire, adjustment, liquidation, reorganization, mortgage and loss-of-lease sales under "closeout sales." Other cities include must-vacate, moving-to-new-location and bankruptcy sales in this category.

Closeouts: Though differing in content and complexity, most close-out statutes say:

• A license or permit must be obtained, for a fee, from the municipal clerk or designated official of the locale where the sale will be held. This must be done several days or weeks before the sale.

• A sale can run only a limited time, usually 30 to 90 days.

• Extensions of sales usually are allowed, primarily if all designated merchandise wasn't sold. An additional license and fee usually are required. The length and number of extensions vary.

• An inventory of merchandise to be sold must be submitted with the application for a sale permit Wares not on the list can't be sold.

• New or additional merchandise can't be added to store stock for 14 to 60 days before the sale or during the sale.

• Closeout advertising must follow a specific format and/or contain specific wording.

• A business that held a closeout sale may not conduct business at that location for an extended period (usually a year) after the sale.

Penalties for violators usually involve a fine (often from $100 to $500) and/or imprisonment (usually 30 to 60 days) for each violation. Usually, each day a sale is held in violation of a closeout statute is considered a separate offense.

Promoters: A very few closeout statutes also deal with sales consultants or promoters hired to conduct such sales.

A good example is the closeout sale statute of Connecticut, a leader in regulating business practices and consumer protection. It defines who or what a sales promoter is, requires annual registration for a state license, tells what an agreement between a promoter and a closeout sale licensee must include and cites the types of improper behavior that can cost a promoter his or her license. These include "conduct...likely to mislead, deceive or defraud the public" or state consumer protection commissioner; engaging in untruthful or misleading advertising; or violating any provision...relating to closing-out sales."

Conviction of misconduct—following a hearing by the consumer protection commission—can bring a stiff penalty. Connecticut levies civil penalties of up to $500 per offense, with each item of merchandise sold deemed a separate offense.

Other sales: Most other types of sales—such as retirement, new management, inventory reduction, special promotions and grand openings—don't have individual statutes. State or local consumer and/or pricing regulations cover them. At least 13 states have laws on retail advertising and pricing. Others use state consumer protection laws and agencies to regulate sales and prevent fraud.

A good example of how states can apply such laws to retail sales is Iowa, which has conducted a three-year study of retail advertising and pricing to devise new guidelines for its Consumer Fraud Act. The proposed guidelines have provoked some opposition from retail groups but, if approved, would require retailers to:

• Document all price comparisons and sale claims for at least a year.

• State the last day of a sale in all ads for it.

• Stop offering merchandise at a sale price after the specified end of the sale.

• Order a sufficient quantity of an advertised sale item to avoid running out.

• Sell up to 30% of an item's inventory before the rest of that merchandise can be put on sale.

A number of other states' consumer protection rules or guidelines contain similar provisions and also:

• Bar non-stop "sales" by requiring that goods sell at regular prices for a specific period before going on sale.

• Prohibit inflated markups or discounts.

• Forbid using the word "wholesale" in retail prices or sales, or using manufacturer's suggested prices as the "regular" prices for merchandise.

Tougher: In recent years, many states have strengthened enforcement of these laws and investigation of retail sale, ad and pricing claims, prompted by questionable discount pricing and non-stop "sales."

Connecticut, Ohio and Massachusetts have gotten tougher with violators of their comparison price advertising statutes, while Georgia's Consumer Affairs Office regularly reviews ads by merchants for compliance with its Business Practices Act. And since 1988, New York, California, Maryland, Colorado, North Carolina, Pennsylvania, Illinois and New Jersey—to name a few—have filed successful legal complaints against allegedly deceptive pricing, advertising or sales by such major national or regional retailers as Sears Roebuck & Co., Boscov's, R. H. Macy, Rich's (owned by Federated Department Stores Inc.), May Department Stores Co., Wanamaker's , J.C. Penney Co. and WalMart.

Challenges: States aren't the only ones fighting questionable sales practices. In recent years, New York City has challenged Sears for allegedly violating its consumer protection laws. Los Angeles, Orange and Sacramento counties in California sued May Department Stores for allegedly false advertising (prompted by jewelers who questioned the validity of May's discount pricing). Brian D. Shore, a jeweler in Rockford, Ill., sued two department store chains— Marshall Field & Co., Chicago, and H.C. Prang Co., Sheboygan, Wis.—for using allegedly deceptive pricing and ads for gold jewelry for three years.

The JVC has toughened its fight against phony pricing through its Truth in Pricing panel and with friend-of-the-court briefs supporting government agencies and others who bring legal action against deceptive pricers.

Nor is it only big guys who are nabbed. In 1991, Gold and Silver Jewelers of Topeka agreed to a demand by the Kansas Attorney General to stop using questionable pricing in its ads. In California, the state ordered Jewelry Jewelry Inc. of Sacramento to institute a price-control program to ensure that advertised price reductions are reliable and accurate. Both firms also had to pay substantial amounts to the states. In Kentucky, a federal judge voided an eight month liquidation sale of Hatfield Jewelers, Louisville, because it violated the state's going-out-of-business law.

These examples show that a jeweler can't afford to ignore or overlook federal, state and local government regulation of sales practices. Nor should a jeweler try to blame any violations that occur on a professional hired to conduct the sale. If you own the business, you're legally responsible for what it does or doesn't do for its sales.

Sources: Claiming you didn't know that the law forbids bringing in new merchandise for a lost-our-lease sale or that grand-opening ads must include the last sale date will get little sympathy from enforcement officers. Ignorance of the law is no defense.

Who enforces statutes governing sales, pricing and ads depends on where your business is located. Different states have different systems for dividing state and local responsibilities and powers. In many areas, enforcement of retail-related issues is often handled by municipal or county officials rather than at the state level.

"The state usually has general consumer protection statutes which set broad policy, and local government [regulations] fill in the blanks and go into more details," explains Jeanne Mejeur, policy specialist for the National Conference of State Legislatures. Indeed, she says, "a lot of local ordinances get involved with retail [issues]."

Retailers can consult several sources to learn the rules that govern pricing and sales. These include the municipal administrator, the county Better Business Bureau and municipal or county offices that issues licenses and permits. Also consult the municipal, county or state consumer affairs bureau. These usually are part of the county attorney or state attorney general departments.

Case Study

Tom Thielman has had his business ups and down, and that has given him occasion to use a sales consultant for different reason at his two Finely's Jewelers stores near Rolling Hills Estates, Cal.

In 1989, as economic worries grew and as customers started to avoid one of his stores during a major renovation of a nearby mall, his cash flow decreased. Deciding to close one store to cut expenses, he called Silverman Jewelers Consultants for help in running a consolidation sale. "I couldn't do it fast enough," says Thielman. He reduced his work force form 35 to 13 and chopped store space from 13,000 to 4,000 sq. ft.

The sale and the cutbacks helped for awhile, but in April 1990, he filed for protection from creditors under Chapter 11 of the U.S. Bankruptcy Act. He called Silverman again for help in running a bankruptcy/reorganization sale. The proceeds enabled him to work with some creditors, but business didn't pick up and, in late 1991, he decided to close his remaining store. He called Silverman again.

The going-out-of-business sale was scheduled to end Jan. 10, so results weren't known at JCK press time. But Thielman's earlier bankruptcy-reorganization sale offers an interesting look at the process of working with a sales consultant.

Help on the way: To climb out of Chapter 11, Thielman knew he would have to acquire and sell more merchandise. But few lenders extend credit to a business in Chapter 11. "Since our credit had suffered," he says, "Silverman was responsible for the disposition of the merchandise, and that allowed us to obtain more from vendors."

Stuart Fetter, executive vice president at Silverman's office in Mt. Pleasant, S.C., says he would have preferred that Thielman not seek bankruptcy protection. "Anytime anything goes into Chapter 11, a lot of money that would go to creditors ends up going to lawyers," he says.

Regardless, the filing created the time needed to conduct the sale. At first, creditors were hesitant, says Thielman, but most were willing to cooperate during the sale. "They were more assured of being paid after the sale than they were before we were in Chapter 11," he says.

Fetter projected Finley's would sell the equivalent of one year's volume during the six-week sale. (The firm's sales volume is confidential.)

In preparing for the sale, Thielman mounted all loose goods to make his inventory as salable as possible. A few memo goods also were brought in to fill out the selection. California allows this for all but going-out-of-business sales, Fetter says.

"We bring it in directly from a third party or from the jeweler's own vendors," he says. The number of items brought in for the sale was small because Thielman had been stocking goods under a working relationship with Silverman following the consolidation sale held in 1989.

Ad plan: Once the sales goal was set, an advertising plan was created. It featured ads in the *Los Angeles Times* before and during the sale; advertising cost 3%-5% of the estimated sales volume.

Silverman created the ads in-house. "We didn't like the wording on some of them," Thielman admits, calling a few "garish." But after several alterations, he approved them all. "They captured the customer's attention and got people in [the store]."

Thielman paid to place the ads and for postage on memo goods delivered for the sale. He paid for Silverman's services on a declining percentage basis: Silverman received 15% of net sales for the first two weeks of the sale and 5% in the final month.

Though the sale reached its stated sale goals, earnings through 1991 weren't strong enough to climb out of Chapter 11. Late in the year, as creditors prepared to force the firm to sell assets, Thielman decided to call it quits and turned to Silverman for help with the final sale.

Overriding State Law

Federal bankruptcy court can override state regulation of liquidation sales, as jewelers in Albany, N.Y., learned recently. New York state law says no new merchandise can be brought in for a liquidation sale. But a federal bankruptcy judge allowed Silverman Jewelers Consultants to bring in new merchandise for jeweler Steven Kretser's Christmas-time liquidation sale. Judge Justin H. Mahoney, concurring with the bankruptcy trustee, said this would raise the most money for Kretser's creditors.

The state jewelers association opposed the plan and gave the judge a petition signed by local jewelers. They and the Jewelers Vigilance Committee said the sale would mislead consumers and draw off business from local jewelers hard-hit by recession. *The Daily Gazette,* a local paper, also questioned the judge's decision, saying it would primarily benefit liquidator, not the creditor, and "could push a few...struggling [jewelers] over the edge themselves."

Nancy Connell, spokesperson for the state attorney general, says New York had "no option" but to accept the judge's order. Not only do federal courts supersede state law, but New York's own general business law allows "the order of a court of competent jurisdiction" to override it. Thus, "the bankruptcy court can order something at variance with the [state] law," says Connell.

Still, a bankruptcy court order *isn't* absolute. Joel Windman, JVC general counsel and executive vice president, says a state can appeal a bankruptcy court decision to the U.S. Court of Appeals. He contends that FTC guidelines on deceptive pricing apply in such cases and that the judge exceeded his authority in his order.

Local jewelers and the state did have some say in the sale's conduct: Mahoney approved a state request that ads say the sale included new merchandise and that the new wares be displayed separately from other merchandise.

This was little comfort to Albany's jewelry community. "My biggest concern is that allowing this will have a domino effect," says Albany jeweler David Adams, who represented the state association at the Kretser hearings. "Many jewelers hanging on by their thumbs will be hurt and may go bankrupt." And that would mean more liquidation sales, raising the issue anew.

Sales Regulation Information Sources

You may consult a number of sources to learn about national, state and local regulation of retail sales.

The closest source is our own attorney. Another is a regional Better Business Bureau. And law libraries of local colleges should have copies of Federal Trade Commission guidelines on pricing.

After that, contact your municipal administrator's office (mayor, township or borough manager), municipal attorney or municipal clerk.

At the county level, contact the head of the consumer affairs or consumer protection department or the district attorney's office. Also check whether the county or state has a Business Regulation department that might handle such queries.

Sources at national, state and territorial levels are listed below (current as of February 1992):

NATIONAL

Council of Better Business Bureaus,
4200 Wilson Blvd., Arlington, Va. 22203;
(703) 276-0100.
Council of State Chambers of Commerce,
122 C St., N.W., Suite 330, Washington, D.C. 20002;
(202) 484-8103.
Chamber of Commerce of the United States,
1615 H St., N.W., Washington, D.C. 20062;
(202)659-6000.
Federal Trade Commission, Sixth St. & Pennsylvania Ave., Washington, D.C. 20580; (202)326-2182 (Public Affairs), (202)326-3238 (Consumer Protection).
National Institute of Municipal Law Officers,
1000 Connecticut Ave. N.W., Suite 902,
Washington, D.C. 20036; (202)466-5424

STATES/D.C.

Alabama
Attorney General: Montgomery, (205) 242-7300.
Consumer Protection: Montgomery, (205) 242-7300.
Alaska
Attorney General: Juneau, (907) 465-3600.
Consumer Protection: Anchorage, (907) 279-0428.
Arizona
Attorney General: Phoenix, (602) 542-4266.
Licensing & Enforcement: Phoenix, (602) 542-1610.
Arkansas
Attorney General: Little Rock, (501) 682-2007.
Consumer Advocacy: Little Rock, (501) 682-2007.
California
Attorney General: Sacramento, (916) 324-5437.
Consumer Affairs Department: Sacramento, (915) 445-4465.
Colorado
Attorney General: Denver, (303) 866-5005.
Consumer Counsel Office: Denver, (303) 894-2121.

Connecticut
Attorney General: Hartford, (203) 566-2026.
Consumer Protection Department: Hartford, (203) 566-4999.
Delaware
Attorney General: Wilmington, (302) 571-3838.
Consumer Affair Division: Dover, (302) 571-3250.
District of Columbia
Corporation Counsel Office: Washington, D.C., (202)727-6248.
Consumer Affairs Section: Washington, D.C., (202) 727-3500.
Consumer & Regulatory Affairs Department: Washington, D.C., (202) 727-7170.
Florida
Attorney General: Tallahassee, (904) 487-1963.
Business Regulation Department: Tallahassee, (904) 488-7114.
Georgia
Attorney General: Atlanta, (404) 656-4585.
Consumer Affairs Department: Atlanta, (404) 656-3836.
Hawaii
Attorney General: Honolulu, (808) 548-4740.
Commerce and Consumer Affairs Department: Honolulu, (808) 548-7505.
Idaho
Attorney General: Boise, (208) 334-2400.
Business Regulations Division: Boise, (208) 334-2400.
Illinois
Attorney General: Springfield, (217) 782-1090.
Consumer Protection Division: Springfield, (217) 782-1090.
Indiana
Attorney General: Indianapolis, (317) 232-6201.
Commerce Department: Indianapolis, (317) 232-8800.
Iowa
Attorney General: Des Moines, (515) 281-8373.
Consumer Protection: Des Moines, (515) 281-5926.
Kansas
Attorney General: Topeka, (913) 296-2215.
Consumer Protection Division: Topeka, (913) 296-3751.
Kentucky
Attorney General: Frankfort, (502) 564-7600.
Consumer Protection Division: Frankfort, (502) 564-2200.
Louisiana
Attorney General: Baton Rouge, (504) 342-7013.
Uniform Commercial Code Division: Baton Rouge, (504) 922-1314.
Maine
Attorney General: Augusta, (207) 289-3661.
Consumer Fraud Division: Augusta, (207) 289-3661.
Maryland
Attorney General: Annapolis, (301) 576-6300.
Consumer Protection: Annapolis, (301) 576-6550.
Massachusetts
Attorney General: Boston, (617) 727-2200.
Consumer Affairs & Business Regulation Office: Boston, (617) 727-7755.
Michigan
Attorney General: Lansing, (517) 373-1110.
Consumer Protection: Lansing, (517) 373-1140.
Minnesota
Attorney General: St. Paul, (612) 297-4272.
Consumer Services: St. Paul, (612) 296-2306.

Mississippi
Attorney General: Jackson, (601) 359-3680.
Consumer Protection Division: Jackson, (601) 359-7063.
Missouri
Attorney General: Jefferson City, (601) 751-3321.
Public Protection: Jefferson City, (601) 751-3321.
Montana
Attorney General: Helena, (406) 444-2026.
Legal & Consumer Affairs Unit: Helena, (406) 444-3553.
Nebraska
Attorney General: Lincoln, (402) 471-2682.
Consumer Protection Division: Lincoln, (402) 471-2682.
Nevada
Attorney General: Carson City, (702) 687-4170.
Consumer Affairs Division: Las Vegas, (702) 486-4150.
New Hampshire
Attorney General: Concord, (603) 271-3655.
Consumer Protection Division: Concord,
(603) 271-3641.
New Jersey
Attorney General: Trenton, (609) 292-4925.
Consumer Protection Office: Newark, (201) 648-3622.
New Mexico
Attorney General: Santa Fe, (505) 827-6000.
Consumer Protection Division: Santa Fe,
(505) 827-6060.
New York
Attorney General: Albany, (518) 474-7330.
Consumer Protection Board: Albany, (518) 474-3514.
North Carolina
Attorney General: Raleigh, (919) 733-3377.
Consumer Protection Section: Raleigh, (919) 733-7741.
North Dakota
Attorney General: Bismarck, (701) 224-2210.
Consumer Fraud Division: Bismarck, (701) 224-3040.
Ohio
Attorney General: Columbus, (614) 466-4320.
Consumer Protection: Columbus, (614) 466-8831.
Oklahoma
Attorney General: Oklahoma City, (405) 521-3921.
Consumer Division: Oklahoma City, (405) 521-3921.
Oregon
Attorney General: Salem, (503) 378-6002.
Pennsylvania
Attorney General: Harrisburg, (717) 787-3391.
Consumer Protection Division: Harrisburg, (717) 787-9707.
Rhode Island
Attorney General: Providence, (401) 274-4400.
Consumer Protection Unit: Providence, (401) 274-4400.

South Carolina
Attorney General: Columbia, (803) 734-3970.
Consumer Protection: Columbia, (803) 734-9458.
South Dakota
Attorney General: Rapid City, (605) 773-3215.
Consumer Protection Division: Rapid City, (605) 773-3215.
Tennessee
Attorney General: Nashville, (615) 741-6474.
Consumer Affairs Division: Nashville, (615) 741-4737.
Texas
Attorney General: Austin, (512) 463-2191.
Consumer Protection Division: Austin, (512) 463-2070.
Utah
Attorney General: Salt Lake City, (801) 538-1015.
Consumer Protection Division: Salt Lake City,
(801) 530-6619.
Vermont
Attorney General: Montpelier, (802) 828-3171.
Public Protection Division: Montpelier, (802) 828-3171.
Virginia
Attorney General: Richmond, (804) 786-2071.
Commerce Department: Richmond, (804) 367-8519.
Washington
Attorney General: Olympia, (206) 753-2550.
Citizens Affairs: Olympia, (206) 753-6780.
West Virginia
Attorney General: Charleston, (304) 348-2021.
Consumer Protection: Charleston, (304) 348-8986.
Wisconsin
Attorney General: Madison, (608) 266-1221.
Consumer Protection Division: Madison, (608) 266-2426.
Wyoming
Attorney General: Cheyenne, (307) 777-7841.
Consumer Affairs Division: Cheyenne, (307) 777-7891.

TERRITORIES

American Samoa
Attorney General: Pago Pago, (011-684) 633-4163.
Public Information: Pago Pago, (011-684) 633-4191.
Guam
Office of the Governor: Agana, (671) 472-8931.
Puerto Rico
Justice Department: San Juan, (809) 721-3084.
Commerce Department: San Juan, (809) 721-1451.
Virgin Islands
Justice Department: St. Thomas, (809) 774-5666.
Licensing & Consumer Affairs Department: St. Thomas,
(809) 774-3130.

That 12-Letter Word

Editorial ◆ *November 1991*

Depending on necessity and personal preference, the person running a company can take all sorts of actions if business falls off.

Cost-cutting generally comes first. Little things such as turning off unneeded lights. The travel and entertainment budget is another likely candidate. So are new carpeting and furniture.

After this, it gets more serious. A freeze on plans for the new branch store. No new merchandise purchases unless the piece is practically presold. Then the freeze extends to new hires. Finally come the layoffs.

All of these proven ways to make a company better able to survive hard economic times.

They have something else in common: they're all negative.

A survival plan that relies too much on "don'ts" is unhealthy. You need positives to balance negatives and, in selling, the key positive is productivity.

If business in your community truly is in a deep recession, it's probably next to impossible to get a person to increase sales by 20% or 30%. But even in a recession, there are unending opportunities for sales of jewelry (birthdays and anniversaries keep coming no matter what) and there always are people in any community who seem recession-proof. It's a question of identifying them and tempting them to buy. That's where superior sales skills come in.

Productivity isn't just a question of making more sales; it's also a question of identifying potential buyers and then making the sale. It's a question of creativity. Of knowledge, both product and psychological. Of enthusiasm.

Maybe the person in line to be laid off can't be transformed into a top producer. But it's worth trying hard to find out. If the attempt fails, the answer isn't necessarily to let him or her go and leave a gap in your sales force. Hire someone better instead.

For some reason, productivity is a 12-letter word many jewelers find distasteful. It's almost as though it's bad taste to suggest that people be held accountable for their output. Consider what the magazine's retail panel has to say on the subject. Asked to rate various staff characteristics, 83% of panelists said their employees' loyalty was either very good or excellent. But only 46% had such nice things to say about their productivity.

This is not to say that many of these jewelers don't wish their salespeople were more productive. They do. But too often, they have no formal plans that set sales goals nor regular, formal review sessions with employees to see whether they're meeting their goals.

Some jewelers, particularly those with multiple stores, measure performance closely and constantly, of course. The president of one midsize western chain had this to say: "Production is [our] No. 1 [concern]. We measure sales by the hour, the day, the week, the month, the year!" This man knows exactly what's selling, who's selling it and how much profit each sale brings in.

Such intensity could be out of place in a smaller operation. But setting sales and other goals (on such issues as tardiness, absenteeism, customer service, educational achievements and so on) are not only practical but sensible for any store. The goal setting will be meaningless unless there is a review process to check whether the goals were met and if not, why not.

The formality of the program can vary a lot. In some larger organizations, it's very cut-and-dried with detailed written evaluations and complex scoring systems to rate performance. In a small store with only a few full-time employees, it is and probably should be much more informal. Goals still should be written at the beginning of the year (or whatever reporting period you use). This involves commitment in a way that a spoken agreement never can. The review also should be informal, a time not only to see how well goals were met but also time for employer and employee to bring up any issues they've had on their minds. The process, by the way, is a great way to encourage frank and fair discussion with family as well as non-family staffers.

One final point. No process that measures sales goals is complete unless it contains incentives. If non-producers stand to lose their jobs, then top producers must see a bigger paycheck or some other reward.

Credit Where Credit Is Due

January 1991

When a customer wants to spend $1,000 on a watch at Orin Jewelers in Garden City, Mich., owner Orin Mazzoni is confident he can upgrade the sale to $1,500 or even $2,000. To make the sale, he gives credit where credit is due: to credit.

"I can easily finance the balance by approving the customer for our private-label credit card," he explains.

But Jeweler David Craig Rotenberg, owner of David Craig Jewelers, Newtown, Pa., found his customers weren't interested when he offered to finance purchases interest-free for one year. Despite extensive promotion of the credit offer last year he received no response. Not surprisingly, he hasn't considered offering his own private-label card.

Between these two extremes are thousands of independent retailers juggling their acceptance of credit with what they can afford, what their customers want and what's available. The choices range from major national consumer credit cards such as MasterCard, Discover and American Express to in-store credit with a private-label card or other financing.

Each type of credit program has advantages and disadvantages. Credit limits and lengthy application processes associated with national consumer cards can hamper sales, for example. And retailers say they often have to wait too long for reimbursement. But in-store credit programs can be considerable workload and can strain a jeweler's resources.

A hybrid of these services—national private-label credit cards especially for jewelers—has begun to attract attention. A growing number of firms offer jewelers a nationwide credit program with faster and easier credit approval, reimbursement and record-keeping. They also assume the bad-debt risk.

The question jewelers must ask is: "Can this boost my profits?"

Mazzoni answers yes. He bolstered his credit arsenal with Artége and Diamonds Unlimited credit services—two of the most recent entries in the market—when his bank discontinued its private-label service in a merger last year. He wanted to continue with a private-label card because in the five years he had the service through the bank, he signed up more than 4,000 customers—1,500 of them active users. He estimates these cardholders account for 15% of sales at his three Detroit-area stores.

Now he expects to sign most of these customers to Diamonds Unlimited, a service begun in July 1990 by Stuckey Diamonds Inc., Houston. He uses the Artége card more selectively, offering one- or two-year financing packages to customers interested in lower interest payments with preset payment schedules.

National consumer cards: Credit in most retail jewelry stores centers on national consumer credit cards. A recent JCK reader poll indicates nearly all jewelers accept MasterCard or Visa. About 79% accept American Express

and more than 73% accept Discover cards. About 30% offer in-store credit, and about 10% accept Diners Club and Carte Blanche cards.

Retailers who accept credit cards say they account for 30% of total sales on average, though some claim as much as 90%. Major cards account for about 83% of credit sales.

Meanwhile, jewelers who offer private-label credit (via a card or other in-store credit service) say it accounts for about 40% of their credit sales.

Convenience: Retailers who use only national cards call customer convenience the primary reason.

"We get more impulse buyers using them," says Jennie Lee Ellis, gemologist at Ellis Jewelry Inc., Gunnison, Colo. The store is a family operation (her father owns it and is the only other employee) in a college town and winter resort. Tourists often call after leaving town to order, on credit, an item they saw while browsing at the store. Credit cards account for only 5% of total sales, but Ellis say she wouldn't be in business without them. "Any retailer who tries to survive on cash alone is fooling himself and cheating himself," she says.

With a small store, however, she pays higher-than-average rates to process her Visa and MasterCard sales. With under $100,000 annual volume, her discount rate (the fee charged by the credit card company) is a high 3.5% of each purchase. "To me it's worth it because of the convenience and because I get the cash right away," she notes. Larger retailers pay rates of about 2%.

American Express rates are higher—too high for Ellis. "It's not worth it because of the fees," she says. "And I have to write a deposit and send it through the mail to them. We wouldn't see the money for weeks."

Paul Cohen, owner of Continental Jewelers in Wilmington, Del., says he doesn't like American Express because of the way it has marketed jewelry. American Express recently agreed to pay damages to several hundred cardholders to settle a lawsuit in which several Pennsylvania retailers alleged the firm misrepresented diamond quality in sales brochures. "We might lose one sale a year because we don't have the card," says Cohen. "But it hasn't been a liability."

Still, the majority of jewelers accept American Express cards. In Newtown, Pa., Rotenberg's store does so much business on American Express cards that it qualifies for a lower discount rate. Nearly half his sales are on American Express or Visa cards.

In-house credit: The mixture of in-house credit and national credit card use varies from store to store. Some retailers prefer the sometimes healthy profits gained from extending their own credit. If a jeweler can borrow money from the bank at 12% interest as a preferred commercial customer, for example, he then can lend the money to customers at 18% interest. Others prefer to let Visa or MasterCard handle the paperwork and take on the risk of bad debt.

Cohen at Continental Jewelers falls into the latter group. "We don't push credit," he says. "Part of me says we can use in-store payments as a profit center, but we'd rather keep that credit line for other uses."

Cohen says the use of credit as a primary means to create sales can have a negative impact on long-term profits. "In economic crunches, you are going to become your own banker," he warns. "Suddenly, you may not be collecting and will have to reduce the growth of your receivables. You can charge all the interest in the world, but it won't be worth it if you aren't getting paid."

On the opposite side of the spectrum is Dale Briman, owner of Briman's Leading Jeweler, Topeka, Kan. He prefers in-house credit at his two stores.

"It's a profit center as long as we can afford to handle it," he reports. Briman says he works closely with his bank and has never paid more than prime rate for financing. About 45% of his total sales are from an in-store credit program that he calls a contract sale.

To quality for the program, a customer need only have a major credit card in good standing. "That's enough to give him credit up to $2,000," he says. Briman then sets up a repayment schedule, generally for 12 months, and provides the customer with a payment book, which requires less paper handling and lower labor costs than monthly statements. If a contract-sale customer becomes delinquent, Briman follows up with a collection schedule. A few frequent buyers receive monthly statements and agree to pay off a balance in less than three months.

During the last months of 1990, Briman Added the Artége card to his credit lineup. Though he hadn't signed up any customers by November, he planned to use it to help customers finance more expensive purchases. The card offers customers a low interest rate (10.8%) and helps Briman avoid extending credit beyond the profit point. "You have got to be careful not to overload with accounts receivable," he says.

For jewelers only: To serve jewelers who seek the best of both worlds, a growing number of firms offer private-label credit services nationwide. Last year alone, Artége of Dallas, Diamonds Unlimited of Houston and Jeweler's Choice of Farmington Hills, Mich., joined Jewelry Express of Southfield, Mich., and Beneficial Corp.'s Bencharge of Peapack, N.J., in the national jewelry credit card market.

While Bencharge has been available to retailers of all stripes for more than eight years, the entrance of Jewelry Express three years ago stirred up interest in jewelry-specific credit cards.

But interest doesn't guarantee success. The card vendors face a huge majority of retailers whose use of national credit cards is unwaveringly loyal and whose suspicion of new forms of credit is intense. Still, many jewelers indicated to JCK they may consider private-label cards in the future.

Jewelry Express, which recently altered its fee schedule to accommodate its growing retailer base reports about 3,000 cardholders. Artége and Diamonds Unlimited each report about 500 users. Jeweler's Choice has 175 users.

Bencharge hasn't calculated the number of jewelry stores among the 4,500 retailers using its service, but Marketing Director Stephen Allan says they place in the top 10.

Advantages: Major selling points of the private-label companies are higher and faster credit approvals and lower discount fees than offered by national consumer credit-card services. Diamonds Unlimited, for example, provides a personal computer to the retailer to hasten the application process, says President Jim Stuckey. Paula Shaver, owner of Diamonds Plus jewelry stores in Jonesboro and Paragould, Ark., praises the on-screen application "form" and the high approval rate of the Diamonds Unlimited service. In September, she says, she made an additional $23,000 in sales using the service and qualified the users for up to $80,000 in credit.

Other firms provide a credit-card processing terminal through which applications can be approved or denied. At least one firm is experimenting with faxing applications for approval.

Nearly all private-label firms will approve a minimum credit amount in minutes (generally $1,000 to $2,000), but the criteria for acceptance vary. Some retailers prefer very high acceptance rates (nine out of ten, for instance) while others want only select, low-risk cardholders. Jewelers should consider which strategy would fit best their stores' financial structure and quiz credit-card firms about approval rates and amounts.

Jewelers also should consider how much they pay the major credit-card companies in discount fees to process credit-card purchases. The fee drops as credit-card sales volume rises, but independent jewelers may not do enough business to qualify for a reduction. However, private-label firms, under an agreement with major card companies, can process major card purchases at lower rates as a volume user. "It's possible that some retailers may sign up just to take advantage of those low discount fees," says Barry Scholnick, head of operations at Artége. His firm's card, which started by offering credit to buyers of art works, has been working with state jewelry associations to secure customized rates for member retailers, he adds.

Other advantages include quick reimbursement (one or two days), no need to worry about bad debt and some firms' willingness to customize financing packages for specific purchases or for a promotion. Thus, the retailer may offer a zero-interest, first-year financing promotion to customers who use the private-label card. The retailer agrees to pay a higher discount fee for use of the card at a lower interest rate.

In addition to the financial incentives, Cohen cites the marketing value of a private-label card. "Every time the person pulls out a wallet to buy something and the card with our name on it flips out, it's a reminder," he says. Most card companies will imprint the retailer's name and the customer's name on the card.

Traditional marketing services also are available. Many of the firms provide full media kits, including camera-ready ads, point-of purchase displays, promotional mailers and statement stuffers.

Proving ground: Despite features to entice jewelers, private-label card companies still have to prove themselves to most retailers. While many private-label card users point to higher sales volume and greater sales per card, others are not quite sold.

Rotenberg, at David Craig Jewelers, says he has received information about the various cards available, but remains uninterested. "I can offer the companies big sales, but not high volume," he observes. Considering the start-up costs associated with the cards, he says the expenses would outweigh the advantages.

But those who use national private-label cards appear to be staying with them. Shaver says she signs up two to three new customers each day to her store's private-label card. She does point out that she sells jewelry, not credit. But when a customer is interested in buying, she says, the private-label card is there to help close the sale.

Preparing For Recession

January 1991

Businesspeople have grown pretty pessimistic about the economy, says Dr. George Lucas, associate professor and interim chairman of the marketing department at Memphis State University, Memphis, Tenn. "But retailers who manage their resources wisely can survive, and some will even do quite well," says Lucas.

Doing well this year requires becoming a better overall business person, he says. But how should you go about this?

BDO Seidman, a New York-based accounting and consulting giant, advises you to reduce costs, improve inventory management and improve cash flow. The firm offers these tips to help you along the way.

Cutting costs
• Remember that your primary goal is to increase profitability. Be sure a cost reduction never results in lower revenues.
• Close all unprofitable operations, eliminate any low margin items and make sure that promotional costs sufficiently benefit the business.
• Hold the line on compensation increases for your employees and lay off any excess personnel. Provide training to improve employee efficiency.
• Offer incentives that encourage cost-cutting and lift morale as employees feel a sense of participation.
• Consider retaining a property tax consultant to negotiate a reduction in property tax assessments and a risk management firm to minimize risks and assess insurance requirements.

• Determine whether you can reduce your firm's telephone and fax costs by switching long-distance vendors.

Inventory management
• Keep track of all inventory, which types sell fastest and how much time to allow when ordering more so you're neither out of stock nor holding a piece in the safe for weeks at a time.
• Improve sales forecasting to better anticipate what items you need when.
• Remember that cost-savings associated with volume purchases should justify the cost of holding the additional inventory.

Cash management
• Keep credit policies stringent enough to minimize bad debt losses, but flexible enough not to restrict sales.
• Put your credit policy in writing and make sure employees enforce it.
• Mail billings promptly and make sure all information—from the amount to the address—is correct to avoid delays. Charge interest on late payments.
• Pay your own bills early enough to take advantage of early-payment discounts, but not so early that you can't take advantage of temporary excess cash by placing it in short-term investments.
• Consider an integrated inventory control, invoicing, accounts receivable and payable computer system.

Cooperative Advertising: Twice The Bang For Half The Buck

October 1990

The mention of co-op advertising usually brings one of two responses:

"It's great—twice the bang for half the buck!" Or "What a headache! All that paperwork. You have to use their ads and you have to wait forever for your money!"

These responses capsulize the benefits and drawbacks of cooperative advertising, which involves a retailer and manufacturer splitting ad costs toward the mutually beneficial goal of selling more product.

Used properly, co-op advertising can generate a great return for the jeweler, says John L. Davis, president of Longines-Wittnauer Watch Co. It's a win-win situation, adds Andrew Kohler, president of the A.B. Kohler Co. ad agency in Parsippany, N.J. The retailer and the supplier both benefit.

And 90% of respondents to a recent JCK Retail Panel poll have used co-op advertising in the past three years. But many say there's plenty of room for improvement in how the programs work.

How they work: Co-op plans vary by manufacturer. Typically, though, a plan allows for a 50-50 split of all ad costs up to an amount equaling 5% of a retailer's annual purchases from a supplier. If a jeweler buys $10,000 worth of merchandise, for example, he is entitled to $500 (5% of $10,000) in advertising money from the supplier. The supplier pays half the cost of each ad until he's given the jeweler $500.

If the jeweler places two ads that cost $500 each, for example, the supplier pays $250 per ad. If the jeweler places one ad that costs $500, the supplier pays $250 and credits $250 toward a future ad. (If the jeweler doesn't run another ad in an allotted time, the credit expires.) If the ad costs $1,500, the supplier's maximum obligation remains $500, and the jeweler has to foot the remaining $1,000.

So it's easy to see how co-op ads help the supplier trying to attract more dealers. If two suppliers have a similar product, a savvy retailer likely will choose the one that offers co-op. Why? That supplier, in effect, offers a discount on ad services and also demonstrates a commitment to moving product.

Retailers speak: Even if retailers have complaints about co-op programs, they say they're well-worth the headache. Of the 90% of JCK panelists who have used co-op, none plans to stop. Fifty percent say the availability of co-op funds *does* influence them to buy a particular line. And only 5% say they've had any truly bad experiences with co-op programs.

But there is room for improvement, starting with communication, say the panelists. Their most-often-mentioned complaints center on a lack of creative freedom, followed by complicated paperwork and/or a long wait for reimbursement.

Many suppliers require co-op participants to use the materials provided. For some jewelers, this can be a problem.

"Co-op advertisements and ad slicks tend to make you look like all the other stores using the same material," says W. Stephen Brown of Brown Goldsmiths & Co., Freeport, Me. "It is challenging to meet the requirements of co-op or to use ready-made ad slicks and still maintain a unique image." Brown, a predominantly custom jeweler, says that running the same ad as his competitors would damage his image of offering unique merchandise.

Panelists also say some co-op ads are hard to customize to include their store name.

"The ads cannot be modified easily enough," says Lou Castiglione of Gem Jewelers Inc., Gloversville, N.Y. "It's mostly advertising product, not the store." Castiglione says manufacturers should realize the importance of adding the store name to personalize ads.

Kohler suggests a simple custom touch: put the same border around your co-op ad slick that you use around your other ads. It helps to identify you, and most manufacturers won't object as long as it's in keeping with the ad image. Kohler does caution, however, that a major reason to use co-op programs is to associate your store with the prestige of a national brand. So in some cases, you may want to forego the border to keep the image of the national ad.

Leeway: Restrictions aren't always the case. Brown admits there is room for creativity in some co-op programs. And Daniel Moyer of Moyer Jewelers in Carmel, Ind., says some firms are quite open to creative ideas, adapting marketing philosophies that have been successful in a jeweler's market. In Moyer's case, it was billboards. Outdoor advertising works well in his market, he says, so he persuaded a co-op supplier to change its rules and allow for billboard ads. This fall, he has two large boards on major thoroughfares in Indianapolis.

Don't be afraid to ask about other alternative means of using co-op money. Some manufacturers agree to cosponsor community, charity or sporting events, or to advertise in small local publications or playbills.

Scott See, co-op manager for Rolex Watch, recommends such sponsorship. "We've found that jewelers who sponsor community events get many, many more bangs for their bucks," he says. "It generates unbelievable goodwill and free publicity."

Complexity: Panelists also complain about the complicated paperwork associated with co-op programs. That shouldn't be a problem, says Diane Hornberger, advertising director for Krementz & Co., Newark, N.J. Krementz practices what it preaches: it requires only a tearsheet of the ad and proof of payment.

"We're very forgiving," Hornberger says. "If they do it wrong, we accept it and just ask them to do it another way next time."

Kohler advocates steering away from complicated programs. He admits that some manufacturers make their programs complicated deliberately so retailers won't use them. But those manufacturers miss out on the advantages of selling more product thanks to name recognition from co-op ads, he says.

Several panelists also have had problems collecting co-op money from manufacturers. Most co-op plans require the retailer to foot the initial bill, then submit proofs and invoices for reimbursement. Hornberger says Krementz sends all reimbursements within a month of receiving the proofs. Unfortunately, retailers say not all manufacturers are as conscientious. Kohler stresses that though some suppliers may be slow in paying, that's not an inherent problem with co-op itself. He notes, too, that many suppliers have to deal with slow-paying retailers.

Some suppliers offer credit toward future product purchases instead of cash reimbursement. This is entirely acceptable, even if it doesn't help the retailer's immediate cash flow. But suppliers who offer credit in lieu of cash should spell this out in the initial agreement so retailers aren't caught by surprise.

Whither thou co-op? Co-op funds can be used in any form of media the manufacturer and retailer agree upon. Print advertising is the top choice, with almost all manufacturers interviewed by JCK indicating they offer prepared ad slicks. But a jeweler must determine what works best in his market, then work with the manufacturer to make sure the money is spent wisely.

Ad slicks usually leave blank spaces for the jeweler to add his logo and store information. Even though some panelists say there's not enough space, it's not difficult to add an inch or two to a newspaper ad—especially if you change the border.

Some manufacturers offer broadcast-quality videotapes, making TV ads more affordable for smaller stores. Such tapes allow time at the end for the retailer's tag.

For radio, "local sound" is important so consider allowing the local station to produce the commercial, say marketing experts. Many stations will create the ad for free with the purchase of ad time. Naturally, you must submit the finished ad to the supplier for approval before running it. Get the approval in writing.

One print ad option gives the appearance of advertising on a national basis. Many national magazines are published in regional editions, with some of the ads changing from region to region. A supplier may pay $20,000 to place a merchandise ad in every issue, for example. This covers the cost of breaking down all color on a page into the three primary colors (red, yellow, blue) plus black. There is one page negative, or plate, for each color. The red, yellow and blue plates remain the same in every edition, but the black plate containing the store's name can be changed at a cost of about $1,500 (which the jeweler normally pays). Consumers are impressed because the jeweler appears to be advertising nationally, though the store name appears in only one edition.

Marketing experts advise a multi-media approach when advertising, backing up newspaper ads with radio, radio with direct mail, and so forth. And if you're on a limited budget, alternate weeks of heavy frequency with weeks off. If you can afford to run 10 radio spots a month, for example, schedule five in one week, none the next, five the next and none the next. Listeners who hear the ad one week and again in two weeks perceive that they've heard it in the interim, as well.

Alternatives: Not all suppliers stick to a standard advertising reimbursement, and not all are bound to traditional media. Rolex Watch and Martin Jewelers Westfield in Westfield, N.J., for example, teamed up to sponsor the opening concert of the Westfield Symphony Orchestra's 1989 season. Jeweler Davia Freeman felt this would be the most effective way to stress her store's ties to this affluent community. She approached symphony officials with the idea and found that for $14,000 the concert could be hers. Rolex was skeptical at first, but agreed to pay half the cost after Freeman presented a detailed marketing plan prepared by the symphony.

Rolex and Martin Jewelers Westfield were mentioned in paid ads placed in the concert programs and the community newspaper, in a direct-mail campaign conducted by the symphony and in much of the free publicity generated by the concert. The co-op program not only met Freeman's goal of stressing her ties to the community, but it won a Silver Peacock Award in JCK's 1990 Excellence in Marketing competition.

Other suppliers offer services, such as sales training, to retailers who buy their products. Aurion International, Van Nuys, Cal., offers to arrange a one-day, in-store sales training seminar conducted by noted sales trainer Leonard Zell. Aurion first figures 10% of its sales to the retailer during the program period, then pays half that amount toward the seminar, up to a maximum $1,300. The jeweler also pays Zell's travel and accommodation costs.

Aurion President Bob Sears says a well-trained staff is a store's No. 1 asset, and this program is a way for his firm to help clients in return for their support.

Catalog and flier programs are another popular co-op venture. Typically, a manufacturer prints a catalog of its merchandise and offers it to retailers for use as a direct-mail piece. Some manufacturers offer the catalog at no cost with the purchase of a certain amount of merchandise. Others provide a limited number of fliers for free and make additional copies available for purchase. Still other firms charge a nominal or even a not-so-nominal fee. Regardless, most catalogs have a space where the jeweler can add the store name.

The importance of catalogs and fliers as direct mail has grown as families get busier and have less time to spend shopping in stores. James Porte, president of the Jewelry Marketing Institute, New York City, says a catalog is a necessity—not a luxury—for any jeweler who wants to stay competitive in the marketplace. And the key to remain competitive is learning how to get the most for the money. Can you afford *not* to take advantage of co-op programs?

Why A Retirement Plan?

November 1987

How much should employees be paid? More important-ly, how much should *your* employees be paid? And how should you go about establishing a pay system which is fair to them, yet economically feasible for you?

A compensation plan must:

• Attract quality employees to your business;
• Motivate them to perform;
• Satisfy them enough to keep them with your firm;
• Be cost effective for you.

Perception is the name of the game, say Steven E. Gross, vice president of Hay Management Consultants, and Bruce J. Goodman, a consultant with the Hay Group. All objectives of a successful compensation plan are based upon employees' perception of that plan. They must *perceive* that they're being compensated fairly, and that the plan is consis-tent. Otherwise, even the most generous compensation pack-age will fail to achieve its objectives. The following blue-prints for a compensation plan are based on an interview with Gross and Goodman.

The four objectives

1. Attracting quality employees: Is your compensation plan competitive with the marketplace? How do you stack up? Above average? Average? Below average? Can your employees make more money elsewhere doing the same job? Are other employees within the organization being paid the same for doing the same?

2. Keeping quality employees: Do your employees per-ceive your compensation plan to be fair and consistent? If the monetary compensation is lower than at other, similar business-es, what other benefits are offered to keep employees with you?

3. Motivation: Does your plan motivate your employees to perform? Is pay linked to performance? Are there rewards for good performance and, conversely, are there penalties for poor or non-performance? Is there a chance for advancement?

4. Cost effectiveness: How does the plan work into your budget? Is your payroll/profit percentage too low? Too high? You have to pay what you must to keep quality employees, but not more than you can afford.

Setting up your plan

The cardinal rule is: Put it in writing!!! Whether it covers 7 employees or 7 million, every compensation plan—regard-less of what it offers—must include a *formal written policy*. A written policy gives both employer and employee a point of reference—and if legal disputes ever arise, the formal written plan may be your best defense.

Issues and answers: Before trying to establish a com-pensation plan, an employer must answer some questions. ¯

1. What sort of business is involved? Is it a high-volume, low-markup mass merchandiser? Is it in the middle? Or is it a low-volume, high-markup specialty store? The type of busi-ness affects the type of employees needed and, subsequent-

ly, how much they are paid. Car dealers can make money selling Chevrolets or Mercedes, but their clienteles are differ-ent and their sales staffs have different images. There also is a big difference in the number of cars each dealer must sell to make the same profit.

2. Should he have full-time or part-time employees? Which would be more cost-effective? Does the store have enough traffic to warrant all full-time employees, or will it be adequately staffed by well-scheduled part-timers? Can he find adequately experienced part-time help? Using part-timers can cut the cost of benefits offered, but be careful about schedul-ing them for almost full-time hours. Legal problems can arise if an employee works full-time hours but receives part-time benefits and compensation.

3. What skill levels are needed in employees? Would four experienced employees bring better results than two experienced and two inexperienced employees? At first glance, the answer seems obvious, but remember that expe-rienced employees must be paid accordingly. Can less-expe-rienced employees be trained to perform some of the tasks that more experienced employees now handle?

4. How much time does the owner/manager want to spend in the store? Does he want to take a more or less active role in day-to-day operations? This is a determining factor in answering the two previous questions and in setting the prop-er experience and compensation levels for employees.

Once an employer has answered these questions, he is ready to begin building his compensation package.

How much? How does an employer determine an employee's worth? Gross and Goodman say experience is the most important factor to consider. Look at the size of the job, and consider three major points:

• The skill level and/or technical know-how needed to do the job;
• The problem-solving abilities needed for the job;
• The accountability of the person doing the job. For what is he responsible?

Always compare the *job*, not the employee, stress Goodman and Gross. How well the employee performs the job also determines how he is compensated, but compare the job itself first to get a basic idea of what its salary should be. Establish salary ranges, within which each employee is paid based on his performance. Ranges should be based on competitive pay and on the value of the job internally.

To establish ranges, Goodman and Gross suggest you:

1. Determine what everyone's duties are. Put them in writing.

2. Determine the value of each position, based on the content of the job. Evaluate the position, not the person holding it. There may be different levels of the same posi-tion, i.e., senior and junior sales executive, etc.

3. Assign a value to each position, after weighing the skills needed to fill it. In a jewelry store, skills taken into account may include sales, knowledge of gemology, jewelry repair or design skills, supervisory, buying abilities, etc.

4. Total up the weight of each position and rank them in order from low to high. This is the framework for a salary structure. The highest job gets the most compensation, the lowest gets the least. The others fall in ranges in between. Goodman and Gross admit that this doesn't always work as simply as it seems. There are many exceptions; thus a former manager may be paid at a managerial level although he is semi-retired.

5. Compare salaries paid for these positions in similar organizations. Compare duties, not titles. For instance, a manager with the owner on-premises has different duties than a manager with the owner off-premises. The former may even compare in duties with a senior sales associate at another store. Another instance is a manger of one store vs. a manager of three. All are called manager.

6. Once a valid comparison has been made, next determine what the firm is willing to pay. Will it be an average payer (compared to similar firms in the area)? A top payer? Below average? What do other firms offer in terms of benefits and perks? If a particular firm doesn't offer the same benefits or perks, it may have to pay higher salaries; conversely, if it offers more, it may be able to get away with less cash compensation.

Other factors must be considered a well. Gross and Goodman point to location as a determinant, offering this hypothetical example comparing two jewelry stores in metropolitan Philadelphia. One is in the Gallery at Market East—not in the worst part of Philadelphia, but not in the best, either. Its after-five clientele is much different from its daytime shoppers. The other outlet is in the Granite Run Mall in the affluent suburb of Media, Pa. The mall attracts a typical upper-middle class suburban clientele. Commuting distance aside, in which store would most employees prefer to work? And what would entice them to work at the other? This point shows that comparisons cannot always be made on a cash-to-cash basis alone.

The basic conflicts of most compensation plans come from the way employees vs. management view them. Each feels he is responsible for the store's profitability, and each is—but in different ways. Often, employees lose sight of the manager's risks or his years of service and experience. The compensation plan must adequately meet both employee and management needs.

Performance, motivation and compensation

How can an employer motivate his employees to perform? Variable pay is the answer, say Gross and Goodman. Money is the most powerful incentive, and commissions and/or bonuses provide the impetus for an employee to work harder. Commissions and other incentives provide an immediate gratification that year-end bonuses don't. On the other hand, a year-end bonus may amount to more money than the immediate forms of compensation. Gross has found a combination of both to be the most effective means of motivating employees. Goodman says that in either case, the more employees know about their pay system and the better they understand it, the more likely their employer is to achieve the desired results from them.

Promotion and job advancement are another powerful motivator. How does an employer determine when a promotion is warranted?

Again, Gross and Goodman stress the cardinal rule: *Put it in writing.* Each employee should have a written job description. Employees need to know what is required of them. If they and management both know, then they can be fairly evaluated on the basis of how well they perform their tasks.

Promotions need to be real—more than just a new title. A real promotion involves a different job, more responsibility and more compensation.

All employees should be formally evaluated on a regular basis. Gross and Goodman recommend two levels of formal evaluations—one for clerical-type help and one for management. Further, they suggest that both be evaluated at least once a year, and clerical help possibly more frequently.

Formal reviews should be documented. In case the employer needs to fire the employee, a documented poor review may be adequate proof in a court case, especially if the employee in question is over 40 or a member of *any* minority group (including women).

Documented reviews also link salary increases to performance. Goodman and Gross oppose flat across-the-board salary increases, either in percentages or dollars. They suggest working within the established pay ranges. After the ranges are established, employees can be paid according to performance. Less experienced, low performers are paid at the bottom of the range, above average employees at the top. The rest fall in between. Salary increases are tied to performance and where an employee falls within the range. An outstanding employee with less experience, now at the bottom of the range, should get a larger increase than an average employee at the top of the range.

Profit-sharing is another means of motivation. Employees who have a share in the firm are more likely to work to bring about its success than those who haven't.

Other small motivators can contribute to good employee relations. Store discounts, free parking, an extra afternoon or day off all are little things that make an employee feel valued. Let the employees feel involved. Ask for suggestions about what would motivate them.

Last but not least, positive reinforcement is always a classic motivator. Compliment employees on a job well-done, but don't overflow with constant praise, or it becomes meaningless. Be honest but not fawning.

Benefits: Hidden compensation

Once pay scales and salaries have been determined, next decide what benefits will be offered. Gross and Goodman recommend that benefits be designed to meet the needs of the individual employees. A 45-year-old head of household with two children has different needs than a single 25-year-old professional. But, as a general rule, they suggest the follow order of importance for benefits:

1. Medical insurance. This is any employee's most critical need. Without it, a simple accident could wipe out most of his or her savings. There are different degrees of coverage, as well as HMO's and other employee-contribution plans. If a small retailer alone cannot afford the cost, he may be able to get in on a group plan offered by a professional association. Several of the state JA's offer such plans.

2. Life insurance. This is relatively inexpensive for an employer to provide, and many employees are grateful for the coverage. Again, group plans may be available.

3. Retirement provisions. Typically, most retirement plans are designed to give the greatest benefit to those at the top of the ladder. The federal government is attempting to eliminate some abuses and require plans to be less biased in favor of highly paid employees. For example, the employment period required for vesting in a pension plan has been cut to five years, down from ten. Many employers allow eligibility after much less time.

Pension plans also are being made more portable, to protect younger people who often job-hop in search of advancement.

401K plans have become popular over the last five years. These allow employees to save money before taxes, with a matching (or lower) contribution from the employer. Some employers contribute fifty cents to each dollar of employee contribution. Whatever the ratio, Goodman and Gross agree that the plan is psychologically worth more to the employee if he has to make a contribution of his own.

The four deadly sins

Any of these four "deadly sins" is detrimental to the health of any compensation plan.

1. Giving away the farm—i.e., paying more than you can really afford.

2. Overstaffing. Make sure that you have adequate staff to cover your needs, but don't hire two people when one will do.

3. Paying too little. Employers who do so suffer many internal problems which, in the long run, cost more than higher salaries. They suffer more employee pilferage (or major theft), particularly if their merchandise is highly desirable and small in size. Jewelry obviously is a prime target; it's easier to slip out with a necklace than a television set. Employees who are underpaid feel they're justified in the theft. They work hard and—since they don't think they're being fairly compensated for these efforts—feel they *deserve* that piece of jewelry.

Underpaying also results in high turnover, which has its own costs. The biggest is time. It takes time to search for a new employee. It takes another employee's time to train the newcomer. And until a new employee fully settles into the store routine, his time is spent less productively than that of an established employee.

Sales also will be lost while the replacement is being sought and trained—and the new employee may not turn out to be as good as the experienced employee he replaced.

4. Keeping unproductive employees. Firing an employee is perhaps one of the hardest tasks an employer will face—especially if the non-performer is a family member. But, keeping the non-performer on the staff is worse. It de-motivates other employees when a non-performer receives a full salary while everyone else does the work. It isn't fair to the non-performer—who might be happier or more successful elsewhere—or to the store owner/manager, who only hurts himself and his profits. Sever the employee. Don't linger.

Gross and Goodman advise payment of severance compensation, based on experience, tenure, etc.

A word of caution: Make sure the reason for firing an employee is genuine (and documented) nonproductivity. Otherwise you leave yourself open for a lawsuit. Formal, written job descriptions, evaluations and warnings can save a heap of trouble.

Have You Tried MBWA?

Every manager's dream is a motivated, cheerful, productive sales staff that so turns on customers they'll buy and buy and buy again.

But how to build such a group?

Bill Boyajian, president of the Gemological Institute of America, has some expert ideas on the topic and he shared them with an overflow crowd during GIA's first-ever GemFest East held during the Jewelers of America summer show in New York City.

Good communication between manager and staff is critical and the best, said Boyajian, is MBWA—"Management by walking around." This policy gives the manager an oversight of store operations and opens up conversations. How an employee receives an ensuing message is far from simple. Sixty percent of any communication, he said, is transmitted through body language, 30% through *how* the message is given and only 10% through the spoken word.

The GIA chief next spelled out the rules a good manager should operate by and the characteristics he or she should have. First the rules:

Let people know what to expect.

Follow up on what's being done.

Support those things that are well done.

Then the eight features of a good manager:

Integrity.

Industriousness.

Ability to get along with people. (Here Boyajian drew a distinction between the "people manager" who is at ease with a staff and enjoys people contact and the "administrative manager" who is good at things; he said they play complementary roles.)

Imagination, an appreciation of what's new and different.

Leadership.

Common sense.

Ability to make, and admit, mistakes.

Ability to motivate.

This last characteristic is, of course, complex and Boyajian had a list of tips that he said will help inspire salespeople. Among them:

Use quotas, goals and non-monetary incentives.

Split commissions and offer team commissions.

Offer a bonus pool for group productivity.

Involve employees in your operations.

Involve them in decision-making such as deciding what to buy:

Encourage training to further education and knowledge.

Invest time and money in your people.

Encourage a friendly, positive atmosphere.

Help salespeople develop a pride in their work.

Boyajian said there must be accountability so that performance can be measured. To start with, a store must have clear policies and procedures to guide workers. Once those are in place management should expect, among other things, a staff that shows up on time, that gives eight hours' work for eight hours of pay, that is well groomed, of nice appearance and healthy and one that has a consistently good attitude. "Attitude is so important," said Boyajian. "At GIA, what we look for in our people are attitude, loyalty, judgment and performance."

How To Buy Diamonds To Increase Profits

September 1987 Part II

Buying diamonds can be just as important to a jeweler's bottom line as selling them. Buying right requires knowledge, initiative and effort. It can keep you ahead of the price competition, which rules today's market.

Here are some key buying points from diamond dealers and successful retailers to help you offer better value at a competitive price.

1. Limit memo purchases. Diamond dealers everywhere prefer cash and are willing to knock 10% to 20% off most goods for money up front. That's a savings which can be passed on to help you stay competitive with the discounters.

Ed Bridge of Ben Bridge Jewelers in Seattle, Wash., offers this rule: "If you know you can sell it right away, pay cash. If it's something you don't normally carry and it's expensive, get it on memo."

Memo still has a place with the large or unusual stone, which would require a heavy up-front investment with no prospect of a quick sale.

Wholesaler Marc Broff in Pittsburgh, Pa., has one other suggestion for jewelers: Use memo to offer customers a choice. If a customer wants to see a 3-carat emerald cut, ask for three of them and let the customer have a choice. Better yet, make one a new radiant cut (which is a rectangle with more flash than traditional emerald cuts) to offer an even wider choice.

2. Continually shop suppliers. Not everyone offers the best price and selection all the time. Should jewelers stay with their local wholesalers, shop 47th Street in New York City or go overseas?

There's no set answer. Bridge has a multi-store operation and swears by his Seattle distributors: "If you're a volume buyer with a good, long-term relationship, you have the leverage to get good prices anywhere."

On 47th Street, some retailers have joined the Diamond Dealers Club because of its "negotiable" environment. Diamond dealer Mike Rapaport says prices are often better in the Club because of its extreme competitiveness.

Buying in the Club or any of the bourses isn't recommended for volume buyers "because it would take forever to make up parcels of sizes and qualities you need, if you're picky about the stones you buy," explains wholesaler Broff.

Buying overseas in Israel and Antwerp can save money—as much as 10% on goods under a carat—but again, the key is volume. Only volume users (at least $100,000 per trip, is the consensus) who know diamonds and the market should attempt this regularly.

3. Examine your goods. Be certain they are accurately graded and well-made. The only way you can be sure is to know diamonds or have a buyer who does.

Most dealers assemble parcels by a range of quality grades, e.g., H-J color, VS_1 and VS_2 clarity. (In plain talk, VS is totally eye clean.) Check the stones with a loupe under fluorescent light to be sure they all fall within the stated range, especially if you are dealing with a supplier for the first time. Some dealers offer low prices and take their profits by salting the parcel with much lower grades. Pick out the stones you're unsure of. And if it's a big stone, double check the grade with the dealer's master stone set.

Remember, when examining a parcel, spread the stones evenly on a white desk blotter. Diamonds tend to look much yellower when they are bunched together in a parcel.

Diamond prices vary greatly by quality and cut. Stores with a quality image strive to buy stones in the G-H color range and VS clarity rating.

Stores stocking goods below these qualities generally are forced into a tradeoff between color and clarity. Which to choose? That depends upon customer tastes. In general, it's best to go with better color in small goods and pear, heart or marquise shapes. (The points of these fancies tend to magnify body color.) Clarity should be stressed in big stones and emerald cuts where inclusions tend to be more visible.

Poorly-made stones carry huge discounts compared to those of a fine cut because cut can greatly affect the beauty of a stone.

4. Beware of low prices. Bridge's rule: "Don't use price as the sole comparison. You may be getting only what you're paying for, no more. It's like the retailers who offer 50%-off."

Rapaport elaborates: "Many times you'll see parcels—say quarter caraters—selling way below the prevailing price. Often times these are 'rejection' goods."

Rejection goods are just that. It means other customers tossed them out of parcels they were buying because of some defect, such as an off-center culet, misaligned facet or crooked table. When the dealer accumulates a number of such stones, he assembles them into ultra-cut-rate (40% off or more) parcels.

"Many times the problems are subtle," says Rapaport, "They're not big black inclusions or cuts way out of symmetry. You really have to look at them."

On the other hand, retailers can use rejection parcels for special price promotions when they have to go head-to-head with the discounters.

5. Know what you want. Be very specific about the size, quality and price range of the goods you are seeking. It saves you and your suppliers a lot of time, and it is the only way to get true price comparisons.

"If you're not sure of what you want, it's difficult to know whether or not you're getting a good price," notes Bridge

Another caveat from Ray Perlman of Jewelcor Merchandising in Wilkes-Barre, Pa.: Don't buy just because you see a bargain. It's no bargain if you can't use it.

To get a better idea of what to buy, jeweler Bridge suggests charting by size and quality the types of diamonds sold in your store. He says customer preferences evolve over the years.

6. Know the market. "Remember, there is no such thing as 'list price'," says Perlman of Jewelcor. "Prices of certain qualities fluctuate with the demands of the market. You can be a GIA grad 10 times over, but if you don't know the market, you won't get a good price."

There are, of course, many diamond price lists around. But they are usually just general guides, says Perlman, who notes that actual prices may vary 10% to 20% depending upon demand at the moment. There are certain times when some goods aren't selling, and dealers are willing to discount them more easily. Sometimes 3-5 pointers may be hot while 10-pointers go begging. Diamond companies will make good deals on 10 pointers. There are certain times when the market is slow all around: Late December, April and June, just before the major shows. The worst time to buy is in the fall when everyone else does. Selections become limited; terms are tougher and prices are firmer.

7. Rules for mounted goods. Some manufacturers offer various quality levels to suit their clients' needs. Stone quality is much more difficult to judge in a mounting so be certain the supplier is as accurate and selective about diamonds as you are. Spot check the solitaires if you're not sure. Manufacturers' big customers can get more "custom" service to suit their needs, such as stones without certain types of inclusions.

Bridge says there's usually no price advantage between loose or mounted goods but, like many traditional retailers, he prefers to mount his own. "We can be pickier that way."

8. Other sources. Buying diamonds from estates and at auctions can offer bargains for those who want to supplement their inventories, says wholesaler Broff. However, it's difficult to make such goods an inventory mainstay because searching them out can be time consuming.

Broff says the big old mine cuts are the best bargains. There are a lot of them, which can be bought cheaply off the street or from auctions. Jewelers can mount these into fine antique pieces, containing less desirable or broken center stones, or can recut them into more modern shapes. In both cases the value of the stone is substantially increased.

When It's Time To Borrow

November 1980

Debt financing has become a major source of operating capital for jewelers.

Despite high interest rates, jewelers increasingly depend on commercial lenders for funds to buy inventory, expand their businesses, or improve their stores.

"The need for outside money has become a primary function in running a jewelry store [because of] sharply increased costs" of merchandise and expansion, says Donald W. Green, of M.L. Green and Sons, Mt. Clemens, Mich.

"As the business grows, I find I spend less time being a jeweler and more time on finance."

JCK's poll of Retail Jeweler Panelists found 52% borrowed money for their business between July 1978 and July 1980. More than two-thirds said their borrowing needs are as great as or greater than during the last major recessionary period five years ago.

The number of borrowers is similar to a 1979 survey by *Management Accounting* magazine showing about 52% of capital held by all American small businesses came from debt financing.

JCK polled its panel to see how member finance their businesses: If and why they borrowed; what sources they use; the effect of the recent credit crunch on business; and ways of coping.

The results contain some surprises:

• 48% hadn't borrowed since July 1978, and several haven't for many years;

• Banks, not suppliers, were the favorite sources for financing. Less than 5% use suppliers for financing.

• Despite recession and soaring interest rates, about 13% borrowed to expand their businesses.

• 86% have no formal, written cash management or cash flow analysis plan, though many cited ways to limit outside capital.

• Less than 5% used the financing services of the Small Business Administration or other federal agencies.

Breaking the borrowing habit

Almost half of *JCK*'s Panelists haven't borrowed for at least two years.

For some, there is no need. "All our borrowing is handled by the parent company, Zales, thank the Lord," said a grateful Leon David, president of Corrigan Inc., in Houston, Tex.

Others, like Paul Vining of Vining's in Tuscaloosa, Ala., credit lessons learned in management seminars.

"Better financial and inventory management thanks to *JCK*'s workshops," as well as tight controls on expenses and payroll have actually lessened the store's borrowing needs, said Vining.

But the steady cost rise of bank loans has been a powerful deterrent to borrowing. One prominent Texas jeweler notes banks "are too tough and require so much collateral, that unless absolutely necessary, we operate on a cash basis, or possibly terms from a supplier."

An Illinois jeweler, though, is unwilling to rely solely on his established suppliers. "If they are unwilling to extend seasonal credit, we find new suppliers," he said firmly.

'Be conservative'

Many jewelers who haven't borrowed for years cite a hard-nosed, tight-fisted fiscal policy.

"You have to be conservative and careful," says Ed Winkler of Savanna, Ill. "You don't spend money as soon as it comes in. You don't extend more credit than you can afford without borrowing on accounts receivable."

Gorden E. Smith, of Robert's Jewelry in Lakeland, Fla., a jeweler since 1924, stopped borrowing money forever in 1968. "I got so teed off at what it cost then to borrow, I decided to live within my income," he said. "And I've done very well."

He cut back on non-fixed expenses, eliminated his own credit program in favor of Visa and Mastercharge, and bought less inventory more frequently. His opposition to borrowing is so complete, Smith doesn't even use is suppliers for credit.

Surviving without outside financing is a matter of attitude, he says. "You have to decide whether you want to compete with the big boys and have four or five stores, or run your own business your own way," he said. "I want one store that I can make my living from." The fiscally conservative approach "is the only way a fellow can survive today," he said. "Be cautious in buying. Watch the balance between incoming cash and expenses. And don't overexpand."

Banks for borrowing

Borrowing *JCK* panelists call banks the best, quickest, and most reliable source of funds, despite high interest rates and collateral demands. Almost 85% of the borrowers checked banks with suppliers, family/friends, and other sources (such as the SBA) each getting less than 5%.

Almost two-thirds of the borrowers (67%) used bank financing only once in the two-year period of the survey (July 1978-July 1980), and 11% went twice in the same period.

Another 22% used bank financing three or more times, with several going "many" times. This may include using the line of credit which many jewelers have at banks for inventory purchases, and informal contacts between jewelers and bankers, rather than formal loan agreements.

Slowed growth in the jewelry industry was apparent. Many deferred expansion because of high credit costs.

As one Illinois jeweler told *JCK*, "In normal times when interest is below 10%, I'm in and out of the bank twice a year. But over 10%, I never go near the place."

Some jewelers also reported sharp sales declines—notably in the Detroit area and those parts of the South affected by closing factories or drought.

Yet, despite the recession, about 13% (or one-fourth of those with bank financing) used outside funds to add another store or branch, despite paying 1% or 2% above the prime rate.

Expansion was the prime reason for longer-term loans. Of those with one to three year notes, about 15% used the funds to expand. That doubled to 33% of loans longer than three years. Inventory purchases and remodeling were other reasons for long-term borrowing.

Most borrowers (43%) took out short-term notes (less than a year), and 58% of these were to buy inventory.

Inventory loans ranged from $3,000 to $500,000, with the average about $65,000. Loans for expansion ranged from $100,000 to $500,000 and averaged $225,000. Remodeling loans averaged $90,000.

What did they all use for collateral? About 22% had "signature" or unsecured loans, give only to very credit worthy customers, while 12.5% had guaranteed loans. A lucky 6% claimed their "personal reputation" (based on decades of stable business) was sufficient collateral.

Others had to put up buildings or homes (16%), assets, including inventory (22%), or stock (6%).

Little help from their friends

Family, friends, and suppliers don't usually demand collateral, and conventional wisdom says these are prime sources. But only a couple of panelists cited family and friends. Why so few?

"They're the hardest to deal with. Everything gets too personal," said one prominent Key West, Fla., jeweler. And one in Illinois, perhaps thinking of lost tax write-offs, grumbled that family financiers "won't take interest."

More surprising was the 5% rating suppliers received as financing sources. Supposedly these are retail jewelers' prime credit sources. As one state association official told *JCK*, "God bless our suppliers. They're one of the greatest sources of my financing."

Yet, a few jewelers disagreed. "I don't like being obligated to someone I'm buying merchandise from," said a Detroit area jeweler, while one in Pennsylvania said "notes to suppliers are like begging."

Since jewelers rely so automatically on suppliers, they may not consider this "borrowing" in the same sense as a commercial loan. But the low response also may indicate chillier relations between suppliers and jewelers due to cutbacks in payment terms and increased rates by suppliers since the economic squeeze.

What about the future? Jeweler borrowing certainly will grow. With the recession supposedly easing and interest rates lower than earlier this year, a number of panelists (including some who haven't borrowed for years) say they plan to borrow in the next few months. Their reasons: Inventory purchases, debt payments, business expansion.

Funding: Where to Go Besides the Bank

To most jewelers, there is only one source for outside financing: The bank. As one California jeweler told *JCK*, "The bank is impersonal and easy to negotiate with. I've never even thought about any other source."

But there are other sources. Here are some:

- **Nonprofessional investors:**
Well-to-do investors looking for a tax shelter.
- **Limited partnership:**
One or more persons contribute capital without management liabilities or responsibilities. They deduct partnership losses from personal income tax.
- **Commercial finance companies:**
These loan on collateral, rather than a firm's history or

potential. Accounts receivable financing is most popular, but they also make loans based on equipment or inventory.

• **Factoring:** Outright purchase of accounts receivable, with credit collection responsibility, not a loan but a purchase at 60% to 80% of the full value of the accounts.

• **Life insurance companies:** Offer policy loans, commercial mortgages, even unsecured loans for customers and non-customers.

• **Consumer finance companies:** Provide personal loans for any personal need, including small business financing. Some also give "signature loans," unsecured lending, only to customers with superior credit ratings.

• **Savings and loan companies:** Make loans on commercial, industrial or residential properties to customers and non-customers.

• **Farmers Home Administration:** Despite its name, makes guaranteed term loans to small, nonfarming businesses in rural areas (less than 50,000 people and not near any city), but only if applicants can't get funds elsewhere. Unlike the Small Business Administration (SBA), it has no loan ceiling limits.

• **Small Business Investment Companies (SBIC):** More than 300 SBICs, under SBA authority, provide venture capital, management assistance and risk loans which commercial banks might deny.

• **Minority Enterprise Small Business Investment Companies (MESBIC):** Part of SBIC program, these specialize in equity funds, long-term loans and management assistance to small businesses owned by socially or economically disadvantaged persons.

• **Minority Business Enterprise (OMBE):** Helps small businesses having operating problems and difficult outside financing. Directed primarily at minority businesses but aids nonminority businesses.

• **Women in Business:** SBA national outreach program for prospective and established women business owners.

• **Small Business Administration:** Has a number of programs to provide lending or management assistance at no cost to the user.

• **State Business Development Corporations:** Some 33 states have institutions to stimulate business and employment, and grant loans which commercial banks can't.

• **Employee loans:** Employees loan back bonuses to the company at an interest rate between that of their savings accounts and that which the firm would pay a commercial lender.

But jewelers can also raise revenue without recourse to funding agencies.

Some suggestions:

• **Social security savings:** A worker's share of Social Security taxes isn't subject to taxation if paid, rather than withheld, by an employer. Taking advantage of this can reduce overall payroll costs.

• **Equipment leasing:** Though used mainly by large firms, small ones can too and avoid frozen capital. Equipment and furniture can be rented from banks, finance companies, or equipment leasing companies. Money saved on purchases goes into the company. Lease payments are deductible, though tax depreciation benefits are forfeited.

• **Refinancing:** New mortgage is written on current, increased value of property, with the owner getting the cash difference between old and new mortgage loans.

• **Finders and financial consultants:** Determine a client's need and appropriate financing sources. However, there are con-men in this business who take the fee and do no work. Consult banks, stockbrokers, accountants or the local SBA office for advice.

• **Bartering:** Several hundred barter clubs in the U.S. and Canada trade goods and services among members.

• **Short-term cash investments:** Rather than in non-interest checking or low-interest savings accounts, put money into short-term higher interest investments like money funds or CDs.

• **Reduction of expansion purchases:** Stock new branches of stores from excess inventory in older stores to balance inventory and reduce overall stock levels.

• **Surrogate purchasing:** A small business manager can join other businesses in negotiating volume discounts on items both use (i.e. office supplies, materials).

• **Sale of stock:** If a firm is large enough, sell shares to get funds. Conversely:

• **Selling off inventory:** Special sales of normally slow-moving inventory, especially if tied to a gimmick or seasonal theme, provide needed, quick funds.

Chapter 6

INVENTORY MANAGEMENT

Successful Stores Get The Most Out Of Their Product Mix

Keeping Perspective

Editorial ◆ *August 1994*

Near the corner of 55 St. and Eight Ave. in New York City is an unprepossessing 15-ft.-wide storefront that offers take-out food service. Sometimes it's open, sometimes it's not. A regular customer says the kindest word to describe the owner is gruff. "You have to know what you want right away," says the customer. "This guy has a bit of a temper. If he knows you, he'll usually give you a few extras. But he doesn't like first-timers."

The service offers only one item: soup. But it's very, very good soup. It's often highly spiced. It comes in a number of varieties. And this store is always crowded with everyone from office workers to busy executives. They love the soup.

What we're talking about here, of course, is product. Product is the core of any retail business. But I wonder whether some jewelers have forgotten this very basic fact. No matter where you go, no matter whom you talk to, if the conversation turns to business, it almost always seem to focus on one word: service.

"Service is what sets me apart." "I offer the sort of service that no department store can match." "Why buy a piece of jewelry from a TV set? There's no personal service."

We've all heard comments like these. There's no question that good service can set one business apart from another, especially if all other parts of the business are much the same. Superior service adds the gloss to a business that's already superior to its competitors in all other areas.

But devotion to top service should never blind an owner to the business's other needs. There's a dangerous possibility this could happen in jewelry retailing. Jewelers focus so much attention on service that, in many cases, they don't focus on the product itself.

May it's time to think soup.

It's almost an axiom today that when you buy merchandise, you should pick what your customers like—not what you like. But some people still don't get the message. Too many jewelers still buy an item based on what they have to pay for it rather than what they can get for it. If

you concentrate instead on how to sell an item before you buy it, then you're forced to consider your customers. This has two benefits. First, you'll likely end up with merchandise that will sell. Second, if you feel confident you can judge your selling price, then you can make more profitable buying decisions because you'll know your margin at the moment of purchase.

That's the thoughtful way to buy in the view of most smart retailers. But noT enough jewelers do so. The outcome is an abundance of stock that doesn't move, either because the price is not right or, more often, because customers don't want to buy it.

Obviously, you buy merchandise because you want to sell it. A recent poll of the JCK Retail Jewelers Panel showed that jewelers are hungry to find new, salable items. Many add or drop a half dozen or more suppliers each year in their search for products that will jump off their shelves. The problem is too little systematic research on what customers want.

The best way to find out is to ask. I wonder how many jewelers from time to time invite a group of customers to come into the store after hours to discuss merchandise. This is a time to ask what they like and dislike and why. How do they feel about prices and values? Publications routinely ask their readers for this sort of input.

It's also sensible to reorder an item that sells well—provided, of course, that you know it sells well. In some stores, that piece of information may take weeks—even months—to surface.

The basic issue is that without salable merchandise, you won't stay in business. It's critical to know what sells and what doesn't. It's critical to know your customers' tastes. It's critical in a crowded jewelry market to have merchandise that's not in each competitor's store. In short, it's critical day-in and day-out to make your merchandise your primary concern.

Then add good staff and good service and wonderful displays to complete the package.

Diamonds:
Still A Jeweler's Best Friend
(How To Fight The Margin Squeeze)

June 1994

Selling more diamonds but enjoying it less.

An indepth look at jewelers' diamond business confirms that profit margins have been shrinking for more than a decade. Diamonds have been "commoditized" as competitors ranging from discount outlets to "upstairs" retailers sell stones based on the Rapaport price list, clinching wavering sales with grading reports from the Gemological Institute of America or other "certificates."

Yet more than ever, diamonds remain the basic staple of the jeweler's business. As one store owner puts it: "Diamonds are the closest thing we have to a necessity in this business: everybody needs an engagement ring."

JCK met with a number of jewelers—some with large stores, some with small ones. Each has found ways to sell diamonds successfully in an age where comparison shopping is the rule and "commoditization" the reality. These jewelers' success stories prove there is no one right way; they win by combining buying acumen, proper inventory practices, expert salesmanship and a reputation for integrity. Here's a more detailed look.

Importance of buying: Despite heavy competition, you can increase profits from diamonds through savvy buying and inventory policies. Successful diamond retailers agree on one key point: you should stay with a few trusted diamond suppliers. Playing the field for bargains is out.

Diamond sales grew mightily throughout the 1980s, even during the recession-plagued early years of the decade. But the number of diamond dealers grew even faster, resulting in unbridled competition that continues to this day. Dealers from all over the world took to calling, faxing or even cold-calling jewelers and promising to undercut their regular suppliers.

This allowed retailers—particularly those with excellent credit ratings—to comparison-shop dozens of dealers, constantly moving their business to those with the best prices and most generous terms. Many simply bought from whoever offered the best deal at the moment, without regard to past relationships or loyalty.

Tom Tivol of Tivol Jewels, Kansas City, Mo., one of the leading upscale independent stores in the U.S., says he had more than 200 diamond suppliers on his list at one point. But he decided to go back to a few trusted, loyal diamond suppliers and now is an ardent supporter of retailer-supplier partnerships as a cornerstone of successful retailing.

He is not alone. Most other successful diamond retailers have followed a similar path for several reasons:

• De Beers' Central Selling Organization has kept supplies of most sizes and qualities of diamonds extremely tight—below market demand, in most cases. As a result, many types of goods are hard to get. Diamond suppliers invariably reserve their choice goods for regular, prompt-paying customers.

• There are fewer "surprises" in diamond grading when the stones come from the same vendors. Retailers say all diamond houses have quirks when it comes to grading, but staying with a few trusted vendors affords consistency and accuracy.

• Consistent service. A few good dealers who process orders accurately and quickly with well-made, correctly graded stones give retailers a strong defense against discount competition.

• The "favor bank." Dealers are much more inclined to give breaks to regular customers. These include first calls on bargain parcels, "picking rights" from parcels, free memo for short-term deals and promotional help.

• Saving time and money. Because retailers deal regularly with known sources, many fewer diamonds have to be returned because they were graded improperly or were wrong for the customer.

Getting what you want: Phillip Forrester, owner of Gainesville Jewelry, Gainesville, Ga., believes the rewards of working with one or two key suppliers are much greater than the savings gained from bargain hunting. "You get much better service because they are keyed in to the type of stones you use and keep a lookout on the market for them. You won't get off makes. You won't get misgraded stones. You get what you want."

Forrester's sales total $6 million yearly in two locations (in an area with about 100,000 people), and he's a voracious diamond buyer. He says he sells 400 to 500 carat-plus diamonds yearly, enough to persuade one Israeli diamond manufacturer to dedicate a portion of his production specifically to Forrester.

While enjoying the rewards of working with fewer dealers, you still get calls from other dealers trying to drum up sales. But you have to be careful. "We get at least 10 calls a week from diamond dealers wanting to sell us H or G color stones of good make, but when they ship them, they're usually something else," says Brenda Roberts. She's manager of Diessl Jewelers, Independence, Mo., a 60-year-old, full-service downtown jewelry store that boasts it was President Harry Truman's jeweler.

Roberts strongly believes that fewer is better. "If my supplier gets special prices on a parcel that's right for us," she says, "he calls us first and passes the savings on to us as well." She notes another benefit of being selective: "Sometimes a supplier will take care of you if you've gotten hit with some big unforeseen expenses and cash becomes short. It's hard to put a price on that kind of help."

However, dollars do count so there still is a place in some stores for diamond dealers who make cold calls. "Sometimes you get offered a deal you simply can't walk away from," says Mary Hayes of Hayes Jewelers, Mobile, Ala., who started her store 12 years ago and has since become one of the city's best-known jewelers. "My usual supplier in New York is good, but a great deal is a great deal."

How much on memo? Memo is the most controversial area of diamond retailing. One camp believes in owning as much stock as possible; another believes in getting diamonds on memo and saving cash for more profitable merchandise. Owners of larger stores with fat cash reserves believe buying inventory outright is the only way to do business. Some of them argue that jewelers who rely heavily on memo use it as a substitute for effective inventory and cash flow management.

The primary benefit of owning diamond inventory is obvious: it's much cheaper in the long run. Most diamond dealers now charge a 15%-20% premium for long-term memo (stones that aren't sold immediately, aren't part of a special retail promotional deal and are used to fill showcases). Tom Tivol offers one more benefit to owning diamond inventory: "Retailers have much more incentive to sell diamonds they own than those owned by their diamond vendor." But even jewelers who like to own their own goods concede memo has its place. Phil Forrester, for example, owns 90% or more of his diamonds. Yet he uses memo to get unusual stones he normally doesn't carry or during special promotions where vendors bring in goods for quick sales. "Again," he says, "it's good to have the trust of a few key suppliers because you can usually get much better memo terms if you are a steady customer and reliable payer."

The other side: Jewelers with smaller diamond volumes and cash reserves say memo is crucial because diamonds have the lowest profit margin of any product category. They prefer to direct their cash into merchandise that makes more money. Moreover, growing numbers of jewelers believe that shrinking margins make owning large stocks of diamonds impossible. Most of these rely heavily on memo, some of them for up to 80% of their stock.

"The days of stocking 1-ct. diamonds are dead. Dead," declares Carl Weimer, who has owned Hirzel Fine Jewelry in affluent Menlo Park, Cal., for several years. "They're hard to get, they're expensive and they carry the lowest markup of anything in my store except, maybe, watches. In short, we can't afford to carry lots of diamond inventory because the margins just aren't there."

Adds Leonard Brown, a jeweler who has a small store with a big clientele in the heart of San Francisco's financial district: "I realize I'm paying a premium, maybe as much as 20%, for memo. But I can't justify tying up so much cash based on the diamond markup I'm getting."

Like others in his situation, Brown keeps a representative sample of memo diamonds in his showcases and gets more via overnight shipping services if needed. Indeed, jewelers agree that overnight shipping has revolutionized the diamond business. Now they can let dealers and wholesalers hold stones until there's a call for them.

But there is a limit. Overnight shipping is too expensive to use too often or for very small stones. "It works if you don't abuse it," says Brenda Roberts, "reserving it mainly for larger, costly goods."

Save by buying direct? Some jewelers try to save money by buying at the source. But while diamonds under 2 cts. often are cheaper in the manufacturing centers of Tel Aviv, Antwerp or Bombay, few jewelers believe it's worth going there on buying trips. Travel is expensive, and leaving the store isn't always possible.

The general rule: prices are about 5% lower in these centers, so you need to buy $100,000-$125,000 worth of diamonds per visit before the savings begin to outweigh the travel expenses.

Critics also say this is an inefficient way to buy diamonds. Says Tom Tivol: "You have to take so much time to sit in the offices and sift through the papers and loupe enough stones to get lucky. I think that time can be better spent by staying home to find customers, train staff and manage your business."

How much is enough? When discussing diamond inventory, quantity is a constant area of disagreement.

At one extreme are jewelers who believe in having almost everything for every potential customer. The explosion of fancy cuts and colors in recent years has added to these jewelers' inventory burden. "Customers are demanding their choices so we do have to stock more," says Mary Hayes in Mobile, Ala. "Years ago, we just had round diamonds. Today, we've got all kinds of shapes, many more different qualities, and now there's champagne and cognac. You have to show them all."

These jewelers say they would lose a sale if they had to ask a customer to come back the next day. Others who keep moderate inventories disagree, saying few diamond customers buy on the first visit anyway.

"Diamonds are the most comparison-shopped thing in a jewelry store," says Joseph Montanari, a jewelry designer who has a retail and custom manufacturing operation in Kansas City's Westport area. "Rarely do customers—even longtime ones—simply walk in and buy. They usually expect to come back because they aren't planning to buy on the spot."

Whether or not you stock diamonds heavily, you need to know your market and your customers' tastes. "You have to *listen* to customers—they'll tell you what they want," says Brenda Roberts. "It's up to you to have it or get it, not try to sell them something else. This is your best guide to what and how much to stock."

H. David Morrow, manager of training and education for the Diamond Promotion Service, sums up this diamond inventory debate with these questions for jewelers:

• Does your inventory conform with customers' perceived image of your store?

• Does the average price of your diamond inventory correspond to the price of your average diamond sale?

• Do you carry sufficient numbers of diamonds to entice consumers to look at your diamond counter?

• Do you have sufficient inventory to back up your diamond jewelry promotions?

The questions are part of the DPS training program, "Diamond Rules."

Margins—how low is low? You've bought wisely from a small number of respected dealers. You've done your best to assemble a diamond inventory that strikes a good balance between owned and memo goods. Now how do you price the merchandise?

Margins for diamonds have been shrinking in the past two decades. In the 1950s, when discounters were less of a problem (at least in the jewelry business) and fair-trade laws ruled out predatory pricing, loose diamonds were sold at keystone markup. A decade ago, 60% was the average. Now, diamond margins range from 20% to 50%, according to the jewelers polled for this report. Tom Tivol argues that "margins have to be there for diamonds. I would say 40% to 45% is the minimum."

One jeweler describes it this way. "I used to have a sliding scale: under $500, 2X; $500-$1,000, 1.9X; $1,000-$2,000, 1.7X; $2,000-$5,000, 1.6X; and up to $10,000, 1.5X. Now I can no longer use a fixed markup structure. I still try for a two-time markup on smalls. But if it's anything over $1,000, I can get only 25% to 40%."

Some jewelers say they still make a respectable markup (50% or more) on smaller loose diamonds under a half carat. This margin is possible because of less competition in these goods from so-called upstairs retailers and wholesale-to-the-public operators who concentrate on larger stones with GIA grading reports at below retail prices.

Every jeweler polled says consumers routinely bring in a *Rapaport Report* and demand prices listed in it, saying other retailers sell at those prices or less. What few consumers know is that prices in the *Rapaport Report* generally are about 25% above actual transaction prices and as much as 40% higher than similar quality stones of fair or poor make or with inclusions or laser drills in very visible locations.

"The *Rapaport Report* more than anything else has dropped profit margins in the diamond business," says Joseph Montanari, the Kansas City jewelry designer. "Consumers are aware of it and use it. In fact I had a customer call me to quote numbers from the report and tell me what my margin ought to be. This tells us clearly that the margins are no longer there for diamonds."

But they can be. Custom mountings and designs make comparison shopping impossible on finished pieces. Superior sales techniques that dwell on quality and cut can make a big difference. For mall jewelers, the precedent exists to ask landlords to exempt low-margin transactions from normal percentage charges.

Georgie Gleim, who has four stores catering to an upper-scale area around Palo Alto, Cal., says she's revamping her diamond department to help recoup margins. Besides adding more custom design, she's increasing her efforts to buy estate diamonds and going back to selling more Ideal Cut diamonds.

Gleim's has long been known for fine estate pieces and "often they come at much better prices than what we pay vendors for similar goods," she says. "And Ideal Cuts allow us to offer a different product from the upstairs dealers and other competitors." Nonetheless, she says, "it's dispiriting that profits from diamonds now have to come from increased volume, not high margins."

The critical last 18 inches: The last, and most important, line of defense against shrinking diamond margins is a very well-trained sales force.

All jewelers polled agree on this point. Tom Tivol admits to being almost evangelical about the need for a well-trained sales force, saying it's the only way to break the downward cycle of shrinking margins and price competition. (He says his own margins have remained stable for the past 15 years.)

"If your sales associates know diamonds and how to sell them," he says, "you can beat the so-called commodity clients who are concerned only with carat weight, grade and price. If someone comes in with a *Rapaport Report* looking for a certain stone at a certain price, many salespeople will get defensive and lose the sale. A well-trained salesperson will engage the customer in conversation and show him how the *Rapaport Report* and GIA reports don't address diamond make or the location and nature of inclusions, which can have a profound effect on the price and appearance of a diamond. I can't stress it enough. A well-trained sales staff is the key to keeping your diamond margins.

"I agree that it's a much tougher business today, but diamonds are still the most important gem to American jewelers, and jewelers *must* learn to sell them."

Competition from Upstairs

Many jewelers feel the worst-case competition is an "upstairs" retailer who advertises prices "10% above Rapaport."

Diamonds routinely sell for an average 24% *below* Rapaport's listed prices, allowing the upstairs retailers an average markup of 34%, better than many jewelers get these days. Off-make stones carry even higher discounts from the Rapaport list.

Diamonds with grading reports from the Gemological Institute of America and diamonds with better makes carry lower discounts, but the potential for high profits remains.

Jewelers who compete successfully with these upstairs operations stress good make and explain the difference to customers.

How to Beat the Markup Limits

If competitors with low prices limit your diamond markup, consider making up some of the difference with these money-saving options:

• Save 15%-20% by buying your inventory rather than holding it on memo.

• Save the 6% or more in so-called "mall tax" by moving to a strip shopping center or downtown site where rent isn't based on a percentage of sales.

• Save 1%-3% by paying vendors promptly and avoiding late penalties.

• Save 10%-35% by augmenting inventory with estate diamonds.

Here's one more tip for dealing with competitors: offer custom-design services using diamond shapes and colors that your competitors don't have.

Inventory Control:
A Diet For Fiscal Fitness

February 1994

Keeping a proper inventory is much like a healthy diet—you must take in what's good for you and keep the fat to a minimum. Jewelers—who face tight cash flow, limited credit and pickier customers these days—no longer can stay healthy simply by filling their cases with anything and assuming someone will buy it.

Instead, they must strike a balance between a lean, well-managed inventory and bare, unappealing showcases. They must also balance between focusing on their best-selling pieces and narrowing inventory so much they have nothing to entice customers back.

That's tough to do. To help, JCK sought advice from some leading "dietitians" who help jewelers stay fiscally fit and from jewelers who themselves have learned how to remain lean yet offer enough of the right merchandise to ensure repeat business. The specifics of a fiscal fitness plan vary from store to store, just as caloric requirements vary from person to person. But the basic theories are the same:

1. Jewelers must have a good inventory-tracking system that can tell them quickly what sells, what doesn't and how long a piece sits in a showcase before a customer buys it. (Many manual and computer inventory-tracking systems are available for the jewelry industry. Which one a jeweler chooses is a matter of personal preference, as long as it supplies all the information needed. This article assumes jewelers already have an effective tracking system in place.)

2. Jewelers must know their market, know their competition, be willing to adjust their thinking and maintain reasonably good relations with their suppliers, especially by making timely payments.

Here, then, is a basic "fiscal workout" for jewelers.

OUT WITH THE OLD

An effective inventory plan begins with getting rid of old merchandise that's not selling. Such goods tie up cash that could pay for faster-selling pieces, they occupy valuable shelf space and they give regular customers who see them repeatedly the idea that business isn't very good.

Look in your showcases and identify the slow-sellers. There is some disagreement of what constitutes "slow." Contrary to popular belief, much inventory sells within two months of purchase, says Don Greig, management consultant with the Gemological Institute of America's Advanced Retail Management Systems (GIA/ARMS).

"We consider a fast-seller to be merchandise that sells within four months of when you stock it, giving at least a three-time stock turnover per year," he says. "After inventory has been with you for more than 12 months, efforts must be made to replace it with fast-selling lines."

Some experts say merchandise is old if it's left after the particular season for which it was bought. Others give merchandise a year—or two Christmases—and still others allow three or four years. Almost every jeweler has at least a few pieces that have hung around longer than an obnoxious houseguest. But some jewelers' cases may be even more cluttered than Granny's attic.

Greig says jewelers should appreciate the beauty of fine jewelry, but when it comes time to manage inventory, they must look at it as money invested. And that investment must bring in adequate returns. "Fifty percent of the inventory of most jewelers is over 12 months old," he says. "This means that half their valuable selling space is taken up by stock that doesn't sell. The cost of holding this stagnant inventory is half the rent and other overheads, and it also takes up salespeople's time cleaning and displaying it. Slow moving stock must be kept to a minimum."

Greig says the average jeweler has an inventory turn of one or less. If half of the inventory is more than a year old, the other half must turn twice to give an overall turn of one. In most cases, 90% of sales come from inventory that is less than six months old, so jewelers can increase their chances of making a sale by offering fresh merchandise.

Fast movers, slow movers: A good way to find out which merchandise is "old" is to track stock turn—the cycle that begins when you buy a piece from a supplier and ends when a customer buys it from you. A one-time turn means you buy and sell a piece within a year. A two-time turn means you buy and sell the piece, replace it and sell it again within a year.

Is there an early warning sign that you have too many old pieces? If sales in one department—or even storewide—are strong in one given period and weak the next, it may be you've sold the things that customers want and are still offering things they don't. In the meantime, your open-to-buy won't allow you to buy enough of the popular pieces because you're sitting on all this excess.

Once this excess is moved out and the open-to-buy freed to buy more popular pieces, sales should be much more stable and profitable. Profits come from both stock turnover and markup. A $100 piece that sells for $200 brings $100 profit. But if the same piece turns three times, you've made $300 on that same $100.

Dale Perelman, president of King's Jewelers, a chain based in New Castle, Pa., compares a piece with other items in the department and usually drops it if it doesn't make his list of top 30 or 40 sellers. Comparison reports also work for Mayor's Jewelers, a 19-store guild operation based in Coral Gables, Fla. Steve Shonebarger, Mayor's vice president and general merchandising manager, compares pieces by class and vendor.

Gary Gordon, president of Samuel Gordon Jewelers in Oklahoma City, Okla., and Jack Woolf, vice president of merchandising for Barry's Jewelers in Monrovia, Cal., look intensely at how a piece turns in relation to expectations for the category. Gordon, a certified public accountant, devised a system to assess turnover by category, for example. If a piece meets its assigned ratio, it's a good mover; if it doesn't, it's a slow mover.

These jewelers agree there is no single formula for determining turnover performance. Most expect different turn ratios for different products. Typically, lower-priced products (such as gold chain) are expected to have a much faster turn than higher-priced ones (such as a diamond necklace). But if you have a high-end clientele, there's no reason not to expect a good turn on costly items.

Another factor to consider, says Greig, is that a product with a low markup must turn faster to achieve the same level of profitability as a piece that costs more and turns less. A product with a 50% markup, for example, must turn twice as often to achieve the same profit ratio as a product with a 100% markup. This is called gross margin return on inventory (GMROI).

For Gordon, determining how each product should perform involves looking at the history of the product or product category, learning about the marketplace, deciding how dedicated the store is to promoting that product and evaluating the sales staff's opinion on how it will sell. Yes, Gordon has assigned overly ambitious turn ratios only to find out the product didn't move as fast as he'd predicted. In most cases, he discovered it was because the product (usually a high-end watch line) started very slowly and took some time to catch on. Once these products did catch on, he says, their turn ratios came much closer to the original expectation.

Perelman, meanwhile, says inventory seeks its own level of sales. "We try to push winners rather than try to make losers into winners," he says.

Losing the fat: What do you do with leftovers in the inventory meal? Options include a "blowout" sale, an ongoing cleanup system, moving pieces to other stores and altering or breaking apart merchandise. Here's a closer look at each option.

1. The blowout means mark 'em down and move 'em out. But it's not quite that simple. Any clearance should be well-planned, well-promoted and in keeping with a store's image. A high-end store can send its customers engraved invitations announcing a once-in-a-lifetime savings event. A lower-end store can use attention-getting media spots and in-store banners.

The key to such sales is to offer realistic markdowns. Experts advise not selling anything for less than cost because it compromises credibility and makes customers think you're desperate. But neither should you set sale prices to include carrying and labor charges involved in cleaning and storing a nonseller. Those charges will be recouped quickly when you bring in faster-selling merchandise, they say.

Russell Cohen, president of the Greensboro, N.C.-based Carlyle Jewelers chain, says there's still money to be made in blowout sales, even at lower markups. "If you're not making any money [operating your business], you're pedaling but not going anywhere." Cohen also believes in a one-time discount instead of a series of markdowns, "which requires a lot more attention and raises costs."

Do confine your discounts to what customers haven't been buying, cautions Greig. Your strength is in what they do want, and they're already buying it at the current price

level. Your weakness is in what they don't want, and lowering the price offers a new enticement.

2. Some jewelers have an ongoing cleanup system. Gary Gordon offers an "item of the week"—an older piece he's trying to move. Because he advertises it only with in-store signs, customers often stop by just to see what's on special. Greig suggests older pieces are good for giving verbal discounts. Be honest, he says. Tell the customer you'd like to make room for new merchandise and offer 10% off the price. If the customer asks for a lower price on a popular piece, say "I'm sorry, I can't give you a discount on that one, but I have some pieces I'd like to move and I can give you 10% off on one of those."

3. Work an exchange with your suppliers. Many suppliers offer "stock balancing" programs which allow you to exchange merchandise for more popular pieces or more seasonal ones (leftover Christmas goods for Valentine's Day designs, for example).

Indeed, seasonal adjustments are critical for improving inventory turn, say retail consultants. The Seattle, Wash.-based Ben Bridge Jeweler chain does "huge adjustments" for each season because different seasons require different merchandise, says President Ed Bridge. "Christmas represents 35% of yearly sales overall, but in some categories, it's 50% and in others only 10%," he says. "We make our adjustments based on past history and current market conditions. We don't call them right all of the time, but this is the best we can do."

Dale Perelman says seasonal adjustments—with massive direct mail campaigns—are a large part of his open-to-buy budget. These mailers are planned for the Christmas and spring gift seasons, with a smaller mailer for Valentine's Day.

But keep in mind that many suppliers are reluctant to offer exchanges to accounts who don't pay on time or who regularly return high percentages of goods taken on memo.

4. Move pieces to other stores, if possible, or even work an exchange with noncompeting jewelers.

At Melart Jewelers in Silver Spring, Md., the managers of all 21 stores meet periodically for an internal "jewelry show" of pieces that haven't sold, says senior buyer Steve Wiczek. "These pieces are then 'purchased' by managers of stores in a different area who think they can sell them," he says. "Quite often we find they can move pieces that sat at other stores."

Several times a year, Gleim the Jeweler hosts an organized-by-category merchandise swap for its four northern California stores, says President Georgie Gleim. Personnel from each store bring all merchandise in a given category (pearls, diamond rings, etc.) and anything—whether it's a best seller or slow mover—can then be tried in another store.

Other store executives say that after Christmas or another holiday, they research what sold best at individual stores to get an idea of different customer preferences. Then they shift inventory around to stores that seem to have the best chance of selling it.

5. Break apart old merchandise. Add or change a stone for a new look. Or just melt the gold and remake the piece into something else entirely. Jewelers with the skills to create special-order jewelry have the advantage here.

Whatever you do, pay attention! It's easy to lose track of slow-moving items even when the paperwork is up-to-date and right in front of you. "There are still many times we think an item is selling well until we really look at the figures and find it's not so popular any more," says Terry Chandler, vice president of the Paducah, Ky.-based Michaelson Jewelers chain. "You really have to pay attention."

IN WITH THE NEW

Now that the fat is gone, it's time to build some muscle with an inventory that's consistently profitable. Jewelers agree that arriving at exactly the right mix is part science and part seat of the pants.

The first rule: buy what your customers want, not necessarily what you like. If customers don't find what they want in your store, they'll find it somewhere else.

The second rule: don't narrow your stock to only a few best-sellers. If you do, you'll find less repeat business than you'd like. You need fresh pieces to keep customers coming back. But keep track of how much you need and when you need it because overbuying robs you of needed cash.

Tight credit makes acquiring new inventory a challenge today, and bankers say the situation won't improve soon. They want their clients to generate as much revenue as possible from business operations (i.e., strong cash flow) before looking for credit. Memo remains available, but it's expensive—adding 15% or more to the cost in many cases—and suppliers have become much more cautious about who gets goods and a lot stricter about returns.

But with careful planning, it needn't be painful.

Science: Let's begin with the science of inventory building. How much you should buy is determined by your open-to-buy, a term that refers to the amount of money set aside to buy the pieces needed for a given time period based on projected sales, less the amount already on hand. (For a detailed discussion of open-to-buy, consult JCK's *Jewelers' Inventory Manual* .)

John Michaels of Michaels Jewelers in Waterbury, Conn., says a proper open-to-buy plan is essential to a successful inventory control program. "First, you need a very good inventory tracking system that tells you what you have and what you've sold," he says. "That way you know right away how much you can buy.

"Second, you need a plan. Sit down with your accountant, if necessary, and figure out how much you can afford to buy and how much you will need on memo. Use the open-to-buy plan to develop an inventory budget so you can buy what you have to buy, *when* you need it.

"Third is *discipline* in staying with the plan. If you don't have a good inventory tracking system or don't have the discipline to stay with the plan you've developed, you're likely to run into cash-flow problems."

Again, the key is to buy what you need, not what you like. Identify what the customers want, not what you think they want, says Greig. And remember you don't have to replace everything you've sold. If you sell seven diamond rings and two were from old stock, replace only the five quick sellers. Use the extra money to clear debt or try new merchandise.

Greig also suggests buying less at a time and turning more. For example, if you buy 12 of a certain popular model of watch and sell all 12 in a year, you've made a one-time turn. But if you buy one or two of the watches, reorder each time you sell one and sell it 12 times, you've made the same money without tying up the resources necessary to buy 12 at once.

Just as an occasional food binge or other indulgence makes life (and merchandise) interesting, you sometimes can deviate from a strict open-to-buy regimen. "Sometimes we have to take a gamble that a certain piece will get hot," says Ed Bridge. "We allow our buyers some flexibility so we don't carry the same things everyone else has. Of course, we don't just take a shot in the dark. We first look at our sales trends, what our competitors are doing and regional trends to see which pieces have that potential."

Mayor's, meanwhile, evaluates how merchandise is selling each month, says Steve Shonebarger. If a category is running 20% or so ahead of plan, more money is made available for it. Mayor's also keeps a close eye on the GMROI for each category.

At Samuel Gordon Jewelers, Gary Gordon deviates from the open-to-buy plan when his salespeople say a new product is hot and they're getting requests for it. This happened recently with Victorian slide bracelets.

"We did go over our open-to-buy for that," he says. "I look at it as the law of supply and demand. If the demand is there and you have the money, take a gamble."

Not all jewelers want to add money to the total open-to-buy in such cases. Some—such as Ben Bridge Jeweler and Gleim the Jeweler—prefer to maintain the same total, so they divert money from other categories to add new merchandise in a particular category. Gleim, for example, often diverts open-to-buy to its big estate jewelry department.

The empty wagon: One oft-voiced complaint by suppliers today is that many jewelers no longer stock a lot of merchandise. Instead, they order something for overnight delivery when a customer requests it. Diamond dealers call this "trying to sell from an empty wagon."

Successful retailers agree this just-in-time system—which sprang up with the proliferation of overnight delivery services—can be valuable if used properly. But they say too many jewelers try to get by on special orders for bread-and-butter pieces. "In this business, just-in-time is often a day late," says Michaels. "Consumers want things now, and if you don't have what they want in the store, they have the option to go elsewhere."

Richard Laffin of The Management Growth Institute, Wellesley, Mass., believes jewelers should keep as many basic pieces in stock as possible. "It's true that financing is tight, but interest rates are also quite low, which means carrying charges are lower," he says. "At the same time, returns on sales are fairly high today, so financially it's well worth keeping pieces you know you can sell."

Some jewelers use special orders mostly to entice customers to come back the following day, though this works only with pieces not readily found elsewhere. "If someone is looking for a 5-ct. diamond or something else we normally don't stock, we say we'll special-order it," says Russell Cohen of Carlyle Jewelers. Customers, he adds, are unlikely to find such a stone in a competitor's stock.

Many jewelers with fully computerized inventory control systems say they use computerized vendor refill programs. The jeweler's inventory tracking system is on-line with the supplier's computer so that when a piece sells, a replacement is ordered automatically. This keeps good-selling items in stock and saves time and paperwork, but experts offer one caution: be certain you can override the system to avert reordering poor-selling pieces you just dumped in a blowout sale.

Memo: Ordering goods on memo—where the jeweler has a specified time before paying for or returning merchandise—is a valuable ace in the hole in special cases but never for basic goods, say consultant Laffin and jewelers Perelman and Shonebarger.

Bridge, who keeps memos to less than 10% of goods on hand, says it makes more sense to buy "because we get better prices [than memoed goods] and we can offer customers better value. But we do use memo for pieces we're experimenting with or things we normally don't stock."

Shonebarger uses memo from suppliers with whom the company has had a longstanding relationship or to test-market goods. Longstanding suppliers often will negotiate the memo price and give the firm a piece at regular sales rates. When test marketing, if memo goods sell quickly, he'll buy them outright for the next season. "I advise stores to use memo only for slow turns of 0.5 or less." And because there's no investment in memo, he adds, jewelers can work with shorter markup.

Michaels, on the other hand, is a firm believer in memoed inventory to help "live within our budgets." But he says the *amount* taken on memo is less important than *what* is taken on memo. "Jewelers who take too many pieces they can't sell make a real strategic error," he says. "The surest way to lose credibility with suppliers is to return half or more of the merchandise taken on memo for Christmas. Those who do that a few times will find they won't get much memo anymore."

Supplier relations: Good supplier relations are crucial to effective inventory control. Jewelers with good payment histories will find many of their suppliers willing to be flexible.

Ask yourself if you're getting the best possible terms from your suppliers. "Make a list of the things you want from each of your suppliers—such as January dating, stock balancing or even financing [many have unused co-op ad funds] and show it to all of them," says Laffin. "If necessary, play one off against the other."

Jack Woolf of Barry's Jewelers, for example, requires major suppliers to ticket merchandise, a time- and labor-saving advantage.

Perhaps the most important service a supplier can offer a good customer is financing. The reality of today is that jewelers must finance a good portion of their inventory needs, says Laffin. And suppliers are more amenable to jeweler financing than banks. "If there's a real problem, banks don't want jewelry, they want money," he says. "Suppliers, on the other hand, will usually take goods back."

Seat of the pants: OK, you can figure out how much to buy, but that doesn't answer the question of *what* to buy. This is the seat-of-the-pants—and often most exciting—part of inventory buying.

Melart's Wiczek compares buying in 1994 with buying in 1984: "Ten years ago, we put in two large orders each year and sold off what didn't sell at the end. Now it's like flying an airplane; you have to make constant adjustments in altitude, speed and the like."

"Good buyers have vision," says Perelman. "They like to experiment, and they have a good understanding of how to tell a fad from a trend." Buyers also should watch inventory tracking systems to see what customers are already buying, keep up with fashion and political trends, study the demo-graphics of areas within shopping distance of their store and visit competitors' stores frequently to see what really moves. Russell Cohen at Carlyle says his buyers regularly visit competitors' stores and their own stores to compare product mix. Buyers then meet to exchange what they've learned, which helps them to keep up with local and regional trends.

Once you know what merchandise your customers already buy, how can you be sure what other types will interest them?

"Beats me," says Perelman. "That's what makes a good buyer; they know when to take a chance."

"Dart board," jokes Georgie Gleim. She tries to safeguard against major goofs by making a contingency arrangement with the vendor allowing some recourse if the line doesn't sell within a specified time.

Jewelers can benefit from looking at new lines frequently—many say they see a new line once or twice a week. And they ask their sales staffs for input. "Not only are they the ones who are going to sell it, but they're the ones out there in the trenches in the best position to say why a particular piece or line won't sell," says Gordon.

Other Gordon buying policies include:

• An all-female buying team. "Ninety percent of jewelry sold in this country is for women to wear, so I feel they are the best to pick it [to be offered in the store]," he says.

• When a sales representative visits the store and the staff isn't busy with customers, all buyers are asked to look at the line and compare opinions.

• When walking a trade-show aisle, Gordon and his staff walk with heads down and eyes on cases, not on the people behind the cases. "Once I started doing that, I saw more jewelry and more different things than I ever had in my life," he says. "I made much more progress because I didn't have to make conversation with everyone who caught my eye."

Barry's Woolf suggests asking support staff for feedback. "Professional buyers are overexposed to merchandise, but the *customers* aren't," he says. "We take new merchandise back to the credit department, the accountants, the payables department—people who don't see it all the time."

History is a good barometer, too, says H. David Morrow of the Diamond Promotion Service. But keep good records and use good judgment. If you sold one very unusual design, don't order a lot more of it unless you're reasonably certain you have other customers interested in very unusual designs. Look at the overall picture, says Morrow. "You can just look at some pieces and know that it's not your market. Other times you think it's worth taking the chance and customers say 'yes!'"

Other tips for deciding which merchandise to buy:

• Distinguish between fad and trend. If one customer asks for a specific item, order it for that customer. If several customers ask for a specific item, think about adding some to your inventory. As examples, Perelman points to mood rings and pink ice as fads, tennis bracelets as a trend. When in doubt, start small.

• Ask your suppliers what sells in other areas that may go well in yours. Greig of GIA/ARMS says most suppliers will try to give you honest information if you've built a good relationship with them, but you should treat their input with some caution. The fact that a supplier sells large quantities of certain lines may mean that jewelers are buying it, but not necessarily that consumers are doing so.

• Test-market pieces you're not sure about. Try pieces in different seasons, in different stores. "For us, spring is our testing season because we like to stay with proven-sellers in the fall," says Cohen. "We work closely with suppliers, using a mix of memo goods and goods we've purchased. We monitor sales for three to five weeks, then purchase for fall inventory any that sell well." Some chain jewelers test-market products in the fall as well as the spring, but only in selected stores in regions where their buyers believe they will do best.

• Check the markets for quality estate and custom-made jewelry. Estate jewelry often can be acquired at much lower prices than new goods and can be sold at a higher percentage markup. Remember that only a small percentage of available estate jewelry will likely appeal to your customers. In other words, don't buy a piece just because the price is "right." Apply the same quality and design standards that you use for new merchandise.

Non-profit merchandise: After all this talk about the importance of profit, is there room in your store for things that aren't highly—or at all—profitable?

Greig says yes, but with extreme limitations. Jewelers stock some items to present a certain image—even if the items aren't big sellers. But it makes no sense to stock a lot of this merchandise if customers can't find what they came to buy in the first place.

"If they want to buy four or five watches, they don't need to see 600," he says. "You can see what they want by what they've bought."

Jewelers agree that loss-leaders, image-builders and traffic-builders all have their place. So what if you're taking a 10% markup on a popularly priced line of fashionable sterling jewelry, asks Gordon. Teenage and young working women who buy sterling now will likely be shopping for engagement and wedding rings in a few years. And some jewelers carry certain high-end lines—even if they're not particularly profitable—because it would hurt their image in the eyes of some customers who expect that caliber of product.

"I personally don't believe jewelers should lose money on anything," Morrow says of loss-leaders. "Eventually, they're going to get caught in it. They're in business to make a profit, and customers know that." However, Morrow, a former retailer, does believe in keeping certain items for traffic-building. When he had his own store, he kept a 5-ct. diamond engagement ring that turned only three or four times in 20 years. But it helped to sell other engagement rings because once customers saw it, he says, they were more inclined to spend a little more money.

Some products just add ambience to the store. Giftware turns maybe one-half time, says Perelman, but it enhances the look of the store. Why not put the money that might have been spent on decorative objects into salable decorative objects?

Building a Basic Inventory

If you were to open a new jewelry store and had $500,000 to spend on inventory, how would you use the money? JCK asked a selection of leading jewelers—independents and chain stores—and came up with the following guidelines.

There is no one-size-fits-all inventory formula. Engagement rings and bridal sets are the mainstays of some stores, while others don't even carry them. Mall stores often stock goods attractive to instant-gratification-minded shoppers; downtown and freestanding stores often carry a more diverse mix with great success.

Virtually all jewelers JCK polled for this chart serve a middle-class to slightly upmarket clientele with two exceptions (one is a carriage-trade store, the other appeals to a working-class clientele).

This breakdown is a basic beginning. You should fine-tune and adjust the mix to suit your needs. Note also that this breakdown is for jewelry only.

TOTAL INVENTORY BUDGET: $500,000

DIAMONDS, LOOSE: $20,000 to $100,000
(mostly for diamond engagement rings).

DIAMOND JEWELRY: $120,000 to $315,000
• Diamond engagement ring and bridal jewelry: $30,000 (downtown store), $40,000 to 50,000 for mall stores (one store specializes in bridal jewelry and allots $125,000 to the category). Also, mall stores carry more diamond engagement rings because mall shoppers have a more "instant" mindset.
• Other diamond rings (average $1,500 to $3,000 at cost): $22,000 to $80,000.
• Earrings: $22,000 to $25,000 (downtown or freestanding stores were at the higher end).
• Bracelets: $22,000 to $30,000 (mall stores were at the higher end).
• Brooches, etc.: $5,000 to $14,000 (mall stores were at the lower end).
• Necklaces: Up to $25,000. "These are usually memo items since they are generally quite costly. Perhaps two or three pieces of owned inventory in downtown."

COLORED STONE JEWELRY: $50,000 to $100,000
• Rings—Emerald, ruby, sapphire: $17,500 to $40,000. Birthstones and other gemstones: $17,500 to $20,000.
• Earrings and brooches/pendants—Emerald, ruby, sapphire: $17,500 to $50,000. Birthstones and other gems: $17,500 to $20,000.
• Generally, freestanding and downtown stores had a higher percentage of "unusual" colored stone jewelry (i.e., tanzanite, indicolite and so forth) than mall stores.

GOLD JEWELRY: $75,000 to $120,000
• Rings: $10,000 to $16,000.
• Chain: $20,000 to $40,000.
• Bracelets: From $5,000 to $30,000.
• Earrings: $10,000 to $20,000.
• Designer pieces (including nonchain necklaces): $10,000 to $30,000.

PEARL JEWELRY: $11,500 to $40,000
• Promotional: $1,000 to $1,500.
• Strands: $10,500 to $25,000 (80% uniform sizes; 20% in graduated sizes).
• Mabe or South Sea pearls: $5,000.

OTHER: BRIDAL SETS, $10,000 to $50,000

Made-to-order Profits

Wouldn't it be nice to have an endless variety of jewelry to suit any customer? Even nicer to know the jewelry is presold or your inventory is guaranteed to be profitable?

Indeed it is. That, says jeweler Jeff Thompson, is the benefit of specializing in semicustom or made-to-order jewelry. Thompason, owner of Trinity Gold & Diamonds in Oklahoma City, Okla., stocks thousands of mountings and loose gemstones at all times. "One of the reasons I like custom or semicustom jewelry is because the pieces stay sold," says Thompson, for whom assemble-to-order jewelry accounts for 40% of sales. "We almost never have a return, and the word-of-mouth advertising increases with every piece we sell." Customers call the piece "their" design, he says.

What about the inventory management aspect of assemble-to-order jewelry? "We almost never have a return, and the word-of-mouth advertising increases with every piece we sell." Customers call the piece"their" design, he says.

What about the inventory management aspect of assemble-to-order jewelry? "The buying itself is profitable because I buy thousands of mountings at a time, thousands of colored stones at a time," he says, stressing the advantage of volume discounts.

He also is bonded and licensed by the state to buy used jewelry, another good and inexpensive source of fine stones. He generally reserves memo for stones over 1 ct. or when he doesn't have an exact match for a particular stone in stock.

To the materials charge, Thompson adds $30 an hour for wholesale customers, $60 an hour for retail customers. He doesn't have an exact match for a particular stone in stock.

Most customers will comfortably spend $300-$600 when they buy a piece of custom or semicustom jewelry, he says, a little more in November and December.

Profit comparison: How does unfinished inventory perform compared with finished jewelry?

"Both have their fast-moving pieces and both have their duds," Thompson says. But having an odd mounting or stone in stock is advantageous "because when a customer does want it, we can say 'now,' not 'two weeks from now.'"

Profit margins are about the same as for finished jewelry, but the customer base is vastly different, he says. This customer is better educated, travels more and has grown up with jewelry in the family. Thompson hasn't analyzed turn ratios for his assemble-to-order pieces, but says they are very profitable.

Chick Leach, vice president of administration for Stuller Settings, Lafayette, La., feels that assemble-to-order jewelry has a faster turn than finished jewelry in most stores. Its biggest advantage, he says, is the flexibility and the ability to give customers exactly what they want.

To make sure retailers can make assemble-to-order pieces quickly, Stuller has set a goal to deliver any piece within 24 hours of an order. Many Stuller clients use brass sample kits to show consumers, then order the gold or platinum pieces as needed. Stuller also supplies a selection of merchandising materials such as ad slicks, radio spots, postcards, banners, buttons and a ring giveaway program for jewelers who want to hold custom jewelry events in their stores.

Selling success: Rings account for about 85% of sales in Thompson's assemble-to-order department. Of those rings, about 60% are diamond and 40% colored stone. Most of this jewelry is handmade (Thompson has a local source for casting), and most is gold, though he works more and more with platinum.

Generally, pieces are completed in five to seven working days, though very simple pieces can be ready sooner and more complicated ones may take up to two weeks.

Thompson attributes his success at assemble-to-order jewelry to two sources: his supplier and his staff. "You can't have it without a supplier like Stuller with 24-hour service. Your supplier is on your team just as much as your sales manager.

"And you *have* to have a fully trained staff." He often teaches a "Fast Five" lesson, a five-minute presentation on a particular topic condensed from a magazine training comes "just by osmosis," he says with a laugh.

He also stresses that his staff members present the facts and allow the customers to draw their own conclusions. "If we say we can do a piece tomorrow, we do it tomorrow. The customer draws the conclusion that we're good enough to do it," he says. "We don't comment about a particular stone; we put it under the scope and let the customers look. When they ask about black spots, we can teach them about quality."

Planning For Profits

April 1993

Here's a true or false quiz.

1. I'm so on top of my inventory that I know, or can find out by computer in minutes, what I have in stock.

       True ❑   False ❑

2. I know which items are selling well and always reorder on time.

       True ❑   False ❑

3. I know all my slow movers and have great plans to get rid of them.

       True ❑   False ❑

4. My sales goals are now in place for the rest of the year.

       True ❑   False ❑

5. To make my goals I'm already finalizing plans for the special promotions I'll need to boost sales.

       True ❑   False ❑

6. I'm also starting to plan what merchandise, at what price points, I want to include in my fall catalog.

       True ❑   False ❑

7. To make sure I'll get all the help I can, I've checked the co-op and other merchandising packages my suppliers are offering this year.

       True ❑   False ❑

8. I've been digging through the store records to help plan what merchandise to buy and, of course, I've also checked customer wish lists and asked my salespeople for their input.

       True ❑   False ❑

9. I've also taken a good look at this year's incentives for my sales staff and I'm confident my new package is a real winner.

       True ❑   False ❑

10. Last but not least I've done such a good job on my buying plan that I don't anticipate any cash flow surprises.

       True ❑   False ❑

Score yourself one point for every true answer. If you score eight or more, you're in good shape. If you score less, you better read on.

It's April already!

The economy finally is turning around.

If you haven't checked recently on the 1993 sales goals you set last fall, this surely is the time to take a new look at them.

That's what the following report is all about: helping jewelry stores to sell more by better pre-planning—and make more money as a result. This is a back-to-basics report. It's one that requires you to start with homework, then go on to crystal-balling and planning with a stress on the probable—but with an open mind that the wonderful may be possible.

Here are some critical issues that you as a jeweler must consider:

• What's the present state of your inventory? Where are the holes? What's moving well? What's stagnating? What's a dead dog? And, of course, how are you going to answer these questions?

• How about your customers? Any changes going on that you should include in your planning? Any bad news on plant closings or layoffs in your market? Any good news on new or expanded plants and new hiring?

• What are your buying plans? Have you done the research needed to determine what you should buy, which price points you should favor and from whom you should buy?

• What plans have you to meet your sales goals? Are you ready with some good crowd-drawing promotions? How about your pre-Christmas catalog? Have you drawn up a list of goodies, such as co-op ads, that your suppliers have available?

• How is your sales staff doing? Is it producing the sales it should? How well do you measure performance? What new sales incentive plans have you put in place? Are you satisfied with your sales training program—provided you even have one?

• Are your plans realistic? Will you have enough cash—or credit—to pay for all the merchandise you want to order? Does your bank know about your plans and when and how much money you may want to borrow during the rest of the year? Have you talked with your suppliers? Are you ready to negotiate terms, delivery dates, return privileges, discounts for early payments and so on?

These are all questions for which any serious business should have answers.

Basic information: You can't decide what you're going to buy unless you know exactly what you have in stock and therefore what you want to add to stock.

Inventory reports come in many forms, ranging from very sophisticated to nonexistent. In most jewelry stores they fall somewhere in the middle. The critical issue to remember at all times is that these records have one fundamental purpose: to provide information that accurately parallels the actual situation in your store. Bells and whistles are wasted if this purpose is not fulfilled.

Two forms provide all the information needed for your inventory records—the purchase order and the sales slip. The information they contain is then held for reference and analysis on the inventory form.

Here's what the purchase order should record:

1. Store name and address.
2. Ship to address if different from the store's.
3. Vendor or supplier name and address.
4. Vendor or supplier number.
5. Date of order and store order number.
6. Anticipated delivery date(s).
7. Cancellation date.
8. Store item number.
9. Vendor or supplier item number.
10. Description of merchandise.
11. Number of units ordered.

12. Cost of merchandise, both unit and total.
13. Freight items: FOB, store or vendor.
14. Discounts and allowances.
15. Method of shipment.
16. Special instructions.
17. Store's authorized signature.
18. Vendor's or supplier's authorized signature.

The sales slip is your other major source of information. Here's what it should record:
1. Store name and address.
2. Customer name and address.
3. Date.
4. Units sold and item number (even though the sales tag is attached to the store sales slip, the customer must receive a copy which includes the item number in case there's a return).
5. Item description.
6. Unit price.
7. Total price.
8. Customer number (if used).
9. Salesperson.
10. Amount of sale.
11. Tax.
12. Sales slip number.
13. Type of transaction:
    a. cash sale.   b. credit card sale.
    c. charge sale.   d. received on account.
    e. layaway.   f. refund/return.
    g. repair.
14. Other information, such as discount, etc.

The third document in this sequence is the inventory record itself. It should provide, for each unit, the balance on hand, the quantity on order (if any), the quantity received, the quantity sold, the quantity returned to the vendor, the quantity returned by the customer and the quantity cancelled. The record also should provide, at a minimum:
1. The item number.
2. Description.
3. Unit cost.
4. Normal markup percentage.
5. Normal retail.
6. Supplier name.
7. Other sources for the item.
8. Other information such as advertising allowances, special supplier discounts, etc.

Assessing open to buy: As you get ready to plan your buying for the summer bridal season, back-to-school promotions and fall and Christmas holidays, the store inventory record is a critical tool. It tells which items are moving, which are stagnant, which should be reordered and which should be cleared out.

One of the first steps is to get rid of the dogs. Your salespeople are bored with them. So, probably, are your regular customers. Getting rid of them will please both groups—and provide ready cash to buy new merchandise.

Of course, dumping the dogs often carries some pain. They may well be items you bought because you liked them, not because you thought your customers would. Or you might have bought them because they seemed to be doing well in a competing store—but they died with you because you cater to a more upscale (or downscale) group. In any event, the nonsellers must go.

Chances are they'll have to be marked down to move. But don't cut prices automatically. Putting the items in a new store location may help. Or try a spiff for the sales staff. If you do cut prices, always remember that you're in business to make a profit so plan any cuts judiciously. Markdowns can be habit forming!

Updating the sales forecast: Let's assume you've assessed your in-house inventory and done all that's needed to get it into shape. Before you can firm up buying plans you need to update your sales forecast for the year.

Many factors are involved here. Some are beyond a store owner's control—for example, the state of the local or national economy, the activities of competitors and the strength or weakness of current suppliers. But even if the owner can't influence these factors, he or she can react to them positively.

Then there are factors the store owner *can* control, such as advertising and promotions, store staff and layout, service to customers and merchandise mix. The sales staff, merchandise mix and owner's ambitions also can combine to influence (if not totally control) another factor: inventory turn. This issue of controllable and noncontrollable factors was the central theme of an article in the February issue, written by Joseph S. Romano, president of Scull & Co. He built a case to show that a typical jewelry store, with annual volume of $1,000,000, could improve net operating income from $60,000 to $210,000 by improving turnover (from 1.0, a typical jewelry store figure, to 1.5), cutting expenses, marketing more efficiently and selling more productively. The figures are not blue sky. They're based on observable performance at various stores in the Scull group.

Here's a quick scan of some key matters to consider in making a realistic forecast.

• Store history. This is an obvious source of information. If sales totaled $X from June through December last year, is it reasonable to assume history will repeat itself this year? Yes and no. If all other factors—such as advertising, promotions, customers and competition—stay the same, sales should, too. Changes in any of these areas almost certainly will change sales patterns as well. But knowing what *did* happen is very helpful in predicting, and planning for, what *will* happen. For example, changes in the economy can make a big difference in customer well-being and confidence. If confidence is down, the store owner may decide to increase his advertising and promotion budget significantly to counteract it.

• Merchandising. This vitally important area needs a lot of attention. Let's just consider four possible promotions that you might add this year. Each could have a major impact on your sales—and your merchandise buying plans. The details are supplied by JCK Senior Editor Hedda Schupak, the magazine's principal marketing writer.

Fourth of July sale. Red, white and blue jewelry. Obviously calls for ruby, diamond and sapphire. But also consider spinel, tanzanite, blue topaz, lapis and garnet. The range of stones allows for jewelry in many price ranges. Also consider colonial-style sterling giftware.

Suggested events: Try a special shopping evening for government or service workers only, with appropriate discounts. Hold a special "American designer spotlight" featuring jewelry from American designers. Or feature a display of jewelry containing only American gems.

Celebration for August brides. June still may be the number one month for marriage (10.9% of the total at most recent government count) but August is close behind (10.7%). For stores which want to help the bride and groom celebrate, there's obviously a good market for wedding bands (we assume the engagement ring was purchased earlier).

But opportunities for other sales abound, as well. There are the traditional gifts of pearl necklace, earrings and/or bracelet for the bride and a fancy watch for the groom. Then there's a long list for the bridal party: pearl stud earrings, pearl pendants, traditional or freshwater pearl necklaces, fine writing instruments, cufflinks, key tags, tie tacs and more.

It's back to school again. Once more, there are opportunities galore to sell earrings, in every style and price range. Also class rings (if you stock them), pens and pencils and charms in all varieties, especially ones depicting school activities—a cheerleader's horn, musical instruments, etc.

There's also the chance to reach a wider audience of grownups. How about a sale directed to parents: "Gee, Mom, you made it through the summer! Reward yourself!"

Men-only pre-Christmas event. Many stores run such specials, generally evening affairs with, perhaps, wine and cheese and a tempting array of jewelry. Put some of these items on your shopping list: diamond jewelry (anniversary bands, tennis bracelets, stud earrings and earring jackets); convertible jewelry (more gift for your dollar); designer jewelry, especially as an ensemble sale; pins; gemstone jewelry and pearls; gold jewelry, going beyond the basic gold chain. And how about a few pieces for the male buyer to spoil himself—such as gold cufflinks or something appealing in diamonds?

Finally, if you're a jeweler who really thinks ahead, even now you should be planning for early 1994 as well as the rest of 1993. An example: If you want to run a crowd-pulling Valentine's Day promotion, it's not too soon to launch a search for some truly innovative pieces.

• Your customers: Here's the centerpiece of any buying plan; if the customer doesn't buy what you buy, you're in deep trouble.

Inventory records will show what customers bought last year and, unless there's been a radical change in your customer base, last year's best sellers should continue to sell, unless they were faddy pieces.

What about items your customers asked for that weren't in stock? Do your salespeople keep a regular log of such requests? And how about customer wish lists? Both are great sources of ideas for items you should put on your shopping list.

It's also useful to check out local competitors to see which jewelry items their customers seem to favor. Some may well be appropriate for your store. The new product sections of industry magazines are another major source of ideas. Suppliers' advertising also provides a very useful guide.

The main point is that as you plan your buying—for immediate sales, to prepare for upcoming promotions and special events, for your catalog if you use one, and for your

longer-range needs—you need a very clear idea of what you want to buy. Much of your buying probably will be directed to known vendors, but it's critical to be open to new sources.

Your suppliers: One of the most common complaints suppliers make about their customers is that so many retailers fail to take advantage of the help they offer.

In planning your selling year never overlook what your suppliers can do for you. In some cases the goodies are so good that you may want to sign up with a new source just to take advantage of its merchandising program.

The help comes in many forms. Co-op ads are one of the most under-utilized, suppliers often say. Be sure to check what's available and to discuss with the supplier how best you can use the cash the company has set aside for its program. Many vendors also prepare statement stuffers and other literature that can offer customers a colorful come-on.

Supplier firms can help in other very practical ways, too. As a long-standing and/or important customer a jeweler can qualify for special privileges on deliveries, terms, returns and so on. These issues can be critical in the planning process.

The jeweler who wants to get first pick of new merchandise and who needs to know that the right goods will be delivered at the right time to coincide with store sales goals must plan well in advance. Early commitments help both parties. The jeweler knows wanted merchandise will be delivered on time with the right payment terms; the manufacturer, with firm orders in house, can schedule production smoothly.

Preparing the sales staff: Buying decisions have been made. Commitments are in hand for deliveries and terms. Promotions have been conceived, developed and are scheduled. The ad program is in place. What about the sales staff? Is it ready to do the job?

The newest Jewelers of America "Cost of Doing Business Survey" reveals some startling differences in sales performance among jewelry stores. In those with annual sales of less than $200,000, sales per employee totaled $66,000. In stores with annual sales of $400,000 or more, sales per employee totaled $124,000. Even more startling is the difference in sales per square foot of selling space. In the lower-volume stores it is $202, according to the JA figures. In the higher-volume stores it is $678.

Store volume alone can't explain such differences. The quality of the sales staff also has to be a factor. And it is a critical part of the entire planning process to look as closely at staff performance as it is to set sales goals or plan promotions. This is difficult in a small store with its "family" atmosphere between owner and employee. But it has to be done realistically and objectively. Nonproducers should be encouraged and trained to do better and, if they can't perform, be replaced.

Good training is a must. Today so many different national, state and local organizations provide training seminars that there's really no excuse for a store owner not to involve his or her sales staff.

Selling incentives also need to be examined as part of the planning process. This involves a fresh look at base pay—salary vs. commission—and such incentives as bonuses, spiffs and so on.

233

It's important, too, to involve the staff in the planning as much as possible. After all, who knows the customers, their likes and dislikes better than the people who are on the selling floor every day? Their input can help shape the owner's buying plan. If someone has good reasons to recommend, for example, that you stock more colored diamond jewelry, then that person is going to be really enthusiastic when it comes to selling the product.

Is it affordable? The best buying plan in the world won't work if cash isn't available to make it work. So, along with the sales goals and the buying plan, you also need a cash flow plan.

Cash flow is quite straightforward, says Richard F. Laffin, author of the *JCK Jewelers' Inventory Manual* (source for much material in this article). The jeweler must project such things as cash sales, receipts of cash from accounts receivable, cash expenditures for operating expenses and for payments to suppliers.

Then it's a case of matching total projected spending with total cash available to see if there's a balance on hand or a deficit for each month. This calculation maps out the projected cash needs for the entire year. The jeweler then can decide how to raise cash to meet projected deficits for any month—by short-term borrowing, accelerating collection on receivables, arranging to defer payments to suppliers for a short time, or running a sale.

Laffin comments: "With a cash flow analysis or plan, we can see where action has to be taken or changes have to be made. Before long we'll find we are managing our cash posi-

tion rather than being managed by it . . . We have to update our cash flow as actual transactions take place just as we do on our sales forecasts and buying plan. These are all management tools; we have to do the managing."

To work up a cash flow analysis a jeweler needs to know:
1. His or her estimated beginning cash balance.
2. Forecasted sales.
3. Percent of sales for cash and for credit.
4. Average number of days for receipt of cash on credit sales.
5. Dollar amount of recurring expenditures such as payroll, rent, utilities, etc.
6. Dollar amount and timing of nonrecurring expenditures such as taxes, vacation payrolls, etc.
7. Payment terms for purchases.

Early planning of purchases does pay off. It means the jeweler can match merchandise and sales goals more efficiently by careful scheduling of deliveries. It means fewer last-minute hassles (though there'll always be some). It means advertising programs can be laid out well in advance. It means there's more time to get the staff prepared for special selling occasions and there's more time for them to alert their favorite customers about incoming merchandise.

"There are some risks in making early buying commitments," says Dick Laffin, "but the benefits far outweigh the disadvantages."

Why Pay 29% More?

Editorial ◆ May 1988

Croppers' Farm Market in Guthriesville, Pa., my local food store, was selling brown eggs for 89 cents a dozen in early April. Large whites were a bargain at 69 cents. But I bought the brown eggs anyway.

Why pay 29% more for one egg than another of the same size? *Simply because I like the look of brown eggs!* Further, I still retain a fragment of a childhood memory which tells me that brown eggs are fresher—a thought my wife ridicules.

All right, you may say, although we're talking about a 29% difference in price, we're still only talking about 20 cents in cash—and 20 cents is no big deal. But let me report on another purchase where the cash amounted to some thousands of dollars.

A little over a year ago I wanted to buy a new car. I planned to trade in a well-liked but aging Chevy hatchback for something similar. Chevy, it turned out, had discontinued the model. Nissan, on the other hand, did offer a hatchback in the style and size I wanted—at a price about $3,000 more than I'd thought about paying. I bought the Nissan because it was just what I wanted. What's more, it's so superior in performance to the Chevy that it's worth every extra dollar it cost.

The moral of these stories is obvious. Price is *not* the most important consideration in every sale. Many other factors influence the buyer, too. There's hardly a store owner in the business who doesn't recognize this, at least in theory. But a horrifying number of owners, and their employees, have become so obsessed with price that they can think of little else.

JCK editors reporting the on-the-road series which began in the January '88 issue have made us all acutely aware of this truth. No matter where they've gone—to the Midwest, the South and the Southwest, so far—the dominant concern of the jewelers they've visited is discounting by competitors, and how to combat it.

Much of the talk and many of the strategies are defensive. Simply put, the philosophy is "If they cut prices, then we've got to cut prices." Say, for example, you and a nearby competitor offer the same brand of watch, with the same model number and the same features, but your competitor charges 20% less. Your price obviously makes little sense. If a customer, with minimum inconvenience (the *minimum* is important), can save $20 to $50 or more, he'd be daft not to.

But there are all sorts of ways to persuade a customer that he should shop at your store anyway, not your competitor's.

Let's start with markup. Many jewelers worry over it, most often relating their price to keystone. Is it brave, and sensible, to go to keystone plus 10 or keystone plus 20 or 30? When do you go to keystone minus 5?

One thing is sure. The customer couldn't care less what your markup is. He doesn't know your cost and isn't interested. But a huge amount of jewelry store pricing is predicated on the belief that the customer *does* care. That means a huge amount of jewelry store pricing is based on bad thinking.

Right now, the whole thrust of pricing is "What can I charge?" Doesn't it make more sense to ask "What is the customer willing to pay?" True, there are shoppers who buy on price alone. Some are inveterate bargain hunters, for whom haggling is a highly developed art form. But more often, they are people of such limited means that financial survival depends on bargain buying. It's a hard but realistic fact that such people will never make a jeweler rich.

Most of those who buy a jeweler's merchandise do so because it's appealing, beautiful, unique, exciting and—at more rarified price levels—a statement of success. These customers base a decision to buy on perceived value and ability to pay, not on whether the jeweler is making a minor or major profit.

Successful pricing, then, really depends on how well you know your customers and how well you can choose merchandise that will appeal to them. Once you know you can offer something the shopper really wants, mark-up becomes a secondary consideration. Obviously, the more appealing the items you can offer which your competition *can't* offer, the easier it becomes to make the sale.

If you can put the pricing issue into perspective, you'll have more time to address all the other factors that produce success. As our on-the-road series shows, many jewelers thrive in price-competitive markets by concentrating on their strengths. These stores offer customers a wide variety of merchandise, and aren't scared to display some fresh and unusual pieces along with the bread-and-butter items. They often choose to be specialists—in appraisals, in colored stones, in unusual timepieces, in estate jewelry, in custom design.

The value of professionalism cannot be stressed too much. This doesn't mean you and your salespeople have to deliver a gemological speech each time you offer a gemstone for sale. It does mean your staff must have the self-confidence that comes from knowledge and be equipped to answer any gemological question a customer may ask.

Service is critical, too. When you can handle any service problem that arises—whether it's a repair, a replacement or a sale on behalf of a customer—then you turn a shopper into a customer, probably for a long, long time. Maybe a couple of generations.

Pricing Strategies: Tips From Top People

February 1988

"A price war is truly one of the most dread things in business."

So declared John McCartney, president of Pricing, Planning & Profit International in Dobbs Ferry, N.Y., at a special two-day conference on pricing held in New York City in early December.

Most price wars start when one or more companies make price their No. 1 concern; they often end with the weak or unprepared forced out of business and everyone's profit margins damaged.

McCartney said those involved in a price war should think in military terms.

It's easier for a market leader to stay No. 1 than to become No. 1," he said. But a leader under attack must "attack" itself often to uncover its weaknesses before others do. Questions the leader must ask include:

Do the new competitors, those on the offensive, feature more extensive merchandise? Do they offer quicker repairs? Are their hours better? Do they concentrate on price competition to the exclusion of all else?

A jeweler who isn't the community leader has a tougher time, said McCartney. Information may be his best weapon. "Be smarter than the competition," he said. "Know them without letting them know you. Control information about yourself."

This jeweler should "attack" the competition on a narrow front, stressing service or repair or unusual merchandise selections. By de-emphasizing price, a business may be spared the costly sacrifices that often come with a price war.

"A fine jeweler entering a price war and playing the price game is going to erode his image," said McCartney. "He may get business but it won't be the top-end business he once had."

The fine jeweler who *doesn't* get into a price war may do himself a real favor. "The high-price segment is small enough that the right jeweler can defend it successfully," said McCartney.

Throughout the two-day event, sponsored by the New York-based Pricing Institute, dozens of marketing, management, advertising and accounting experts hosted almost 50 seminars on effective pricing strategies. Some points relevant to the jewelry industry:

"How much is it?"

These words can scare the commission out of even the most aggressive salesperson. An unexpected answer can frighten away the most interested customer.

"It's the moment of truth," said Ron Brown, a marketing consultant from Tenafly, N.J. "The buyer should not be surprised when he learns the price."

Customers must have a perception that jewelry is worth what it costs. If they think a piece is too expensive or too cheap, the store's advertising message (in product and image advertising) isn't working properly.

Salespeople must be familiar with store advertising, know the prices and specials quoted and make sure the customer isn't confused with contradictory information.

Price deals, in addition to hurting profits, can damage customer relations and kill a store's high-class image.

A jeweler can't make sound decisions on pricing unless he or she knows how price-sensitive customers are. Example: Items regarded as having premium value—such as sports cars, posh credit cards and jewelry—can benefit from carrying high price tags.

A customer may be ready and willing to pay more for a diamond than the store owner is ready to charge. (A classic jewelry store problem is the salesperson who is more scared of closing a high-dollar sale than the customer is of paying the money.) There are simple ways to discover customers' attitudes toward price. First ask them.

"Do some research," Brown suggested. "Talk with customers and find out their perceptions of the cost of gold and diamonds in your store." And be ready for changes in perceptions. Repeated media coverage of fluctuations in jewelry commodities—such as gold and diamond prices—can affect consumers' perceptions, said Russell S. Winer, associate professor of management at Vanderbilt University in Nashville, Tenn.

Try a questionnaire. "It doesn't have to be full blown. Maybe just ask a few questions after a sale, at the point of purchase."

By quizzing customers over a period of time, for example, you can develop a feeling of how sensitive they are to changes in the price of gold.

Try to find out, too, what customers think an item *should* cost. Then try to tailor inventory to meet those expectations. Example: If your gold jewelry retails in the $500 to $1,000 range but enough customers think a gold jewelry item should retail for between $200 and $300, add some items in that price range to your stock. Conversely, you may need to add more expensive items.

Narrowing the difference between perceived and actual prices is a wise strategy, said Brown. "Then the salespeople can focus on other aspects of the product."

What factors most commonly provoke a price squeeze? George Leaming, principal consultant for the Western Economic Analysis Center in Marana, Ariz., identified four majors:

• New and aggressive competitors.
• Declining consumer demand.
• Higher consumer price sensitivity.
• Internal pressures to make sales.

What to do if a price war breaks out?

Maybe it's best to do nothing, said Leaming. "Prices should not be cut out of fear," he said. "In some cases, low-ering them can be fatal." (Extreme example: "Knee-jerk" price cutting over six years in the copper industry that ended in 1986 with only six of 11 major producers surviving.)

If action must be taken, here are some possibilities:

• Price bracketing, where a product category is divided into higher- and lower-priced models. Said Robert Green, owner of Lux, Bond & Green in Hartford, Conn. (and president of Jewelers of America), "We can take a style and differentiate the quality with the size of the stones we use. You can have different price points for the same look."

• Bundling—or selling a package, not just a product. Here's the time to talk about warranties, rights to trade in a diamond toward a bigger and better stone, special services, etc.

• Market segmentation. "We do it all the time," said Green. "It's a matter of finding out who your market is and gearing merchandise for that market." Earrings are particularly easy to segment, he added. "You can market to a more mature audience, to working women and to the young market."

• Cut costs so you can survive with lower margins.

Don't Just Cut Prices

Jewelers can remain strong without cutting prices. Here are some market conditions that often cause discounting, along with some non-price responses.

Condition: A general decline in demand for product affecting all sellers in the area

Tactic: Hold prices steady as long as possible. Determine why demand has decreased. Revise sales incentives from piece commission to a structure based on contribution to overall company profitability.

Condition: Increased competition in the market. More retailers or newly aggressive approach by one or more

Tactic: Determine impact of competition on sales and profit. Cut prices only as a last resort. Price by variable discount. Emphasize the temporary nature of any sale.

Condition: Customers are growing more price sensitive.

Tactic: Desensitize customer. Educate and promote other aspects of the product, including the four C's, style, selection, service, uniqueness, honesty.

When Action is Needed

If a price war is declared in your market, don't adjust your prices. Consider these options:

• Bracket prices. Divide each product category into two or more new categories, pricing one above your current level and one below. Maintain current price on original product.

• Bundle. Provide additional products or services along with the item. For instance, offer free lifetime cleaning or a par of earrings with purchase of a necklace.

• Segment market. Split your customers according to their interests and purchasing power. Identify preferences in style, color, brand and price, then appeal to those preferences.

• Reduce operating costs—without affecting apparent quality of business.

Five Steps
To A Better Inventory Mix

September 1987 Part II

Divide and profit.

That's the key to developing a successful mix of diamond inventory at the right price points, say many jewelers.

Categorize your diamond inventory, then watch closely to see what turns best and which items are snails. Use that information to buy and budget.

Here's how jewelers do it.

1. Back to basics. First, you need lots of "bread & butter"—such basic constant sellers as engagement rings, anniversary rings and earrings.

Stock this merchandise in sizes and styles popular in your specific market. As Murray Rose, co-partner of Long Island's four-store Rose Jewelers chain, explains, "merchandise mix is based on a store's personality." Whether you cater to yuppies or to cattle-growers, be sure your diamond inventory reflects the tastes of your customers.

2. Trend spotting. Include a generous portion of popular fashions in the rest of your diamond shopping list.

Out in Columbus, Ohio, "Style and trends are very much a part of what we do," says Bill Argo of Argo & Lehne. "A year ago, diamond necklaces with more diamonds were the in style, so we bought a lot of those. Now, pins and brooches are coming back, so we're looking more at those."

How do you know what will be hot and what to stock? Easy: Keep your eyes and ears open to a variety of sources. Pay special attention to what customers ask for, what's advertised heavily in the trade, and what vendors seem to be promoting, especially at trade shows.

Argo finds out about trends by reading the trade press and such consumer fashion magazines as *Vogue* or *Town & Country*, while Rose periodically visits "some of the trendier stores."

3. Be systematic. Once you have an idea of what to stock, organize your diamond inventory records by specific category and price range. This will tell you what's turning at what price level—a good indication of what's hot in your store.

List each type of diamond jewelry (stud earrings, engagement rings, etc.) under specific price ranges: Up to $500, $500-$1000, $1000-$2000, $2000-$3000, and $4000-plus, for example.

"We found people come in with definite price limits in mind [when buying jewelry], and these seem to be the cut-off points," says Diane De Scenza, vice president of marketing for De Scenza jewelers in Boston, Mass. Such a specific breakdown tells her "how many to buy in each category, rather than take a stab in the dark."

4. History lessons. Monitor daily activity in each product and price categories. Keep careful records, on computer or manually. Rose Jewelers, for example, enters every piece of diamond jewelry in a ledger book by description and department, removing it when sold, reordered or replaced with a similar style. Get daily sales breakdowns, review inventory frequently and solicit staff input on what's selling.

5. Buying smart. All this information serves several purposes.

It helps you buy right. "We know the price ranges where we sell the most, and emphasize that by stocking diamond pieces in them," says Argo.

It helps you set goals. "Last year, tennis bracelets were big," says De Scenza. "We doubled our budget for them, and increased our sales 300% at Christmas."

It provides nuts and bolts data for inventory budgets. Rose explains, "If one of our stores get a twice-a year turn on earrings [selling for] under $250, and sells 50 pairs a year, it should have 25 in inventory. If they cost $100 wholesale, that means we should allot about $2500 for them."

It keeps inventory mix current and consistent. "Watching our total figures," says Arnold Bockstruck of Bockstruck Jewelers, Minneapolis, "ensures we don't get stuck with a lot of merchandise we can't move, or have 60% or 70% in any one category and almost nothing in another."

Chapter 7

SALES PROMOTION

---

*Tips That Could Make
Even A Salad Sizzle*

Buy & Win

November 1994

Lifestyle Vacation Incentives, a travel agency in Palm Harbor, Fla., offers a program in which jewelers give customers free travel vouchers with the purchase of jewelry above a specific price. The voucher gives them free airfare to a choice of nine destinations. Customers pay for their own hotel accommodations at rack rates (the published rates for the hotel), but are given a choice of rates for high or low season. The agency also offers a series of land packages in which customers receive accommodations at various resorts instead of airfare.

Destinations are Orlando and Ft. Lauderdale, Fla.; Honolulu, Hawaii; Nassau, Bahamas; Montego Bay, Jamaica; Acapulco and Cancun, Mexico; San Diego, Cal.; and Phoenix/Scottsdale, Ariz.

Jewelers across the country have used the program with great success, says David Boerngen, national marketing director of LVI. For example, David Rogoway, president of La Rog Jewelers in Portland, Ore., used the program successfully four times in his three stores (April, May and December 1993 and March 1994). La Rog Jewelers kicked off the program with a heavy radio advertising campaign and has enjoyed a 30% increase in engagement ring sales since then.

"Radio is really the best vehicle to advertise this promotion," says Rogoway. "We went with rock-and-roll stations because the promotion is geared to a younger demographic, bridal. We tried an older demographic but it wasn't as strong." Rogoway will run the promotion again shortly and will advertise it on television.

The promotion also gave Rogoway a chance to clear away many unclaimed layaways. "We sold $25,000 in one weekend in one location just clearing out layaways," he says.

Rogoway says many jewelers have called him about the promotion. His only caution: train your staff thoroughly. "Be sure they know about the destinations, how the program works and so forth." He also gets the staff in the mood by offering them trips as sales awards.

Other jewelers report similar success stories. John Steinla, manager of the Hagerstown, Md., branch of Melart Jewelers, says the promotion helped to make several important sales. In one case, the store gave a customer a trip instead of a discount to win a big sale.

LVI's Boerngen says his program has been used by jewelers of all sizes, from chains such as Carlyle & Co., Finlay Corp., Karten's Jewelers, Barlow & Eaton Jewelers, Service Merchandise, Luria's and the Diamond Park division of Zale Corp. to independent stores such as Lee Michaels in Baton Rouge, La., and Glennpeter Jewelers in Schnectady, N.Y.

LVI recently unveiled a new package of four days and three nights in Las Vegas, with a choice of the Excalibur, Sahara and Palace Station hotels.

Performance Group/Lifestyle Vacation Incentives, 1314 Tampa Rd., Suite 126, Palm Harbor, Fla. 34683; (800) 456-0907 or (813) 787-1920.

Phone home: Preferred customers at Greffin Jewelers in Minneapolis, Minn., can earn discounts and free long-distance telephone calls with a beginning purchase of $200 or more.

With the first purchase, customers receive a Greffin Jewelers Preferred Client Savings Card imprinted with the store logo and a diamond design graphic. The card gives them 20% savings on all future jewelry purchases, a 10% discount on all jewelry repairs done in the store and 10 free minutes of long-distance calling time via AmeriVox to anywhere in the U.S. and Puerto Rico. After the 10 minutes are up, customers can activate the card into a debit calling card at a rate of 30¢ per minute. Basically, it works like many European phone cards, with the user buying time in advance and using it as needed. It's an auxiliary phone card and not a replacement for current phone service.

"With the AmeriVox card, customers buy time in $20 increments charged to their Visa card," says owner Greg Greffin. "The advantage is that there's no surcharge like there is with AT&T, MCI and Sprint." Customers who make frequent calls from public phones can set up their accounts so they are refilled automatically (they receive 30 free minutes each time they refill their account). The more the customer uses the card, the lower the rates per call.

Greffin Jewelers unveiled the promotion May 1 with the tag line "Call Your Mother on Mother's Day, On Us." The store has given away more than 100 cards so far, mostly to new customers.

The main advantage for the retailer, says Greffin, is that the cards keep the store name in customers' wallets. Greffin says the promotion has generated quite a few sales, both from using it as a closing tool for a first-time sale and then later when customers return to use the discount.

His cost for the promotion was $700 for 100 personalized cards with 10 free minutes of calling time. This included a one-time charge of $100 for artwork. He's now making the program available to other jewelers across the country, with a certain degree of geographic exclusivity. Interested jewelers may call Greffin at (612) 825-9898.

"By itself, this promotion isn't going to change the world for you, but it's one more way to make sure customers come back," he says.

The Atocha Treasures
& Other Promotions
That Make Sales Sizzle

November 1994

Without much thought, jewelers often refer to the few months after New Year's Day as "the dead season." It's a "slow time," they say; "consumers are broke."

With a little more thought, however, retailers can convince consumers that winter and early spring are an excellent time to buy jewelry.

"You'd be surprised at how many people have money left over from Christmas," says Larry Hirsch, owner of Westerly Jewelers, Westerly, R.I. "And many people actually receive cash for the holidays."

Hirsch is among the jewelers who keep their promotional hats on after Jan. 1. Taking a cue from department stores, bars, airlines—wherever promotions are standard operating procedure—they ignore the fact that overall first-quarter sales are the lowest of the year (retail jewelry stores wrote only 4.8% of their total 1993 sales in January, 6.0% in February and 5.5% in March, according to the U.S. Department of Commerce).

To get you thinking about business life after the holidays, the following pages offer examples of promotions you can use or adapt for your store. They range from simple (a spring cleaning sale) to sumptuous (The Ultimate Platinum Party). Some relate to specific dates or events (the Super Bowl, Valentine's Day); others are appropriate at any time of year (the Atocha Event). One is tied to a fairly rare occurrence (opening a new branch store); another to a common one (repairing jewelry). All feature ideas that can help you warm up consumers' interest during the chill of a new year.

ATOCHA: TREASURES FROM THE DEEP

Are you captivated by sunken treasure? Do you dream about pulling a heavy gold chain and emerald-encrusted crucifix from the sand on the ocean bottom?

This is the spirit of the Atocha Event, a promotion based on the discovery of gold bars, coins, jewelry and gemstones in the wreckage of Spanish galleons off the coast of Florida (see "Treasure Trove").

You can bring this fantasy-turned-reality to your store to increase sales and enhance your visibility in the community. "The results are nothing short of phenomenal," says Kate Peterson, training director for Littman Jewelers of Edison, N.J.

How it works: In a nutshell, an Atocha promotion involves several months of planning and staff training culminating in a three- or four-day in-store event. Organizers bring

in authentic Atocha pieces (some for exhibit only, others—mostly gold and silver coins—for sale) and reproductions of originals found in the wreckage.

Two companies offer Atocha promotions; one is Treasure Group International of Sebastian, Fla., which is authorized by Atocha expedition leader Mel Fisher and the Fisher family. Its clients have included Littman Jewelers; Fox's Gem Shop of Seattle, Wash.; and Shreve & Co. of San Francisco, Cal.

Not every retailer can put on the Atocha promotion. TGI studies a store and its market extensively to decide whether it can support the promotion. The typical client is an American Gem Society, guild or independent jewelry store. Only recently did TGI start to work with chain stores. "We had to sell Littman to TGI as a viable business relationship," says Peterson. "We had to convince them of our level of commitment and our resources directed at the event."

While the promotion itself is free, there are some impressive preparation costs and requirements. The jeweler first must agree to submit to TGI's promotion formula. The costs include:

• Hiring a public relations company to publicize the event.
• Arranging and paying for the transportation and lodging of TGI staff and security for the Atocha treasures.
• Providing for rigorous historical and sales training for staff members so they blend in with the TGI staff during the promotion itself.

Having the store professionally decorated is an optional expense.

Jewelers who have hosted the promotion suggest budgeting $15,000-$25,000 for the expenses noted above.

The other company that offers Atocha promotions is Sinclair Educational Archaeology Services of Key West, Fla. SEAS is led by Jim and Lisa Sinclair, who were archaeologists during the original Atocha expeditions. Many of the original divers also are involved in SEAS. Its clients include Altobelli Jewelers, Hollywood, Cal.; B.C. Clark Jewelers in Oklahoma City, Okla.; and Gleim the Jeweler in Palo Alto, Cal.

"It's much more than another retail sales event," says SEAS President Lisa Sinclair.

SEAS, which also provides exhibit-only and for-sale items, provides media kits to promote the event. It also provides information packages that jewelers may use to present Atocha seminars for service clubs, museum organizations and schools. More than 150,000 school students have listened to Atocha seminars in the past four years, says Sinclair. She credits events such as these with generating enormous good-will for jewelers who host them.

Georgie Gleim praises the promotion and says the four months of planning that preceded it were well worth the effort.

Results: The results can be dramatic in terms of sales and image. Jewelers say the promotions can generate more than $100,000 in sales if it's held during the summer, more than $250,000 during the fall as the Christmas sales season nears.

And because the treasures are genuine, Atocha promotions lead to free publicity, too. Littman, for example, which worked with TGI, got coverage in three regional and local newspapers, was filmed by a cable TV channel and was the subject of radio coverage in metropolitan New York City.

To get even more value out of the promotion, Peterson offers these suggestions:

• Commit to two or more Atocha promotions using similar or identical mailing cards, posters, etc.

• Choose your best salespeople to participate in the event. "We held a lottery to see who could be a part of it," she says.

• Make sure you follow TGI's time line and suggestions precisely.

Quantifiable results can be measured in sales. "What can't be measured is the amount of goodwill you generate," says Peterson. "Atocha is a community service exhibit; it makes us feel we are returning something to the community. We gave people a chance to touch adventure, history and beauty."

Treasure Group International, 1626 Seahouse St., Sebastian, Fla. 32958-6061; (407) 589-1082. Sinclair Educational Archaeology Services, P.O. Box 5927, Key West, Fla. 33045; (305) 292-1847.

TURNING KISSES INTO SALES

In the spring, a young man's fancy lightly turns to thoughts of love." So wrote English poet Alfred, Lord Tennyson in 1842.

While love really knows no season, the official bow to love is just around the corner. Valentine's Day, Feb. 14, is a perfect day for men (and women) to express their feelings with a (jewelry) token of love.

Continental Jewelers Inc. of Wilmington, Del., took advantage of that fact and injected a little romance in 1992 with a "Count the Kisses Contest." The concept was simple: customers had to guess the number of chocolate Hershey Kisses in a large jar. And while people were in the store to guess the Kisses, they could see a line of sterling and vermeil 14k and 18k Hershey Kiss pendants and earrings by J&C Ferrara Co.

Preparation: Because contests need prizes, local non-competing businesses were solicited to participate in exchange for listing their names on advertisements for the promotion. Gamma Communications agreed to provide a first-prize limousine ride and overnight stay and breakfast at a local hotel. Cuisine's restaurant donated a $100 gift certificate for the second-prize winner and $50 certificates for third, fourth and fifth prizes.

The store's Chrysa Cohen then bought advertising on radio and in newspapers. The ads ran for two weeks during the promotion (20-30 radio ads each week and two ads in the local newspaper).

With the prizes and advertising set, Cohen filled a large transparent jar with Hershey Kisses (only she knew they totaled 1,000). Then the jar was decorated and placed on a front counter in the store. Beside the jar were entry blanks with space for the entrant's name, address and telephone number and the Hershey Kiss estimate. In addition, the store was decorated with a Valentine's Day theme.

"The contest generated a great amount of fun and excitement among employees, and they conveyed that feeling to our customers," says Cohen.

The cost of the promotion was minimal because the advertisements were built into the store's regular ad budget and the only material costs were for the entry blanks, jar and Hershey Kisses (which employees happily consumed after the contest).

Results: The promotion attracted a lot of people who ordinarily wouldn't have come to the store, says Cohen.

Sales of the Hershey Kiss jewelry soared, she says. During the promotion, the store sold 123 small and 17 large sterling pendants, 26 small and two large vermeil pendants, 13 pairs of small sterling earrings, one pair of small vermeil earrings, five small and one large 14k pendant, one small 18k pendant and two 14k and sterling pendants.

"We should have purchased more heavily initially," she says. "After Valentine's Day, we received orders for a dozen or more pieces."

In addition to the sales, the promotion provided a lot more mailing addresses for future promotions.

And last, but not least, there were five very happy contest winners destined to become dedicated Continental Jewelers shoppers.

Who says love is not in the air?

THE ULTIMATE PLATINUM PARTY

When Samuel Gordon Jewelers of Oklahoma City, Okla., throws a party, people in town take notice.

Before he opened his current location in 1990, President Gary Gordon threw a giant barbecue/block party in the soon-to-be parking lot. Another year, he invited jazz musician Joe Morello and his quartet to play for customers. This year, he turned down the music, moved the party indoors and served red wine and hors d'oeuvres instead of red sauce and ribs.

The Ultimate Platinum Party, as the evening of September 9 was called, featured a cocktail party and a fashion show sponsored by the Platinum Guild International. Dancers from Ballet Oklahoma wore platinum-colored costumes and platinum jewelry and performed on special pedestals built for the evening. Local models who mingled among guests wore the latest in platinum jewelry and evening fashions from Balliet's, a clothing boutique in Oklahoma City. The highlight of the evening was a prize drawing for a pair of platinum earrings designed by Valerie Naifeh, Samuel Gordon Jewelers' in-house designer, and a bottle of Angel, the new fragrance by Thierry Mugler, donated by Balliet's.

Many of the jeweler's showcases were turned over to platinum jewelry designers Michael Bondanza, Steven Lagos, Simon Sobie and Namdar. Balliet's filled some other showcases with handbags by designer Judith Lieber and other evening accessories. William Goldberg, Alan Friedman, Oscar Heyman and 15 other high-end jewelry manufacturers sent merchandise on consignment for the event, at a total retail value of about $4 million.

The night of the party, a Friday, the 400 or so guests who attended the event bought merchandise worth in the six figures, says Gordon. Ten percent of all proceeds from the event were donated to Ballet Oklahoma.

The planning: The Ultimate Platinum Party capped a four-day Platinum Week at Samuel Gordon Jewelers. Planning began in February, growing out of Gordon's desire to hold a fashion show in the store. He contacted Laurie Hudson, president of Platinum Guild International USA Jewelry, to ask if she could bring the fashion show she'd presented at several industry shows into his store. Coincidentally, says Hudson, the Platinum Guild International headquarters in Europe had just asked her to choose one retailer to host the PGI fashion show.

Gordon was an ideal choice—he has media presence, an upscale image and a store large enough to handle the crowd.

The planning began to pick up steam. Gordon initially wanted Balliet's to lend clothes in return for a "courtesy of" credit. But when he met with Balliet owner Bob Benham, they recognized the opportunity for a crossover promotion. For example, Gordon sent Valerie Naifeh to Balliet's store a few hours every day of Platinum Week to sell and discuss platinum jewelry. Designer Michael Bondanza gave a luncheon presentation at Balliet's the day of the party, which Gordon says led to the sale of several important Bondanza pieces that night.

Wednesday through Friday, meanwhile, two house models from Balliet's walked around Gordon's store modeling clothing and platinum jewelry.

The two stores conducted cross-training sessions for employees so Balliet's salespeople could suggest/sell jewelry and Gordon's staff could suggest/sell clothing. At the party, a few Lieber handbags, Nicole Miller accessories and three dresses were sold, along with jewelry.

Gordon arranged for the jewelry designers and was in charge of security and food; Balliet's helped to offset the cost to some degree.

Town & Country magazine got involved, too. Gordon initially contacted the magazine hoping for editorial coverage of the event. The magazine responded with a letter telling its subscribers in Oklahoma about the event and urging them to contact Gordon for an invitation. It also donated 500 copies of the magazine, which were given out at the party along with a "goody bag" containing a fact card about Samuel Gordon Jewelers, a Jewelers of America consumer brochure about platinum jewelry, a "platinum" pencil, "platinum" coin candy, a perfume sample courtesy of Balliet's and a polishing cloth imprinted with Samuel Gordon Jewelers' logo.

Gordon and Balliet's have discussed the possibility of future projects based on the success of this one. Gordon is dedicated to a major promotion benefiting a civic organization each September, and now he hopes Balliet's will share that vision.

SUPER BOWL, SUPER SALES

While their husbands watch two football teams vie for national supremacy on Super Bowl Sunday, women in Westerly, R.I., stream into Westerly Jewelry in search of a winning price for jewelry.

For the past five years, Westerly Jewelry has held a Super Bowl Sunday sale and invited "football widows" to a one-day promotion that promises prices 50% below normal. Every item in the store is included in the five-hour sale, says owner Larry Hirsch.

"We often have a big inventory after Christmas, so we give true percentage-off these items," he said. The sale is an effective clearance event for older merchandise and draws a great deal of traffic. "People actually wait in line to get in before we open," says Hirsch.

Some customers are Super Bowl Sunday regulars, but the sale also attracts a lot of first-timers, thanks to heavy advertising on cable TV and radio. Last year's newspaper advertisement urged "football widows" to take advantage of the store's "option play. . . You won't have to sit at home with the smelly cigars, looking at the couch potato with the two-day-old beard and watching guys beat each other up on television over a little oval pigskin."

Now that the sale has become an annual event, some customers wait until January to buy anything, admits Hirsch. "That's up to them," he says. "But maybe some of them would go somewhere else to buy [if the sale didn't exist]."

Sales increase: Do people buy or browse during the sales? Total January 1994 sales were at least 25% higher than the figures for January just before the promotion started, says Hirsch. "And that's a conservative estimate."

Of course, there are fixed expenses behind the scene. Hirsch says advertising costs aren't too high because he uses cable instead of network TV and because media rates drop after New Year's Day. (He says his store's advertising budget for the entire year is conservative and rarely exceeds 3.5% of annual sales.)

But staffing the store on a Sunday does take a big bite out of the budget. Not only does Hirsch pay double-time, but traffic requires 18 staff members instead of the 10 who work on a typical January day.

"It's well worth it," Hirsch says. The sale generates cash flow early in the year to cover new purchases and pay for employees to attend trade shows in search of goods. "It's the best sale we have all year," says Hirsch.

Hirsch recognizes he may be pioneering the early-year sale. "This is during the time of year when most people are pulling in their horns and saying it's the dead season," he says. "I say it's the time to do the advertising and a good time to boost revenue."

SPRING CLEANING-UP

When Dunbar Jewelers of Yakima, Wash., was preparing to move to a new location after 100 years in its original store, owner Pat Gilmore pulled jewelry from boxes in the attic and put them on sale. He videotaped the entire procedure to use in TV ads for what he dubbed the store's first Attic Sale.

Eleven years later, Gilmore still gathers older merchandise for a two-week sale in mid-March. Because the new store doesn't have an attic, the sale has been renamed for the ritual of spring cleaning.

"The employees wear aprons and cleaning rags in their pockets," says Gilmore. "We decorate the windows with cleaning solution and jewelry to make it look like we are doing our spring cleaning."

Like the original Attic Sale, the Spring Cleaning Sale features merchandise at least one-year-old and covers all categories of jewelry. No jewelry is brought in just for the sale.

The promotion is advertised in newspapers and on radio at a total cost of about $500, says Gilmore. "We are a small store in a small town," he notes.

The newspaper ads are one-column and have the look of a classified ad. They note "25% off" and then list the actual items, their original prices and their "spring cleaning" prices. The ads also remind consumers that the sale is a once-per-year event and that stock is limited.

Labor costs are low; because the period generally is slow for his two goldsmiths and one watchmaker, he doesn't have to hire additional skilled labor. A part-time sales clerk occasionally helps out during the promotion.

Timing is critical, says Gilmore. Through trial and error, he has determined the very best time is a two-week period starting March 15. "We are careful to include two pay dates, which generally means we continue the sale through April 2 or 3."

The promotion fills a gap between Valentine's Day and Mother's Day but is over before the April 15 income tax deadline, a day he describes as "not good" for selling jewelry.

Results of the promotion: Gilmore says March totals are doubled thanks to the sale of $15,000-$20,000 worth of older merchandise. Diamonds are the best-seller by far, he says.

"We do have a few regulars who wait for the sale to purchase," says Gilmore. But he prefers the regulars shop at his sale rather than go elsewhere, even if they only come in once a year.

REPAIRING FEBRUARY BUSINESS

During the 1980s, Valentine's Day sales were the heart of February's business at Erik Jewelers in Tonawanda, N.Y. But when consumers pulled back as the country plunged into recession in the 1990s, co-owner Jann Anderson began to search for alternatives to the annual heart-fest.

The store specializes in custom-made jewelry, so Anderson decided to bolster its Valentine's Day offerings with a repair and service promotion. "We started to offer a certain percentage off repair work brought in that day," she says.

Anderson notifies 5,000-6,000 customers of the repair/service promotion through a customer list that goes back five to seven years. "These are the people with jewelry most likely to need service or repairs," she says. To be sure she reaches the customers, Anderson sends all promotional mailers with a request for address correction. Anderson says this is a costly service offered by the U.S. Postal Service, but one she feels is a bargain in the long run. "It updates our lists—which is critical."

It works. "We do a lot of business with remounts and our other sales pick up, too," she says. In fact, much of the sales boost can be attributed to new purchases (or redesigns) for customers who haven't visited the store in several years but return to take advantage of the promotion.

She notes that not all jewelers can earn money by increasing their repair load. "Repairs cost more than most jewelers realize," she says. If a jeweler doesn't have the staff, training or space to do repairs, holding a repair/service special would be counterproductive. Late or sloppy repairs can drive away potential purchasers and are likely to turn off current customers.

But as a custom-jewelry shop with a large number of bench workers and designers, Erik Jewelers has had little trouble meeting the sale traffic demands.

Now an annual event, the repair special has built up a formerly ebbing February bottom line. "It's not land-office business in terms of a lot of money," says Anderson. "But it makes our February a lot more livable than if we sat around and waited for [a standard sale at] Valentine's Day."

PERSONAL SHOPPER RINGS UP PROFITS

February is a better month than January to sell diamonds, says Robert Perdrizet, owner of Creative Jewelers, Danbury, Conn. But last March beat them both, thanks to Perdrizet's annual Antwerp Diamond Buying Program.

The promotion is straightforward. Creative Jewelers spreads the word via radio ads that Perdrizet will spend almost a week in Antwerp, Belgium, and personally select any diamond for a customer. The customer first talks to Perdrizet or an assistant and describes what he or she wants, places a down payment and lets Perdrizet do the shopping.

"This works out well for us and for customers," he says. "They get exactly what they ordered and we look good as a direct diamond buyer." Customers like the idea that Perdrizet "eliminates the middle man" and sells at lower prices.

The promise of a lower price in Antwerp is realized largely because Perdrizet simply adds each preordered diamond to his list and then deals with familiar companies on his annual trips. Generally, he leaves Saturday and returns Wednesday, with only three days out of the store.

He takes preorders primarily for diamonds that will be set into engagement rings at Creative Jewelers. In fact, the purchase price for the Antwerp Program customer includes placing the stone in a standard four-prong or six-prong setting. While a setting is not required, thus far no one has purchased only a loose stone.

Perdrizet has offered the program since 1986, trying various months to determine which yields the most orders. Recently, he has concentrated on the first quarter of the year with promising results. On average, diamond sales increase 55% during the month he travels to Antwerp. The average number of preorders per year is 15, and the average size of the stones is .86 ct. He estimates he needs five preorders to break even.

Next year, he plans to link the program to Valentine's Day to see whether the generally good sales period can be extended or enhanced.

Last year, he had a long list of preorders during a period that may surprise some retailers—after April 15. "I think that some people were willing to buy because they had the IRS out of way," he says.

For six weeks before Perdrizet leaves for Antwerp, he advertises the promotion in five radio spots each day on two radio stations—one rock and one "contemporary."

In addition, employees telephone potential Antwerp Program buyers from an extensive list of customers throughout the year. "Many tell us they aren't ready this year but ask us to let them know before the next trip," he says. "We are sure to call them until they are ready."

A TIVOL PARTY

Tivol Jewels, which has had a single store in Kansas City's upscale Country Club Plaza since 1957, opened its first branch in July. And that, thought the owners, was ample cause for an elegant party at Hawthorne Plaza, their new home in Overland Park, a south Kansas City suburb. Here's how it all happened.

Branching out: "It was never my intention to have a second store," says President Thomas S. Tivol. "It wasn't part of the business culture of my family to be a multi-store operation."

But like many other cities, Kansas City has seen its suburbs grow over the years. Tivol's realized during the 1980s that many current and potential customers were moving to outlying areas, where they often formed new shopping patterns and developed loyalties to new stores. Many no longer were willing to drive back in to the Plaza.

"The number of trips they made to the Plaza decreased enough that we felt we had to open a second store," recalls Tivol. "We did studies that supported that conclusion. But business was great and we were growing so much in the original store that we chose not to expand then."

The Tivols also were waiting for Kansas City to develop another high-end shopping area like the Plaza, supported by a major department store. But nothing came along. At the time, they turned down a spot in the new Hawthorne Plaza, a strip center built in the late '80s in the central corridor of prosperous Johnson County, Kans. The center lacked a department store, though it featured very fine retail stores.

In the early '90s, Tivol took another look. Hawthorne Plaza had one free-standing pad available, which was what Tivol wanted. Negotiations were completed in late 1992, an architect was hired and work started.

Off and running: The new store opened undramatically on July 15. "We felt a midsummer opening should be done softly," says Tivol, "since so many people are out of town and the Kansas City weather is hot and humid."

September was chosen for the huge official opening party. Tivol hired a Kansas City company called A Special Event, which does major business meetings for Fortune 500 and international firms, to make all the arrangements. These included a big circus tent in front of the store, creatively decorated and filled with food, music by Atlantic Express and dancing. Party-goers could go directly from the tent and under a canopy into the store. Hundreds were on hand to do just that.

Tivol did no advertising for the grand opening; in fact, it rarely does do much for its major in-store events. Some are for a very limited clientele, some for a more general audience. But most are considered thank-yous for current customers rather than occasions to attract new ones. "It's important," says Tivol, "to continue to develop client relationships, even if they've been shopping with you for decades."

This event started with a private party on Friday, September 16, lasting from 8 p.m. until the small hours of the morning. Invitations went to a select mailing list of about 1,500 people; more than 600 accepted. Most of those who did so actually came; some who didn't also showed up.

On hand to greet them were representatives and merchandise from many of Tivol's top vendors. (The list included A link, Ambar, Asch Grossbardt, Baume & Mercier, Michael Bondanza, Luca Carati, Cartier, Henry Dunay, Ebel, Kurt Gaum, William Goldberg, Lagos, Mikimoto, Nova, Rolex, Gregg Ruth, Jeffrey Stevens, Tiffany, Unigem, Vacheron Constantin, Jean Vitau, Raymond Weil and David Yurman.) Tivol's own salespeople were told not to sell or

even to take things out of the showcases. They were there to make people feel welcome. ("Of course, if somebody asked, we'd show them a piece," says Tivol.)

The party continued on Saturday morning—once again with the party tent, food and live entertainment. The store was open to the public, of course, but Tivol also sent invitations to its larger general mailing list. Most of those who came in that day were from the firm's current clientele; many had been invited to the party the night before and came back to buy.

"The events introduced us to south Kansas City," says Tivol, "but this also turned out to be a terrific weekend for business, although it wasn't really intended for selling."

"We have more than 250 new clients since opening in July— people who had never been to our Plaza store and are excited about having a Tivol's in their neighborhood. If you have a well-known name, a name for quality, a lot of people may want to shop with you. But they have their own shopping patterns, so you have to go to them."

PERENNIAL PEARLS

Never underestimate the power of a repeat promotion. That's the philosophy behind an annual March pearl promotion at Gudmondson & Buyck Jewelers, Columbia, S.C.

Customers come to expect and appreciate the promotion, seeing it as a good opportunity to choose exactly the pearls they want, says Krista Buyck (pronounced bike) Birchmore. "We bring in a selection of pearls from three suppliers," she says. "They are in hanks [not strung] so customers are free to choose the pearls and the length they want. Then we string and clasp them while they wait."

The promotion also gives customers an opportunity to examine and understand different pearl qualities. "When you spend time with people and explain the differences between pearls, they gravitate toward the better qualities," she says. "The pearls basically sell themselves."

How it works: The promotion lasts 10 days and focuses on pearls that retail for $400 to $2,000 when strung. The pearls are sold at full price. And while customers are in the store, Buyck Birchmore is ready to encourage add-on sales with a good stock of pearl earrings, rings and bracelets.

The event is promoted in a two-column-by-8" advertisement in the local newspaper; it runs once on the Sunday before the event starts and once on Thursday or Friday. The ad pictures a hand holding a strand of pearls. Buyck Birchmore also sends postcards to selected customers and names culled from the membership lists of a symphony, art museum and churches. "Knowing the right names in the community is very helpful," she notes.

She uses the same strategy when advertising a similar fall pearl promotion that coincides with local college football games. "If our South Carolina Gamecocks are playing, we know we'll have some great foot traffic," she says.

While some may think that repeating a promotion will dampen customers' enthusiasm, Buyck Birchmore says sales consistently rise 25% during the pearl events. That, she says, proves her point that people *are* comfortable in buying when they know what to expect.

Holiday Selling:
What You Need To Know

September 1994

As the holiday selling season approaches, jewelers hope to find demand for all their product lines picking up. Jewelry from basic bridal to high fashion designer, materials from gold, silver and platinum to diamond, pearl and colored stone, along with watches and clocks, fine writing instruments and tabletops—all have a place on customers' "to buy" lists.

Many weddings and anniversaries fall in the final quarter of the year. So, of course, does the Christmas shopping season. As crowds and business increase, chances are that many stores will take on part-time workers unfamiliar with much of their merchandise. And even experienced sales associates may find themselves pressed into duty selling product lines they don't normally handle.

That's why JCK is offering this product refresher course. It includes basic information on major jewelry store merchandise categories, explaining both features and benefits. For quick reference, a "reason to buy" box lists several key characteristics that sales people may want to stress when discussing each product with customers.

DIAMONDS: SYMBOLS OF LOVE

In cold clinical terms, a diamond is crystallized carbon, the fundamental building block of all matter on earth.

In cold business terms, a diamond is the fundamental building block of a jeweler's inventory; an engagement stone is one of the few "necessities" he or she can offer.

But few people buy a diamond for cold, hard reasons. They buy them to express love and commitment. According to N. W. Ayer's Diamond Information Center, the first betrothal sealed with a diamond was Maximilian of Austria's engagement to Mary of Burgundy in 1477. Today, more than 75% of all brides in the U.S. receive a diamond at their engagement.

Why has the diamond taken on such symbolism? Back to the cold, hard facts. It's the hardest substance known (the word diamond comes from the Greek *adamas*, meaning unconquerable), the product of tremendous heat and pressure caused when the earth was still being formed. Geologists estimate that most diamonds are at least 1 billion years old.

Diamond also has a very high refractive index. In simple terms, this means the stone sends out all of the light entering it in a brilliant array of flash and color. The flash or fire is called **scintillation**, while the overall light coming from the diamond is called **brilliance**.

And diamonds are rare. It's no accident the first known diamond betrothal involved a royal family. At that time, diamonds were found only in a few places in India, making them so valuable that only royalty could afford them. Deposits were found later in Brazil, but these gems also were inaccessible to all but the very wealthy.

An African diamond rush in the 19th century launched the modern diamond trade. Since then, diamonds have assumed a different type of rarity. There are sufficient quantities to satisfy the middle classes of the world. But to extract each carat ($1/142$ of an ounce) of diamond, more than 100 tons of soil and rock must be dug and processed. Fewer than half of these carats are suitable for jewelry; the remainder are used in industry. The vast majority of the gem carats are small diamonds, the kind used in most cluster rings and popularly priced tennis bracelets. The carat-sized diamond is still fewer than one in 25,000, and top qualities are rarer still.

These statistics comprise one reason why diamonds cost what they do. Another reason is the cutting process. Generally half or more of the diamond is lost when cutters fashion the rough stone into a beautiful gem. And cutting is very difficult, exacting work. First, a bruter determines the basic shape of the stone. The bruter is the person most familiar with rough diamonds and the best one to determine how to get both maximum size and maximum beauty.

When the bruter is finished, a blocker rounds out the entire piece. Then the brillianteer adds the facets that give the diamond its fire and brilliance. The bruter and blocker must take great care to get the most from the diamond while following scientifically determined proportion guidelines. A slight miscalculation may leave the diamond looking dull and lifeless. The brillianteer must ensure that all facets (58 in the traditional round brilliant cut) line up perfectly or risk losing the fire that makes a diamond so special.

This is all very costly, time-consuming work.

Is it worth it? Television and other media periodically run negative reports about jewelers who overstate the quality of the diamonds they sell. As a result, some consumers worry whether they will get their money's worth.

The basic fact is there is no magic source where any jeweler can get similar quality diamonds for less money than his competitors can. The price of most diamonds is regulated by De Beers at the rough level (De Beers controls about 80% of the world's total rough supplies) and by intense price competition between cutters and polished dealers at the wholesale level. Therefore, jewelers who claim they can buy and sell at much lower prices than competitors probably are buying and selling much lower qualities. In short, as with any product, you get what you pay for.

Determining value: The value of diamonds is determined by the familiar 4Cs—carat weight, color, clarity and cut. Some consumers may prefer one "C" over another, but all are very important in determining the stone's value. Here's an explanation of each:

• Carat weight is the best-known indicator of diamond value. As mentioned above, a carat is $1/142$ oz., or 200 milligrams. It takes its name from carob seeds, which ancient societies used to measure gemstones because of their consistent size and weight. Some dealers use the term "points" to express hundredths of a carat (25 points for a quarter carat, for example). But Federal Trade Commission guidelines require jewelers and their staffs to use the term carat when describing diamond weight to customers.

• Color refers to a diamond's body color. Most diamonds worn today are considered colorless, though that description covers stones ranging from truly colorless to light yellow or brown. Completely colorless diamonds are quite rare and quite beautiful because there's nothing to mute the light coming from them, resulting in beautiful display of fire and brilliance. Diamonds with very, slight body color—the type offered in most better jewelry stores—can be nearly as beautiful because it's almost impossible to tell the difference if the diamond is viewed face up.

The Gemological Institute of America created the most widely used color grading system, starting at D for completely colorless and going through the alphabet as body color darkens. Most better commercial grades run G through J. Lower colors can be attractive and are more affordable than their colorless counterparts.

At the end of the alphabet, starting at Z, the scale of value and desirability swings upward again if a diamond has an attractive body color. These are called fancy colors and come in virtually every hue. The most common are yellowish brown, which at their best offer warm, golden or orange shades called champagne (for the lighter fancies) and cognac (for the darker hues). Yellow diamonds with no modifying colors are called canary stones because of their resemblance to the songbird. These are quite scarce and carry premium prices. Rarer still are the pinks and blues.

Many people have seen the world's most famous blue diamond—the Hope—at the Smithsonian Institution. On a less grand scale, blue diamonds do turn up occasionally; most have a grayish undertone or pale body color. These can be attractive and relatively affordable, though blues with truly deep colors command lofty prices. Australia's Argyle Diamond Mine, meanwhile, turns out a few choice specimens of pink and purple-pink diamonds each year. It also produces a limited quantity of lighter pinks.

• Clarity is the measure of a diamond's internal characteristics—or inclusions, to use a more negative term. All diamonds have some internal characteristics. Those with characteristics so tiny they can be seen only with a microscope are called flawless on the GIA clarity scale. The next lowest clarity grades—VVS (very, very slightly included), VS and SI (slightly included)—are given to diamonds with inclusions visible only with a 10X jeweler's loupe. Most better commercial stones are VS or SI clarity. Diamonds with inclusions visible to the unaided eye are graded I for imperfect. Stones graded I_1 generally are attractive because their inclusions aren't obvious. I_2 and I_3 stones—often used in more affordable jewelry—can be very attractive when the inclusions are hidden under a prong.

Recent innovations have helped diamond cutters to improve clarity. Laser beams can burn out black inclusions, leaving a clear "tunnel." While this improves the diamond's appearance and makes it more salable, it rarely raises the clarity grade because the cutter merely substitutes a slightly larger white inclusion for a dark one. Lasering is fairly common and must be disclosed to the buyer.

More controversial is fracture-filling, in which surface fissures are infused with a clear material. Stones so treated are still relatively rare because the fillings can be removed and because many jewelers and consumers don't like the idea of owning a diamond that isn't quite "pure." On the upside, filled diamonds sell for much less than similar-looking untreated diamonds, and most fillings will last a lifetime if cared for properly. The treatment must be disclosed.

• Cut ties together the other three Cs. Cutters unlock the beauty hidden in a rough diamond by polishing it to bring out life and fire, eliminate as many inclusions as possible and preserve as much carat weight as possible. In a well-cut diamond, light enters through the table at the top, bounces inside between facets, then is reflected back out through the table. If a diamond isn't cut properly, the light "leaks" out of the bottom facets, giving the diamond a dull appearance.

Unlike the other "Cs," there's no specific grading system for cut. Most people regard the round brilliant cut as the norm, but other cuts—called fancy shapes—have been growing in popularity. The most popular fancy shape is the marquise (an oval with pointed ends), then the pear (an oval with one pointed end), the heart, the oval and the rectangle (also called emerald cut). Other fancy shapes include square cuts, called princess or Quadrillion (which has a slightly different facet arrangement); triangles (called Trillions, Trilliants and Trielles); and baguettes (long flattish rectangles). A number of new diamond cuts have come on the market in recent years, including the Fire Rose, developed by De Beers' researchers. In addition, lasers have been used to cut diamonds into virtually any shape imaginable.

COLORED GEMSTONES: A SPECTRUM OF POSSIBILITIES

Iolite. Never heard of it? Neither have many other people. But don't console yourself just yet.

A purplish-blue gem often referred to as a water-sapphire, iolite is steadily climbing the ranks of gems that people seek and buy. More and more designers use it—and it's little wonder. Iolite—or cordierite, as some call it—is beautiful, rare and a bargain.

Many other gemstones also have joined emerald, ruby and sapphire in the spotlight. Fire agates, spinels, andalusites, peridots, morganites, sunstones, fire opals, tourmalines. This virtual smorgasbord is filled with unique gemstones with special characteristics that may coincide with your customer's fancy.

Which ones can you sell? First take a good look at your existing colored stone inventory and decide what sells best. To find out what else your customers crave, try a little experiment. Invest in a rare, beautiful and unusual gem—one you don't normally stock—and show it to the customers. Maybe this is *just* the "new" gem they've been long looking for! They will think they've found something unique and will feel unique themselves.

What makes your job easy is the variety of colors to choose from.

Emphasis on color: Imagine a world in which you could see only varying tones of black and white. Not a pleasant prospect, surely. Gone would be the romance of flowers, greeting cards, jelly beans and—of course!—gems. In colored gemstones, color is the most important factor by far. Enthusiasts often overlook obvious inclusions as long as the color is brilliant and saturated.

Emerald is a classic example. It's often permeated with inclusions, but as long as the color is saturated and the inclusions don't imperil durability, all is well. Size may not even matter, if the color can be see across a dimly lighted room. If the gemstone is well-cut and proportional, that only adds to the mystique and allure.

Remember that beauty often sells itself. If customers walk into your store and request pink sapphire jewelry, show your very best pieces first. Their planned budget may not concur with your prices, but they may be willing to spend more for the right stone. This is known as selling up.

Once you've shown a jewel, have the customer try it on. Now it's time to romance the gem.

Romancing a gem: What does romance mean to you? Does it conjure up images of warmth, feelings of comfort or of being appreciated? Does it speak to you of love?

Romance may encompass one or many of these feelings and is a sensation that people tend to seek. Gemstones have come to symbolize these sensations and now are given as gifts on special occasions in a person's life: graduation, promotion, engagement, anniversary, birthday and for myriad holidays. Giving a colored gem as a present says you feel very special about the recipient.

Most people who hold a gemstone in their hands want to know where on earth something so beautiful and precious was produced. Tell them! If you're showing a tsavorite garnet, tell about Tsavo National Park in Kenya, Africa. Suggest that the customer can own a very special piece of Africa. Appeal to your customer's sense of adventure when you tell about tourmalines extracted from the rugged Hindu-Kush range or the spinels found in Burma. You might even stir patriotism when you tell about America's unique gems.

Relate the incredible journey and process most gems go through to reach the final faceted state in a jewelry store. And if a gem has special optical characteristics—such as the star effect in sapphire or change of color in alexandrite—show these off.

Don't overdo it: Be careful, however, not to turn off customers with incessant babble. It's equally important to listen to them. Since they're about to spend their hard-earned cash, they deserve the opportunity to comment or reflect also. It's important to know when to be quiet and let the customer get in touch with the jewel. This "art of the pause" gives a customer space and the feeling of not being pressured to buy.

Some things you must say, of course. It's important to disclose any enhancements or treatments the gem may have undergone. If you do this properly and in a straightforward manner, this explanation can actually become a selling point. Acquaint yourself with the various treatments and be in close contact with your supplier regarding enhancement information on specific gems. Disclosure terminology and your ability to inform consumers are of paramount importance.

Sell even after it's sold: You've concluded your sales presentation, the customer likes the gem and is at ease. In short, all objections to writing the sale have been removed. It is time to say: "Which of these gift wraps do you like?" or "Your new tourmaline ring looks just splendid on your finger!" Suggest that the gemstone will give the customer years of satisfaction and pride. By this time, you should be working on a sales receipt and inquiring how the customer wishes to pay.

Find a good reason (or reasons) to compliment the customer on the choice of gems. Suggest how it should be worn and explain about care of gemstones, particularly soft or brittle ones. Obviously, this involves preparation and knowledge on your part.

After you've sold the gemstone, follow up by calling the customer to see how he or she and family members like the piece. Ask whether you could call when you get another unique or rare gem in the store. Above all, show that you are the jeweler of choice when it comes to color.

PEARL: THE QUEEN OF GEMS

Sir Geoffrey Henry, the prime minister of the Cook Islands, recently described a pearl as the result of an oyster trying to scratch an itch. Henry, whose South Pacific nation produces high-quality ocean pearls, then went on to say these gems from the sea—like fine wines—can be treasured for their great variety.

Until this century, pearls were called the queen of gems. Because they were found only in the wild and only one oyster shell of many thousands contained a pearl, they were rare indeed. Today, these are called natural pearls.

Early this century, Japanese technicians discovered that inserting a tiny piece of oyster shell mantle and a round bead could cause an oyster to secrete materials to cover the bead and create a beautiful cultured pearl within a year or two. Since then, cultured pearl industries have sprung up throughout the Pacific, creating a variety of pearls and making them available to almost anyone.

Types of pearls: The major categories of pearls are akoya, freshwater, South Seas and mabe.

Traditional Japanese akoya pearls, produced by oysters in the oceans of southern Japan, are a staple of any pearl wardrobe. Akoyas generally range from 5mm to 9mm in diameter and come in subtle shades of white, pink, lavender, gold and blue.

Freshwater pearls—produced by mussels living in rivers and lakes in China, Japan and the U.S.—offer a wide range of price and appearance. Let's look at these pearls by country.

China has become an important pearl producer in recent years on the strength of the small, irregularly shaped pieces the trade likes to call "rice crispies." These are very affordable and very versatile because they can be layered or twisted into endless varieties. Many of these are dyed, adding even more versatility. A new variety of Chinese freshwater pearl is nearly round and ranges from 3mm to 5mm. Pearl dealers often call these "potato" pearls because their color resembles the inside of that vegetable. These are often sold as less-expensive substitutes for akoyas. But they possess a different type of beauty and should be considered a different product.

In Japan, the freshwater pearl industry centered on Lake Biwa is nearly gone, having been overwhelmed by development and pollution. (Incidentally, it's against Federal Trade Commission guidelines to call freshwater pearls "Biwa pearls" unless they really came from that area.)

In the U.S., several pearl farmers have been creating freshwater pearls in interesting shapes for jewelry designers and for necklaces and bracelets aimed at consumers who want to go beyond the basic pearl strand.

White and black South Seas pearls are the Cadillac of the pearl industry. They were once so rare that they were sold only in the salons of the world's "ultra-jewelers." Now, however, they are becoming a favorite of jewelry designers, who value their unique beauty and varied shapes. They range from 9mm to 18mm and can cost many thousands of dollars, depending on size and quality.

Most white South Seas pearls are produced in Northern Australia and the sparsely inhabited Indonesian islands. The costliest whites are perfectly round, without blemishes and with high luster. However, jewelry designers have made interesting use of the off-round shapes, called "baroque," to create "natural" looking strands and jewelry. Though called "white," these pearls also come in varying shades of yellow to a brilliant, exquisite gold that is growing in popularity all over the world.

Most black pearls come from French Polynesia (of which Tahiti is the main island) and the Cook Islands. As with the whites, the large, perfectly round black pearls command extremely high prices all over the world, though there's been a surge of interest in the baroques and lighter colored goods. Though called black pearls (and coming from the large black-lipped oyster), their colors range from silver and greenish silver to deep green black (essentially black). All of these colors have their special appeal in the hands of talented designers who have an appreciation for Mother Nature.

South Seas pearls also are closer to nature than most other pearl types because they usually are sold without treatment of any sort. (Akoyas and freshwater pearls are usually bleached to achieve a uniform color, then tumbled to improve their luster and shape. Some are dyed to achieve the pinkish color popular among many American consumers.)

South Seas pearl farmers also produce mabes, which are half pearls grown in a shell around a dome-shaped core. Most mabes are used in earrings, though designers have been fashioning them into necklaces and other types of jewelry of late.

Quality terms: Besides the five basic types of pearls (akoya, freshwater, white South Seas, black South Seas and mabe) are quality terms that customers will want to understand.

• Shape—Rounder is still better, though off-round and "baroque" shapes have been gaining popularity.

• Color—In akoyas, pinkish white reigns supreme, followed by white. Blue, silver and lavender are also popular and yellow has found favor among some consumers.

• Luster—The shine of the pearl. High-luster pearls are the most desirable.

• Orient—This is the hardest to define because it's a combination of luster and the subtle undertone colors that play when pearls are moved around in the light.

• Nacre—The layered substance that surrounds the nucleus. Nacre should be sufficiently thick to ensure the durability of the pearls.

PRECIOUS METAL JEWELRY: FROM THE MINE TO THE SHOWCASE

Gold

A walk though any good museum will show the timelessness of gold. Our ancestors revered the metal and fashioned it into jewelry, including ankhs (symbols of life) that still look beautiful and wearable 5,000 years later.

The same properties that attracted our ancestors to gold still make it perfect for jewelry today: it's attractive, easily worked and very precious.

When a woman acquires her first piece of fine jewelry, chances are it's karat gold jewelry. But before it can be fashioned into jewelry, gold has to be mined, traded and alloyed with other metals for durability. Here's a closer look at these factors.

Gold is rare in a relative sense. There's enough for jewelry and industrial demand, but a lot of ground has to be moved and processed to get to it (one ounce of gold per five tons of ore is a fairly rich mine). With some mines running 7,000+ feet deep, the cost of extracting the nearly microscopic bits of metal often exceeds $325 per ounce. That's 80%-90% of gold's general trading price in world markets today.

World governments used to trade gold at an official price of $35 per ounce. When free trading was legalized in the early 1970s, the price quickly rose to about $100, then rode a speculative boom to more than $800 by the end of the decade. Since then cooler heads have prevailed, allowing gold's price to function more on the basics of supply and demand than as a hedge against war and financial disasters.

Nearly all gold in jewelry is alloyed with other metals to make it durable enough for everyday wear. The degree of fineness (or percentage of gold) is expressed in karats, with 24 karats equaling 100%. Most jewelry sold in the U.S. is 14 karat (58.5%). About a quarter of it is 18 karat (75%). The lowest legal karatage in the U.S. is 10 karat (41.6%).

The other metals alloyed with gold vary, depending on the color the manufacturer desires. The most common is yellow gold, which consists of copper and silver in addition to gold. White gold, popular for setting diamonds and colored gems, also includes copper, zinc and nickel. Pink gold has added copper, while green gold has silver, copper and zinc. The varied colors come only from the alloys. Gold itself is an element and its color and quality never change regardless of where it was mined or processed.

Jewelry production: Once the metal is ready to be made into jewelry, the factors of design, labor, production and marketing come into play.

The majority of gold rings, brooches and pendants are produced by casting. This process creates a wax "tree" from a mold. The tree may contain up to 24 models of the ring to be produced. The tree is then encased in plaster of paris and placed in an oven that melts out the wax (this is called the lost-wax method). Molten gold is forced into all spaces once occupied by the wax. When the gold cools and hardens, the plaster is removed, then the gold jewelry is removed from the tree for finishing and polishing. The technique is exacting because manufacturers must ensure the gold alloy is uniform and must prevent air bubbles that would create porosity and brittleness in the finished piece.

Much mass-produced gold jewelry is made by stamping—very similar to the way coins are minted. Many popularly priced earrings, charms and pendants are produced this way.

A newer production process called electroforming creates very lightweight designer jewelry pieces. This process begins with a wax model which, after a very light copper coating, is immersed into an electrolyte bath. This bath contains suspended gold and acids that help the gold to collect onto the models and also help to dissolve the copper plating. After several hours in the bath at low, then high amperage, the pieces are spun to ensure a uniform, smooth finish. As many as 72 pieces can be done at a time, but electroforming is still expensive because it requires an investment of $100,000+. However, the process allows designers to create very light, seamless pieces with very flowing lines, not always possible with older techniques.

The karatage—such as 14k, 18k, or the decimal equivalent (.585 or .705)—is stamped into many pieces of finished jewelry. Since 1982, the legal tolerances are .003 below the decimal equivalents (this is called plumb gold). Before 1982, the tolerance was a half karat, so some older jewelry may be 13.5k instead of 14k. By U.S. law, all jewelry carrying such quality marks also must include the maker's trademark.

Platinum

Platinum, the rarest and most valuable of the three basic precious metals, is the "comeback kid" of the jewelry industry. Jewelers and jewelry manufacturers have rediscovered platinum and are making it one of the fastest-growing categories of fine jewelry.

During the 1920s and 1930s, Cartier, Van Cleef & Arpels and other top jewelers created magnificent platinum jewels. But then platinum became so valuable to industry that its use in jewelry in the U.S. and Europe declined to a mere trickle (it remained popular for jewelry in Japan).

Several years ago, the Platinum Guild International began to promote the metal's properties. Platinum's cool color complements fine white diamonds as no other metal can and also sets off the vivid colors of rubies, sapphires, emeralds and some other colored gems.

PGI also began to work with designers and manufacturers to create new and different products and to train goldsmiths how to work with the metal. Platinum has different qualities from gold: it is whitish gray, has a much higher melting point and is much stronger (most platinum jewelry is 95% pure metal).

Platinum also is much rarer, with annual production totaling only about 6% of gold's production. Two platinum mines in South Africa provide about three-fourths of that total.

The fact that platinum jewelry is pure, precious metal (the 5% alloy is usually a platinum-group metal such as palladium or iridium) makes it much more expensive than comparably sized gold jewelry. To make it more affordable, some jewelry manufacturers are working to develop 50% platinum alloys.

Silver

Silver, the most common and least expensive of all precious metals, has also experienced a renaissance. Big, bold, silver jewelry is now in vogue as a fashion accessory. And some designers have started to blend silver with myriad other materials, ranging from traditional lapis and onyx to the more adventuresome such as Lucite®.

Silver's relatively low cost ($5 per ounce, compared with $375 for gold and $400 for platinum) allows jewelry designers much more freedom to create interesting and affordable pieces.

Hundreds of years ago, silver was worth much more when compared with gold. When Spanish invaders conquered the Inca and Aztec empires, for example, they were looking for silver as well as gold. And silver was the chief ingredient in most coinage for centuries, until its price rose above the face value of most coins in the 1960s.

The photography industry then became the largest user of silver—until last year. In 1993, more silver was used for jewelry and flatware (221.6 million ounces) than by the photography industry (195 million).

The leaders in silver production are Peru and Mexico, contributing about one-third of world totals. The U.S., Canada and Australia are also important producers.

The vast majority of silver jewelry is sterling, meaning it contains 92.5% silver and 7.5% copper. The legal tolerances are the same as for gold and platinum. Some sterling jewelry is plated with gold of at least 120/millionth of an inch to create vermeil (pronounced ver-MAY).

DESIGNER JEWELRY SETS THE STYLE

Designer jewelry is a relatively new segment of the jewelry market. The term is used to describe the expression of style by a particular jewelry designer or group of designers.

Jewelry makers all follow basically the same manufacturing procedures, just as clothing makers all follow basically the same sewing procedures. However, the designer garment or designer jewelry is meant to be an artistic statement spoken in textiles or precious metals and gems.

In many cases, designer jewelry—like designer garments—is set apart by the amount of handwork that goes into it. But hand-fabrication alone does not a designer piece make. A strand of South Seas pearls can be knotted by hand and a gold chain can be made by hand. While they may have excellent quality, they are not necessarily "designer."

Designer pieces have a definite personality. In fashion, it can be minimalism á la Giorgio Armani and Calvin Klein. In jewelry it can be Michael Bondanza's flexible platinum and gemstone bracelets, Cartier's panthers or Elsa Peretti's stark simplicity for Tiffany. All these designs are identifiable and carry the signature style of the artist.

Designers put a lot of research and development into each new design. Mass manufacturers more often restyle existing ideas, perhaps adding a dangle here, a gemstone there, or simply creating a similar style in a cast or stamped version so it can be produced in volume. This doesn't necessarily make the mass-produced piece any less salable or attractive, but it isn't on the same level artistically.

Even designer jewelry has different levels. At one end is the artisan who creates each one-of-a-kind piece. Next is the designer who creates the design, carves the wax, works with a silver sample to create the prototype and then turns it over to other workers to go into production. This designer may employ a small group of workers or may contract production out to casters and polishers. Finally, there are big-business designers who simply oversee the work produced under their names. They have input into the styling of the collection, but don't actually sit down and design anymore.

Consider the following analogy: an original Picasso painting (the one-of a-kind jewel) vs. a numbered lithograph (limited-production jewelry line) vs. a poster (generic, mass-produced jewelry items).

Selling tips: Here are some tips for selling designer jewelry:

• Merchandise designer jewelry by collection. It's best to keep each designer's jewelry separate, showing a small collection instead of just one or two pieces. Remember you're selling the concept as well as the merchandise. Also, it's difficult for a customer to get a firm grasp of the designer's artistic sense from just one or two pieces.

• Use name plaques, different display units and special props to differentiate your designer goods from your regular merchandise. Little groupings also connote specialness and exclusivity.

• Designer jewelry often can be distinguished from its mass-market counterparts by special clasp or hinge treatments, intricate texture detailing and design, hand-finishing, a designer's signature, a finished back.

• Usually, the designer jewelry customer is a woman. Industry experts agree that women are driven more by design than men, are willing to spend a little more to get a design they like and are more willing to go out on a design limb. But some men do look for the unique to express their taste in gifts or know that their special lady prefers unique and unusual jewelry.

• To spot a potential designer jewelry customer, look for people who are well-dressed with a strong sense of style. They may be dressed to the nines or in jeans and a T-shirt, but the clothes will be excellent quality and even the simplest outfits will somehow look different on these customers. Look for quality in shoes, belts and handbag or briefcase as well.

BRIDAL JEWELRY: BUILT-IN PROFIT

Weddings are big business for jewelers.

Seventy percent of all engaged couples sealed their commitment with a diamond engagement ring in 1993, says the Diamond Information Center at N. W. Ayer, De Beers' U.S. advertising agency.

And they paid an average $1,597 for the ring, up 23% from 1992. The DIC attributes the increase in part to growing consumer acceptance of the two months' salary guideline (the cost of an engagement ring should equal two months of the groom's salary). Further, most consumers polled said they expected to spend far more on an engagement ring than they actually did.

After the engagement ring comes the wedding ring. This can be a simple gold or platinum band or intricately designed and diamond- or gem-intensive.

Statistics aside, it's important to know who buys what in terms of bridal jewelry. Younger brides often prefer a classic solitaire, whereas older and more sophisticated brides may be more inclined to choose a design-oriented style.

Design is an increasingly important factor in bridal jewelry, if trends at recent jewelry shows are any indication. Walk through the designer gallery at any major jewelry trade show and you'll see many jewelry designers have added engagement and wedding rings to their collections.

This growth in designer bridal jewelry can be attributed to couples waiting longer to marry; they can afford to spend more and have been exposed to more in terms of style and

experience. Additionally, many of today's marriages are remarriages. Such couples tend to spend more than first-timers because they can afford to and because the groom wants to give his new wife a better ring than he gave his first wife or a better ring than her first husband gave her.

Selling advice: Here are some tips for selling bridal jewelry:

• Good "grooming." Remember that, in most cases, the actual customer is the groom.

• In some cases, however, couples shop together. The bride is more likely than the groom to put the brakes on spending. To overcome this objection, remind the couple this is a once-in-a- lifetime purchase and that they wouldn't want to look back and be sorry they didn't spend a little extra for the ring they really wanted.

• There are two kinds of price objection. Sometimes, the couple just can't afford a certain ring and will most likely say so in no uncertain terms. When that's not true, however, sales experts say the resistance can be overcome by holding their interest and convincing them of a ring's value.

• Unless a couple says right away what they're able to spend, begin a bridal sale by showing the best you have. If the couple reacts with "sticker shock" ("$5,000?? We were thinking more like $1,000"), a good response is, "Let's ignore price for a moment and concentrate on finding a style you like. After we settle on the style you want, we'll find one in your price range." Most customers find this idea reasonable, especially if they know you can order a style they like in their price range. This doesn't limit them to choosing from what you have available in their price range. And it often leads them to spend a little more when they see something they really like.

• When couples are taken with an engagement or wedding ring, get it on their fingers as soon as possible. It helps to create ownership if they see themselves wearing it.

• When the couple seem uncomfortable looking at anything out of their set price range, move to their price range immediately. However, you may show them *one or two* pieces that are no more than $250 more than their stated price. Preface it by saying you know it's a little more, but thought they might like to see this style.

• Consider selling diamonds and mountings separately so customers feel as though they've bought a "custom" ring. Or let real custom rings be your bridal niche, especially if you're fighting tough discount competition.

• The best way to ward off discount competition is to know exactly what the discounter sells and be prepared to show why your rings are a better value. This includes educating your customers about the 4Cs and what gives a diamond its value.

• Consider adding services such as a lifetime guarantee, free delivery, a decorative jewelry box and a free home ultrasonic cleaning machine.

• Remember that not all couples want a matched set of wedding rings. Often the bride will opt for a diamond wedding band while the groom prefers a plain gold one; sometimes the reverse is true.

WATCHES: MORE THAN TELLING TIME

If there is one product in your jewelry store that almost sells itself, it's the watch.

The reasons are numerous. Virtually every U.S. consumer wears one. In fact, surveys show that Americans now own an average of three to four watches.

Watches also are one of the few branded products in a jewelry store—one that your customers know and ask for by name.

In addition, watch companies spend millions of dollars annually in marketing, advertising and promoting in the U.S. to attract consumers.

And watches are fun, functional and trendy. It's been a long time since they were only time-tellers. Today's watches are designed to be durable fashion, sports and lifestyle accessories. They're status symbols, hot collectibles, high-tech multifunction marvels and stylish eye-catchers.

"With the advent of new watch fashions and distinct watch styling for different lifestyles and activities, the potential for repeat business is enormous," according to one watch brand's instructions to its retail clients. What's more, a growing number of watch brands are adding jewelers as outlets or designing collections for the jeweler's market.

Timely background: The $10 billion global watch industry produces almost 1 billion watches and watch movements annually. One fourth are sold in the U.S., the world's largest and most lucrative watch market.

The major watchmaking industries are in Switzerland, Japan and Hong Kong (much of whose work is now done in China). But there are also strong industries in France and Germany and developing ones in Taiwan, China, Thailand and India. In sheer numbers, Japan is the top watch producer (40%), followed by Hong Kong (20%) and Switzerland (18%). In value of watches made, Swiss watchmakers claim 54%, followed by Japan (22%) and Hong Kong (9%).

In the past two decades, the watch business has changed dramatically. The inexpensive, easily produced and precise quartz watch movement, created by the Swiss but first used commercially by the Japanese, replaced mechanical movements and radically altered the industry and market. It paved the way for watches as trendy fashion and lifestyle accessories and as multifunction high-tech marvels.

More recently, mechanical watches have regained popularity as highend handcrafted timepieces, while midprice and highend brands have lowered prices to make their watches more accessible to consumers, especially young adults.

Selling tips: Watch customers are predisposed to buy a watch when they come to your store. But they may be unsure what type of watch they want, in part because of the wide variety of brands, types and styles on the market now. Here are some tips that will help you help the customer make a choice.

• Ask who the watch is for. Is it for the customer or is it a gift for someone else? Women buy the majority of watches, often as a gift for men. It also helps to know the wearer's age and interests (hobbies, profession, etc.).

• How will the watch be used? Will it be used primarily at work, with evening wear, for a casual lifestyle or as part of an active, sporting lifestyle? If the customer isn't sure, ask about the intended wearer's hobbies and interests. A weekend sailor may enjoy a yachting watch, while a gardener may want a sturdy strap model designed for casual wear.

• Ask about style preferences. Does the customer want a watch with a bracelet or a strap, with classic or trendy styling?

• Emphasize features that benefit the wearer. This makes the customer focus on the value of the watch rather than its price. In more expensive watches, explain features that account for the difference in price (an 18k-filled case instead of stainless steel, the addition of a perpetual calendar, etc.).

• Narrow the choice. Let the customer try on a couple of watches with the features specified. Start with more expensive models; the customer's comments will help you determine his or her budget.

• Emphasize the value of buying the watch from an authorized dealer who can provide guaranteed after-sale service and support.

Watch basics: Depending on how it displays time, a watch is **analog** (a dial with hands to show minutes, hours, seconds); **digital** (numbers displayed on a liquid crystal panel) or an **analog-digital combination.** Most watches are analog.

There are two types of watch movements (the device that "runs" a watch): **mechanical** and **quartz**.

The mechanical movement (or *ébauche* as it is sometimes called) has only mechanical parts and is powered by a spring connected to gears and a balance wheel. There are two types of mechanical movements: hand-wound (connected to the mainspring) or self-winding (also called automatic) by the wearer's wrist action. Mechanical watches are accurate to within an hour per year and require servicing every two to three years.

A quartz movement uses an electronic module powered by a battery. In analog watches, there is also a mechanical section (including a "stepping motor" continually activated by electrical impulses from the module's integrated circuit and a gear train that transfers that to the hands). In digital watches, the digital displays receive impulses directly from the circuit. Nine out of 10 watches are quartz.

Quartz movements are accurate to within a minute per year; most need battery changes every two to three years. However, a small but growing number of quartz watches use lithium batteries that last five to 20 years.

Generally, mechanical watches are more expensive than quartz watches; most high-end watches are hand crafted mechanicals.

In addition to the movement and dial, a typical watch has a case enclosing the movement; a protective transparent crystal that covers the dial, usually made of plastic or mineral glass (chemically tempered glass, hardened and scratch-resistant); a bezel, the protective rim holding the crystal over the dial; and a band (strap or bracelet) that holds the watch on the wrist.

Watch words: Here are some watch terms you may need to explain to customers:

• Caliber. The diameter and factory number of a watch movement.

• Crown. A small knob or button on a stem (usually at the 3 o'clock position on the watch case) that sets time and can perform other functions. Chronographs usually have three buttons for their functions.

• Functions. These are activities a watch performs in addition to telling time. They can include day/date, moon phase, alarm and seconds hand.

• Shock-resistance. The ability of a watch to withstand an accidental fall or bump without being damaged. The government says a watch must be able to withstand a 40" fall to a hardwood surface without damage and a gain or loss of no more than 60 seconds a day to qualify. It is illegal to call a watch "shock proof."

• Subdial. A small circular "face" on the dial showing seconds, dates, moon phases, dual-time, chronograph or other functions.

• Watchband. Holds the watch on the wrist. There are three main types: **bracelets** (block, link, mesh and wire mesh metal bands most often made of stainless steel, gold, goldplate, gold-tone or a combination; the latter is called two-tone); **expansion metal bands** (which stretch to fit easily over the hand and onto the wrist); and **straps** (made of leather or synthetic materials in a wide variety of styles and colors).

• Water resistance. A federally approved term to indicate the amount of pressure a watch can withstand under water without leaking or losing accuracy. It is illegal to call a watch "water proof." Water resistance isn't permanent; gaskets around the crystal and stem must be inspected periodically. General water resistance means a watch can withstand minor moisture (such as rain or hand washing), but shouldn't be worn for swimming. Watches that are water resistant to 50 to 100 meters can be worn for bathing, showering or swimming in shallow water. Those resistant to 150 to 200 meters can be worn for recreational scuba diving, swimming and snorkeling. Professional diver watches can be worn to 300 to 1,000 meters for deep-sea activities.

Types of watches: The categories of watches available to consumers keeps growing. Here are some of the most popular:

• Chronograph. In addition to telling time, a chronograph can act as a stop watch, measuring intervals of time (start, stop and return to zero) down to fractions of a second.

• Diver watch. Designed to withstand deep water pressure, these watches have a screw down crown (so it can't be pulled into a setting position under water) and a unilateral, rotating bezel that shows how long the diver has been down. Diver watch styling has become popular, creating a new category of "sport-look" watches.

• Fashion watch. This term describes colorful, trendy watches, often designed to complement popular fashion trends.

• Perpetual calendar. These watches have a calendar function that automatically keeps track of days, dates, months (including February and 31-day months) and years (including leap years) without adjustment. Perpetual calendars are preset for periods ranging from decades to several hundred years.

• Skeleton watch. The movement in this watch is exposed to view through a transparent face and/or caseback.

• Sport watches. These are designed for active wear, especially swimming, and are water-resistant to 50 meters (165 feet) or more. Many watches are designed for a specific sport, such as flying, diving, sailing, yachting, fishing, golfing or climbing. Chronographs, a category of sport watches, can be used in timing a number of speed sports, such as car racing, boating or track.

• World time watches. Also called travelers' or travel time watches, these enable travelers to keep track of times at home and in one or more other time zones.

• Jewelry or dress watches. These are designed for evening wear and look like fine jewelry with a watch. Upscale models use real gemstones and precious metals.

WATCHBANDS: PRACTICAL, FUN, EXOTIC

Behold the lowly watchbands. Often set off to the side of a counter or even stored out of sight until a customer asks for one, they rarely get the support they deserve. Yet watchbands account for an estimated $44 million in annual bread-and-butter business in the U.S. And vendors say the figure could be higher if retailers made even minimal effort.

True, watchbands aren't diamonds or gold, though you can get them made of both. But their margins—up to triple keystone—are proportionally higher. And more than half the jewelers who sell watchbands do most of their business in bands selling for more than $20, according to a recent JCK poll.

Watchbands are practical, fun and exotic; they help to pay the bills during slow business periods; and they are great add-on sales. Almost everyone must buy one sometime.

Promoting watchbands with the same enthusiasm you promote gold chain or engagement rings or watches is smart business, say many jewelers. Remember that if you don't carry watchbands, your customers will go to another store where they might also find a piece of jewelry they like.

What is a watchband? Simply put, the watchband is an attachment that holds a watch on the wrist. Watchbands come in a spectrum of colors, styles and materials, ranging from synthetics and leather to platinum and karat gold, and at retail prices ranging from a few dollars to $100 or more.

There are three main types:

• Metallic bracelet. These come in several styles (including block, link, mesh and wire mesh) and often are stainless steel, gold, goldplate, goldtone or a combination. The latter is called two-tone.

• Strap. These can be leather (calf being the most popular) or synthetic materials (including cord, plastic and nylon) and come in a variety of styles and colors. Straps are popular attachments for sport watches and are ideal for fashion watches. Consumers often change straps of inexpensive quartz watches to suit their wardrobe or activity.

• Expansion bands. These stretch to fit over the hand and onto the wrist and are especially popular in the U.S. Though once made only of metal, they now also come in versions that have the look of leather.

Selling tips: Here are some guidelines on how to sell watchbands:

• Display your watchbands in your watch department or near the cash register. Make use of displays that vendors offer for use on countertops, in counters or in windows. Many of these make your selling job easier by showing which band is suited to what type of watch.

• Create watchband customers. When you sell a watch, include a coupon for a 10% discount on a replacement band or offer a minimal discount on a new band when someone brings in an old one as a trade in. Create add-on sales. When customers come to buy a watch or to have some jewelry serviced, encourage them to look at their watchband and suggest getting a new one—or two.

• Offer a variety of colors, widths and styles. Target bands to specific lifestyles, such as sports, evening wear or children.

• Know your watchband customers. Men buy more than half the bands sold in jewelry stores (ages 30-39 comprising the largest segment of this group).

• Cultivate a specific market. Some watchband suppliers have added jewelry bracelet collection for women's watches, for example. And the popularity of chronographs and sport watches has created demand for hefty straps and sport watchbands. Some band suppliers even offer gift packets of watchbands.

• Promote style. More than half the jewelers (53%) recently polled by JCK said this is what matters most to watchband buyers. Only 25% said material and 12% said price. More than 50% of watchband customers are buying for themselves, so ask whether they will use the band mostly for casual, active, business or evening wear.

• Be prepared. The heaviest selling season for watchbands is November and December. Lay in a good supply of bands and promote them as part of your full service. Highlight exotic fashionable and unusual bands.

• Romance the product. Promote affordable elegance. Talk about the exotic leathers. Encourage customers to upgrade the look of their watches with gold-filled or even gold bracelets.

CLOCKS OFFER OPPORTUNITIES

Clocks are naturals as home and office accessories and as gifts.

Of special interest to jewelers is the fact that the upscale end of the market—primarily mantel and table clocks—is growing. While the total U.S. clock market (excluding clock radios) has shrunk (from 37.6 million sold in 1990 to 32.7 million in 1993), the share of clocks retailing for more than $51 grew from 6.4% to 9.1% in the same period.

The average U.S. household now owns more than six clocks, most of them other than bedside alarm clocks and clock radios. And most Americans buy at least one new clock a year.

Clocks come in as many styles as there are consumer tastes, from traditional to contemporary, and in price points from very affordable to luxury.

The most popular case materials are polished brass and wood, such as walnut, oak or maple. Also popular are crystal, porcelain, lacquered and "metalized" or hot-stamped finishes.

And the most popular type is wall clocks—accounting for about a third of the market—though desk and mantel clocks have steadily increased their share in recent years.

Selling tips: Here are some ideas to help you sell clocks:

• Emphasize the clock's features and benefits. Consumers identify style and features as the major factors in choosing a clock, according to industry surveys. So point out styling, craftsmanship, precision (most clocks use state-of-the-art quartz movements) and special features that make them a stylish and functional addition to a home or office.

• Promote variety. Everyone knows there are mantel, wall, desk and grandfather (long-case) clocks. But how about grandmother clocks (smaller than grandfather clocks), picture frames clocks (with a picture on one side and a clock on the other), clocks with crystal cases, clocks designed as trendy home furnishings, clocks with world time zones, exquisite luxury timepieces, nautical clocks, clocks with Mickey Mouse and other popular cartoon figures, avant garde clocks, clocks that glow in the dark, bedside clocks that "talk," and clocks for kids? And that's just a few.

• Stress value. When consumers spend money these days, they want value and quality. They are willing to pay a little more if they know a clock is a well-made, state-of-the-art timepiece that will enhance their home or office for years to come.

• Promote clocks when people are most likely to buy them. The biggest clock-selling season is April to June, in time for graduations, weddings, Mother's Day and Father's Day. The next biggest season is the year-end holidays.

• Clocks also are popular components of corporate incentive award programs. Cultivate local businesses, country clubs and schools. To keep them coming back, offer free plating and engraving.

• Specialize. Find a clock niche no one else in your area serves, such as artistic luxury-price clocks, grandfather clocks or nautical clocks.

• Promote after-sales service.

• Stock according to your market. Stock more expensive models if you serve an affluent market, less expensive models for middle-class markets.

• Show your clocks. Put those with moving parts such as pendulums and revolving balls in your window. They catch people's attention.

Clock mechanisms: Three types of mechanisms "run" a clock:

• Quartz. These work the same way as quartz watches (see the watch section). Quartz clocks are either analog (dial and hands) or digital (liquid crystal numerical display). Most clocks have quartz movements.

• Mechanical. The two main types are **spring-driven** (also called key-wound and spring-wound), in which a key is used to wind a mechanical mainspring that powers the clock as it unwinds, and **weight driven,** in which the gravitational pull of heavy weights powers the movement. This is used in floor clocks and some wall clocks.

• Electric. These clocks are plugged into an electrical outlet for energy to run the motor. Electrical clocks can be analog or digital.

Clock words: Here are some words you may need to explain to customers:

• Bezel. Front section of clock case, including the rim into which the crystal is set.

• Case (also called the cabinet). Contains the clock movement and houses the dial face.

• Chapter ring. The outer ring of the clock face in which hours are marked.

• Crown. The top of a clock case (not to be confused with the stem of a watch case).

• Crystal. The protective transparent covering of the dial.

• Finial. A decorative element, usually brass or wood, on top of a clock cabinet, especially on mantel or long-case clocks.

• Lunar dial. A "window" on some clocks showing the phases of the moon.

• Minute track. A zone (either on the dial rim or its center) divided into 60-minute segments.

Clock types: Here are other major types of clocks:

• Alarm clock. A desk or table clock that can be preset to ring, buzz or play a melody at a specific time. A travel alarm is compact, often with two or more time zones.

• Anniversary clock. So called originally because it needed winding only once a year. Now it's best known as an anniversary gift. Characteristics include a glass dome or a brass and glass case with four small balls or weights that rotate horizontally.

• Carriage clock. A small rectangular clock, often brass, with glass sides and a hinged handle on top. It was first created for Napoleon's officers after a tardy general caused him to lose a battle.

• Chime clock. A clock with a chime mechanism that plays on the hour and, in many models, quarter-, half-, or three-quarter-hour intervals, in mantel and wall versions. They often have a silencing switch.

- Cuckoo clock. This originated in southern Germany (not Switzerland, as commonly assumed), which remains the primary source. The cuckoo clock is usually a replica of a small house made of wood or wood-like material and decorated with carved animal figures. A "bird" pops out and chirps on the hour and half hour.
- Decorator clock. A generic name for a variety of wall clock designed to complement home and business interiors.
- Grandfather clock. Also called long-case or floor clocks. These combine detailed cabinetry with weight-driven chime movements in a wooden case 72" to 84" high. A grandmother's clock is smaller.
- Nautical clock. A replica of navigational devices that tell time and also navigational/nautical functions. The case is usually round and brass.
- Schoolhouse clock. Originally designed for early American classrooms, this clock (usually wood) has a round or octagonal case and a lower pendulum cabinet.
- Tambour. Also called a Napoleon clock, the shape of this mantel or desk clock reportedly resembles the shape of Napoleon's hat (thin edges rising to a high rounded center).

WRITING ORDERS FOR WRITING INSTRUMENTS

When seated at the diamond counter with a smartly dressed, successful business executive, the retail jeweler noticed one piece of the picture missing. The executive was wearing a fine timepiece, sported a jeweled wedding band and pocketed a hand-crafted leather appointment book. But when making notes about a ring, the customer pulled out a disposable plastic pen that barely scribbled.

Mental note made, the jeweler decided to discuss fine writing instruments with the customer during a subsequent visit. Fortunately, the retailer carried a wide selection of writing instruments—enough to meet the needs of such a clearly demanding customer.

Would you be able to take advantage of the same sales opportunity?

High potential: If inventory is available and employees are informed, the potential for a sale is high. Fine writing instruments have long been a favorite gift for corporate and personal reasons. Now more and more people buy them for themselves. The reason may lie partly in what some people see as a more conservative way to accessorize.

"Men are running out of accessories," says Wayne Kingland, vice president of marketing for Montblanc USA, Bloomsbury, N.J. "Although neckchains and cuff links are still very much available, many men today take a more conservative approach." He believes men have three main accessories: fine timepieces, personal leather products (key chains, agendas, card holders) and fine writing instruments.

Of course, women also buy fine writing instruments, and manufacturers offer models specifically for them. In fact, customers in search of a writing instrument today have a wide variety of choices, says Harold Rosenberg, vice president of sales/carriage trade, at Waterman and Parker, Boston, Mass.

In addition to pens as accessories, many customers also are interested in the "culture" of writing, says Kingsland. Using a fine writing instrument for personal and business correspondence indicates a high personal interest in the sub-

ject, he says. "With automation, it's easy for anyone to generate a well-typed letter," he says. "But a handwritten note shows that the person has taken the time to be personal and to present a high touch—as opposed to high-tech." (Kingsland also suggests that jewelers offer choice stationery with their fine writing instruments.)

Selling tips: As with jewelry, customers need education about writing instruments, says Rosenberg. Here are some tips:

- A customer may not know that a rollerball offers a somewhat smoother ink delivery than a ballpoint, which uses a thicker ink. Demonstrate the difference.
- Does the pen use a twist mechanism or a push button? It makes a difference to some customers.
- With a fountain pen and many twist pens, the cap is an integral part of the design that you should explain.
- Circumference also makes a difference. Larger hands often prefer pens with greater girth or with heavier counterweight for better balance.
- Jewelry manufacturers encourage retail salespeople to wear jewelry so customers see how it looks. The same rule applies for pens. When taking notes or writing orders, use a fine writing instrument in an attempt to pique consumer interest.

Display: Many manufacturers of fine writing instruments offer showcase displays that make efficient use of shelf space while showing a range of pens and pencils. In most cases, several pens are shown in their own sleep package while most of the line is shown out of the package. Create an interesting corner by adding an opened diary with calligraphy or stylized writing.

Also take advantage of the nameplates, mirrored displays, counter signs, window signs and advertising material offered by manufacturers, says Rosenberg.

Concentrate on a line of writing instruments that best fits your store image and clientele, say manufacturers. While many luxury lines offer affordable versions of their pricier models, be careful about underselling your image. A low-cost pen that's also sold at a nearby mass merchant could undercut your guild image.

A jeweler known for original and exclusive jewelry should keep abreast of limited-edition writing instruments offered by leading manufacturers. These often include diamond accents and fine enamel and lacquer finishes on gold, platinum or stainless steel.

HELP CUSTOMERS SET A FINE TABLE

Picking tableware is a pleasurable task. Many customers choose it as they begin a new life together. Or when they are redecorating and want new china to go with a new dining room. Or when they finally can afford to buy the dinnerware they didn't get for their wedding.

But choosing tableware can be a daunting task, with hundreds of styles and patterns to pick from. In addition, many brands are discounted widely. Consider these tips to make your selling task easier:

- Begin by helping customers assess their needs. Some good questions to ask: Will the dinnerware be used more often in formal or casual settings? Is this a first dinnerware purchase, a fill-in or a replacement? How is the home decorated—is it traditional, contemporary, country? What's the color scheme?
- Tastes change. Customers may opt for something bold, dramatic or thematic, only to tire of it in five years. If

customers admire a certain pattern but aren't sure of its long-term appeal, suggest they buy just a few pieces—such as a bowl, candlesticks or pitcher—then choose a more enduring style for the dining room.

• Explain patterns in groups: floral, geometric, solid color bands, all-over color, one overall motif or pattern applied to the entire surface. Does the customer prefer a traditional pattern, a contemporary pattern, a simple pattern, a busy floral?

• Select a color family. Does the customer prefer earth tones, pastels, white or rainbow bright? Will there be a gold or platinum band around the edge?

• Choose a shape for the cups and bowls. Will it be coupe (rimless) or deep-rimmed?

• Remember that dinnerware doesn't have to match. Many people choose coordinating patterns to mix and match for different uses and courses of the meal. One of the easiest ways to mix and match is to begin with the dinner plate and then choose pleasing combinations of color, texture and pattern for the remaining dinnerware.

• Be able to explain the different types of china to your customers.

Earthenware is formed from clay and fired in a kiln without the addition of glass-like material.

Stoneware is made of clay to which a fusible stone—such as sand or ground flint—has been added. This allows the clay to be fired at a higher temperature. The finished product is harder than earthenware.

Fine china, or porcelain, is the most glass-like variety of china. This is due to a combination of kaolin clay (fine white clay), feldspar and flint, along with other elements particular to each manufacturer. Fine china is fired at very high temperatures, allowing the elements to vitrify into a hard, nonporous ceramic. Its strength allows dinnerware to be formed into thinner, more delicate shapes. Fine china is translucent when held up to the light and rings clearly when tapped on the rim.

Bone china is a form of fine china to which bone ash has been added for a bright white color. Because the process was developed and is used primarily in England, bone china is often called English china.

The rest of the table: A well-set table includes flatware, hollowware and crystal or glassware. Here are some pointers for selling each:

• Flatware includes eating and serving utensils. Sterling silver is the most elegant and expensive choice. Many women have a silver pattern chosen for them at birth. Pieces are added for significant events throughout their lives so that when they marry, they are well on their way to a complete collection. Sterling is high-maintenance, requiring polish to remove and prevent tarnish.

Silverplated flatware has a base metal core electroplated with layers of silver. The look and designs emulate sterling, but at a much lower cost. It also must be polished, but frequent use helps to prevent tarnish for sterling and silverplate.

Stainless flatware comes in many designer styles. The color is cooler (bluer), and the price is only a fraction of sterling.

• Hollowware simply means accessory serving pieces such as bowls, vegetable dishes, candlesticks, coffee and tea services and trays. Hollowware can be made from china, sterling, silverplate, stainless or crystal.

• Crystal refers to brilliant, clear, high-quality glass with lead added. Lead content varies by manufacturer; 24%

lead is considered "full lead" crystal but some manufacturers add up to 30%. The best way to tell the quality of crystal is the "ping" test. Fine crystal produces a clear ringing tone when tapped gently. The clearer and longer the tone, the better the crystal.

To choose a crystal pattern, first set the table with the china and flatware the customer likes. Discuss the options available, such as a cut or clear pattern. Clear patterns can be more expensive than cut or etched patterns because it takes a great deal of skill to blow a perfect stem, whereas tiny mistakes can be covered up with cutting or etching. Stemware, by the way, simply refers to glasses with an elongated stem.

Figurines and collectibles: Some jewelers also offer a selection of fine figurines or collectibles in their tableware departments. They can be a good source of incremental sales because figurines echo the owner's interests and hobbies, making a very personal gift.

Figurines come in all shapes, sizes and themes—from cats to canaries to children. They are made in porcelain, crystal, silver, brass, fine wood or even carved gemstones.

If the customer is interested in collecting figurines of a certain type, this can ensure repeat sales.

Reasons to Buy

REASONS TO BUY DIAMONDS

• They symbolize love. Diamonds are a traditional symbol of betrothal and love. They're they very essence of the beauty and timelessness of love.

• They are beautiful. Diamond's unique properties create fire and brilliance no other gemstone has. Cared for properly, they'll always do so.

• They are versatile. Single-stone engagement rings aren't the only diamond pieces consumers want to see. New shapes and different colors are the perfect option for consumers who value tradition but want something unique.

• They are durable. They're the hardest substance known to man and can be handed down from generation to generation. Like the saying goes—diamonds really are forever.

Care and cleaning

Believe it or not, many consumers complain that their diamond has "lost its sparkle." In a way, they're right. Oil from soap, hand cream and skin coats diamonds and cuts the light that travels through them. In a jeweler's showcase, dust and other air pollutants can have the same effect.

The solution to this problem is regular cleaning with a commercial jewelry cleaner or ammonia and water. Dip the diamond jewelry into the solution, scrub gently and thoroughly with a soft brush (hard bristles won't harm the diamond but may scratch the gold setting), rinse in clear water and dry with a lint-free cloth.

While diamonds are virtually unscratchable, they can be chipped or broken by hard knocks so they should be removed for manual labor, including gardening. If a diamond is chipped, it can be repaired or repolished by sending it to a cutter who specializes in such work.

REASONS TO BUY COLORED GEMSTONES

- Colored gems add diversity and exur jewelry collection.
- This is a chance to buy your own birthstone! You will find that your birthstone often is available in a great array of colors and varieties.
- Colored gems are easy to wear because you can tie the various colors in with trends in fashion.
- Looking for a one-of-a-kind look? Colored gemstones speak of your individual sense of style and beauty. They add to your unique nature.
- Colored gems often combine beautifully to make statements that are multicolored, dynamic and eye-catching.

REASONS TO BUY PEARLS

- They're versatile. Pearl jewelry can range from a single magnificent South Seas pearl mounted on a pendant or ring to affordable multilayered strands of small freshwater pearls. These strands can be natural colored for evening wear or dyed any color for more casual wear. Traditional round akoya pearls are a near necessity for formal evening wear. Add-on pendants or fancy clasps that can be removed and used as a brooch transform an elegant strand into a fashion statement.
- They're fashion-makers. Affordable dyed strands of freshwater pearls can be found to complement every color in a woman's wardrobe. Baroque pearls are combined with gold and other gemstones for unique designer pieces. And even traditional strands can be doubled or tripled with a jeweled clasp or cameo.
- They're "green." Because pearl oysters and mussels are very sensitive to environmental conditions, pearl farmers take great pains to preserve the ecology of their regions.

REASONS TO BUY PRECIOUS METAL JEWELRY

- It's timeless. Gold and silver have been prized for their beauty and rarity for thousands of years and continue to be today.
- It comes in all price ranges. Precious metal jewelry is available at price points that will suit every budget.
- It's a perfect gift. No one ever has to worry about getting the right color or style; nearly everyone loves precious metal jewelry.
- It's versatile. Nothing combines timeless appeal with current fashion like precious metal jewelry. It goes with everything—and never goes out of style.

CARE AND CLEANING OF PRECIOUS METALS

Gold and platinum are among the world's most tarnish-resistant metals. They can be cleaned easily with jewelry cleaner or a mild detergent.

Some consumers complain that their gold jewelry leaves a black smudge on their skin. This doesn't come from the gold itself, rather from the skin's own oils reacting with the gold alloys. Customers should be able to prevent the smudge by cleaning the jewelry frequently.

Silver does tarnish because it reacts to particles in the air (sulfur, in particular). This tarnish is a microthin coating, not deterioration, and can be wiped away easily with silver polish.

REASONS TO BUY DESIGNER JEWELRY

- It's unique, setting the wearer apart and saying "I have taste and appreciation for fine art."

- A customer can find one (or several) designers whose style matches her own.
- A jeweler can help a customer to become a collector.

REASONS TO BUY BRIDAL JEWELRY

- It's a tradition that dates back centuries. In modern times, many couples don't even consider an engagement "official" without a ring. And the wedding ring symbolizes marriage to everyone who sees it.
- The marriage ceremony itself often states "with this ring, I thee wed," thus making it rather awkward to get married without one.
- The ring will last at least as long as the marriage.
- Jewelry is just about the only part of the wedding day attire that will be worn again. Wedding rings will be worn every day for the rest of the couple's lives.

REASONS TO BUY WATCHES

- They're fashionable. Today's watches are designed to be as stylish as they are durable and functional. In fact, many jewelry designers have added watches to their collections.
- They're versatile. Today's watches offer a variety of functions and designs to suit every need, taste and lifestyle.
- They're durable. Today's watch is water resistant (from crystal to strap), shock resistant and just plain tough. Many have stainless steel cases and bands and mineral crystals that are chemically hardened and scratch-resistant.
- They're fun! Many watches are designed for specific activities, including flying, boating, fishing, golfing, climbing and racing. In addition, a variety of models feature trendy and popular cartoon characters at prices ranging from $25 to $5,000.
- They're collectible. Once a prerogative of the wealthy, watch collecting is become a popular hobby of mass-market and midprice watch buyers. In addition to Swatch and Fossil watch clubs, a number of other popular brands regularly produce limited-edition watch series with collectors in mind.
- They're affordable. Good quality, well-made watches are available at virtually any price point. Indeed, a number of mid- and upscale watch brands have lowered their entry prices or added more affordable collections to attract new, younger customers.

REASONS TO BUY WATCHBANDS

- They are practical. A new strap or bracelet gives a watch new life and is an economic alternative to buying a new watch.
- They are healthy. Many of today's watchbands are antiallergic and water-resistant.
- They are available in a variety of styles—from conservative to fashion-forward—in many materials—from inexpensive synthetics to leather and precious metals—to suit any watch.
- They are fun and exotic. Genuine leather straps come from a variety of animals, including shark, boar, lizard, alligator, ostrich and calf.

REASONS TO BUY CLOCKS

- They are versatile and varied. There are clocks to suit virtually every taste, style and need.
- They make ideal gifts. They come in all shapes, sizes and functions and are appropriate for any gift-giving occa-

sion. Many desk clocks, for example, are sold to women seeking that elusive "great gift for the man who has everything." And others—such as anniversary clocks—are designed specifically for landmark occasions.

- They are ideal for corporate and incentive award programs.
- Clocks are stylish and elegant. Wall, desk and mantel clocks are designed to complement and enhance home or office decor.
- They are efficient and functional. Most of today's clocks use state-of-the-art quartz timekeeping technology, guaranteeing accuracy to within one minute per year.
- They travel. In today's on-the-go business world, compact travel clocks with alarms, time zones, radios and lighted dials are indispensable.
- They are collectible. More and more clockmakers have created models designed for collectors, including miniatures and limited editions.

REASONS TO BUY FINE WRITING INSTRUMENTS
- They help your customers to make a more complete style statement.
- They appeal to people interested in the "culture" of writing.
- They offer gift options at a variety of price points, from the highly affordable to the astronomical.
- They are on a limited list of accessories for men.
- They provide an opportunity for add-on purchases,

including wood and gold or goldplated pen holders and choice stationery.

REASONS TO BUY TABLEWARE AND FIGURINES
- A table set with fine china is a wonderful way for your customers to express themselves, their tastes and their graciousness to guests.
- Assuming it's properly cared for, fine tableware is a worthy heirloom. Many women are sentimentally attached to their mother's or grandmother's china, silver or crystal; often such patterns are discontinued, but can be located with a bit of searching. If you are able to locate the pattern, chances are you've captured a lifelong customer. If you can't successfully locate the pattern, you can help the customer find pieces to coordinate and fill in the set.
- It's a way to set yourself apart. While a great deal of tableware is discounted, a great deal isn't. Focus on carrying patterns from manufacturers that don't allow discounting and that aren't carried in every department store in town. Customers, too, will feel special if they have china that isn't advertised at 50% off every week in the newspaper.
- Figurines are decorative works of art, enhancing customers' homes and echoing their personalities. They're a natural for collecting; owners often concentrate on pieces by the same artist or with the same theme.
- Figurines make excellent gifts and can increase in value with time, especially if they are limited editions.

JCK Management Study Center: Putting Your Message Into The Marketplace

July 1994

CREATIVE AD CAMPAIGNS HEAT UP SALES
The first step is to advertise.
The second step is to advertise.
And so is the third.
So say advertising experts, who add that jewelers all too often feel no need to advertise even when their profits are stagnant or dwindling. By not advertising, say these experts, jewelers become their own worst enemies in the competition for consumer attention.
"Retailers will throw open the doors, then sit back and wait for people to just file into their store," says Shelly Kuehn, president of Jewelry Pro-Motion, Dallas, Tex. "Instead, they should give the public a good reason to come into their store."

Further, say the experts, some jewelers who do advertise use a scattershot approach, missing opportunities to reach the very targets they want to hit. Because today's consumers have more options than ever when spending disposable income, jewelers need to know how to put their message into the marketplace with creative, targeted, goal-oriented advertising.
And creativity is crucial. A distinctive look, a special quality, a hook of some kind should connect jewelers' ads with their stores in the minds of consumers.
JCK asked the experts to explain why this type of advertising is so important and tell how to develop and launch effective ad campaigns. Next, seven jewelers tell how their creative, innovative advertising campaigns captured consumers' interest—and dollars. Then, finally, come lists of tips

259

related specifically to TV, radio, print and direct mail advertising and public relations.

Why advertise? Amazingly, a number of retailers still question the need to advertise at all. They use all means of rationalization to justify a meager or nonexistent ad budget. "Business is good enough" and "It costs too much" are common examples.

Also common are retailers who advertise occasionally, see no immediate gain and conclude that all advertising is a waste of money.

But advertising experts and other jewelers see it differently. They say the out-of-sight/out-of-mind axiom is even more prevalent as today's busy consumers balance family and work schedules and grow more disenchanted with shopping. If you don't remind consumers you have the perfect accessory for that new dress or the perfect gift for that upcoming event, they very well may buy something from another retailer whose advertising did catch their attention.

Once you concede that advertising will help keep your store in the public mind, organize your thoughts so you can develop an effective campaign. The major considerations:

• Set aside time to develop a goal-oriented, long-term advertising program.

• Set aside enough money to see the program through to completion.

• Remember that while individual ads may feature a particular piece of merchandise or service, the important thing is to keep your name and message clearly etched in the public mind.

Setting goals: We've mentioned goals. They can be anything you wish to accomplish. Here are some examples:

• Realize immediate sales of a particular item.

• Create the appropriate image for your type of store.

• Revamp your image to appeal to a different kind of consumer (perhaps you want to move upscale, for example).

• Introduce your store to new residents or visitors.

• Remind potential customers you offer a certain type of jewelry (class rings, diamond anniversary jewelry, etc.).

• Simply let consumers know where you are located, your hours of operation and payment terms.

• Link your store's long history to the community ("75 Years on Main Street").

• Differentiate your store from others in the area ("The store for affordable karat gold jewelry").

• Feature a service (such as watch repair) in addition to a product.

• Announce a change in management and/or policy ("We now take American Express").

Getting started: Once you set your goal and are ready to develop a campaign around it, answer a few basic questions, says H. David Morrow of the Diamond Promotion Service.

First, is your goal to advertise specific products? If so, are the products already popular with your customers? Do your salespeople know what is being advertised and have they been given a sales goal? Are the goals attainable? Are prices appropriate to your customer demographics.

Can you achieve your goal with your targeted audience? For example, are engagement rings likely to stir interest in the many retirement communities your store may serve? Do the single men and women in your community read the newspaper in which your engagement ring ad appears? Have

you found out which radio stations and newspapers interest students at the local college? Do you have the goods that either of these specialized groups are likely to buy?

The latter questions assume you know your customer base. While a long-term goal for any advertising campaign is to increase the number of regular customers, it's critical that you know who already shops in your store. Gathering such demographic data can be as simple as compiling a list of recent sales and separating customers into groups based on items purchased, price categories, frequent customers, males, females, gift- or self-purchasers. Add to the list by asking all customers to fill out a postcard with space for name, address, birthdate and anniversary date.

You also must update the list periodically. If you send a direct mail piece using a list that hasn't been updated for two years, many of the pieces will be returned because the customers have moved. And that could lead you to assume—incorrectly—that direct mail is a failure as an advertising method.

Proceed with the plan: Once you've set a goal and defined your customer base, devote time to planning what medium, what approach and what frequency of advertising you will need to achieve that goal. If you have time to do it yourself, fine. But some will need to obtain professional help.

Skilled local marketing and advertising agencies can put a novice on the right track or expedite a veteran's prepared plans. They know the best printers and photographers and may have a better idea about exactly where ads should be placed and for how long.

Finding an advertising agency can be as simple as consulting a telephone directory. But a more efficient method may be to ask around within the business community. Is there a nearby business with an advertising campaign you admire? Ask the retailers who they work with.

Whether in-house or not, an advertising plan needs to have a budget and a schedule. "The typical allocation for advertising is 5% of gross sales," says Kuehn. At that amount, a good campaign can operate during the entire year and begin to show returns over the long run. "But realistically, I think most jewelers spend closer to 2%." She encourages jewelers to aim for the higher figure.

The amount has to cover all production costs (photography, printing, paper and videotape) as well as postage fees, ad placement costs, agency fees, employee time (if required) and insurance (if you have to ship merchandise to be photographed).

Retailers also should take advantage of the co-op dollars and materials offered by their suppliers, says Don Reisfeld, president of Morton Advertising, New York, N.Y. Suppliers often provide photographs and camera-ready advertisements featuring their goods. Some go as far as to provide assistance and materials for radio and television advertising.

In addition, advertising material is available from some industry organizations, including the Diamond Promotion Service, Jewelers of America, the Platinum Guild International USA Jewelry Inc. and the World Gold Council.

Stay on schedule: Retailers often determine when to advertise based on when they sell the most jewelry. But this can be dangerous. "Jewelers often want to use all their ad dollars during one time of the year [November and December]," says Kuehn. "That's a big problem because they are advertising when the consumer has less time to look at ads and buyer traffic is already strong."

All jewelers should advertise for Christmas, she says, but huge promotions are probably unnecessary. Instead, more of your ad budget may be better spent during slower periods.

A schedule also ensures consistency. A hit-and-run strategy, where one or two ads are used at odd times during a year, can confuse consumers. "Jewelers can create a cycle effect, where consumers expect certain sales at certain times of the year," says Kuehn. If the jeweler breaks the cycle, it may take months or years (and added expense) to regain the momentum built up during the previous ad campaign.

RADIO ADS BREAK THROUGH THE CLUTTER

Business: Adolf Jewelers, Richmond, Va.

Goal: Create an unforgettable image to separate the store from other local jewelers in consumers' minds.

Strategy: Use offbeat, "non-jewelry store" ads.

Result: Holiday business was up 25% and continues to attract new customers.

Ron Adolf had a two-edged problem in 1992. He was tired of doing his own advertising work for his jewelry store—Adolf Jewelers. And he wanted somehow to set his independent, $1 million-plus-yearly store apart from two dozen other jewelers in his market.

His solution: hire an agency to create an advertising campaign, built primarily on radio, to "break through the clutter of jewelry advertising."

He chose Barber Martin & Associates, a local agency with some national accounts. The agency had hired a radio ad sales representative with whom Adolf had worked closely, so the agency and Adolf were on the same wavelength from the start. They agreed Adolf had to break away from the norm—nothing he did in advertising should look or sound like typical jewelry store ads.

Planning the campaign: First, agency representatives visited Adolf's store—without the sales staff's knowledge—to see how customers are treated and to get a feel for the business. They were impressed. When they walked in, the staff was friendly and helpful.

So their first suggestion was to add a logo—the store's first—to all packaging and ads to reflect that atmosphere. Instead of a usual slogan such as "The Diamond Store" or "Your Hometown Jeweler," Adolf's logo says "Relax. We'll try to make you happy." Because many people are intimidated about going into a jewelry store, says Adolf, the slogan "tells them they don't have to be nervous."

Next, they agreed that radio would be the primary advertising medium because it can target certain audiences and costs less than TV advertising.

Then Barber Martin & Associates, consulting with Adolf, went to work on the ads themselves. The first series of five radio spots (for a 30%-off sale) ran in late 1992. They targeted the gift purchase market and used a fictitious interviewer asking people about their purchases for the holiday season. In one ad, for example, the interviewer questions a man who bought his wife a vacuum cleaner for Christmas. The radio spot was supported by a half-page newspaper ad showing a large vacuum with the caption: "Nature abhors a vacuum and so does your wife. . . Buy her the ideal gift at Adolf Jewelers."

Adolf admits now he was "scared to death" when he launched the campaign. "Here I was going into my biggest season using ads about vacuum cleaners!" he says.

But he needn't have worried. Even in a weak economy, the ads contributed to "unbelievable" traffic and a 25% increase in holiday sales over the previous year, he says. And it wasn't once-in-a-lifetime luck. The store ran the ads during the 1993 Christmas season and posted another 25% gain.

Benefits: Adolf credits the ads for keeping consumer interest strong all year. "I have a store that is busy from the moment I open in the morning until I close at night," he says. "We always have traffic, and I'm in a strip center so we're a destination store—people come here looking for us."

The ads have had impact beyond sales. ZIP codes from outside the store's usual customer area are showing up on sales slips more often. And periodical public surveys by Barber Martin & Associates find Adolf is the one name people cite first or second when asked to name any jeweler they recall from advertising. (The agency also tracks competitors' advertising, seeing who spends how much, when and on what media.)

The ads also have gained recognition for Adolf in the jewelry industry. The company won first place in JCK's 1993 Excellence in Marketing Contest.

The cost: Adolf budgets well over $100,000 a year for advertising, most of it for radio. "I'm constantly on radio," he says. "If you just go on and off, spending a few thousand for a couple of weeks and then are off for 12, you're just throwing your money in the trash."

The cost of using an agency? "I'm spending the same amount of money now, but the agency is doing the work, and doing it much more effectively than I did," he says. Adolf typically launches about 10 new four-to-six-week campaigns each year. General sales and store image ads are targeted at people ages 18-55 while those for engagement rings are targeted at ages 24-40.

Adolf uses only major radio stations and newspapers—he does no secondary advertising in local newspapers and stations outside of Richmond. His agency found that anyone who reads local newspapers or listens to smaller radio stations also uses the bigger ones.

His latest radio ad announcing a two-for-one sale is getting lots of response. The announcer repeats every line. It's a simple gimmick—but unforgettable. "It's even ticking off some people who are tired of hearing it repeatedly," Adolf says with a chuckle. "But it brings people in; business is unbelievable right now."

PERSONAL TOUCH ATTRACTS A YOUNGER CROWD

Business: Tivol's, Kansas City, Mo.

Goal: To increase traffic, especially younger customers who might be intimidated about entering an upscale, prestigious jewelry store.

Strategy: Heavy use of cable TV ads during the Christmas shopping season, supported by newspaper advertising.

Result: Success! Business has grown and the store has had to enlarge its product mix to include merchandise suited to the increasing number of younger customers.

"I've worked with ad agencies for 31 years and hate 'em all! But if you can show me how to sell diamonds in the newspaper, I'll love you." With these somewhat intimidating words, jeweler Harold Tivol kicked off a relationship with his new advertising agent, John Muller of John Muller & Co., Kansas City, Mo.

The year was 1982. The two men conversed about the diamond and jewelry businesses at length. Muller was impressed with Tivol's charm and humor, as well as his breadth of knowledge about the jewelry market. In fact, he knew from the beginning that Tivol would have to be part of the ad campaign.

"The whole concept for the newspaper campaign sprang from Harold's vivacious personality," Muller says. The concept was simple: show no jewelry, only Harold Tivol in tones of black and gray against a white background. "In one ad, he leaned against the edge of the ad. The accompanying text was in large type and had a very eye-stopping effect." Even though no jewelry or diamonds were shown ("diamonds tend to look terrible in a newspaper," says Muller), the message was clear: Tivol's is about jewelry and diamonds.

Focus shifts: Four years into the print campaign, the focus shifted to trying to get the Tivol message to younger consumers. Tivol's reputation and business bond with the older, wealthier generation was solid, says Muller. But the upscale, conservative-looking store with a highly visible armed guard seemed to intimidate potential younger buyers. (Now the guard is less visible and the store has acquired a more open, inviting atmosphere.)

The goal was to cultivate the same bond with the younger generation that existed with the older one. Think of it as sowing seeds for sophisticated jewelry buyers of the future. To that end, Muller asked Tivol to participate in the television commercials. "At first he refused to be seen on TV," says Muller. "But we persisted, because we felt his sense of humor and character could be combined in an ad that would truly intrigue people. We wanted to show the public that Harold's is a face you can trust and like."

Tivol finally agreed when told he wouldn't have to speak in the commercial.

Ad development: Several TV ads were designed to break down the intimidation factor. They start similarly, with what appears to be a strongly backlighted planet against a blue background. "The Planets," a dramatic composition by 20th century composer Gustav Holst, plays while the viewer's attention becomes riveted on the supposed "planet." No planet. It's the top of Harold Tivol's bald head, with the camera then panning down to Tivol's irrepressible grin. Further panning reveals the product in Tivol's hands, all as the music builds to a crescendo.

"What we were looking for was positioning and tonality," Muller says.

The ads run on cable TV only. Muller estimates it costs the same amount to run an ad 10 times on cable TV as it does to run it once on network TV, allowing for higher frequency. Also, cable TV tends to attract younger viewers, exactly who Tivol's wanted to reach.

The TV ads have been running for seven or eight years, from late October through Christmas, and are supported by a newspaper campaign that continues after Christmas. Minor variations allow for different products.

Reasons for success: Muller labels the ad campaign a success for several reasons. "The 'Harold personality concept' reflects what the store stands for, and that has not changed,"

he says. "In fact we believe the campaign is successful because we haven't jumped around. The ads have had a cumulative effect."

The success has been quantitative, too. "More kids with jeans come into the store," he says, adding that Tivol's has increased its product mix as a result. "Now the mix goes down the scale, attracting younger customers who will turn into future seasoned buyers."

In addition, people talk about the campaign even after it ends. In April, for example, a customer told Tivol he'd seen him recently on TV. It's more likely the customer saw Tivol in a recent print ad and mentally made the connection to the TV ads that ran four months earlier!

And business is still growing. Vice President Jim Kriegel says business has tripled in volume since Tivol's first contracted with John Muller and Co., and he credits the agency for much of that growth.

As for the future, Tivol's will open its second store July 15 in Overland Park, Kan. Ads prepared for the grand opening are similar to the Christmas ads. Says Kriegel, "We are using the same strategy—building today's younger customer into tomorrow's buyer."

VIDEO WINS RAVE REVIEWS

Business: R.F. Moeller Jeweler, St. Paul, Minn.
Goal: Increase diamond business.
Strategy: Create an infomercial videotape to be given to prospective diamond customers and to support existing advertising.
Result: Business is up 40%, and the average diamond ring sale is up 51%.

One of the most successful videos now showing in the Minneapolis-St. Paul area isn't a Hollywood blockbuster. But it is getting rave reviews, recognition in the film industry and—most importantly—lots of diamond sales for its producer, R.F. Moeller Jeweler. The six-minute infomercial features the independent jewelry store and its diamond business and is given free to all prospective diamond ring customers (plus any other customer who requests one). In the first six months, the store gave away more than 300 copies.

The effect of the video? Total store receipts for the year ended April 30 were up 40%, and the average diamond ring sale rose 51% (from $2,247 to $3,400). "A significant portion of those increases was in the last half of the year and was directly due to the videos," says President Mark Moeller, who oversees the store's advertising and conceived the video promotion.

Moeller can be sure about the video's impact because the store closely tracks its diamond sales on computer. Since the video handout began, he says, "we literally don't lose a diamond ring sale."

Full advertising menu: R.F. Moeller Jeweler has an extensive advertising program, including the opening full-page ad in the jewelry section of the Twin Cities' telephone directory *Yellow Pages*, newspaper ads, "a good deal" of direct mail and local cable TV ads. (Moeller recently approved a $20,000 deal to run 3,000 spots over three months this summer on a rotation basis on 12 channels, including ESPN, CNN, CNN Headlines, TNT, USA and Discovery.)

"But just putting ads in newspapers and on TV isn't enough," says Moeller. "They bring people through the door. But we like to put something in customers' hands that they can't get from any other jeweler."

So Moeller fulfilled his long-time dream of creating a promotional video that his diamond customers could view at their leisure and that salespeople could use to close a sale and generate new ones. "Business and customer schedules can be so hectic that you can't always get your points across," he says. "The video is something that customers can take home, plug in and get the whole story in just six minutes. It reenforces what we say in a sales presentation and lays the groundwork [for a future sale]. Besides, do you know anyone who takes a video home and *doesn't* watch it?"

The creative process: The chance to create the video came when Moeller, who is vice president of the Twin Cities Muscular Dystrophy Association, met Joan Steffen, a popular news anchor for TV station KARE, at a fund-raiser. Steffen's husband, Joe Brandmeier, is an award-winning filmmaker with a video and film production company called Moving Pictures Inc.

After Moeller chose Moving Pictures to make his video, officials of the film company met with him within a week, listened to his concept, observed store operations and produced a script that he approved. Consulting Moeller each step of the way, Moving Pictures filmed 10 hours worth of material and edited it to a six-minute video with narration by Steffen.

The video combines black-and-white documentary-style coverage of a store staff meeting with color footage of employees and customers. "It talks about our history, our service and employees, and it presents the case why you should buy from us," says Moeller.

The project cost $12,000, which included 100 copies of the video. All work—including scripting, filming, direction, editing and post-production work—was done by Moving Pictures. The cost was reasonable and competitive, says Moeller. Depending on content, length and the film company, a professional video production can cost $2,000-$5,000 per minute. Duplicates cost $2.50 to $3.50 each, though the average cost shrinks as the number ordered increases, says Moeller.

Planning, impact: All Moeller advertising is carefully planned and adheres to a decision in the late 1980s to be *the* jeweler for diamonds and to make that fact the cornerstone of marketing campaigns, says Moeller. "You can't just do $20,000 cable TV ads or $12,000 videos overnight," says Moeller. "We plan advertising and the budget a year ahead and know how much we can allocate for diamond rings, for example. From that comes the money for cable TV, video or the *Yellow Pages*."

Interestingly, Moeller spends the least of his advertising budget in the yearend holiday season. "It's better to be dominant in the market in the first 10 months—when you get better buys out of season and fewer competitors are advertising heavily—than at the end of the year. If they hear my name all year, they'll remember it at year's end."

The video's impact on business has been dramatic, says Moeller. In addition to the 40% increase in diamond engagement ring sales and the 51% increase in average price, Moeller's market is expanding. For the first time in the store's history, customers from outside the local ZIP code now outnumber those from within. "People don't throw these videos away," he says. "They give them to their friends, who pass them to their friends." He expects to give out 5,000 copies and estimates the video will have a shelf-life of three to five years.

The video also has won recognition in the film industry. In April, it was a top winner in the annual Telly Awards, a national competition that honors outstanding, non-network film and video productions and cable TV commercials. Moeller's video was chosen from some 7,900 entries and such competitors as MGM and Jim Henson Productions.

Moeller and Moving Pictures have since created a video to promote Moeller's estate jewelry wholesale business—The Registry Ltd.—to retail jewelers around the country. A third video—a half-hour infomercial on how to buy a diamond, for use in direct mail and/or on cable TV—is under consideration.

ESTATE JEWELRY CATALOG BLOSSOMS INTO A WINNER

Business: Bromberg & Co., Birmingham, Ala.
Goal: Expand business in estate jewelry.
Strategy: Create a high-quality catalog for regular customers and other affluent residents.
Result: The catalog has become a general marketing tool that broadened the estate jewelry business, contributed significantly to annual growth during a recession and now accounts for at least 5% of store business annually.

Estate jewelry has been important to Bromberg & Co. for decades. "Everyone sells jewelry, but when you sell estate jewelry, you're selling something special, something with a story you can talk about," says Vice President John K. Bromberg.

In fact, each of the company's six stores has at least one 8'-long showcase filled with estate jewelry. And in the fourth quarter, before yearend holidays, the company assembles a $3 million estate jewelry show that travels to each of its stores, located in four markets.

To promote this show, Bromberg and his brother, William, decided to publish a catalog six years ago.

Quality look: The first eight-page issue set the format for its successors. "The key is to create a book with a long shelf life, not something that looks like a throw-away flier," says John Bromberg. That means high-quality paper, top-notch photography, informative descriptions—and a minimum of product photos. "Some catalogs are jammed with hundreds of items, which is confusing to the reader. For us, less is more."

The catalog features items that are already in the stores. "Many retailers think that in order to have a catalog, they have to get fancy stuff to show in it," he says. "But that's an additional cost and is unnecessary. We put in the things that make Bromberg what Bromberg is."

The Brombergs developed this concept and then assigned the photographic and production work to a local agency whose two partners were friends of the family.

The catalog was a winner professionally and business-wise from the start. The first edition won an Addy Gold award in a statewide advertising competition sponsored by the Montgomery Advertiser Federation (and is still proudly used by Bromberg & Co.'s ad agency in its own promotion packet). More importantly, customers responded enthusiastically. Indeed, one customer waving a just-published copy knocked vigorously on the door before the store opened in order to buy two of the most expensive pieces in it!

Bromberg & Co. also uses newspaper and radio advertising. But the catalog has grown steadily in importance and has changed in the process. What began as an eight-page catalog showing only estate jewelry now has 30 pages and shows all types of jewelry. Estate jewelry takes only one page these days, but it's always the first or second page. John Bromberg handles the jewelry section of the catalog while his cousin, Paul Byrne, oversees the tabletop section.

Year-long project: Work on the catalog begins in January when top management makes preliminary decisions on what to include and how to present it.

Local agencies are asked to submit bids to produce and distribute the catalog. An agency is selected by February, primary photography begins in April, galleys are reviewed and corrected between late June and August, printing begins in September and the ad agency mails the catalogs the fourth week of October.

Each catalog will cost Bromberg & Co. about 90¢ to produce and mail this year (postage accounts for about 35% of the total). That's down from $1.50 the first year (despite higher production and postage costs) because suppliers whose products are in the catalog now provide more co-op money to produce it.

The company mails about 25,000 copies of the catalog. The total includes 20,000 people on Bromberg & Co.'s regular customer list as well as names from mailing lists of area residents with annual household incomes of $70,000+.

Evaluating the catalog: The Brombergs measure the success of their catalogs in several ways.

One is the volume of telephone calls to order merchandise from the catalog using the toll free and local phone numbers listed inside.

Another is the support the catalog business provides, especially in difficult times. During the late 1980s and early '90s, when recession sent sales sliding for many jewelers, Bromberg & Co. enjoyed annual increases of 10% to 20%. "We've no doubt that the catalogs were significant contributors," says Bromberg.

Then there's the walk-in traffic. "People come in—catalog in hand—saying, 'I want to buy this,'" he says.

Bromberg doesn't have specific figures, but he estimates the catalog contributes at least 5% of annual business.

INFOMERCIAL DEMYSTIFIES CUSTOM DESIGN

Business: Roman Jewelers, Flemington, N.J.

Goal: Increase custom design sales.

Strategy: Create an infomercial explaining the custom design process to potential customers and present custom pieces as unique and desirable.

Result: Seventy percent of new customers are people who have seen the infomercial.

Roman Jewelers is located in an outlet town known for price promotions, but it's definitely at the other end of the retail spectrum. It caters to a local, affluent clientele that shops for distinctive, one-of-a-kind jewelry.

The store had advertised its services with 30-second commercials on cable television station C-TEC. "They were inexpensive to make and the coverage was good, but every few months they needed to make another one," says Ken Greenberg of C-TEC. Store owner Roman Shor and C-TEC considered other options and decided on a 30-minute

infomercial—enough time to explain the store philosophy, its merchandise and its focus on custom design.

Working with C-TEC, Shor literally produced his own show. "He's a natural producer," says Greenberg. "He instinctively knew how to get the best results."

Filming: The infomercial was filmed in the store. Lydia Smilek of C-TEC acts as host and introduces Shor, who gives a short history of the business his grandfather began 100 years ago in Minsk, Byelorussia, and which the family moved to the U.S. in 1980. Shor then turns over the show to Smilek and his sales specialist, Allyson Berlin.

This segment of the video answers concerns a new customer might have about shopping at the store. For example, Berlin discusses the store's quality- and service-oriented philosophy, gives Smilek a tour through some of the showcases, then summarizes the buying/selling process. She explains that customers are asked to describe their jewelry needs, then are shown different materials, methods and features that would best fit those needs. Berlin also stresses that whenever possible, the store encourages customers to wait while jewelry is repaired or when stones are set into new mountings.

The video also focuses on products in some detail. One example: Berlin demonstrates the versatility of a pearl necklace with a "mystery clasp" (a small bolt anchored to a pearl that screws into the adjacent pearl for a seamless appearance). Several such clasps are set into the same necklace so it can be quickly turned into two shorter necklaces or necklace and bracelet.

Smilek also interviews several satisfied customers, some of whom show jewelry that Shor designed for them.

Custom focus: The customer accolades introduce an educational section of the video that explains the custom-design process from sketch to finished product.

As a customer explains that she wants an old diamond set in a more contemporary piece, Shor sketches a design with baguette and round side stones. The customer approves the design, and the camera follows the creative process to the backroom, where an employee meticulously carves a wax model, pours the investment and casts the ring along with other models. Closeups show how the stones are set, how the prongs are tightened and how the ring is polished.

The video closes with a recap of the store's commitment to quality and customer service and a short introduction of the entire staff. The parting words from Shor: "Come to Roman's as a customer, leave as a friend."

Good response: The infomercial has aired four times weekly for several months. The response? The store's custom-design business has increased dramatically since the infomercial began, says Lucy Shor, head of promotions.

"Seventy percent of our new customers are people who have seen the infomercial," she adds.

Shor declines to reveal specific figures, but she says the infomercial was "well worth the cost." It was so worthwhile that the store plans to run another infomercial focusing on engagement rings and remounts.

THE VALUE OF CREATIVITY

Business: JayMark Jewelers, Birmingham, Ala.

Goal: Enhance awareness of the company's seven stores and stimulate sales, including a campaign to boost Christmas 1993 sales.

Strategy: Develop creative print and television advertising to differentiate JayMark from competitors.

Result: JayMark feels that television advertising has defined its image and accounts for much of its success.

JayMark Jewelers knows the value of creative advertising and plans its campaigns carefully—and often. In fact, Marketing Director Margaret O'Neil communicates weekly with Bill Attaway of Attaway Advertising, Hoover, Ala., which has handled the account since JayMark opened in 1981.

Together, O'Neil and Attaway develop print ads four to six times a year and direct-mail campaigns eight to nine times a year for the business, which O'Neil describes as a credit operation whose customers are interested mostly in lower-priced merchandise.

Direct mail campaigns—using the company's mailing list—feature booklets with coupons that customers can redeem for dollars off a purchase—a jewelry advertising technique that JayMark and Attaway say they pioneered in their area.

To reach new customers, JayMark relies on "marriage mail." This type of advertising gives several retailers a chance to save money by placing individual ads or coupons in one envelope per household in a given region. The retailers share mailing—and sometimes design—costs.

But most notable about JayMark's advertising strategy is the use of television commercials. Attaway says JayMark develops 30-40 commercials each year, accounting for more than 70% of total advertising.

JayMark makes television commercials for Christmas, Valentine's Day, Mother's Day and Father's Day. In fact, any holiday is a reason to celebrate with a commercial! When there isn't a convenient holiday, JayMark creates one—such as "Christmas in August." The company also advertises high-impact sales, wild weekend sales and popular seasonal events such as a January Clearance Sale and a Spring Diamond Sale.

National recognition: JayMark's unique advertising was recognized in 1993 when the television commercial "Christmas Magic" was chosen as a national finalist in the retail category of The Vision Awards for advertising. The competition selects the best local and regional television commercials created by advertising agencies.

The 30-second commercial featured a computer-animated toy train running around the base of a Christmas tree. Each car on the train displayed a part of JayMark's four-part slogan: "Best Service, Best Terms, Best Selection, Best Price." The animated opening was followed by product shots (seven versions featured different merchandise). The animation resumed to wrap up the commercial. "Christmas" ran Nov. 8 through Dec. 23 on all local television stations during the morning news, daytime soaps, prime time and late night. In fact, it could be seen as many as 30 times a day during the preholiday season.

Simultaneously, JayMark ran commercials for a high-impact sale, a one-day sale and a wild weekend sale.

The evaluation of the success of the commercial was straightforward—sales figures. JayMark set and reached its holiday sales goal. Customers also offered positive feedback, with many saying they enjoyed the animation.

Development: Planning and production of a commercial such as "Christmas" take four to six weeks. A concept and script are developed and given to the computer animator.

Animation time varies, but Attaway estimates two to three weeks. All of the product shots are done at the production house and usually take no more than one day per commercial.

The pieces—voice-over, product shots and animation—are brought together at the editing stage. Attaway often edits an entire commercial series in one day.

Hints for working with an advertising agency? While the agency usually develops the ideas and follows through with production, says Attaway, the jeweler and advertiser must work as a team. "We all need each other," Attaway says of the merchandiser, managers, sales team and ad agency.

A WELCOME KISS

Business: Lee Michaels Fine Jewelry, Baton Rouge, La.
Goal: To break into Baton Rouge's established community and become its "family jeweler."
Strategy: Gain recognition by using well-known community residents in billboard ads.
Result: Not only has Lee Michaels become the jeweler of choice, but Baton Rouge's well-known and respected residents now wonder out loud if *they* will ever be chosen to appear in the ads.

When Texas native Lee Michael Berg opened his first store in Baton Rouge 16 years ago, most residents were in the habit of driving 80 miles to New Orleans to buy fine jewelry. He found it difficult to crack this established Southern buying pattern until he contacted Dianne Allen and Associates, an advertising agency in Baton Rouge, in 1979.

Berg and the agency decided their initial objective should be to elevate the store's name and profile rather than focus on jewelry itself. When Berg related a story about a real-life customer who surprised his wife with a gift from Lee Michaels and got a big kiss in return, the idea for the "kiss-man" campaign was born.

"We decided to focus on the image of Lee Michaels Fine Jewelry by associating the store with a very well-known, respected and loved individual from the community," says Al McDuff, a partner and creative director at Dianne Allen and Associates. The idea was to create billboards showing a black-and-white photo of the individual with a big red kiss mark superimposed on his cheek and the words: "All I said was . . . 'It's from Lee Michaels.'"

Successful launch: The honor of being the first kiss-man went to bachelor Milton Womack, a successful building contractor. Womack had high public recognition because of his business and because a Baton Rouge community board had just honored him with a Golden Deeds award for his fund-raising and general philanthropy. "Getting him to participate was considered a major coup because he is shy, retiring and discreet," says McDuff. "He was the very last person Baton Rouge ever expected to see on a billboard, but he was the very best person for it."

The campaign was launched in 1981 and involved two media:

• A single billboard on a central interstate highway for 60 days beginning in November. "We chose a billboard because we could show the portrait and kiss larger than life," says McDuff. "Also, the interstate has high visibility. It runs right through Baton Rouge, so residents use it going to work or just getting around town."

• A one-time four-column-by-12" ad in a Sunday edition of Baton Rouge's *The Advocate* newspaper.

A new kiss-man is chosen each year. Other notables have included a dentist, an engineer and another contractor—all well-known in the community. Womack reprised his role in 1983, this time with his new bride, the only time a woman has appeared in the campaign.

Breaking the ice: Response—measured informally by comments by customers, employees and the owner's friends—has been phenomenal, says McDuff. In fact, people often ask how they too can become the kiss-man.

The campaign also broke the ice with Baton Rouge's entrenched families. Various segments of Baton Rouge society have turned to Lee Michaels as their family jeweler.

The campaign has been so successful that Berg and McDuff now have time to concentrate on separate projects to promote products. The product ads run in newspapers and most are directed at men. One series, titled "A Lee Michaels Christmas Hint for Men," shows a variety of Christmas gifts men might give their wives. As you scan down one of the long and narrow ads in this series, you see a blender, then a mixer, then a food processor, all with the word "NO" printed beside them. At the bottom is an elegant chain with the words, "You really know how to stir things up," and the red kiss mark.

When developing ad campaigns, Berg takes a hands-on approach in formulating the concept, then gives the agency room to work, says McDuff. The relationship seems to work. The company's success, generated in part by the ads, has led to substantial growth. In fact, it now has five jewelry stores in Louisiana and one in Mobile, Ala.

As successful as the ads have been in establishing the company's presence in the community, Berg feels it's also important to be involved personally. He takes part in fund-raising activities for the Baton Rouge Community Fund for the Arts and serves as president of the Arts and Humanities of Baton Rouge and co-chairman of the United Way fund drive.

Practical Tips on Advertising

Here are some practical tips to help you apply the theories of advertising to your business. The advice covers advertising on radio, in newspapers and magazines, on television and with direct

MAKE WAVES WITH RADIO ADS

How do you create an most effective radio campaign? Pick the most popular station in town and place your ads in the most popular time slot, right?

Not necessarily. The most popular station in town may not be your customers' favorite; nor may they listen during the most popular time of day. While results can never be guaranteed, here are some guidelines to help maximize your exposure and minimize your expense with radio advertising:

1. Examine a station's demographics carefully. The station may tell you it's tops with the 25-54 age group, but that represents a vast difference in ages and spending habits. Find out whether most of the listeners are closer to 25 or 54. Also,

remember that "upscale" spans more than classical. Baby Boomers who grew up on rock 'n' roll or jazz are entering their prime spending years and have diverse musical tastes.

2. Frequency is the key to radio advertising. You can't advertise once a week and think everyone will hear you. Budget for frequent repeats of your ad or don't bother with radio.

3. Cluster your ads. A week of heavy frequency followed by two weeks off is much more effective than the same number of spots spread over three weeks. With this system, people tend to perceive they've heard your ad even when they haven't.

4. Consider longer spots. A 60-second spot costs only 20% more than a 30-second spot and gives you more time to grab listeners' attention, make your pitch and not lose them. Listeners generally count the *number* of commercials between songs rather than the length of each one.

5. People are dial flippers. Try to blanket your market with ads so people hear you on several stations.

6. Consider the purpose of your ad. If it's an image-builder, consider a preemptive spot, meaning your ad can get bumped to a different time than originally scheduled. This option is quite a bit cheaper than guaranteed time.

7. Use guaranteed time if you're advertising a specific event. A preemptive spot that bumps your big sale ad until the end of the day of your big sale isn't a very good value.

8. Commit to your campaign. Be willing to go with it for at least six months because people have to get used to hearing you on the radio, accept you and then consider going to your store. If you have a small budget, try one week of heavy frequency each month for six months.

9. Look for freebies and other ways to be mentioned on the radio. Sponsor a charity event that regularly gets media coverage, especially a pet project of the radio station such as Toys for Tots or food for the homeless.

10. Know your target market. All radio stations know who *they* reach; it's your job to know exactly who *you* need to reach.

PRINT MEDIA OFFER ATTENTIVE AUDIENCE

One advantage of print advertising is that you can assume anyone who buys a newspaper or magazine intends to read it. People can listen to the radio or TV while doing something else, but most of them don't read and try to do something else at the same time. Here are some tips for effective print advertising:

1. Circulation is important, but look beyond the numbers to get the true picture. Each newspaper and magazine should have a circulation statement that tells not only *how many* people read it, but also *who* reads it. Also consider whether the publication is paid circulation (people who pay for a publication intend to read it) or whether it's distributed free (how many of the free publications you receive in the mail do you toss without reading?).

2. If you're choosing between two newspapers, decide which one has readers who most closely resemble your customers?

3. Where do most of a publication's readers live? If they live in the western suburbs and your store is in the northern suburbs, you may not want to advertise there unless you have a product so unique that people are willing to make the drive.

4. Consider those little neighborhood newspapers and shoppers guides. Though often free, these publications are read because their content is specific enough to be of interest to readers. And their ad rates are lower than major metro publications.

5. Frequency is crucial in print, which is why less-expensive publications may be beneficial. The day you place an ad is important, too. Generally, Sunday and Friday are prime editions, as is the day when most supermarkets run their coupons (frequently Wednesday or Thursday).

6. Many suppliers offer co-op ad funds and ad slicks to which you can add your name. The ratio of who pays what varies. A publication's co-op ad manager usually has lists of suppliers who offer co-op programs, including jewelry suppliers.

7. Camera-ready ad slicks are not necessarily co-op ads; they may be part of a co-op program or may be a value-added service from the supplier. Feel free not to use any you don't think are attractive, but those you do use can help to keep down your art costs.

8. Newspaper and magazine ads are sold by the amount of space they take up. Newspapers are generally sold by length and column width, magazines by page or fraction thereof. You will usually have little, if any, control over placement. But outside of main news sections, you may have a better shot at getting where you want. Ask whether the publication can guarantee section if not place.

9. Ask about the demographics of each section (readership and the cost of ads vary from section to section). A $100 ad in the classified section may net you better results for some things than a $2,100 ad in the main news section. An about-to-get-engaged male may be reachable in the stock market or the sports section; a self-purchasing career woman may be interested in the stock market or the style section.

10. Always ask for the best position available. You may not get it often, but if you never ask, you are virtually guaranteed to be buried in the gutter.

11. Know your target market. All newspapers and magazines know who they reach; it's your job to know exactly who *you* need to reach.

HOW TO ADVERTISE ON TV ON A BUDGET

Television probably isn't the first thing that pops into your mind if you have a small ad budget. But it may be less expensive than you think. You don't necessarily have to sponsor the Olympics or buy time on the top-rated *Seinfeld*. Here are some guidelines for less-expensive TV advertising:

1. Rates change according to season. The lowest rates are in midsummer and midwinter; the highest are in fall and during the yearend holidays.

2. The most cost-effective time is January to March when people are more likely to stay in and watch TV (at least in cold climates).

3. Frequency is important—cluster a lot of your ads in a short time frame, then take time off.

4. Unlike radio, 30 seconds is plenty of time for a TV spot because you're combining audio and visual stimulation. Even consider a 15-second spot. Well done, with one very simple message, it can be effective.

5. Your ad must be professional. An amateurish or obnoxious ad is more of a turnoff than an enticement.

6. Leave family members and yourself out of commercials unless you're truly talented, have television experience or are willing to take enough lessons to learn to appear professional on camera.

7. Contact various industry associations for prepared television spots to which you can add your store name in a voiceover. Many are exclusive to a market.

8. You can try to get freebie mention on television the same as radio, but it's much tougher. Try to get involved with the station's pet causes. Volunteer your staff to answer telephones in the evening or donate goods to give away for the local Public Broadcasting Service station telethon.

9. Consider nonprime-time ads. People watch TV before they leave for work in the morning, some work second or third shift and others are addicted to daytime soap operas or eat lunch in a restaurant with a television.

10. Know your target market. All television stations know who *they* reach; it's your job to know exactly who *you* need to reach.

THE ADVANTAGES OF GOING DIRECT

Direct marketing can be highly effective—if *your target base is good*. Here are some guidelines to make your next campaign work:

1. Developing the target list is crucial. You have several options: buy a list, rent one or create your own. Creating your own is the most important, of course, but you can supplement it with other sources.

2. Keep all receipt records and ask all shoppers to sign your mailing list.

3. A computer will help to keep everything straight.

4. Address each piece of mail by name, avoiding "resident" and other anonymous greetings.

5. Keep your list sorted by shopping habits such as spending ranges, frequency of visits and how recently they've been in. A customer who never spends more than $300 probably won't be interested in a mailing for jewelry starting at $3,000. Someone who comes in once a year probably should receive only your Christmas mailing. And customers who used to visit more often may have moved (do you have a catalog with an 800 telephone number?), experienced a family crisis (divorce, illness, loss of job) or found another jeweler that suits their needs better (what does the competitor have that you don't?). A friendly telephone call saying, "Hi, we haven't seen you for a while and would like to invite you to see our new collection of custom jewelry" can give you some answers.

6. Get consumers past the obstacle of opening a direct-mail envelope by using a big, glossy four-color postcard. If you use an envelope, include something three-dimensional—such as a pencil or cubic zirconia for a "guess the real diamond promotion." Few people can resist opening an envelope with something nonflat inside.

7. Update your customer list constantly. A list peppered with names of people who don't respond wastes money that could be spent mailing to better targets.

8. Use first-class postage to ensure that undeliverables are returned to you. It's important to do this at least a few times per year to clear your list of people who have moved. Also use first class for invitations to special events. Bulk mail is OK for mass mailings.

9. Telemarketing can be effective, even though it has reached new lows with computers instead of people calling during dinner. When you call a customer, it should be like a telephone call to a friend, with you calling to see what's new and to remind him that his wife's birthday is coming up (information gleaned from your customer list). Read the local newspaper for comings and goings of residents, send

welcome-home notes when they return from a cruise and send congratulations for an award received, a high school or college graduation, an engagement and so forth.

10. Effective targeting is especially crucial in this category.

THE VALUE OF GOOD FREE PUBLICITY

Good, free publicity can be invaluable in promoting goodwill. Here are some ideas to help you get started:

1. Learn to recognize a good public relations opportunity and how to create one where none exists. This is no harder than being observant.

2. Keep up with all major charitable events in your community. Donate gift certificates because the winner will visit your store and will likely spend more than that amount. However, make the amount meaningful so it seems like a gift, not a discount.

3. Donate a product and tell the organization its retail value (the organization doesn't have to know the donation costs less on your books). Don't know where to start? Get a list of all major philanthropies in town and send a letter saying: "We have some limited amounts of products to donate for charitable purposes." Stand back for the response.

4. Make it a point to honor outstanding citizens. Run a contest such as "Why My Mom/Dad is Best" or "Most Romantic Anniversary" and give the winner some kind of product.

5. Create a speaker service and offer to talk to a wide variety of groups. A church group may like to hear about the Biblical histories of gemstones, while a medical group would be interested in their supposed medical properties. High school physics classes may like to learn about diamond cutting, social studies classes about gem mining. You'll have to do some homework, but you can recycle your talks for different groups in different towns.

6. Remember the theory developed by marketing expert James Porte: C = MSU, which stands for Creativity = Making Stuff Up.

VIDEO TIPS

Mark Moeller offers these tips to jewelers who may want to create videos for their stores:

1. Look around. Check out business film and video production companies in your area. Good sources include the telephone book and local business associations such as the Chamber of Commerce and Rotary.

2. Don't be cheap. Professional photographers who make videos of family gatherings and weddings generally charge only $1,000-$2,000, but Moeller says they're not qualified to produce a sophisticated, professional film about a business.

3. Get references. Ask to see what other work a company has done and for whom. "Better yet, ask to see a copy of their own promotional video, if they have one," he suggests.

4. Be involved. Whatever company you chose should consult you throughout the production process. The company that Moeller chose was responsible for production and artistic content, but actively sought his input at every step.

Picking an Agency

John K. Bromberg offers these guidelines in choosing an advertising agency:

1. Hometown agencies know the local market, the people, what you want and how best to present it. And they're close enough for you to work with them.

2. Ask for copies of an agency's own promotions and names of some customers. Your chief concern is that they have the experience and ability to do what you want.

3. Money is a factor. Don't be cheap, but don't ignore the low bids either.

JCK Management Study Center Quiz

Advertising is not a definitive art or science; for every "general rule" there is an exception. It may depend on budget, on a particular store specialty or some demographic quirk. This quiz, a baker's dozen, is designed to uncover the most likely correct answers in the most commonly observed situations.

1. What is the single most important goal of advertising?

a. To sell specific pieces of merchandise
b. To announce sales and other special events
c. To keep your name and message before the public
d. To build your customer base

2. When buying merchandise, what is the most important factor in deciding what to stock?

a. To buy high design pieces which will catch the eye of window shoppers
b. To make sure the style and price points match your customers' needs and buying power

c. To try out merchandise which you hope you can persuade customers to buy
d. To give your store an upscale look

3. When deciding which media to use for your advertising, what is most important?

a. To know that most 25- to 34-year-olds watch an average of five hours of TV a day
b. That over-55s get most of their news from newspapers
c. To be sure the customers you want to reach read, watch or listen to the medium you choose
d. To get the best deal on rates

4. Typically, about what percentage of your gross sales should you spend on advertising?

a. Less than 1%
b. More than 10%
c. About 5%
d. About 3%

5. When is the best time to commit the majority of your advertising dollars?

a. At least 80% of the money should be spent in November and December

b. Spending should be concentrated on five or six major "events" during the year

c. Spending should be consistent throughout the year, maybe skipping the last two months

d. Money should be split about evenly between bridal season and Christmas

6. What is the typical cost per minute to have a good video made?

a. Between $5,000 and $6,000 b. Around $500

c. Between $2,500 and $5,000 d. About $10,000

7. What is the key to success with radio spots?

a. Making sure you hit morning drive-to-work time

b. Targeting young people

c. Staying clear of stations that play elevator music

d. Maintaining high frequency in concentrated periods

8. How much more should you normally expect to pay for a 60-second radio spot rather than a 30-second spot?

a. Twice as much

b. About 50% more

c. About 20% more

d. About the same if you give the station some free merchandise

9. What is a preemptive radio spot?

a. One where your time slot is not guaranteed

b. One where no one else can take that time spot

c. One where you may be bumped but get double time for compensation

d. One where the amount you pay is determined by when the spot runs

10. At what times of the year can you normally expect to get the lowest cost TV time?

a. Throughout the year, in mid morning hours

b. In mid summer and mid winter

c. Immediately after Easter

d. Immediately after Memorial Day

11. Why should you use first class mail for your notices to customers?

a. It guarantees more timely delivery

b. Customers appreciate that you care enough to go first class

c. The cost makes you determine who really should get the mailing

d. The Post Office will return all undelivered mail, allowing you to update your mailing list

12. Why should you donate gift certificates rather than gifts to good causes?

a. The person receiving the certificate has to come into your store to redeem it

b. It doesn't make you look "cheap" by giving away merchandise

c. The gifts you give often are dogs that won't sell and won't do much for your image

d. Certificates are easier to issue

13. What is the first crucial aspect of newspaper advertising?

a. The circulation figures

b. The placement of the ad on the page

c. The placement of the ad in a particular section

d. The newspaper's readership demographics

(Answers to Quiz can be found at the end of this chapter)

Jewelers Try Coupon Advertising

Lynn Clark Bergman ◆ *June 1994*

Jewelers across the nation are discovering the value of a relatively new form of direct mail advertising: cooperative coupons targeted to specific local neighborhoods.

This advertising option—rising quickly in quality, value and popularity—features special coupon offers from many local businesses. The cost of each mailing is shared by all participating companies—jewelers, doctors, restaurants and others. This results in a cost far lower than a business would pay to do an equivalent solo mailing. Including postage, the cost is less than 4¢ per home.

Statistics from Donnelly Marketing & McCann-Erickson Inc. show that more than 70% of all consumers use coupons, with more than 25% using five or more a week. While only 57% of men use coupons, 83% of women do. Direct mail redemption rates are 25% higher than those for newspaper and magazine coupons.

Jewelers often consider direct mail and newspapers their most affordable advertising option. Large chains, mall stores and some smaller jewelers as well use additional radio and cable television advertising, but many independent and local jewelers can't afford them.

269

Direct mail offers certain advantages—including specific market targeting—and the cooperative coupon version of direct mail adds the benefit of shared costs. Most jewelry stores are successful with cooperative direct mail ads because:

- They create exciting offers that will attract a variety of new and existing customers to the store.

- They effectively target selected neighborhoods with the income levels the store wishes to attract.

- They help keep a jewelry store's name and logo out in the neighborhood constantly, which is the key to successful advertising, says Chris Taylor, owner of Taylormade Jewelers, Glen Rock, N.J. When potential customers desire to buy jewelry, they will think first of the jewelry store whose name is most familiar to them.

Best deal/best value: It isn't always best to stress the jewelry in a cooperative coupon program, says Taylor. Coupons touting a discount may work well for pizza, where everyone wants the best-value deal. But with jewelry, people may assume a discounted price is equivalent to discounted quality—even if the quality is the best.

Taylor recommends taking a backdoor approach to advertising jewelry sales by coupon. By discounting less expensive items—"$2 Off Any Watch Battery" or "$2 Off Any Jewelry Repair"—you appeal to almost everyone, says Taylor. Most people wear a watch that will need a battery replaced at some time. And people often have a broken necklace or earrings lying in a jewelry box waiting to be repaired—all they need is a reminder. By implementing these everyday coupon offers in your direct mail advertisement, you will increase your store traffic.

Some aggressive jewelers—such as Taylormade—even offer a free jar of jewelry cleaner with no purchase necessary. Other jewelers give jewelry cleaner free with any other purchase or offer $2 off. While "free" consistently proves to work best in attracting new customers, the other options work, too.

Taylor consistently advertises with Super Coups Direct Mail Advertising Co. His Super Coups consultant advises him to include an assortment of offers on the same coupon in the same mailing to attract a variety of people. His "$2 Off Watch Battery" coupon usually brings in about 150 to 180 men each, and many women respond to the discounts and the freebies. He also makes offers of "$1/3$ Off Crystal or Gold Chains" and "$10 Off Any Purchase of $50 or More" to encourage existing customers to visit and to attract new ones.

"It's important to change some of your offers every time you mail," he says. "It will keep people from getting bored with the same old ad, yet it keeps your name out there in the neighborhood."

By taking advantage of attractive coupon offers on everyday necessities such as repairs, watch batteries and jewelry cleanings, people grow comfortable with visiting their local jeweler. Then when they get engaged or go shopping for special occasion or holiday gifts, they will look no further than the same local jeweler with whom they have built a personal rapport.

Consistency pays off: John Leonard of Wolfe Jewelers, Denville, N.J., started to advertise with cooperative direct mail two years ago. He mails four times a year to 30,000 homes within a 3- to 5-mile radius of his store. A direct mail consultant helps him to target his mail offers to the house-

holds with the best profit prospects. "This is the best way to take advantage of your local market," he says.

Leonard says he had unrealistic expectations of phenomenal redemptions the first time he advertised, even though the consultant gave him a realistic goal. Though he was disappointed with results on the first attempt, he tried a second and third time, finally breaking even and learning the importance of repeated name brand recognition. "This is the key to direct mail advertising," he says. "It really does take a few times to get your name out there and for people to respond."

Today, Leonard is flooded with customers for the first two weeks after each mailing. The traffic levels off, then picks up again as customers rush to take advantage of the redemption period a few days before it ends.

Here are some tips that Leonard offers first-time co-op coupon direct mail advertisers:

1. Stick with it! Consistency and repetition are the keys for building any successful advertising campaign. Consider the first few mailings a long-term investment in your business. It will pay off in time. Some jewelers who get discouraged quickly with direct mail advertising advertise only when they are overstocked or just once a year—in time for the holiday season. Quality advertising works best on an ongoing basis while building recognition.

2. Keep it simple. Simplicity is very important and very effective. Many advertisers try to put too much copy into their ad. The busier the ad, the more confusing it is. It helps to use a variety of offers within the same ad, but remember to keep it simple. For diversification, change the offers each time you mail your coupon. This keeps customers from getting bored with the same coupon. Your direct mail representative often will help with everything from what to offer to the layout.

3. Shop around for quality. Research a high-quality local cooperative direct mail firm with very colorful and very full envelopes. It is best to find a company that can meet your needs in everything from artwork, design and printing to mailing, with the postage costs included in the price. There are excellent direct mail companies out there. Interview several coupon providers, and don't hesitate to ask other local businesses for recommendations to start you in the right direction.

Adding the polish: How you advertise with coupons is as important as using a reputable company to target the most profitable areas for your business and to keep your name and logo in the neighborhood. Just as you would polish your best gems for the most dazzle, you also need to polish your advertisements for the most appeal to consumers.

The "quality" combination of color, cut, clarity and carat weight makes a diamond beautifully unique and valuable. For direct mail coupon advertising, the quality combination comprises simple copy, the best offers, targeted markets and attractive, full-color layouts to attract customers' attention.

"Full color is an effective and attractive feature in cooperative direct mail coupon advertising," says Julie Richter, owner of Diamond Designs, Milwaukee, Wis. "It portrays the high quality image I want for my jewelry store."

Studies have proven that people are three times more likely to respond to a color advertisement than a black-and-white ad. For jewelers, it's important to remember that people have a difficult time visualizing the beauty of a sapphire or ruby ring or a sparkling gold chain when it is printed in black and white. Jewelry seems more desirable and tangible when illustrated in color. Recent market research shows that ad recall after 24 hours is almost 70% for full-color ads and 41% for black-and-white ads.

When preparing an advertisement, you may choose from your own custom photographs or from the direct mail company's stock photograph library. Most major direct mail companies have a remarkable number of photos in every imaginable category. These photo libraries not only help you create effective ads, they also save you the expense of hiring a photographer.

Institutional advertising: Richter uses coupons for "institutional advertising" rather than offer special deals. She doesn't discount any services or jewelry. Instead, she uses the direct mail package as a way to send out her "display" advertisement with the purpose of building her store's image and boosting its name recognition throughout the community.

"I can't get quality four-color advertising to 20,000 homes any more affordably than this!" says Richter.

Jewelers should not expect a stream of trackable customers to beat down their doors when using institutional advertising because people have no discounted offers to ask for, Richter emphasizes. Yet it is important to promote a high-quality image consistently.

It's also important to remember that few customers will come to your store as soon as your "institutional" ad hits their mailboxes because there is no incentive to come in "today" or respond to any specific offer. Yet display advertising is an effective and important way to build name recognition.

Some jewelers worry about the ethics of advertising free or discounted services or merchandise, Richter notes. Some question coupon advertising itself. High-quality jewelers don't want to look "cheap," so many are reluctant to offer "Free Jewelry Cleaner" or "$2 Off Repairs" just to get clients in the door. But there are effective ways to use cooperative direct mail advertising without compromising ethics or image.

Repetition advertising: Mike Kalmus of Kalmus Jewelers, Parsippany, N.J., uses an occasional newspaper ad during the holiday seasons. But for years he has relied on direct mail as his most effective advertising resource. "There are three reasons it works for my jewelry store: repetition, repetition, repetition," he says. "I keep my name out there all the time and am always attracting new and regular clients."

He says he has tried every imaginable offer in his direct mail programs and found the best ones for building new store traffic are "repairs, repairs, repairs." While specific jewelry offers, watch sales and percentage-off gold jewelry offers work, he says repairs are among the most effective hooks for gaining new customers. But don't limit yourself to one offer. "You need a combination of two to three offers so you have something that will appeal to everyone," he says.

Once a repair customer is in your store, then you, like Kalmus, can try to turn the visit into a jewelry sale.

Valuable guidelines: Glen Liset, national vice president of sales for Super Coups, offers the following tips for cooperative direct-mail advertising:

• Create annual direct mail advertising budgets. Annual advertising agreements with your direct mail company will help to reduce the cost of your overall ad budget. Consistency and repetition are the two most important keys to any successful advertising program.

• Use dollars-off rather than percentage-off. Unless something is 50% or more off these days, the percentage sale price has no perceived value—"$10 Off" is better than "10% Off." Show true value in savings by listing your regular prices. But be certain the item has been offered at the regular price as long as local and state consumer protection laws require before being marked down.

• Introduce name brand lines. Use your top brand names—such as Rolex or Seiko—when making offers in your ad. Use a "$2 Off Jewelry Repair" offer as an opportunity to list which brands you carry. Customers may be sparked to buy a new watch or a new necklace even though they are responding to the repair offer. However, list only the brands you wish to highlight; your ad will appear too busy if you list every brand you carry.

• Use lots of color. Colorful ads ensure better redemption rates. Studies show that consumers prefer full color ads 3-to-1 over black-and-white or two-color ads. Full-color ads reportedly have 300% greater impact and increase redemption rates by 30% to 60%.

• Use quality photos. People tend to be attracted by the photos first, then read the headlines, then search for the specific details of an offer. Use photos of sparkling jewelry or romantic couples.

• Use bold headlines and strong logos. Present a specific focus of whatever jewelry or "back-door" offer you are presenting. Be aware that both men and women use coupons these days.

• Order coupon overruns. To get more mileage and more value out of your coupon advertisement, buy a thousand or more extra coupons and give them to your neighboring business associates. Encourage them to return for some other item or service, too.

• Shop around for quality direct mail services. Interview several coupon providers. Evaluate the quality of their ads, their expert services and their ability to provide a complete package, including marketing advice, artwork, typesetting, printing, addressing, postage and mailing services.

To find a local cooperative direct mail service near you, contact the national headquarters of these three leading North American companies:
Money Mailer, (800) 624-5371.
Super Coups Direct Mail, (800) 626-2620.
Tri-Mark, (800) 874-6275.

12 Ways To Boost Christmas Diamond Sales

October 1993

All customers have two basic things in mind when they walk into a store: what they want to buy and how much they want to pay for it.

Which is uppermost in their minds?

Wrong. It's the first, because that's the one they haven't decided yet.

Customers usually have a much firmer idea of what they're willing to spend than what they want to spend it on, say sales experts. A man may have budgeted a specific amount—say $1,000—to buy his wife *something* for Christmas. Your ability to transform this vague *something* into a specific gift idea can make the difference between a so-so Christmas sales season and a strong one.

What's the best way to help customers choose a jewelry or watch gift? Try the game of *show* (have a variety of merchandise and show it) and *tell* (communicate, talk to customers, ask them who they're buying for and what they like). More specifically, consider these 12 Christmas sales tips from industry experts.

MOTIVATE BROWSERS

A gem in the hand is worth two in the case.

"How many people in this world have ever worn a 2-ct. diamond?" asks Bill Farmer, a jeweler in Lexington, Ky. "And how many jewelers keep their larger diamonds in their safes until someone asks to see them?"

The first question is rhetorical, he says, but the answer is a very small percentage. The second question isn't rhetorical, and the answer is a very large percentage. Farmer's point is that jewelers should put a 2-ct. stone in a customer's hand and explain that very few people have ever worn one. "That makes them feel very special," he says.

Marketing consultant Jim Terzian says this strategy works even with less spectacular pieces for two reasons:

• It focuses their attention on a particular piece, turning a passive browser into an active shopper.

• It gives the sales associate some direction. If the customer likes it, the associate can show similar pieces. If the customer doesn't like it, the associate can go in another direction. "Remember to listen to what customers say because they'll lead you to the 'right' piece," says Terzian.

Another tip: don't start your "show" with low-priced merchandise. It's more difficult to get customers to move up in price than down.

SPARK BURNED-OUT SHOPPERS

Who hasn't encountered the glassy-eyed, disgruntled customer who thinks he or she has seen everything? How can you make this sale?

"Nobody ever leaves a bazaar empty-handed," suggests one jeweler. While most jewelers will cringe at being compared to a bazaar, those who show a wide variety of merchandise stand a much better chance of selling some of it.

Farmer, for example, keeps a selection of loose fancy shaped diamonds in the half-carat to three-quarter-carat range in his showcase. "People like to look at them, and this shows them they have a choice," he says. "We also keep some emerald cuts in the case because many people have forgotten them."

Communication is as important as selection because it breaks the ice and helps to narrow the choices. First, ask who the customer is shopping for and try to find out what that person would like, says Terzian. Then ask, "What's the best thing that will happen when she or he unwraps a gift they truly love?"

This shifts the salesperson/customer relationship from adversarial to a partnership—finding a gift that will produce that outcome.

It's also helpful to offer a refuge from the pre-Christmas mayhem. If a customer looks haggard, offer a chair and some refreshments, then say, "Sit down and relax! Tell us what you're looking for and we'll bring it to you."

"You'd be surprised at how grateful shoppers are to get out of the Christmas rush," says David Morrow, manager of training and education for De Beers' Diamond Promotion Service. "In addition, if sales associates help to keep up their customers' spirits, it often raises their own at a time when everyone is pretty frantic."

NUDGE THE FENCE-SITTER

Try not to let customers leave before you get some indication of what they're looking for or why they're going out empty-handed.

Since customers often don't know what they want, you should be ready to help them narrow their focus and then show some jewelry that fits that focus. If a husband is shopping for his wife, for example, ask if she's blonde or brunette. Does she like colorful clothes? What are her favorite jewelry pieces?

When customers can't decide between two pieces, don't let them leave without making a decision. "Ask what they don't like about a particular piece," advises Morrow. "Chances are they'll pick the one they like the least [if only slightly] and describe a defect. Put that piece away and focus on the other."

NEGOTIATE ON PRICE?

"It's important to sell product, not price," says Sam Arnstein, a sales trainer based in Seattle, Wash.

But if price is a problem and there's some room to deal, some jewelers favor the blunt approach. They'll ask: "What would it take for you to buy this piece today?"

"They might just tell you," says Robert Wood, sales manager at Kahn Jewelers in Pine Bluff, Ark. "Once they do, you can work with them, if what they tell you is reasonable."

What if it's not reasonable? Don't close off negotiations, says Arnstein. He offers this scenario involving a customer who says a $2,000 piece of diamond jewelry is too expensive.

Associate: "What did you have in mind?"

Customer: "$1,000."

Associate (keeping his or her cool): "Why so low?"

Customer: "It's all markup, isn't it?"

Associate: "If it were all markup, everyone would be in the business . . . diamonds basically come from one source and everyone pays nearly the same. And you can check the gold price in the business section of the paper. It's too competitive to allow excessive markups."

At this point, the sales associate should use some confidence-builders ("We've been in business for years and stand by what we sell." "We offer a 30-day return policy." "We offer the best price for the quality of diamonds in our jewelry."). The associate also should review credit options to make it sound like an easy purchase.

"In the end, the guy who offers $1,000 on a $2,000 piece may end up settling for $1,950 if you handle him right," says Arnstein.

'I JUST DON'T WANT TO SPEND THIS MUCH!'

The customer says a piece costs more than he or she wants to spend. Sales experts say you should determine whether it's really more than the customer can afford, or whether it's a self-defense mechanism that seems to click on when some customers—especially men—enter a jewelry store.

This can be done gracefully. Begin by saying, "Let me ask you to clarify. Is it that you think the piece itself is overpriced or is that price just more than you want to spend today?"

If it's more than someone can afford, show a less expensive piece. However, if the customer simply hadn't planned to spend that much but can afford it, discuss trust (value for price, cheaper doesn't always mean a better buy). It's important to talk about value and confidence *before* the customer turns to leave so it doesn't appear to be a last-ditch effort, says Arnstein.

If someone really loves a piece and is certain the prospective recipient will, too, they'll find a way to buy it. Discuss financing, credit cards and any other options that will make it easier for customers to take the jewelry home with them.

But remember, you often can avert this situation altogether by asking a customer how much he or she wants to spend at the outset and sticking to that range. Don't hesitate, however, to show one or two slightly more expensive pieces, explaining, "I know this is a little over your range, but I thought you might like to see it because it's a beautiful piece [or it just came in or it's a new kind of cut]."

EVEN REGULARS NEED STROKING

In these uncertain times, price may become an issue even with regular customers. Listening again becomes the key. "If a regular customer holds back, don't keep trying to sell," says Arnstein. "Ask what's bothering him. He may tell you his business is slower or his company is laying off. In this case, stress how you can work with him and review the payment and return options and service."

Also, it never hurts to reiterate confidence-building phrases such as, "You know we've worked well with our customers for many years, so we'll be here if you need us" or "You know you're getting the best value for that price and quality."

WHEN ALL ELSE FAILS, TAKE THE BULL BY THE HORNS

Want to keep browsers from walking out the door? Trip them, then tie them up until they buy something. That's one jeweler's tongue-in-cheek solution to dealing with reluctant buyers and tough times.

But would-be customers sometimes do manage to get out the door. What then? Or what if it's getting close to Christmas and some regular customers haven't come in yet?

Call them or drop them a note.

Bill Farmer offers a service called Farmer's Fit-up. "I listen closely all year long to what women shoppers tell me they like," he says. "Then when Christmastime rolls around, I call their husbands and tell them what their wives looked at." His Fit-up data base includes finger size, anniversary and birthday dates, description of jewelry items already owned and of those they would like to own. The Fit-up extends even to moderately priced pieces in the $400-$500 range.

"Many men appreciate this," he says. "They're busy and don't always have the time or inclination to get caught up in Christmas shopping, and this is something their wives are guaranteed to like. I can have the gift wrapped and delivered with no problem." What if the husband already has bought a Christmas gift? Farmer points out this would make a good anniversary gift.

Morrow adds, "It's amazing how many people appreciate when people call them with such suggestions, and it's doubly amazing how many jewelers and associates are reluctant to do this. They think it's beneath them, like dragging people in off the street."

GET 'BE BACKS' TO COME BACK

When tough-guy actor Arnold Schwarzenegger promises "I'll be back," he keeps his word before the movie is over. But how many customers who say they'll be back really do return?

Robert Wood, the sales manager at Kahn Jewelers, gets the departing customer's name and address, then sends a thank-you-for-stopping-in note, hoping this will encourage a return visit. (One word of caution: "We don't send these notes before Christmas because we don't want to give away to spouses that a husband or wife was in our store looking for a Christmas gift.")

"We also give a written assurance that we offer the best price for quality," says Wood. "In case they are going to check out the discounters, then know there's a difference between price and value."

If you can't get the customer's name, offer a brochure on colored stones or a business card that will keep your name and merchandise on their minds once they get home. "On the brochure, write the price and stock number of a piece the customer looked at so the sales associate and the customer can better remember it," adds Morrow.

One jeweler Morrow knows goes one step further: If a customer seems seriously interested in a fairly expensive piece, he takes a Polaroid photo of the jewelry and his logo to give as a reminder.

COUNTER INCESSANT PRE-CHRISTMAS SALES

Plan your own pre-Christmas sale, but make it an event so it stands out from the competition.

While sale prices should be one feature of the event, also offer interesting things to do and see. Start with a by-invitation-only evening reception with refreshments and agree to donate a certain percentage of sales from the event to a charity. "The charity will usually reciprocate by contacting its board of directors or providing their names and addresses so you can invite them to attend the reception," says Morrow.

Invite stone dealers and jewelry designers to attend, and feature their merchandise in ads for the event.

Hold the event very early in December to get a jump on competitors and to ensure that suppliers still have a good selection, says Farmer. "Early December is just before they start memoing everything out, so you can get a really good selection if you promise to have everything back within 48 hours or so," he says.

'I SAW THIS ELSEWHERE FOR HALF YOUR PRICE'

The price-vs.-quality issue is obvious in discussions with customers about discount pricing. Less obvious is your store's "brand name."

First, the less obvious point. Begin with your store's reputation for integrity and longevity. Then say, "When your wife opens the package and sees our store logo on the box, chances are she'll smile and give you a hug even before she sees what's inside. That's what we stand for."

On the obvious point, offer a written guarantee that you will sell a specific piece of specific quality at a specific price and will subject it to independent verification by a gemological lab or reputable appraiser. Ask the customer to take the guarantee and see if X Jewelers will sign the same pledge, says Terzian. "Many jewelers won't make a written pledge if they're misrepresenting the quality of their diamonds," he says.

Morrow suggests constructive retaliation rather than bad-mouthing a competitor who misrepresents quality. "A customer may say he saw a G VS diamond in X Jewelers' case and it's half the price of yours. Tell him you carry this quality also and ask him to pick it out in your showcase." This little exercise shows the customer he's at the mercy of the jeweler when it comes to diamond grading, so he must deal with someone trustworthy.

When shoppers are motivated only by price, there's little you can do. But Morrow suggests you might say, "If you truly believe you are getting the same quality from X Jewelers, then you shouldn't pay me more." He says, "Sometimes that starts them thinking."

TREATMENT ISSUE

Many customers who come into a jewelry store are cynical or even hostile because they've seen TV reports about undisclosed treatment of gems, overgrading of diamonds and other unethical conduct.

"The big mistake most jewelers and sales associates make is to brush off these questions by saying they don't sell such goods," says Morrow. "Consumers are intelligent. They know when they're being brushed off or patronized just for the sake of a sale."

Morrow's remedy: straight, honest, intelligent explanations. "Explain how stones are treated and what such treatments do. Show them if there's a microscope available, and take the time to answer questions." This will help to dispel the cynicism and hostility.

Terzian says sales associates also can have the owner or manager sign his or her name on the store receipt. "This says the store stands behind the quality it advertises," he says. "Also stress the store's refund and replacement policy to help bolster trust."

CHRISTMAS COMES ONCE A YEAR; DO CUSTOMERS?

Many jewelers see more new faces during the Christmas selling season than the rest of the year combined. "This is a great chance to turn people into regular customers," says Morrow. "More than just being satisfied with their gift, they'll remember if they were treated patiently, intelligently and in a friendly way at a time when everyone is acting rushed and harried."

Hold a meeting for employees—everyone from the receptionist to the manager—just before the Christmas selling season begins and remind them how important hospitality and courtesy can be.

It's old stuff, Morrow admits, but it's easy to forget in the rush of Christmas. "Customers won't forget, however. They'll be back if they remember they were treated well."

Promotion Ideas For Women

August 1993 Part II

• Establish a tie-in promotion with a quality clothing retailer. Any customer who spends above a certain amount at the clothing store would receive a gift certificate to your store and vice versa.

• Try the same approach with the best local hair salon. Offer a gift certificate for a haircut with the purchase of a pair of earrings over a certain price. The salon would give women who get a haircut or other styling a discount certificate redeemable at your store.

• Don't neglect the time-honored idea of having, or being a part of, a community fashion show. Start with community women's organizations, but don't forget other groups that need fund-raising ideas.

• Target print advertising in any section of the newspaper, not just fashion or food sections alone. Women do read news, business and sports.

• Display jewelry the way it's meant to be worn, not just on a display pad. Put cuff links on a blouse, or a pin on a scarf. Take some of your display dollars and spend them on good apparel props instead of trays.

• Pull good-looking ads from upscale fashion publications and use them as display props.

• Make sure your staff is dressed up to par, in whatever is appropriate for your market, and make sure it's the best quality they can afford.

• Merchandise your store by life-style. Group your jewelry selections according to who's most likely to buy it. Just as you would show a group of $500-$750 diamond engagement rings separately from $3,000-$5,000 rings, separate your other merchandise by general market. Visible pricing is a key element to attracting the female self-purchase market. So if you're not comfortable with total visible pricing, then at least put a sign in the case giving a fairly tight range ("from $250 to $500").

Show ensembles and different kinds of pieces in each range, as well. You don't want the woman with a small budget to feel that all she can afford in your store is a tiny chain bracelet or some small earrings. Even Tiffany has attractive jewelry for about $100.

• Donate a gift certificate to a charitable cause, especially if the charity's fund-raising committee is made up of women. A gift certificate costs you only half the face value of the jewelry, and many women will be inclined to spend even more than the certificate (and hopefully tell their friends about the nice experience they had in your store).

• Make sure your store hours are conducive to professional women's shopping needs. What's the point of trying to attract them if your store is open only during the hours they're at work? Make sure, too, that your store has easily accessible parking and that women feel safe walking to and from. Offer escort service from store to car, especially after dark.

• Don't forget the little touches that mean so much. These are what customers remember. Offer coffee, tea and ice water in attractive glassware. Decorate your store's bathroom nicely, fill it with scented soaps and guest towels, and allow customers to use it. (If security is a problem with allowing customers in the bathroom, rearrange your stockroom so that it isn't.) Fill your store with potpourri, flowers or anything else that gives a delicate, subtle scent.

Promote Gold For Bigger Profits

May 1993

Karat gold jewelry is a primary product in most jewelry stores. But apart from endless percent-off advertising, there's a gaping hole where good gold promotions should be.

It doesn't have to be that way. Gold responds very well to promotion, says Christine Yorke, merchandise manager of the World Gold Council. Why, then, do so few jewelers focus on promoting it? Does gold sell itself?

In fact, basic gold (chain, hoop earrings, etc.) does sell itself, say jewelers. "People pretty much know what gold chain is and whether they want one," says Mary Blumenthal of Corinne Jewelers, Toms River, N.J.

Beyond the basics, however, is another story. Jewelers interviewed for this story say they benefit from specialized display, promotion and merchandising of designer, custom and other non-basic gold jewelry.

Overall, these jewelers generally don't promote gold jewelry as a category. "We advertise the store, our custom work or the designer," says Jaime Pellissier of Pellissier, Greenwich, Conn.

Scott Cusson of Brinsmaid's in nearby New Canaan says marketing by designer is the way to go. "So many discounters do it [advertise] by weight, etc.," he says. "We try to take the high road and promote the designer as the vehicle to sell gold jewelry." He also has promoted specialty gold, which he defines as high karat gold, imported gold or new looks such as deep matte textured gold.

Greg Mendel, proprietor of Kern Jewelers, Burlingame, Cal., has a slightly different view. He promotes gold jewelry, but not by designer name and never with a price. "I want our advertising to sell *Kern's*, not a designer name," he says. "I want people to buy designer jewelry here because they are in Kern's and they trust Kern's."

At Corinne Jewelers, Blumenthal normally uses image/product promotions, not gold-specific. For Valentine's Day, however, she planned a "Sing to Your Sweetheart" promotion in which men were invited to call radio station WOBM and sing to their wives or sweethearts on the air. Those chosen by the station to sing received a 14k gold heart link bracelet by Gori & Zucchi worth about $100 retail. One of the five winners was chosen to receive the grand prize—a 14k gold and diamond heart designed by Corinne Jewelers.

"All five winners came in to pick up their bracelets, two bought additional jewelry and listeners who got a kick out of the promotion came in to see what we were giving away," she says. "It was the best Valentine's Day in the history of Corinne Jewelers!"

How to display: Non-basic gold jewelry isn't always displayed the same way. Jewelers say they display designer gold jewelry separately from other gold jewelry and non-designer gold jewelry by category (earrings, chain, etc.).

At Pellissier, for example, 10 of the store's 14 cases have designer jewelry or custom pieces. At Brinsmaid's—in addition to separate displays for designer jewelry and category displays for non-designer jewelry—Cusson assembles little collections. In a small case—perhaps a window, display a cube or island away from the designer and category cases—he highlights a few pieces that work well together, such as a pin, earrings, necklace and bracelet.

Corinne Jewelers also merchandises higher-end gold, such as the Kurt Gutmann line, separately from lower-end merchandise. "Throughout these tough times, the one thing that has sold consistently is high-quality, high-design gold jewelry," says Blumenthal. "When customers see the difference between something like a Gutmann and by-weight gold, they opt for quality. Even if they can't afford it, they put it on layaway or they wait until they can."

Adds Pellissier, "Gold sells only if you show something worth having. You sell the quality, the design."

Why promote? "Jewelers sell gold, but they don't *focus* on it," says Jack Carpenter, vice president of the World Gold Council. "It's always on the last pages of a jewelry catalog; it's always one of the last counters in the store."

But WGC research shows gold jewelry is the best way for jewelers to increase profits, says John Calnon, WGC's director of merchandise planning. Each dollar invested in gold jewelry inventory has the power to yield more profit than any other jewelry category, says WGC. A 1992 study done for WGC by Management Horizons showed that gross margins were 60.5% for gold jewelry, 51.4% for diamonds and precious gemstone jewelry and 42.7% for watches. The same study found that annual inventory turn is 3.0 for gold jewelry, 2.6 for watches and 1.7 for diamonds and precious gemstone jewelry.

Gold jewelry sales also are virtually recession proof. During the economic downturn of the past two years, gold jewelry sales have held steady or risen slightly while sales of other product categories dropped.

How can you focus on gold jewelry? WGC has developed a "Build Your Business Out of Gold Program" that teaches how gold jewelry can help to increase a jeweler's profits. (An advertising section detailing the program will appear in JCK June and will be available at Jewelry '93 in Las Vegas.)

WGC also is working to build consumer desire for gold through introduction of the Goldmark trademark and advertising campaigns titled "Treat Yourself" in 1990, "How Do You Symbolize a Feeling?" in 1991 and "Gold Shivers" in 1992. The 1993 program is under development. All campaigns are targeted at women, the primary purchasers of gold jewelry.

How to sell: According to WGC research, women buy 64% of all gold jewelry sold (43% for themselves, 21% as gifts for other women).

Gold is democratic, says Calnon, meaning good-quality pieces are available in a wide range of prices. The average retail price for gold jewelry is $88, says WGC. "It's definitely a lower price point than other jewelry categories," says Calnon. "But the secretary who buys $19 gold earrings feels just as good about her purchase as the executive who buys a $3,000 bracelet."

And once a woman buys a piece of fine jewelry, she will feel more comfortable at higher price points for future sales.

Another factor to consider is shopping style. WGC's Christine Yorke says women are used to shopping in a certain manner—namely browsing—and many jewelers don't accommodate this shopping style. "Jewelers need to re-create the shopping experience that most women are comfortable with," she says. "A woman buying a suit is used to going to the rack, looking through the selection and seeing at a glance what is available in her style, size, color *and price*. A lot of jewelers are against visible pricing, but most women want to know what they're dealing with up front."

Putting one or two pieces in the showcase and keeping the rest in the vault is another mistake, says Yorke. Women don't want to waste a salesperson's time asking to see other pieces if they're not sure they'll buy, she says, and they're afraid they'll feel pressured by taking the salesperson's time.

"I don't think you can 'sell' a piece of jewelry to a woman any more than you can sell a piece of clothing to her," says Yorke. "All you can do is validate the decision she's already made to buy." If you "sell" a woman something she hasn't already sold herself on, adds Yorke, chances are better than average the item will come back.

That brings up another factor: the return. In a department store, a woman can buy a suit, take it home, decide it just doesn't work and feel perfectly comfortable bringing it back, knowing the return will be accepted without question or comment. A jeweler can use a liberal return policy as a valuable selling tool; women who are unsure about the piece or the price are more likely to buy if they know they can bring it back with no hassle and no guilt.

Additionally, encouraging a woman to take a piece home to try with her wardrobe often results in a sale. It helps her to develop a sense of ownership and seeing how the piece works with different outfits increases its value to her.

Gold Promotion Ideas

Special events that focus on gold jewelry are a good way to build traffic and name recognition. Here are some ideas:

1. Create an eye-catching display of Italian gold. Fill a window or highlight case with different sizes and shapes of dry pasta, then drape the jewelry in and around it.

2. Carry the theme further by holding a reception with an Italian theme. Get posters and slides or a video of Italy from a local travel agency. As the slide show or video runs continuously in the background, invite customers to sample Italian food from a restaurant or hire a caterer who can make pasta on the spot. Call the Italian Trade Commission at (213) 879-0950 for ideas and interesting information about Italy's jewelry-making tradition.

3. Work with a travel agency on a joint promotion. Anyone who buys Italian gold jewelry in your store would be entered in a contest for a free trip to Italy; anyone who books travel to Italy through the agency would receive a gift certificate for gold jewelry from your store.

4. Move back in time for a "solid-gold" '50s sock hop. Send record-shaped invitations, dress your staff in '50s apparel and play '50s tunes on a rented jukebox. Serve burgers, hot dogs, milkshakes and popcorn.

5. Celebrate the start of the Gold Rush, which began with the discovery of gold at Coloma, Cal., on January 24, 1848. Re-create the event in your store by getting gold slivers (perhaps some sweepings from your bench), mixing them with sand and inviting customers to "pan" for gold. They could keep what they find or "cash it in" the old-fashioned way. Weigh the gold and let them redeem it for X amount of dollars off on a gold jewelry purchase. Send invitations done in an old-fashioned typeface, design your ads in poster style and dress the staff in saloonkeeper costumes.

6. Bake a 14-carrot cake. Sponsor a contest in your community to see who makes the best carrot cake and give the winner a gift certificate for a piece of gold jewelry. Invite the public to sample the cakes and browse the store, then donate a percentage of the day's gold jewelry sales to a local food bank.

Do Freebie Promo Gimmicks Work?

June 1992

Ever wonder how effective those calendars, pens and other advertising freebies you give to customers are? Wonder no more. They can be very effective.

Customers tend to keep and use these advertising aids, according to a recent survey by Specialty Advertising International, Irving, Tex. Thus, they are a good way to reinforce a company's name and image, according to SAI.

The survey found that 68% of 305 shoppers randomly polled in Chicago, Los Angeles and New York City were wearing, using or carrying free caps, pens, key tags, matchbooks, tote bags, shirts or sunglasses bearing company names, messages or logos. Of these shoppers, 81% easily recalled the business's name or message before showing it to the pollster.

"The shoppers' ability to remember the advertiser is due to the fact that these items are useful, therefore continually seen by the owners," says C. Ronald Schwisow, SAAI chairman.

Indeed, 49% of the shoppers had kept the items for at least a year, 23% for more than two years. "A promotional item that is useful is bound to be retained for a significant length of time," says Schwisow.

In addition, the survey found that 88% of the shoppers received their promotion freebies from businesses in their hometowns. "Businesses that target customers locally . . . recognize that success is often achieved when relationships are built and maintained," says Schwisow.

Rating the Impact of Promo Freebies

57% of recipients use the products or services of the advertiser whose name is on the item.

57% appreciate having the items given to them.

55% say the items are useful

53% feel positively rather than negatively toward the advertiser.

49% are aware of the advertiser's name, logo or message on the item.

42% remember the person who gave the item.

No People, No Sales

Editorial ◆ *July 1991*

You don't have to be a genius to know that if more people walk into a store, it becomes more likely that someone will buy. That's the basic reason for a mall location.

It's equally true that if fewer people walk in, sales volume drops. That's bad news for jewelers, a lot of whom seem to be suffering from extreme traffic drought right now. Therefore it seems a good idea to come up with some traffic-building thoughts and it's fine with me if you think up better ones of your own. The main thing is to do something positive.

Whatever your choice, the idea should excite and cheer up people—including you and your staff, as well as your customers. When everyone's in a good mood, good things tend to happen (you and your staff make money, the customer is happy with a purchase). Here are some ideas that may work for you.

1. Invite your best customers' children who've yet to reach their teens to take part in an art contest (draw and color a gemstone, a gold mine, a piece of jewelry?). Recruit independent judges, put the finalists on display and announce the winners at a special showing; give the winners a small jewelry gift. Expect a lot of parents to show up and consider the potential for media coverage.

2. Cooperate with other jewelers in your community to run a joint advertising campaign. Eight American gem Society jewelers in the Philadelphia area tried this before Christmas 1989 and Bill Shepherd of Wayne Jewelers & Silversmiths says they did well enough to put the plan on their regular schedule.

3. Stage a trunk show that's heavy on pizzazz and good values; well done, this can really bring in customers and dollars. Andy Johnson of the Diamond Cellar in Columbus, Ohio, an aggressive, single-store operation, invited four major suppliers to an open house last fall. In three days he attracted more than 1,500 customers and had sales totaling well into six figures.

4. Identify the most ritzy retirement community in your area and arrange to put on a special showing of special jewelry— then wrap up your presentation with plenty of lore and romance. These folk often have enviable income and net worth and they're quite prepared to pamper themselves with some nice jewelry—if properly tempted.

5. Sponsor an American gemstone display. Right now the public still is enjoying a post Gulf War euphoria of patriotism and there's nothing wrong with taking part in it. Put together a showcase full of California tourmaline, Idaho opal, Arizona peridot, Montana sapphire and try for at least one of those unique American stones, the beautiful, blue benitoite. A collection like that has got to be a traffic-puller—and don't forget to have information on hand about the only working U.S. diamond mine at Murfreesboro, Arkansas.

6. Hold a forecasting contest. Invite consumers to forecast the hottest day in August in your town and the top temperature that day (use the local radio station as the judge—and try to get one of its talk-show hosts, if it has one, to talk up the idea). Participants have to fill in a blank in your store and all are invited to hear who won. Reward the winner with a sunshine stone, a pretty heliodor. (If you prefer black humor, try an irradiated topaz.)

7. Launch a sustained young people's campaign. Too many jewelers don't pay enough attention to young people but you can't cultivate good contacts too early in a potential customer's life. Try to adopt a local school. Arrange class presentations. Encourage store visits. Offer part-time jobs. And be sure to involve parents and faculty. A campaign like this can do much more than help the kids overcome the threshold resistance they feel a jewelry store presents ("It's too expensive for me!"). It builds traffic, creates some sales now and promises many more in the future.

Why not make your next staff meeting a brain-storming session for ideas on how to build store traffic? Be sure to involve everyone—sales, back office, part-timers and managers. You may get some impossibly blue sky ideas; you're also sure to get some real winners.

Anatomy Of A Trunk Show

July 1991

Imagine emptying your store, rearranging the furniture, serving up cases of champagne and dancing between the showcases. Sound ridiculous? Maybe not, once you add two key elements—your customers and a well-known jewelry designer. Put these all together and you're bound to create an event that serves your customers and your bottom line.

The designer trunk show, or personal appearance, feeds into the latest desire of consumers for more personal connection to their stores and goods. Every other fashion medium promotes its designers. Clothing designers do major productions in many department and specialty stores. Accessories designers often hold workshops. Even nouveau-chic food designers (chefs to you and me) make personal cooking appearances in book stores and housewares departments.

Customers like to get to know the face, and hands, behind their favorite jewels. Often the designer becomes your best salesperson, especially of high-ticket items, because he or she knows the work best. The designer can explain the philosophy behind the design, the gemstones' attributes, the gold karatage, the workmanship. This extra detailing can clinch the sale.

Here's how you can do it—a step-by-step anatomy of a trunk show.

DECISIONS—THE FIRST STEP

Decide which designer(s) you'd like to showcase. Invite either someone whose work you sell particularly well or someone whose designs you're sure will do well once introduced in your area.

You can shoot for the stars (Henry Dunay, Jose Hess, Michael Bondanza, Whitney Boin, Lagos Inc., David Yurman, et al) or go for a relative newcomer and experiment together. "I do about 25 appearances a year," says Yurman. "I get to develop a relationship with the store's sales staff and get close to the market. The trunk show allows me the chance to make it more than gold and stones for everyone."

One-person shows are good, but group shows of two or even three designers covering a range of price points can be even more effective. Choose your purpose; what customers do you want to reach?

But be cautious: more is not always better. Larger groups of designers can be counterproductive. "When customers see more than three designers, they can feel like they're being herded in to see a group of New Yorkers open their cases," warns veteran trunk-show host Tom Tivol of Tivol Jewelers in Kansas City, Mo.

But to prove there are no hard-and-fast rules, Florida-based Mayor's Jewelers invited *nine* designers to its Coral Gables store one evening last December. The evening turned into a party worthy of newspaper coverage. And the following day, almost all of the designers worked behind the counters helping customers.

Be clear on your intent from the start. Tivol stresses the distinction of hosting the party as a way to thank clients for their patronage, welcome them to the store's family and extend one more effort to please them. Court your designer clientele, says Sam Getz, president and chief operations officer of Mayor's Jewelers. Make them feel like members of a private club so they'll want to attend your special events, he says.

Designer details: It's the presence of the designer, not a salesperson or representative, that makes the difference with crowd turnout and at the register, say retailers.

Whichever designer you choose, book early. The most popular party season is mid-October through December, and designers start to fill their Christmas dance cards as early as June or July.

Also figure out early just what merchandise the designer will bring. Do you want the whole line, only the finest pieces, just the conservative styles, etc. This is the chance many of your customers have been waiting for; they'll have all the pieces they could want from their favorite designer right at their fingertips! Often designer jewelry customers act more like art patrons. They want to view, appraise, appreciate and collect the work. Be careful not to limit their possibilities with your own limiting beliefs. Don't get bogged down thinking "this is too big, small, expensive, progressive, etc., for my clients."

Thursday and Friday usually are the best party days for private cocktail receptions; Saturday afternoons are great for open-house events. Trunk shows can be two-day affairs. These start off with an invitation-only evening party for the best customers, followed by an in-store event the next day to build traffic and excite newcomers.

PRE-PARTY PLANNING

Invitations should be mailed four to six weeks in advance. They can be as simple as postcard notes or as elaborate as engraved invitations. Don't forget to invite local politicians, dignitaries, celebrities and media along with your regular client roster. You never know who'll show up, so stack the publicity deck in your favor. Local TV stations and columnists are must-haves—they do the party circuit for a living!

You can expect about a 20% return (considered a high response) on your invitations. The more targeted the event, the higher the response. If you invite only Henry Dunay groupies to a Dunay party, for example, you'll get a better turnout. For private parties, keep in mind the size of your space, and shoot to fill to just below capacity. People will file in and out; some come early and stay an hour, others come later and take up the slack. Most retailers agree the right number is between 75 and 100, but quality is more important than quantity. Invite the cream of your crop, the customers who spend and spend on design.

For the open-house day, you're interested in maximum exposure. Ads, postcards and phone calls will help to create the crowds. For preshow publicity, ask local newspapers and magazines whether they're interested in interviewing you and the designer. Also ask whether they need to borrow any jewelry for upcoming fashion layouts, stories on Christmas gift suggestions, holiday specialties, etc.

Depending on your budget ($3,000 to $5,000 is the expected range for the entire production), you should contact caterers and other services four to six weeks in advance. Refreshments can run the gamut from wine and cheese to full bar and hot hors d'oeuvres. A waitstaff is the key to elegance. But the finishing touch is a valet parking service, says Tivol. This way, customers know they're welcome guests from the moment they arrive.

You also can hire musicians—from one violinist to a string quartet—and models to mingle in the crowd wearing some of the designer's goods.

To add to the ambiance that good food, wine and music create, try candles, potpourri and a light touch of holiday decorations. Tivol also suggests dressing in black tie to up the ante even more.

The last decorations you might want to consider are promotional material for the designer. Examples are counter cards, name plaques, designer biography-artist's statement, pamphlets and jewelry photographs in silver frames or blown up poster-size.

If the event isn't invitation-only, place ads in local newspapers. The ads should be large enough to show the jewelry and designer, as well as tell a bit of the designer's story. You may need as long as six to eight weeks to plan, design and execute the ad. If you're uncertain how to proceed, get help from a local ad agency or public relations firm. The expense of doing everything just right should pay off on the balance sheet.

AT THE EVENT

Once clients alight from their cars, they are your guests for the evening. Your store should shine as an establishment dedicated to their well-being, enjoyment and desires.

Someone from the staff, preferably the owner or manager, should greet everyone at the door. By name! Thank them for coming and invite them in as if they were honored guests in your home, suggests Tivol.

A waiter should be nearby to offer refreshments, then the guests should be left on their own for a while to mingle and enjoy the party. You don't have to show them any merchandise, says Bruce Weber of Miss Jackson's Precious Jewels by Bruce Weber in Tulsa, Okla. They never seem to have a problem gravitating toward the jewelry on their own, he says.

Weber and Tivol take different roads to the same goal. Tivol concentrates on the long-range benefits of happy, familiar customers; Weber counts on the sales made at the event as a success marker. But they agree that success means keeping your eye on the bottom line and looking toward future possibilities. But let's get back to the party, which need not be an all-night affair. In most cases, 7-9 p.m. is long enough. Add another hour if you're having an extra-special evening. Or invite a few select clients to dinner with the designer after the party. A little more investment on your part can really clinch an important sale.

You also might need to supply extra security for the party and for the time the jewelry is in your care.

Often the designers pay their own way—travel, hotel, insurance, shipping. But some—especially up-and-coming designers—will require your help.

The evening serves many purposes for the designer. "You get to talk to the customers, hear what their lives are like, what their needs are, how they speak, what they look like," says designer Michael Bondanza. These conversations are fodder for a designer's creative mill—providing outside input missing from the secular world of bench, factory and trade show. "I think about them when I'm working," he adds. "I'm not working in a void that way."

Bondanza, like many other designers, does as many special appearances as his schedule allows—about 10 a year. Several designers do more than that, including Henry Dunay, Jose Hess, David Yurman and Steve Lagos.

Relative newcomer Paul Klecka also values the interactive feedback from the customer. And he likes the chance to build stronger ties with the store owner and sales staff. "They support me with sales; it's my obligation to come when they call."

Says Getz of Mayor's, "Like in clothing, designer names play such an important role. I think the marketplace is calling for it."

But exclusivity is a big deal. "If I'm going out on a limb to name these items, they have to go out on a limb to protect me," said Getz. "It's a two way street; the designers need to keep in mind the interests of the retailer who's promoting their name. They need to not make it easy for the customer to shop around, or else the name becomes a brand to be shopped."

WHEN THE PARTY'S OVER

Even if the cash register rang consistently during the evening—and Tivol stresses expecting no immediate returns—the following days are valuable sales events, too.

Many customers will call or visit the store to pick up a piece they saw at the party. Some were too timid to buy on the spot; others have been thinking about the jewelry, or the designer, ever since the party and won't be complete until they own the trinket they fell in love with that night.

And depending on timing, there's a gift glut that may take a week or so to kick in.

Whatever the customers' rationale, you can be prepared by doing some party homework. Have your staff make notes at the end of the evening. What did Mrs. Jones like? What did Mr. Smith say would be nice for his daughter? Who was interested in the one-of-a-kind designs? Who wanted several sterling pieces for office gifts?

What did people ask for that you didn't have? What did they like about the event, the decorations, the designer, the food? Store all these side comments for future reference. You'll have a better handle on what your customers want and expect from you by collecting off-the-cuff party chat.

Tivol and his staff are on the phone for several days after a big party. They call just to say thank you—not to ask what a guest liked or what they wanted to buy. This lets people know they're more than a sales receipt to you. Inevitably, a customer will ask about a certain piece of jewelry when you call.

Often the designer will leave the line, or some additional merchandise, at your store for a day to a week after the event. This enables you to create additional excitement and sales. Ads about the collection and reviews of the party by local media will keep the spotlight focused even after the designer leaves. An educational channel also might be interested in taping a show when the designer is in town and broadcast it later. The fantasy jewels shown during Mayor's designer blow-out even produced a few minutes of party action on the local news—complete with designer comments and jewelry inspection.

Fashion shows and informal modeling can take place anytime—you can put on a show in any barn and have it turn out well.

Creativity is the key to unlocking promotional doors. You can create unlimited possibilities just by looking at what's never been done before and what you can do differently. And by calling on the support team you already have on the bench—your suppliers.

Trunk Show Checklist

Four months in advance
- Contact designer.
- Schedule dates.
- Decide on type of event; start a journal of plans and ideas.
- Contact ad agency/public relations firm.

Two months in advance
- Plan and execute ads.
- Order invitations.
- Order promotional materials.
- Write press releases.
- Contact caterer, musicians, valet parking services, coat checkers, etc.
- Buy decorations.

One month in advance
- Mail invitations.
- Send press releases.
- Hire photographer.
- Finalize menus, beverages, musical selections.
- Finalize designer's travel schedule—airport transportation, hotel accommodations, merchandise transport.
- Contact security company.

Early in show week
- Place ads.
- Make last-minute phone invitations.

- Contact local newspapers and magazines.
- Be sure you have promotional materials in the store.
- Hold a staff meeting. Educate everyone about the designer, the event, how to be with the guests, etc.

Early the evening of the event
- Decorate the store.
- Set up the bar, kitchen area, coat check, entry way, valet area.
- Display the designer's goods in cases and windows.
- Lay out promotional materials, ashtrays, coasters.
- Get the sales staff together right before the doors open; be sure everyone is excited!
- Dress staff in jewelry by the featured designer.
- Assign one person to be door-greeter.
- Line up musical tapes or check that the musicians are ready.

During the evening
- MINGLE!
- Keep in touch with staff—they're everywhere you're not, with customers, watching the bar, the waiters, the door.
- Let the photographer know what photos you want (of special clients, the designer, your staff).

End of the evening
- Thank everyone for coming.
- Congratulate staff for excellent performance and get feedback.
- Pack the jewelry and secure the store.
- Clean up (or leave for morning), or use a service.
- Take the designer and staff (and selected clients) to dinner.
- Make arrangements with photographer for film development and picture printing.

The next day
- Finish clean-up.
- Start thank-you notes or calls.
- Keep momentum up if you're doing a follow-up event in the store. Displays, promotional aids, decorations all can stay put.
- Have staff follow up on potential sales from the previous evening (make notes, call people who asked that items be held, send additional photos or ideas to interested buyers).
- Send thank-you note to the designer.
- Order photo prints; send party shots to local newspapers for party coverage.

Maximum Exposure, Minimum Bucks

August 1989

You already know advertising is key to building business. You've heard it a million times. Nonetheless, your budget just won't accommodate a major media blitz.

Cheer up. Quality is more important than quantity in achieving effective exposure. What you should do is learn how best to use the resources you have and take advantage of free publicity opportunities.

First, decide how much you can spend on advertising, then explore how to get the most return on your investment. Study demographics to determine where your ads will do the most good. Demographics are statistical pictures of a given population, including income, education, occupation and spending habits.

With this information, you can begin to match which customers will be attracted to which type of ad and which media. Do your customers listen to classical, country-western, pop or easy listening radio stations? Do they watch daytime or prime-time TV programs? Do they pay more attention to the world, national, local, life-style or sports sections in newspapers?

Finally, is one medium enough? Can you back up newspaper ads with radio spots? Can you use direct mail to support radio ads? Following are the advantages of radio, TV and print media ads, and some hints of how best to use them. (See related story for ways to get across your message outside of media ads.)

Radio

Radio advertising is relatively inexpensive. But savvy planning is necessary to get the most for your money.

The most-listened-to station isn't always the best choice. Its rates may be prohibitive, and other stations may have more listeners who would be receptive to jewelry ads. Every station has demographic information about its listener base, and most offer it freely.

Also, ad rates vary according to time of day. A station's demographic profile will help you to choose which time slots have the most listeners you want to target.

Ask questions. A station may rank No. 1 among listeners ages 25-54, for example, but that covers a wide range of ages and spending habits. Find out whether most of the listeners are closer to 25 or 54. They are vastly different groups.

Once you decide which station and which time slot suit your needs, you must decide how often and how long your ads will run.

Frequency is important. It's more effective to advertise heavily for a week than do it sporadically. If your ad is an image-builder, you can get away with lower-cost advertising (for example, frequent repetition during a lower-priced time

slot such as early evening). Another option is a preemptive spot, allowing the station to bump your ad and use it later. But if you're running a timely ad about a sale, spend the extra money for a guaranteed time. Also, consider heavy short-term advertising on different stations because many radio listeners are dial-flippers.

Sixty-second ads are best for radio because they allow time to grab listeners' attention, make your pitch and spur them to action without losing them, says Gavin Stief, general sales manager of WKSZ-FM, Media, Pa.

A 60-second spot is 14 typed lines. Ask the radio station whether it offers copywriting services or ask the sales representative for help—many of them are creative copywriters. Keep your message simple and tasteful, and avoid the dialogue format—it's too confusing.

You may think you could cut the cost in half with a 30-second spot. But a 30-second spot generally costs 80% of a 60-second spot and offers much less time to sell your product. Also, listeners tune out radio stations they perceive to have too many commercials. For example, listeners perceive four 30-second commercials to be twice as long as two 60-second ones, even though they take the same time.

Other hints for paid radio ads:

• If you can afford to have a little musical tune created, do so. It sets your ad apart.

• A good image-building campaign has to last longer than a week. For a small budget, Stief recommends frequent ads one week per month for several months.

Finally, you sometimes can get free publicity by sponsoring a community activity. The Federal Communications Commission requires all radio stations to donate time for public service announcements. You can qualify by sponsoring events involving, for example, high school sports, handicapped children, animal protection, benefit marathons or collections for the disadvantaged. Many shoppers like to patronize stores that appear to care about the community. One caution: check with the station to be sure you comply with FCC rules.

Television

Firms with small ad budgets often don't even consider TV. But it's not as expensive as you might think.

Naturally, prime time costs top dollar. But you may be able to reach your buying public at other times for a great deal less. For example, KYW-TV 3, the NBC affiliate in Philadelphia, ran a summer promotion in which $1,500 per week bought a 30-second spot on the daily noon news broadcast. A 30-second spot during late night can cost as little as $100, says Jim Gallagher, a KYW account executive. (For the record, a 30-second spot on *The Cosby Show* costs $18,000 to $20,000.)

Rates change seasonally. Generally, they're lowest in midsummer and midwinter, and highest in the fall and during the holidays. The best time for retailers to buy TV time is January through March, when ad rates are lowest and audience number are highest, says Gallagher.

TV stations, like radio, have information on listener demographics and run public service announcements. But TV stations get more requests for public service ads so the competition is stiffer. Be persistent; call the station for its criteria and to learn about its pet projects. Also, appearing on or donating merchandise to TV fund-raisers can give you quite a bit of good exposure. And don't forget public television stations, which generally attract an affluent market.

When creating a TV ad, remember it must be utterly professional. An amateurish production is more turn-off than enticement. Work with station personnel, an ad agency or jewelry organizations that offer prepared commercials. The World Gold Council, De Beers and other have designed commercials to which your store name and logo can be added. Don't let your ego get in the way; unless you have true performing experience and talent, stay behind the camera.

TV commercials should be 30 seconds. Unlike radio listeners, few TV viewers will pay full attention to a 60-second commercial unless it's spellbinding. (That, however, is as rare as pink diamonds!)

Print media

The newspaper is one of the most successful means of retail advertising. While glossy magazine ads do much to build desire, the immediacy of newspaper ads brings customers into the store.

The cost varies greatly from small town to big city. But whatever the cost, you want to achieve the best return on your investment of time and money.

To make sure the newspaper reaches the people you want to reach, review its audited circulation statement, demographic information and readership studies. Remember the *New York Daily News* may have a higher circulation than *The New York Times,* but the readerships are quite different.

Don't discount neighborhood papers and shoppers' guides. People read those things! Their rates should be considerably lower than big papers, and you can target very specific markets with high frequency. People who live in the neighborhood are likely to support local merchants, even if initially for the sake of convenience. Friday, Sunday and food editions generally have larger circulation than other days. But if you're running a special event, you'll need ads a few days beforehand regardless of edition. Frequency is important in print, too.

Ask your suppliers if they sponsor co-op ads, in which you and the supplier split the cost of ads featuring his products. Co-op programs differ from prepared ad material offered by suppliers; make sure you understand this difference. Ad managers at newspapers often have lists of manufacturers with co-op programs.

The newspaper's rate card should tell you all you need to know about cost. Ads usually are sold in standard ad units. (SAU's) or by measurement—generally 14 lines per column inch. For example, an ad that's 100 on 3 (100 lines, 3 columns) would measure about 7" deep by 5" or 6" across.

Ads can be sold on a one-time noncontract basis or by contract. Contracts can be based on frequency or the number of lines per week or month.

You will have little, if any, control over your ad's position in a newspaper. Outside the main news sections, you should have a better chance of getting the ad into the section you want, if not the exact position. Always ask your ad representative for the best placement within the section. Rarely will you get it; all advertisers make the same request. But not asking virtually guarantees you won't get it.

Preparing the ad: Many suppliers offer camera-ready ad slicks, and the newspaper will add your store name and/or logo for a fee. Or you can pay an agency or the newspaper to design the entire ad.

Keep the ad simple and clean, including pertinent information such as prices, hours, address, phone, store logo and product pictures if you choose.

If you hire the newspaper to design the ad, it usually does a speculative layout free, charging only after you approve the final layout. Regardless of who does the ad, you *must* allow enough time (at least two publishing days) to proofread and correct any mistakes before deadline. Newspapers don't give a lot of credit for mistakes in ads. For example, if the price of your top loss leader is misprinted, it could cost you thousands of dollars. But the newspaper will see the misprint as only 5% of the total ad and refund only 5% of your cost. Be 100% happy with the look of your ad *before* you OK it!

Newspaper freebies: If you do anything noteworthy, write a press release and send it to your local papers. But be warned it must be unusual or newsworthy—editors are pros at sniffing out free advertising in disguise. Worthy examples are an exhibit of antique Mayan jewelry, an exhibit of works by local high school metalsmithing students or honoring a community member at a special event. You would have a tougher time justifying an article on a three-day exhibit of one designer's products that you hope to promote. You could try to submit such a story after the event, when it would seem less like free advertising.

Editorial mention is much easier to obtain in a small town than a big city. Small-town papers keep up with the comings and goings of community residents and merchants. They may even print a picture of you at the Jewelers of America show—which you can use to begin a new season promotion.

Here are two sample press releases:

BEFORE THE EVENT

Students in the Metalsmithing and Jewelrymaking course at Anytown High School will exhibit their work at Joe's Fine Jewelers, 123 Main St., Anytown, Feb. 7-9. Finished pieces will be on display, and the students will demonstrate their craft live at 11 a.m. and 1 and 3 p.m. each day. Refreshments will be served.

The jewelry course is a joint effort of the school's art and industrial skills departments. Art instructor Lynn Johnson teaches design and sketching techniques; industrial shop instructor Mike Mallone teaches cutting, soldering and shaping techniques for precious metals. Students participating in the course must take two semesters of art and design and one semester of basic shop training first. This is the fourth semester for the jewelrymaking course; three of its previous graduates are now apprenticed to noted jewelry designers.

The works on display at Joe's Fine Jewelers are not for sale. A design contest will be held, to be judged by the employees of Joe's. The winner will receive a $500 scholarship to further his or her education in jewelry design.

AFTER THE EVENT

Noted jewelry designer Marty Smith displayed his latest collection at Joe's Fine Jewelers last week. The collection includes brooches, pendants, necklaces and bracelets featuring colored gemstones set in 18 karat gold. Smith is famous in the jewelry industry for his innovative designs combining fantasy-cut gemstones and textured metals. All pieces are available for sale.

Smith was on hand for two days to answer customers' questions and to demonstrate his design technique from rough sketch to finished product.

"Marty Smith's pieces are living proof that unusual designs, aside from being conversation pieces, can enhance the beauty of the materials and the wearer," said jeweler Joe Adams, store owner.

The Smith display was part of a monthly series of designer exhibits at Joe's Fine Jewelers. From Feb. 10-13, the store will feature designs by Susan Jones, who has won awards for her work in sterling silver.

Joe's Fine Jewelers is located at 123 Main St., Anytown.

The first press release is designed to build traffic, but it's a public service announcement and has nothing to do with selling. The second press release combines the news of the designer's visit with a gentle advertising pitch for his works and the continuing designer program.

Magazines: Magazine advertising should appeal to a more specific market than newspaper ads. Newspapers attract readers from many walks of life; magazines usually attract readers with specific interests.

A magazine ad can be used to convey urgency, such as for a month-long promotion, but usually it's used to build desire. Check the magazine's demographics and readership the way you would a newspaper's.

Magazines usually sell ads by the page or a fraction thereof and have corresponding rates. You may have more control over ad placement, and it's much easier to use color in a magazine than in a newspaper. Magazines tend to be a little more lenient than newspapers about credit for mistakes in ads, but be just as careful with proofreading. Check the magazine's credit policy before you buy.

Other publications: You also can advertise in a multitude of church and school yearbooks, association and club newsletters, town-watch bulletins, convention guides and other publications.

These ads are more of a goodwill gesture than anything else, but people whose organization you support are more likely to support you. In most cases, rates are low, and you may be able to take a tax deduction for a charitable contribution.

If you advertise in a city guide or a convention flier, you might pick up business from out-of-towners. Don't discount them—you never know when they'll be back. They also have friends who may pass through your town, and rest assured they'll be asked where they picked up such a lovely, unusual piece of jewelry.

Last, but not least, are the *Yellow Pages.* Jewelers are divided in their opinions on the value of *Yellow Page* ads, but it doesn't hurt to research how many potential customers they reach. Large ads tend to be expensive, though, so make a thorough assessment of your budget before committing to one. Do ask about the coupon section in your local directory.

Recommended reading

The best publicity efforts in the world will be useless if you don't capture the attention of media personnel. Newspapers, magazines, radio and TV stations are deluged with organizations that feel their cause is the most newsworthy. How can you grab their attention?

Study books that instruct how to produce professional publicity announcements, how to make sure information is really newsworthy and how to make yourself stand out from the crowd. Browse through the *Jewelers' Book Club Catalog,* available from JCK and also head for your public library.

Two good references are *You Can Spend Less and Sell More* by Bill Witcher (available from the Jewelers' Book Club and reviewed in the August 1988 JCK) and *A Layman's Guide to Successful Publicity* by Oscar Leiding (Ayer Press, Philadelphia, 1976). This should be available in your local library.

Ad agencies

The words "ad agency" usually conjure up visions of Madison Avenue and millions of dollars. Not so. Small-town agencies often don't cost a fortune, and they already know what kind of ads work in their locale.

Tell the agency exactly how much you've budgeted and stress that you want it used in the most effective way possible. The agency should be open to your ideas and you to theirs. If your budget is limited, an agency that's heavily committed to making a big name for itself or using only the most visible and expensive media may not be right for you. Find one that understands your goals and will help you attain them.

No agencies in town? Try a college marketing department — your advertising plan may become the senior class project.

The jeweler's other promotional choice

Radio, TV, newspaper and magazine ads are an effective way to promote your quality products and service. But you should support them with other promotional activities. One is public relations, a first cousin of advertising.

Community involvement is crucial to good public relations. One option is to donate merchandise or a gift certificate (of a meaningful amount) to charity auctions. A gift certificate serves a triple purpose, getting your name mentioned, drawing the winner into the store and giving you a chance to persuade the winner to buy a more expensive item.

Build good relations with future customers by donating a pen-and-pencil set to the high school valedictorian and a medallion to the most valuable football player.

When someone displays outstanding civic responsibility or heroics, honor him or her with a luncheon and piece of jewelry. If someone else decides to honor the person first, donate a medallion, an engraved watch or a gift certificate. Or you can set up an annual award contest, with the public voting for the most outstanding community member. Check the potential winners carefully to be certain they're deserving.

Create a speaker service and target your talk to the audience. Teach a women's group how to select colored gems to fit their complexions, tell a church group what role gemstones played in Biblical times or regale a medical group with a humorous look at how gemstones were once used for healing. Give elementary student simple explanations of pretty stones, teach middle-school social studies students about gem industries around the world and show high-school physics students a slide demonstration about gemstone cutting while they're studying light refractions. Check Jewelers' Book Club titles and read JCK for ideas.

Two Michigan jewelers have had great success with their speaker services. Bruno Tews, manager of Du Puis et Fils in Lansing, used elegant engraved counter cards to publicize his service. It took a bit of time, but word got around and now quite a few of his employees have been asked to speak. John Godfrey, a jeweler in Battle Creek, is an old hand at public speaking, running special seminars for engaged couples, addressing civic and church organizations and teaching gemology to high school students.

Here are some other ideas on how to attract customers and keep them coming back:

• Direct mail. Direct marketing can be very effective, provided your market base is up-to-date *and* properly targeted.

Joan Phillips of the Direct Marketing Association says your marketing list—whether bought, rented or developed on your own—must be updated continuously. And a computer is essential, she adds, because each piece of mail should be addressed by name. "Dear Resident" is unacceptable.

You've probably heard a 1% response rate is considered excellent, but that's only in very general, widespread mailings. A local jeweler who targets his "happy birthday" discount to customers who will soon observe birthdays may see a response approaching 80%.

Remember also that different occasions call for different types of mailings. Some are appropriate as statement stuffers, others call for an engraved invitation. And if you're mailing to potential customers, rather than actual customers, there's a trick to keep them from discarding the envelope without opening it. Enclose a small prize such as a plastic pen or keytag. The expense is greater, but who can resist opening a three-dimensional piece of mail?

Ask your post office for its free brochure on mailing rates. The cheapest rate isn't always the best. Undeliverable mail is returned if sent first class but not if sent bulk mail. You need those returns to keep your database current. On the other hand, if you are doing a mass mailing to potential customers and time isn't of the essence, take advantage of lower bulk mail rates.

• Postcards. A postcard with a four-color glossy picture on one side and a message on the other is very elegant—and effective. People may toss out a direct-mail envelope without opening it, but most will read a postcard. Also, postcards are cheaper to mail and have an image of immediacy, because they often advertise limited-time specials.

• Newsletters. Some jewelers produce their own newsletter with informative articles, colorful anecdotes and other information. Echols & Son in Tifton, Ga., and Earth Resources in Appleton, Wis., invest a great deal of time and effort to their newsletters, with good results.

• Thank you. Jewelers are divided on whether to follow up each purchase with a simple thank-you note. It seems the obvious thing to do, but one thank-you led to a divorce. The purchased piece was intended for a paramour, but the spouse intercepted the thank-you note. A discreet way to determine whether it's OK to mail a note to the house is to ask about sending "follow-up paperwork"—such as written guarantee, insurance or cleaning information.

• Telemarketing. People cringe when they recall the pushy people—and now push computers—who phone to hawk their goods. But it's different for jewelers. You already know your customers, you probably know their children's names and how many pets they have. You don't call to push merchandise. You call to see how everyone is, and incidentally, to remind the customer his wife's birthday is in two weeks and you have a beautiful amethyst necklace that suits her coloring exactly. Get the picture?

Your sales staff should compile information on customers, including upcoming birthdays, anniversaries, graduations and marriages. Also, make a welcome-home call when customers return from a trip, and send sympathy card should the need arise. Let them know they're more than customers, they're your friends.

• Point of purchase. OK, you've enticed the customer into the store, but now you need a subtle reinforcement to help with the buying decision. Point-of-purchase advertising can help. It might be as simple as a personalized counter mat or as elaborate as an interactive video terminal. One example: a freestanding sign highlighting your credit terms can be the make-or-break decision for someone who has more desire than ready cash.

Check with suppliers, as well as local retail display and sign shops. Also consider recruiting local art students to create an individual look for your store, and take advantage of any employees with good handwriting. Of course, make sure your point-of-purchase material is in line with your image, and keep it subtle. Remember that interpersonal communication between your staff and customers is still the key to sales.

• Names. You've made the sale, and now you should keep your name in front of the customer long after he or she leaves the store. Your name is (or should be) on your boxes and bags already. Now give a personalized jar of jewelry cleaner or polishing cloth with each purchase. If you prefer to sell such items, give a small sample and sell larger sizes. But put your name on both.

For special events, give decorative jewelry boxes with your name on the inner lid instead of the outside. That way, people are more willing to display the box and will still see your name when they open it. Two more suggestions: personalized pocket calendars with gift-giving dates marked, and refrigerator magnets in the color and shape of birthstones.

• Around town. Paint the town with your name—on billboards, on park benches, on parking meters and on trash can placards, especially if you donated the can to the city. For some clever billboard ideas, read what Lee Michaels Jewelers in Baton Rouge, La., did in "How Deep South Jewelers Fight the Price Squeeze," JCK March 1988.

• Friend to friend. Word of mouth can be the most powerful—and the most destructive—form of advertising. You pay nothing for it, but it can bring you much business. Or cost you much business. Statistics show that people tell eight to 10 others about a bad experience, and only one or two about a good experience. All your advertisement and public relations efforts will be wasted if your sales staff and service aren't the best. If your financial resources are slim because your salespeople are lacking, sink what you have into training them. Once they are knowledgeable, skillful and service-oriented, business will pick up and you'll be able to afford an ad campaign to attract even more customers.

Staff Up For Christmas

September 1988

STAFF UP FOR CHRISTMAS

Your sales staff may be dynamic and diligent, positively gushing with stamina and charisma. But the holiday season can overwhelm even the best selected and trained staff. As Christmas approaches, and the level of traffic in your store increases, be fair to your employees and yourself. If necessary, hire some extra help to lighten the load.

Map out your needs on paper

List your store's holiday hours and identify how these differ from your normal schedule.

Decide how many people should cover the floor at all times.

Decide what skills and types of people you need for specific duties.

Decide who can open and close the store.

Identify the major selling days to plan coverage accordingly.

Using the last few years' holiday sales figures, determine how much you can afford to spend on holiday help. One guideline: December salaries should not exceed 10% of December sales.

From the information you've derived, decide *exactly* how many people you can hire.

Where to find extra help

Back-up employees who have filled in for full-timers on vacation or sick leave.

Children of friends.

Customers whom you've gotten to know.

Senior citizens, especially if they have been involved in retailing. Find them through services for older people (such as the local Association for Retired Persons) and church groups.

High school seniors and college students, found through school placement services or through ads in school newspapers.

Temporary help found through a state employment agency.

Picking ideal part-timers

Look for:

A genuine smile.

A pleasant demeanor.

A well-groomed, neat appearance.

Maturity.

Self-confidence without being overly aggressive.

Good eye contact.

Enough energy to handle a fast-paced sales environment.

Good posture and walk.

A sincere desire to help the customer.

Ability to follow directions.

In students:

High grade-point average.

Membership in extra-curricular activities and/or National Honor Society.

No holiday travel constraints. (Plans to go home for the holidays?)

Using and training part-timers

Part-timers should be used to free up experienced personnel for more important sales. Plan to use new employees to sell gold chains and charms or gift items such as pens, sterling, porcelain and crystal. Use them, too, for gift wrapping, manning the cash register and light bookkeeping.

It's important that your new part-timers be informed enough to handle the simple sales that come their way. It's also vital that everyone be prepared for the inevitable Christmas con artists. Use your own established store policies to train them. Here are some suggestions of what to cover.

On security:

• Watch suspicious characters closely. Wait on one customer at a time. Show one piece of jewelry at a time. Don't turn your back on the customer. Never allow a customer to handle loose stones. Examine each piece before returning it to the tray.

• Communicate any suspicions to other employees. (Many stores use a pre-planned code word or comment to alert others of trouble.)

• In case of robbery, remain calm, do not do anything unless told to, and only push hold-up button after robbers have left.

Before selling, part-timers need some product knowledge as well as tips on how to approach a customer and even write up a sale:

• Some product basics:

The difference between carat and karat.

The 4 C's.

The differences between 14k and 18k; the meaning of gold filled and sterling silver.

The names of colored stones and beads you carry.

Styles and lengths of gold chains you carry.

How to read the carat weight on a diamond tag.

How pearls are graded.

The type of watches you stock (analog vs. digital) and how they work.

• Some selling basics:

Use an active greeting—"Hi, what can we do for you today?" or "Did you have something particular in mind?" Avoid the bland, "May I help you?"

Remember that customers are never "just browsing" a week before Christmas. They're looking to buy. So ask leading questions to focus in on a few items.

More money is spent at Christmas than at any other time of year. So don't be afraid to suggest a higher-priced item first.

Use emotional words in describing the merchandise. But be sincere—and never lie.

Move quickly and efficiently. Five or ten small sales take little time and add up quickly. Big sales should be left to more experienced employees.

Don't be too eager to use newly-learned jewelry terms. Stay away from technical points and be ready to turn over a customer to more experienced salespeople when needed to close a sale.

TRIM THE STORE

A clean, attractive store is as important as a star salesman. Uninviting displays, clutter and grime can chase customers away before they've even seen your merchandise. So look carefully at the shopping environment you offer.

Spruce up

Clear out the clutter of odd-sized boxes from your cases; replace them with uniform trays. Check whether the floor boards in your showcases are soiled or faded. If so, recover them as well as the case backgrounds.

Do your walls need repainting or repapering? What about the carpeting? It may still be good, but probably needs a cleaning.

Indeed, be sure to clean the store thoroughly before the Christmas rush begins. This will make daily maintenance easier during the hectic period.

Remember to wash the outside of your windows, polish display cases and vacuum carpets daily.

Throughout the day, empty ash trays and check the cleanliness of restrooms.

Plan your decorations early

Order as soon as possible, preferably sometime in the summer. Often decorations, especially those manufactured overseas, take more than three months to arrive. (Don't be in too much of a rush to put the decorations up, however. Wait until other merchants have done their decorating; don't be the first.)

Remember that Hanukkah comes in December, too. Tasteful recognition that Christmas and Hannukah are religious holidays may be in order, depending on your clientele and community.

Choose a central theme

This makes decorating much easier. Consider your clientele (young? older? upscale? sporty? fashion-forward?) and pick a theme that seems most appropriate to them. Incorporate that theme in your exterior, windows, selling floor, lighting, signage, key traffic points and staff identification.

Think about hiring an interior designer to give you a special look you can use for several years.

This is especially helpful when you have more than one store. Using a central theme for all branches distinguishes your stores from the rest.

Be sure to contact designers early, you may find they often are booked by the fall.

In order to find a designer in your area, contact the American Society of Interior Designers, (212) 944-9220.

Involve employees

If you don't use a professional designer, put an employee with a demonstrated "flare for display" in charge of choosing and installing decorations. Don't try a committee approach; too many opinions produce an uncoordinated look.

But make the decorating itself a party. Involving all of your employees in the process is a productive way to get a head start on the holiday spirit.

Above all, don't overdo it. Decorating is important, but too much is *too much*.

Make your decorations proportionate to your store size, window size and jewelry. To check your window displays, one designer recommends this method: stand in front of the window, close your eyes and then open them. What do you see first—the jewelry or the display? If you see the decoration first, the window is overdone.

PICK YOUR SALES WINNERS

Good Christmas sales require merchandise pre-planning. What should you buy? And from whom? Here are some tips on choosing a supplier plus a rundown of hot jewelry prospects for the holidays.

Choosing a supplier

Allow yourself enough time, especially when using new suppliers around the holidays.

Look at the spring lines at trade shows.

Gather suggestions from fellow jewelers. Discuss problems and gather information.

Use trade publications to see exactly what's out there.

Ask about services—delivery terms, repairs, warranties, memos, terms, packaging, advertising, catalogs and exchange policies.

Be prepared for holiday hits

Notice what type of jewelry young people are wearing.

Follow fashion magazines, or fashion trade magazines and newspapers. Most of these provide fall fashion forecasts in the spring or summer. Check what merchandise your suppliers are carrying.

Find out how fast your suppliers can get merchandise to you upon demand. If something is hot, you'll want it in a hurry.

Keep track of items your customers request that you do not carry. If an item pops up a number of times, try to order it.

Hot jewelry for the 1988 holidays

Fancy stones.

Pink, purple, green and yellow stones—amethyst, tourmaline, tanzanite, tsavorite and citrine.

Cabochon cuts.

Gold—high karat, bold but lightweight, not blocky.

Silver—with colored stones, with gold, with colored gold.

Large pieces with delicate filigree, curvy lines.

Victorian jewelry.

Pearls strands of all lengths.

Pearls mixed with colored stones—a Chanel-look.

Big-on-the-ear button earrings.

Full and dangling earrings with interest on the ear as well as what hangs below.

Men's jewelry for women—pocket watches, tie tacs and tie bars.

Swingy, long, open-link chains.

Bold rings.

Bangle and open-link chain bracelets mixed together.

Colorful beads in red, green and purple, and in gold and silver.

Big brooches for coats.

Charms.

Watch pins.

Braided necklaces and bracelets.

Watches with big faces, chronographs, watches on chain link bracelets, men's watches for women.

Tabletop gift ideas for '88

Mix-n-match separates, especially in contrasting colors.

Dinnerware and silverware with a holiday motif.

Glassware, candlestick holders, paperweights, salt and pepper shakers with a holiday motif.

Crystal or opaque glass perfume bottles with a unique design, or a traditional style with sterling accents.

Dinnerware in sophisticated, traditional patterns, floral patterns and muted pastels.

Accessory items produced in the same pattern as dinnerware—jewelry trays, small boxes, paperweights.

Traditional vanity gifts with sterling—make-up brushes with sterling handles, jewelry trays and boxes, sterling-handled hair brushes and combs.

SPREAD THE WORD

You've got the goods. Now how do you find customers to buy them? Try advertising, in all its myriad forms, including catalogs and even promotions. Here's what to consider.

Plan holiday advertising

• Analyze what you did last year. What worked—and didn't work? How did sales figures relate to the ads used? Which ads looked the best? Which were the most informative? And what did your competitors do that worked particularly well?

• Define your image, and incorporate it in everything you do. Keep one image and one identity. The most effective advertising is consistent; it must set your store(s) apart from the rest.

Jewelers of America suggests five image categories: Exclusive, inexpensive, innovative, conservative and mass market. Decide where you store fits.

Choose priorities. Advertise services that are special *to your store.*

• Let your customers help you. Ask them when they make a decision to buy a jewelry gift. This helps you decide when to begin advertising and ask what brought them into your store.

• Focus your efforts. Decide what merchandise you want to push and at what times during the holiday season. Make sure to have enough to back up what you advertise. Let your suppliers know what you're pushing. Ask for a 30-day memo.

Don't forget old stock, either. Rebox it, retag it and make it exciting to your staff.

• Budget your dollars. First estimate your potential Christmas sales volume. Figure on spending 5% to 8% of that on advertising.

Use newspapers for holiday ads, but don't forget two other cost-effective media. Radio zeroes in on specific audiences and times. Direct mail reaches working people who don't have time to shop.

Check with your suppliers to see who offers cooperative advertising and promotional support to stretch your budget.

Consider devoting 1% of your ad budget to employee incentives.

• Assess your print ads:

Is the copy clear, direct and to-the-point?

Does it include the name of the store, the address, all necessary directions to find the store, hours you are open and phone number?

Does it stress the special services you offer?

Is the layout distinctive? Will it attract your readers' attention?

Is the ad uncluttered? Is the white space effective?

Will the photographs reproduce well? If not, would line art be a better choice?

Overall, does the ad project your store's image?

Profitable promotions . . .

Help the customer remember you.

Set you apart from your competition.

Give people a reason to stop in your store.

Make your store more fun for your customers—and for your staff.

Offer something unusual and imaginative for your customers to see and do.

Offer something free.

Teach the customer something.

Make customers feel good about your store and themselves (e.g., donating to charity in the customer's name for each purchase made).

When planning a promotion, decide what you'd like it to do for you.

Decide whom you want to reach.

Develop an interesting event.

Decide how to promote it—newspapers, magazines, TV, radio, direct mail? Is any free editorial available, and how can you get it?

Plan advertising and public relations.

Consider that you may need extra security, extra help or longer hours from your staff.

Will it be necessary to obtain extra merchandise or displays?

Prepare a realistic budget for all of these extra costs.

Prepare a timetable to keep your self on schedule.

If necessary, check your insurance company's requirements early enough to act upon them.

The catalog approach

Christmas catalogs are a perennial favorite with many jewelers. You can produce your own. It'll be exclusive, matching your store image and merchandise perfectly. It'll also be time-consuming and expensive. Manufacturers' catalogs offer an alternative, with some shortcomings.

• Do-it-yourself. Consider hiring a professional to help you , especially if this is your first catalog. It may cost more initially, but could end up saving you aggravation, time and money in the long run.

Set a schedule, allowing time to:

Do a layout.

Photograph merchandise.

Order inventory.

Write good copy.

Check and double check proofs.

Print, label and mail the catalogs.

• Let others do it. When using a supplied catalog, ask yourself:

Is the merchandise of the quality you carry in your store?

Is there enough product range? It's fine to feature diamonds because they spark consumer interest, but don't let customers forget you offer other goods, too.

Are the price points appropriate? (A catalog should offer competitive price points, with a range of approximately $20 to $2,500—the bulk of it falling in the $250-$300 range.)

It's important to stock enough merchandise to back up a catalog, but make sure not to over-buy. Try sending out a fall flyer to see what's in demand. Merchandise which is left over can be marketed in a spring flyer.

Make sure your staff is very familiar with the merchandise in the catalog, as well as prices, sizes, availability, and back-order status. Call a meeting and go over the items, so your salespeople become experts.

It's in the mail

You may decide to distribute your catalog through the mail or have it inserted in a local newspaper. Newspaper insertions are generally cheaper, but sending through the mail is said to have more impact.

Be aware of your competitors. When are they mailing? Mail order houses and department stores generally send their catalogs earlier. Many jewelers prefer to send theirs in mid-November.

Target the mailer. Not every mailing piece needs to go to every customer. If you've maintained your records, you will know who buys what.

An up-to-date mailing list is vital to any direct mail effort. Existing customers should be your target. They already know you; keep them trusting you.

Gather the customer's name and address from each transaction. Tell the customer you want to add his/her name to your preferred mailing list.

The sales receipt will include a description of the items sold. Use this to record and classify what your customer buys so you can target them for specific sales or promotions.

Use the date on the sales receipt to keep track of frequent or infrequent buyers. Mail a letter to customers you haven't seen for a while. Invite them back into your store. Entice them by offering a discount with the letter, or a free polishing. (Remember to include the value of the service on the card.)

Consider sending a thank you note to customers who have recently purchased something in your store.

Store information on a computer to save time. A computer also allows you to produce labels when you're ready to mail. If you don't have one, a card file will suffice. Many computer software programs designed for jewelers can store birthdays, anniversaries, previous purchases and a "wish list."

Target new customers on your list soon after Christmas. Mail them a note and tell them your staff would love to assist them with their future jewelry needs.

STAY IN CHARGE

During the busy Christmas season, it's easy to ignore or overlook basic management duties. It's even more important than usual to stay on top of things. You should hold staff meetings to keep employees informed and enthused. You must stay calm and healthy, no matter how hectic things get. And you must keep an eye on credit so that your business actually reaps the rewards for the goods it sells.

Call a meeting

Use staff meetings to:

Go over all merchandise, especially new items or items you are pushing.

Let your buyers talk to your staff and explain why they were "excited" about picking certain items.

Stress your philosophy of doing business.

Make clear your goals for this season.

Reinforce a positive attitude by being positive yourself.

Give some professional sales training.

Reinforce "team effort" and "co-operation" to your employees.

Make every employee, from sales associate to clerk and bookkeeper, feel needed.

Give employees a chance to express ideas.

Cover any bonus or incentive programs. Make them exciting.

Go over all the services you offer—gift wrapping, bagging, repair services, exchange policies.

Let various "in-house" experts—the engraver, the bridal consultant, the repairman, the watchmaker—explain their areas of expertise.

When planning a meeting, hand out typed agendas a few days beforehand to give employees a chance to prepare. Supply audio/visual aids to reinforce your messages. Offer some refreshments. Put out coffee and donuts 15 minutes prior to the meeting to get everyone there on time.

Go beyond the in-store business by urging your staff to relax on lunch hours, exercise and maintain outside activities to clear their minds. It will only improve their attitude and productivity.

At least once a week hold meetings with managers only. Discussions should include everything from emergency procedures to day-to-day business activities.

Be of good cheer

Get lots of rest.

Exercise and have outside activities which relax you.

Leave personal problems at home.

Allow the opportunity for a busy and financially profitable season to motivate you.

Motivate your staff in mid-November by treating them to a nice dinner, a champagne party or a holiday kick-off extravaganza. Their excitement for the upcoming season will benefit your mood and profits!

Set *realistic* objectives for yourself each day. Meet as many as you can, but don't overdo it.

Don't spread yourself too thin—delegate a share of responsibilities to other employees.

Don't waste time worrying about things you cannot change.

Regardless of the pressure that is on you, treat your employees with respect and understanding. They will treat you the same in turn.

Will that be cash?

• Don't be so anxious for holiday sales that you are lax about issuing credit. Obtain:

The full name of the applicant, no nicknames. If it is a single account you may not ask for information about a spouse.

A telephone number. Use it to verify residence, and keep it to contact the customer for collection purposes, if necessary.

The applicant's employment status, position, salary, length of time with the company and previous employment. If unemployed, question his sources of income.

Information on the applicant's banking status—checking and savings accounts, as well as loans outstanding.

References from other credit sources.

Note: The applicant does not have to reveal any income obtained by child support, alimony or separate maintenance, such as welfare. Under federal law, you must inform the applicant of this. It's best to print it on the application.

• Thoroughly investigate the information provided.

Check all references.

Contact your local credit bureau.

Look for good signs: stable employment, prompt payment of rent or mortgage, home ownership, and keeping checking/savings accounts.

Recognize bad signs: frequent moves, numerous job changes, and no bank accounts.

• If you decide to grant credit:

Notify the customer and the salesperson immediately.

Give the customer a copy of the retail charge agreement which he has signed; this is required by the federal Truth in Lending law. Keep a copy for your file.

If you decide to grant credit of less than the amount requested, ask for a larger down payment or have the salesperson suggest a lower priced item.

• If you deny credit:

Under federal law you must inform the applicant within 30 days of receiving the credit application.

The applicant must receive the notification in writing. According to the Fair Credit Reporting Act and Equal Credit Opportunity Act, you must state specific reasons why the credit was not granted.

• Regardless of how busy you are, keep records.

Keep a file of the original interview, the credit investigation and the decision. Federal law states these must be kept for 25 months for those denied credit.

Keep a ledger sheet or computer file of all monetary transactions.

If the customer deviates from the credit terms and the payment is delinquent, be firm, but maintain a friendly attitude.

• Be careful when accepting other forms of credit.

When accepting major credit cards, first check the credit card company's cancellation list. Then make sure to get authorization for every transaction, through a machine or by calling the credit card center. Write the authorization number on the sales receipt.

When accepting checks, get all the information possible, including a credit card number (check it the same way you would if it were a credit card transaction), ask for picture identification and make sure the signature on the check matches the signature on the identification.

How To Profit Without Price-Cutting

April 1988

A certain Tupelo, Miss., jeweler competes head-on with 70% discounters.

Though the competition is fierce, not once does she utter that nasty four-letter word: SALE.

She is an American Gem Society jeweler, and she doing just fine, thank you.

How is she making it? How do ethically minded retailers survive amidst the discounters?

By attitude and action. AGS jewelers don't waste time dreaming up ways to beat discounters at their own game. Instead, they maintain an upbeat attitude and concentrate on good, clean, often innovative marketing methods. They succeed by selling quality goods and services to informed consumers.

But how do they attract today's price-conscious consumers in the first place?

A recent JCK survey of AGS jewelers identified at least six major marketing strategies, built around promotion, service, advertising, display, sales staff and public relations.

Discounting and a focus on price were not listed; indeed, they're excluded from AGS standards.

The following pages offer some marketing tips and tactics that have worked well for AGS jewelers. Chances are you've already used a few; many are improvements on tried-and-true salesmanship. But others are unique eye-catchers, image-builders and educational campaigns that might spur your business.

PROMOTION

Service enticement

Throngs of customers, braced for a sub-zero Connecticut January, stood clutching dusty jewelry boxes at Michaels Jewelers in New Haven. Some came to have rings resized for $6 or watch batteries changed for $1.99. Others came to have pearls restrung, chains shortened or stones reset.

It was Service Week at Michaels. The event, held each September and January, enlivens a normally slow time for jewelers and builds good-will. Customers who drop off jewelry for repair during Service Week often return for more substantial purchases. That, says partner John Michaels, is the reason for the event.

Begun last year, the promotion was almost *too* successful. A few managers considered the heavy traffic unmanageable, even though the firm put five jewelers on duty at each of its 13 stores for the event.

Michaels certainly didn't want to drop an event that drew so many people. So rather than try to elicit new orders during Service Week, staffers now delay their sales efforts until customers return to pick up merchandise dropped off for repair.

About 70% of Service Week customers are new to the store, Michaels estimates. And enough of them return to recoup the low margins taken on service fees. (Fees during Service Week are 10% off the normal price, but that's not mentioned in the one newspaper ad run several days before the event. The ad just shows prices, not discounts or comparative prices.)

Well-trained employees are the real key to a successful service promotion, says Michaels. "The objective here isn't just selling. It's to give the customer a positive, professional experience with a jeweler."

'T' time on campus

Carl Schmieder of Otto Schmieder & Son Jewelry, Pheonix, Ariz., has done his share of promotions—from T-shirt contest to local jewelry design competitions. All these promotions have one thing in common: Non-price orientation.

Schmieder promotes two ways. Internally, he motivates his staff to improve selling. Externally, he motivates the public to come in and buy.

One promotion was designed to foster his firm's name recognition among college students. Schmieder developed a contest in which students were encouraged to color—in any way they chose— T-shirts he had printed with a design that included his store's logo.

About 400 shirts were given away; about 100 students came to the store on judging day wearing shirts they had colored. Schmieder enlisted an art professor to help judge.

Prizes awarded in six categories included a diamond ring, several watches (older models) and gold-filled jewelry.

The promotion generated publicity and considerable foot traffic at a total cost of less than $1,000, including prizes and T-shirts (about $1.75 each), says Schmieder.

Too much time

A few years ago, Leroy and Louise Walker had a lot of time on their hands. The couple, owners of Walkers n' Daughters Jewelers, Bismark, N.D., had ordered nine full-size grandfather clocks but received 18.

The Walkers displayed one of the 18 in the window of their main downtown store and announced that all would be sold by silent auction. A minimum starting price was included on instruction cards for customers. About three weeks later, the bids were pulled and the clocks were sold.

"We got about the same price for each that we would have received selling them," says Louise Walker.

The Walkers had parlayed a warehouse clearance measure into a promotional event.

Caution: A few years later, the Walkers held another silent auction with less than satisfying results. Louis Walker theorizes this type of promotion was too specialized to generate interest more than once at the same location.

Bingo bash

When an entourage of women in fur coats gathered for a party at Carl Bussell's Diamond Room, standard chit-chat was supplanted by cries of "Bingo!"

Most of the 75 attendees that evening were Bussell's regular customers. A few were potential customers. All were invited to play Bingo and celebrate the opening of Bussell's new fine jewelry store in Bryan, Tex.

"It was kind of a non-plush activity for a plush jewelry store," says owner Carl Bussell. "Bingo gave the evening a fun focal point."

He mailed 500 invitations (which looked like Bingo cards and contained his logo), and he rented the game equipment for only $15.

Three times during the evening, Bussell gave away door prizes: Pearl necklaces and earrings worth about $400 each.

The store, now supported by low-key radio advertisements, has prospered. Sales for December exceeded sales the previous December.

PUBLIC RELATIONS

Wagons, ho!

To reach the newest prospective customers in town, Larry Hug sends out the Welcome wagon.

Hug, owner of Hug Jewelers in Cincinnati, pays Welcome Wagon International to deliver his message to each new homeowner in the affluent Wyoming district of the hilly southern Ohio City.

Welcome Wagon hostesses visit newcomers with a smile and endorsements from local businesses. The cost is $1.65 per call, and Hug says it's money well spent. Hug estimates he gets about 50 new customers each year through referrals by Doris Deardurff, the Welcome Wagon hostess in his area.

Deardurff also invites each new family to pick up a free jar of jewelry cleaner at Hug's store. The name, address and telephone number of the newcomers are forwarded to Hug for promotional mailings. That information is for use by the jeweler only and cannot be sold, says Deardurff.

As a loyal Hug customer for 33 years, Deardurff is well acquainted with the store's services. Deardurff has introduced Hug's store to hundreds of potential customers in her 30 years with Welcome Wagon.

A recommendation from a long-time resident such as Deardurff is appreciated particularly by people interested in buying jewelry and people who may have changed insurance agents and need jewelry appraisals.

Wizard of words

When Patty Witt of Way-Fil Jewelry, Tupelo, Miss., wrote about the "magic of crystals" for her weekly newspaper column, a crystal ball could not have predicted the response.

"I got all types of calls," says Witt. "One woman wanted me to meditate with her." Others just offered compliments.

The 7- to 8-inch column costs Way-Fil's owner $50 each week.

Witt's photo appears with her column, and the recognition is good business. She gets one or two calls every week about her column, and people even stop her while grocery shopping to chat about her latest topic.

Officially speaking

Linda Brantley, owner of Trein's Jewelry Store, gains recognition and prestige through her community service.

She is a member of the Dixon, Ill., Chamber Board, which advises the city council.

Also, Brantley, a talented freelance photographer, touts her community through a slide show she prepared herself. By word of mouth, she manages to stay booked for showings of her 20-minute program to area associations. The program's last slide, of course, plugs a good local spot to buy fine jewelry—her store.

SERVICE

Offering the extras

It's difficult to "sell" service, says Patrick Gilmore of Dunbar Jewelers, Yakima, Wash. Still, Gilmore and many other AGS members rely on service-oriented extras to keep customers coming back. At no charge, Gilmore offers gift wrapping, presentation boxes, diamond guarantees, staff jewelers and watchmakers, sizing, engraving and fusing of wedding sets.

In addition, any item sent out for repair is checked thoroughly to ensure a clean, proper job before it's returned to the customer. Sloppiness at this point will lose business overnight, says Gilmore.

Selling with class

Bill Lieberum finds advertising difficult in New Hope, Pa., an area with 18 regional newspapers and "zillions of little phone books."

So he sells by word of mouth—usually his own. The owner of Bill Lieberum Fine Jewelry teaches classes up to four nights per week for interested diamond buyers. All customers are welcome at the two- or three-hour classes, which often have just one or two students.

Classes are strictly educational. "I don't sell the stone the night of the class," he says. "They are not pressured to buy anything."

Students sometimes visit other stores after the class, but Lieberum says almost all of them come back to buy from him. "I've had some employees say I'm crazy for doing this," he says. "But then they see that it works."

No-gimmick refund

If Donald Thoma's customers don't like what they buy, they can return it and receive their money back within 30 days. Period.

Thoma, president of Williams Jewelry Inc. in Bloomington, Ind., says that differs from many other retailers' policies. "Some will take the stone back if your appraisal isn't bigger than the purchase price," he says. But none will hand back the full purchase price outright, he says.

The few items that are returned to his store typically are the result of a hasty gift decision, he says.

The guarantee is unconditional and extends to every item in the store, as well as some services. Because it is standard policy, it is a permanent promotional device and an effective sales tool.

"An AGS store should be impeccable in standing behind merchandise," Thoma says. "You have got to be a good loser sometimes to be a good winner."

Responding to need

John Nowlin of Nowlin Jewelry, Lake Jackson, Tex., describes his store's full service in terms of solving customers' jewelry needs: Repairs, appraisals and answers.

Nowlin's sister, Cherie McBride, tells this story of a sale won because of service. A customer bought a Rolex at the store after seeing the same watch in Houston for $500 less. He didn't try to deal, and explained he was willing to pay more because Nowlin employs someone who can repair Rolexes. The Houston store did not.

Nowlin's advertising emphasizes its service and features write-ups on the in-house repairmen. "Many customers come in for repairs on jewelry they bought elsewhere," says McBride.

Visible location

From his small, second-floor shop at the edge of town, Robert Hallett did a good business selling custom-made jewelry. Then he moved downtown to a street-level shop about four years ago, and his business got even better. "Suddenly, we were no longer word-of-mouth," recalls Hallett, owner of Robert Hallett Goldsmiths, Oakmont, Pa.

The new location greatly increased his walk-in business, with many customers shopping for "off-the-shelf" items. As a result, Hallett began to stock pearls, watches and other items he doesn't manufacture.

"It would have been difficult to meet the demand and increase our stock with our work alone," says Hallett, who has been making jewelry since he was in high school.

Today, goods from outside his own shop comprise about 50% of his showcase and 25% of his sales. By carefully choosing the items he stocks, Hallett has increased sales 30% each year since his move and maintained his reputation as a high-quality, custom jeweler.

ADVERTISING

A date in Georgia

In Americus, a small south Georgia town, movies are big business. So what better place to appeal to local youths than on the silver screen?

Ronald Scott, owner of Scott's Jewelry, saw the potential and created a screen advertisement to corner the teen market over popcorn and romance. "We get the couples while they're sitting together, holding hands, and we show them engagement rings," he says.

The 30-second spot, which shows the store's interior and personnel, focuses on items of particular interest to young people, such as class and engagement rings and bridal merchandise. The ad cost $650 to produce and $120 per month for a one-year contract at the theater.

Scott is assured of the ad's reach when customers tell him, "I see you're in the movies" or "I didn't know you were a movie star."

'Let's talk'

"A discount is like an overcoat. It has to be put on before it can be taken off."

So says one jeweler tired of public misconceptions about jewelry. The sage quote is part of a radio advertisement Howard McCoy produced for his McCoy's Jewelers in Carlsbad, N.M.

In the ad, McCoy asks whether 30%, 50% and 70% discounts are truly bargains. After the quote comparing discounts with overcoats, he advises listeners to learn more about selecting fine jewelry by reading the Better Business Bureau brochure titled "Tips on Buying Jewelry," available at his store.

The ad ran throughout December 1987 in cooperation with the New Mexico Retail Jewelers Association. The feedback was heartening, says McCoy. One typical comment from his customers: "It's about time someone started telling the truth about all of the so-called sales."

People are interested and listening, McCoy says. Stay tuned.

That lovable face

Most Kansas City residents know jeweler Harold Tivol. His smile and trademark bald head have been splashed across clever newspaper and magazine advertisement for four years.

But Tivol balked when his advertising agency suggested he use his high recognition factor in television ads. "I had always thought of car dealers selling things on television," says Tivol. The agency, Muller and Co., eventually persuaded him to do the TV ads, and the first in a series of seven premiered on local stations in November.

"They turned out to be the most successful ads we've ever done," concedes Tivol. In the first three weeks of the campaign, Tivol says, more than 388 new customers visited his single mall location. Many did more than just browse. His firm's average sale was $1,500 to $2,000, so the cost of the ads ($30,000 plus agency fees) was more than covered.

The ads feature an educational message. Prices, sales and other standard ad fillers are eschewed. Meanwhile, Tivol stocks good merchandise and offers more education in the store. For instance, if a customer suggest he can get a similar piece for a better price at a discount store, Tivol teaches a mini-lesson.

"If it's a diamond, I'll sit down and explain that the other store is probably only dealing with color and clarity," he says. "I'll tell them that cut is more important as far as beauty and value are concerned.

"As long as you continue to tell the truth, promote and advertise properly and have the right merchandise, you have to be successful."

DISPLAY

A good sign

Gustave Julian uses sign language to stir up interest in the fine jewelry at his Parma, Ohio, store.

Perched in his showcases are 30 small signs describing the adjacent stones in terms that go beyond cost, cut and color. "I research the stone and explain something particularly interesting about it," he says.

Julian has used signs since he opened the first of his two stores in this south Cleveland suburb 45 years ago. The signs often turn browsers into buyers because they are conversation starters. "If you start a conversation, you've got a chance," he says.

The signs at his tsavorite and chrome tourmaline displays explain how similar the stores are in appearance to emeralds, which he also stocks. One sign explains that tsavorite, a "green garnet, is the color of the very finest emeralds. But more durable and far less costly. Emeralds are found all over the world. Tsavorite is found only in the Tsavo Basin in Tanzania and only since 1965, whereas emeralds have been known for centuries."

Signs are not a new idea, notes Julian. AGS has recommended using them even longer than Julian has been in business. But few jewelers take the time to provide more than cursory information about the stones. Julian gives subtle, occasionally scientific, descriptions to de-mystify the origins, color, style and history of the stones.

Spinels, for example, are said to have "the same hardness, luster, etc. as rubies and sapphires and are found in the same color range. The Black Prince Ruby of the British Crown Jewels was found to be spinel after several years of being considered a ruby."

The signs are hand-written on fine paper and slipped into clear L-shaped, free-standing picture frames of various sizes. Most measure 5 by 7 inches, depending on the amount of information Julian has collected about the item.

Catching the eye

Bob Haines does windows—displays, that is. He has a knack for dressing windows in a way that almost forces passersby to enter his store, The Diamond Shop in Lewiston, Idaho.

"Sometimes I feel bad," says Haines. "I'll see someone rushing by, obviously in a hurry, and he or she will stop and come back to the window. They have to see what the new display is all about."

Haines is quick to credit MariAnn Coutchie, a former instructor at the Gemological Institute of America, who taught him the important role that window displays can play in attracting customers. Today, Coutchie is a thriving jewelry store design specialist in Woodland Hills, Cal.

Current events often inspire Haines, who recently turned over his business to son Michael but will remain as consultant. When President Nixon visited China in the summer of 1972, his window featured a look at the Far East. Mixed in was jewelry that matched the foreign feeling.

More recently, when William "Refrigerator" Perry was making news as the largest linebacker to tackle the NFL, Haines' window made a splash with its whale theme.

"Show products in a way customers don't expect," he explains. "You're only limited by your own imagination."

Open forum

At E.P. Watkins Jewelers, Durham, N.C., the entire sales staff gets involved in display themes. Each month, a specific type of jewelry is highlighted.

A couple of years ago, the store's bookkeeper picked up a packet of plastic colored stones at a local five and dime. The plastic pebbles were sprinkled playfully throughout showcases, says owner Edward Watkins. Though obviously phony, the pebbles stirred up interest in the real thing.

"My colored stone sales have increased 40% in the past two years," says Watkins. And it all began at the five and dime.

Love, honor and display

Warren Hyman is married to the fanciest, best-looking showcase in New Britain, Conn., store.

"My wife carries jewelry well," he boasts. "And it is so much easier to see it actually on somebody."

He and his wife Ray both wear jewelry from the store, and they encourage their salespeople to do the same.

Wearing pieces can create excitement about them that a showcase display can't muster, Hyman says. He wore a Seiko Mickey Mouse watch for two days and sold a half dozen to customers who may not have seen the model in the showcase.

Sometimes a man just needs to see a piece on a woman before he decides to buy, says Hyman.

A doctor once came to the store to buy a $6 lighter. After browsing, the doctor asked Ray for a gift suggestion for his wife. "She showed him the tennis bracelet on her wrist and he liked the way it looked so much he bought it," says Hyman. "That was a $12,000 sale."

Ask a Silly Question . . .

JCK asked AGS members to complete this phrase: "When a potential customer tells me he can get the same item for less cost at Sam's Discount, I tell him . . . "

The overwhelming majority of jewelers say they would tell the customer how the two items differ in quality, service and price. "Take a good look at my article," began a typical reply. "Let me explain its qualifications so you can knowledgeably compare."

Some respondents had a slightly more offbeat response. "You can have a hamburger at MacDonalds or you can have one at the 21 Club," wrote one jeweler.

Another offered more food for thought: "You can eat your steak at curbside from a street vendor or have your steak at a beautiful restaurant."

A third quoted Ben Franklin. "At a great bargain, pause awhile."

Others were content, perhaps successfully, with tried-and-true clichés. "All that glitters is not gold," and "You get what you pay for," they said.

One jeweler said simply, "My customers don't say that."

Ham Takes A New Look
At His Market

March 1988

Jezebel Jewelers, a mythical Main Street store, is a continuing JCK case study of management problems and solutions. Last year, repairman Hamilton Waltham and his partner, Ebenezer Cheribel, bought the store from long-time owner Hiram Jezebel. Now Waltham must find ways to turn around the money-losing business.

Ham spent some sleepless nights wondering how to make his new store a success.

How, he asked himself, could he be sure he had the right inventory? Where could he find new customers? How should he improve his advertising approach?

One day, after work, he went to Cyrus Smuckmann, a friend and fellow jeweler in a nearby town, for advice.

"What you need," said Smuckmann after listening for 20 minutes, "is a good marketing plan, based on sound market research."

Ham looked puzzled.

So his friend explained. A market plan, he said, tells you how to sell your merchandise and to whom. Market research simply means collecting facts about your community and customers, then drawing business conclusions from them.

"It takes the guesswork out of merchandising," Smuckmann said.

"I can't afford a marketing consultant," Ham objected. "Besides, I know this community."

That, said Smuckmann, is what Hiram Jezebel thought. "But if he had, the store wouldn't have gotten into the hole it's in. Are you *positive* you know your customers and what they want?"

"Well, sure . . . I think," said Ham.

"Look," said Smuckmann, grabbing a yellow pad and a pencil from his desk. "You can do your own market research. And you don't need much cash, just some time and creativity. Let's do this by the numbers."

1. Who are you? First, be clear in your own mind about the type of business you are and want to be. A guild store with upscale clientele? A mom-and-pop store, stressing service and repairs? A local chain of independent or mall stores? A specialist in diamond rings, tableware, watches?

Your location obviously affects this; it influences the customers you get and the merchandise you stock. Are you downtown, in a mall or on a side road? Is the surrounding area prosperous or declining economically? Is there enough parking?

And don't forget store appearance or staff performance, added Smuckmann. Do they conform to what you want your store to be? Does the interior have a specific, identifiable style? Is it dark and uninviting? Do the walls need painting? Are outside signs weather-beaten? Are salespeople friendly and informed? Is service prompt and reliable?

"Get outside opinions," said Smuckmann. "Invite a couple of non-competing jewelers, or retailers, or members of the Rotary to observe your operations. Then take them to lunch and get their comments.

"Do the same thing with a few select customers, and ask *their* view of your staff, service, ads and merchandise."

2. Where are your customers? "Knowing where customers live tells if you're getting the type you want, or are overlooking any. And that helps when you buy inventory and plan advertising," said Smuckmann.

"Obviously," said Ham dryly. "The question is, how do I find out?"

There are several easy ways to do it, said Smuckmann:

• Credit slips. Periodically review charge accounts (at least a month's worth) for addresses, frequency of purchases, most popular merchandise and price points. Chart results on a large local map (with different colored pins to indicate frequent or occasional customers) and in inventory records.

• Customer/purchase surveys. For a week, have a staff member interview customers as they leave. Note gender, age, type (i.e., student, businessman, homemaker) and purpose (purchase, non-purchase, repair or service work). Ask about addresses and customer satisfaction. Keep each interview *short* (a minute or less) to ensure every customer is polled.

If a staffer can't be spared, hire a temporary worker or a student from a nearby college, said Smuckmann. Or, simply have salespeople jot on sales, credit or repair/service slips the basic information (gender, approximate age and type, purpose).

"You'll get a good idea of how many and what type of people come into your store and why," said Smuckmann.

• License plates and phone number show who comes to your immediate market area (including other stores on the street or mall). Have a staffer jot down license numbers at specific times (after work, Friday evenings, Saturday mornings). Some states' plates list towns. A few states give information about drivers, on request, if you have the plate number.

Phone numbers—available on checks, credit slips, credit applications and sales slips—can give similar information just for your store.

• Ad response. Marketing experts suggest you occasionally use coupons (which readers bring in for a small discount, a free gift or service) in printed ads to find out which ads reach which customers. In TV or radio ads, use "limited time only" blurbs for the same offers.

3. Who are your customers? "Of course, these methods give you only general information about where your customers live and what sells," said Smuckmann.

"You can supplement that with loads of specific facts about current and potential customers—everything from income and family size to which roads have most traffic. With information like that, you can effectively plan inventory and marketing strategy. And the best part is, that information is available at little or no cost from sources near you."

• Federal and state census data offer statistics by age, sex, race, housing, income and many more categories. These statistics are broken down by state, region, metropolitan area, even—in some categories—by local city blocks.

Many business and economic census statistics from state and federal agencies are updated annually, and sometimes monthly.

County planning commissions are an ideal source for census, population and economic data. The county commission not only collects statistics produced by federal, state and regional agencies. It also does its own research on specific municipalities. Just tell the commission librarian what you need.

College and municipal libraries also carry federal census data.

• Local or county chambers of commerce have lots of information, periodically updated, for hometown businesses about the local market.

• Industrial development agencies can provide facts on housing, labor and the economy.

• Check local newspapers and business journals for listings of new businesses, bankruptcies, real estate transactions and building permits. Charted over a period of time, these provide a profile of activity and change in your area.

• Many utilities, especially electric companies, have departments which give businesses (no matter how small) data on regional population, taxes, labor force and communities.

• Advertising or business departments of local media or banks can provide overviews of community trends and changes.

• Municipal officials (such as the township manager) or agencies (like zoning boards) know about zoning or tax changes affecting your business.

4. Check the other guys. "You can't plan marketing strategy without knowing what the other guys are doing," said Smuckmann. "So you or one of your staff should systematically shop your competitors."

Compare merchandise, promotions, service and prices.

Pay attention to what you offer that they don't or can't (i.e., parking, trained gemologists, more colored gems, convenient shopping hours, delivery service, 24-hour repair).

Keep a record of your advertising and theirs.

"With such information, you're better able to set yourself apart from the herd in merchandise, service and promotions," said Smuckmann. "Try it."

What he learned: Ham took Smuckmann's advice and did some basic market research over the next couple of weeks. Here are some findings.

• City officials and the local chamber of commerce told him city council planned to revive Lenzville's deteriorating downtown business area, where Jezebel Jewelers is located. Much of Main Street would be turned into a pedestrian shopping area, with a large downtown parking garage and more specialty stores. Ham realized that these developments would benefit his firm in the long run, by making the area more attractive to shoppers. But in the short run, he'd have to adapt advertising and increase promotions to offset the inevitable decline in customers during reconstruction.

• A review of census data at the county planning commission indicated 40% of the area's population would be under 25 by 1990. Young families had moved to new tracts north of town during the past decade, and more affluent older couples had delayed families until set in their careers. A check with the school districts confirmed census data: More students were coming into schools.

For Ham, that suggested more opportunities to sell graduation gifts and school rings; more bridal-related sales; new markets for specific advertising and direct mail promotions, and the chance to create long-term customer loyalty early.

• Customer surveys and a review of credit charges showed that most were older, long-time, primarily blue-collar customers. Jezebel was attracting few of the more affluent residents and young-marrieds. Ham realized he should start cultivating those markets through advertising, promotions and direct mail.

• Census figures showed areas where affluence was higher than average. They also revealed a sizable (16%) Hispanic community. ("Perhaps I should add a Hispanic employee," Ham thought.)

• A check showed that no jewelry stores advertised in newspapers at the local colleges (four-year George Lenz College and two-year Lilo County Community College), although some department stores and catalog houses did. That revealed another market which could be reached at less-than-usual ad costs.

• And what about competition? The local economic development authority and a review of statistics on local business patterns showed 30 other jewelry stores or jewelry retailers within a five-mile radius, down from 35 in 1983. There also were 15 general merchandise stores, including three department stores in the mall and a department store and catalog showroom within a few blocks of Ham's store.

Ham's spot check of jewelry stores in the regional mall and smaller shopping centers showed most were open from 9:30 a.m. to 9:30 p.m. daily, until 10 p.m. Saturdays and 5 p.m. Sundays. Ham realized he might have to rethink his store's 9-to-5 hours, and later staff schedules.

The 10 Basic Rules Of Public Relations

September 1987 Part II

You need a strong marketing program to be successful jeweler. Your advertising dollars will stretch farther when they are backed up by a realistic public relations campaign.

To promote your store and its image, you must develop a good relationship with your local media. They're always looking for an interesting, timely story. And when you present your story ideas and publicity releases professionally, you will increase the chances of getting coverage in the local media.

Here are the basic rules of publicity, developed by the Diamond Information Center with the Diamond Promotion Service NW Ayer:

1. Maintain regular contact with fashion, jewelry and design-oriented reporters. Find out who they are by asking your local advertising representatives. Keep a list of their names, titles and telephone numbers close at hand. Your ad rep can introduce you to the editorial staff, but once the introduction is given, *never* try to use your advertising as clout to get editorial space.

Also, remember that getting to know their work helps you know them. So develop a working relationship with them. Start by inviting them to a business lunch. Remember, one "courts" the press.

2. Learn the format for writing a press release. Adhere to the format closely. Writers are sticklers for grammar and form. Watch for spelling and typographical errors. And remember, they want news—facts, statistics, trends—not an advertising message.

3. Issue regular releases. Releases sent to the media on topics relating to your business will keep editors informed of your activities. Occasions that mean big business to you are good subjects for general interest stories. Valentine's Day, Mother's Day, May-June engagements, graduation, anniversaries and Christmas are "holidays" that can be turned into "news." For example, you may have a large selection of diamond heart-shaped jewelry for Valentine's Day. Use that fact in a story about how Valentine's Day began and/or the history of the first gift received in its honor. You then have the makings for a timely article that isn't commercial.

4. Make your releases timely. Nothing is as boring as old news. Learn your editor's deadlines for material and give him/her plenty of time to write the story from the information you provide in your press release. Editors work under tight deadlines and need your cooperation. A general rule of thumb is to have the release to them four to six weeks prior to when the article is to appear.

5. All photographs should be captioned. Including photographs with your press release increases your chances of getting coverage on your store or product. It's important to deliver a clear, uncluttered picture of the main topic of your release.

If you're talking about engagement rings, be certain that your model conveys the image you want and that, without being blatant, your ring is a "standout." A newspaper or magazine isn't likely to use a picture where too much is going on.

6. Maintain your files. Never release your last copy of anything. Compile a scrap book of releases and photographs.

You'll be addressing the same people again and again. It's important to stay fresh, and this will help you with story ideas for next year.

Another key reason for keeping files is that too often what seems new, isn't. You'll avoid repetition, which can embarrass you or make you look less credible to the media.

7. Be informed. Keep a record of stories which have appeared in local newspapers, magazines, radio and TV.

By staying informed of the news in your industry, as well as current trends in consumer buying, you'll avoid the "head in the sand" syndrome.

You'll be on top of what's happening, which will keep your promotions and releases right in step with the times.

8. Check the copyright on material that is not original. If you're quoting from a book or magazine, or even an excerpt from a news commentary, give credit where credit is due. Call editors and producers to be sure you have a "go ahead." It may take time, but you can avoid legal entanglements easily by doing homework.

9. Host special events, parties and jewelry exhibits. Events can generate publicity as well as goodwill in your community. Make sure fashion reporters, including radio and TV people, are always on your guest list. And remember to send captioned photographs of your events to your local papers. They are always looking for "social" notes, even if they cannot send a reporter to cover the party.

10. Work at maintaining good relations with the press. Always have a courteous manner and positive, friendly attitude. Keep your standards high, maintain your professionalism.

If you are positive in your approach, you are bound to see editors turning to you more and more. Your store will be their regular source for information about diamonds and diamond jewelry.

How To Hold A Remount Sale

September 1987 Part II

Diamonds may be forever, but their settings can go out of style.

Many jewelers take advantage of this fact to build business through remount sales, putting stones from old jewelry pieces into new settings.

Special remount sales can build a great deal of traffic and sales if conducted correctly. Here are some tips on how to do it from Michael O'Mahoney, vice president of Mayors' jewelry store in Miami, Fla.:

1. Decide how you want to conduct the sale. Do you want to do it yourself or go through a supplier?

If you do it yourself, you must get adequate supplies of ring/earring/pendant mountings and be certain sufficient benchworkers are on hand to serve customers quickly, without your having to take the piece in overnight.

2. Start four weeks in advance. Hold a sales meeting to explain the benefits and procedures of a remount sale to your staff.

Get them excited about the idea. This is extremely important because their work will make the event successful.

3. Promote the sale. Call key customers and mention the remount sale to everyone who comes into the store. Also send out notices and set up in-store posters, showing styles available. Advertise the sale a week in advance.

4. Set goals for your staff. Ask salespeople to make specific appointments. If every salesperson makes just one, the

sale should succeed. Appointments are especially important, O'Mahoney explains, because "the close rate is tremendous.

More than 80%. When people walk in with their jewelry, they're virtually pre-sold."

Plan to give incentives, such as spiffs, to each salesperson for appointments that are kept.

5. Stay informed. Hold weekly meetings to assess progress of appointments and to keep the enthusiasm going. O'Mahoney emphasizes that enthusiasm and teamwork are crucial to make a sale work. "If the staff is keen on the idea, they will make appointments and go all out to make it successful."

6. The day before. Have your staff call customers who've made appointments to remind them of the time and place. (If the customer doesn't show up at the appointed time, wait one hour and then call, explaining the benefits of the remount sale.)

7. During the sale. Put benchworkers near the window to attract on-lookers. Serve refreshments to put some fun into the event.

8. Limit your sales. Schedule no more than four remount sales each year. More than that dilutes the effort.

The good thing about remount sales is that they can be run anytime, even in the slowest part of the year. They don't have to be tied to a holiday or special event.

How To Develop An Ad Plan

August 1987

If you're like most retail jewelers, you want to advertise, but don't know where to begin. You don't know how to spend your ad dollars efficiently. And you're probably uncomfortable talking with ad people because they speak a different language, tossing around terms like CPMs, dayparts and SAUs.

But you *can* make advertising work for you. Just start with a plan and treat advertising as an investment, George Eversman told American Gem Society members at their annual conclave. As vice president and executive director for the De Beers account at N. W. Ayer, he has years of experience planning ad campaigns for jewelry. Thus the program he led on developing and implementing retail advertising was packed with practical advice for jewelers.

Once you decide to advertise, said Eversman, there's no real end. It's a circular process in which you constantly evaluate where you are, why you are there, where you want to be, how to get there and what, if anything, you should change.

Here's the short course in advertising that Eversman and N. W. Ayer staffers Jean Connolly, Hugh Meenan and Jeff Odiorne presented to AGS.

Where to start: First, determine your image. Who are your current and prospective customers? What is your competition? And what is your niche in the marketplace?

Next, decide where you would like to be. Perhaps you want to upgrade your image and sell more quality jewelry. With that advertising objective in mind, you're ready to develop a strategic ad plan.

Where should you advertise? Your message has to run in the right place to be effective. You need to set a media objective—what you want your ads to do for you. You'll want to reach the largest group of the right people for the least amount of money. Use your advertising objective to develop your media objectives. For example, if you want to increase sales of quality jewelry (advertising objective), ask yourself:

• Who is your target audience, in terms of income, education and age?

• When is the best time to reach it—all year or during key months or weeks?

• Where is your trading area?

• How much communication do you need? The amount will depend on the difficulty of your message. A sale is a rather simple one, but building a reputation for quality jewelry takes much longer. The amount of communication you need also is determined by the size of your audience, their awareness of your store and the ads placed by your competition.

De Beers uses these objectives:

Advertising objective: Sell quality

Target audience: Adults with household incomes of $50,000+

Geography: Total U.S., skewed to high-income zip codes

Seasonality: Year round

Communications: Emphasize repeat exposure

Once you know your media objectives, the next step is to set your ad budget. It's usually between 2% and 10% of sales. If you want to do something involved, such as change your image, you'll have to spend more.

Evaluating media: Now you're ready to check the advertising options available, using the 4 Cs of media evaluation. These are composition, coverage, cost per thousand (CPM) and concept.

Composition refers to purity, how much of the audience is useful to you. The general purity factor for adult households with incomes of $40,000 is 22% for TV, 37% for magazines, 29% for radio, 30% for outdoor and 35% for newspapers.

Coverage means the size of the audience, how many people see or hear your ad. For example, if the *Chicago Tribune* goes to a third of Chicagoans, you'll have a coverage rate of 33%.

To determine how many of the right people see your ad, combine the coverage and composition rates. Let's say the *Chicago Tribune* reaches 300,000 of a total 900,000 people in Chicago. That means an ad in the Tribune reaches 33% of all Chicagoans. Since you know that adult households with incomes over $40,000 comprise 35% of all newspapers' circulation, your *Chicago Tribune* ad will reach 105,000 people (35% of 300,000) in your primary target audience.

Next, balance cost of the ad against the size and quality of the medium to find the actual *cost per thousand* people (CPM). For example, if a $1/4$-page costs $6795 in a newspaper going to 518 (thousand) people, divide $6795 by 518 to get your CPM of $13.12.

Also evaluate concepts when choosing a medium. Look at what surrounds your ad: Other ads, editorial, listings, etc. Try to schedule your ad next to editorial, especially editorial of interest to those you are trying to reach.

Television: TV is the second largest medium, but the most influential. The average household watches 7 hours and 48 minutes of it daily.

Why should you advertise on TV? Here are the pros and cons:

• Pros—It will give you a dramatic presentation with sight, sound and motion. TV is also intrusive; it commands a viewer's attention without the viewer having to do anything. With TV you can build awareness quickly, have the potential to reach a large audience, give creditability to your product and appeal visually to the viewer.

• Cons—TV time can be very expensive, up to $7000 per second. Plus, production costs are high. Research has shown that only a small percentage of upscale viewers watch TV. The CPM for all viewers is $6.12 for TV and $6.15 for newspapers. However, the CPM for upscale viewers is $30.48 for TV, but only $13.71 for newspapers—less than half. In addition, TV is cluttered with lots of other ads and has a limited geographic flexibility because of its far-reaching signals.

When choosing TV, scatter your ads among different time slots. For example, if you advertise only in the early morning, you will reach about 30% of the audience. But if you advertise in late night, early morning and sports slots, you will reach about 60% of your audience.

Be careful when choosing your TV advertising time. Remember that a quality environment, determined by the type of program, makes a difference.

Cable TV: This is a fast-growing advertising means. About 46% of all households have cable TV, up 26% since 1980. Meanwhile, network share of market dropped 10% from 1981 to 1985. Cable is especially popular in the suburbs where it reaches 55% of the people.

Cable gives your advertising the dramatic presentation, intrusiveness and visual appeal that you'll find on network TV. Some other advantages of cable: Ability to select upscale audiences, more opportunity for creativity and geographic flexibility.

Be careful of cable, though. It has a high CPM. The average CPM for network TV is $6.12, while the average CPM for local cable TV is $36.72. And you may run into problems with program quality and production.

Buying television: First you must gather information. Before calling stations, you need an idea of when you intend to advertise, and which programs and dayparts (time slots), you are *not* interested in: i.e., kids' hours, most game shows, daytime, unless your target is all female.

Contact sales representatives for each station in your market and request the following information for the time of year you intend to advertise: Program listings for requested dayparts, compositions for your target for requested dayparts, target ratings for requested dayparts, cost per :30 (30-second) unit and target CPMs.

Next, narrow the field. Eliminate dayparts or programs with very low ratings or improper environment and those that are too expensive (high CPMs) or have too much waste (low-target comps).

Now you can begin to negotiate rates. It is perfectly acceptable to go back to a sales representative and tell him you have negotiated better CPMs from another station for comparable dayparts/programs. Name the other station, but do not reveal its unit costs. Attempt to get a better price.

The last step is to put it all together. Schedule spots by station, program and day-of-week, using the following general guidelines: No more than three spots per week per individual program with spots spread among various time slots.

A minimum weekly schedule might be two or three spots during prime time, five spots during the day, three spots during the news, four spots during fringe, and five spots during late night. If you want to reach people quickly, you'll need more spots. But if your message, such as building a quality image, is a long-term one, you can use fewer spots.

Before you place an order, discuss in detail any merchandising programs with each station. You should have specific ideas in mind when you call, so that you can lead the discussion. Ask about sponsorships, billboards or even coverage. Be sure you end up with a clear understanding of who will be responsible for financing and administering every aspect of the merchandise package.

Newspapers: This is the single most important medium for retail advertising. It gives you rapid audience accumulation: All the people who are going to see your ad usually do so within one or two days. Newspapers also lend a timeliness to your message and it requires only a short lead time to place an ad.

When selecting newspapers, consider these drawbacks: Cost, low-quality reproduction because of the paper and printing methods used, broad-based audience, clutter from other ads, flat circulation throughout the year and same daily readership.

Your ad's position on the page does not affect readership, according to a Newspaper Advertising Bureau survey. But size matters. A quarter-page ad has an ad read index of 141, while a full-page has an ad read index of 350, even though a full page costs four times as much.

Position in a section also matters. The first and last pages of each section are best. Next are the pages nearest the front.

The particular section in which your ad runs affects its readability. For example, the sports section has a higher readership among men than women, while sections oriented to women have higher performance indexes for women. General news has an equal performance index for men and women.

Color matters a great deal because it calls attention to your ad. Full color increases readership 113% for men and 69% for women.

Some newspapers also offer zoning or targeting. You can buy ads in sections released in your area for single market coverage.

Evaluating newspapers: Speak to the salespeople at each newspaper in your market; they are your best sources of information. If you do not know or aren't sure of all the newspapers that cover your market, check the local Chamber of Commerce and Newspaper Advertising Bureau.

For each newspaper, obtain the following information:
- Standard Advertising Unit (S.A.U.) rates. Most daily newspapers in the U.S. use the S.A.U. system. The standard column width is 2 ^{1}/16 in.; measurement and billing of advertising is based on that standard column inch.
- Circulation figures. Is the circulation paid or is the paper given away? If free to readers, how is it distributed? Are there any controls on who gets free copies, or are they bulk-shipped to locations to be picked up by anyone?
- Readership studies, if available. Publisher's proprietary research on who reads his newspaper in terms of age, income, profession, etc. This is the composition data.
- Coverage data. Be specific with regard to the area you wish to cover, your trading area. If a substantial portion of

copies are going well beyond the distance you think your customers are willing to travel, that circulation is wasted.
- Copies of the paper printed.
- Color capabilities. If you are considering color ads, find out if the newspaper can do them. Ask to see examples of color ads that have run in the past. Find out what the premiums are over black/white ads. Are there limitations on the size of ads that run in color?
- Compare the editorial of newspapers you are evaluating. Are there significant differences? Is one more likely to be of interest to your customer as you understand him?

Radio: This can be an effective medium for jewelry advertisements. About 99% of U.S. homes have five radios. The average person spends three hours each day listening to the radio. The average market has 25 stations.

In addition, radio station audiences are targeted. Album-oriented rock stations have more teen listeners, while classical or all news stations attract more upscale adults.

Radio also makes your ad immediate and timely, and it is affordable. Radio's CPM for adults is $4.75, while TV's is $600. For adults aged 18-34, radio is even more cost effective with the radio CPM $4.50 and TV's $20.

Radio does have some drawbacks. The buying can seem difficult. Radio usually is a background medium with low attention levels. And it can be cluttered with other ads.

Evaluating radio stations: First, gather audience data by contacting a sales representative for a large station in your market. Ask for the following information from the latest *Arbitron* book (issued quarterly with listening data on previous quarters):
- Station share of listening for your demographic target,
- Station rating for your target in all dayparts,
- Compositions for total listening in all age breaks to get a sense of how each station skews by age. Some stations tend to have older or younger listeners.

Rank the stations in your area according to the share of your target market that listens. Ideally, you should consider enough stations to achieve 50% share of the listening audience in your demographic target.

Next list the daypart ratings (percentage of your target audience listening in each time slot) for each of these stations, starting with the highest ranked. For example:

Station	Dayparts*	Daypart demo rating
WAAA	6-10am	2.4
	10am-3pm	1.2
	3-7pm	2.0
	7-12pm	.7

* Monday-Friday

Continue to the next ranked station and repeat the process.

Now that you've collected this information, you're ready to negotiate rates. Determine the number of 60-second spots to run each week. Consider 10 minimum and 20 the maximum on any one station. The more spots you buy on a station, the lower the cost. Generally stations offer different costs by number of spots—10X plan, 15X plan, 20X plan, etc. Obtain cost per 60 seconds by daypart and CPMs for your target audience from each station sales representative. Don't put all of your ads into one daypart.

The number of stations you select depends on whether you want to emphasize reach (use several stations) or repeat exposure (fewer stations).

Also ask about added impacts from sponsorships and special reports done by the radio station.

Now you're ready to put it together. Consider the composition of your target market, when a station's audience skews young or old (a too young audience won't buy much more than engagement rings) and the proper format when choosing stations.

Schedule spots by station, daypart and day-of-week with the following in mind: A minimum of 10 spots per week per station, a minimum of two dayparts per station, and a maximum of three spots per day per daypart.

Call the stations you've selected and give them an idea of the size of schedule you have in mind. Then get commitments on merchandising before you place the order.

After your ad runs, ask for post analysis (affidavits that you got a fair rotation in the daypart and that your spot aired in the correct daypart with promised audience share). Be sure to listen to the station to determine if the station changes its format after you sign the contract.

Outdoor advertising: Choose this medium to give a broad awareness to your product at a low cost per person. It also allows you to use local and innovative copy. To make effective use of outdoor advertising, your message must be simple.

Drawbacks to this medium can include the physical environment surrounding your message, the fact that ads lack intrusiveness and the overall cost is high.

You should know a few things when buying outdoor advertising. The location provides all targeting for your market. You usually have to contract for a 30-day minimum. Ask about showing (percent of the market that will see your ad) and individual locations available.

• Types. The poster panel and the painted bulletin are the two standard structures in outdoor advertising. Most are built on leased property and are rented to advertisers by independent outdoor advertising companies.

• Reach. Daily exposure opportunities are measured according to the showing size of the bulletin. For example, an average #50 yields daily exposure opportunities equal to 50% of the population in a given area. The #50 should reach over 80% of all adults in that area in one month. More than half are reached the first week. That instant impact makes outdoor advertising ideal for product introductions, store openings or promotional events where timing is critical.

• Frequency. Because of its continuous presence, outdoor advertising can produce high frequency levels. A typical #50 showing has an average exposure potential of 15 times in one month.

• Constant presence. Outdoor is seen all day, every day.

• Audience demographics. Outdoor advertising audiences have upscale characteristics. While the medium reaches every population strata, Simmons Market Research Bureau shows it has above average performance in the younger, affluent and working market.

• Selectivity. Outdoor is flexible. An advertiser can tailor showings to reach an ethnic audience, shoppers near a mall, students near a college, or sports enthusiasts near a stadium.

• Reinforces any media schedule. Without increasing your budget, outdoor can be added to any schedule to strengthen a campaign through improved audience delivery, higher frequency (repeat exposure—your ad is seen over and over) and more people reached per dollar.

Buying outdoor advertising: First select the markets you want to reach. Remember that location is everything.

After selecting markets, look them up in the *Buyer's Guide to Outdoor Advertising*. There, you'll find the outdoor company for each market as well as the cost of poster panels and bulletins in those markets.

Try to contact the outdoor company at least 90 days before you want your ad to appear. This helps you assure that space is available for your campaign.

Although your own ad agency usually designs artwork for an outdoor campaign, some outdoor companies have art departments to assist in ad design. Remember that posters take time to be printed. A simple screened poster requires approximately 21-28 days for printing time; a full lithographed poster (with color separations) requires 45 days. Poster paper should be at the outdoor company 10 days before the posting date. For painted bulletins, artwork must be at the outdoor company 60 days before the start of the contracting period to assure accuracy in the rendering.

Some facts to consider: The scale is different for posters than it is for design. There is an additional charge for extensions/ embellishments on bulletins. If one outdoor company represents a number of selected markets, you may wish to contact the national representative for that company. Outdoor buying services that will implement your campaign are available. Agency commission for space is often 16 2/3%.

Magazines: This medium offers several advantages to retailers because upscale, prime-prospect consumers read a lot of magazines. About 97% of persons with $35,000-plus household incomes read an average of more than 11 issues per month.

By demographics, magazine reading is heaviest among people 18-44 years of age, college-educated, $50,000-plus income, and professional/managerial occupations—the exact opposite of television viewing.

The average magazine copy has 5.32 adult readers. Each one spends an average of 58 minutes reading the magazine. And each reader see the average page 1.7 times.

In addition to a desirable audience, magazines offer reasonable ad cost, excellent color reproduction and product display, and a good fit between editorial and ads. They usually have a long life and provide merchandising and promotion support.

However, magazines lack intrusiveness, require a long lead-time to schedule ads and have a slow audience accumulation. Many markets have few local magazines, which leads to geographic waste.

To overcome the lack of intrusiveness, try for a good ad position. It's most important that your ad be placed next to editorial. The table of contents, a great position which attracts 40% of readers, often does not require an extra premium. Cover positions, however, are more expensive. Some advertisers, like De Beers, do not think the premium prices are worth the cover position.

Research studies show *no difference* in readership of ads in the front or back of a magazine, or between left- or right-hand pages.

Evaluating magazines: Magazines themselves are the best source of information. If you don't know all those in your market, check the local Chamber of Commerce, the magazine Publishers Association in New York City and *Standard Directory of Periodicals* (available in city or university libraries).

Request the following information of each magazine being considered: Readership study (composition and coverage data on readers, sometimes called a reader profile), circulation figures, rates for the ad size you intend to run (the more ads, the lower the rate should be) and copies of several issues. Most larger city publications will offer to send you a media kit. Be sure it at least contains the above information.

Consider these questions:

• How much of the magazine's circulation is in my trading area? Do many copies go to people too far away to ever be customers? If so, can I buy just the circulation I want (some magazines sell geographic-zoned editions).

• Is the circulation paid for? As many magazines are given away free as are paid for by their recipients. Among free magazines, ask how they are delivered. Are they bulk shipped to stores or supermarkets, where anyone can pick one up? Are they mailed to individuals who must meet some kind of qualifications, e.g., doctors, members of a social society, symphony subscriptions, etc.?

• How well is the magazine written? Is it graphically appealing? Will it complement your advertising? What other kinds of advertisers are in the magazine? Read a few issues and ask yourself if the image you have of your customer fits the audience the magazine appeals to.

• Before you commit to a schedule, discuss any merchandising, such as mailings or counter cards.

Direct marketing: This is an expensive medium, which requires professional assistance. Its CPM is $200 to $500, compared to $12 for magazines. So be sure you know what you're doing when you take this approach.

Why use direct mail? It's proactive, reaching out to customers; it is very segmented by target, with little waste; it can offer different messages to different customers; it allows you to tell a complex story, and its results are measurable.

Direct mail does have some problems. It does not give you a broad reach. There is a lot of clutter in consumers' mailboxes, producing a negative reaction and making it difficult for your message to stand out. There also can be a problem with quality control.

Direct mail is best when used for very specific messages, such as a store opening, promotion, sale, etc. It works best with general media support, but it can stand alone.

To implement a direct mail program, start the project six to nine weeks before the event. Allow at least two weeks for mail delivery. Ideally, the consumer should receive it one week before the event. Keep a database of customers with as much information on them as possible.

The average response rate for direct is about 3%, but it can be 10%-20% if the offer is outstanding, or if the piece is especially creative.

A Very Short Course in Media Math

Share of audience: The number of homes or people tuned to a particular program. It's expressed as a percentage of the total number using their TV or radio sets when the program was on the air.

Example: If six out of a total of ten homes have their TV sets turned on during prime time (8-11 p.m., EST) and three of those six homes are viewing *The Cosby Show,* then that program has a 50% share of audience.

Homes viewing program (3) divided by total viewing homes (6) equals rating (50%).

Ratings: The percentage of the universe tuned to a program. Example: Three homes out of a 10-TV home universe are viewing *The Cosby Show.* Therefore, the program has a rating of 30.

Homes viewing program (3) divided by total viewing homes (6) equals share (30%).

Cost per thousand: This is the universal media yardstick for measuring efficiency. The audience is always expressed in terms of standard units, such as homes, men, women, etc. It is the cost of any media unit divided by the estimated audience, in thousands. CPM is best used to evaluate options between media of the same kind.

Example: A network TV 30-second spot costs $90,000 and delivers an audience of 13.4 million adults aged 18-49 at a CPM of $6.72.

Ad cost ($90,000) divided by audience size in thousands (13,400) equals CPM ($6.72).

Magazine total audience: This is the total number of readers per copy. Example: A magazine has a circulation of 6,096,000, but 4.18 readers read each copy. That gives the magazine a total audience of 25,481,300.

Circulation (6,096,000) times readers per copy (4.18) equals total audience (25,481,300).

Television viewing audience: This is the total viewing audience for a television show. Example: A TV show reaches 27,745,700 homes where an average 1.468 viewers watch that show. That gives the show a total audience of 40,730,700.

TV homes (27,745,700) x viewers per homes (1.468) equals total viewing audience (40,730,700).

Homes using television: The percentage of all TV homes having their sets turned on at a particular time. Example: If six out of a total of 10 TV homes have their sets turned on during prime time (8-11 p.m., EST), the HUT level for prime is 60%.

Homes using TV (6) divided by TV-home universe (10) equals HUT level (60%).

The Premium & Award Market: Extra Butter For The Jeweler's Bread

June 1987

Thirteen billion dollars—that was the total 1986 sales volume for the premium/incentive/award industry (collectively called the presentation industry). There is room for retail jewelers to carve a niche in this lucrative market, but the jeweler who does must be prepared to take a different approach to selling.

For starters, profit margins are much lower (usually about 20% over cost; keystone is virtually impossible), timing is crucial and business rarely just strolls through the front door. But, jewelers who have gone after this business are basking in its potential. It may not be their bread and butter, but it's certainly a little extra butter on the bread.

Presentation business, explains Tibor Kentey, national sales manager of Bulova Watch Co., requires little if any monetary investment. Each order is a "sold order," meaning merchandise comes in the door and goes right back out again. Inventory, if the jeweler chooses to build one, consists of sample items or a few extra pieces kept from each order to help a customer in a bind.

The presentation business enhances a jeweler's full-service reputation and helps regain some profits lost to discounters. It also boosts his regular business. After all, if a jeweler can fill a customer's corporate jewelry needs, why should he turn elsewhere for his personal jewelry?

There are several facets to the presentation business. There are advertising specialties, business gifts, premiums, incentives and awards, the aspect with which most jewelers are familiar. Awards themselves fall into different categories. Jewelers most commonly provide service awards—given for retirement, number of years of employment, community involvement, etc. Incentive awards, designed to motivate employees, frequently are used in sales situations. Safety incentives encourage employees to take extra precautions, and usually reward lengths of accident-free time.

Today's marketplace is changing. Many companies are trimming staff, while trying to increase productivity. This makes incentive awards a natural. The jeweler who sells only length-of-service awards is selling himself short, says Stuart Marcus, vice president of sales for supplier Gold Lance.

Getting started: Community involvement is key to building incentive sales. So is a spotless reputation, says Greg Emerick of Mann's Jewelers in Rochester, N.Y. Memberships in local civic organizations and the chamber of commerce are important; they help establish the jeweler's reputation and offer a place to network and generate business.

Start small, advises Marcus. "Don't head right for AT&T."

Typically, jewelers start with people they know. Wayne Madere, vice president of Jules Madere, Baton Rouge, La.; Brady Rockey, manager of Kiess Jewelers in Coldwater, Mich., and Tom Cook, president of Tom Cook Jewelers, Daytona Beach, Fla., did. All are active in their communities and have built a nice following by serving fellow businesses. They looked for small and medium-sized local businesses—banks, hospitals, schools, industry, sales or service-oriented firms, even other retailers. Gold Lance's Marcus particularly recommends car dealerships. They spend about $100 a month per salesman for incentives, he says, and jewelry is a favorite choice.

Supplier support: When contacting suppliers for presentation products, ask what support and education they offer. Many suppliers have well-developed programs, and will send out a sales rep to make presentations, accompanying the jeweler on sales calls, etc. Bulova, Gold Lance and R.Q.C./Rembrandt are among the larger, better-known suppliers in the industry offering such programs. Bulova has a free series of booklets on safety, incentive and service award programs and corporate anniversary celebrations, entitled "A Simple Guide to Running a . . . [safety award program, incentive award program, service award program, corporate anniversary celebration]." These are designed to educate the jeweler about running a presentation business and the consumer about building a presentation program.

Gold Lance offers ad support materials, information sheets, how-to-do-it brochures and a staff of representatives who will visit the jeweler. Rembrandt, whose presentation business is tailored strictly for the jeweler, has prepared a special sample kit for demonstrations. The firm also will affix a logo to any product the customer chooses.

The products: Many products already carried by an average retail jewelry store are suitable for incentive use—especially those which can be customized with a logo or an engraving. Jewelry, watches, clocks, pens, trophies and plaques, desk accessories, silver, giftware, crystal and china are used, although many jewelers steer away from customized china.

The quality level of products varies with the customer's need. Rembrandt, for example, does most of its award business in 22k gold over sterling, says general sales manager Kathy Koening. But, karat gold and gemstone pieces are frequently requested.

What should a jeweler expect when he places an order? And what will he be expected to do?

First, the jeweler should provide a clean piece of artwork from which to make the design. The art may have to be stylized or manipulated a bit to meet manufacturing specifications, but the original should be the best possible.

There usually will be a charge for the tool, die, screen, mold or whatever is used to customize the product. Die charge policies vary with the supplier. Rembrandt, for example, has a one-time charge for making the tooling and requires a deposit. After the tooling is made, Rembrandt requires no more up-front deposits. It has minimum piece requirements only on orders for base metal products, which Koening attributes to the difficulties of working with brass.

After the initial order is placed, most suppliers send a sample back to the jeweler for correction and/or modification. Again, there may be charges; that varies by supplier. It's a good idea to have the customer check the piece at this point, but be sure he's aware of any modification charges.

Once the piece is approved, it goes into production and the finished product is delivered. Gift boxing and/or wrapping is negotiable, but most jewelers prefer to package pieces themselves to reinforce their store's name.

The sale: Some jewelers aggressively seek incentive and award business; other don't. "If a jeweler opens in the morning, closes at night and only has a few [presentation] samples in a showcase, that's the amount of business he'll get," says Kentey.

If he just wants to offer the service, he can get by with a few sample pieces, word-of-mouth references and his good reputation. He doesn't need a separate sales staff or division. But to make the market a viable source of profits, he must invest time and effort. "The jeweler has to get out of the 'sit-behind-the-counter-and-wait-for-someone-to-come-in' mentality. He has to get aggressive," says Stuart Marcus.

Mann's Jewelers of Rochester, N.Y., does a large volume of presentation business—about half of it aggressively sought. The other half comes from referrals. Mann's, now a leader in the field, took 40 years to build up its reputation, explains corporate sales director Greg Emerick. Its aggressiveness has paid off; several major Fortune 500 corporations number among its incentive accounts. An outside salesperson handles incentives only, while Emerick and store owner Irving Mann also work closely with the incentive business.

Graubart's Jewelers in Schenectady, N.Y., doesn't have enough staff to send someone out in the field to sell incentives. That's a common problem in small stores.

"If we had a few more good people on the floor," says Herschel Graubart, "I could go out and get the logo business. It's out there. We could do another $15,000-$20,000 a year." Graubart feels strongly about having only family members sell incentives. The store's reputation is what sells incentives, he explains, and the Graubart name is key.

One selling point to stress is the continuity of a piece of jewelry. Using Stuart Marcus's example, if a car dealer spends $100 per month per salesperson for incentives, he can start by awarding a gold ring for a certain number of cars sold. Each additional goal achieved would earn the employee a 5-pt. diamond for that ring. A 5-pt. diamond would cost the dealer about $60—considerably less than the $100 he was prepared to spend—while the jeweler can make triple keystone on it. The jeweler also gets to set the diamond in the ring, reinforcing his reputation for service. The same can be done with a watch, a gift item, etc.

Advertising: Jewelers disagree on the value of advertising for incentive business. Greg Emerick says it hasn't brought in as much business as outside sales and store reputation. Jim Hayden, owner of Hayden's Jewelers in Liverpool, N.Y., uses direct mail (with follow-up calls), and vows it brings in business.

If a jeweler wants to advertise in print, the best vehicles are a local business newspaper, the community newspaper's business section and chamber of commerce guides. Word of mouth, instore or window displays and direct mail (statement stuffers) also bring results.

The competition: Competition for the incentive dollar can come from premium/incentive or advertising specialty distributors, who almost always will undercut a jeweler's price. "If a jeweler keystones and wins the program this year, he's opening himself wide to undercutting next year," warns Koenig. Competition also comes from large manufacturers whose corporate divisions solicit incentive orders directly from the end user.

A jeweler can't get keystone, but he can make up the difference in volume. He can counter price objections by stressing his reputation, quality, service, onsite repairs and product knowledge.

The problems: Jewelers' biggest gripe about presentation business is that customers often don't understand the time involved in custom work. On repeat orders, the problem can be eliminated by calling customers on a regular basis to remind them to reorder. Time can be a problem for manufacturers, too. S. Joseph Neally Jr., national sales manager of Bulova's presentation division, feels the onus is on the supplier to deliver the goods, but that jewelers should be aware of the time needed to prepare them.

One supplier to both the retail jewelry and premium incentive industries says his biggest problem with jewelers is small orders. They don't understand the manufacturing process, he says, then want to know why they can't get a discount on only a dozen.

Reputation is everything: It can't be stressed enough that reputation is the jeweler's most important asset. The whole presentation industry is built upon trust, delivery, credibility and reliability, emphasizes Neally. If you don't come through once, you won't be trusted with business again.

"The customer is always right," says Bob Smyth, vice president of Albert S. Smyth, Timonium, Md. That may be a cliché, but if a product doesn't come out the way the customer expected it to, you either do it over or apologize and eat the order, Smyth says. Luckily, he adds, this isn't a common occurrence.

The main thing to remember—beyond service, reputation and product knowledge—is that, as in any other business, building good presentation sales takes time and patience. Retailers report slow but steady growth. "It's a long term investment," says Neally, "but there's a real benefit to the retail jeweler."

Anatomy Of A Promotion: How Cartier Launched A Collection

March 1987

Promotions pay off any time of year. Holidays and traditional gift-buying occasions offer natural tie-ins—but every other jewelry outlet in town will take advantage of them, too. Scheduling your promotion during a quieter time will guarantee greater attention—and attendance.

Every promotion needs a focal point. Look for something notable about your store, your business or your merchandise that you'd like consumers to know about. Perhaps you'd like to share the arrival of an exciting new jewelry collection with your customers.

You want all your favorite people to come see it. Every element must be perfect. Invitations must arrive before other commitments have been made, yet not so early they're forgotten. The champagne must retain its bubbles and the hors d'oeuvres their freshness. Yet with all the festivities, the purpose of this celebration must remain foremost in the minds of your guests.

Here's how one store did it.

Panthers add punch: When New York's Cartier heard its new "Collection '86" was to arrive from Paris, the firm's public relations department leapt into action. Launching the 81 specially-created jewelry designs called for champagne, paparazzi and . . . panthers.

Why panthers? They represented the predominant Panther Theme present in Cartier's collections for nearly a century. They came as last-minute surprise guests and heightened media interest before the event.

Cartier's PR department, headed by Camilla Mackeson, had just five weeks to organize this "champagne preview." Two months would have been better, says Lori Rhodes, assistant PR director.

Listed below are the steps Cartier took before its promotion. Smaller retailers may not be able to rent panthers or mimic the full extravaganza described here. But with a bit of imagination, any store can adapt these ideas to fit its image and clientele. And the general approach applies to any promotion.

The steps

• *Goal:* To create broad awareness of the new jewelry collection's arrival. Selling was secondary; the real pay-off would come from future purchases inspired by the event (delayed response, word-of-mouth).

• *Plans for achieving goal:* Build excitement and desire for the new designs by gathering long-term clients and area press at an exclusive preview.

• *Merchandise:* 81 designs, created by a special team of Cartier artisans in Paris to mark Cartier's 140th year. "Collection '86" was divided into four themes—Panther, Pearl, Diamond and Yellow Gold. Panther pieces included both actual sculptures of the animal and abstract representations. The collection's brooches, necklaces, earrings, bracelets and rings were priced from $2,100 to $200,000. Most fell between $18,000 and $25,000.

• *Location:* Cartier hosted the preview on its second level, above the selling floor. Using this gallery area, which usually exhibits antique Cartier merchandise, allowed the firm to hold the preview during the day, yet maintain an air of exclusivity.

• *Setting the date:* Cartier hosted clients and press separately on two different days. Media day allowed for interviews and snapshots, with Cartier's public relations people readily available. On the following day, salesmen took center stage to interact with clients and explain jewelry details.

The event was scheduled during regular business hours (11 a.m. to 5 p.m.) to better highlight the pieces on display. Evening events, explains assistant PR director Rhodes, tend to emphasize store image more.

• *Theme:* Every promotion needs a theme. It provides decoration ideas and sets the tone. Cartier's selection of the panther theme was relatively easy: "The special beauty and magic of this feline has captivated generations of Cartier designers," explains the promotion program.

• *Decorations/atmosphere:* A live model dressed each day in a different $10,000 floor-length gown by designer Arnold Scaasi. (The dresses were borrowed; mention in the program was Scaasi's payment. Special insurance covered possible damages.) She sat in an old-style high-back chair in front of an enlarged artist's rendering of an Egyptian woman with a panther at her feet.

Guests were invited to register in a sign-in book like those often displayed at weddings. This is a good way to keep track of better clients. Addresses and/or last names may have changed since they were last contacted. And those invited may bring friends whose names can be added to the client list.

• *Contracts:* None, because the merchandise belonged to Cartier. When jewelry is not already owned, the retailer may be able to obtain it on consignment.

• *Invitations:* These were sent about two weeks in advance. Time had to be allowed to design the invitation (including color selection, wording, layout), then find a quality printer. The order's size, time of year and general business climate will affect the time needed for printing. Check this as early as possible to avoid last-minute panic.

• *Who's invited:* All area press, including local television, both daily and monthly fashion magazines, wire services and newspaper editors—in all, roughly 200 media people—were invited.

Nearly 1500 client names were gathered from salesmen's informal customer lists and orders for repair work. This took a good bit of work, admits Rhodes, assistant PR director. A previously compiled, updated client list is an asset.

• *Security:* Two security guards were hired (approximate cost: $200/two days) to monitor traffic on the second floor. Guests were required to present their invitations to the guards before admittance. Additional insurance was not needed as merchandise belonged to the store.

Obtaining insurance on goods not owned can be tricky. Depending on merchandise value, insurance companies may set conditions for coverage. Discuss it *at least* one month before preview date. Complying with conditions (hiring guards, arranging transportation to and from offsite vault) may take time.

• *Hiring help:* Needed were one butler, to circulate with refreshments; one human model and two panthers, to demonstrate the jewelry, and a hair/makeup artist to prepare the model for the public. Some were found through networking, people who knew people. The model was the sister of a professional model. Although she'd never modeled professionally, she had the defined bone structure and dramatic appearance Cartier wanted. Her fee was substantially less than a professional would charge.

Finding the panthers presented the greatest challenge. The local zoo couldn't help. Finally the animals were discovered at the Dawn Animal Agency in New York City. The agency, which rents animals for special occasions, also serves as a shelter for abandoned and abused pets. Delivery, use and return of the panthers totaled $4,000 for two days.

• *Press kits:* A press kit typically provides an overview of the event. Included might be one or two pictures of jewelry on display, a brief history of the store and a description of merchandise (noting special qualities). Cartier's press kit was quite elaborate, with slick red folders containing pictures and a program featuring special information about the collection.

Smaller retailers who have no PR department can make an impression without getting so fancy. A single sheet of information with an interesting snapshot can go far with the local media.

• *Programs:* A program of events, which forms part of the press kit, can also be given to customers. It explains the event's purpose and provides basic, intriguing information about the merchandise. Cartier's program cover offered a smaller version of the wall poster used as backdrop for the model. Mentioned inside were all who assisted in the event.

Several brief paragraphs described who creates Cartier designs, the themes used in designing and some background on the panther creations.

• *Refreshments:* "Champagne" evokes a feeling of class and importance. This champagne preview had both—plus plenty of bubbly with trays of catered pain brioche (tiny, sandwich-like hot ham-and-cheese pastries).

Base the quantity on your anticipated attendance. Hors d'oeuvres represent hospitality, and are not meant to replace a meal. As for libations, less-than-full glasses are a sophisticated signal that guests best sip.

• *Media alert:* Two days before the preview, media were alerted that "photo opportunities" would be available. The message, hand delivered to all invited press, revealed that two panthers as well as a human model would be present to demonstrate the jewels. A follow-up phone call from Cartier further encouraged press attendance.

A "media alert" is a good idea for smaller retailers, too. Phone calls may do the trick. Keep in mind that the press must constantly rearrange priorities and wants to be sure time devoted to your event will be well spent. A last-minute "must attend" notice (reminder) creates that necessary urgency.

• *Presenting merchandise:* Both model and panthers demonstrated the jewelry. At irregular intervals, "when one of us got tired of seeing one of the pieces or no guests were in the room," designs being modeled were switched. Jewelry not being worn could be viewed in the various eye-level display cases situated about the gallery. One such vitrine featured original sketches, mold-forms and wax sculptures of Cartier's panther.

• *Results:* Nearly 500 clients and 100 media people visited the preview. Though actual selling was played down, two pieces were purchased during the event. Several other purchases closely followed. When the preview was over, Cartier received editorial coverage in various media, further spreading word of the new arrivals. Print advertising also was placed in local newspapers.

Adding it all up: Now hang on to your party hats! This preview cost $10,000 total. New York City, of course, is not the cheapest place to host a party. Security guards in the Big Apple cost more than in most other towns; so do top caterers. But with a bit of imagination, it's possible to trim expenses without sacrificing novelty.

One sure way is to involve sponsors. You might ask a new caterer in town to contribute free hors d'oeuvres; in return, you'll mention the company in your program. Do the same with the specialty dress shop where you select the model's clothes.

As for the model, look around you and ask friends. A local agency may have eager young talent willing to work for modest fees. And, although panthers may not be feasible (or reasonable at $1,000 each per day), other live pets might stimulate interest.

Ten Steps
To Better Colored Gem Sales

February 1987

To develop a strong colored gem department, you need a commitment to education and inventory . . . plus patience. It may take as long as two years for your department to produce the way you want it to.

This guide to setting up a department is based on conversations with many jewelers and colored stone experts. They recommend the following 10 steps.

1. Be sure at least one person on your staff has a gemological education. The Gemological Institute of America and the American Gem Society offer classes in colored stones.

But don't stop after just one gem course. You must make a commitment to education by continually taking more courses and following gem industry news.

Then you must try to see many different varieties and qualities of colored gemstones. Plan to attend the Tucson gem shows held each February, where you'll see the largest display of both gems and minerals.

This process will teach you what factors affect a gem's price and enable you to buy well.

2. Study the market. If you plan a serious venture into colored stones you must:

• Know which price points sell best. About half of all pieces sell for $50 or less and four in five sell for $300 or less (these figures come from JCK's continuing research on consumers' jewelry buying habits). Clearly this represents a good impulse market. But don't overlook the one piece in five that sells for more than $300—often much more.

• Know how well this jewelry sells in jewelry stores. Jewelers are losing share of market. As recently as six years ago, they made more than half (54%) of all colored stone jewelry sales; today the figure is closer to a third (34%), according to JCK research.

But they still sell a lot. Colored stones account for roughly 8% to 10% of total volume for a "typical" jewelry store, government figures show.

• Know the competition. Discount and department stores offer the biggest challenge, though jewelers still outsell each of these competitors by a margin of better than two to one. While men tend to spend more than women when buying colored stone jewelry, women are more likely to shop in a jewelry store.

To find out who's selling what in your community, shop the competition. Find the gaps. Are all types of jewelry—rings, earrings, pendants, pins, bracelets—offered? Are they traditional or more fashion-forward pieces? What are the price points? What types, sizes and qualities of colored stones are available?

• Use all this information to help you decide which stones, which types of jewelry and which price points you should stock.

3. Give method to your buying. To decide how much inventory you need, first forecast your annual sales volume, advises David Barry of Management Growth Institute in Wellesley, Mass. Then figure about what percent of the total will come from colored gemstone sales.

If you've never done big business in this type of jewelry, you'll have to make some educated guesses. Consider all known market factors. Also consider how special promotions will affect sales and the response you can expect from your sales staff. Jewelers of America, the American Gem Society, the American Gem Trade Association and others have useful training material.

Let's say that after checking all available facts you decide you can sell $12,000 worth of colored stone jewelry in the next year. You expect a 1.5-time turnover. Here's how Barry figures your inventory needs:

$12,000 (projected sales) / 1.5 (turnover goal) = $8,000 (average inventory requirement)

Remember that the average inventory requirement is computed at retail. If you use a keystone markup, you'll need to purchase $4,000 worth of inventory.

4. How should you invest these dollars? Shelly Kuehn, executive director of the American Gem Trade Association, suggests dividing inventory dollars into thirds. "You'll have a nice selection of gems at a variety of price points," she explains. Here's her breakdown:

• Put one-third into relatively inexpensive pieces containing citrine, amethyst, chrysoprase and other similarly-priced gems. This gives you affordably-priced jewelry for impulse buyers.

• Allow another third for what Kuehn calls "the great look-alikes to get an 'Oh my!' reaction from customers." You can achieve this effect with lesser-known stones that mimic the colors of ruby, emerald and sapphire. Try some nice rubellite, garnet, tourmaline and blue topaz. This selection will help start a conversation with customers.

• Put the last third, Kuehn suggests, into something "real pretty so that the jeweler can say to himself, 'I like it, I can sell it.'"

5. Finding the right mix of color to please both you and your customers requires trial—and error!

The most important thing is to see *a lot* of color. Jewelry shows are the best starting place. Tucson—with its multiple displays of colored stones of every quality, variety and price—is ideal, but *any* show is good. Look and compare. Look and compare again. Then buy.

Suppliers can be a great help. Garth Garnett of Simm's Inc., a Bernardsville, N.J., store, offers this suggestion:

Narrow down your prospective suppliers, then ask these vendors to send you, on memo, a parcel of stones containing the sizes, prices and qualities of specific gems you want to sell. Compare each supplier's parcel for quality and price.

Be honest in your approach, Garnett cautions. Let the supplier know that you're trying to build a colored gem department and that you want to find out about his merchandise. Follow this procedure in the slow months.

Don't be afraid to stock gemstones that may be unfamiliar to the average customer. But be sure you and your staff know all about them.

Be a trendsetter. The most recent poll of JCK's Retail Jeweler Panelists (results were published last month) shows that the sapphire, ruby and emerald Big Three still are the bread-and-butter stones for a majority of jewelry stores. Adding something different can make your store stand out as a merchandise leader.

Still, the easiest way to ease into new inventory is to choose gems that people already know, says Garnett of Simm's. He chose birthstones, stocking natural gems instead of the more common synthetics. The move, he says, gave Simm's a definite competitive edge.

But don't let a good idea get out of hand. It's easy to overbuy if you lack sales records or don't use them. Simm's, for example, bought the same amount of each birthstone, even though its sales records showed that peridot (August's birthstone) was a slow seller. If you are unsure about where to order heavily and where lightly, pick colors you and your salespeople like, says AGTA's Shelly Kuehn. It's always easier to be enthusiastic about and to sell what you like.

6. Keep up with gem and fashion trends. Follow the jewelry trade magazines and consumer fashion magazines, such as *Vogue, Harper's Bazaar* and *Town & Country,* to find out what will be hot. Plan to offer gems that coordinate well with the colors used in clothing.

Study clothing fashions to determine what types of jewelry will be needed, says David Coll of Montclair Jewelers, Oakland, Cal. "If low necklines are shown, pendants will be popular," he explains. "Pins and brooches are used with high necklines."

Don't overlook coordinated jewelry suites. With four-piece ensembles of rings, necklaces, earrings and bracelets, you'll create repeat sales, says jeweler Michael Hayes of Carl Mayer Jewelry Co., Austin, Tex.

Always track what competitors lack and what customers ask for.

7. Early on, consider the relative merits of stocking loose and mounted goods.

When building your department, carry more mounted goods, says Garth Garnett; they're easier to sell. "You can back up that [inventory] with loose stones of equal size." Calibrated (standard) sizes allow you to offer the customer a different color if that's what she wants, he adds.

Once you've developed a reputation for colored stones, you may want to specialize more in loose goods. But that move could require in-house manufacturing to be cost-effective.

8. Good records are vital. Once you start buying gemstone jewelry, keep a ledger, advises Samuel Kind of La Vake Jewelers, Princeton, N.J. Record carat weight, shape and cost per carat of each gem, including mounted goods. Also assign some quality rating to the gem, using an established system or one you develop. Just be consistent in assigning values, Kind says. This helps you learn about and keep track of qualities and prices.

9. Stress sales training. Colored stones are a blind purchase for most customers, so they want to feel they're getting fair value. Here knowledgeable salespeople can reassure customers and make the big difference.

Use knowledge as a sales tool. Folklore will help you romance a colored stone sale. And gemological knowledge lets you discuss technical issues with customers who demand it.

Education also give you an edge over stores with no gemologist. When considering an important purchase, consumers will go to the most knowledgeable in the field, say jewelers.

10. Educate the public. While developing your department, let consumers know you have something new.

Plan to increase colored stone advertising and promotions, say Shelly Kuehn and jewelers interviewed for this story. One low-cost method: Have your gemologist speak to civic groups about gems and jewelry.

Finally, stick with it. It *will* take about two years to build your reputation. Or as jeweler Michael Hayes would say, "No guts, no blue chips."

How To Improve Your Diamond Sales

September 1985

Diamonds remain the key to most jewelers' success. Anything that boosts diamond sales means more money in the bank. The following ideas—ranging from diamond windows to men's jewelry boutiques, from sports tie-ins to sales incentive contests—have helped build other jewelers' sales. Some of them might work in your store.

Large diamond values: When the diamond cutter who supplies B.C. Clark in Oklahoma City, Okla., went on vacation, store owner Jim Clark used a substantial quantity of the cutter's stones for a "two-carat and larger" diamond promotion.

The large stones, in a variety of shapes, were promoted during the usually slow month of July via a television and newspaper advertising blitz, says Clark. TV spots used close-up camera work to show the merchandise, some of it from the store's own inventory. Clark promoted the event as a sale, but didn't use price comparisons. Instead Clark, ad spokesman for the firm, described the "exceedingly good values" that were available for a short time only. Clark says the stones were priced at a close margin. The event was "a real plus," he says. It created sales that normally wouldn't have been made during July.

Lecture giver: Bill Shepherd of Wayne Jewelers & Silversmiths, Wayne, Pa., says every one of his diamond customers gets a five-minute lecture on the GIA grading system before a diamond ever comes out of a case. "I want to be sure that we're talking the same language," he says. To get diamond customers into the store, Shepherd emphasizes diamonds, which account for 25% of his business, in two-thirds of his newspaper ads. "We don't run promotions," he says, "so we've got to hammer at it constantly."

Quality presentation package: Jim Barnes of Bill Barnes Jeweler, Victoria, Tex., was concerned about his store's sales presentation of carat-plus diamonds. So he hired a consultant and purchased a copyrighted presentation program for him. "It stresses color, clarity and proportion," says Barnes. "It's basic stuff. But how many times do you really see a quality selling presentation by a diamond salesman?" To promote large stones, Barnes uses the De Beers quality diamond ads, plus direct mail advertising to qualified buyers. "We know who they are," he says. "There's only 50,000 people here and we've been around for four generations."

If you've got it, flaunt it: Mark Fleishner, owner of Lauray's Jewelers in Hot Springs Ark., bills himself and his staff as diamond experts. "We advertise in all media, including direct mail, and always refer specifically to our knowledge of quality diamonds," he says. Before touching a diamond showcase, all Lauray's staff members must complete the Diamond Council of America Diamontology course. Along with expertise, Lauray's emphasizes services. "We want our customer to know that we know more than the discounter and that we are here for our customer."

Display's the thing: For Murray Rose, owner of Rose Jewelers in New York, displays are essential selling tools. "In the four small towns where our stores are located [on eastern Long Island], windows play an important part" in selling diamonds. Each store has a "major window" designated for diamond displays. Every month, that window sports a different theme, but the merchandise in the displays changes every two weeks to keep the interest of passers-by. A recent one was "Rose diamonds come in many different shapes." Another emphasized large stones, with a special display of one-carat diamond engagement rings of various grades, sizes and shapes. "A window display like that with 25 or 30 pieces has an impact, especially in a small town," says Rose.

Inside the store, the first showcase to the right of the entrance is always a diamond display case. Research by the firm, working with its architect, found that customer traffic "flows that way," says Rose.

Every Rose Jewelry store also has a small, comfortable "diamond room," complete with gemological equipment,

which a salesperson—always a trained gemologist—can use to sell hard-to-convince customers. But a very important feature is what the room doesn't have—doors. That's because of the psychological effect on sales. "Our diamond rooms are always open," explains Rose, "because customers don't want to feel trapped." A feeling that they're being forced to buy can actually hinder a sale, "especially in a small town."

Show-and-sell: A tray of diamond rings is "the backbone of our diamond business" says Herb Levine president Van Cott Jewelers in Binghamton, N.Y.

"The average diamond customer is very confused" by various jewelry promotions and selling gimmicks, says Levine. "First-time buyers, especially, don't understand diamond value in terms of quality, cut and clarity. They don't know they can get a large diamond with poorer cut or clarity, or a smaller one with better cut, for the same price."

That's why his salespeople use "The Van Cott's Diamond Solitaire collection" to explain the differences to customers.

The collection is a 12-inch tray with three rows of diamond rings. Each row offers the same-size diamonds—in a range from 1/6 carat to 3/4 carat—but in a different quality and naturally, price. Thus, a customer can choose a 1/3-carat stone selling for $595, $795 or $995. Or for that $995 price, he can get either a 1/3-carat or a 3/8-carat diamond. This approach helps the customer learn about differences among diamonds "and lets them decide what *they* want to concentrate on—clarity, size, cut or price"—in making a purchase.

The firm has to make sure its stores keep a full collection of rings in the given sizes, prices and quality in stock. It also has to invest time in explaining diamond quality differences, which can take longer than a normal sale.

But, says Levine, the technique has been "very successful, and customers tell us they appreciate the fact that we take the time to explain these things to them." That not only makes sales but builds customer loyalty, especially with first-time buyers.

The Wight stuff: A weekly column in the local newspaper wins friends and influences customers for Wight's Jewelers in Ontario, Cal., says manager Don Riffe.

Some of the articles come form AGS's *Gemwise* subscription service, but most are written by owner Don Wight or Riffe, often based on ideas staff members offer at their weekly sales meetings or on questions from customers.

The column is "information-oriented, not sales oriented," says Riffe. "We want to build a link with customers, and let them get to know us. So, we provide informative facts, folklore, warnings about deceptive price mark-offs, diamond color and cut, cleaning diamonds, jewelry design, and so on.

"We know it brings business into the store," he says. "We've had people tell us they read the column every week." And that familiarity "breaks down the threshold of [customer] resistance. Because people read it, they feel like they've already been here or know us"—which makes selling easier.

'A true sale': Special sales can turn the summer doldrums into hot profit days. That's what happens at Christensen Jewelers, a three-store Las Vegas, Nev., chain, during its annual three-week July diamond sale. Goods then are discounted up to 30%.

The "30%" figure wasn't picked out of thin air. The firm conducted "a very expensive survey," which found most people "consider anything [marked down] more than 50% as a lie and anything under 20% as too 'chintzy', " says Wayne Christensen, a partner in the family firm.

Prices are dropped only during the promotion and return to normal afterward. "Customers look forward to this. They come in days before—and after—to check the prices. They see it's a true sale, not a con. That, plus our reputation, makes it successful."

How does the firm do it? "Buying power and contacts," says Christensen. "We buy diamonds inexpensively, especially now when the diamond market is soft, particularly for large diamonds. Second, we buy a lot of stuff off the street. Some we mark up to regular prices, others we tear down" for the stones.

Also successful was the firm's "Special Purchase" promotion last year. Christensen's ordered 75 quarter-carat-and 75 half-carat diamonds of the same color and clarity ("H colors, S1 or better"). They were put in two lucite trays, with a card marked "Your choice." The half carats sold for $699 each; the quarter carats for $299. "Customers could look through them, pick out the ones they wanted, and look at them under the "scope" says Christensen.

The firm sold two thirds of them, plus the mountings.

Join the club: The Diamond club has provided Wight's jewelry store in Ontario, Cal., with a steady flow of diamond jewelry sales, customers and cash flow. No, not the Diamond Club in New York, but the store's own. The idea is similar to a Christmas Club (without, of course, the interest rate) where people put money aside now for a later purchase.

The set-up is simple: customers pay $3 to join the club, plus a $2 weekly fee. The money is put in individual accounts for use in any department in the store, even repairs. "However, we emphasize diamond purchases, especially one carat or more," says owner Don Wight.

Each club is limited to 130 members and lasts 38 weeks. At the end, members use the money to buy something or have it set aside by the store as a layaway credit until they do.

Club membership makes customers eligible for weekly drawings for a $150 saving on the purchase of "anything in the store with diamonds in it—earrings, watches, rings, whatever," says Wight. (Winners have to drop out of that club, though they can join the next.)

"It's a can't lose situation for both customers and us," says Wight. Customers save up for a purchase; get a chance for big savings, and can join new clubs as often as they want. And the store gets "additional cash flow, added diamond sales, and customer traffic [because] people come in weekly to pay their $2 and for the Tuesday drawings."

Wight has been running diamond clubs for several years. "We're on our 60th club now, and usually have three a year," he says.

The idea does "involve a lot of work getting the first two or three going, and a lot of bookkeeping," says store manager Don Riffe. But once the program starts, "it's self-perpetuating, brings in business and creates good PR for the store." And, adds Wight, "we find that once a customer has been in a club, they want to join again."

Motivation: Incentive sells diamonds for Karten Jewelers, and it works on both customers and salespeople. In April, for example, the 10-store chain, based in New Bedford, Mass., promoted one-carat stones for $1995, with each buyer getting a free weekend for two at a Marriot Hotel in Boston, Mass. In addition, every salesperson who sold

three or more such stones won a free weekend at the hotel, says Joy Prenda, the firm's diamond buyer. Karten promoted the sale heavily on radio and TV, and Marriot provided rooms free in return for the advertisement.

The results? "Sales for the month were up 35%," says Prenda. Indeed, Karten sold so many, it had to pay for more rooms than those originally provided by the hotel!

The jeweler has tried the one-carat promotion two ways, says Prenda—with a free hotel stay for both customers and salespeople, and just for customers. "We found we have more success when there's an incentive for the salespeople, too," she says.

In June, Karten offered its salespeople a dinner-for-two at a fine Boston restaurant if they sold two stones, and dinner plus limousine service to the restaurant and back if they sold three. The result: Sales for the month increased 45%.

Such incentives are "very important", says Prenda. They give salespeople added motivation to make big sales, and "increase healthy competition" among them.

Leaving their mark: Some customers buy diamonds for something they *can't* see: A permanent laser-inscribed identification number or message on the diamond girdle, invisible to the eye but clearly seen under 10X magnification. That's what Herb Levine of Van Cott's Jewelers, Binghamton, N.Y., has discovered.

"This is very appealing to many customers, especially those who are nervous" about losing a stone, leaving jewelry in a store to be repaired, or having it stolen, he says. Each diamond's number is registered and customers get a certificate with the registration number from the jeweler to file with their insurance.

The laser-inscribing technology is currently available from Lazare Kaplan International in New York and the Gemological Institute of America in Santa Monica, Cal.

Wrapping up sales: There are ways to promote such basic items as diamond stud earrings without tacking a "50%-off" sale sign in front of the store.

Evelyn Hesch at Costa Findings in New York says that earring jackets help spur diamond stud sales by offering variety—a set of studs can be used with several jackets to create a jewelry wardrobe.

"We have found that jackets spur gift sales of stud earrings because many men aren't sure whether or not their wives will like them. So they buy several different jackets to go along with the studs to be sure of getting something they'll like."

Hech says that earring jackets can also accompany a jeweler's remount promotion.

"We make many jackets which take very small diamonds so if someone wants to break up a ring with melee and a large center stone, the center stone can go into a new ring and the earring jackets can take the melee," she explains.

Scooping the competition: A diamond room, set up like a laboratory, makes a lot of sales for Stanley Jewelers and Gemologists, N. Little Rock, Ark. Owner Lloyd Stanley says he's convinced that once a customer looks at a diamond through his microscope, he's made the sale.

"They may not buy from us that day, but they'll come back and buy from us." Stanley says his store sells diamonds that are more expensive than his competitors'. He's able to do so because customers can see the difference in quality and cutting through the scope. "If we forget to show the diamond through the scope, the chances of closing the sale are lessened."

Pavé diamonds: Anita Fiedler of Treasures in Jewelry Scarsdale, N.Y., has found a way to boost her diamond sales by hooking them up with colored stone and pearl sales. Colored stones are increasing in popularity, but customers don't understand that type of jewelry as well as they do diamonds, she says. So, to make the customer more comfortable with a large colored-stone ring, the store will put pavé diamonds around it. "Customers understand that and we make a nice sale out of it," she says. Similarly, she is stringing diamond sales out of the popularity of pearls, too. "We'll sell a long strand of pearls with a round diamond clasp. The customer can then wear the clasp in the front if she wants."

Men's diamond promotions: A local sports team with a strong following has been one of the keys to the success of G.M. Pollack & Sons' men's diamond jewelry business.

Pollack, headquartered in Portland, Maine, began running full-page ads in a magazine distributed at Portland Mariners pro hockey games.

The ads featured a well-dressed man with a diamond jewelry wardrobe saying "Show the world you've made it." They included a sweepstakes drawing coupon. Those who filled out coupons and deposited them in one of Pollack's five stores had a chance to win $1500 worth of diamond jewelry. Reminders to fill in the coupons were broadcast during the game over the stadium sound system.

"We had thousands of entries," says Stanley Pollack, president. More to the point, sales of men's diamond jewelry doubled.

Since then Pollack's has gone deeply into men's jewelry, establishing 'men's boutiques' in each store and advertising them in the local newspapers.

"It is a separate section with special decoration and a whole case full of inventory," says Pollack. He says it's worked out very well.

"I believe De Beers [which has been promoting men's diamond jewelry heavily]. We've just begun to tap the men's jewelry market. But we have to promote to get it. It won't just come to us."

In fact Pollack's has become so identified with men's diamonds that when it ran a loose diamond promotion-heavily advertising a 1-ct. loose diamond for $1495—four people bought stones and mountings the first day. Three of them were men.

To tell the truth: While some jewelers swear by their microscope, Jack Kellmer Co. of Philadelphia dismisses it totally. "We don't use it because we think it confuses the customer," says manager Jules Silverstein. Instead, the store relies on truth and quality to sell diamonds. "Over 50 years we've built a reputation. It's like Tiffany and Cartier. People don't question them. And we've been able to do the same thing by telling the truth about our product and explaining the value of what [a customer] is getting." The sales staff is trained in the GIA grading system because, as Silverstein says, "it's the Bible of the industry." But the staff does not overwhelm the customer with highly technical information. "Customers tend to be very upset by that."

Selling to salespeople: Most retailers think only of the public when they want to build diamond sales and traffic. Not Grunewald & Adams. The three-store Arizona firm also promotes its wares to salespeople in other stores in malls where it is located, usually through the malls' tenant newsletter. The jewelry firm benefits in two ways: It gets the interest and business of outside salespeople—who are shoppers, after all, just like anyone else—and they, in turn, encourage their own customers to shop at the jewelry store.

The attraction is a reduction on purchase costs. "We tell them that if they shop at our store, they get a 15% savings on any purchase because we appreciate them as salespeople and they're part of our business," says Al Bouley, the jewelry firm's general manager. "And anyone they send here also gets a 15% saving."

Bouley finds that satisfied sales clerks who buy from Grunewald & Adams usually "turn around and tell their own customers about us and our fine jewelry, which make *them* want to come."

Because of this idea, which the firm has used since January, "all three stores are 25%-30% ahead of last year," says Bouley.

TLC: Show customers you care. It keeps them coming back, says jeweler Michael Delmonte of Carle Place, N.Y. Thus, before a recent multi-million diamond sale, Delmonte mailed copies of his newspaper ad promoting the sale to 8000 customers on his mailing list. Afterward, he sent postcards to those who made purchases, thanking them for their patronage.

Why the fuss? A key to success is "making customers feel they picked the right people to do business with," says Delmonte. A direct mail effort like this not only subtly tells them Delmonte is a successful retailer who is "on top of things, but also says, 'You are a valued customer to me,'" he says.

That attitude affects the entire store's operations, even apparently unrelated elements. "If a salesman needs a haircut, I don't let him wait on customers until he gets one," says Delmonte. "We want to do everything we can in appearance, in service, in quality of merchandise to show customer's we're totally dedicated to them. Anything that can be offensive to them [in a store] simply shows that a retailer didn't care enough about his customer" to correct it.

How To Make That Big Sale

December 1984

Successful sellers of big-ticket merchandise sell themselves first, their jewelry second.

Why?

Because jewelry is a blind item for many customers. The person who is going to spend $30,000, $50,000 or $100,000 wants to know whom he's spending it with, says Durward Howes III, B.D. Howes and Son, Pasadena, Cal. The buyer wants to know not only that his jeweler is honest, but that he knows what he's talking about.

Jeanne Larson, director of retail sales at The Collector in Fallbrook and La Jolla, Cal., sells herself and her store by educating the customers.

"If you want to show a customer that you're honest, trustworthy and giving good value for the money, education is first and foremost," she says, "Educate people on all the factors that affect the price of a stone. Show them why one stone is better than another. Get them to read, to go to museums, encourage them to learn as much as possible about the gem they're considering. Educate them on design and wearability, too," she says. "A lot of customers need help on how they an wear a piece, what their options are." The more *customers* learn, the more they'll appreciate the *jeweler* who knows his or her stuff.

"We must build up the sort of trusting relationship that our parents and grandparents had with the merchants with whom they dealt," says Leonard Prins, Prins & Volkhardt, Stafford, Pa. "If I say something is a good value at $40,000, my customers believe me."

It's critical that your career mean more to you than any one sale, says Douglas Cooper, F.J. Cooper Inc., Philadelphia. You must project that philosophy to each and every customer.

Appearances count, too.

When Douglas Cooper first opened his store on Philadelphia's Chestnut Street, he made it a point to create one that didn't look like any other. In fact, in the beginning, Cooper admits, the store was far more grand than the amount of inventory it held. But people were impressed by what they saw and it wasn't long before the stock—and the sales—matched the decor.

The Collector shops in California make customers pause, stand back and look, too. The moment shoppers walk in they *know* this place is different. The professionalism of the operation is reflected in the stores' "look."

Who's who of gem buyers

Often—but not always—the buyer of the big piece is someone you've dealt with before, either on a business or a personal level. These individuals may have bought from you before. Or, you may know them socially, through community activities or they may be friends of friends.

Once in a while, though, they simply walk in off the street. Jeanne Larson says The Collector does a lot of business from tourist traffic. She tells a story about a man from New York who came to southern California for a vacation. He came into her store and fell in love with a $20,000 emerald ring. "I didn't know him and he didn't know me," Larson explains. Her employees, however, gave him a thorough education in emeralds. The man left the store, came back in 48 hours and bought the ring. He shopped for such a piece in both New York and Chicago. But he bought from The Collector because he was impressed with the layout of the store, the quality of stock, the knowledge level of the employees and the amount of time they were willing to spend with him.

A two-way street

It works in reverse, too.

Just as your customers want to know you, it's imperative that you know your customers.

Jewelers must be familiar with their clients' taste and lifestyle. Customers don't always know what sort of piece really suits them, so jewelers take it upon themselves to make certain pieces customers buy are appropriate. For example, if a woman wears a piece that doesn't fit in with her friends and lifestyle, she may end up feeling foolish and dissatisfied and be angry with the jeweler.

"Sometimes you really have to pick a potential customer's brain to find out what she's like," Larson admits. "Know their friends, too," advises Leonard Prins. "You don't want them all to end up with the same sort of piece!"

What's more, jewelers say, you must be able to communicate with clients on their level. There is the occasional client who wants his jeweler to be subservient, but most, jewelers say, want to feel that their dealing with an equal.

"If a man comes in for a fine emerald ring, for example, I have to be able to talk to him about more than emeralds," explains Durward Howes. I have to be prepared to converse as his equal on other things, such as fine food, fine clothes, fine automobiles, or maybe about travel."

"They must view you not only as knowledgeable and honest, but as someone they like, too," Cooper adds.

Serve them all your days

The jeweler who wants the "big" clientele must be prepared to be on call, practically 24 hours a day. Leonard Prins says he's received calls from clients as late as 2 a.m., and as early as 5. Clients spending a lot of dollars may want a lot of service. It goes with the territory.

What's more, the jeweler can't expect to stand behind his counter and have the big sales flock in. More often, the sale is finalized outside of the store.

If a woman is considering an important jewel it's only natural for her to want to see it with her wardrobe and in the environment in which it will often be worn. Sometime, if he thinks customers are really interested, Prins will make the appropriate insurance arrangements to leave a piece or two with the customer for a few days. This way she can be sure that the piece is really what she wants.

Sometimes, though, customers simply don't have the time or just don't want to go into the store. In this case, with hardly a second thought, jewelers go to them.

What's more, some jewelers say that if a good client expresses interest in a piece, and the jeweler feels the piece is right for that customer, they won't sell it to someone else until they're sure that first client has decided against it. "If I'm sure the client was interested, and a month or so goes by and I've heard nothing," Prins suggests, "I might tactfully call and tell him that if he's still considering the piece I'll hold on to it for him."

Prins encourages customers by maintaining a standing offer to buy back anything his customers are unhappy with. "You save good customers that way," he insists. "Besides, service is the first thing we give," he says.

The sales presentation

The first step in Jeanne Larson's sale presentation is to determine what sort of stone the customer wants. Sometimes she knows, sometimes she doesn't, Larson says. She starts by showing a selection of gems. Often the shopper will come in and say *she* wants a particular color. Then Larson or her staff shows the customer her options among stones that come in the color she likes.

Once Larson determines the type of stone, she works on shape and size.

Then, she'll talk to the customer about what she wants to do with it. Does she want a daytime piece, or one for the evening? Or perhaps a piece that can do double duty?

"When you're working from loose stones and you can start from scratch in terms of design, you have many options," Larson explains.

If a customer seems to have trouble visualizing a finished piece of jewelry, Larson will show her items from stock, or renderings and photographs of pieces she's done before. Sometimes she'll even do a wax for a customer to try on.

"I like to play up the romance and intrigue of the exotic places that the stones came from, too," Larson adds. She talks about how they were formed, how rare each and every gem really is.

Douglas Cooper begins the presentation of a spectacular piece by building excitement. Unless he senses the customer is in a hurry, Cooper will start the conversation on other matters. Since he has a reputation for selling exceptional pieces, he knows his customers are anxious to see what he has. He likes to prolong their suspense. Often he'll start out saying something like, "I just can't decide which piece to show you first." Or he'll reach into his pocket to pull out a jewel, then register shock because it's not there. He quickly reassures the anxious customer by "finding" the piece in another pocket. Cooper smiles and the piece makes a grand debut.

He'll place the piece in the customer's hand. "If I'm sure it will fit," he says, "I encourage the customer to put it on." He wants the customer to know that the jewel she's admiring is rare and precious, but that it's nothing to be scared of.

Cooper says sincere enthusiasm is one of the most important aspects of presenting the spectacular piece.

"When you're selling something that you truly believe is one of the rarest, or the most beautiful, that you've ever seen, you're enthusiastic," Cooper says. "You love the piece; you're genuinely involved with it. That enthusiasm is infectious.

"People appreciate uniqueness and rarity." Cooper continues. He explains that different people require different approaches. You have to determine which emotion will reach each customer, he says.

For some, beauty and rarity is enough. They want to buy jewelry simply for the joy of wearing it.

Others want more. With a more pragmatic customer, for example, Cooper might employ the rarity factor, but he goes about it in a different way. You'll enjoy it now, he might say, and down the road it will be an important part of your estate. Just think how much more it will mean to your heirs than the usual stocks and bonds. Over the years your children will see the pride of ownership you have in this piece. You'll pass on something of great value, to be sure, but in addition it will be something they've watched you love and enjoy all of these years.

Leonard Prins often starts off a sales presentation by showing a customer an unusual colored stone—a golden beryl, for example—and asking if he knows what it is. The customer often will guess diamond or sapphire. Prins say, but rarely will he know what he's looking at. "When I tell him, he's fascinated," Prins points out. "He can't believe that stones come in so many colors." And can't wait to see more.

Fascination is a big part of Prins' sales presentation. He tells customers every, little detail he knows about a piece of jewelry. He'll tell where it was made, how he happened to find it, what it is. "The more background and story we have to go with a piece, the better," he says.

Closing the sale

Closing on a big piece is especially tricky. The experts agree you must never let your customer see that you really want to make the sale. The presentation must be so good that the customer feels he simply "must have" the piece. Let the customer complete the close for you.

"The customer must have a desire for the piece to start with," caution Durward Howes. "If it's what he wants and the price is right, he'll buy."

Cooper says sometimes it's acceptable to give a gentle push. If he showed someone a piece in his office, for example, and the person seemed very interested but didn't make a move to buy, Cooper doesn't pursue it... right away. If he sees the customer later, somewhere else, he might casually inquire, "Do you think that you'll put that piece into your collection?"

Prices

Do customers look for deals on big pieces?

Many do—the first time.

"If I ask $60,000 and let a customer have it for $50,000, then he may think he could have gotten it for $40,000," says Howes. "That makes for unhappy customers. I want people to be happy with what they buy from me."

Cooper agrees wholeheartedly.

"I offer my best price the first time," he says. "I'm convinced that my customers would lose respect for me if they felt they could haggle."

The basics

Successful sellers of big-ticket jewels generally agree on the basics:

• Know your product. Know what it is and know that it's priced correctly.

• Love your merchandise and convey your enthusiasm.

• Know your people. Know how to communicate with them.

"We all love the merchandise," Larson says of herself and her staff. "We all collect it ourselves. We get as much joy and excitement just seeing it in stock as we do selling it. Our customers can see that. For us the love and excitement are a big part of our success."

"You must have love and you must have the knowledge," Cooper says. "One without the other is worthless."

Ye Reap What Ye Sow

The jeweler can't stand by and wait for affluent clients to come into his store. "It's our job to seek them out," Durward Howes explains. There simply aren't that many $50,000-plus customers around.

The important client often is born of a social relationship. He or she may have served with the jeweler on the hospital board, or they may have both been involved in organizing a charity function.

Larson says she is very involved with both charity and educational groups in her area. "We're constantly doing functions of one sort or another for them," she says. When the Salk Institute had a fund raiser, for example, Larson staged a jewelry fashion show during the cocktail hour.

For the local charity ball, she designed a tsavorite and diamond necklace and donated it to the charity.

"This sort of thing gets you lots of exposure... with the right people," she insists.

The right kind of dinner party is another wonderful way to meet potential clients. Leonard Prins says it's not at all unusual for him to attend a party and have one of the guests approach him and say, "I've heard so much about you. May I stop in?"

Cooper says he always follows up on likely prospects whether they're local or not. Often he'll meet someone from out-of-town when he gives lectures or charity shows, or through another client. If the person shows interest in what he has, he'll often say, "Well, it just so happens that I'm going to be in Palm Beach (the person's home town) next month. I'd love to stop in and say hi." If his offer is accepted, Cooper stops in and of course has a few special pieces with him. His hosts are flattered that he has come and often show him off to their friends as an expert.

It's a self-perpetuating process.

Word of mouth is the jeweler's best means of gathering an important clientele. "Get a hold of one or two good clients, and you'll find they have friends," Howes says. "Once you get yourself in that league, and once people know that you tell the truth, word gets around." Clients will start to seek you out.

'I Can't Buy Now Because'

September 1982 Part II

Before dealing with some of the more common statements a customer may make in order to delay buying now, let's first look at what the customer is really telling you and how you should react.

Seeking reassurance: The customer would like to buy the item but wants another reason to do so.

Action: Give the customer the reassurance he wants and ask him to buy.

General or vague: The customer has another question to ask but doesn't know how to phrase it.

Action: Probe deeper to get the question from the customer. There's a silent objection here that has to be dealt with.

Stall: the customer would like to put the decision off and hopes the sales person will let him do so.

Action: Put a little pressure on the customer to buy now. Either the customer will agree to buy or will come up with a specific reason not to which the sales person can answer.

Smoke screen: The customer gives a reason not to buy which is not the real reason.

Action: Get the customer to tell you the truth by continuing to ask questions.

Valid: The customer has a true reason for not buying. Most of the time the valid objection, no matter how it is

phrased, is, "I'm not yet convinced that this particular item is worth the dollars I have to spend to own it now."

Action: Try to overcome the objection. If you can, you have a sale. If you can't you still have the option of moving to another item and selling it.

Now let's look at some statements a customer may make. Try to determine what he's probably saying (in parentheses) and then let's come up with a suggestion on what the sales person may say to overcome the objection.

1. "$550 seems like a lot of money for this." (Give me some reassurance that this is a good value or I don't have that much money with me.)

Suggestion: First find out which is the real objection with a question. "Do you mean that $550 is a lot of money today?" If the answer is "Yes," explain the options available. Down payment, balance on credit; lay away; use of credit cards, etc., and ask which method the customer wants to use.

If the answer is "No, it just seems like too much money," reassure the customer on the quality, workmanship, enjoyment she'll get, etc., and ask the customer to buy.

2. "I want to think about it." (I still have another question.)

Suggestion: Probe a little deeper with a series of questions. "Is the mounting the style you want?" "Are we in the right price range?" "Do you like that style?", etc. If the customer gives you a series of "Yes" answers, ask "Well, is there any other reason you don't like it?" Here a "No" is your clue to close the sale.

If you get a specific objection to any question, deal with it.

3. "I heard that XYZ brand is not as good as some others." (Reassure me that this is a good brand.)

Suggestion: Reassure the customer but first ask this question, "Oh? Would you mind telling me where you heard that?" Perhaps the customer knows of a specific case where someone had trouble with XYZ. If this is the case, reassure the customer that you will stand behind the item.

On the other hand, maybe the customer feels that in general XYZ is not as good as another line. If this is the case, agree. For more money you have the same type of product which is better and you would be glad to show the customer if he wants. However, reassure him that in this price range this is an excellent value.

4. "I'm not sure this is worth $1200." (Reassure me that the value is here **and** that I can be sure your pieces are fair.)

Suggestion: Point out the advantages of doing business with you, your reputation, reliability and fairness in pricing. Then reassure your customer that the item is, in fact, priced fairly and ask for the sale.

5. "I saw the same item advertised for 20% less." (Smoke screen. Will you give me something off if I buy?)

Suggestion: If this is valid, you ask yourself, "Why is she here?" You can be a little aggressive here. "Oh. I missed that ad. Could you tell me who it is? I'm always interested in what my competitors are doing." If the customer names a store, you now know what you are up against. Point out differences in quality, advantage of your store and ask the customer to buy.

If the customer can't remember or the ad is for a store 100 miles away, you don't have to worry about this particular objection. Again you can point out the advantages of doing business with you and try to close the sale.

6. "I'll bring my wife in. After all, she has to wear it." (I need reassurance that she will like it and if she doesn't that she can exchange it.)

Suggestion: Emphasize that of course she'll like it and if she doesn't she can certainly exchange it.

7. "I didn't want to spend this much." (This may be valid or may be asking for reassurance on the value.)

Suggestion: Try once again to convince the customer that this is an excellent value, emphasizing the beauty, enjoyment, etc. Ask for the order. If the customer still says, "No," you can now ask him how much he wanted to spend and go from there to another item.

8. "It's not really what I had in mind." (I have another question.)

Suggestion: Ask a series of questions trying to find out what she doesn't like about the item. Once you get a specific objection, deal with it. If there is no specific objection, ask her, "Is there any other reason you can't take it today?"

9. "This is the first store we've been in. We want to look around." (We're stalling. Convince us we should buy from you.)

Suggestion: First get their agreement that they do want the item and put the question to them that what they really want to do is assure themselves of the best value for their money. The sale now hinges on whether or not they'll buy from you or someone else. Again shift to the advantages of dealing with you. If you can't convince them of this, your next step is to make sure they'll return before deciding.

Depending on store policy, there are several things you can do to insure they will return or (in the first option), buy now. Here they are in a decreasing order of effectiveness.

A. "I agree that you should compare us with other stores. The best way to do that is to have this with you. Why don't you take this with you, pay for it, and if you find something you like better, bring it back in 48 hours and we'll refund your money." (Stores that do this find that 98% of the people who agree keep the item. Of the 2% that come back, at least half wind up buying from you.)

B. "I know you want to look around. I want to be sure this will be here when you come back so I'll hold it for you. However, I will need a small deposit—refundable of course if you find something else. Is that agreeable with you?" (They'll at least return to get their deposit.)

C. "Of course you want to shop around. I can hold this for you if you'll promise to let me know what your decision is when you come back." (A moral obligation to return is not too strong but it is better than nothing.)

D. "Here's my card. Please ask for me when you come back." (No obligation on their part. You just hope for the best.)

10. "I can't afford it." (Probably valid. I'm not convinced this is worth the price to me.)

Suggestion: There's a classic approach to this used by many good sales people. "I know it seem like a lot of money right now. Tell me, if you could afford it, would you take it today?" A "No" answer leads you into some other objections that you'll have to deal with although the primary objection is still "I can't afford it." a "Yes" answer closes the sale if you can work out the details on how he's going to pay for it. You still have the option to go to a lower price range.

Certainly there are more objections a customer can raise than the ten we've covered here. We would suggest that you have your people make a list of all the objections they hear for a one or two week period. You'll find the same ones coming up again and again. Isolate those that are most common and make sure everyone in the store can deal with them. Once you've done that, you should see your sales start to increase.

Some general rules on handling objections.

1. Never argue. You'll probably win the argument but lose the sale.

2. Deal with specifics. General or vague objections are tough to deal with.

3. Reassure the customer. Most of the time that's what the customer wants.

4. Deal with the objection and ask the customer to buy.

Remember there's no reason for a customer to object unless he's thinking of buying. If you've removed the obstacle, the customer should be ready to buy.

Answers to JCK Management Study Center Quiz:
(Questions can be found on page 266)

PUTTING YOUR MESSAGE INTO THE MARKETPLACE

This report prepared by the *JCK* staff appeared in the July 1994 issue. The quiz answers:

1. c	8. c
2. b	9. a
3. c	10. b
4. c	11. d
5. b	12. a
6. c	13. d
7. d	

Question #5 which asked about the best time to commit the majority of your ad dollars, posed the problem here. Most people answered c ("Spending should be consistent throughout the year, maybe skipping the last two months.") While spending all the money in the last two months, as some jewelers do, is a bad idea, skipping November and December entirely is not a good alternative. The best answer of those given says spending should be concentrated on five or six major "events" during the year.

Chapter 8

MARKETING

Understanding Demographics And Niches Spells Success In The Marketplace

Birth Of An Era

Editorial ◆ *May 1995*

What forces are going to shape the jewelry business over the next few years? Who will be the major players? Who will win? Who will lose?

For the past six months, JCK's editors have been seeking answers to questions like these. The results of their research are described in a special report in this issue. In some ways, the findings are not too startling. The report says publicly what many in the industry have said privately for some time. But if you stop and think about the findings for a while, you realize the report is really a statement that we're passing through some watershed years.

The industry truly will be very different by the turn of the century.

If our forecast—really a forecast by more than a score of industry leaders and specialists—is right, traditional jewelers will lose about $2 billion in sales to other retailers of jewelry. The principal gainers will be mass merchants who sell at rock-bottom prices and those who sell jewelry via TV home-shopping programs and computer networks.

The prime losers will be traditional jewelers who offer no special reason—in merchandise, price or service—for consumers to shop with them.

In a way, this is a generational issue. Much of the strength of the "modern" jewelry industry dates from the late 1940s and early 1950s, when thousands of World War II veterans took advantage of the GI Bill to get a start in this industry. Most of them chose retailing.

But now, nearly half a century later, many of the stores these veterans—primarily men—started have gone out of business or soon will. Many owners have no successors. Too few are ready or able to operate successfully in today's more competitive and sophisticated market.

One thing our report reveals clearly is that the human element will continue to set winners apart from losers. Our business world may seem dominated by computer experts, financial analysts and cold-hearted bean counters, but knowledge about people and markets, along with sheer personality, still are what make the real winners.

GIA's Bill Boyajian puts it succinctly: "The segment of the industry that will lose ground can be classed less by category than by those who do not educate their people versus those who do." Further, when we asked our group of leaders to identify the most critical issue facing retailers of jewelry in the next few years, overwhelmingly they picked finding and training good employees.

The downside of our report—loss of market share, the demise of many small and middle-of-the-road jewelers—is harsh. But it's also a fairly realistic look at the real world.

This is not a putdown of the traditional jeweler—far from it. The outlook is outstanding for the truly fine jeweler who specializes in unusual merchandise, offers excellent service and is a skilled businessperson. You might say we are seeing a return to the jeweler's real roots, to an era when craftsmanship is the premium setting winners apart.

The explosive growth of and interest in so-called designer jewelry is part of this trend. Look back just 15 or 20 years and think what an innovation it was to have a handful of high-design jewelry makers at the New York JA show. Next month at The JCK Show in Las Vegas, The Design Center will have about 140 exhibitors. This end of the jewelry business is thriving.

So is in-store custom design. Almost every leading independent jewelry retailer in the country now makes a substantial amount of its own merchandise. This is not just a desire to be more competitive; it is a celebration of the jeweler's craft.

These jewelers will own a goodly share of the market. So will a number of the high-volume outlets, whether stores, TV networks or computer networks. It's common for some jewelers to sneer at such competition, pointing to shortcomings in quality or deception in pricing and marketing. That's stupid. Sure, some high-volume merchandisers cut a few quality and ethical corners (as do some jewelers), but they also know how to run a business and how to court customers.

It's a waste of time for the small independent jeweler to berate mass merchandisers; they couldn't care less. The independent should try to see what business savvy can be learned by watching how the majors run their day-to-day operations.

We are at the end of an era. It was good and it lasted for 40 years or so. Now we're entering another era. I'm optimistic it can be a time of high hope, performance and profit for the traditional jeweler. The opportunity is there to be grasped; those who do not grasp it probably will fail.

Where Will Consumers
Buy Their Jewelry In 1999?

May 1995

In this final decade of the 20th century, jewelry retailing in the U.S. is undergoing more change than it did in the preceding 90 years. Merchants who were marginal sellers of jewelry just a few years ago—or who didn't even exist—now crowd the market. Pressure to capture the consumer's patronage and dollars is intense.

It's likely to become even more so. Giant retailers such as Wal-Mart, Service Merchandise and J.C. Penney have catapulted themselves into major players and are ambitious to grab an even bigger share of a relatively slow-growing market. TV shopping, at least in the eyes of those who control it, is still in its adolescence. And the potential of computer on-line shopping, extolled by many as the true future of retailing, is just in its infancy. Even jewelry suppliers are getting into the act as more open their own retail outlets or consider doing so.

Where does all this activity leave the traditional jeweler?

There is no definitive answer. But after a six-month study of the market, involving well over 100 personal or telephone interviews and a written poll of the 500+ members of the JCK Retail Jewelers Panel, it's possible to draw a pretty clear outline.

The traditional jeweler, who owned 60% of the total jewelry market as recently as 1982, saw that share drop to 48% by last year, according to estimates by some key industry leaders. They further predict the figure will shrink to 42% by 1999. Since one percentage point of market share represents between $325 million and $350 million, the dollar stakes are very high.

Our study makes possible some educated guesses of where, in addition to jewelry stores, consumers are likely to shop as we enter the 21st century.

Jewelry retailing will be split conclusively. At one extreme, the market will belong to the jeweler who offers unusual, appealing, high-quality products, superb service, a skilled and attentive staff and an attractive shopping atmosphere. The other end will belong to the merchant who offers convenience and attractive, middle-of-the-road merchandise in an unthreatening location at very competitive prices. Quality will not be of prime importance in this market; perceived value will be.

The retailer who fits neither profile is going to be in trouble; hardest hit will be the independent store run by an individual whose love of jewelry far exceeds his or her business savvy. In this list, count many typical Main Street and Mom and Pop jewelers. Those who die, says Dr. George Lucas, professor of retailing at the University of Memphis, will "lack sufficient capital to invest in sophisti-

cated inventory control and management systems required to run businesses efficiently." Those who try to compete on price are equally at risk, he says. The big merchants can outgun them on any deal.

Price is a critical issue in how the industry is reshaping. Indeed, it's the basic marketing tool for high-volume operators. "Today, if you don't have the right price, you're not in the game," says J. Richard Blickstead, president of Wal-Mart's jewelry division and former chief operating officer of the Peoples Jewellers chain in Canada. It may be put less bluntly at the high end of the market; the customer willing to spend $30,000 or $40,000 for a particular piece of jewelry won't haggle over minor shifts in dollars and cents. But the high-end jeweler more than ever stresses value. The mantra-like message: the item may cost a lot but it's worth it.

Equaling price in importance to the jewelry customer are convenience, quality and service, according to the select group of industry leaders questioned at length for this report. The problem is that except in the rarest of cases, the four elements have a built-in contradiction. The store that offers rock-bottom prices can't afford the best in quality and service. The store that stresses convenience—promoting speedy shopping, 10:00 a.m. to 10:00 p.m. hours daily and so on—to some extent is unlikely to put a premium on service.

The reality is that today's jewelry retailers must choose. Some—mainly the mass merchants—pick price and convenience. Others—mostly guild jewelers—pick quality and service. These are not exclusionary choices, of course. The mass merchants give at least lip service to good service and improved quality, and often try to achieve the best quality price will allow. Some high-end stores try to be more competitive on price and more accommodating on convenience. But in practice, we come back to the high-low split. It's not possible, and often not desirable, to try to be all things to all people.

More pressure: The competitive pressures facing traditional jewelers from mass merchants, TV home shopping and an exploding home-delivered catalog business are heightened by another key factor: the nation has become "seriously overstored and overmalled," in the words of Michael D. Roman, chairman of Jewelers of America. The figures certainly bear him out.

The number of retail stores of all types has grown 28% since 1980, outstripping U.S. population growth by a ratio of almost 2-to-1; that ratio is even higher for jewelry stores. In the same period, the number of shopping malls has grown from about 22,000 to almost 40,000. Put another way, there was one retail store for every 186 people in 1980 compared with one store for every 167 people today.

This store-to-customer ratio makes holding existing customers a daily challenge and attracting new ones even harder. This is especially true for traditional jewelers because they're in an industry bedeviled by sluggish sales. In raw numbers, jewelry store sales just about doubled between 1980 and 1994, reaching $16.6 billion last year. But discounting inflation, the growth for that 14-year period totals only 24%—less than 2% a year in constant dollars.

It's tough to make money in such an economic climate. JA's Michael Roman points out that a typical jewelry store's pretax net profit was a lowly 6.5% of sales in 1993, the latest year for which figures are available. The figure for the highest profit companies was 11.5%.

Comments the University of Memphis's George Lucas: "There are too many people selling jewelry and other products in the U.S. That will keep margins down and force retailers to look for more efficient ways to buy. This situation will continue for some time and probably get worse."

ASSESSING THE PLAYERS: INDEPENDENT JEWELERS

The small independent jeweler, the much-dissected Mom and Pop store, clearly is the most vulnerable member in the overall jewelry community. Four of every five industry leaders questioned for this report expect these stores' share of market to decline, often drastically, over the next few years. More than half the independent jewelers on JCK's panel agree.

The reasons are simple enough. These stores often lack good management and sales skills, have no real handle on their inventory and can't afford the marketing efforts that could build sales. "Most of these jewelers don't have a game plan," says Stanley Marcus, former owner of a successful group of jewelry stores in New Jersey and now a consultant to the industry. "They tell their banker, 'If we have a good Christmas, everything will be OK.' That's not good enough. They have to have a plan."

Additionally, such stores often face succession problems. As their name implies, they are family businesses, but they're rarely successful enough to support more than Mom and Pop. And when the time comes to take over, children often are reluctant because they see a demanding job that promises few rewards. The stores that do survive will be specialists (concentrating perhaps on repairs), serve a market bypassed by the competition or do business with loyal customers who feel a special bond with the owner.

The future of what might be called the middle-of-the-road jeweler is harder to predict. Defining the business itself is the first issue. The store probably handles a significant volume of repairs; does maybe a third of its business in diamond jewelry with a stress on engagement rings, tennis bracelets retailing for $400-$700 and inexpensive multistone pieces; carries basic karat gold jewelry; and stays with the tried-and-true in colored stone jewelry. The store probably carries few watches, perhaps a few popular brands that retail between about $100 and $300. Location? It's probably in the shopping district of a small town or a suburban strip shopping center. The cost of doing business keeps most of them out of malls.

One of the more supportive voices for this group comes from Michael Frieze, chief executive of Boston-based Gordon Brothers and a specialist in dealing with troubled retailers. "I've a strong feeling that if the customer is interested in buying a nice product with some design," he says, "then the independent

jeweler will be a major player." The middle-of-the-road jeweler is equipped to meet such needs. But the store must be able to offer more than a nice product. The price has to be realistic—not carry what Stanley Marcus calls "an insane" 3.5- or 4-time markup—and the staff has to be equipped to sell the product.

George Lucas of the University of Memphis tells a revealing story about shopping for a piece of jewelry for his wife's Christmas present. "The salesperson in a nice jewelry store repeatedly showed us items my wife didn't care for," he recalls. "They were so similar and the salesperson obviously didn't listen to us. I decided if I'm going to be jerked around by know-nothing salespeople, I might as well go to a discount place and save money in the process. They [the discount store] had everything displayed. We just picked up what we wanted and told the salesperson."

Price and salesmanship. A good jeweler can work with price objections, but untrained salespeople can kill the business. Comments William E. Boyajian, president of the Gemological Institute of America, "The segment of the industry that will lose ground can be classed less by category than by those who educate their people versus those who do not."

High hope at the high end: Just as much as the small Mom and Pop jeweler seems on most people's lists as a sure loser, the smart, imaginative independent with exciting and varied inventory is regarded as a sure winner.

One reason is that the polarization of the jewelry market into relatively vibrant high and low ends with an uncertain and financially strained middle reflects a similar pattern in U.S. family life. The economic upheavals of the past few years have split the population into a nation of have's and have not's. The strong upmarket independent retailer will do well in the next years catering to the have's, says Andy Johnson of the Diamond Cellar in Columbus, Ohio, one of the most successful independent jewelers in the country. He identifies the have's as "those who have developed investment income or are professionals with good income."

The upmarket independent jeweler builds business with service and cultivation of customer relationships. "An independent store gives clients individual attention," says Joseph A. Rosi Jr. of Joseph A. Rosi Jewelers, a 45-year-old family business in Harrisburg, Pa. "It has salespeople who know and work with clients. It creates customer confidence through after-sale service."

The right merchandise also is vital. Some stores specialize in the unusual—in colored diamonds or elegant, expensive watches or jewelry created by a big-name designer. Many create their own jewelry, designing pieces to match the taste and budget of an individual customer. At Underwood's Jewelers in Fayetteville, Ark., the leading store in its region, the owners estimate their custom-made jewelry accounts for about half of a substantial annual dollar volume.

Not only do better stores carry what their lower-priced competition does not, they also make a point of *not* carrying what the competition does. "I see the high-end independent vacating the lower-end goods," says Harvey B. Brown, a former jewelry manufacturer who now is director of merchandising for ViaTV Network, a TV home shopping concern that also offers specialty programs.

Certainly the jeweler who works at the high end has little trouble competing with those who operate at the other end of the scale. Stanley Kahn, a jeweler in Pine Bluff, Ark., is a good example. Pine Bluff has two Wal-Marts, one perched at each end of town, and most businesses between them have closed. Not Kahn. "We compete against the Wal-Marts by not paying attention to them," he says. "We sell completely different products; we're known for high-quality and higher-priced pieces. People here know us and trust us as they have for many years."

But independent jewelers—high, middle and low—face competition from more than just the likes of Wal-Mart.

ASSESSING THE PLAYERS: THE JEWELRY CHAINS

Next to their own kind, independent jewelers view jewelry chains as their next most important competition. This study raises questions about just how important a role these chains will play as the century nears its end.

There's no doubt many of them have gone through gut-wrenching trauma since the mid- to late-1980s. Zale, Barry's, Merksamer, Glennpeter—all in and out of bankruptcy reorganization. Sterling acquired by Ratner (now Signet), itself a troubled British company. Kay absorbed by Sterling. These have not been easy times.

Those who've been tested by bankruptcy say the experience strengthened them. They say they're leaner, more focused and more knowledgeable about their markets and the merchandise they need to meet those markets' needs. They're optimistic about their futures.

Their optimism is shared sparingly by the industry leaders and jewelers whose input shaped this report. While the industry group forecasts growing share of market for jewelry chains at all levels—local, regional and national, with the regionals enjoying the best potential—independent jewelers are much more skeptical. They see the local and regional chains growing slightly while the nationals' market share declines.

"We're seeing a more sophisticated [jewelry] customer and I'm not sure the chains know that," says Blaine Orr, assistant manager of Pilcher Jewelry Co. in Mexico, Mo., a family-owned business with two stores that was founded in 1868. "This is a customer who takes more time to learn about a product, who is more mobile, who goes from store to store. The problem for the chains is that they usually have people behind the counter who are just warm bodies filling space, without much [product or sales] knowledge."

Orr hits the target in the center when he draws attention to staffing problems. Those taking part in this study indicate hiring and training a good sales staff comprise the single most critical operating issue they face. "It is absolutely essential to be able to recruit and train good salespeople," says John Belknap, former chief financial officer for Zale Corp. and now a strategic planner for the company. "It is the single most important ingredient in store management." Belknap concedes that building a good staff is more difficult for a chain than for a local jeweler with an owner-manager who can act as a day-to-day mentor. "A large chain will have lots of [training] resources and sophisticated programs not available to local jewelers," Belknap adds, "but those really aren't a substitute for a good mentor. When you have stores all over the country it's difficult to do that."

JA's Michael Roman estimates the annual turnover for salespeople at chain stores is 20% and can run as high as 50%.

Jewelry chains face other problems. Most of their stores are in malls and, with few new malls under construction or being planned, they face a dearth of new markets. Moreover,

escalating mall costs mean some chains "can't afford the real estate any more," says Willis R. Cowlishaw, former chief executive of the Zale Fine Jewelers Guild and a consultant to the industry for the past decade. "As a result, you're going to see more downsizing of the big chains."

You also may see fewer chain stores in malls because landlords don't like them as much as they used to, Cowlishaw adds. "Jewelers are not as productive as they could be. The landlords don't want to cut the jewelry pie any more than it's cut now." A factor in these stores' declining appeal is the sameness of the merchandise they offer—merchandise that often barely exceeds the quality of jewelry offered by discounters but certainly costs more.

The big chains have closed more than 500 stores since their financial troubles hit in the late 1980s. According to some observers, the blood-letting is not finished.

While the outlook for large chains may be questionable, that appears less true for small (up to 10 units) and regional (usually fewer than 100 units) chains. The regionals are particular favorites of our leadership group, with almost three in four forecasting growing market share. A very clear vote of confidence for the regionals came in mid-March when Berkshire Hathaway, the investment firm run by the legendary Warren Buffett, acquired Helzberg Diamond Shops. Helzberg, one of the bigger regionals with 148 stores, is widely regarded as one of the best-managed companies in its class. In the under-100 store category, that title is readily awarded to the Seattle-based Ben Bridge chain.

Interestingly, Helzberg was one of the first chains to experiment with a larger-than-normal store to cater to changing customer needs. The idea is catching on in the industry. Sterling now has four Jared superstores and an ultimate goal of 100, though that target is some years off. Lorch Diamond Centers with 56 stores and 22 leased departments has opened its first Goodwin's Jewelry Superstore in its headquarters city of Birmingham, Ala.

"The biggest change [in retailing] is the superstore—whether it be in jewelry, electronics, books or office supplies," says Robert Keller, president of Lorch. "It is simply a response to the changing retail environment. The reason for [their creation] is that we're all working harder to give customers a reason to leave home and come out and shop."

ASSESSING THE PLAYERS:
MASS MERCHANT DISCOUNTERS

These juggernauts offer the most immediate threat to the traditional jeweler, especially the small-town jeweler who lacks distinctive merchandise and remains wedded to a minimum keystone markup. But when megaretailers offer diamond engagement rings at $1,299 and a reasonable selection of ruby, emerald and sapphire jewelry for around $450 along with basic 14k pieces—as does Wal-Mart, for example—you're looking at real competition for sizable numbers of jewelers, both independents and chains. The ambiance at Wal-Mart may not be romantic, but the prices are very competitive for the qualities shown.

Among the biggest players in the field are such discounters as Wal-Mart, Kmart, Target, Service Merchandise, Venture and such lower-end department stores as Sears Roebuck and Montgomery Ward. All make a point of stressing bargain prices, though they prefer to talk in terms of value rather than price.

They share a common obsession with margins—by product category, by line and by item. They monitor sales scrupulously, always seeking the hot item that will take off, in their own stores or in a competitor's. Return on investment is a constant concern.

Many of them also share a concern that while the size of their jewelry operations makes them very big fish in the jewelry industry, they are pretty small fish in their own companies, which sell a multitude of different products. Because buying, stocking, selling and marketing are so different for jewelry than for shoes, toasters or T-shirts, the people running the jewelry operations in such massive companies worry that management doesn't understand or appreciate them. Gordon Brothers' Michael Frieze, for one, questions the management commitment. "There's great potential there," he says. "But will the companies commit the resources? Will they live with the slow turns, the big inventories, the need to have better-paid staffs?"

The answers to these questions will have a huge impact on how big a force mass merchants continue to be in the jewelry market. They'll also have a huge impact on the traditional jewelers who compete with them.

The quality question: Meantime, many of these companies say they want to upgrade the quality of the jewelry they offer—though it still seems price usually wins in any battle with quality. It's an open question how the customer feels. Frieze says the lure of the price-off notice remains very strong. "Consumers understand that markups are phony, but they still shop when the item is 50% off and they don't when it isn't." Many agree with him.

But there's also a growing feeling in the retail trade that significant numbers of consumers have had it with tissue paper gold that lacks any substance and diamonds that look, in an unpleasant but accurate description, like frozen spit. A veteran marketer of Far Eastern goods to the U.S. market says that "customers are tired of the Bangkok and Chinese crap. They're becoming more quality-conscious and, hopefully, they'll be willing to pay more."

One important question: "Will existing market forces allow the huge retailers to upgrade?" The way they buy suggests they may not.

A number of Asian jewelry manufacturers say they turn out the quality of goods they do because U.S. buyers demand products that can be sold at a low price point. The supplier who's producing a diamond pendant to retail at $29.95 or a ruby ring to retail at $69.95 or a 1-ct. total-weight tennis bracelet to retail at $149.95 can't pay much attention to quality. What's more, it's common for major retail buyers to demand even lower prices once they have a manufacturer committed as a prime supplier. Because of such practices the retailer may be able to pare the margin on such items to 10%-20%—certainly lower than the big discounters' usual low margins—but the products will indeed be junk.

"The manufacturers hate being ground down by the big retailers," says G. Peyton Kelley, an executive with the Bangkok-based jewelry manufacturer Bijoux d'Amour, which prides itself on the quality of its goods. Because the U.S. business is important, many Asian producers are willing to go with the flow. But at least some of the more quality-minded manufacturers are either pulling out of the U.S. market (concentrating instead on Japan and Europe) or considering ways to reach the U.S. consumer directly. Direct selling catalogs are one option.

In any debate on mass merchant jewelry prices you must keep one salient fact in mind. By the very nature of their operations, they can and often do offer genuine low prices. A look at Wal-Mart, the biggest of them, shows how.

Wal-Mart lives by a basic formula: low overhead permits low margins, low margins permit low prices, low prices permit good value. It all starts with a Spartan way of business life that rejects any frills and applies to everyone from the cleaners to the chief executive officer. "Our team works hard to keep down costs, which we believe gives us a competitive edge," says Rick Blickstead, president of the jewelry division. "We have a low expense structure. All the money we save goes into the stores."

The low expense structure means, among other things, that "there are no company cars, no auto expenses and when we travel we stay at the Red Roof Inn and sleep two to a room," he says. That's pretty hard living for a division head whose operation sold more than $1 billion worth of jewelry and watches last year. Between a half and two-thirds of that falls in the fine jewelry category—diamonds, other gemstones, karat gold jewelry and watches. Fashion jewelry accounts for the rest.

"We're working very hard to increase quality," says Blickstead, "and we've just hired a manager of quality control. Quality for quality, we're as good as anyone else." He says his buyers are merchandising better quality diamonds, though the company still must carry a promotional line. The Wal-Mart superstore near company headquarters in Bentonville, Ark., has a number of cases with colored stone and diamond jewelry (diamond rings in "good," "better," and "best" qualities range in size from fifths to thirds and in price from $199 for a "good" fifth to $599 for a "best" third).

A diamond engagement ring marked at $1,299 comes with a valuation appraisal of $2,550 from the International Gemological Information division of the International Gemological Institute in New York City. "That's what they say it's really worth," a saleswoman explains.

Return to sender: The emergence of mass-market retailers—whether in stores or by way of television—has created a relatively new jewelry-industry phenomenon: merchandise that comes back to the supplier.

This occurs in three main situations. The buyer may have an agreement with the seller that merchandise that doesn't sell will be returned, for credit or for alternate merchandise. This is a so-called "guaranteed sales" agreement.

Second, the buyer may return merchandise without any agreement. He says, in effect, "I don't want these goods. They aren't selling. If you want to continue to do business with me, you'll eat them."

Third, the buyer may simply have taken the merchandise on consignment. What sells is paid for, sometimes after a long delay; what doesn't sell goes back.

In the past few years, unsold merchandise—much of it promotional-type goods—has been going back to suppliers by the ton. Neither individual retailers nor the TV sellers will disclose figures on returns, but informed industry guesses say they run from a low of 10%-20% to a high of 50%. One cynic describes a scenario that runs something like this:

A home shopping channel sends back 2,000 items. These are refurbished and sold at a suitable price to a mass merchant which, in time, returns 1,000. After another refurbishing, the goods are sold to a warehouse club which, in time, returns 500. These are sold to a liquidator at rock-bottom prices. The liquidator either scraps them or sells them to a retail jeweler looking for a real bargain.

Retailers who do return goods aren't particularly happy about it; they'd rather sell them. And they're not ready to be branded as the bad guys. They argue that a number of suppliers have only themselves to blame because they force-fed the goods to the retailer in the first place. Says one: "When times were good, they didn't mind a 20% return because they were selling so much. But when orders were cut in half and they got the same returns, they couldn't handle it."

Wherever the blame lies, the supplier is the real sufferer. In fact, some suppliers have been so overwhelmed by the return of goods they counted as sold that they've been forced out of business. Others are just hurting. At least one major U.S. manufacturer now has 60 staff members whose sole function is to rehab returned merchandise. This is not a situation with winners.

ASSESSING THE PLAYERS: THE DIRECT SELLERS

Bypassing the usual distribution channels and selling directly to the consumer is one of the hottest of all retailing issues today. Most obvious here is the TV shopping channel that goes right into the consumer's home; this already is a huge market. The two top players, QVC Network and Home Shopping Network, between them sell about $1 billion worth of jewelry merchandise a year.

Jewelry sales through catalogs are booming; they account for another $1 billion or so yearly. And, although almost impossible to pin down, there's a growing business in manufacturers who sell direct to the public, either through their own retail outlets or through private office transactions.

Finally, a whole new era of direct selling by way of computer is just beginning.

Just about everyone polled for this report expects TV home shopping's market share to grow over the next few years. The industry group asked to estimate current and future market share for various jewelry sellers is most optimistic about TV's growth opportunities. The group estimates TV sellers accounted for 4% of the total jewelry market in 1994 and should account for 7.5% by 1999.

In the midst of all this euphoria over shopping via TV are some non-believers. They say the early excitement of home shopping programs is wearing off and that TV channels will never be able to break the $200-$400 price barrier consistently. They also say major suppliers to TV channels are tired of having to eat the high number of returns. One supplier complains that certain stations, which he won't identify, have asked to have planned shipments delayed by three to four months. Looking to the longer term, critics wonder whether computers will replace TV screens as the primary home seller.

Some evidence supports such caution. Late last year, for example, Fingerhut canceled a much-ballyhooed plan for a 24-hour TV shopping channel after escalating costs chilled financing plans. The Home Shopping Network early this year reported disappointing results for its final 1994 quarter, ended Dec. 31. Sales of $301 million were up a meager 1.6% from the 1993 period, while operating net was down significantly. At QVC, while final net of $67 million for the year ended Jan. 31 was up 12% from the year before, the company lost more

than $37 million on new ventures that did not take off as well as expected. Total revenues were up 14% to $1.4 billion.

TV lacks the personal attention that many service-conscious shoppers like. Some also feel there's a real or implied stigma in being a TV shopper. But any new medium that can go from zip to more than $1 billion in sales within just five years is a major player.

ViaTV Network's Harvey Brown ticks off a list of pluses. TV offers more product than a typical store, he says. It searches out and experiments with new products—often being a leader that jewelers follow. It allows the customer to make choices without any pressure. It provides a huge audience. And it offers security (more and more shoppers are fearful of crime, especially after dark).

One of the biggest pluses, says Brown, is that those who present jewelry on TV are far more qualified than most jewelry store salespeople to inform and educate the customer about it. Jeff Taraschi, senior vice president of jewelry merchandising at QVC, hammers home this point. "TV's great strength is its ability to convey information about the product," he says. "The single biggest deficiency in retailing is the unwillingness to pay for good help. The average jeweler doesn't make the commitment to consumers to make them shop with him exclusively."

Taraschi dismisses the idea of a price barrier that TV shoppers are unwilling to cross. "I truly think price will become less important," he says. "We have not found any price resistance." He won't set any upper limit, but says he can see no problem selling a piece of jewelry priced at $3,500 provided it offers good value.

The QVC executive also dismisses jeweler complaints about the quality of merchandise offered on the network. He concedes there have been some problems in the past, particularly with herringbone chain priced in the $49-$59 range. But he says QVC today is a stickler for quality—a boast that suppliers to QVC sustain. Taraschi also says he's sure consumers will be willing to pay higher prices to get higher quality.

Meet your maker: One of the most surprising findings in this JCK study was the pervasive belief that we'll see more manufacturers selling directly to consumers and more of them opening their own retail outlets. At the same time, of course, more and more retailers are making their own jewelry. How far this blurring of the lines between maker and seller will go is unclear. But it seems unlikely it will reach the proportions it has in Asia, where the distinction between manufacturer and retailer is almost academic.

Members of the special group questioned for this report believe—by a margin of more than 2-to-1—there will be more vertical integration, with major companies controlling a product all the way from production to the final sale to the consumer.

QVC's Jeff Taraschi is one who sees more suppliers opening their own retail businesses. "It will come with [consumer] disillusionment with retailers and how they train their staffs," he predicts. Some others see it happening because of *supplier* disillusionment with retailers who don't pay their bills. During the great jewelry-retailer bankruptcy shakeout at the end of the 1980s, many failing companies stiffed their suppliers for a lot of dollars.

Getting a handle on just who does such selling—other than some well-known jewelry designers who do it openly and successfully—is next to impossible. One major bank with a large jewelry industry business says 20%-30% of its customers have some sort of direct-sales outlet. But the bank was unable to persuade any of these companies to talk with JCK for this report—even when they were promised anonymity. Mostly, manufacturers see these outlets as a cheap way to get rid of returns or pieces that didn't get past quality control.

Consultant Willis Cowlishaw says he's had more calls in the past two years than in the previous five from manufacturers who've asked him to find a retail store they can buy. But total calls number only 15-18 a year, and very few follow through when they learn the full costs of operating a retail outlet, including inventory, staffing, rental costs and so on. Cowlishaw dismisses the majority of the inquiries as "mostly talk. These are people who've been hurt and they're looking at their options." Gordon Brothers' Michael Frieze also has heard about suppliers who are considering going retail but he adds, "It's a lot of talk, little action."

Some of the most direct action in this area took place in the fall of 1993, when a group of manufacturers opened a jewelry outlet mall called the Direct Gold and Silver Outlet in Attleboro, Mass. The prime goal of the organizing manufacturers was to raise money for a local hospital and a downtown business association through the sale of discontinued lines. Jewelers in the area were upset, however, when the outlet ran ads with the headline "Prepare to meet your maker; we've got prices to die for."

The outlet closed this January because of lease problems and not because of slow business, as some jewelers thought, says Bob Schriever of Najarda Pearl, one of the participating companies. "It was a great place to sell returned items," he says. "Before this outlet, we had no good way to sell off merchandise that wasn't selling." Schriever also used the outlet to testmarket new lines.

Plans originally called for the outlet to reopen at a new location in February. The opening was postponed and, as of late March, no new date was scheduled.

Some companies involved in the Attleboro outlet were shy about publicity. That's certainly not the case with jewelry designers who have their own retail outlets—among them John Atencio with six designer boutiques in Colorado, Etienne Perret with a store in Maine, Diana Vincent with one in Pennsylvania and, most recently, Steve Lagos, also with one in Pennsylvania. Some jewelers who carry designer lines worry they'll face direct and unfair competition from "the manufacturer." However, studies in the apparel and shoe industries, both flooded with outlet stores, show the opening of a brand-name outlet actually *increases* business at nonoutlet stores carrying the same lines, thanks largely to the added exposure and prestige.

Perhaps jewelers should have greater concern about high-end catalogs, many of which carry jewelry—including some very expensive pieces. Bill Dean, a catalog industry consultant in San Francisco, was quoted in *The New York Times* in March as saying, "Catalogs are now too common a way for too many high-income people to shop to consider it a low-end business."

The *Times* article was about the revitalized Gump's store in San Francisco and its stepped-up catalog sales, which this year should surpass the store's expected volume of $21 million and are projected to reach $75 million to $100 million within five years. The company with a controlling interest in Gump's also controls, through other connections, such luxury goods makers as Sulka, Dunhill, Cartier, Mont Blanc, Baume

& Mercier and Piaget. Dean indicates these connections raise the interesting prospect of yet more high-end catalogs.

When do shoppers go on line? Despite all sorts of hype among the lap-top set, shopping by computer will be more curiosity than reality for the foreseeable future. This doesn't mean computers won't bring buyers and sellers together, by e-mail or telephone, to conclude business deals. That already happens in the jewelry world on the RapNet and Polygon networks. But reaching out to consumers in their homes is another issue.

There are three principal reasons why. First, not enough consumers have the necessary equipment. Second, a lot of bugs still must be worked out. Third, security is a concern; few consumers will flash their credit card numbers on the Internet or any other computer network that can't guarantee privacy.

"Computer on-line probably will be a major force in retailing some day, but it won't be as soon as many predict," says Walter Ife, director of operations for the Diamond Promotion Service. "Right now there's a huge learning curve and acceptance to deal with. But when it gets here, it will be really big. Many kids today grow up with computers as first nature, not second nature. They'll be used to computers, and they'll do a lot of shopping that way. This could transform retailing in 30 years."

ASSESSING THE PLAYERS: THE REST OF THE TEAM

There are other competitors, of course. Department stores. Pawnshops. Military PXs. Among them, department stores have the largest share of the jewelry market, an estimated 8% last year. Those polled and interviewed for this study expect that share to hold even or shrink a bit. Walter Ife, for one, sees it going down "because the medium to higher end of the market will be concentrated in more traditional jewelry stores, largely because of the trust and service they stand for. Also, department stores are less committed to jewelry as a business. Departments that don't yield the right returns can be given over to others that will, cosmetics, perfume and so on."

Pawnshops, as JCK documented last year, are making a bigger stand in the jewelry business, but they're still relatively small fry. Our panel members see only modest sales growth and little if any change in market share for pawnshops. And with military bases closing left and right, PXs are in clear decline.

A more silent form of competition could gain strength: the upstairs diamond dealer. "These are in every major city now," says consultant Cowlishaw. "In Dallas alone there must be 100. A lot of these are people who worked for Zale and retired early or were let go. They've got diamond connections; they can sell out of a briefcase." These dealers can work on paper-thin margins and still make money; many specialize in carat-plus stones. With so many cut by the big chains in the past few years, there's no shortage of these entrepreneurs. They're one more indication that this is a changing market.

AND THE FUTURE?

Jewelry retailing will remain in a state of flux right into the 21st century. There almost surely will be more contractions and consolidations, as there will be in all retailing. Last year, for example, Gordon Brothers helped to close down about 1,500 retail outlets, perhaps 10% of them jewelry stores or other retailers stocking a lot of jewelry. In all, these stores carried about $1 billion in merchandise. There will be more such closings.

There probably also will be more newcomers. And there's little doubt that by 1999, the main activity in jewelry sales will be concentrated in fine jewelry stores dealing with the high end and in high-volume sellers—whether stores or TV stations—dealing with the low end.

That leaves the middle ground. Nature, as they say, abhors a vacuum, so someone will have to serve this market or at least the portion not taken by the high end reaching down or the low end reaching up.

The jeweler is the logical one to do so. To succeed, this jeweler must meet some nonnegotiable terms. He or she must run a tight, well-managed business, be different enough from the competition in some specialty to be a desirable destination, have a truly competent and welcoming staff, know exactly what market the business wants to serve and know how to buy, mark up and sell the right merchandise for that market.

There's a rich jewelry market promised for 1999. The challenges to capture a share of it are big, exciting and more than a little scary.

Ben Janowski of Janos Consultants in New York City was an editorial adviser for this project, providing insight on market trends and helping in the preparation of a questionnaire sent to 22 individuals chosen for their experience or special knowledge of the industry. The share-of-market figures in this report are based on answers from these individuals or, where so identified, on replies from the 500-member JCK Retail Jewelers Panel. Here are the 22 people who served on the industry panel:

Ed Anderson, Princess Pride Creations, Chicago, Ill.
John Belknap, Zale Corp., Irving, Tex.
J. Richard Blickstead, Wal-Mart, Bentonville, Ark.
William E. Boyajian, Gemological Institute of America, Santa Monica, Cal.
Harvey Brown, ViaTV Network, Wynnewood, Pa.
Thomas Chatham, Chatham Created Gemstones, San Francisco, Cal.
Hans Clapper, Wright & Lato, East Orange, N.J.
David Cornstein, Finlay Fine Jewelry, New York, N.Y.
Willis R. Cowlishaw, Dallas, Tex.
Michael Frieze, Gordon Brothers, Boston, Mass.
Jonathan Goldman, Frederick Goldman Inc., New York, N.Y.
Walter Ife, Diamond Promotion Service, New York, N.Y.
Robert Keller, Lorch Diamond Shops, Birmingham, Ala.
G. Peyton Kelley, Bijoux d'Amour, Bangkok, Thailand.
William Levine, William Levine Inc., Chicago, Ill.
Nathan R. Light, formerly of Sterling Inc., Akron, Ohio.
Marvin Markman, Suberi Brothers, New York, N.Y.
Michael Paolercio, Michael Anthony Jewelers, Mount Vernon, N.Y.
Etienne Perrett, Etienne & Co., Camden, Me.
Jeff Taraschi, QVC Network, West Chester, Pa.
William Thompson, A.A. Friedman, Savannah, Ga.
Jacques Voorhees, Polygon Network, Dillon, Colo.

Boomers And Aging: Good For Retailing

May 1995

As baby boomers reach their 40s and 50s, mass merchants may suffer while specialty retailers such as jewelers benefit, according to G.A. Wright Inc., a management consulting company in Denver, Colo.

In a recent report on retail trends, President Gary A. Wright says younger consumers (ages 20-30) historically have accounted for the highest level of consumer spending while older ones (50-60) have had the lowest. And because population studies have shown the older group will grow 15% and the younger one will shrink by the same percentage from now through the year 2000, some retail analysts have predicted a contraction in retailing.

Wrong, says Wright. "Spending on merchandise won't decline" and here's why:

• Consumer spending is vital to the economy, so expect government stimuli.

• An aging population means fewer entry-level workers and more reliance on immigrants. Hence, more reason for foreigners to move to the U.S., meaning more new consumers.

• Lifestyle changes and preventive health care are keeping people healthy and working longer, increasing their spending ability.

• The oldest baby boomers will turn 50 next year and are entering their peak earning years. In addition, more women have returned to work and are climbing the corporate ladder. They have more to spend.

Another error, says Wright, is that large discount stores will become the predominant retail venue. Wright cites other studies finding that discount retailing has entered a consolidation phase, "indicating the rapid growth is over." In addition, consumer interests and needs are more diverse at age 55 than at 25, he says, so smaller, specialized retailers will have the advantage.

Taking advantage: Retailers should consider several measures to take advantage of the situation, says Wright. Among those especially relevant to independent jewelers are:

• Make customers welcome and comfortable. A consumer behavioral study by Yankelovich Partners Inc. and LAR

Management Consultants finds consumers entering a store "want to be greeted in such a way that it is clear they are welcome and then they want to be left alone. If they need help, they want it to be available, attentive and knowledgeable."

• Find out about your customers. Where do they live? What are their lifestyles? What media reaches them? Where else do they shop? What are their incomes? What merchandise and services do they like? Gathering such information isn't hard; trade magazines regularly provide articles on do-it-yourself market research.

• Create a comfortable environment to shop. For example, provide a rest area with chairs.

• Entertain the customer. "With so many shopping options, the customer is inclined to go where she is most entertained," says Wright. Fashion shows, special events, contests, creative decor, music, merchandising, refreshments, demonstrations and lighting are some of the elements that can make shopping fun.

• Build value through good, hassle-free service.

• Satisfy customer demand for information about products, pricing, location, availability and service through advertising, personal communication and point-of-purchase materials.

• Look at your store's environment. Is it designed and engineered to differentiate it from the competition?

• Use computer technology to track customers prone to return merchandise (and take them off the preferred customer mailing list).

• Use the telephone and mail for "relationship marketing"—developing personal communication with customers. "Though it appears expensive when compared with newspaper or radio costs, it reaches the customer most likely to shop with a personal and compelling message, providing a lot of bang for the buck," says Wright.

• Make merchandise easier to see and find. Two-career couples have less time to shop.

Of Men And Money

April 1995

One of the major trends in the past 20 years has been the rise of the male shopper, says *Gentlemen's Quarterly* magazine. The rising number of dual-income households has provided not only more money to shop, but also more need to split the duties of shopping.

And men's shopping trips aren't limited to necessities such as groceries and gifts for someone else. While marketers have paid much attention to the women's self-purchase market, *GQ* has found a growing men's self-purchase market. The "1995 *GQ* Jewelry and Watch Study" offers some interesting information about this market.

Among 1,000 *GQ* readers surveyed in September, for example, 41.2% of the respondents said they would buy a watch for themselves in the next 12 months. Nearly a third (31.9%) indicated they would spend more than $1,000 (17.6% plan to spend $500-$999, 49.6% plan to spend less than $500). And while jewelry industry surveys historically show that men own two or three watches, the *GQ* readers own an average of five watches.

The survey also found that many of the respondents are interested in giving watches as gifts. In fact, 85.5% said they had already done so (59.5% to a wife/partner, 28.7% to a girlfriend/ significant other and 27.1% to a parent). However, they paid less for watches given as gifts than for those for themselves.

GQ readers also seem to know that jewelry makes a great gift. Nearly all respondents (95.2%) said they have bought jewelry for someone else (74.1% for a wife/partner, 52% for a girlfriend/significant other and 40.7% for a parent). Nearly half the respondents (45.7%) spent more than $500 on a jewelry gift, and 23.7% spent more than $1,000.

Contrary to stereotypes of males being helpless at gift selection, 79.2% of these men bought watch gifts on their own, while only 20.8% consulted with the person receiving the gift. For jewelry, an equally impressive 78.9% bought the gift on their own, with 21.1% consulting with the recipient.

The best news? More than two-thirds of the respondents (67.1%) plan to buy jewelry as a gift in the next 12 months. Of those men, 24.3% plan to spend more than $1,000. Here are some other findings from the study:

• In descending order, respondents were most likely to give a jewelry or watch gift for a birthday, Christmas, anniversary, Valentine's Day, wedding, other.

• Asked where they shop for jewelry and watches, 80.3% said independent jewelry stores and 54% said department stores (exceeds 100% due to multiple answers).

• Asked where they seek information on buying jewelry and watches, 63.0% read magazine ads, 50.9% look at store displays, 44.6% ask friends and family, 43.9% read articles in magazines, 39.8% rely on salespeople and 37.4% look at catalogs.

• These men are an educated, affluent, professional group in the prime of their earning years. By age, 2.0% are 18-24, 31.8% are 25-34, 39.8% are 35-44, 23.9% are 45-54 and 2.1% are over 55. By marital status, 51.9% are married, 32.2% have never been married and 15.6% are widowed, divorced or separated. Just over 92% are employed in professional, technical, managerial, executive or sales positions. Household incomes exceed $75,000 for 68% of the respondents, range between $50,000 and $75,000 for 22.7% and are below $50,000 for the rest.

They Care Enough:
Jewelers Who Help Others

December 1993

At this time of year, we celebrate ancient festivals of light that brighten our own lives with love, hope and joy—and remind us that such light is to be shared, not hidden. In that spirit, JCK once again presents stories of jewelers big and small whose good works brighten their communities.

These works come in all sizes and shapes. Support for hometown arts, galas to raise money to fight devastating diseases, a summer-long program to revive an entire community, collecting toys or providing a start in life for needy kids—these and other projects were initiated by the retailers described on these pages.

Doing good has obvious benefits for business: it builds customer loyalty, a store's public image and employee morale. But most jewelers do good in their communities simply because it is the *right* thing to do.

A business has a responsibility "to give something back to its community," says one jeweler. "There's more to life than just getting a paycheck," adds another. "There are myriad opportunities to do good."

Of course, doing good takes commitment, planning and hard work, as these jewelers explain. So sit back for a few moments and read about jewelers who make a difference in their hometowns. Then think about spreading some light of your own.

TREASURE HUNT AROUSES A COMMUNITY

Mix compassion, pirate lore, jewelry and a strong sense of civic duty and what do you get? "The Captain Whitworth Treasure Hunt," a charity promotion spearheaded by Whitworth Jewelers, Kingston, N.Y.

Jery Whitworth, who did bench work for his wife Valerie's store, had dreamed for years of creating a grand promotion to combine business and entertainment, boost tourism and benefit a worthy cause. That would be a tall order for almost anyone except Whitworth. Those who know him say he is tenacious and a visionary.

"You don't find many people as generous and crazy as Jery and with a real commitment to the community," says Pat LaSusa, director of the Community Rehabilitation Center (CRC) near Kingston. Adds Bud Walker, retail advertising manager for the *Daily Freeman*, Kingston's newspaper, "Only Jery had the vision and commitment to make this project work, to take the leadership role and to put his own name and business on line for the community."

Whitworth contacted Walker in early 1990 with his ideas, and the store and the paper decided to sponsor a fund-raiser to benefit CRC, a 42-year-old non-profit affiliate of the United Cerebral Palsy Association. They chose CRC because it helps

thousands of men, women and children and its state and federal funding was declining. Whitworth, Walker and LaSusa formed a committee, and the Whitworths got the treasure-hunt idea going by donating jewelry valued at $10,000 retail.

"Jery got everyone involved—the city, the mayor, the council, the media, even the Marine Corps.," recalls Valerie Whitworth. "A project like this requires a lot of organization. It took $1^{1}/2$ years of planning, with meetings several times a week, sometimes with one or two per morning. But if you don't put anything into the community, you won't get anything out. The best way a business can help its community is to help those who can't help themselves."

Community effort: In all, some 200 business, government, civic and police representatives in two counties donated time, money, material, merchandise, services and ads. (No other local jeweler supported the project.)

What evolved was a 10-week summer 1991 promotion called "Captain Whitworth's $10,000 Buried Treasure Hunt." The program kicked off June 1 with Heritage Day. The event featured an armada on Rondout Creek led by the *Black Pearl* pirate ship carrying swashbuckling swordsmen and Capt. Whitworth himself, with an air attack by restored World War I planes from nearby Rhinebeck, N.Y.

Throughout the promotion, people could buy a card and key (for a $2 donation to CRC), then try their luck at opening any of many locked treasure chests holding $500 in gift certificates from participating businesses. (Whitworth, Walker and other volunteers built the chests from wooden pallets.) Cardholders also were eligible for a special treasure hunt at the promotion's end. Weekly drawings offered $175 in gift certificates.

The promotion ended with a Saturday afternoon treasure hunt in a sports stadium. Spectators cheered as 10 finalists dug through sawdust to find small treasure boxes containing three grand prizes of jewelry, three second prizes of family vacations to Disney World and runner-up prizes of vacations at local resorts.

Each week, the *Freeman* printed a tabloid supplement featuring reports on CRC, its "wish list" of equipment, the promotion and clues for the final treasure hunt. These were distributed to 28,000 households in two counties. Local TV and radio also offered extensive exposure.

Cost vs. benefits: The cost of it all is hard to pin down. Whitworth Jewelers donated $10,000 worth of jewelry and spent $5,000 on advertising. But Walker says the donations of all participants are added in. The event attracted public and regional attention and won regional and national awards, including the Hudson Valley Marketing Association Eclat

Award for Excellence, the 1991 United Cerebral Palsy New York Public Service Award and the 1992 United Cerebral Palsy Association's National Award for Commitment to Excellence.

More important than the awards, though, are some continuing benefits:

• Public awareness—as well as more than $20,000 and donations of sophisticated equipment worth thousands of dollars—for CRC. "We gained many new clients who were unaware of CRC before this campaign," says LaSusa. "We also developed a strong network of volunteers and businesses that still support our events."

(Whitworth's treasure hunt concept has been repeated—on a much smaller scale—by cerebral palsy organizations in Pennsylvania and California.)

• Goodwill for area businesses that participated in the project, says Walker, as well as a unity among the businesses and business organizations.

• More widespread recognition of Whitworth Jewelers. "We reach a much broader community today because our name was out there [in the media] every day for months," says Valerie Whitworth. The project also projected an image of a business deeply involved in its community.

(Postscript: Jery Whitworth's humanitarian impulses, his attraction to challenges and a long-standing but unfulfilled interest in medicine have led him out of the jewelry trade and back into cardiovascular medicine, which he studied years ago. He's in his first year of residency. Valerie Whitworth is now chairperson of the area's United Way, and her store is a sponsor of the CRC golf tournament, this year donating a $10,000 gold necklace as a "hole-in-one" prize.)

PARTYING WITH A PURPOSE:
STERLING FIGHTS RP & AIDS

Sterling Inc. is well-known as an innovative retailer and the second largest jeweler in the nation. It's less well-known for its active support of local and national charities, netting almost $3 million in three years.

And it all began with frozen turkeys.

For years, Sterling gave each employee at its Akron, Ohio, headquarters a turkey for the holidays. Then some employees began to ask that theirs be given to the poor instead.

Over the years, this blossomed into a variety of good works. In addition to donating turkeys (or, if the employee chooses, the monetary equivalent) to a hunger center in Akron, Sterling also works closely with the United Way and the American Heart Association and sponsors needy families at Christmas. Proceeds from an October gala celebrating Sterling's new Jared Galleria "category-killer" jewelry store in Akron, for example, went to aid children and elderly residents who might otherwise get nothing on Christmas Day.

Sterling officials and employees also collect coats for the homeless, send aid to flood victims, donate school supplies for needy children and take part in an annual Walk for Cystic Fibrosis in Akron. All employees are encouraged to get involved with their communities.

But the charity that gets much of Sterling's corporate attention is the RP Foundation, which seeks causes, cures and treatment for retinitis pigmentosa, a genetic eye disease in which the field of vision narrows progressively, often to the point of blindness. Sterling's management and employees have

a special interest in the disease: the firm's chairman, Nathan R. Light, is one of 2.5 million Americans afflicted with RP.

Sterling's major RP fund-raiser is an annual dinner called "A Party with a Purpose," now held during the JCK International Jewelry Show in Las Vegas. In the event's first two years, proceeds went exclusively to the RP Foundation. In 1992, Sterling added two charities: the American Foundation for AIDS Research (AmFAR), which is dedicated to AIDS-related research, preventive education and policy development, and Mothers' Voices, a grass roots organization founded in 1991 by Ivy Duneier, wife of jewelry designer Clyde Duneier, to promote compassion and respect for people with HIV and AIDS.

The trade's response to "Party with a Purpose" has been gratifying, says Pattie Light, director of special projects. This year's event raised $1.2 million.

Sterling also places canisters year-round in all its stores to collect change for the charities ($43,000 in the past year). Store managers are urged to encourage their malls' owners and mall associations to allocate some of the money they donate annually to charity to the RP Foundation.

Sterling also provides a day-care center, physical fitness center and quit-smoking classes for its employees. Unlike some companies, though, Sterling neither seeks public attention for its good works nor exploits them for business advantage. "We don't seek publicity for anything we do," explains Pattie Light. "That would defeat the purpose of doing something with pure motives."

NEIGHBORLY CARE CREATES A FUND-RAISING GIANT

Neighborly concern for a dying boy grew into what is now the largest single muscular dystrophy fund-raising event hosted by any U.S. business.

It began in the 1960s, when Harry Zimmerman, founder of Service Merchandise, moved to Nashville, Tenn., and befriended Billy Sandler, a young neighbor who suffered from MD. When Billy died at 17, Zimmerman made a lifelong commitment to raising money and educating the public about the neuromuscular disease. He helped form one of the first national chapters of the Muscular Dystrophy Association and his efforts inspired Service Merchandise stores and employees to hold their own backyard fund-raising carnivals, a staple during MDA's early years.

Service Merchandise set up a voluntary payroll deduction program for MDA donations in 1972 and became an MDA national corporate sponsor in 1978. In 1986, the firm formed an MD support committee to "learn from successes of individual stores, replicate and share those ideas with the chain, and organize and grow our overall corporate support," says Greg Winnett, assistant vice president of community relations.

That same year, Nashville announced it would honor "Mr. Harry's" contributions to the city with Harry Zimmerman Day. "We saw that as an opportunity to create a black-tie dinner for our favorite charity and to co-honor Mr. Harry at the same time," says Winnett. Unfortunately, Zimmerman died before the event, but the dinner went on as scheduled and was later renamed for him and his wife.

The impact from the dinner and the organized coordination of fund-raising efforts was almost immediate. Service Merchandise raised $400,000 in 1985 and $800,000 in 1986. This year, the firm will donate more than $2.7 million to MDA.

329

The money comes from three main sources:
- Voluntary employee payroll deductions, which raised some $340,000 between August 1992 and July 1993.
- In-store fund-raising events, this year including a Shamrock Sale (March), Seed Sale (April), Diamond Dig (May), Flag Promotion (June) and Christmas Tag sales (July). Proceeds from these events and in-store canisters raised an estimated $850,000 for MDA this year.
- The annual Mary and Harry Zimmerman Memorial Dinner, now the single largest MDA fund-raiser in the U.S., netting a total of more than $7 million over seven years. This year's dinner at the Opryland Hotel in Nashville attracted 2,000 people and raised $1.2 million. The firm presents two awards at the dinner. The Harry Zimmerman Memorial Award honors celebrities and businesspeople who raise money for or educate the public about muscular dystrophy. The Service Merchandise Leadership Award goes to a leading researcher in the fight against MD.

Support from its vendor community and sound business principles are essential to the company's fund-raising success, says Winnett. "Our expenses never exceed 15% of money collected and are often much less," compared with 30%-40% for some fund-raisers.

Service Merchandise and the employees at its 373 catalog showrooms also are involved in the United Way, collect food for needy families and participate in the Salvation Army's "Angel Tree," a program in which people donate Christmas gifts for children and elderly people who might not receive one otherwise. The firm also encourages its store managers and salespeople to be involved in their local communities.

Though Service Merchandise doesn't do its good works for public praise or reward, the good works "pay untold dividends by creating customer loyalty and community good will," says Winnett. They also build employee morale, "breaking their daily routine, building team spirit and fostering better attitudes."

ART FOR ART'S SAKE

If you read the list of patrons for virtually any cultural event in Houston, you'll likely see the names of Mr. and Mrs. I.W. Marks or I.W. Marks Jewelers at the top along with such giants as Exxon and Conoco.

For nearly 20 years, I.W. Marks Jewelers has forged alliances with established and emerging arts organizations in Houston, providing sponsorships, volunteers, product and service donations and advertising tie-ins and grants. In addition, President Irving Marks sits on the boards of Houston's opera and symphony orchestra.

Marks' interest in the arts grew from simply attending events. Later, local arts organizations approached him for some funding, and the rest is history.

"I saw a real need for it," he says. "Big business's support for the arts is waning in favor of the environment and other issues." Marks also is acutely aware of dwindling government funds. "I think it behooves small and medium businesses to support the arts," he says. "If other companies would support them as we do, there'd be no need for government support."

Some 1992 I.W. Marks projects:
- Underwriting Houston Symphony Orchestra concerts, the orchestra's opening night ball and the cost for printing 250,000 symphony tickets.
- Funding of Houston Grand Opera performances and Opera Ball and inviting prospective business supporters to performances and post-performance cast parties. This year, the firm underwrote performances of *Elektra* and *Madame Butterfly*, capped by a Japanese garden-theme cast party.
- Funding of Opera-to-Go, an educational outreach program that develops future opera audiences.
- Sponsoring the I.W. Marks Master Class Series, which brings Houston's professional artists into the community for one-on-one dialogues with audiences and young artists. For example, Marks brought Edward Vallela, a principal dancer with the New York City Ballet, to teach students about the ballet.
- Funding of the annual Musicfest, which awards scholarships for future musicians and entertainers.
- Underwriting a series about Texas music on Houston public television station KUHT and sponsoring classical music programming on public radio station KRTS.

Marks' interest in the arts has not gone unnoticed. The store received a national 1993 Business in the Arts Commitment Award, given by the Business Committee for the Arts and *Forbes* magazine. The award recognizes businesses that have provided exceptional support to the arts for at least 10 years, through a variety of philanthropic and business initiatives. Marks is proud of this recognition—it's the third time his store has received the award, which usually goes to Fortune 500 companies.

UNDER WATER

As Marvin and Margo Radloff of Stone Bros. Jewelry attended the Heart of America Jewelry Show this summer, flood waters converged on their Alton, Ill., store. It was, in their words, "buried under two feet of a mixture of the Mississippi, Missouri and Illinois rivers, making it into a 'gook' that is almost impossible to describe."

The board of directors of the Heart of America show took matters in hand, starting the Radloffs on the road back home with a $500 donation. (The Heart of America show also donated $1,000 to the Salvation Army of Kansas City to help with flood relief there.)

The Radloffs counted themselves among the lucky. "We anticipated some flooding and moved quite a few things up and out of danger," says Marvin Radloff. In fact, damage was limited mostly to carpeting, fixtures, boxes, displays and the electrical system. The flood did damage about 40 watches, but vendors Seiko, Pulsar and Longines-Wittnauer refurbished them. Sy Kessler Co. of Dallas even called Radloff to ask if he needed any help. He couldn't think of anything, but Kessler sent a supply of watch batteries, a battery case and a gold tester anyway, all free.

However, the flooding did hurt business. "We lost business for three months," says Radloff. "Before the flood, no one could come downtown because the streets were blocked with sandbags. Then we had 2 feet of water that took a week to recede, then we had to clean up."

Four or five employees worked day and night to clean the store, then new carpeting was installed and repairs were made before the store could open again. But business isn't back to normal; Radloff says he'll be happy to make 50% of what he did last year.

GIVING IT BACK

Harry Levitch says that when he was a youngster, everyone was poor. He came from a family of eight and realized early that being successful would require hard work and perseverance. He vowed that when he did succeed, he would help others get off to a good start.

Levitch worked hard all through school, studied law—primarily at night—and graduated with honors. But he loved the jewelry industry, so he went to work for a Memphis jeweler and eventually opened his own store—an exclusive business that now does $1 million a year in sales.

So it was time to give back, time to make a difference. Levitch contacted the principals of schools in the Memphis area, seeking children who needed a helping hand. Race and religion were unimportant.

When kids came to school with threadbare clothing or bare feet, he provided clothes, shoes, glasses and medical care. When their families had no heat or nothing to eat, he provided coal and food. It was a simple idea with a simple solution: provide kids with what they needed to work hard in school so they could become successful.

After using his own money for a number of years, he asked his B'nai B'rith lodge to help support the project. Lodge members liked the idea and the B'nai B'rith Student Aid Fund was established around 1965, with Levitch as its chairman. Today, the fund helps as many as 300 students each year. The idea has even spread to a few other B'nai B'rith lodges throughout the country.

NO MORE GAGS

For the past five years, the 55 employees of B. Sanfield, Rockford, Ill., have given to charity the money they would have spent on Christmas gag gifts for each other. The money, along with a matching amount from the company, goes to Park Pantry, a volunteer organization in Love's Park, Ill., that feeds needy families.

Lee Hartsfield, owner of the 21-year-old jewelry and floral firm, suggested the idea to his employees. They responded enthusiastically as a way to do something worthwhile instead of spending money on frivolous gifts.

At a Christmas party the Sunday before Thanksgiving each year, employees contribute their share and Sanfield writes a check to match the employees' contributions. The money then goes to the pantry in plenty of time to buy and distribute food before the holiday.

CHARITY ALL YEAR 'ROUND

Needy people are needy all year, not just in December, notes Susan McCoo, owner of The Capital Craftsman Inc., Concord, N.H. So McCoo got involved with five Parent-Child Centers, which provide year-round child-abuse prevention programs and parent-training for mothers in need.

About 300 low-income mothers take part in Parent-Child Center self-help programs geared toward getting families back on their feet. Counselors strive to show them ways to deal with issues and frustrations in a healthy, nondestructive manner and encourage them to discuss their problems and learn to help each other. The mothers are taught to choose toys such as crayons and blocks because they make a child use his or her imagination. Toys that promote violent behavior are discouraged.

McCoo, also a registered nurse, encourages her customers and employees to donate toys, games, clothes, furniture, food and money toward the project. And recently, her firm organized a golf tournament that raised $2,000 for the project. Winners received handmade gifts donated by the store, which sells American-made handcrafted jewelry and gifts. Last year, the firm donated a weekend's profits and had a $1 raffle for a handmade quarter-carat diamond ring.

UPDATE ON JCK'S 1992 DO-GOODERS

In last year's inaugural report on charitable deeds in our industries, JCK featured a host of jewelers who had supported or launched special events in their communities. This year, we checked back with a few of these jewelers whose projects are ongoing.

Jack Land is vice president of store operations for Melart Jewelers, Silver Spring, Md., by day and Santa's elf by night. Now he's back in his basement fixing hundreds and hundreds of broken toys so underprivileged children will have a present on Christmas morning. He says things are "rolling right along."

Last year, he gave away about 1,000 toys through the Colesville (Md.) Council of Community Congregations. This year, the organization only needs about 800 toys, a mere "drop in the bucket" for this industrious elf.

But Land is a little concerned about the future of his toy shop. He gets the broken toys from stores in malls where Melart has branches and from flea markets, but the supply is dwindling. His basement holds a two- or three-year backlog now, but he's keeping an eye on the future.

Dolores and Harold Dunker, whose doll-dressing contest made many little girls happy last Christmas morning, have hosted another doll contest in their store, Michael's Jewelry, Fremont, Neb. At press time, the Dunkers expected more than 200 dolls to be submitted by the Nov. 13 deadline. The dressed dolls were to be judged and then displayed for two weeks inside the store before being given to the Salvation Army for distribution to needy children.

New this year was a separate division for dressing teddy bears for little boys. Other divisions of competition were infant/small child dolls, period costumes, general and a special division for contestants under age 18. The winning dolls in each division were to be sold, with proceeds going to the Salvation Army.

Fred Feldmesser, the Massachusetts gem dealer who has spent many years bringing the magic of gems and jewelry to critically ill children, continues his work with the Starlight Foundation of New England and Children's Hospital in Boston. This summer, he took on a new project, spending 10 days as a volunteer counselor at Paul Newman's Hole in the Wall Gang camp for seriously ill children.

"I met kids from the inner city, and it was the first time I realized that these kids might not die from leukemia but from violence," he says. That infuriated him. Upon his return from the camp, Feldmesser went to work to combine the resources of the Starlight Foundation, the camp and a program in Boston called "Facing History, Facing Ourselves," which deals with the issues inner-city children face in school and life.

Meanwhile, his Freddy Rocker project, centering on a character he created to teach sick children about gems and minerals, is moving along well, garnering interest and support from both the kids and the business world. He tells this story of Freddy Rocker's impact: When a child gets out of the hospital, he or she is instructed to call Freddy Rocker for a one-on-one trip to the Peabody Museum at Harvard University. Freddy and the child have lunch in the curator's office, then tour the gem and mineral collection. One of Freddy's young patients was so enamored of the subject that he re-created the Peabody Rock Museum in his bedroom at home in Maine. He appointed himself curator, his best friend assistant curator, and printed up business cards for the museum: "Tours, 10 cents; Super-tours, 15 cents. Discounts for kids under 5."

Good Tips for Good Deeds

• **Pick the right charity**. The Internal Revenue Service recognizes more than 900,000 U.S. charities. Add churches, Boy Scout car washes and the like and the number tops 1 million! How do you choose one to support?

Ask your staff for suggestions. If you can't agree on a specific cause, offer a payroll deduction program in which employees can donate to their favorite charity. Other sources for advice include the Better Business Bureau, Chamber of Commerce, consumer affairs offices and the advertising directors of local news media, which often cosponsor charity benefits. "If you can get a media partner, you have it made," says one charity agency official.

• **Narrow your choice** to one charity, when possible. This prevents dilution of your efforts and donations and builds up a relationship between the business and that charity.

• **Research the charity** to be sure you are comfortable with it. Tour its offices, meet its officials and learn about its work in the community. Information on many charities is available from several sources, including:

1. *The Annual Charity Index* and *Give, but Give Wisely*, both published by The Council of Better Business Bureaus' Philanthropic Advisory Services, 4200 Wilson Blvd., Suite 800, Arlington, Va. 22203. The *Index* ($12.95) gives the name, address, purpose, financial reports and salaries of officials of more than 200 major charities. *Give, but Give Wisely* rates more than 200 major charities according to CBBB standards. It costs $2, but is free with each order of the Index.

2. *The Wise Giving Guide* is published by the National Charities Information Bureau four times yearly. The free guide evaluates close to 400 charities according to the NCIB's detailed standards and identifies those that don't comply. NCIB, 19 Union Sq. W., Sixth Floor, New York, N.Y. 10003.

3. The Conference Board has information about seminars and publications on business support of and donations to charities. The Conference Board, 845 Third Ave., New York, N.Y. 10022; (212) 759-0900.

• **What, why and how**. Support can take a variety of forms, including collection canisters in your store, sales with proceeds going to a charity, sponsorship of a community event and donations of service, time or merchandise. You may want to start your own event, such as a marathon, dinner, concert or event honoring a local celebrity.

Whatever your game plan, set realistic, attainable goals. Raising a million dollars for a hospital may be unrealistic, but a fund drive for a needed piece of equipment isn't. Remember that charities also need donations of merchandise, services, equipment and volunteer time.

• **Plan and organize**. No general goes to war without calculating the cost. Neither should a business planning to help a charity. Several jewelers and directors of philanthropic groups suggest you begin preparing for a charity promotion no less than six months in advance. This allows time to estimate costs, contact people on your mailing list, develop promotional literature, create a media plan and prepare your staff and store.

• **Keep a tight rein on expenses**. A fund-raiser in which most of the proceeds go to pay operational costs is of little value to any charity. Apply sound business principles to maximize the money you can collect. How much you spend on a charity promotion depends on how much you want to make. The Council of Better Business Bureaus says a charity should spend at least 50% of what it collects on its cause. Charity directors say expenses should be less than 25% of the total.

• **Consider the business advantages of good works**. If the value of helping others isn't enough incentive to support good works in your community, consider some other facts. In addition to tax benefits, supporting public service or charities boosts customer goodwill and employee morale. Most charities publicize their business supporters and working with high-society events for high-profile charities will give you a chance to build up your mailing list of affluent residents.

Reaching Catalog Shoppers

November 1993

More two-income families with less free time combined with a lagging economy and anti-'80s consumption fervor may be deflating interest in going downtown or to the mall to shop.

If this has affected your business, you may want to consider launching or increasing catalog sales.

But first, you'll need to know what sets catalog shoppers apart. That's the focus of a new study of 150,000 catalog and direct mail shoppers that Impact Resources conducted for the business consulting firm of Deloitte & Touche, New York, N.Y.

In a nutshell, the study found that catalog shoppers are better educated (more than two-thirds attended college, compared with only half of noncatalogers), earn more (more than half earn $30,000-$99,000 annually, compared with 38% of noncatalogers in this range) and buy more electronics than those who don't use catalogs.

Here are some other tidbits from the study:

• While catalogers and noncatalogers rank shopping motivators in much the same order—selection, price, quality, location and service—quality is more important to catalogers.

• Catalogers spend a few minutes more each day than noncatalogers with TV, radio and newspapers and are more likely to pay attention to sale solicitations by phone, mail, billboards and transit ads.

• Women outnumber men among catalog shoppers 58% to 42%.

• Twenty-five percent of catalog shoppers are in the populous 35-44-year-old group; only 17% of the noncatalogers are in this group.

• The percentage of married consumers is higher among catalog shoppers—57% compared with 45% of non-catalog shoppers.

• More catalogers own homes than rent, and 66% of them live in houses rather than apartments.

Reaching For The Middle Market

October 1993

Every community has affluent customers who are largely unaffected by economics. It also has customers who shop for the lowest price—period. But there's another customer: the one who *is* affected by economic shifts, has a house mortgage to pay off, two kids to educate and eventual retirement to consider. This customer considers a few hundred dollars a good chunk of change, but he or she will spend that much if a product is appealing enough.

Shoppers who will spend $200-$700 for a piece of jewelry often come back time after time and spend a bit more with each visit. They comprise an important market for many jewelers, who need to work to protect it.

But just who are these customers, what will bring them into your store and what tempts them to buy?

Defining the customer: Jewelers interviewed by JCK say middle-market customers most often are women, especially at the lower end of the price range. These women usually buy jewelry for themselves or as gifts for another woman. In many cases, they earn their own income and feel comfortable spending some of it on jewelry. Jewelers say that if they're not employed outside the home, they might divert money left over from grocery budgets. Once they decide they want a piece of jewelry, jewelers say they rationalize and budget a way to pay for it. Easy credit or layaway terms will help to finalize their decision.

Young couples comprise the next most common customer in this middle market, say jewelers. They're fairly recently married (within a few years) and can't afford much, but the husband does want to buy a nice gift for his wife. Randi Cooper, a jeweler in Wichita, Kan., finds many young professional men in their mid- to late-20s shopping in this price range.

In addition, the very young portion of the bridal market (late teens to early 20s) finds this price range appealing. But this segment is dwindling as couples wait longer to marry, says Martin Stein, president of Silver Spring, Md.-based Melart Jewelers. (In overall sales, Stein has noticed a strong market for jewelry selling for under $1,500 and over $4,000, but a real drop in between.)

Differences exist even within the $200-$700 market. The breaking point for female self-purchase customers seems to be around $300. Below that amount, women can absorb a purchase from their own earnings or their "mad" money, says Cooper. Above it, the purchase tends to become a family decision, say Cooper and Jeff Thompson, president of Trinity Gold & Diamonds, Oklahoma City, Okla. "I can relate to that," says Cooper. "Women want to have a sense that 'it's my money, not his.'" Once the price rises to $400-$700, however, it becomes more of a male gift market or a couple together, she says.

Impulse vs. intent: What drives the middle market to buy jewelry—impulse or specific intent? Some of both, say jewelers.

Melart Jewelers' 20 stores generally are in shopping malls. They attract some middle-market customers who are looking specifically for jewelry and others who just want to buy something—which may turn out to be jewelry or may be something else.

These browsers present a special challenge, says Stein, because he first must persuade them to buy jewelry rather than clothing or a stereo, and then persuade them to buy it at Melart. "When a customer says 'I'm going to look around,' we know there's a good chance they won't be back," he says. "So we try to show them that jewelry is a good hedge against inflation, it doesn't depreciate in value and it can turn into an heirloom."

He also explains that a woman will get more use out of a piece of jewelry than a piece of clothing. As Cooper says, a $1,000 St. John knit suit may be in the Goodwill box four years from now, but jewelry lasts a lifetime.

Convincing middle-market customers of jewelry's value isn't a real problem, say jewelers. Middle-market customers may gasp if a piece is beyond their budget, but few complain that it's overpriced. Instead, they usually speak up and say that X dollars is more than they planned to spend and they are looking for something in the Y price range.

One particular challenge arises as some regions emerge slowly from recession. Robert Grant, an American Gem Society jeweler in western Massachusetts, and Starr Bragg, president of Bristol, Bragg & Young, Alcoa, Tenn., say many middle-market consumers have started to look at houses, furniture and major appliances that they put off buying until now. "We noticed last Christmas that our big customers bought homes and house things," says Bragg. "But at least we know they'll be back. The husbands came in and bought small items, saying 'next year, it'll be a different story.' "

Dale Perelman, president of the Kings Jewelers chain based in New Castle, Pa., says competition for discretionary income depends on the market. "In bridal jewelry, our biggest competition is other jewelers," he says. "For jewelry in general, it can be cars, houses, anything. We're fighting for fewer available discretionary dollars and we're fighting a psychology that says 'recession.' "

Creative financing: Making jewelry easy for a customer to afford is important in the middle market. Jewelers say credit plans are the most effective marketing tool they've found. Their customers find it much easier to absorb a $25-per-month charge than a bill for $300 or $400.

Many jewelers tell JCK they offer in-store credit and various payment options. Melart, for example, has six options ranging from 90-days-same-as-cash to traditional revolving charge accounts.

At Bristol, Bragg & Young, middle-market customers take advantage of an in-store credit program, and often look around at other items when they come to the store to make a payment. "When they get down to their last $75 or so [on the account balance], they're getting ready to make another purchase," says Starr Bragg. Women are particularly prone to use "creative financing" and put a piece on layaway or budget it out, she says. Men are more likely to pay for it outright.

In-store credit isn't the route for every jeweler. Sissy Jones, chief executive officer of Sissy's Log Cabin in Pine Bluff, Ark., offers two options. She'll arrange bank financing for customer purchases. Or she has a year-long layaway plan in which customers pay monthly installments without interest and "visit" their jewelry while paying it off. Most customers redeem their purchase well before the year is up, says Jones, and visiting the piece keeps their interest level high.

Even jewelers who don't offer credit realize its potential. Andrew Grant Inc. doesn't offer it, but the firm's Robert Grant says many people ask for it, and he admits it's a marketing tool he'll eventually need to compete.

What they buy: Colored gems and gold are big sellers in this price range, as are promotional-quality tennis bracelets. Engagement rings and sets, of course, are popular with the younger segment of the bridal market.

But semicustomized jewelry is responsible for 80% of sales in this range at Trinity Gold & Diamonds. "We were getting so many sales in the $300 range that we had to stop and ask ourselves why," says the firm's Jeff Thompson. "Much of it comes because a customer has some kind of jewelry that isn't right and wants it changed." Reasons vary from divorce to modernizing Grandma's heirloom ring to fixing broken jewelry.

Thompson stocks thousands of 14k gold mountings, thousands of gemstone heads and thousands of loose gemstones. He has three full-time goldsmiths on staff to do while-you-wait work. He says his assemble-to-order philosophy has many advantages. Customers like to be involved in the design of the piece. They like not having to wait several weeks. And they like the savings he passes on from not having to stock a lot of finished jewelry, then wait for it to sell. In most cases, he says, the assemble-to-order pieces cost no more (and sometimes less) than finished jewelry.

Selling techniques: Selling to middle-market customers differs from selling to some other groups. Most jewelers don't try to sell them up, for example. It's important that they know they won't be pressured into spending more, says Thompson.

Some independent jewelers feel it's hard for them to appeal to a customer who regularly shops at warehouse clubs and discount stores, says Randi Cooper. "I don't think they feel comfortable in my store," she says. "If I knew why, I'd tell you. So we try to make people feel just as good whether they're spending $25 or $25,000."

Allen Kessler of Burbank, Cal., says many of his customers are elderly and remember when a strand of pearls or a really fine watch cost $150. Now they get "sticker shock." In addition, he competes with the nearby jewelry marts in downtown Los Angeles and has to convince customers they don't necessarily get a bargain there.

Despite the competitive problems, jewelers who sell to the middle market say they're not about to abandon it. The bread-and-butter market is still "the heart of it," says Perelman, adding that many jewelers have built their businesses solidly on this middle ground.

Study Draws Portrait Of Home Shoppers

October 1993

Picture someone who shops via TV. A widow who splits her waking hours between the television and tending to her numerous cats? An insomniac who enjoys the "company" of a bubbly shopping show host and rarely visits a store?

Think again. Customers who shop in retail stores and those who shop on TV have a lot in common, according to a study by Impact Resources and Deloitte & Touche, New York, N.Y. To know what this could mean for your jewelry business as home shopping grows more popular, you first should know what type of consumers buy from TV shows.

The Impact Resources/Deloitte & Touche study gathered such information by surveying 6,000 regular TV shoppers and comparing them with a market average on such factors as age, marital status, profession, income and fashion preference.

Age, marital status: TV shoppers are younger than you might think. Almost half of the TV shoppers surveyed are 25-44. Forty-four percent are married, 27% have never been married and 8% are widowed (the rest are divorced or didn't answer the question).

The largest TV shopper group comprises professionals (13% of all TV shoppers interviewed) and managers (11%). While that's below the market average (18% for professionals and 12% for managers), the percentages are very close.

Income, education: The average household income of TV shoppers is $34,900 vs. a market average of $38,000. In the lower income categories ($30,000 and below), consumers are more likely to be TV shoppers than market-average consumers. But in the higher income categories ($75,000 and above) the percentages are very close: 9% of market-average consumers and 8% of TV shoppers earn that much. What do these figures mean to you? TV shopping appeals to consumers at both ends of the income scale.

Thirty-four percent of TV shoppers completed only 12 years of formal education (compared with 31% of the market average), while more than 27% went on to study one to three years in college (compared with 30% of the market average).

Fashion orientation: The TV shoppers are more likely than the market average to look for familiar labels (47% vs. 33%). And while consumers in the market average lean toward conservative/traditional looks, value and comfort before fashion, TV shoppers lean the other way, according to the study.

How to reach them: The two leaders in home shopping—QVC of West Chester, Pa., and the Home Shopping

Network of St. Petersburg, Fla.—take in $2.2 billion in sales annually, with jewelry accounting for nearly half the total. If you want to attract some of these sales yourself, here are some hints on marketing to TV shoppers:

• Regular TV shoppers are more likely than the market average to listen to sales solicitations on the phone (27% vs. 13%).

• Regular TV shoppers are more likely than the market average to read mail advertisements (50% vs. 40%).

• Regular TV shoppers are more likely than the market average to buy from catalogs and other direct mail (44% vs. 12%).

How TV Shoppers Compare with Market Average

% of TV	% of market	shoppers average
Married	44%	49%
Never Married	27%	25%
Widowed	8%	8%
Ages 25-34	26%	4%
Ages 35-44	22%	21%
Ages 65+	11%	16%
Professional	13%	18%
Manager	11%	12%
Laborer	12%	9%
Homemaker	11%	9%
Salesperson	10%	8%
Retired	2%	16%
Familiar labels are important	47%	33%
Prefer latest trends	26%	16%
Prefer conservative look	29%	33%
Prefer value over fashion	29%	35%

Source: Impact Resources and Deloitte & Touche, 1993

Marketing To Attract Women

Suzy Spencer ◆ *August 1993 Part II*

"When Lynn Steinhauer divorced a few years ago after more than two decades of marriage, she expected to feel lost and lonely. Instead, she enjoyed the peaceful pleasures of an empty house and a table set for one. Now Steinhauer eats what she wants, comes and goes as she pleases, and spends the money she wants without reproach."—The New York Times

How will Lynn Steinhauer spend her money? On heavy gold earrings? On a choker? On a pendant or a bracelet? Or on her home, her car, her clothing?

There's a good chance she and other women—married, divorced, widowed or never married—would be more inclined to spend their money on fine jewelry if they became more familiar with it. This should be of particular interest to retailers as more and more women gain financial independence—or at least greater financial resources.

The early 1993 *New York Times* news service article quoted here said a growing number of divorced women are showing an indifference to remarriage, especially if they've gained financial and sexual independence. In fact, societal changes in the past 30 years have given women in general a greater sense of independence.

But is it really worthwhile to market to women? After all, they may buy lots of gold jewelry, but it's all lower-priced, isn't it? And they certainly don't buy diamonds. Or do they?

Statistics compiled for N.W. Ayer on behalf of De Beers reveal that women buying for themselves accounted for 20% of women's diamond jewelry unit and dollar sales in 1991. That added up to more than 2 million pieces worth more than $1 billion; the average price for this jewelry was $483. By comparison, husbands spent an average $727 when buying women's diamond jewelry as a gift, male friends spent $419, and other gift buyers spent just under $300. (These figures do not include diamond engagement or wedding rings bought before the marriage.)

While women often spend less per piece of jewelry than men, they still can spend a fair amount. At Walzel's in Houston, Tex., for example, women can easily spend $5,000 at a time. Yes, says owner Cherryll Walzel, the chance of a woman buying a diamond for herself is pretty small. But when a woman, usually older and single (by death or divorce), does buy a diamond at Walzel's, it's in the 7- to 8-ct. range.

And the growth potential for the woman's self-purchase market is enormous. While most women receive a pretty limited number of diamond engagement, wedding and anniversary rings over their lifetime, there's no reason they can't keep buying diamond earrings, necklaces, pendants and bracelets.

Of all women's gold jewelry sold each year, women buy 43% of it for themselves and 21% as a gift for another woman, says The World Gold Council. Women also buy sterling silver and platinum jewelry, and Pat Henneberry of the Diamond Promotion Service says they often help to pick out and sometimes even chip in for their engagement and wedding rings, also.

In Oklahoma City, which jeweler Gary Gordon calls "a melting pot of divorced people," women readily buy diamonds for themselves—as long as the diamonds aren't heart-shaped or set in a ring that makes the wearer look "attached."

At Glenda Queen Union Street Goldsmiths in San Francisco, women—married and single—buy diamond earrings, pendants and tennis bracelets. "Women have more disposable income these days," says Glenda Queen. "The divorced woman definitely spends money on jewelry." In fact, Queen does a profitable business in what she and her customers term "freedom rings"—new rings made from old wedding stones.

Market-wise: So how do you market to women? Jewelers JCK spoke with stressed three essential points:
• Market yourself as the fashion-forward jeweler.
• Focus on the product, not the price.
• Attract them when they're young.
Let's look at each aspect in more detail.

Fashion-forward: A woman who buys jewelry for herself is a fashion-conscious person, says jeweler David Rotenberg of David Craig Jewelers Ltd., Langhorne, Pa. It's crucial that the store atmosphere be comfortable to women and make a fashion statement. Personnel must be fashion-forward in dress, posture and knowledge. Every aspect of Rotenberg's store, from the scent of potpourri to the white Leatherette displays, is intended as a "silent seller."

Without a doubt, fashion is important, say Liz Chatelain and Michele Silbar of the Champagne Diamond Registry. "A woman knows the difference between fashion and tradition," adds Chatelain. Every woman should have certain traditional pieces, such as a strand of pearls, a good watch and good all-gold earrings, she says. But once she has her basic wardrobe of classics, she's ready for some more fashion-forward pieces. They must be fashionable without being overly trendy, however, or women will worry they'll soon go out of style.

Elva Valentine of Valentine's Jewelry & Accessories outside Scranton, Pa., points out that women, particularly those entering the job market, want direction because they don't have time to study fashion. They expect a jeweler to know what's new, what the magazines and designers are showing.

Glenda Queen always stocks at least three avant-garde pieces, though she knows they may sit on the shelf for a year. While there, they attract attention and stimulate interest. Queen has her employees wear the pieces, too, and when they finally do sell, the style moves so rapidly for about two years that she can't keep it in stock. Right now, she can't stock enough big, long, gold chains and huge gold bracelets to be worn stacked.

Product, not price: Jewelers such as Valentine and Alice Barlow of Earth Resources in Appleton, Wis., see differences in male and female shopping behaviors. If a woman is going to buy a present (for herself or for a man) she typically shops for a while. She tends to find something she likes and then worry how to pay for it. A man often waits until the day he needs something (on his wife's birthday, their anniversary, Christmas Eve), then comes in with a general price set in his head. He's more concerned with finding something that day at a price he likes.

When Gary Gordon focused his marketing efforts on men, he promoted price and value. Now that he markets to women, too, his newspaper ads feature an oversized photo of a product. The ad copy talks about the product's attractiveness, desirability and emotional prestige. His ads tout the designer or the thrilled response of the wearer and her friends. Price is never mentioned.

Price is mentioned at the point of sale—obviously. Some women have a guilt factor, says Valentine. To get them to buy, she breaks down the purchase price into acceptable bites. So much down, so much over 90 days, particularly if the price is over $500.

Jewelers such as Valentine also say non-working wives sneak from their grocery money to make jewelry purchases. Indeed, Gordon derived an ad campaign that promoted charge accounts payable with leftover grocery money.

And at David Craig, some women have come in to upgrade gifts from their men, never tell the men about the switch and pay the additional cost out of the grocery money.

But when it comes to single working women, says Valentine, "She'll buy herself anything and just budget it out." She treats herself and is systematic about it. She'll buy one piece now and have her next purchase already chosen.

Age: The third point, say jewelers, is stock lots of gold and sterling silver jewelry to hook female customers when they are young. And always remember women's tendency to buy in gradually increasing price increments. Elva Valentine pierces ears for young girls, and Gary Gordon stocks sterling silver and encourages women to shop for jewelry as enthusiastically as they do for clothes. Once they buy sterling silver, he says, they are interested in sterling and gold, and then gold, and then . . .

"The younger they are, the less you have to convince them of anything," says Valentine. A 25-year-old woman makes her own decisions, she says. A 50-year-old woman is more likely to feel something's wrong with buying jewelry for herself. She may feel guilty about not spending the money on a family-oriented purchase or may simply never have thought about buying jewelry for herself.

Cherryll Walzel agrees that the 50+ woman isn't spontaneous about buying jewelry. But Walzel adds that if a woman is over 50 years old, widowed or divorced, and sees a piece she wants, she'll buy it.

Merchandising: This all means that jewelers need a wide assortment of styles for all styles of life—married, single, divorced, working or full-time mom. Full-time moms need jewelry that is durable. Working women need tailored jewelry. And many of today's women want designer jewelry, especially if it's designed by women, says Valentine, because a woman knows what feels good on the body.

Glenda Queen stocks lots of gold, particularly gold earrings, and holds after-hours workshops to teach professional women how to buy good jewelry. "Some of these women are in their 40s and have never tried to learn about buying jewelry," she says. She has her customers play dress-up with fine jewelry, and that breaks the fear/intimidation factor. They'll buy a neck chain, then earrings ($250-$2,000), bracelets, etc. "Once you sell them one good piece of jewelry," she says, "they come back for more."

Store atmosphere also is important. Every aspect of Walzel's in Houston is an artistic statement. Paintings on the walls, sculptures and antique mirrors all encourage women to come into the store to admire the art. The women then see—and buy—the jewelry.

Once a year, Gary Gordon organizes focus groups of women to discuss what they like and don't like about his store. These focus groups have changed everything from what's in the candy dishes to the music that's played to the jewelry he offers. And he rewards local dress shop, furrier and beauty salon employees for referrals with "Samuel Gordon Bucks." Every time one of those employee referrals results in a sale, the employee receives Samuel Gordon Bucks, a gift certificate for purchases at his store. Gordon also employs a woman designer and promotes her as "the woman's designer."

"Women, women, women," he says, "you belong at Samuel Gordon Jewelers."

There's one other thing that belongs at Samuel Gordon, as well as some other jewelry stores that cater to women—child care. Gary Gordon hires college students trained to work with children to keep them entertained while their mothers shop. Elva Valentine keeps a box of toys for the kids and a television with a VCR. Sometimes she plays jewelry tapes, other times children's tapes. And often, the mothers are ready to leave before the children are.

Community ties: One last absolute in marketing to women is to be a leader and a friend.

Through community benefits and social gatherings, Nelson Holdo of Asanti Fine Jewellers in Pasadena, Cal., establishes solid relationships with the few key women in his community who are considered fashion leaders. He becomes "their jeweler" and their friend, and this reputation brings him their followers, at least 20 to each woman.

Cherryll Walzel is very involved in the arts. This is important to her business because most of her customers attend the ballet and the opera, and many are art collectors. She regularly features a particular artist's work in her store. Customers are invited in to meet the artist—who may be a painter, sculptor, musician or jewelry designer. Once she even brought in a special show of linens, though she doesn't carry giftware. She sold $15,000 worth of linens and obtained four new jewelry customers (each with a first purchase in the $5,000-$6,000 range). Walzel also hosts a breakfast or luncheon in her store once a month for no more than 20-25 people, who may be board members of a charitable organization or a professional women's group. She cooks the food herself and serves it on her own china and silver, establishing herself as a caring and concerned community leader who also sells fabulous jewelry. "You have to be a leader in your community," she says.

Will It Play In Portland?
Understanding Regional Tastes

Cathleen McCarthy ◆ *August 1993 Part II*

Once upon a time, there was no such term as "regional marketing." Stores simply catered to local demand because that's what kept them alive. Then came the big chains: McDonald's and Sears, Zale and Gordon among them. Their success with homogenized merchandising seemed to render regionalism obsolete.

This concept of merchandising-to-the-masses dominated U.S. marketing for years. But now the retail scene is changing once again—because of recession and because consumers are choosing stores that save them time by catering to their specific needs.

"Homogenized retailing worked only when you were trying to achieve an economy of scale, when retailers wrote with a big pencil and were able to use that clout to demand efficiencies and translate them into lower prices," theorizes jewelry marketer Jim Terzian. "But economies of scale in our marketplace work less and less well and are available in fewer situations."

Department stores and jewelry stores alike now realize that efficiency and volume discounts don't matter if the customer doesn't want the products offered. In addition, volume discounts are becoming less frequent and less generous.

Nordstrom is one of a new breed of department stores that practices specialty merchandising, tailoring the mix to suit the demands of individual stores. J.C. Penney also charts regional differences among its fine jewelry departments. Merchandise managers use a core assortment plan, then tailor that assortment to their individual market, says Don McKean, the company's jewelry merchandising manager.

Contrast that to some of the big jewelry chains that offer virtually the same merchandise in all their stores. These stores are suffering as baby boomers demand individualized service and recession makes consumers more reluctant to buy anything not suited exactly to their tastes.

Whether these tastes vary from region to region is a matter of disagreement among some jewelers, but one thing is clear. Women are more attuned than men to fashion trends, thanks to the millions of dollars spent annually on women's apparel advertising. So jewelers can benefit from keeping tabs on tastes and trends as women become bigger jewelry buyers.

Regional differences: fact or fallacy? Some in the industry say demand varies from store to store but not region to region. Others believe even store-to-store variation is a matter of salesmanship.

"I don't believe in the regional concept," says Steven Lagos, a jewelry designer in Philadelphia, Pa. "You can have a salesperson who is hot on a product and suddenly that store sells more than another," he says. "But as for regionalized demand, information [transmission] and transportation have gotten so big and so fast that everyone gets the same message at the same time. Whether you live in the East, South or Midwest, you're watching the same TV, reading the same magazines, getting the same output. My top 10 selling pieces are my top 10 everywhere."

The same thing is true for Gantos, a women's apparel chain based in Grand Rapids, Mich. "Basically, the same thing seems to work from region to region," says Linda Marr, the firm's fashion jewelry buyer. "If I see a style that is doing well, the stores not selling it are more likely to be from the lower-volume groups than from a particular region." Rather than track sales by region, Gantos looks for the common denominator. "In a chain with so many stores, it takes less time to find the common denominator that sells everywhere than to differentiate according to region," she says.

"If that works for you, Mazel Tov!" responds Joel Garreau, an editor at the *Washington Post* and author of *Edge City: Life on the New Frontier* and *The Nine Nations of North America*, which blew a big hole in the homogenized merchandising theory in the 1980s. National advertising campaigns such as those for Campbell's Soup, which had suffered inconsistent results from region to region, were successfully revamped according to Garreau's theory.

It's true that after World War II, the developing highway and air travel systems and communications technology helped to blur cultural differences that had set regions apart from one another. But the technological revolution had the curious side effect of creating separate "nations," each operating somewhat independently, Garreau told JCK. "The center of the universe is no longer New York or the Northeast because power, money and influence have been dispersed," he says. "If you think there is no difference between the way the world works in Los Angeles or New York, you haven't been to one or the other place in a long time." Take, for example, the surge of interest in regional cultures and cuisines such as Cajun and Southwestern, Ethiopian and Vietnamese.

As jewelry designer Paul Klecka puts it, "Life-styles vary tremendously in different parts of our country. This country has a diverse geography, and that creates a big impact on people's life-styles."

The big and small of it: How does this translate to consumer demand? On the uppermost level of design, a common factor exists in major cities worldwide. "In major cities, people tend to share an interest in certain designers," says Laurie Hudson, president of the Platinum Guild International USA Jewelry Inc. "It's in the outskirts that you notice different preferences in fashion, lifestyle, economic situation and demographics."

Henry Dunay has noticed the same thing while tracking his jewelry designs carefully for two decades. "You will always have some women—whether in Boston, Chicago, Los

Angeles or Dallas—who will buy high fashion," he says. "But there are overall taste differences between Chicago and Los Angeles. I'm talking about the mainstream woman, the one you can always count on to buy another little piece."

Dunay says regional variations have little to do with state boundaries. "There's a difference between Dallas and Houston. There's even a difference between Oklahoma City and Tulsa, Okla. Tulsa is a religious, extremely conservative town and Oklahoma City likes a little excitement. They want their jewelry big and flashy."

The breakdown: Before making further generalizations, let's loosely define the boundaries of Garreau's nations-within-a-nation theory and take a look at their individual jewelry markets.

• New England (Connecticut, Maine, Massachusetts, New Hampshire, Rhode Island and Vermont). The New England woman-of-means tends to dress simply and tastefully, Dunay says. "She values quality, nondescript quality, but not fashion. In Boston, they'd rather put their money into a house than a pair of earrings, and if they do, it's often a very simple Tiffany style."

• Pacific Northwest (coastal strip that stretches from San Francisco to Vancouver, Canada). Jewelry marketers frequently compare the Pacific Northwest to New England. "The San Francisco Bay Area and Boston's Back Bay are areas where education and cultural knowledge carry more prestige than visible symbols of success," says Terzian, "and that translates into jewelry. The preference is for quality over quantity, a small, flawless sapphire instead of a carat-heavy one that wouldn't pass GIA standards."

Glenda Queen, owner of Union Street Goldsmiths in San Francisco, says her customers travel and are exposed to a huge cluster of designers. "You have to stretch harder to titillate them, to show them something they haven't seen before," she says.

This region also includes Portland, Ore., headquarters for Nike, Adidas and many computer companies. As fortunes are being made, so are jewelry sales. And the tastes reflect those in the rest of the Pacific Northwest. Nick Greve of Carl Greve Jewelers, Portland, says women in his city like exceptional products. "Women come into my store wearing Escada, carrying Chanel bags and wearing great shoes," he says. "We do well with Michael Bondanza and Lagos. Enamel jewelry is strong also, and anything exceptional. It doesn't have to be understated or small, but we don't sell a lot of flash-for-the-cash, like the big cheap diamond."

• The Breadbasket (primarily the Midwest). Agriculture is still the primary source of revenue, though most Midwesterners aren't farmers any more. Still, they retain a certain earthy practicality. "The Breadbasket has built an enviable, prosperous, renewable economy," Garreau writes. It is the "North American nation most at peace with itself . . . stability here is a virtue."

CNN fashion show broadcasts can generate disdainful amusement here, as can many of the fads embraced on the coasts. In fact there's a certain prejudice against the coasts, Terzian says, and it's reflected in jewelry buying through a rejection of form over function. "Fashion doesn't hold much sway in the Breadbasket," he says. "Here, first and foremost, you have to offer value for the money."

With the exception of Minneapolis, where a thriving music industry attracts a "hipper" element, even young Midwesterners avoid trendy fashion. Urban Outfitters buyer

John Hoffman, who buys for three stores in Minnesota college towns, says Midwesterners are more into basic merchandise. If they pick up on a trend, they pick it up in accessories. It's less a matter of price than of not wanting to feel foolish walking down the street. "Not wanting to stand out is a very important thing there," he says.

This sense of propriety does not indicate a weak market for fine jewelry, however. On the contrary, market reports in recent years show Midwest demand to be a safe shore in a turbulent economic climate. "It's not that they buy more," Terzian says. "They're simply the most consistent. The coasts have suffered more ups and downs, while the Midwest has showed a slow, steady growth pattern. Many suppliers tell me their Midwest customers are their most loyal, and that's a vital and scarce commodity."

Another fallacy about the Midwest is that the rejection of form over function means bad or even dull taste. "I find the highest demand for my work in the Midwest," says designer Barbara Westwood. "Retailers know and understand their customers there, as opposed to the driving population here in southern California or Arizona, where we often have no idea who the customer is."

Market experts say there are some differences in product preferences. For example, while Rolex watches are big sellers in Dallas, Midwesterners might be more likely to buy a Timex, says Susie Watson, Timex's fashion analyst.

"We're strong nationwide, but more so in suburban and rural areas. The Heartland has always been good for Timex. There's something about it that Midwesterners relate to more than an urban crowd. Maybe it's that Timex has the same personality as a Midwesterner: reliable, long-lasting, honest and inexpensive. And I can say that because I'm from there," she says with a laugh.

• Mexamerica (the Southwest U.S.). Ray Tracey, a Santa Fe designer, says it best: "It's mañanaland: 'I'll get around to it tomorrow.' People here are real casual—they take time to stop and smell the roses—and that's reflected in the jewelry they wear. The jewelry here is casual with a lot of Indian and Spanish influences."

Mexamerica is one region where J.C. Penney sells more silver jewelry than gold. While the American Indian influence remains strong, designer jewelry created and worn here reaches far beyond the silver-and-turquoise cliché. Sante Fe designers such as Tracey and Danny Romero use faceted diamonds and gold in their inlay work and often feature such stones as sugilite and coral in their high-end jewelry.

Many designers target Southwest resorts for their most conspicuous pieces. "My bolder look always goes down to the resorts like those in Arizona," Barbara Westwood says. "Customers in resorts are generally treated with the finest and highest style because that's what gets their attention when they're away from home. When a person is on vacation and browsing, they will purchase more exciting design because of the mood they're in."

Southern California, technically a part of Mexamerica, demonstrates the regional preference for bright colors and bold statements, especially in San Diego. But Los Angeles, as a major business center, moves faster. Los Angelenos jump on trends with the speed of a New Yorker and the brazenness of a Southwesterner. "The result is some schlocky stuff," says Glenda Queen, who grew up in southern California. Adds Terzian, "L.A. is where the bumper stickers read, 'The one with the most jewels wins.'"

The recession has tempered the bigger-is-better mentality somewhat. But splashy still reigns. "So the earring is this big instead of that big," Dunay reasons. "It's still glitz."

• Dixie (the Southern U.S.). Retailers say jewelry trends hit the South two to three years after they hit the coasts. "The South is a little more conservative," says Harry McCloud of N.S. Co., a manufacturer in Tucker, Ga. "Styles run more along classic lines than far-out designs."

One difference between Midwestern and Dixie women is that the latter tend to be more clothes-conscious and more "done" in terms of hair and make-up.

Garreau agrees. "You won't find sweats in a jewelry store in the South like you might in Denver, where women make a point of being studiedly natural," he says.

Retailer Bill Underwood of Fayetteville, Ark., says if he jumps the gun on a trend, he sits on his inventory for a couple of years. He typifies the jewelry designed for his store as "modern but not far out," with a heavy use of sapphires, emeralds and rubies. Modeling his store after Tiffany has stood him well for several decades.

• Miami. Most people in the industry refer to Miami apart from the Dixie South. Garreau sees it as the capital of a "nation" he calls the Islands, including the Caribbean. "The Miami aesthetic is not so much glitz as gold," says Henry Dunay. "Jewelry sales have become more conservative because people are afraid to walk the streets with their jewelry. They're foregoing the $10,000 pair of diamond earrings for a $5,000 gold pair."

He refers to Miami's upper crust, but the Cuban/Hispanic taste for gold infiltrates all levels. Don McKean offers similar observations about J.C. Penney's south Florida sales record. "Hispanics seem to like gold better than diamonds," he says, "so we sell a lot more gold merchandise."

• The Foundry (roughly the mid-Atlantic states). The common element is industry, particularly steel, and a history connected to Europe. Major cities here struggle to integrate what Garreau calls "widely different personalities and cultures and ethnic groups," so the region's jewelry tastes aren't well-defined.

National marketing strategies often are based on the tastes and demographics of this region. J.C. Penney doesn't tailor its merchandise mix in the Northeast; the recommended assortment works there—"no demographics assumed."

Two exceptions are Manhattan and Washington, D.C., both of which Garreau calls "aberrations" with an international, often transient population. Says Dunay, "In New York City, you have a tremendous number of people from Europe, Mexico, South America and so many other influences. To have a jewelry store there, you have to offer a wider span of jewelry styles than in Chicago."

Targeting a region: When discussing regional differences, it's important not to oversimplify. Even the smallest town has a variety of humanity. And where demographics vary, so should the merchandise mix.

J.C. Penney has 21 stores in Chicago and several different jewelry assortments among them. "In an affluent northern suburb called Northbrook, we do a bigger diamond business," Don McKean says. "In the Brickyard, a mall in Northwest Chicago where there are more ethnic and lower-income groups, we sell more gold and watches."

To further complicate matters, the U.S. has a very mobile population. Not only do we travel for business and pleasure, we move frequently. Still, different regions have been found to have overall preferences and personalities that you should take into account when formulating a marketing strategy.

Barbara Westwood caters to such differences by allowing jewelers to customize her pieces to suit the tastes of their clienteles. "We offer a designer mounting line that the retailer can reorder with his stone-of-choice, making it a one-of-a-kind piece," she says. "In New England, a jeweler might choose a half-carat round diamond, in Beverly Hills a 3-ct. diamond and in Wyoming a colored stone. It can be easily customized to fit the region and also price points without invalidating the integrity of the design."

In addition, fine design and craftsmanship are regionless as well as timeless, and a well-positioned brand name doesn't hurt either. Tiffany, for example, says its lines sell equally well everywhere. "Our designs range from traditional to contemporary," says Tiffany spokesperson Susan Sussman. "We merchandise to about 100 jewelry accounts across the country, but in different depths from different categories. I think it's more the individual buyer's sense of merchandising than regional preferences."

Klecka sums it up best: "Different regions focus more on different items, but consistency in a designer's work and in a brand name goes a long way in overcoming the diversity in regions and taste levels."

10 Steps To Assessing Image

August 1993 Part II

1. Don't be misled by what a woman wears. In the movie Pretty Woman, Julia Roberts' character enters a tony Beverly Hills store dressed in her hooker's outfit. The sales staff (female, by the way) snubs her and escorts her out—even though she's ready to spend thousands of dollars. Roberts returns to the store wearing a designer dress and is greeted warmly. Naturally, she takes revenge and walks out.

2. That being said, there are ways to form a general idea of your customer's income, taste and self-value. Observe the consistency of quality of what she wears.

3. Pocketbooks are one good barometer. A woman wearing jeans and sneakers but carrying an expensive handbag probably has some money to spend. Visit upscale department or luggage stores and look at the top-line pocketbooks

(including Coach, Dooney & Bourke, Mark Cross, Bally, Louis Vuitton and Gucci). Then look at some moderately priced lines such as Liz Claiborne and Etienne Aigner. Also look at lower-end bags so you'll know how to tell the difference.

4. Look at her shoes. Familiarize yourself with better, designer-type shoes (such as Stephanie Kelian, Manolo Blahnik and Ferragamo); popular moderate lines (such as Nine West and Naturalizer) and budget-priced shoes. How much a woman spends on shoes and bags can indicate her attitude toward spending and her income and taste levels. Check also to see whether the quality of her shoes is consistent with the quality of her bag, suggests Edna Jacques.

5. Look at her clothes. Set aside personal style and assess their quality. Is the fabric frayed or covered with "pills" or "fuzz"? Natural linen will be somewhat (or very) wrinkled. Cotton has either a crisp look if it's woven or a comfortable, solid look if it's knit. Good-quality woven or knit wools are virtually ageless, maintaining their shape and texture for years. Natural silks—indeed most natural fibers— flow and drape softly against the skin. Remember that good natural fibers tend to be more expensive than their man-made cousins, but poor-quality natural fibers exhibit the same tendencies as cheap polyester.

6. Learn to recognize good workmanship in clothes. Are plaids or stripes matched at the seams? Are her clothes clean and pressed? Does the garment fit properly? Are the colors consistent? Is the garment in good repair? Does her outfit look pulled together, well-accessorized and coordinated? Visit the best clothing store you can find, as well as moderately priced shops and budget stores. You're not there to make a value judgment, only to learn how to recognize which market your customer comes from.

7. Look at her hair. If her hair is well-cut, it swings in unison, the edges are in sync and it falls back into place when she moves her head. Good hair care isn't cheap, so this is another indicator of a woman's personal standards and income level.

8. Listen to her manner of speaking. Do her speech and choice of words indicate she's well-educated?

9 Watch her gestures. Generally, women from higher socioeconomic backgrounds tend to "occupy less space," says Anne Ginsberg. They move with smaller, more graceful movements—as if they went to finishing school and were taught to walk with a book on their heads. They also are far less likely to fuss frequently with their hair, make sweeping dramatic gestures or pull at their clothing in public.

10. Remember there are exceptions to every rule! Like the Pretty Woman example, a woman decked out in polyester stretch pants may have just received a bonus at work and want to treat herself to jewelry. The best rule of thumb? Treat every woman as though she's a long-lost relative about to leave you $10 million!

Meet The Future...
And It Is Female

August 1993 Part II

Come meet the average American.

In 1990 (the last Census year), says *American Demographics* magazine, the average American was a 32-year-old woman who stood 5'4", weighed 143 pounds, had brown hair, was married with one child and worked in a technical, sales or administrative job. She wore a size 10 or 12 dress and size 7 1/2 B shoes; she also wore jewelry every day, and she bought most of it herself.

That last trend is growing, according to a recent poll of the JCK Retail Jewelers Panel on the subject of the women's self-purchase market. Indeed, 84% of the panelists said that in the past five years, they've noticed a moderate to significant increase in the number of women buying jewelry for themselves.

The World Gold Council already knows the significance of this market—almost two-thirds of all women's gold jewelry sold is bought by women, and the council's prime target market is working women ages 18-54. The Silver Institute says women also are the primary buyers of sterling silver jewelry. And the self-purchasing woman is the target market for Argyle's champagne diamond jewelry.

"I think the women's self-purchase market is the largest growing segment [of the jewelry market] outside of bridal," says Liz Chatelain, vice president of Argyle's Champagne Diamond Registry.

To understand the power of this market, you first must understand the cultural changes that have occurred since the beginning of this century—especially in the past 50 years.

In 1940, the average American was a 29-year-old male with a ninth-grade education who could be fairly certain to find a solid factory job with which he could support a family. In 1890, the average American was a 22-year-old male farmhand whose wife was not allowed to vote!

But in the past 20-30 years, societal attitudes toward women have shifted. The "traditional American family" is commonly thought to be a nuclear family consisting of working father, stay-at-home mother and 2.2 children. In truth, this family structure was an anomaly that occurred as the nation grew into the Industrial Age and peaked in the post-World War II era amid great prosperity and little foreign competition. Traditionally, most American women have always worked, though it was on the family farm until industrialization divided spouses into the roles of bread-winner and bread-baker.

As economic pressures forced more and more women to take jobs outside the home, society developed a picture of the Superwoman successfully juggling multiple roles. While this perfect Superwoman is largely a myth, many women do have to do double or triple duty as paid worker, wife and/or mother. Some say women have made great strides in the workplace in the past 20 years, while others, such as author Susan Faludi in her best-selling book *Backlash: The Undeclared War Against American Women*, argue that women have lost ground in their fight for equality.

Whether they're being paid, promoted or treated equally, it's certainly true that more women are in the work force, more women do control their own finances and, most importantly to you, more women feel they need not wait for a man to give them jewelry or permission to buy it. Women have more choices available to them—and less social pressure to conform to what's "proper"—than ever before.

Women and your bottom line: Is selling jewelry to a woman really so different from selling it to a man?

"Absolutely!" says David Morrow, manager of training and education for the Diamond Promotion Service. "A man buying jewelry for a woman wants to express his feelings and to make himself look good in her eyes and everyone else's eyes. A woman simply buys a piece of jewelry because she likes it. And she would like other women to compliment her taste, the same as when she buys a dress."

Other industry experts concur. Chatelain points out that men buy jewelry for a variety of reasons from romance to power, but women buy jewelry to reward themselves. And they're coming to feel it's perfectly OK to spend discretionary money on jewelry without feeling guilty that they should have spent it on the family. (Note the use of the word discretionary—this is money available after the household expenses are paid.)

The whole shopping process differs between men and women just as much as the reason for buying. For starters, design affects women far more than men. "When selling to a female, jewelers should know that design is the primary motivator," says Christine Yorke, merchandise manager of the World Gold Council. "She's looking for a specific style and is generally willing to go out of a set price to get the style."

Women also go out on a design limb, she says, while men tend to be much more conservative and stick to tried-and-true classics.

The importance of aesthetics even carries over into sport watches—a traditionally male market where function has been prized over form. Pamela Fields, president of TAG Heuer, says the company noticed that sales to men and women were almost equal, especially in the Sports Elegance line [the most feminine style it offers]. "We slapped our foreheads," she says. "We were attracting women even though we weren't promoting or advertising to them."

Now the firm has targeted women for a major marketing effort. "I think aesthetics and fashion drive the female purchase more than pure function," says Fields. But don't think for a minute that function is lost on females, she cautions. Women don't want to give up the functions for which they bought a sport watch, they just want it to look nice—and so increasingly do men. "Ugly just doesn't cut it anymore," says Fields.

Instead, WGC research shows women usually seek "updated classics." They want fresh, interesting design, but they also want to love that piece of jewelry for a long time.

Apparel-jewelry connection: Is there a connection between apparel and fine jewelry?

Traditionally, not a lot, says Yorke. It's not connected the way apparel and costume jewelry are. But there is one very crucial connection: shopping behavior.

Women are used to browsing, she explains, and jewelers need to understand that. Some women, like most men, know what they want, go to a specific store, buy the item and leave. But many women enjoy shopping as a leisure activity, comparing prices and merchandise and seeing what tempts them to buy. Even they are becoming increasingly pressed for time, however, so efficient service is more critical than ever.

Jewelers who want to succeed in the female market need to replicate the apparel shopping experience as closely as possible, says Yorke. This requires visible pricing, a liberal return policy and an understanding of women's learned shopping behavior. It's also important that jewelers wear what they sell.

WGC is a strong proponent of visible pricing and of making it easy for women to see merchandise in a showcase without interference from a salesperson. This theory is carried out in two Gold Stores, which are prototype stores devoted specifically to selling karat gold jewelry and testing WGC theories. These stores display merchandise in a "shopper-friendly" environment, at eye level with visible pricing, which invites browsing.

On the other hand, Alan Master, national director of training and education for the Diamond Promotion Service, feels that giving a visible price range (for example, "from $150 to $500") is enough to show the customer that "there's something here for me."

Visible pricing is just one element of the typical apparel shopping experience, which includes being able to look freely through the garments on the rack, find the right size, mull over the style and compare prices mentally—and privately.

This brings up another difference in selling to male or female customers. Women like to have time alone, says Yorke, whereas men tend to prefer assistance. "When a woman is left to herself, she can convince herself to spend more," says Yorke. "The salesperson is there to provide reinforcement to a decision that's already been made and, by talking about quality or workmanship, can seal the sale." Of course, a salesperson should be available to answer in an instant any questions that will help to satisfy a woman's need for information.

Wearing what you sell also is important in building desire in female customers. Retail experts from jewelry and apparel firms concur that you are the best advertisement for your merchandise. National apparel chains such as Banana Republic and The Limited require sales associates to wear the current season's fashions, and make it easy for employees to buy them.

Jewelry experts agree. Toni Lyn Judd, a designer representative, tells her retail clients to wear a jewelry uniform. "I fervently believe that jewelry should be worn. I make a little contest among my clients. I tell them to pick two ensembles from the case, make an index card to check them out in the morning and back in in the evening, then see how many pieces they sell. I wager they'll sell more than 50% of it."

She also says most consumers don't have a good way to see jewelry and fashion together. People in the industry are used to seeing it at jewelry shows, but the average consumer needs the jeweler as a role model.

Morrow adds, "If I knew salespeople were going to a special function in town, I'd want to make sure they were wearing my jewelry. I'd do whatever it takes on my jewelers' block policy to make this possible. It's a form of advertising!"

Finally, adds Yorke, a liberal return policy is a strong selling tool for women. "Even if you spend $1,500 on a suit at Saks or Bloomingdale's, if you get home and it doesn't work, you can take it back." Make your return policy known, otherwise customers will feel uncomfortable asking about it. "Reassure a wavering customer that she can bring it back if it doesn't work with her wardrobe," says Morrow. "Don't wait for the customer to ask."

Many jewelers worry that a woman will buy something, wear it for an event, then bring it back. It happens, says Morrow, but most women who want a piece of jewelry want to own it.

Politically correct: The one thing women don't need is permission from their husbands to buy jewelry—or to have a jeweler suggest that they do.

"It's a respect thing, and it goes two ways," says Andrew Johnson of the Johnson Family Diamond Center, Columbus, Ohio. "Do I think a woman should confer with her husband if she's going to spend a lot of money on a piece of jewelry? Sure! But at the same time, if her husband is going to spend a lot of money on a piece of stereo equipment or a power tool, then I think he should confer with her!"

Chatelain of the Champagne Diamond Registry says the only person who needs to approve of the piece is the one purchasing it. Suggest she take it home, tell her that her husband will love her taste and reassure her of her own gut feeling. Chatelain also points out that "big ticket" is relative – a husband may feel perfectly comfortable spending more than $100 on tickets for a ball game, so there's no reason for a woman to feel she can't reward herself with a piece of jewelry. And if a woman feels she wants to confer with her husband first, she'll tell you.

Be certain never to talk down to your female customer. Her buying decision may depend more on the design of a piece than the intrinsic value of its metals and gems, says Yorke, but that doesn't mean she isn't concerned with quality and workmanship.

"Whether the customer is male or female, they need information," says TAG Heuer's Fields. If a jeweler gets too technical, a woman's eyes may glaze over [and so may a man's], but don't talk down to her, she says. "Jewelry may be more of an emotional purchase than a sport watch, but in either case, the customer needs to fall in love with the product," she says. "If you spend $15, you don't need to love the product. If you're spending $1,500, you'd better love it. Nobody needs a $1,500 watch!"

The bottom line, she says, is to build trust and not treat women in a patronizing or offensive way. These customers have intelligence, money, decision-making power and a desire for respect. They're also free to walk out of your store and into your competitor's.

What Women Spend

Here's what panelists say a typical woman customer spends on a piece of jewelry for herself.
- Less than $150—20.5% of panelists.
- $150-$300—37.3% of panelists.
Most often cited figures: $200 or $250.
- $300-$500—23.3%.
- $500-$1,000—12.0%.
- $1,000-$2,000—5.6%.
- More than $2,000—2.8%.
- Other respondents gave wide ranges, such as "from $50 to $50,000."
*Percentages are approximate because some respondents gave more than one range.

Source: JCK Retail Jewelers Panel

Style, Female Appeal Crucial To Bridal Sales

Suzy Spencer ◆ *July 1993*

Women are becoming more involved in the purchase of their engagement and wedding rings. At David Craig Jewelers Ltd. in Langhorne, Pa., for example, women often choose the engagement rings. "The man is just there for the checkbook," says owner David Rotenberg.

A December 1992 Cahners Research study commissioned by *Modern Bride* magazine backs that up, and adds this information:

- 65% of the women surveyed selected their engagement ring—with or without their fiancé present. In only one-third of the cases did the fiancé pick the ring alone.
- 89% of the respondents had input in the selection process.
- Style was the most important factor in selecting the engagement ring. Eighty-one percent of the respondents called it "very important."

• Price was less crucial, with fewer than 50% saying it was "very important." In fact, guarantee and retailer reputation were more important than price.

• The respondents' engagement rings averaged almost $2,800 and their wedding rings slightly more than $700.

• The diamonds in the engagement rings averaged 1 ct. t.w.

• 57% of the engagement rings were solitaires, 55% of the rings had a round center stone and 23% had a marquise center stone.

• Style was the most important factor in selecting a wedding ring, as well.

• Women and their fiancés visited an average of five stores when shopping for an engagement ring; 43% bought their rings at an independent jewelry store and 30% at a chain jewelry store.

• More than three-quarters of those surveyed got their engagement ring style ideas from stores.

• 53% bought their wedding ring at the same store as their engagement ring; 31% bought their engagement and wedding rings at the same time.

• More than three-quarters of the respondents planned to give their fiancés a wedding gift. Nearly a fifth of those gifts were to be a wedding band with diamonds; another fifth would be watches.

• The average cost of the groom's ring was slightly more than $400 without diamonds, almost $950 with diamonds.

• $400 is the average top price a bride is willing to pay for her groom's watch.

• More than 27% of the respondents planned to give their bridal party a gift of fine jewelry.

• Average annual incomes were $26,700 for the respondents and $32,100 for their fiancés.

New Faces:
The Fight For Market Share

June 1993

As department stores and jewelry chains retrench from the overleveraged Eighties, new retail sources are tapping into the jewelry market.

Alternate sales channels such as warehouse clubs and televised merchandising have attracted scores of jewelry buyers in the past five years. Discount stores and discount department stores continue to add jewelry to their wide merchandise mixes. And catalog and catalog showroom jewelry sales operate as efficiently and effectively as chain-store jewelers.

These retailers clearly compete for the same dollars sought by jewelry retailers that sell charms, 10k and 14k gold chain and earrings, moderately priced engagement rings and wedding sets. Many jewelry retailers have battled discounter tactics creatively. Some have joined their ranks; others have carved new niches, expanded their target markets and cut costs in order to compete.

Market share: How much jewelry do these alternative sources sell? The totals aren't always clear, but it's certain they're selling more than ever, say industry observers.

If jewelry stores still command the 53% share of jewelry sales reported in 1987 (the most recent figures available from the U.S. Census Bureau), then jewelers accounted for roughly $14 billion of the estimated $26 billion U.S. jewelry market in 1992. Put another way, outlets other than chain or independent jewelry stores sold at least $12 billion worth of jewelry last year.

But the 53% market share reported for jewelry stores in 1987 may have changed. Many industry observers expect that when official government figures are updated to 1992, they'll confirm that non-jewelry store jewelry sales have cornered a bigger share of the total market.

Consider the following:

• Last year, Service Merchandise, the catalog showroom giant that dominates its market for jewelry sales, filled nearly $1 billion worth of jewelry orders.

• At the same time, the two major televised shopping networks, QVC Network, Inc., and Home Shopping Network, together sold more than $1 billion worth of jewelry. Jewelry is by far the largest single sales category for each network.

• Few warehouse clubs even existed five years ago. Now the more than 600 outlets nationwide may sell up to $640 million worth of jewelry each year.

• In each of the past two years, the retail channel reporting the largest increase in sales of karat gold jewelry has been the "discount store" group—up 8% to $792 million in 1991 and up 10% to $871 million in 1992, according to the World Gold Council.

Growth of discount outlets: So-called discount stores account for only about 10% of all karat gold sales. But discount and catalog showrooms combined sold $2.25 billion worth of karat gold jewelry—more than did independent jewelry stores, according to the World Gold Council.

This doesn't include karat gold sales at QVC or HSN, which the council does not yet quantify. Using a conservative $500 million estimate of karat gold sales at these two networks (neither keeps separate statistics for karat gold sales) brings total sales at television, discount and catalog retail outlets to $2.75 billion, topping the council's figures for chain store jewelers.

To be sure, many traditional jewelry stores wouldn't stock much of the gold jewelry sold though discount stores, catalogs and television programs Still, the proliferation of discount outlets and their increased interest in all types of jewelry, not just gold, has many in the industry watching carefully.

Here's a closer look at alternative sources.

DISCOUNT STORES

Low price points are clearly the fuel for growth at discount stores such as Wal-Mart and Kmart, says Ed Anderson, vice president of sales at Princess Pride, Chicago.

"Their buying is no different than the large jewelry chains," he says. But their retail prices can be lower and national marketing muscle stronger because they operate under tighter margins, enjoy higher volumes and place jewelry alongside scores of other merchandise categories (clothes and hardware, for instance).

A list of the top 25 discount retailers compiled by *Discount Store News* last year includes names that some jewelers consider primary or secondary competition—particularly for low-price-point volume goods. Wal-Mart and its subsidiary Sam's Club, Target, Kmart and Montgomery Ward are joined by Service Merchandise (No. 12 with $3.4 billion in sales in 1991; 1992 sales were $3.7 billion).

All discount stores enjoyed strong growth in recent years, particularly during the recession, according to the Management Horizons division of accounting firm Price Waterhouse. However, discount store annual sales growth should slow from 5.2% in each of the past five years to 2.7% in coming years, according to the firm's *U.S. Retail Outlook to 1997*.

The largest companies—Wal-Mart, Kmart and Target—will continue to boost their market shares at the expense of many other traditional discounters. However, other formats, including warehouse clubs, are expected to gain ground, too, according to the report.

WAREHOUSE CLUBS

Mingled in among the top 25 discounters are five membership warehouse clubs: Sam's Club of Bentonville, Ark.; Price Club of San Diego, Cal.; Costco of Kirkland, Wash.; Pace of Engelwood, Colo.; and B.J.'s Wholesale Club of Natick, Mass.

Warehouse clubs, which typically operate in facilities exceeding 100,000 sq. ft., keep prices as low as—or lower than—typical discount stores through bulk buying, low overhead and tight margins. They sell "memberships" for a small annual fee to individuals as well as to groups such as credit unions, schools, churches and businesses. A member-customer has access to merchandise in the store.

In all, some eight major firms now operate nearly 600 wholesale club outlets nationwide. Last year, these clubs sold an estimated $32 billion worth of merchandise. While jewelry remains a small part of overall sales (estimates range from less than 1% to 3%), that still adds up to between $320 million and $960 million in 1992.

None of the clubs would give sales breakdowns, but some estimates are possible. Sam's Club (owned by Wal-Mart) and Pace (a subsidiary of Kmart) sell karat gold, silver, watches and a few fashion accessories supplied by Jan Bell Marketing Inc., Sunrise, Fla. Last year, Jan Bell sold $116.6 million worth of goods to its largest customer, Sam's Club. Pace, Jan Bell's second largest customer, bought $38.1 million worth of goods from Jan Bell, its only jewelry supplier.

Estimating a retail markup of 12%-25%, these two clubs alone could have combined jewelry sales of $173 million to $193 million. Because Sam's may buy from additional jewelry firms, these estimates likely are conservative.

Jewelry sales at the clubs are likely to catch up to catalogs soon. Even if they don't add more merchandise, an increase in the number of outlets (at least 100 are expected to open this year) is likely to spur overall jewelry volume.

Low-margins: John Calnon, World Gold Council director of merchandise planning, agrees that growth will continue at the clubs, primarily due to their value appeal and their ability to operate by selling high-turnover jewelry at very low margins.

Manufacturers say the clubs—and their discount-store cousins—operate at substantially lower margins than the typical jewelry chain store. The clubs don't disclose retail markup, of course, but several jewelry manufacturers offered estimates ranging from 10% to 25% over wholesale cost.

But low margins and low operating expenses (including consolidated shipping costs, lower wages and spare display) are only part of the equation. Equally critical is the club or discounter's ability to negotiate costs with manufacturers. Unlike most independents and many jewelry chain stores, the warehouse club or discount store often can take advantage of higher volume/early payment schedules that invariably shave several percentage points off the final purchase price.

And because the discounter's target market is limited in most cases to buyers of jewelry priced at $99-$499, the firm's needs are clear. Unlike a retail jeweler—who seeks to appeal to several groups of customers—the discounter need not use multiple vendors for its jewelry.

Pricing advantages are not a given, however. One major vendor says a mass merchant may have a long list of custom demands, including prepackaging, prepaid freight, stock balancing, marketing assistance and labeling. Any of these demands can increase the price the vendor charges a store, regardless of size. In fact, adds the vendor, a larger chain store with greater demands may be charged more for certain items than a small retailer.

CATALOGS/SHOWROOMS

Catalog and catalog showroom jewelry sales leveled off in 1992 after several years of decline. A major dip occurred when Best Products Inc. of Richmond, Va., filed for Chapter 11 bankruptcy protection in 1991. The following year, the World Gold Council said karat gold sales by catalog showrooms rebounded a modest 0.3% to $1.4 billion.

Service Merchandise Co. ,Inc., Nashville, Tenn., dominates the category with nearly $1 billion in jewelry sales. Though jewelry sales as a percentage of overall sales dropped slightly in 1992, better inventory management and higher margins keep gold and diamond jewelry at the forefront of the firm's reputation. Self-dubbed "America's Leading Jeweler," Service Merchandise operates 372 stores and does, indeed, sell more jewelry under one name than any retail source in the U.S. Charles Septer, the firm's divisional senior vice president of jewelry merchandising, says some new lines will be added this year, though the current mix of bridal diamond and karat gold items will remain largely intact. Popular prices range from $150 to $500.

While Best works toward reorganizing and Service Merchandise continues to expand, L. Luria & Son Inc., of

Miami Lakes, Fla., is moving away from the catalog showroom business. President Peter Luria calls his new prototype store in Suniland, Fla., a specialty discount retailer. During the next five years, the remainder of the 52-store chain will be modeled after the prototype (see sidebar).

Luria's jewelry sales for years have been third largest among the major catalog showrooms, says Jean Coticchio, president of the National Association of Catalog Showroom Executives. For the fiscal year ended January 30, 1993, Luria reported that jewelry accounted for about $87 million of its $235 million in total sales. Total sales increased 13.5% from the previous year.

Among catalogs with substantial jewelry sales, manufacturers cite Fingerhut, Cos., Inc., of Minnetonka, Minn.; Spiegel, Inc., of Downers Grove, Ill.; and Ross Simon of Cranston, R.I.

Arthur Kapplow Jr., vice president of merchandising-jewelry, for Fingerhut, estimates that $750 million to $1 billion worth of jewelry is sold through catalogs nationwide. At Fingerhut, jewelry provides 7% of overall sales, or about $105 million of the $1.5 billion total in 1992.

With a 7,000-sq.-ft. jewelry vault, the firm's inventory and investment in jewelry rivals that of a medium-sized jewelry chain. A computer system tracks all jewelry sales and helps the firm keep inventory records and test new styles.

Fingerhut's standard catalog contains 10 pages of jewelry, but customers also receive six jewelry-only catalogs each year. The firm stresses a monthly payment plan, but doesn't advertise specific "sales" or discount prices. "I think the customer is starting to get tired of seeing the big discounts, the big markups and the markdowns," says Kapplow. He adds that while many discounters have been quite successful in the past, he sees "value pricing" as the trend of the future. He points to Wal-Mart and Home Depot, among others, as successful practitioners of value pricing.

TELEVISION SHOPPING

Jewelry is by far the best selling merchandise category at both major nationwide television shopping networks.

Jewelry accounted for 45%-46% of total sales in each of the past three years for QVC Network, Inc., of West Chester, Pa. While the sales figures don't distinguish between fashion and fine jewelry, most of the firm's sales are 10k to 18k gold jewelry. In 1992, QVC reported sales of $1.07 billion; jewelry sales totaled about $481.5 million. Diamonique, a simulated gemstone jewelry firm owned by QVC, accounted for $67.1 million of the total.

Home Shopping Network, Inc., of St. Petersburg, Fla., says 49% of its sales are jewelry. In the fiscal year ended Aug. 31, 1992, HSN recorded $1.1 billion in total sales, about $537.9 million of it jewelry.

OTHER SOURCES

The U.S. Army and Air Force have combined retail exchanges that sold about $7 billion worth of goods in 300 general merchandise stores worldwide in 1992. Jewelry and watch sales accounted for 3.5% of the total, or $245 million. Currently, more than 10 million military personnel are eligible to buy at the exchanges.

As a sales market, military exchanges often are considered an out-of-the-ordinary retail channel. As one manufacturer quips, the exchanges operate in "another world" where pricing is not dictated by standard market forces. Firms that manufacture for the military praise its high quality standards and careful buying procedures.

The Navy, which has a separate exchange service for its personnel, is reorganizing its retail service. Representatives were not available for comment.

There are still other jewelry sales outlets, including retailers who illicitly market their services as "wholesaling to the public." State attorneys general, assisted by legitimate retailers and the Jewelers Vigilance Committee, have attacked the problem with some success. Still, sales via this channel remain significant in various markets. N.W. Ayer, the U.S. advertising, marketing and research firm for De Beers, estimate such sales at $232 million annually for diamond jewelry alone, based on figures from 1988 to 1990. The total likely will be much greater when updated later this year.

The same study also estimates diamond sales by any remaining retail channels, including noncatalog mail order, sales from friends or employers, private dealer and foreign sales. Each is estimated at $116 million to $232 million, representing 1%-2% of all diamond jewelry sales.

From Catalog Showroom to Specialty Discounter

Though Hurricane Andrew destroyed much of L. Luria & Son, Inc.'s, South Miami store last year, it also created an opportunity for owners of the 52-store catalog showroom chain.

Executives decided to push ahead by a full year their plan to begin changing from a catalog showroom to a specialty discount store operation. The hurricane-damaged outlet was a perfect spot to develop a prototype.

"We had 71 days to get it ready," says Peter Luria, president and chief executive. "We had people work two shifts, seven days a week so the store would be ready to open by November 21, just in time for holiday shopping."

The new store was an immediate hit and helped to boost the firm's overall sales for the year to $235 million, up 13.5% from the previous year.

The new format, to appear in existing and new stores over the next five years, will allow shoppers to navigate wider aisles in a larger selling area. Though the prototype is 28,000 sq. ft., other new and renovated sites will measure 40,000 sq. ft. New stores already are being planned for Cutler Ridge Mall in Dade County, Sawgrass Mills Shopping Mall in Broward County, St. Petersburg and Hollywood. All Luria stores are in Florida.

The new stores will stress Luria's history and reputation as a source for jewelry. Though Luria sells a wide line of consumer goods—including housewares, gifts and electronics—jewelry remains its top merchandise category. In fact, jewelry comprises 37% of sales—a higher percentage than at any other major catalog showroom.

Jewelry departments in the new stores will be 25% larger and will remain in a dominant position, says Luria. While most other departments will be self-service, jewelry departments will be full-service, complete with staff jewelers and polishers. They will showcase more styles of karat gold and diamond jewelry and more watches (Luria doesn't sell costume or gold-filled jewelry). The firm's most popular jewelry items this year: gold chains, freshwater pearls and low-priced tennis bracelets.

The change: Why change from a catalog showroom to a specialty discount retailer? Luria says the potential for growth of catalog showrooms is limited. A major reason is that customers have less time to shop, and less time to wait for items to be delivered from a catalog showroom's stockroom. The prototype store averts the wait.

Even before the prototype store opened, Luria took a step toward becoming a specialty discount operation by distributing its catalogs in stores rather than through the mail. "Many older customers buy from the catalogs and, for bridal goods, they represent the variety we offer," Luria says. "But catalogs are less important than they used to be. They aren't flexible." Direct mail, newspaper inserts, radio and television allow advertisement of newer goods that may have been acquired too late to include in the catalog.

In addition, the firm saved $1 million by not mailing the catalog. Luria will continue to produce the catalog because it hopes to start a mail-order service in several years.

Consumers Shop Less, Demand More

April 1993

Consumers in the 1990s will narrow their shopping destinations and limit their time in stores because of more shopping options and less time, according to a poll conducted for the National Retail Federation by Mimi Lieber at LAR Management Consultants and Yankelovich Partners, Inc.

Thirty-two percent of consumers polled said they spend less time shopping than two years ago; 45% spend the same amount of time and 23% spend more time.

Other findings:

• Customers with higher incomes and those with children tend to shop more often.

• Customers older than 30—especially those 50-74—are more likely to shop less. Retirees said they visit department stores more than any other type of outlet.

• As consumers earn more, they increase the number of types of stores where they shop.

• Women are more likely to frequent clothing boutiques; men are likely to go to a category or specialty store.

• Younger shoppers are more likely to shop at clothing boutiques and factory outlets.

The study also identifies five primary shopping types:

• Price Hounds (22% of respondents), who constantly search for the lowest price.

• Low-interest Shoppers (22%), who typically don't find shopping exciting.

• Brand Bargain Hunters (20%), who still cling to the status brand names of the 1980s but seek good buys.

• Quality Service Enthusiasts (19%), who expect high levels of service.

• Disenchanted Shoppers (17%), often men who have given up on finding an enjoyable shopping experience.

From these categories, three are most likely to regularly visit a specialty store such as a jewelry store: Quality Store Enthusiasts, Brand Bargain Hunters and Disenchanted Shoppers. These customers rate service among the most critical factors that determine where they shop, the study adds.

Where Customers Shop

TV shopping network—5%
Factory outlet—22%
Warehouse store—30%
Discount store—33%
Mail-order catalog—36%
Clothing boutique—37%
Regional dept. store chain—51%
Specialty store—58%
Mass merchant—70%
National dept. store chain—70%

Source: National Retail Federation Consumer Behavior Study

Winning Customers With Custom Design

November 1992

Jewelers nationwide are responding to a clear and growing consumer interest in custom-designed pieces. In fact, two-thirds of jewelers polled by JCK in August say consumer interest in one-of-a-kind pieces has led to increased sales in their stores.

The interest in a unique "look" is a reflection of the heightened buying power women are exerting in the jewelry marketplace, according to many retailers. Coupled with recent fashion trends that focus on more colored stones, fancy diamond cuts and alloyed or metal mixtures, customized goods are poised for growth, they say. Retailers who have seen increased requests for custom jewelry often point to "greater fashion awareness" or "a different attitude" to explain why women—and some men—are more likely today to ask for an item not displayed at their showcase.

The prominence of designer names throughout the fashion world also has generated awareness of the appeal of a distinctive look. Increasingly, customers show retailers photos from fashion magazines and request jewelry of similar—though not exact—appearance.

"Basically, the people we design for are thrilled to death to have something different," says Jann Anderson of Erik Jewelers, Buffalo, N.Y., whose store is known as a custom-order shop.

Who buys and why? Custom-designed pieces now account for 13% of a typical jeweler's sales, according to the JCK poll.

According to many retailers, women over 35 constitute the largest segment of the customers who buy this jewelry. Their interest lies primarily in the following areas:

• Exclusivity. Many already have their wedding rings and are searching for a "signature" piece, generally another ring or a pendant, that generates a stronger individualized fashion statement. "It seems that every customer wants something different," says Robert Shay, owner of Galperin Jewelry in Charleston, W. Va. Special-order business at Galperin Jewelry has increased steadily in recent years and now accounts for more than 25% of total annual sales volume. Shay even hired an additional bench jeweler to help with the increase in custom orders in the past two years.

•A new look for old jewelry. "Many are just tired of the rings they inherited," says Terry Dickens, manager of Harteen & Stocker, a jewelry firm in Iowa City, Iowa, that earns 15% of its total sales from custom-ordered items. "About 75% of the rings we make are custom-ordered." Though many of these are simpler remounts, much of the custom work involves adding colored stones or side diamonds in a new setting.

• The appeal of having something that is handmade. Of course, it's critical that the jeweler be able to translate the customer's design ideas into a finished piece, says William Kingoff, owner of two Kingoff's Inc. stores in Wilmington, N.C. "Many customers want to talk to the person who is making their piece," he says. Adds Dickens, "People like the idea that they have some involvement in creating the piece."

Creating the design: While a few customers enter their local jewelry store with a specific design in mind, most are unaware of what can be accomplished by a talented jeweler, says Dickens.

"Half know what they want, others are completely blank," he says. Often, consumers in the latter group are easier to satisfy because they are willing to discuss the pros and cons of different designs, resulting in a piece that is accepted relatively early in the design stage.

"I treat the customers as if they have an idea of what they want," says Ruth Gillam of Gillam's Originals, Marshalltown, Iowa. "But nine-tenths of them really don't."

Jewelers advise that even if a customer seems sure about the design he or she initially inquires about, each detail should be discussed carefully.

Gillam says designers at Studio Designs, her store's parent firm in neighboring Waterloo take the customer's ideas and sketch several workable prototypes. A finished piece can be delivered in less than two weeks on average, she adds.

Christopher Heffern, owner of Elleard B. Heffern Inc., St. Louis, Mo., creates a wax model. "It gives the customer a good idea of what the piece is going to feel like one it's made," he explains. About 25% of Heffern's items are custom-ordered.

Growth market: While only a small percentage of jewelers have cultivated a reputation as a custom jeweler—as Gillam and Heffern have—traditional retailers say they realize the potential growth of their custom jewelry services.

Paul Cohen, owner of Continental Jewelers in Wilmington, Del., says only a few customers have requested truly original designs in the past year. Most who express interest generally want a remount. Still, more customers do ask about new designs than in years past, he says.

To meet and cultivate that interest, Cohen recently hired a full-time jeweler who can render wax carvings and is a proficient setter and caster. Early last year, he bought a complete casting facility to expand his ability to create customized jewelry.

"Most of the growth we have seen in the demand for custom design is a result of our sales staff presenting it as an option," he says. Most customers still fear that a customized piece will be prohibitively expensive, he says. But with five full-time staffers who are trained to help a customer with a custom-designed piece (and assure them of its affordability), Cohen expects sales of such items to expand in the near future.

Independent edge: The ability to crate custom design jewelry isn't limited to independent jewelers, but they're the ones who seem to attract most custom orders. The reason: independent retailers are more likely to have a jeweler and/or designer on staff who can create the piece more quickly.

"They go to a chain store and are told [a custom piece] could take eight to ten weeks," says Dickens. "We can do it in 10 to 14 days."

Many smaller chain stores (and some independent stores) work closely with contractors and effectively compete in the custom-design market. But larger chains with limited flexibility and purchasing knowledge often appear less prepared to handle such requests. "The chains just don't attract this type of business," says Kingoff. "They don't have the people in their stores who do the buying so they don't understand how pieces fit together."

Another factor for independents is direct competition—or, more accurately, lack of it. "There are fewer jewelers in the area who do custom design," says Eileen Eichhorn of Eichhorn's Jewelry Store in Decatur, Ind. "Two independents in the immediate area who used to do it retired, and three others have changed careers." As a result, 40% of her annual sales now involve custom-designed jewelry.

With fewer independents vying for an increasingly active customer base, retailers with a reputation for creating designs are drawing new customers.

"We are now the oldest jewelry store in Wilmington," says Kingoff, whose store was founded 72 years ago. In recent years, several area jewelers who specialized in custom work have closed and their customers now have come to rely on Kingoff's Inc.

Concerns: While the prospect of a growing niche in the jewelry market is attractive to most retailers, many are quick to note the numerous problems associated with customized orders.

Customers can have unrealistic expectations regarding the finished product, retailers say. "Sometimes they ask for odd-size stones to be channel-set or they have other impossible design requests," says Randall Chambers of Chambers Fine Jewelers Inc. In Ft. Worth, Tex.

Adds Robert O. Evans of R. Evans Jewelers in Bozeman, Mont., "One of the greatest difficulties is getting the customer not to use every chipped small or worthless stone in Aunt Tillie's old ring."

Customers often have a difficult time visualizing the final three-dimensional piece from a two-dimensional piece from a two-dimensional sketch, retailers say.

To avoid disappointing the customer, not to mention wasting bench time and materials, you must make your own vision of the piece clear early in the design process. Indeed, a few jewelers we queried have given up on custom design because the labor costs tipped profits into the red. Rejection of finished pieces and extended design times generally take the blame.

To counter these adverse possibilities, jewelers offer the following suggestions:

• Provide a wax model or use similar-looking jewelry to keep customers expectations realistic.

• Keep a talented designer on staff or be sure one is easily accessible.

• Be certain that sales clerks understand all design and manufacturing processes needed to satisfy the demanding buyer of custom jewelry.

• Thoroughly explain to customers the processes used to create the jewelry and let them see your jeweler working at the bench. That will help them to understand why the cost increase as a piece becomes more customized.

With these basic concerns addressed, jewelers say they can generate the custom-design goods they find increasingly in demand. For those of you who stop at remounts, perhaps a new niche in custom design—with a little extra effort—can become a new profit center.

Commitment:
The Key To Moving Upscale

September 1992

For an established retail jeweler caught in today's all-too-common downward price-quality battle with discounters, the best solution could be to move upscale.

Repositioning your store to a more upscale market may not require $10,000 chandeliers or a new staff sporting foreign accents. But it does require a total commitment. Without it, the effort will come to naught.

Much of the commitment is financial, certainly. But it can be done on a budget if you're willing and able to devote the time and energy, pay attention to detail and change the way you do business.

How it's done: There are two schools of thought on how to move upscale:

• The Rebirth.
• The Gradual Move.

Rebirth involves scrapping as much of the old operation as possible and starting anew. This may entail total remodeling, new inventory and maybe even a new location. While drastic and expensive, "It's best to make a statement, not just stick your toe in the water and hope the public believes you" says Dr. George Lucas, who heads the marketing department at Memphis State University, Memphis, Tenn.

The Gradualists believe an abrupt change may rankle old customers and look phony. "'Ladder' your way up to keep your old customers while you attract new ones," advises David Morrow of the Diamond Promotion Service, New York, N.Y.

The two views actually apply to different situations. When Lucas speaks of rebirth, he refers to stores that have suffered from owners' neglect or moved downmarket with a vengeance in the past decade. When Morrow speaks of gradual change, he addresses independent jewelers who are still well-established, but lack a definite focus on the image they want to portray and the market they want to serve.

The former group should not change gradually, say the experts, but the latter can. The steps required for the two types of transition are similar.

Forming a plan: First, says Morrow, "compare the customers you have with those you want." Conduct a demographic study of your market or look at your records. Where do your customers live, what do they buy and for what occasion? Do they come in for repairs and second-opinion appraisals? Do they ask you for advice, then buy elsewhere?

Armed with this information, you're ready to develop a plan outlining changes you must make in four areas—inventory, decor, staff and advertising/promotion—to reach the customers you want.

Throughout the planning process, remember your mission is not only to attract upscale consumers. You also must ensure repeat business by winning their loyalty through service and their trust through professionalism, says Lucas.

"It won't help much if you try to do one without the other," says Richard Baum, a retail analyst at Sanford Bernstein, a New York brokerage house. "The whole package must work together."

Here are the four elements of change you must consider.

INVENTORY

You don't have to junk everything in your showcase in favor of a few $30,000 pieces. But you must make some changes.

Make two lists: one of merchandise you sell on the basis of design, quality, uniqueness or prestige, the other of items you sell on the basis of price or "price-off."

(When making the lists, remember that price and quality aren't the same thing. "There are plenty of well-designed, well-made, very distinctive items selling for $100 or less," says Morrow. "Tiffany has pieces selling for less than $200, but they are very high quality and very distinctive.")

Once you've completed the lists, hold a blowout sale to get rid of everything that's inappropriate for your new upscale image. "Keeping low-quality jewelry in inventory will send confusing messages to customers," says Lucas. "That's the last thing you want to do because it will undermine your image and credibility."

Any merchandise that's a little better quality but still not in keeping with your new image can be cleared out more slowly.

New inventory: Choose new inventory with extreme care, advises Baum. "Presumably, the retailer has done his homework and knows the demographics he's working with." The younger affluent set, for example, looks for more fashionable, design-oriented pieces than the country-club set, which looks for larger single-stone items.

Check many sources at trade shows and elsewhere. "Look at as many lines as you can," says Morrow. This may require a fundamental shift in your buying strategy. "If you're accustomed to naming a price and telling a supplier to match it, you'll have to change," says Lucas. "The emphasis is on value, not price—big price concessions usually mean quality reductions and that will defeat your purpose."

Instead of negotiating on price, persuade suppliers to:
• Help train your staff in how to present the new pieces properly.
• Host special promotions such as a trunk show at your store.
• Provide displays, professional advertisements and even cooperative ad funds.

Prepare for customers: Here are some other ways to initiate your move upscale:
• Arrange for designers with national reputations to make personal appearances at your store.
• Set up a custom-design department where customers can design their own jewelry.
• Feature period jewelry; many such pieces offer reasonably priced beauty-on-a-budget. But homework is essential to avoid pitfalls.
• Establish a designers' section or boutique within your store. Designer William Schraft of Millburn, N.J., says jewelers who go into the designer market can get away from the price/discount market more easily and establish themselves as a brand-name store that stands for integrity. Designer sections should carry collections to give customers a better feeling for a designer's style. And you must work closely with the designer. "It's a more personal business because you are selling a name as well as jewelry," says Schraft. "The more you know about a designer, the more you can impart to the customer."

Review: Periodically, you must review what's selling and fine-tune the new inventory mix. "No matter how much homework you've done," says Morrow, "there will be a certain amount of guess-work about what will appeal to your customers and some pieces that won't move well."

But before getting rid of any new lines, evaluate whether you advertised and promoted them properly. You may decide all that's needed is to feature them in a new campaign.

Meanwhile, Lucas warns that jewelers moving upscale will alienate some customers, especially those who always demand bargains and deep discounts. But the alienation of less affluent customers can be minimized by stocking new, affordable merchandise of higher quality.

"Let's face it. You're not going to keep the people who will buy only 75%-off," says Lucas. "You will keep those with only $200 to spend if you offer them something nice and can explain the difference between price and value."

STAFF

Staff training and motivation are important when moving upscale.

Least costly and most important is getting salespeople to replace high-pressure sales with personal service, taking time to talk with customers about their desires and educate them about a piece.

"If you evaluate and pay your staff by how quickly they 'process' customers, you'll undercut your efforts and alienate your staff," says Lucas. "And if you tell your staff to take more time with customers but continue to pay them for volume sales, you'll send conflicting signals."

"This takes an entirely new mind-set," says Lucas. "I can't say that enough."

Education: Upscale customers demand information about products they buy, so salespeople must be able to provide it. This could require a substantial investment in time and tuition on your part, says Lucas, but it's necessary if you move upscale.

Morrow agrees, saying salespeople should be taught the basics about gems, jewelry production and watches so they can properly explain these to their customers.

Then they should be taught how to apply what they've learned in sales situations. Whatever program you choose be sure it stresses personal service over volume sales, says Lucas.

Training can range from formal courses at the Gemological Institute of America to in-store sessions run by suppliers, say experts, but there should be no skimping and no end. "You've got to assemble a professional, career-oriented sales staff because there are too many choices out there for consumers to endure ill-trained or unhelpful sales staff," says Lucas.

A professional staff also requires more autonomy from the boss. "Let sales associates be professionals, not sales clerks," he says. "Allow them to make decisions regarding returns and check cashing."

In the end, notes Lucas, professional sales associates earn their keep by establishing a rapport with customers and bringing in repeat business.

DECOR

Richard Baum, the retail analyst from Sanford Bernstein, says sprucing up your store decor is part of establishing credibility with upscale consumers. It shows your commitment to moving upscale and should provide an atmosphere conducive to shopping for a luxury product.

The extent of this project depends on your decor. If the last redo was in 1968 and all the showcases have chips and scratches, a complete facelift is necessary.

"Worn fixtures and drab interiors may work if customers think there are bargains to be found," he says, "but not for a store trying to project a quality image."

If the interior is serviceable, then a thorough cleanup may suffice, says Baum. Additional lighting may brighten things up and give the appearance of a more extensive refurbishment.

Here are some other options, some of them inexpensive:

• Refurbish or replace worn cases. Then rearrange your inventory to make a statement, putting your newest, most exciting pieces (not necessarily the most expensive ones) in the prime spot. Don't move the cases unless you plan to replace the carpets, too.

• Redo your windows and feature themed merchandise in window and interior displays. Get rid of all price-off displays and signs.

• Spruce up entrances with fresh flowers, advises Joan Parker, vice president of N.W. Ayer's Diamond Promotion Service. "You'd be surprised how much they improve the look of the store."

• Is the store sign your father ordered in 1955 still there? You may not have to replace it if it was tasteful when new. But do repaint it and replace letters that may have fallen off. No neon.

• Are your interior signs dusty? Do they uphold your image? Replace hand-lettered signs with professional ones.

Don't delay: All these changes should be made quickly, says Lucas. "You must make the show of total commitment. Even if you can't afford a total makeover, you must do the basics so you don't confuse customers by offering quality merchandise in a shabby store."

Attention to detail also is important at this stage, says Parker. For special events, hire a calligrapher to do invitations and offer quality refreshments. "Quality has to be consistent or you'll lose credibility with upscale consumers."

To make sure you've attended to all details, Lucas recommends "management by walking around." Walk around your store and look at everything a customer would notice, he says, from the dust on the displays to the goods in the showcase.

Now, the key question. "If I have to choose between paying for a major renovation and a sales training program, which takes priority?"

Without exception, the answer is sales training.

ADVERTISING/PROMOTION

The final step, to be done only when everything else is in place involves advertising and promotion. "You can't advertise a better mousetrap before it's in the store," says Baum. "To do so would destroy all the faith and trust you want to build."

First, end all discount and price oriented advertising and concentrate on two areas:

• New and exciting merchandise that no one else has.

• Service and longevity ("We've been your family jeweler for 75 years. . .")

Review where and how you advertise. Is your current medium appropriate? If not, find one that can deliver the audience you want. Once the advertising is in place, start adding more exclusive, costly pieces, but vary them with reasonably priced, distinctive items to avoid alienating longtime customers.

Develop plan: Morrow says a well-planned advertising plan is essential to establish and maintain your new image. "You can't just plan by making a budget," he says. "This type of campaign [image rather than product] requires a unity of approach that will establish a definite image in the minds of consumers."

Several months into your new ad program should come a new element: explaining price vs. value. This is more difficult because you'll have to do it in a few words. A professional ad agency can help.

Suppliers and marketing agencies such as the Diamond Information Center, World Gold Council and Platinum Guild can help by providing ad programs. "We've all seen clients who lost a lot of sales to discounters and downtrading," says one quality-oriented diamond dealer. "Most of us would rather sell better stones, and we don't mind helping clients do so."

Lucas cautions that image advertising is a slow, long-term investment. "It's not like running a sale declaring: 'Watches: Regular price $250, now $175' then counting how many people come in to buy them," says Lucas. "The results of image-advertising will be a long time coming in."

Indeed, experts warn that moving upscale is not a quick fix to a competitive problem.

"Don't forget that the upscale field is very competitive as well," says Baum. But it's a sure way to escape the downward spiral of declining margins, declining quality and declining service."

Getting Your Message To The Affluent

September 1992

When you consider how best to advertise to and communicate with the affluent, think of the ever-widening circles produced when you throw a stone into still water.

• One-on-one communications. In the center of the circle, place your most targeted and intense efforts to reach the affluent. These should include writing personal notes, making phone calls and calling on clients to alert them to special lines or new pieces in which they might have an interest. Jewelers and other marketers who are experts on connecting with the affluent believe that such one-on-one communications, undertaken at just the moments when customers are in the mood to buy, are absolutely essential for successful selling to all segments of this market, from old line wealthy to nouveau riche.

• Networking and public relations. In the middle circles, establish your wider networking efforts These would include socializing; volunteer work for charitable and civic events; and in-store promotions benefiting local arts groups, hospitals and other organizations patronized by the affluent. These actions establish you and your store as community-minded and committed to good causes. They also provide you with a ready way to meet the movers and shakers in your town, many of whom are affluent.

• Traditional advertising. On the outer rim, place your print, television and/or radio ads, your regular in-store promotions and your major direct mail catalogs or pieces. These put your name and merchandise in the affluent eye and increase your general reputation as a store with higher quality goods.

All three ways in which successful jewelers reach out to the affluent are important. That is, important if you hope to sell to that part of your community. "The affluent are very sophisticated consumers, and the jeweler's image and reputation must be able to withstand their scrutiny," says Andy Kohler, president of A.B. Kohler, Montville, N.J. His ad agency advises jewelers concerning their communications needs. "Jewelers need to consider a wide span of communications efforts, some of them quite subtle."

Following are the stories of six jewelers who successfully lure the affluent by using the various communications tools described above. Because what you say to the affluent is almost always as important as how, where and when you say it, each profile also illustrates the different messages marketing experts believe attract and impress the affluent.

VIDEO TRAVELOGUE:
'I SEARCHED THE WORLD FOR THESE PIECES'

Underwood Jewelers, Fayetteville, Ark.

The problem: many of Underwood Jewelers' affluent prospects are too busy or live too far away to shop in the store. Print ads and direct mail pieces just don't draw enough of them in.

The creative solution, suggested by Craig Underwood, vice president of the store his father founded: bring the merchandise to them, via a lavishly produced video.

The video features spectacularly filmed jewelry; the strong, reassuring voice of Craig's father, President Bill Underwood; photographs of Bill Underwood selecting jewelry and gems in exotic locations around the world; and all the messages affluent customers like to hear. Among them:

• "We are a family-owned, second-generation jewelry store."

• "We hold the highest credentials in the industry."

• "There are only 250 gem labs like ours in the U.S."

•"I personally selected these diamonds . . . I hand-picked these sapphires in Bangkok where they are mined . . . I selected these pearls from a pearl farm in Kobe, Japan . . . it took 15 years for us to find a goldsmith in Northern Italy who makes these gold collars by hand."

• "We travel the world markets to buy directly from the source and give you the best value—no middleman or importer is involved."

• "This piece is made by hand—one-of-a-kind—by our own designers."

• "This is the same kind of French enameling found on Fabergé eggs—almost a lost art."

Such "romancing" of jewelry to appeal to the affluent comes naturally to Bill Underwood, who was an early believer in the power of television and who still writes his own scripts for the commercials the firm produces twice a year.

Underwood, dissatisfied with the work of professionals who filmed earlier commercials, has gradually bought all the camera and special effects equipment he needs to produce his own at the store. "It takes a jeweler to know how jewelry pieces look to their best advantage," says Underwood. "You don't need trick lights or filters to make jewelry look good."

Did the video produce the desired effect: more sales to the affluent? Overwhelmingly, says Bill Underwood. "It's the best marketing we've ever done," he says. "People told us they watched the video more than once, and a large percentage of viewers invited others into their homes to view it. We made sales to people who hadn't even received the video! Wives would often watch it first, then view it again with their husbands to show what they like. Most of those men would never have time to shop but they appreciated finding the right thing that their wives would like.

"Apparently what impressed a lot of viewers the most was that they received their very own copy. Many people think of videotapes as very expensive, because most commercial videos cost a lot to buy. They felt privileged to be one of the people to get this from us."

Underwood made sales to affluent prospects the store had been trying for years to reach through print and direct mail. Some were prominent professionals who lived as far as 200 miles away and had never been in the store. "One man told me, 'I had no idea we had a jewelry store with those credentials,' and ordered three items sight unseen. He's still never been in the store," says Underwood.

ADVERTISING TO THE AFFLUENT: LOCATION, LOCATION, LOCATION

Lee Michaels Jewelers, Baton Rouge, La.

Lee Berg, owner of Lee Michaels Jewelers, has been rewarded for his faithfulness to newspaper advertising for his stores in five markets: Baton Rouge, Lafayette, Hammond and Shreveport, La.; and Mobile, Ala. "Though newspapers never guarantee it, when Lee says, 'I want Tiffany placement,' nine out of ten times he gets it," says Diane Allen of Diane Allen Associates, the advertising and public relations firm that keep the Lee Michaels name in the public eye.

What's Tiffany placement? If you've ever read the New York Times, you're familiar with the treasured spot Tiffany claims regularly in the newspaper's first section: first spread, right page, mostly upper right side. Day in and day out, New York readers can count on seeing the store's simple elegant ads. For readers of the Sunday editions of major newspapers in Louisiana and Mobile, Ala., Lee Michaels is their Tiffany.

The jeweler's ads follow the Tiffany pattern. "A single piece of jewelry, a few sentences of copy, the store's logo and the same two columns by 7" size each time," says Allen.

Though format, size and placement remain in a pattern, Berg, with Allen's help, is constantly reinventing the message to draw in the well-heeled. In fact, the local affluent community often figures prominently in the newspaper ads, as well as on billboards and other media. "We want to establish the position that we, and they, are associated with the best," says Allen. One campaign for anniversary diamonds featured local prominent couples photographed in sports or evening clothes. Underneath was a stunning piece of diamond jewelry. A small amount of copy, in list form, detailed events from their marriages, such as "Doubles Matches. Charades. 8-Track Tapes. Two a.m. feedings. Mardi Gras Mambo. PTA Meetings. Lite Food. Road Trips. The Bump. Your Love Survived Them All . . . The Anniversary Diamond. A brilliant celebration of a loving marriage."

Another successful ad campaign aimed at the affluent features prominent businessmen with a red kiss planted on one cheek. The copy says "All I said was . . . 'It's from Lee Michaels.' " Allen says fellow businessmen call Lee Berg and ask if they can be in the ad campaign.

For television coverage, says Allen, Lee Michaels Jewelers is more interested in the time slot, television's version of location, than in the ads' content. "With television, we sell sizzle, not jewelry," says Allen.

The firm buys syndicated ads, then places them at crucial spots during short breaks on network TV at 10 p.m. and 10:25 p.m. EST (9 p.m. and 9:25 p.m. in Lee Michaels' markets). The firm has been able to buy 10-second spots rather than the customary 30-second spots for these short breaks, thus saving money and still appearing during prime hours. The company also buys time during the 10 p.m. news (11 p.m. EST), which Berg believes is the news that upscale peo-

ple are most likely to watch. "Affluent people are still working during the earlier news," says Allen. The firm also places ads during key sporting events such as the Kentucky Derby, the U.S. Open and Wimbledon.

To garner publicity for the stores, Berg and Allen also have put together affluent crowd-pleasers, such as a rare appearance by porcelain sculpture designer Helen Boehm at the opening of the company's Mobile store and a demonstration by a diamond cutter.

Berg also buys program ads, and offers other support for charity events. For a program called Project Wildflower, which is organized by the affluent to put wildflowers along interstate highways, Berg advertised that if anyone bought a certain piece of jewelry, he'd donate a percentage of the sale to the project. "Lee believes that he has to give back to each community where his stores are located," says Allen. "If you want to reach the affluent and be successful it all goes back to the community."

USING PICASSO TO REACH THE 'NEW' AFFLUENT

J.E. Caldwell Co., Philadelphia, Pa.

Picture a table covered with African-inspired linens and set with angular, nonmatching plates drenched in sun-burnished oranges, reds and yellows; glassware in exotic colors and shapes; and all this complemented by African sculptures.

Or what about tableware all sporting bird motifs, from teacups with hands made of outstretched wings to dinner plates decorated with a fine relief of feathers? These are complemented by flatware featuring squiggly lines and cage-like bars.

For most people in Philadelphia, the venerable J.E. Caldwell Co., jeweler to generations of the conservative wealthy, would be the last place you'd expect to find such avant garde design. Yet these tables, among others, recently spent the summer at Caldwell's Philadelphia flagship store as part of a promotion honoring the Philadelphia Museum of Art's summer-long exhibit of Picasso still lifes.

The tables, designed by Art Museum curators and using existing Caldwell stock, reflected various themes in Picasso's art, such as his love of African art and bird motifs. Rosenthal tableware, designed by commissioned artists, and contemporary Kosta Boda stemware figured prominently on many tables. The promotion garnered much press, locally and regionally.

"The affluent are changing," says Eileen Rosenau, the public relations executive who helps Caldwell plan such publicity-minded promotions. "It's not just the old wealthy anymore. You have corporate types and young professionals now. And they've been shocked to find out that Caldwell's carries such avant garde things." The exhibit has forced these affluent segments to take a whole new interested look at the store they thought was too stodgy for their design-oriented tastes.

Over the years, Caldwell has found the affluent are devoted to supporting the arts. For this reason, many of Caldwell's recent promotions have tied in with museum exhibits, including the city's Franklin Institute and Swedish Museum. Such joint promotions garner much approval from Philadelphia's prominent arts supporters. "Many people went back and forth from the Picasso exhibit at the Art Museum to our tables," Rosenau says.

That the affluent approve of Caldwell's jazzier image was proven to one Caldwell executive who, on her train ride home from work, overheard two obviously wealthy women raving about the Picasso-inspired tables. Praising the store's attention to Picasso-like details, one said: "They even have live bugs on one table!" The executive not knowing what to think, quickly hurried to the table in question the next morning. It turned out that a wooden log used as part of the design on one table had carried some ants inside! Fortunately, Caldwell's patrons didn't seem to mind at all.

WE ARE FAMILY: THE VALUE OF TRUST

Crescent Westwood Jewelers
West Los Angeles, Cal.

When the affluent clients of Crescent Westwood Jewelers opened the direct mail piece sent by the store this summer, they saw more than beautiful merchandise. They also were introduced to the newest grandchild in the Friedman family, the same family that has owned and operated the store for 46 years.

"Our clients are used to us knowing about their lives, and we share ours with them," says Linda Abell, who works in this family-run store with her brother David (father of that new baby) and their parents, Sunny and Leonard Friedman. "When we make a sale, we make a friend."

The Friedmans' frequent overseas family buying trips often provide amusing family photos that are used for window displays and promotions. "We might show one of the family being pushed into a pool," says Abell, who is a graduate gemologist and vice president of the firm. The joke photos are placed alongside other photos showing the Friedmans searching for fine and unusual loose stones. The message this conveys appeals to well-heeled buyers eager to know that their jeweler goes to the source for the best stones and prices.

This emphasis on family and friendships with customers is joined by a third communications element that Abell says appeals to their affluent client base (which includes such wealthy communities as Bel Air, Beverly Hills and Brentwood and the entertainment industry in West Los Angeles). "We call our customers 'clients' because the trust they place in our advice is similar to that in the attorney-client relationship," says Abell. All communications from the store, from personal phone calls to direct mail pieces, emphasize the Friedmans' role as "advisers" to their clients.

The friendship and closeness such efforts produce make it easier for the sales staff to reach out to the affluent through frequent phone calls. "Our clients are never unhappy that we called. They really appreciate it, especially if we call enough in advance of a special occasion to plant the idea of a gift of jewelry," says Abell. "It give them something to think about, and more often than not, we make a sale."

Crescent Westwood Jewelers also uses traditional print ads to "keep our name out there," says Abell. "Since much of our business is from referrals, we want such people to know our name and reputation when they are referred."

The ads, like most ads that appeal to the affluent, feature lots of white space surrounding a small amount of merchandise. "We're not trying to sell a specific piece as much as to get our image as a high-end store, with 10 gemologists on staff, in an environment of honesty and integrity," she says.

The firm also sponsors private party promotions, with an exclusiveness that appeals to their affluent customers. To introduce Argyle Diamonds' champagne diamonds, for example, the store was closed to the public, and the staff dressed formally for a champagne and hors d'oeuvres reception.

SUPPORTING THE ARTS, HELPING HOSPITALS

Henne Jewelers, Pittsburgh, Pa.

Henne Jewelers saw opportunity in the young professionals moving to Pittsburgh as the city became a high-tech computer software center.

The store, which had always supported the arts through program ads for the Pittsburgh Symphony, also began to advertise in the playbills for the Pittsburgh Broadway Series and the local pops symphony. "We realized that our older affluent audience that attends the Pittsburgh Symphony knew us well, but these newcomers did not," says John C. Park, vice president of Henne Jewelers.

The ads, which feature a simple photo of a single piece of jewelry, stress such store qualities as longevity (more than a century in business), long support of the cultural arts, an on-premises custom goldsmith and unique services, including estate jewelry appraisals. "We try to tell about us with 75% of the ad," says Park. "Only 25% is devoted to product."

The store also began a yearly tradition of bringing in a sought-after designer for a one-day buying event. A percentage of sales for the day is donated to a local hospital auxiliary. "The affluent like one-of-a-kind pieces, and they like the idea of hearing the story behind the piece they're buying," he says. "With our event, they get to meet the designer and even order custom-made pieces," says Park.

Formal invitations, addressed by hand, are sent to all those on the hospital's auxiliary board, as well as to another few hundred of Henne's most regular customers. "Our affluent customers like to know that they're helping the hospital," says Park. "They like the idea of contributing to a cause."

VALUE OF ONE-ON-ONE COMMUNICATION

The Redmond Corp., Greenville, S.C.

"I have a friend who jokes that anytime two or more people are gathered for lunch, Redmond is there," says John A. Redmond, who reaches the affluent in his community in a unique way.

He has no store to speak of, just an office he's hardly ever in and a secretary.

He never advertises or sends direct mail.

He never sponsors in-store promotions, because he keeps most of his inventory out of the office in a secured location for insurance reasons.

Instead, he spends his time meeting people through socializing (hence, all the lunches), doing volunteer work for a number of church and civic groups, and visiting his clients in the privacy of their homes or offices.

"I have one client, an extremely wealthy woman who is almost a recluse," he says. "She likes to buy jewelry at the holidays for almost everyone in her family, as well as for her secretary, her maid and others. So I go over there and sit in her music room, where she offers me cheese and crackers and something to drink, and I show her my jewelry."

Nice work if you can get it, eh? Redmond didn't always do business this way. Seven years ago, he was in partnership with another jeweler, running a very nice American Gem Society store with a storefront and the usual 9-9 hours. Then he decided to go out on his own to sell one-on-one. Soon, the people he was getting to know through volunteer work became his customers.

"When they got to know me, they found out that I'll sell them things they won't see someone else wearing," he says. "It will be the best value possible, and I won't take advantage of them." Now the majority of Redmond's clients come through referrals.

"I like the community work, which I could never find the time for when I worked in a retail store," says Redmond. "Not only am I helping my community, I'm getting the camaraderie I once had at the store. We're all on a first-name basis. Today, for example, I had lunch with some CEOs. We're working on an education project together."

Redmond also gives talks for garden clubs and women's groups, usually consisting of a slide presentation on a period of jewelry, such as Victorian or Edwardian, or a category, such as diamonds or colored stones. He tell anecdotes about estate jewelry he's seen and then opens up the floor for questions. "Just about everyone has a story about the diamond she inherited from Aunt So and So," he says.

In addition to his community contacts, Redmond makes it his business to sell his services to affluents whom many other sellers ignore. "A lot of very successful people have what look like modest businesses, such as trucking," he says. "They may work out of very seedy warehouses filled with 18-wheelers that need washing. The owner may wear blue jeans and sit in an office with no air conditioning and a linoleum floor. But he has a Cadillac and a house in the mountains, and it's all paid off. No one ever paid him any attention until me."

Redmond also calls on minority businesspeople and professionals. "No one seems to approach them, either," he says.

Redmond makes copious notes about his clients' tastes, the pieces they're longing for and their special occasion dates. Then he calls them at the right moments with an offer to come over and show what he's got. "The men who buy for their wives love this service. They don't want to have to leave their offices or get dressed up on a weekend to come to a jewelry store," he says. "I show up at the office and let them select a piece, then bring it back beautifully wrapped on the specified day."

"One of the best ways I demonstrate my service is by listening to what people have to say about their tastes and wants. Many jewelers do too much talking. If you listen long enough, you'll hear all you need to know to make a sale."

Messages that Attract the Affluent

In all of a jeweler's communications and advertising to the affluent, certain messages and themes hit home. They are:

• Trust, the jeweler as professional adviser, akin to a lawyer or a stockbroker.

• Good value, as in "we went to the source and cut out the middlemen," not "70% off" which turns off the affluent.

• Exquisite design, in classic styles or in avant garde interpretations.

• Unusual or unique styles.

• Meticulous service with tremendous emphasis on catering to the individual.

• Community involvement, whether through promotions that help charitable or civic organizations or through individual efforts to serve on boards, planning committees and so on.

• Romancing of jewelry, through exotic or historical facts or by promoting the international character of jewelry via stories of overseas adventures to obtain certain pieces.

Get Expert Help

"Most jewelers shouldn't expect to do sophisticated public relations to the affluent on their own. They should work with a local public relations firm," says Joan Parker, director of the Diamond Information Center, New York, N.Y. "Jewelers will find that on a project-by-project basis, it's not that expensive and prices are negotiable. I'd estimate between $1,000 and $3,000 per project depending on the market and the services desired."

Along with hiring public relations firms, many jewelers also use the services of ad agencies to plan formal advertising. Here are some advantages of hiring outside help:

• Advertising agencies can help you sort through the mind-numbing blur of media choices to come up with the right ones to connect you to the affluent. They have statistics on your local market, they know how to buy lists for direct mail campaigns and they know the local media and what segments of your market they reach.

They can also can help you plan less obvious advertising strategies and, sometimes, public relations.

"Half of our services are intangible," says Andy Kohler, president of A.B. Kohler & Co., a Montville, N.J., advertising and public relations firm. "We help jewelers identify the image they're trying to project. Sometimes, we decide not to develop an ad at all. Ads are only part of the picture when you're trying to reach the affluent audience."

• Public relations experts can help you plan well-thought-through promotions, from the idea through the event, with press coverage into the bargain.

"When it comes to the affluent, everything has to have style," says Parker. "From the invitations to the food, flowers and color scheme, it takes a lot of thought and planning."

In addition, says Parker, public relations experts can help you get media training so that when the TV camera comes calling, you're up to the job.

Both kinds of experts also can be a tremendous help with the technical details of ad production and proper contacts for press releases.

To find an advertising and/or public relations firm, you can go several routes. First, pay attention to great promotions, ads or newspaper and magazine stories aimed at the affluent in your area. Then try to find out whether the retailer relied on expert help and if so, who supplied it.

You also may contact the Diamond Information Center, which keeps a ready list of local public relations experts who are familiar with the ins and outs of promoting jewelry stores, says the DIC's Parker.

If you decide to go it on your own, you might want to consult a four-part series of informational packets prepared by the Diamond Promotion Service and called The Diamond Marketing Series.

Though the emphasis is on selling diamonds, the information is relevant to pitching all kinds of jewelry store products to the affluent. The series includes "Direct Marketing," "Media Buying," "Publicity" and "Window Display."

Get To Know
The All-Star Customer

Jim Terzian ◆ *September 1992*

Forbes magazine calls it "the trickle-up phenomenon."

As a society grows richer, it tends to produce larger fortunes. America now has 101 billionaires and more than 1.5 millionaires—people who have amassed a net worth of $1 million or more after the value of their primary residence is adjusted to compensate for regional differences. More than 1,000 have reached the $100 million mark, while several tens of thousands have exceeded $10 million.

These groups are both exclusive and elusive. Marketing firms rarely research small and eclectic consumer segments, irrespective of their staggering assets. But one thing seems clear: there are almost as many types of affluent individuals as there are affluent individuals. Different ages, employments, family situations and consumer behavior patterns segment the marketplace into hundreds of subtypes.

From within this blur of buyers emerge seven distinct groups that are prime potential customers for fine jewelry. These are the retail jewelry industry's all-star customers. See how many of them are also yours.

EXECUTIVE CLASS

Today's business elite are also today's financial front-runners, as *Forbes* magazine's July 20 focus on billionaires demonstrates.

With a net worth of $6.4 billion, Bill Gates heads both Microsoft and *Forbes'* list of the country's richest people. He's followed by Metromedia's John Werner Kluge at $5.9 billion and the five principal heirs of Walmart's Sam Walton—Alice, Jim, John, Helen and S. Robson—coming in at better than $4.7 billion each.

Business, it appears, has been very, very good to owner-executives and their families. More of the very wealthy classify as members of the executive class than any other group we will describe.

America's corporate, professional and entrepreneurial chiefs, on average, are skilled executives and personable individuals, 40-60 years old, married with two kids (now out of the house) and a mortgage that is no longer burdensome. They like the good life, rewarding themselves with its perquisites more liberally than their parents did. But they're still most comfortable with a conservative consumer attitude. If their parents have money, it's just beginning to be inherited and added to the estates their children will one day receive.

Chief executives at large firms do far better than the $125,000 annual income we established as a minimum for consideration here. CEOs of 25 major corporations saw their average annual compensation increase 171% to $2.67 million in the 10 years preceding 1991, according to a survey by

Hewitt Associates, a benefits and compensation firm. Though they make excellent money, however, members of this group seldom total their net worth at more than seven figures. The principal family breadwinner plans to continue working for some time to come.

In 1989, people ages 45-65 spent $1.23 trillion overall (according to the statistical abstracts) and accounted for proportionately more than their share of the $14 billion that the U.S. Commerce Department estimates American spent in jewelry stores in 1991. And when the affluent executive buys, he expects the retailer to reflect his business values of quality and service.

Taking time: Because it was one of the things he sacrificed on his climb up the economic ladder, the executive values time with his family. Attorney Bruce Sikorsky and his wife Jane typify the established executive family of the '90s.

Bruce is a principal of a San Francisco area law firm. His extensive experience and higher hourly fees ensure that his time goes to difficult cases and better heeled clients who demand he alone serve them. Younger attorneys (including his son, a graduate of Berkeley's Boalt Law School) carry the bulk of the load. Jane no longer works for the associations she once helped to manage, so the couple now can spend time together in a way they haven't done since they were in their early 20s.

Accepting "an offer they couldn't refuse" for a house bought 20 years ago, they recently relocated to a smaller but more luxurious three-bedroom home in a multi-million-dollar development 18 miles away [homes in elite communities sell today for about three times their 1980 prices, despite the slowing housing market]. They used the remaining profits to buy a condominium on Maui.

Beyond some high-tech entertainment electronics, his golf clubs and his second-hand Rolls Royce, Bruce hasn't spent much that isn't real-property related. He like to play golf and relax in Hawaii, so he uses his significant earning power to buy leisure time. Accustomed to fiscal conservancy while raising two children, Jane allows herself a new Corvette every four or five years, buys new clothes when she finds something that really catches her eye and lunches in fine restaurants with friends. Otherwise, her checkbook gets limited exercise.

But this is changing. Increasingly, Bruce and Jane buy more, and what they buy is well-designed and of very high quality, with price now a secondary consideration. The Sikorskys found their current jeweler 12 year ago based on a friend's recommendation for a repair. The jeweler, not Jane, maintained the relationship and now handles all the family's business at home. Vacationing three to four times a year on Maui, Bruce and Jane also Frequent a small firm there that specializes in designer jewelry; they've bought four pieces on the past few trips.

In addition to the pieces brought in Maui, Jane has many gold earrings, none overly large, a number of fine rings, a gold and diamond watch and a couple of bracelets. Bruce wears only his wedding band and gold Rolex Presidential, unless occasion demands cuff links. Between them, they can spend $7,000- $17,000 a year on jewelry, but they have the basics and what they buy now is creative work that captures their aesthetic interest.

The jewelry Bruce buys for Jane is intended to show materially both to his wife and to his social circle how much she means to him. The most notable difference form years past is the price tag. When Bruce buys, he spends an average $3,000.

Disposable income: "Our biggest-spending customers are in their 50s, are settled in their careers, have more disposable income and like the finer things in life," reports Craig Underwood of Underwood Jewelers in Fayetteville, Ark. "They like the quality and the service and the prestige. They want to show off their success, but in subtle ways; they will wear, but not flaunt."

Says Hank Siegel of Hamilton's Jewelers in Lawrenceville, N.J., "They travel or they run in a particular social circle that allows them to show off the latest special treats they bought for themselves. We do a lot of target marketing to these groups, including direct mail and specific product advertising. Often times when a special piece comes in, we call them before it ever goes in the case."

Not all of these corporate elite live in urban areas. The July 1992 issue of American Demographics magazine focuses on four categories of the often-ignored rural rich: suburban refugees with urban jobs, equity-rich urban expatriots, urbanites with rural second homes and wealthy rural land owners. "America's urban markets may be big and rich, but they are also saturated with competition," says the magazine. "The number of potential customers is much smaller in [rural] towns, but so is the number of competitors."

Adds Mike Grant of Steve Schmier's Jewelers in Tahoe City, Cal., "The executive elite respond to something they don't see everywhere, something well made with rich, beautiful stones." And who wouldn't?

DINK A DO?

Here is a question to test your market awareness quotient. Do more married-couple households contain children or not contain children?

If you answered "not" you are right. In summaries of the 1990 census released this year, the U.S. Census Bureau announced that for the first time in history, the majority are childless. This is good news for zero-population growth advocates and even better news for retailers of high-dollar consumer products. The money these couples once would have spent raising children, they now will spend on themselves.

These couples are part of the baby boom generation, born between 1946 and 1964. (One note of caution before we proceed; because the term baby boomers is popular, many retailer mistake them for members of the executive class, but only a few have made it there yet.) Boomers have made family decisions that differ significantly from their par-

ents'. In the late 1970s, demographers noticed a large percentage of boomer women delaying marriage and motherhood to get through college and begin careers. While the total number of households increased more than 14% between 1980 and 1990, the number of married couples with children living at home rose only 1.2%. Going back to 1960, almost half (47%) of all households were headed by married parents. Thirty years later, the figure had dropped to 26%.

Why are families choosing to be childless? They give quite a few reasons; most can be summed up in four general answers:

• A desire to be free to do what they wanted to with their lives.

• Cash. Children are expensive, and many would-be parents realize they either won't have the money necessary or want to do other things with it.

• A decision to delay having children until they are older (sometimes waiting too long).

• A serious question in the minds of many middle- and upper-class adults about their competency to raise kids.

Whether or not to have children is so serious a decision that failure to agree was cited in a Northern California study as the second most common reason for relationships ending.

Money to spend: Most 35- to 44-year-olds are struggling with life's greatest expenses: kids in high school or entering college, big home mortgages and time-consuming workloads that force them to pay others to do work they might otherwise do themselves. Yet this age group, which accounts for 15% of the population, takes in more money each year than any other—and spent $906.6 billion in 1989.

The members of the group best positioned to spend it are DINKs (Dual Income, No Kids). The Urban Institute calculates parents spend $150,000-$230,000 in the first 18 years of a child's life—and that's before college. Families with children average more than two, so not having children can add up to $2.1 million in after-tax assets by retirement time.

The U.S. Census Bureau reports that married couples without children under 18 at home accounted for 24% of all household spending in 1990. They place a high priority on vehicles, homes, vacations and entertainment.

DINKs by choice: Kevin and Laurie De La Fountaine are DINKs by choice. Having bought out the partnership that established his fire-protection technologies firm, Kevin now spends 10 to 12 hours a day, 4.5 days a week, running the company. In her corporate financial management position, Laurie gets away less than Kevin does, working 11 hours a day in busy seasons, seven hours a day in lighter times. They decided before meeting 3.5 years ago they didn't want children.

Kevin and Laurie, who earn $163,000 a year, married last fall and bought a four-bedroom house in Southern California. They own most of the adult toys that nay family working so much could find time to play with, including three cars, two VCRs, a living room full of modern furniture and two espresso machines. The toy they are thinking of picking up next is a 29-ft. sailboat.

Most often the DINK population chooses to buy modern jewelry that makes a strong statement of their success without being overpowering. For Kevin's birthday, Laurie gave him a gold and steel Rolex quartz watch. For a wedding ring, Kevin gave Laurie an invisibly-set princess-cut diamond band of about 3.5 cts. t.w.

They have yet to settle on one jeweler because of the competition for time to shop and because the marketplace offers so many choices.

Dramatic increase: "In the past two to three years, there has been a dramatic increase in the two-person, two-income family; they have more income, they like to have fine watches, a big diamond, and fine gold and colored stone jewelry," says Tim Braun, manager of precious jewelry for Neiman-Marcus in Houston. "Usually they hang around with people like themselves. They want to have a little more than the Joneses."

"We have close rapport with our clients," Braun says. "They have a lawyer, they have a doctor and they have a jeweler. We become their jeweler. That's the kind of relationship we like to build with our client.

Maria Frasca, who owns M. Frasca in Palm Desert, Cal., does more dollar business with DINKs than any other kind of client. "The women tend to buy just as often for the men as the men buy for the women," she says. "The women earn almost as much as their husbands do, so they can spend. They will buy him a diamond ring, chains and bracelets."

By the time they reach the end of their child-bearing years, many of these two-person families will become parents. U.S. government reports reflect a change in attitude: in 1976, 22% of childless women between 30 and 34 expected to be mothers eventually; by 1990, 41% expected to have children.

Tim and Sue Masood are trying to decide whether to have children. He is an engineer, she a critical-care nurse, they have a bought a house and built their asset base, but not yet made the final decision. "Part of the process of deciding to have kids is committing to the care of lives that cannot take care of themselves," he says. "It's an awesome responsibility, and though we have put some money away, we haven't come to a final conclusion."

Should they remain childless until their middle 40s, DINKs take on the appearance of any other executive-class family, substituting nieces, nephews and pets in their affections for children they never had. One thing that doesn't change is the joy found in giving gifts—sometimes moderately expensive.

"We had a gentleman who came to interview us for an architectural magazine," reports Eve Alfillé, the owner and driving force behind the Eve Alfillé Gallery in Evanston, Ill. "The next day he came back, brought his wife and got her a $6,000 necklace. We almost fainted. But we are getting used to it very rapidly."

WHERE THE GREEN IS BLUE (COLLAR)

If your average take home pay is $37,500 a year over 40 years, how much money will you have earned by the time you retire? America's wealthy blue-collar workers are beginning to find out. They're also beginning to prove that it's not how much you earn but how you plan to spend it that makes a difference in the marketplace.

The shrinking and stressing of the middle class over the past two decades has dealt both good and ill to the classic American worker. Blue-collar but highly skilled, he and she have worked hard, saved diligently, raised a family and paid for one house and several cars, the latter often in cash.

Let's define the middle class as all families earning $18,500-$55,000 annually (the 1991 poverty level for a family of four was $13,500 a year). For almost any five-year period between 1970 and 1990, 7% of the population moved above

the $55,000 level by the end of the period. And many of them continued to move to above the $75,000 level.

Why does $75,000 make any difference? There are two reasons:

• It's the highest income bracket ($75,000+) that federal agencies report regularly.

• For the less expensive life-style of North America's blue-collar families, $75,000 may well provide as many discretionary dollars as $125,000 provides in the same size executive-class home.

Differences: The house is a big part of the difference between blue-collar and executive-class family fortunes. While the newly purchased executive-class home averages 3.5 times the family's annual pretax income, blue-collar workers spend closer to 2.25 times.

Clothes and cars also differ significantly. An executive typically spends $2,500-$4,000 a year to renew and maintain a wardrobe, about $650 of it in dry-cleaning bills. Most blue-collar employees have roughwear work clothes that cost far less and can be laundered at home. Their wardrobe spending, including dress clothes, averages closer to $1,000 a year.

Executive families often feel each adult deserves one very nice car, an average $6,388 per year to own and operate plus $1,500 for insurance. Blue-collar families usually have one extra car or truck (often it's bought used), and each new car or truck costs less than three years worth of an executive's annual car budget. Because they buy more conservatively and keep their cars longer, blue-collar families pay about half what executives pay for insurance.

For these reasons, a number of blue-collar families are spending as much or more on jewelry and other luxuries as their higher society counterparts by the time they reach their late 40s.

The wealthy blue-collar worker serves in the type of position for government and industry that higher level sergeants and chief petty officers do in the military. They are business's non-commissioned officers. Foremen and plant floor managers, office administrators and tenured civil servants, truck drivers and shipping chiefs, these are the people how make America go. They do their most productive work from ages 25 to 55 and are estimated to make up 6.79 million of the 101 million households in the U.S. and Canada. Many jewelers see themselves as part of this group.

Rewards of hard work: Garth & Donna Swordman live near the Mississippi River and have worked all their lives. A high-span bridge painter, Garth makes extra money for the danger involved and gets time off when the weather is bad. Donna works as a critical-care nurse now that the kids are out of high school and living on their own. Each earns $40,000-$48,000 a year and has job seniority and wages that will continue to rise. With a refinanced low-value mortgage (the house cost $128,000 eight years ago) and low living expenses, they have a lot of money left at the end of the month. What doesn't go into the bank, they play with.

Their eldest son is having the time of his life competing with Dad to see who can acquire and adapt the most decadent boat. Geoff's journeyman status on the job site and lack of family responsibilities mean he can spend as though there were no tomorrow. And he sometimes does. Recreational vehicles, fishing boats and other competing purchases all vie for the family's attention. Because they don't face many bills each month, Donna can indulge in her favorite hobby—buying jewelry.

The engagement ring Garth bought her was small and not very well made, but she wouldn't trade it in for the world. Remounted now as the side stone for a larger center, she also has several matching pieces, a good number of colored stone rings, many earrings (most with stones) and a fine quartz watch.

Garth has never worn a wedding band for safety reasons. But last year, Donna saved up money and surprised him with a diamond ring to wear when he's not working. He resisted at first but now wouldn't give it up. He also wears a nice diver's watch on weekends (he uses a beat-up, paint-speckled watch for work).

When they found out that a jeweler in town sponsored the kids' Little League team, they visited the store and became regular customers. They now consider him a friend of the family and recommend him to others. The jeweler has a great concern for detailed workmanship and a dislike for fancy pricing schemes. Like many other blue-collar workers, Garth and Donna wouldn't have it any other way.

Shopping habits: "They start with one decent piece and then build from there," Jeffrey Samuels says of blue-collar customers at William Jeffrey's LTD in Mechanicsville, Va.

"One husband was looking for a 14k watch with sapphires and diamonds all the way around it the first time he bought form me; the second thing I sold him was a Gumuchdjian Fils sapphire and diamond ring for over $3,000," he says. "This guy is typical blue-collar; he likes the Cleveland Browns, drives a Ford and is a big Jack Daniels drinker—just a regular kind of guy.

A number of jewelers report their wealthy blue-collar customers buy bi-monthly. When a piece costs less than $1,000, they often take it with them; if it costs more, they commonly put it on lay-away until an occasion or an over-powering urge causes them to pay it off. A few turn out to be big spenders. One of Samuels' customers spent $18,000 last year. The average is closer to $5,000 annually for the upper-end factory worker.

Don't discount blue-collar taste. Diane Wiggins, a former JCK editor who went on to join a trucking magazine, once commented that she never saw so much expensive and tasteful men's jewelry as she did at a trucking industry convention.

Moreover, tradition and sentiment become important. Where those in the executive class want to trade up their engagement ring center stones and the new rich say the bigger the better, working class often says no. "It would make me feel funny," says one blue-collar mother.

Explains Wally Vieregg, president of Walters and Hogsett Jewelers north of Denver, Colo., "My middle class customers work hard, save their money and then buy the item they want. They are inclined to support their hometown merchant. And they want quality, service and selection—the same old things I would have told you in 1950; not everybody offers you that."

The wealthy blue-collar worker also appreciates a retailer being honest and thorough when explaining about a piece of jewelry. "Not a lot of them stop to think about why lightweight jewelry fall apart because they think that's all there is," Vieregg says. "They don't know the difference because they have never had better made jewelry before."

ETHNIC MARKETS

This past summer's riots painted some American ethnic populations as dangerous, vengeful and impoverished in the eyes of the television-viewing world. Very small numbers of America's non-white population took part, but the camera doesn't distinguish population percentages and rarely shows the forest for the trees.

The much larger but undiscussed side of this story—a hard-working and entrepreneurial side—came to North America to build a future and a fortune they couldn't get at home. Many have succeeded, becoming America's ethnic millionaires.

Cesar Viramontes may be the Spanish translation for Horatio Alger. Profiled in the December 1990 *Fortune* magazine as a self-made millionaire, he also typifies the high-end ethnic potential. Viramontes built a small El Paso laundromat into a $3.8 million personal net worth, washing jeans for Levi Strauss to five them the faded look.

Born in Mexico and now living in a 6,000-sq.-ft. house worth more than $250,000 in southwestern Texas, he says he has more than enough income to take care of his eight children. So he gives heavily to the Roman Catholic Church and a local prep school. He says he can live comfortably on $250,000 a year, but the business grosses $23.5 million annually. This leaves a lot of room for luxuries.

The ethnic affluent of the U.S. and Canada are typical executive-class and blue-collar wealthy with one difference: they are still influenced by the cultures in which they were raised.

There are many ethnic Americans. Minorities make up 22% of the total U.S. population, broken down roughly as 1% Native American, 3% Asian, 11% African American and 8% Hispanic. But neither these ethnic groups nor the remaining 78% Caucasian majority are homogeneous groups. The divisions help to identify general groups, but cannot guide a marketer in understanding the different ethnic cultures.

North American Caucasians include Western Europeans, Scandinavians, Teutons, Eastern Europeans, Mediterraneans and Slavs. Hispanics are made up of Mexicans, Puerto Ricans, Cubans, and a wide variety of South Americans. Iberians cross into both categories. Asians include Asian Indians, Chinese, Japanese, Koreans, Vietnamese, Filipinos, Hawaiians and a host of peoples less well represented in the population. And Native Americans comprise Aleuts, Eskimos and each tribe that still inhabits the lower 48 states, including large groups of Sioux, Navaho and Iroquois.

Every one of these groups has a different culture, defining consumer patterns, approved and disapproved uses of money, and tastes in jewelry. Though we cannot provide details on every group, we offer two examples to show the kinds of information you may want to gather about those living in your community. Armed with this information, you can build a much stronger relationship with potential clients.

Analytical approach: For the analytical approach, we examine the Mexican-American buyer.

Question: How many of the world's three largest Spanish-speaking populations are in North America? Answer: Two. Mexico City and Los Angeles. Spain's capital city Madrid comes in third!

Even Wall Street has become interested in Hispanic businesses, noticing in the past year that firms listed in the Hispanic Business 500 were up 10%, compared with a 1.8% drop in the Fortune 500.

Hispanic business owners have done very well, becoming a large part of the high-end ethnic market, but certain subgroups have exceeded others. In terms of minority-owned businesses per 1,000 individuals, Mexican-Americans own 18.8 businesses, Puerto Ricans 10.9, Cubans a powerful 62.9 and other Hispanics 22.9. As a retailer, it helps to understand that these groups see each other as different; that they look, sound and behave differently; and that they have very different economic profiles. You cannot market successfully to them in the same way.

Some further comparisons:

• The median family income of a Cuban American is almost $10,000 higher than a Puerto Rican's, though large numbers of both groups came to the continental U.S. about the same time.

• Nearly 19% of Cubans over age 25 have been through college, compared with only 10% of Puerto Ricans.

• Mexican Americans comprise 60% of U.S. Hispanics, Puerto Ricans 12% and Cubans only 5%. So if your business has nothing to do with New York or Florida where the Puerto Rican and Cuban populations are concentrated (respectively), you may want to focus your information gathering on Mexican-Americans. Professional golfer Lee Trevino likes to tell his listeners, "When I started out they call me a poor Mexican. Today, I'm a rich Spaniard. I just don't know when I changed."

Many well-to-do Mexican Americans feel the same way. Latin cultures tend to define people in large part by how they wear their success. This includes the well-to-do Mexican-American, who shows the same taste and buying behavior as his or her rich southern relation. "The Mexicans have a tendency to flaunt it more and are more price-conscious, but will spend a lot of money," says Tim Braun, who does a lot of business with affluent customers for Neiman-Marcus in Houston. "Their pieces have a splashier look, and they like big collections of jewelry." Mexicans are not interested in lowering the price, but they want good value. When Mexican or Mexican-American customers see something 20%-30% off, they realize it should not have been that high to begin with and won't do business with that store, he says.

Qualitative approach: To demonstrate the value and use of a qualitative approach, consider the Greek-American community's buying behavior.

The Greek Americans of Upper Darby, Pa., and the Chicago suburbs own fairly modest homes. But don't assume these communities aren't well-to-do. They exhibit passions for expensive and well-made clothes, furs and jewels. Both groups are aware of their personal appearance when in public and consider jewelry an important possession.

The Orthodox Greek Church has provided a strong foundation on which Greek-American communities can build their identities. For these groups of family-oriented people, the traditional gifts surrounding life's ceremonies play important cultural roles. When those ceremonies are baptisms, weddings and anniversaries, the gifts are jewelry.

Generations not far removed from their country of origin are especially eager to live up to traditional practices while proving they can make it in America.

Eve Alfillé, the Evanston, Ill., gallery owner, tells of a new customer, a young Greek dentist who is getting married in the Orthodox Church. The groom's family traditionally gives the bride a piece of coin jewelry before the wedding. "He could get this very inexpensively in Greece," says Alfillé. "But he

wants something special, so he is having us make a bracelet from old Greek coins. Why he is having it made here, I don't know. But he's turning out to be a very good customer."

Bridging a gap: Sensitivity to cultural traditions isn't easily quantified, but it's a good bridge to communities that value their origins.

Most discernibly ethnic Americans, naturalized or citizens from birth, know relatives in the "old country." Many still speak with accents, especially if raised in the heavily concentrated ethnic barrios and ghettos of inner cities. And it is still possible to be born, live and die in the U.S. without ever learning a word of English; in Canada an important minority of cultural preservationists strongly advocate French instead.

Because many ethnic Americans have a strong drive to raise themselves up from lower or middle class to the pinnacles of financial success, retail jewelers have a good reason to seek out the career winners in these communities.

WOMAN POWER

She is affluent, she is in charge and she buys much of her own jewelry. With eight women running for the U.S. Senate and more than 100 competing for seats in the House, it's no wonder commentators have dubbed this the Year of the Woman.

In JCK's September 1989 Part 2 issues, we introduced you to the average American: a 32-year-old woman with brown hair and brown eyes, 5'4", 143 pounds, married with one child and working in a technical, sales or administrative job. Her engagement ring was size 6 and cost about $800.

Since then, she has become a little more female (females account for more than 53% of the total population) gained three pounds and half a ring size, and aged only six months every year that has gone by. But the big differences in the average American:

• While she is still married, she has yet to have any of the two children she will have.

• She still performs many of the same jobs, but she is much more likely to be in management.

• Her engagement ring now carries a $920 price tag and she is more likely to have contributed toward its cost.

In command: The high-income woman is very much in command and comfortable with it. She may or may not work. As with her feudal predecessor, she's still expected occasionally to defer to a man of equal standing (something it rankles her to do), but every man and woman beneath her on the business or social scale knows right where they stand.

Nearly 25% of the executive work force is female, contrasting sharply with less than 13% in 1980. Many more small-business owners and divisional managers are women than they were even three years ago.

Pay equity remains an issue; women still earn less for the same work than men, but legal rulings are narrowing the gap. Because they may find themselves lower on the totem pole, many women have gravitated to jobs that pay by performance rather than by time-influenced fixed scales. In many of these cases, they outperform men in the same jobs.

Women are on their way to becoming richer than men. The wealthiest woman in the world, not counting the Queen of England (whose assets also run part of the government), is less affluent than only two men. Married-couple finances disguise who currently spends what on significant purchases among more normal households. But longevity coupled with increasing pay equality will lead to women controlling most families' wealth before the year 2025.

As women's affluence has increased, so has their willingness to buy their own luxuries; indeed, women buy more than half their own jewelry. Women often make what they consider a fashion purchase or buy an addition to their wardrobe. If married or engaged, however, many women still want buying significant pieces to be a two-part decision.

Women buying for themselves can spend a good deal of money, but they most often spread it over many pieces and several purchases. Women who have yet to buy or be given much jewelry gravitate first to diamond stud earrings, a strand of pearls and a ring for the left hand (most often containing colored stones, statistics show). Once the basics are in hand, they buy the styles they enjoy—choosing earrings, pendants, pins and bracelets, in that order of volume.

Rings are a very strong market, but men do most of the buying. Single divorced women buy rings sparingly for themselves; engaged and married women normally select pieces, then buy them with their mates or have their mates buy for them. The woman who buys herself many rings is the exception.

While the less affluent buy mostly commercial jewelry, women who are highly educated, who are in positions of social or business authority, or who wield considerable financial strength prefer designer jewelry in direct proportion to these three conditions. Many select from one to three designers to collect, artists whose styles reflect their own. Large and specially cut stones play their role here, proving very popular even when highly priced.

Living well: Alison Babas directs the marketing department of a midsized manufacturing firm headquartered in downtown Atlanta. With a piece of the company and a vice presidency, she typifies the affluent woman. Thirty-six and recently married, she doesn't have to work, but chooses to continue her career. She hasn't decided how she will handle the pregnancy she and her husband plan for next year.

Alison and her husband, Dave, live well in this regional capital; nothing they can afford is difficult to get. Both drive European sedans and both have car phones. As befitting her station, her wardrobe is tailored, moderately expensive and immaculate. The same is true of her jewelry. Alison's wedding set is tasteful and conservative, but much of her other jewelry, especially the earrings she always buys for herself, are more striking. When she's contemplating a major jewelry purchase, she looks first, then takes her husband along for the final consideration.

Willing to spend: "In my salon, I have easily a 5-to-1 ratio of women to men," says Neiman-Marcus's Tim Braun. "Years ago, women wouldn't buy for themselves. Now perhaps because they are working, they think nothing of spending $5,000-$10,000 without going home and asking their husbands."

Braun's clients are a bit more affluent than most. Many jewelers interviewed for this report put similar sales at $2,500-$6,000. As with any customer, it's important to support a woman buying for herself, especially when taking such a decisive step appears to be new to her.

"Male jewelers often don't buy pins big enough because they don't think they will sell," says Wally Vieregg, the jeweler near Denver, Colo. "They don't understand that you need a big pin if it's going to go against cloth and show up." He

once told a woman to take a larger 18k pin home to try it with her outfits. "The next day she put it on lay-away," he says. "She said, 'Thank you for making me take it home. I never would have bought it otherwise.'"

The largest group of women overlooked by jewelry marketers today are those in their 20s. While marketers adore baby boomers, throwing millions of dollars in advertising at these supposedly big spenders, the Roper Organization finds that younger women are more likely to splurge on luxuries such as designer lipstick and expensive handbags. The research, commissioned by Conde Nast's *Mademoiselle* magazine and reported in *The Wall Street Journal*, points out how managing executives can be overly attracted to larger dollar pools and bypass lucrative smaller markets where women buy for themselves.

Wider perspective: With a perspective afforded him by an international, national and regional clientele, Maurice Grunberg, chief executive of The Princess Jewels Collection in Beverly Hills, Cal., sees another aspect of women's self-purchase market.

"The European, the Asian, the African and Middle Eastern women are more independent in following their impulses without having to pick up the phone to consult with their husbands or fathers," he says. Perhaps because jewelry choosing and buying is part of a woman's role in those cultures, he continues, "it is truly their own decision. The American woman is far more reliant on her mate for approval and seldom will make a big purchase without consulting him."

Adds Deanna Haimoff of Haimoff and Haimoff, a chain of fine jewelers in resort hotels in Hawaii and San Francisco, "She will buy earrings, but I don't find a lot of women buying themselves rings."

She relates these observations of male-female jewelry buying patterns: "Many times it is obvious the husband doesn't know what his wife is spending. She may spend a couple of thousand dollars on clothes and he never says a word because he doesn't see the bills. But if she comes in and looks at a $300 ring, he will ask if she really needs it. If she spends the same amount on a pair of earrings, he is never going to notice."

You shouldn't read his report and conclude that sex-based distinctions are all but gone. Many prevail and show no signs of impending mortality. Yet women, especially affluent women, are demanding and receiving equal roles in American economic and social life, and that change has affected the jewelry industry in a positive way.

"I bought my husband a Cyma for his birthday," Maria Frasca tells JCK. "He hated to think I would buy him jewelry, but after he wore it a couple of times and got a few compliments, he likes it!"

OLD MONEY: THE AFFLUENT ELDERLY

Dwight Eisenhower understood age. Referring to a rocking chair that had graced his grandfather's porch, he said, "I'm saving that rocker for the day I feel as old as I really am."

With plenty of money to live on, plenty of world to see and, hopefully, a couple of decades left to do it in, most well-to-do Americans over 65 act younger than any 56-year-old store manager two days after Christmas. About 978,000 households headed by an adult over 64 still have incomes topping $75,000 a year, a number that will increase to 1.75 million by 1996. This sizable market is the cruise industry's most important customer group and one of the hotel/resort industry's greatest interests, taking three times their share of vacations.

361

Older people aren't planning to give up on life or each other: two thirds of all Americans 55 and up are married, one third of those over 74 still live with spouses, and those now age 75 can expect to live 10 more years if they're men, 12-plus if they're women. Don't write off these customers because they are old or depleting their resources.

PSI's John DeMarco notes that most "established" senior-citizen millionaires are "actively" living off their investments, no longer too concerned with building assets. They make up a good part of the 10%-20% of this country's 1.5 million millionaires who DeMarco computes to be right on the edge, at the risk of any stock market fall or Congressional tax enhancement that would push them down into the simply well-heeled category. But few of them worry about it the way they once did. Their largest expenses—including homes, children and a small fortune in earned income taxes—have been paid.

Many retirees, though not millionaires, were successful during their working years and enjoy sizable bank balances. Whether they wore a white or blue collar, earned moderate or high income, career workers are big retirement winner; pensions begun 40 years ago and set aside before corporations started to play games with their employees' accounts now yield impressive monthly stipends. And almost one in five people ages 65-75 has yet to totally retire.

Disposable income: As a general group, the elderly are excellent clients with considerable disposable income. The 33 million Americans 65 and over spent $472.7 billion in 1989; while they had higher health-care costs, almost every other expense category required less than before. Consequently, those ages 65-74 averaged $20,704 discretionary dollars annually, higher than any group under 45.

This past year, the same group bought more than 1.5 times its share of jewelry sold by dollar value (based on extrapolation from government statistics). High-performance sedans and exquisitely appointed living rooms may have held more attraction at 35 than at 70; jewelry is—if anything—more appealing now.

Though only 13.4% of the population, those over 65 will account for slightly more than 21% of the total dollar value of jewelry sold in 1992, based on past years' experience, and more than 22% of the total amount spent for jewelry and watch gifts.

The affluent elderly show themselves quite willing to spend money when and where they get treated as respected customers with well-educated tastes, preferably where they feel they know somebody personally.

"Many of our older, affluent customers bought a lot of jewelry from us in the '70s and '80s and, of course, they come back," says Tim Braun, adding they account for 15%-20% of his business at Neiman-Marcus in Houston. They buy sophisticated watches and larger and bigger stone jewelry, he says. Instead of pavé and clusters, they want to trade in for a single stone. They have arrived, he says, and they realize that quality is more important than quantity.

Attitudes: Some retailers are inclined to discount or become exasperated with older clients who seem too concerned with an item's "high" price; this is only natural on both sides.

Remember that many older customers genuinely are taken aback by the cost of jewelry. They established their sense of worth when a dollar bought far more; when they return to the market after a prolonged absence, they're not in tune with costs. Consider when you go into a toy store today. Isn't it amazing how toys you grew up with are so much more expensive and much less well-made? Everything in a jewelry store may seem that way to an older person, especially when $35-an-oz. gold is now spot priced around $350.

The men and women who turn 65 this year were just babies during the great Depression, but the people who raised them taught well. The elderly of America who learned the Depression-era mentality of savings and self-reliance put away very healthy nest eggs. Now they're being affected by modern mentalities that say it's OK to do a little for yourself, and they have the means to do it.

Many older customers still like gifts and vanity pieces. The vast majority have very conservative tastes, but don't misunderstand this to mean small or exclusively estate in style or only diamonds, rubies, sapphires and emeralds. Classic designs and modern adaptations of traditional themes are very popular with them. Unfamiliar stones capture their attention and delight their senses. Many a jeweler who has had the patience and tact to re-educate an older client in a way that enhances his or her dignity has gained a lifelong friend. To quote one jeweler of the couples he sees, "They buy together and they buy big."

Buying behavior changes: Consumer behavior among wealthy men changes after retirement. These ex-business leaders with good decision-making skills and fine taste have looked at men's jewelry over the years but rarely bought any. They generally felt their corporate lifestyle or business environment prohibited wearing anything more luxurious than cuff links and a watch. Once over 60, however, retired men tend to visit jewelers with their wives and start to let down their guard, indulging their tastes by buying a ring or chain.

Another change in buying habit is prompted by exposure. "Our older clients travel, they go on expensive vacations, they see jewelry on the trip and they want to know if we can get it for them, too," says Hank Siegel of Hamilton's Jewelers in Lawrenceville, N.J.

One of the strongest reasons the elderly buy jewelry is to obtain some quantity of immortality as they near the end of their lives. The affluent are especially this way. "Buying a quality piece of jewelry that can be passed down, something they can leave behind to three, four or five generations to ensure they will be remembered," motivates many of Craig Underwood's customers.

For Norma and John Kelly, home is Kentucky in the summer and Arizona in the winter, reflecting a pattern common with those wealthy enough to own two residences. Having grown up in the blue grass country and prospered each time his business dealt with horses, John has put away a "tidy sum." A housewife all her adult life, Norma is justifiably proud of her husband's and children's achievements.

They feel they worked and saved for all those years so they now can spoil their grandchildren, entertain friends, treat each other a little now and then and take two vacations annually. John has never really had jewelry, save for his watch, wedding ring and a few pairs of cuff links and matching tie bars. Several of the links and bars bare equine motifs. So the last time they went to a jeweler, Norma insisted he try on a ring with a horse theme. When she isn't around, he admits he likes the idea and thinks it befitting of a gentleman who has done well in business; he will probably get one this year.

Norma, on the other hand, collected plenty of jewelry over the years. Most pieces have smaller stones and go well with her simple diamond necklace. But now that they are splurging a bit, Norma wants a nice ruby surrounded by small but high-quality diamonds set in 18k gold. It will be an heirloom that one of their grandchildren will wear one day. And maybe it's time to trade in some jewelry she's had for years. A few better pieces would please her more.

Traveling twice a year and living in two places, the Kellys have many jewelers to choose from, but they almost always buy from one in Arizona and one in Kentucky. They just aren't sure they're comfortable with the rest and don't want to be disloyal.

"The affluent elderly need a little bit more professional and sincere, touchy-feely kind of jeweler," says Jeffrey Samuels of William Jeffrey's LTD in Mechanicsville, Va. "They need a jeweler who is going to spend a lot of time with them. A lot of jewelers have taken the chairs and benches out of their stores and gone to all stand-ups. I will always offer somebody a chair."

Good customers: Harold Tivol of Tivol's in Kansas City, Mo., wants any customer who will come into the store. But his best customer, he candidly admits is the well-provided-for widow.

"Here she is going to get what she wants and we are going to make her happy," he says. "My best customers will buy every month, every two months or every three months, where your average customer will buy once every two to three years. These are mostly older people, the retirees who have done well in business."

Few jewelers do anything to get the affluent elderly customer they wouldn't do to develop their overall client base. This means developing a reputation, merchandising and marketing correctly and making themselves available to the clients they want to serve.

"When they are interested in fine jewelry and are in Kansas City, where we are strong in the market," says Tivol, "it's pretty difficult not to come to us."

Adds Samuels, "When people bring in a repair, they want to tell you the history of the piece. They want to tell you when Aunt Bessie's ring was handed down, why it was handed down, all about it. And instead of rushing them along and saying 'OK, OK, what do you need done to it?' we listen to the whole story. It makes them feel very comfortable.

"They have plenty of jewelry already, so nine times out of 10, they come to get something fixed. A repair for an affluent elderly leads to a sale for an affluent elderly. That's when we get the chance to shine."

REALLY OLD MONEY: THE ELITE

Some money isn't just old, it's antique. But while the social elite of the past century competed to outspend and out-display each other, today's conservators of their ancestors' affluence are very, very private people. Thus when *Forbes* focuses on billionaires, listing the 64 wealthiest individuals, it also catalogs 33 family fortunes tipping the 10-digit scale without mentioning given names. Here the 19th century lives again in its descendants; the Du Ponts, the Rockefellers, the Hearsts and the Mellons continue to enjoy inherited preeminence.

Serious money, it is said, doesn't grow on trees, it breeds. Looking at the top of the social pyramid, you see many established names who have made tremendous fortunes through business in recent years. That's not an optical illusion. Money has to be cultivated to grow, and only today's

business will do that fast enough to please the socially advantaged. They have an edge. Through intermarriage and family friendship, they maintain a network of connections that positions them to take maximum advantage of financial situations and business opportunities. It's rare for the new men of business success to be unknown to the social register. H. Ross Perot may have risen to wealth from a poor beginning, but almost every other family worth close to $50 million or more got there with help from earlier generations.

Accustomed to wealth: As a couple, Charles and Alison Maison illustrate the gracious scion of success. With bank accounts begun by their respective great-grandparents and property handed down through the family, they call Manhattan home and spend as much time as they can in Oyster Bay.

Younger but no less affluent than the executive elite they regularly associate with, they were raised to a tradition that's rapidly disappearing. As children they were taught to dance at cotillions, to ride at select stables and to come out in only the right debutante society (to which one is invited, usually the group in which your mother made her debut) or to join the correct gentlemen's clubs. At school they learned squash, tennis, golf, plus rowing for Charles and ballet for Allison.

By the time they went to boarding school, they had learned to jump and hunt, knew how to sail and ski, and probably could navigate Europe's capitals better than their chauffeurs. They know the Maine coast and Martha's Vineyard, the Napa Valley and Catalina, Corpus Christi and West Palm Beach, the heights of Toronto and the straits of Mackinac. Pebble Beach has its attractions, Vail and Aspen their appeal, but Myrtle Beach is the U.S. location that allows them to relax. And that's just in the U.S.

Charles went to the select college his family has attended for generations, taking classes in a number of buildings named for relatives and studying under professors who were grateful to the family for funding their chairs. Alison met Charles at college again, having actually known him from the numerous Christmas parties and spring events of their preteen youth. She still keeps up regularly with her sorority sisters.

They share the limo in the city; it has become a practical necessity for a family that still needs to make social engagements on time. Charles is a senior member of the family firm, which is managed by his younger brother, Nathaniel, the real businessman.

There are few idle rich anymore, and the Maisons will not be among them. The $3.5 million brownstones on the Upper East Side and larger weekend "cottages" would disappear if family fortunes weren't actively maintained. While they see ostentatious displays of wealth as a sure sign of insecurity or poor breeding, everyone is concerned with money. It's not the amount; $30 million or $300 million doesn't matter. Once one has enough, one doesn't talk about it. But it will disappear in the blink of an eye if not well-cared-for.

Their jewelers: Two types of jewelry firms successfully cater to the old-money community.

The first type, those working to establish themselves as the jeweler in a given area, maintain a large, refined selection of very fine jewelry, typically $1 million or more in inventory. They pay close attention to developing an atmosphere in which their customer will feel comfortable. And they make it their business to provide whatever their best customers need in the way of jewelry and service.

The second type is already an established jeweler and, over the generations, has become an institution in the lives of the clientele. These jewelers don't need the same large selection or investment in inventory. Having attained a position only they themselves can lose, they make customized service and consultative sales their specialty. Their clients depend on them for advice and counsel.

Both types of firms must offer unparalleled quality at a very fair price to stay in business, and both count many customers among their personal friends and social acquaintances.

Greenwich, Conn., has long been served by this second type of firm. As one resident puts it, "Betteridge Jewelers has been here since God made Greenwich."

"They come to us because they trust our judgment, our sensibilities and our taste level to supply them with the best possible materials and workmanship for the best possible price," says the firm's Randy La Pointe. "We know the difference between a Kashmir sapphire and a Ceylon sapphire, and they may not. They do know there is something to be known.

"Our customer base is very loyal; they've been doing business with us, if not for generations, then for some time. The community has come to respect us for what we do. I think it's more of a guidance thing than anything else—they look to us because we know what is right."

A customer typically will offer an idea of what he's looking for, give some parameters, then trust the jeweler to do what is right.

Two firms in Denver, Colo., are working to become this kind of jeweler. Neither is over 25 years old ad the race is far from over, but one will probably end up the jeweler for the social elite.

Brian Foster, owner of one of the two stores, remembers how his firm got started doing business and traveling in "the right set."

"You won't like the answer," Foster says. "We were already there. My mother and the other investors were part of the Colorado social scene. They could create the needed word of mouth that starts this kind of business."

Other jewelers agree that they had to be "in on the scene" before they could make any headway. But that's not all. "Yes you have to be a member of the country club, but people are there to relax and don't want to be caught in the lobby and solicited for business," he says. "You have to meet people constantly; they need to want to come see you."

Why do people come to see Foster? "We have fun, oh God, we have fun!" he says. "When people come in feeling down, they go out feeling good. When they come in feeling good, they go out feeling better."

How many jewelry stores will order pizza and share it with a customer right on the counter? "And when we get new designer jewelry in, like Ronna Lugosch's mobius bracelet [4.25 ct. t.w.]," he says, "everybody tries it on. Within a few days, three people want it.

"You do whatever it takes. I will never lose an engagement ring sale. They shop around, they come back; if I have to, I cut the deal right next to the bone. If all else fails, ride the margin to cover the goods. I make 99% of my wedding sales. And from then on, they are mine for life."

La Pointe and Foster agree that price enters into every purchase, but that it's always secondary. They also agree that these people need to be befriended, not broadcast to. "We do advertising, but it's not to get big numbers of people in," says La Pointe. "It's more to keep our name out in the public."

Asked about merchandise, La Pointe and Foster say they stock the best. "Not glitz, but a variety of fine jewelry with lots of goods in it," Foster says, "including, fine gifts, china and crystal as well as Oscar Heyman."

International outlook: International in outlook and shopping practices, old-money customers spend a multitude of currencies in top cities around the world. In these cities, they are known. Personalized leather may come from Gucci, luggage from Vuitton, and Cartier would be pleased to receive madam at her convenience when next she is in Paris. Old money is very quality-conscious, knowing that anything worth having is worth having made well. Companies with discretion that prove conspicuous only in the quality of their customer service attract this client.

"International people are the same everywhere," says Maurice Grunberg of the Princess Jewels Collection, Beverly Hill, Cal. "The very, very wealthy are far too demanding for the average jeweler. These are very well-traveled, extremely sophisticated people, and they are not going for the gaudy or the simply flawless; they want something unique.

"The national, international and regional client is truly a pearl that has to be treated as a rare pearl. Creativity in providing for them is a must."

Eve Alfillé says the socially elite often make their first visit to her gallery in Evanston, Ill., when they're looking for an elegant gift that a traditional jeweler may not have. "Then they see things for themselves which they will send their husbands to purchase when an occasion comes, and the relationship begins," she says. "We work very hard to please our customers."

To keep them requires some effort, says Tim Braun of Neiman-Marcus. "Sometimes, these families are too busy to come to the salon, and they like to be catered to in their home," he says. "They feel more comfortable at home."

Old-money customers also may be interested in redesigning a piece they inherited but never use and aren't likely to pass down. The diamond from Great-Aunt Martha's hideous brooch, God rest her soul, would make an excellent tie tac for junior to wear at graduation.

Reaching the market: Very few forms of advertising seem to work when targeted at this client. If just anyone can find it in the marketplace, why should the social elite respond? *Town and Country* and the *New Yorker* generally are successful in reaching this market because they report on its social happenings; *The Wall Street Journal* is a good vehicle because these clients use it as a business tool.

Also helpful are personal and financial support of the cultural activities and charities in which the socially prominent participate. Ever sit in the audience waiting for the philharmonic or opera to begin? Old money reads those programs, too.

Jewelers who regularly serve the social elite say they are very gracious. Where new money often and sometimes rudely demands discounts, old money treats the retailers it patronizes as professionals. A carriage-trade customer who finds out afterward that he was taken advantage of generally stops patronizing the firm and tells his friends why. If you want large markups and high margins proceed to the world of the nouveau riche. Old money didn't get old by being foolishly spent.

Like any other desired client, the socially elite can be sought out; salespeople do it 24 hours a day. Their names are found in social registers, yacht club listings and executive guides. But they protect themselves; you may have to become a member to get the list, though a friend who is a member may be willing to help.

What makes the difference is adjusting your life-style to theirs and inserting yourself into their circle. There are many sacrifices involved in changing to this life-style, not the least of them financial. But there are many rewards. The jeweler who does so successfully will act as consultant to many wonderful people from whom the dollars are available if the product is right. And the jewelry you deal with will be the best in the industry—works of art that deserve public attention. Why else did you get into this business anyway?

THE FUTURE FOUR

Beyond the seven distinct demographic groups whose affluence and interest in beautiful jewelry make them important to jewelers, there are four more groups often considered too poor, too unknown, too difficult to please or too flighty. But they can be the future for many in this industry.

THE NEXT GENERATION

The younger end of the baby boom and its immediate successor ages 20-30 make up 16.4% of the American public. Few in this large group have reached their prime earning years yet. But a small percentage already does very well thanks to trust funds, inheritances or early high-paying careers.

Yet many industries ignore this market in favor of older buyers. Businesses that do pursue it typically find captive audiences and lock up much of a young person's disposable income.

Many are tied up with high mortgage and car payments. But the fact they can afford these payments indicates considerable discretionary income once everything is paid off. Getting them interested in jewelry before they have the money available is often the key.

Most never own a valuable piece of jewelry until they get married. But having been raised in the media age, young consumers create long and detailed wish lists, coupled with high expectations for immediate gratification. The desire to own fine jewelry is not hard to develop in them.

"I sell a tremendous number of watches to young executives who want to establish themselves," says Tim Braun of Neiman-Marcus, Houston. "the 25- or 30-year-old who wants that important watch or diamond, who may earn $100,000 plus, is fashion-conscious and society-conscious and buys a certain level and quality of jewelry that can be recognized by his peers. "

Electronic advertising: The young market responds well to electronic media advertising.

"We have over 200 commercials because we make our own here," says Craig Underwood of Underwood Jewelers in Fayetteville, Ark. "We target different ads to different markets: executives through CNN, married women through daytime programming and young people through MTV and VH1. Our results are good."

This younger group is essential to most jewelers' business future.

"I'd love to get more of the 20 - to 30-year-olds because the 60-year-olds have almost everything they really need; you have to renew the market," says Eve Alfillé. "When I have a young man buying a wedding ring, I plant the seed. I jokingly say, 'You realize you are tying yourself down to a whole lifetime of birthdays and anniversaries.' Usually it's the first time he has thought about it."

John Wendt, senior vice president of L'Oreal, put it this way in a *Wall Street Journal* article: "We've got to broaden what we stand for and attract younger customers, users just starting to form habits and buying trends that may last for years. Success with those customer goes a long way toward insuring the success of your business."

GAY AND LESBIAN POPULATION

With the onset of the AIDS crisis, an epidemic never confined solely to the homosexual community, the general public became much more aware of people who are gay and lesbian. Yet when asked, most jewelers say they know little about the gay population, wouldn't know when a gay person comes into their store and consequently never recognize what this segment of the market buys.

"Gay men are much less inhibited about wearing jewelry," says Eve Alfillé. "They are typically professionals, doing well, are often interested in the jewelry we design and will buy it for their partners. Once they do 'come out of the closet,' they indulge themselves and wear some very nice things. I target advertising in the gay newspaper that caters to the more professional, more upscale gay population."

Jonathan Summit, a partner in Opera Jewelry Inc., Provincetown, Mass., does a significant part of his business with the gay community. "The desire for diamonds in the gay community both from gay men and gay women is pretty strong," he says. "They like quality jewelry and they like integrity in the people they deal with—a lot."

He does a big business in commitment rings. "When a couple decide they are going to make a commitment to each other, they buy each other rings. A lot of times, they want matching rings, but that can be a sensitive issue. When they are with family, if they are not 'out,' that is an issue.

Gay women are very relationship-oriented, he says. "They tend to travel in groups a little bit more, are very supportive of each other in decisions like this and encourage each other—which is a little different than a straight crowd would be," he says. "If they like you and your merchandise, they will support you and you will have a line of their friends coming in who are in the same circumstance."

Many gays are more affluent than their straight counterparts, but exact figures are difficult to come by. "It's an absence of documentation," said Sara Craig of Overlooked Opinions, a marketing firm in Chicago that surveys gay consumers, in the April issue of American Demographics. Interviewing 25,000 self-identified gay men and lesbian women, Overlooked Opinions found that 81% of the men dine out more than five times a month, 17% of the women read a book every day and 56% of gay couples have household incomes exceeding $50,000. The median age of the male gay population, estimated at 10% of men overall, is 37; the median age of the female gay population, estimated at 4%-6% of the female population, is 35.

NATIONAL & INTERNATIONAL SET

In today's rapidly shrinking world, many a jewelry customer shops in places far from home.

For Europeans, Asians and Arabs, buying in the U.S. means taking advantage of favorable exchange rates and encourages holiday-like consumerism.

Traveling gives many overscheduled Americans and Canadians the chance to spend time with friends and family, and buying jewelry may happen because it's one of the few times they can shop together.

Because of their regular access to jewelry from the most exacting producers, these clients demand high material quality and exceptional deign. Platinum, 18k gold, VVS/G diamonds and richly colored, imperceptibly included gemstones have nearly become the standard. The competition that existed among the wealthy of past eras to exhibit large, expensive, overpowering jewelry has given way to very valuable but discreet, refined, unique pieces. Understated elegance rather than ostentation satisfies this customer's demand.

Referring to Robert Leser's flexible 18k and diamond cuffs and necklaces, Shirley Dwyer of R.H. Teel in the Fairmont Hotel in San Jose, Cal., indicates her customer's preferences: "These are the fine materials and great designs my customers are looking for. The executives who live here and the people who stay in the hotel want something they can take home as a gift that will really get attention."

Service is held to the same high performance standard. "We keep [these clients] by doing just about anything they want," says Mike Grant of Steve Schmier's Jewelers in Tahoe City, Cal. He recalls a couple who came to the store on a Thursday and wanted a very fine three-stone ring. He rose at 4 a.m. Friday to carve a wax model and, before they left town on Sunday, the ring was ready. "That's service," he says. "I have to get them while they are here."

Just as the jewelry for this clientele makes a subtle statement, so should the advertising. "This is not the type of business you want a herd of people coming into," one jeweler confides. "You are dealing with the very select, and you acquire a reputation for the very select; no other type of advertising works." In some cases TV and magazine advertising are counterproductive. "We stay in touch with them either by phone or by mail, and that has been the most important thing in building and keeping this client," says Tim Braun.

NEWLY RICH, NOUVEAU RICHE

The preceding variations suggest the rich are not a static group of old-money families limited to the Du Ponts or Rockefellers. Every year, a good number are replaced in the top 1%, and some of the new ones acquire their wealth in a very short time.

Those who acquire money without any previous experience with financial comfort come in a wide array of employments and upbringings. But they seem to behave in one of two ways: the majority seem bent on going for broke, the others spend a small portion and use the rest to develop and enviable estate. When looking at jewelry, they often are as interested in how jewelry can further their advancement as they are to receive an award or enjoy giving a gift.

This important minority of newly rich men and women—including many lawyers, brokers, financiers and commercial real estate executives—go to work daily side by side with associates whose money bears a better pedigree. They strive to fit in.

Steven Gower, for example, couldn't pronounce Breguet to save his life or even make an informed choice between buying a Vacheron and a Constantin. But before making an important sales presentation wearing a watch that didn't enhance his reputation or his employer's he found out.

Where the minority of Newly Rich plan to be old money in generations to come, Nouveau Riche are more concerned with looking the part and living the lifestyle now. This style of new money can be divided into two groups, the short-term customer and the "who knows how long it will last" variety.

"There is a new couple I am working with now," Jeffrey Samuels reports. "He has been a bachelor for a long time, owns his own company and all of a sudden she's got money. She write checks for $4,000 and doesn't think about it.

"You know," he marvels, "settlements, accidents, all of a sudden they get this big, huge check. They come in with this money market account just burning a hole in their pocket. My feeling is, ride this train while it lasts because it isn't going very far."

Then there are the newly created fortunes growing at such a pace that their owners are justified in spending vast amounts without worry. Media celebrities, sports stars, corporate raiders and certain land developers come to mind. "When it comes to jewelry," says Susan Monk of the North Boston's Quadrum, "new money needs to express its new success." These customers often feel it is very important to have the newest things, to be right up with fashion.

How they spend: Boulder, Colo., has its share of newly rich, especially those whose engineering and start-up ventures have made good.

"The new money feels it has to go off and shop the world, to be romanced by the big guys, so it doesn't spend at home right off the bat," says Walter Vieregg of Walters and Hogsett Jewelers. "Once they are used to the comforts of having this money, they start buying locally. Service is still the main ingredient of the small independent jeweler, and that brings them in."

Adds Deanna Haimoff of Haimoff and Haimoff, Hawaii and San Francisco, "The newly affluent need to be educated a little more than other wealthy customers. They were not raised with [fine jewelry], so why this stone is a little more and things like that need going into."

Maria Frasca of M. Frasca, Palm Desert., has a lot of the same customer. "The new rich don't have family jewels, so they buy them." she says. "They tend to buy mostly diamonds because they don't really understand colored stones. They like cutting-edge stuff, but they want diamonds." She says they also want to deal. "But they do it all on my say [not knowing what a good deal is]," she says. "They don't shop, they are here to buy."

While new-money millionaires come from all walks of life, statistics give the edge to venture capitalists, financial and securities brokers, media and sports celebrities, niche marketers and cutting-edge technology entrepreneurs. Most often, the successful individual leveraged money, time and effort, and the leveraging blossomed.

The new-money millionaires typically are married and have one to two children, and one person in the household still works. The new rich feel less loyalty than old money; if a merchant goes out of his way for them, they feel that's what they've paid for.

Specialty publications concerning high-dollar activities are one of the most direct ways to reach these customers. *The Robb Report,* several golf publications and a number of the Conde Nast group of magazines are good examples.

For newly rich who grew up expecting a working life and now find themselves combating excessive time or emotional troubles, retail therapy proves a popular relief. Expensive new jewelry bought on a whim, we have been assured, works miraculous cures.

WHO DO YOU HAVE?

One of the soundest business management practices any retailer can invest time in is a periodic analysis of the client base.

A thorough look should reveal the following:
• Who your principal and secondary customer types are and could be.
• What kind of products and services they demand.
• Whether you're getting to these customers and meeting their needs.
• Whether you are making a profit at it.
• Equally important is to identify the following:
• What activities distract you from these primary tasks.
• What client groups and services expend your resources but don't move your company and profits in the right direction.
• What activities and products sap your times and strength without helping you to reach your goal.

LAST THOUGHTS

Those who depend on old customer bases without compensating for changes find some of their clients moving on to other retailers and the rest with fewer and fewer discretionary dollars to spend.

If you want to know more about these well-heeled targets of retail opportunity, we suggest the following reading:
• *Forbes* magazine catalogs the richest of the rich, the 400 wealthiest people in the world. The 11th annual edition this fall will include brief biographies on the top 101 affluent. Preceding it is the July 20, 1992, issue titled "The World's Billionaires," covering only those 291 who could make the cut.
• *Fortune* magazine periodically includes a section on wealth.
• Dow Jones publishes *American Demographics,* a monthly magazine that delves into the mysteries of the U.S. Census Bureau's figures and comes up with insights you would otherwise pay market-research firms thousands of dollars to produce.
• *The Wall Street Journal,* recently reorganized to make finding marketing material much easier, is the daily diary of the American dream. It only occasionally requires that you hire an MBA for interpretation.

(Author's note: Many of the potential customers interviewed for this article were reluctant to be quoted and spoke on the condition they not be identified. Because so much valuable information came to light, each customer profiled is a composite of two or three people and is given a fictional name. This provides a more complete view of the customer type and maintains anonymity. The jewelers quoted here are real people, each one of them more than happy to help and be quoted. Our thanks and full credits go to each of them.)

Reaching The Corporate Boardroom

August 1992

Richard Kessler was frustrated. During his 10 years as a retail jeweler in Menomonee Falls, Wisc., he had enjoyed working with customers and selling them the perfect gift. But he often didn't see many of those customers for a year or more after the sale. Could he create more repeat business, he wondered?

Three years ago, he found the answer hidden in the local hospital. Its personnel director, a Kessler customer, was unhappy with the firm that had been supplying the hospital's service award pins. After repairing a few broken pins for the hospital, Kessler offered to design a new one himself.

"They loved it," he says.

The hospital asked Kessler to take over its awards program. Then the hospital volunteer group hired Kessler to

design its annual award pins. And soon afterward, Kessler was working on award and gift programs for Miller Brewing Co. and Outboard Marine Corp., two corporate giants in nearby Milwaukee, as well as other firms.

"Now many recipients of these awards purchase jewelry in our store," he says.

Corporate course: Corporate sales account for 10% of Kessler's $350,000 annual sales volume. "The business is growing right underneath us," Kessler says. "We are way up this year, and much of it is from corporate gifts."

Kessler is one of a growing number of smaller independent retailers to start corporate service award programs. While most retailers sell sporadically to businesses in need of a special gift or awards, some have organized separate departments and formalized the procedures to solicit and retain corporate customers.

A corporate award is generally a pin, ring, desk accessory, pen, charm, watch or clock that typically is given to an employee to commemorate superior service, attendance, safety or sales performance. These awards, which often contain the firm's logo or other corporate symbol, are commonly referred to as incentive gifts.

Other popular programs involve gifts given to employees on significant anniversaries, at board meetings or at retirement. Timepieces, silver tableware, jewelry, pens and engraved crystal are the most popular gifts for these occasions, though some retailers have widened the selection to include luggage, clothing, electronic devices and even fishing gear.

Large established retailers such as Tiffany & Co. and Cartier Inc. typically manufacture their own gift selections. Smaller independents often order from jewelry and gift manufacturers such as Anson Inc. in Providence, R.I.; B.A. Ballow & Co. in East Providence, R.I.; A.T. Cross in Lincoln, R.I.; Jostens Inc. in Minneapolis, Minn.; RQC Ltd. in Buffalo, N.Y.; Talisman in Grand Rapids, Mich.; O.C. Tanner Jewelry Co. in Salt Lake City, Utah; Tropar in Florham Park, N.J.; and a host of emblematic jewelry, gift accessory, watch and clock firms.

Right for the retailer: Businesses and wholesalers buy a large percentage of their corporate gifts and awards directly from manufacturers. But independent retail jewelers are in an enviable position from which to reach into corporate boardrooms across America.

"This is a business for independents," says Paul Dlouhy, sales representative at Talisman. The firm was founded four years ago as a division of the Terryberry Co. to meet increased demand from jewelers selling corporate gifts and awards. Dlouhy says local jewelers can more easily customize an award, incentive or gift program than can a large national company. Retailers can visit the client corporation and ask the right questions about its needs, budget and future plans.

Herman Ginsberg, owner of Herman Ginsberg Jewelry, Cedar Rapids, Iowa, discovered that large manufacturers and wholesalers often miss opportunities that retailers can spot easily. About two years ago, a large chemical firm called Ginsberg after failing to find what it needed form a manufacturer, several national department stores and a wholesale outlet. "They needed 1,450 pens in two days," recalls Ginsberg. "The first manufacturer they called turned them down because the order wasn't large enough, and the stores didn't have the correct model."

The chemical firm then chose a pricier pen and called Ginsberg. "I put them on hold and called the manufacturer," he says. "The pens were shipped overnight." The same firm has since ordered numerous items from Ginsberg. "I couldn't believe that all those big-shot firms couldn't have done the same thing."

The pen incident was a good omen for Ginsberg, whose family business has been in Cedar Rapids since 1930. Now he actively courts corporate business and has built it to about 10% of total sales. Daughter Julie Brusen is the store's chief salesperson.

"We sell to trucking firms, engineering companies, charities and even IBM," he explains. The best-sellers are cuff links, lapel pins, watches and rings. Like Kessler, Ginsberg considers repeat business one of the attractions of the corporate client.

Research first: "Any jeweler can go to these companies, find out what makes them tick and use that information to customize a program," says Douglas R. Harris, owner of Douglas R. Harris Jeweler in Gastonia, N.C. His retail store had been in business for five years in 1987 when Harris started to investigate the corporate gift potential in his area. Though he had received numerous customer inquiries and occasionally provided awards and gifts to country clubs and other organizations, he had never formalized his programs.

"We discovered we had about 30 Fortune 500 firms nearby," says Harris. "Many of them told us they were having difficulty servicing their incentive items like watches or clocks."

He also found that most of his store's jewelry and gift suppliers had a corporate division to help him with customized or large-scale orders.

In 1987 alone, six inquiries were quickly turned into corporate accounts. Now, his three-person corporate sales division services 40 firms, including several of the largest textile firms in the nation. About 25% of his firm's $650,000 annual sales volume comes from the corporate sales division.

Emphasize expertise: Harris says jewelers can put their expertise to work quickly when seeking corporate business. "With a background in jewelry, china, crystal, silver, watches and service, a retail jeweler can tear up the competition," he says.

In a few cases, the task was simpler than expected. "We analyzed [the awards] other firms were selling to corporate clients," he says. "What many of the local businesses thought was 14k gold was actually goldplate, and synthetic stones were common. Nobody ever checked it before."

Harris, like an increasing number of retailers, extends the range of corporate gifts to include non-traditional items such as pearl necklaces, 14k and 18k gold chains and earrings, telescopes, art prints and even rifles and hunting knives.

"When we ask what they want as a gift, the answer is always 'Something I can't or wouldn't buy for myself,'" he says. Hunting accessories, including a knife from a local manufacturer, are popular among area mill employees. Harris emphasizes locally made items, which has won the appreciation of import-wary textile workers.

Becoming known: Corporate gift sales have led the overall store growth of more than a few retailers in recent years. Michael C. Fina, a retailer based in New York for 57 years started a corporate division 15 years ago. Today, the division produces half the firm's total sales. On the West Coast, retailer Prestige & Co. of Portland, Ore., has seen similar growth.

The ball started rolling, appropriately enough, in 1989 when Kareem Abdul-Jabbar received a handcut handpolished glass backgammon set inlaid with gold and platinum leaf just before his last game with the Portland Trail Blazers. Prestige & Co. commissioned the set from artist Kathleen Miesen Meehan at the request of the Trail Blazers. "We received some very good press coverage for that," recalls Prestige President Eli Kassab. Though Jabbar's backgammon set was one of a kind, Prestige today offers chess, checkers and other board games of similar design (and varying cost) to corporate gift clients.

Since 1989, several large local companies such as Nike, a prominent boat manufacturer and advertising firms have joined the Trail Blazers as Prestige clients. The corporate division now has three full-time employees and accounts for nearly 30% of total sales.

Kassab attributes much of the growth to careful planning and an individualized approach to gift-giving. For each client, Kassab or an assistant visits the person in charge of buying gifts and inquires about the male-female ratio of the group, hobbies they may have in common and their ages. "If a recipient plays tennis, you don't give him golf equipment."

Making deals: Kassab also encourages firms to trade or buy products from their own corporate customers to use as incentive gifts - which Prestige then wraps and presents to the employees. "We advise them how to put this together, but we don't deal with their suppliers," he says. "We don't charge a fee, but we hope the employees will buy from our store in the future."

While most of Prestige's sales involve traditional items such as watches, clocks, pens, desk sets, jewelry and leather goods, Kassab has noticed a trend toward brand-name crystal with discreetly inscribed corporate names and toward electronic items such as radios or Watchman. "We just delivered 80 'world time' radios by Sony to a customer," says Kassab.

The key to reaching this market, he says, is in the hands of nearly any jeweler with an approach appropriate to local businesses. "If the jeweler presents himself nicely," says Kassab, "he can cater to just about anybody."

Spreading the Message

Three jewelers share some hints on developing a corporate gift business:

• Elie Kassab, president of Prestige & Co., Portland, Ore., advertises his corporate gift department in the Yellow Pages section of telephone books. To solicit board members, he also sends direct mailers to the president's executive assistant. To reach new clients for incentive or reward gifts, he targets the purchasing agent or personnel director.

• Richard Kessler, president of Richard Kessler Jewelers, Menomonee Falls, Wisc., sends direct mailers to customers he knows are involved in corporate gift purchases. He includes a hand-written note pointing out that, as a jeweler, he can offer service and has direct access to a wide range of gift suppliers. "And when anyone comes in the store wearing a corporate pin or ring, I ask them where they got it and if they like it," he says.

Fina Expands with Brand Names

Michael C. Fina Co. has sold jewelry at 580 Fifth Ave. for 57 years, longer than any other of the building's tenants. Its prestigious location—the ground floor in a prime building at the core of Manhattan's jewelry district—is the key reason the firm's corporate division was founded 15 years ago and today leads overall growth.

"We got into the business by accident, strictly because of where we are located," says Vice President Charles Fina, who runs the business with his brother, George, the firm's president.

"Executives from all the top firms would come in for a gift for themselves, then ask us to find a gift for a retiring employee. Or someone at the United Nations would buy a gift for a visiting dignitary," he says. "Then suddenly, these people would come back with an order for 200 gifts."

But the division's 25 employees aren't content to wait for business to walk through the door. They actively solicit firms of all sizes, primarily in metropolitan New York. The corporate division outgrew the Manhattan site and moved to Fina's Long Island City distribution site in 1982. Last year, the division accounted for 50% of the firm's total sales, says Fina.

Merchandise mix: Fina emphasizes that anything stocked in its store is available to corporate customers. Fina also will obtain any other requested item and add it to a corporate gift program, including clothing, camping equipment, electronic equipment and even tools. "It's not all what we may have wanted to sell," Fina explains. "But the customer may want to diversify his program."

A typical Fina program might include a four-color catalog that displays gift selections for anniversaries or service awards. Fina prepares the catalog, mails it to the appropriate employees and handles all shipping and ordering.

In addition to anniversary gifts and service awards, Fina is called on to provide gifts to be distributed at board meetings and conventions, as incentives for sales and quality-awareness programs and for retirements, which have increased as companies try to save money by encouraging early retirements.

What do companies request most often? Cameras, video-cassette recorders and other electronic equipment are fast-growing gift categories, but at least 75% of Fina's orders are more traditional gifts such as watches, silverware, clocks and jewelry. Fina emphasizes name brands, including Waterford, Movado, Rolex, Concord, Bulova, Howard Miller, Wittnauer, Kirk Stieff, Lladro and Mont Blanc. "If it sells in the store, it must be popular," says George Fina.

Because corporate clients want to present their employees with popular items, Fina's corporate division keeps a keen eye on retail sales. The programs are reviewed annually and changed every two or three years to replace less popular items.

"Right now, pieces like black onyx necklaces are not selling like they were two or three years ago," says Charles Fina. Pearl necklaces and gold chain are perennial favorites, he adds, and in recent years, engraved crystal and Waterford crystal clocks have been in strong demand.

Can any retailer start a corporate division? Yes, says Charles Fina. "I think the small jeweler has a very big advantage: personal contact with the corporate president."

Wanted ASAP: More Traffic

Editorial ◆ *July 1992*

Every now and again, when you face a difficult issue, it's a good idea to go back to fundamentals.

In jewelry retailing right now, the difficult issue is easy to identify. Too few people are buying. The clear solution is to get more people into the store because more customers will almost guarantee more sales.

That's fundamental number one.

Fundamental number two relates to productivity. Any store owner who tolerates an unproductive staff has only him- or herself to blame if sales goals are not met. A sub-fundamental here is that any store owner who doesn't constantly measure sales productivity is asking for trouble—and sadly a disproportionate number of jewelry store owners fall into this category.

Consider this fact. A JCK study a few years ago showed that six out of every ten people who walk into a jewelry store walk out again without making any purchasing decision—of new merchandise or of some store service. In other words, only four in ten do make a purchase. That's a pretty low conversion rate.

But look what happens if just one of those six non-shoppers can be persuaded to shop. The conversion rate goes to five in ten, an increase of 25%! If this new customer buys at the same pace as existing customers, then sales go up 25% as well. Not bad. Not bad at all.

The next obvious question is how do you convert more lookers into shoppers. First you must get them into the store. In the short term, good promotions or special events will do the trick. But the store that's in the business for the long haul must do more. It needs a well-defined strategic plan spelling out what image it wants to cultivate, which customers it wants to target and where it wants to go.

Let's assume, perhaps rashly, that such a plan is in place. Next, to be sure that salespeople are properly prepared, they must know which types of customer you want to attract and what merchandise you have to tempt them. Still very basic information.

Let's start with customers. It's the boss's job to identify them and then help the sales staff learn about these shoppers and how to cater to their needs. Today, the boss has a lot to learn and a lot to pass on, because we're seeing some radical changes in the consumer market.

Today's prime jewelry customers are older. These famous, former baby-boomers now are moving into middle-age. On their way there, many acquired a taste and appetite for jewelry. But most are no longer the free-spenders of the 1980s who earned, accurately enough, the reputation of a generation which shopped 'til it dropped.

Middle age—already here or fast approaching—often brings financial success but it also bring mortgages, the cost of educating children and a sense of mortality that prompts thoughts of saving money towards retirement needs.

These shoppers not only are more frugal, but also more conservative than they were a decade ago. As members of the first generation to be exposed to television from childhood on, they're also more susceptible to persuasive advertising than earlier generations.

It's critical that salespeople be aware of these changes and be comfortable with such shoppers. It's critical, too, that the store owner stock merchandise that meets their needs and thus brings them into the store.

Discounting won't do it. True, price shopping can appeal to sophisticated, well-educated consumers just as much as to bargain-hunters on a very tight budget. But the right merchandise for the right value is more important than a 50%-off tag for the sort of shopper who is or can become a jewelry-store regular.

Many jewelers have made significant shifts in their inventory so they can offer customers merchandise which offers real appeal and is relatively immune to comparison-price shopping. Witness the larger share of showcase space going to custom-made, estate and unusual colored stone jewelry. It's notable, though that willingness to diversify product is rarely matched by willingness to diversify prices. Jewelers often reject well-made items at modest prices (under $100 retail) as "just not right," yet this may be just what's needed to build traffic.

So we're back to traffic—that fundamental that must exist if sales are to be made. Jewelers who know their customers and what they want, can impart that information to their sales staff and then motivate salespeople to greater productivity are going to get good traffic. And then they're going to make the sales that underpin a successful business.

High-End Gifts Set You Apart

July 1992

Selling high-end giftware is much like selling jewelry, says Anne Glass, merchandise manager of the tabletop department at Maier & Berkele, Atlanta. But don't think of these items as just giftware, she says. Regard them as works of art.

The rewards will come in the profit. Indeed, high-end giftware is profitable enough that the jewelry department at Maier & Berkele is taking another look at "us in the back," Glass says with a laugh.

The keys to selling high-end giftware ($500+ retail), say retailers, are product knowledge, knowing customers and their needs, top-notch service and tantalizing displays. Of these, product knowledge is most crucial. Customers expect a salesperson to know more about the product than they do. Many salespeople, in turn, assume the customer is an aficionado of the product and therefore knows more. This isn't necessarily true, says Nancy Clark, director of marketing for Chase Ltd., Ridgefield, Conn.

"Even if the salespeople never use these things, they must know how to set a table correctly," she says. "They must know how to properly care for linens, how to properly polish silver and so forth. Customers who don't know how to do these things rely on the salesperson to teach them"

Unfortunately, says Clark, much of the retail world hires at minimum wage and can't attract people knowledgeable about the products they will sell. However, jewelers who have built a successful profit center on high-end giftware hire experienced salespeople.

"Our entire staff has experience from working at places like Tiffany's or the Birks chain," says Vern Kagan president of Smart's Jewelers, Lincolnwood, Ill. "We don't have turnover and we don't have to train new people."

Customer contact: The selling process is largely intuitive, says Clark, and jewelers agree the low-key approach is the only way to sell high-end products. These are products people can live without, as Clark points out, so selling them takes a special approach. Her trick is to present a product not just for what it is, but rather as something to be used in the customer's home. You can rhapsodize about the handmade, limited-edition aspects of a product, she says, but that's not why customers buy. They buy because they can see themselves using it at home.

Begin by initiating an easy conversation about the beauty of the piece, admiring it with the customer on the same side of the product. This isn't a sales pitch or a "selling conversation"; it's more like a casual conversation in a museum. Sales happen by osmosis, says Clark. Say how lovely the product might look with a particular interior, and get the customer to visualize the product in his or her own setting. Gentle probing will reveal what you need to know about the customer's decorating style.

Notice body language, says Clark. Customers who like a piece will touch it; those who don't touch it feel some barrier (break that barrier by placing the piece in the customer's hands) or simply aren't interest (try another style).

Once you've determined what a customer likes, keep a record. Glass says her staff maintains careful records so they can call customers when new pieces arrive that might interest them.

Creating a niche: James Alger, a gemstone sculptor and wholesaler of pieces by other gem sculptors, says the salesperson's reaction to a piece is important. A salesperson must have genuine interest in order to generate interest and enthusiasm in the customer. "It won't work if a salesperson has the attitude that 'I don't like it, but I think I can sell it,'" he says. "Wrong. He has to like it."

Alger says gem carvings are a natural for jewelry stores that define themselves as selling beautiful things that come from the earth. He adds this is an excellent niche for independent jewelers to develop. "There's no reason to let The Nature Company [a retail chain devoted to products from nature] take all the market," he says. "You've been selling things from the earth for a while. Here's a great way to differentiate yourself from mall jewelers."

But again, sales people must have strong product knowledge in order to set a store apart. They must learn everything about the product in order to have confidence in themselves and to exude a sense of authority, says Clark. They should be able to discuss why a piece is so valuable, what effort went into making it and what inspired the designer to make it, adds Edwin J. Rosenblatt, director of marketing for Iris Arc Crystal, Santa Barbara, Cal.

At Fahrney's Pens in Washington, D.C., for example, President Jon Sullivan, makes certain his sales staff is thoroughly versed in how pens work and why certain features are or aren't necessary. "When you're selling a pen that's over $500, it may be sterling, lacquered, even solid gold, but that doesn't mean it's going to write any better," he says. "We want to make certain the customer is comfortable with the pen." For example, a left-handed customer needs a quicker drying ink and finer point to avert smudging. A person who does a lot of writing may find a fatter pen more comfortable than a thinner one. "We don't want to change the way people write," he says. "We want them to have a pen they're comfortable using."

How can you keep up with product knowledge? Many high-end jewelers take advantage of seminars offered by gift and collectible vendors. At Maier & Berkele, for example, a supplier training session preceded a recent Fabergé egg event.

Show and tell: How the product is displayed also counts. High-end gift and tableware should not be stuck on a shelf, say jewelers interviewed for this story. It should be set up as though in use. This means in table settings, on bookshelves, on a desk and so forth. Put together pieces that make sense, so people can envision them in their homes or as gifts, says Clark.

Rosenblatt stresses the importance of proper merchandising. Crystal, for example, is best shown under halogen lighting to maximize its reflective and prismatic qualities. Products also should look like they belong together. "Make sure that other lines merchandised along with your high-end gifts are also tastefully done and of similar quality," says Rosenblatt. If you mix high- and low-end merchandise, it cheapens the value of both and makes customers wonder whether they can believe what you tell them about the high-end product.

Maier & Berkele's Anne Glass adds that a display should sell itself. People should come in, like the table setting and buy the whole thing, she says. Bridal registries notwithstanding. Glass finds that upper-end giftware tends to be more of a self-purchase than a gift item. She also finds a lot of decorators shopping for interesting objects d'art for their clients.

Trunk shows are another way to display a variety of high-end gift and tableware. Maier & Berkele not only hosts several supplier trunk shows a year, it conducts its own mini trunk shows at local clubs and events.

For a trunk show to be effective, says Rosenblatt, it has to offer at least one of three things:

1) Something unique and new enough for people to want to show up.

2) The artist in attendance.

3) Something free.

Which of the elements you choose depends on the kind of traffic you want to generate, he says. A free gift or gift-with-purchase is the best way to generate lots of traffic. Seeing something unique or meeting the artist is more likely to attract a certain demographic group, such as the affluent customers.

Collecting: Another aspect of high-end giftware is collectibility. Salespeople should key into whether a customer collects certain brands or types of giftware or is interested in starting such a collection.

Sometimes all it takes is a push, says Glass. "Tell a customer, 'I know you were interested in the Limoges animal boxes. Would you like to see the new ones coming in?'"

Vern Kagan of Smart's Jewelers takes another approach with his high-end giftware business. He aims for the corporate market by carrying 60 prestige brands of watches, clocks and writing instruments. He packages them in expensive wooden jewelry boxes and mounts clocks on a museum quality wooden base with a plaque for engraving.

"Many other jewelers' price points end where ours begin," he says bluntly. Smart's advertises it business on a national basis in papers such as the Chicago Tribune and The Wall Street Journal. "Your average jewelry store has 200, 500, maybe 1,000 families it does business with," he says. "But because we have a wider reach, we can stock this kind of merchandise and not sell it from a catalog."

He also points out the corporate market yields cross-over business. "We deal with decision-makers on a corporate level," he says. "Who do you think they think of when they need something on a personal level?"

Service factor: Whether you're selling pens or crystal, collectibles or carvings, you need top-notch service.

Service isn't just gift wrapping, stresses Nancy Clark of Chase Ltd. It means "gracefully solving problems," she says.

Service involves spending hours teaching a bride how to choose china, silver and crystal, setting a table over and over again, says Anne Glass.

Service means taking the time to learn everything there is to know about the products you sell, adds Vern Kagan.

Selling high-end gifts isn't for everyone. A jeweler whose customer base is predominantly lower end may want to start very small. But it is a good way to distinguish your store form the competition. "Each jeweler has to find a niche," advises Kagan. "Work from your strengths, be they watches, repairs or whatever. Start from there and it will develop."

New Wave Retailing

July 1992

Innovation. That's the best way to describe retailing of the future, says Carl Steidtmann, chief economist and vice president of Management Horizons, a business research division of Price Waterhouse.

The hallmark of future retailing, says Steidtmann, will be innovative "New Wave" retailers who create new rules, new roles and new relationships that tradition-bound and debt-burdened retailers will find hard to follow.

"Innovation lies at the heart of retail success," he says. "Marketing, merchandising, supplier relations, human resources, organizational structure and technology are all seen by New Wave retailers as a process of continuous improvement, not as goals in and of themselves."

Steidtmann offers several thoughts for retailers who want to "Ride the New Wave":

• Consumers won't be driven by price alone. The value equation includes quality, differentiation, convenience and service.

• Focus on the productivity of space, inventory and people. The combination of low inflation and stagnant real growth means that margins will shrink. Productivity gains provide the only path to improving profitability.

• Focus on and develop a few key categories. Become a destination store in these categories.

• Tailor marketing programs to match consumers. Advertise, promote and close the sale at the point of purchase.

• When it comes to salesmanship, keep it simple, keep it focused, keep it consistent.

• Intensify development of computer systems that increase efficiency in every aspect of our business.

• Close marginal stores and redirect the investment dollars.

"Not since the beginning of the 1981-'82 recession has the business environment for retailing look so bleak," he says. "For retailers who are finding sales and profitability growth difficult in this new business environment, the choice is simple: innovate or die."

Mature Market: Spectrum Of Interests, Wealth Of Opportunity

September 1990 Part II

If someone were described as self-indulgent, extroverted, healthy, fit, fashion conscious and open to life's ever-changing possibilities, what age would you guess he or she was? Probably not over 50, if you're honest. Like most of the population—especially if you're under 50—you may be adhering to out-dated notions of what being over 50 means. Do descriptor phrases such as "watching every penny," "declining health," "dowdy" and "set in their ways" ring a bell?

These attitudes could cost you a great deal of business, especially if you ignore or insult the 50+ population in your sales and marketing efforts. Here's why:

The mature market buys a lot of jewelry and watches. In 1988, the most recent year for which statistics are available, people over 55 bought more than $2 billion worth of the $10 billion spent on jewelry, according to the U.S. Bureau of Labor Statistics' Consumer Expenditure Survey. They also accounted for 18% ($364 million) of the total spent for new watches.

In addition, they accounted for 21% ($511 million) of the total amount spent for jewelry and watch gifts.

This doesn't even count the money spent by people ages 50-54 (who are included in the survey's 45-54 age group). This group has the highest average household expenditure on jewelry: $2.1 billion.

The size of the 50+ population is enormous. There are 64 million Americans over age 50, fully 26% of the population, or one in three adults.

The growth of this age group is enormous also. Experts who study the 50+ population say that by the year 2000, the group will have grown 18.5%, compared with only 3.5% for the group under 50. By 2020, the 50+ population will be swollen to 112 million, or 38% of the population. Put another way, every day, 6,000 more people join this age group.

The mature market's discretionary income is impressive. Nearly half of all discretionary dollars (what's left over after the bills are paid) in the U.S. are commanded by people over 50, according to *A Marketer's Guide to Discretionary*

Income, published by the Consumer Research Center of the Conference Board and the U.S. Census Bureau. One reason their purchasing power is so great is that as a group, they have little or no expenses for children or mortgages, says Jeff Ostroff, author of *Successful Marketing to the 50+ Consumer* (Prentice-Hall, 1989). And purchasing power in the 50-64 age group may be best of all, he says. Most of these people are still earning wages but spending less on debt.

The net worth of people over 50 is significant. As with the population overall, a small percentage of mature buyers (12%) earn more than $50,000 (an income number at which discretionary income begins to rise dramatically). But experts at the Consumer Research Center of the Conference Board predict that the number of $50,000+ incomes in the mature market will rise to 21% by 2000. Income doesn't tell the whole story, however. This group's net worth (total assets minus unsecured debt) amounts to 70% of the total net worth of all households, as well as 77% of the nation's financial assets, says the Conference Board. Ostroff says that 50+ consumers own 80% of the money in savings and loans and two-thirds of all money market accounts. They also make 40% of all stock and bond purchases.

These numbers tell more about a 50+ consumer's spending power than his or her income alone. That's because many older members of the mature market are retired and their incomes are low. But all those years of saving, investing and low debt have added up to significant net worth.

Older people who aren't retired, especially those who are in or approaching the 65-74 age group, may have three sources of retirement income. These sources are Social Security, private pensions and income from assets such as real estate or stocks. This is the World War II GI generation, says Charles F. Longino Jr., director of the Center of Social Research in Aging at the University of Miami in Coral Gables, Fla.

They enjoyed free college tuitions and low-cost home loans, and they spent many of their wage-earning years during a time of unprecedented economic expansion. They also were around to see a cost-of-living escalator clause attached to Social Security benefits and to see their pensions become more secure under federal law.

In addition, many of them invested in assets such as securities and real estate when an economic boom began after the war. All of these add up to powerful spending resources for many in this generation.

Planning the strategy: Targeting the mature market requires a two-pronged approach. To go after the high-end big spenders, you'd use many of the same techniques suggested in the chapter on the affluent. As that story relates, the average age of people earning $100,000+ hovers around 50, so you're likely to find many of your most affluent customers in the mature market. Marketing research organizations have studied the life-styles of older, big spenders intensively to help their clients target the market.

Still, many people over age 50 aren't wildly affluent. This doesn't mean they don't buy jewelry. It just means they spend less per purchase than their more affluent counterparts. The 1988 Consumer Expenditure Survey, for example, showed that 50+ consumers in lower income groups generally spent one-third to one-half the amount spent on jewelry by older consumers making $40,000+.

But the numbers of people in this age group are the big story. Chances are an increasing number of 50+ customers will be walking through your doors in the years ahead. So if you want to make lots of sales, learn how big your local 50+ market is, then draw its members to your store by catering to their needs and not offending them with patronizing, outdated notions of what it means to grow older. Here's how.

Finding the market: Does your area match national statistics in terms of the size and spending power of the mature market? Is the 50+ population larger? Smaller? Finding the answers to those questions can help you to decide how much to target this audience. Begin by asking your county planning commission whether it has prepared reports from U.S. Census Bureau data that classify people in your area by age groups. Next, find out the income levels of the local mature market. You also can identify high-spending "Empty-Nesters," specific net worth and disposable income levels of older consumers through the services of a marketing data company such as CACI Marketing Systems, Fairfax, Va.

Into the store: Capitalizing on the mushrooming older market isn't as easy as it may seem. You may believe that by stressing a life full of leisure activities, for example, you'll draw a lot of seniors. After all, don't seniors have a lot of time?

Not so for many, especially the not-retired group. And the ones who do have leisure time don't like to be reminded of it, says David B. Wolfe, founder of the National Association of Senior Living Industries, Annapolis, Md. It "goes against the deeply ingrained work ethic of our society," he says. This is just one example of the kinds of traps into which jewelers can fall when trying to attract the older market.

Here's a list of assumptions to avoid and positive attributes to stress when advertising, sending direct mail, speaking before older consumers or telemarketing to them.

1. Don't talk about age. Any way you do it, you'll make it sound like you've lumped older people together into one monolithic group whose members think and act alike. To the contrary, people over 50 have a spectrum of interests, desires,

needs—just like people under 50. In fact, an older individual's interests may be just the same as they always were. "I get just as excited about life as I did 50 years ago," says Bill Nusser Sr. of Hands Jewelers in Iowa City, Iowa, an acknowledged member of the 50+ age group. "I don't feel any different."

Categorizing people by their age also makes them think that you think they're old. Yet most older people "simply don't think of themselves as old," says author Ostroff. Statesman Bernard Baruch said, "Old age is always 15 years older than you are," and studies show he was right on the mark. A study by Cadwell Davis Partners, a New York ad agency, found that 40% of people over 60 thought that getting old happened to people over age 75. Don't risk insulting older buyers by referring to their "advancing years."

2. Don't make older people feel invisible either. Just because you're not referring to their ages doesn't mean you shouldn't show pictures and graphics of older people in your ads and promotions. To the contrary, the American Association of Retired Persons says older people often feel like an invisible generation because they're so often missing from ads and promotions of products they're interested in.

But don't portray them in stereotypical poses or settings, such as nodding off, rocking, knitting, baking cookies, whittling, wearing out-of-style clothes or only in the company of other old people, very young children or people of the same sex, says the AARP. How *should* you portray them? Think about how you'd portray a younger person interested in fine jewelry: stylishly dressed, dancing, having fun with members of the opposite sex alone and in groups, shopping, dining out, playing sports, traveling and working at a paying job or as a volunteer. And don't forget to portray a variety of age groups mixed together—remember that 50+ consumers want to be recognized as still being part of mainstream life.

3. Stress the fashion aspect of jewelry—style and design are still important. Aesthetically oriented older people don't lose their taste for style just because they grow older, according to *55 PLUS: Volume II,* a study of the mature market from Management Horizons, Dublin, Ohio. And though some older people may have somewhat less interest in the latest high fashion (don't throw out your classic line of jewelry), a significant portion is fashion-conscious, says Management Horizons. An AARP study of mature Americans indicated that nearly half of the women and 38% of the men give a high priority to accessories. And 28% said they have a strong need to keep up with new products on the market.

4. Stress social events and get-togethers to counter the notion that older people are isolated. And while you're at it, keep in mind that romance isn't dead in this age group. A whopping 57% of the respondents to the AARP poll said they regularly attend parties and social gatherings, while 46% said they give a high priority to community activities. Over a quarter of older Americans regularly attend sports events, movies, museums and concerts.

5. Stress personal growth and new experiences. "Marketers should not think that older people of any age are 'finished products,'" says the NASLI's Wolfe. Don't be afraid to suggest something new to an older person, adds Ostroff. He cites a study showing that 75% of 50+ people surveyed had tried a new brand within the past year.

6. Stress aging attractively. Increasingly, people over 50 expect to continue to look good—but looking good doesn't mean looking 20. There has been an increasing celebration of the beauty growing older—no doubt fueled by the baby boom generation as it ages, says Ostroff. A recent *People* magazine special issue on the 50 most beautiful people in the world also celebrated the beauty of older people, including 60-year-old Audrey Hepburn and 81-year-old Jessica Tandy—neither of whom attempts to hide signs that her face is aging.

7. Play up the special relationship that older people have with their children and grandchildren. Many jewelers interviewed for this article mentioned the power of this link. Not only do mature consumers buy gifts for these significant family members, they give serious thought to who will inherit the fine jewelry they buy for themselves. Earl Dempsey of E. Dempsey & Son Jewelers, Sacramento, Cal., says his older customers buy a steady supply of add-a-pearl necklaces, 16th birthday gifts and 21st birthday gifts. "And when they buy for themselves, they often buy a second or third piece in duplicate so they'll have something to leave for both daughters, or for a daughter and a daughter-in-law," he says. "They're very aware of the estates they're going to leave."

Services: Don't forget that people over 50 grew up before the regrettable era of "self-serve," says Ostroff. They remember what it was like to have knowledgeable salespeople and plenty of after-sales service. They also remember what it was like to get a lot of value for their money. Catering to these two central desires should be the cornerstone of your store's approach to the 50+ population. For jewelers, this should be a somewhat easier task, because fine jewelry can be positioned as a product that has high durability and quality.

Here are some ideas on how to cater to the 50+ market:

1. Hire mature salespeople. They understand what you mean by customer service, product knowledge and value, says Ostroff, and they have a rapport with customers of their own generation. You'll also be capitalizing on future employment trends, he says. Think about the numbers we presented at the beginning of the article: the population segment under 50 will increase only 3.5% in the next 10 years. But 50+ Americans will swell by 18.5%, providing a larger and more active pool of potential employees.

2. Be ready to convey a lot of information about your merchandise—this is a consumer-oriented crowd. The explosion of magazines, newsletters and other publications aimed at older people has raised their level of knowledge about a variety of goods and products, says Ostroff. You'll need to prepare your staff to answer questions, impart more information about product features and develop policies for handling customer complaints. You also may want to offer printed information about your merchandise that they can absorb at their leisure.

3. Stress the soft-sell sales approach. People over 50 don't appreciate hard sells, says Ostroff. To appeal to their increasing savvy and healthy skepticism, Ostroff says, you should mention the cons as well as the pros of the piece you're selling. Open house-type presentations of your merchandise can help also. They give mature consumers a chance to look over your merchandise in a low-pressure atmosphere.

4. Don't forget special service for the very elderly. The number of people age 75 and up will grow an enormous 26% in the next 10 years. Some of them could contin-

ue to be very good customers—if you provide services that cater to their needs. Decreased mobility among some in this age group will require that you go to them. Some jewelers offer to market and sell products through the mail, even to customers who have moved to retirement communities far from their original stores. Eileen Eichhorn of Eichhorn's Jewelry Store, Decatur, Ind., says she has hired a marketing firm to find out where her retired customers have moved. "I'm targeting them because they have a loyalty to the jeweler that younger people don't have," she says. "I'm regularly doing business through the mail to customers in Florida and Arizona. I send them snapshots or they just tell me to send something because 'you know what I like.' They very rarely send it back." Eichhorn says such customers have even referred her to friends in their new communities.

5. Make your store accessible to older people who need special accommodations. Such features may include wheelchair access, wider doorways, more chairs and the like. Jewelers often include such adaptation in remodeling efforts. Eichhorn, for example, is building in two private showrooms where older customers will have a comfortable place to sit and think about a piece.

Ralph M. Fava Jewelers: Rewards of a Lifetime

When couples are young, the address and the automobile are more important than jewelry, says Ralph M. Fava, owner of the jewelry store that bears his name in Little Falls, N.J. But when they've been married 40 or 50 years, priorities and attitudes change.

"If the woman likes a pin and there's a necklace that's compatible, they're apt to buy both," says Fava. "They buy for themselves, but also with an eye to leaving the jewelry to their children and grandchildren. They may even buy two pieces at a time, so there's a piece for each grandchild.

"We also do business with people who have married again in older years. These are very special types of relationships, very sweet and romantic. They're very attached and they buy lots of diamonds for themselves."

Older people buy just about every type of jewelry in a range of prices, he says. "They have a vast range of interests, from the designs of their youth to new designs," he says.

Fava says his store reaches the older audience in a variety of ways. Direct mail goes out four times a year to affluent areas where the population is older. "I might enclose a letter talking about new merchandise we have, and because many of these people are friends, I usually send regards to spouses and inquire about children and grandchildren," he says. "We've found direct mail to be very effective—sometimes people come in a year later with one of our brochures in hand. We also call people on the arrival of new pieces that we know will be of interest to them."

In addition, the store features private showings specially designed for older customers. "Older customers take their time, they're not in a hurry," he notes. "Younger people are louder and they're always in a hurry—there's a certain hysteria in their body language that's tiring to watch."

Hands Jewelers: Jewelry for the Dessert Crowd

"If you'll forgive the expression, it's hard to target the over-55 audience—it's so gray," says Bill Nusser Jr., chief operating officer of Hands Jewelers, Iowa City, Iowa. "That is, you can't pigeonhole it as well as yuppies or blue-collar types."

But there are some commonalties. "They want quality, reliability and service to back it up," he says. "And they have lots of disposable income."

Nusser is especially adept at marketing to the most affluent mature. "Jewelry is dessert for them," he says. "They've gone through clothes and travel phases and whatever else the rage is. Now they want to indulge in things that will last."

Jewelers have to court the mature, he says. If they don't trust you, they won't shop in your store. "You have to develop a personal relationship, get to know them and their children," he says.

Sometimes it's difficult to judge who the big spenders will be. "The pickiest, most difficult, crabbiest customers can become the best spenders," he says. "I had a very crabby customer who was disgusted because we didn't have in stock a South Sea pearl ring she wanted. I called her when we had the rings, but she didn't like them and thought they weren't the right price. I called a month later to say I had more pieces to show her. I said I'd make a sacrifice—it wasn't much, but it was enough. 'Now is the time to buy,' I told her. She did—and now she spends $15,000 to 20,000 a year with us."

Older people are skilled at disguising their needs, says Nusser. "You have to be persistent and patient with them," he says. "If a customer is a little recalcitrant, don't blow her off. Even if she doesn't buy, she might bring her friends in if she's had a positive experience—sometimes out of guilt for not buying anything herself."

He says some older people think of Hands Jewelers as part of their family. "They come in every week to look around, buying maybe twice a year," he says. "They bring us cookies and stay and talk.

"Older people may feel they don't have much time left—even if they're still robust. You have to help them to pamper themselves—work it into your sales approach."

Nusser says that Hands Jewelers reaches the affluent mature market mostly through phone work (salespeople keep blue sheets on customer likes and price ranges) and private parties to show off such items as Lazare Kaplan's diamond jewelry line. "We had that party at an outside location. It was very beautiful, very low-key," he says. "We were very picky about who came—everybody knew everybody." Nusser and his father, Bill Sr., are involved in community activities and the social scene, so many attendees at their parties are friends.

What kind of jewelry does the mature market like? "Every kind of merchandise there is," he says. "People over 60 have very open minds—they've seen all the phases: deco, retro, nugget jewelry from the '60s and classic lines.

"People who think older people are deadends are just not right. I have a customer—a professional woman who is bizarre, strange, eccentric—but she's spent $300,000 to $400,000 in our store over the past 10 or 15 years. Older people can become lifelong customers and very big spenders."

Mature Market: What They Read, Watch and Listen to

If you're trying to aim your sales message at the mature market through the media, spend your dollars on the best formats.

Depending on your goals, each one of the major media formats may appeal. Print ads, for example, might be best if you're trying to convey information about your store, its merchandise or your services. That's because older readers can control the rate at which they take in the information, says Jeff Ostroff, author of *Successful Marketing to the 50+ Consumer*.

Television might be appropriate if you're trying mainly to convey visual images of jewelry.

Your local print and broadcast media and your ad agency probably can give you accurate statistics about what your local mature market reads, listens to and watches. But here's a general look at media habits nationwide, gleaned from on article on the subject in *American Demographics* (October 1989).

Newspapers
• Older Americans are 13% more likely to read a newspaper than the average person.
• 90% of the nation's top newspaper editors say older readers are their most consistent audience.
• 47% of newspapers run a regular column on aging.

Magazines
Magazine categories which they like and read include:
• Travel-leisure.
• Health and fitness.
• Literature and science
• Home-oriented.

Radio
• 70% of older Americans tune in some time during the day. Eighty-three percent listen sometime between 6 and 10 a.m.; 50% listen in the evening.
• Older people are 37% more likely than others to tune in all-news format stations.
• They're 24% more likely to listen to news/talk shows, 40% more likely to listen to an easy-listening station and 32% more likely to listen to a nostalgia station.

Television
• Older Americans generally prefer news, sports and talk shows to other programming.
• They're 30% more likely to watch "Meet the Press" and 22% more likely to watch Phil Donahue.
• They're likely to tune in between 4 and 11 p.m.

Otto Schmieder & Son: Stressing Value to Educated Customers

Value is a prime concern to residents of Sun City, Ariz.

"Before we opened our store here 10 years ago, we did some market research," says Carl Schmieder, president and owner of Otto Schmieder & Son. "We found the residents were extremely liquid, with moderately high incomes. The average home was paid in full within five years and down payments were typically two-thirds of the purchase price. It's a very conservative clientele, very concerned about cost and value."

Schmieder says value is an extraordinarily important component of his marketing thrust. "Because many of our customers are retired, they have time to comparison shop."

The merchandise mix at this store differs somewhat from the firm's other two stores. "We don't have as much demand here for high fashion or large gold jewelry," says Schmieder. "We don't have many traditional engagement ring sales, but we do sell a lot of second marriage rings. Diamond bands and elaborate wedding rings are popular."

Because of the value issue, he says, the employees spend a lot of time educating customers about the value of pieces, explaining about the cost of gems, for example.

"To keep in touch with this market and draw people in, we send out a newsletter four times a year," he says. "Newspaper advertisements are also effective here—though not as much as in our other locations."

The salespeople keep in touch with customers by phone. And the store sponsors sales of special interest to this market; for example, remounts and extra diamonds.

"The store was designed with the mature market in mind," says Schmieder. "Jewelry is displayed in sit-down cases, with comfortable chairs. We also have wider aisles to accommodate walkers, wheelchairs and crutches."

'I Am Woman Hear Me Roar In Numbers Too Big To Ignore'

September 1990

Come meet the average American.

According to *American Demographics* magazine, she is 32 years old, has brown hair, stands 5'4", weighs 143 pounds, is married with one child, and works in a technical, sales or administrative job. She wears a size 10 or 12 dress and size 7 $1/2$ B shoes. She wears jewelry every day, and she bought most of it herself. Her engagement ring is most likely a size 6 and it cost about $800.

Looking at each half century, this is the first time the average American is female. Fifty years ago, the average American was a 29-year-old male who, with a ninth-grade education, was fairly certain to find a solid factory job that would enable him to support a family. One hundred years ago, the average American was a 22-year-old male farmhand.

The jewelry industry has been doing its own research on Ms. America. And it's found that *American Demographics* is right on target about women and jewelry. The World Gold Council says that in 1988, women bought 58% of all the karat gold jewelry sold. And now, the Gemological Institute of America estimates that women buy almost two-thirds of all karat gold jewelry sold.

Cultural swings: To understand this formidable market, it's important first to understand the cultural changes that have taken place since the turn of the century and, in particular, in the past 30 years.

Today's woman is portrayed often as a "Superwoman," perfect in a multitude of roles—executive, wife, mother. Though the myth is exaggerated, women *have* changed considerably and have many more choices available to them.

Two decades ago, a typical TV commercial breakfast cereal might have portrayed a housewife urging her harried, professional husband to put down his briefcase and have a nutritious breakfast. Now the same commercial may show a harried, professional woman dressed for work and trying to feed and keep track of a busy family while listening to her husband urge her to slow down and eat a good breakfast. Even the Betty Crocker emblem has been updated to reflect a more career-oriented than kitchen-oriented woman.

Here's a simple compare-and-contrast exercise to illustrate the evolution of women in the past 30 years.

Consider two favorite TV families: the Cunninghams of the 1950s-themed sitcom *Happy Days* and the Huxtables of the very-1980s *Cosby Show*. Look at the differences between Marion Cunningham and Claire Huxtable and how each might get a new piece of jewelry:

• Both families are upper-middle class, own a large, pleasant home and have a fair share of amenities in that home, including TV and various other gadgets suitable to the time. Both drive nice cars and both put several children through college.

• The Cunninghams live on Howard's salary as a hardware-store owner. Housewife Marion stays home and bakes an endless supply of cookies. Her character is portrayed as a lovable ditz whose little "problems" (such as PTA politics) are silly. Howard is the supposed authority figure in the family. If Marion disagrees, she contrives cutely to get her way. She usually wins.

• If Marion wants a piece of jewelry, she'll likely have to wheedle and cajole Howard into buying it for her.

• The Huxtables are both professional—Cliff an obstetrician and Claire a lawyer. Both salaries help to pay for the household, where the kids are expected to do a fair share of chores. Cliff is the supposed authority figure. If Claire disagrees, she tells him bluntly and they hash it out. Claire usually wins. (OK, some things never change!) Claire seldom bakes cookies and isn't portrayed as silly.

• If Claire wants a piece of jewelry, she'll most likely go to a good jewelry store, select the piece she wants and buy it.

Marion is going the way of the dinosaurs, Claire is the "new" American woman, and she might walk into *your* store today.

Everything new is old: Marketers who think this Claire-type woman is new are wrong, says *American Demographics*. Actually, she's very old. She's been working since the last century, though then it was most likely on a farm. The typical *Happy Days* American family (i.e., father breadwinner and mother homemaker) actually is an abnormality that peaked a few decades ago. This rapid industrialization in the first half of this century changed the way America worked, generally forcing spouses into two roles—breadwinner or bread-baker. But the post-industrial society is blurring those lines again, and the pendulum is swinging back to the way things were: to the two-earner family. Of course, there are differences this time around.

Today's working woman is likely to be much better educated than her earlier counterpart. The National Center for Education Statistics says today's average American woman has nearly one year of college, up one year from 1970 and twice the education the average American had in 1890.

The return of dual-earner marriages is due also to the changing structure of the job market, adds *American Demographics*. In the 1940s, the labor force was predominantly blue-collar manual or service labor. Since the mid-'70s, it has grown increasingly white-collar—often technical in nature. According to the U.S. Census Bureau, the largest job growth is in the health, service and technical fields—areas that generally attract women.

Other cultural changes, both economic and social, also are responsible for the infusion of women into the labor market. Economically, two incomes are a virtual necessity for many families, particularly ones that wish to buy a home or send children to college.

When Howard Cunningham of *Happy Days* built a large home in a nice neighborhood, educated three children and took the family for nice vacations in his new DeSoto—all on the income of a small shopowner—it wasn't too far from reality. Today, that house and the kids' education would require a healthy salary from Howard as well as a pretty penny from Marion.

For others, the economic necessity is more psychological than actual—one income would house and feed the family, but two incomes provide the better cars, the computers, the vacations, and so forth.

Socially, the feminist movement has made it acceptable for women to seek a fulfilling career and demand self-actualization and enrichment beyond the confines of the home. Along with this are some important shifts in attitudes about motherhood.

Three decades ago, a woman usually dropped out of the work force when the first child arrived, unless extreme circumstances forced her to continue. Today, many working women postpone motherhood until they establish careers, often waiting until their mid-30s before starting a family. When they do have children, most have only one or two,

and most return to work as soon as possible. Some choose not to have children at all—another option that has become socially acceptable. All told, the trend toward delayed or non-motherhood and smaller, dual-income families means more disposable income for many women.

It's also acceptable for a woman to buy herself things that a decade or two ago were supposed to be received as gifts: perfume, furs and jewelry.

Dealing with women: Salespeople have to be careful not to let society's past prejudices affect their attitude toward women customers, warns GIA's new "Fine Jewelry Sales" course.

The delineation of "traditional" sex roles blurs even more where love and money are concerned, says GIA. A couple entering a jewelry store together are not necessarily married, or even engaged. They might be living together with no intention of pooling their resources, or they might be married with no intention of pooling their resources. More than half of all married women, especially those in higher income brackets, have their own checking accounts.

Treating a successful professional businesswoman like a '50s housewife can kill a sale; if women feel they're being patronized, they'll shop elsewhere. Be careful, too, when using titles. Some women prefer Ms., others hate it. The quickest solution is simply to ask. Most women won't be offended and will appreciate the gesture.

Other ways jewelers can help to boost their reputation with women shoppers is to be sensitive to their needs. Women's shopping habits have changed. John Godfrey, a Battle Creek, Mich., jeweler, once observed, "Traditionally, men had limited time to shop. They carried a list, they got what they wanted and they got out of the store. Women on the other hand, had time to browse. That is no longer true. Now the women, too, have a list and limited time to get it done."

Jewelers must cater to these needs, say marketing experts. Convenience is a priority for reaching this market, so you must have evening and weekend hours, hire enough staff members so customers don't have to wait and offer credit options and flexible payment plans.

But perhaps one of the biggest keys to successfully reaching the women's market is to make an appeal based on life-style rather than gender.

Focus on life-styles: Don't assume that because a woman is a woman, she will behave in a certain way, says *Communications Briefings* magazine. Income, education and interest are far more indicative of behavior than gender, so try to think of your female market in terms of the people they are, not just the fact they're female.

For example, says the GIA, women who earn $25,000+ comprise an elite group. They are more sophisticated than the average woman and twice as likely to have a college education and a professional or managerial career. But while the U.S. Census Bureau shows a significant percentage of the female population falls into this income bracket, don't be fooled into thinking this is Everywoman.

The bureau's 1988 figures show the largest percentage of female-headed households (with or without children) have incomes under $30,000 and one-fourth have household incomes under $20,000.

In a special report on the women's market, *Advertising Age* magazine asked company executives about the success of ad campaigns. Some financial executives said their direct-mail campaigns failed miserably because, though the product was good, the implied message was "this is for women." When they stopped keying the message to *women* and started keying it to the women's *life-styles,* returns picked up substantially.

Here are some more suggestions on reaching the women's market, courtesy of *Communications Briefings:*

• Don't perpetuate the Superwoman concept. Show women living diversified lives, but remember that most women don't identify with perfection in every role.

• Don't always depict working women with a briefcase and suit. Women hold a wide range of jobs.

• Be informative and treat women with respect, intelligence, warmth and humor. Remember they are sophisticated consumers who are interested in a product's quality and benefits and your integrity.

What they're buying: In addition to karat gold, the GIA estimates that by the mid-1980s, women were buying about half of all diamond jewelry sold and almost three-fourths of all colored stone jewelry.

Jewelers report that women generally are more comfortable buying earrings, bracelets, pins and necklaces than rings.

Women's attitudes about jewelry differ from men's. Men tend to buy jewelry based on the intrinsic value of the piece; women, while interested in the piece's value, are more likely to choose a piece on the basis of how it suits their style and personality. Women, for that reason, are more likely to buy designer or more stylish pieces.

Linda Meyer, president of J.E. Caldwell Jewelers in Philadelphia, has observed this for several years, sometimes even to the point where a couple argues over which piece to buy. In one incident, a woman wanted a designer necklace and earring set, but her husband insisted on a traditional diamond solitaire. The couple left without purchasing either.

In terms of price, World Gold Council statistics show that women tend to spend less per piece, but they buy more frequently than men. This trend is substantiated by a number of jewelers, including Meyer. Men tend to think of jewelry in terms of a gift for an occasion, whereas women buy throughout the year.

Much of the jewelry women buy is not for themselves; in fact, the World Gold Council says much of the karat gold jewelry bought by women is destined to be a gift. Most often, the recipient is her husband.

Whatever the reason, the fact remains that today's woman has a much different attitude than her mother and grandmother. Tradition dies harder in some places than others but, by and large, women have taken control of their destiny and they're the ones who will decide where and when they'll buy jewelry.

Karten's Jewelers: Treat Yourself to Real Gold

The power of the women's self-purchase jewelry market is incredible, says the World Gold Council. That's why the council focuses on working women in its ad campaigns, and why Karten's Jewelers of New Bedford, Mass., has twice featured the council's "Treat Yourself" program.

The "Treat Yourself" program enables jewelry retailers to create their own in-store promotions to attract women customers. It was developed to help retailers create an integrated themed promotion, on small or large scale. It's based on a collection of merchandise that a retailer puts together from his or her own inventory.

The kit contains scripts for local radio and TV spots, newspaper ad slicks and an array of coordinated black and gold collateral material, including posters, counter cards, case signs and tags. The entire package is available to retailers for $100.

Karten's first used the program last fall. The results were so good that it repeated the program in April and May, boasting a 14% increase in gold jewelry sales those months.

"It was one of the few areas of business that was up," says Dorrie Hatfield, vice president of merchandising. "Business was down overall, but gold jewelry sales were up."

Karten's advertised the promotion on prime-time network TV (time was bought in cooperation with the World Gold Council), on radio during peak driving times and in two newspaper ads.

Hatfield says the typical woman customer at Karten's fits the WGC's demographics for women who buy gold. The women are between 25 and 50, with middle to high household incomes. They most often buy earrings, chains and heavier bracelets. The price range: $95 to $800, averaging $400 per sale.

Michael Barlerin, the World Gold Council's chief executive, says the "Treat Yourself" program was developed after research showed that women buy themselves nine "treats" a year, but that less than one treat was gold jewelry. "We decided to develop a program that would help the jewelry industry to capture its fair share of these women's dollars."

The message of the "Treat Yourself" program is simple: "Sometimes the best things you do, you do for yourself. The 'Treat Yourself' collection, real gold jewelry. For you. From you."

Chupp Jewelers: Women are the Driving Force

"If it weren't for women, there wouldn't be a jewelry business," says Leland H. Chupp, chairman of Chupp Jewelers in Lafayette, Ind. "I don't think that's really changed much since I started working in the jewelry business in 1929."

Women have always been the driving force behind jewelry sales, he says. But he admits he's seen some significant changes in women's lives and attitudes since he opened his own store in 1946.

In the early 1970s, he says, women began to buy more jewelry for themselves as they joined the work force. At the same time, the feminist movement chipped away at the belief that women should receive their jewelry from men. Today, he estimates that more than 75% of his sales are to women.

Chupp does very little advertising—to women or anyone else. He attracts women to the store in other ways. "Everything in our store is geared to women—our color-coordinated decor, our eye-catching displays, our varied merchandise," he says. "We talk to them and we read, read, read to keep up with what they want. We try to anticipate trends and keep up with fashions."

One of his biggest selling points: an all-female sales staff headed by his wife, Martha. He says women have an automatic rapport with each other, and that women are more likely to be honest with other women.

In addition, Martha's social contacts and networking abilities have brought a lot of women to the store.

What do women look for? Price, service and brand names, he says. They are particularly price-conscious in this traditionally conservative area. But they also demand service and are willing to pay a bit more for it.

What do women buy most often at Chupp Jewelers? Gold chain.

Selling Tips from Industry Organizations

From the Diamond Information Center...
MORE THAN 1.3 MILLION women age 37 or younger hold a management or administrative position and by the mid-1990s, close to 80% of all women under 45 will be working outside the home. To accommodate this potentially huge market for fine jewelry, you can:
* Change your hours to make shopping more convenient.
* Cater to women in terms of fashion, design and color.
* Plan special events to attract women.
* Create special credit incentives.

From the Cultured Pearl Association...
FOR WORKING WOMEN, pearl chokers (single or multi-strand) are part of the corporate look. Also popular are fashionable pearl and precious metal brooches and single pearl studs or maybe earrings.

Price points for the market range from $500 to $3,000.

Most women prefer to shop for pearls in a catered environment. As in the business world they live in, they seek clear and concise answers to their questions about pearls. Discuss price options thoroughly while retaining finesse and style. Avoid the hard sell—people get enough of that at work and will resent it in a store.

Offer corporate discounts and advertise in corporate newsletters. Your advertising should stress success, style and value.

From the Sterling Silversmiths Guild of America...
BECAUSE MANY WOMEN delay starting families in order to concentrate on their careers, they often are high-earners by the time they become pregnant. They contribute to the fact that baby goods are one of the steadiest and most profitable segments of the sterling business. Display the merchandise in a prominent location.

In fact, if space allows, set up a separate baby goods alcove.

From the World Gold Council...
HOUSEHOLD INCOMES of working women are growing. One out of four working women lives in a household earning more than $50,000. The discretionary income of women who are employed averages $29,095 per household and $8,457 per person.

To help reach this market, the World Gold Council produces TV commercials and cooperative trade programs.

Upgrading:
The Key To Survival In the '90s

June 1989

Jewelry retailers will have to upgrade their image and service if they are to survive the competitive 1990s.

That's not a point for debate, say business analysts. Changes in the marketplace will require jewelry retailers to aim more at the affluent market and depend less on the middle class. They'll have to sharpen product knowledge, offer more convenience and otherwise set themselves farther apart from mass merchandisers—even if it means charging higher prices, say analysts.

Jewelers who don't change with the times are headed for trouble. They may find themselves victims of a major shakeout among U.S. retailers that many analysts believe is on the way.

Changes coming: First, let's look at the changes that will make upgrading necessary. The rich will get richer, says Fred Posner, N.W. Ayer executive vice president. Families in the top 20% income brackets will have more discretionary income than

ever, he says. But much of it will come from husband and wife both working. "These families will have much less time at their disposal, so they will want convenience," says Posner.

To ease their buying decisions, customers will demand better quality and more distinctive products. "Q.S.B.—quality, service, branding—will be the critical trends for luxury retailing in the '90s," says Posner.

At the same time, the middle class will lose much of its formidable spending power because of increased expenses. "Many middle class couples put off until their 30s having children and buying a house," says Posner. "Now they have high mortgage payments and the prospect of paying enormous college tuitions."

The middle class has been the driving force behind the explosion of retail growth in the past 15 years, says Posner. So when middle-class spending declines, so will the retailers who serve it.

The growing number of retailers contributes to the problem, says Dr. George Lucas, associate professor of marketing at Memphis State University. Consider, he says, that the U.S. has more than 14 sq. ft. of shopping center space for every man, woman and child—double the amount 15 years ago. "Slices of the retail pie are getting thinner as more and more competitors are entering the market," he says.

Too many retailers wooing too few customers resulted in price competition. Many well-known, respected retailers have cut costs on the very things they built their reputation around—service and quality. Now they may have trouble surviving in a climate of slower retail growth, says Lucas.

Four categories: Lucas divides retailers into these price/service categories:

• Low price/low service. This style of operation has a good chance of survival but requires more volume and financial resources than most jewelers have.

• Low price/high service. Many small retailers cut prices to compete, but this ultimately cuts too deeply into profits. It's not viable in the long run, he says.

• High price/low service. Many larger retailers—including some large jewelry chains—have fallen into this trap, says Lucas. They focus on short-term gains and ultimately destroy their image. To survive, they need to forego short-term profits and restore service, or lower prices to compete with discounters. "Continued operation under this strategy requires the retailer to take faith in P.T. Barnum's assertion that a sucker is born every minute," says Lucas.

• High price/high service. Most retail jewelers must position themselves in this category. Lucas sees a strong opportunity in the high service niche, especially as service suffers while some retailers chase lower prices. But filling the high-service void requires a concerted effort from everyone, particularly management, he says. It also may require a renovation and maybe a move.

How to upgrade: tips from experts

If you need to upgrade your operation, says Lucas, first identify your current niche and the one you want.

Jewelers should target households with annual income of $50,000-plus, says James Buck, senior vice president of PSI, Tampa, Fla., a consulting firm on the affluent market. This fast-growing group has the most disposable income.

Buck acknowledges the lower segment of this market may be caught in a price squeeze. But the segment still is crucial to any jeweler's upgrade plan. "Right now, 40% of all spending among affluent consumers comes from those in the $50,000 to $75,000 bracket," he says. "These people can't be ignored."

Also focusing solely on the super rich can cause problems, he says. They're rare and prefer to be discreet, making them hard to find.

Ground rules: Many jewelers believe they already offer the service and merchandise that attract their target market. But that perception doesn't always jibe with reality because too few stores have a strong identity or memorable service. Lucas says recent studies found that 70% of mall shoppers couldn't even name the store they were in, including jewelry stores. "That's amazing when you stop and think about it," he says. Nothing set those stores apart from any others.

How can you stand apart? The affluent are diverse, says Buck, but here are some common ground rules to attract them:

Provide a professional, well-trained, well-disciplined sales staff. "The affluent consumer wants to know what he or she is buying," says Buck. "If they can't get good answers to tough questions, they'll go elsewhere."

Sales personnel must be knowledgeable enough to justify the higher prices that high-service operations must charge, says Lucas. They must be able, for example, to explain why one diamond is worth much more than another.

De Beers conducted a survey on $1,000+ diamond jewelry purchases and found that 82% of all buyers of such jewelry rely on the jeweler for help. "The level of trust is very high in that price range," according to the survey report, "so jewelers exert a strong influence on buying."

The staff also must want to help the customer. Lucas offers this personal anecdote, which stems from a recent trip to buy diamond earrings: "I went first to a price-oriented store. The staff wasn't very helpful... so I went to a 'full-service' jeweler whose staff really knew what they were doing. They took the time to work with me and acted like they were interested in me, not just my money. Not only did I buy my earrings from them, but I remember them and I'll go back."

This last factor is critical, he says, because specialty retailers depend on repeat customers for their long-term survival. "Customer loyalty isn't high where price is the only motivator. In those cases, buyers are loyal to the lowest price," he says. "But a high level of service fosters loyalty to a store."

It also fosters more customers. According to the De Beers survey, 19% of all purchases of $1,000+ diamond jewelry were made in stores recommended by friends or relatives.

• **Feature value and distinctive designs.** A majority (55%) of respondents to the De Beers survey said they set no price limit when shopping for expensive jewelry. Their main concerns are value ("is it worth what I'm paying?") and design. In fact, design has motivated many of them to buy expensive pieces or trade up to a more costly piece. "Consumers are drawn to retailers who offer something distinctive," he says. "They remember them because their goods aren't the same old things available in every mall."

Lucas suggests keeping loose stones, design books and a benchworker so customers can design their own jewelry.

Also rid your store of any inventory that's not appropriate to your image, says Alan Master of the Diamond Information Center. "Otherwise," he says, "you defeat your own purpose."

Tailoring a store image to the affluent can be done in several ways, he says. First, a marketing firm or the marketing department of a local university can organize focus groups of affluent consumers who say what they like and don't like about your store. Next, track what your affluent customers buy, and ask them what they'd like to see more of. Finally, keep enough stock on hand to offer a choice. "Product mix should be relatively narrow but deep," says Lucas. "Wide and shallow is the way of the mass merchandisers."

• **Offer convenience.** Convenience will become even more critical in the coming decade, says Buck. Dual-income families may have more disposable income, but they'll have less time. Store locations and hours must accommodate their busy schedules.

If the store isn't convenient to where the affluent live or work, move it. This is particularly true in a declining downtown business area. "Very few people will spend 30 minutes driving to a store, then spend 20 minutes looking for a parking space." says Buck. "I can't stress enough the importance of a convenient location."

Moving is easier said than done, admits Lucas. Some retailers see moving into a mall as the best way to gain exposure to a lot of potential customers. But mall stores also can mean expensive leases, loss of business freedom and the undesirable possibility of ending up between stores that don't fit an upscale jeweler's image.

"It's important to remember that a lot of mall traffic is mindless—people just wandering from store to store with no specific objectives," he says. These shoppers wouldn't be wandering around a mall if their intention was to buy an expensive piece of jewelry, he says. The De Beers survey backs him up. More than 90% of all $1,000+ diamond jewelry purchases were made by people who never considered any other gift.

Casual mall shoppers also can deter serious buyers by monopolizing the sales staff.

If not a mall, then where?

"Most upscale neighborhoods have convenient strip centers. They're a good bet if the neighboring stores have a good image," says Lucas.

If there are no suitable strip centers, consider building or finding a new store in a convenient location: near a mall, in an affluent neighborhood with good road access or along a popular commuter road.

Regardless of location, the store must reflect your distinctive image. Replace shopworn fixtures and furniture. Also give customers a good impression by setting a showcase with one or two distinctive pieces near the door, says Dave Morrow of the Diamond Information Center. "That will tell the customer who you are right away," he says.

• **Know how to reach the affluent.** Perhaps the most critical part of reaching the affluent is finding them. Local, state and federal government offices usually have demographic information. The real estate pages of local newspapers are a good source to find expensive housing areas.

Once you determine your target areas, determine their ZIP codes and mount a direct mail campaign, says Master. The mailing should be distinctive enough to entice people into your store, and should stress your store's personal and professional services.

Also promote your store in area business centers, says Master. "That's where the executives are," he says, "so it makes sense to reach them there." Some jewelers even take pieces to offices for private sale.

When designing ads, remember image as well as product, says Judith Langer, who heads Langer Associates, a market research firm in New York. She mentions Rolex as having one of the most successful status-oriented ad campaigns. "Rolex ads imply the product's status and class without stating it overtly," she says. "The implicit message 'You know and we know our product has status. We don't have to say so.' "

Once designed, the ads should be placed in the media most likely to reach your targeted customers. Local publications and radio and TV stations can provide demographic information on who they reach.

Consultants agree that specialty stores will thrive in the 1990s if they carve their own niche. "But it takes a great deal of effort," says Lucas. "And most importantly, follow through. It's not enough to say you're service-oriented. You have to make every one of your staff believe it before it will happen."

The Full-Service Store

Here is a checklist for successful full-service, niche-oriented specialty retailing offered by Dr. George Lucas, associate professor of marketing at Memphis State University:

Management structure. Decentralized. Delegate a great deal of decision-making responsibility to mangers in contact with customers.

Product/inventory mix. Distinctive or custom-made. Be capable of creating product to customer specifications.

Marketing orientation. Research to determine the most appropriate merchandise. Coordinate this with the proper in-store image, and sell this image through promotion and advertising.

Location. Very important. Convenience is a key to the high price/high service retailer.

Product mix. Narrow and deep. To be knowledgeable and maintain adequate inventory, limit the types of products offered. But offer a wide selection of each type chosen.

Stock turn. Because of the depth of products offered, inventory turnover should be *relatively* slow, but not excessively so. Profitability comes from margins on each item, not from high-volume turnover.

Promotional emphasis. Advertising and promotion must stress high-service image and professionalism. Personal and knowledgeable service must be up to the promises made in the advertisements.

Store orientation. Long-run customer satisfaction. A successful high price/high service store develops a sizable group of loyal customers. Introduce enough new products to induce customers to return regularly.

Vendor relationship. The buying staff must work closely with vendors. Vendors often help store personnel with sales training, product information and selection.

How Much Is This Couple Worth To You?

March 1989

Kevin swathed the small, velvety box in tissue paper. Then, carefully, he tucked the precious package in the oversized pocket of a brand new terry cloth robe.

The robe was an early Christmas present, or so he told Christine. When she snuggled into it, slipping her hands in each side pocket, she felt the tiny bundle.

"The rest is history," Kevin says, laughing. "Corny, huh?"

The diamond engagement ring in that package symbolizes the new life that Christine, 22, and Kevin, 25, will share after their wedding in June.

Further, that ring with its half-carat, marquise diamond hopefully marks the start of a lifelong relationship between the happy couple and the jeweler who sold it.

Have you made a similar sale recently?

If so, will the couple return to your store, for wedding bands? For attendants' gifts and crystal for their home? Will you sell them anniversary rings two, 10, 20 years down the road? And for icing, will the couple introduce your store to family and friends as a gift center?

Attracting the bridal market can produce a festive year, and future, for you. Even better news: this decade is producing more marriages than any other in U.S. history, says *Modern Bride.* The magazine projects a total 24.8 million marriages in the 1980s. That's up 11% from the 22.3 million recorded in the 1970s.

Marriage, it seems, is rad; it's hot, happening, "in."

And the "in" crowd is spending big. "As more couples marry at an older age, they're able to put more money into their wedding," says Bruce Thiebauth, president of Bridal Fair, a national trade show group that licenses its name and promotional efforts to local media. "But this doesn't lessen the parents' load. Couples simply find more ways to spend the extra money."

Here's how. In 1987, couples spent $2.1 billion on engagement rings and $1.1 billion on wedding rings, according to a study by *Modern Bride.* This market also spent $680,000 for gift watches and other jewelry.

Add to that $1.7 billion for tableware and table accessories, which the study says represents 25.7% of all national retail sales in the tabletop group. All told, the bridal market annually spends $21.4 billion on 143 different products and services, according to the study.

To get your share of this profitable market, learn what turns bridal customers like Kevin and Christine on and off; learn what they need and want from you, their trusted jeweler. Then take advantage of sparkling sales and heady add-ons.

Defining the couple: To attract engagement ring shoppers, you must know who they are. Pinpointing an identifiable market will help to focus your efforts.

Typically, today's wedding couple will bring home about $40,800 a year, states Bridal Fair's Bruce Thiebauth.

A study of *Modern Bride's* readers reveals a full 90% of brides and 96% of grooms are employed. Both typically are college-educated, with 85% of brides and 80% of grooms having spent some time acquiring higher education.

The median age of today's bride is 25.2 years, meaning half of all brides are older, half younger. That's up from 23.3 in 1985.

More broadly, the woman's bridal market is defined as ages 18 to 34, says Nancy Robey, diamond engagement ring account supervisor-brand management group at the Diamond Information Center.

This market includes all brides, regardless of how many times they've been married. It's divided into young brides (ages 18 to 24) and older brides (ages 25 to 34). The division affects engagement ring sales in two ways:

• The older bride is more inclined to choose design-oriented, fancy shapes than the younger one, who most often prefers the classic solitaire. The older bride's preference perhaps indicates a higher level of confidence and more defined sense of self, says DIC's Anne S. Payne, diamond engagement ring brand manager.

• The older bride tends to receive a diamond engagement ring costing about 65% more than a younger bride's ring, says Robey.

And don't forget the groom. He's older, too (median age is 27.4, up from 25.5 in 1985) and much more involved than ever in marriage and household planning, say bridal market experts. For this reason, you must try to attract men and women, not just women.

Many involved in the bridal market are doing just that. For example, Howard Friedburg, publisher of *Modern Bride,* says many of the magazine's features have been geared toward bride *and* groom in the past few years. "Men won't buy *Modern Bride,* " says Friedburg. "But many couples share parts of the magazine," such as finance-related articles, that lend themselves to discussion.

The National Bridal Service, Richmond, Va., also recognizes grooms as a force to be reckoned with. Its booklet *Make Room for the Groom,* available to members at 85¢ each, includes chapters such as "It's the time of your life," "Rings 'n things," "Financial responsibilities" and "Suggested gifts for the wedding party."

Though grooms traditionally have been left out of wedding preparations, you shouldn't ignore them. The groom typically spends more for a ring than his future wife anticipates. In fact, many a bride has persuaded the groom to spend less, says Robey. The bride whose top priority is

383

design, doesn't want him to overspend. The groom, who thinks first of quality, fully intends to spend what's necessary on his bride's lifetime diamond, says Robey. Be prepared to confirm the groom's higher cost expectations.

Shoppers in the know: Christine, a magazine journalist, and Kevin, an engineer for AT&T, did a bit of browsing together for their ideal engagement ring.

During Christine's last semester at Penn State University, she and Kevin occasionally window-shopped in local malls. They never intended to buy in those stores because of "concerns about quality and price." Christine felt that salespeople in those stores focused on making a sale rather than assistance.

When the decision was made, Christine wasn't present, leaving to Kevin the when, where and what of ring selection. And Kevin was prepared.

"At the time, I knew the difference between diamond grades, how the size of an inclusion affected things. Generally, I knew what the terminology meant," says Kevin.

Most of his diamond knowledge came from colleagues. "Kevin's the kind of person who has to know everything about a product before he buys," says Christine. "He'll get books...ask friends."

He got some information from jewelers, but mostly they just confirmed what he already knew. "By the time I was ready to buy," he says, "I had decided that color and cut were more important than size."

More and more couples are taking the time to educate themselves before buying, and that's an advantage to jewelers wanting to sell a quality diamond. But there is a down side. "The education is good and bad, depending on what information they got," says Jeffrey Hurwitz of Colonial Jewelry Co., Federick, Md. "The less-educated [jewelry store employees] often give out misinformation, and once the couple has a certain idea, it's hard to change that perception."

Also, this new breed of buyer demands more of your time. "He wants to spend so much more time looking," says Hugh Rader of C.R. Rader, Macon, Ga. Yet the additional time is a fair tradeoff for the higher ticket sales Rader now reaps. His average engagement ring sale has nearly doubled from the $3,000-$4,000 of five years ago.

Making the sale: "The jeweler wasn't trying to sell me a diamond," Kevin says of his purchase experience. "He was more like a friend, explaining to me what I needed to know. If I bought there, fine; if not, that was fine, too."

The approach worked, and the sale was made.

Most jewelry stores have their own ways to attract and sell to engagement-ring shoppers. But three elements are universal, say many jewelers and suppliers. They are:

Salesmanship. Salespeople must be knowledgeable about diamonds and must sincerely want to help the customer, says Hurwitz. Given today's educated consumers, a salesperson's approach easily can make or break a sale.

Selection. Styles and needs change. Jewelers wishing to attract bridal market business must keep up with what's happening design-wise. "Bridal customers generally shop three to four stores before buying," says Jonathan Goldman of Frederick Goldman Inc., New York City. "Jewelry stores with a varied selection will automatically get the attention of bridal customers."

Value. Educated shoppers must perceive the price as reasonable, relative to value. Regardless of financial standing, no one wants to feel he or she paid too much.

Making the sale is the bottom line. But making the bottom line bigger is even better. To that end, the Diamond Information Center offers these tips on maximizing your sales potential:

• Talk with the couple. Where do they work? What are their hobbies? Get information that gives you an idea of their life-style and how much they have to spend.

• Focus on the diamond's price rather than on the mounting or completed ring. To keep the focus on the center diamond, show fancy stones.

• Don't sell sets. A set typically earns you 25% less than two pieces sold separately.

Hugh Rader, of C.R. Rader, offers this tip for going beyond the average engagement ring sale. Don't try to talk the customer up in price. Instead, for example, show a $7,000 2.5-ct. alongside a $19,000 2.5-ct. "I let the product sell itself," he says. "Sometimes they'll say, 'I can't stand that $7,000 diamond,' or maybe they'll decide they need something in between."

Bill Shepherd of Wayne Jewelers & Silversmiths, Wayne, Pa., usually starts with a high-ticket item, for example a $20,000 2-ct. diamond. "Is this within your budget?" he'll ask. The approach impresses, says Shepherd, and it doesn't limit the sale.

Drawing customers: But how do you get bridal market customers into your store to start with? Bridal jewelry manufacturers and suppliers on the whole feel many of their retail customers don't take full advantage of available marketing material. "Many aren't marketing-oriented and are too tentative about pursuing aggressive programs," says one leading jewelry maker.

Greg Clapper of Wright & Lato, East Orange, N.J., describes an exception, a jeweler client on the forefront of bridal jewelry success. The keys to this client's success include:

• Aggressive advertising.

• Special sales with a casual—yet professional—approach to add-on business.

• Straight talk to the consumer.

• No high pressure.

In addition, says Clapper, the jeweler offers a good selection in a wide price range.

Jeff Levitt of Alfred Levitt & Son, New York City, agrees that a strong media presence is important for jewelry retailers. "Year-round advertising creates an identity in people's minds as an engagement ring specialist," he says. Levitt & Son provides, among other items, ad slicks you can use to promote bridal sales.

Another approach is to advertise at local business places. Soon-to-be-groom Kevin planned to visit Jewelers Row in Philadelphia. But he never got there. Charles Boyer Jewelers, near Reading, Pa., placed a 15%-off coupon in a newsletter circulated where Kevin works. "I thought that if I really liked the jeweler, with the discount, the price would be about the same as in Philadelphia." He did like Boyer Jewelers and chose Christine's ring there.

What they buy: A diamond usually takes center stage in engagement ring sales. Ninety-two percent of engagement rings sold feature a diamond as the primary stone, according to a 1986 DIC study. The average expenditure is $1,770 and the average center-stone weighs .38 ct., according to the study.

There's a trend toward more diamond- and gemstone-intensive mountings that enhance the featured stone. The larger the diamond, the more elaborate the mounting, says Colonial Jewelry's Hurwitz.

But with all the design-oriented mountings available, the bottom-line remains traditional, says Suzanne Gould-Maggin, fashion editor of *Modern Bride*. The classic solitaire setting is still the cornerstone of the business.

If trendy brides want "different," they get more—more side diamonds, or sapphires or rubies. Or they get bigger stones.

Trends to watch are a growing interest in the emerald shape and in white gold and platinum, says Gould-Maggin.

As for wedding bands, the big news is diamond-intensive. The bride indulges in this type most often, while the groom typically prefers the simple gold band, says DIC's Robey. Still, some diamond bands are surfacing for grooms.

Manufacturer Jeff Levitt and some others foresee growth in diamond bands for men. "But they'll require the right styling to be successful," says Levitt.

As for the matching wedding band set, "[It'll] always exist, but I'm not sure the more sophisticated, urban girl will want it," says Gould-Maggin. The DIC says the West and Southwest do well with matching designs.

Y'all come back: Kevin and Christine will select their wedding bands any day now, and they plan to return to Boyer's. Most couples do buy their bands at the same place they bought the engagement ring.

"I'd say 75% of the time, I sell [engagement ring customers] bands as well," says Hurwitz. This typically occurs three to six months after the engagement ring is bought, he says. "It seems couples are waiting longer to get engaged, but once they do, the marriage comes soon after," he says.

To ensure couples return to you, suggest they stop back to have the diamond checked and/or cleaned. At that time, show them your wedding bands.

Don't stop now: No occasion equals a wedding in opportunities to stimulate add-on sales. So says Gary Wright, president of the National Bridal Service.

When this aggressive leader envisions a couple buying a ring, he doesn't see just two people and one sale. "For each couple, we also see, hopefully, 10 attendants, the couples' parents and about 200 guests," Wright says, eyes twinkling. Each one of these people either gives or receives a gift, or both, because of the wedding. How many of these sales you capture is limited only by your perception of the possibilities.

Take the tabletop department. "The jeweler says it's not profitable," says Wright. "That's wrong. If they ran their diamond department the way most run their tabletops, their diamonds wouldn't be profitable either. If they treat it right, they'll get a good return on their investment."

A good return is $5,000 on tabletops/gifts for each engagement ring sale, he says. "[A jeweler] should sell more than he got for the ring," he advises.

Such success requires some effort. First, you must consciously make the transition from ring sale to tabletops. Begin immediately after selling an engagement ring, says Wright.

For example, an NBS member can give the couple the association's glossy, colorful 1989 *Wedding Guide and Preference Awards*. This tells them about some finer things, including china and crystal. In addition, the member can introduce the couple to his onstaff bridal consultant, says Wright. The jeweler who has no bridal consultant may introduce the couple to his foremost tabletop authority.

Christine will definitely register a tabletop pattern. But the lucky retailer will be a major department store, not a jeweler. She's not opposed to the latter; she's just not certain how a local jeweler could help the many relatives and friends who live far from her home.

There is a way to handle this, says Wright. "First, you must build a reputation as the source for bridal services, so a bride still wants to be registered with you," he says. Then encourage the bride to pass the word that phone orders and shipping merchandise are no problem if the buyer lives out of town.

More gifts: Sometimes a bride wants to surprise her groom with a wedding-day gift. And the groom may want a gift for his bride, perhaps arranging to have it placed in their honeymoon suite before they arrive. Quite possibly, neither will think of these gifts unless the jewelers makes the suggestion.

Such a suggestion often is a delicate issue and not always appropriate if both the bride and groom are present, says Colonial Jewelry's Hurwitz.

Pearl strands are most popular for the bride, he says. Other suggestions are gold or diamond earrings or a watch, adds *Modern Bride's* Gould-Maggin.

For the groom, the bride may want to invest in a gold watch, says Wayne Jewelers' Shepherd. Now also is the time for him to acquire gold and onyx cuff links, says Gould-Maggin. If the bride doesn't buy them for him, maybe he should splurge on himself.

The bride and groom also traditionally give tokens of appreciation and affection to each member of the wedding party. The total expenditure for attendant gifts averages $165 per wedding, says Bridal Fair's Thiebauth. The figure climbs to $240 for the typical formal wedding, in which an average 10 attendants are on hand, says Modern Bride. Shepherd says his customers typically spend $20 to $50 on each attendant's gift.

While the numbers are low, compared with most jewelry sales, these items are relatively easy to sell. The customers are already in the store to buy rings; all you have to do is make a suggestion about gifts.

"Couples may have the perception that a jeweler is too expensive for gifts," says Thiebauth. Not true. Besides, most brides are more in need of convenience than bargain prices. Make the couple feel special, tell them what products you have available, then let them browse, says Thiebauth. The jeweler who caters to engaged couples will win the sales, he says.

Stock traditional attendant gifts. This means letter openers, key chains, money clips, pens, 14k gold tie tacs and engraved pocket knives for men.

Women's gifts range from cultured pearl bracelets to pearl pendants. Don't forget, the gift may be going to a future customer; will Christine's maid of honor tie the knot next year? Just in case, package each present for impact.

Also appropriate are suggestions for gifts going to mothers and other special guests.

The National Bridal Service suggests couples give jewelry, crystal and silver.

Year-round sales: The best news on this market? It's a year-round business, says Nancy Youngbeck, *Modern Bride's* promotion manager. Unlike Valentine's Day, Mother's Day and Christmas, the rush isn't seasonal, an important tip when planning your commitment to the bridal market.

June, the fabled month to tie the knot, accounts for 11.9% of U.S. weddings. But May, July, August and September aren't far behind, each with more than 9%.

October and December have more than 8% each, and March, April and November have more than 7% each. At the bottom of the list are January and February, with 5.5% each. But remember, we're talking about a $21.4 billion market— plenty to spread around.

In addition, bridal market sales are staggered—first engagement rings (18% are bought in December), then wedding bands, then attendants' gifts. And somewhere in between are tabletops and other gifts.

Want the business? It's out there. Sometimes, all your customer needs is a little nudge.

"I thought of getting Kevin a watch," says Christine. But on the subject of wedding gift-giving, she adds, "I'm not really sure of the procedure." Anyone care to assist?

Haves And Have Nots

Editorial ◆ *October 1988*

A major trend is developing at the retail end of the jewelry industry. It's the widening gulf between the haves and the have nots. The haves are prospering; the have nots often are struggling just to survive.

Each group has distinct characteristics. The haves are true professionals. They buy and display exciting merchandise, mixing designer goods and one-of-a-kind pieces with their regular best-sellers. They are sound mangers. They know the importance of tight inventory control, of good cash management, of putting together an ambitious business plan and making it work.

They're very people-oriented. They place a top priority on hiring good staff, then training members properly. They believe in education. They also know how to motivate and, when the need arises, to inspire. The people-connection extends fully to customers. The business of these professional jewelers is built on the bedrock of good service. They interpret "service" as going the extra mile to recognize and meet customer needs.

Store size is irrelevant. Among the haves are businesses with 20 stores and 200 employees and others with one store and two employees. You don't have to be big to be the best.

The have nots are equally recognizable. Too often their sales counters are stocked with the same lookalike, bread-and-butter goods found in a score of competitive stores within the same shopping area. The usual defense? My customers won't buy that one-of-a-kind stuff. Were they ever asked, ever tempted?

These stores are run by slipshod or seat-of-the pants managers. They may concede that professional management is a good idea—but not for them. They've no time to live in such an ideal world. The same goes for hiring, training and the whole compensation package. Each is given short shrift as business is conducted on a day-to-day, largely unplanned schedule. It's not that the intent to improve operations is missing; only the will and determination.

This nonprofessional jeweler, who has a legion of colleagues, is living in a dangerous retailing world. This is one where too often price is the critical selling tool. It is full of big, efficient and ruthless competitors who can out-price-cut, out-manage, out-advertise and out-promote the small independent who has nothing truly different and distinctive to offer potential customers.

This split between the professional and the get-by jeweler is probably as old as the jewelry business itself. What's different today is the nature of the competition. Today it seems that *everyone* is selling jewelry. Pick up almost any mail-order catalog from almost any type of retailer and you'll find at least some jewelry for sale. You can buy jewelry at Kmart, at Blommingdale's at mall kiosks, at street-corner stands, even in some gas stations. If you want to stand out in that crowd, you'd better be different.

The urgency of this need to be different is what's so important now. The haves recognize this; the have nots fail to do so. Unless the have nots wake up to reality, they're going to find themselves playing a very minor role in the future of jewelry retailing. If cut-throat competitors don't drive them out of business, angry consumers will. We have yet to see the full force of consumer awareness strike the jewelry industry, demanding an end to shoddy appraisals, illegally marked karat gold, misrepresented diamond grades and undisclosed colored stone treatment. When this force strikes, as it will, heaven help the jeweler whose business lacks a sound ethical base and who is not prepared with total knowledge of his product.

The real jewelers, the haves, are prepared. They know not only how to attract customers and encourage them to buy. They and their staffs also know how to answer the toughest customer questions.

This elite corps of jewelers thankfully numbers in the thousands. It's always risky to make sweeping prophecies, but I'm convinced that its members are poised to lead the industry into a period of immense success. There's a host of demographic statistics to show that a generation of consumers born to good things can and probably will spend heavily on jewelry right through to the turn of the century and beyond. These jewelers don't need to be licensed to sell, as some have suggested. They'll survive and prosper because they match honesty with ability, a combination that breeds consumer trust.

Many of today's have nots still can join this group, if they're willing to raise their management, selling and gemological skills to the needed level. Such efforts will take great commitment. The outlook for those who don't want to make that commitment is bleak. If the competition doesn't get them, some consumer protection agency most likely will.

What's In A Name?

September 1988

"Jezebel!"

Ham Waltham looked up in surprise from the merchandise order he was writing in the store office and saw his irascible cousin and partner, Ebenezer Cheribel, standing in the doorway.

"Jezebel!? What kind of a name is that for our jewelry store?" Ebenezer demanded.

"Well, Eb, it *was* the name of the former owner and the name of the store when we bought it," replied Ham.

"But why keep it?" demanded Ebenezer. "Just think of the negative connotations! I'm keeping my promise not to interfere with how you run this store as long as it makes a profit. But give some thought to changing the name, OK?"

Such outbursts were typical of cousin Ebenezer. Still, he had a point. Ham really had never thought about the store's name. It was called Jezebel Jewelers all the years he worked there as watchmaker for owner Hiram Jezebel. Then Waltham and Cheribel bought it. All that was involved with that purchase, shaping up the staff and drafting marketing and advertising plans left little time for worrying about something so obvious as a name.

Getting advice: So where do you get advice on changing a name?

Ham asked his accountant, Gelda Numerouno.

"Me," she answered.

Numerouno explained that a firm's accountant or banker often has contacts with business consultants (who can advise on when and why to change a name) and with ad agencies (who can do market research and handle name and image changes).

She also suggested chatting with the company lawyer and other business acquaintances—senior employees, fellow merchants, longtime customers. "A proverb says wisdom is found in many voices," she said.

Ham asked whether he would need a business consultant just to change the name.

"It depends on how important it is to your business plans and store image," Numerouno responded. A consultant, she warned, can cost several hundred dollars just in consultation fees.

Small firms have other options, she said, such as a state university with a business advisory and/or education program. Another possibility, she said, is the national Service Corps of Retired Executives (SCORE), an adjunct of the U.S. Small Business Administration. SCORE, which has offices in hundreds of towns, offers free counseling to small businesses. Counselors are retirees from various businesses; inquirers are matched with someone from their trade.

Important asset: Ham called the local SCORE office in Lenzville (listed under "Small Business Administration" in the U.S. government section of his phone book). He made an appointment to see Wally Wiser, retired vice president of a local department store.

Ham told Wally he needed advice on changing his store name.

"You're in good company," said Wally. "Just last year, for example, 1,753 companies changed their names, 27% more than 1986's record."

Ham asked why so many changes.

Wally handed him a magazine interview on the subject with Joel Portugal of Anspach, Grossman Portugal Inc., a leading New York-based identity consulting firm. Ham read the section Wally pointed to:

Portugal: *"Corporate naming is very important; a name is one of the most important assets a business has.*

Q: *Is a business name the same as its identity?*

Portugal: *No. Too often, people confuse name with identity and image. A store's identity is what makes it unique. It is its personality, its character, its distinctiveness. It's what a business does to differentiate itself from other businesses. A store's image is what customers and suppliers see, how they view it.*

Q: *And the name?*

Portugal: *The name, hopefully, captures and reflects that identity. It reinforces what you try to do in your business. A name like Jones Fine Jewelers conveys a sense of personal business service, while one called Smithtown Jewelers says, "We're a part of your community. Trust us." Such name personalize the business instead of institutionalize it. But you have to live up to the name.*

You also want to be sure it doesn't conflict with the identity you're creating for your store. If you're opening a children's toy store, for instance, you don't want to use a stuffy boring name.

Why change? "OK," said Ham. "So when or why would a jeweler want to change his business name?"

Wally detailed the following instances:

• In the case of mergers, acquisitions and new owners. A new owner often wants to stamp the business with his own identity. For example, if a regional chain specializing in diamond jewelry buys an old-line store, a name change could reflect new management and a new image and inventory.

• When heirs join the business. Adding "& Son" or "& Daughter" reflects family pride and underscores the continuity and stability of the firm.

• When a business moves or expands. A name change can reflect a change in image, location and operating style. Changing location and name at the same time rather than separately can save money.

• When the owner wants to upgrade the store's image or account for a changing market or new operating style. Franklin & Buchannan, an old-line, long-established downtown jeweler in a nearby city, offered a good example, said Wally. Over the years, its carriage trade clientele dwindled and the neighborhood changed. The owner wanted to create a younger—though quality—image to attract up-and-coming executives and professionals. A local ad agency conducted a survey and found that young people considered the store old and stodgy, and the name was intrinsically linked to that.

So when the owner moved the business to a new shopping center in an affluent area outside town, he decided to change the name. He wanted a name connected with the old firm which reflected a new identity to attract a new market. The new name: Franklin Fine Jewelers.

When not to change: "Aren't there reasons for a store to keep its name?" Ham asked.

"Sure," said Wally. "A store's reputation and goodwill. If your store—or one that you buy—is well-known and profitable and has a good reputation, it's probably wise not to change the name.

"That's why you'll often find big firms *don't* change the names of established stores or chains they take over in new markets. They're buying not only the buildings and merchandise, but the goodwill those stores have established in the community, as represented in that name."

Ham thanked Wally for the advice, then dropped in on Smiley Burke, head of a small ad agency, for tips on picking a name.

Smiley said some of the best names are those that stick in people's minds. One example is Walkers n' Daughters Jewelers in Bismarck, N.D. Another is Ten Window Williams Jewelers in Eureka, Cal.

But it doesn't have to be unusual. Chambers Jewelers in Fort Worth, Tex., changed its name to Chambers Fine Jewelers to set itself apart from local gold and silver exchanges.

Good names also can describe your business or service, said Smiley. An Albuquerque, N.M., jeweler calls his store Butterfield Personal Service Jewelers. A Freeport, Me., jeweler changed its name to Brown Goldsmiths & Co. In fact, says owner Stephen Brown, "before we incorporated in 1982, we changed our name three times to meet our growth and changing image."

However, you don't want a name that gets lost in the crowd. One California jeweler refused to use "diamond" or "gems" in his store name. Many surrounding discount stores did so, and he didn't want to be associated with them.

A store's name also can refer to its location. That both identifies you and helps customers find you. One example is Robbins Eighth & Walnut (at the corner of Eight and Walnut streets) in Philadelphia. Another is Montclair Jewelers in California. When the store moved from Oakland, where it had been named for its owner, it took the name of its new home town. Because Montclair is known locally as an affluent area, much as Rodeo Drive is in Los Angeles, there's no need to add "fine jewelry" or "diamond jewelry" to the name.

Smiley said even a bad name sometimes can be useful. "If you have an unwieldy name, play off it somehow. Turn it into an advantage, especially if it's already well-known."

To change or not: With those facts in hand, Ham did some research of his own.

He took an informal poll of other merchants, his banker, some lawyers, his staff and some longtime, trusted customers. He said he was thinking of changing the store's name and wanted their opinions. He also had his senior staff members question vendors and customers.

Then he met again with his accountant. "If I change the store name, how much will it cost me?" he asked.

"That's up to you," Gelda said. Hiring a consultant or ad agency to create a new store identity can cost hundreds or thousands of dollars. By choosing the name himself, Ham could save a lot of money. But he'd still have to pay for a new store sign, business cards, stationery, packaging, checks, invoices and inventory forms.

"You also may want to print up new brochures to send to longtime customers announcing the name change, or tie it in with a promotional event to bring more customers into your store," Gelda suggested.

She advised checking with company lawyer Perry Flatbush about legal aspects.

Legal issues: "Well," Perry harrumphed when Ham stopped by his office, "you have to file a legal notice that you're changing your name.

"Generally, if you change your *corporate* name, you have to file a short document, usually just a page, with the state's secretary of state. You should be able to get a copy of the form from the county courthouse.

"If you're just altering your *business* name, then you only have to file a certificate stating the change with the town clerk or county courthouse, depending on state law. The document is usually called a 'doing business as,' 'fictitious name' or 'trade name' certificate. You can get them at the town hall, county courthouse or even stationery stores."

Ham asked Perry to explain the difference between a corporate name and a business name.

Perry looked at his client for a long moment over the top of his thick glasses. Then he patiently explained that a corporate name is the formal name the state keeps on record. Only under that name may the company do all legal acts, and only under that name can it sue and be sued. It may or may not also be the business name under which the company operates and by which it is known to the public.

"If you change your corporate name, you may want me to do a legal search to ensure there are no claims or patents to the new name," he said. "It's not unlike a title search to ensure there are no liens against a property you buy. But it's not necessary for just a change in business name."

"OK," said Ham. "What's all this going to cost me?" "Very little," said Perry. "In fact," he added in a rare moment of altruism, "You can do it yourself and save my fee. It costs no more than $20 to $40 for a corporate name change, and less than $10 for a 'doing business as' certificate."

As for a legal search, said Perry, the secretary of state will usually inform the applicant if the corporate name change is approved or not. For a change in business names, he added, most town halls or county courthouses have a list of existing business names that can be checked.

And the name is..: The informal survey by Ham and his staff showed the store was well-known, in part due to its unusual name. A few people, who didn't associate it with the former owner, thought it quirky to name a store Jezebel. But there were no strong negative feelings. Ham did find that some people thought old Hiram Jezebel was still in charge.

Ham and Ebenezer decided they wanted the store name—but not the corporate name—to reflect the new ownership. But they didn't want to lose the community goodwill and reputation the existing name was generating, via such strategies as buying uniforms for the Lenzville Little League and offering its annual Jezebel Trophy.

Besides, even Ebenezer had to admit the name is easy to remember and has certain promotional possibilities. Thus, they could develop humorous advertising or even a cartoon logo for ads Ham planned to run in the local college and military academy newspapers. The ads would feature class rings, engagement sets and jewelry for young men.

So six months after Ebenezer raised the question, the two partners, with the concurrence of their staff, picked a new name for the store. The winner: Jezebel's Fine Jewelry.

Critical Issues Revisited

Editorial ◆ *June 1987*

Just a year ago I wrote about four critical issues facing most jewelers. All centered on the question of not misleading customers . . . about gem treatment, appraisals, diamond grades and the actual weight of the diamonds in total-weight pieces.

These were and, to varying degrees, still are critical issues. But some of last year's urgency has dissipated thanks to considerable publicity about the issues and to greater understanding of how to deal with them.

All four issues deal with correcting common or uncommon wrongs—non-disclosure of treatment, inadequate appraisals or deceitful diamond practices. In other words, they deal with negatives. It's very important to realize there are *positive* critical issues, too.

Here are six, all related to business practice. You should:
Know your market,
Identify the customers you want to reach in that market,
Direct your advertising and promotions to those customers,
Have distinctive merchandise to sell them,
Have a superior staff and
Be a good manager.

The list may seem so obvious that it's not worth discussing. But is that really true? Too often we take the simple things for granted Let's look at this list as a refresher course, if nothing else.

Know your market. Name any market in the U.S. today which hasn't changed somewhat over the past year and significantly over the past five years. That's an almost impossible task.

Consider just the very obvious changes. New housing (with new residents who could be new customers) was built. A factory was opened; another closed. High school enrollment fell. Two retirement homes sprang up. A regional mall is under construction 10 miles out of town.

There are many less obvious changes, too. The anchor in your mall is part of a chain with new owners. How will its merchandise change? Its promotions? There are more service jobs in the area, but they don't pay well. Downtown parking is getting tougher to find. A spurt in the crime rate has curtailed evening shopping.

The details obviously vary from market to market. What's important is that *something* is changing. Why not sit down with your staff for an hour and list everything that's changed in your market in the past year or two? You may get a few surprises.

Target your customers. Not everyone shops in your store. Who are your ideal customers? Rich old ladies? Young people? Successful businessmen? People who like new and exciting merchandise?

You must make that decision. Then you must be sure they know you want them. A couple of years ago we talked with a jeweler who was sure many of his regular customers were lawyers and other professionals. When he analyzed his charge accounts, he discovered that most of his regulars actually were low-spending housewives from a neighboring development.

Advertise and promote to reach these customers. Knowing who you want to reach makes it much easier to spend advertising dollars wisely. If you choose print, be sure you know what target customers read. If you don't know, ask them. The same goes for listening and viewing, assuming radio and/or TV are affordable in your area.

It's easier to target your promotions when you have a good idea that turns your ideal customers on.

Offer distinctive merchandise. Competition to sell jewelry is more high-pressure than ever before. Everyone-and-his-friend seems convinced that selling jewelry as a mainline or a sideline is a great way to make money. Clothing stores, hi-tech catalogs, TV hosts, coin stores, outside-the-office peddlers—all are into the act. Not to mention regular department and discount stores.

One of the best ways to stand out in the crowd is to offer something no one else has. It can be an unusual stone, or a special design, or in-depth selection of high-fashion goods. But it must be something. This doesn't mean there isn't room for bread-and-butter lines. But the jeweler who relies on bread and butter alone won't be with us long.

Have a superior staff. That thought should be a mantra, repeated again and again. Without the right staff, you have little chance for real success. Think of all the things you want to see in a salesperson when you shop . . . enthusiasm, courtesy, knowledge, helpfulness, nice grooming. Those are customer needs.

The store owner has needs, too. He or she wants all these characteristics plus good judgment, loyalty and high productivity without high pressure. It's not easy to find such paragons but they do exist. To the jeweler who says, "I can't afford to hire the best possible staff," the answer is "Today you can't afford not to."

Be a good manager. Know what's going on in every aspect of the business. Keep informed. Listen well. Be ready to delegate—and give authority along with responsibility. Be firm but fair. Be frugal in your spending but not stingy. Always strive for personal excellence and expect the same of those who work for you.

The store that scores an A on each of these issues will have a very good year this year . . . and next year.

389

Naughty Or Nice:
What's Your Christmas Image?

September 1986 Part II

One fourth of all jewelry sales over and half of all diamond sales occur during the Christmas-selling season

Are you ready to get your share?

You are, if you know your image. A successful store needs a specific image to attract specific customers.

"It's basic marketing," says David Barry, president of the Management Growth Institute. "A jeweler can't serve all segments of the market. He or she has to make a statement, to have an image that appeals to some segment. If a jeweler doesn't appeal to anybody, ultimately he won't get new customers, and will be on the way out."

Here's how to find out what your image is, and some ideas of what to do once you know.

Who are you? First, decide what type of operation you are, or want to be. A neighborhood, mom-and-pop store, emphasizing personal service? An expanding firm, with mall stores throughout the area? A specialist known for expertise in colored gems? Set specific goals.

Your image will be influenced by:

1. Store location. It affects what type of customers you get. Is yours downtown, in a suburban mall, a neighborhood, on Main Street or a side road? Is the area prosperous or declining economically? Is there sufficient parking? Is the population growing, declining, changing?

2. Store appearance. As soon as customers walk through the door, they have an image in mind. What does yours say? Is it inviting—or forbidding? Does it have a specific, identifiable style?

Consider color, carpeting and lighting. Does your store look dark and uninviting? Do your walls need a new coat of paint or some decoration? What about showcase layout. Does it "guide" customers through the store? And don't forget the outside: Is paint peeling? Are windows dirty? Do your signs look faded and weather beaten?

3. Your market. It's vital to image-making since it affects inventory and marketing strategy. Is yours a young market interested in bridal and engagement sets? Or is it the 40-plus crowd, who are more likely to buy big-ticket items?

Outside help: To help define your image, don't just rely on your own perceptions. Consider:

1. Outside evaluations: Ask fellow (non-competing) jewelers or retailers for advice. If you don't belong to a PEG or Scull group, invite a few members of the local Rotary or Chamber of Commerce to observe your operations. Then take them to dinner and get their comments. Or, invite a few select customers to lunch for *their* view of your staff, service, ads, and merchandise.

2. Market research. An easy, in-store project is a staff survey of customers and purchases. Another is reviewing recent charges and sales slips to learn where you draw customers from—and don't—and what sells.

More detailed demographic information is available at little or no cost from local, county or regional planning commissions; chambers of commerce or industrial development agencies; federal census records; utilities, and local media ad departments.

3. Competition. Periodically shop your competitors. Compare merchandise, promotions, service, and pricing with yours. Note what you offer that they don't or can't, i.e. good parking, trained gemologists, a large supply of colored gems, convenient shopping hours, delivery service, 24-hour repair. Tell the public about your pluses in your promotions and advertising.

When to change: In analyzing your store, you may find that the customers' perception of your image differs from yours. Change to theirs.

When Richard Potasky Jewelers Inc. opened 13 years ago in Dayton, Ohio, it catered to the upper-class market, with contemporary, high-ticket items. As it opened more stores in malls and shopping centers around town, a review of clients and purchases showed "our customer was, in fact, the blue-collar person," says James A. Sparks, vice president of operations. Market surveys confirmed it, and Potasky changed marketing and inventory accordingly.

Image builders: Once you decide who you are, pay special attention to:

Employees: Staff performance is what most consumers mention about a store's image. How do yours measure up Are they well-trained and friendly?

Are your salespeople suited for your market? The Potasky chain is very conscious of how salespeople affect its image. Sparks "won't hire some fast-talking salesman" more suitable for a discount store, nor what he calls a "Tiffany-type" with a slightly elitist attitude, because neither appeals to the blue-collar worker.

Ads and promotions. What do yours say about you? Keep your market in mind when designing ads and promotions. For example, Potasky's primary customers are blue-collar people, aged 25 to 50. So, most of its radio ads are on country-western and easy-listening stations, not rock-and-roll.

Packaging. Boxes, bags, pouches, wrapping paper are tools that remind customers of your store after they leave. Do yours bear your store name and logo? Are they gaudy or stylish? Is wrapping free or do you charge?

Image conscious: The owners of J. Duffey Fine Jewelers in Phoenix, Joseph and Patti Duffey, have given serious thought to the store's image.

The Duffeys wanted a store for affluent customers, one that's "casually elegant, not intimidating, with a different look," says Patti. She created that look, aided by an interior designer friend. That meant no western motif or crystal chandeliers.

The result: A store where walls and showcases are curved, not cornered—"so people don't feel closed in." There's a 350-gallon salt water aquarium in the center—"to create a relaxed feeling." And the color scheme uses soft pastels. The interior design is so effective it was recently featured in a Phoenix fashion magazine, which goes to the very affluent clientele the store wants.

J. Duffey's reinforces its image in other ways. Showcases are lined with ultrasuede, the same as in its gift boxes. It features custom jewelry, avoiding a traditional look. This jewelry store serves iced tea and wine to customers, offers them delivery service, and makes private appointments for special ones.

The store advertises in local publications for the affluent community. And the Duffeys are active in municipal social events, such as fund-raisers for cancer research or the Phoenix symphony.

All of it, says Patti Duffey, is to "make us unique, to be like the Tiffany's of Phoenix. [We want] people to say, 'Oh, you bought that at J. Duffey's'."

Six Tips for a Better Christmas

A Christmas marketing plan should be part of your fall merchandising strategy.

Include these ideas in your Christmas plan:

1. At the summer trade shows, note what vendors offer in holiday promotional support, unusual merchandise, and special holiday services, such as overnight deliveries.

2. Compose holiday strategy by September. Review last year's final quarter results. What promos and ads drew the most business? When did they run? What merchandise had the best and worst sales?

Set overall holiday sales goals, by department, product, and/or employee.

3. Make an October-December calendar to schedule your holiday activities, such as mailings, meetings, and late ordering.

4. Target the merchandise you want to push and at what times during the holiday season.

Don't forget old stock. "Repolish it, retag it, rebox it and get your staff as excited about it as new merchandise," notes Art McElfish, R.J.O. Inc. president.

5. Include your staff in your Christmas marketing plan. Hire extra staff early, and hold training sessions.

6. In December, concentrate on point-of-sale business. On the last day before Christmas, suggests the National Retail Merchants Association, start Christmas clearances.

Make Ads Part of Your Plan

Be sure to schedule advertising and promotions for the holiday season.

Plan which audiences to reach; what ads to run, when and in what media; and budget expenses accordingly.

Use newspapers for holiday ads, but don't forget two other cost-effective media. Radio zeroes in on specific audiences and times. Direct mail reaches working people who don't have time to shop, notes Michael Roman, Jewelers of America's chairman.

Stretch your ad dollars with as much promotional and ad support as you can get from suppliers.

Schedule several in-store events and promotions to call attention to your store. You should have at least one a week.

Contact associations and suppliers for promotional event ideas and booklets.

How to Stand Out in the Ad Crowd

Millions of gift ads will entice consumers this Christmas. Still, jewelers can be the shining stars.

Here are four strategies to make your ads successful this Christmas season:

1. Repetition. Tell your story often enough, and it becomes common knowledge. Create a slogan—ABS jewelers, the Diamond People—and use it often in your ads.

To make this strategy work faster, demand that your newspaper ads appear in the same spot each time, and that your radio ads are broadcast at the same time.

2. Domination. Be a big fish in a small pond. Choose an advertising medium—billboards, weekly newspaper, radio station—and become the biggest jewelry advertiser in it.

3. Saturation. Combine your slogan from the repetition strategy with the image-building of domination. Instead of dominating a single advertising medium, you'll saturate a market area. One caution: You must have enough resources to make a big impression in each medium.

4. Fascination. Whatever your stategy, add some fascination to your Christmas ad campaign. You'll be noticed in the crowd. Offer in-store exhibitions of the biggest, the best or the only collection of items related to jewelry.

Chapter 9

LAWS & REGULATIONS

Playing By The Rules Is A Winning Formula

Note: Due to ongoing changes in the nation's laws, we recommend that you consult with your attorney to get the latest legal interpretations and rulings before you take action based on any information in this chapter.

How To Avoid Problems At Take-In

William Hoefer, Jr. ◆ *June 1994*

What happens when a customer leaves a watch with a jeweler for repair and it's lost en route to a repair shop? Simple answer, right? Ordinarily, an insured retailer who fills out the standard repair form feels safe from liability beyond the value declared on the form. In most cases, this is accurate.

But try telling that to the New York retailer whose take-in slip was so incomprehensible that a court considered it non-binding. Or try convincing the retailer who showed a customer a slip of paper that appeared to limit liability but who was held responsible anyway because the customer didn't sign it.

These are extreme cases of everyday concern to retailers who take in jewelry and watches for repair. Most retailers use legibly written take-in slips, and most are sure the customer signs on the dotted line. So in general, the jeweler (known as the bailee in legal parlance) is not considered to be liable for goods left by a customer (a bailor) unless the jeweler was negligent during some phase of the take-in and delivery process.

This applies nationwide except in a few states, most notably California, where a jeweler is considered to be the "insurer" of goods left for repair. To guard against liability, a California jeweler without insurance must have a customer sign a statement acknowledging that he or she knows about the lack of insurance.

Who's liable? Let's look at three types of situations involving liability: jewelry left for identification or repair, jewelry "farmed out" to someone else for work and third-party repairs.

In situations where customers leave jewelry for identification or repair, any agreement—written or oral—is generally binding. But the liability of either party depends on what the agreement states. For example, if a jeweler says he'll send a ring for identification to a laboratory in New York but sends it to a lab in Los Angeles instead, he can be held liable in the event of a loss. Why? He didn't do what he agreed to do. The lesson: if a retailer agrees on a course of action, there should be no deviation from it. The customer must first agree before a plan is changed.

In the case of "farming out" repairs, law generally used to favor jewelers. A California court once ruled that because contracting for repairs is common in this industry, the jeweler need not inform the customer about it.

But wait! A contradictory court ruling in New York several years ago said jewelers must inform customers if items are repaired off-premises. This was based on the prevalence of theft as pieces are transferred between businesses. The New York court cited a jeweler as liable when he didn't tell a customer where his watch was to be repaired. According to the written decision, to fail to inform the client is "the legal equivalent of error by omission. Robberies of expensive jewelry are more prevalent in today's society. A consumer should therefore be told when an expensive piece of jewelry will not be repaired on premises so that an intelligent choice can be made whether the jeweler should be given possession under the circumstances."

I suggest telling clients about all work done outside the store and workshop. This is required if the store displays a sign that states "all work done on premises." The same applies to appraisals if the jeweler sends items to dealers for opinions.

Who's liable if an item is lost or stolen after it was sent to a third party for repair? Again, laws aren't the same in every state, but the retailer generally isn't liable unless he or she violates a specific agreement with the customer. Let's take a look at an actual court case that illustrates the point.

In California, a customer brought a brooch to a retail jeweler and asked that a missing stone be replaced. The retailer sent the brooch to a wholesale repair company for repair. The wholesale repair firm sent the brooch and a replacement diamond to a diamond cutter for the actual work. The diamond cutter locked the brooch and the diamond in his safe. The next day, however, the diamond cutter discovered the items had been stolen from his safe.

The court decided the retailer wasn't liable because he never stated that repairs were done on the premises and because he had no reason to worry about the item's safety—given the good reputations of the wholesale jeweler and the diamond cutter. Further, considering that the items were locked in a vault, said the court, neither the wholesaler nor the diamond cutter was negligent. The customer didn't collect damages from any party involved.

Appraisers should note this case refers specifically to repairs and may not apply to appraisals.

Insurance: The insurance industry tells us too many jewelers are underinsured or uninsured for loss. While generally risky as a business practice, lack of insurance alone doesn't automatically invite a lawsuit if items are lost. However, if a customer asks about insurance, the jeweler must tell the truth. If a piece is lost when a retailer who said he had insurance really had none, he'd be held responsible for the loss.

Retailers without insurance should never display a sign that says anything like "Our insurance company does not allow us to show more than three items at any one time." Though we could find no actual cases, a court would likely view such a sign as misrepresentation because the retailer had no insurance to begin with. Fraudulent practices invite damages.

A jeweler with insurance should let customers know about the extra precautions taken to care for their items. To have insurance makes good business sense and will increase customers' trust in a jeweler.

William D. Hoefer owns Hoefers' Gemological Services, San Jose, Cal., and is a trained paralegal. His book Advanced Appraisal Methodology *is set for release later this year. He is not an attorney. Readers should contact their own lawyer with questions regarding the opinions seen here.*

Do's and Don'ts of Take-In

Do notify the client if you are going to change what was promised.

Do have the client read and sign anything that would be considered an agreement, such as a take-in slip.

Do be prudent. Take care of a client's items.

Do inform the client that responsibility for sentimental items is limited to actual market value in case of loss due to your negligence.

Do inform the client that it's customary for dealers to insure items at wholesale, if that's what you will be doing.

Do make language on take-in slips readable and understandable.

Do make it clear if the value on the take-in slip was rendered by a clerk by stating so on the slip.

Do note on the take-in slip any noticeable damage or inherent flaws visible on the item.

Do have a statement on the take-in slip that upon further investigation, preliminary examination conclusions may change. The word "agreement" or "contract" should be part of the limiting conditions as listed on the slip.

Do not post signs about insurance if you have no insurance.

Do not promise any client services you will not perform.

Do not take items to another person or location if the client has asked you not to.

Do not allow the client to use default value on the take-in slip if you know the item to be of much higher or much lower value.

Do not repair items beyond your skill unless the risk is explained beforehand.

JCK Management Study Center: You, The Law & Your Employees

Tom Tivol ◆ February 1994

OF EEOC, ADA, OSHA & MUCH MORE

The law is a source of frustration or worry to many jewelers. Laws too often symbolize Big Government at work, whether in Washington, D.C., or a state capital. The people who make the laws too often are seen as legislators who fail to understand the particular problems of small business—the sort of business that a typical jewelers runs.

Because legal issues can be vexing and difficult to understand and comply with, many people tend to shy away from them. But the law can be a jeweler's valuable ally. It provides a discipline for the business, a discipline which can shape a management style. Moreover, most laws affecting relations with employees and customers offer clear guidance on what to do.

Like the laws or not, learning about them is mandatory. It's timely to learn now because so many new laws—and modifications of older laws—have been passed in recent years. These laws and changes affect moment-to-moment operations within a retail jewelry store.

Equal Employment

The Civil Rights Act of 1964, 42 U.S. 2000e *et seq.,* commonly known as **"Title VII,"** prohibits discrimination in employment on the basis of race, color, religion, sex and national origin. It does not protect sexual orientation, although some states do.

Claims of discrimination are investigated by the Equal Employment Opportunity Commission (EEOC). Most states have similar antidiscrimination laws, with agencies established to enforce them. In states where such agencies exist, complaints of discrimination usually are filed jointly with the state agency and the EEOC. Through a work sharing agreement, the EEOC and the state agency determine who will investigate and pursue the charge; the other agency generally adopts the findings of the one that conducted the investigation.

This law prohibits employers from basing hiring and firing decisions, and setting terms and conditions of employment (including wages, working hours, benefits, etc.), on race, color, religion, sex or national origin. It is sometimes hard for retailers to accept the fact that the requirements of the job itself, not the experience or background of the applicant, are the basis for pay distinctions. For example, you cannot pay a male and female salesperson who do the same job at different rates unless it is due to a bona fide union-related seniority system, which is not applicable in the jewelry industry. (This area also is covered by the **Equal Pay Act, 29 U.S.C. § 206,** which applies to gender-based discrimination only.)

You may, however, pay all of your salespeople on a commission basis, permitting them to earn whatever they can through their efforts. Then the fact that a woman might earn less than a man in any given month or year will not be considered discrimination, as long as nothing else you do makes it difficult or impossible for her to reach the same sales level.

Employers often have difficulty with the initial job interview. Women sometimes are asked if they plan to have children, or what arrangements they have made for child care—questions that men are rarely asked. Asking those questions makes it appear that you are willing to discriminate against the woman because of her child care obligations, and that could be prohibited sex discrimination.

Freedom of Religion

Claims of discrimination on the basis of religion often arise when employees are assigned to work on their Sabbath, particularly when their religion prohibits performing any work on the Sabbath. Employers are required to accommodate their employees' religious practices, as long as doing so does not impose an undue hardship on the employer. Undue hardship is determined on a case-by-case basis.

What is a reasonable accommodation for AT&T may not be reasonable for a small employer. However, even if you are small, you must attempt to accommodate your employees' religious practices. This may involve adjusting schedules, perhaps by letting the employee trade days off with others so he or she need not work on the Sabbath. However, if you have only three or four salespeople in a store, the others may be unable or unwilling to take over all of the weekend work so their fellow can take off every Sabbath. Requiring them to work for that employee on the weekend day then might create an undue hardship on your business, which would not be required.

Sexual Harassment

Sexual harassment is a major issue for employers right now. Since the Anita Hill/Clarence Thomas hearings, claims of sexual harassment filed with the EEOC have increased enormously. The U.S. Supreme Court recently determined that a woman does not have to suffer severe psychological injury to be able to sue her employer for sexual harassment.

The EEOC's guidelines on sexual harassment in the workplace state that unwelcome sexual advances, requests for sexual favors and other verbal and physical conduct of a sexual nature will be considered harassment under these conditions: When submission to such conduct is explicitly or implicitly a term or condition of an individual's employment. When submission to or rejection of such conduct by an individual is a basis for employment decisions affecting that individual. Or when such conduct has the purpose or effect of unreasonably interfering with an individual's work performance or creating an intimidating, hostile or offensive work environment.

The Supreme Court's decision confirmed that these guidelines will be used to evaluate claims of sexual harassment. It held that a claim of an abusive work environment

may be maintained if the employee reasonably perceived the environment may be maintained if the employee reasonably perceived the environment as abusive and if a reasonable person would find the conduct hostile or abusive. Employers are responsible for the sexually harassing actions of supervisors. When the employer knows or has reason to know of the conduct, it also is responsible for sexual harassment by co-workers, clients and others. Many employers do not understand that they can be liable for condoning discriminatory or harassing actions by their customers.

The EEOC recently issued guidelines similar to those relating to sexual harassment which deal with harassment on the basis of race, national origin or other similar factors. An employers' liability for this type of harassment is the same as for sexual harassment. That is, if a supervisor, co-worker, client, vendor, etc. engages in harassment, the employer will be held liable if he knew or should have known that the harassment was taking place but did nothing to stop it. Every employer should distribute a clear, written antidiscrimination and antiharassment policy to all employees—and enforce it.

Ethnic Discrimination

Claims of discrimination on the basis of race usually stem from failures to hire, disciplinary actions and discharges. However, they may be related to harassment in the workplace as well.

After the Iran hostage crisis, and again during Desert Storm, claims by Iranians, Iraqis, Lebanese and other Middle Easterners of national origin discrimination became commonplace. They alleged that employers refused to hire them and that they were harassed and taunted in the workplace by co-workers who called them offensive names and demanded that they "go home to [their homelands]."

Similar claims have been brought by persons alleging discrimination on the basis of Polish, Israeli, Mexican and similar ethnic backgrounds. This type of discrimination is prohibited by Title VII, just as is sex, race and religious discrimination. Customer preference (for example, a preference to be waited on by a man rather than a woman, or by a Caucasian employee rather than a person of color) is not a defense.

The remedies available to employees for Title VII violations are quite broad. **The Civil Rights Act of 1991** expanded those remedies considerably. An employee who can persuade a jury that an employer discriminated against him or her on the basis of one of these prohibited factors can obtain an award of back pay, compensatory damages (including sums for inconvenience, humiliation, loss of sleep, loss of appetite, etc.), punitive damages (of up to $300,000, depending upon the size of the employer), reinstatement and attorneys' fees.

Age Discrimination

The Age Discrimination in Employment Act (ADEA), 29 U.S.C. § 621 _et seq.,_ prohibits discrimination in employment against persons over 40 years of age. Remedies that an employee can obtain through a lawsuit include backpay, front pay, reinstatement, liquidated damages and attorneys' fees.

There is no upper limit on the ADEA, although when originally enacted it protected employees only up to the age of 65. Now, an employee cannot be forced to retire at any age; you cannot reduce an employee's salary or benefits because of his or her age, and you cannot treat that employee any differently than you would any other employee.

When an employer terminates an employee, it often enters into an agreement with the employee whereby it pays some extra severance pay in exchange for the employee's release of potential claims. **The Older Workers Benefit Protection Act** changes the procedure with respect to release agreements with persons over 40. Persons in the protected age classification must be given at least 21 days to decide whether to execute the release, with an additional seven days after execution to change their minds and void the release. To be effective, a release must contain specific language confirming that the employee was given this additional time and was encouraged to consult an attorney. A settlement that does not meet all these requirements is not binding on an employee.

Americans With Disabilities Act

The Americans With Disabilities Act (ADA), 42 U.S.C. § 12101 *et seq.*, currently covers employers with 25 or more employees, but effective July 26, 1994, that drops to 15 or more employees. The ADA not only prohibits discrimination against employees and applicants based on disability (or a perceived disability), but also requires employers to provide reasonable accommodations for an applicant's or employee's disability.

The ADA defines a disability as a "physical or mental impairment that substantially limits one or more of an individual's major life activities; a record of such an impairment; or being regarded as having such an impairment." Temporary conditions, such as broken bones that are expected to heal normally, are not disabilities. Disabilities include such conditions as seriously impaired vision or hearing, loss of a limb, confinement to a wheelchair, diabetes, heart conditions and back ailments, and can include mental illnesses such as depression, schizophrenia, etc.

An employer is not permitted to inquire whether an applicant (or employee) has a disability. This will affect pre-employment interviews. An applicant (or employee) may self-identify a disability and request an accommodation, if one is needed to assist in doing the job. Such accommodations can be as simple as changing an employee's schedule, or may involve purchasing equipment such as TDD's (telecommunication devices for the deaf) or specially designed workstations. The extent to which an employer is required to provide these accommodations is decided on a case-by-case basis, with the employer being obligated to provide the accommodation as long as it would not constitute an undue hardship.

An employer may require a pre-employment physical, but only after an offer of employment has been made and only if all persons hired for similar jobs must submit to such examinations. The results of an examination cannot be used to deny employment to a newly-hired employee, unless the disability would present a serious and immediate danger to the employee or others in the workplace. Current alcohol and drug addiction are not considered disabilities, although recovering alcoholics and drug addicts undergoing treatment who are not currently using alcohol or drugs may be protected.

Employees are protected from discrimination based on the history of a disability, such as a prior heart condition, diabetes, etc. Finally, employees are protected from discrimination on the basis of a perceived disability. The most common example of this is an employee who is believed to be homosexual. That person may also be thought to have AIDS or be HIV-positive. Such employees are protected from discrimination, even if they are not actually homosexual, do not have AIDs and/or are not HIV-positive.

Retailers have additional obligations under the ADA to accommodate customers and potential customers. These accommodations may include ramps, handicapped parking spaces and similar measures. All new construction, as well as changes to existing buildings, must comply with the ADA. Where physical changes are not feasible (stairs must be climbed, aisles are too narrow for wheelchairs), retailers are expected to come up with alternative ways to make their goods available to customers. Advocacy groups for the disabled can suggest simple adaptations you might never have thought of. Both landlord and tenant are expected to comply with the ADA.

Family and Medical Leave

The Family and Medical Leave Act of 1993 (FMLA) applies to employers with 50 or more employees within a 75-mile radius. A jeweler who operates a smaller store outside the 75-mile radius does not have to comply with this law in that location, but as a practical matter, many employers elect to give its benefits to all employees.

Employees are eligible to take family and medical leave under this act if they have worked for the employer for at least 12 months, and have worked at least 1,250 hours during the prior 12 months. (The 10% highest-paid employees may be exempt, which means that if they take the leave, the employer need not keep their jobs open. However, these are the key employees whom a jeweler can least afford not to take back.)

Employees may take up to 12 weeks of unpaid leave for the birth, adoption or foster-home placement of a child; the serious illness of an immediate family member (spouse, parent or child); or a serious illness of the employee. Spouses working for the same employer get a total of 12 weeks between them, in most cases. An employer may require an employee to use up paid leave (such as vacation or sick leave) as part of this 12 weeks of family and medical leave. This leave may also be taken intermittently for such things as physical therapy appointments, chemotherapy, etc. The employer can require an employee to provide certification of his or her medical condition.

For all practical purposes, an employer must continue health insurance for an employee who is on leave. An employee can be required to pay the premiums, but if they are not paid, it is unwise for an employer to cancel the insurance since the employee must be returned with the exact coverage he or she had before taking leave, and cannot be subjected to any waiting period or limitation for pre-existing conditions. The employee must be returned to the same job held before taking the leave, and must receive any general wage increases or improvements in benefits granted to other employees during the leave.

Employees generally must give 30 days notice of intent to take this leave, unless an emergency arises. In general, the law will be construed as to require employees to give "reasonable" notice under the particular circumstances. The law will be enforced by the Department of Labor.

Polygraph Testing

The Employee Polygraph Protection Act, 29 U.S.C. § 2001, *et seq.*, prohibits most polygraph testing in employment situations. Pre-employment screening is prohibited except in a very few industries (not including ours). Tests can be administered only to employees who are reasonably suspected of workplace theft or other incidents causing the employer economic loss.

Even if you suffer an economic loss through theft, you cannot test all employees. For example, only employees who had access to money or merchandise at or around the time it was stolen can be tested—not employees who were not working at the time (if the time can be determined). Employers must post a notice supplied by the Department of Labor which explains to employees their rights under the Employee Polygraph Protection Act.

Wage and Hour Laws

The Fair Labor Standards Act (FLSA), 29 U.S.C. § 201 et seq., and other wage and hour laws require, among other things, that employers pay their nonexempt employees a minimum wage (currently $4.25 per hour) plus, with very few exceptions, time-and-a-half their regular hourly rate of pay for all hours worked over 40 in any workweek. Certain classes of employees can be exempt from overtime, but the rules are strict, and the burden is on the employer to prove that an exemption meets the law. It is not unusual for an employee to say he or she prefers to be treated as exempt, but unfortunately, they have no say in the matter. A jeweler will have relatively few exempt employees.

This law is administered by the U.S. Department of Labor. A special section of the statute relates to retail employees compensated principally by commission. These employees may be exempt from overtime pay if: (1) their regular rate of pay is more than 1.5 times the minimum wage and (2) more than half of their compensation for a "representative" period (which may not be less than one month) represents commissions.

If you do not pay on a commissioned basis, your employees generally are entitled to 1.5 times their regular pay for all hours worked over 40 in a week. Employees who voluntarily come in early, stay late or work through lunch are entitled to overtime once they put in more than 40 hours. While "comp time" is allowable in lieu of overtime in some circumstances, the law is tricky here, and many employers get themselves into serious trouble by not checking it out thoroughly in advance.

Failure to comply with these requirements can result in payment of back pay, liquidated damages(equal to the back pay assessed), an injunction and sometimes even criminal penalties. The secretary of labor may bring suit on behalf of employees who failed to receive minimum wage or overtime payments as required by FLSA.

States also have minimum wage and wage-payment laws in addition to child labor laws. Each state is different; you should make sure your pay practices (and your practices with regard to hiring people under age 18) comply with these state laws.

OSHA

The Occupational Safety and Health Act, 29 U.S.C. § 651 et seq., is administered by the Occupational Safety and Health Administration. It requires employers to provide safe workplaces for their employees. Investigations can be triggered by individual complaints or can occur randomly.

In addition to the general requirement of maintaining a safe workplace, employers must have certain written programs, including a hazard communication program, to advise employees of any potentially hazardous materials that may be present in the workplace. OSHA administers rules concerning exposure to chemicals and fumes in confined spaces, including chemicals that a jeweler might keep on his or her premises. (Note that these chemicals also may be subject to local fire codes.)

OSHA violations can be very expensive: the penalty for a willful violation can be as high as $70,000. OSHA has regional offices and, if an employer wishes, will send a representative to help make sure a business complies with OSHA requirements.

Handbooks and Contracts

In most states, the employer or the employee can terminate employment "at will," unless a written contract governs the length—as well as other terms and conditions—of employment. Employee handbooks sometimes have been considered contracts, as when the employer promises in the handbook to discharge employees only for "just cause." Similarly, some courts have held employers to the terms of their employee handbooks—such as provisions for severance pay, vacation pay, sick pay, etc.—on the ground that the employer promised or contracted with the employees to provide these particular benefits.

Having an employee handbook is often a good idea; it is a nice, easy way to acquaint your employees with your practices and policies. And it gives your employees consistent rules to work under. To avoid creating a contract, however, you should couch your policies in general terms and include a disclaimer that the handbook is not a contract. It is essential that you be consistent in applying the handbook to all employees. If your handbooks states that the company will *always* do something, you may have obligated yourself to always do it that way, even if the handbook includes a disclaimer saying it is not a contract.

Handbooks often improve management consistency because the rules are clear for everyone to read. It's important to include some sort of procedure for solving problems. Such a procedure (for example, discussing the situation with a supervisor and, if not resolved, with the store manager or owner) can often resolve problems before they become so major that they lead to employee termination or to litigation.

Another important aspect of an employee handbook is a policy against harassment, including sexual harassment. Publishing (and, of course, enforcing) such a policy provides an employer some protection if an employee subsequently claims sexual harassment without ever having brought it to the attention of the company.

A handbook also helps explain to employees what is expected of them. For example, customer confidentiality is one of the most important services in our business. We do not permit employees to reveal confidential information about customers or about our commission structure; we terminate them if they do so. Explaining this in the handbook lets every prospective and new employee know that this kind of behavior will not be tolerated. Thus, we often can avoid problems before they might otherwise arise.

This is one area where a retailer would be foolish to proceed without legal advice. State laws on employment at will and other issues normally covered by handbooks vary dramatically. The jeweler who operates in more than one state must be sure that the handbook is acceptable under all laws.

Performance Evaluation

If you give your employees performance evaluations, you must be consistent and honest. You should evaluate employees only on job-related matters, and preferably only on criteria that are objective. For example, evaluating an employee on "attitude" often can get you in trouble. Attitude is very subjective and open to wide cultural variations. It cannot be objectively measured and often, in the past, represented an avenue for racial and ethnic discrimination. Sales quotas, on the other hand, are objective and job-related.

I suggest that you have your attorney review your evaluation forms, and that you teach all persons who perform evaluations how to do them consistently, fairly and on time. You owe it to your employees to operate this way, and it will protect you as well.

Supervisors often feel uncomfortable giving an employee an average or less than average evaluation. However, if you aren't going to do honest evaluations, don't do them at all. Many employers have incurred liability by trying to defend the termination of an employee who performed poorly, only to have the plaintiff's attorney shove a raft of above-average evaluations before the jury. The supervisor who gave them didn't want to upset the employee or have to defend the evaluation when the employee complained it was not accurate. (Most employees believe, regardless of the effort they put forth or the errors they make, that their performance is "above average.")

An untruthful evaluation tells an employee nothing, and puts an employer at risk. While employees have attempted to sue employers for defamation or libel based on "unsatisfactory" evaluations, to date no court has permitted any recovery on this basis.

Drug Testing

No law requires an employer to engage in drug testing. However, many employers wish to do so, to protect their property and employees and to reduce potential liability. Government contractors are subject to the **Drug Free Workplace, 41 U.S.C. § 701 et seq.,** which requires the employer to commit to providing its employees with a drug-free workplace, but makes no provision for drug testing.

Pre-employment testing is common, and it does not violate the Americans with Disabilities Act (ADA). Testing an employee "for cause," that is, when his or her behavior leads an employer to believe he or she is under the influence of drugs or alcohol, is also common, as is post-accident testing. Random testing, the most invasive and offensive type, is rarely used unless the employer is engaged in safety-sensitive or dangerous work.

Many states regulate how an employer may do drug testing; you should seek legal counsel before implementing any program other than pre-employment testing. If you engage in pre-employment testing and decline to hire an applicant because his or her test was positive, you need not provide the results of the test to the applicant or permit him or her to retest. Your obligations to provide this information to employees may vary, depending upon state law and, in certain cases, whether you are engaged in safety and sensitive work that would be covered by certain federal laws.

Confidentiality

Confidentiality of customer information is very important. Our employees have access to information about our customers and our business that we have a right to protect.

If you have an employee handbook, you should stress in it the importance of confidentiality and explain that employees who divulge confidential information will be discharged. If you do not publish a handbook, you can post a policy requiring confidentiality and distribute copies to your

employees. Be sure that you take the same disciplinary action against all employees who violate such a policy, to avoid potential claims of discrimination and favoritism.

Many retailers want to protect customer information, such as client lists, even after an employee has been terminated. This sometimes can be accomplished through a confidentiality or noncompete agreement, although the courts generally are reluctant to enforce such agreements.

Fair Credit Reporting Act

The Fair Credit Reporting Act, 15 U.S.C. § 1681 et seq., deals with credit checks and how information may or may not be used. Generally, such information can be used specifically to decide whether or not to advance credit to an applicant. For example, you get a report on a potential customer from a credit bureau which says the customer is behind in his payments and owes money all over town. You absolutely have the right to refuse to do business with that customer. The law also requires you to tell the customer that credit has been denied, and of his or her right to ask for the reason.

Revolving Charge Accounts

Laws govern in-house charge accounts as well as "revolving" accounts on which you charge interest. Revolving credit accounts must comply with state usury laws. Examples of such usury laws in Missouri and Kansas can be found in the Retail Credit Sales Act, Mo. Rev. State 408.250 et seq. (Missouri), and the Uniform Consumer Credit Code, as adopted, K.S.A. § 16a-101 et seq.

Truth in Lending

Reg. Z (12 C.F.R. § 226 et seq.), which was issued to implement the Truth in Lending Act, requires extensive disclosure on credit forms, invoices, etc. of all finance and interest charges. This regulation tells you when disclosures need to be made and what they must include.

Equal Credit Protection Act

Reg. B, which was promulgated under that part of the Consumer Credit Protection Act commonly known as the **Equal Credit Opportunity Act, 15 U.S.C. § 1691 et seq.,** contains, among other things, provisions which protect spouses and others from being "forced" to co-sign or guarantee debt for any charge accounts. It also allows an individual to decline to list the credit of a spouse (or parent) if he or she doesn't want to.

Say a man wants to buy a $5,000 ring and the jewelry store decides it will not extend credit without a co-signer. The store cannot require his wife to be a co-signer, but it can say that if the man wishes to purchase the ring on credit, he must have a co-signer, who need not necessarily be his wife. The jewelry store is not precluded from having the wife be a co-signer, but it's up to the customer to decide what additional security or guarantee to offer. The jeweler then can decide whether to accept what the applicant offers.

Reg. B also prohibits denying credit if that decision is based upon race, color, national origin, sex, marital status or age. If credit is refused, you must notify the applicant and explain the basis for denial.

Customer Privacy vs. IRS

As mentioned earlier, it is our store's policy to keep information about customers and transactions strictly confidential. Sometimes, however, disclosure is legally required, so we cannot guarantee total confidentiality to customers.

For example, **§ 60501 of the Internal Revenue Code** requires reporting of receipts of over $10,000 for one or more "related" transactions. You must file Form 8300 with the IRS within 15 days of receipt of funds, telling the name, address and taxpayer I.D. number (social security number) of the customer. Many people don't know that the term "cash" in this section recently was broadened to include sales for cashier's check, traveler's check, money order or bank draft, or equivalents, Temp. Reg. 61.6050I-1(c)(1). The penalty for not filing Form 8300 is up to 10% of the amount to be reported, and five years' imprisonment, plus a fine of up to $25,000 ($100,000 for a corporation).

That particular law does *not* require reporting of cash transaction of less than $10,000. I've known of jewelers who choose not to keep records of other transaction so they will not end up having to produce records to a court in the case of a customer's divorce, probate proceedings or IRS audit. I feel a jeweler puts himself at far greater risk by not keeping records of all transactions, since he'll need them to support his own tax returns. IRC § 6001 and Reg. § 1.6001-1(a). If you are audited and can't show where the money came from, IRS will use "net worth" type analyses to reconstruct your income. So it is not only a legal obligation, but also in your best interests to keep accurate records of all transactions.

You and your customers can take some comfort that the information in these filings will remain confidential (to everyone but IRS) under another code section, § 7213, which allows substantial penalties (including punitive damages) against IRS for victims of willful or negligent disclosure.

Assisting Tax Evaders

Beware of the customer who wants your help in turning unreported cash (such as gambling winnings) into goods. You could be exposed to a $100,000 fine plus three years' imprisonment under IRC § 7206 for making a false statement or, worse yet, to the same penalties as the customer you accommodated as an "aider and abettor" (18 U.S.C. § 2) or "co-conspirator" (18 U.S.C. § 371), or both!

Representations & Warranties

Jewelers are no different from other retailers in their exposure to claims that they misrepresented merchandise. You at least can control written representations by making sure that a trained supervisor reviews all sales tickets, receipts for goods left with you and appraisals. You might also wish to consult your attorney about drafting warranties or "disclaimers" for your forms.

Allegations about oral misrepresentations are harder to deal with because they ultimately come down to the gray area of credibility, and businesspeople generally are uncomfortable with leaving their fates in the hands of juries. The salesperson accused of making the statement often is no longer in your employ, which places you at a disadvantage.

Legally, there is a distinction between "puffing" and misrepresentation, but it often is tough to tell. What if the customer says she was told that she's buying a "lifetime" watch, that a diamond is "the hardest substance in the world," that a golden sapphire will never fade, that a treated emerald won't lighten.

By training your sales staff carefully, you can reduce the number of problems with such remarks. I have found

that we need to probe the customer for his or her unspoken expectations, to avoid the problem of "I said X but you heard Y." For example, a few years ago I told a customer that she could wear an expensive gold watch everyday. After three years, she came back to show me that the bracelet's gold links had spread and were, in fact, ruined. It turned out that her "everyday" activity was teaching horseback riding, which exposed the watch to extremely abnormal stress. I replaced the bracelet at my expense, but learned not to tell people that they could wear such items "every day."

Manufacturers' warranties such as watches can present their own problems. A jeweler who repairs the watch himself in order to accommodate an impatient customer may be voiding the manufacturer's warranty. Consumers often think that any retailer who sells a certain branded object is required to honor a warranty regardless of where the item was purchased. These issues should be discussed with your attorney, although most complaints about representations and warranties come down to judgment calls by the jeweler: Is the accommodation requested worth it in terms of maintaining customer relations?

Summary

Philosophically, I feel that legal issues—while sometimes vexing and difficult to interpret—are much easier to comply with than the general challenges of finding customers and selling them beautiful jewelry at good profit margins.

I also feel that jewelers, like some successful businesspeople, have an underlying fear of what will happen if they disclose too much about legal issues to their employees. They follow the old rule that "if the employee gets too knowledgeable, it can hurt me."

I don't agree. I think it's time to call employees into your office and say, "This is 1994. We have entered a new age. And I want to bring ABC Jewelers up to par, not only with legal issues, but with ethical ways of maintaining good communication between all employees and management.

"We're going to begin a series of discussions about legal issues. We're going to talk about overtime. We're going to talk about harassment. We're going to talk about the older worker law. We're going to talk about the Family and Medical Leave Act, the ADA, polygraphs and workers' comp. We're going to talk about these so that you as the employee and I as the employer can become knowledgeable.

"We're going to work out a way that all of us can understand these very difficult and rapid legal changes. We'll do so because we want this business to run well, within the bounds of the law, and so that you can feel comfortable when you have a question about the behavior and performance we expect of you and how we regulate that."

This is the way to define integrity in a company and remove any underlying anxiety about coming clean with your employees. And don't think you need a law degree to get a lot of this information. A very average business mind and a few hours of reading will clearly outline the simple principles involved. Then, for the more vexing issues such as employee handbooks, contracts of employment and First Amendment problems, consult an attorney occasionally to make certain you are complying with federal and state laws.

It May Not Be Fair

You want to hire two salespeople. Looking over the applicants, two stand out—a man who works for a good store in the state capital, 90 miles away, and a woman who's just graduated from college with a business degree and is looking for her first job.

You hire them both and assign them to general sales. Because the man has 20 years' experience, had to relocate and has a family, you decide to pay him $30,000. Because the young woman is taking her first job, you pay her $20,000.

A few months later, at a staff outing, the young woman discovers that the salesman from the state capital is earning much more than she is. She asks her supervisor for an explanation and he tells her that the man's greater experience justifies a higher salary. The woman says that seems fair.

But a year later, when talking to an attorney friend about her job, she tells him of her conversation with the supervisor. The attorney tells her that what she considered "fair" a court might consider illegal, under its interpretation of the Civil Rights Act of 1964.

If the man and woman were doing the same work and each job carried the same job description, a court probably would rule against the company. To justify the man's higher pay, his responsibilities should be *significantly* greater than the woman's and the job descriptions should define the differences in responsibility clearly.

Don't Ask

You, the employer, sit down to interview Judy Essex for the job of staff gemologist. You establish that she has a G.G. from GIA, worked at the diamond counter in a leading San Francisco store, and has six years' experience in the business. It's important to you to learn more about her personal side because you have a small staff and want to hire someone who's a good "fit" with your present team.

Employer: "Judy—you don't mind me calling you Judy, do you?—I notice you signed the application letter you sent, 'Judy Essex.' I guess that means you're a Ms. Right? I'm sort of old-fashioned and never can get used to that."

Judy Essex: "Don't let it bother you. I'm used to signing just my name. No special reason. But it would be Mrs."

Employer: "Oh, you're married. And your husband . . . ?"

Judy Essex: "He's a computer guy. Works for Telegraphic Industries."

Employer: "Great, great. It must be a busy time for you both since you're so new in town. Do you know any people here, have any family?"

Judy Essex: "Do you mean children?"

Employer: "Well, I was thinking more of other relatives. But you have children?"

Judy Essex: "Yes, two boys. Three and five."

Employer: "That's a great age for kids. Full of life. It must be a real handful taking care of them."

Judy Essex: "We manage."

Employer: "I'm sure you do. You seem to be a very capable person."

Question: If you decide not to hire Judy because, to your thinking, she has no feel for colored stones although they're an important part of your inventory, are you vulnerable to a charge by Judy's attorney that you violated EEOC law by asking personal questions about issues not related to the job?

This is No Joke

You're a good boss. Because you want your staff to feel appreciated, you have a "party night" once every year—dinner at a nice restaurant where they have a pretty hot combo and dancing. You're not a dancing man, so you go home right after dinner.

Along with the dinner, you also foot the bar bill.

Well, late in the evening Sam Swinger who's one of your sales stars, is getting pretty high and he asks Suzy Strict, your secretary, to dance. Suzy doesn't drink and she doesn't like jokes about sex. But Sam could care less at this point, tells a couple raunchy stories and, to be honest, comes on to Suzy fairly strongly.

Suzy walks off the dance floor, grabs her coat and takes a cab home.

The next morning Suzy complains to you about Sam's behavior.

You're sympathetic but you know that Sam is much more important to the business than Suzy so you tell her, "Suzy, you're making too big a deal out of this. Sam was only kidding around. After all, he's a married man."

You also tell Suzy that there's not much point her complaining to you. The restaurant incident, if it happened at all, happened after business hours and away from the store. She should be an adult about the whole thing and forget it.

Suzy is so mad she quits her job, hires an attorney and sues you for sexual harassment. Will she win her case? You better believe she very well could.

Sick or Disabled?

Doris is a sad sack. She gets coughs and colds. She has a bad back. She's been known to get migraine headaches. She has problems with her family—her mother's a hypochondriac, and if her kid hasn't got chicken pox he has strep throat.

But Doris is a whiz at the diamond counter when she puts her mind to it.

So you live with the little problems.

Then one day Doris comes to you and says she's suffering from stress. Well, you try to cheer her up. You tell her to take a couple of days off. But she insists this isn't a normal sickness. She just feels worn out and has a feeling of being constantly stressed out. She also says she's talked about her condition to a friend who's a nurse, that this friend told her she qualifies for disability leave.

Disability leave for not feeling good?

This may seem unreasonable to you as an employer, but under the Americans with Disabilities Act which went into force in mid 1990, or the Family and Medical Leave Act passed in 1993, Doris may well qualify for special consideration.

Ask for your attorney if you're in doubt.

When a Volunteer Isn't

Joanna is your pride and joy. She's always at work 15 minutes before she has to be, and if there's an extra chore to be done she'll cut short her lunch hour to do it—or stay after hours if necessary.

The extra time rarely runs into big numbers. Usually it's a matter of 40 minutes here, an hour there. Things like that. So it doesn't seem to be the sort of extra effort that calls for overtime, although Joanna is a nonexempt employee and should get either cash or comp time for extra work beyond her normal 40-hour week.

Joanna feels the same way. She loves the job, hasn't any big family commitments to rush home to at store closing time and is more than willing to work until the job is done.

But as an employer you can't just look the other way if an employee is willing to work extra hours without extra pay. That's a no-no. Federal wage and hour laws make it clear that there must be just reward for qualified overtime, even if the employee doesn't specifically ask for it.

If Joanna leaves your employ and later decides to sue you for unpaid overtime, or if you ever get audited by the Department of Labor, you may find it a very costly business.

Being Nice or Being Smart

In your store, your long-time employees are considered "family."

This can be a problem when you sit down with them for their annual review—a process you dislike very much but one that's so highly recommended by your state association that you do it. The truth is that in these reviews you don't tell the truth. Rather than talking frankly with these oldtimers about their shortcomings and asking what they can do to overcome them, you gloss over their faults in a wishy-washy way.

Certainly that's what you do with Tom, 50 years old and with you for 28 years. You know he's sloppy about security. Sometimes you've heard him being brusque with a customer. But, hey, that's good old Tom. You don't say anything and you don't bring up the issues at evaluation time.

But then Tom really messes up. So you fire him—and he hires a lawyer who sues you for age discrimination. The attorney says that firing for a first offense is ridiculous, that it's clear you just want to get rid of a higher-paid, older worker. You reply that this was no first offense, Tom has been messing up for years. Well, says the attorney, you explain to the court how come, over the many years he's worked for you, you never mentioned any of this to Tom.

Was There a Contract?

You finally took the plunge and put together that employee handbook that's been on your "Things to do" list for years. Your attorney gave you good advice on how to write it and stressed that it should carry a disclaimer saying that existence of the handbook does not represent a contract with the employee.

One of the book's big advantages is that it helps you maintain consistency in dealing with the staff. But you'd better be sure you are consistent.

Consider this situation.

Maggie is a wonderful salesperson who wrote more than $1,000,000 in business last year. One evening at a party, she runs into her favorite customer who, in the course of conversation, says, "Maggie, you're the most wonderful salesperson I've ever dealt with. I hope they pay you well!"

Maggie replies, "Oh they do! With the commission I get I'm very happy." Your store manager who attended the same party overheard this conversation.

The manager reports the matter to you and reminds you that the handbook says the penalty for revealing any salary information to a customer is cause for immediate discharge. There's no gray area. But Maggie is a very valuable employee so you give her a warning and drop the issue.

Two months later Mitch, another salesperson, has a customer who's undecided about a piece of jewelry and says she'll think about it and come back. "Please don't come in on Wednesday," Mitch says. "That's my day off and I don't want to miss you because we're paid on commission."

The manager overhears the comment and tells you about it. You're not pleased with Mitch's performance so, invoking the handbook, you fire him.

Later he sues you for breach of contract because you applied different standards to Maggie. He may win.

JCK Management Study Center Quiz

1. John and Suzy do the same sales job and have identical job descriptions. Will you incur legal risk if you:

a. Pay John $1,000 a year more because he has 20 years' experience and Suzy has none? (No, as long as you consistently pay more for years of experience.)

b. Pay John more because he has a wife and two children, while Suzy is single? (Yes.)

c. Pay John more because both he and Suzy are paid on commission and he produces many more sales dollars than Suzy? (No.)

d. Pay John more because he has additional responsibilities which include opening and closing the store and because he can make decisions about discounts for himself and other salespersons? (No, but you should change his job description to reflect the additional duties.)

2. Harry has been fired and he is now threatening to sue you based on alleged sexual harassment. Would the following four situations he details be likely to be found sexual harassment?

a. You, the store owner, often take women salespeople to lunch, but you've never taken Harry or another salesman to lunch? (No.)

b. The store has a strict written dress code for men but none for women? (No. This could be sex discrimination, but not sexual harassment. In addition, it probably is not serious enough to lead to a finding of liability.)

c. The female office manager told some risqué jokes at an after-hours staff get-together at a local bar. The manager laughingly told you that Harry is a prude because he seemed so uncomfortable. Because you didn't want to further embarrass Harry, you ignored the incident. (Yes, this could be sexual harassment, even though it occurred outside of working hours, but a single incident will rarely be enough to result in the imposition of liability.)

d. A secretary uses obscene language from time to time. Harry has complained to her and to you about the offensive language, but you have done nothing. (Yes, if it is frequent and offensive and you are aware of the problem but do nothing.)

3. The Americans with Disabilities Act became law on July 25, 1992.

a. Will that law ever effect employers with as few as 19 employees? (Yes, in fact, it now covers all employers with 15 or more employees.)

b. Can you give job applicants physical or mental examinations in connection with the application process? (No, these examinations may only be conducted after a conditional offer has been made.)

c. Emily, once a great salesperson, is getting older now and suffers from arthritis, which occasionally causes her to miss work or need to go home early. When you suggest she should retire, she asks you to reschedule her working hours so that she can deal with the arthritis problem. Can you solve this personnel issue by making her take early retirement? (No. This probably would violate not only the ADA but also the Age Discrimination in Employment Act.)

d. Can stress-related illnesses be considered disabilities under the ADA? (That is a close question, but the safe answer is "yes." There are several pending cases that may clarify the issue, but it may be a couple of years before they are decided on appeal.)

4. Wage and Hour Laws cover base pay and overtime pay requirements.

a. Suzy is a wonderful secretary, always willing to go that extra mile. To help finish a special promotion, she works two hours after her normal quitting time and tells you, "It was fun. Call it a labor of love." Is it legal to take her at her word and not pay her overtime? (No.)

b. All your salespeople work strictly on commissions. Tom has a terrible week and his commissions add up to less than minimum wage for that week. He says you have to make up the difference between his earnings and the minimum wage. Do you? (Yes. Retail sales employees, even if paid on commission, are not exempt from minimum wage requirements. Employees paid on commission are exempt from overtime pay as long as their regular rate of pay, computed on the basis of earnings, is at least one-and-one-half time the applicable minimum hourly rate for that workweek.)

5. Dealing with older workers can be a difficult proposition.

a. Harry, who is 42, has given you a lot of grief and isn't too hot a salesman. When he blows yet another big sale, you fire him. He sues you for age discrimination because you fired him when he was over 40. Is he likely to win? (No, unless he can show that employees under 40 years of age who also aren't very good and who have blown big sales were not terminated.)

b. Because your small staff is "family," you find it hard to criticize anyone. But one day you face the fact that Gerry is dead wood and you let him go. Gerry, who is 55, says that in his 25 years with the business, you never told him you were unhappy with his work. He sues for age discrimination. Does he have a case? (Probably.)

c. You and Alice, who is 51, agree that it is time to part company. She's a good gemologist but not a good staff fit. You agree on a severance package and she signs a release in connection with the severance agreement, but you don't advise her that she has 21 days to consider the offer and consult an attorney or that she has 7 days after signing the agreement to change her mind. Several months after leaving she sues you for age discrimination. Can you get the suit kicked out of court because she signed an agreement that she wouldn't sue you? (No, because you didn't follow the OWBPA [Older Workers Benefit Protection Act].)

6. Sometimes you don't have to have an individual contract with an employee to have an agreement. If you have a company handbook you may find the written word is even more binding than you thought.

a. Your handbook spells out in detail conduct that can lead to dismissal. When Jane, who is one of your best salespeople, breaks a rule, you let her off with a warning. But when Sam breaks the same rule a month later, you dismiss him—because the rule was listed in the handbook as cause for discharge. Sam sues, charging that your rules are not applied consistently. Does he have a case when the suit goes to court? (Probably, but not on the handbook. It would most likely be brought as a Title VII sex discrimination suit, since Jane, the female, was treated more favorably than Sam, the male.)

b. Your handbook says that you follow a policy of progressive discipline including a verbal warning, a written warning and, as a last resort, discharge. George, a repairman, is consistently late to work and often absent on Mondays. When he fails to show up one Monday and a customer repair job doesn't get done, you lose a good customer. So you fire George. He sues you because you promised in the handbook that you would follow progressive discipline and you didn't do it. Is there a chance he can bring this kind of claim? (Yes, in most states.)

Gemstone Justice: How Scam Victims Can Strike Back

William Hoefer, Jr. ◆ *July 1993*

In April, a municipal court judge in San Mateo, Cal., ordered a Canadian firm to settle a lawsuit filed by two U.S. men who said they were victims of a gem investment scam.

It was the first time in recent memory that a gemstone scam lawsuit reached beyond the seemingly impenetrable Canadian border. To do so, the U.S. plaintiffs used the Hague Convention, an old and often-overlooked international agreement, to enforce the court's decision. The case may serve as a model to the thousands of gem-scam victims trying to retrieve money they sent to Canadian and other foreign gem "investment" firms.

Of course, each gem scam involves different degrees of financial loss, and some foreign gem investment companies disappear soon after a sale. But even when the dollar loss is high and the firm remains active and identifiable, victims often are frustrated by reports of red tape, high costs and low success rates when taking legal action against foreign firms. In reality, crossing the border with a lawsuit is not the high hurdle many might imagine.

The Peterson cases: The April court decision resulted from a lawsuit filed in San Mateo Municipal Court in 1991 by Milton Peterson and his son, Ronald, both of Belmont, Cal. The Petersons alleged that Euro-Can-Am Trading of Toronto, Ontario, misled them when they paid $8,937 for a 6.77-ct. "golden" sapphire. The Petersons tried to return the stone for a refund, in accordance with a sale agreement, but the firm wouldn't accept the stone or return the money.

In response to the suit, Euro-Can-Am sent a representative to the municipal court. The court ordered the two sides to meet with an arbitrator to reach an agreement. The resulting agreement required Euro-Can-Am to refund the purchase price and pay court costs in return for the sapphire.

"To my knowledge, this has never been done with a gemstone case," said Charles A. Connors of San Francisco, the Petersons' attorney.

Progress also has been made on a second Peterson lawsuit, filed in 1991 against Global Royalties Ltd., Mississauga, Ontario. This suit alleged that Global Royalties misled the Petersons regarding the value of—and the firm's intent to resell—a 20.3-ct. sapphire for which they paid $90,000.

The same court ruled that Global Royalties owes the Petersons $300,000, including $150,000 in punitive damages. Connors said collection procedures were under way in Canadian courts, though the company had not responded to the suit or the ruling.

Border crossing: The legal channel that Connors used in the Peterson litigation is based on a century-old international agreement called the Hague Convention, which allows individuals or corporations in one country to sue those in another country.

To use the convention, the victim follows procedures only marginally different from filing a suit in the U.S. To ensure a solid case, the victim should handle the evidence and the necessary appraisal process with care.

While the gem generally is appraised before the lawsuit is filed, I will address the legal procedures first. But let me start with a word of warning: I am not an attorney. I am only presenting information on one course of action. Laws vary from jurisdiction to jurisdiction and are modified frequently; you would be prudent to seek professional advice before acting.

Serving the papers: To take advantage of the Hague Convention, you first must file a lawsuit (also known as a complaint) in your local court. (If you seek more than $50,000, you may file in federal court.) Then the defendant must be served with notice of the complaint so he knows he's being sued and can prepare to defend himself.

Laws regarding how a defendant is served notice vary from state to state and country to country. Some require an attorney or government official to serve it. Each country that signed the Hague Convention (including the U.S., Canada and most European countries) must have a central authority through which lawsuits from other countries are directed (a foreigner suing a U.S. citizen or corporation contacts the U.S. Department of State).

A U.S. citizen suing a foreign citizen or corporation must obtain Form USM 94 from the U.S. Marshal's Service (see telephone book under U.S. Department of Justice), complete the three-page form, then send it to the central authority covering the city where the defendant is located. (Canada has a central authority for each of its 10 provinces. In the Peterson case, the central authority was the Sheriff's Office, Ontario Court, Haileybury, Ontario; (707) 672-3395. The cost was $50 in Canadian currency. Allow eight weeks for it to be served.)

Before serving a suit in Canada, call the central authority and ask whether the suit should be in French or English. In Ontario, it must be in English.

No country that signed the Hague Convention can refuse to comply with it, though some may reject requests involving certain objects such as arms. In such cases, the

405

country must inform the plaintiff promptly. If the deadline to reply to a complaint passes without comment, the plaintiff may ask the U.S. court for a default judgment in his favor. That's what happened in the Peterson vs. Global Royalties case.

A final issue, referred to as "minimal contact," involves the length of time any corporation is active in a particular state or province. But this would have limited effect in gem suits and is beyond this article's scope. Contact an attorney if you wish more information. For a more detailed discussion of the Hague Convention, see *International Lawyer,* Vol. 24, No. 1, Spring 1990.

Appraiser's role: Appraisals of the value of a gemstone bought from foreign "gem investment" firms demand a more complicated narrative format than usual, as explained below.

In addition, the gem value should relate to the approximate date of the transaction, not the date of the appraisal. It doesn't hinder the appraisal process to include current value, but retroactive or historical values are imperative. If several transaction dates are involved, the appraisal will need to report the valuation dates that correspond to each gemstone involved.

Marketplace selection: Usually, the selection of marketplace depends on the market where the stone was bought. But if the vendor claimed the stone was sold at wholesale, the appraiser needs to research comparatives in the wholesale market. If the marketplace was conveyed verbally, all possible marketplaces should be researched. Gemstones are sold in retail, wholesale and collector markets—to name a few—so each must be researched for transactions that can be used to form an opinion on value.

The most powerful methodology is the market data approach. An opinion based on actual sales transactions, on or about that date, is the best approach. The value still must be based on the market where the gem was bought.

Appraisals rendered in anticipation of litigation must be the appraiser's opinion as to value. Price guides can be used as guides only, not as a main source of market price information.

The appraiser and the plaintiff's attorney should avoid agreeing there are "investment" gemstones. Investments pay dividends or interest; "capital appreciation" is the preferred description. "Gemstone investment" firms are careful to mention their involvement as investment counselors, and some even try to make their claims seem authentic by saying securities laws prohibit them from taking advantage of the investment they are "brokering." But the appraiser should not reinforce the myth that gems are investments.

Plastic seals: Should an appraiser break the plastic seal encasing the gemstone? No. Simply state in the cover letter's limiting conditions that the seal has not been opened, therefore, the critical assumption as to weight, quality and identification was derived from the accompanying laboratory report or sealed card's description. State there is an element

of doubt and that proper identification and authentication can be achieved only if the gemstone is removed. Follow the guidance of your client's attorney or a court order.

Market value definitions: The most difficult aspect of rendering the appraisal report is matching the market value definitions to the cause of actions in the civil complaint. I call this the Broad Market Value Rule.

A civil lawsuit often has multiple causes of actions. Examples include fraud, breach of warranty, misrepresentation, negligent misrepresentation, breach of contract, fraudulent detainment and negligent torts. Each cause has its own market value definition, as developed through judicial opinions and other legal documents. Definitions vary from state to state.

Research will show which market value definition is appropriate. The retailer-appraiser should be well-versed in the definitions and research methodology and should check state civil codes or other relevant legal statutes. Many appraisers use the IRS market value definition, but be aware it has no jurisdiction in courts outside the federal tax court system. (Some states—such as California—have adapted the IRS values into their own codes.)

This research is critical because there is a very real risk of not being allowed to testify if the opposing counsel convinces the judge you don't have the proper market value definitions.

But more than just choosing the correct definition, the appraiser must also understand it, research all judicial opinions and render an appraisal in full compliance. In most fraud cases, value is based on the so-called out-of-pocket rule—the difference between the price paid and the actual value. Breach of contract would refer to the anticipated value if the breach had not occurred. Research marketplaces such as wholesale, collector and gem shows are open to the public.

Because most Canadian firms involved in recent scams claim to be investment firms, the argument could be made that they have assumed the position of a fiduciary. In California, that changes what the plaintiff can seek in damages. Instead of sticking to the out-of-pocket rule, the plaintiff may sue for compensatory damages that equal the difference between the actual value and the value if all the seller's claims about the gemstone were true.

Most states apply the latter rule, called "benefit of the bargain." Unless the fiduciary connection can be proven, however, California requires the out-of-pocket rule. If unsure which rule prevails, include both methodologies in the appraisal report.

Advice: Victims should consider suing scam artists and do it as soon as possible. Statutes of limitations vary, depending on the cause of action.

And while the jewelry industry works to halt the cross-border fraud, until it succeeds, victims can use the Hague Convention to fight back.

How To Hire Under New Disabilities Law

May 1993

Businesses with 15 or more workers should begin now to prepare to comply with hiring provisions of the Americans With Disabilities Act of 1990.

The provisions go into effect July 26, 1994 (firms with 25 or more workers have had to comply since July 1992). It's not too soon to prepare, says Philip Rosen, an employment and management lawyer with Jackson, Lewis, Schnitzler & Krupman of New York, N.Y. Rosen participated in Jewelers' Court, a mock trial involving ADA issues at the recent JA International Jewelry Show.

He suggested that employers take the following steps to implement ADA:

1) Train your interviewers. It's illegal to make pre-employment inquiries into an applicant's disability, so interviewers must not ask questions such as, "Have you ever had a back problem?" Instead, they should ask essential function-related questions such as (for a position that requires heavy lifting), "Can you lift 50 pounds?"

2) Review employment applications and other company forms. Prohibited inquiries may not be made orally or in writing. For example, some application forms ask, "Do you have any physical or mental disabilities which would affect your ability to perform your job?" However, any question that seeks information about an applicant's physical or mental condition could result in a liability and must be removed.

3) Do not make medical judgments. Many employers reject applicants with readily apparent disabilities as a result of a good-faith belief the person would be unable to do the job. ADA requires that you make the determination based on whether the person can perform "essential functions" of the job. For this reason, you should carefully list these functions to determine whether the applicant can perform them. A physician's opinion is accorded greater weight than a layperson's.

4) Revise or develop job descriptions. Because a job description can be considered evidence of "essential functions," it should define these functions of the job. Employers must make reasonable accommodations for "essential functions."

5) Review job standards criteria. In addition to intentional discrimination, employees and applicants can prove disability discrimination by showing that a company policy or job criterion that appears to be neutral actually has a disparate effect on the disabled. To avoid this problem, list only the standards that are essential to performance of the job. Non-essential standards that would have the effect of screening out the disabled (lifting, hearing, etc.) may result in liability and must not be used.

6) Review pre- and post-employment medical examinations. ADA prohibits traditional pre-employment medical exams. Exams may be administered only after an offer of employment is made. All employees in the job classification must take the exam, and the information obtained during the exam must be collected on separate forms, maintained in separate files and otherwise treated as confidential medical records.

7) Centralize your applicant and employee screening system. If a number of people in your firm have the authority to hire and make other employment decisions, different standards and criteria might be applied to different individuals. To ensure that consistent, lawful employment practices are followed, it's best that one person who understands the many employment laws be given final review authority.

8) Develop procedures for maintaining and disclosing confidential medical records. Employers who require medical examinations and maintain medical records must develop appropriate procedures to maintain confidentiality.

9) Consider modification of drug testing programs. Drug testing programs may have to be modified if they aren't restricted to illegal use of drugs.

10) Train supervisors on reasonable accommodation for employees returning to work, including those receiving workers' compensation. Current employees returning to work from disability leave may require reasonable accommodation. Special issues may arise where the return to work involves workers' compensation. Supervisors must know how to handle employees returning to work under these conditions.

For more information, call Rosen at (212) 697-8200 or call federal ADA assistance programs at (800) 466-4232 or (800) 949-4232.

How Gem Enhancement Turns Ugly Ducklings Into Swans

May 1993

Tanzanite. It's one of today's most popular gemstones, numbering among its virtues a velvety royal purplish-blue that no other gem—synthetic or simulant—can duplicate. Yet untreated tanzanite is a dowdy brown that wouldn't excite anyone. That's why all commercial material is heat-treated, a process that transforms it into a real swan among gemstones.

Does this ill-remembered fact interfere with tanzanite's popularity? Hardly. Tanzanites have been on best-seller lists at such world events as the Tucson Gem and Mineral Show for a decade. Not bad for a gem discovered only 25 years ago in Tanzania. Or for a gem whose natural color is routinely tampered with—indeed changed—by humans. Even natural gemstone purists who scoff at enhanced goods admit that "this is how a tanzanite ought to look!"

What about other gems, such as emeralds, rubies and sapphires? It's widely known—but rarely discussed—that the "Big Three" gems also are enhanced routinely. True, treatment doesn't always change the colors of these stones as radically as it does tanzanite's. Instead, it may help to deepen colors, diminish inclusions and imperfections or improve durability.

Gordon Austin, gemstone specialist at the U.S. Bureau of Mines, says most gem species undergo a wide range of treatments. "Very high-grade rubies, perhaps no," he says. "But almost all else in ruby, emerald and sapphire is treated. Close to 100%. Even beyond that, aquamarine and other beryls and some tourmalines are all treated to clean up the color or hide the inclusions."

The goal of all treatments is the same: to make gems more beautiful or durable—and, of course, more salable.

This is where controversy over gemstone treatments is born. You may agree it's fine to "complete" gems in areas where nature failed to do the job properly. But what happens to the gem's value compared with natural, untreated counterparts of similar appearance? How should prices be set? And what about disclosure of treatment? Failure to disclose can deceive the customer and lead to charges of misrepresentation. But how much technical detail can the seller disclose without turning off the customer?

There are other questions. Even if jewelers want to disclose all treatments fully, how can they detect them? And how do treatments affect a gem itself? Do they alter its overall stability? Will the enhancement fade or disappear over time?

Gem treatment has received plenty of industry attention in recent years. But new enhancements constantly surface, bringing with them new sets of questions and the need for new identification techniques. This article discusses all types of treatment now applied to gems and answers the questions their use produces.

DIAMOND TREATMENTS

Coatings or backings: Since, like most jewelers, you undoubtedly carry diamonds, you're probably familiar with some of the main treatments that affect diamonds—and diamond prices.

The hardest known natural gem material, diamond has grown in value more than any other gem over the years. So it's not surprising that we continually strive to improve the quality of this scarce commodity. Diamond treatments can be traced back to the mid-1500s, when Benvenuto Cellini discussed backing and coating in his *Treatise on Goldsmithing*.

Backing (where a reflective, usually colorless, metal is painted behind the gem in jewelry) is uncommon today because it's fairly easy to identify and because more effective treatments have been developed. Coating, however, is still around. Diamonds sometimes are coated with a colored substance such as ink or food or fabric dye. This either changes the perceived color of the gem or actually modifies it. Diamonds treated this way likely boast fancy or even the more desirable intense-fancy colors. But treatment of this kind, if not properly disclosed, may signal the seller's intent to deceive.

Coating can be identified under a microscope by viewing the pavilion side, which reflects the color into the body of the diamond. Seen in reflective lighting, coatings often exhibit an irregular, unnatural surface. Color may concentrate where dye accumulated and may actually chip or flake off in some areas.

Coating isn't used too often today because it may fade or wash away. Newer treatments tend to be more sophisticated, often involving an irradiation laboratory.

Fracture filling: The difference in price between an I and an SI_1 clarity diamond can run into the thousands of dollars, depending on size. So many a gem dealer undoubtedly has dreamed of boosting the clarity of diamonds. In the late 1980s, Zvi Yehuda of Ramat Gan, Israel, developed a form of treatment that does just that by disguising inclusions.

The catch: the diamond must have fractures that reach the surface, such as bearding on the girdle, feathers or even laser drill holes. Yehuda developed a way to introduce a substance (a special high-lead-content form of glass) into these fractures. The substance works best when its own refractive index (R.I.) most closely approximates the gem's R.I. The adhesive substance between the walls of the fracture literally helps to hide the fractures.

Is this legal? Yes, as long as the process is disclosed properly to the buyer.

While the treatment improves clarity, however, it often decreases the color grade because the diamond appears slightly more yellow. Stone setters also complain that the filling sometimes leeches out under high temperatures during mounting.

The Gemological Institute of America's Gem Trade Laboratory and other labs will not grade Yehuda-treated stones. However, GIA did develop ways to identify the treated material. GIA's quarterly journal, *Gems and Gemology* (Summer 1989), noted these gems often show yellow or blue and sometimes pink or purple "flash effects" in the fracture-treated areas under a microscope. When stones are properly lighted and then tilted and swiveled, a trained eye may locate the telltale interference colors in the fractures. The microscope also may reveal trapped bubbles where the substance did not completely fill the fractures.

GIA tests show that fracture filling holds up to ordinary care and handling. But great care must be taken not to "sweat" out any of the material when using a jeweler's torch, as in mounting or retipping.

Irradiation: This is one of the most controversial diamond treatments, due in part to the fear that gems we wear might be radioactive. But the Nuclear Regulatory Commission ensures the safety of the wearer by strictly controlling the maximum amount of radioactivity a gemstone can have.

The effect of radiation on diamonds was discovered at the turn of the century when radium salts were used to alter diamond color. This method is now out of favor (and illegal) because it does produce residual radioactivity.

Today, three types of nuclear facilities irradiate diamonds and other gemstones: nuclear reactors, gamma-ray facilities and linear accelerators. The latter are used most often, says Dr. Chuck Ashbaugh, manager of radiation testing at GIA. Gems treated by this method have no residual radioactivity and thus are safe to wear. Irradiated diamonds tend to turn a variety of colors, including green, blue, yellow, orange and pink.

Irradiation is difficult—sometimes impossible—to detect by conventional gemological methods. This is especially true of greenish diamonds. A Geiger counter will detect radioactivity, but there rarely is any because diamonds can no longer be treated legally with radium salts. It's easier to detect treatment when irradiation and annealing (see "Heating" below) are combined—except in the case of green diamonds; a spectroscope can help with most fancy yellow and reddish diamonds. Naturally colored blue diamonds contain boron and are natural semiconductors of electricity; irradiated blues are not. "Finally," says Ashbaugh, "though this is obviously not diagnostic, much of the separation can be done with the eye. Most of the time, irradiated diamonds just don't look right."

Laser drilling: With laser technology, we now can surgically remove unsightly dark included crystals. The laser burns a minute tunnel through the diamond's surface and down to the embedded crystal. In the process, laser heat often vaporizes the offending inclusion. If it doesn't, treaters finish the job by flooding the channel and included crystal with hydrofluoric acid.

GIA says this treatment doesn't change a stone's clarity grade. Still, it *looks* better, which is thought to make it easier to sell. Laser drilling sometimes can be detected with the naked eye and then confirmed by a microscope; the new channel stands out in high relief against the surrounding diamond. Technology can even take care of that, through impregnating laser drill holes Yehuda-style to reduce the channel's visibility.

Heating: Irradiated diamonds often are heated or annealed, as well. This step helps to modify the irradiated color, sometimes even returning a diamond to its original color. Most often it helps to turn blue diamonds green. Detection, although difficult, can be done via spectroscope and by noting heat damage through a microscope.

RUBY & SAPPHIRE TREATMENTS

The U.S. Bureau of Mines estimates that more than 95% of corundum—the mineral of which ruby and sapphire are varieties—is treated. You and your suppliers should know how to detect the various forms of treatment so you can disclose them to buyers.

Heating: Rubies are heated to improve their transparency and/or color. Ruby sources in Burma and Vietnam most often heat-treat to remove rutile silk found in natural stones. Heat treatment followed by controlled cooling allows rutile traces to go into solution with the corundum host, producing greater transparency. Similar heating followed by a different cooling process may allow the silk to reform, giving asteriated (star) rubies more pronounced rays. Heating also removes the purplish component in rubies, resulting in a purer red.

The same principles apply to blue sapphires, which often are heated to increase transparency in rutile-clouded stones or to develop asterism in star stones. Most commonly, however, heat treatment serves as a catalyst to cause color. Heat dissolves the milky rutile in "geuda" sapphires (milky white stones from Sri Lanka) into the corundum itself. The titanium component in rutile causes the resulting blue coloration.

Yellow and green sapphires (which owe their coloring to iron and titanium) often are heat-treated as well. The treatments reportedly help to saturate the yellow to orange colors.

Ted Themelis of Gemlab Inc., Clearwater, Fla., who has written several articles and a book *(The Heat Treatment of Ruby and Sapphire)*, says other colors can be obtained as well. He says an understanding of the material, its source and the nature of its impurities suggests how a stone will respond to treatment. "Parameters such as temperature type, oxygen and processing time—as well as the heating and cooling cycles—are of vital importance, too," he says. "These parameters dictate the nature of the way in which corundum is prepared for treating, what sort of equipment is used to do the job and how the gems are treated and later cooled."

Heat treatment tends to leave a few telltale clues. It may cause discoid fractures to develop around inclusions. Faceted surfaces may exhibit a charred appearance where the treatment's effects could not be polished away. Silky rutile inclusions in corundum often appear broken or irregular.

Diffusion: Many labs that heat-treat corundum are only a few steps away from diffusion treating. This treatment literally has been reborn in the past two years. A form of surface diffusion—in which a very thin surface layer of colorless corundum is treated to show blue—has existed for some time. But the high temperatures this process requires often scarred and sintered the material, and repolishing removed much of the color.

Recently, a new breed of "deep-diffusion" gemstones appeared on the market. The once-thin layers of color-induced corundum had grown thicker (from 3mm to 3.5mm of penetration). Repolishing was less likely to destroy the thin layers of diffusion.

Diffusion, according to the Summer 1990 *Gems & Gemology*, involves coating colorless or near-colorless corundum with a titanium and oxide compound, then exposing it to extremely high temperatures—ideally 1,700°C, or higher, nearing corundum's melting point. This allows the compounds to seep into the atomic lattice of the gem, causing a bluish color.

Diffusion-treated blue sapphires are common in the market. Experts say other colors have been produced as well (using other compounds, such as chromium), though no commercial quantities are yet available. Diffused multicolor corundum (especially reds) may be a product of the future. Themelis, who experiments with ruby color diffusion, explains: "The process requires ultrahigh temperatures, around 1,850°, in a controlled environment and stabilized atmosphere. What is key about red corundum is that the color penetration be deep enough that after repolishing, it can still be classified as ruby. Most of the colors achieved after repolishing are only saturated pinks." Other experts say the process is costly and not yet commercially feasible.

Detection of diffused sapphires depends on their appearance. They've been described as having a strange "watery appearance." When they're immersed in methylene iodide (a heavy liquid) with a diffused back-light source, the concentration of color is seen at facet junctions. And repolishing after treatment leaves areas of deeper color diffusion. Diffused sapphires also often show discoid inclusion fractures like those seen in plain heated sapphires.

Glass-filled fractures: Fractures or pits in ruby or sapphire are filled with glass to increase the gem's weight and soften its exterior appearance. While the treatment is fairly common, it's also relatively easy to detect. Bubbles—not found in rubies—often can be seen through a microscope in the area of the glass filling. And because fillings often are polished to the level of the ruby facets, reflected light will illuminate inconsistencies where the two materials meet (such as polishing marks in the glass but not in the ruby). Immersing the stone in methylene iodide makes the glass fillings show up in high relief against the rest of the gem.

Dyeing: This enhancement is seen most often in rough material—primarily rubies—at the source. The dye permeates into the crystal, giving it a richer appearance. Using colored oils in this way is considered a form of deception because the buyer will polish away the dye (and enhancement) at the faceting station. Test crystals with a cotton swab and a small amount of acetone; this usually removes the color.

EMERALD TREATMENTS

Emeralds are among the most commonly treated gemstones because of their popularity over the centuries and because of the nature of the material itself. Even the best-quality emeralds tend to have inclusions and minute fractures that often reach the surface. This characteristic makes the gem susceptible to so many treatments that selling an oiled emerald has become a standard trade practice. All who understand emeralds take such oiling for granted—with some exceptions.

Oiling: The trade considers emerald oiling acceptable as long as the oil isn't colored green (dyed). Because of this widespread acceptance, disclosure is rare.

Ron Ringsrud of Constellation Gems, Los Angeles, who wrote about treatment in Colombian emeralds in the Fall 1983 *Gems & Gemology*, notes that emerald oiling occurred as far back as ancient Greece. Today's method of impregnating an emerald with oils probably is little different than it was in those days. Oil treaters often use Canada balsam or cedar wood oil, whose R.I. of 1.512+/- is close to emerald's 1.577-1.583; this helps to hide the oil in the emerald's surface-reaching inclusions. The oil is heated to diminish its viscosity, then inserted into the emerald's fractures by a vacuum process.

Oils in emerald can range from obvious to difficult to detect, depending on the size of the inclusion, the amount of oil and the relative success of the operation. A microscope often will reveal bubbles in the oil. More difficult cases can be identified by the way the oil fluoresces. Oiled areas may stand out when the emerald is immersed in water or heavy liquids, with diffused light transmitted from behind.

Even moderate changes in temperature can cause oil to seep out of an emerald. Great care is required when cleaning or mounting it in jewelry. Canada balsam also may dry out over time, after which the stone should be cleaned and oiled to restore its former beauty.

Fracture filling or impregnation: The advent of epoxy-like resins such as Opticon revolutionized the art of filling emeralds. Most dealers and jewelers agree this treatment is rapidly becoming quite common. The principle is the same as in oil filling, but the mechanics are different.

Opticon's R.I. (1.545) is very close to emerald's, so fractures filled with it are barely visible. The resin also hardens over time, which improves the gem's stability and durability.

Various types of resins are used. A number of labs around the world offer fracture filling. Some claim they don't use resins or plastics at all; what they do use remains a secret.

Detection of filling is difficult. Robert Kammerling of GIA discussed fracture fillings during the 1991 GIA International Gemological Symposium. He noted that some bubbles in the resin can be seen under magnification; whitish, granular areas also may be seen. But one of the most diagnostic features is a telltale yellow or blue flash effect—an iridescent plane at the point of contact between the beryl and the resin.

OTHER GEMS & THEIR TREATMENTS

Irradiation: The treatment of topaz is one of the field's most remarkable developments of the past 15 years. Natural untreated blue topaz is rare, while irradiated and heated blue topaz abounds at gem counters and shows everywhere. These stones start as dull, colorless pebbles and end up with strongly saturated colors ranging from slightly greenish blue to deep blue, depending on the type of irradiation and treatment used. They carry such names as California Blue, Sky Blue and London Blue, a subtle clue to their depth of man-induced color.

Typically, topaz is submitted in mass quantities (several thousand carats) to a licensed linear accelerator or gamma-ray laboratory or to research reactor facilities that use neutron radiation. Linear accelerator treatment often is used after neutron irradiation to produce a darker, more commercially desirable color. Irradiated topaz is brownish, so heat-treatment usually is needed to arrive at the final color.

Dr. Chuck Ashbaugh of GIA's radiation testing lab says the NRC closely monitors residual radioactivity in topaz, especially that treated in the U.S. Only people licensed by the NRC to sell or distribute irradiated topaz may market the material. U.S. gem organizations follow the rules by asking their members to disclose that any irradiated topaz they sell was released by an NRC-licensed facility.

Some colorless or yellowish topaz changes to a deeper golden yellow or brown upon irradiation. There is no residual radiation effect.

Other gems commonly are irradiated, but they carry no residual radiation and thus pose no danger to wearers. These include some beryls, such as morganite, and some corundums, such as yellow sapphire. However, these yellow sapphires tend to fade when subjected to heat or light.

Certain rubellites (reddish tourmalines) commonly are irradiated to enhance the saturation of color. There is no known way to detect irradiated rubellite, because it also occurs naturally in deep saturated colors.

Gamma ray facilities also irradiate freshwater cultured pearls, which turn an astonishing and unnatural array of iridescent colors ranging from deep greens to magentas and blacks.

Some quartzes such as smoky and rose also have been irradiated to deepen their color or produce new and unusual colors. In his book *Gemstone Enhancement,* Dr. Kurt Nassau discusses the possibility of producing certain bicolor amethyst/citrine from originally colorless material.

Heating: Controlled heating—from simple to sophisticated, using porcelain crucibles, Bunsen burners, electric and gas ovens—is by far the most prevalent method of treating gems today.

Some organic gem materials such as amber or ivory have been heat-treated since Biblical times. Amber loses some of its cloudiness when properly heat-treated; its color saturation also may deepen. The same effect is noted in carefully heated ivory, which can assume an "antiqued" look.

Amethyst may fade with heat or turn yellowish or brown. Citrine, the yellow quartz, sometimes turns a reddish "sherry" color when heated.

Heating rock crystal produces very convincing emerald and ruby simulants. The heated quartz is cooled rapidly in water so it "crackles," producing an array of minute, intercrossing, surface-reaching fissures into which colored dyes are inserted. This method of producing simulants reportedly has actually fooled a few experts. Crackling and color-inducing dyes sometimes are used in other gem materials that lack color saturation, such as pale corundum crystals.

Aquamarine is among the most famous of heat-treated gems. When slightly greenish-blue beryl is heated, an oxidation-state change removes the yellow component (iron) and increases the perceived blue. Should the component be man-

ganese (which produces pink morganite), certain heat treatments will induce a deeper red beryl.

Heat treatment produces the changes described under specially controlled conditions with oxidizing or oxygen-reducing environments specially designed for certain gems. No one should attempt to treat gems on his or her own without guidance or proper knowledge of the procedures.

Coating, bleaching, dyeing: Dyeing was discussed briefly in the previous section, which brings up an important point. Treatment methods often are combined to produce the desired effect.

Use of dyes or coatings on single-crystal gems has fallen largely out of favor because detection methods have grown more sophisticated. However, certain porous gem materials that aren't single crystals take dyes very well and aren't always easy to detect.

Chalcedony, a cryptocrystalline form of quartz, varies in porosity. Thus some banded agates take well to a variety of dyes. Pioneered in Europe, colored agates are now commonplace and inexpensive throughout the world. Chalcedonies that have been dyed black are universally known as "black onyx" and often thought of as untreated material. The correct name, however, is dyed black chalcedony.

Dyed jadeite is difficult to detect. Jadeite and nephrite usually are heated first, a step that's said to "open the pores of the jade." Then the dye is introduced, most commonly to produce the popular green (imperial green, of course) and lavender material. Acid-bleaching to remove brown staining in cracks of jadeite is a more recent development. This is done before dyeing, because the bleaching process is said to weaken the structure of this aggregate gem. Bleaching is followed by a polymer impregnation.

Treated jadeite isn't always easy to detect because dye concentrations aren't always apparent, even under magnification. Natural, fine-green jadeites tend to show sharp chromium lines in the spectroscope, whereas dyed material has a broader band at 640-670nm in the spectroscope.

Being aggregates, or conglomerate stones, jadeite, lapis lazuli and turquoise all are susceptible to dye as well as wax, paraffin or even epoxy impregnations. These help to "stabilize" the more crumbly material and saturate the underlying color.

Dyes are applied to other organic gem materials as well, including coral, pearl and ivory. The intent is to intensify the desired color or make it more uniform. Cultured pearls, ivory and some coral also are bleached in peroxide solutions to make the body colors more uniform. When black coral is bleached with a peroxide solution, it turns a lovely golden color that is more salable in Central and South America.

Carbon treatment: Opals frequently are carbon-treated by one of two methods. "The first, used on porous material from Mexico, involves heating the fashioned stones in a paper bag with manure, or other such substance, that is then burned, depositing dark carbon particles just below the stone's surface," say Cornelius Hurlbut Jr., and Robert C. Kammerling in their book *Gemology.* "A related treatment involving similar material from Andamooka, Australia, involves soaking [opals] in a sugar-rich solution, followed by placing the stone in sulfuric acid to 'carbonize' the sugar, that is, deposit out dark particles."

Both treatments are superficial and may be detected by a very fine "pinfire" play of color seen against a dark background.

PRICE DIFFERENTIAL

In an ideal world where seller and consumer know all the facts about gem treatments, the buyer benefits by getting more bang for the buck. The gemstone he or she buys looks good and hopefully will mount and wear well with time. And because it's known the stone was treated, it should cost somewhat less than an untreated stone of comparable quality.

But how much less? This varies with market demand, availability and cost of treatment, degree of acceptance by buyers and price of rough. With so many variables, and so many types of gem material involved, it's impossible to make blanket statements about price. So let's look just at ruby, emerald and sapphire. Richard Drucker of Gemworld International, publisher of *The Guide* price manual, says his surveys suggest the following parameters (reprinted with permission).

For non-oiled or non-Opticon-treated emerald:
- Commercial grade: little or no effect.
- Good to Fine: up to 10% or higher than treated.
- Fine to Extra Fine: up to 20% or higher than treated.

For non-treated rubies and sapphires:
- Commercial: little or no effect.
- Good to Fine: up to 10% higher than treated.
- Fine to Extra Fine: up to 20% higher than treated.

Remember, these rules of thumb are not necessarily true for all gemstones. Even among corundums, prices may vary widely. A diffusion-treated sapphire may sell for $1/6$th the price of a natural sapphire of the same color. The question is moot for tanzanites and blue topaz, because virtually all are treated. Irradiated fancy-color diamonds actually are more expensive than diamonds in undesirable natural yellowish colors, but irradiated stones can't match the prices of natural deep yellow or other fancy colors.

WHAT MUST YOU DISCLOSE?

A surprising number of gem dealers admit that even they have been burned by buying a treated gem they thought was natural. So both dealers and retailers generally agree that consumers must be told *something* about gem enhancement to avoid fraud and deceit. But they disagree about just how and how much to tell. There's a fine line between informing consumers and turning them off with too much technical jargon.

The problem is universal. In fact, disclosure will be one of the main topics of discussion at the next International Colored Gemstone Association Congress, to be held in Israel in June. ICA Vice President Israel Z. Eliezri points to the need for a "worldwide unified policy for the disclosure of gemstone enhancement treatments."

Many feel that current disclosure regulations, as contained in the U.S. Federal Trade Commission "Guides for the Jewelry Industry," are sufficient. Others support revisions formally proposed in June 1992. (The new wording: "It is an unfair trade practice to sell or offer for sale any gemstone which has been enhanced by coating; application of colorless or colored oil; irradiation; surface diffusion; dyeing; heating; by the use of nuclear bombardment; or by any other means, without providing a description which informs the purchaser that said gemstone has been or may have been enhanced; and disclosure that a change in color or tinting is not permanent if such is the fact.")

FTC attorney Suzanne Patch says much of the proposal is little changed from the current "Guides." Still, the revisions attracted 260-270 comments—some more than 100 pages in length—when they were opened to the trade for comment last year. "These comments must still be tabulated, reviewed and evaluated by the commission," says Patch.

Among the many organizations that sent comments was the American Gem Trade Association, which hopes to fine-tune much of the FTC disclosure language. But the AGTA proposals have met with some controversy. Martin Bell of Rio Grande, Albuquerque, N.M., for example, says some of the proposals go too far. "Regarding diffusion-treated sapphires, the words AGTA proposes seem to be designed to restrain trade in this product category," he says. "The specific mandated wording is lengthy and hard to remember. It seems unlikely that salespeople on the road or at trade shows will bother to write the complete text on invoices. We should have rules that are easy to comply with if we want them to gain acceptance."

It's important to remember that today's consumers tend to be better-informed than those of 20 years ago, so it pays to have an equally well-informed jeweler/gemologist on the premises. The ability to explain in simple terms why most gemstones are treated, with some particulars about the gem in question, is vital. Salespeople also must keep gem treatment in mind during the take-in procedure, to prevent possible lawsuits.

To help meet this need, a coalition of industry groups published *The Jewelers Information Manual For Gemstones, Synthetic Stones and Imitation Stones,* a guide to the various enhancements seen in gemstones. The coalition comprises the American Gem Society, American Gem Trade Association, Jewelers of America, Jewelers Vigilance Committee and Manufacturing Jewelers and Silversmiths of America. For more information, contact a coalition member or ask GIA for a brochure titled *Radioactivity & Irradiated Gemstones.*

WHAT NEXT?

New gem enhancements present both a threat and a promise. The threat is that they'll pass undetected by dealer and jeweler, ending up in the hands of uninformed consumers. The promise is that plentiful supplies of beautiful, affordable material will be available to more people.

Whether you consider treatment good or bad, you can be sure it's here to stay—and that new forms will continue to appear. Here are some to look out for.

There's a potential for the coating of thin diamond films on other gem material, says Dr. Emmanuel Fritsch, GIA research scientist and manager of research. "Whether it will be done commercially remains to be seen," he says. "I'm not concerned about diamond coatings of CZ, nor am I concerned about adding weight [by depositing a thin film on the diamond] in diamonds. Nobody is pursuing that route, and will not in the future, unless a lot of money is invested in development of this technology."

Instead, he says, more will be done to develop and expand on older treatments such as dyeing and polymer impregnations. He also expects new techniques from Asian countries, where he says the development of treatments has flourished because regulation isn't as strong as in the U.S. "Some of these innovative treatment styles already have presented us with challenges in identification," he says.

New treatments described by GIA include the microscopic gold coating of quartz (the "aqua-aura" technique), which gives colorless quartz a bluish, iridescent color. Recent findings suggest this gold deposition technique has been tried on colorless corundum and may appear on other gems as well. The technique does have some telltale features. When examined in direct light, blue to purple iridescence appears on the surface of the stone, particularly in the pavilion area.

Other experts expect the future to bring some interesting developments in the diffusion of corundum. One obvious goal is an inexpensive way to diffuse red into corundum. "It has been done, but not on a commercially feasible basis," says one gem treater who prefers to remain anonymous for security reasons. Others say diffusion still isn't deep enough to produce the deep red colors desirable in ruby. However, gem treaters throughout the world continue to try.

Untreated Gems
The following gemstones are not treated:
- Alexandrite
- Andalusite
- Apatite
- Benitoite
- Charoite
- Chrysoberyl (alexandrites or cat's eyes)
- Feldspars (some spectrolite, labradorite and sunstone)
- Garnet (all varieties)
- Hematite
- Iolite
- Rhodochrosite
- Rhodonite
- Sodalite
- Spinel
- Sugilite

The Lanham Act In Action

January 1991

With the Federal Trade Commission currently taking little action, the Lanham Act has become a primary tool against misrepresentation in the jewelry industry. Since the law was revised in late 1989, no fewer than seven lawsuits have used it as a foundation in cases involving misrepresentation.

By late October, at least two of the cases had been settled, two were being negotiated, one was nearing a court date and one was being defined by the courts and the parties involved. A seventh was on hold due to a bankruptcy filing.

Though most of the defendants battle on, the issues generated by their cases have cast a bright light on trade practices that few in the jewelry industry were willing, or able, to combat with previous laws. Even more critical, according to legal experts, is the growing feeling that jewelers no longer need to stand by helplessly while unfair trade practices undermine their business.

"There is greater awareness in the industry of the ability to prosecute acts of unfair competition," says Roberta Jacobs-Meadway, a trademark and copyright attorney who has represented the Jewelers Vigilance Committee and the Cultured Pearl Association of America in five of the seven Lanham Act lawsuits filed in the past year.

In addition to creating awareness, she says, the seven suits also make firms "less inclined" to cross the line into misrepresentation. JVC General Counsel Joel Windman agrees. "I think people are going to think about it a second time before committing acts of violation—if they are smart," he says.

Federal law: The act, a federal law established in 1947, was strengthened in 1989 to give any retailer, wholesaler or manufacturer the legal backbone to sue any other firm that it believes is misleading or falsely representing itself or its goods.

A critical change in the revised act allows for awards that include legal fees and compensation for any monetary loss brought about by the misrepresentation. The act used to be unclear as to whether the jeweler could receive damages from violators.

In the past, damage awards were most likely for trademark infringements. Misrepresentation suits often ended with an order to cease the offending action, period. The difficulty of obtaining damages in these and other instances inhibited businesses from filing lawsuits at all.

The 1989 revision also brought misleading advertising, false pricing and deceptive business practices more clearly into what traditionally had been an arena for trademark-related disputes.

Taking the lead: Before the revision, trade organizations such as the Jewelers Vigilance Committee were doing most of the work. Attorneys general aided the battle on the state level, scoring important though scattered victories.

"Without the act, we would be relying on the FTC or using our own right to take action under the Stamping Act," Windman says. "It [the revised Lanham Act] gave us the ammunition to fire back."

While the JVC has taken the lead in using the Act, there are promising signs that word has spread beyond the New York-based industry watchdog.

Jacobs-Meadway, a partner in the Philadelphia law firm Panitch, Schwarze Jacobs and Nadel, says awareness of the act got a boost when Jewelers of America denied booth space to Vitale Inc. of Dallas after the firm was named in a Lanham Act suit in 1990.

Since then, the Cultured Pearl Association of America and a group of retailers led by B. Sanfield Inc., Rockford, Ill., have filed unrelated Lanham Act-based actions that further spread awareness of the Act.

Close to the heart: Though the CPAA action was settled in August, the B. Sanfield Inc., action may be the case that brings the Act closer to retailers hearts.

The suit, filed June 28 in U.S. District Court in the Northern District of Illinois, alleges that two large department store chains Marshall Field & Co. of Chicago and H.C. Prange Co. of Sheboygan, Wis. used misleading advertisements, sales and prices to sell gold chains.

It was the first time a retail jeweler used the revised Lanham Act against other retailers for allegedly deceptive ads. If successful, it could open the gates to similar suits nationwide. "Some visible and noted successes would generate interest," says Brian D. Shore, the attorney representing B. Sanfield Inc.

Lee Hartsfield, chief executive of B. Sanfield Inc., initiated the suit after Illinois approved a strong truth-in-pricing law in June 1989, says Shore. The law is similar to those in states where consumer protection agencies have successfully battled department stores that used false discount advertising. "The revised Lanham Act added steam," Shore says. The chance to tackle the department stores head on, as well as the added potential for a financial award, gave greater focus to the entire issue, he says.

Tide shifts: A jeweler's victory in a class-action suit (filed in 1988 before the Lanham Act was revised) against American Express may have started the tide flowing.

As part of the settlement, American Express agreed to make refunds to cardholders who bought jewelry inferior to what it had advertised. It's too early to assess the fallout from that victory. But Mark Cuker, the attorney who represented jeweler William Lieberum of Warminster, Pa., and others in the suit, is cautiously optimistic. "A clear [deceptive pricing] victory against a retailer may change the practices of other retailers," he suggests.

His major concern, shared by Shore, is whether enough retailers are willing to cast the first stones. "Retailers have their hands full running a business, and there is still reluctance to get involved in legal issues," he says.

Some also fear becoming the defendant in a similar case, he says, noting that many jewelers have used discount pricing over the years.

Windman adds that retailers also need to be wary of venturing into other legal complications when acting alone or even as a group. "You are dealing with competitors, and that means you are dealing with restraint of trade," he warns.

In addition, a business owner could misuse the law by trying to force an honest competitor out of business.

Still, Windman doesn't foresee retailers rushing to use the Act as a competitive ploy. "The potential for abuse is present with any legal process," he notes.

But most retailers will continue to be the beneficiaries of the Lanham Act, not its victims, says Jacobs-Meadway. "The benefit spreads up and down the line," she adds. "Anytime action is taken, it restrict unfair competition and alerts people to those problems in the industry."

Windman notes that action taken against suppliers helps to shield retailers. "The cases we have pursued will help avoid confusion and misrepresentation and keep the retailer from looking like a fool," he says. "Who is the consumer going to sue when something is misrepresented to the retailer? Not the supplier."

The Act may have appeared just in time, he notes. Historically, periods of economic slowdowns invite dishonest operators who prey on businesses looking for a better price. Armed with the Lanham Act revision, Windman is more ready than ever to play hardball.

Taking Action

Retailers who feel they've been damaged by a firm that is misrepresenting its products or conducting what appear to be unfair trade practices should keep a good record of the violations, then contact a lawyer.

As a group or individually, retailers first should try to resolve the matter without litigation, says Roberta Jacobs-Meadway, an attorney representing the Jewelers Vigilance Committee in Lanham Act suits.

If official letters and direct confrontation fail, a cause for action using the Lanham Act may be appropriate. With legal fees and damage awards now an integral part of the Act, retailers have a better (though never guaranteed) chance of recouping losses and expenses if the court decides the misrepresentation of fraud is clear.

But a clear case relies on solid evidence. While retailers are not detectives, most know when they are being treated unfairly and can collect examples that show the problem. In a discount pricing battle, for example, it takes more than a few "for sale" fliers to prove the case, says JVC General Counsel Joel Windman. "A continuous group of ads, not just one or two sales, is needed to show there was never an original sale price," he says.

Windman invites retailers to contact his office with complaints about pricing or other misrepresentations of products or services. "When we receive a number of complaints about an individual or a firm, then we can become involved."

Private Right To Act Against False Advertising Strengthened (Lanham Act)

Roberta-Jacobs Meadway ◆ *March 1990*

Effective last November, federal law makes it much easier for a honest jeweler to fight back against competitors who misrepresent what they sell. The change comes about because of significant revisions of the 43-year-old Lanham Act.

The revised act, in sum, now provides a viable basis for action against companies that habitually underkarat, companies that falsely represent the quality of gemstones offered for sale, companies that seek an unfair competitive edge. These actions may be brought up by individual companies or by companies having a common interest or by trade associations such as the Jewelers' Vigilance Committee. Each may act to protect his own commercial interests and the buying public from those who operate by sharp practice as well as outright fraud.

Since 1947 Section 43(a) of the Lanham Act has given any person, including a company, the right to sue a competitor who falsely represents or describes goods it sells or services it renders in commerce.

The prohibition against false representations and descriptions extends not only to statements which are literally false, but also to claims which have a tendency to mislead or deceive. By way of example, to advertise a diamond as "the finest there is" implies the stone is D flawless. If the stone is of lesser quality, but the grade is not disclosed, customers who see the ad may be very dissatisfied with their jeweler who cannot provide a D flawless stone at the advertised price. While the stone may be a "fine" stone, or the finest there is for the advertised price, the advertisement has a tendency to mislead which is likely to injure competitors of the advertiser. If the advertisement is distributed through the mail, or published in a newspaper such as *The Philadelphia Inquirer*, it is not difficult to establish the impact on interstate commerce which is a prerequisite of action under the Lanham Act.

For a variety of reasons to be discussed later, however, the act was not considered an appropriate legal recourse for small independent businesses, such as those run by most jewelers. The true value of the revised act, from the jeweler's point of view, is that it strengthens Section 43(a) to better serve its intended purpose—namely promotion of fair dealing to protect competitors as well as consumers from deceptive trade practices.

The language of Section 43 15 U.S.C. 1125 as amended is:

(a) Any person who, on or in connection with any goods or services, or any container for goods, uses in commerce any work, term, name, symbol, or device, or any combination thereof, or any false designation of origin, false or misleading description of fact, or false or misleading misrepresentation of fact, which—

(1) is likely to cause confusion, or to cause mistake, or to deceive as to the affiliation, connection, or association of such person with another person, or as to the origin, sponsorship, or approval of his or her goods, services, or commercial activities by another person, or

(2) in commercial advertising or promotion, misrepresents the nature, characteristics, qualities, or geographic origin of his or her or another person's goods, services, or commercial activities, shall be liable in a civil action by any person who believes that he or she is or is likely to be damaged by such act.

This dovetails with the amendments which relate to monetary remedies in 15 U.S.C. § 1117:

(a) When a violation of any right of the registrant of a mark registered in the Patent and Trademark Office, or a violation under Section 43(a), shall have been established in any civil action arising under this act, the plaintiff shall be entitled, subject to the provisions of Sections 29 and 32 and subject to the principles of equity, to recover (1) defendant's profits, (2) any damages sustained by the plaintiff, and (3) the costs of the action. The court shall assess such profits and damages or cause the same to be assessed under its direction . . . If the court shall find that the amounts of the recovery based on profits is either inadequate or excessive the court may, in its discretion, enter judgment for such sum as the court shall find to be just, according to the circumstances of the case. Such sum in either of the above circumstances shall constitute compensation and not a penalty. The court in exceptional cases may award reasonable attorney fees to the prevailing party.

What this means is that any person, including a jewelry manufacturer, wholesaler or retailer who believes that he or she is likely to be damaged by a false or misleading representation or description by a competitor has standing to bring a claim under Section 43(a), and may secure an injunction against continuation of the deceptive conduct. The plaintiff may also be awarded the violator's profits attributable to the false representations, any damages he has sustained that may be established, and, most importantly, may receive from the violator his reasonable attorneys' fees incurred in the prosecution of the action.

Limitations: Section 43(a) of the Lanham Act, did not become a significant vehicle for action against false and misleading representations and descriptions except for major consumer goods companies for a number of reasons:

• The statute initially was narrowly drawn and initially read to reach false designations and representations as to the geographical origin of products.

• The statute was unclear as to whether any relief other than an injunction against continued false representations or descriptions was available. By its language, the provisions of the act providing for awards of damages, profits and attorneys' fees were limited to cases of infringement of registered marks, and did not extend to other violations under the act. The cost of litigation, without the prospect of any financial return, certainly discouraged the filing of suits by individual businesses against competitors engaging in false and misleading representations and descriptions.

• There may have been some concern as to what was meant by the requirement of interstate commerce.

As a result, it has generally been left to trade associations such as the Jewelers' Vigilance Committee to bring the private cause of action where the Federal Trademark Commission has failed or refused to act, since there is no private right of action under Section 5 of the Federal Trade Commission Act.

The purpose of the Lanham Act, and particularly the purpose of Section 43(a), is remedial. Thus, when the Trademark Review Committee—established by the United States Trademark Association to review the Lanham Act on the 40th anniversary of its passage—reviewed how the courts have interpreted the section and how companies have used the section, it was recognized that it was appropriate not

only to clarify the statutory language to accord with judicial interpretation, but—as noted earlier—also to strengthen the section to better serve the intended purpose: promotion of fair dealing to protect competitors as well as consumers from deceptive trade practices.

The revision of Section 43(a) proposed by the Trademark Review Committee would have added a provision expressly making omission of material information from advertising a violation of the act and also making a violation the use of a designation or representation likely to disparage or tarnish a mark used by another or to dilute the "distinctiveness" of another's mark.

During the legislative process, the provisions with respect to material omissions, disparagement and tarnishment and dilution were deleted because of first Amendment considerations. The advertising community, in particular, expressed the fear that even truthful comparative advertising could be subject to suit and that it would be impossible to advertise a product without so many qualifications and caveats as to preclude effective advertising.

While the express prohibition of material omissions was deleted, precedent which may continue to develop establishes that material omissions may violate Section 43(a) where the representations made create a false or misleading impression which would be dispelled by the information withheld: that is, that the stones are not D flawless or that the stones are not offered by an affiliate of an international cartel.

Hands Off:
When Friendliness Goes Too Far

October 1988

"Excuse me, cutie." Wilson Sharpe stroked his hands across Ophelia Goodbodie's back as he passed her at the gift counter. "I need to get some gift wrap."

Ophelia stiffened. Her normally cheerful face tightened and her sunny smile faded. This was too much. When she first began to work for Jezebel's Fine Jewelry, she thought Wilson, the diamond salesman, was one of those "too charming" types, but she didn't mind his attention at first. After 1 1/2 years, however, she considered his sexist comments and innuendoes more annoying than charming.

But right now, Ophelia was more worried about Wilson's hands than his words. Today's incident was just one of too many times recently when his hands were where they shouldn't be. She was almost afraid to be in the store alone with him.

Wilson disappeared into the back room in search of the gift wrap. Ophelia glanced around the store, fidgeting nervously with a silver bowl. Only Wilson's customer was in the store, but with no other employees up front she couldn't

leave the counter unattended. Suddenly, with a sigh of relief, she spied Henrietta Creekee, a long-time Jezebel's salesperson, returning from an errand.

"Please," she called to Henrietta. "Watch the store for me for just a moment until Wilson gets back from wrapping this customer's purchase." Henrietta, noting tension on Ophelia's face and urgency in her voice, glanced toward the wrapping room. She occasionally overheard Wilson's remarks to Ophelia, and correctly guessed he was the source of the pretty girl's distress.

"Of course, dear. Is everything all right? You seem rather distressed," she said gently.

"I'm OK. I just need to take care of something," Ophelia said.

Time to act: Ophelia knocked timidly on Hamilton Waltham's door. She wasn't quite sure how to approach her boss. She didn't know whether Ham was aware of Wilson's actions toward her, or even whether he would believe her.

Maybe he was one of those men who thought women "asked for it" by being provocative. In either case, Ham and Wilson were friends; this wouldn't be easy.

"Come in," called Ham.

Ophelia stuck in her head. "Do you have a moment?" she asked.

Ham really didn't, but her tone of voice caused him concern. He put down his pen.

"Of course. Come in, sit down. What's on your mind?" he asked.

Ophelia fidgeted with her skirt, wrinkling it between her sweaty palms. Where did she begin?

Ham noticed her distress. "What's wrong, Ophelia? It must be something big."

Suddenly, it seemed easier.

"It is," she said. "It's Wilson. He has a habit of making these sly remarks every now and then. Maybe he doesn't really mean anything and maybe it's just his way to flirt around. But some of his comments are starting to upset me."

"Yes, I've overheard him," replied Ham. "I've asked him before to please tone down his banter."

"Well, that's not all," she rushed on.

Ham caught his breath. Uh, oh, he thought. He leaned forward and looked at Ophelia intently. "What are you saying?"

"Well, he hasn't really . . .well, I mean . . . ," Ophelia worried with her skirt a little more.

"What exactly has he been doing? I want to know everything!" Ham barked.

Ophelia looked up in alarm. Seeing her expression, Ham quickly assured her he wasn't angry with her, but was extremely concerned.

"Well, he's been sort of touching me a lot, and I don't think it's quite right."

"Touching you how? And when? And where?"

"Well, if he has to pass behind me at the counter, and he wants me to move over a little, he sort of rubs my back instead of just tapping my shoulder. And once or twice, I swear I felt his hand brush against my . . . umm . . . rear end. That kind of stuff."

"How long?"

"About a month now."

"Why didn't you come in sooner?"

"Well, at first I thought it was just coincidence, since it didn't happen all the time. But then it got bolder and more frequent and I realized it wasn't coincidence. I know he's a friend of yours, and I didn't want to make a big deal until I was sure it was really happening."

Ham sat back thoughtfully. "Did you ask him to stop?"

"No. I know I should have, but I still feel like he's a boss or something, and I was really uncomfortable talking back to him."

"Well, I guess I can understand your reluctance, but friend or not, he's still an employee. If he's stepping out of line, it's my responsibility to know about it. And I want you, young lady, to remember that I believe in fairness and honesty. That is Jezebel's way of doing business with the customer and it's my way of doing business with my employees!"

"I know. But this is awfully awkward!"

"Yes, I know it is. And for the record, yes, I have been a little concerned about Wilson's attitude. But I had no idea he had gone that far. You'd better believe I'm going to speak with him!"

"And for future reference, Wilson may be senior staff member, but he is not your boss. If he needs to be told to get in line, then tell him exactly that," Ham said emphatically.

"Thank you," Ophelia responded. "That's a relief. But truthfully, I'm dreading having to work this Saturday—Wilson and I will be the only two here."

"He won't bother you. I can assure you that."

"Not now, he won't, I'm sure. But it's still going to be awkward, since he'll know I came to talk to you."

"Don't worry about that. I'll handle it."

Confrontation: Wilson closed Ham's door, wondering about the unusual summons. He was a little uneasy; rarely did a request for a private word in the office mean good news.

"Sit down, Will," said Ham. "I've had a little news that is very disturbing. I've asked you before to please stop making sexist remarks and to behave yourself around the ladies."

"Has a customer complained about me?" asked Wilson, alarmed.

"No. Ophelia has. She says you've been making passes at her recently. I know you've always liked to flirt. But she finds some of your comments offensive, and she says your hands are wandering."

"I haven't touched her! Except maybe to ask her to move or something. Why, I would no more lay hands on her than on my own daughter. If I've ever touched her, it was just to get her attention. It certainly wasn't meant any other way."

"Regardless. I want whatever you are doing to stop immediately. You're a valued employee and a trusted friend, Will. I don't want to have to take disciplinary action. But unless you watch your hands, I'm going to have to.

"Now, let's consider the matter closed. You two are working by yourselves on Saturday, and I assured her there will be no reason for her to feel uncomfortable—either because you're flirting with her or because you're avoiding her. I want business as usual, and let this be the end of the issue."

Saturday came and went without incident, as did the next 1 $^1/_2$ months. By October, thoughts were turning to Christmas. Ham was planning selling strategies and decorations, and a bonus incentive plan was in place. Business was brisk, thanks to his new holiday layaway promotion. Indeed, all was well or almost all.

Wilson was in top form, selling more diamonds than ever and feeling on top of the world. Whistling a jaunty tune, he slid his hands over Ophelia's hips and gently moved her aside. "Excuse me, sweetie, but I have to get a bag right where you're standing," he said.

Ophelia, stunned, jumped out of the way. She reddened, hoping none of the customers had seen Wilson's hands. Nobody seemed to notice.

As the day wore on, Wilson's hands continued to wander. Ophelia resolved to speak with him about it at the end of the day. If he didn't stop, she would tell Ham. After closing, as Wilson was putting rings into the safe, Ophelia approached him.

"Wilson, I didn't appreciate your comments today. And I prefer that you kept your hands off me!"

Wilson, shocked, straightened. "Come on, Ophelia, you can't honestly believe I'm trying to put the moves on you. Why, you're no older than my daughter! I'm sorry if I insulted you somehow, but believe me, it wasn't meant in any way other than a simple, polite gesture." He looked hurt.

Ophelia was confused. She felt badly about hurting Wilson's feelings. Maybe he really *didn't* mean anything maybe it was just his nature. That night, over a cup of hot chocolate, Ophelia told her mother about the problem.

"I remember Wilson from high school," said Mrs. Goodbodie. "He had a silver tongue then, and it seems he hasn't improved much since. I never much cared for him myself, but a lot of girls just ate up his charm like a cat with a cream crock. You watch yourself. Did you talk to Mr. Waltham? He seems like a fair sort of fellow."

Ophelia told her mother about the talk she'd had with Ham in August. Her mother advised her to go to Ham again, and to call Rosalynn Tibbets, a lawyer and longtime family friend. Mrs. Goodbodie thought Ophelia could use some legal advice, and Ophelia agreed.

Legal advice: Roz looked at Ophelia. "It seems that if this Wilson Sharpe doesn't change his tune, Hamilton Waltham could have some trouble."

"Ham? I just want to stop Wilson, not make trouble for Ham!" cried Ophelia.

"I know," Roz responded. "But he is responsible for making sure Wilson ceases harassing you. If he doesn't take action to stop it, you could take legal action against him. Sexual harassment is a violation of Title VII of the Civil Rights Act of 1964. Federal guidelines list three criteria for determining whether certain behaviors constitute sexual harassment."

The guidelines:

1) If an employer explicitly or implicitly makes submission to his or her advances a condition of employment.

2) If the employer bases employment decisions such as raises or promotions on whether the worker submits to his or her advances.

3) If such conduct by the employer constitutes an unreasonable interference with the worker's job performance or creates an intimidating hostile or offensive work environment.

"Now," continued Roz, "sometimes improper conduct is verbal, such as abusive or derogatory comments or demeaning jokes or slurs. Sometimes it's physical, such as outright assault or physical interference with normal work or movement. And sometimes it's visual, such as hanging offensive posters in the lunchroom.

"Also, illegal harassment doesn't always mean a man harassing a woman. It can be the other way around, or it can be two people of the same sex. The law applies in all cases."

She explained their state's procedure for sexual harassment cases. She said a harassed employee in Oklahoma should first confront the perpetrator's immediate supervisor. If not satisfied, the employee should go to that person's supervisor, and so on up the ladder. If the problem isn't resolved at the top level, the employee has several options.

If the business has 15 or more employees, the person can file a complaint with the local Human Rights Commission or Equal Employment Opportunity Commission. Complaints usually are made against *the company,* not the individual accused of harassment, but the individual is named in the complaint. Oklahoma doesn't award punitive damages in harassment cases. (Workers in other states should inquire about their state's policy.)

Oklahoma businesses with fewer than 15 employees such as Jezebel's fall outside the commissions' jurisdiction. Thus the employee must file a harassment suit in civil court.

"You say you've gone to Ham once, and he warned Wilson. Was it a verbal or written warning?" asked Roz.

"I don't know. Verbal, I think. It was behind closed doors, so I'm not really positive," Ophelia said. "But the store's discipline policy is a verbal warning the first time, a written warning the second, then probation and then you're fired."

Roz digested this. "Well, it seems that Ham enforced discipline according to store policy. He has taken care of his responsibility so far. At this point, you have to go back and tell him there's still a problem. After that, if he doesn't cooperate, you come back to me. I also recommend that you keep written documentation of each event as it happens—what is said or done, where and when and whether there were witnesses."

She got up to walk Ophelia to the door. "Unfortunately, laws against this sort of thing don't change some people," she said. "There are a lot of old dogs who just won't learn new tricks.

"It's miserable for the person being harassed. And sadly, even with a legal way to fight back, it's still often the victim who suffers. It's uncomfortable to keep working for people you've sued, and new employers frown on hiring people who file lawsuits. It just stinks."

Repeat performance: Two weeks later, on a Monday morning, Ophelia unlocked Jezebel's front door and turned off the burglar alarm. As she hung her coat in the wrapping room, she heard the front door open and saw Wilson enter with coffee and a bag of donuts.

"Wilson! What are you doing in here so early?" she said as he walked toward her. "You don't usually work on Mondays!" Ophelia's stomach knotted. He knew Monday was her day to open the store and that she usually worked alone until noon.

"Came in to get some paperwork done, honey. Thought you'd like to have a little breakfast with me," he said, waving the bag of donuts temptingly.

"Thanks, Wilson, but I'm not hungry. Mom made me a nice big breakfast before I left home."

"Aww, come on. At least keep me company while *I* eat, then."

Ophelia shifted uncomfortably. "No, Wilson, I have to get to work," she said in a low voice.

"Come on, cutie, you're not still scared of me now, are you?" Wilson somehow managed to sneer and look endearing at the same time. He chucked her under the chin.

Ophelia drew back, alarmed. Wilson was blocking the only entrance to the wrapping room and she was trapped. She glanced nervously around the room, spotting a pair of scissors on the counter. She relaxed visibly.

Wilson read her thoughts. "Hey! Whoa there, babe. No need to get violent! I'm just trying to be friendly. If you don't want a donut, I'll save it for someone else!" He stepped back. Ophelia darted out and began to ready the store for opening.

Later, as Wilson left for lunch, Ham arrived. He was in a great mood. A visit with his accountant proved that his plans were working—store profits were up nicely from the previous year. He was too engrossed in thought to wonder why Wilson was in on a Monday. Whistling merrily, he strode to his office. Ophelia was right on his heels.

"Good morning, Ophelia! What can I do for you? Hey, who's minding the store?" Ham suddenly remembered that Ophelia was the only one who worked Monday mornings. He was very strict about not leaving the counter unattended at any time.

"It's Wilson again."

"What's Wilson again . . . oh, no! He's not even supposed to be in here on Mondays!" Ham now remembered passing his diamond salesman.

Quickly, Ophelia related the morning's incident. Then, sensing that Ham wanted to be alone, she returned to the counter.

Ham slammed his fist on the desk.

"He's going to find himself on the street in a minute! But I can't lose him during the holidays!! What am I going to do?" Ham was fully aware of his position and of the fact that Ophelia could very easily bring a lawsuit against Jezebel's. The legal costs alone would just about finish the business, not to mention what the publicity would do!

Tempers unleashed: "Wilson!! Come into my office!" Ham, too angry to worry about professional demeanor, bellowed across the store.

"Hey, where's the fire? Let me finish adding these figures!" Wilson called back.

"NOW!!"

Wilson shrugged, ambled over and stuck his head around Ham's doorjamb. "Yes, master?" he joked.

Ham was in no mood for jokes "SIT DOWN!" he shouted.

"Hey, no need to holler. My hearing is fine! Who put a bee in your hat today?"

"What the hell did you think you were doing with Ophelia this morning?"

"What? Nothing! I offered her a donut, that's all! She got all huffed up. Thinks I'm gonna rape her or something. I tell you, Ham, that girl's got a real complex! Man, this women's lib stuff makes even old-fashioned courtesy illegal!"

Ham clenched his fists behind the desk. This was no time for a major dispute, not with Christmas a mere eight weeks away. He took a deep breath.

"Wilson, what you call friendly can be offensive to others," said Ham. "I've told you before that some of your remarks are sexist and inappropriate, and I've told you about Ophelia. Do you realize how much trouble she could make if she decided to sue you, me or the store?"

Wilson fidgeted. Lawsuits! He hadn't thought about lawsuits. He admitted he was a flirt and that he really didn't take Ophelia seriously. He thought she was a harmless place to practice his charm.

Ham shoved a piece of paper across the desk.

"What's this?" asked Wilson.

"It's a written warning. It spells out all the charges Ophelia has made, and states that you have been warned to cease and desist. Sign it."

"Wait a minute. This has only her version of the story!"

"It also has yours. It is not an admission of guilt to her charges, but it is an official warning that your behavior will have to change. Now sign it!"

"And if I don't?"

"You'll be signing employment applications elsewhere."

Wilson glared at Ham, grabbed the pen and signed.

"Good. I'm glad you did sign. You know you're more than just an employee and how much I rely on your ability. Now, just please be extra careful with your charm, especially around Ophelia."

"Whatever you say, boss. I still say she's too sensitive, but if you want me to walk on eggs, then eggs it is."

Better times: One evening a few months later, Ham locked the door and trudged through the twilight snow to his car. He smiled to himself Jezebel's had had a record Christmas season, an innovative cleaning and repair promotion was helping the store through the midwinter slumps and he was looking forward to delivery of his spring merchandise. He had lots of new plans, and the staff was eager to begin them.

The Wilson-Ophelia incident seemed long buried. Wilson had even taken it upon himself to apologize for his behavior. In fact, his whole demeanor had undergone a subtle change. He was still as charming as ever toward female customers, but there was a new respect in the way he addressed them. His increased sales proved that respect was a key element to selling.

Hiring?
The New Immigration Law
Affects Your Business

July 1987

Your ancestors may have come over on the Mayflower but, if you're an employer, the Immigration Reform and Control Act of 1986 (IRCA) affects you as much as any illegal alien.

Why? The IRCA—which aims to stem illegal immigration by making it a crime to hire unauthorized aliens says it's up to *you* to verify in writing that your employees are authorized to work in the U.S.

And Uncle Sam isn't kidding. In June, the Immigration and Naturalization Service (INS) began issuing warnings to employers violating IRCA. After Sept. 1, repeat offenders face fines escalating to $10,000 and six months in jail for each violation.

419

Here's what you, as an employer, must know.

What must I do? Employers must complete an Employment Eligibility Verification statement ("Form I-9") for each new employee hired after *Nov. 6, 1986* (the date the law was enacted).

This must be done for temporary as well as full-time workers.

The form must be signed by the employee, who states under penalty of perjury that all information he has provided is "genuine," and by the employer, who states under penalty of perjury that the worker, "to the best of my knowledge, is authorized to work in the United States."

Are any businesses exempt? No. Every firm, whether it be a Mom-and-Pop jeweler or IBM, must comply. Only "casual" workers such as babysitters or domestic help in a private home are excluded.

Does IRCA affect only foreign-born workers? No. Everyone hired after Nov. 6 must be checked. Otherwise, employers violate IRCA's anti-discrimination clauses, which also prohibit bosses from firing or not hiring people simply because they speak a foreign language or "look" foreign.

When must I do this? Form I-9 must be completed no later than three days after a person starts work, or before the end of the first working day for anyone hired to work less than three days.

A new Form I-9 isn't necessary for anyone rehired within a year, provided that person is still authorized to work in the U.S.

Do I keep the I-9? Yes. An employer must keep a Form I-9 on file for each employee, available for inspection any time (with three days notice) by the INS and/or Department of Labor.

INS and DOL officers may inspect or take such files (provided they leave a receipt for each I-9 form) without providing a subpoena or a warrant.

How long do I keep an I-9 on file? Three years or for one year after an employee leaves, whichever is longer.

What must employees do? They must have documents establishing their identity and proving they're authorized to work in the U.S.

These can be a U.S. passport; an INS Certificate of Citizenship; an unexpired foreign passport stamped "processed for I-155" or a Form I94, with an unexpired work authorization stamp; an Alien Registration Card, with a photo, or an unexpired INS work permit.

If they don't have any of these, they can use a combination of other documents, including (to prove work authorization) a Social Security card (unless it says it's not valid for U.S. employment); a birth certificate from any state; a Report of U.S. Citizenship Abroad, from the State Department; or a Form I-94, with an employment authorization stamp and (to prove identity) a state-issued driver's license or ID, with photo, or a Notice of Discharge from the U.S. military.

The employer may, if he chooses, make copies of these documents to attach with an employee's Form I-9.

How does this affect the way I hire people? During interviews you may ask job applicants if they're U.S. citizens. If not, ask if they're lawfully authorized to work in the U.S.

Where do I get a Form I-9? The INS was expected to mail them to all tax-paying employers in June. They're also available from INS regional offices and Border Patrol offices. Or the Government Printing Office (Washington D.C. 20402, (202)783-3238) is selling them for $13 per 100.

What do I do with employees who are illegal aliens? They may be eligible for legal resident status if they've lived in the U.S. since Jan. 1, 1982. Urge them to seek aid from the INS and provide them with documentation of their work history. (Such records, says the INS, only establish an applicant's eligibility, and won't be used against an employer.)

If the person was hired before Nov. 6, 1987, you aren't subject to penalties, though the person is.

If hired after Nov. 6, you face no penalty *if* they apply for legalization and seek interim work authorization from the INS while the case is pending. They must do so by Sept. 1, and it should be noted on the Form I-9.

Otherwise, if you knowingly hire an illegal alien, you face stiff sanctions.

What are the penalties for violating the IRCA? Employers who knowingly hire an illegal alien will get a warning. After that, they face civil fines up to $2,000 per worker for a first offense; up to $5,000 for a second; up to $10,000 for a third. Fines keep climbing for repeat offenders, who also face a six-month jail term. And after May 31, 1988, there will be no warnings.

Where can I get more information? Call your regional INS office. Check the telephone under "Ask Immigration." Write the Immigration and Naturalization Service, 425 Eye St., N.W., Washington D.C. 20536. Attn: Employer Facts. Or call (800) 777-7700.

Chapter 10

SECURITY & INSURANCE

*Protect Your Employees,
Yourself And Everything
You've Worked So Hard To Achieve*

Employee Violence: Are You Prepared?

May 1995

Jewelers are well aware of the risk of violence during a holdup. But recent years have seen an increase in another type of workplace violence: attacks by other employees or ex-employees.

The good news is that employers can take some measures to minimize the risk of employee violence on the job, says Jack Jones, a licensed industrial psychologist and vice president of research for London House, a leading developer of human resource assessments.

Here are his suggestions:

• Implement pre-employment screening. Thorough pre-screening can alert employers to job candidates who might be prone to violent behavior at work. The interview procedure should include background checks that could uncover a history of on-the-job violence and drug screening.

• Create anti-harassment policies. "We tend to think of employee violence in terms of rape and murder, but even incidents of vandalism or arguing with coworkers and customers are aggressive acts," says Jones. "Employers should promote a culture in which there is zero tolerance for any form of violence. Companies should create and enforce policies that explain the repercussions for committing a violent act.

• Train managers to recognize high-risk employees. All managers should understand the psychology of aggression and be able to recognize the warning signs. Managers with good listening and conflict-resolution skills are better prepared to calm a disgruntled employee before he or she becomes violent.

• Establish a threat-and-incident management team of employees to plan how to handle threats of violence.

• If violence occurs, employees should know what to do to help an injured person, what emergency telephone numbers to call for police and ambulance, and how to calm traumatized customers.

"Employees spend the better part of their day at work," says Jones. "They need to feel a sense of security and that their employers are concerned about their well-being."

London House, 9701 W. Higgins Rd., Rosemont, Ill. 60018; (800) 221-8378, ext. 3349.

Knock Knock: Most Jewelers Open The Door To Theft

March 1995

A 1994 Labor Day weekend burglary of Tiffany's in New York City unnerved some jewelers. "If Tiffany with all its security can be robbed, what chance do the rest of us have?" asked a jeweler interviewed on a TV news show.

But it was violation of a simple security procedure—not Tiffany's sophisticated security equipment—that gave thieves access to the store. A security guard, who wasn't part of the plot, simply opened the door and let them in.

Incredible? Maybe not. JCK wondered how common it is for jewelers to ignore such simple security procedures as keeping the door locked after closing and doing background checks on new or promoted employees. We polled more than 400 U.S. retail jewelers—from mom-and-pop stores to multi-million-dollar chains—and reviewed the results with John Kennedy, president of the Jewelers' Security Alliance, and Ronald R. Harder, president of Jewelers Mutual Insurance Co.

The results of the poll shocked the experts and showed that many jewelers make themselves easy targets by ignoring common-sense precautions. The results have "serious" implications, says Kennedy, because business people who respond

423

to such polls tend to be serious and know what they should be doing. "If these people aren't taking basic security measures," he says, "then lapses in security among jewelers in general are more serious than indicated by these [results]."

Here are highlights from JCK's poll.

Knock, knock: The Tiffany incident occurred because a security guard let in a fellow employee and two companions after the store closed. Two out of three jewelers polled (68%) say they do the same thing. That shocks Harder and Kennedy. "It's extremely dangerous," says Kennedy. "I'm surprised that so many people can be so lax [because that] frequently is how and when robberies of jewelers occur."

One in five jewelers say they would open the door for a utility or repair person, one in three for a postal employee and more than half for "a customer" or a security or police officer. Many of the jewelers contend this isn't as foolhardy as it might seem. They say they'd open the door only if they knew the individual or if the person could show identification.

Kennedy sees it differently. ID cards can be stolen or faked, he points out. The Tiffany incident proves that simply knowing someone doesn't guarantee security. And even if a jeweler opens the door for a trusted friend or staff member, any thief who is lurking outside has a chance to push the person aside and run into the store.

A number of jewelers agree. A third say they never let in anyone, no matter who it is, before opening the store or after closing it. One Texas jeweler says emphatically that if his "employees aren't in here by 8:55 a.m., they are locked out until the cases are loaded."

That's the type of rigid rule that JSA recommends.

Two by two: Three out of four jewelers say they always open and close the store with at least two people. "Having one person open while another watches from nearby really does deter 'bad guys,'" says Kennedy. "Everyone should do it."

But the fact that 24% say they don't disturbs Harder. "That's dangerous," he says. "Doing it alone leaves you or that staff person open to robbery or a hostage situation."

Some jewelers's staffs aren't big enough to double-team openings and closings. But even they can reduce risk, says Harder. "Ask a nearby merchant to watch when you open and close," he suggests. "And consider where you go in and out. Where is the store located? What's its exposure? Is it a back door? Can other people see you?"

Merchandise: Waiting until after you close the store to put away merchandise is a commonly accepted security rule of thumb. Yet almost half (45%) of the jewelers polled start before they close for the day. Do a few minutes either way really make a difference?

Yes, say Harder and Kennedy.

"Removing a percentage of merchandise not only leaves less available for sale," says Harder, "it also concentrates much of your merchandise in a small area and [leaves you open for] a possible large loss."

Adds Kennedy, "Nothing should be put away before closing. If you do, you not only have merchandise out [of the cases and vulnerable], but you also give [thieves] access to your open safe or vault. This is a terrific time for a robbery, theft or distraction theft."

Most jewelers polled put most or all merchandise away each night; half say the maximum value of any single item left overnight in a showcase is $250 or less. That's firmly within Jewelers Mutual guidelines. "We like to see all diamond merchandise, rings, gold chains—any high-value piece—put away," says Harder. "Anything under $250 can stay out."

While what goes in the vault each night depends on a jeweler's insurance requirements and inventory, Kennedy says it's smart to put away as much as possible. "If the jeweler does leave expensive things out overnight," he says, "then he needs extra protection against people who will try to break in."

Protection: Virtually all respondents have safes (and vaults) and alarm systems. After that, a gap develops in security equipment. Just over half of JCK panelists have video surveillance cameras and shatterproof window glass. One in four has buzz-in doors; one in seven has shatterproof showcase glass.

Harder and Kennedy say all jewelers should use video surveillance and showcases with shatterproof glass on the top and sides. "[The glass] is cost-effective and a great deterrent to robberies, thefts and smash-and-grabs," says Kennedy.

Personnel checks: Virtually all jewelers polled check the information that potential employees provide about their previous employment. And three out of four do background checks on people they hire for, or promote to, supervisory or managerial positions.

JSA strongly recommends both procedures. "Anyone who has access to valuable goods should have some background checks done [if they are promoted to a managerial post or higher]—even if they've been around 10 or 15 years," says Kennedy. "Today, you can hire services with computerized links with state courthouses to do background checks."

When it comes to written security procedures, barely half the jewelers polled (49%) have them. Interestingly, almost the same number believe their employees know the procedures "very well."

Even though most jewelers review such procedures with their staffs once every quarter or more, Harder finds it "disturbing" that only half have actually put them in writing. "When you put these guidelines in writing, it's concrete and specific," he says. "Everyone—including new employees—knows exactly what to do."

Written guidelines don't have to be long, adds Kennedy. A couple of pages are sufficient to spell out what your staff should do when opening or closing the store; taking out, showing and putting away merchandise; reacting to an emergency such as a robbery; and reacting to the presence of a suspicious person in the store.

The toll: In view of other findings, it's not surprising that one in three jewelers (34%) says he or she had at least one merchandise loss in the past year.

Burglaries and armed robberies together accounted for a third of these losses. Distraction thefts and smash-and-grabs produced a majority. But most surprising, and unsettling to the experts, is that 20% of jewelers polled blame their losses on "mysterious disappearance."

"That's very significant," says Harder. "If one in five jewelers can't even explain a [merchandise] loss, then something's wrong with those security procedures. They're not as effective or defined as they possibly can be.

"There's enough loss in a jewelry store business without 'mysterious disappearances' that could be prevented with more attention to security."

Part-Timers 'Out-Steal' Full-Timers

January 1995

Part-time retail employees commit more internal thefts than full-timers, and their thefts are more costly to employers, according to a study by Reid Psychological Systems, an employee testing company in Chicago, Ill.

The nationwide study asked more than 15,000 employees about their thefts of cash and merchandise in the previous three years. The differences between part-time and full-time employees were substantial.

Part-timers stole 33% more cash from their employers (an average $414 vs. $311). They also took 47% more in merchandise than full-timers ($368 vs. $251). On average, this means each part-timer accounted for combined merchandise and cash losses of $782 over the three years, 39% more than the $562 for full-timers.

And these figures are likely to be understated because the survey focused on admitted thefts, says Reid President Stephen Coffman.

"This study clearly confirms that employers need to be on guard against theft by part-time workers," says Coffman. "Employers who count on employees to handle cash and merchandise need to reevaluate their screening procedures for part-time as well as full-time employees in order to find solutions to employee theft and other counterproductive behavior."

Experts Debate Use Of Guns

October 1994

Should a jeweler buy a gun to use in defense against robbers?

No, according to John J. Kennedy, an attorney and president of the Jewelers' Security Alliance, New York, N.Y.

Yes, if he or she so chooses and prepares properly, according to Emanuel Kapelsohn, an attorney and president of the Peregrine Corp., a defense consulting company in Bowers, Pa.

Kennedy and Kapelsohn debated the emotional issue in a seminar titled "Should I Carry a Gun?" held during The JCK Show, held in Las Vegas in June.

"This is a question of life or death," said Kennedy. "JSA is 100% against jewelers having guns. Not only can they result in injury or death to the jeweler, but may also subject you to civil and criminal liability."

Homicides in jewelry-industry robberies in the past decade total 221, he said, and only 30% of the dead were robbers. The rest were jewelers, customers and other innocent bystanders. And most of the robbers who died were killed by police, not jewelers.

In 1993, 273 retail jewelry stores were robbed and 138 of the cases involved violence. Of the 16 jewelers who were injured or killed, 11 resisted, three didn't resist and the resistance was uncertain in two cases. "Should you resist or cooperate with the robber—that's the key issue," he said. "We believe you should cooperate. If you do, your chances of not getting hurt increase dramatically." Kennedy cited a national study done for the National Association of Convenience Stores that showed 82% of people who actively resist an armed robber are killed.

But he stressed it's not a numbers game, rather a matter of life and death. Putting faces to the statistics, Kennedy showed videotapes of real armed robberies and related a story about a California incident last year. A jeweler, his wife and his 11-year-old son were in the store when an armed robber entered. The jeweler reached for a gun, but the robber fired first, killing the wife and son but not the jeweler. "Before the jeweler reached for the gun, there was absolutely no indication the robber was going to shoot anyone," said Kennedy. "The jeweler has to live with that the rest of his life."

He advised jewelers who think they are a quick-draw to remember that an armed robber already has a gun drawn and pointed. His advice in the event of a robbery:

• Obey the orders of the robber. Don't say or do anything—even raise your hands—unless told to do so.

• Don't try to disarm a robber, reach for a concealed weapon or reach for a holdup alarm. Assume the robber will shoot without hesitation.

• Expect to be threatened. "I'll kill you if you make a move" is a typical threat. Expect it. Keep calm.

• Expect to be forced into the backroom or bathroom. Expect to be tied up or handcuffed and told to lie on the floor. Do as you are told.

425

A different view: "It's extremely common for people in the jewelry industry to keep and carry guns," said Kapelsohn. "But it has been largely a taboo subject."

He agreed with Kennedy that gun use is not a numbers game, but he urged jewelers to consider not only the odds of being shot but also the consequences. When training smaller police departments, Kapelsohn often gets questions about the need for training and is asked how often a police officer is shot and killed. "'Just once,' I reply."

Kapelsohn told of a robbery in a Windsor, N.C., market last year during which robbers emptied the cash register and safe, forced employees and customers to lie two deep, and shot some in the head and slit the throats of others. "If compliance with a robber will most likely secure your safety, by all means do it," he said. "But in cases like this, it doesn't suffice.

"I am not here to recommend that anyone keep or carry a gun—that's an extremely personal choice," he said. "What I am here to do is to say that a firearm is one of many, many options in a total plan of self-protection and self-defense. And if you make the choice to keep a gun, there are certain responsibilities you have to accept."

Those responsibilities include training in safety, the law of self-defense, marksmanship/gun handling, tactics and the legal liability of gun use. In addition, you have to prepare yourself mentally for the ethical, moral and emotional considerations of using a gun against another person. And you have to accept the responsibility for safety, good judgment and competence in gun use.

He also cautioned: "The only reason you should ever think of using a gun against another human being is in defense of your life or some other innocent person's life—not defense of property."

To avert the need for a gun in the first place, Kapelsohn advised:

• Deterrence. The starting point for defending yourself should be deterring robbers by the layout of your store, by your business habits, by the locks on the doors, by alarms, by cameras, by the way you admit people into the store, by the hours you're open and by managing the number of people on the display floor at any one time. "You don't have to make it impossible to rob your store," he said. "You just have to make it harder to rob your store than the store down the street."

• Avoidance. If it's dangerous to make a cash deposit at a certain time at a certain bank, choose a different time or a different bank. Avoid situations that are most likely to result in a threat.

• Study. Know when you can and can't defend yourself before it happens. Can you successfully defend yourself against someone with a gun to your head? "Of course not," he said. "But when you say no normal person with normal training can possibly effectively defend himself against criminals, that's just not true. Scholarly studies show that 1 million to 2 million private people use guns to successfully defend themselves against criminals each year."

When should you resist? "The time to resist is when the robber has already started to hurt people," he said. "Once you let someone tie you up, you have relinquished all options to protect yourself.

"No one is in a better position to decide what risks you're willing to take than you. There is no professional on the face of this earth who can supplant your right and your ability to make that choice. The basic rule of thumb is to do what you think is most likely to result in your safety and the safety of your loved ones."

How To Spot And Stop Distraction Thefts

September 1994

Sneak thefts by trained thieves occur in scores of U.S. jewelry stores and result in losses of more than $2 million annually, says the Jewelers' Security Alliance, New York, N.Y.

Often, the retailer doesn't know a theft has occurred until the thieves have left the store. It's only when merchandise is missed or when daily surveillance videotapes are reviewed that the theft is spotted. Even then, many such crimes go unreported because jewelers assume it's an internal theft or the amount is covered by insurance, says JSA.

Yet such thefts can be deterred. It's a matter of knowing how the thieves work and being alert, says Robert J. Frank, manager of JSA's crime section and a former New York City police detective. "Most criminals know more about

your business than you know about theirs," he says. "Security is a state of mind. If you and your people are looking for them, you can outsmart them."

Distraction thefts: As many as 3,000 people in the U.S. are members of jewelry theft gangs, say the U.S. Department of Justice and the Federal Bureau of Investigation. These gangs—numbering anywhere from several dozen to hundreds—have two primary functions:

• Distraction thefts in jewelry stores.

• Thefts from traveling salespeople and others who carry jewelry on the road.

Almost all gang members are South American, primarily from Colombia, say authorities, but also from Peru, Ecuador and Chile. (Some Russians may be working with them on the West Coast, add the authorities.) "There is evidence" the gangs may be connected to Colombian drug lords, says Frank. And a few may be linked to South American terrorist groups.

The gangs are so well-organized that many tour the country on a circuit, committing several thefts over a few days in one town, then moving on when word spreads about their presence.

They have a strict chain of command, says Frank. Bosses are called "dons," their lieutenants "hombres." Each boss has as many as half a dozen hombres. Each hombre may control three to six groups of "workers," who do the actual thefts.

Bosses and hombres split proceeds from the thefts, while workers are paid a daily wage. Workers never meet a boss.

"These aren't poor aliens from across the border who steal to eat, though they are trained to say so, if caught," says Frank. "They are well-trained, well-paid professional thieves who live well in South America and enter the U.S. with fraudulent documents."

Job descriptions: Each worker has a specific job assigned by his hombre, who picks the target, decides what to steal and how to do it. There are four jobs:

• The "distractor"—and there may be several—enters a store first and distracts the clerk's attention away from the area where the theft will occur.

• The "stall" distracts any other salespeople who come on the sales floor.

• The "cannon," "pick" or "jostler" commits the theft, often audaciously. He will lean over, quickly duck under or go behind a display case to steal a tray of jewelry or open a showcase when no salesperson is looking.

• The "mule" receives the jewelry from the cannon to carry immediately after the theft.

The hombre usually stays outside the store and quickly arranges bond and bail if his workers are caught.

While gang members have very little formal education, they are trained to steal in a "crime school" (authorities believe at least one school has relocated from South America to Canada) and get hands-on training in malls in the continental U.S. and Puerto Rico.

The thieves are nonviolent, at least in sneak thefts (see sidebar). No violence has been reported against a jeweler or jeweler's staff in so-called distraction thefts in several years, says JSA. Bosses and hombres know violence would bring charges far more serious than larceny if a worker is caught. And the more serious the charge, the more likely police will be able to persuade the worker to reveal the name of his hombre in exchange for a lighter penalty, says Frank.

Male gang members are taught to be nonviolent in a brutal way. During training at crime school, an instructor punches the student unexpectedly in the face. Those who don't fight back can stay in school. In fact, a broken nose is one sign law enforcement officials use to identify a gang member.

(Following JSA policy, however, Frank and other JSA officials stress that if violence does occur, "if a weapon is pulled or used during a theft, *don't* resist.")

Spotting theft gangs: JSA identifies several characteristics of distraction thieves that jewelers should be aware of:

• They usually target small stores with small staffs. They case a store first—often using a child or teenager, alone or with an adult—to check the location of security cameras, the number of clerks and where high-end items are kept.

Alternatively, a group leader may come in first to pick what to steal before giving others a signal.

• They are 25 to 45 years old. The group may include one person as young as 10 or 12 for on-the-job training.

• Women involved in the gangs usually wear clothes with subdued colors, carry large purses and wear scarves or sweaters with which they can change their appearance. Men may carry a man's purse, briefcase or garment bag or something similar with which to conceal their actions or transport stolen items.

• They use vans or station wagons (borrowed or rented with fraudulent documents).

• They enter a store one at a time, within a few minutes. Be suspicious if five to seven Hispanic customers suddenly enter your store individually, especially if there were none previously. They usually enter during a slow time or when only one or two clerks are on the floor.

• Be alert to efforts to distract clerks and/or determine where high-end items are kept. One example: a female gang member tells a salesperson she must replace a large diamond lost from her ring, though close inspection may show the mounting never had a stone. "When the clerk goes to the diamonds, the gang immediately knows where they are kept," says Frank. Distractors then insist they need help in other parts of the store, leaving the cannon free to commit the theft.

• Be suspicious of customers who seem to signal each other with subtle hand, leg, eye or head signals.

If you have suspicions, simply refuse to do business, says Frank. Have an internal alert word or phrase—such as, "Has Mr. Clark's ring arrived yet?"—to call all your staff onto the floor. And make a point of calling police and saying, "There are some suspicious people here."

"If you stonewall them, they will leave immediately," says Frank. "And remember, always keep your showcases locked." In addition, notify JSA, police and your local network of jewelers.

Getting violent?

While members of jewelry theft gangs are generally nonviolent inside jewelry stores, authorities fear some may be getting more violent outside.

In-store distraction thefts aren't the only jewelry crime these groups commit. They also follow and rob salespeople and jewelers on the road. Since mid-1993, there has been "real violence" against traveling salespeople, says JSA's Robert Frank. At least one salesman was killed in November 1993 in San Francisco, for example.

Authorities suspect violence is committed by a small segment of the theft underworld, mainly Peruvians who may have links to the Shining Path terrorist group in Peru. The authorities think this segment also may be responsible for some recent violent thefts and armed robberies, not all of them against jewelers. Here are some guidelines to protect yourself:

• Be alert when salesmen visit your store. They may be followed by a gang member—often a young person—who will confirm the target *is* a traveling salesperson, then return to cohorts who commit the theft later. The young person may enter the store or watch from a window.

• Conduct business with traveling salespeople in your office or other out-of-sight section of the store so they don't have to display their wares on the counter.

• Ask an employee to check that nothing unusual is going on outside. ("A van with four or five heads watching the store would be unusual," says Frank dryly.) If anyone follows a salesperson when he or she leaves, contact them immediately. (JSA recommends that all traveling salespeople carry a cellular telephone.)

• Traveling salespeople should lock up their lines overnight with a local jeweler instead of taking them home or to a motel.

• Be careful yourself. "As soon as they identify someone as a jeweler or salesman, they assume every bag carried has jewelry in it and try to steal it," says Frank. "When you leave the store at night, don't carry anything that might have jewelry in it."

Shoplifters Take $7 Billion Yearly

April 1994

Retailers attribute a third of their retail shrinkage (loss) to shoplifting, says the 1993 National Retail Security Survey. Jewelers report the highest shrinkage rate.

The nationwide survey of 386 firms—ranging from supermarkets to jewelry stores—found that 1.88% of the $1.1 trillion in non-automotive retail sales in 1992 was lost to inventory shrinkage. That translates to more than $20.7 billion, with shoplifting accounting for $6.96 billion or a third of the total, says the study.

Retailers reporting the highest shrinkage rates were jewelry and optical stores, listed as a single category (4.93%), followed by auto parts stores (3.07%), recorded music/video stores (2.67%), discount stores (2.52%) and apparel stores (2.51%).

The study found that closed-circuit TV and electronic antishoplifting tags continue to gain popularity as shoplifting deterrents. Close to 40% of those interviewed now use electronic security tags. Almost 49% use CCTV; 20% of them plan to use it even more.

But survey respondents said eagle-eye employees remain the best deterrent. Of the shoplifters caught in 1992, sales-floor employees reported 57.7% of them. Security guards detected 26.1%, electronic surveillance showed 9.8% and other shoppers reported 4.3%.

Overall, retailers blamed 40.7% of their losses on employee theft. The most successful methods of combating this, they said, included coworker tip-offs, security audits and electronic surveillance. However, retailers prosecuted only 43.5% of the dishonest employees who were caught in the survey year, compared with 59.3% of shoplifters from the outside.

The survey was underwritten by Sensormatic Electronics Corp., which supplies loss prevention systems. It was conducted by Dr. Richard C. Hollinger, head of the Security Research Project of the University of Florida, with input from the University's Center for Retailing Education and Research, the National Retail Federation and Loss Prevention Specialists Inc.

Security Guards: Easing The Fear

March 1994

For some jewelers, all the closed-circuit television cameras and door buzzers in the world can't ease the gnawing fear that their next customer could be a smash-and-grab burglar or, worse, an armed robber.

And while many retailers feel safe when following procedural advice from their insurance company and the Jewelers' Security Alliance, others prefer an added element: security guards.

Deterrence is the primary reason jewelers hire uniformed guards for their store, according to a recent poll of the JCK Retail Jewelers Panel. While only 8% use guards every day, 20% do so for special events and sales. Of the total 28%, three in four hire uniformed and armed guards. The same number feel the guards' presence has prevented crime in their stores.

"When we have a sale or event, there are just too many people in here for us to watch," says William Kingoff of Kingoff's Inc., Wilmington, N.C. Kingoff hires armed guards through a local detective agency, but requires that they not use their guns. "We don't want to risk hurting anybody."

Smart advice, according to JSA. An armed guard can become a liability if he or she is the "hero type" and decides to use a weapon. "You can have some violence and, at the very least, the robbers could take the gun," says Robert Frank, manager of JSA's crime section.

If you're thinking of hiring a security guard, says Frank, you first should assess your specific needs. If you have more customers than your employees can watch, or if your store layout hampers visibility, security guards could be the answer. If robbers travel in a gang in your city, however, a guard won't deter them.

If you determine a guard could help deter crime, ask your insurance company for its requirements, then call local law enforcement authorities for advice. Local police can suggest authorized security agencies and advise on how to hire a full-time guard. In addition, police in many areas of the U.S. are authorized to work off-duty as security guards. (In the JCK poll, 17% of jewelers who employ guards use off-duty police.)

You also should check with your state government regarding laws and licensing involving security guards. Beginning this year in New York, for example, a state law requires retailers who hire their own guards (and don't use a registered agency) to obtain a license. The law has strict provisions regarding training, fees and licensing and applies to any company that hires a guard.

For more information, contact your state government (listed in the telephone book) or JSA at (800) 537-0067.

Watch Out For Robbers With Mace

October 1993

Robbers used Mace or a similar substance to disable victims in a number of recent jewelry-store thefts, says the Jewelers' Security Alliance. In Tulsa, Okla., for example, three men sprayed clerks with Mace, then fled with 22 expensive watches. Police caught two of the suspects shortly afterward.

Mace is a chemical mixture in aerosol form that causes burning eye pain and respiratory irritation when sprayed in the face. To reduce the likelihood of all types of robberies, including those involving Mace, JSA offers these tips:

1. Use buzzers to admit customers.
2. Use and properly maintain store video surveillance equipment.
3. Spread valuable goods on display among different cases.
4. Keep particularly tempting goods in the safe.
5. Display merchandise in smash-resistant cases.
6. Don't admit anyone except employees to your store before or after business hours.
7. Be vigilant for people "casing" your store and report suspicions to police and to JSA.
8. Develop a neighborhood alert system to share warnings with other local jewelers.
9. Have at least two employees in the store at all times.
10. Don't open or close the store alone. One person should lock or unlock the doors while the other watches from a safe distance.

How Much Security Is Enough?

September 1993 Part I

How much security is enough?

Every jeweler should ask that question—when starting in business and as the business grows and the market changes. To find some answers, JCK recently talked with security and insurance experts. We described four types of independent jewelry stores and asked the experts to suggest the security and insurance coverage each ideally should have, based on factors such as size, inventory, sales and location.

On these pages, Thad L. Weber, a veteran jewelry store security consultant, provides most of the specific suggestions on security coverage. John Kennedy, president of the Jewelers' Security Alliance, tells what JSA believes each jeweler should have. Gary Draheim, vice president of underwriting at Jewelers Mutual Insurance, and other JMI underwriters outline basic insurance and security coverage. And Tom Prevas, another veteran jewelry store security expert, offers general input.

These suggestions are intended only as guidelines to help you plan or review your coverage. Individual needs vary from store to store and are affected by factors such as locale, population and merchandise.

The makeup of a store and its community greatly affects security and insurance needs. The price of insurance coverage also varies from state to state or town to town and with different levels of average inventory cost and off-premises exposure. But there are some specifics every jeweler should consider in planning and budgeting for security coverage, say the experts:

• UL testing—Use only equipment (including safes, alarm systems and break-resistant glass) tested, certified and rated by Underwriters Laboratory Inc., a 99-year-old non-profit product-testing organization and leading developer of safety standards for products (see sidebar, "Defining UL").

• Location—A jeweler with a street entrance has "somewhat more exposure" than a mall jeweler, for example, and must pay more attention to door and window protection, says Prevas.

• Inventory—You will need to know your average cost per item and your inventory price range in planning store security, says Prevas. This information helps to define a store—primarily low-end, middle market or high-end. "The needs are different for a store with an average cost per item of $50 and little high-end merchandise than one averaging $500 per item with items priced up to $30,000," he says.

• Motion detectors—It's "prudent" for a jewelry store to have motion detectors in every room and enclosed area, says Prevas. "These increase the probability of detecting a burglar no matter where he enters; limits his ability to move around undetected; and reduces the likelihood that he will be waiting inside the store when you arrive in the morning and turn off the alarm."

• Alarm systems—The store premises and the safe(s) should have alarm coverage. The safe should have "complete" protection (all six sides). "A contact on the door isn't protection, just supervision," says Prevas. "It simply tells the alarm company if the door has been shut at night, not if it's locked."

• CCTV—Experts say all jewelers should have properly installed and maintained closed-circuit video surveillance and recording equipment. Experience shows that CCTV deters robbery, says Prevas, but also provides evidence for police and is a management tool and record of daily activities for the store owner. He warns against installing dummy CCTV set-ups for appearance sake because "robbers can spot a fake system right away."

• Safes—Experts recommend a high-security UL-rated safe with complete protection. "This is a good time to buy a safe," says Prevas. "Because of the economic slowdown, there are a lot of safes on the market; you can buy new or used ones at very good prices." For example, a waist-high TRTL-30x6 that costs $5,000-$7,000 new can be bought used for $3,000-$4,000.

But Draheim cautions not to buy too much. "There is a point at which adding more security really doesn't add value or make the store any more secure," he says. Security and insurance consultants can help you determine where this point lies.

Following are examples of four types of independent, non-chain jewelry stores with the experts' recommendations for security and insurance coverage. Insurance is based on estimated minimal security needs; estimated costs are based on what each store can reasonably afford.

MALL STORE

This store is in an upscale mall between two major highways in a thriving middle-class suburban community. The area has another mall nearby, as well as some freestanding stores and smaller shopping centers.

The store has 850 sq. ft., annual sales of $1 million-plus and $400,000 in inventory that includes high-quality engagement and wedding rings, gold chains, gold and diamond jewelry, two watch brands (one mid-priced line, one high-priced Swiss brand) and some designer merchandise.

For the year-end holidays, it adds up to $250,000 in merchandise. It has five full-time employees and two part-timers and is open 10 a.m. to 9 p.m. seven days a week.

Security: The security system should include the following (all costs are approximate):

• Safes—A TRTL30x6 ($11,000) and a TL30 ($3,000). An alternative would be a Class 1 modular vault ($20,000).

• Burglary alarms—Six-side coverage of safes and a UL-rated AA system for the premises with central-station monitoring. Motion detectors in sales and alarm control box areas. (Total, $2,500 for installation, $1,500-$2,000 for annual maintenance.)

• Hold-up alarms—Two buttons plus pendants (an alarm disguised as a pendant worn around the neck) for use only after robbers leave ($500).

• CCTV—Three to four cameras (two for high-value merchandise cases, one for the entry and one for the other cases), a recorder, a switcher (to switch between camera views) and a monitor ($4,000).

• Showcases—Break-resistant glazing material—such as Plexiglas or Lexgard—for high-value merchandise cases (several hundred dollars per case).

Insurance: JMI underwriters' suggestions for this store are based on minimum security of a TRTL-15x6 safe with 90% of the merchandise in the safe when the store is closed; a UL-rated 2 or 3 AA alarm for the premises; complete protection UL-rated AA alarm with line security for the safe; and motion detectors in the sales and alarm control box areas. CCTV may or may not be used. The suggestion presumes high-end merchandise is displayed in cases farthest from the doors; that photo ID may be required before showing the merchandise; and that store management stresses "proper floor coverage, security awareness and safe selling methods." Based on these presumptions, the store should have:

1. Jewelers' block policy with annual premium of $5,000-$6,000 that would include:

• On-premises coverage limits of up to $400,000, with $250,000 peak season coverage during the holidays; $40,000 on show windows. Deductible: $5,000.

• Off-premises coverage of $25,000 for product in possession of employee; $50,000 in possession of owner; $15,000 for goods left at another jewelry dealer for repair or other reason; up to $25,000 for U.S. Postal Service shipments; and up to $15,000 for Federal Express and United Parcel Service shipments. Deductible: $1,000.

2. Business owner's policy with estimated and annual premium of $900-$1,000 that would include:

• Property loss of up to $40,000 on furniture and fixtures; $10,000 on money; and $2,000-$3,000 on glass.

• General liability of up to $1 million for bodily injury to third party and property damages; an additional $1 million "umbrella"; $5,000 for premises-related medical payments. It also would cover employee dishonesty and loss of income.

Also consider coverage of receivables, computers and improvements to rental property.

(Note: This insurance proposal presumes the store has a properly trained staff, uses proper key control, follows the JSA manual, stays current with JSA flash bulletins and always has two people open and close the store.)

DOWNTOWN STORE

Located on Main Street, this store serves a city of 60,000 that has seen better days. In fact, several stores on Main Street are empty.

The store has 1,200 sq. ft., annual sales of $150,000 and $97,000 worth of inventory that includes family and birthstone rings, baby jewelry, some karat gold and gold-filled jewelry, a few engagement and wedding rings and two popularly priced watch lines. It cut staff recently from five to three and is open from 9:30 a.m. to 6 p.m. Monday to Saturday.

Security: The security system should include the following (all costs are approximate):

• Safes—A UL-rated TL30 ($3,000).

• Burglary alarms—Complete protection, UL-rated AA coverage for the safe and UL-rated 3AA coverage for the premises with central station or police-department monitoring. Motion detector. (Total, $1,500 for installation, $1,000 for annual servicing.)

• Hold-up alarms—Two buttons (price included with the cost of the burglary alars).

• CCTV—One camera to cover high-value cases and the entry and a monitor ($1,200-$1,500)

• Showcases—Secure (lock) tops of showcases (included with cost of showcases).

• Doors/windows—Grill insert for entrance door when store is closed ($300).

Insurance: JMI underwriters' suggestions for this store are based on minimal security of a non-UL rated two-hour fire safe weighing 750-plus lb. without wheels, with 80% of merchandise in the safe when the store is closed; a 3A alarm system for the premises installed by a non-UL certified alarm company and partial (door and front face coverage only); an alarm for the safe with digital communicator; all UL-rated equipment installed to UL specifications, with annual maintenance contract. The store should have at least:

1. Jewelers' block policy with an estimated annual premium of $900-$1,500 that would include:

• On-premises coverage limits of $100,000 with peak season coverage as needed and $10,000 on show windows. Deductible: $500.

• Off-premises coverage limits of $10,000 for travel and $10,000 for goods left with another jewelry dealer. Shipments should be sent First Class registered mail and insured through the U.S. Postal Service. Deductible: $500.

2. Business owner's policy with an estimated annual premium of $350-$500 a year that would include:

• Property ($20,000 on furniture and fixtures, $5,000 on money, $2,000 on glass and $1,000 on signage).

• General liability ($1 million for bodily injury and property damages, $1,000 for medical payments and coverage for loss of income).

The experts also suggest possible coverage of receivables, computers and improvements to rental property.

(Note: This insurance proposal and the two that follow presume the store has a properly trained staff, uses proper key control, follows the JSA manual, stays current with JSA flash bulletins and always has two people open and close the store.)

COMMUNITY OR STRIP CENTER STORE

This store is in a suburban shopping center facing a parking lot that fronts on a road. It has 900 sq. ft., annual sales of $325,000 and $175,000 in inventory that includes engagement and wedding rings, gold chains and gold jewelry, some standard bread-and-butter jewelry, two well-known mid-priced watch brands and some giftware. It has three full-timers (owners and daughter), a part-timer (high school student) and is open 9:30 a.m. to 5:30 p.m. Monday to Thursday and Saturday and to 9 p.m. Friday.

Security: The security system should include the following (all costs are approximate):

• Safes—Two UL-rated TL30 safes ($6,000).

• Burglary alarms—Complete protection, UL-rated AA coverage for the safe and UL-rated 3AA coverage for the premises with central-station or police-department monitoring. Motion detector. (Total, $2,500 for installation, $1,200-$1,500 for annual servicing.)

• Hold-up deterrents—Two buttons plus pendants ($500).

• Showcases—Secure, bolted tops that can't be forced open and a system in which the keys can't be removed until the case is locked. Break-resistant glazing material for high-value merchandise cases. (Several hundred dollars per case.)

• Doors/windows—Grill inserts for after-hours for entrance door and show windows ($1,000). "Man trap" entrance ($1,000).

Insurance: JMI underwriters' suggestions are based on minimum security of a UL-rated TL-15 safe with 80% of merchandise in the safe when the store is closed; 3A alarm system for the premises and partial A system for the safe; installed by a UL-certified company with monitored opening and closing. (Note: monitoring must be requested). Based on these presumptions, the store should have at least:

1. Jewelers' block policy with an estimated annual premium of $2,000-$3,000 that would provide:

• On-premises coverage limits of $175,000 with peak season coverage as needed and $20,000 for show windows. Deductible: $1,000.

• Off-premises coverage limits of $25,000 for travel; $10,000 for goods left with another jewelry dealer; $25,000 on shipments insured through the U.S. Postal Service; and $10,000 for shipments through Federal Express or UPS. Deductible: $1,000.

2. Business owner's policy with annual premium of $450-$650 that would include:

• Property ($20,000 on furniture and fixtures, $20,000 on money and $2,000 on glass or $1,000 on signage).

• General liability ($1 million for bodily injury and

property damages, $5,000 for medical payments and coverage of loss of income.)

The experts also suggest possible coverage of receivables, computers and improvements to rental property.

FREESTANDING STORE

Located on a main road leading to a popular lake resort, this store has a side parking lot and landscaping. It's a half mile from a major mall and minutes from a couple of nearby towns.

It has 1,100 sq. ft., annual sales of $700,000 and $320,000 of inventory that includes bridal rings, gold chains and jewelry, some bread-and-butter jewelry, three midpriced watch lines and some giftware. It's open 10 a.m. to 9:30 p.m. Tuesday to Saturday, the same as the nearby mall.

Security: The security system should include the following (all costs are approximate):

• Safes: A UL-rated TRTL-15x6 ($6,000-$8,000).

• Burglary alarms: Complete protection, UL-rated AA system for the safe and a UL-rated 2AA system for the premises with central-station or police-department monitoring. (Total, $2,000 for installation, $1,200-$1,500 for annual maintenance.)

• Hold-up deterrents: Two buttons for use only after robbers leave. (The price is included with the cost of burglary alarms.)

• CCTV: One or two cameras (viewing high-value merchandise cases and entry), a recorder and a monitor ($2,500-$3,000).

• Showcases: Secure, bolted-down tops that can't be forced.

• Doors/windows: Grill inserts on entrance and show windows for after-hours windows ($1,000). Buzzer system to enter the store ($100).

Insurance: JMI underwriters' suggestions for this store are based on minimal security of a TL-30 with 80% of the merchandise in the safe when the store is closed; a 2A alarm system for the premises and partial (door and front face only) A system for the safe with digital or radio communication; all UL equipment installed by non UL-certified company to UL specifications and an annual maintenance contract. Based on these presumptions, the store should have at least:

1. Jewelers' block policy with estimated annual premium of $3,500-$4,500 that would provide:

• On-premises coverage limits of $325,000 with peak season coverage as needed and $30,000 on show windows. Deductible: $2,500.

• Off-premises coverage limits of $25,000 for travel by employee and $40,000 for travel by owner; $15,000 for goods left with another jewelry dealer; $25,000 on shipments through the U.S. Postal Service and $15,000 on shipments through Federal Express or UPS. Deductible: $1,000.

2. Business owner's policy with estimated annual premium of $900-$1,200 that would include:

• Property ($30,000 on furniture and fixtures, $10,000 on money, $2,000 on glass, $1,000 on signage).

• General liability ($1 million for bodily injury and property damages; $1 million "umbrella"; $5,000 for medical payments; and coverage for employee dishonesty and loss of income.)

The experts also recommend considering coverage of receivables, computers and improvements to rental property.

Defining UL

Security and insurance consultants say jewelers should use only UL-rated and UL-listed equipment. But what is UL and what do its ratings mean?

UL stands for the Underwriters Laboratory Inc., an independent non-profit product-safety testing and certification organization based in Northbrook, Ill. It has evaluated hundreds of products, materials and systems in the interest of public safety since 1894 and is a leading developer of international safety standards for products.

The UL Listing mark (a circle containing UL with a ® under the U) is the most widely recognized UL safety certification program. A UL Listing mark on a product means samples were tested and evaluated according to nationally recognized standards.

UL ratings, meanwhile, define a product's characteristics based on UL tests. Following are the UL ratings for safes, alarms and bullet-resisting materials, plus explanations provided by Steve Schmit, associate managing engineer in charge of testing and auditing burglary alarm equipment at UL; Sara J. Payne, UL spokesperson; and UL documents.

Safes: UL safe ratings are TL-15, TL-30, TL-30x6, TRTL-30, TRTL-15x6, TRTL-60, TRTL-30x6 and TXTL-60.

The letters indicate the tools to which a safe is resistant. TL means resistant to common hand and power tools. TR means resistant to cutting and welding torches. TX means resistant to explosives.

The numbers 15, 30 or 60 indicate the minimum minutes a safe will withstand attack.

The "x6" means all five sides and the safe door have been tested and can resist entry for the indicated time. A rating without "x6" means only the door and front face are protected from attack.

Burglary alarms: Due to the variety of types of burglary alarm systems (local, bank, vault, police, residential, etc.), UL alarm codes have different meanings, depending on the system. As far as jewelers are concerned:

• A single letter—A, B or C—refers to response time by a guard or police from the central station after the alarm is received. A=15 minutes, B=20 minutes, C=30 minutes.

• Double letters—AA, BB and CC—refer to the degree of extra security features protecting a system's lines to the central monitoring station. AA is the highest.

• The numbers 1, 2 and 3 refer to the extent of protection that an alarm system provides a retail premises.

• "Partial" (door and front face only) and "complete" (all six sides) refer to the extent of alarm protection of a safe.

• Certification means a system is installed in accordance with the highest UL standards by a UL-listed alarm service company using UL-listed equipment and that the firm has given the owner a service contract to maintain it. UL may audit a certified system to ensure it was installed properly and is serviced regularly; UL randomly audits 20% of certified installations annually. An alarm owner with a UL-certificate may get a better deal with his or her insurer.

Note 1: Not all companies are UL-listed, even if they install UL-listed equipment. Only 1,300 alarm firms out of about 14,000 are UL-listed.

Note 2: UL-certified installation—which may be somewhat more expensive than regular installation—must be requested, even from UL-listed firms. Don't assume that because you use a UL-listed firm that you automatically get a UL-certified installation.

Bullet-resisting materials: This rating applies to materials, devices and fixtures used to form bullet-resisting barriers such as showcases. UL defines "bullet-resisting" as protection from "complete penetration, passage of fragments of projectiles or spalling [fragmentation] of protective material to the degree that injury would be caused to a person standing directly behind the bullet-resisting barrier."

THE RATINGS:

• **Medium**—small arms (weapon, Super 36 automatic; barrel length, 5"; ammunition, metal case).

• **High**—small arms (weapon, .357 Magnum revolver; barrel length, $8^1/_4$"; ammunition: lead).

• **Super**—small arms (weapon, .44 Magnum revolver; barrel length, $6^1/_2$"; ammunition: lead).

• **High**—rifle (weapon, 30-06 rifle; barrel length, 24"; ammunition, soft point).

For more information, contact Underwriters Laboratory, 333 Pfingsten Rd., Northbrook, Ill. 60062-2096; (708) 272-8800, ext. 43436 or 42128.

JSA Recommends

Rather than make individual proposals for the four stores in this article, the Jewelers' Security Alliance says all of them ideally should have the following:

1. A UL-rated TRTL30x6 safe.

2. Properly installed and maintained video surveillance and recording equipment.

3. The highest UL-rated (AA is best) alarm system available in the geographic area.

4. Jewelers' block insurance (consult insurance carrier).

5. A fire alarm and/or sprinkler system, as appropriate.

6. Pull-down metal security gates inside the store.

7. Inventory control system (consult insurance carrier).

8. Showcases that are break-resistant and from which the key can be removed only when locked.

9. Check references and do appropriate background screening of prospective employees.

10. Sufficient external and internal illumination of the store at night.

11. An alert system, in the store and with neighboring jewelers.

12. Established written policies for security and regular employee training.

In addition, JSA say the mall store and freestanding store each could use an unarmed, uniformed security guard, and that the downtown, strip center and freestanding stores should have buzzer systems to control entry.

Reduce Home Crime Risk

April 1993

At-home thefts are a significant problem for jewelry sales representatives and retail jewelers, says the Jewelers' Security Alliance. In fact, 10% of all sales rep losses involved at-home crime in 1992.

Most of the crimes occur in urban areas and generally involve professional gangs of thieves who are South Americans, says JSA President John Kennedy. "It is a significant, troubling [trend]," he says. JSA is concerned enough that it issued a special alert in February to warn jewelry salespeople, retail jewelers and their staffs and provide tips to reduce the risk of at-home robberies.

Above all, Kennedy says, salespeople and jewelers should assume they are a target and under surveillance by criminals at any time. Once criminals identify a jewelry salesperson or jeweler, they "keep that person under surveillance for days, waiting for an opportunity [to strike]."

Common sense precautions can reduce the risk. Most of the following tips apply to sales reps, but are useful for retail jewelers, as well.

1. Don't take jewelry lines home. Though some suppliers forbid this, many allow it or even make it company policy.

Such a policy should be "seriously rethought," says Kennedy. Homes are less secure than a vault, and keeping jewelry lines at home puts the salesperson's family at risk. In one recent case, thieves forced their way into a salesman's house while he was out jogging, threatened his wife with a gun and tied her up, did the same to him when he returned and then fled with two lines of jewelry he had brought home. Another salesperson who took lines home had them stolen three times—at home—in recent years.

2. Arrange to store your lines overnight with jewelers locally and when you're on the road, says Kennedy. (Alternate so you don't use the same jeweler every night.)

3. If you must take jewelry home, take precautions. Review the security of your house. Do all windows have locks? Install a burglar alarm. Add an electronic garage door opener so you don't have to get out of your car in the driveway, where many thefts occur. Don't leave doors unlocked, and don't let strangers in the house.

4. Never leave jewelry unattended in a car or car trunk. The time it takes to open a trunk and grab a sales case is about as long as it takes to read this sentence. If you must

leave your case in your car, buy a car alarm and have a locksmith install chains in the trunk to attach to the case.

5. Drive defensively. Never go straight home, and don't use the same route each day. Take evasive action periodically to see if you are followed. For example, drive down a one-way street. Pull into a fast food or grocery store parking lot and then leave again. Drive around a block several times. As you do, check whether the same vehicle appears behind or in front of you. If so, drive to the nearest police station.

6. Start a neighborhood watch program. Ask neighbors to keep an eye on your home, as you will for them, and report suspicious individuals, vehicles or events to you and/or the police.

7. Keep your name, job and/or address out of any directories or publications with public circulation, such as those of school PTAs, churches or synagogues and local business groups.

8. Don't discuss your business in informal social situations, such as parties, bars or golf courses. People to whom you talk may be trustworthy, but what about all the others within earshot?

9. Put your business address—not your home address—on your car registration and driver's license. In many states, such motor vehicle data is public information and available to anyone with the license plate number of a driver.

10. Never answer telephone or door-to-door surveys. You don't know these people and have no guarantee they represent the organizations or agencies they claim to. Even answers to apparently innocuous questions can provide crooks with useful information.

11. Get to know a local police officer. "It's wise to establish a relationship before something happens so you have someone to call for advice, report suspicions to and speak with if something does happen," says Kennedy.

12. If you are the victim of a theft—at home, in your store or on the road—don't resist. That can get you, your staff, your family or innocent bystanders injured or killed. Instead, says JSA, comply with the robbers' demands and then, when they have left, contact police.

Security Products Offer New Ways To Fight Crime

December 1992

Crime rates and costs may be rising, but jewelers trying to protect merchandise from crooks can take heart. Many security products are declining in price while increasing in sophistication, becoming ever more effective in deterring crime.

That's what JCK found when it asked makers and vendors of security products and services about trends in their industry. A lot is going on. Indeed, two in three expect major changes during the '90s in a variety of retail store security equipment and services—including closed circuit television, alarms, showcases, safes and honesty tests.

"The security industry is in flux, with advances in technology occurring rapidly," says John Villella, marketing manager for Burle Industries Inc., Lancaster, Pa. "Products will change, become better, smaller, faster, more efficient and more flexible."

Here is a look at some trends to watch.

CCTV: Closed-circuit television surveillance is changing most in cost and use, say experts. That's largely because strong consumer demand for camcorders, whose technology is similar to CCTV's, has enabled manufacturers to improve the solid state imaging technology used in both.

The result is state-of-the-art CCTV cameras whose versatile and reliable "digital" technology permits many features. These cameras are more compact (some as small as cigarette packs), easier to conceal from customers and employees,

with longer life than earlier cameras and no decline in picture quality as years pass.

"With advances in technology, video security is becoming more precise and customized to individual store needs," says Villella.

Systems are easier to install than earlier ones and cost less, too. A CCTV camera that ran $1,000 five years ago, for example, today is about $350. Prices will continue to fall in this decade, though more slowly, predict security experts.

The next step, they say, is integration of CCTV technology with store computers (also digital-based), opening up new opportunities for store operations and security. By the end of this decade, says Stan Rosoff, president of Security Resources, Fairfield, Conn., many stores' security and operations systems—including CCTV, fire and burglary alarms, cash register, sales records, video verification of alarms, inventory control and so on—will be computer-controlled.

"Interfacing CCTV and computer [technology] will give a jeweler access to information previously unavailable to him," says Jack Schultz, president of Gem Security Consultants, Chicago, Ill., which is creating such a computer-based system for a small jewelry chain.

Safes: Locks, the basic element of safes, are changing. Electronic locks (i.e., digital keypads) are beginning to replace mechanical ones.

"They are just as hard [for crooks] to get into, but easier for jewelers to operate and change," says Ray Wilson, vice president of Wilson Safe Co., Philadelphia, Pa. "If a jeweler fires someone, for example, all he does to change the lock is punch in a new combination, rather than call in a locksmith."

Vendors say such locks reduce internal theft and unauthorized use of safes. Many provide computerized audit trails of unauthorized attempts to open a safe; some even shut down after a few such unsuccessful attempts.

Electronic locks fit most safes; they cost about three times as much as mechanical ones (i.e., $180 versus $60). Though used mainly by retail chain stores now, safe and lock dealers expect more jewelers to add them in the next few years.

Crooks' technology also is affecting safe design. Burglars, for example, have adopted the fiber optic scopes created by medical research. A flexible mini-fiberscope inserted into a safe keyhole or through a drilled hole lets a burglar "read" locking mechanisms. So, more safe makers have or are designing features to counteract them. Most use hardened sides to prevent drilling holes. At least one has an anti-fiber optic keyhole cover.

Lighter-weight safes are coming, say some vendors. Mike Kasper, marketing manager of Safes Unlimited, Clifton Park, N.Y., says these are "as secure but more affordable [than heavier ones today], and usable on higher floor levels."

Requirements for safes also will get tougher. Some suppliers expect low-security safes (those lacking six-sided protection or electronic protection) to dwindle. And Craig Collins, president of Harwood Protection Industries Inc., Woodbridge, Va., predicts more jewelers' block insurance carriers will urge jewelers to upgrade to higher-rated safes because of rising losses sustained by major carriers.

Meanwhile, Underwriters' Laboratories—which tests and rates safes—has begun a program to reexamine all UL-listed safes, vault panels and doors every seven years. Use of new techniques and adherence to more stringent requirements will be included. Those not passing will lose the UL-listing until they comply.

Alarms: Wireless technology is strengthening alarm systems' reliability, say suppliers.

Outside the store, long-range radio signals now provide backup to phone lines which alarm firms use to transmit to and from central monitoring stations. Indeed, "long range wireless reporting will become more important in coming years as phone lines become less reliable and subject to tampering," says Brian Rockett, marketing manager of AES Corp., Peabody, Mass.

Inside, "signal grade transmission (direct wire) alarm systems will be increasingly replaced by more efficient and maintainable microprocessor-based systems," says E.G. Lestardo, president of Holmes Protection Inc., New York, N.Y. "Wireless technology will become more acceptable as the systems and detectors' reliability and aesthetics improve."

Alarm verification by monitoring stations will improve, too, with two-way audio and video transmissions, say experts.

Meanwhile, computer chips used in alarm sensors now can distinguish between "real" and "false" causes of alarms, says Richard Cantor, president of Amerigard, New York, N.Y. Many false alarms are "environmental," he notes, caused by such factors as vibrations from an air conditioner, heat from a photocopier or even movements of a cat.

Expect, too, more use of vehicular and personal alarm and tracking systems by jewelers in transit to prevent or frustrate kidnapping, adds Lestardo. Several applications already are in development.

Showcases: Unlocked showcases and smash-and-grabs are two serious problems for jewelers, but new products help deter them.

Case locks are evolving. One mechanical model has a variety of internal configurations (and matching keys) which a jeweler can change periodically. Use of electronic locks (i.e., digital keypads or sensors which respond to electronic "keys") is growing, too.

There are more alarms for individual showcases, triggered when a case door is opened or left open. The alarm usually sounds until it is reset or the case is closed. But at least one firm, Stajer Corp., Lowell, Mass., offers an affordable, attachable device which not only distinguishes between a closed door and a locked one, but also sounds a low alarm if a door is unlocked and no salesperson is near. It resets itself when the door is locked. Units can be wired to a central station to monitor each showcase. Some firms also offer pressure sensitive mats which beep if a salesperson leaves an unlocked case.

Security experts expect to see more wireless alarm technology (including infrared, ultrasound and digital equipment), and fewer wired systems (such as cord or glued-on ones).

Laminated glass, which is tougher than tempered glass and less likely to break helps deter smash-and-grabs. The price is reasonable: about 10% of the total for a five-foot case costing $1,600.

Harwood Protection Industries offers another deterrent—a hinged showcase "hood." The tough, lightweight polycarbonate material can be custom-made. Each costs $300-400, is fitted in moments and attached with steel shackles. It can withstand attacks by hand tools for at least 15 minutes, and stores flat when not in use.

Showcase design also is changing. There are new ways to hinder removal of glass tops, including aluminum extrusions, tighter security clips (to hold glass) and silicon inserted between the glass and the case.

Two-way mirrors are more important in case design, says Terry Irby, vice president of marketing for Berg Store Fixtures, Lynbrook, N.Y. Indeed, almost all jewelry-store layouts it now does include a mirror/showcase combination, generally in the diamond room, at the checkout counter or in the office. "Constructed as an integral part of the showcase, [the mirror] draws little attention to itself, maximizes the selling and merchandising area and lets the retailer attend to administrative functions in his office while watching sales area from a concealed location," says Irby.

Tags: Product tags which deter shoplifters and internal theft are becoming essential security items. Electronic tags, for example, trigger an alarm at the exit unless deactivated at checkout.

Two recent ideas are the Fluid Tag and the Accent Tag from Security Tag Systems Inc., St. Petersburg, Fla. Both are based on "benefit denial"—discouraging theft of merchandise by damaging it. Shoplifters or thieves break or damage jewelry or watches if they try to remove Accent tags; they spill ink if they tamper with Fluid tags. These tags are small, lightweight and don't prevent customers from trying on merchandise. The retailer uses a compact "detacher" to quickly remove tags.

Making a product unusable and/or unsellable is "a far more effective deterrent than risk of apprehension," says Robert L. DiLonardo, marketing manager for Security Tag. And "making it extremely difficult to remove the tag [is] a physical impediment that also deters shoplifters."

"Benefit denial" tags are becoming a major method of deterring theft, says DiLonardo, and will "displace to some degree" use of electronic tags and lockable fixtures, especially in jewelry categories.

Tests: Internal theft costs retailers $1.4 billion a year, says the annual Retail Loss Prevention Survey by Ernst & Young, an international accounting firm. It adds that one in five job applicants is "high risk" (likely to rob employers). That's why more retailers are using honesty tests to screen applicants. Two out of five in Ernst & Young's poll already do; another one in five will add to them soon.

The "test industry" is changing, too. Recent federal and state laws—such as the 1988 act limiting polygraph use and 1991 additions to the civil rights act—restricted what can be used in the tests. Smaller firms that violated such laws, couldn't comply or create test alternatives have closed. The result: More retailers are going to established vendors for reliable, scientifically valid pre-employment tests.

These firms also have been refining or expanding services. Thus, P.O.S. Corp., Chicago, Ill., added hotlines which clients' employees can use anonymously to report crimes, such as internal theft, at their companies. And Reid Psychological Systems, Chicago, Ill., exclusive supplier of honesty tests to Jewelers of America and the Leading Jewelers Guild, is adding programs which provide test results more quickly.

These programs use such new technologies as voice-activated scoring (the phone caller tells results to a "listening" computer, which scores the test); Intelligent Fax (a completed test faxed to Reid is returned, corrected, within seconds); and a computer program, available to jewelers with personal computers, which they use to score tests themselves.

Entry: Buzz-in entryways, which keep people from entering until checked by store personnel, are now a familiar part of jewelry stores. The next addition may be walk-through weapon detectors, like those at airports.

Many precious metals users, including jewelry manufacturers and mints, already use detectors to reduce internal theft. Now, use by jewelers to spot weapons-carrying robbers is "growing significantly," says Peggy Forster of Protective Technologies International, Salt Lake City, Utah. And it will keep growing due to unstable social and economic conditions, says Mal Schwartz, general manager of Infinetics Inc., Wilmington, Del., which pioneered detector technology. "A jeweler can ill afford armed guards," he says, "but can afford this."

A basic system starts at $2,400; the most sophisticated ones go for $30,000 or more. But suppliers says costs will drop as advancements in electronics and computer management improve the performance of detector systems.

"The '90s technology is making weapons detectors more capable, more cost-effective and [better] able to tolerate site adversities [which can cause false alarms or static]," says Schwartz.

How To Shrink Shrinkage

April 1992

The most effective "tools" to reduce retail inventory shrinkage are your own employees.

So finds the 13th annual Survey of Retail Loss Prevention Trends by Ernst & Young, an international professional services firm serving the retail industry. The survey is sponsored by the International Mass Retail Association and *Chain Store Age Executive* magazine. The latest survey was based on 1990 statistics and released in late 1991.

Shrinkage is defined as shoplifting, employee theft, paperwork errors and unexplained losses. Fine jewelry ranked eighth among 12 types of merchandise when listing shrinkage as a percentage of sales—3.1%. That's an improvement over second place and 4.71% the previous year. Fashion accessories and costume jewelry firms had the highest losses both years.

How are companies fighting shrinkage? Four out of five (83%) firms surveyed explain their anti-shrinkage efforts to employees and indicate the employees' role in these efforts. Most firms rated these employee-awareness programs as their most effective loss-prevention measure.

"Awareness programs are the heart and soul of many loss prevention initiatives today," says Burnie Donoho, senior adviser to Ernst & Young's retail industry services section and a former president of Marshall Field department stores. "They also are becoming more elaborate. To reach young sales associates, more retailers use rock videos, comic books and in-house radio stations [to explain program details], and some offer loss-prevention incentives such as lottery contests and monetary awards."

Nearly two-thirds of the firms surveyed (63%) use incentives to reduce shrinkage. Of these, 64% combine monetary and non-monetary awards. The rest use monetary awards only. Three-fourths of the firms with incentives reward employees who identify dishonest coworkers, 60% offer rewards for reporting shoplifters and 58% offer incentives for reducing shrinkage in a department or store. The average individual employee award is $176.

The survey also found:

• Firms that take physical inventories on a regular basis have a lower shrinkage rate than those that don't.

• Three-fourths of the companies surveyed have a stated goal to reduce shrinkage. These goals average 1.84% of sales—12% below the actual retail shrinkage percentage that retailers reported for 1990.

High-risk hiring: The survey also examined retail hiring practices. Nearly half the respondents (47%) administer honesty tests to applicants; one job applicant in five (21%) falls into the "high risk" category. A majority (61%) reject any such applicants. But a third (36%) say they consider high-risk applicants if they have other qualifications.

Those using the tests believe they help reduce inventory shrinkage (93% say so), reduce employee turnover (72%) and improve employee productivity (51%). "Unless lawmakers force retailers to stop using these honesty tests, as was the case with polygraph testing, we are going to see a rise in their use," says Stephanie Shern, national director of retail industry services for Ernst & Young.

Retail Jewelers Are Top Target Of Telephone Credit-Card Scams

December 1991

Jewelers have become "a principle target" of telephone credit-card scams, says Richard Collier, senior director of security and risk management for MasterCard International. Officials of the Jewelers' Security Alliance and the Secret Service, which investigates the federal crime of credit-card fraud, agree.

They say many current scams can be traced to inmates of state prisons in Pennsylvania, though prisoners in Florida, New Jersey and Alaska are also suspected of placing fraudulent phone orders with jewelers.

The problem isn't new; JSA reported it in 1989. What is new, say officials, is the significant increase following the Persian Gulf war ("soldiers" claiming to be ordering gifts for loved ones) and approaching the year-end holidays during an economic downturn.

Problem for jewelers: Fraudulent credit-card phone sales are "a continuing, growing problem for jewelers," says James B. White, JSA executive director. While there are no specific figures for the jewelry industry, White estimates individual losses average $2,000 to $10,000. Phone frauds as a whole, including those against retailers, cost $1.2 billion a year, says the Secret Service. One ring of inmates in a Pittsburgh, Pa., prison alone reportedly ordered millions of dollars worth of merchandise last year from retailers in 30 states.

Independent jewelers and dealers in electronics are the "principal targets" for phone fraud because they sell expensive merchandise that can be fenced easily and quickly, says Collier. Also, independent jewelers are less accustomed to phone orders than chains or mail-order firms, and thus less suspicious of phony callers.

Networks: "These people are very glib," says Collier, "and they have an extensive network of confederates outside [prison] who provide numbers and collect the ordered merchandise." One Chicago-based ring, broken up by police in July, had 50 people in several states who found legitimate card numbers by sifting through trash from restaurants and retail stores for discarded credit-card receipts, says the *Chicago Tribune*.

Even when criminals are jailed, they can continue the scam, say fraud-control authorities. Unlike federal prisons, state and county prisons do not restrict or monitor phone calls by inmates. Doing so, argue civil libertarians, would violate inmates' rights. Collier adds that the Pennsylvania Attorney General's office told him it would be pointless to prosecute prisoners already serving long jail sentences.

Controls possible: Even so, some efforts are being made. Collier recently urged Pennsylvania's Commissioner of State Correctional Facilities to attach a message to all inmate phone calls saying the call is coming from a state prison. He hoped to have a response by Christmas. Some law enforcement officials also have suggested moving suspected callers to a federal prison, where phone use is restricted. Congress also is studying ways to strengthen the law against credit card fraud.

Meanwhile, phone crooks continue to sting jewelers all over the country. They usually call several retailers in one area over a couple of days (getting names and phone numbers from prison phone books or the telephone company). Then they shift to another area before anyone gets wise. A recent flurry occurred in West Virginia. Frank Petrolik, a jeweler in Keyser, W.Va., for example, took two phone orders for $5,000 of merchandise in two days in October from callers claiming to be soldiers. A few weeks later, he learned the legitimate card holder hadn't placed the orders, and he was left holding the bill.

The scam: The scam works like this:

Someone phones a jeweler, give his name and says he is calling from another city or a military base. He says the jeweler was recommended to him by friends or relatives, then he places an order to be delivered for a holiday, birthday or anniversary. In the "military" version, the caller says he's a serviceman shipping out (or returning) who wants something for his wife, mother or girlfriend. (One Pennsylvania jeweler even gave a caller a discount, believing he was a serviceman going to the Persian Gulf.)

The caller gives a credit-card number, the jeweler checks with the credit-card company and the company gives the authorization because it's a legitimate number. The caller asks to have the gift sent overnight to the alleged recipient. Often the caller asks for the tracking or routing number of the delivery form "in case there are any problems" or "to make sure they deliver the right gift to the right place." Once the crook has the tracking number, he calls the delivery service and has the package rerouted to a different address, where a confederate signs for it, fences it or exchanges it for drugs.

Within a few weeks, the real cardholder has notified the credit-card firm he didn't make the purchase, and the jeweler is left holding the bill. The jeweler has little recourse other than to contest the bill with the bank handling his credit-card business.

Be wary: You should be cautious if a caller who wants to place an order:

- Seems to be in a hurry.
- Is unconcerned about price.
- Can't or won't give his home address and/or phone number, if you need to call him back.

- Asks that the package be sent to an adress other than his own.
- Insists the package be sent overnight.
- Asks for the tracking or routing number on the delivery form.

If you suspect a credit-card order is phony, immediately contact the Secret Service office in the area. The number usually is listed on the phone book's inside front cover. Also, call the Jewelers' Security Alliance at (800) 537- 0067 (New York) or (800) 227-9251 (Los Angeles).

If your store does take phone orders as a customer service, follow these tips to prevent being stung, says White:

- Accept phone orders only from customers you know.
- Ask the caller for his address and phone number. Check with the verification service that credit-card companies provide retailers (for a small fee).
- Ship *only* to the billing address on the credit card.

Another option guarantees you won't be hit by fraudulent phone sales: don't accept any phone orders. After all, says White, "taking a credit-card order by telephone *is* a great risk."

Frank Petrolik agrees; he has already instituted that policy. "I'm not going to be burned again," he says.

Closed-Circuit TV: This Unblinking Eye Scares Crooks

December 1991

"Camera surveillance? Who needs it?!"

That's what almost half the jewelers in recent JCK poll said, and the actual number of disbelievers may be even higher. Suppliers of closed-circuit TV surveillance systems say most jewelers lack CCTV. And the Jewelers' Security Alliance says the absence of CCTV is most common in Mom-and-Pop stores.

Why? Anti-CCTV jewelers simply believe they don't need it. Many say their security is adequate or that their small town or small store is, as one says, "risk-free." One in three also cites cost as a reason for not installing the unblinking camera eyes.

Brother, are these people wrong!

Information from jewelers with camera surveillance and from jewelry trade groups strongly indicates CCTV *does* deter thefts. Further, if thefts do occur, it provides information that often helps capture the crooks.

Deterrent: Among the findings of JCK's poll:

- 53% of panelists have CCTV.
- 74% of those who do have it believe CCTV prevents thefts. "The real advantage is as a deterrent," says Georgie Gleim, whose three stores in Palo Alto, Cal., area have CCTV.

"If someone is casing stores, I want enough visible security so they go elsewhere."

Says Iowa City jeweler BIll Nusser, "I wouldn't be without it." His CCTV recently helped to nab a crook with a stolen credit card. "It prohibits all but the most cunning internal theft."

- Almost two thirds (60%) of panelists with CCTV have been *robbery-free* since their systems were installed (1985 is the median year for getting their first systems).
- Of CCTV-equipped stores that have been robbed since 1989, at least a third provided police with CCTV evidence leading to arrests.

The files of Jewelers Mutual Insurance also suggests CCTV deters crime. In 1990, 91% of policyholder losses—armed robberies, sneak thefts, grab-and-runs and ring switches—were in stores *without* CCTV. This figure has risen annually as more jewelers add CCTV.

JMI is such a believer that it gives a reduced premium to policyholders for the first year they have CCTV. In some high-crime areas and in stores where JMI believes CCTV would have prevented a loss, such a system is *required* if the jeweler wants to maintain the policy. (However, serious theft alone can be a strong persuader. Several jewelers who were interviewed for JCK's September 1991 crime report added CCTV after suffering substantial robbery losses.)

Even without JMI's urging, it's smart financially to install CCTV. "The jeweler's block policy is experienced-rated," says JMI President Ronald R. Harder. "If a store has losses, its insurance cost rises higher than one with CCTV where losses are deterred."

The Jewelers Security Alliance concurs. CCTV systems "reduce losses by deterring crimes," says a recent JSA report. "A suspect entering the store and observing he is 'on camera' may be deterred from criminal activity and move to a less well-protected retailer."

CCTV has additional advantages, according to JSA, CCTV dealers and jewelers. It can:
- Identify those who commit crimes.
- Record events for later review.
- Screen people as they enter the store or sensitive areas.
- Spot internal theft.
- See "blind spots" (unseen by staff) in the store.
- Be used to train employees in proper sales and security methods.
- Spot weakness in security procedures and violations by staffers, such as leaving out jewelry trays.
- Monitor employee behavior on the sales floor.

HOW TO BUY A VIDEO SURVEILLANCE SYSTEM

Before shopping for a CCTV system, know what you want from it.

"Think through the entire system," says Richard Cantor, president of Amerigard Alarm & Security Corp., New York City. "Establish a clear reason for having CCTV. Determine how it will be operated. Examine various equipment configurations. Then consider pricing limits and alternatives." Unfortunately, he adds, "jewelers usually reverse this procedure, approaching it from the standpoint of cost rather than objectives."

Cameras: Many jewelers with a CCTV system use one camera, but this may not be enough. "It depends on a store's layout and factors such as the location of high-value showcases," says James B. White, president of JSA.

While needs differ, a typical jewelry store probably needs two to five cameras, says CCTV suppliers, JSA jewelers polled by JCK. Important camera locations to consider, they say, include:
- Entrances/exits.
- Cash register, point-of-purchase or payment section.
- Sales floor.
- High-value showcases and areas with the most expensive items, such as a gem room, diamond counter or luxury watch area.
- Safe or vault area.

Cantor says camera locations "depend on the purpose for which they are intended." You'll need a different arrangement depending on whether the CCTV is supposed to deter hold-ups, prevent internal theft, screen customers entering the store or keep watch inside a vault.

What to buy: Comparison shop. Buy quality, brand equipment from a dealer with a reliable reputation.

Look for "commercial-grade" equipment, not cameras intended for home use.

Don't go to your discount, mass merchandise or home video store because it's cheaper. Many jewelers—out of naiveté or to save money—buy the wrong type of system, says Bud Wilkey, president of Video Surveillance Systems, Ashland, Ore. "They purchase systems from discount stores because they cost only a couple of hundred dollars," he says. "They may be cheaper, but they're not commercial grade. They're housed in plastic and don't have the technology or durability [for business situations]. They're better for watching the nursery!"

Commercial-grade CCTV systems are made with tougher materials and are more durable. "They're work-horse systems created specifically for industrial or commercial use, designed to operate 24 hours a day, day in and day out," says Wilkey.

Home-use VCRs, for example, are built for non-continuous use, says James Ridenour, senior products manager for Wells Fargo Alarm Systems, King of Prussia, Pa. "You turn it on for a couple of hours, then off. But commercial-grade VCRs are built to operate continuously, for hundreds of hours, non-stop. If you use a VCR made for home use [in a commercial setting], it must be serviced more often and replaced much sooner" than a commercial one.

UL listing: Look for VCRs and monitors with an Underwriters Laboratory listing, adds Ridenour. (A UL committee that includes JSA's White is drafting standards for CCTV cameras.) As with safes, the listing means equipment meets UL standards. Not all CCTV equipment is UL-listed.

Get an easy-to-use system. Have the dealer explain clearly what it does, what its parts are and what it means to your security.

Don't worry about knowing *exactly* what you need. Most dealers will discuss your needs (by phone, if they are mail order firms); many will even survey your store, check lighting conditions, floor plans and layout, and prepare a proposal for you with recommended options and costs.

Cost: A basic system (including installation) can run from $1,000 to $10,000 per store, depending on the number and type of cameras and other equipment. Most cost from $1,000 to $5,000.

There are options other than outright purchase. Francis Call, a jeweler with 11 stores in the Phoenix, Ariz., area, finds that lease/purchase is best. Leasing and service support cost him $2,000 a year per store; the equipment was paid for in three years.

Also, check with your insurer. "Ask if [CCTV] will reduce insurance premiums and by how much," says Bill Shepard of Wayne Jewelers & Silversmiths, Wayne, Pa. "It may help to make the expense worthwhile."

Remember, too, that maintenance costs are minimal initially and reasonable thereafter if the system is serviced regularly.

After-sale: Ask the dealer if a service contract is available, says White. "If so, is it [effective] only when there is trouble or does it include periodic inspections?"

Get a list of other retail customers from the dealer and ask them about the product and service support. How fast does the dealer respond to problems? Does he have backup equipment when yours is being serviced?

Even if you have a service contract, check your CCTV daily or at least weekly to ensure it's in good running order and your cameras are in focus. Surprisingly, many jewelers told JCK they only do this "as needed" or "if there are problems." But by then it's too late

"This a common error," says White. "A number of robberies haven't been recorded due to jewelers' negligence. The system was broken and not repaired. There was no tape in the VCR, or it was turned off!" Indeed, a jeweler in JCK's poll says he had no tapes of a robbery at his store because his staff forgot to turn on the CCTV that day!

Testing: Before permanent installation (by you or your dealer), put up the cameras temporarily and view the monitor and VCR tapes, say jewelers with CCTV systems. Are the pictures sharp and clear? Does the camera show what you want? If not, you may want to use a wide-angle lens, a zoom lens for close-ups or a pan/tilt device. Are lenses clean and focused?

Look for blind spots, such as out-of-sight corners and areas hidden by showcases or pillars. You may need to reposition the camera or add another one. White adds that dropped ceilings, partitions and posts limit a camera's view.

Are your cameras too high? When Davenport, Iowa, jeweler John Benson was robbed of $20,000 in merchandise in December 19090, his CCTV got the thief on tape—but the man wore a wide-brimmed hat that obscured his face. Benson has now lowered his cameras to see "below hat-brim level."

Lighting affects video images, and this affects how useful they are to you and police. Check the image in low, normal and high lighting situations, Is lighting adequate or must it be improved for a clear picture? If your system is on 24 hours a day, use cameras that provide sharp pictures under low light.

WHAT CCTV INCLUDES

A basic CCTV system includes:

• One or more cameras (and camera mounts). Many come with 16mm lenses, though wide angle (6mm, 8mm, 9mm) and zoom are available. Most are black and white, which is cheaper than color. However, some professionals say color CCTV gives more detailed pictures

• One or more monitors. This "TV set" shows what the camera sees. At least one is needed for every four cameras, unless you use a sequential switcher (see "Accessories" below).

• A videocassette recorder. This records what the camera sees and the monitor shows, making a complete record of what happens for later review. It's an essential part of a jeweler's CCTV, says the Jewelers' Security Alliance.

There are two types of commercial VCRs: time-lapse and real-time. Time-lapse VCRs recorded with brief breaks—from a second to several minutes, depending on programming—between pictures. A time-lapse VCR can record hundreds of hours on a tape that can be viewed in less than two hours. Real-time VCRs record non-stop.

Buy VCRs with a time/date generator. These imprint the exact time on the tape, says Jim Pusateri of Forest Security Systems, River Grove, Ill. "Without a day/date stamp, a tape is useless in court," he says.

• Videotapes. These go in the VCR to record what the CCTV sees. Blank tapes can be bought wherever prerecorded ones are sold. Various grades are available; security professionals advise buying the top grade ($6 to $9 a tape); these last longer and give better pictures. Keep tapes two weeks before reuse to allow time for review, says JSA, especially if a crime was committed.

• Accessories: These include zoom lenses for close-ups and pan/tilt devices, which move a camera up, down or sideways. For multi-camera systems, there is a quad splitter, which divides a monitor screen into four parts to show the entire operation at once, and a sequential switcher, which shows each scene in quick succession.

BASIC CLOSED-CIRCUIT TELEVISION FOR JEWELERS

JCK asked a dozen suppliers of CCTV equipment to suggest basic systems for two types of jewelry stores. Here's a synopsis.

Store #1: Downtown, Main St., 1,600 sq. ft.

Cameras: Two to six.

Other equipment: A time-lapse videocassette recorder and a quad splitter or a sequential switcher.

Total cost (including equipment, installation and accessories): $1,100 to $10,000, with most in the $2,000 to $5,000 range.

Approximate annual maintenance cost: $100 to $500, depending on cameras and level of service.

Store #2: Mall, 1,000 sq. ft.

Cameras: One to four.

Other equipment: Time-lapse VCR, video monitor and a quad splitter or sequential switcher.

Total cost (including equipment, installation and any accessories): $750 to $7,500.

Approximate annual maintenance cost: $65 to $1,200, depending on cameras and level of service.

Crime Against Jewelers: Ever More Violent

September 1991 Part I

"I knew I was going to die!"

Jeweler Janella Sims recalls clearly the gun barrel touching her head as she sat, as ordered, with her head between her knees in the bathroom of her Hokes Bluff, Ark., store.

The gunman, one of the two robbers, pulled the trigger. The only sound was a 'Click.'

Fortunately for Sims, the gun jammed, but she took another pistol whipping before the two men fled on that Dec. 14 afternoon.

Jeweler Duyet Dinh Vu, a 42-year-old Vietnamese immigrant, wasn't so fortunate. Shortly after 4:30 p.m. on Dec. 29, two teenagers locked his two young daughters in a bathroom, then shot and killed Vu, whom they had beaten and tied, after he managed to pull a concealed weapon and started firing. His family has since sold the store, Gold Port Jewelers in Westminster, Cal.

Under attack: These are just two casualty reports from a domestic war zone that reaches into every one of the 50 states. Today the nation's 40,000-plus retail jewelry stores are under sustained attack by criminals whose only common bond is their lust for quick riches, in cash or easily-fenced, high-value jewelry. They are white, black or Hispanic; race is irrelevant. They are polite or crude, well-dressed or wearing dirty jeans. And, increasingly, they are vicious.

Armed robberies of jewelry stores rose 24% last year, and violence occurred in one out of three, says the Jewelers Security Alliance, with 30 people killed. That's the most jewelry store fatalities since 1980's bloody tally of 46.

Faced with this onslaught and fearful of its consequences, many jewelers are tightening security, with the major chains setting the pace. Yet, for every jewelry store with an alert, well-trained staff there are many more where security precautions are lax, ineffectual or non-existent.

One key message emerges from interviews with chain-store and other security experts, local police and the FBI: Many jewelry store robberies could be averted simply by adopting and following good, basic, common-sense security procedures.

"The human element is a big factor in and the cause for most losses," says Kevin Valentine, vice president for loss prevention of Sterling Inc., the second largest U.S. jewelry retailer with about 1,000 stores. If more jewelers followed their own security procedures consistently, he says, "many losses would not occur."

Prepared: Regrettably, too many jewelers don't take adequate precautions until *after* a robbery, say jewelry industry and law enforcement officials. Many don't even know the person to call at the local police or at mall security in an emergency nor have they any personal contacts with police.

"People don't want to discuss security ahead of time," says Sharron Nelson, executive director of the Pacific Northwest Jewelers Association, which is actively developing security programs for its members. "But the crime problem isn't going to get better, just worse.

"Jewelers must learn to be pro-active, not reactive. The better prepared jewelers and everyone else in the industry are, the better the chances of keeping it [crime against jewelers] under control."

COMMON SENSE SECURITY REDUCES ROBBERY LOSSES

More jewelers should use common sense, not guns, to prevent robberies or reduce losses.

That's the conclusion of law enforcement, security and jewelry store security experts whom JCK interviewed for this special report.

Too often, they say, jewelers ignore common sense precautions. They're understaffed at critical times, display too much expensive jewelry in one place, don't use verbal alert codes or don't report suspicious characters. Many don't even know or post the name and number of police or mall security to call in an emergency. Even worse, they violate their own security policies, letting in customers after closing to make an extra sale, for example, or turning off buzz-in locks because it might slow down business.

Do most jewelers know what to do before, during and after a robbery?

One store manager, who echoes many others, puts it succinctly. In an actual robbery, she says, "no one knows how they'll react. Instinct takes over."

But foreknowledge and good in-store training can prevent that—and save lives and merchandise—say security experts.

WHAT YOU SHOULD DO BEFORE A ROBBERY

• Consider the safety of your location. Are security costs rising to an unacceptable level? If so, at least consider a move to a safer location.

• Don't "stretch" normal opening or closing hours to make an extra sale. This is when you are most vulnerable to attack, say security experts.

At least two employees should open the store, with one watching the other from a short distance, such as across the street, says the Jewelers Security Alliance (JSA). The observer should have quick access to a phone. An approach by anyone to the person opening the store should be regarded as a threat, and the observer should call police immediately, says JSA President James B. White.

Once inside, keep store doors locked while taking merchandise from the safe to showcases and window displays.

Closing time is even more precarious. The staff is hustling to wrap up the day's business, the safe usually is unlocked and merchandise is neatly concentrated ready for overnight storage.

"Lock up at a specified time religiously, even if customers are in the store," says White. "Absolutely no one should be let into the store after closing time." That includes apparently upstanding citizens who appear at the door after closing saying they need a gift for a forgotten birthday or anniversary.

One employee should stay at the front door after closing to let out any customers still in the store. Doors should be relocked immediately after each leaves.

• Always aim to have at least two adult employees in the store and visible to customers at all times.

If that isn't possible, protect yourself by investing in appropriate security equipment, i.e., buzz-in locks, surveillance cameras and riot glass.

• Have regularly scheduled in-store security training.

All employees should know and discuss your plans for crisis situations. Sterling Inc., for example, requires a review of security procedures at least once a quarter at its stores' weekly staff meetings. Security procedures, including what to do during a robbery, are reviewed and role-played by all staffers.

"If you do this constantly, covering all situations, it's likely you and your people will know exactly how to react to a holdup," says Kevin Valentine, the chain's vice president for loss prevention. "This should also be part of the orientation of every new full-time and part-time employee."

Invite law-enforcement authorities to discuss proper procedures in hostage, holdup and other crisis situations. Hold a similar session with the store's alarm company to clarify its procedures (such as requiring employees who want to enter the store during non-business hours to sign in at the alarm office).

Jewelers Mutual Insurance also suggests an employee or employees be made responsible for daily security checks, such as checking showcase glass and motion detectors.

• Be alert to suspicious, untypical consumer behavior, especially if it seems your store is being cased. Spotting such behavior should be a subject for staff training and review in staff meetings for both managers and employees.

Act on your suspicions. The old adage, "Better safe than sorry," certainly applies. Use in-store security alert codes and notify police and/or security.

• Have an in-store verbal alert system for suspicious customers and situations. Be sure all your employees know these security code words or phrases.

These alert the staff and any in-store security that something isn't right. For example, "Has Mr. Jones picked up his special order?" can actually mean "I have a suspicious person here. Call security."

Such an alert warns sales floor staff to spread out to pre-assigned positions (near the entrance, in front of the counters, etc.) and watch the suspicious customer. A pre-assigned individual (usually in the office) should call police or security.

• Get to know your mall security people and police. *Ahead of time,* learn the names and numbers, and whom to contact in an emergency. Post an emergency list next to all phones.

• Limit the amount of merchandise you display in windows and display counters. Don't exceed your insurance limits. This is especially true if your store doesn't have shatterproof riot glass.

"The more there is in a window, the more likely a store will be a target," says Valentine. Indeed, a survey among convicted robbers found the amount of money or merchandise available in a store was their top concern.

Jewelers Mutual recommends displaying valuable merchandise at strategic sites around the store rather than in one place.

• Don't exceed your insurance requirements or misrepresent your inventory. It will certainly affect your claims and coverage if you are robbed.

Jewelers carry higher inventories at peak seasons. Most insurers allow for the differences, but you must state the amounts clearly and not exceed them. "If the adjuster requires a full inventory and determines there was more on the premises than was recorded, he can deny the claim," says Carol Basden of Basden Risk Management, Birmingham, Ala. You also must tell the insurer when you increase inventory, change address, trim staff or alter any other item covered in the insurance contract, says William Herrbold, vice president of claims at Jewelers Mutual.

• Minimize risk by showing very high-end merchandise by appointment only, suggests Edward McGunn, chairman of McGunn Safe Co., Chicago, Ill.

• Show only one piece of merchandise at a time. Show only what is necessary.

High-ticket merchandise like loose diamonds should be shown only in a designated room, such as the diamond room, says Ann Cranford, vice president of operations for Carlyle & Co. Jewelers.

• Keep some inventory in stock as backup to prevent being "wiped out" if robbed, suggests Cranford.

• Ask for identification, where appropriate. Demand it of delivery people, sales representatives and visiting vendors.

Also consider asking for ID when showing very high-end jewelry and retaining it until the end of the presentation. If a customer refuses, you refuse service.

"Demanding an ID when showing expensive merchandise—even if the customer objects—can deter someone from robbing your store," says Tom Jones, vice president of operations of Littman-Barclay Jewelers, the 112-store Northeast chain which has such a policy.

Both Cranford and Valentine add that stores which use buzz-lock entries should have an identification policy for who is admitted. "Admitting any strangers without question or identification can be dangerous," says Cranford.

• Don't violate your own security procedures. Follow them consistently. Don't bend rules or make exceptions. Train your staff—part-time and full-time—to follow them consistently. Repeated experience in the jewelry industry shows that ignoring one's own precautions is dangerous and provides the foot-in-the-door which robbers need, says Cranford.

WHAT YOU SHOULD DO DURING THE ROBBERY

• Keep calm and do as you are told. (Good staff security training helps here.) Expect to be threatened, tied up, handcuffed and/or made to lie on the floor.

• Obey a robber's orders exactly. Don't say or do anything—not even raise your hands—unless told to do so. Freeze until the robber tells you to do otherwise.

• Don't do anything that creates risk to yourself or others.

"Too often, prudent conduct gives way to emotions," says the JSA's James White—and that's when a incident can turn violent.

Sterling has a written policy covering holdups which notes that store managers and assistant managers "are responsible for the protection of customers and employees. Do nothing that will compromise the safety of them."

• Don't resist robbers. Security experts are virtually unanimous in this. Make no threatening, violent responses. Do what they say—and only what they say—without question.

"Life is more valuable than merchandise," says Carlyle's Ann Cranford. "There's no way to predict the outcome of the situation" if you resist.

• Don't reach for a gun. It may seem a natural reaction, and many jewelers keep a gun in their store for protection and the psychological security it provides.

But, say jewelry store security experts, the odds are almost always in favor of the armed robber—who usually won't hesitate to use his weapon.

"If you pull a gun, you must be prepared to use it," says one veteran industry expert. "If you do, you should know *how* to use it"—and be prepared to accept the consequences of your action. These include your own possible death or injury, the same for an employee or customer and possible criminal charges and/or financial liabilities against you from injured victims or their survivors.

• Don't push an alarm button or any other alarm device during a holdup. Any move can provoke a violent response from a robber. Also, if police arrive at the store during a robbery, "you have a potential hostage situation," says Valentine.

Push the button only after robbers have left, Sterling tells its people.

• Don't get cute with armed robbers. Don't try an obvious stall when they demand cash or merchandise.

• Carefully observe characteristics of robbers and their accomplices (i.e., physical appearance, hair color, weight, height, clothing) and their vehicle, if any (color, style, license). These will aid police in catching and identifying suspects.

At staff meetings, review what employees should look for. For example, Sterling gives employees standardized pictures of a man and a woman, with notations of basic things to observe (physical appearance, height, weight, appearance).

• Don't pursue robbers when they flee. There is a risk of harm to you or others, and such action can leave your store unprotected.

"It just isn't worth it to fight or chase a gunman for merchandise," says Littman-Barclay's Tom Jones. "That's what insurance is for!"

WHAT YOU SHOULD DO AFTER THE ROBBERY

• Immediately write down any characteristics of robbers which you and your employees observed for use by police. Such procedures are already used in the banking industry. Sterling requires employees to fill out and submit incident reports within 24 hours of any loss (including robbery, shoplifting, smash-and-grab, internal theft). Copies go to police, the district manager and insurance firms.

• Armed robberies almost always bring media and consumer attention. This can interrupt your business's efforts to recover quickly and can hurt sales.

Have one person (manager or owner, or a corporate spokesperson) designated to deal with media and customers' questions. Tell other employees not to discuss the situation with the press.

20 Tips to Deter Robbers

Jewelry store security experts who reviewed JSA's list of robberies in December 1990 at JCK's request offered these tips on improving basic store security:

• Have a regularly scheduled review of store security procedures at store staff meetings. All full- and part-time employees should know them.

• Be alert to untypical customer behavior. It may indicate your store is being cased.

• Don't "stretch" normal opening or closing hours to make a sale.

• Have a policy for buzz-lock doors on who gets buzzed in and who does not.

• Have in-store staff security codes and be sure all staff members know them.

• Report suspicious persons and activities. Don't wait or ignore them.

• Know and post emergency phone numbers ahead of time.

• Don't have fewer than two employees in the store at all times.

• Use security cameras and shatterproof glass to deter crime.

• Don't ignore your own security procedures or bend the rules.

• Ask for ID when showing expensive merchandise and hold it until the end of the presentation.

• Show only one piece at a time.

• Follow a robber's instructions exactly.

• Don't do anything that creates risk for other people.

• Don't hit an alarm button while a crime is in progress.

• Don't reach for or use a gun.

• Observe details of a robber—physical appearance, type of car, license—for police use later.

• Don't get cute with robbers; don't try an obvious stall.

• Don't pursue a criminal.

• Know how to deal with media after the event.

Robbery & Burglary Defined

Robbery and burglary are forms of theft, which is the taking of property without the owner's permission with the intent of not returning it.

Burglary of a business involves the breaking and entering of the premises after business hours. Usually, there is no confrontation with the victim.

Robbery, on the other hand, is theft through force or intimidation and involves confrontation with the victim.

Well-equipped

Certain security equipment can help jewelers, especially those with small staffs or high-risk locations, deter or frustrate robbers.

Surveillance cameras: Surveillance equipment can be a deterrent. Last year, 80% of armed robbery claims filed with Jewelers Mutual Insurance occurred in stores *without* surveillance equipment. Would-be thieves often go elsewhere when they spot it.

A panning camera at the entrance, especially in malls, monitors people entering the store as well as any standing just outside casing it.

Use TV equipment which gives high-quality pictures. (Low-quality equipment which gives poor—sometimes unusable—photos is a recurring problem, say law enforcement officials.)

Be sure your surveillance TV functions properly and has a regular proper maintenance schedule. Cameras should be checked regularly to ensure they cover the store's high-value area and are in focus.

Glass: Use shatterproof laminated riot glass in windows and display cases. Sterling Inc., which does, recommends using glass at least a half-inch thick.

Such glass, which contains a layer of plastic, won't collapse when struck, and can take many hits. It is available at most glass suppliers, and cost has come down considerably in recent years.

However, say experts, be sure the glass is attached properly to display window frames or it may fall out when hit.

Buzz-in locks: Ease of access and escape is the second biggest concern of retail store robbers, according to a recent survey of 241 convicted robbers in five state prisons conducted by the Athena Research Corp.

Jewelers Mutual Insurance says buzz locks can be effective for the "high-risk jeweler who uses [them] wisely," according to a spokesman. However, insurance firms may or may not award credits for the use of buzz-lock doors when drafting a policy.

If you use buzz-lock doors, say security experts, devise specific procedures governing their use. These should cover who is and isn't admitted, if identification is required and when—if ever—the lock isn't used. Be sure all your staff knows and follows these procedures without exception.

Mirrors: Install mirrors in strategic places around the store if your store is short-staffed or if there are blind spots where customers can move out of view of salespeople.

Time locks: Time-delay locks can prevent up to 75% of attacks on safes during robberies, says Edward McGunn, chairman of the McGunn Safe Co. in Chicago, because a crook won't wait for the timer to kick in so the safe can be opened.

Some experts dispute this, saying an unstable crook or one high on drugs may act rashly if told that a safe can't be opened right away. However, says McGunn, "overwhelming statistics [show] the risk of robbery is reduced with a time-delay lock."

A clear in-store advertisement that the safe has a time-delay lock can be a deterrent. However, warns McGunn, don't post such a sign if your safe *isn't* equipped with such a lock.

"A crook may sense you're lying, and this is when violence can occur," he says.

In Case You're Cased

The same guy has been in your store twice already. He says he wants an expensive diamond for his wife, but something isn't right. He's looking too closely at too many things throughout the store and isn't paying attention to the salesperson's conversation.

You're being cased, and you know it. You feel helpless and apprehensive because you know the next time you see him, he may have a pistol pointed in your face.

What do you do?

Tip-offs: First, be alert and know what to look for.

"A store manager should know what the natural habits of customers are, and a good jewelry salesperson should be able to perceive what is natural and not natural in a jewelry transaction," says Kevin Valentine, vice president for loss prevention at Sterling Inc. "When things seem unordinary, then be suspicious."

Here are a few tips from the Los Angeles Police Department and jewelry store security experts on how to spot someone casing you.

Be alert to:

• Lone individuals or a man and woman posing as a couple, the most usual way in which would-be robbers case jewelry stores.

• Customers who seem to interested in looking over the store, or seem to be checking out surveillance camera locations. Take note, too, if they seem to examine showcases. They may, for example, tap on the glass.

• Customers who ask to see expensive merchandise, but seem disinterested in the salesperson's explanations.

• People who stand outside the store before entering or after leaving.

• Customers who linger in the store a long time, without buying, and seem to be waiting until other customers leave.

• Customers who dress or behave in an unusual manner or wear clothing which can hinder recognition of their features. Examples would be people who don't remove their sunglasses or a wide-brimmed hat during the entire time they are in the store.

Staffers: The next line of defense is a well-trained staff.

Everyone in the store must be trained to recognize suspicious people and to alert other staffers, usually with an innocuous-sounding code word or phrase such as "Has Mr. Smith picked up his special order?"

Then, says James B. White, president of the Jewelers Security Alliance, the staff should spread out discreetly to various posts in the store, including the back room and near the entrance. This puts some staff out of the potential range of fire; gives others a better opportunity to sound an alarm; enables those by the entrance to check license numbers and/or accomplices after the casing suspect leaves—and lets the suspect know he is under suspicion and being watched.

Discourage them: If you are suspicious of a customer, tell that person that new merchandise is coming which may interest them and that you'll contact them when it arrives. Then, ask for a business card or address and phone number. Note very carefully the person's reaction to this.

Jot down a brief description of the person immediately after he or she leaves, and note—if possible—the description of the car driven, if any, and get the license plate number.

Alert police and/or mall security as well as your staff. All too often, jewelers don't report suspected individuals or activity because nothing happened, say security experts. When they do make a report an FBI agent involved in loss prevention recently told JCK, "it is much after the fact.

"There is," he said, "a lack of communication between jeweler and police. But if someone seems suspicious to you, they'll probably seem suspicious to the police."

"If you're *really* sure you're being cased," says JSA's James White, "give it a shot and call the police. They may not bother, but they may come right out—even in New York."

As proof, he cites the case of one Manhattan jeweler who called the police after a suspicious customer came to the door at closing, trying to talk the jeweler into buzzing him in. Instead, the jeweler called police and furnished a description of the man, says White.

"It turns out the description fit a suspect who had just robbed a jewelry store a few blocks away," he says. "So the police came right out."

Jewelers can help their case by visiting local police stations to meet officials, explain what they do and tell when their most vulnerable times are (opening and closing). They also can cement relations with police by inviting them to present security lectures at store staff meetings.

Organize: Jewelers also can help themselves improve defenses against would-be robbers.

"I remember being cased once and calling the police," recalls Santa Barbara, Cal., jeweler Dick Kern. "The first thing they asked me was, 'Has a crime been committed?' I told them, 'Not yet,' and they said they weren't interested."

But Kern says there's an easy way for any jeweler to get help, even if it isn't an armed police squad guarding your door: Organize an alert network.

Chances are, says Kern, of Churchill Jewelers, the suspect will case other stores in the area as well—comparison shopping, if you will. So Santa Barbara-area jewelers have organized a "Fan-out" telephone network to alert one another to suspicious characters.

Here's how it works: If a jeweler thinks he's being cased, he waits until the person leaves, then phones the team leader. That's another jeweler designated by the group to put the network in action. The jeweler gives the team leader a description of the suspect and any other details he's noticed.

The team leader than calls three colleagues, each of whom calls three others. The entire network of 42 members can be warned within a few minutes. (As a double-check, the team leader calls the last name on the list 30 minutes later to be sure everyone was warned.)

With warnings, jewelers can take better precautions if the suspect comes to their stores. These include refusing to buzz the person in or keeping closer watch on him or her. Jewelers also can jot down the suspect's license number and type of car.

"Normally jewelers in the same area don't even want to talk to one another," Kern says. "But we've got a good organization [The Watchmakers and Jewelers Guild] which meets monthly and has formed good lines of communication."

It's an idea which more jewelers are adopting. At least three states—Oregon, Washington and Oklahoma—have or are setting up security alert networks for their members.

Remember, Malls are Vulnerable, Too

Security in a mall may differ from that for a downtown or strip center store, but there's no greater immunity from crime, say security experts.

Too often jewelers who move into a mall let down their guard, because they feel the threat of crime is lower. That's particularly true if they've just left an area of rising crime.

"That's a major mistake," says James B. White, president of the Jewelers Security Alliance. "There are many, many holdups at malls. Malls have no access control and some criminals are very brazen.

"We've even had reports of holdups in leased departments in department stores where there were hundreds of people around. So jewelers who feel safer in a mall are kidding themselves."

Differences: There are two main differences between mall stores and stores located elsewhere, say security people.

First, as noted, it's impossible for mall stores to restrict entry; the malls themselves are wide open and so are most of the stores inside. That makes them more vulnerable than downtown and strip center stores, which can install "access control" devices (mainly doors with buzz-in locks).

Second, however, mall stores are located much farther from parking lots and highways than downtown or strip stores. That makes robbers' escape routes longer, too.

The rule that jewelers are most vulnerable at opening and closing times applies especially to mall stores. The smaller crowds in the mall at such times make those long escapes much easier.

ID: Except for these two major differences, jewelers who operate both mall and non-mall stores generally apply the same security precautions to both.

Craig Ashe, head of security for 12-store Corbo Jewelers, based in Rutherford, N.J., says there are slight differences in risk between Corbo's mall stores and strip or downtown stores. However, they aren't significant enough to require different security measures.

"We're a bit less concerned with holdups at malls because it takes a long run to the parking lot," he says. "So we're more on the lookout for sneak thieves."

One Corbo control method is to take IDs from customers shown any item selling for more than $2,500 ($1,500 in some stores where they believe security risks are higher). The IDs are held until the item is returned to the case, Ashe says.

Usually sneak thieves work in pairs, he explains. One creates a diversion, like dropping a $20 bill or asking the time. Meanwhile, the accomplice looks at a piece of jewelry with the intent of grabbing it and running, or switching it with a fake.

"That's where the ID requirement comes in handy," he says, noting every store posts a sign with this policy. "Studies have found that many thieves don't carry IDs so we make it a policy: No ID, no merchandise. We think it's a good deterrent."

In malls: Among malls themselves, security differs widely, says Thomas Jones, vice president for operations at Littman-Barclay Jewelers, all of whose 112 stores are in malls.

For example, "Some malls hire off-duty police as armed security guards. This can deter armed robberies," he says.

445

Jewelers should be aware there are differences and make a point of learning the security precautions in malls where they now have or plan to put a store, says the Littman executive.

"We discuss a mall's security precautions with its management," he notes, "but we have never pulled out of a mall because they've been too lax."

While armed robberies are traumatic and tragic, and grab-and-runs are a nuisance, most of Littman's security hardware is directed against internal theft, he says.

"We've installed security cameras in some of our stores," he says, "but in most cases, it's where we have discovered inventory shrinkage."

Tips: Here are some security tips that apply to any mall.

• Install a panning camera at the store entrance. This monitors not only people entering, but also those who might be just outside casing the store.

• Be sure all salesmen show their lines in the back office, not in the store area. This reduces the possibility of grab-and-run thefts. It also keeps the salesmen from being targeted and followed by would-be thieves.

• Install strategically-placed mirrors if your store is short-staffed, or if there are blind spots where customers can move out of view of most salespeople.

• Have salespeople and mall security (if possible) present at opening and closing. Above all, keep the gate at the entry to your store closed until all inventory is locked in the showcases or safe.

Insurance Policy Perils: Read The Small Print Or Else

May 1991

With a revolver aimed at his face, Robert Trainer, owner of Trainer Jewelers Inc., Waverly, Ohio, did exactly as told. He lay on the floor, his wrists and ankles bound with tape, as a well-dressed young man rifled his store's safe and showcases that Saturday afternoon, March 5, 1990.

"Got any boxes for this stuff?" the thief yelled; Trainer answered no. Satisfied with his take, the man left. Trainer, who turns 70 this year, ripped free of the tape, freed an employee who had been bound and pushed an alarm button.

Police arrived within minutes. Though shaken, Trainer gave them a rough estimate of the loss that day, then contacted his insurance agent first thing Monday morning. The insurance adjusters asked questions about the robbery, checked the security system, took inventory and reviewed Trainer's tax forms from the previous two years.

"They were businesslike and polite," he says. "I felt they were very fair." Within a month, he received a $62,500 check from his insurer, Jewelers Mutual Insurance Co., to cover the loss.

No kid gloves: Howard Posin, owner of Howard's Diamond Center, Wheeling W.Va., tells another story. After his store was burglarized the night of March 28, 1987, Jewelers Mutual instructed him to take inventory to help determine the extent of loss. "It took six people four days to research through the past 10 years of invoices to come up with these figures," says Posin.

But when the adjusters arrived, he says, they refused his inventory figures. "To our surprise, they refused all help and began to take inventory from our retail prices," he says. This resulted in a much higher total inventory value than if the adjusters had used the invoice prices. The difference was critical because the in-safe warranty of Posin's jewelers block policy required that 86% of total inventory (by value) be placed in the safe at night. Based on the higher inventory value, however, he had only 74.6% in the safe the night of the burglary. Because of this violation, his claim for $74,000 was denied, says William Herrbold, vice president of claims at Jewelers Mutual.

Furthermore, says Herrbold, the figures Posin supplied failed to account for many items not stolen. (The adjustment process requires full inventory figures to be sure the in-safe warranty was complied with.) Jewelers Mutual says it gave Posin a chance to refute the adjusters' figures. "He didn't change them at all," says Herrbold.

Posin denies that he violated the warranty and says Jewelers Mutual never gave him a chance to refute the figures. He sued Jewelers Mutual, which tried to have the suit dismissed because it was filed more than a year after the burglary (a clause in his jewelers block contract said any legal action must be taken within 12 months of the loss). The West Virginia court denied the motion for dismissal, and the parties settled out of court three years later for what amounted to less than half of Posin's loss.

Strict enforcement: These two cases—polar opposites in the world of jewelers block insurance—demonstrate the importance of understanding the claims process. Most jewelers concede the need for insurance. They understand that they need a minimum level of security and procedural guarantees to get coverage. But far fewer realize that insurance firms require much more from retailers than just a signature on a policy. Because handling the claims process well can be critical after a burglary, JCK contacted insurers and policyholders for advice on how to avoid problems.

First and foremost, you must recognize that you'll run into great problems if you underestimate how strictly an insurer adheres to its jewelers block policies. Unlike auto and personal insurance, jewelers block insurance is narrowly defined and subject to legal agreements that, if made haphazardly, could leave you shouldering the very loss you thought your policy would cover.

Insurance agents present themselves as a friend of business and, in fact, do provide critically needed services. But insurance firms are in business to make money. And they can't make money by covering losses for jewelers who have violated provisions of their own policies.

Herrbold explains it this way: "We have an obligation to pay [the policyholders'] claims, and we have an obligation not to pay the claims that aren't covered. If we paid every single claim—covered or not, fraudulent or not—we wouldn't be here today."

Most claims handled by major insurers of retail jewelers are settled in timely and equitable fashion. Two major carriers of insurance for retail jewelers—Lloyd's of London and Jewelers Mutual—say they have low claim-denial rates despite an increase in the number of claims in recent years. Since 1987, Jewelers Mutual has received 4,387 claims and denied 396 (a 9% claim-denial rate). Many of the denied claims were from jewelers who knew they may not have been covered, says Jed Block, corporate secretary and communications director for Jewelers Mutual. "We encourage retailers to file claims in any loss—even if the agent or the jeweler is relatively certain there is no coverage," he says. "If we can find coverage, we'll cover it."

Lloyd's of London brokers in the U.S. say very few claims are denied, though they decline to offer statistics. "I don't think that's a statistic that is kept," says Howard Herzog, vice president of the Jewelers Block and Fine Arts Insurance Division of Alexander & Alexander of California Inc., a Lloyd's of London broker in Newport Beach, Cal.

Avoiding problems: How can you best prepare for a problem-free claims process?

"The most important thing is inventory—precise, documented inventory," says Art Cafiero, an agent at United International Adjusters, a New York City firm that sells insurance to jewelers for Lloyd's of London. Disputed inventory figures are among the most common reasons that insurance firms deny claims.

Adds Herrbold, "If retailers keep a perpetual inventory record, day-to-day figures, they know exactly what they have in the store. That's the ideal situation."

The minimum record-keeping suggested by Jewelers Mutual and most insurance companies is part of many retailers' basic accounting procedures. The basic steps include:
• Making a detailed and itemized inventory once or more each year. Items should be described in a manner that they can be traced to their original source (purchase invoice with stock number). The value of each item, inventory date and total inventory value should be included.
• Maintaining invoices of items purchased.
• Keeping a record of the cost of component parts of assembled items.
• Keeping a record of sales receipts that can trace a sold item to the listing of the physical inventory and the original source document.

"In keeping copious records, you protect yourself against a potential loss," says Jan Wilson, president of Aldo Brionis Fine Jewelers, Tampa, Fla. Masked gunmen tied up Wilson while ransacking her store in an upscale mall in May 1989. She says the insurance adjuster was sympathetic and, because of her perpetual inventory records, he was able to settle her claim in less than a month.

Quick settlement of a claim is important, says Carol Basden, owner of Basden Risk Management, a Birmingham, Ala., firm that insures jewelers through Jewelers Mutual and Lloyd's of London. "The initial trauma of an armed robbery is bad enough," she says. "You don't want to have to wade through 18 months of paperwork, too."

Trouble spots: Neither do you want to be notified that your claim is denied. When that happens, say insurers and retailers, one of the following is usually the reason:
• Exclusion from coverage. Several types of losses typically aren't covered under the standard jewelers block policy, including employee dishonesty and losses from unattended vehicles or property at trade shows. Such occurrences sometimes can be covered at additional cost. But buyer beware: additional coverage can be very specifically defined (see the Gemring Corp. section of the accompanying story on lawsuits).
• Violation of in-safe warranty. You must keep a minimum percentage of inventory in your safe when the store is closed. Generally, the higher the percentage, the lower the insurance premium.
• Misrepresentation of inventory. Jewelers carry higher inventories at peak seasons. Most insurers allow for the differences, but you must state the amounts clearly and not exceed them. "If the adjuster requires a full inventory and determines there was more on the premises than was recorded, he can deny the claim," says Basden. You also must tell the insurer when you increase inventory, change address, trim staff or alter any other item covered in the insurance contract, says Herrbold.
• Quality of safe (generally also a warranty condition). Your safe must not have a lower rating than noted on your insurance application. Insurers are emphatic about highly rated safes because statistics prove their usefulness. (New TL-30-rated safes cost about $3,000; higher-rated versions can exceed $20,000.)

The size of the safe is also important. "With a larger safe, more merchandise can be put away at night in the safe and the insurance costs can be lowered," says Herzog.
• Fraudulent claims. "Fraud against insurance companies is a major problem and we are not immune," says Herrbold. Though no figures are available, Basden adds that many of the larger fraudulent claims are from manufacturers and can be traced to a dishonest employee. Insurers deny coverage in the case of fraud, though recent court decisions have required payment to third parties, such as customers who bring jewelry in for repair, then lose it through the fraud.
• Loss of items in for repair. More than inventory is at stake in a burglary. You could lose a valued customer if an item he or she brought in for repair is stolen. But if your coverage is sound and the piece was identified properly when brought in for repair, says Herrbold, insurers will replace it. Most insurers recommend a repair envelope that creates three copies of the repair form. The customer signs the form and either assigns a value or agrees that you are

liable for only $75 if the item is lost. (Nearly every jewelers block policy requires the customer to first apply his or her personal jewelry insurance to the loss. Occasionally, the adjuster or the jeweler will negotiate a replacement cost with the customer directly, or the jeweler will replace the item at his own expense.)

Understanding complexities: To avoid these trouble spots, you need a clear understanding of your policy provisions. But policies and the contracts that bind them are complex. Too often, retailers sign without realizing the policy is a legal contract. The answers to such queries as "Do you take a complete, written, annual physical inventory of all your stock at least once a year?" and "The maximum value of all your stock during the last 12 months did not exceed $—" are legally binding once the contract is signed.

In many states, the contract is considered a warranty, and any violation can be grounds for denying a claim. Other states down-grade the contract to what is called a "representation." In this case, the violation must be "material to the loss" to be used as a reason for denying a claim. For example, if you violate a warranty requiring two employees in the store during business hours, that can't be considered in a claim resulting from an after-hours burglary. The violation is not material to the loss in this case, says Block. Ask your agent which interpretation applies in your state.

Many insurers now offer easy-to-read versions of standard policies. Examples include Jewelers Mutual's "Easy to Read Jewelers Block" and "Jewelers Pak" (which combines jewelers block and business owner policies). "Most companies are issuing easy-to-read policies," says Gerald Scattaglia, principal examiner for the New York State Insurance Department. "In personal lines [auto, home] they are being forced to; commercial lines are doing so voluntarily for the most part."

Finding a knowledgeable, helpful agent also goes a long way toward avoiding problems. "The policy is only as good as your agent—how he explains it to you and how good you read it," says H. Mark Fleischner, owner of Lauray's—The Diamond Center, Hot Springs, Ark.

Basden cautions that the number of agents and brokers experienced with jewelers block policies is limited. "If the jeweler has to explain what memo goods are or what keystone is, he needs to be careful," she advises.

Good sources of advice on insurance are other local retailers and local or state jewelry associations. In addition, Jewelers of America will refer retailers to appropriate Lloyd's of London or Jewelers Mutual representatives, says David Kelley, chairman of the JA Insurance Committee and a jeweler in Weatherford, Okla. "We don't recommend; we make sure retailers have several people to talk to about insurance," he says.

Soft market: During periods of stress—such as in recessions, crime waves and price fluctuations—jewelers are apt to take heavy losses. This translates into heavy hits on their insurers, which can affect everything from cost to requirements to availability of coverage.

During the high-gold-price, high-crime days of the late 1970s and early 1980s, thefts increased so rapidly that insurers had trouble keeping pace. That's why Jewelers Mutual, for one, temporarily stopped writing policies in many high-crime states. Conditions that made insurance very difficult to obtain then are tempered today by lessons learned over the years, say insurers. Instead of banning policies in high-crime areas,

insurers have stiffened security requirements and some charge considerably higher premiums than in low-crime areas.

Basden notes that an increase in the number of insurance sellers means lower prices in the 1990s. But she adds a note of caution. "Insurers will become enamored with the jewelry industry and put together a nice package and make it cheap," she says. "Then they'll take their first big loss and go home." She advises retailers to be aware how long a prospective insurance firm has been in the industry before signing up.

The strongest on a nationwide basis have been Jewelers Mutual, American International Group and Lloyd's of London, says Al Nagelberg, vice president of JH Albert, Needham, Mass. JH Albert is an independent risk management consulting firm that works with large retail chains to assess insurance needs. Others—such as St. Paul Fire and Marine, Chubb, Hanover and scores of regional firms—also have policies with jewelers. (One longtime regional insurer, American Universal Group of Providence, R.I., was declared insolvent early this year, leaving about 100 jewelers block policy-holders searching for new coverage.)

If you have questions about insurance in general or about a specific insurer, contact your state insurance commissioner. The commissioner's office will tell you how long the firm has been licensed in the state, its financial footing and whether anyone has filed complaints against it.

NO STRANGERS TO LAWSUITS

In the insurance business, lawsuits are part of the territory. Disputes erupt, complaints are filed and court dates are set. "Lawsuits in the jewelry industry are probably about as common as in any other industry," says Carol Basden, owner of Basden Risk Management Inc., Birmingham, Ala. "If a jeweler is denied coverage, and it's a substantial loss, there will be a lawsuit."

William Herrbold, vice president of claims for Jewelers Mutual, adds that for an insurer to deny a claim and risk litigation, "It has to have a very good reason."

Jewelers Mutual and Lloyd's of London both have entered courtrooms in recent years. Lloyd's brokers won't discuss lawsuits or say how many exist. But the firm was hit in January with what may be the largest "bad faith" lawsuit award in U.S. history. A jury in Alaska awarded a restaurant owner $60 million in punitive damages because Lloyd's canceled a claim after fire destroyed the business.

Jewelers Mutual openly responded to questions JCK posed about litigation. Five lawsuits are pending over disagreements with retailers in the past four years. During this period, the firm received 4,387 claims and denied 396 for a denial rate of 9%, says Herrbold.

Retailers who have been to court with Jewelers Mutual are invariably miffed by the experience and say the firm uses extensive legal maneuvers and delay tactics to wear down opponents. Evidence from recent lawsuits suggests that, at the very least, the firm is no pushover when defending itself against lawsuits.

"We felt from the first day that they had no intention to pay," says Keith Sutton, owner of jewelry stores in Evanston, Wyo., and Park City, Utah. Jewelers Mutual denied a $40,000 claim filed after an armed robbery at the Park City store in June 1986.

Jewelers Mutual said Sutton violated policy warranties requiring two employees in the store during business hours and that doors remain locked each morning until all jewelry is on display and the safe is locked. Sutton admits the violations, but says he understood from his agent that he would receive a portion of his claim nonetheless. Jewelers Mutual petitioned the local court to decide who was correct. The jury found that Sutton violated the locked-door warranty, but also said the warranty was ambiguous. It awarded Sutton $35,000 of the original $40,000 claim. "It cost us $20,000 to defend ourselves, so what we got out of it was a moral victory," says Sutton.

Herrbold admits the jury's message was "You're a little right and a little wrong," but he says Jewelers Mutual prefers consistency in dealing with policyholders. "We are a mutual company and we cannot overlook the terms of the contract." He adds that jewelry retailers won't receive partial payment for partial compliance to any insurance policy.

On the road: In California, meanwhile, Gemring Corp. of Los Angeles thought it was safe with $75,000 worth of coverage for each of its sales representatives for losses on the road. Then as a Gemring salesman walked away from his car to pay for gasoline on April 28, 1987, a thief jumped in and drove away with the jewelry case inside. The salesman made an attempt to stop the car but he was thrown to the ground.

Jewelers Mutual denied Gemring's $75,000 claim, saying the policy clearly states salespeople must always "attend" their vehicles when jewelry is inside. It also dropped the salesman from coverage. Gemring sued in 1988. Jewelers Mutual tried to have the suit dismissed, saying it violated a contract requirement that any suit "be commenced within twelve months next after discovery by the insured of the occurrence which gives rise to the claim." U.S. District Judge William Matthew Byrne declined to dismiss the suit, saying "the language of the policy limiting the time to bring suit in this regard is ambiguous."

Since then, the clause has been reworded to specify that suits must be filed within one year after the loss. In addition, some states allow lawsuits one year after the initial claim is denied.

After more than two years, Gemring settled out of court for $45,000.

Delayed settlement: In September, Paul Isaac, owner of Fox Jewelers, Beaufort, S.C., and Jewelers Mutual settled a claim resulting from a burglary at Isaac's store in Hilton Head 3 1/2 years earlier. The settlement followed a lawsuit in which Isaac charged the insurer with bad faith and delay tactics in his claim for $140,000.

Jewelers Mutual contended that Fox Jewelers hadn't bought enough insurance. The policy said the average daily balance of customer goods was $5,000, but the adjuster determined they exceeded $129,000.

The insurer also had trouble establishing the amount and arrangements for settlement because:
- The store's log book listing consignments and customer goods was stolen in the robbery (the log reappeared four months later).
- Customer claims continued to come in after Isaac filed suit.
- South Carolina law is unclear on who has rights to proceeds from the policy. The law doesn't say whether the money should be given to the jeweler or prorated and divided among memo holders and customers who lost jewelry in the robbery (Isaac had already paid customers who lost items).

With a jury already called in state court Sept. 4, 1990, Jewelers Mutual settled on a $172,500 payment rather than risk an adverse ruling. "Our recourse to an adverse reaction would have been to appeal," says Herrbold. "The appeal and retrial would have cost at least $100,000."

Date in court: In a suit scheduled for trial in March or April, Charles Ellenwood Jewelers, Dallas, alleged bad faith, breach of contract and other claims against Jewelers Mutual in connection with an armed robbery May 26, 1988.

Ellenwood sent proof of loss to Jewelers Mutual Aug. 3, 1988. The insurer denied the claim the following October, saying the firm violated policy warranties by opening its doors before its stock was placed in locked showcases and by not taking inventory quarterly.

Ellenwood sued in February 1989, but the case was delayed until May 1990 when Jewelers Mutual amended its answer. The insurer claimed one robbery participant (who was convicted) said in April 1990 that the robbery was planned and carried out with Ellenwood's help.

Ellenwood and his attorney, William Clay, deny that allegation and call it another "tactic" being used to deny the claim. Clay says the alleged mastermind of the robbery denied any involvement with Ellenwood. Herrbold says Jewelers Mutual has telephone records to back its case. But Clay sums up, "It's his [the alleged mastermind's] word against a convicted felon's."

Appointment With Trouble

May 1991

More jewelers, gemologists and jewelry salespeople than ever are finding that selling important pieces by appointment can be a lucrative source of income. Unfortunately, more criminals than ever are taking advantage of this privacy to work their trade, says Carol Basden of Basden Risk Management, Birmingham, Ala.

For some dealers, these have been appointments with murder.

Basden advises jewelers to avoid such transactions altogether. But she offers some do's and don'ts for those who insist on continuing them:
- Do restrict such deals to longtime customers. Some professional criminals may buy one or two smaller pieces to establish a relationship, then lure you into a trap with a much bigger sale.

• Do restrict such appointments to a bank vault or other secure place with guards and security cameras. Be sure you are covered walking to and from your car and be sure you're not followed.

• Do be as invisible as possible. Don't discuss your profession in public. It's tempting to try to impress people or pick up business with tales of big diamonds, but it's also very risky.

• Do get special insurance for goods that you'll carry out of the store. You'll be less likely to offer "fatal" resistance if they're insured.

• Don't do business after hours.

• Don't carry a gun. It provides a false sense of security. The criminal will use his before you can defend yourself.

U.L. Safe Ratings: What They Mean

September 1989

TL-15—The safe will resist entry for a total working time of 15 minutes when attacked on the door only with common hand tools, picking tools, mechanical or portable electric tools, grinding tools, carbide drills and pressure-applying devices or mechanisms.

TL-30—The safe will resist entry for a total working time of 30 minutes when attacked on the door only with common hand tools, picking tools, mechanical or portable electric tools, grinding tools, carbide drills and pressure-applying devices or mechanisms.

TL-30X6—This new rating, which Underwriters Laboratories began to test in July, indicates the safe will resist entry for a total working time of 30 minutes when attacked on any of its six sides with common hand tools, picking tools, mechanical or portable electric tools, grinding tools, carbide drill and pressure-applying devices or mechanisms.

TRTL-30—The safe will resist entry for a total working time of 30 minutes when attacked on the door only with common hand tools, picking tools, mechanical or portable electric tools, grinding tools, carbide drills, pressure-applying devices or mechanisms, abrasive cutting wheels and power saws, oxy-fuel gas cutting or welding torches—(quantity of gas consumed in one test limited to 1,000 cubic feet, combined total oxygen and fuel gas).

TRTL-15X6—The safe will resist entry for a total working time of 15 minutes when attacked on any of its six sides with common hand tools, picking tools, mechanical or portable electric tools, grinding tools, carbide drills and pressure-applying devices or mechanisms, abrasive cutting wheels and power saws, oxy-fuel gas cutting or welding torches (quantity of gas consumed in one test limited to 1,000 cubic feet, combined total oxygen and fuel gas).

TRTL-30X6—The safe will resist entry for a total working time of 30 minutes when attacked on any of its six sides with common hand tools, picking tools, mechanical or portable electric tools, grinding tools, carbide drills and pressure-applying devices or mechanisms, abrasive cutting wheels and power saws, oxy-fuel gas cutting or welding

torches (quantity of gas consumed in one test limited to 1,000 cubic feet, combined total oxygen and fuel gas).

TRTL-60—The safe will resist entry for a total working time of 60 minutes when attacked on the door only with common hand tools, picking tools, mechanical or portable electric tools, grinding points, carbide drills, pressure-applying devices or mechanisms, abrasive cutting wheels and power saws, oxy-fuel gas cutting or welding torches (quantity of gas consumed in one test limited to 1,000 cubic feet, combined total oxygen and fuel gas).

TXTL-60—The safe will resist entry for a total working time of 60 minutes when attacked on the door only with common hand tools, picking tools, mechanical or portable electric tools, grinding points, carbide drills, pressure-applying devices or mechanisms, abrasive cutting wheels and power saws, oxy-fuel gas cutting or welding torches (quantity of gas consumed in one test limited to 1,000 cubic feet, combined total oxygen and fuel gas), and nitro-glycerine or other high explosives.

Testing procedures: According to an Underwriters' Laboratories test engineer interviewed last year, the bulk of U.L. testing involves physical attack on walls and doors. Penetration is recorded when a 2-sq.-in. hole is created with cutting torches and tools. Other tests performed:

• A jamb test, which focuses the attack on the gap on the hinge side of the door, generally considered the weakest point on a safe.

• A mechanical check on the safe's bolt work. This includes the dead bolts—non-moving hardware on the hinge side of the door—and the live bolts, which move when the safe handle is turned.

• Tests involving specific attempts to pick and release the lock mechanism are performed separately, and may be contracted out to specialists. The locks are usually Group 2-listed and have undergone a series of picking tests.

Specialized equipment is not used during testing; all the tools used are readily available to the public.

According to U.L. spokesperson Natalie Miller, the company tests only prototype models, not every safe produced.

A comprehensive follow-up program includes field representatives who make unannounced factory inspections to ensure that every product is built to the specifications of the test model. These spot checks can be as often as daily and are performed at least four times a year per manufacturer.

Fire ratings: Fire ratings are based on the maximum allowable temperature in the safe interior. A class 350 safe means the interior cannot exceed 350° Fahrenheit during the fire exposure test. Class 350 safes are designed to protect paper documents, class 150 safes protect magnetic tape and photographic film and class 125 safes protect floppy disks.

In addition to the class rating, the safes are given an hourly rating (30 minutes to four hours), indicating the time the device can withstand a standard fire of controlled extent and severity.

Guns: Yes Or No?
The Jeweler's Ongoing Dilemma

December 1988

The gun control issue is back in the headlines. Heavily-armed drug dealers regularly outgun police forces, with innocent bystanders caught in the crossfire between rival gangs.

But the wildfire of drugs is not the only catalyst for gun control. Several violent incidents have captured public attention recently. In January five children were killed in a Stockton, Cal., schoolyard when a crazed Patrick Edward Purdy sprayed the crowd with a semi-automatic AK-47. On May 9, Alfred Hunter III, charged with killing his wife, stole a small aircraft and strafed Boston with a semi-automatic weapon for more than two hours.

Such cases have brought the issue of ordinary citizens arming for self-defense to the forefront of gun-control debate. Citizens certainly seem to be armed: roughly 70 million Americans own 140 million rifles and 60 million handguns, according to recent estimates from the federal Bureau of Alcohol, Tobacco and Firearms.

Armed robbery is a serious concern for many retailers and businesspeople. A vicious new breed of armed robber, the "drug-crazed thief," incites more fear than any professional thief or con man. Some see firepower as the only effective way to protect assets.

Statistics make it clear that crime is on the rise. The 1988 U.S. Uniform Crime Report shows violent crime up more than 5% from 1987. A total of 1,560,000 incidents were reported nationwide—an average of 4,274 such crimes every day of the year.

JCK recently asked its retail panelists how they feel about retaliation and weapons in the store. An overwhelming majority (75% of the 159 jewelers who responded) do not keep weapons in their stores and regard retaliation as unwise and dangerous.

The few, the proud, the armed: A militant minority of armed jewelers does exist, however. Of the 40 who do keep firearms in the store, three flat out disagree with the official Jewelers' Security Alliance position of no retaliation coupled with quiet compliance as the safest way out of a holdup situation.

All three indicate they would not hesitate to fight back in any holdup situation in which the robber showed force or a weapon. All are well-trained in the use of firearms. Two are JSA members; one belongs to the National Rifle Association.

The NRA member, Michael Ellenstein of Rogers Jewelers in Evansville, Ind., has this to say: "To sit passively by and let someone take my possessions or my life is not acceptable. It's ridiculous to think the government is going to protect me."

Some feel safer with guns: Most of the armed jewelers indicate that their gun has always been there and basically is not used. Some add that although they don't intend to use it, their staff feels a sense of security knowing the gun is behind the counter.

Despite these "the gun is just there" attitudes, only six respondents in this group say that retaliation could *never* be justified and would never be attempted.

About half of the armed jewelers agree wholly with JSA's no-retaliation position. An equal number have mixed feelings about fighting back. Most of the latter say retaliation would be justified only in a life-and-death situation, or when the "perfect opportunity" presented itself.

Different notions of this "perfect opportunity" generally involve turning the tables and getting the jump on the robber. One jeweler writes: "If an assailant is holding a gun on you, it would be foolish to go for a weapon. But if it were a situation when opening or closing and the gunman approached from a distance, it might require different action."

Richard Sather, who manages Sather's Jewelry in Evanston, Wyo., and works as a police deputy, touches another common thread. He explains that a holdup situation warrants retaliation only when "using a weapon will not further endanger the lives of customers, employees or bystanders."

The drug-induced growth of violent crime would spur several respondents to fight back. "Because of today's drug use," says one jeweler, "criminals are not non-violent, but extremely life-threatening." Mark Moeller, a certified gemologist appraiser from St. Paul, Minn., agrees that "it isn't the professional you worry about, but the drug-crazed thief."

Most don't pack guns: When JCK surveyed its panelists in 1976, 68.5% said they kept no weapons in the store.

That's still the majority view (today's 75% figure doesn't represent a significant change, given the size of the survey).

Jewelers most often attribute their refusal to keep firearms in the store to a general feeling that guns only invite and create a danger instead of helping to prevent it. These jewelers are content with electronic security systems and see no point in initiating a shoot out over the loss of inventory.

'Dead wrong': The high number of unarmed jewelers is welcome news for James White, president of the Jewelers' Security Alliance. White is "1000%" against retaliation and says that "store owners who point to rising crime as justification for arming and fighting back are dead wrong."

White says that although the numbers are distressingly high, incidents of jewelry store robberies involving violence have remained essentially the same since 1985: 22% of robberies involved violence in 1988, 27% in 1987, 21% in 1986 and 29% in 1985, according to JSA statistics.

The number of jewelers killed during robberies also has remained fairly even. There were 19 deaths in 1988, 12 deaths in 1987 and 15 deaths in 1986. As of May of this year, 10 jewelers had died during holdups.

Retaliation is a losing proposition in any situation, White says, because the robber has the jump on the employees and customers from the moment he enters the store. His gun is already drawn and it must be assumed he is ready and willing to use it. He also may be packing a concealed weapon, which can be even more dangerous.

Sudden moves, like reaching under a counter or to a holster for a gun, can only exacerbate an already tense situation, White says. Twelve panelists spell out their fear that an attempt to fight back might trigger violence from a holdup man who otherwise planned to grab the goods and get out.

Other options: Jewelers Mutual Insurance statistics indicate that video surveillance equipment is the best deterrent against all daytime (during open hours) losses. In 1988, 80% of daytime losses incurred by JMI clients occurred in stores without cameras or other surveillance equipment.

Both JMI and JSA also point to electronic lock doors, which allow store personnel to grant or deny someone access to the store, as effective holdup deterrents.

Jed Block, director of JMI communications, notes that JMI has no official stance on retail jewelers arming themselves, though it fully agrees with JSA's no-retaliation position.

Block feels, however, that guns are effective deterrents and notes that if JMI policy forbade clients to keep guns in their stores, it could become known that jewelers insured by JMI were unarmed. This knowledge could leave them vulnerable.

"Whether or not a jeweler has firearms in the store usually does not affect coverage," Block says, "and it is something JMI does not inquire about when drafting a new policy."

Guess Who Could Be Robbing You Blind

December 1988

Did you hear the one about a jeweler who learns some jewelry is missing and assumes it's lost? Need a punch line?

If his employees do steal, he'd "rather not know about it."

Then there's the jeweler who hires well-known, wealthy women because "they have no reason to steal." No punch line needed here.

Sound like "Saturday Night Live" spoofing "The Twilight Zone"?

No spoof. The attitudes are real, and they're hazardous.

Retail employees steal $10 billion to $20 billion from their employers each year, says *Thieves at Work*, a research book published in 1988 by the U.S. Bureau of National Affairs. The problem is rampant, and the retail jewelry business is no exception.

But take heart. You can catch employees who steal, and there are ways to avoid hiring a thief.

Common problem: First, let's look at some statistics gleaned from a JCK survey of retail jewelers. Eighty-seven percent of the respondents have experienced employee theft, 67% of them at least twice and 24% within the past 12 months.

What's stolen the most? Jewelry topped the list (mentioned by 78%) followed by cash (58%). "After one employee left, our register started balancing," says one Texas jeweler.

Also on the list are selling to friends below price (42%), private selling to customers (36%), embezzlement (23%) and stealing from store suppliers (6%).

"Employee theft is a big problem," says James B. White, president of the Jewelers' Security Alliance. In fact, the Jewelers Mutual Insurance Co., in cooperation with JSA, hopes to release a film next year on how to deal with employee theft.

Many jewelers could write the script from personal experience. For example:

• In Albuquerque, N.M., a jeweler's employee stuck an envelope containing jewelry in his pocket. When the store owner sought the jewelry days later, the employee said he'd forgotten about the envelope. His wife washed the pants containing the envelope, he said, and the jewelry got lost!

• In California, an employee used a supplier's courtesy of below-cost price for personal use to buy an expensive watch. Then he sold it "at a nice profit" for himself, says the jeweler. (The employee was never given another raise and eventually quit.)

• Some thieves get more than a slap on the wrist. "One of our administrative personnel was skimming money from daily cash business receipts," says Bill Shepherd, Wayne Jewelers & Silversmiths, Wayne, Pa. The confronted employee paid restitution and was fired.

Many inside thefts are suspected, but unfortunately, never traced to one person. "Our five-stone color grading set disappeared without a trace. We could pinpoint the day but not the occurrence," says a jeweler in Maine. "We now are very careful about the whereabouts of all loose stones."

Who's to blame? Were these jewelers simply unlucky? Did they go wrong in hiring? Or was it their management style? Each case is different.

"A thief has an advantage over you because he spends all of his time and effort thinking how to outsmart you," says Jack Spector, a certified public accountant quoted in the May 1987 issue of *Motor/Age*.

You *can* reduce the thief's advantage, however. It helps to understand his mindset. Some psychologists say stealing is pathological behavior, evidence of a person's lack of character. Regardless of psychological causes, says JSA's White, two factors are always present when an employee steals: opportunity and inclination.

Various situations create opportunity, including:

• Economic pressures on employees. However, *Thieves At Work* concludes only a small percentage of workers steal from employers to solve economic difficulties.

• Little commitment to the firm, especially among part-time and younger employees.

• Job dissatisfaction. Some workers feel they are entitled to make up for low pay by taking merchandise or money. Sometimes, the theft satisfies a desire for revenge on the store.

Preventive hiring: While psychologists and research analysts wrestle with the why of worker theft, jewelers deal with the result.

"We hire only highly educated, top-strata people from our area, a town of only approximately 120,000 population," says C.R. Rader, a jeweler in Macon, Ga. "We know most, if not all, our employees or their family before hiring."

Meanwhile, an Indiana jeweler thought he would be safe in hiring the daughter of a jeweler in another town when she moved to his area. "We learned she just about ran her father's store," he says, "but she couldn't get all our money to the bank." Store deposits often decreased when she took them to the bank.

Here are some tips on hiring honest employees:

• Confirm resume information. Check the previous employer's phone number through a telephone book or directory assistance to make sure it's not a phony number with a phony employer at the other end. Once you reach the previous employer, discuss any concerns and ask whether he would rehire the applicant if given a chance. If he wouldn't, you probably don't want the applicant either.

• Check the applicant's credit standing. Randall Chambers of Chambers Jewelers Inc., Fort Worth, Tex., asks past employers if they hold any outstanding bills against the applicant. He also researches the applicant's credit standing through a national credit checking firm. "If the applicant can't meet obligations to debts, I consider that irresponsible," he says.

• Consult consumer reporting agencies. Under the Federal Fair Credit Reporting Act, agencies may furnish consumer reports to potential employers. Reports usually contain information about a person's creditworthiness, general reputation, personal characteristics or mode of living, says the National Retail Merchants Association (NRMA) in a handbook titled *Apprehending and Prosecuting Shoplifters and Dishonest Employees.*

• Ask state or local police whether the applicant has been convicted of any crimes, says JSA's White. Policies vary by state, but conviction records generally are available to employers who have a signed release waiver from the applicant.

Remember that a conviction itself isn't always just cause for denying employment. A court is most likely to approve a denial of employment if there is a clear relationship between the nature of the crime and the duties of the job. The NRMA strongly urges retailers to contact their attorneys to discuss laws on information privacy, denying employment and handling of information gathered about applicants.

• Screen employees, but remember lie detectors no longer will be a screening option come Dec. 27. After that date, federal law will prohibit businesses from using polygraphs to screen job seekers or randomly test employees.

A few retailers responding to JCK's panel say they will sorely miss polygraphs. Most said they will turn to paper tests to weed out the dishonest. JSA highly recommends this option, but opinions vary on how well these tests pinpoint who is most likely to steal.

Build loyalty: As soon as you choose a new employee, strive to make him or her feel like part of the team. This helps to build accountability and loyalty to your business.

At Olson Jewelry, owner Karl Johnson likes to hire someone he's familiar with, and he discusses possible employees with his staff. The team feeling starts the moment a new worker arrives at the door. Johnson's choice for his first new full-timer in 12 years apparently met with staff approval—the new employee "was greeted with shouts and hugs by our present staff."

Set a good example for new employees—and long-timers. One jeweler relates his management style to childrearing. "As with my children, I stress honesty and exhibit it in my actions," says James O'Bryant of O'Bryant Jewelers & Gemologists, Maumee, Ohio. The key is showing, as well as telling.

A jeweler in Maine adds, "I make it clear that honesty begins at the top. We're careful to buy stamps from the business for personal mail and make sure, subtly, that [employees] know it."

Don't give your employees a reason to want to steal. Pay fair wages and treat them with respect. Salespeople at a smalltown jewelry store in Alabama are taken to dinner anywhere they choose when the store's monthly inventory is 100% accurate. That keeps everyone conscious of where they place jewelry, says the owner.

Keeping track: Employee theft accounts for a whopping 42% of all retail shrinkage, according to a 1986-'87 survey of more than 100 retailers by Arthur Young & Co. for the National Mass Retailing Association. That being said, you can never check inventory too often.

Numerous inventory systems exist, the most sophisticated being computerized lists of jewelry in-house. The regularity and consistency of these systems result in prompt discovery of theft and often deter it.

A lot of smaller jewelry operations haven't invested in this type of system, however. Most jewelers readily admit they make few inventory checks. Most common are annual storewide surveys, with twice-yearly or monthly checks on merchandise valued at $500 and up. Is that often enough?

No, says JSA's White. Inventory must be checked daily if employees are to get the message, he says. Certainly this is not always practical for small operations, he admits. But jewelers must try harder to develop frequent checking systems.

Not all jewelers are lax. Some in the JCK survey check everything daily; others check a different showcase or department daily. Several conduct weekly, unannounced spot checks, and one asks a different employee to do the check each time. Choose a system that works best for you, but choose one and use it.

When it happens: Let's assume you've covered all the bases; you diligently screen applicants and create an atmosphere of honesty for your staff. But one bad seed arrogantly ignores your controls and disappears with a gemstone. Do you have any recourse?

Possibly. If your insurance policy includes a rider for employee dishonesty, you may be able to claim the loss. In the past, employers would bond individual workers. Today, says Bill Herrbold, vice president of claims for Jewelers Mutual, jewelers may opt for staffwide coverage against employee dishonesty.

The option sounds great. But the store owner must prove the theft was internal. "This requires more than a shortage on inventory," says Herrbold. Types of evidence typically considered acceptable proof include a signed confession, altered paperwork, a film of theft or an eyewitness.

One upnote: you needn't bring a criminal charge against an employee in order to claim internal theft.

To help determine the specific nature of a loss—employee theft rather than shoplifting—White advises jewelers to control access to certain areas. Often only one or two employees need access to areas around the safe, the workshop or other designated places. Outsiders such as repairmen should be restricted from certain areas or accompanied by a responsible employee.

Closed-circuit televisions also help in classifying a loss. Employees needn't know you're watching them as well as shoppers.

Confessions: When you can't determine whether a loss is due to inside or outside theft, a high-pressure atmosphere might help to flush out the culprit. At Michaels Jewelers, Waterbury, Conn., a daily inventory showed that some loose diamonds were missing. An intensive daylong search initiated by the store manager turned up nothing but anxiety for everyone involved. By day's end, a young salesman approached the manager. "I've got to talk to you," he said. The search was called off and the manager, inexperienced in handling confessions, called owner John Michaels. "When confronted, [the young salesman] fell apart and confessed," says Michaels.

Michaels declined to give specifics of how he obtained the confession, but he said a jeweler must be careful of the legalities involved. "Before charging in, talk to an attorney," he says. "If you don't talk to an attorney, you had better be very, very experienced in handling these situations."

The salesman promised to return the diamonds the next day, and Michaels said that would bode well for him with police. Michaels even tried to help the man. "I said we'd support him," he says, adding the man was a nice person who'd grown up in a bad environment. "We had some feeling for him."

But three days later, the diamonds still had not been returned and the salesman was missing. "That's when we called the police," says Michaels. The diamonds eventually came back via mail. Authorities reviewed the man's background and offered him accelerated rehabilitation, which demanded family counseling.

Thief outsmarted: At Continental Jewelers, Wilmington, Del., a thief on the payroll lasted just 10 days. "He probably would have been around much longer had we not been tipped off by another area jeweler," says owner Paul Cohen.

The other jeweler said the man came to his store offering to sell a diamond estate ring, and he remembered seeing him in the store previously boasting that Cohen had hired him. Meanwhile, twice-daily inventory checks revealed first one ring, and later more jewelry missing from Cohen's store. Cohen rearranged employee assignments to pinpoint the person responsible and hopefully secure some evidence. At that point, his fellow jeweler called.

"Immediately, I went down to [his] store and identified one ring as ours," says Cohen. The jeweler also had a paper from the transaction bearing the employee's signature. "From there I drove straight to the state police barracks," Cohen says. "They arrested the guy that day."

The estate ring and two others were returned to Cohen. Other missing items couldn't be traced to anyone. The sentence: six months' probation.

"I'm sorry for society," Cohen says, adding the light sentence doesn't help much in the war against employee theft. But he and other jewelers continue to fight.

Follow through: When something is discovered to be missing, Michaels Jewelers follows a strict procedure. The manager takes a complete inventory, and an owner is called into the store within 24 hours. An insurance investigator comes to the store to question employees. In stores with closed-circuit television, film is viewed, and a paper test is administered. "It never fails," says Michaels. "Within a month, someone leaves employment here." In cases where specific evidence is gathered, Michaels promises to prosecute.

Jewelers should never accuse an employee of wrongdoing without solid proof, or they become open to a lawsuit.

At L. Luria & Son, a Florida-based catalog showroom, months of suspicion and surveillance recently were ended when the suspected employee was caught leaving work with $30,000 in diamonds, says assistant state prosecutor Fred Kerstein. Diamond buyer Michael Sunshine was convicted of grand theft, largely because he was caught redhanded, says Kerstein.

But even before Sunshine's arrest, a paper trail had begun. It started when another employee noticed that internal paperwork procedures weren't being followed. The employee alerted superiors, and a security check began immediately.

"A paperwork trail must be documented every step of the way," says Kerstein. "In this case, the employee was in a position of trust. He was responsible for both the paper trail and checking to make certain the paper trail was flowing correctly."

Sunshine was sentenced to a year and a day in jail and four years of probation. He also was ordered to cooperate fully with L. Luria & Son to uncover vulnerable areas that made possible a theft of this magnitude.

Luria employees spent countless hours documenting and cross-referencing proof of the theft. Does nailing thieves always involve enormous amounts of time and red tape? Many times it does, says John Michaels. One of several owners of the 13-store Michaels Jewelers chain, he doesn't lose time at the register or with customers when he has to appear in court. "For the guys who need to be in the store, it's difficult," he concedes. "But unless you're firm, you're a toothless tiger."

Insurance:
Flexible Life Preserver

September 1988 Part II

Insurance can be the life preserver for a family business in the turmoil following the death or disabling of an owner or key person. At such a time, liquid assets are needed quickly to cover debts, taxes and stock purchases to stay afloat.

Life insurance proceeds can provide ready cash while the rest of an estate is tied up in probate. Life insurance also is free of income tax and can be free of estate tax with proper planning, says the financial firm of Merrill Lynch, Pierce, Fenner & Smith.

In addition, certain property insurance products are important to the healthy continuity of a business and protection against large shock losses, says Carol Basden, program manager for the special accounts division of Hilb, Rogal & Hamilton Inc., a national independent insurance agency.

If you're the new owner of a family business, take a few minutes to review these basics and see how you measure up. If you're preparing a successor, this would be a good time to go over insurance concerns with him or her. The following insurance programs can benefit family businesses.

• Life insurance on shareholders and partners usually funds buy/sell agreements (also called stocked redemption plans). Each policy covers the value of the shareholder's stock; total coverage should equal the value of the company.

A company can use proceeds from the insurance to buy a person's shares if he or she dies or withdraws. If the insurance doesn't cover the full cost, the balance is paid in installments to the seller or his or her heirs.

• Key man insurance covers the life of an important officer (such as an owner) or a key employee vital to the efficient operation of a business (such as a watchmaker or jewelry designer whose loss through death would affect profits).

"I find banks like companies to have key man insurance in place as an added guarantee in applying for loans, so there will be additional cash in the company in the case of turmoil," says the head of a regional jewelry chain who took office when his father died suddenly.

It also "quiets fears of vendors who get nervous on the death of a principal and want to be paid off instantly," adds a Midwest jeweler.

The size of the policy can be based on the assumed loss of profits or tied to the amount of debt such a loss would incur, says George Nolen, southeast area manager for Hilb, Rogal & Hamilton.

• Disability coverage (a form of health insurance) for a key officer or essential employee provides income for that person if he or she is disabled and can't work. This is the one type of insurance most small firms overlook or ignore. But Nolen says it's especially important in a business that has no key person to keep it operating if the owner can't work.

• Overhead insurance provides money to pay operating costs—such as rent, salaries and equipment costs—if the owner is disabled. The costs are paid for up to two years. For example, if the owner is in the hospital for a couple of months, and the watchmaker is essential to the business operation, overhead insurance will provide money to pay the watchmaker's salary.

• Comprehensive all-risks coverage, like jewelers block insurance, covers serious inventory losses from robbery, theft or burglary. "It can happen anywhere, anytime to anyone," says Basden. "Not many businesses can sustain the shock of losing much of their inventory in one incident," especially during a period such as succession in a family business.

• Employee dishonesty coverage (also called fidelity insurance) protects against internal theft.

• Business interruption insurance covers the loss of profit if a business is closed due to a catastrophe such as fire, tornado, windstorm, fire or bodily harm to the owner.

• Deferred compensation insurance defers taxes on the earnings of a policy until retirement and is a good vehicle for key person coverage, says Basden.

How much?: The company takes out these policies, pays the premiums and usually is the beneficiary. But how much insurance should a company buy? Nolen says the size and type of policy (term, whole or universal life insurance, for example) depend on these factors:

• How much the company can afford to pay.
• The value of the company.
• How much is needed to cover the property in question.

A buy-sell agreement, for instance, should cover the firm's worth. Key man and business interruption policies should cover anticipated losses. All-risk should cover the value of the property.

Here's an example of how one firm has used insurance. Nelson and Magnolia Jones (pseudonyms for the owners of an actual Midwest store) and their long-time manager, Darryl Haus, are the only stockholders in a company whose book value is about $490,000. In a stock purchase agreement to sell the company to Haus, the Joneses set the per-share price at $1,500. At the time the agreement was signed, Mr. Jones owned 160 shares, Mrs. Jones owned 86 and Haus owned 26.

To meet the obligations of the agreement, the company has a life insurance policy on Mr. Jones for $240,000; on Mrs. Jones for $130,000 and on Haus for $50,000. Haus also has a disability income policy in case he is incapacitated or to buy out his shares if he is unable to work for more than a year. In each case, the company is the owner and beneficiary of the policy.

In the event of the death of any shareholder, the company will buy that person's stock within 30 days of receiving his or her life insurance proceeds.

Tips: When buying insurance, compare costs (including averages over a period of years).

Look at the ratings of various firms. Best Insurance Company Ratings, an independent service used by the insurance industry, annually rates insurance firms after reviewing their solvency and financial strength. Those rated A+ or better (such as A+ 6) are the strongest financially; those rated C are the weakest.

For advice and information about business insurance or companies, consult your certified public accountant, financial adviser or attorney; your state insurance commissioner's office; and, of course, your insurance agent.

"Go with an agent you can trust," says Nolen.

Jewelers & Crime: The Ongoing Battle

July 1988

Randy eyes a tray of gold bands and some watches in the jewelry store window. Heart racing, he fingers the lone bill in his pocket. Could this be your window?

Randy has been watching it covetously for nights now. His appetite has been whetted and tonight it will be satisfied. Will you pay?

Randy finds a brick in the alley. Heart pounding, he mutters, "Now! Do it, now!" The glass shatters, an alarm blares, then Randy grabs his booty and darts behind the building into darkness. Minutes later, a squad car arrives.

Jewelry and crime: Beauty is the jeweler's stock in trade, but his merchandise requires that he contend as well with the ugliness of crime. Crimes against jewelers have grown in both number and variety over the decade. Thus it's ever more vital that jewelers keep informed on crime trends, know how to discourage crime and know what to do if they become victims.

For example, the crime Randy committed in the opening vignette is called a 3-minute burglary. It's so named because even though an alarm sounded, and police responded immediately, Randy disappeared too quickly to be caught. The jeweler could have averted this loss by removing merchandise from his display window at closing time.

Three-minute burglaries accounted for 123 (or 41%) of the 300 burglaries committed against jewelers in 1987. But this approach to crime isn't new. It was used in 40% to 42% of burglaries against jewelers in 1985 and 1986. And in the Jewelers' Security Alliance notebook of bulletins, insert B-19—dated 1977—outlines this hit-and-run crime in elementary fashion.

Criminals occasionally do devise new ways to get their goods. One example is the smash-and-grab gang robberies that began in Los Angeles, Cal., about eight years ago. In these attacks, a gang of young, black males smashes showcases and grabs high-priced jewels while one member threatens violence. Rarely is anyone injured, says JSA president James B. White, though sometimes a shot is fired. Armed with a gun, the thieves need only demand that cases be unlocked and contents handed over, he says.

Gang leaders seldom participate in these attacks. It's believed new members are constantly being trained for new attacks. Though such robberies have spread to neighboring states (some have been reported even in Texas and Virginia), the gangs continue to concentrate on Southern California.

Feeling the crime: Crimes against jewelers involve more than just lost inventory. One loss, one shattered window or one nutty gunman can devastate your business, or you.

Colorado jeweler John Cubitto recalls a $130,000 robbery at his store in February 1987. Two men wearing ski masks entered when the store opened. One approached Cubitto and pointed a .44 magnum at his head.

"My first thought was that this wasn't real," he recalls. "I didn't believe it. The barrel seemed five times the size it really was." When he looked down the gun barrel and saw the bullet, Cubitto snapped back to reality. While afraid for his own life, he was even more concerned for the safety of the saleswoman and customer also in the store. The victims followed JSA recommendations to do as robbers instruct, make no sudden moves and not argue.

No injuries resulted, but emotions were potent. "Immediately after the robbery, I felt very angry and revengeful, which I understand is a common reaction" says Cubitto. Sleepless nights followed. "I was reliving [the robbery] for six months."

Shortly after this robbery, Cubitto had a locked entrance installed, and he doesn't hesitate to use it. "It makes a point," he says. The release often is pushed before good customers ever realize the door is locked and become offended.

Crime realities: What are the chances of facing crime in *your* store? Over the past five years, jewelers have experienced an annual average of 300 burglaries (the high was 360 in 1986), 300 robberies and an unknown number of other crimes such as shoplifting, switching, bad checks, etc. White says figures aren't available for this third category of crime, but that it "happens all the time."

If industry crime continues its current trend, you—as one of 39,209 jewelers nationwide—stand a one-in-65 chance of becoming a victim. That's not counting those unspecified thefts that "happen all the time."

But many jewelers ignore the odds when it comes to protecting their business. Some strut their trust like Oz's lion, who believed a badge of courage would make him invincible.

"I'm the wrong person to talk to [about security]," said a Pennsylvania jeweler located in an upper-income community plaza. "I break all the rules, show too much jewelry at one time. I just don't think about it; I trust." His display windows contain thousands of dollars worth of wedding bands and silver designs after hours. "We've been lucky," he concedes.

One brush with crime can change that trusting attitude. Indeed, most jewelers who've experienced 3-minute burglaries take precautions against repeat scenarios. They install metal bars and shatterproof glass, empty all display areas and/or install showcase covers.

Violence: Unfortunately, some people never get a second chance.

Twelve people died in jewelry store robberies in 1987—a five-year low. The dead were salespeople, owners or security officers—not robbers. Inappropriate action or inaction by the victims frequently provoked the deaths, says White.

In 1983, 27 people died in 325 robberies. The number of robberies hovered around 280 over the next three years, with 16 deaths in 1984, 20 in '85 and 15 in '86.

Injury was inflicted in 24% of jewelry store robberies in 1983, 32% in 1984, 29% in 1985, 21% in 1986 and 27% in 1987.

Overall crime figures released by the U.S. Bureau of Justice aren't encouraging. Violent crime rose 12% nationally in 1986 (the most current data available).

The bureau says that nonresidential robberies totaled 63,284 in 1986, up 14.9% from 1985. Nonresidential burglaries totaled 990,708, up 12.9% from 1985. (Robberies involve violence or threats against someone; burglaries don't.)

As long as national crime rates climb, a jeweler's chance of escaping crime is increasingly slim. But there is good news.

JSA figures show that informed and alert salespeople can and do prevent crime.

The Jewelers Mutual Insurance Co. is so confident of that claim that it makes JSA membership a priority for its policyholders.

All of JM's block policyholders automatically are enrolled in JSA at the insurance company's expense.

Look out, Randy!

Crime-tackling tips

To avoid smash-and-grab burglaries, empty all showcases and display windows each night. If you can't empty every case due to lack of storage space, the Jewelers' Security Alliance recommends using showcase covers to protect merchandise.

In the event of a robbery, remember to follow all orders of the gunman, reminds JSA. Also, don't try to disarm the gunman, don't push a holdup alert button and expect to be threatened and tied up. Keep calm and remember that one wrong move could lead to violence.

After A Burglary: How To Pick Up The Pieces

December 1987

Every day of the week, every week of the year, a jewelry store is burglarized. Whose will be next? If it's yours, are you prepared for the financial stress, emotional woes and plain hard work involved in recovery?

The struggles are real:

• A Maryland jeweler, who settled out of court on a suit against his alarm company, barely came out ahead after paying his lawyer.

• A Colorado jeweler, who lost $500,000, was blamed for sky-rocketing insurance rates and made the brunt of jokes by area jewelers.

• A Virginia jeweler lost her complete inventory record along with her jewelry.

There's no way to forget the anguish and anger of experiences like these, but there are ways to ease the pain.

Develop a strategy for surviving burglary that's as thorough as your defense against one. Otherwise you chance hassles with insurance claims, extensive property damage and the frightening realization of vulnerability. You could even, like one jeweler, be sued by the burglars.

Protect what's left

Immediately after a burglary, think first about saving what's left, says James White, president of the Jewelers' Security Alliance. This is no time to mourn over long-gone jewels; if you're not careful—and haven't already lost everything—you could be hit again. Criminals aren't too proud to strike while you're down.

This is especially true of smash-and grab losses. Burglars waited just three nights after their first attack to smash once again through the door of Billmeier Jewelry in Saginaw, Mich. Only following round two were metal bars installed.

Ask yourself, "What happened? What went wrong?" If burglars breached your safe, they obviously defeated the alarm system. How? You must find out so you can correct the flaw.

But be a smart sleuth; prowling around alone in the dead of night is not recommended. Ask an armed guard or police officer to go along when you check for cut lines or tampering outside the store.

It's important to get your security system working again. If this is temporarily impossible, then someone—the jeweler or a hired security guard—must stay in the store until security's restored. If you must stay overnight, lock all doors and keep the lights on. Inform local police of your situation and request regular surveillance.

Decide before a loss occurs just who will handle this responsibility, and who will act as alternate. If you're number one but are out of town, has someone else been assigned to play substitute? If you choose an armed guard, which security company will you turn to?

One Maryland jeweler depends on off-duty policemen. He did try armed guards after a 1971 burglary, but recalls, "They would get bored in the middle of the night, prop the door open and go for a walk. The off-duty officers present themselves well, are well trained and professional." Stop by your local police station or talk with officers you know to find one willing to do the work.

And keep quiet about your loss. Sometimes jeweler are so relieved when burglars overlook a lot of hidden jewels that they share their joy with the press: i.e., "They weren't so smart. They missed a million in diamonds."

Not for long! "It's like telling the world what's left to steal," says JSA's Jim White.

Add protection

Your insurance company may require that you upgrade protection after a break-in. Even if it doesn't, you'd be wise to do so before another loss. Most members of JCK's Retail Panel who report being hit by smash-and-grab crooks say they've since installed iron gates and/or unbreakable glass in front doors and display windows. The reasoning: Anything which slows down burglars may encourage them to choose another target.

If your safe was broken into, it may be inoperable. Contact your safe company to arrange for a replacement, if necessary. You may have to rent a safe temporarily until you can buy one.

Showcases and windows that are empty after hours offer one of the best defenses against a "three-minute burglary." Jewelers who've been victimized by this crime always had something on display. Although the merchandise often was of little value, it still tempted someone to shatter a door, a window or even several showcases.

If possible, put everything away! To do so, you may need a second safe. It's worth it for your peace of mind.

After suffering a $600,000 burglary, Albert Smyth Co. of Timonium, Md., bought several safes to put inside the walk-in vault. "It spreads out the risk," says owner Robert Smyth, Jr., because it takes longer to crack several safes instead of just one.

For added protection, Albert Smyth also subscribes to several alarm stations. The firm decided it needed back-up protection from multiple stations after its alarm service failed to respond to a trouble signal at the time of the burglary.

Is all this protection cost effective? Robert Smyth thinks so; he's determined not to suffer a similar loss.

Tracking inventory

How do you determine what was taken in a burglary—and what it was worth? Police often ask for an immediate estimate of your loss. Can you provide an accurate estimate on short notice?

Good inventory records not only protect you when filing loss claims, but also make good business sense. Recording what is and isn't moving helps you develop a solid buying plan, forecast sales and measure turnover. That's a strong case for accurate records!

An inventory record—whether on paper or computer—typically should include a description of the item; style number; inventory code (unique to *each* item); unit cost; % markup; retail price; supplier, and alternate source. Leave space to add information as needed.

List in chart form for each item: Date of activity; whether the item is on order, has been received or sold; how many are in stock, and any other additional comment, such as a special discount price. To stay organized, you must keep track of purchase orders and sales slips, and continuously update your records. Total time expended per item is approximately 11 minutes.

Record keeping may be done daily, twice a week or weekly, as desired, says *JCK's Jewelers' Inventory Manual,* which guides retailer through every phase of setting up an inventory system. However, Jewelers Mutual prefers that jewelers keep daily records.

It's important to keep two copies of your inventory records. When burglars took $500,000 worth of jewelry from Facets in Norfolk, Va., owner Mary Jo LeFevre was thankful she had a second record stored on computer disc and tucked safely away at home. The burglars had stolen her office copy, which listed approximately 1800 items.

Are you covered?

Before you file an insurance claim, compare your deductible with your loss. If you lost $3000 in a burglary, but have a $5000 deductible, no claim is even necessary. That's often best with minor losses anyway, if your business can comfortably cover the expense. A claim typically causes insurance rates to jump and may cost you more, over a period of years, than absorbing a small loss yourself.

Higher deductibles generally mean lower premiums. Try to set your deductibles as high as the business can withstand, says Jewelers Mutual's Bill Herrbold, vice president-claims. Deductibles may dip as low as $500, with the sky the limit on the high end. Some large corporations, with numerous stores, have deductibles in the $200,000 range.

Insurance may be of little value on small claims. Where it really pays off is on total, or near total, losses. There is no guarantee against such losses, so don't consider this an area for cost-cutting.

If a claim is in order, determine whether you've complied with all underwriting requirements. If you haven't, your claim may be denied. Avoid this unexpected heartache by reading requirements carefully and following them—before a loss.

Typically, your insurance requires that you:
• Maintain the alarm system listed on your contract. Maintenance includes paying monthly service bills and informing your alarm company of any malfunctions in your system as they become apparent.
• Maintain the safe and/or vault described on the proposal. This includes maintenance of the alarm system set up specifically to protect it.

• Lock the required percentage of merchandise by value in your safe or vault after hours. The amount required is determined by nature of stock.

• Report an accurate inventory figure to your insurance company. This is critical, says Jewelers Mutual's Herrbold. Often jewelers report less inventory in an effort to save money on insurance. But this could result in either total claim denial or slower than usual payment from insurance.

Insurance typically covers the jeweler's merchandise, memo goods and at least some portion of customers' merchandise on the premises for repair. When a claim is made, a specified percentage goes to each group. If the jeweler doesn't have enough insurance, distribution becomes difficult, says Herrbold. But since coverage is the jeweler's responsibility, he may find himself on the short end of the stick when the money is handed out.

If you've met all the requirements, you will be paid. That payment generally is based on what you originally paid for the merchandise, however. If you've owned items for a long time, your replacement cost may differ significantly from the insurance company's reimbursement.

The good news is that at least one insurance company (Jewelers Mutual) offers a "valuation clause endorsement" which allows you to add a percentage of the original cost to the claim. Though it's a good clause to have, you do pay for it. Paying an annual premium that's roughly 8% to 9% higher allows you to add 10% to a claim. Adding a higher percentage boosts your premium even more.

Be aware that personal jewelry and jewelry belonging to employees is not protected under your burglary/robbery insurance. To protect such items—which may be in your store for remount, repair, etc.,—you can:

• Buy a personal articles policy through your insurance company; or

• Check your own or your employees' homeowners' policies. Most cover such articles while in the care of a jeweler. But don't make assumptions. Even if a homeowners' policy does offer this coverage, it may not cover the entire cost of extremely valuable jewelry.

Friends or foes?

Beware of strangers, customers, suppliers and even local law enforcement officers who enter your store after a burglary. While some will lend a supportive hand, others may be far less sympathetic.

After losing $40,000 in a smash and grab, a Midwestern jeweler was further humbled by a local con man who claimed to be an undercover agent with the state Bureau of Crime. "He sweet-talked us out of $75 he said he needed to buy back the merchandise he'd located," recalls the jeweler. Insurance didn't pick up the tab.

At Hands Jewelry in Iowa City, Iowa, a nighttime smash and grab led to a $26,000 loss—and a perhaps more tragic event in the light of day. Several days after the incident, a Hands' sales clerk spotted a woman shopping downtown—wearing a missing one-of-a-kind designer necklace. The clerk followed the woman to her car and recorded its license number.

Hands' owner, William Nusser, Sr., was then also Iowa City's Civil Service Commissioner, responsible for hiring, promoting and firing police and fire department personnel. He gave the woman's license number to the police department, which called him in later that day. The car, Nusser learned,

belonged to a policeman whom Nusser himself had hired. That officer had been the first to arrive at the store the morning after Hand's smash and grab.

When confronted, the officer admitted stealing the necklace from the crime scene. "In Iowa we have a presentence investigation, where the victim is asked what he wants done," says Nusser. "I requested they *not* put him in jail. He'd put enough guys away; [the inmates] would've killed him." The officer was a casualty of his job, claims Nusser. The sentence: Parole.

If you can't trust the "good guys," don't be surprised by the bad. After a $500,000 burglary at Zerbe Jewelers in Colorado Springs, Colo., one of the suspects filed suit against the store. The burglar, it seems, wanted back the jewelry he possessed when arrested.

"When informed that we had invoices and that perjury conviction would make him eligible for a life sentence for habitual criminal, he dropped it," says Charles Zerbe, owner.

"Document everything!" says Mary Jo LeFevre. This includes repair work brought in by customers. Unless you know exact stone sizes and quality, jewelry left for repair may become something much better in the minds of customers who file claims.

Who's at fault?

After a substantial loss, it's not uncommon to feel anger and the need to focus it on someone. That "someone" may be the burglar(s) or, in some cases, the alarm company hired to protect your store.

Occasionally, culprits are caught. From there, any of several scenarios may follow. Gilbert Davidson, Jr., of Klar Brothers Jewelers in Muskogee, Okla., was surprised and impressed when police caught his burglar in the early morning hours. But even more surprising, says Davidson, is that the suspect was tried and set free!

An officer left the police station, located just 85 yards from Klar's, at 3 a.m. As he walked around the corner, he saw the suspect throw a brick through the jeweler's front window and grab some gold ring mountings on display. The suspect fled, with the officer in pursuit. The chase lasted several blocks, with the suspect disappearing once before the officer caught him. The captured man was both out of breath and carrying Klar's jewelry.

A cut-and-dry case? Not really. Davidson claims the trial's jury foreman was a notable Muskogee hoopster who at one time had played ball with the suspect. Somehow, the suspect went scot free, and that's all Gilbert Davidson knows, not having attended the trial. "The police were livid," he adds. The suspect had a reputation in town for dealing in stolen goods.

Other jewelers who report more favorable results spent anywhere from two hours to two days to lock away their bad guys. Graham Rees of Rees Jewelers, Richmond, Va., views his time spent positively. "Forty years for [the burglar]; two hours for us!" he says.

Sometimes the guilty verdict doesn't seem quite enough, however. A man found guilty of the $500,000 burglary at Facets was sentenced to 10 years in jail plus 30 years' probation. The sentence is considered "harsh for a 'first time offender,' " says owner Mary Jo LeFevre. But she's not satisfied. "This man has been arrested, but never convicted, in as many as a dozen major burglaries." And according to a Jewelers Mutual newsletters, many offenders are released early due to prison crowding. Up to 70% of those released repeat the same crime, says JM.

Then there's the alarm company. Did it wait too long before calling police? Did it fail to contact the retailer? Sometimes the alarm company charged with protecting a jewelry store fails to act in the best way to thwart a crime. When this happens, do you:

a) let it slide;

b) sue the pants off your alarm company;

c) negotiate in private?

There's no pat answer, since each case is different. Settlement often is made out of court, says JSA's Jim White. While payment may not be less in private settlement than required in court, your chances of "winning" are far greater.

A lawyer representing Albert Smyth Co. and one representing its alarm company spent two years in private litigation before agreeing on a sum of money for the jeweler. After Smyth paid off its lawyer, roughly $20,000 was left— yet the firm lost $600,000 in the burglary.

So why settle out of court? "We would have tripled our legal fees going to court," says Robert Smyth. And even if the store had been awarded full damages, the alarm company wasn't solvent enough to pay, he says.

Before seriously considering a lawsuit, make sure you are clear on all facts: What happened? Who's responsible? What's your chance of recovery? Then prepare yourself for battle.

Your first hurdle is the disclaimer, part of any alarm company contract. Here's an excerpt from a typical one:

". . . Contractor [alarm company] is not an insurer . . . ; . . . the Contractor is being paid for the installation and maintenance of a system designed to reduce certain risks of loss and that the amounts being charged by the Contractor are not sufficient to guarantee that no loss will occur; that the Contractor is not assuming responsibility for any losses which may occur even if due to contractor's negligent performance of failure to perform any obligation under this Agreement . . ."

An additional paragraph, from the same contract, states:

Even if the liability is proven, ". . . on the part of the Contractor, such liability shall be limited to an amount equal to one half the annual service charge provided herein or $250, whichever is greater. The sum shall be complete . . . paid and received as liquidated damages and not as penalty . . ."

Some alarm companies allow customers to increase their liability fee by paying a higher service fee. This seemingly puts alarm companies in the insurance business, says Les Gold, managing partner of Shea & Gould, and legal counsel for the National Burglar and Fire Alarm Association. However, the option is available.

If, after considering all the facts, you feel action against your alarm company is warranted, rest assured the situation isn't hopeless. Some jewelers who've fought the contract have won.

However, decisions vary by state, with some states more prone than others to decide against alarm companies. And, as is typical with court proceedings, the process is long and exhausting.

One of the first cases in which a jeweler successfully sued his alarm company was filed in 1972 and took nearly five years to come to trial. But the wait was worthwhile for Richard Accolla, the Miami jeweler involved. He filed jointly, as Mr. Richard's Originals Inc., with Jewelers Mutual Insurance Company against Burns Electronic Security Inc. and Lloyd's of London.

Historically, claiming "gross negligence" (conduct which would probably and most likely result in injury to people and property) has been more successful in overriding a contract's disclaimer than has been the charge of "simple negligence" (con-duct which a reasonable and prudent man would know might cause injury to persons and property). That was true in this case.

The court said the alarm company's $250 limit of liability clause was sufficient to prevent Accolla and JM from recovering damages against Burns for acts of simple negligence. But it held that the firm couldn't contractually limit its liability for gross negligence, which it ruled the plaintiffs had proven.

The Florida Supreme Court found the alarm firm failed to perform the three basic duties of a burglar alarm company upon receiving a trouble signal at the central station. The three:

• Call police;

• Send a guard;

• Call the customer.

While those duties were not stated outright in the contract, both parties conceded that expectation of having all three fulfilled was reasonable.

A finding of gross negligence was handed down against the alarm company and the jeweler awarded $200,000 in damages.

What's yours?

Can you positively identify your property if it's located? Use of retail trademarks, while time consuming is the best solution. When, as sometimes happens, jewelry is found with the tags still attached, unique tagging or coding can help prove ownership. Again, detailed inventory records may pay off. Provide copies to law enforcement and the Jewelers' Security Alliance.

In 1981, Phoenix Ariz., jeweler Darrell Olson used his detailed list of stolen jewelry and a bit of luck to recover all but a third of $628,000 in stolen merchandise. He simply sent a copy of the list, which included a 53-carat brown diamond, to the Jewelers' Security Alliance.

When an Iowa jeweler was offered the goods, he smelled trouble and called his local police. The police, in turn, contacted the FBI. When the local FBI agent called JSA, Olson's list of jewelry was matched to the offerings in Iowa. The Feds moved in.

Reclaiming stolen merchandise doesn't happen overnight, says JSA's Jim White. The items are held as evidence throughout the prosecution. Then the owner get a chance to reclaim, not always an easy task. However, retail losses are easier than domestic because of the specific numbers involved. If inventory records show you had three of X item, five of Y item and ten of Z item, and that's what was recovered, you've got a pretty solid case.

Starting over

The fallout from burglary lingers on. Customers who lost jewelry in your store may feel more comfortable with another jeweler. And local retailers may be less kind-hearted than hoped. "We were 'bad mouthed' around the region as being solely responsible for general rate increases," says Charles Zerbe in Colorado Springs, who lost $500,000 in a 1982 burglary. "They'd walk up to me at trade shows and say, 'So *you're* the S.O.B . . .' "

Where did they get this news? Straight from the insurance company, jewelers told Zerbe.

Then there's the one where burglars cut through the ceiling to get into a jeweler's vault. The punch line? "Anyone drop through your ceiling lately?!" Ha! Ha! Even today this Midwestern jeweler get ribbed about the rip-off, but he's not laughing. "I feel it's kind of callous," he says.

On the other hand, most suppliers are very helpful, say retailers. You actually may be bombarded with calls from suppliers just wanting to "help." A Texas retailer says suppliers were "sympathetic, but offers of help were more of the nature to sell me replacement goods." In that case, you can always say no.

One Virginia jeweler was annoyed when suppliers with whom she had never dealt began shipping unsolicited merchandise. Fortunately this situation appears to be rare.

Generally, jewelers have good reports about supplier support. Sometimes, memo goods meant the difference between "business as usual" and closed doors.

Survival Under The Gun

July 1987

A man enters your store. An instant later you're staring down the barrel of his .357 magnum. "One move and I'll blow your head off!" His words, meant to scare, are more effective than you ever imagined.

Your heart does doubletime. You think of the holdup button, just beyond your reach. If only you could get to it, just one small shuffle sideways, lean into it and . . . BOOOMM!!

Playing hero is a deadly game. It's not just your life you're putting on the line; everyone else in the store may be jeopardized, too. The Jewelers Security Alliance repeatedly issues bulletins telling jewelers what to do in a holdup. These rules make sense, and can save lives:

• Obey the gunman's orders.

• Do *only* what you are told.
• Do not attempt to disarm a holdup man.
• Do not reach for a concealed weapon.
• Do not press the holdup button while a gunman is on the premises.
• Expect to be threatened.
• Stay calm!

Playing hero is taboo. So is screaming . . . and running. And every store must play by these rules.

Coaches say a team is as strong as its weakest player. When that "team" comes face to face with a deadly force, no player can afford to break. One scream, or one false move, could cause a gunman to pull the trigger.

When that happens, everyone stands to lose.

How To Shop For A Safe

December 1986

"Safe: A place or receptacle to keep articles (as valuables) safe," states Webster's. Concise, but misleading in its simplicity. To the jeweler, a safe is a complex, costly creation which safeguards the heart of his business. Here, then, are 21 facts Webster's didn't cover. The list offers soon-to-be safe shoppers better understanding of so vital a "place."

1. Cost: Safes aren't cheap but you get what security you pay for. A jeweler may spend anywhere from $4,500 to $10,000 for a safe protecting inventory valued between $250,000 and $1 million. Safes at the lower end of the rating scale—offering protection from tool attack on the door only for a testing time of 30 minutes (TL-30)—cost approximately $4,500-$4,800. Safes at the higher end—offering torch and tool resistance on all six sides for a tested attack time of 30 minutes (TRTL-30X6)—will cost about $8,500-$10,000. (Prices are for safes with 11 cubic feet internal capacity.)

Expect a wide range of prices within each rating category. Price variances reflect a difference in construction and/or materials. Ask the dealer to explain to you *why* style "A" costs more than "B." Reasons exist but it's up to you, the

buyer, to evaluate the relative importance of any differences. Worth remembering: Safes bought before Dec. 31, 1986, will qualify as investment tax credits. This potential savings deserves immediate consideration since tax reform kills that deduction beginning Jan. 1, 1987.

2. Insurance demands: Insurance underwriters need some type of formal guideline to use in recommending safes, says Bob Zivkovich, assistant vice president-underwriting at Jewelers Mutual Insurance Co. Underwriters' Laboratories Inc. (UL), Northbrook, Ill., the non-profit independent firm which tests safes, provides those guidelines. The ratings UL attaches to deserving safes carry clout with insurance firms.

The type of safe an underwriter requires is a compilation of security factors. Included are inventory level, store location and nature of stock, but there are no golden rules. Ultimately the decision's a judgment call.

An underwriter may offer the retailer options, such as buy one TRTL30X6 or two TL-30s to store the same amount of inventory.

3. UL ratings: A safe's performance rating is based on its ability to withstand various levels of attack. A safe has succumbed to attack when its door has been opened or a hole of a specified size has penetrated the surface being tested.

Most attacks are made on obsolete safes with no UL rating. Thus the jeweler who invests in a modern, UL-rated safe already is beating the odds.

Again, safes made differently, or of different materials, may earn identical UL ratings. Alisha Goldman, international safe expert and director of International Safe Distributors, is one of several manufacturers who feel some safe designs are superior to others with the same rating.

Example: People often forget to use the keylock or turn their combination dial. A safe in which the key *must* be used for opening and closing prevents this mistake, notes Goldman.

4. Inventory levels: Jewelers Mutual's Zivkovich urges retailers to consider these minimum rating guidelines: Inventory worth $250,000 or less warrants a TL-30 rated safe; $250,000 to $500,000, a TRTL-15X6; $500,000 to $1 million, a TRTL-30X6.

Inventory valued at more than $1 million calls for more than one safe. Because it takes time to break into a safe, a burglar often can tackle only one or two. Thus the jeweler with multiple safes may be able to open for business the day after a burglary using his remaining inventory.

5. Location/neighbors: A location's vulnerability to burglary plays a significant role in what safe will be required. Insurance companies reason that stores located in metropolitan areas run a greater risk of being violated than those in rural areas.

Other location considerations include upper or ground floor, mall or strip store and general crime rate of the neighborhood. These factors help dictate the underwriter's requirement.

6. Nature of stock: How desirable is the merchandise? Is it relatively easy to fence? Easy to melt down? If so, maximum security may be a must.

7. Weight/installation: A safe's finished weight is an important consideration for stores on upper levels. Have the flooring checked for adequate support. The distributor sometimes will handle this task.

Both TL-15 and TL-30 rated safes must either weigh a minimum of 750 lbs. or be equipped for anchoring to something less easily moved (a larger safe, concrete blocks or the floor of the premises where the safe is to be located). Instructions for anchoring are to be included with the safe.

Safes rated TRTL-15X6, TRTL-30, TRTL-30X6 and TRTL-60 must weigh a minimum of 750 lbs. (Anchoring devices may not be substituted for weight.) TXTL-60 safes must weigh at least 1000 lbs.

8. Construction: The body of a safe may be cast in one piece (called composite construction), which offers fewer areas of vulnerability. Or it may be welded together, as required by some superior materials. Each method offers benefits.

The safe body and door may consist of various materials. Concrete, with its relatively low cost, is popular. The type used for safes has greater tensile strength than concrete used for other commercial purposes. While perhaps the least sophisticated material being used in safes today, concrete still is considered effective.

Also used are aluminum, copper, steel and materials invented specifically for safe construction. At least one company holds a patent on its unique mix. Good materials will resist cutting and/or drilling and dissipate heat.

9. Locks/combinations: All safes are required to have a combination lock. These have three rating levels: 1R (highest), 1 (middle) and 2 (lowest). Combination locks on TL-15 and TL-30 safes may have any of the three ratings. All higher rated safes require a 1 or 1R combination lock; these are manipulation proof.

Typically, safe manufacturers also equip the door with a keylock. Jewelers Mutual advises use of the two locks together. "There are people out there who can manipulate a combination if they want to," says Zivkovich. The keylock strengthens the barrier against would-be thieves.

Also required is a relocking trigger to protect the combination from direct attack. The small device triggers a catch for the bolt which prevents opening. This device is directly connected to the combination's interior.

Additional relocking mechanisms are available. The number of mechanisms a safe has depends on specific make and manufacture.

Typically these "backup" relockers are located away from the combination and keylocks. They are activated if a severe blow shatters a plate of glass positioned between the door's outer wall and the main locks. The shattering causes tension on a thin wire which in turn affects the backup. Bolts shoot out from all sides of the door into the body of the safe. If relockers are randomly placed, as in some models, burglars won't know where or how best to continue the attack.

10. Internal security/key control: An employer should control access to the safe tightly. The key and dial combination protect the lifeblood of the business.

Do not write combinations on a card to be kept in the executive desk or even taped to the underside of a desk top or drawer. Burglars have caught on to these tricks, says the Jewelers Security Alliance (JSA).

Make certain those closing the safe turn the combination dial several complete revolutions. Safe burglars know that some "lazy employees" move the dial only a few numbers from the last digit in the combination series. That's so they need move the dial only a few digits when opening in the morning. JSA suggests putting a second employee in charge of turning the dial after the safe has been closed.

When any employee who knows your current combination leaves your employment, change that combination. This has less to do with the employee's integrity than with the common practice of keeping combinations on a card tucked in the wallet. If the wallet were lost or stolen, the combination would fall into the wrong hands.

11. Merchandise in safe: Consider storing your most valuable items on the safe's bottom rack, advises Richard Krasilovsky, president of Empire Safe, distributor of the ISM line. Most attacks occur in mid and upper areas of safes, he says. Burglars reaching in through a hole may knock shelving down, covering merchandise on the bottom and making it extremely difficult to reach.

12. Fire protection: Ability to withstand fire is a vital consideration. Don't assume fire protection is included. Ask.

Underwriters' Laboratories has established three classifications which express the degree to which a safe will protect contents from destruction by fire:

- Class A: Four-hour protection of contents against fire at 2000° F.
- Class B: Two-hour protection of contents against fire at 1850° F.

- Class C: One-hour protection of contents against fire at 1700° F.

Most materials resist heat penetration to a point. Beyond that, certain materials hold up longer. Steel, being a conductor of heat, offers little protection. Concrete dissipates heat, thus offering greater resistance.

13. Alarm systems: A good alarm system, though a necessary part of a jeweler's insurance contract, plays a lesser role in safe requirements than some would think. The merits of a safe must stand alone, says Zivkovich. "A good alarm get response. A good safe buys time for that response."

However, when setting up interior alarm protection, consider covering every side of the safe, including the bottom! Burglars have attacked safes by coming through the floor or the wall behind it.

14. Size: Know what you need. Safes come in a range of sizes, the most common being internal capacity of 11 cubic feet. There is no sense in buying a safe large enough to hold *everything*, only to learn that contractually it may store only a portion of your inventory.

How large are the trays to be placed inside? In some cases manufacturers will custom build a safe to meet interior size specifications.

15. Service: There is little room for a safe to fail in daily operation, but what if . . . ? What if you get to the store and cannot open the combination lock? What if the keylock won't turn? Ask the manufacturer about service: What is the response time? What are hours of availability? Who foots the bill?

Mark Lacka, owner of Lacka Lock & Safe, suggests having boltwork greased every five to ten years (combination and keylock or self-lubricated). No matter how old the safe, the company that sold it should handle this detail, he says.

16. Trade-ins: First make certain the old safe won't be useful as a secondary storage unit. If you opt to get rid of it, look farther than your dumpster. Manufacturers willingly purchase used safes, though the payment is minimal. Selling it yourself is more lucrative. However there's a trade-off in time and hassle.

17. Warranty: Know your safe's warranty. Look for a minimum one-year guarantee on parts, labor and material. Longer warranties on parts also may be offered.

18. JSA membership: Membership in the Jewelers' Security Alliance can earn jewelers 3% credit on the crime portion of a Jewelers Block Policy premium. Most companies that provide insurance for jewelers are involved in the program.

JSA carries this prestige because of the security awareness it consistently provides to jeweler members. Annual dues range from $40 to $250, based on the stock inventory of applicants.

19. Purchase options: Leasing a safe requires less money upfront. But be very careful, warns Jack Schultz, owner of Gem Security Consultants, Chicago. "A jeweler could easily end up spending *a lot* more," he says, before the lease is through. Different types of leases exist. Some result in a much higher end expense than others. Confer with an accountant before signing up.

Secondhand means trouble if a jeweler buys an older foreign-made model without a UL label. Although the seller may say its rating is "equal" to a specific UL rating, insurance agents may not agree. Get approval.

For the best price on secondhand safes, consider the classifieds. Used safes sold through distributors demand a higher price. In some cases, little to nothing is saved through buying secondhand.

20. Consulting: Security consulting firms can offer guidance, often free of charge. They need to know exactly what your insurance company requires so check that out first. Also seek advice from jeweler friends who recently made such a purchase. Are they happy with their selection? Any areas of disappointment?

21. Suppliers and distributors: Ask about the manufacturer's history. How long in existence? What is the track record for its products in actual attack situations?

Don't ignore foreign-made safes, which often are praised for quality. They too must submit to UL tests to compete in the U.S. market. But there may be a trade-off in speed of service. Learn avenues of recourse before problems arise.

Insurance companies sometimes offer advice on where to buy a safe. The recommendation may be valid, but don't consider it gospel. Most distributors admitted having "heard of the practice" of kickbacks, though none would speak on the record. Be sure to check all options.

Stop The Shoplifting Plague

March 1985

Most shoplifters aren't all that clever and scare easily in the face of vigilant store surveillance. Yet statistics compiled by the National Coalition to Prevent Shoplifting show that for every dollar stolen in a robbery $300 worth of goods is shoplifted. And the problem is escalating. Total shoplifting losses topped $24 billion in 1984, up from $16 billion in 1980. One million-plus shoplifters were arrested in 1983, up 30% from five years ago.

Jewelers, who keep most precious merchandise under lock and key, often think they're immune to the classic sneak theft from open self-service shelves. But plenty of items—from high-ticket giftwares to designer leather goods— are exposed in jewelry stores. And salespeople often show an appalling disregard for showcase security. During a holiday rush, they'll leave cabinets open and unattended, keys dangling in locks or lying on counters. Such carelessness is an open invitation for shoplifters—who may become your best repeat customers.

How can jewelers reduce their losses? Traditional options include a permanent full-time guard; roving security personnel (increasingly popular and cost effective for groups of smaller stores); additional sales staff and one or more part-time guards. The latter may be semi-retired security officers hired just for the holiday season or whenever the problem gets especially bad. There are equipment options, too: Peep holes, fisheye or two-way mirrors and electronic surveillance such as CCTV.

But the battle against shoplifters can be fought successfully with only imagination and common sense. The key is to establish an obvious, ongoing security presence to convince potential shoplifters, it's not worth the gamble. Making them think they'll be caught is as good as actually catching them.

Creative sign writing is one inexpensive deterrent. A warning sign that says "Shoplifters will be prosecuted to the full extent of the law" impresses only honest customers. A thief reasons that if no one is looking, he won't get caught.

A more effective sign would read, "We reserve the right to use concealed electronic devices against shoplifters," or "1250 people caught shoplifting in Chester, Pa., were all convinced no one was watching," or "We thank our many loyal customers who have reported shoplifters. Together we have caught 136." Signs must emphasize the certainty of getting caught.

Subliminal messages, an unconventional technique, have proven effective in influencing behavior. No laws prohibit use of this technique in retail outlets. Some stores that have tried it reported a 30%-40% reduction in shrinkage. A positive reinforcing message can be repeated (below the threshold of hearing) on cassette tapes through a store's music or public address system.

A store's best anti-shoplifting weapons, however, are the eyes and minds of its employees. Indeed, stores too small for a full-time guard or elaborate electronic surveillance have little else to rely on.

Employees must be made responsible for protecting merchandise. This requires that they be keenly observant. Staff members take periodic vision breaks from work, but usually just look at the floor. Instead, teach them to look up and make eye contact with customers. This will discourage shoplifters, catch some in the act, help recover merchandise and build honesty awareness among personnel. As a plus, it's also good customer relations.

"Training them to meet, greet and speak with customers is the first step," says Lawrence A. Conner, author of the book *The Shoplifters are Coming*. "Afterward you can teach them, to look for shoplifters."

One effective drill helps develop alertness. Inform your sales staff that "next week someone in a blue pinstripe suit [or red dress, etc.] will come into the store. When you see that person, contact me." Wait a few days, then send your target through the store in a way that passes the maximum number of personnel.

Initially only one or two employees may notice the target shopper. But if you repeat the drill periodically, results should improve. Try building a monthly incentive program around these exercises. Make a big fuss over the winners with some (noncash) recognition such as certificates (i.e. the "Eagle Eye Award") coupled with dinner or free movie tickets.

Location security

Try to pinpoint and eliminate blind spots—such as alcoves or behind pillars and high cabinets—where shoplifters can work without being seen. Walk through your store and

ask yourself where you would feel safe concealing merchandise. Make a floor plan and mark every spot, numbering them from least to most vulnerable. Then ask other personnel to walk through; they may come up with different blind spots.

Armed with this data, you now can eliminate, or at least reduce the dangers of, blind spots through a mix of the following measures:

• Add a ceiling, wall or display case light to reduce shadows and increase visibility in a blind spot.

• Make security part of staff thinking and store routine. For example, have employees go past serious problem areas on their way to the lounge, stockroom or other areas frequently visited.

• Install ordinary mirrors, but make them look like security windows so shoplifters notice them.

• Make each salesperson responsible for a specific aisle, showcase, etc. Be sure he/she watches everyone in that area.

Suppose you or an employee witnesses a customer concealing merchandise. Author Lawrence Conner recommends that you:

• Note the suspect's age, sex, weight, height, race and dress.

• Alert another employee to act as standby (near a telephone) just in case.

• Approach the suspect and confront him/her by pointing out firmly and politely, "I need that gold chain [or watchstrap or whatever] that's in your front left pocket back." Be specific so the thief can't deny it. Add, "I would prefer to handle this matter without calling the police but, either way, I must get the merchandise back. Please come with me."

• Get the shoplifter to accompany you to a quiet office. Do not touch or back the shoplifter into a corner. Move alongside, not behind or in front of the offender.

• Request identification. (Once you have the I.D., you've got control). At the slightest sign of a problem, secretly alert your standby to call the police, step aside and then maintain visual contact.

• Make up an incident report; ask for the return of other merchandise and get a signed release of liability (to protect the store against future legal action).

• Either release the shoplifter or call the police (mainly when the suspect refuses to return the item; exhibits loud or threatening conduct; is a repeat offender; has taken unusually high-priced merchandise or refuses to be detained or sign a release.)

A warning and release approach (i.e. "I'm gonna let you go this time..." or "If you ever do this again...") causes more harm than a failure to prosecute. Such unilateral pledges to forgive and forget give shoplifters the impression they've talked you out of arresting them. It's like giving them a license to steal and turning them loose on the retail community.

Shoplifters Anonymous (SA), a shoplifter rehabilitation group suggests another approach; Controlled Release. It produces the kind of anxiety felt during police arrest... but without actual arrest.

Under this plan, you have shoplifters read and sign a letter before releasing them. It says, in part:

"Our action in releasing you at this time does not mean that we have waived our right to file a criminal complaint... Our review of the facts in this case will be completed [within 60 days]. If we decide to initiate prosecution, you will be notified by the police or the court... Do not call the store to discuss the details or inquire about the status of this matter..."

SA president Lawrence Conner claims the letter kills any elation by mimicking the arrest and prosecution experience. "Shoplifters will read it, then have 60 days to sweat it out. While they wonder whether or not they'll wind up in court, they'll have plenty of time to consider the consequences of their stealing."

Most retailers know better than to resist during a armed robbery, but often think they can boldly collar a shoplifter who appears unarmed and nonviolent. How do you know for sure the thief won't run, throw a punch, even pull out a knife or gun?

Few retail salespeople or managers are either trained or inclined to handle any "rough stuff." That's fine. You still can stop shoplifters without arresting them by using "passive intent." Stand aside—even allow the thief to get away—at the slightest risk of bodily harm to store personnel or customers. Give him what he wants. The moment the thief steps outside the store, police or security can make the arrest.

If Fire Strikes...
What Do You Do?

April 1983

Within 24 hours after you read this report, some 140 businesses in stores and offices around the United States will go up in flames. The yearly damage to these businesses is about $650 million, according to the latest statistics from the National Fire Protection Association. And these numbers represent only a tiny portion of total fire losses around the country each year.

The jewelry industry was hit recently when fire destroyed the headquarters of the American Gem Society. Though AGS staffers were back in business within 24 hours after the blaze, the society's loss is estimated between $150,000 and $250,000. It also lost its entire archives.

Iowa City, Iowa, jeweler Bill Nusser also suffered a severe fire recently. He lost all his computer records as well as his office building.

Despite these recent losses, jewelers are pretty lucky when it comes to fire. Jewelers Mutual, Neenah, Wis., says it had only 21 fire-related claims in 1982. The Jewelers Board of Trade, which records fires, also says they're not a big problem. And, when fires do occur, the damage is more likely to be caused by water and smoke than by flames.

But it still pays to be prepared. This report is a primer on fire safety. It includes:

- Choosing a building that resists fires.
- Preventing fires inside the store.
- Protecting employee and customer safety.
- Equipment to detect and deter fires.
- Insurance to help you get back in business again.

Choose a Fire Resistant Location

There are two goals in fire resistance, says Dale McCleary, Underwriters Laboratories. (UL rates building materials for fire resistance.) You want to prevent an outside fire from spreading to your store, and a fire in your store from spreading around you and outside to others.

If you're in the process of choosing or building a new store, the following checklist offers some fire safety guidelines.

- Familiarize yourself with your city or town building codes, which will require certain fire-resistant standards. But remember, these are just minimum standards, says Harry Walsh, chief of fire prevention for the Philadelphia Fire Department. You can do a whole lot more.
- Is the building made of highly fire resistant materials, such as brick, concrete or stone? This includes walls, floors and roofs.
- Are stairs, elevators, public hallways or other shafts enclosed in fire-resistive partitions or enclosures?
- Do you have fire-resistive doors? UL says fire doors can contain flames within the areas they protect. This keeps them from spreading.
- Does the building have a sprinkler system? If your store is in a small building with a low occupant load, it probably does not, says Chief Walsh. But they're still a good idea. "They're a silent firefighter that's always there," he says.
- What's the electrical system like? The National Fire Protection Association says fires of electrical origin have been the leading type in stores and manufacturing properties for the last ten years. Are there enough outlets for your use? Are all fuses of proper type, size and in good condition? Can you turn off electrical currents at night? How old is the electrical system in the building? Is it modern enough to handle all the modern conveniences, such as air conditioning, extra lighting and neon signs?
- Are all entrances and fire exits unobstructed? Are they clearly marked and lighted? Are emergency stairs in good repair?
- What's the basement of the building like? If you're sharing the building—what are your neighbors storing down there? Are storage areas separated by substantial partitions from furnace rooms and other hazardous areas?
- Who are your neighbors? Are they as fire safety conscious as you are? Find out, or start a fire safety campaign in your neighborhood or building. Also, note the types of establishments surrounding your store. Stores that use lots

of flammable chemicals, or restaurants, where cooking fires start, are more susceptible to fire, making them less desirable as neighbors.

Prevent Fires in the Store

Inhabiting a fire-resistant building is only the first step in avoiding fires. Conducting a fire-prevention survey and inspection of your store also is essential. Here's how to go about it. For more information, contact your local fire department. It may help you conduct a fire safety survey.

Electrical

Since electrical fires are the leading cause of store fires, this should be your first concern. Check out the age and durability of your overall electrical system.

• Do you overload outlets? "If you need to use more electrical outlets, put in more wall sockets," says Philadelphia Fire Dept. prevention expert Harry Walsh.

• Are your cords protected from damage? Check that they are not in the way of people or equipment traffic where fraying may result. If they are frayed, have them repaired or replaced.

• Repair any loose connections, broken plugs, switches, or outlets.

• Don't hide electrical outlets under rugs.

• Treat anything that smells overheated as a potential fire. Investigate all strange smells.

• Use a wire guard cage on light bulbs that could get broken. Keep hot bulbs away from dripping water, oil, and combustibles.

• If you do jewelry repairs and/or custom work, assign someone to check all appliances at the end of the day. They should be unplugged when not in use. Keep appliances clean. Dirt makes fire.

• Lubricate motors and keep them clean. Don't overload them and keep them away from flammables.

• If a small electrical fire starts, sound the fire alarm, shut off the power source fast and use a fire extinguisher designed to fight this kind of fire (see equipment section). If the fire gets bigger, get out, and close all doors.

Flammables

• Cleaning fluids and other solvents used by jewelers are highly flammable. Keep them away from open flames.

• Keep flammables in approved metal safety cans. Never use glass containers.

• Use solvents in well-ventilated areas.

• Keep an extinguisher designed to fight chemical fires nearby (see equipment section).

General housekeeping

• Remove papers and other ignitable rubbish regularly and frequently.

• Keep repair and jewelry-making areas extra clean and well organized.

• Never pile up rags or other ignitable materials.

• Never let storage areas, like basements and attics, get dirty or cluttered. Keep smoke or heat detection devices in them.

• If you use portable or space heaters during the winter, be very careful. They should be secure from tipping, safely mounted and kept ventilated.

• Passageways should be keep clear of obstacles.

• Fire doors should be unlocked and operating freely.

• If you use open flames for any reason, keep them away from flammables, curtains, papers, etc.

Smoking

• No smoking signs should be marked clearly.

• Ashtrays should be provided so that smokers can extinguish cigarettes safely.

• Do you dispose of cigarette butts carefully?

• If you don't permit smoking, are there designated areas where employees can smoke?

• Prohibit smoking in flammable and storage areas.

• Do you keep matches away from sources of heat?

Equipment to Detect and Fight Fires

Jewelers can purchase various equipment to detect and fight fires. Most can be tested by Underwriters Laboratories, so when shopping, look for UL's label.

Detecting fire

Smoke detectors sense rising smoke from a fire and sound an alarm. There are basically two types of detectors, each senses smoke in a different way.

Photoelectric smoke detectors use a photoelectric bulb that sends forth a beam of light. When smoke enters, light from the beam is reflected from smoke particles into a photocell and the alarm is triggered.

Ionization chamber detectors contain a small, safe radiation chamber source that produces electrically charged air molecules, called ions. When smoke enters the chamber, it causes a change in the flow of ions, triggering the alarm. The Federal Emergency Management Agency says both are effective in detecting smoke.

Since smoke rises, a smoke detector should be placed on a ceiling. Be sure to use them in basements and other storage areas. Consider wiring them into your burglar alarm setup, so if a fire starts at night, your central station can notify the fire department. The hookup cost is very low.

Heat detectors also are used to warn of fires. But they should always be a supplement to a smoke detector, says the Federal Emergency Management Agency. Why? Heat detectors must be close to a fire to set off an alarm. They also can totally ignore a smoldering fire that is putting out lethal amounts of smoke and toxic gases. But heat detectors are useful in areas that are too hot or cold for smoke detectors to function properly, such as furnace rooms, unheated basements and unheated storage areas.

Fighting fire

For small containable fires, the fire extinguisher is an essential store item. UL rates extinguishes for four classes of fires. Class A: Quenches ordinary combustible fires caused by wood, cloth, paper, etc. Class B: Quenches flammable products and grease fires. Class C: Quenches electrical fires. Class D: Quenches combustible metal fires.

Separate extinguishers can fight each type of fire, or retailers can purchase a multi-purpose extinguisher that will fight A, B, and C class fires (the most common ones).

UL also uses numbers on its A and B class extinguishers to indicate the extinguishing potential of the device. The higher the number rating on the extinguisher, the more fire it puts out.

When buying a fire extinguisher, ask the dealer how to have it serviced and inspected. Recharge it after any use. A partially used one may as well be empty, says the National Fire Protection Association. Extinguishers should be kept away from potential fire hazards and near an escape route.

The NFPA also uses an acronym, PASS, to help consumers remember how to use a fire extinguisher. *Pull* the pin. *Aim* the extinguisher nozzle. *Squeeze* or press the handle. *Sweep* from side to side at the base of a fire until it goes out. Then shut off the extinguisher.

Sprinkler systems are the other main way to fight fires. They are expensive, but fire fighters say they can pay for themselves in insurance premium savings and the costs of a huge fire loss. "Sprinkler systems are 98% effective in controlling and extinguishing mercantile fire," says Harry Walsh, chief of fire prevention at the Philadelphia Fire Department. Walsh says sprinkler systems can be hooked up as fire notification alarms to the fire department. In fact, in any Philadelphia building required to have a sprinkler system, when it activates it must notify the fire department.

If you already have a sprinkler system, check it frequently, says the NFPA. Are all the valves open, plainly marked, easily accessible? Are any sprinklers obstructed by partitions, high-piled stock, etc.? Are any sprinkler heads coated with paint, corroded or otherwise inoperable?

Protecting records

UL also tests equipment to protect records, such as computer tapes and papers. It's a good idea to keep duplicate sets of these items outside the store, however, in case papers and tapes are out of their protected file drawers or safes when a fire occurs.

It's important to make the distinction between fire safes and burglary-resistant safes. A fire safe will protect against heat and flames, a burglary-resistant safe may not. Also, a fire safe will not protect merchandise or papers from a burglar's tools and torches.

UL's Dale McCleary says most burglary-resistant safes tested by the lab are not tested for fire-resistance. Unless they are specifically designed to fight fire, McCleary says, burglary-resistant safes can act like ovens because of the heavy metal used in their construction. Jewelers should check with safe dealers if they want a safe that combines burglary and fire resistance in one unit. (UL does test one safe in both categories.)

Among the equipment UL rates for fire resistance are file drawers, file room doors, insulated record containers, safes, and vault doors. UL rates all these for their protection of paper records, under a Class 350 rating system.

UL also has a Class 125 and Class 150 ratings for insulated record containers used to store magnetic tapes, like computer records and discs. (Safes, vaults and other filing equipment are not tested for their protection of magnetic records.)

Insulated record containers and safes also are tested by UL for their durability when buildings collapse.

UL can give a dual fire and burglary resistance rating to one of the safes it tests for fire resistance. The Class 350 safe that resists fire for two hours can also be classified tool-resistant to burglars, under UL's TL30 burglary-resistant rating.

Protect People

• Install smoke detectors so that you have an early warning system. It could give you, your employees and your customers time to get out.
• Make a floor plan of your store, showing all possible exits from each room. Distinguish between regular exits and emergency ones that can be used if regular exits are blocked by fire or smoke.
• Develop a signal for danger that is only used in fire situations.
• Hold fire drills regularly—at least once a year. Plan a specific outside meeting place, i.e. the mail box across the street. Take attendance to be sure everyone got out. Tell all employees to close doors behind them.
• Stress to employees that they should get out, not try to save merchandise.
• Make sure exit signs are clearly marked.
• Employees should be able to assist customers in getting out.
• Teach employees how to use fire extinguishers, and when (only when the fire is quite small).
• If there are elevators in your building, stress that they are not to be used during a fire. The elevators should contain signs indicating this. Make sure everyone knows where the stairs are.
• Teach employees that if they are caught in smoke, they should crawl instead of walk.

Insurance: Getting Back in Business

Fire damage to jewelry store merchandise is covered by most jewelers' block policies. But jewelers also should consider purchasing furniture and fixtures coverage, which will take care of fire, smoke and water damage to showcases, lighting, machines and other items.

Jewelers Mutual offers this coverage in its Special Multi-Peril policy. Insurance Company of North America also offers a standard fire policy to cover such claims.

Like crime loss claims, fire loss claims will be settled a lot more smoothly if a jeweler keeps a detailed and accurate inventory. Take inventory of furniture and fixtures, too.

Jewelers also should consider buying business interruption insurance. This policy covers continuing expenses while a disrupted business is getting back on its feet. It pays rental fees on a new store and furniture. It pays key employees' salaries while the business is halted. Most importantly, a jeweler can get coverage for lost profits. The lost profits figure is determined using the store's profit figures from the same period the year before.

Plan In Advance To Prevent Kidnapping Extortion

January 1983

A Fayetteville, Ark. jeweler arrives home at 9 p.m. and is met in the driveway by three gunmen who hold him, his wife and son hostage all night. Early the next morning, one thug holds the jeweler's wife and son hostage, while the other two drive the jeweler to his store, using his car. There they scoop up $300,000 worth of merchandise, leave the jeweler handcuffed and take off in his car. His wife and son are unharmed.

A Little Rock, Ark., jeweler is forced to hand over $100,000 while his wife and child are held hostage in his van outside the store.

In three other separate cases, all in small towns or cities, jewelers' wives are called by men who say they are from the phone company. The wives are asked to keep their phones off the hook for 45 minutes so that the phone company can correct some trouble on the line. The jewelers then are told that their wives are being held hostage and unless they turn over jewelry immediately, the wives will be harmed. When the jewelers call home to check, they find the phones busy. Not wanting to take a chance, they *turn over the goods.*

"A jeweler has to recognize the distinct possibility that he and his family are potential victims," says James B. White, Jewelers' Security Alliance, New York. The above cases are from JSA files. The Alliance currently is preparing a kidnap/extortion manual for its members. Whether a real kidnapping has occurred, or an extortion threat has been made and the jeweler is not sure if a victim is being held, jewelers should have a plan worked out in advance, says White.

In the first two cases—essentially robberies where hostages are taken—jewelers should follow the instructions of the robber to keep everyone safe.

But in the last three cases, it gets trickier. "You've got to try and find out if the extortion threat is a hoax," says White. According to William Herrbold, claims manager at Jewelers Mutual Insurance Co., Neehan, Wis., jewelers block insurance will usually cover losses only where a kidnap actually has occurred. There is a separate kidnapping and extortion insurance policy, offered through Marketing Management Inc., a Pelham, Ala., insurance marketing firm. But this special policy also covers only actual kidnaps—not threats.

The American Bankers Association, the New York police department and the Jewelers Security Alliance all issue advice on planning in advance of kidnap/extortion threats. Here's a summary of their suggestions:

• Vary habitual routines. Take different routes to work. Don't always arrive and leave at the same time. Tell your family to do the same.

• Don't let your family or yourself give out details about your business or personal life. Criminals often pretend to be requesting information for business directories or social registers.

• Keep your home well-lit and securely locked. Don't ever open your door to, or admit strangers. Don't put your name on the house or mailbox. Park your car in secure and lighted areas. If you notice suspicious persons, jot down the license plate number and make of their car, then call police.

• Tell your children's schools to notify you immediately if your child doesn't show up for school on time.

• If your spouse or child receives a call from the phone company telling them to leave the phone off the hook, or unanswered, for some technical reason, tell them to hang up and call the phone company to verify. Telephone repair service can be reached in most cities at 611. Or call the operator. Even if the request is legitimate, your family should arrange an alternative way to keep in touch with you.

If you are taken hostage

• Don't be a hero. Accept the situation and be prepared to wait.

• Follow all the captor's instructions.

• Try to be friendly, but not phony. Speak only when spoken to, but make normal eye contact (not staring). The captor is less likely to harm someone he is looking at.

• Don't make suggestions to captor. If the suggestion is a bad one, the captor may think you are trying to trick him.

• Be patient, even though it may seem that police are doing little to gain your freedom.

• Don't try to escape unless you are absolutely certain you can make it safely.

• Remember descriptions of the captors for use by police.

If a threat is received

• Have a plan worked out in advance. If you receive a threatening call, a signal should be pre-arranged with a co-worker. While you keep the caller on the line, that person can immediately begin locating family members whom the caller says are being held. To prevent phone sabotage, install a second unlisted phone at which family members can be reached if the main home phone is out. Also, have neighbors' numbers on hand and call them.

• While you keep the caller talking, have your co-worker call police and the FBI. Under the Hobbs Act, Congress extended the FBI's jurisdiction to encompass nearly every kidnap/hostage extortion affecting commerce.

• Keep calm. Assure caller of your cooperation. Try to determine if the call is a hoax; ask to speak to your spouse, child, etc. If the captor says no, ask for color of hostage's eyes, clothes, etc. Prepare a personal descriptive information file on yourself, spouse, children and key employees—i.e. anyone who could be a kidnap target. Keep in a safe, but easily accessible place.

• If you are allowed to talk to the victim, have a pre-arranged code so that you can be sure you're talking to the person you think you are.

• Ask the captor questions to prolong the conversation, such as, why are you doing this... how much money/jewelry do you need, etc.

• If a payoff is discussed, attempt to arrange a simultaneous exchange of money/jewelry for hostage.

Chapter 11

COMPUTERS

Machines Can Expand The Potential Of Humans

Choosing Computer Software For Your Business

May 1995

Back in the late 1970s, when my company got its first computer, things were very different. Hardware and software for these minicomputers cost in the six-figure range. The monitors alone cost as much as a high-end personal computer does today, and they were black and white. You had to pay someone to program the computer, and you had to pay a programmer to make any changes you wanted later.

Well, times have changed. Personal computers and networks have replaced minicomputers, and inexpensive software can be bought off the shelf. It sounds wonderful, doesn't it?

It is, but there are drawbacks. Most software programs are not databased (a collection of data arranged for ease and speed of search and retrieval). More importantly, you never get exactly what you want when you buy software off the shelf and you can't change it when your needs change, even if you hire a programmer.

You can buy software developed specifically for jewelers, however. And the past couple of years have seen the development of Windows-format, databased software that allows you to create and modify your own custom programs without learning the complicated "languages" programmers use to tell computers what to do. This kind of software is called relational database or database management system—DBM for short.

Power, flexibility: DBM systems are incredibly powerful and flexible. Here are some operations we perform with our DBM system.

1. Order-entry orders, print orders and invoices. The system automatically prints mailing labels and invoices for each order, calculates charges including C.O.D., looks up and prints the applicable United Parcel Service zone and determines where the merchandise is in which warehouse. We can approve a credit card purchase at the time of order, and we can fax invoices and quotes directly from the computer screen at the click of the button.

2. Purchase orders, inventory control, accounts payable. The DBM system calculates, writes and prints checks, automatically filling in the appropriate information in the correct areas (supplier name, date, amount in numbers, amount in letters and to which invoices the check applies). It also tracks our checking account, showing what checks have not cleared yet, their total value and the balance in the checking account. Labels for the envelopes of bills being paid are printed automatically; labels for suppliers who provide self-addressed envelopes don't print.

3. Accounts receivable. Everything is displayed on one screen. As checks are deposited, the invoices against which they are deposited disappear from the screen (they're not lost or deleted, just not displayed). C.O.D. orders are sorted by C.O.D. number so they are a cinch to locate. Statements are produced at the touch of a button.

4. Product and sales analysis. Because of the nature of database applications, you can sort information virtually any way you want. We have some set reports for regular product and sales analyses. But we also require some one-time reports, which take anywhere from just a few seconds to 10 minutes to produce.

5. Charts. We produce charts with our system primarily to display sales analysis information. Quite a few chart formats are available (bar charts, pie charts, two- and three-dimensional, for example), and custom modifications are very easy to perform. A word of caution: charts such as three-dimensional multicolored versions require a lot of computer memory and could cause your system to crash (the screen freezes and you have to restart the computer) if your graphics resources are inadequate. It doesn't hurt the computer, but it can be very frustrating.

6. Letters. We don't use our DBM system for this, but you can write letters for advertising, bill collection and other purposes. The system automatically inserts the customer name and address and the contact name in the appropriate spots.

7. Product labels. We have a separate program for product labels and are reluctant to use our relational database program for this purpose. But it easily can print the appropriate number of labels for a particular product. Bar coding is no problem.

8. Deleting data. Database programs save everything until you delete it. Periodically, you will want to condense or delete old data. We have not had our program long enough to need this, but it's easy to do.

9. Changing reports and displays. It's easy to add, delete and alter data. You also can change the appearance of the screen by moving data displays or changing colors. You can even change the way you access data. All can be done very easily and quickly.

10. Security. The system offers several levels of security.

11. Finding data. One thing I really like about DBM systems is the ease of finding information. If someone calls and identifies himself as Joe, I can call up all our customers with that name in a few seconds. For a guy like me with a poor memory for names, this is a godsend.

Drawbacks: As you can see, DBM systems are almost infinitely flexible. As your company changes, you can easily and quickly change your software to meet the new needs. But like all software, DBM systems have some drawbacks.

For starters, they require a lot of resources. Our DBM system requires about 15 MB (MB is an abbreviation for megabyte, which is a unit of storage). That can be a tremendous drain on the computer; at times it's difficult to run word-processing with heavy graphics and the DBM system at the same time.

In addition, DBM systems are not an out-of-the-box-and-you're-up-and-running software. They give you the tools to create your own programs, but you first have to learn how to use the tools. You could hire an outside consultant to do it for a few hundred dollars, but is this an expense you want to pay every time you'd like to make a little change?

Perhaps explaining our experience will make you less hesitant. We chose MicroSoft Access as our DBM system (I'm not qualified to offer an opinion on how this compares with similar systems). For security reasons, I set up the program rather than have an employee do it. I read the 800-page instructional manual in my spare time over a month. That gave me an overview understanding of how the whole thing works.

It took another month of not-so-spare time to actually set up the program. Quite frankly, every time I mastered a particular part of the program and went on to another, it was like jumping into the deep end of a pool without knowing how to swim. However, Microsoft Access is very user-friendly. Those few times when I just couldn't figure out what I was doing wrong, Microsoft's technical hotline was there to help me solve the problem over the telephone. If you like puzzles and other kinds of problem-solving games, you may actually find setting up a DBM system fun.

Once the program was set up, we had to transfer the data from a previous software. We bought software called Monach for Windows just for this purpose. Monach is easy to use and comes with the best-written manual I have ever seen. I had expected no problems with the data transfer, but was I ever wrong! The program we used before MicroSoft Access was written with little traps and bugaboos that made it extremely difficult—if not impossible—to extract data and get out of the program. (I suppose that's one way for software companies to keep their customers buying upgrades.)

The net result was that we couldn't extract the data electronically. Instead, we had to spend about 200 hours entering it into the new system by hand. That was expensive and extremely annoying, but well worth it.

We began to use the program as soon as some of the data were entered (we didn't have to enter everything first). To my surprise, almost no debugging was required. One reason is that DBM systems use primary tools that write the programming for you. If you make a mistake by using the wrong tool, the system just won't let you move on until you do it correctly. As of the writing of this article, we've been using the program about eight months. We still make little changes and additions as needs arise.

DBM systems are not for the fainthearted; they require courage and tenacity. But they are a powerful and flexible tool for any business regardless of size. They are well worth the investment of time and money.

The Revolution Is Here

April 1995

Threshold resistance is a common consumer disease when it comes to visiting a jeweler. Savvy store owners, of course, work effectively to dispel it. They eschew forbidding columns and marble faces that can chill. They advertise and display merchandise that is not only appealing and exciting but also affordable. They train their staffs to be warm, friendly and helpful. And they get out into their community to project on a one-on-one basis the message that their stores are a pleasant and rewarding place to shop.

You'd think the sort of person who can overcome a potential customer's threshold resistance would have no trouble dealing with his or her own threshold resistance—not to jewelry stores but to computers. But it seems this is no easy task. I can think of a number of highly successful jewelers who are scared stiff of computers. They regard them as complex, failure-prone, mysterious and expensive devices they'd rather not have to deal with.

My sympathies lie with those who either hate or fear these machines. A few years ago when the publishing world said goodbye to decades of tradition and turned to the computer, most of us in the business went through a period of mental upheaval and adjustment. Once we made the move, there was no turning back.

Nor can there be any turning back in the jewelry business. Computerization is a nonnegotiable unless a jeweler runs such a small and simple operation that pencils and typewriters can handle all the day-to-day chores. Such a jeweler has to be content with smallness and simplicity; significant growth is only a remote possibility.

The special report on computers in this issue spells out many of the reasons why a well-programmed and well-managed computer system is critical. The principal one is simple: such a system allows a jeweler to make more money.

There's much more to it than that, of course. The computer is a tool—and should be regarded as no more than a tool—that will enhance efficiency when used properly. I know jewelers who, three months after their fiscal year has ended, still don't know whether they made or lost money or by how much they were up or down. How on earth can these jewelers make intelligent buying and other management decisions for the new fiscal year?

Such talk probably seems akin to baby chatter to businesses already making good use of computers. But based on responses we've received from the JCK Retail Jewelers Panel, for every three jewelers who even have a computer in their business, there's a fourth who hasn't taken that basic step. No matter how the experts may feel, there's still room for a lot of discussion of computer ABCs.

Our special report is designed to appeal to nonstarters, beginners and experts. For the first two groups, there are some useful Computer 101 facts and figures on the value of having equipment that will complete in hours chores that used to take days. Case histories show how various jewelers put their computer technology to good use—and it's important to note that we're not always talking about large, sophisticated operations.

We offer the experts food for thought more than operating facts. This is where the report turns to the future, which in some cases is almost at hand because change is taking place so quickly. The two key areas we look at are online networks and imaging. What's happening in both areas is little short of mind-boggling. Only a year or so ago, Polygon and RapNet were the only two networks jewelers were likely to know or be able to deal with. Today, the number is expanding rapidly; it seems only a matter of brief time before jewelry and jewelers will have a serious presence on the Internet, an international computer network.

Imaging, the ability to transmit pictures from computer to computer, also is a burgeoning art and science. Quality is improving as finer definition shows more detail and true color.

What the future will bring, and how soon, is immensely exciting and a little frightening. If you think you've seen changes in technology in the past five years, it's nothing compared to what we'll see in the next five. This will bring a profound change in the way retailers and consumers shop. Those who aren't ready for the changes, mentally and physically, will be in trouble.

The Real Computer Payoff: More Profit

April 1995

The revolution is over: the computer has captured the jewelry store with dramatic effects. Thousands of jewelers have become more efficient, gaining a tighter grasp on operations and sales and—in consequence—becoming more profitable.

"It has improved our lives immensely," says Allan Herrud of Langdon, S.D., whose watch repair business doubled thanks to computerization. "I don't think we could get along without it now."

But while computers help many jewelers as a bookkeeper, merchandiser and analyst, their full potential as profit-builder—especially with jewelry design and networking—has yet to be realized.

These are some findings of a JCK poll of hundreds of jewelers nationwide. Full results of the poll are detailed in this special report, "The Real Computer Payoff: More Profit."

The report also looks at how some jewelers use their computers for daily tasks such as inventory control, shows how a jeweler can be successful with a $250 used computer and looks at the quickly growing industry of retailing by computer.

The report includes easy-to-use lists of computer networks with services for jewelers and computer software providers, not to mention a look at a new fashion fad: computers chips as jewelry.

Essential: No question about it: the computer has become an essential tool in the daily business life of most U.S. retail jewelers, regardless of size.

Three out of four jewelers in the study (77%) use computers in their business operations, and half of them plan to upgrade or add functions to their systems in the next 12 months.

Computerization is so extensive that virtually everyone polled—including those without a computer themselves—say most of their colleagues use them. In Yakima, Wash., for example, Pat Gilmore of Dunbar Jewelers estimates at least 75% of his peers have computers and "most of us. . . brainstorm [via computer] on better use" of them.

And many of those who don't use a computer now soon will: two out of five (42%) say they will add one within the year.

Order or chaos? Jewelers aren't unanimous in their use or praise of computers, of course. A few are downright disgusted. "The learning curve is tough," says one New England jeweler who went on-line with a computer last year. "I may write a book called *Automation: 10 Easy Steps to Chaos.*" A Florida jeweler who added a computer in 1993 agrees, declaring, "hardware is great, software is a disaster." There are a few holdouts against these modern contraptions, but they are the exceptions. The overwhelming opinion of jewelers polled is that a computer is an effective, work-saving business tool they can't do without.

This computerized takeover of jewelry store management has occurred in a relatively short time. It began slowly in the 1970s with major chains and then picked up speed in the 1980s with regional chains and large independents.

Recently, the trot has turned into a stampede, with many jewelers having gone on-line since 1990.

The biggest influence on many to plug in and turn on wasn't the wonders of modern technology but the oldest form of data transfer—word of mouth. More than a third say the advice of other retailers led them to buy their first computer. Toss in the counsel of friends, relatives and accountants, and the figure rises to almost half of those polled.

Office manager: Once jewelers install a computer, most of them turn over basic business operations to the electronic marvel. The most common use: inventory management. "[We have] accurate, up-to-date inventory information by department, by vendor and by store," says Dale Briman of Briman's Leading Jewelers, Topeka, Kan. Adds Phil Lemon of Lemons Jewelry in Waynesboro, Va., precise sales and stock information from the computer "has improved our inventory control and reduced our inventory levels."

Also near the top of the list are such routine office tasks as accounts receivable and payable, direct mail, customer and vendor lists, tag printing, sales analysis and various reports.

One in five of the jewelers polled buys software off the shelf. Just over half use software designed for retail jewelers, while a third use software designed specifically for them. Inventory and appraisal functions are the two leading categories of customized software among the jewelers polled.

Dramatic impact: The impact of computerization on business operations has been dramatic. Almost every jeweler polled say computerization has improved their efficiency, and two out of three say it has done so "greatly."

In Southfield, Mich., for instance, jeweler Lew Silver says the computer cut paperwork by 60%. And Pat Gilmore of Dunbar Jewelers adds that the billing process used to take 2 1/2 days, but now, with computers, takes two hours at most.

The resulting freedom from so much paperwork gives jewelers and their employees more time for selling, for displays and for business planning. Many also cite the "timeliness," "speed" and "convenience" of having instant detailed information—whether it be verifying a customer's purchase or six-month sales data on quarter-carat diamond rings. As jeweler Harry Levitch of Memphis, Tenn., puts it, "Everything is available at a finger's touch."

Even more significant is the "control"—an often-repeated word in the poll—that computers give users. "We no longer fly by the seat of our pants," says Don Kelsheimer, a jeweler and computer enthusiast in Casey, Ill. "I know where I am financially everyday." Adds Craig Benson, manager of John Rich Jewelers in Mentor, Ohio, "We have a better idea now of how much money is invested in various categories, which departments are more profitable than others and which vendors' merchandise moves better."

In short, says jeweler David Coll of Montclair, Cal., "computerization has given me a better picture of how my store is doing."

In turn, that helps jewelers to plan for the future. "Being able to analyze, compare and generally have concrete data on hand ... helps us be smarter and plan better," says George Robey of Sibbings Jewelry in Dubuque, Iowa.

Profits: The bottom line of all this is—a better bottom line. Four of five jewelers say computerizing their operations has improved their profits at least a little, and many of them say it has "helped greatly."

Still, most jewelers polled haven't progressed beyond the management basics to more imaginative, and profitable, uses of their computer. Few of them use their computers for jewelry design or computer imaging (showing and adapting jewelry to customer preferences), two functions that could boost sales. Though imaging technology can be expensive (running into several thousand dollars), design software is affordable for virtually any jeweler who wants to do custom work.

Another untapped business opportunity is the computer network. A network is basically a collection of computers linked through cable or telephone lines. There are literally thousands of networks worldwide (including Internet, the largest global web) and hundreds in the U.S. A number of these are designed specifically for jewelers, including Polygon (which allows trading among jewelers and offers Jewelers' Security Alliance information), GIA Net (established by the Gemological Institute of America), Diamond Network, The Registry Ltd. (for estate and period jewelry) and RapNet (providing diamond market information).

Only one in four jewelers polled belongs to one or more computer networks. The fact that only 67% have a modem—a device that would connect them to a network—is a factor. But even those with modems don't always use them fully. One West Coast jeweler, for example, uses his modem only to communicate with his software supplier—about twice a year.

Maybe the revolution isn't completely over yet. The computer has taken over the office, now jewelers must learn how to use it to fatten their profits.

SELLING ONLINE: THE ADVENTURE GROWS

Just when you thought you knew all the ways to sell jewelry, along comes another: the home computer.

Online shopping turns a personal computer into a cyber-mall of retailers connected to a widening web of networks.

"Electronic shopping is going to change the way consumers shop, and retailers will have to adjust the way they do business," says Daniel Porter, president of RFS North America. RFS services the private-label credit cards of thousands of retailers around the world and is working on "electronic store" technology for them.

Enthusiasts say computer home shopping could rival TV home shopping within a few years. And like any shopping center, this electronic mall has room for smaller retailers, as some jewelers already know.

Ballooning demand: Shopping by computer isn't new. The CompuServe computer network has been selling merchandise for at least a decade. But online shopping has grown substantially in the past 18 months as consumer demand for home computers balloons and computer makers shift focus from business-only to home and entertainment services.

About 7 million personal computers (PCs) were sold in the U.S. last year, and at least that many will be sold this year. In the next decade, say industry experts, the number of U.S. homes with a computer will rise from 33% to 50%.

What makes PCs so popular? They are increasingly "user friendly" (easy to use), offer multimedia features (full-color pictures, sound and video), and have sophisticated telephone modems that connect them to a global web of computer networks and services, including on-line retailing.

The multimedia features make computer selling increasingly attractive, say vendors. Instead of just words describing a product, consumers now see it in full color. "When the color pictures of our inventory jump up on the screen, people [expecting a text-only presentation] seem startled," says Douglas K. Hucker, president of The Registry Ltd., the estate and antique jewelry division of R.F. Moeller Jeweler in St. Paul, Minn. The Registry launched an online service last year and already has more than 100 retail clients.

Some retailers—including Ross Simmons, Tiffany and Brendle's—have even put their catalogs on CD-ROM (computer disc-read only memory). Consumers simply slip the disc into their home computer to see pictures of the merchandise and text describing it.

But while more and more vendors are testing this new marketplace—selling everything from chocolates to cars—shopping by computer is still a tiny drop in the $2 trillion retailing sea. Only 6% of U.S. computer owners now use any online service, and total annual sales from online shopping is under $200 million, says Matthew Kursh, president of eShop of San Mateo, Cal., which makes technology that enables retailers to sell to computer users, either directly or though a network.

That's peanuts compared with the $3 billion dollar TV home shopping industry. But analysts expect 25% growth in online retailing within five years. "It's a small business now," says Kursh. "But consumers are looking for easier, better ways to make purchases and increasingly use computers to do it. We expect electronic shopping will grow rapidly during the rest of this decade."

Kursh concedes online selling won't replace walk-in retailing or catalogs, but says it will "easily compete with and probably eclipse TV home shopping" in annual sales volume by the end of the '90s.

Footholds: Not surprisingly, some big retail names, including some in TV shopping, already have deep footholds in this new electronic marketplace. For example:

• eShop is creating an "electronic marketplace" for AT&T's Persona-Link online service. Other major retail clients—including Lands' End, Hallmark and Tower Records—are working with eShop on their own online "stores."

• GE Capital Services' Retailer Financial Service division recently made a "significant investment" in eShop. RFS is the world's largest provider of private-label credit cards, servicing some 300 major retailers and thousands of smaller ones worldwide. The company "intends to help [them] become actively involved in electronic home shopping by facilitating the design and launch of electronic shops using eShop technology," says a spokesperson.

• The Home Shopping Network, which reaches 60 million U.S. households, recently bought Internet Shopping Network, which offers computer products to Internet's 25 million users worldwide. ISN has created an online "store" on the Prodigy computer network (with 2 million users) called the HSC Outlet Net. HSN plans to "greatly expand" ISN this year and may sell space to other merchants. "[Merging] the TV and the PC is an area [of retailing] that is coming closer and closer," says HSN Vice President Louise Cleery.

• QVC, the world's largest TV home retailer (50 million homes in the U.S., 17 million in Mexico and the United Kingdom) will soon launch "Q-online," a computer shopping service that will offer more merchandise than its TV service.

• CompuServe, one of the oldest computer networks, offers its 11 million users "Electronic Mall" (with 120 merchants, including J.C. Penney).

• America On-Line, another leading network, has "CompuStore," with a quarter million items from dishes to furniture.

• Richard C. Marcus of Neiman-Marcus retail fame and developer Kenneth H. Hughes have created Shopping IN, an online network in the Dallas area that features upscale merchants.

Jewelry on-line: Jewelry is an important part of this burgeoning industry. It will be a major category on HSN's expanded ISN and already is in HSN's Prodigy "store." In fact, it quickly sold out of its initial stock of jewelry ($20 to several hundred dollars retail) after "opening" in October.

Even retail jewelers themselves are looking at online retailing. Sterling Inc., the second largest U.S. jeweler with 880 stores, has been studying the possibility and will likely add it within five years. "Times are changing and so are consumer buying habits," says Executive Vice President Steve Holden. "People want shopping that is not only easier but less time-consuming."

(Zale Corp., the largest U.S. jeweler, is rebuilding its market after exiting bankruptcy protection two years ago and won't give serious attention to online selling until the late '90s, says a spokesperson.)

Online retailing also attracts smaller retailers who want to reach a larger audience without adding a store or printing a catalog, says Kursh. The Registry Ltd. of St. Paul, Minn., is one example. Mark Moeller of R.F. Moeller Jeweler launched The Registry as a wholesale division in 1982; the online service started in 1994. Douglas K. Hucker, president of The Registry, describes the computer service as "an on-line catalog with vivid photographs, current news items, education information and a discussion group, available to users at no charge. Though the market is minimal now, says Hucker, "I expect we'll be selling a mountain of jewelry in five years."

Moeller plans to put his store online through The Registry this spring. "This is the future of retailing," says Moeller. "It won't replace holding and touching pieces, but it will pique [consumers'] interest and expand horizons beyond belief."

In Chicago, meanwhile Steve Quick Jewelers offer estate and custom-made pieces to potentially millions of network users via Chicago-Electric. Quick was "pleasantly surprised" by initial on-line inquiries and made several sales in the first weeks after he went on line in October.

And in Dallas, Tex., Castle Gap Jewelry, a four-store company specializing in American Indian jewelry, joined Shop IN in October, offering items retailing from $18 to $200. Computer users pick Shop IN from a list of services on the computer, choose "Jewelry" from the on-screen menu and then see digitized color images and descriptions. Keyed-in orders are sent to Shop IN, which faxes them to Castle Gap.

During its first four months online, says Charlotte Bennett, Castle Gap co-owner and vice president, the company received at least a dozen orders from online shoppers. The customers were all new and were the type her company seeks: "sophisticated consumers looking for unique pieces." While a dozen orders aren't many, "no one has ever done this before, so we had no idea of what to expect," says Bennett. "We're pleased so far, but it will take time to develop this."

Some problems: Online shopping isn't all black ink and roses. Some vendors complain that older computers can't offer detailed graphics quickly or don't have sophisticated enough modems to receive improved programming. And it's taking longer than assumed to get the bugs out of some new computer technology.

There's also concern about protecting data, including credit-card information, from computer-sophisticated thieves. The Internet—linking some 30 million computers worldwide—has had problems with thieves who know how to circumvent its security systems. Bank of America, Citicorp Bank, Wells Fargo, the First Interstate Bank and operators of online retail services are trying to create more sophisticated encryption technology to frustrate such break-ins and thefts. They're also working on technology to let users make payments directly to stores and banks on their computers.

Quick, Hucker, Moeller, Bennett and Holden are excited about the potential of on-line retailing. "We have a tremendous opportunity to get in on the bottom floor," says Bennett. "This is the wave of the future."

PUTTING 'CONTROL' BACK INTO INVENTORY CONTROL

Many jewelers say computers have helped them to put control back in their inventory control.

"With manual records, inventory management was very difficult," says Rob Panowicz, a jeweler in Olympia, Wash., who computerized in 1989. "We had to track each piece of merchandise through years of paper trails and couldn't really replace fast-moving items on a regular basis. A salesman would sell us something to replace an item we sold the week before—and we'd forget we had it [in stock] for five years."

Computerization forced Panowicz into a regimented approach to inventory. "We broke down our merchandise into finer categories," he says. Wedding bands, for example, are now categorized by plain or carved, color, metal quality and metal width instead of just plain or carved. "This makes it easier for us to compare what's selling and to compare costs among vendors," he says.

Panowicz says computerized inventory control offers other benefits, including:

• Better customer service "because we now have a better chance of having in stock what customers look for."

• Lower holding and financing costs and better margins.

• Higher sales volume and lower inventory costs at the same time. "That's essential for survival in the '90s. In fact, without the computer, I'm not sure we would have survived."

The edge: Dan Danford, a jeweler in Madison, Wis., and a former Zale Corp. vice president, agrees that jewelers need computers for profitable inventory control. "The jewelry business has become so complex that jewelers need an edge," he says. "Computers can provide it."

When Danford bought his business from his employer in 1992, the computer wasn't being used effectively to track price points or turnover. "Strong sales categories weren't being replenished in a timely manner," he recalls.

He upgraded the computer system and customized an off-the -shelf inventory program to track such specifics as turnover by price point, vendor and merchandise category "We now take our 15 best lines and track them every two weeks to see how they're turning, then reorder merchandise," he says. "We don't wait for the salesmen." One example: the computer quickly showed that an initial order from Southwest jewelry manufacturer Kabana turned 80% in 40 days, justifying its addition.

Now Danford is taking electronic inventory control a step further with bar code scanning equipment—including tag printer and handheld scanner. He says the $15,000 system will pay for itself within a year by significantly reducing the time necessary to take inventory and eliminating human error.

The complete upgrade was expensive—about $50,000. But the store's annual volume jumped from $1 million to $2.4 million in just two years, and Danford attributes much of the gain to the computer.

Danford concedes that computers still "scare" many jewelers who have done business for many years without them. But this 28-year jewelry retailing veteran offers a word of advice: "I'm not a computer whiz. I got one and 'played' with it to see what it could do. Once you start to use it, you feel more comfortable and learn new ways to use it as you go along. I'm proof that you can teach an old dog new tricks."

SUCCESS WITH A $250 COMPUTER

Many small jewelers assume they must spend thousands of dollars to computerize their business. Nonsense, says jeweler Don Kelsheimer, owner of the Bird's Nest, which he operates with his wife and a staff of four part-time salespeople in the small farm town of Casey, Ill.

With a used IBM personal computer he bought for $250 at a computer fair and about $200 of off-the-shelf software, Kelsheimer successfully tracks inventory, turnover and repairs; produces appraisal reports, a newsletter and mailing labels; and generally keeps his finger on his store's financial pulse.

"The idea that computers and software are just too expensive is false," says Kelsheimer, a self-taught computer buff who paid $1,500 for his first computer in 1990 and now teaches evening classes in computer use at a junior college.

Why would a guy who knows so much about computers not buy a state-of-the-art model to run his business? "Because I'm not wealthy, and because I can do the same things with my [used] IBM PS2 and color monitor," he says bluntly.

Finding a good used computer is as easy as ABC, says the former high school teacher:

A. Familiarize yourself with computers so you know what you want from one. Go to a newsstand to buy computer magazines that explain what new models can do, rate hardware and software, and offer news about the rapidly changing computer industry.

B. Get advice from a local computer guru, someone who "knows and does things with computers." It may be a store salesman, teacher, relative or other retailer. Or ask at schools, computer stores or newspaper offices for the name of a local computer user group.

C. Shop around. Check newspaper ads and telephone books for computer or electronic stores that sell used computers and visit computer fairs. "There is a constant market [of good used computers] from people who upgrade to more sophisticated hardware" he says. When buying a used computer, be sure to ask for any manuals or support materials.

Drawback: One drawback with used hardware is it may not be sophisticated enough to use jewelry design or imaging software. "But a small-town jeweler can get along fine with what's available in basic store-management software," says Kelsheimer. "I find most mom-and-pop businesses don't want to do everything at once. They add as they go along, starting with inventory, then on to accounts receivable, mailing lists and then a total accounting package."

Computerization has had a significant impact on Kelsheimer's own business. "Before, we flew by the seat of our pants," he says. "Now I know where I am financially everyday. I know who owes me and who I owe. And when someone has a problem with a product, I know where it came from." A customer once lost the stone in an emerald ring. Kelsheimer returned the ring to the supplier, who said it wasn't his product. "With my [computer] tracking, I was able to tell him when I purchased it, the invoice number, how much I paid for it and when I delivered it to my customer. With that information, the supplier was willing to admit he had made a mistake in his first assessment of the ring," Kelsheimer says dryly, "and he replaced the emerald."

MORE TIME FOR BUSINESS

Computerization has had a significant effect on the watch repair business at Herrud's Jewelry, a store with a staff of five in Langdon, S.D. (population 2,200). "It not only has made life a lot easier," says owner Allan Herrud, "but I don't think we could get along without it now."

The immediate impact of computerizing Herrud's watch repair business in 1990 was on recordkeeping. "We do a lot of trade work," he says. "To handwrite all those records took umpteen hours." Since computerization, the store has nearly quadrupled its trade accounts (from 10 that accounted for 25% of total revenue to 36 that account for 40%).

In addition, salespeople now have more time to work on sales and displays, he says.

Herrud couldn't find an off-the-shelf computer watch repair program, so he had a computer-programmer friend design one for him. The cost: a couple of hundred dollars. When someone brings in a watch for repair, the salesperson gives it a "Herrud number" and enters that in the computer along with the account name, number, description and condition at time of take-in, the date in and when it was invoiced out. Information can be retrieved instantly for any reason.

The store also invoices through its computer, an IBM 426.

While many jewelers start their computerization journey with inventory control, Herrud took a more ambitious path with repair tracking, accounts payable and receivable and a newsletter.

Based on the success of the watch repair program, Herrud now plans to expand his computer use by adding a bridal registry and possibly inventory control.

PROFITING FROM LISTS

Customer lists. Every jeweler has one, but not everyone gets the most profit out of them. Computers can help by keeping accurate, easily accessible records of what and when customers are likely to buy.

Consider Krista Birchmore, co-owner of Gudmondson & Buyck Jewelers in Columbia, S.C. Birchmore, a former president of the South Carolina Jewelers Association and a computer user since 1988, divides her list into three categories:

• Group A comprises regular customers who spend more than $1,000 a year in her store.

• Group B comprises those who spend less than $1,000.

• Group C has the names of people she would like to have as customers but doesn't yet.

Under each customer's name are address, telephone number, place of work, finger size, ZIP code, whether married or single and a place for notes such as likes/dislikes ("likes emeralds"), anniversaries, birthdays and other relevant marketing and sales information.

When she gets new emerald jewelry in the store, for example, she calls up the category "Likes Emeralds" and calls everyone on the list. When a woman shows interest in something during the year, Birchmore makes a note in her computer then calls the husband at Christmas time to suggest the item as a gift. "I call those notes my 'Santa Claus' list," she says.

You can do the same manually with index cards. "But that takes a lot more time," she says. "With a computer, I just pull up what I want whenever I want it."

A brand-new computer will give Birchmore the capability to personalize letters. "I'll be able to follow up on past purchases, such as writing a letter to newlyweds on their first anniversary or reminding customers about upcoming anniversaries or birthdays."

Immediate effect: Birchmore has used a computer in her business since 1988. Edwin Larosa, owner of Ayens Inc. in Clifton, N.J., just bought his last summer, but it has already affected his business. "Before, we didn't know who our customers were unless we looked into our [manual] files," he says. "Now we ask the computer for reports on who bought what and for how much. If we have a $5,000 piece, for example, we now send a mailing to all those who the computer says can afford it" based on past purchases. He uses the computer to customize the letter so the customer thinks it was prepared just for him or her.

Early this year, Larosa invited his 60 best customers (those who the computer said spent $5,000 in the past year) to an appointment-only visit at which they could receive discounts. He expected a 20% response but was pleased with the 50% turnout—and everyone who came bought something.

The computer also has cut the time he spent on paperwork, giving him more time to sell. In fact, his sales volume has increased at least 30% since he computerized.

Meanwhile, jeweler Dan Danford of Madison, Wis., uses his computer to target specific markets. "For example, we track ZIP codes of those who make $2,000 purchases or more and then send them circulars on upcoming estate jewelry shows," he says. "That's better than having to guess who may or may not be interested."

The computer also comes in handy in Danford's effort to expand his market beyond his mostly upscale clientele in the university town. "We want to expand our market to include customers who spend only $200 to $400 annually," he says. "We concentrate on them when we are looking at a promotion such as a remount event. [This precision targeting] gives us a better return than across the board."

IN THE CHIPS: COMPUTER BITS AS JEWELRY

Using computers to design and sell jewelry isn't unusual. But making jewelry from computer parts? It's one of the latest cybertrends.

Intel Corp. of Santa Clara, Cal., the world's leading maker of computer chips (tiny pieces of silicon embedded with trillions of tiny circuits that perform computer tasks), used to discard defective chips. Now Intel gives the chips to Silicon Valley Ware Inc., a small promotional products company in Mountain View, Cal., that sets them into jewelry.

Silicon Valley Ware is headed by designer Diane Emerson, who suggested the idea to Intel and who designs the jewelry. In a test project last year, chip jewelry was created for Intel employees and business contacts. The test was so successful that the jewelry is now available to retailers.

Silicon Valley Ware's Pentium jewelry collection comprises earrings, key chains, cuff links, bracelets and lapel pins that retail for $20-$25. The collection debuted this past fall (including a day-long event at Nordstrom's) and now is available in several dozen university and museum shops across the U.S. "We've had a lot of requests from people who run jewelry stores, art galleries and such who want to [carry the collection]," says Emerson.

Emerson and an Intel spokesperson say they are committed to a permanent retail marketing program to generate consumer awareness of technology.

Meanwhile, Connie Perry, a craftsman-entrepreneur in Somerset, Mass., has created CeeDeez, a line of jewelry made from pieces of recycled compact discs and computer chips. The pins and earrings in the line retail for $5-$15 and debuted at the CD-ROM Expo in Boston during the fall.

Perry, who has been doing this for five years, gets her discarded CDs and chips from friends and business companies, sometimes in a barter exchange for creating corporate art for them.

The line is sold in some art stores and in the Boston Computer Museum.

Why would anyone wear computer chips or CDs as jewelry? Emerson and Perry cite their uniqueness and beauty as one reason. "It's a conversation piece, and the intricate circuitry and interesting light reflection hold people's eyes," says Emerson. Adds Perry, "They're so lovely to look at; it's like looking at a rainbow."

NETWORKS WITH JEWELERS IN MIND

Computer networks link users who have common interests or purposes. They offer all sorts of services, from shopping to stock prices to information about the Bible to debates about *Star Trek* movies.

To connect to a network, you need a personal computer and a modem, a small device that links computers via telephone lines or cable. You'll pay the regular telephone service charge for each call plus a network subscription fee, if there is one.

Each network usually provides the communications software you'll need to "log on" and use a particular service.

There are hundreds of computer networks in the U.S. and thousands throughout the world, the largest being the Internet, linking some 30 million computers around the globe. Of special interest to jewelers, though, are networks designed especially for them and for businesspeople in general. Here's a sampling (keep in mind other networks are being developed all the time):

Appraisal Profession On-Line. This network has been providing appraisal information since mid-1994 to appraisal professionals, government agencies, the banking industry and legal industries and the general public.

The American Society of Appraisers developed the network. ASA members have unlimited free access to ASA directories, course applications, even calendars, special interest forums, bulletin board information and surveys.

Other member services include an employment opportunity database, public auction schedule, on-line news, surveys, e-mail (global via Internet), resource bibliography and discipline-specific information.

DOS-based communication software will support graphic imaging. The software and service are free except for pay-for-use features. To obtain a copy of the software call (703)478-5500 or download it from the services file library. You may use any communication software to connect to the network; the modem connection number is (703) 478-5502. The network is available also though the Internet by dialing apo.com.

Appraisal Profession Online, P.O. Box 17265, Washington, D.C. 20041.

Deep Discount Network. DDN is an electronic marketplace for buying and selling products. It features search, retrieval and communication capabilities in a Windows environment and gives manufacturers, resellers and retailers access to diverse markets and products, enabling them to buy and sell merchandise quickly.

Information requests include brand names, physical condition, quantities available, prices, payment terms and how to get samples. Buyers refer to Offers-to-Sell to find deals or locate specific items and Requests-to-Buy to list their own product needs. Sellers list their own Offers-to-Sell, look at Requests-to-Buy to find items from other companies or look at the general buying and selling interests of other companies.

Members contact each other via DDN's e-mail or automated fax, search through member profiles, observe buying activity and form groups of buyers or sellers for private dealing. Products can be listed anonymously, and purchse offers can be made privately.

The service costs $50 monthly. Deep Discount Network, 1939 Newark-Granville Rd., Granville, Ohio, 43023; (800) 434-2798.

The Diamond Network. This relatively new network enables jewelers to trade diamonds, colored stones, watches and other merchandise by computer.

Manufacturers and trade services can buy full-screen advertising that appears when users log on. Multiple-location companies may lease private conferencing so employees can communicate with each other and with customers. Software manufacturers can use the service to provide on-line demonstrations for potential users. And trade magazines can provide timely information to subscribers.

Future plans include improved color, sound and full motion video, an industry directory, on-line ordering, live chat between multiple users and access to the Internet (see below).

Users connect to The Diamond Network with any communications software by setting their modem to 8-N-1 and dialing (619) 788-7008. To view on-line graphics, users must have an IBM-compatible 286 or better, VGA monitor and mouse. The communications software is provided free.

The subscription fee is $19.95 monthly. Conference set-ups and full-screen advertising are $199 monthly. Diamond Network, 1530 Main St., Suite #3, Ramona, Cal. 92065; (619) 789-2048.

GIA Net. The Gemological Institute of America launched this computerized education/information center in 1986. It now has more than 2,300 users and is being upgraded with a graphical user interface (a Windows-like environment) and features designed to make it more flexible and user-friendly.

GIA students receive complimentary access so they can chat on-line with their instructors, get information from the library, work on GIA courses and read current news.

An enhanced service is provided to paid subscribers, who can retrieve GIA documentation and current and past trade articles. A GemLink option provides limited access to the Business Discussions and Appraisal channels of Polygon, another industry network.

GIA also uses the network to communicate with its overseas facilities.

GIA Net is a DOS platform, but can be accessed by most other computer systems. GIA provides free communication software to users with IBM-compatible systems. This package can read all information on the network, including graphics. Other operating systems can use generic communication software to access the network, but may not be able to see graphics or some file formats.

The basic service is free to GIA students. The extended network is $60 yearly for students and alumni, $75 for anyone else. Gemological Institute of America, 1660 Stewart St., P.O. Box 2110, Santa Monica, Cal. 90407; (800) 421-7250, ext. 292, or (310) 829-2991, ext. 344.

The Internet. This is the world's largest conglomeration of computer networks and users, including government and university networks and smaller, specialized networks such as those listed above, all capable of exchanging information. The global service has more than 30,000 networks, with an estimated 1,000 added every month.

The Internet has no governing body or controlling group, though the Internet Society, a nonprofit group based in Reston, Va., promotes its usefulness. It started as a U.S. military project in 1969, designed as a decentralized communications network connecting defense researchers with the Pentagon and with each other. In 1986, the National Science Foundation spurred nondefense use of the network by creating NSFNet, connecting five supercomputer centers for research use. Universities gained access to this network and provided it to students. With the addition of several large commercial networks and many smaller ones, the network evolved into the Internet.

You gain access to the Internet through access providers who charge a fee to "surf" (or roam) the system. These providers can be private businesses, educational facilities, libraries or government agencies. With the advent of easy-to-use communications software, the Internet is growing rapidly, especially as a commercial selling tool. Users can view images in catalogs, download free software and "talk" to each other via e-mail.

Recently, the Internet has come under attack by thieves who know how to circumvent current security systems. These individuals break into networks and steal information, including credit-card numbers. Until more sophisticated encryption technology is put in-place, networks will be easy prey for this kind of theft.

For a free list of Internet access providers, call InterNIC Information Services at (800) 444-4345.

JewelNet. This network offers members of the jewelry trade a computerized way to buy, sell and trade diamonds and jewelry. Features include diamond, watch and jewelry inventories as well as spot metal prices, buy/sell classifieds and a Jewelers Forum with news of interest to the industry. Subscribers also may conduct business conversations with each other.

The network recently added graphics so dealers and retailers can view items before buying.

JewelNet costs $49 per month. JewelNet, 21 Charles St., Westport, Conn. 06880; (203) 226-3367, fax (203) 226-7633.

Polygon. This network, established in 1983, is a trading and communications network for the jewelry industry. It features channels grouped into four major categories: Jewelry, General Merchandise, Communications and Private Networks. Most channels are used to buy or sell merchandise, including diamonds, colored stones, watches, antiques, coins, electronic and photographic equipment, guns and musical instruments. Others are for business and appraisal discussions, conversation, announcements, security and news.

The Jewelers' Security Alliance, Jewelers of America and *National Jeweler* magazine all have independent channels through which all Polygon subscribers can receive their latest information. Polygon and JCK also are studying how they might work together.

Polygon also has private network channels for the American Gem Trade Association, the Women's Jewelry Association, the Accredited Gemologists Association and the Canadian Jewelers Association. Only members of these organizations can send or receive information on these channels.

One of Polygon's most popular services is the CertNet database of diamonds. Suppliers list their diamond inventories and retailers search the listings to find the diamonds that suit their customers needs.

Polygon also offers GemLink, which provides limited access to GIA Net, the on-line information/communication system of the Gemological Institute of America.

In a joint venture with *National Jeweler*, Polygon also offers the ability to send and receive full-color images of items available for sale.

Polygon provides communications software for IBM-compatible and Macintosh computers. Plans are near completion to make Polygon accessible through the Internet.

The fee is $95 monthly or $950 yearly (Polygon offers an introductory year-long subscription of $475). Polygon Network Inc., P.O. Box 4806, Dillon, Colo. 80435; (800) 221-4435, fax (303) 468-1247.

RapNet OnLine. This network links diamond and colored stone traders and offers an outlet for industry news and discussion. It was developed by Martin Rapaport, well-known for his expertise in the diamond market and publisher of the *Rapaport Report*.

RapNet provides information and buy/sell bulletin boards. Topics include Diamonds (buy/sell), Gems, Estate Jewelry, Rough (buy/sell), Appraisals, News and TalkLine. Messages can be sent and received, sellers can choose to list their stones confidentially, markup can be built in to the sell listings and sell files can be updated.

An area on Pricing includes the *Rapaport Report* price indications for diamonds. The latest prices for round and pear-shaped diamonds are updated automatically when a user connects to the network. An available price calculation program shows the price indication and discounts for particular stones.

RapNet requires an IBM-compatible computer running DOS or Windows, a hard disk with 5 megabytes of free space and a modem. The system supports high-speed modems and can transmit up to 38,400 baud rate.

The subscription fee is $300 yearly. Rapaport Diamond Corp., 15 W. 47 St., New York, N.Y. 10035-3306; (212) 354-9100.

The Registry Ltd. Estate and antique jewelry are the focus of this network, launched in 1994. It is a free service to the jewelry trade (users pay for the telephone connection, of course) and will soon be available through the Internet.

The Registry Ltd. offers a catalog of windows containing color graphics, descriptions, prices and ordering information to buy and sell estate and antique jewelry. It also provides education information on industry topics and news items and includes a conference option for user communication.

The Registry runs on IBM-compatible and Macintosh computers and comes with communications software tailored to each system.

The service is free. The Registry Ltd., 2073 Ford Parkway, St. Paul, Minn. 55116; (800) 328-1179, fax (612) 698-0316.

SOFTWARE MANUFACTURERS

Following is a list of software developed for the jewelry industry, including individual features and the name and address of the developer/distributor.

The list is organized alphabetically into five groups—retail management, manufacturing, appraisal, brokerage and miscellaneous—based on the main purpose of the software packages. The list comprises companies that responded to JCK's requests for information; other companies also offer software designed for jewelers.

RETAIL MANAGEMENT

APPRENTICE, CRAFTSMAN & JOURNEYMAN SERIES
Company: Applications Systems Corp., 30 Winter Street, Boston, MA 02108; (617) 426-2918, fax (617) 451-2352.
Cost: Start at $695 single store operation +
Operating System: IBM (DOS) and compatibles.
Features: Point-of-Sale, Inventory and Imaging.
Training and Support: Is available at company headquarters.

BUSINESS PARTNER P.O.S. & ACCOUNTING
Company: Abbott Software, P.O. Box 1318, Maggie Valley, N.C. 28751; (704) 926-2892, fax (704) 926-8400.
Cost: $895.
Operating system: IBM (DOS).
Features: Accounting, inventory, sales and customer services.
Additional: The company also sells Tag-It Version 5.0 for $199.95, a tagging program.
Training and support: Unknown.

DMS FOR JEWELERS
Company: Services on Software, 540-506 Exchange St., Geneva, N.Y. 14456; (315) 789-7365, Compuserve 71240,3405.
Cost: $895 for entry level, $1,895 for two-user system, fully integrated, with training.
Operating system: IBM (DOS) and compatibles.
Features: Two levels of security per module, accounts payable/receivable, inventory, sales, barcoding, point of sale, tax tables, import and export capabilities and customer services.
Training and support: Can be used by beginners; technical support on toll-free telephone number for a fee.

FREQUENT BUYER PROGRAM
Company: Abbott Software, P.O. Box 1318, Maggie Valley, N.C. 28751; (704) 926-2892, fax (704) 926-8400.
Cost: $250.

Operating system: IBM (DOS) and Windows.
Features: Marketing.
Additional: The company also sells Tag-It Version 5.0 for $199.95, a tagging program.
Training and support: Unknown.

INSTORE LINK
Company: STR, 6800-A W. Snowville Rd., Cleveland, Ohio 44141; (216) 546-9510, fax (216) 546-9516.
Cost: $50,000.
Operating system: IBM (DOS) and Windows.
Features: Corporate headquarters multistore data link.
Training and support: None needed.

INSTORE PLUS
Company: STR, 6800-A W. Snowville Rd., Cleveland, Ohio 44141; (216) 546-9510, fax (216) 546-9516.
Cost: $3,000.
Operating system: IBM (DOS).
Features: Accounting, inventory, sales, and customer services.
Training and support: Unknown.

JCS6000 RETAIL JEWELER'S SOFTWARE
Company: Gemprint Computer Systems, 24 W. 500 Maple Ave., Naperville, Ill. 60540; (800) 621-2002 or (708) 355-1116.
Cost: $1,495+.
Operating system: IBM-compatibleS.
Features: Accounting, inventory, sales, customer services, repricing of gold, tag printing and ability to track weight, color and clarity of diamonds. Bar coding and imaging are optional. Multiuser and Multistore capabilities.
Training and support: Can be used by beginners; one-year support on a toll-free telephone number and updates are included.

JEM RETAILER PLUS SUPER VERSION 8.0
Company: JEM Integrated Technologies, 9460 160 St., Surrey, British Columbia, V4N 2R6 Canada; (604) 582-7639, fax (604) 582-2749.
Cost: $2,995.
Operating system: IBM (DOS).
Features: Accounting, inventory, sales and customer services.
Training and support: Unknown.

JEMS (JEWELRY MERCHANDISING SYSTEM)
Company: BIS Computer Solution, 2428 Foothill Blvd., La Crescenta, Cal. 91214; (213) 245-3691.
Cost: $20,000 to $200,000.
Operating system: IBM (DOS) and compatibles; all UNIX systems.
Features: The system consists of a number of fully integrated applications that provide control of jewelry merchandising, internal operations and accounting. Functions include serialized inventory, bar coding, integrated point of sale with back office, service/work orders, sales analysis, sales ticket processing, credit and collections, accounts payable/receivable, financial statements, appraisals, mailing list, payroll and office automation, including word processing and e-mail.
Training and support: Can be used by beginners; training and support are available.

THE JEWELER
Company: IBIS, 3637 Main St., Stratford, Conn. 06497; (203) 377-7100, fax (203) 261-9665.
Cost: single user, $1,950; multiuser, $2,450.
Operating system: IBM (DOS) and compatibles.
Features: Accounting, inventory, sales and customer services, including point of sale, inventory management, bar coding, repairs, custom manufacturing, appraisals, target marketing, customer profiling, charge accounts, accounts payable/receivable, check writing and general ledger. Professional appraisal documents can be created to include images.
Training and support: Can be used by beginners. Upgrades and modem support are included in the package price and are $250 per year thereafter. A half day of training is provided to customers within a two-hour drive; otherwise, training can be arranged for a fee plus expenses.

JEWELERS INFORMATION MANAGEMENT SYSTEM 5
Company: D.A.T.A. Inc., 303 S. Main St., Lombard, Ill. 60148; (708) 627-DATA, fax (708) 627-3285.
Cost: $2,500; a full accounting program option integrated with JIM V costs an additional $1,000.
Operating system: IBM (DOS) and compatibles.
Features: Accounting, inventory, tag printing, bar coding, video imaging, reports, repairs, sales and customer services.
Training and support: Can be used by beginners. Support and quarterly updates are included for one year; continued support and updates are provided for an annual fee equal to 10% of the license fee. Training is provided at no charge at D.A.T.A. headquarters; fee required for on-site training.

JEWELMAN
Company: Jebco, 6730 E. Alabama Rd., Woodstock, Ga. 30188; (404) 924-3141.
Cost: $195.
Operating system: IBM (DOS) and compatibles; Commodore 64 or 128.
Features: Prices colored stones in various qualities, shapes and sizes. The software prices mounting by wax or metal weight and gold chains in various styles and lengths. Features allow you to account for higher or lower karatage and to estimate weights of colored stones and diamonds.
Training and support: Can be used by beginners; no training or support is available.

THE JEWELRY CONTROLLER
Company: Haggard's Technical Services Inc., 432 N. Market, Shawnee, Okla. 74801; (800) 352-5240, fax (405) 273-5353.
Cost: $2,495; leasing is available at $131 per month, ($249 for a multistore operation).
Operating system: IBM (DOS) and compatibles.
Features: Point-of-sale invoicing, accounts payable/receivable, perpetual customer history, inventory control, repair tracking, password protection, multiple price levels, user-defined SKU numbers and departments, layaway and assembly tracking, management reports, memo goods tracking, cash drawer support, bar-code scanners, imaging, general ledger, payroll and customization.
Additional: The company also offers data conversion services; inventory, customer and vendor data can be converted and loaded into the program. In addition, the company

offers the Digital Image Capture Station, a turnkey system that is used to capture, store and print color images of jewelry. The images can be linked to The Jewelry Controller so images of inventory and memo goods can be viewed at the point of sale or on inventory control screens.
Training and support: Can be used by beginners; training is available onsite or at company headquarters.

THE JEWELRY SHOPKEEPER
Company: Compulink, 3300 Overland Ave., Suite 201, Los Angeles, Cal. 90034; (310) 204-5121.
Cost: $2,295; networking is extra.
Operating system: IBM (DOS) and compatibles.
Features: Accounts payable/receivable, inventory by weight/piece, loose stone tracking, assembly, tag printing, core tracking, custom work and repairs, point-of-sale system, financial statements and customer services.
Training and support: Can be used by beginners; training and support offered by phone or modem.

JEWELSOFT
Company: PC Consult, 2269 S. University Dr. #201, Davie, Fla. 33324; (800) 577-1799.
Cost: $795.
Operating system: IBM (DOS) and compatibles.
Features: Inventory, sales and customer services.
Training and support: Unknown.

JEWELWORKS/MAC
Company: JewelWorks/MAC, P.O. Box 2136, Rancho Santa Fe, Cal. 92067; (619)756-9911 phone and fax.
Cost: $2,500 single, $3,000 multiuser.
Operating system: Macintosh.
Features: Accounting, inventory, sales and customer services. Detailed inventory records and history for completed item, makeup and loose stones; complete line-by-line customer and vendor histories; detailed repair tracking and comprehensive reports.
Training and support: Can be used by beginners; training is offered through an 800 number; onsite training available at additional cost.

JIMS
Company: Onasco Systems, 4660 S. Inca St., Englewood, Colo. 80110; (303) 781-7926.
Cost: $4,000.
Operating system: IBM (DOS) and compatibles.
Features: Accounting, inventory, sales and customer services.
Training and support: Unknown.

KEEP IT SIMPLE (KIS) SOFTWARE
Company: Keep It Simple Software, 7705 Wadsworth Blvd., Arvada, Colo. 80003; (303) 425-4849.
Cost: $3,295, multiusers add $595.
Operating system: IBM (DOS) and compatibles.
Features: Accounting, inventory, sales, payroll, appraisals, repairs, setup options, spreadsheet interface, backup program and customer services.
Training and support: Three day onsite installation and training costs are $995; support and optional updates are $495 annually.

MICA IV ACCOUNTING SOFTWARE
Company: MICA Accounting Software, 2349 Memorial Blvd., Port Arthur, Tex. 77640; (800) 448-6422, fax (409) 983-5106.
Cost: $6,780.
Operating system: IBM (DOS) and compatibles.
Features: Accounting, inventory, sales and customer services.
Training and support: Unknown.

REGISTER-MATE
Company: Register-Mate, 16885 Dallas Pkwy., Suite 300, Dallas, Tex. 75248; (214) 732-0700, fax (214) 732-8060.
Cost: $139.
Operating system: IBM (DOS) and compatibles.
Features: Accounting, inventory, sales and customer services.
Training and support: Unknown.

RETAIL JEWELRY SOFTWARE
Company: Jewelers Software Group, 130 Baker Hill Rd., Second Fl., Great Neck, N.Y. 11023; (516) 829-8182, fax (516) 829-8419.
Cost: $15,000.
Operating system: IBM (DOS) and Windows.
Features: Accounting, inventory, sales and customer services.
Training and support: Unknown.

RETAIL JEWELRY PARTNER
Company: Ultimate Solutions, 7720 Lankershim Blvd., North Hollywood, Cal. 91605; (818) 765-8551, fax (818) 765-5841.
Cost: Single user, $999; multiuser, $1,499.
Operating system: IBM (DOS) and compatibles.
Features: Accounting, inventory, sales, customer services and user-defined fields for inventory, appraisals, ring/gift tag printing, point of sale, commissions (split), imaging and more.
Additional: The company also offers a wholesale/manufacturing software system, a metal manufacturing module named Goldpro, an imaging system called Jeweltrace, a counting instrument called US1 Microlaser Counting Instrument and a PRO Windows/DOS SBT Platform used to customize features of all the programs for users of large systems.
Training and support: Can be used by beginners; training is offered via modem, telephone or onsite.

RETAIL MANAGER
Company: Retail Science Corp., 2882 Cleary Ave., Metairie, La. 70002-6807; (504) 838-6888, fax (504) 887-5291.
Cost: single user, $1,995; two users, $2,995; three or more users, $3,995.
Operating system: IBM (DOS).
Features: Accounting, inventory, sales and customer services, store management, bar coding and imaging.
Training and support: Can be used by beginners; training and support are available.

SOFTGEM
Company: Gemological Research Corp., 60 E. Third Ave., San Mateo, Cal. 94401; (800) 443-6638, fax (415) 579-5710.
Cost: $5,995.
Operating system: IBM (DOS) and compatibles.
Features: Accounting, inventory, sales and customer services.
Training and support: Unknown.

STEPSTONE MANAGEMENT
Company: StepStone Jewelers Database, 861 Sixth Ave., Suite 829, San Diego, Cal. 92101; (619) 238-2382, fax (619) 234-6020.
Cost: $995.
Operating system: IBM (DOS), Windows and compatibles.
Features: Inventory control, tag printing, bar codes, customer histories, repairs, layaways, point of sale, accounting, accounts payable/receivable, check writing, general ledger, inventory imaging, multiuser connections and multistore with polling communication.
Training and support: Can be used by beginners; support and training provided with a toll-free telephone number.

SYNTONIC JEWELERS INVENTORY/ACCOUNTING
Company: Syntonic Systems, 80 Eighth Ave., Suite 901, New York, N.Y. 10011; (212) 989-8787, fax (212) 989-9515.
Cost: $13,500.
Operating system: IBM (DOS) and compatibles.
Features: Accounting, inventory, sales and customer services.
Training and support: Unknown.

TRIPLE KEY
Company: Golding Technologies, P.O. Box 55253, Seattle, Wash. 98155; (206) 362-4581, fax (206) 363-4398.
Cost: $695.
Operating system: IBM (DOS) and compatibles.
Features: Accounting, inventory, sales and customer services. The software automatically integrates and updates point of sale, mailing lists, inventory and accounts receivable/payable by entering a single transaction.
Additional: Golding Technologies also offers computer-aided-design software. ScanDesign is a drawing library, color imaging and sizing application for $695; TechDesign is a host program containing drawing libraries, color images, digitizer tablet and auto-sizing capabilities for $599. Jewelers Clip Art provides custom-drawn jewelry images for use in newsletters and ads.
Training and support: Unknown.

WINJEWEL
Company: WinJewel Co., 3065 N.W. Hurletwood Dr., Albany, Ore. 97321; (503) 967-0225 or (619) 265-1140.
Cost: $2,950.
Operating system: IBM (DOS) and compatibles running Windows version 3.1 or later.
Features: Bookkeeping, point of sale, inventory control, budgeting, checkbook, accounts payable/receivable, repair and bookkeeping. Bar coding and video capture of inventory require specialized hardware.
Training and support: Can be used by beginners with an understanding of jewelry and store operations. Training is provided by telephone or on-site. Support is by telephone.

MANUFACTURING SOFTWARE

ASSET BUSINESS MANAGEMENT SYSTEMS
Company: Asset Software Publications, 39-19 Morlot Ave., Fair Lawn, N.J. 07410; (201) 796-5862, fax (201) 796-8180.
Cost: $5,592.
Operating system: IBM (DOS) and compatibles.
Features: Accounting, inventory, sales and customer services.
Training and support: Unknown.

JEWEL BYTE SYSTEM
Company: Big Byte Solutions, 340 E. 65 St., New York, N.Y. 10021; (212) 486-6062, fax (212) 755-6902.
Cost: $5,000.
Operating system: IBM (DOS) and Windows.
Features: Accounting, inventory, sales and customer services.
Training and support: Unknown.

THE JEWELER'S SHOWCASE
Company: M2M Corp., 1001 N. Federal Hwy., Suite 202, Hallandale, Fla. 33009; (800) 991-4367, fax (305) 457-4368.
Cost: $1,500.
Operating system: IBM (DOS) and compatibles.
Features: Inventory.
Training and support: Unknown.

JSG MANUFACTURING JEWELER SOFTWARE
Company: Jewelers Software Group, 130 Baker Hill Rd., Second Fl., Great Neck, N.Y. 11023; (516) 829-8182, fax (516) 849-8182.
Cost: $25,000.
Operating system: IBM (DOS) and Windows.
Features: Accounting, inventory, sales and customer services.
Training and support: Unknown.

POWER JEWELER
Company: LS Software Systems, 419 12 St., Lakewood, N.J. 08701; (908) 367-7164, fax (908) 370-9083.
Cost: $15,000.
Operating system: IBM (DOS) and compatibles.
Features: Accounting, inventory, sales and customer services.
Training and support: Unknown.

SILVER ONLY
Company: Ultimate Solutions I, 13263 Ventura Blvd., Suite Six, Studio City, Cal. 91604; (818) 905-5191, fax (818) 905-1920.
Cost: $3,600.
Operating system: IBM (DOS) and compatibles.
Features: Accounting, inventory, sales and customer services.
Training and support: Unknown.

APPRAISAL SOFTWARE

JEWEL MATE
Company: Streight Jewellery Products, Three Central Ave., Como (Sydney) New South Wales 2226 Australia; (61-2) 528-2489, fax (61-2) 528-2489.
Cost: $3,000.
Operating system: IBM (DOS) and compatibles.
Features: Printed appraisals, auto stones weight calculator and valuation assistance.
Training and support: Unknown

THE JEWELRY JUDGE
Company: The Jewelry Judge, 252 James St. S., Suite 201, Hamilton, Ontario L8P 3B5; (905) 577-4140, fax (905) 577-4148.
Cost: $500 startup (software with 50 appraisals).
Operating system: IBM (DOS).
Features: Jewelry Judge newsletter, monthly price information and updates, access to Help Desk (BBS), printed appraisals, auto stone weight calculator, valuation assistance and watch information.

Training and support: Can be used by beginners; training and support are provided.

QUANTUM LEAP APPRAISAL SOFTWARE
Company: Quantum Leap, 3309 Juanita St., San Diego, Cal. 92105; (619) 265-1140, fax (619) 286-7541.
Cost: $1,695; leasing available.
Operating system: IBM (DOS) and Macintosh.
Features: Access to *The Guide* pricing publication, automatic calculation of gem weight and depth, "pick lists" that can be customized in writing insurance documentation and appraisals, merging of addresses into letter of transmittal and layout customization to match your store's stationery.
Training and support: Training is provided and technical support is available through a toll-free telephone number. User groups meet aT various industry trade shows.

BROKERAGE SOFTWARE

THE DIAMOND DEALER
Company: Genesis Software Designs, 444 Park Ave. S., New York, N.Y. 10016; (212) 889-9191 phone and fax.
Cost: $3,000.
Operating system: IBM (DOS) and compatibles.
Features: Accounting, inventory and sales.
Training and support: Unknown.

MISCELLANEOUS SOFTWARE

THE ADAMAS ADVANTAGE
Company: Adamas Gemological Laboratory, 320 Place Lane, Woburn, Mass. 01801; (617) 935-5430 phone and fax.
Cost: $995, which includes free upgrades for one year.
Operating system: IBM (DOS) and compatibles.
Features: Gemstone plotting and gem identification database, diamond and colored stone analysis and a color graphics package that provides three-dimensional drawings based on parameters such as table size, crown height and star facet length.
Training and support: The software requires an intermediate level of computer expertise combined with graduate gemologist knowledge.

GEMDATA
Company: P.G. Reed Consultancy Services, 16 Green Park, 91 Manor Rd., East Cliff, Bournemouth, U.K.
Cost: About $60.
Operating system: IBM (DOS) and compatibles.
Features: The software is designed to identify gems before evaluation and/or appraisal. It includes gem and crystal identification, gem comparisons, refractive index tables, specific gravity values and gem calculations. The latest update includes more diagnostic information on inclusions, spectra, pleochroism, luminescence and enhancement treatments.
Training and support: Can be used by beginners; the company offers yearly updates at about $10.

GEMVISION WORKSTATION
Company: GemVision, 1049 State St., Bettendorf, Iowa 52722; (319) 355-6272.
Cost: $29,500; leasing available.
Operating system: IBM

Features: Jewelry design software, color video camera, high-resolution monitor and photograph-quality thermographic printer combine to create quality images onscreen. This complete system enables jewelers to present ideas to customers for new pieces and repair work.

Training and support: Can be used by beginners; four days of on-site training and installation are included in price, as are a one-year free warranty and telephone or modem support.

How Do You Use Your Computer?

Inventory control—86%
Receivables/payables—81%
Direct Mail—70%
Customer lists—58%
Tag printing—50%
Order & vendor status—49%
Appraisal records/reports—47%
Point of sale/inventory—46%
Payroll—45%
Repair tracking—29%
Newsletter—18%

Bar coding—11%
Computer imaging—8%
Jewelry design—4%
Other—14%

What functions will you add or changes will you make to your computer in the next 12 months?

Upgrade—30%
Inventory control—29%
Bar coding—8%
Tag printing—8%
Imaging—7%
Repair tracking—7%
Customer lists—6%
Receivables/payables—5%
Appraisal reports—4%
Newsletters—4%
Direct mail—3%
General—3%
Jewelry design—3%
Checkwriting—3%
Payroll—2%
Other (including point-of-sale, order status, budgeting, advertising, cash management, scanner, modem and networking)—10%

Playing Tag With Bar Codes

November 1993

Gun in hand, John Benson eyes his target, squeezes the trigger and, blip, scores a direct hit!

Blip? That's the sound of a laser bar-code reader registering the data printed on a small barbell tag wrapped around a ring in Benson's showcase. The code will be entered into the inventory system at Dallas Gold & Silver Exchange, Dallas, Tex., where Benson is chief financial officer.

"It's an extremely accurate way to conduct inventory and keep track of the 4,000 items we stock," says Benson. In the past year, more jewelers have discovered that the accuracy of bar codes has made the systems cost-effective, say industry sources.

The initial investment has dropped by hundreds—even thousands—of dollars in the past two years, spurred by lower priced laser and CCD (charged coupled device, using technology similar to a home video camera) readers and bar-code printers.

In addition, the need for greater inventory control is more a necessity than a luxury for today's competitive jeweler. "Banks are interested in seeing that your inventory has been carefully managed," says Chandru Nambiar, director of sales for Kassoy Automated Solutions, Hicksville, N.Y.

Bar codes allow inventory to be taken faster and more accurately than by hand. While a clerk can easily transpose a number while keying in an item code, bar-code readers cannot.

Benson says he can complete his monthly inventory much more quickly than before. "It used to take four or five people six to eight hours to take inventory," he says. "Now three people can do it in $2^{1}/2$ hours."

Benson hasn't quantified whether the bar-code system has paid for itself yet, but he expects good results. "We can readily identify inventory shrinkage, and we have a more accurate reflection of the cost of sales," he says.

Deciding factors: Bar codes can be used to track inventory and, as part of a larger management system, at the point of sale. If inventory is the primary objective, point-of-sale use isn't required, says William Baccich, president of Retail Science Corp., a Metaire, La., firm that sells jewelry management and accounting software.

Regardless of use, many retailers had trouble justifying a bar-code system until prices for readers and printers started to drop: "It depends on volume, but a single store owner is often squeamish about a $2,500 printer," says Baccich. But considering that similar printers cost about $8,000 five years ago, the lower prices have attracted more than high-volume or chain stores (still the primary users.)

Today, retailers with more than one store or those with annual sales of $750,000 comprise the starting point for most of the interest in bar-code systems, says Baccich. Smaller retailers benefit also, he says, but those with very small stores or low turnover often consider the tags unnecessary or find the investment too costly. Also, many retailers prefer to hand-tag their items as part of a "personalized" image.

The basics: For inventory purposes only, the basic system requires a bar-code printer, precut tags, code reader (CCD, laser gun, wand or stationary), personal computer and accompanying software. The software can be used by the store's own computer or can be supplied by the tag vendor.

Many jewelers also buy a portable data-collection terminal. This device looks much like a hand-held computer or calculator and attaches to a bar-code reader. It's taken to a showcase to scan items, then the information is transferred to a personal computer.

Baccich says laser bar-code readers cost about $2,000 two years ago but now are about $500. They come with varying levels of technology, he cautions, and retailers should not choose based on price alone. He says several good quality CCD scanners are available for about $700.

Bar-code printers generally cost $2,300-$4,900, depending on their versatility and print clarity. Some retailers prefer tags large enough for codes with letters and numbers and three lines of descriptive wording on the reverse side. This requires a slightly larger tag than a basic eight-digit code offered on smaller tags.

Tags should be made of material that withstands cleaning fluids and regular handling, says Sandy Chow, president of JEM Software Management, Surrey, British Columbia. Tags that meet these requirements are typically mylar plastic, though lower-cost paper tags are available. Prices average $300 per roll of 10,000 mylar tags.

Typically, items are tagged as they arrive from a manufacturer. Each is given a code that's printed as both a bar code and corresponding numeric or alphanumeric code. A clerk can type the code into the software system if the reader can't "read" the bar code because of a scratch or other damage to the tag. But expect this to occur rarely. "I am totally not satisfied if I don't get 97% to 99% accuracy on the first read," says Baccich, who advises retailers to peruse different technologies before choosing a system.

The Personal Computer:
A Jeweler's Tool

December 1991

You can't quite recall her name. This time she's in your store to leave some simple repair work. Last time she spent $5,000. Stepping up to the store computer, you casually ask for her phone number as you type in her repair order. You punch a few keys and her name pops up. You greet Mrs. Jones confidently and ask how her husband George is doing. You know by her expression that she's grateful you remembered. You've made an impression.

This is just one of my experiences as a retail jeweler, and one of the many ways I've found computers can help retailers.

Our single store in a neighborhood shopping district is typical of a midrange, independent operation. My father and I built it from scratch into a half-million-dollar operation. At the forefront of the transformation was a lot of hard work. Right behind and just as critical was help from a tool that many jewelers have been reluctant to accept: the personal computer.

Computer 101: Starting with a home computer, a lowly Commodore 64 that was not compatible with the business world, I soon discovered that even a "toy" computer could become a useful tool. I didn't realize how useful until one day in 1984.

A very good customer stopped by to pick up a high-priced order for her wedding the next day. The order hadn't even been started. I prefer to forget the mood of our conversation, but I remember the lesson. I realized that my bench

jewelers had no way of knowing deadlines except to wade through dozens of repair envelopes and check for the promise date. I vowed never to have to learn this lesson again.

My career as a computer programmer began. Within two weeks, that toy computer was producing a complete printed schedule of my customer's jobs in the exact order they were to be done. Since then, we haven't missed one important job. I still oversee the jewelry store today, but not without the five personal computers at my staff's fingertips.

Let's take a look at what a personal computer can do for your store.

Four basic functions: Gone are the days when marketing was done by guesswork or chance, if at all. Today, jewelers can't sit on the sidelines and wait for business to come their way. They must be assertive and have at their disposal all the information needed to make the best decisions. This information is largely based on control of four basic functions: accounting, inventory, receivables and payables.

• **Accounting:** Computers are very good at certain tasks that many people hate. Adding long columns of numbers, preparing reports and writing anything repetitive are just a few. Liberating yourself and your employees from these chores allows more time for customers or being creative—and making sales. An accounting software program for your personal computer accomplishes this and more.

Even if you have an accountant or bookkeeper, you still have to keep track of all the particulars, including every penny you've received, every penny you've spent and what you've bought with it. You could pay your bookkeeper more to handle every little detail. Or you could handle it yourself instead of running your store. Why not put your personal computer to work instead?

Most small jewelers who are not computerized manage their books on a cash bookkeeping basis rather than with true accounting. Readily available software can provide you with true accounting, giving you better decision-making information, improved accuracy and greater control.

Imagine yourself at tax time. Federal, state and local taxes keep you busy every quarter, if not every month. Working late is great when it brings in money, but pretty unpleasant when you're dishing it out. Go ahead, add that column of figures by hand five times and get five different answers! Or press five keys and get the correct answer in five seconds.

Computers also can help in other ways. Because tax forms take only minutes to complete on computer, you can keep your money in the bank earning interest as long as possible.

If accounting is important to the health of a business, cash-flow management is critical. There isn't a business around, large or small, that cannot benefit from keeping an eye on cash flow. Exactly how much money have you taken in? How much have you paid? Are certain expenses running wild? Are you open to buy? And most important, how much money is left? Your computer can answer these questions in seconds, so you can make quick decisions to solve problems or take advantage of opportunities.

• **Inventory:** "I see you've sold all the goods you bought from me last time," remarks the third salesperson to visit you today. Most sales people want to help and won't oversell you. But now you have the protection of computer-generated reports showing that you don't need any half-carat channel-sets right now—you've still got all three from the last time. But those quarter-carat solitaires have been hot!

Of course, keeping an inventory count accurate also is important. With manual inventory, a sold item might not be recorded for six months, says Mike McKay, a salesman covering the Pacific Northwest. "It takes an hour just for one customer to count by hand what's been sold from my line," he says. Computerized jewelers can summon a printout in seconds. And though you can always make more money, no one can make more time.

Computerized inventory also makes employees think twice about stealing. They know you have a detailed list of every item you carry and know precisely where it should have gone.

Another noteworthy function is the ability to adjust prices with the fluctuations in precious-metal prices.

Most people have heard of the 20-80 rule: 20% of the items you carry product 80% of your revenue; 20% of your salespeople make 80% of all sales. Well-designed software can quickly separate which products, salespeople and customers mean the most to your business. Without a computer, such accurate data would be very difficult to acquire and analyze.

• **Accounts receivable:** Short of taking money to the bank, there's nothing more rewarding than the accurate count of the money you are owed. Accurate accounts-receivable records are imperative. They are an asset shown on bal-ance sheet as well as valid collateral for a loan. But no matter how fabulous they are, your accounts receivable must be accurate and documented to be accepted as collateral.

Computers also can help to determine the potential for profit or pitfall when a customer wants credit. You could take time from your busy schedule to call the references on the credit application. Or you could have your computer dial a database of credit information for a full report in minutes. The fee you pay for the database service will seem trivial compared with the bad debts you save.

• **Accounts payable:** Keeping track of how much money you owe isn't nearly as gratifying as how much you are owed, but it's vital to your business.

Discovery of an honest mistake in accounts payable could save you hundreds, even thousands of dollars, At the computer several months ago, I noticed a $900 difference between a vendor's statement and my computer records. A few keystrokes later, the computer produced a record showing the vendor transposed two numbers. 1 might have noticed it manually, but the computer was a real time-saver. I much prefer to have the computer search through hundreds of invoices in 30 seconds than dig through file cabinets for hours myself.

Appraisals: Appraisals may be one of your most profitable activities, but they can be troublesome to produce. A handwritten appraisal doesn't have much credibility, and typewritten appraisals take a long time to prepare. Typographical errors can be costly—to your image and in legal terms. Sometimes it also can be very hard to locate an appraisal done some time ago.

The computer can help to solve all these problems. It won't relieve you of your legal liability or identify a stone for you, but your computer can reduce the chance of error. Some appraisal programs contain a database of the latest prices for diamonds and colored stones, eliminating guess-work. Using a computer also can reduce the time needed for an appraisal by as much as 70%.

Mailing lists, good will: Jewelers are likely to mention a computerized mailing list as one of their most prized assets. Using a computer-generated mailing list and newsletter, jeweler William Gray of Anjevine Ltd. in Denver, Colo., builds an ongoing relationship with customers and provides them with valuable information. "My newsletter does better than television, print or radio," he says.

Many businesses have built and maintained a mailing list without computers, but it's a time-consuming process.

Bench tickets, scheduling: For repairs and custom orders, computers can generate a claim ticket for the customer and bench ticket for the jeweler while maintaining an internal record for management. At the end of the day, the computer can construct the next day's schedule in 10 minutes or less. All deadlines are checked automatically to be sure they won't be missed. In the morning, your jewelers receive a printout of all jobs in exactly the order they should be done. No questions.

Good order-entry software will double-check that a due date has been specified, that the order has been priced and, among other things, that a clerk's initials have been entered.

In addition, software usually allows you to locate past orders to verify a customer's claim. If an irate customer says he just had the prongs on an item tipped in the past few months and they need tipping again, you can verify the claim quickly. If the computer proves to the customer the work was done more than a year ago, you'll likely be writing a new retipping order.

Computerized jewelry design: Many jewelers have begun to use computers for design work, too. It's particularly impressive when customers can watch a design being modified to their preference. The result often is a quick decision on a design, and the sale is closed. Once the printout is shown to the customer, it goes to your wax maker to begin the production process.

Computerized libraries of stone and diamond shapes are available to get you up and running fast.

Computerizing your business: There are two ways to become computerized. One is to hire a VAR (Value Added Reseller). Professional VARs buy computer hardware to resell and combine with software that meets your needs. They provide it to you in a complete package referred to as a turnkey system—you just turn the key and go. Training is usually included in the price.

Hiring a VAR is the most emotionally painless way to add the benefits of computerization to your store. When trouble comes, and it generally does, the VAR will handle it for you, usually quickly. But all that added value is not free, and it's also not quite that easy. Finding a VAR experienced with jewelers may be a formidable task.

The second way is much less expensive, but requires much more time. It involves buying your computer hardware and software independently, then setting up both so they meet your needs. This sounds easy. But if it were, there wouldn't be any VARs. If you decide to handle the job yourself, put the emphasis on selecting the software.

When the IBM personal computer was introduced in 1981, little software existed for any purpose. Now more than 10,000 software packages perform various tasks that may or may not be of use to retail jewelers. Many of these software programs costs less than $300, some of them under $50. Other programs are very specialized and cost hundreds or thousands of dollars, but they're worth the cost. Numerous specialized software packages are designed to handle the range of retailer functions for jewelers.

Most IBM-compatible hardware has dropped considerably in price in the past two years. Apple Computer also produces several models that are very popular. The Macintosh has continued to grow in sales and shrink in price. Although it has many features that the IBMs do not, Apple's line has not been

as readily accepted into the business world, though this is changing rapidly. A few software packages specifically made for jewelers and applicable to the Apple are now available.

Worth: Is using a computer worth it? Yes, even more now than a couple of years ago. Computerizing isn't painless, but the results are outstanding, especially in saving your most valuable asset: time. The jewelry business is tough and the jeweler needs every competitive edge possible. Truer than ever is this business theory: "If you are not moving ahead, you are falling behind." Using a computer in your business can bring you squarely into the 21st century.

What Computers Can't Do

Despite their versatility, computers do have some limitations. But the first words of warning concern your expectations, not the computer. It's truly amazing—and unrealistic—to see serious business problems solved on a 30-second television commercial.

When reality sets in, computer users realize their machines perform no magic. They merely follow instructions and process the information they've been fed. Here are some guidelines on what to expect:

• Computers are no substitute for people. William Gray, a Denver jeweler, prefers to balance technology with human contact. His newsletter, produced via computer and sent to customers, is one example of this balance. Gray also handwrites invitations to all his store's vendor shows and special events.

• Computers won't always be right. If the proper information isn't entered, the correct data won't come out.

• A computer can save countless hours of totaling and categorizing, but it won't replace your accountant's expertise.

• A computer won't transform your business overnight. The time needed to train your managers and employees depends on the complexity of the software and the service provided by your vendor.

• You can and probably will become computer-dependent if you computerize. And despite what you may hear, a computer won't turn your business into a "paperless office." Computers can spit out reams of paper in minutes. Paper manufacturers love them.

What Computers Can Do For You

August 1989

Last year, Daniel Chandler suffered computer chip gridlock. His fine jewelry store's inventory control, accounts receivable and point of sale software was overburdened. Though he cheered the 20% sales jump during the first half of 1988, his five-year-old computer system was sagging under the added accounts.

"We needed something that was quicker," he said. "It would have been difficult to grow without a faster system."

Chandler, general manager of Galloway & Moseley in Sumter, S.C., is typical of the many already-computerized jewelers who now need more powerful and versatile systems. Meanwhile, an even larger group that still operates with pens and pencils is ready to take the computer plunge.

Both groups need help. Jewelers like Chandler who already use computers often are better able to judge their needs, but still need to find what they're looking for. Chandler himself decided to hire a computer programmer to customize his software. But first-timers are adrift.

Why use it? Many retailers still are leary of computers. Most chains, even small ones, realize they must computerize to compete more successfully. But independent store owners often balk. They may be frightened, put off by the costs, confident they don't need a computer or just too busy to start looking.

"I think the computer has an impersonal image," says Richard Eyerman, president of the Jewelers Software Group, a software vendor from Great Neck, N.Y. Yet computers can personalize your selling by putting information about customers right at your fingertips.

They're more than just a sales tool, however. Computers free store owners from manual chores, allowing them to use their time more efficiently. Computers compile lists, facts and figures in the blink of an eye and recall them instantly. "It is so much easier to let the computer handle the paperwork," says Ed Brown, vice president of software vendor Vance Info Systems, San Francisco.

The number of vendors with software specifically designed for jewelers is growing. Applications such as memos, layaway sales, installment sales and invoices are readily available. In addition, there are all the standard functions offered to retailers—such as accounts receivable, accounts payable, general ledger, payroll, point-of-sale terminals (including barcode technology), purchasing, inventory and mailing lists.

Today's user can operate more quickly, and with fewer keyboard motions, then he could just a few years ago. Larger memory—which allows the computer to store more inventory and data—is standard.

Networking may be even more important for the growing retailer. This feature allows a store to use more than one terminal at a time. A terminal in the office, one in the diamond room and another at the front desk give the retailer easy access to data at all times.

What's available: Computers suitable for retail jewelers fall into several categories.

First are *microcomputers*, commonly known as personal computers. For smaller retailers with fewer than five stores, PCs are as commonplace as cash registers. In fact, sometimes they *are* cash registers, eliminating the need for two separate machines. (Adding a cash drawer and register printer to a terminal allows the sales clerk to check inventory on the same machine used to ring up a sale.)

PCs run the bulk of the retail-oriented software sold by myriad vendors. Nearly every function of jewelry-store operations has an equivalent software program. "The microcomputer has become much more powerful in recent years and that has allowed the programs to be much more useful," says Eyerman.

Jewelers can choose from software that tracks inventory, follows accounts receivable and accounts payable, creates mailing lists, prints reports, letters and appraisal data, and performs a host of other standard tasks. Many software vendors also sell or lease the accompanying hardware. Software-only vendors usually will at least recommend what you should use to operate their packages.

A second major group of vendors sells *minicomputers*, the most powerful type of small business computer. Medium

and larger chains likely use a minicomputer to handle more applications at a more sophisticated level than is possible with a micro. However, the gap between the two types is shrinking; microcomputers now offer features available only with a mini a few years ago.

Finally, there are systems that allow a jeweler to hook into a powerful computer at the computer vendor's headquarters. The vendor installs terminals and printers at the user's site, where data is entered. The data then is sent to the vendor's computer, processed and returned to the user for printing or display. Only a few vendors provide a full range of system services geared to retail jewelers. However, some retailers use similarly conceived off-site payroll or accounting services.

For a list of vendors offering software and hardware for retail jewelers, trade shows, computer magazines, the computer sections of larger book store chains and computer hardware vendors are good sources. Alan Leopold, director of member services at Jewelers of America, will provide information to retailers interested in computer vendors.

But other jewelers probably are the best sources. Talk to retailers of similar size and makeup. Find out which vendor they use and if they are satisfied with equipment and service.

Get details. Try to discover what the jeweler was looking for and whether the vendor provided what was promised. How have employees taken to using the system? Is it getting good reviews from the staff? Where are the problem areas? Is there a thorough service contract?

When you contact a vendor, ask about its history. How many retailers use its services? Call several of them. Does the company continually develop its software to keep up with technological advances?

Successful installations can tell you a lot. The following short case studies show how six jewelry firms have used computers to boost profits and facilitate growth.

More brides=more profits

A year and a half ago, 500 brides-to-be registered at the gigantic Albert Smyth Co., Timonium, Md. This year 2,000 have signed up, filling Smyth aisles with gift buyers.

Vice president Robert Smyth Jr. does not attribute the business boom to an increase in marriage vows. Instead he points to a powerful IBM System 36 and the 60 terminals scattered throughout his 30,000-sq.-ft. store.

"I don't credit the computer with making the growth, I credit it with making the growth possible," he explains.

Smyth's computer allows him to advertise a toll-free bridal registration telephone number and handle the calls easily. Registered brides go into the computer file immediately. Then when gift buyers come in and ask for the bride's "wish list," they get a computer printout of her favored items. The list also tells if an item is in stock, what it costs and whether it has already been purchased for the bride.

"Customers are more likely to buy something in stock rather than special order it," Smyth says. "And it is much easier to complete sales over the telephone this way."

The firm—which sells equal amounts of fashion jewelry, giftware and diamond jewelry—has enjoyed annual sales increases of 10%-20% for the past five years or more. This year, Smyth expects sales to top $15 million.

"At some point, a manual inventory system just wouldn't let that happen," he says.

That point actually came in 1982, when an overloaded card-filing system resulted in some lost records and overlooked repair jobs. Computerization started with an IBM system 34 and a single terminal. Today the computer is an integral part of every operation. All sales are recorded immediately at the point of purchase, with inventory updated at the same time. Each of the 100 employees can call up any item in inventory and read its status and price to a customer in seconds.

Part of the system's appeal is its user friendliness, Smyth says. Clerks get little formalized training because data retrieval is so simple. When bridal gift buyers ask clerks if they have information on a certain registrant, clerks can safely respond, "I do."

Installing software to get things done

When Rob Panowicz consolidated his two Olympia, Wash., retail stores five years ago, he had a single bookkeeper tally sales. At each day's end, she would add up the receipts, hand balance the total, then enter it into a general ledger. A simple PC portable would keep track of overall totals.

But both portable and bookkeeper were straining. "About a year ago, it was becoming apparent that some things weren't getting done," recalls Panowicz. First, bookkeeping began to take a lot of time. Second, inventory control suffered. "We were less and less able to tell what was turning and what wasn't."

A simple general ledger program, similar to those used by thousands of small businesses, would solve the bookkeeping problem, he reasoned. The abundance of generic programs promised plenty of choice for computer novice Panowicz.

But as he investigated accounting programs, Panowicz spoke with jewelers using inventory control software. He was impressed by their ability to solve many of the same problems he faced in his store.

Panowicz began comparing inventory and general ledger programs. He spoke with six major vendors, read reports and spoke to other jewelers. After narrowing the field to three vendors, he finally chose one.

He settled on a hard disk system with two terminals. It's fully integrated, meaning each sale is recorded automatically and inventory records are updated immediately. When a sales clerk inquires about a piece sold the previous day, the computer will note that the sale occurred and tell whether additional pieces exist in inventory.

By the end of summer, Panowicz plans to put another feature of the $30,000 system into action: the ability to target mailing lists to select groups of customers. Specifically, 500 customer anniversary dates—gathered during the store's 40th anniversary celebration last year—are being fed into the computer. Once the data are entered, Panowicz can send mailings describing anniversary bands to these customers at the appropriate time.

"The computer system meshed perfectly with what we are marketing," he says. Earlier this year, information from the Diamond Promotion Service and his store's own research convinced Panowicz that the Olympia area is full of potential anniversary band buyers. "We decided to go after them," he says.

The computer will create mailing labels for customers whose anniversaries are pending. The mailers will describe two categories of bands: those in the $1,000-$2,000 price range and those over $2,500. Because he's targeted his buyers

and now has a computer to speed up the marketing process, Panowicz expects a very healthy 41st anniversary at his store.

Adding a personal touch

It was William W. Thraves' less-than-perfect memory that prompted him to buy a personal computer for his Seneca, S.C., store. He wanted to send more letters to customers on birthdays and anniversaries. These personal notes serve as a helpful reminder for spouses and parents to purchase special gifts.

But with 500 customers on his list, "I couldn't remember everyone's name, let alone their anniversaries and birthdays," he admits. Worse yet, his book of names was listed alphabetically and it took extra effort to isolate the dates of special occasions.

A local computer dealer helped Thraves purchase and develop a program that would update and sort a mailing list. He bought a hard disk computer with a single terminal and a printer. Total cost: $3,000.

Thraves now can print out a list of customers who have birthdays the following week. He can write a full-size letter to a wife about her husband's birthday and a husband on his wife's. Both spouses receive letters about anniversaries.

"I write personal notes on the computer so I can see what they were interested in the last time they were in the store," Thraves explains. These notes are used when it's time to send out a letter.

Having all the information in one easy-to-access location saves time and lets Thraves reach everyone on his list without extensive manual labor. "But I didn't buy it just to help me do work, I want it to make some money," he adds.

And it does. Each month, Thraves estimates the letters produce about four additional sales, ranging from $50 to $3,000.

He sells more earrings, too. His "earring club"—which allows members who buy five pairs of earrings to get one free pair—is now computerized. Thraves handles lists and letters for the club in much the same manner as the special-occasions mailings.

Overall, Thraves' $3,000 investment had paid off handsomely, he says. "And we haven't even tapped into what the computer can do." His next project: adding an inventory and accounting program to replace the manual methods he currently uses.

Linking a chain at the point of sales

As retail chains move beyond the 10-store barrier they begin to eye the computer behemoth, the mega-system capable of operating a small city. Bigger may be appropriate, but growing businesses all too often overestimate the need for capacity to handle future expansion.

But once you grow to, say, 80 stores, you certainly need a huge system, right? Not necessarily.

Merksamer Jewelry Co., a rapidly growing 84-store chain based in Sacramento, Cal., was a rapidly growing 22-store chain just two years ago. In early 1987, management decided it needed better financial reporting than it was receiving from its stores in the field.

"We were running at least a week behind the facts," says Doug Streifling, manager of data processing. "We never had a comprehensive picture of the dollars and cents."

At the time, each store would compile the day's receipts manually and send them to the Sacramento headquarters. There the data were painstakingly entered by hand into the firm's IBM System 36 minicomputer. Sometimes the financial department got a grip on what was selling one or two weeks later. But daily reports were needed.

Streifling wanted to install a system that would grow with the company. The chain, recently purchased by Australia's Hooker Corp., was set to add 13 stores by the end of 1987, and further expansion would have to include the computer system. (Note: Hooker recently announced that it will sell Merksamer.)

The priority was to retrieve data for each store immediately and put it into daily reports for each manager. At Merksamer's, individual store inventory is minimal and kept relatively standard throughout the chain. So a manager doesn't need full inventory reports. "But we did want to give that store manager a full snap-shot of each day's sales, who made them, what the cost was and how it was paid," says Streifling.

Merksamer chose to give each store an IBM personal computer, linked it to the main computer with a modem. At the same time, the IBM System 36 at the Sacramento headquarters was upgraded to a larger System 38.

The system, installed by software vendor STR Inc., Akron, Ohio, gave Merksamer point-of-sale reporting ability in computer terminals that double as cash registers. Data from each sale is recorded during the sale in the PC. Every morning before opening, the main computer in Sacramento dials into each store's PC and in just five minutes retrieves the previous day's sales information.

"They went from a two-week process to an overnight process," says Scott Lines, president of STR. By the end of 1987, the system was running in all 35 stores.

As data is received from each store, a complete sales report of the day's activities is created and sent to the store. The store manager can check each salesperson's activity against the company's goals. "Sharper salespeople also use the report every day to see how well they are doing," Streifling adds.

He decided against the networked system (where each store can communicate by computer) favored by some chains because he felt the cost was excessive and the payback limited. He also kept the system lean by minimal use of inventory software for each store, though each store can retrieve inventory numbers when needed.

"The system was designed for high speed data entry," says Lines. "There aren't a lot of added keyboard functions." And while some chains install a separate cash register and PC, his system combines the two.

The end result of this streamlining was low installation cost. The STR system cost Merksamer $5,000 per store, including a PC, printer, modem and software.

Though the system can compile customer data, only the main office now keeps a complete file. Each store does, however, keep its own list of credit customers and many keep individualized customer data. "That is on our agenda of enhancements to the system," says Streifling.

Soon he plans to start notifying each store, via the daily report, of stock shipments as they are delivered. And bar coding, used by many chains nationwide, can be added to the system easily, as can most other PC-based software programs.

The flexibility of this point-of-sale, PC-based system makes it easy to hook a new branch up to the computer, says Streifling. All that's needed is a modem, a PC, a printer and the software (copied from the main office, per licensing agreement with STR).

Removing dust collectors

Ara Simoniam's three Rochester, N.Y., stores, The Source of Gold and Silver, do well with a variety of rings—to the tune of $2.5 million in sales in 1988. And Simoniam thought colored stone and diamond cluster rings were pulling in their share of the sales.

Then he took a look at the facts—via a computer inventory system that will list the sales history of any item during any specified period of time. Simoniam found that cluster rings had been in his showcases for exactly 1,219 days—more than three years. During that time, nine different styles were displayed—yet few customers bought them.

"I checked the inventory and we still had plenty," says Simoniam. "We didn't get a good turn on them."

Simoniam phased them out over a period of time, then utilized the showcase space and purchasing energy for something that did turn. Again checking his computer, he found that signet rings and onyx and diamond rings were selling very well. "They'd last 30 days in inventory and then we'd have to reorder them," he says.

Simoniam has invested more than $45,000 in his computer system. Maintenance and service costs another $550 each month. He considers the money well spent; indeed, the investment has paid off many times over.

"Prior to the computer we would go through the inventory cards and look to see how something sold," he recalls. "When a vendor came in, we would buy based on whatever that vendor had. Now we try to order without the vendor there at all. . . except for new items."

This newfound purchasing power contributed to The Source's 50% sales increase over the past four years. The ability to track inventory has been enough of a sales booster that Simoniam hasn't yet found time to use his powerful system's other features, such as accounts receivable or general ledger. But he's about to add a printer and a terminal in each store and link all three by modem. Where he used to compile the three stores' receipts at the main store, Simoniam soon will transfer data over phone lines (via modem), speeding the process considerably.

Who needs a bookkeeper?

In 1987, Olsen Jewelry's 88-year-old bookkeeper became ill. Eventually she left the Fort Dodge, Iowa, store and was never replaced.

Owner Karl Johnson found that he and partner Lloyd Hambleton could crunch the same numbers—and then some—with an Apple Macintosh personal computer Johnson used at home.

All general ledger calculations, which had been done by hand, could be completed much more quickly on the computer. So Johnson brought his Mac into the office and soon found another use for the machine: tracking sales and purchases.

"We used to do that with an older model computer that was limited to 32 characters per line," he explains. (That early model TRS computer had been in the store since 1979, though the bookkeeper never used it.) "I would have to print four pages and tape them together to get a useful report." The Mac, however, printed the entire sales report on one page, with fewer hassles.

Hambleton, soon the primary computer user, began adding new applications, including payroll and purchasing. Doing payroll checks for the store's nine employees by hand took all morning; the computer could calculate and print them in less than 15 minutes. The same applied to supplier payments.

Johnson advises jewelers who want to add a computer to "keep it simple and cheap." He certainly can attest to the time and money saved by his original $2,300 investment. For starters, the firm has eliminated the yearly salary for another bookkeeper—important to a store that grosses under $500,000 a year.

And they've had some fun, too.

"I don't mind sitting down and punching in a few numbers," Johnson says. "It's not as damn dull as writing the thing by hand."

Should I Computerize?

Retailers consider computerization for a variety of reasons. Some seek a more efficient inventory system; others have marketing and sales in mind. But in most stores, streamlining day-to-day operations undoubtedly is the computer's greatest contribution. Every basic procedure the business routinely handles can be transferred to computer. With proper training and equipment—and a little patience—each can be done more quickly and accurately.

Step one, if you're thinking of computerizing, is to take a good look at your business, says Peter Sandor, a consultant at Sandor Associates, a Merrick, N.Y., management consulting firm. Analyze your basic information and record-keeping needs. Check whether your current operations provide:

- Information needed to manage your inventory. Do you know what is in stock when you need to know it?
- Reliable sales analysis. Are you able to tell what is selling and what is not?
- Dependable gross profit information.
- Accounts payable record keeping.
- Monthly profit and loss data.
- Collection of data at point of sale.
- Accurate cash controls.

If you are not getting a majority of these items, it may be time for you to computerize.

Shopping for Software

Once you've decided to computerize, you need software. The type of software purchased generally narrows your hardware choices. Many vendors sell hardware with their software; others simply advise what is best and let you make the arrangements.

A confusing number of vendors offer applications you'll need. When shopping for software you will use for day-to-day operations:

- Look for designed programs, not customized software. Customized software can be the ideal—indeed the only—solution for some computer experts with very specialized needs. But most retailers will do better to adjust some internal procedures to meet the requirements of existing software than to create software to suit their particular methods.
- Locate software that has a track record of successful, continually operating operation in similar-sized firms.
- Get a complete hands-on demonstration of the software. Make sure the demo uses "live" data similar in size and scope to your firm's files. If you plan to have more than one person use the system, try a system with multiple users.
- During the demonstration, look for ease of use and speed of response time. Check that the software answers your information and record-keeping needs.
- Get references from at least five other users. Ask each about ease of conversion (changing from the previous system to the new software). Ask, too, about quality of training, follow-up support, ease of use and reliability.

In detail, determine what services are standard, including:
- Access to future updates and enhancements.
- Amount of on-site user training.
- Software installation and conversion assistance.
- After-conversion on-site or telephone support.
- Length of guarantee against system bugs.
- Hardware requirements.

Be sure to obtain every vendor commitment and warranty in writing.

Selecting Hardware

The data storage requirements of your software, and the number of users who will operate the system, determine your hardware requirements. Find out if your software supplier will help you select and install the hardware. It generally is better to deal with a single source for both hardware and software. These arrangements are often referred to as "turnkey" computer systems.

Don't overbuy, but allow for growth in terms of data storage capacity and hardware speed. Project your business growth and buy equipment that can expand with your firm.

Buy name-brand equipment on the leading edge of current technology. This helps ensure future availability of maintenance and replacement parts as well as compatibility of new generation equipment.

Computer equipment manufacturers' warranties generally run for 90 days. Purchase an annual on-site maintenance contract from a major computer hardware maintenance company that will service your computer manufacturer's initial warranty and pick up thereafter.

Chapter 12

YOUR BUSINESS PLAN

Facing The Future Requires More Than Just A Sense Of Direction

Your Business Plan Highlights: A Summary

September 1993 Part II

Who am I? The company description. Kronos Jewelers is a single-store operation located in its own building in the northern suburbs of Utopia, Central State, USA. It sells a medium to high-end range of merchandise with a strong emphasis on diamond engagement rings. Repairs are an important part of the business; more than half of the customers who come into the store are there for a repair transaction. The business is owned by David and Effie Onassis and has a total of 14 employees. The mission statement declares that the company's goal is to operate at a profit sufficient to provide for its principals and offer suitable opportunities for its employees.

Who are my customers? There are four primary groups of customers: those shopping for engagement rings; an older generation in the market for anniversary rings and other gifts; customers who visit the store for repairs; and people who are attracted to the store by advertised "specials" and who belong to no particular demographic group. A major concern of the owners is how to convert more of the repair customers into jewelry customers; the present philosophy is to move repair customers in and out of the store as quickly as possible, thus building a reputation for efficiency. The owners realize they have to change that way of doing business.

Meet the competition. There are at least a dozen competing jewelers in the Utopia market. Kronos feels that where it competes quality-for-quality with other stores, it has a distinct edge. It would like to compete at the highest end of the market but lacks the right merchandise. In spite of a generous advertising budget, a limited consumer poll in the company's market area revealed that some competitors appear to be better known than Kronos—a finding that concerned David Onassis.

Market strategies. The company invests heavily in advertising, spending more than 7% of gross revenues. This relatively high commitment is somewhat offset by low occupancy costs in its stand-alone location; in a mall location, by contrast, ad costs usually are lower because the mall location helps bring in traffic but rent is much higher. Kronos also uses its engagement ring sales techniques to attract customers whom it hopes will develop a life-long loyalty. Appraisal services help attract more affluent customers. A new sales accountability program is being used as a direct strategy to increase sales.

Operations. A new buying plan has yet to produce desired control of inventory. This has led to cash flow problems. Lack of time (or determination) to develop suitable computer programs adds to difficulties in inventory control, in having access to timely financial information and in building really informative customer mailing lists.

The people factor. Kronos Jewelers is run as a family-style business. In addition to the owners, there are four managers—for sales, services, repair and custom work and back office. The owners want to project an image in their market of being efficient and professional but at the same time being a warm and pleasant place to shop.

What does the future hold? The owners anticipate steady growth in both sales and profits. Profitability will be increased by raising margins and carrying more store exclusives. The owners want their staff to share in their success, planning to reward high performers with salary increases and to add new benefits as they become affordable. They plan to expand geographically using the low tax rate in their state to attract new customers from neighboring high-tax states. They have no plans to open another store.

The money picture. Sales in the fiscal year ended last June 30 were almost $1.3 million, a 25% increase from the year before. The owners have a modest forecast of reaching $1.5 million by fiscal 1996; they probably will do better. Net after taxes totaled $36,886 in fiscal 1993; it is forecast to increase to $90,788 in fiscal 1996. Largely because of unplanned buying Kronos has continuing problems with cash flow, which has delayed payments to vendors though in the end all bills always are paid.

Who Am I?

September 1993 Part II

Why does a company need a business plan?

There are a number of good reasons.

A plan is critical if you must go to a bank or some other lender for funds; serious lenders want to deal with well-prepared borrowers.

A plan is a critical management guide. It is the touchstone against which management should measure all important decisions. At the plan's core is the company mission statement and any actions taken by anyone in the company should further the stated company mission.

A plan offers old and new staff members an understanding of the company for which they work and gives an insight into management's goals and ways of fulfilling them.

A plan offers management the opportunity to review people, products and services once a year to assess what is right, what may be wrong, and what should be changed or improved.

One of the greatest rewards a jeweler can get from preparation of a business plan is the preparation itself. It forces the company president to look critically at every single aspect of the business. Properly done, it demands answers to questions. Questions about staffing, inventory levels, margins, cost control and about projects that were started with good intentions but, somewhere along the way, lost their focus or justification. Questions, indeed, that call for answers about every aspect of the business.

Some of the information that goes into a good business plan seems so obvious that a reasonable person might ask, "Why include it?" The simple answer is that a good plan is a complete plan.

Thus the plan should start with a number of basics:

• The company name.

• How it is organized—a corporation, a partnership, a sole proprietorship?

• The names of the principals, with their titles.

• The location of the company—and of individual stores if it is a chain operation.

• A brief company history. It should inform those with whom it is shared—whether lender, investor or staff—what sort of company this is, how it was started and by whom, how long it's been in business, what are some of the milestones it has marked since its birth.

• A review of the main products and services. Rather than just saying " diamond jewelry," it should say "diamond jewelry retailing generally in such-and-such a price range and using such-and-such quality stones."

• Financial status. This should be a statement about sales volume, profitability, gross margin, cash flow and significant outstanding debt.

Two other very important elements need to be added: the mission statement and a description of how the principals hope and believe their business is perceived by customers and potential customers.

The mission statement should be relatively short and focussed on essentials. Such a statement for a jeweler might read:

"The purpose of this business is to provide a good living for the owners and employees by offering customers quality products and services in a congenial setting."

Or it might be considerably more elaborate.

"The purpose of this business is to:

• Provide the owners with enough profit to live a good lifestyle; to purchase the company building and related real estate; and to fund a comfortable retirement.

• Grow enough to justify the creation of four branches to provide business bases for the principals' four children.

• Provide superior compensation to all key employees.

• Become the dominant retailer of jewelry in its target markets through the sale of high-quality merchandise.

• Exemplify in all its operations the highest standards of ethical and honest behavior in dealing with both suppliers and customers."

How the mission statement is worded and its length are matters of individual preference. What's not negotiable is the importance of the message. This statement should reflect a truly serious attempt by the principals to get down on paper exactly what role they want their business to fulfill. Over time the goals may change; some firms write a new mission statement each year, though that seems extreme. However, once goals are set they should become a daily reality for everyone in the business.

How the company appears to others may or may not relate directly to the mission statement. For example, the mission statement quite rightly will have profitability as a key ingredient. But it's unlikely that the owner wants customers to think of the store as a profit source! It's another matter if the statement says the owner wants the store to specialize in high-quality jewelry and/or wants to conduct business at all times ethically and honestly. Obviously he'll be delighted if customers view the store as an ethical seller of high-quality merchandise.

What image do you want to project to the public? Is the image so clearly defined that you can write it down and include it in the employee manual—assuming, of course, that you have such a manual? What have you done to find out if customers' perceptions of your store match your own? Really, it's not that difficult to find out. Simply ask!

As we go through the case history of Kronos Jewelers we'll find that at times what the owners believe about their business doesn't always match up with what others think. These contradictions probably are true to some extent for most businesses—and for most individuals.

Now it's time to let the owners of Kronos Jewelers tell their story.

Kronos Jewelers Asks: Who Are We?

David Onassis: "Okay, the company is Kronos Jewelers, a retail jewelry business located in the northern suburbs of Utopia. It is a corporation with two principals, myself and my wife. As far as the mission statement goes, the purpose of the company is: "To turn a profit sufficient to provide the principals with the ability to have financial successes and at the same time provide opportunities for employees.""

"We're a continuing business. It was founded in 1955, moved to the northern suburbs in '59. It operated in a strip center until '89, then moved into its own building close by.

"As far as products and services, we carry diamonds, colored stones and karat gold jewelry as our primary product lines; these probably compose about 70% of our business. We're not very big in watches or in giftware; together these total maybe 4% of our business. Repairs are about 15%-18%, with other general merchandise categories making up the balance.

"We stock jewelry retailing from roughly $100 to about $4,000- $5,000. Store wide, our best sellers are probably between $200 and $750; we're reasonably strong between $750 and $2,000. Our average engagement ring sale is $3,000.

"My parents started the business as some sort of partnership and then bought the partnership out early on. But they rooted the business in providing service, ethics and integrity; they instilled that in us. That philosophy continued as the business moved from parent to child. I joined the business full time in '75, when an opening was available.

"I actually had decided in my teens that I didn't want to be in the business, and did a number of other things trying to find my way. But, by the time I turned 18, I realized this wasn't so bad. I went to mom and dad and said I'd like to join the business, but they said there wasn't any opening and I'd have to wait. I did, for a year, until a position opened up on the sales floor. I worked up from there.

"Then my parents separated. My father thought he could keep the business, but my mother decided she wanted it and said, 'If you want to leave, go ahead. We'll buy you out.' That forced me to grow into things a hell of a lot faster than anyone had expected. There really wasn't anyone to fill in some of the roles my father did, although we had a good management staff at the time. I found myself thrust into having to do marketing plans, advertising and things like that.

"We decided to open a branch downtown in the late '70s, but closed it a year and a half later. Great timing with interest rates going through the roof! We did it then because we had some key management people we were afraid we'd lose if there wasn't a place for them to grow. That was a tremendous learning experience that cost us a sum of money.

"The problem was interest rates. We had to do it mostly on borrowed funds. Interest rates then were about 9% maybe 9.5%."

Effie: "And we anticipated, what with inflation, they might go to 12%. We didn't know we'd be hitting 17%-18%. It just sucked up any money that we had available for promotion. And also the downtown building we moved into didn't do anything to help."

David: "Yes, they were supposed to open up this major retail center and it never panned out. That had an impact. And I wasn't particularly responsive to suggestions that might have helped, not willing to make the decision quick enough to do something. So we looked at it and cut our losses. We probably did it just in the nick of time. If we'd gone another year, my guess is it would have pulled us under. And within a year of closing it, we lost both those management people. With no hard feelings."

Effie: "But you got me."

David: "Yeah."

JCK: "Just what are you looking for in terms of personal success, of the sort of business you want to run, and of how you relate to your employees and your community? What sort of business is this? And are reality and what you want at all close?"

David: "If you ask Effie and me that, you may get two different answers."

JCK: "Okay, let's start with Effie. How would you like somebody in your community to describe this business? As a nice, friendly, family sort of business? As a fashion-forward or aggressive go-get-it business?"

Effie: "All of the above."

David: "Yeah. But what I would be most proud to be associated with would be 'crisp, professional, forward thinking, successful.'"

Effie: "But friendly, warm, down-to-earth, a nice, comfortable, pretty place to be. I think we want to be all of that. And can we be? I think so."

David: "Absolutely. I think you can have a warm, friendly, inviting atmosphere, provide professional service.'

Effie: "Be fashion forward, and forward thinking, progressive."

David: "And not just in fashion, but progressive from a business standpoint so that other business people in the community look to you and say, 'Here's the epitome of success.'"

Effie: "But how close are we to that? As far as how we're thought of in the community, I'd say we're more than halfway there. I think we and our staff need, as individuals, to get out there more. I think once they're in, people feel good about the store. But we need to reach out more, make it better known that we are special and different."

How Is The Industry Doing?

September 1993 Part II

The jewelry industry, like any other, is constantly evolving and changing. The store owner must be aware of these changes; to ignore them can be disastrous.

The business plan is the ideal place-of-record to acknowledge change, assess its impact and commit to actions that will allow the jeweler to take advantage of opportunities change will bring.

Let's look at some of the most challenging industry developments—those that already affect everyone in the industry and those that soon will.

Competition. This single word carries more import that any other in retailing today, and definitely so in jewelry retailing.

The principal reason is obvious. Jewelry can be, stress "can be," most profitable. If you don't believe that, look who's selling it today:

• Traditional jewelry stores, both independents and chains. In spite of some well-publicized failures and departures, the total number of jewelry stores stays high because new faces always seem ready to replace old ones that disappear. They may be small and unknown when they start, but who knows which among them will be the giants of tomorrow.

• Just about every mass merchant in the country. Include in this list Wal Mart, Kmart, J.C. Penney, Sears, Target, Venture. The list goes on and on.

• Major department and specialty stores. Add Bloomingdales, Saks Fifth Avenue, Nordstrom, Bullock, Neiman-Marcus, Macy's.

• The warehouse clubs—Price, B.J.'s, Sam's, etc.

• Literally millions of catalogs for apparel, appliances, gift and museums, all of which offer jewelry as a side- or main line.

• TV home shopping networks.

This is incredible competition! What's more, if it changes in the next five years, it's only likely to get more intense. Further, while much of it is centered in lower-priced and lower-quality merchandise than most independent and many chain jewelers carry, that should not be considered reason to be complacent or to ignore such competition. Just as many jewelers have upgraded their merchandise and their stores over the past couple of decades, so also will many of these new competitors upgrade. The difference is that they'll do it in an accelerated manner. Consider, too, that today almost all of these outlets offer consumers diamond engagement rings, a jewelry-store staple. Consider what that proliferation of outlets already has done to engagement ring margins.

What then does the traditional jeweler do to cope with this competition both successfully and profitably?

That's up to individual store owners. Their options are as varied and as extensive as a Chinese menu. Most center, however, on developing some specialty, on catering only to a very clearly defined market. The challenge is to make the focus narrow enough to be a real specialist yet broad enough to do enough business to prosper.

In refining existing marketing strategies or defining new ones, jewelers should consider:

Location. Does your style of business need high traffic or do you cater to the destination shopper? If you thrive on traffic, you're probably in a mall. Is that the best location? How costly is it—really? What about a strip center? They're regaining a lot of lost luster these days, coming back into popularity because of relatively low costs and convenience (you can actually park near the store you want to visit!).

If you're in a center of shopping (any large conglomerate of retailers) but depend on destination-shopper traffic, would you be better off in a stand-alone location?

How about branches? If you have two or three, do you really need them? An increasing number of jewelers are closing branches and consolidating operations in one super headquarters store.

People. "Our most valuable asset"—it's a cliche every CEO uses. For the specialty retailer—and in this context that's any company, no matter what its size, that specializes in the sale of jewelry-store merchandise—it is more true than ever. If you're going to sell an essentially unnecessary consumer product in a cut-throat competitive market you need:

• **Salespeople** who are well-trained, well-informed, skillful, productive, personable, gracious, persistent, dedicated and a pleasure to meet.

• **Benchworkers** who are talented, imaginative, resourceful, conscientious and who can repair and create jewelry on schedule and without undue waste.

• **Accountants** and other back-office staff (bookkeepers belong with Charles Dickens in the 19th century) who are efficient, understand the need for timely financial information and know the advantages of running a truly tight organization.

• **Managers and owners** who know the importance of strategic planning, target marketing and healthy cash flow and understand that smart buying, optimum turnover and well-managed margins are critical keys to profit.

"Get real," you say. "Who has such a perfect staff?"

Probably no one has. But every jeweler should try to acquire one. In the business plan, this means setting goals for hiring, training and compensating the very best. Don't think of this as spending money; think of it as investing in your future.

The future. "People don't change, they only become more so." This is a comment on life by a wise and observant former editor of JCK, Don McNeil.

The business outlook—specifically the retailing outlook—goes one better. It not only changes, but the conditions we have become more so. Thus competition will get tougher. So will finding good people, judged by today's education standards. The manager/owner's job will be more complex and more demanding. Relationships with suppliers will become more demanding, too, as consolidation continues at that end of the jewelry business and as surviving firms become more picky about which retailers they want as customers.

At the same time retailing as a whole will be altered radically by advances in electronic communications and as the so-called video mall emerges from its cocoon to become a reality. The combined power of TV and computer will bring awesome change. To survive successfully in this business world certainly will be possible. But it will take greater thought, greater expertise and greater planning than ever before. Your next business plan should address all of these issues.

Who Are My Customers?

September 1993 Part II

Do you really know who your customers are?

Some years ago JCK put that question to a Pennsylvania jeweler and he laughed. Of course he knew! It took a reporter only a couple of weeks to find out how misinformed that jeweler was.

Since his store was in the county seat, the jeweler was sure most of the lawyers and lobbyists who populated the county buildings and courthouse were his customers. Few were. The same for the rich folks in a fancy new housing development in the immediate area. Few of them shopped in the store, either.

It wasn't that hard to find out who *did* shop in this store. Our reporter simply looked at the addresses on some hundreds of sales slips and asked people who went in and out of the store.

A store owner must know everything possible about customers and potential customers. He needs to have target markets—both geographic and demographic. It's easier to define the geographic area, so let's start there.

Geography. There are various ways to select your geographic limits. You may decide, for example, to target only those customers who have a higher-than-average income.

One simple course here is to drive around your area and select sections with an obvious concentration of expensive real estate. Then you can use direct mail and advertising to aim your store and sales messages at this audience.

A more precise course is to spend some time with U.S. Census data, which includes vast amounts of people information. Much of it is more of demographic than of geographic interest, but consider just one set of Census figures that we collected for Kronos Jewelers, our case-study store. Median family income in its home town is $31,140; 25% of the families have incomes of $50,000 or more; nearly 5% of them have incomes of $100,000 or more.

Basic research such as this can pinpoint certain geographic target areas. Common sense may provide others. Say there's an area within reasonable driving distance (30 minutes? 45 minutes?) of the store which is not now served by a jewelry store. This might be a good market to try to penetrate.

Store advertising also helps define a geographic market. Suppose you combine cable TV, radio and print in your advertis-

ing mix. Which markets do these various media reach? There's little point trying to reach customers who aren't going to see, hear or read your ads on a regular basis. The media themselves usually have detailed information on their audiences.

A third geographic target could be new territory you want to tap, because you think it either is under-served by jewelers now or has the potential to grow into a strong consuming market within two to three years. An early marketing effort could get you in on the ground floor.

Demographics. Here you run into all sorts of variables, since a typical jewelry store will target a number of different demographic groups. The most simple division is men and women; each sex has distinct and often quite separate motivations to shop in a jewelry store. Each also probably is looking for different products in different price ranges.

Deciding which customers you want to reach, therefore, involves a balance of inventory, price, sales abilities, after-sales service, store appearance, location and owner preferences. But in considering all these factors and how they will or will not appeal to customers, you face a fundamental chicken/egg dilemma. Do you chose the customers you want first, then tailor every aspect of your business to reach them? Or do you assess your store's attributes of people and product, then find the customers who would like to shop in such a store?

This dilemma often resolves itself when a store owner elects to seek out those customers he or she feels most comfortable with. Remember, however, that there are dangerous limitations to growth for any store owner who wants to live permanently within a comfort zone.

You may well choose a number of different target customers. One store, for example, might court teenagers because they eventually will become engagement ring customers and, in turn, anniversary gift customers. That same store might also seek to do some corporate gift business because of the many thriving businesses in its area.

So here you have four separate market groups. Can they be meshed efficiently with the store's capabilities? Let's look in more detail:

Inventory. Probably no problems with the engagement ring and anniversary customers. But will the merchandise that appeals to a teen be looked down on by the established customer buying a 25th anniversary diamond necklace? Will the jewelry that appeals to corporate buyers scare away teens?

Price. Some stores successfully stock items that sell for $50 along with those selling for $5,000 because their quality is good regardless of the price. That means there should be no problem in carrying inexpensive inventory to meet the tastes and pocketbooks of teens or young married couples seeking a gift along with high-end, high-cost items—as long as quality is maintained.

But consider price-off advertising, too. How will the four different target markets respond? Will price-off deals combine well with a policy of quality in all merchandise?

Salespeople. This area should be of least concern. A carefully-selected, well-trained salesperson should be able to treat any customer pleasantly and efficiently.

Store location and appearance. You could have real differences. A smart, look-alive operation in a busy mall will be a draw for teens and no problem for most young engaged couples. But such a location lacks appeal for the older and probably more affluent buyer. It is unlikely to appeal to the corporate buyer, either.

How to find them. Let's assume that you want the four different target markets we've identified. How do you find them?

The first place to turn is the U.S. Census. It provides vital information on age, sex, ethnic mix, income, home-ownership, commuting patterns and more for every community in the United States. City- or county-wide statistics are more than adequate for most jewelers. But for those who want even more targeted information, the Census gives demographic details right down to tracts of only a few square blocks.

The local chamber of commerce, TV and radio stations, the newspaper and utilities serving the area all have useful facts and figures about the people who live there. Utilities in particular generally have excellent data on economic development, as do area planning commissions. This information can help you determine where your business has the best chance of growing and where you might consider opening a branch, if such expansion is in your long-range plans.

In summary:

• Any store probably has a number of different target markets.

• These groups of consumers should be compatible enough to be served by existing store merchandise, salespeople and store "atmosphere."

• The groups—and the products and services they need—should be clearly defined in the store owner's mind.

• They should live within an equally clearly defined geographical area.

• Current and potential customers, taken together, should be numerous enough and of sufficient means to provide your store with the level of sales you need.

Psychographics. Once upon a time retailers were satisfied with the kinds of demographic information we've just discussed—facts and figures on customers' jobs, income, types of housing and number of children. That was before the business shrinks moved in. Today the retailer who wants to stay ahead of the competition needs psychographic information, as well.

Simply put, this means finding out what makes your customers tick, what motivates them to buy or not buy, how to reach the hot button—in personal contact and in advertising—that prompts quick reactions.

Observation will produce some answers. You know certain of your customers' preferences: they play golf, they jog, they like foreign travel, they're addicted to a certain color, they appreciate the unusual and so on. You learn about these preferences by listening and observing.

You can learn a lot more by asking. The questions can be part of a casual, across-the-counter conversation or they can be posed in informal and unthreatening questionnaires. Who's going to object if you ask about hobbies, TV viewing preferences, favorites sports, etc.? Once you have the information, be sure to use it intelligently. Computers make it so simple to build, maintain and update customer personal profiles that very few stores can find an excuse not to have first-class files.

Who buys what? When you buy, always make sure you're buying merchandise that meets your customers' needs. It's awfully easy to buy something because you wish your customers would buy it or because you love the piece yourself.

As you'll see read later in this issue, Kronos Jewelers has sometimes fallen into the first trap. Owners David and Effie Onassis have an on-again, off-again flirtation with the idea that they can cater to customers who buy high-style designer pieces. So, from time to time, they buy a few such pieces and put them in inventory—where they stay. In their more realistic moments, the Onassises realize that while they may cater to such upscale buyers some day, today they do not.

Their experience probably recurs daily in stores all over the country because jewelers insist on buying merchandise they rarely if ever will sell. They make the mistake largely because they don't match merchandise and target customers.

This isn't to say you should never take a chance with something out of the ordinary. In every aspect of your business, you must try to identify trends—in clothing, in behavior, in design, in colors, in politics and, of course, in merchandise. If you see a jewelry line that is very different from your normal inventory but seems to mesh with some lifestyle trend in your community, take a chance and stock a few items. But before committing on an order, try to think of customers who might be willing to share your experiment.

Your economy: sweet or sour? In an ideal world, all the people who want jobs have them, all the jobs pay top dollar, and shoppers go shopping confident that they have plenty of disposable income to spend on such desirable luxuries as jewelry.

This is not an ideal world, however.

Peoples' incomes, attitudes and buying patterns directly reflect the state of their personal economics which in turn reflect what's happening to business in their communities. That's very obvious right now, after several years of recession and weak recovery. It's also obvious that a jeweler must temper buying to reflect economic reality.

Traditionally when times are tough, sterling silver jewelry makes a sudden upsurge at jewelry shows. Inexpensive colored stones gain new popularity. Lighter karat-gold pieces begin to show up. All this makes sense, for it allows a jeweler to stock attractive merchandise at lower prices.

But if you do choose to buy some "better value" pieces to match your customers' ability to spend, don't abandon the higher-priced lines you normally carry. Even in hard times some people are not affected financially—only psychologically. They still respond to intelligent selling.

The simple truth is that you must read your market area's business pulse carefully and adapt as needed to keep in step. This is true whether the market is going up or down. Always look for trends; a trend, after all, develops only when enough similar incidents occur. If you can spot the incidents beginning to accumulate, then you'll be well ahead of the trend. Two examples: you hear of one company laying off workers, then another, then another. That's the beginning of a bad trend. Conversely, you hear that the local planning commission has approved one new housing development, then another, then another. Clearly the beginning of a good trend.

As you get ready for a new year with a new business plan, be sure to reasses your target market and the people who live there. If you and your customers should fall out of sync without you realizing it, your business could be in real trouble. Being totally in sync makes a wonderful start for a new year.

Kronos Jewelers Looks at its Target Markets

"I guess I'd say our #1 target would be the young, professional, slightly more affluent engagement ring market," says David Onassis. "I would further describe that as from 22-24 up to maybe 35, from just out of college to making their way into their professional life. They usually have a little bit more disposable income. Sometimes they've just bought a house, though more often they haven't quite gotten to that yet. But they have professional jobs so their cash flow is in a pretty good position—which may explain the higher dollar average of our engagement rings.

"That's one market. The next would be that same group five or ten years down the road. This is the 'second occasion' market, which includes birthdays, anniversaries, holidays. Here price points obviously are lower than our average $3,000 engagement rings. But we believe there is a building element. In their first years of marriage, these customers might get an anniversary gift that's going to be just a couple hundred dollars, but hopefully, as they get to their 20th year, that anniversary gift is going to be a multiple-thousand-dollar gift.

"We don't really target our third market; it just happens to be what our business grew from. That's the repair business traffic, with the shop on the premises.

"A final target is the people we attract when we promote specific, low-price items to pull traffic into the store. The demographics here are often times very broad. An item such as the Hershey Kiss, which retails at $20 in sterling, produces people from 18 to 65 years old, straight across the board. But we hope this is new traffic into the store, so we can make new impressions.

"Blue collar workers might be 25% of our traffic and our trade. It's not a marketing decision to say we don't want the blue collar worker. I think it's a consequence of our corporate decision to not off price. I think blue collar worker is a bit more inclined to be pulled in by off-price advertising. Yeah, I think so. So I think we gave up that market, not because we didn't want them, I'd love to have any market, but I think they are inclined to shop in other places.

"I can't back it up with specific numbers, but I think the loyalty of our customers is extremely high. Extremely high. I was chatting with a client yesterday, who is getting ready to move to Florida, saying we're sorry to see you go, and he said, 'Don't worry, we still have family here. We'll be back for our jewelry. I wouldn't go anywhere else!'

"And that seems to be a common comment. We had one client who purchased an engagement ring. Six months later, the engagement breaks off and he comes back to us. We work with him to take the ring back, at the least cost to him. He felt very good about how we treated him. He moved away, went to North Carolina and two years later, when it was time for him to buy an engagement ring, he called us unsolicited. 'The first place I thought of for an engagement ring was you, David,' he said. 'Can we do anything at this distance?' I said, 'Absolutely.' We virtually closed the sale on the phone. He came up here to pick it up.

"We build this loyalty by focusing on doing what's best for the client even if that sometimes hurts us. Spending ten hours with an engagement ring customer establishes a rapport. It gives a very clear message that we're here, we're going to work with them, we're going to do whatever we need to do to make them feel comfortable. And after 10 hours you have a friend.

"That may seem like a lot of time. But most people seem to walk into our store blindly; they don't know anything about us. Maybe they came on a recommendation, referral, an ad or something like that. If we say outright, 'We're going to sit down and go through a two-hour educational session,' they'll laugh and probably walk away. 'Are you nuts?' they'll ask. 'Give me your spiel in 15 minutes; I've heard it a dozen other places.' But if you weave them into it, before you know it two hours have gone by and they're hooked at that point.

"Some people, maybe two or three out of ten, may be hesitant when you start getting into it and it's obvious they don't want to spend the time. They're not interested in that education. They are tougher for us to sell."

Meet The Competition

September 1993 Part II

Don't ever play hunches when it comes to the competition. Too often they're self-deluding. The best way to find who's really challenging you for customers and sales is to make a serious study.

But before you start checking out other jewelry stores in the market, consider who really are your competitors. Among the possibilities:

Other jewelry stores, including jewelry chains.

Other stores that sell jewelry but for whom jewelry is only one of many different products.

TV at-home shopping services.

Luxury auto dealers.

Travel agents.

The list can go on and on. Each jeweler can put together one that's appropriate for his or her store's market area.

It's very important here to look at competition from other outlets selling jewelry-store merchandise. If you haven't examined this competition in a while now's a good time to do it because, in case you haven't noticed, the marketing of jewelry has changed dramatically in just the past three or four years.

Last year, for example, jewelers sold about $14 billion worth of merchandise. Outlets which don't classify as jewelers—in other words, less than 50% of their total sales come from jewelry—sold about $12 billion worth. That's competition! Included here are catalog showrooms, dominated by Service Merchandise; TV home shopping networks; warehouse clubs; and such mass merchants as J.C. Penney and Sears Roebuck.

Jewelers selling higher-end merchandise, the so-called guild stores, may dismiss this type of competition as irrelevant. Those who shop at Penney's or buy from a TV pitch are not their customers, they say. And today, that's probably true. But tomorrow? Who knows. To ignore such competition could be very dangerous.

The same is true when independent jewelers consider jewelry chains. Many guild independents tend to look down their noses at chain competitors, regarding them as has-beens in the market. The attitude is a reaction to the heavy price-off policies of most chains along with the well-publicized business misfortunes of Zale, Hooker, Ratner and others over the past few years. But the surviving chains are coming back actively and they're as anxious as most retailers to sell the market at the top while keeping what they have at the middle and bottom.

Checking out the competition. There are a number of ways to do this. Perhaps the best is to shop the competition—and if you want an impartial reading of the other stores' relative strengths and weaknesses, hire someone to do the shopping for you. You or your staff can't be objective.

Be sure that whoever does the shopping is comparing oranges and oranges. Have a tally sheet of each facet of your competitors' businesses you want to check and get the same information for all stores.

If you're willing to invest the necessary dollars you can arrange exit interviews with shoppers who have just left a competing store. These will be conducted by a professional research firm used to approaching consumers to ask for opinions. Often they can gather some very interesting facts on how these consumers view the competitors' staff, appearance, pricing and so on.

You also can, as we did for Kronos Jewelers, recruit a polling company to call a random selection of consumers in your market area and ask them about their jewelry shopping habits. Our study, which was very limited in scope, did turn up some information about Kronos and its competitors that contradicted what Kronos' owners believed.

Finally, you can do some of your own sleuthing. Observe what you can about the competitors, talk to your suppliers' salespeople about them, dig for facts when you attend various industry meetings, talk to your local media reps and, of course, talk to your own customers.

The importance of detail. The more precise the information you gather about competitors the better.

Let's look at gold jewelry as an example.

• How extensive are the displays in a particular competitor's store compared with yours?

• How does its merchandise quality compare with yours?

• Is it possible that your competitor and you carry goods from the same supplier? If so, what should you do about it?

• How do its prices compare with yours? Quality-for-quality, is it fair to compare prices? How can you—and more particularly your staff—handle this price/quality issue with customers?

• How does this competitor advertise gold jewelry? Are its ads in any way misleading? How will you handle this issue with customers?

• Does your competitor regularly deal on price? Do you? If so, where does the deal end? If you don't, what action can you take?

Probably not one jeweler in a thousand has the time to handle this sort of detail for all the major product lines and services in the store. But if a competitor is hurting you in some important area—whether it be karat gold chain, diamond engagement rings or mid-priced watches—it's well worth examining that store's tactics in this amount of detail so that you can fight back effectively.

Strengths and weaknesses. It's always good practice to draw up an annual balance sheet of your competitive strengths and weaknesses. You should do the same thing for your principal competitors. Typically, your balance sheet might look like this:

Strengths	**Weaknesses**
High traffic location	Unexciting window
Friendly, professional staff	displays
Wide-range of merchandise	Lack of bite
High-quality merchandise	in advertising
Reputation in the community	Over-impulsive buying
Gemological expertise	Trouble getting
Excellent appraisal service	best margins
Customer loyalty	Weakness in add-on sales

Clearly a list such as this gives you a working set of goals for next year's business plan. Each weakness you identify should be targeted for action and all of your staff must be involved in bringing about change. Window displays and bad buying habits should be correctable right away. A sales training program has to be started to deal with the add-on issue. Improving advertising and margins may be longer-term goals—but once they've been identified as weaknesses they should be addressed right away with both short- and longer-term strategies.

As far as possible, you also should create such balance sheets for your main competitors. Then go to work on those stores' *strengths,* the qualities that may tempt your customers to shop with them. Be sure you have anything they have that attracts customers, and that what you have is better than theirs.

Opportunities, opportunities. The enjoyable side of analyzing where you and your competition stand is that you get a glow from identifying your strengths. But you can't stand pat. Strengths can be transient unless you regularly commit yourself and your staff to improve, not just maintain them.

Ironically, identifying your weaknesses may be even more rewarding. Correcting a weakness offers greater opportunity for business improvement than building on a strength. The staff that works together to solve a problem gets a collective surge of pride when the problem is licked. That sort of pride can translate into many successful sales.

As others see us. Robert Burns, the Scottish poet, said it very well a long time ago (and for convenience sake we'll paraphrase his words into more-or-less contemporary English):

Would the gods
The gift ha' gie us,
To see ourselves
As others see us!

Forget for the moment about other stores that sell jewelry. Just look long and hard at your own. What do you see? Do you think you can embrace that gift of the gods and see your store as others see it? If you can, fine. If you can't, ask others for their candid opinions. It could be an another opportunity to turn a competitive disadvantage into a strong strength.

Kronos Jewelers looks at the competition

David Onassis: "When we think about competition, we like to think that we're marketing to customers who buy the high-ticket, high-design items. We have competitors who do. But maybe it's a matter of ego. Maybe that's not our market. We don't have the inventory to cater to that upper end."

Effie: "Or the clientele."

David: "But we still cross over into their territory, or they into ours, when it comes to the middle-of-the-road market and to engagement and anniversary rings, those things that people have a greater tendency to shop about for. So

who is our competition? Every jeweler in town. Who is our primary competition? It depends on the product line.

"Given a similar product, say engagement rings, and quality for quality, we believe we are competitively priced for the marketplace. When it comes to specific categories like Ideally-cut diamonds, which we sell, we are probably a little bit less than some and dead even with others.

"There's always going to be the guy who will bust it for a buck. You know, he doesn't care and he can have the sale. We as much as tell our client that. Say the client comes in and says, 'I can buy a .5-ct. Ideal cut diamond, G color, VS_1 clarity, for $1,500,' and we know $2,200 is a reasonable retail price in the marketplace and the cost on the thing is maybe $1,400-$1,500. After you have a serious dialogue so the client knows how to verify he's getting the right thing, how can he buy it from us? He's got to buy it from the other source, it's such a good deal. But, short of those oddities, we believe we're very competitive.

"Misrepresentation is a problem everywhere. Some guys are misleading and intentionally inaccurate with quality description. When they have to deal with one of our customers—and they know it because of how informed that customer is—they may back peddle a little bit, maybe work a little bit tighter, maybe even deliver the product at cost so they don't get caught. That's happened once or twice. But we've also come across flat out misrepresentation. We've shopped some competition and found blatant misrepresentation. But there's not much you can do about it. For one jeweler to complain to the consumer affairs department, the attorney general or the media doesn't do a whole heck of a lot.

"What's our competitive edge? We've built a reputation for honesty, integrity, quality. We take time with clients that other jewelers are unwilling to take. We do not discount, and that sets us apart from the other people. It has its pros and its cons, but I think it's more a positive than it is a negative.

"That even carries into our engagement ring sales. I talk with pride—though sometimes at industry functions a little sheepishly—about the $9,100 sale that walked out the door because we wouldn't change the price by $200. People say we're nuts. But through a recession that hit local jewelers hard, where they had two, three and four years of declining business, we turned down a little bit but we turned up before they did. Something's working.

"I think we're satisfying customers. But where we're having a competitive difficulty is in perception of value. That is, by not discounting, we create an impression of high price, though quality is there."

Effie: "We've always had that problem. We've always been thought of as expensive."

David: "That's true. And we've never done anything to address it. I don't know whether we should just say that if people think we're high priced, let's get some extra margin. Or whether we should build into our marketing message that lack of discounting does not mean high price.

"When I read through the comments from the competitive shopping survey I saw one of my main competitors scored high on inventory. My reaction was that they have inventory we don't have and it's making an impression.

"So maybe we'll alter our mix a little bit. But we're not going to go head to head to match inventory with certain places. Maybe later when we have more disposable income to invest in inventory we can try to break into that high upper-end market.

"Meanwhile, there are little things we can do. We can put in higher-style engagement rings, more interesting mountings, maybe display something a little differently so that the walk-in trade sees something that gives an impression. People who come in now spend two hours before they see anything. They have to see sample stones, and go through mountings for a long while.

"One concern I do have is that stores that have been competing with the discounters are finding that they can't, so they're going to come back into our market. We see that starting to happen with one competitor. Their newspaper advertising is going from the big boraxy off-price ad to doing very little off-pricing. I believe it will take a long time for them to change their image and break into what we've earned over 10 or 15 years. But if they stick to their guns, I think they're going to start to cut into our market."

Market Strategies

September 1993 Part II

Marketing and sales are so closely linked they must be considered together. Marketing tells people what you have; sales occur when they respond to the message and buy.

Let's start with getting the message across. It's fairly obvious that most stores follow the same path—a mix of advertising, promotions and public relations—to tell the public about their products and services. Perhaps because it's all so obvious, it's tempting to hurry through the planning, letting formulas take charge when inventiveness and imagination should prevail.

Let's start at the beginning. How many jewelers, in promoting their products and services, tell consumers what they are rather than what they do?

Example: Think how many ads you've seen that say (or shout) that X Jewelers has the most beautiful diamonds in town? Or, if not the most beautiful, then the least expensive? But when did you last see an ad that said, "If you wear a piece of diamond jewelry from X Jewelers, you'll be envied [or admired] by everyone at the party"?

Another example: How many store ads boast that the jeweler offers "professional appraisals"? How few say that "if you get an appraisal from us you needn't worry if you lose your engagement ring. Our appraisal is so accurate and precise your insurance company will be able to replace the lost ring with one just like it."

Never take things for granted. As we said early in this issue, one of the main functions of a business plan is to make you question every single aspect of your business once a year. Few things can do as much to keep your company healthy. So let's go through some elements that can be very helpful in the annual re-examination of your marketing and sales strategies.

How effective is your advertising? First of all, do you know? Let's assume that your advertising is designed to cover all or key parts of your market area. If you use more than one medium, do you have a clear reason for doing so? Is your advertising coverage based on a plan that allows you to reach key present and potential customers—or on how much you can afford to spend?

TV and radio stations and various publications generally can offer demographic guidance on how best to reach the

market you want through your advertising. Are they also willing to help you measure the effectiveness of your ads?

There are simple ways to judge certain types of ads yourself. They may contain a coupon which has to be sent or brought to the store; an 800 number the customer may call for information; or a special offer on a particular product or service. Here immediate response can be judged fairly accurately. But have you tried to check whether an ad for an engagement diamond at a special price draws better from TV than from a newspaper? What about response related to cost?

Response to institutional advertising is even harder to judge. And it can be judged incorrectly. Kronos Jewelers, as you'll find out in the continuing narrative that follows this story, covers its market with a steady diet of institutional ads. Owner David Onassis told us he felt confident this campaign—which consumes an unusually high 7%+ of total revenue—has positioned his store as No. 1 in jewelry consumers' minds. But it seems that is far from so. Consumers polled by telephone placed a number of his competitors ahead of Kronos when they were asked to name jewelers in the market area. Onassis hadn't even regarded some that outscored him as competitors.

Admittedly this was a small study; it drew responses from 100 people in households with annual incomes of at least $40,000. But it was enough to jolt Onassis. Fortunately he's a man who considers glasses half full when others might think them half empty. Once the first shock was over, he called his ad agency to discuss how he might have a greater impact on those consumers who seem to know so little about his store. "What an opportunity!" he said. "If we can get just a few of these people, think of what it would do to sales!"

Which media do you use and why? It depends, of course, on what you want a particular ad to do and whom you want to reach.

The jeweler who knows both his prime customers' demographics and pyschographics will have the least trouble selecting the right media. Cable TV and commuter-time radio probably will be his choice for the engagement ring couple. The newspaper for his price-off traffic ad. Direct mail for the select offering of some new and exciting designs—though personal calls by the sales staff to some of their favorite customers may be more effective here (more on the role of the sales staff later).

The critical issue is to make each decision to spend ad dollars thoughtfully and logically. And be sure to question past decisions continually. If conditions in the market have changed, and change really is a constant, then what worked once may not work again. Or it may. But be sure to think before you act.

How valuable are promotions? The answer should lie in your store records. Marketing records that go back too far—more than seven years, say—serve mainly to collect dust. So much probably has changed since then that the records no longer offer a reliable guide. But current records can be a wonderful help and usually far outperform memory.

Thus if you ran an after-closing-hours wine and cheese party last fall, your records should tell you enough about attendance, the attendees' mood and sales to decide whether it's worth another shot.

Promotions should generate sales. That's their prime purpose. If they don't, they're largely a waste of time and money. You can argue that they open up leads, making newcomers familiar with the store and staff. But if a sale doesn't result within a month or two (and those delayed sales are hard to pin down as a direct spinoff of the promotion), then you might seriously consider using some other way to introduce your store to consumers who have yet to visit.

Always question actions that do not produce measurable results.

Does PR pay off? In a word, yes. Meeting the right people socially can produce great rewards for a jeweler. Bonding creates situations where the consumer will buy from you either from loyalty or, sometimes, from guilt. Who wants to tell his golfing buddy that he bought that gold watch from someone else!

Playing the lecture circuit is good for recognition and recognition certainly can help create sales. (Over-exposure can be a danger, however.) When possible, try to correlate personal appearances at civic clubs or other such places with any sales that result.

It's also possible to do well by doing good. A watch presented to the winner of a local marathon will draw some attention. But it's even better to do things that encourage more news coverage, like the Dallas jeweler who for many years won yards of newspaper space for his annual awards to local citizens who had performed some unusually brave deed.

Marketing and the local economy. Keeping close tabs on what's happening in your community is essential. A blizzard of layoffs in your town will put a freeze on spending and knock the bottom out of consumer confidence. As the recession we've just gone through shows well, even people whose jobs aren't in jeopardy stop spending when the collective mood is bad.

Conversely, upbeat news can send consumer confidence soaring. Any number of different developments can help—more new houses being built, home prices rising, plants expanding, and so on.

A good business plan must address such economic downs and ups. They affect every aspect of marketing, from the merchandise that gets special promotion to the message the store wants to send to its public.

Sales strategies. How you sell is an integral part of your marketing philosophy. While marketing through advertising and promotions may shift with the seasons and the state of your local economy, sales strategies likely will vary less and be more long-term.

Pricing probably is the most critical issue. Are you a one-price store or are you open to negotiations? If you do negotiate, then your business plan should examine the policy at least yearly. Should you negotiate more or less? Might you give your sales staff greater or lesser leeway in making deals?

Pricing also, of course, is a key factor in attracting customers. You should decide early how many sales or other price-off events you want to run during a year and build that into the business plan. You may want to adopt a short- or long-term move to use certain merchandise as a loss leader. Or you may want to make a move on margin. All such decisions must go into your plan. Poor control of pricing, with impulsive changes being made, can affect the business disastrously.

Sales strategies for your staff also should be assessed in the business plan. Your marketing plan certainly will set sales goals and your sales staff must be ready and able to help you meet those goals.

This raises the issues of compensation and productivity. Productivity can include total dollar sales per employee, a salesperson's ability to improve closing skills and such matters as add-on sales. All probably will come up for discussion when you're planning for the year ahead. You may prefer to look at these issues more closely in the operations section of your business plan (as we will), but remember that they must be considered.

Services as marketing tools. To an alarming extent, many jewelers give away services or at least seriously undercharge for them.

The normal justification is, "This is what sets me apart. I provide real services." Following this logic, watch and jewelry repair costs routinely are understated. The jeweler who says keystone isn't enough for merchandise sales rarely would consider taking keystone for a repair charge.

The same is true of appraisals. Some jewelers charge a sensible hourly fee for professional work; others make a minimum charge because this is "a service."

No question that services can be useful marketing tools. Kronos Jewelers, for example, prepares highly professional appraisals which it says attract customers who wouldn't otherwise shop there because the merchandise isn't of the quality and substance to meet their tastes.

In preparing your business plan, it makes sense to re-evaluate the role of service. You may find that you can use your service department to attract more shoppers, make more money—or, ideally, do both.

Kronos Jewelers looks at its market strategies

David Onassis: "Over the years, we've moved out of print and into radio and television, which are much more effective with the engagement ring market. Most of the print ads we run are traffic-building item ads and/or institutional and often are geared toward a slightly older market. Here it's usually a higher-ticket item, a $1,000+ item, anniversary rings and things of that sort.

"The message is that we're going to take time with you. We're not going to rush you through anything. If you want to be rushed, you can go to the other guy.

"We're very specific. Our radio ad is a testimonial type. A young gentleman is talking about his experience in buying a diamond. He's saying something like, 'When Linda and I were looking for a diamond, we didn't know what to do. What did we know about diamonds? It was gimmicks here and sales there, a lot of double talk. It was kind of confusing, but then we found Kronos Jewelers. And Kronos took the time that we needed to make a comfortable, well-informed decision.'

"That ad was structured from comments we got from clients. And we've had response to it. Someone came into the store for about 20 minutes and overheard a conversation we were having with a client about something. He interrupted the sale and said, 'You know, it's absolutely true what you say in your ad. You are taking time with these people, aren't you?'

"In TV, too, we talk about commitment to customers and about taking time to build relationships. About delivering professional services, giving them what they need to make good decisions.

"The one print engagement ring ad that we repeat over and over is simply headlined, 'What are you looking for in a diamond? At Kronos Jewelers we take the time to show you all the facts that you need to know about buying a diamond. No tricks, no gimmicks, just plain, simple facts.' There's a picture of a loupe with a diamond it, and that's it. Every time we run the ad, we get a surge of engagement ring traffic.

"The best advertising is word of mouth. When we spend 10 hours with a client and it results in a sale, they are impressed and they'll tell their friends to at least stop in and learn from us. With a close rate in the 70%-80% range, if we get them in, we've got a real, real good chance of selling them."

JCK: "I've heard one successful jeweler say that his employees can do anything they want to make a sale provided it is in line with the company mission statement. What is your philosophy about the role of the sales staff in fulfilling your marketing strategy?"

David: "Well, you're not going to fulfill anything if you don't have a staff, because two people can't do it themselves. But they need to be given the tools to do the job that you ask them to do."

JCK: "But what job do you ask? Do you explain what your philosophy is, or do they sort of pick this up as they go along?"

Effie: "We rely on them greatly to carry out our objectives. They are very familiar with how we want customers treated, how we want our merchandise priced, and how we want to service after the sale, that sort of thing. That's gone over regularly, though informally."

David: "Our mission statement really just says we want to make sufficient profits for the principals to be happy and to maintain a staff that is pleased, happy and growing.

"I think one advantage our employees have is that we give them the tools to succeed. If we ask them to be top diamond sales people, then we train them on how to sell diamonds. We're willing to provide funding for them to get the education that's needed to help them.

"Can they play with price in order to close a sale? No. One of the philosophies of our store is that the price is what the price is. That's a marketing strategy because it distinguishes us from almost every other jeweler in the country.

When we face a client, we say this is a fair, reasonable price. We can feel good about doing it, and look them square in the eyes, and not be shifty or anything.

"I think our sales staff takes pride and comfort in that fact as well. They can go through the typical explanation of fair price, fair value, comparisons, advantages of the product and service and store, and all of that and some diehard customer will say, 'Let me talk to David. He'll give me a better price.' But our salespeople know that when the client talks to me, the price for that $500 chain is still going to be $500."

JCK: "What are your criteria when you're buying? Do you buy with the idea that you can sell it for 'X' amount, and then compare that with the cost, or what?"

David: "Our buying philosophy has changed, which has a lot to do with Effie's input. When I was doing a lot of the buying, I figured you pay this, you sell it for that based on your standard margin. I didn't look at value or think, 'Will somebody pay more for this?' Now we think, 'Why do we have to sell it for 1.9 over cost when, gee, maybe we can get a 2.3 on it?' We're slowly trying to prop up our gross margin."

Effie: "When we look at merchandise now we do tend to look at what type of margin can we get on it. If we can only get keystone on it, do we really want to have it? How badly do we want it? And how fast will we turn it? We recognize that we can't make a profit with keystone all across the board because such a large portion of what we do is engagement rings, which is a lower margin item."

JCK: "You've identified various markets you want to reach. If you try to stretch into Big City, will you try to attract the same groups?"

David: "We're trying to get our name into the Big City market by using price-pointed items. We want to build a base, a list of names that we can draw on. We're looking for bodies. If we can get the gross profit to cover the costs of the advertising, we'll be happy. Then we can start sprinkling in a few engagement ring ads and measure the response. If only three people come in from the *Tribune* engagement ring ad and two buy, and if our average engagement ring sale is $3,000, we've covered the cost of the ad."

Effie: "Maybe. What's the gross profit on that $3,000 engagement ring?"

David: "Probably about $1,000. So we'd have a gross profit of $2,000. And the ads are about $2,500."

Effie: "No, $2,900. So we need to sell three."

David: "My point, is that if we get those two engagement ring customers from Big City and they are satisfied with what we've done for them, they're going to tell their friends."

JCK: "When you talk about investing eight or ten hours, this presumably is spread over a period?"

David: "Three to four meetings."

JCK: "Does distance become a problem then?"

David: "It hasn't been. We had some people come down for three different meetings before they finally selected the piece, and then they came a fourth time to pick it up. They travelled an hour and half.

"Is it an element? Yes, but people will drive easily 30 minutes to shop for something like engagement rings."

JCK: "Your big strength is in the engagement ring business and yet that probably is one of the most competitive areas where margins are tight. Should you really be stressing them or should you build lines that offer better margins?"

David: "Our engagement rings average about $3,000. Maybe we would be better having our engagement rings average $1,000 but sell more of them, because the margin is better there. However, I think we are competitive.

"We also sell a product that's different than most other people's. When they start selling a product similar to ours, I think we might have some competitive problems, margin problems.

"We stress the make. We know most of our competitors don't do a lot of educating or even discuss cut. We've got a great opportunity to sell an Ideally-made stone versus an off-make stone. We seem to be very successful showing clients that there is a difference and that the difference has value. So we're able to narrow our competition. Instead of dealing with 15 jewelers, we cut it down to two, maybe three, competitors."

Effie: "One thing we have lacked is follow-through after the engagement ring sale, the building of additional sales and the follow-up six months or a year later."

David: "I hate to say it, but maybe we're suggesting that diamond engagement rings are our loss leader. And maybe that's not so terrible. It is an important purchase, an emotional one.

"Engagement rings are about 25%-30% of our business. Consider them our Rolex watch. How many jewelry stores do 30% or more of their business in Rolexes? If you ask why they sell them, it's a status element. Except I think we're more successful with engagement rings, because we know they lead to wedding bands, to attendants gifts and to anniversary products. Generally, these are areas where we do get better margins. If we can make them customers for life, we have a heck of a lot more sales coming.

"We actually have raised margins on engagement rings steadily over the past five years. But if it gets to the point where we have to lower them a bit, that might be OK if we're certain we follow up better, keep those customers and get more sales from them in the next five or ten years. We're selling a low margined item that creates significant customer loyalty in order to build business in other lines with higher margins."

JCK: "Let's look at customer lists. I don't know how fresh you keep your lists, or whether you really know where your customers are."

Effie: "Three or four years ago, we did a zip code breakdown of our Christmas sales lists. Our top two zip codes were the ones closest to us. After that, it was amazing how varied they got. We didn't expect to see that."

David: "We're not targeting particular zip codes now, because the mailing list we have isn't broken down by zip codes. We could do that; it wouldn't be terribly costly. Or we could put all these customers on the computer, with much more history and the ability to break it out in a variety of ways.

"We're strong in our two closest zip codes here and then downstate because our advertising reaches a wide area away from Big City. If we really wanted to cover that market, we'd need to use major newspaper, major radio, at great expense. Here people will travel distances."

JCK: "Let's look at your customer mix again. Is the blue-collar worker essentially a non-customer for you?"

David: "Yes and no. They might be 25% of our traffic and trade. That's not small. But we're not really targetting them because I think they're a bit more inclined to be pulled in by off-price advertising. That's not what we do."

JCK: "How does inventory affect your marketing?"

David: "Our image is built on how we treat people, and how we present professional, knowledgeable information. I don't think it would change if we had different inventory. I think inventory has more impact on what market we want to get. We may have a wonderful image with people who are going to buy a $25,000 piece, but they're not coming to us because we don't have that inventory and they feel we can't serve their needs. But I don't think that has a negative impact on their belief in us as a professional. That client will come to us for professional service. They will come to us for appraisals, or for repair work. But maybe when it comes to buy the $25,000 piece they won't."

Day-To-Day Operations
September 1993 Part II

This is the classic battleground for the spenders and the savers.

You want to invest in a new line. Your spouse (or partner) says, "We can't afford it!"

You want to upgrade the computer software. Your spouse says the investment isn't needed.

You think the store looks pretty good as it is. Your spouse wants to put $50,000 into a total remodeling.

These are big decisions to fall under day-to-day operations but they belong there because their common denominator is that they involve the spending (or not spending) of company cash.

Smaller issues belong here, too. To buy or not to buy new cost-saving light bulbs. New equipment for the shop. Or for the gem lab.

There also are issues not directly related to cost control or spending. Turnaround time in the repair shop. The salespeoples' productivity. Debate on adding or dropping a supplier. Security.

It comes down to a matter of priorities. In preparing your business plan, it is not realistic to include a review of every part of your operations. The best you can hope to do is isolate areas where decisions you make will produce meaningful change. For routine expenses such as utilities, postage, phone bills, etc., the best bet is to check your income statement and, if any of these expenses are obviously out of line, add them to your list for special study.

How sound is your buying? This is a good place to start, for your buying decisions will affect many aspects of the business plan.

Have you a good buying plan in place? If not, then this is a must for your next business plan. There are some good sources to help you; one of the best is the *Jewelers' Inventory Manual* by Dick Laffin, which includes all the basics for setting up a sound buying plan. The book is available through JCK's Jewelers' Book Club. Whatever plan you prepare, be sure the open to buy includes a little mad money to spend on the unexpected. But beware of impulsive buying outside the discipline of your open to buy.

Over-impulsive buying can put you quickly on the slippery road to Chapter 11. One bad buy can wipe out your cash flow.

How you buy is as important as what you buy. Every purchase should be made with profit in mind. The majority of jewelers accept this philosophy, but some still insist on buying an item they think their customers will like, applying a standard markup (generally keystone plus)—and then watching the item sit and gather dust.

They were right that their customers would like the piece. What they failed to address is that their customers would like the piece *at a different price*. The way you should buy involves asking yourself, "What can I sell this piece for? How much will my customer pay for it?" If the difference between cost and proposed selling price is enough to give a satisfactory margin, you buy the piece. If it isn't, you don't. This approach ignores standard markup; instead it focuses on sales and profit.

Supplier relations. Buying and suppliers are naturally related topics. The only really relevant supplier issue for your business plan is whether you want to add or drop any firms.

This is the time to evaluate all suppliers with whom you do business. You should use a standard checklist covering all aspects of the relationship—the quality, depth and price of the supplier line, the availability of co-op ad funds, payment schedules, memo goods available, return privileges, and so on. You also should factor in your relationship with the supplier's salespeople and support people at headquarters with whom you deal.

A number of big jewelry chains told JCK in recent interviews that they're cutting back on the number of suppliers they use. They argue that it's in their best interests to be more important to fewer firms. Every jeweler should consider this point when preparing a business plan.

Productivity and profits. This is a vital area to review. The review can't cover every store operation, but at the very least it should address sales productivity and shop productivity if appropriate.

Jewelers of America's *Cost of Doing Business Survey* is an excellent place to find some helpful basic figures. It provides average sales per employee in various sizes and types of jewelry store. Kronos Jewelers, for example, has a dollar output per employee far below the average for its size—about $85,000 compared with $138,000.

David Onassis defends his lower figure on the grounds that he is "under-saled" rather than over-staffed. Jewelry industry consultants say they hear this argument often. But the issue isn't really whether a particular store has too few sales or too many employees. The issue is that the principals must recognize that they have a problem and should begin to solve it.

There are two alternatives in this case: increase sales or cut employees. Which solution you, as owner, choose is a matter of personal choice. What's not open to argument is that some action must be taken. David and Effie Onassis already have put in place an accountability program for their salespeople which they believe will soon lead to a significant increase in sales.

Productivity in the shop is less easy to measure, largely because the variety of work is so great and can include jewelry and watch repair as well as custom design. But well-kept records probably can provide useful guidelines on average number of jobs completed, turnaround time and quality control. Then there's the separate issue of profitability; repairs and special order work rarely are priced for maximum profit.

The store owner must address these issues in the business plan. There may be stores where the issues don't arise; productivity and profitability already are as good as they can and should be. The business plan offers the less perfect the opportunity to come up with steps that hasten the day when perfection arrives.

Cash flow and cash drought. In an ideal world there's always enough money in the bank to pay all the bills in 30 days—and then enough left over to splurge on some extras.

This is not an ideal world.

Cash flow control ultimately is an issue of self-discipline. Once more, the business plan is the vehicle that can help impose the discipline. The budget is so closely intertwined with operating the business day-to-day that the two must be considered together.

A well-planned and realistic budget forms the financial base for the entire business. If your sales forecasts are accurate and you control your expenses, then you should be able to plan for and expect a satisfactory cash flow. If you have a poor record as a sales forecaster and if you have had lack of discipline in controlling expenses, then this is where your business plan can help.

Look at your past weaknesses and draw up a series of goals that will help you overcome such weaknesses. Put those goals in your plan. Then follow them. If there have been big problems in the past, don't try to correct them all at once. Chip away at them. You may set three-year terms for some goals, and a single year for others. That's fine. There's nothing wrong with letting a new plan inherit some unfinished business from a predecessor.

A critical factor in cost control and budgeting is an accounting system that provides you with fast, accurate and timely information. This is where the computer comes in. This essential business tool must be used productively to be of real value—a matter that may be yet another concern to include in the business plan.

Of leases, remodeling, etc. Many other operating issues obviously exist. If a lease is coming up for renewal any time soon, what the jeweler may want in a new lease automatically becomes part of the business plan.

The same is true if the owner is thinking about relocating the store or going through a major remodeling. Each jeweler must decide individually which items to include; it is all a matter of priorities.

Kronos Jewelers looks at operations

JCK: "Judged by JA operating statistics, you are four or five people overstaffed for the volume you have. What are you doing to correct this?"

David: "We know we're over-payrolled, so we're going through a new process right now to deal with productivity. Our payroll ratio to sales is 4:1. That's nowhere near what it should be. And while it would be very nice to see 10:1 or 12:1, we'd be real happy to see 8:1. My goodness, that would mean with the same payroll dollars we've doubled our business.

"Our salespeople are starting to keep track of their sales and their productivity, which will be the basis for reviewing their success rate. As their success rate climbs, they start to pay us, if you will, and then somewhere along the line they'll get more themselves.

"Our people don't sit around idly wiping a showcase, waiting for someone to come in. They're busy. The problem is that we're paper heavy. We have too much paperwork. I think if we work at it, we can cut down on some of the paper flow and that means some of the jobs that our people are doing. A lot of the paperwork is involved in our appraisal and shop work, where we handle a great volume of work."

Effie: "That's the problem. I know stores that do comparable volume with four salespeople, one of whom is the manager and one's the owner. But if we only had two people to wait on customers and one went to lunch, we couldn't do it because of the number of repair jobs that we take in."

David: "Repairs probably account for 60% of the traffic in our store. It's not 60% of sales, of course. If we could turn some of that traffic into buying, we'd have some great opportunities. But we have to pay attention to what happens in our repair shop. If we start going too slow with our repair work, the prices become too high or quality of work is not appropriate, then we stand to lose major traffic in our store."

JCK: "It seems that if you can convert this add-on business out of your repairs, it becomes worthwhile. If you can't, then maybe you're doing yourself a disservice by maintaining something which creates a drag on your staff and doesn't produce a profit."

Effie: "We talked about that about a year and a half ago, about raising the price to eliminate some of the traffic. Your costs would stay the same but your margin would increase."

David: "Actually your costs would drop because as that traffic diminishes, you have less need of staffing to serve the traffic. I think that's a very good short-term fix, but I would suggest it's a remarkably dangerous long-term problem.

"However, I really don't believe that we have been terribly underpriced. There was a point where we hadn't changed prices for eight years. That's ridiculous, so we are much more price conscious today. Effie says we don't have to be the cheapest in the market. Why do we have to have the cheapest ring sizing? But we shouldn't be the highest, either. We did a major phone survey and sent shoppers into all the competition with repairs, and found out just what was being charged for what work and how long it took, then positioned ourselves right in between."

Effie: "Our turnaround on basic jewelry repairs is a week. It's done on the premises. There's only a handful of places, if that, in North Utopia where consumers can get their work done on the premises and in a week's time. So we're fine there. But we do have some problems with specialty work. That takes two to three weeks."

JCK: "Two to three weeks? I recall taking a special repair job to a nameless jeweler and it was seven months!"

David: "That happens from time to time."

Effie: "Those are the ones I get concerned about because they're often more complicated, higher dollar and a more influential customer. So of course they take three, four, five months."

David: "We're working to improve it. One thing we have improved is appraisals, where turnaround time now is probably four weeks, where a year or two ago it was two to three months, and five years ago you were on a waiting list for nine months before we could even get to it and then maybe it would get done.

"In spite of all that, we still have as much appraisal work as we want. But we're looking at ways to change our procedures. We want to do the formatting and the narratives of the appraisals more quickly, yet still deliver the quality product that our affiliations with professional organizations like ISA and our CGA title suggest.

"We use our computers for the word processing part of our appraisals. But I'm uncomfortable with the appraisal programs I've seen that do pricing for you. I don't like that formula pricing. Nor do a lot of the people I've talked to who are extremely knowledgeable in the appraisal field."

Effie: "We're thinking about offering two levels of appraisals."

David: "One would be done with the appropriate comparables and hard research. The other would carry appropriate disclaimers and explain that because we're taking less time, you the client, the insurance company or any third-party taking this report and accepting the conditions of it also accept that there is some degree of inaccuracy. But it's faster and costs less money.

"We've gotten to the point where our appraisals are 16-17 pages long. Take out two for the preface, that leaves 14-15 pages of support material. Then there's the actual value document itself.

"And that's not boiler plate. A lot of it is narrative that's talking about, 'Okay, we have this old European cut stone. What method of replacement is going be considered if a loss occurs?' Are you going to replace it with an exact duplicate? That means it has to be hand made. That's a hell of a lot more expensive than replacing it with a comparable, which says we go in the market and find something similar though not exact, which is going to be a different value than using a modern equivalent."

Effie: "We used to fly someone out here once every six weeks to do our appraisal work, paid him for his time, paid his air fare, and then had to redo a lot because he was working in a pressure situation and missed a lot. We've cut that expense by having someone trained on staff to do it. Now we're going to offer two levels of appraisals, and charge appropriately for them."

David: "We charge $45 now for the detailed appraisal, but we could charge $100 or $125."

JCK: "We've talked a lot about your strengths. What about some weaknesses?"

Effie: "Some things do affect our ability to compete as well as we might. There are a lot of operational things that we push aside in lieu of other things. We've already talked about staff compensation versus their productivity. And we don't have benefit or procedure manuals. We've started writing a benefit manual several times and been stopped by the legality of it and been fearful to actually complete it.

"We don't plan our cash flow specifically. We don't really look at it monthly. Also we have a lack of buying controls. And we don't have a monthly P&L. We look at it yearly when the accountant gives it to us.

"We're working on over-compensation, the need to get productivity and salaries in line. I have the videotape and the cassette tapes from Harry Friedman's program, but I haven't listened to them. So I don't know if we'll actually get it finished. That would be an achievement for '93.

"The failure to plan cash flow, buying controls and the P&L would be solved by getting our computer up and running. But we keep running into the time element because I'm primarily the one to do the inputting, and I always seem to have other responsibilities that take precedence."

JCK: "How do you set priorities?"

Effie: "Whoever screams the loudest."

David: "Unfortunately, we're still crisis management oriented, though less so today than we were five years ago."

Effie: "For a long time, until two years ago, I didn't have a bookkeeper. I didn't have an assistant to follow me around and clean up after me and follow through on things. Someone who knew everything about the business that I do and would be able to make judgements and decisions. So we're getting better, it's just happening slowly."

David: "And then there's a problem setting priorities. There are a thousand and one things we ought to do to make our business run better and be more profitable, and that in itself creates a problem.

"That's where a business plan is really helpful. We can say, 'Okay, we think that being on the computer is important, but we think that setting a more targeted goal for our marketing is more important.' So we'll spend the next three months taking a really hard look at marketing and developing a marketing plan for the next five years. Then we'll tackle the next thing."

JCK: "Let's take a look at purchasing."

David: "I handle loose diamonds and colored stones, with input, but Effie handles basically everything else. Again with input from staff. You know, everyone may gather around the salesman's line and look..."

Effie: "And help make decisions. So if we come across a colored stone, and we think this could be a fairly good value that we can get a good margin on, we might leave it to Harriet or Linda to make a decision. We're saying they have the okay to do it if they feel it's a good thing to do—or the authority to say no."

JCK: "If you were going to add any suppliers, what criteria would you use?"

David: "The product, product category, who they sell in the market. And then reputation of the company or the character of the salesman. If we're dealing with a company and we like the line a lot, but the salesman is an unpleasant sort of person, that has a major influence on whether or not we consider putting in a line."

Effie: And there are a handful of salesmen I wouldn't let in the door because they harass the sales staff at times."

JCK: "How about your location? You were in a shopping center. Why did you leave it?"

David: "We'd been located in the shopping center since 1959. It had been under one particular owner from out of town for a good number of years. We had an excellent working relationship with that owner. His family partnership sold the shopping center to a local fellow who came to us, although we had two and a half years left on our lease, and wanted us to give up our extremely favorable rates for current rates.

"We agreed to talk because we felt that if we gave up two and a half years of equity in the lease—maybe $30,000-$40,000—we might get favorable treatment that would offset it. Instead, we were presented with an ultimatum, which was: 'You will sign a new lease, you will sign at current rates and, if you don't, two and a half years from now, we won't give you a lease and we'll put you out of business. We'll put another jeweler in your place. That prompted us to ask whether this was somebody we wanted to deal with at all.

"We opted to say no; in effect, we told them to go fly a kite. So we started looking for a new location and fortunately we found one. Then our landlord decided to come talk to us, saying 'We want you to stay. What can we do to keep you here?' They offered us a 20-year fixed-rate lease. But by then, it was too late.

"We're going to own our own building shortly. That has created some financial stress. But it was time for remodeling our old location, so I would have put in at least $50,000, maybe $75,000, for that. And our rent was going to go up. If we combined the payback costs of the remodeling with the increased rent, and its projected increases over time, it would have been close to our current costs of operating this building, with a difference of maybe $1,000 a month. For that difference we own a building, or will soon.

"The beauty of it is that we expected a drop in traffic when we moved out of the shopping center, but actually our traffic and sales increased."

Effie: "Of course there is a lot more expense to owning a free-standing building than being in a shopping center. A lot more time and effort has to go into maintaining a building, just like maintaining a home."

The People Factor

September 1993 Part II

This is the people section of your business plan. It is the place for candid evaluations of all the people who fulfill the role of manger in your store—a very difficult exercise in a smaller business where the owner and possibly his or her spouse form the sole management team. If this is your situation, turn to an outsider for help since candid self-evaluation is next to impossible.

But let's assume the store has more than one manager. Also let's assume that any person who has any management responsibilities falls in this category.

What we need to know first is the management structure:

• Who is responsible for what duties and who reports to whom?

• What are the qualifications needed in each position and does the present holder have such qualifications?

• If not, what is being done to rectify the situation?

• What changes, if any, need to be made in the job description for each particular role?

• What about compensation?

It is a given that there should be a job description for each position in the company. It's also a given in a smaller company that a manager's job description probably is fairly fluid, changing and/or expanding in response to various needs, many of them unanticipated. That isn't an excuse for not having an up-to-date description. You, as owner, need some known yardstick against which you can measure performance. Chances are that if you rely purely on hunches and "personal observation" (namely, seeing the person at work every day) your evaluation will not be fair to the company, to the employee or both.

How well do you know each manager's qualifications and skills? As part of your business plan you should write down all this information. It can have various uses. It gives you the chance to consider whether what you "feel" about each person tallies with the real facts. It may prompt you to change a particular manager's duties or to arrange training to improve a particular skill. And it will be a valuable guide if, for whatever reason, you have to replace that person.

Compensation obviously belongs here. This issue intertwines with the owner's management philosophy and style, for here is where we decide whether we're talking straight salary, salary and bonus, or commission and/or bonus after a draw. It is only reasonable that if a manager is expected to reach certain goals in his or her department or area of responsibility there should be some reward if that goal is reached or exceeded.

Only the owner can decide what the compensation structure will be. As owner, you may want to discuss the issue frankly with your managers.

Rating performance. How do you evaluate performance? Do you use a standardized evaluation form or one designed specifically for your business? Do you keep a writ-ten record? It may sound callous, but in this litigious age a written record is essential.

Do you extend your evaluations to outsiders you use as regular support for the business—your attorney, your accountant, your insurance agent and any other person to whom you may turn for business advice? Clearly you're not going to ask your attorney to fill out a written evaluation form! But you should stop every once in a while and ask yourself if your attorney (or accountant, etc.) provides the service you want and expect, whether this person is responsive to your needs, whether past advice has proven useful and so on.

Let's face it. You're probably paying a lot of dollars to these advisors and you must be sure you're getting value for your money. Your customers expect this of you; in this case you're the customer and you, too, should expect and get the best.

Management style. What sort of business life do you want? If your goal is to run a comfortable, easy-going store where the staff is friendly and "like a family," where the merchandise is okay but nothing special, and where customers like to drop in to chat and are loyal enough to buy their wedding, anniversary and other gifts, that's fine. At least it's fine if you operate in a sheltered market with minimum competition. If the competition is tough you may well smile yourself right out of business.

Or your goal may be to take a million-dollar business to five million within five years. Then you'll be a driven jeweler, pushing for volume where you can get it and setting steep sales goals for your staff.

These are obvious extremes. If you haven't already done so, when you next sit down to write a business plan describe as carefully and accurately as you can what sort of business you want to be. Also, realistically, assess your own management style and your relations with your employees. Do you view them as employees, as friends, as people who can help you make money? As all three?

It's a somewhat high-risk venture, but you also might like to ask your employees to rate you. Let them use a standard evaluation form to make their assessment as objective as possible.

Your management style, whatever it is, determines almost everything about your business—whom you hire, how you deal with them, what you buy and how you price the merchandise, how you'll promote your message to the public and which customers you'll most likely attract.

With so much in the balance, it's well to be sure what your style is.

Kronos Jewelers looks at its people

David: "When my father left the business and I took over a lot of his duties, I had no set qualifications. Just being in the business was it. I was running on the seat of my pants. I attended some management programs and we belonged to a small management group, so I was picking up things. And, of course, I grew up with it.

"As critical as my father was to the business and its plans and future growth, we had only a six-month downturn of about 10% when he left, and then just took off again. That taught me that no one is indispensable. We always try to build a team, people that can pick up for other people, so that our business doesn't suffer if someone's out."

JCK: "You two would be considered the management of the company, now, right?"

David: "No. We have a management team. Linda functions as the floor sales manager; Russ is our shop manager; Harriet is our appraisal services division manager or director; and Susan basically runs the office. She oversees primary bookkeeping and clerical elements, sees that maintenance is followed through on, and oversees the person who handles some of the ordering.

"Russ is responsible for processing the work through his shop and getting it out to the people in the front to get it out to the customers. He orders and maintains inventory for the shop, schedules the work, oversees any other jewelers he may have working for him. We actually run the shop as a separate entity. It's still under one corporation, but has its own P&L and Russ is paid a flat sum plus a share of the net profits.

"Linda is responsible for the sales staff. She sees that they do their job selling, helps them if they're having a problem, handles scheduling. She is critical in implementing our new accountability program.

"Harriet basically runs all the appraisal work and things associated with it, like handling estate merchandise that comes in on consignment. She's responsible for processing and doing a good percentage of the appraisal work and comes to me only when she really has a problem or has some overflow she wants some assistance with. She also oversees the processing of diamond stock. When diamonds come in, she's responsible for verifying the goods against the invoice, checking the grades, applying a retail value to them. And the same thing with colored stones.

"Effie and I fill in on everything else. She is the financial controller person and the overall personnel director that everyone reports to. She does a fair amount of work on implementing advertising and promotion and that sort of thing. I sit back with my feet up."

Effie: "You do long-term strategizing and promoting the whole company philosophy. You're the creative person. You'll say, 'Oh, well, we don't have to do it this way. Can we do it this way?'"

David: "If there is a particular problem with a customer's job, I'll definitely be brought in, either to work with the customer or provide technical support. And I just kind of keep my fingers in everything. Sometimes it's intrusive and a problem; sometimes it's beneficial.

"When I joined the business, I had no formal training. I was a high school graduate, no college. But I went to GIA for the GG program, and then through the AGS program, RG, CG. I'm an ISA member and have gone through four courses. And that would be the extent of my formal education.

"Effie came into the business in 1980. Actually that's where we met."

Effie: "I was looking for a job; I had graduated from high school and there were no plans for college. I was a salesperson. But we started seeing each other and my brain started

working more as an owner, although I was still a salesperson. That caused a lot of conflict with David's mother. So two and a half years later she fired me and I quit at the same time. I went into retail catalog sales with a book company and then into selling ladies' apparel. I managed a mall chain store. It was a nice cushy job. I didn't appreciate it at the time."

David: "And then around 1986, there was an opening. My mother talked about not working as much, and Effie knew the business, had additional retail background and knew the bookkeeping elements. So, she worked into things that much more quickly, and basically took over what my mother had been doing. By that time, we were married."

Effie: "Linda's really the only one with a college background. She did three and a half years, but never graduated. It's all been on-the-job experience. Susan, for example, managed her family restaurant. Harriet has never worked anywhere but here. Her formal education is GIA correspondence courses, the RJ and ISA courses. Linda has taken some GIA courses, though I don't know if she's completed them all. In fact, I'm not certain she ever will. But she is a top salesperson."

JCK: "JA's operating statistics show sales per employee—counting everybody who's full-time, the principals and all—of about $138,000 for a store of your size, where you have about $85,000. So we come back to you being overstaffed. Now this is a matter of philosophy; you can run a business this way if you like, and that's fine."

Effie: "I feel that we're not so much overstaffed as we are undersaled. We don't make that much of an effort to be professional salespeople. A lot of times it's busy in the store and there are people waiting. Our philosophy has always been to take care of a customer as quickly as possible and get on to the next one, instead of saying to that customer, 'By the way, I have something really neat to show you,' and trying to make add-on sales."

David: "And yet we have a philosophy of taking as much time as necessary with the engagement ring customer, 10 hours if we need it. I don't know if we're really going to change how we approach our engagement ring traffic, and that accounts for some of the ratio of sales to hours worked, if you will."

JCK: "Do you encourage salespeople to call customers if they see something nice in the store they think the client might like?"

Effie: "Yes and no. We haven't required or pushed people to do that, but they know that it's a technique that exists to increase sales. Linda took a sales course last fall, that we've just started to implement recently. We're hoping that this sort of follow-up will be a regular occurrence, but up until now, it hasn't been."

JCK: "You mentioned that Harriet spends a lot of her time taking in consignment, logging it, getting into the estate case. Is this justified by the volume and goodwill and whatever?"

David: "It's hard to guess, but I'd say at any one time we probably have 200 consignment pieces in the store. It seems when we get something on consignment it's usually multiple items, not just one. They probably flow in and out at the rate of maybe 5 to 10 pieces a week."

Effie: "And there are probably 50 waiting to be taken care of."

David: "Is it profitable and beneficial? There's a short margin. The top margin on a consignment piece is 45%, except on loose diamonds and loose color that's not beat up; we get a better margin on that.

"So what are we doing it for? Service, reputation. We handle a customer who wants to sell an item as differently as we handle the engagement ring customer. A customer who comes in to sell an item doesn't say, 'I want to put it on consignment.' They come in blindly saying, 'I want to sell. Do you buy?' 'Yes.' 'Then let's talk.' So we will spend a half hour to an hour giving them options. Consignment is one we can provide, but we also encourage them to consider bartering, selling privately, going to auction, trading it out whether with us or with someone else."

Effie: "We've discussed ways to try and make this less labor intensive. Because David primarily does all of this. I would guesstimate over 50% of his appointments are with people who want to sell things. We want to maintain that sense of professionalism and giving them something that no other jeweler will give them, which is information, but not have it take that length of time."

JCK: "If you were talking to another jeweler who'd never done a business plan, what would you tell him?"

Effie: "That he needs to do one, but he needs outside help doing it. I don't think that we as business owners are anywhere near objective enough."

David: "The main benefit of doing a business plan is that you can't get there if you don't know where you want to go."

Effie: "It has helped, and will continue to help us define what we really want and where we want our business to go. I think we are not unlike a lot of business owners who get caught up in the day-to-day stuff. This makes you step back and look at more of the overall picture. But again, I can't stress enough how beneficial the third-party aspect has been for me. Because we come complete with our biases and prejudices."

David: "Over the past five or six years we've talked about developing a board of directors to ask the questions we may not ask ourselves. And while we may not be legally responsible to that board, if we spend our money developing it and giving the directors some sort of compensation and meeting from time to time, we're going to pay a bit of attention."

What Does Your Future Hold?

September 1993 Part II

This is the time to look beyond the next 12 months and to set or reset goals for the future. Perhaps the most important goal is to be sure what your ultimate wishes are—to pass the business on to a child, to sell out to some other jeweler for a nice profit, to close down the business when you're ready to quit.

Your mission statement should help you here—if it does not, then there's something wrong with either the statement or your long-term goals.

What are your goals and your priorities in reaching them?

Making a profit? How big a profit? Will your present merchandise mix give you the margins you need? What sort of money do you want to draw from the business to achieve what net worth by what date?

What level of sales do you want to reach to produce such profits?

Expanding the business? What plans have you to add stores or to add people? How specific are your plans in both areas? What is your time frame?

What steps do you plan to enhance your position in your present market and increase share-of-market? Will you change merchandise mix? Change suppliers?

To what extent will you try to reach into new markets? How and when?

What plans have you to diversify your financial base? Do you want to invest in real estate—and perhaps own your own or other properties? How about new ventures outside the jewelry field? What are they? How and when will you make the move?

What about your goals for your staff? What do you want to do for them that you're not doing now? How will you achieve these goals? When?

How do you want your business to grow? As it is now, only more so? Is your long-term goal to become more of a specialist or more of a generalist? How would you like to be able to describe your business five years from now? Ten years?

For each goal, you need a strategy. Are such strategies in place? If not, when will you formulate them and when implement them?

Finally, what priorities have you set among your many goals? As you set your priorities, what risk factor have you assigned to the achievement of each goal?

Guidelines. In a small, busy company, coping with day-to-day and month-to-month issues tends to occupy so much of the owners' time that thinking in year-long terms becomes a luxury—or a casualty. Thinking about the long term may seem an impossible dream in these circumstances.

But to lose sight of the long term is a cardinal sin.

Just as the whole staff should operate constantly with the store's mission statement as a guiding principle, so should the owners operate with the mission statement *and* the long-term goals as their guiding principles. These goals may not be a part of day-to-day operations, but they should be reviewed regularly. The annual business plan offers the best time and place to do the review and, if necessary, make a change or changes in emphasis.

Kronos Jewelers looks at the future
David: "Looking ahead, I'd like to increase sales volume, and margin. I don't necessarily want to increase employees until we can get more productivity out of our existing employees."

Effie: "I'd like to increase benefits. We don't have a pension plan, and I'd like to have one. I'd like to be able to pay our employees better. Not that we pay them badly. But we have to see performance. Then we can reward them even more. I'd like to increase what they get out of it and maintain employee loyalty."

David: "We have no desire at the moment for additional stores. But I'd like to become more of a dominant force in the market, especially in the engagement ring market. I want to be on everybody's list when it comes to shopping for engagement rings as one place that you must always at least go. That's going to take advertising and promotion."

Effie: "And continuing to improve our engagement ring follow-up, even with people who stop in and do not buy, so there's a continual reminder of Kronos Jewelers."

JCK: "Where is your market going? Is this a strong market? Is it growing?"

David: "I think the Utopia market has been strong in the past and will continue to be. Our unemployment rate of about 5% is much lower than the national average. We have great diversity in our economy, with agricultural, service, and industrial sectors. Of course, there is a major plant due to close, which would cut maybe 3,500 jobs.

"However, that's not in our immediate market. And it's going to hurt some other jewelers more than us. We're located in the corporate heart of the county, with a lot of middle management people. And although companies have been downsizing, we've been surviving reasonably well. I think we've gone through the worst of that downsizing now and it shouldn't get any worse. Then, too, there's an expanding market here in the financial services end, with growing employment. These are more our type of customer.

"We're in a state that is in financially sound shape. We've got fiscally responsible politicians that work together to get jobs done. We haven't had a deficit in years.

"It helps that our sales tax is lower than in nearby states. That brings us a lot of customers. In fact, it's one of our reasons for trying to reach a little bit into the Big City market.

"We don't really advertise it. But we had one guy come in from out-of-state who'd seen our name in a book somewhere. He thought, 'Hey, there's not much sales tax there, so let's go down and see what they can do.' It resulted in a several thousand dollar engagement ring sale."

"*Effie:* "We'd like to break into a higher-end market. But there already are an awful lot of stores in our area that try to gear to that market."

David: "I think we can pick off certain aspects of it. It will take some time and thought, but we can do it without a great deal of investment in inventory. We might be able to access that market by providing a service—namely special design—that some of the other stores aren't as capable of providing."

JCK: "How about the corporate gift market? Do you do anything there?"

David: "No. We've talked about it and I think we might target more aggressively sometime."

Effie: "One problem with getting into that market is that we don't carry a lot of giftware."

JCK: "You've talked about converting more of your repair customers into buyers."

David: "Yes. We probably average somewhere around 150 jewelry and watch repair jobs a week."

Effie: "That doesn't include things like restringing, watch repairs, special orders, battery replacements. It's just stuff like chain solders, ring solders, ring sizing."

JCK: "Is this profitable work?"

David: "We've structured the shop as a separate division and broken out all the appropriate expenses to it, as though it were a separate wholesale trade shop. Russ, our jeweler is paid a salary and a draw and a share of the net profit. It used to operate at a loss before Russ came here, but now we've achieved what looks like a breakeven position and it is our belief that we can make it profitable."

JCK: "Does the repair business generate sales?"

David: "It generates goodwill, word of mouth and occasionally, accidentally, some sales. That's our goal, making more sales off of those repairs."

Effie: "I think our staff's mentality, and that includes me, is to take care of the repair. This customer is just coming in for a repair, so we finish the job, have some nice chit chat and say goodbye. We don't try to do any suggestive selling. And that's something we hope to change."

JCK: "As a business, how do you want to relate to your employees?"

Effie: "There are certain things I would like to be able to achieve for our staff. I'd like them to be a happy, emotionally healthy, growing group of young professionals. I guess I shouldn't say young, but most of them are now. I want them to really like their job, be very excited to come to work in the morning and be well compensated for that.

"Our numbers suggest they are well compensated, but when I look individually, I'd like this person to make $10,000 more a year. I wish I could afford to give her that right now, because I feel she deserves it. And I wish that person could make this amount more a year, because I think she really earns it."

How Am I Doing?

September 1993 Part II

Invite jewelers to a conference and offer seminars on sales training, motivation, marketing and finance. Guess which one won't be well attended? The answer is too easy. It's the one on finance, of course. But financial statements are the corporate skeleton; without that skeleton there's nothing to support the company's flesh and blood.

In this section of the business plan we're including some of Kronos Jewelers' key financials: the income statement, balance sheet and cash flow statements along with payments-to-vendors and open-to-buy reports. The income statements and balance sheets are projected through fiscal 1996; detail is given just for fiscal 1994, which ends June 30 next year.

For comment on Kronos' financial health we turned to Willis Cowlishaw, who not only made all the projections in cooperation with David Onassis but also offers the following comments:

The Cowlishaw report. David Onassis expects to achieve the sales and financial goals that are outlined here.

He knows that "flying by the seat of his pants" is responsible for his current inventory problems. Vendors are playing the role of his banker, as they do for most jewelers in the industry. David has made a commitment to live by the open-to-buy plan in the *future*.

David needs professional help. He's very comfortable selling by appointment; he has not made the commitment to manage his million-dollar-plus business *profitably*.

Having said that, I have to report that fiscal 1993 was a stunningly successful year. Sales increased 24% to $1,298,686 from $1,046,222 in 1992; gross margin improved from 51.9% to 52.3%, a very healthy condition.

Fiscal '93 sales were up 12% over 1991—the best year ever for Kronos Jewelers. Sales were down in 1992 because of the local economic climate. Even so, gross margin increased from 50.26% in 1991 to 51.9% in '92.

Look at additional highlights of the 1993 income statement! Net income before taxes reached $49,181, up from $1,108 in 1992. Interest expense declined from $17,222 to $14,933.

Rent is very low at 2.17% of sales. Marketing costs of 7.5% are high by industry standards. But consider rent and marketing expense together to compare expenses with other jewelers.

This store relocated from a shopping center to a residential/business mixed use area in 1990. The location is not easy to find; definitely a destination store. David will need to commit substantial marketing costs to continue to build customer awareness of the convenience of drive-up shopping.

Total salary costs, including benefits and owners' compensation, are high at 28%. Sales associates are not on commission. A new incentive plan will be implemented in 1994 to improve productivity.

Examine the balance sheet. Ratio of current assets to current liabilities is 2.94—a very strong condition.

Inventory reached an unplanned level of $444,732 at the end of the fiscal year on June 30. This is the wrong time to peak. Accounts payable increased by $40,000 to $140,000 because of the high inventory balance. Turnover of inventory reached 1.39% for 1993—substantially better than comparable industry standards.

Projections for 1994. The sales goal of $1,325,000 certainly is realistic and attainable. Actually, it may be too low with current momentum.

I question the ability to increase gross margin *again* this year. The trend from 1991 through 1993 of 50.26% to 52.3% is very commendable. The 1994 projection of 52.9% will be a real stretch. Operational expenses are based on achieving this goal.

Caution: If the gross margin remains at the current level of 52.3% in 1994, there will be a net loss of $14,000 if all other projections stay constant.

The rent increases from $28,000 to $39,000 in 1994. David bought his building (with settlement in July) and the increase will cover the mortgage and taxes.

Full and proper use of the computer will improve productivity (through improved records, among other things) and reduce payroll. The manual systems now in place must be eliminated.

The cash flow and open-to-buy reports will enable David to manage inventory levels better. He has committed to reduce accounts payable by $50,000 during the next 90 days.

The lack of capital requires that the firm continue to sell diamonds from memorandum. Employees can be directed to sell merchandise from stock to help correct the inventory overage and provide cash for purchases.

Exercise for cash flow management. Cash flow analysis is the single most important financial assessment. It is not about profit. It is about how much money you have in the bank and the amount of money going in and out of your business on a monthly basis.

To help you understand the cash flow of Kronos Jewelers—and your own business—you need to use the figures from three reports: Cash flow projections, payments to vendors and open to buy.

Example: Cash flow for December 1994 shows cash receipts of $301,376. This is a total of cash, credit card receipts and payments on account.

Cash disbursements total $139,611. This includes operating expenses of $80,740 and the cost of inventory of $58,871. The question is: Where does the $58,871 come from? The answer is in the payments to vendors report.

Line 1—Scheduled payments to vendors	$20,000
Line 2—Memo sales	$30,331
Line 3—Purchases	$ 4,608
Line 4—Repairs	$ 3,932
Total	$58,871

Look at the open-to-buy report. It shows memo sales of $30,331 (contracted for in November and paid for in 30 days) and purchases of $4,608 (bought 60 days previously). Repair materials are paid for in the month they are bought.

Thus your ending cash balance for December is $224,077 — cash receipts of $301,376 minus cash disbursements of $139,611 plus the opening cash balance of $62,312.

Select several months of the Kronos cash flow projections and use the figures from the vendors' payment and open-to-buy reports to work out the cash flow. Continue until you reach a comfort level.

Cash flow analysis is particularly important for stores with large inventories or those that sell on credit. You must plan for the slow months and the long time-lag between buying, selling and realizing cash receipts.

Instructions and terminology:
Cash flow projections.
Cash receipts:
Income from sales
    Cash sales include sales made on all credit cards.
    Payments on accounts receivable include layaway deposits and all income collected from sales made in a previous period. Kronos treats all layaways as charge sales.
Cash disbursements:
Expenses
    Cost of inventory. Actual payments made for merchandise, including memo and repair material.
    Operating expenses. Actual payment on items in this category—salaries, rent, marketing, etc. Do not include depreciation.
Net cash flow:
    Opening cash balance. Amount of money in the bank at the beginning of the month.
    Cash receipts. All cash received.
    Cash disbursements. All payments made.
Ending cash balance:
    Cash in the bank after receipts and disbursements.

Instructions and terminology:
Payments to vendors, 1994
    Kronos Jewelers is in a heavy inventory position and owes vendors $140,103. The company has agreed to a 12-month payment schedule and will pay for all *new purchases* within 60 days. Memorandum merchandise will be paid within 30 days of sale.
    Beginning accounts payable: Total, $140,103 (amount paid monthly as agreed)
    Memo: Merchandise sold in the *previous* month.
    Purchases: Merchandise *bought* 60 days previously.
    Repair: Materials purchased *this* month.
    Total: Total disbursement for merchandise and material.

    Conclusion. In summary, Kronos Jewelers is well positioned for continued success.
    • The core business is diamonds.
    • It is a one-price store. The price on the ticket is the sale price.
    • The markup is highly competitive.
    The traditional statement, "If you don't know diamonds, know your jeweler," is what Kronos Jewelers and David Onassis are all about.

Kronos Jewelers looks at its financials
    David: "Our fiscal sales figures will be coming in in just a few days, and probably should show us finishing at about $1.275 million, although we're hoping for $1.3. To be modest, we expect our sales growth for the next fiscal year, 1993-'94, will take us to $1.325. We'll use that figure for budgeting purposes, but push for something greater. Then we look for $1.4 for the next fiscal year and, by June 30, 1996, $1.5 million. That would give us increases of 4% to 7%. But it would be nice if we could hit $1.5 million next year—and it's a possibility if things really go great."
    JCK: "What are your primary plans to increase sales?"
    David: "We expect two things to have an impact on sales. One is trying to get greater productivity out of traffic that's presently coming in. I think it will be fairly easy prospecting if our sales staff will work toward that end. We've started; we're three weeks into the early stages and it's been interesting seeing their reactions to looking at their sales on a weekly basis."
    JCK: "Does everybody see everybody else's goals?"
    David: "Not yet. We'll probably start posting individual sales goals and sales made by the first of the year.
    "The second way we'll improve sales is to increase the amount and/or quality of traffic through our marketing effort. Continuing to devote a strong 7%-7.5% of annual volume to advertising will put us over $100,000 in ad dollars for the coming fiscal year. That's a strong budget, and we feel that we just need to keep pumping.
    "We've seen sales growth. The recession did hit us, but softly. Although the recovery reportedly has been very weak, we've come on quite strong. We've gone from last year's sales of just a million fifty in the trough of the recession to this year's sales pushing $1.3 million. That's a 25% jump in business in this environment."
    JCK: "How about specific merchandise lines? Do you forecast sales growth by line or by category?"
    David: "I've projected sales for our main product and service departments; that would be diamonds, colored stones, watches, gold jewelry, rings, non-karat gold, estate and gift/miscellaneous merchandise categories, plus repairs, appraisals and what not. I've taken this out to fiscal 1995-'96 and it shows an increase across the board.
    "That growth keeps everything pretty much in line with what it represents today as a percentage of overall business —with some exceptions. We're looking at maybe a 30% increase in non-karat gold jewelry over a three-year period. I expect that to come about as a result of some of the direct mail marketing we're going to do. But these are small-dollar parts of the business. Watches may take a jump; we're trying to work out a deal to bring back one line we had a problem with. I see diamond sales going from about $560,000 this fiscal year to $625,000 next year."
    JCK: "Are you doing anything specific with diamonds to produce that?"
    David: "Not really. But I think we'll see our engagement ring business continue to grow, because the more people we serve, the more referrals we'll get. It's almost geometric, one person, two people, four people and so forth.
    "In addition, we've got a fairly aggressive ad campaign oriented toward non-engagement-ring diamond jewelry. It's all tied in to the De Beers co-op advertising effort. I think

the 25th diamond anniversary necklace is going to be important, maybe almost as important as the anniversary ring was. And that's new business for us, because we've done very little with diamond fashion jewelry. There's also the inflation factor. Diamond prices probably will go up a little bit.

"I expect a reasonable jump in colored stones. People like color; it's something they find easy to get excited about. But I'm predicting a rather modest increase in karat gold jewelry."

JCK: "Let's take a look at profits."

David: "As we look at projected expenses for fiscal years 1993-'94 and 1994-'95, we want to see expenses drop as a percent of volume. If we can just keep our profit margin even, obviously we're raise our operating profit if we can cut our expenses. They'll go up in dollars, but anticipating an increase in sales, we hope to reduce expenses from 49.4% of sales this past year to about 48.5% for the 1993-'94 year and then about 47% for 1994-'95.

"The largest expense we have is our payroll. Counting salaries for officers and everyone, it was almost 27% of volume in fiscal 1991-'92. It should be around 26% in the fiscal year just ending, 25% in fiscal 1993-'94, and 23% in 1994-'95. That's a slow move. We'd like to see our payroll ratio to sales go from less than 4:1, as it is now, to 6:1. But as sales go up, we'll have to see some increase in payroll dollars, too.

"I suspect certain individuals will be key to the majority of our sales increase and some other individuals who won't be. It's conceivable those individuals won't necessarily be staying around, though that's not a goal we want to achieve. But if we get more productivity out of our traffic—and it doesn't take a lot to see a 10% increase—we'd be at $1.450 million next year. And then salary could go up $15,000 or $20,000, which would be nice to distribute among the key selling people. That's not a bad increase for their extra effort, yet still keeps payroll at a smaller percentage.

"More importantly, I'd like to see an increase in gross margin. We're about 49% now. I'd like to see that get to 50% as an overall store margin. We need to buy better and intentionally mark up. If the public believes we're high priced and we know we're not, then we have to wonder. Are we paying too much for goods ,because even with a shorter margin it's still high priced for the market? Or do they think we're high priced simply because we don't discount price?"

Effie: "When we've done surveys in the past, the perception has been that Kronos Jewelers is expensive."

David: "But that's usually followed up with, 'They give good service and fine quality.' There's a difference between being expensive and providing value.

"My point is that our increase in gross margin will occur by trying to buy better so we can get better margin, which I think maybe our market will bear."

Effie: "Buying better also means trying to buy items that people can't easily shop, that are more exclusive."

JCK: "What about your suppliers? Do you feel that you've got a good mix of all the people you'd like to have?"

Effie: "Sometimes I think we want higher-end merchandise than we can sell in our store at this time. But I think we have a good mix of suppliers and services."

David: "We're not unhappy at all with our sources; they service us extremely well. They provide us with reasonable values. We have long-term relationships with a lot of them. So when cash flow is tight, if we stretch out payment 60, 90,

120 days sometimes, they are very nice and caring about it and don't bother us at all. That's been built upon meeting obligations and being very straightforward with our suppliers.

"When we looked at cash flow recently, we saw that we had some problems coming up. If we're looking at July and cash is tight now, it's going to be tighter in November. You know it's not going to ease up until we get into December. So we sent letters to our suppliers saying, 'Our books indicate that we owe you this now. We're already 60 days on it. We expect that it's going to be tight. You can anticipate getting payment from us every month. You know we'll make good as we have done in the past on any obligations we have, and we expect to be completely caught up with you by January. But we wanted to let you know.'

"Some suppliers have acted harshly to that; I think it's because they don't understand it. I'm not sure that many retailers would have contacted them that quickly. A couple suppliers we weren't even 30 days with wanted to slow us up. They wanted to hold shipments and things like that. When we talked to them, we realize they thought we were in serious trouble. But we explained, 'No, it's just that we have an obligation to meet payments by a certain time and we know we're not going to be able to and we wanted you to know that.' That has built a good relationship with suppliers. They know we're not going to take the goods and run and not pay."

JCK: "Has this happened because of any shortcomings in your business? Or is it just endemic to the jewelry business?"

David: "I think that is certainly typical of jewelry businesses in general."

Effie: "But it's also because of overbuying."

David: "And if we overbuy in the spring, it's a long time until the next good selling season. We've tried to do something about that. Three or four months in the spring and at least one in the summer were slow months and are now important for us. But it's been at the cost of putting more advertising dollars out, which don't always come back for a year or two."

JCK: "How do you feel about your volume? Is it pretty well managed or are you in danger of overbuying at times?"

David: "Controlling inventory is one of the difficulties that we have. Not that our inventory is that far out of control We sit with inventory between $375,000 and $400,000 with $1.2 million in sales.

"But when you have tight cash flow, as we do, and not a lot of cash reserve, if you overbuy by just $50,000, cash flow is gone."

Effie: "Which can happen pretty easily. I mean, you get excited at a show or when the salespeople come in, and then all of a sudden you bring it back to the store and it sits there for six months."

David: "I don't think we fully like how we've done our budgeting for buying, but we've recognized that. So in the past year we actually sat down and did a fairly hardcore buying budget. We broke it down by 40 some classifications, with projected sales for the season and anticipated gross margins, then we looked at our inventory in those categories and said where we were going to put our dollars. Sometimes it worked, except we opened up a couple of lines that we were not planning on opening. I don't know if that's discipline or being a risk taker."

Action Plan: Things To Be Done

September 1993 Part II

After more than a month of discussing their business with JCK and Willis Cowlishaw, digging into their records for facts and figures, and examining most parts of store operations, David and Effie Onassis had the details they needed for a fiscal 1994 business plan.

Was all the effort worthwhile? Definitely, they said. It helped them decide that they have to commit to certain actions over the next 12 months. In a general sequence of importance, these are:

1. Do a better job of setting priorities. "We operate by crisis management too much," David admitted.

2. Get the computer up and running with all systems at full strength. This will help bring needed efficiency to inventory and financial control, among other benefits.

3. Get a better handle on inventory. Specifically work the year's starting inventory of $440,000 down to $380,000 by year-end. That would put an extra $60,000 in cash into the business.

4. Exercise more discretion in buying. Kronos Jewelers has created some of its own cash-flow problems by buying impulsively. David says impulsive buying isn't all bad by any means. He sees it as a strength for the independent jeweler who can be flexible enough to react quickly to a trend. Chains, on the other hand, he says, are committed to buy by formula. But he says "impulsive" buys must be made with greater attention to customer needs and the firm's general financial picture.

5. Proceed with sales staff accountability program. The plan, introduced earlier this year, records all sales by each salesperson, a new store practice. By the end of 1993, the owners hope to post monthly sales figures for each person, giving recognition to the high (and low) performers. David is confident the staff will respond to the challenge and that the program will lead to much higher sales, not the need to lay off under-performers.

6. Assess the effectiveness of store advertising. David and Effie have been satisfied with their advertising, noting for example that a diamond engagement ring ad in the state Metropolis—some 40 miles away—usually brings "a flood" of responses. However, a JCK-sponsored spot check with consumers in Kronos' market area found the store had low name recognition. David has given a copy of the report to his ad man; they will discuss whether they should change their approach, which is heavily institutional.

7. Do a better job with time management. Appraisals show the greatest need for attention. Today they involve about 75% of the time of someone who has a proven record as a top salesperson. Says *David:* "Appraisals are a very important customer service. They draw in new customers of the type we want to attract. But Harriet, who does the appraisals, could do $200,000 in sales in a year while appraisals bring in only $30,000. We have to consider what's the best thing to do." David also wants to reduce the time he spends taking in consignment items from customers. He plans to put much of what he explains into a booklet which the customer can read before asking specific questions. He figures this should reduce take-in time from 45 to 15 minutes.

8. Do more to appeal to pass-by traffic. Because the store is in its own stand-alone building it gets none of the walk-in traffic enjoyed by a mall jeweler. Yet zoning restricts how bold the store signs may be. David wants to do more to appeal to passers-by.

9. Give new thought to appointing an advisory board of directors. David says that doing the fiscal 1994 business plan was very useful. Would he do another? "Knowing what we learned we'd be crazy not to," he says, but adds: "Will we have the discipline?" He and Effie think the best way to get that discipline is have some outsider impose it. For four or five years they've discussed the idea of having a board of directors. "I like the idea," says Effie, "but one thing we like about having our own business is that we enjoy the autonomy. There's no one there to tell us what to do." David points out that he and Effie, as sole stockholders, can make all the decisions anyway. They also can fire the board if they don't like it. It's not likely they'll act on this issue in the current fiscal year.

Now It's Your Turn (Quiz)

September 1993 Part II

David and Effie Onassis run a successful business. Their reputation with customers is enviable. Their staff relations are harmonious. And their store—which for obvious reasons we could not show—is very attractive. But they have some business problems. They're light on capital. They're heavy on inventory. Their salespeople aren't as productive as they should be. Their advertising isn't as effective as it might be. Their computer isn't being used efficiently. The owners acknowledge these concerns and, as their action plan reveals, they plan to correct them as best they can.

What do you think about this jewelry store, its owners and staff? You've been given a very candid look at how it works. If this were your store, what actions would you take? When would you take them?

We'd like all our readers to answer the following questions:

1. Knowing what you now do about Kronos Jewelers, what three issues are the most critical for the owners to address right away?

2. David has set himself the task of reducing inventory by $60,000, or 14%, over his next fiscal year. What is the best way he can achieve this goal?

3. What advice have you for a store owner with annual volume of $1.3 million who does not get monthly P&L statements?

4. David Onassis says that impulsive buying can be both good and bad; good in that it allows a jeweler to react quickly to attractive new merchandise, bad in that it can overload his inventory. What should Kronos Jewelers do about impulsive buying over the next year?

5. There's a rule of thumb that says a jewelry store salesperson should produce sales equal to 10 times pay. Thus a full-time person earning minimum wage should produce sales of $90,000+ a year. The average at Kronos Jewelers for all employees is around $85,000. What should the owners do?

6. Kronos Jewelers' owners want to convert repair customers to jewelry buyers. How should they go about doing this?

7. The computer system at Kronos Jewelers isn't up and running because, say the owners, they haven't had the time to enter all the necessary data. What do you think of this argument and what should they do?

8. David was surprised to find that his heavy advertising has not made the impression he would like on consumers in his market. What advice would you give him, remembering that his ad budget equals around 7% of revenues?

9. At Kronos Jewelers we have a situation in which an expert who could, according to David, bring in $200,000 a year in sales spends most of her time on appraisals and other services—for revenues closer to $30,000. How should this store deal with the issue of important services that are not big revenue producers?

10. Willis Cowlishaw says David and Effie need professional help to guide them to greater profitability. The Onassises admit they've considered appointing an outside board of directors to get expert advice. What do you think they should do?